AA

The

Golf
Course
Guide

C000024700

HIRE
OTELS

Win a Golf Break for two with AA Lifestyle Guides in association with Shire Hotels

AA Lifestyle Guides has five golf breaks to give away. We invite you to enter one of five free prize draws*. The winner of each free prize draw will enjoy a free golf break consisting of a two night Refresher Break including breakfast and dinner at Cottons Hotel and Spa in Cheshire for two people, plus a free round of golf each at High Legh Park (see entry on page 41)

For more information on Shire Hotels Refresher breaks, call 0800 854290 or visit **www.shirehotels.co.uk**

To enter simply visit www.pspcomp.com, click on the picture of the 2005 AA Golf Course Guide enter the competition code GG05 and complete your details on the form.

Terms and conditions apply. *For postal entry and terms and conditions please see page 491

This 19th edition published 2004

Typeset/repro by Servis Filmsetting Ltd, Manchester

Printed and bound by Oriental Press, Dubai

The cover photographs are held in the Association's own picture library (AA WORLD TRAVEL LIBRARY), with contributions from:
tl Corbis; tc Corbis; tr Corbis; bl Corbis; bc Corbis; br AA World Travel Library/Rick Strange

The Automobile Assocation would like to thank the following libraries for their assistance in the publication of this book.

Corbis ii, iiibl, iiibr, iv, 1t, 1b, 8, 9, 13tl, 13br, 303tr, 303br, 371tl, 371tr, 371br, 398tl, 398br; Photodisc 6

The remaining images are held in the Assocation's own library (AA WORLD TRAVEL LIBRARY) with contributions from the following:
Adrian Baker 303tl; Jamie Blandford 17tr, 398bl; Steve Day i; Roger Moss 5; Tony Souter 17bl; Rick Strange iiibc; Stephen Whitehorne 303bl; Peter Zollier 398tr.

Maps prepared by the Cartography Department of The Automobile Association.
Maps © Automobile Association Developments Limited 2004.

This product includes mapping data licensed from Ordnance Survey® with the permission of the Controller of Her Majesty's Stationery Office. © Crown copyright 2004 All rights reserved. Licence number 399221.

This product includes mapping based upon data licensed from Ordnance Survey of Northern Ireland ® reproduced by permission of the Chief Executive, acting on behalf of the Controller of Her Majesty's Stationery Office. © Crown copyright 2004. Permit number 40064.

Republic of Ireland mapping based on Ordnance Survey Ireland Permit number MP0002104. © Ordnance Survey Ireland and Government of Ireland.

Published by AA Publishing, which is a trading name of Automobile Association Developments Limited, whose registered office is Millstream, Maidenhead Road, Windsor, Berkshire SL4 5GD

Registered number 1878835

A CIP catalogue record for this book is available from the British Library.

ISBN 0749542063
A02068

Contents

How to use the guide

The AA Golf Course Guide aims to provide useful information about a large selection of courses across Britain and Ireland. Golf courses are selected by the AA and their entry in the guide is free of charge. The guide is updated every year as many courses change, close, open, upgrade and add new features. Entries include the contact details for each course, a brief description of the type of course, and details of green fees, leisure, club, catering or conference facilities. AA recommended accommodation follows most entries. To avoid disappointment when visiting a golf course we recommend that you telephone in advance, please do mention the AA Golf Course Guide when you make an enquiry.

1 Town name and map reference
The directory is organised by county then alphabetically by town or village name. Use the atlas or index of course names if you are unsure of the location of a particular course. The map reference includes the map page number and National Grid reference. The grid references for the Republic of Ireland are unique to this atlas.

2 Club name
Where the club name appears in bold italics we have been unable to verify current course details with the club. You are strongly advised to check any details with the club in advance of your visit.

3 Contact details
Address, postcode, telephone, fax and e-mail information is provided where this is available.

4 Description
A brief description of the course or courses is provided, significant features are highlighted.

5 Course statistics
The number of holes, yardage, par, Standard Scratch Score, Course Record and number of club members appear here in italics.

6 Visitor information
Details of booking requirements or restrictions. A small number of courses included in this guide are not open to visitors however we have included limited details where possible for information.

7 Society information
Details of booking requirements or restrictions for societies.

8 Green Fees
Only the most up-to-date green fees are given, including any variations or restrictions. Where green fees are not confirmed we recommend that you contact the club direct for current details. An asterisk * denotes 2004 fees.

9 Credit Cards
Symbols appear for credit cards accepted by the club.

10 Professional
The name of the club professional(s).

11 Facilities
Please see the key to symbols on the left.

---

1 **OXFORD**   Map 04 SP50

2 **North Oxford** Banbury Rd OX2 8EZ
3 ☎ 01865 554924 ▤ 01865 515921
4 **Gently undulating parkland course.**
5 *18 holes, 5736yds, Par 67, SSS 67, Course record 62. Club membership 700.*
6 **Visitors** at weekends & bank holidays may only play after 4pm. **Societies** must contact in advance. **Green Fees** not **8** confirmed. **Cards** ▤ 🗒 💳 **Prof** Robert Harris **Facilities** **9**
10 ⊗ ⊞ ⬛ ♀ ⛳ 🏠 🛒 ⚑ **Conf** Facilities Available **11**
12 **Location** 3m N of city centre on A423 **13**
··

Hotel ★★★ 66% The Oxford Hotel, Godstow Rd,
Wolvercote Roundabout, OXFORD **14**
☎ 01865 489988 173 en suite

☎ Telephone number	🛒 Well-stocked shop	
▤ Fax number	⛳ Clubs for hire	
€ (Republic of Ireland only, the exchange rate between the Euro and Pounds sterling is liable to fluctuate)	🛺 Motorised cart/trolley for hire	
	🛒 Buggies for hire	
⊗ Lunch	⛳ Trolley for hire	
⫸ Dinner	⛳ Driving range	
⬛ Bar snacks	★ AA star classification for hotels	
▼ Tea/coffee	◉ AA Rosette Award (in championship course entries)	
♀ Bar open midday and evenings	◆ AA Guest house classification	
⚐ Accommodation at club	🏠 Town House hotel	
⚒ Changing rooms	♨ Country House Hotel	

Finding a golf course in the directory

The directory is arranged by country and county, golf courses appear alphabetically by town within each county. Country divisions are listed on the contents page and golf courses are listed by name in the index.

12 Conference facilities

Conference facilities are noted where available, as are corporate hospitality days.

13 Location

The location of the club is given in relation to the nearest town or motorway junction. Many golf courses are in rural locations and we are unable to provide detailed directions in this guide, we recommend that you contact the club direct.

14 Accommodation

AA recommended hotel or guest accommodation is provided for most entries. This does not imply that the hotel offers special terms for the golf club. The Star or Diamond rating, Quality Assessment (%) score and AA Rosette award appear as applicable. (See page 2 for more details of the AA accommodation schemes.) Contact details and the number of rooms are given.

Photographs and advertisements

Only golf courses and hotels selected for the guide are able to enhance their entry with a photograph or to take a display advertisement.

Selected highlighted courses

Green boxes in the guide highlight selected courses considered to be of particular merit or interest. These may include historic clubs, particularly testing or enjoyable courses or those in holiday areas popular with visiting golfers. The selection cannot be either exhaustive or totally objective; however it is independent, courses cannot pay to have an entry in the guide, nor can they pay to have a highlighted entry. Highlighted courses do not represent any formal category on quality or other grounds.

Championship Courses

Major championship courses have a full page entry in the guide with more extensive details. A selection of AA recommended restaurants and hotels are given for these courses.

Hotels & Guest Accommodation

Many golf course entries in the guide are followed by details of a nearby AA recognised hotel. In some cases the golf course will be in the grounds of the hotel. Most of the recommended hotels fall within the two, three and four star classifications. Where there is no nearby AA recognised hotel, AA guest accommodation will be recommended, with a classification from one to five Diamonds.

Club accommodation at golf courses

Where courses offer club accommodation the bed symbol appears under Facilities. This is listed as an option for readers wishing to stay at the course, however, unless the club accommodation has an AA Star or diamond classification, the only AA recommended accommodation is the hotel or guest house which follows the entry.

U rating U

Hotel not yet rated by the AA.

Recommendations

If you would like to recommend a new course which does not feature in the guide, please write to: The Editor, AA Golf Course Guide, Fanum House, Basing View, Basingstoke, RG21 4EA.

AA Hotel and Guest Accommodation Inspection

The AA inspects and classifies hotels and guest accommodation under quality standards agreed between the AA, English Tourism Council and RAC. Hotels receive a star classification from one to five stars and guest accommodation establishments receive between one and five diamonds.

AA recognised establishments pay an annual fee, this varies according to the classification level and the number of bedrooms.

The establishments receive an unannounced inspection visit from a qualified AA inspector who recommends the appropriate classification. Return visits are made to check that standards are maintained and the classification is not transferable if an establishment changes hands.

The AA Hotel Guide and AA Bed & Breakfast Guide, published annually, give further details of AA recognised establishments and the classification schemes.

Details of AA recommended hotels, guest accommodation, restaurants and pubs can be found on the AA website www.the AA.com

The Quality Assessment score appears after the star rating for hotels in this guide. This is an additional assessment made by AA hotel inspectors, covering everything the hotel has to offer, including hospitality.

The Quality Assessment score allows a quick comparison between hotels with the same number of stars, the higher the score the better the hotel within the same star rating.

The Top 200 ★

Red Stars are the highest accolade, awarded by the AA to a small number of hotels which are considered to be outstanding. No Quality Assessment score is shown for hotels with red stars.

AA Star Classification

Quality standards you can expect from an AA recognised hotel

All hotels recognised by the AA should have high standards of cleanliness, proper records of booking, give prompt and professional service to guests, assist with luggage on request, accept and deliver messages, provide a designated area for breakfast and dinner with drinks available in a bar or lounge, provide an early morning call on request, good quality furniture and fittings, adequate heating and lighting and proper maintenance. A guide to some of the general expectations for each star classification is as follows:

What you can expect from a one star hotel ★

Polite, courteous staff providing a relatively informal yet competent style of service, available during the day and evening to receive guests. At least one designated eating area open to residents for breakfast. Dinner does not have to be offered. However if an establishment does offer dinner it should be on at least 5 days a week, last order should be no later than 6.30pm, there should be a reasonable choice of hot and cold dishes and a short range of wines should be available. Television in lounge or bedroom. Majority of rooms en suite, bath or shower room available at all times.

What you can expect from a two star hotel ★★

Smartly and professionally presented management and staff providing competent, often informal service, available throughout the day and evening to greet guests. At least one restaurant or dining room open to residents for breakfast (and for dinner at least five days a week). Last orders for dinner no earlier than 7pm, a choice of substantial hot and cold dishes and a short range of wines available. Television in bedroom. En suite or private bath or shower and WC.

What you can expect from a three star hotel ★★★

Management and staff smartly and professionally presented and usually uniformed. Technical and social skills of a good standard in responding to requests. A dedicated receptionist on duty at peak times, clear direction to rooms and some explanation of hotel facilities. At least one restaurant or dining room open to residents and non-residents for breakfast and dinner whenever the hotel is open. A wide selection of drinks served in a bar or lounge, available to residents and their guest throughout the day and evening. Last orders for dinner no earlier than 8pm, full dinner service provided. Remote-control television, direct-dial telephone. En suite bath or shower and WC.

What you can expect from a four star hotel ★★★★

A formal, professional staffing structure with smartly presented, uniformed staff, anticipating and responding to your needs or requests. Usually spacious, well-appointed public areas. Bedrooms offering superior quality and comfort to that at three star. A strong emphasis on food and beverages and a serious approach to cuisine. Reception staffed 24 hours per day by well-trained staff. Express checkout facilities where appropriate. Porterage available on request and readily provided by uniformed staff. Night porter available. Newspapers can be ordered and delivered to your room, additional services and concierge as appropriate to the style and location of the hotel. At least one restaurant open to residents and non-residents for breakfast and dinner seven days per week, and lunch to be available in a designated eating area. Drinks available to residents and their guests throughout the day and evening, table service available. Last orders for dinner no earlier than 9pm, an extensive choice of hot and cold dishes and a comprehensive list of wines. Remote-control television, direct-dial telephone, a range of high-quality toiletries. En suite bath with fixed overhead shower, WC.

What you can expect from a five star hotel ★★★★★

Flawless guest services, professional, attentive staff, technical and social skills of the highest order. Spacious and luxurious accommodation and public areas with a range of extra facilities. As a minimum, first-time guests shown to their bedroom. Multilingual service consistent with the needs of the hotel's normal clientele. Guest accounts well explained and presented. Porterage offered and provided by uniformed staff. Luggage handling on arrival and departure. Doorman or means of greeting guests at the hotel entrance, full concierge service provided. At least one restaurant open to residents and non-residents for all meals seven days per week. Staff showing excellent knowledge of food and wine. A wide selection of drinks, including cocktails, available in a bar or lounge, table service provided. Last orders for dinner no earlier than 10pm. High-quality menu and wine list, properly reflecting and complementing the style of cooking and providing exceptional quality. Evening turn-down service. Remote-control television, direct-dial telephone at bedside and desk, a range of luxury toiletries, bath sheets and robes. En suite bath with fixed overhead shower, WC.

AA Diamond Classification

The AA Diamond Awards classify guest accommodation at five levels of quality, from one Diamond at the simplest, to five Diamonds offering the highest quality. The emphasis for the assessment for a Diamond rating is on guest care, housekeeping, quality and maintenance of all the bedrooms, bathrooms and public areas, rather than the provision of extra facilities.

To reach the appropriate Diamond rating, all aspects of the operation are assessed

♦ Cleanliness and housekeeping

♦ Hospitality and service

♦ Quality and condition of bedrooms

♦ Quality and condition of bathrooms

♦ Food quality

♦ Quality and condition of public rooms

Establishments applying for AA recognition are visited on a 'mystery guest' basis by one of the AA's team of qualified accommodation inspectors. Inspectors stay overnight to make a thorough test of the accommodation, food and hospitality offered. After paying the bill the following morning they identify themselves and ask to be shown round the premises. The inspector completes a full report, resulting in a recommendation for the appropriate diamond award. After this first visit, the establishment will receive an annual visit to check that standards are maintained. If it changes hands, the new owners must re-apply for classification, as standards can easily change under a different regime.

Guests can expect to find the following minimum standards in guest accommodation at all Diamond levels:

♦ Pleasant and helpful welcome and service, sound standards of housekeeping and maintenance.

♦ Comfortable accommodation equipped to modern standards.

♦ Bedding and towels changed for each new guest (at least weekly if the room is taken for a long stay).

♦ Adequate storage, heating, lighting and comfortable seating.

♦ A sufficient hot water supply at reasonable times.

♦ A full, cooked breakfast. (If this is not provided, the fact must be advertised and a substantial continental breakfast must be offered.)

♦ Diamonds are shown as "red" to highlight the best establishments within the three, four and five Diamond rating levels.

AA Rosette Awards

Out of around 40,000 restaurants, the AA identifies, with its rosette awards, some 1800 as the best in the UK. The following is an outline of what to expect from restaurants with AA Rosette Awards

Excellent local restaurants serving food prepared with care, understanding and skill, using good quality ingredients. These restaurants stand out in their local area. The same expectations apply to hotel restaurants where guests should be able to eat in with confidence and a sense of anticipation. Of the total number of establishments with rosettes around 50% have one rosette.

The best local restaurants, which aim for and achieve higher standards, better consistency and where a greater precision is apparent in the cooking. There will be obvious attention to the selection of quality ingredients.

Outstanding restaurants that demand recognition well beyond their local area. The cooking will be underpinned by the selection and sympathetic treatment of the highest quality ingredients. Timing, seasoning and the judgement of flavour combinations will be consistently excellent, supported by other elements such as intelligent service and a well-chosen wine list. Around 10% of restaurants with rosettes have been awarded 3.

Amongst the very best restaurants in the British Isles, where the cooking demands national recognition. These restaurants will exhibit intense ambition, a passion for excellence, superb technical skills and remarkable consistency. They will combine appreciation of culinary traditions with a passionate desire for further exploration and improvement. Around a dozen restaurants have four rosettes.

The finest restaurants in the British Isles, where the cooking stands comparison with the best in the world. These restaurants will have highly individual voices, exhibit breathtaking culinary skills and set the standards to which others aspire. Fewer than half a dozen restaurants have five rosettes.

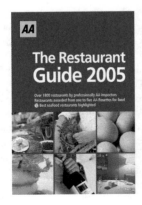

AA

The Restaurant Guide 2005

Over 1800 restaurants by professionally AA inspectors
Restaurants awarded from one to five AA Rosettes for food
Best seafood restaurants highlighted

A Swing and a Prayer

So you have never picked up a golf club. But you've watched the professionals on TV, and your neighbour plays, so you fancy trying the game. Bill Robertson, Editor of Golf Links magazine, takes a wry look at what could be a life-changing decision.

Sir Winston Churchill called it 'a game played with implements ill-designed for the task'. Mark Twain said it was 'a good walk spoiled', while that late, great comedian Bob Hope once claimed: 'I'd give up playing tomorrow, if only I knew what to do with all those sweaters.'

So be warned, golf is a game that can mess with your mind, increase your blood pressure, lower your self esteem, and if all that isn't enough, it can also become highly addictive. Still interested in trying the game? All right, but don't say you weren't warned.

Most people never really intend to take up golf seriously. Their introduction to the game usually comes as the result of a 'fun' knock about on a municipal putting green, often during a family holiday by the seaside. It's all very simple and relaxed. Expectations are low and because of this initial results are often encouraging.

The next step may involve a visit to the local driving range or pitch-and-putt course. Again, at this stage it is still 'only a game'. So what if you miss the ball as often as you make contact with it - after all, it's just a bit of fun. Until one day something very strange and very special happens.

It comes right out of the blue. Amidst all those ill-timed lunges at the ball, through a combination of sheer luck and the law of averages, the golf club actually ends up travelling on the correct line, at the right speed and on the ideal path, which in turn enables the clubface to arrive squarely into the back of the ball at precisely the correct time and place.

The result is a clean, crisp contact that sends the ball rocketing forward and upward in a long, high graceful arc. That small, white orb seems to hang in the sky for what seems like an eternity, before gravity finally pulls it back down to earth where it lands, bounces once and spins to a sudden stop.

Now some people will take the eminently sensible view that this shot was a pure fluke, and continue to enjoy simply 'having a bash' at golf until they eventually get bored with the game and give it up. Others, however, will ask themselves the same fateful question millions have asked before them: 'If I can hit a shot like that once, why can't I do it every time?'

Like it or not, these individuals are now well and truly hooked on golf. At this point there are two paths you can follow. One is the 'self taught' route. This will enable you, at least initially, to make progress quite quickly but in the majority of cases that progress is quite limited. For without a basic understanding of how they were able to hit that first clean, crisp shot many golfers find themselves doomed to spend the remainder of their golfing lives searching frustratingly for golf's Holy Grail – hitting two consecutive straight shots as if they were wearing a blindfold.

Golf, or more specifically the golf swing, is built on establishing a few simple but nevertheless important fundamentals, which include how to grip the club, how you stand to the ball, and then how to develop the correct repetitive swing action. Get these basics right at the start and your golf game will be built on sound foundations rather than on the swing-and-a-prayer approach of the majority of self-taught golfers.

So if you do become well and truly hooked, the second and best path to follow is to book a lesson, or more realistically, a series of lessons with your local golf club professional. And before you ask - no, you don't have to be a member of the golf club to have lessons with the pro. Neither do you have to own your own set of golf clubs, as most pros are usually more than happy to lend you clubs for your lessons. Not only is the club professional the best person to teach you those all-important swing basics, you'll also discover that his long experience and extensive knowledge about all aspects of the game will prove invaluable. For example once you decide that you are really keen to play the game regularly, most club professionals are more than happy to advise you on what type of golf equipment you will need to get started, ranging from clubs to clothing.

After all, it's never too late to start collecting golf sweaters.

Many of the clubs in this guide offer a wide range of options for anyone new to golf. The list below includes those that have told us they have a golf academy.

ENGLAND
CHESHIRE
Portal Golf & Country Club
TARPORLEY

CORNWALL & ISLES OF SCILLY
Mullion Golf Club
MULLION

DEVON
Yelverton Golf Club
YELVERTON

DORSET
Dudsbury Golf Club
FERNDOWN

GLOUCESTERSHIRE
Cirencester Golf Club
CIRENCESTER

GREATER MANCHESTER
Haigh Hall Golf Complex
WIGAN

HAMPSHIRE
Paultons Golf Centre
OWER

KENT
Chart Hills Golf Club
BIDDENDEN

Weald of Kent Golf Course
HEADCORN

Lydd Golf Club
LYDD

Marriott Tudor Park Hotel & Country Club
MAIDSTONE

LINCOLNSHIRE
Boston West Golf Centre
HUBBERT'S BRIDGE

NORFOLK
Barnham Broom Hotel & Golf Club
BARNHAM BROOM

NORTHAMPTONSHIRE
Collingtree Park Golf Course
COLLINGTREE

OXFORDSHIRE
Rye Hill Golf Club
BANBURY

Hadden Hill Golf Club
DIDCOT

Kirtlington Golf Club
KIRTLINGTON

SOMERSET
Wheathill Golf Club
SOMERTON
Oake Manor Golf Club
TAUNTON

EAST SUSSEX
East Sussex National
UCKFIELD

WEST MIDLANDS
Stonebridge Golf Club
MERIDEN

NORTH YORKSHIRE
Romanby Golf & Country Club
NORTHALLERTON

WEST YORKSHIRE
Willow Valley Golf & Country Club
BRIGHOUSE

SCOTLAND
PERTH & KINROSS
The Gleneagles Hotel
AUCHTERARDER

STIRLING
Brucefields Family Golfing Centre
BANNOCKBURN

WALES
DENBIGHSHIRE
Kimnel Park
BODELWYDDAN

NORTHERN IRELAND
LONDONDERRY
Radisson Roe Park Hotel & Golf Resort
LIMAVADY

REPUBLIC OF IRELAND
CO CORK
Fernhill Hotel & Golf Club
CARRIGALINE

CO WEXFORD
St Helen's Bay Golf & Country Club
ROSSLARE

Ignorance of the rules is no excuse!

Golfers Pocket Referee

is the only handy guide which summarises, in simple chart form, all the infringements in the Rules of Golf, from tee to green, and matches them at-a-glance with the penalties they incur.

● There are also diagrams reminding you of various options you have in classic trouble situations, and a useful list of 32 Player's Privileges arising from the Rules. There is also a section on Stroke-Saving Reminders.

● All 18 pages are laminated for weather protection, and are fingertip indexed for quick selection.

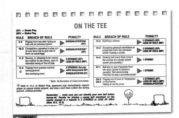

Each section is set out in easy-to-read chart form, and every breach of the rules, matched with its proper penalty, can be picked out at a glance. The Golfers Pocket Referee at 41/2" x 53/4" fits easily into pocket or golf bag

The Golfers Pocket Referee covers all parts of the course:
● ON THE TEE ● THROUGH THE GREEN ● IN THE HAZARDS ● ON THE GREEN ● IN GENERAL PLAY

THE **GOLFERS POCKET REFEREE** CAN SAVE YOU A STROKE, A HOLE OR EVEN A GAME.
ONLY £6.00 PER COPY INC. P & P
TELEPHONE FOR YOUR COPY TODAY 01382 52 52 00
www.golfreferee.co.uk

● Enquiries for bulk orders and or overprinted copies from Clubs, Societies and Companies always welcome.
Golfers Pocket Referee (originally Golf Infringements & Penalties) has been submitted to, and is published with the knowledge of the R & A and USGA. Rule numbers are as contained in the current edition of The Rules of Golf as approved by the R & A and USGA.

ORDER FORM

VISA MasterCard

I enclose my cheque / Postal Order or debit my Visa / Mastercard
Please make cheques payable to: Howard Publicity Services

Name ....

Card Number ....

Address ....

.... Postcode ....

Expiry Date ....

Valid From .... Issue No......................

Tel: ....

Signature ....

Home Club ....Handicap..........

Howard Publicity Services, 17 Manhattan Works, Dundonald Street, Dundee DD3 7PY
This is a high quality product and carries a money back guarantee. If not completely satisfied return the book unmarked within 7 days for a refund. **Please allow 7 - 14 days for delivery.**

Where do I look if I don't have time to book?

Booking a place to stay can be a time-consuming process. So why not search quickly and easily on-line for a place that best suits your needs.

Whatever your preference, we have the place for you. From a cosy farm cottage to a city centre hotel - we have them all. Choose from around 8,000 quality rated hotels and B&Bs in Great Britain and Ireland.

Just **AA**sk.

Hotel Booking Service
www.theAA.com/hotels

You may contact us using a Textphone on 0870 243 2456.
Information is available in large print, audio and Braille on request

The UK's Premier Supplier
of Quality Trophies and Awards

In early 2000 a revolution in golf trophy retailing took place. Using the expanding technology of the Internet, Silvertrophy.com launched an online trophy shop which enabled golfers and tournament organisers to purchase the finest awards from the comfort of their home, day or night. Offering a wide range of trophies to cover all budgets, and with delivery within 5 days of ordering, a new benchmark in service and quality had been set.

No longer would appointments have to be made to visit trophy shops after working hours.
No more waiting a week or two to collect the engraved awards.

Engraving (including logos) can be ordered using the web site's simple-to-use technology and the finished awards are delivered to your address by UPS.

Golf customers love the service and the company has gone from strength to strength, supplying small golf days as well as major tournaments around the world.

Based in Staffordshire, Silvertrophy.com take great pride in supplying the finest handmade English silverware to the UK market. They are able to offer their customers many advantages over traditional trophy shops: convenience, speed of delivery, quality and choice, are all at the top of the list.

Whilst orders are processed very quickly, Silvertrophy.com maintain a very high level of customer service. Whatever the size of the order, customers can be sure of the highest degree of personal attention.

Convenience

With products logically divided into sections, it is easy to find what you are looking for. Every product is illustrated by high quality images that really get over the feel and detail of the range. Full measurements and details of construction materials make it very easy to see exactly what you are buying.

Advice and suggestions for engraving layout are also presented, or you can leave the layout to the skilled team of engravers.

With the web store open 24 hours a day, and the process so simple to use, it is easy to appreciate why the website has become so popular with anyone who organises golf prizes on whatever level.

Ease of use

The Silvertrophy.com online shop is very simple to use. All engraving is ordered online with a choice of letter styles. You can see at a glance how much your engraving costs. Ordering is very easy, the website takes you through each step carefully. As soon as your order is complete a full order confirmation and VAT receipt is e-mailed to you.

Choice and Quality

Silvertrophy.com only supply Swatkins Silverware products. Swatkins Silverware Ltd have been producing golf trophies since 1898 using methods and materials which have hardly changed over time. The whole range of Swatkins Silverware awards are proudly featured in the online shop. All budgets are catered for from a simple 'hole-in-one medal' to handmade silver golf cups which would be at home in any professional tournament. Silvertrophy.com only supply this time honoured brand which commands respect around the world.

Many of the trophies carry a 10 year or even a lifetime guarantee, the quality is so high. The awards are manufactured using traditional methods of metal spinning, soldering, polishing and heavy deposit silver-plating. Each process is carefully carried out by time served craftsmen drawing on over 100 years of experience.

silvertrophy.com
The Hallmark of Success

Security

The online payment system uses the very latest security to guarantee against fraud. Customers can shop with confidence. Our payment system is approved by the following banks: Natwest, Royal Bank of Scotland, American Express, Bank of Scotland, Barclays, HSBC, Lloyds TSB.

Speed of delivery

Silvertrophy.com order processing and dispatch is fast! Most orders are engraved within 2 days of being placed and dispatched the next day by UPS courier.

99% of orders arrive with the customer in 3-5 working days. The dispatch department has a huge commitment to a speedy efficient service. As soon as an order leaves the depot a UPS tracking number is sent to the customers' e-mail address, so they can follow the progress of the shipment and know to expect it the next day.

This is the winning combination:

- Secure and convenient ordering 24 hours a day, with excellent customer support.
- A huge choice of the finest handmade awards.
- Delivery in 1 to 2 days by UPS.

Silvertrophy.com Awarded Official Supplier Status to Faldo Series

In 2001 Silvertrophy.com was appointed the official trophy supplier to the Faldo Series. Nick Faldo established the Faldo Series in 1996 to identify and nurture the next generation of champion golfers in Europe.

Underwritten by Nick, the Faldo Series is a non-profit making initiative combining competition with education and is aimed at young golfers under the age of 21. The schedule includes tournaments at a varied selection of the UK and Ireland's finest championship venues. Competitors also benefit from a series of unique seminars with Nick's hand picked panel of experts on every aspect of the sport.

Past members of the Faldo Series include Nick Dougherty and Zane Scotland, both of whom have gone on to compete professionally on the PGA European Tour. Major partners include Nike Golf and the International Junior Pairs. The Faldo Series also receives backing from the PGA, the Royal and Ancient Golf Club of St Andrews and the PGA European Tour

HRH Prince Andrew and Nick Faldo present the main prizes at the end of play after the final of the Faldo Series on September 3, 2003 held at Brockett Hall Golf Club, Welwyn, England (Photo by David Cannon/Getty Images)

FALDO
SERIES
Official Supplier

England

silvertrophy.com
The Hallmark of Success

ENGLAND
BEDFORDSHIRE

ASPLEY GUISE   Map 04 SP93

Aspley Guise & Woburn Sands West Hill
MK17 8DX
☎ 01908 583596 🖹 01908 583596 (Secretary)
A fine undulating course in expansive heathland
interspersed with many attractive clumps of gorse,
broom and bracken. Some well-established silver birch
are a feature. The 7th, 8th and 9th are really tough
holes to complete the first half.
18 holes, 6079yds, Par 71, SSS 70, Course record 65.
Club membership 590.
Visitors with member only at weekends. **Societies** Wed &
Fri normally booked 6 mths ahead. **Green Fees** £30 per
round weekdays (£38 weekends). **Cards** 🖶 ▭ **Prof**
Colin Clingan **Course Designer** Sandy Herd **Facilities** ⊗
by prior arrangement 🏌 ♣ ♀ △ 🏠 ⛳ 🚗 ♂ **Conf** Corporate Hospitality Days available
Location 2m W of M1 junc 13

. . . .

Hotel ★★★ 69% Moore Place Hotel, The Square,
ASPLEY GUISE ☎ 01908 282000 39 en suite
27 annexe en suite

BEDFORD   Map 04 TL04

Bedford Great Denham Golf Village, Carnoustie Dr,
Biddenham MK40 4FF
☎ 01234 320022 🖹 01234 320023
e-mail: thebedford@btopenworld.com
American styled course with 89 bunkers, 8 large water
features and large contoured USPGA specification
greens. Built on sand and gravel the course is open all
year round.
18 holes, 6471yds, Par 72, SSS 72, Course record 65.
Club membership 500.
Visitors contact in advance, weekends after 10.30am
Societies telephone for details. **Green Fees** £30 per 18
holes (£40 weekends). **Cards** 🖶 ▭ 💳 ▭ 🖬 💷 **Prof**
Zac Thompson **Course Designer** David Pottage **Facilities**
⊗ 🏌 🏌 ♣ ♀ △ ⛳ ↑ 🚗 ♂ ♀ **Conf** fac available
Corporate Hospitality Days available **Location** 2.5m W of
Bedford off A428

. . . .

Hotel 🏠 Innkeeper's Lodge Bedford, 403 Goldington Rd,
BEDFORD ☎ 0870 243 0500 & 01234 272707
🖹 01234 343926 47 en suite

Bedford & County Green Ln, Clapham MK41 6ET
☎ 01234 352617 🖹 01234 357195
A mature parkland course established in 1912 with
views over Bedford and surrounding countryside.
Beware of the brook that discreetly meanders through
the 7th, 10th, 11th and 15th holes. The testing par 4
15th is one of the most challenging holes in the area.
18 holes, 6420yds, Par 70, SSS 70, Course record 66.
Club membership 600.
Visitors handicap certificate required, weekends with
member only. **Societies** welcome Mon,Tue,Thu & Fri,
telephone in advance. **Green Fees** £32 per day, £26 per
round weekdays only. **Prof** R Tattersall **Facilities** ⊗ 🏌 by
prior arrangement 🏌 ♣ ♀ △ ♂ **Location** 2m N off A6

. . . .

Hotel 🏠 Travel Inn, Priory Country Park, Barkers Ln,
BEDFORD ☎ 08701 977030 32 en suite

Bedfordshire Spring Ln, Stagsden MK43 8SR
☎ 01234 822555 🖹 01234 825052
e-mail: office@bedfordshiregolf.com
A challenging 18-hole course on undulating terrain with
established trees/woods and water hazards. Magnificent
views in all directions.
18 holes, 6565yds, Par 70, SSS 72, Course record 65.
Academy Course: 9 holes, 1354yds, Par 28, SSS 28.
Club membership 700.
Visitors must contact in advance and may not play18 hole
course play at weekends except with member. Must contact
in advance. **Societies** must telephone in advance/confirm in
writing. **Green Fees** £40 per day, £30 per 18 holes. 9 hole
course £6 (£8 weekends). **Cards** 🖶 ▭ 🖬 💷 **Prof** David
Armor **Course Designer** Cameron Sinclair **Facilities** ⊗ 🏌
by prior arrangement 🏌 ♣ ♀ △ 🏠 ⛳ 🚗 ♂ ♀ **Conf** fac
available Corporate Hospitality Days available **Location**
3m W of Bedford on A422 at Stagsden

. . . .

Hotel 🏠 Travelodge Bedford South West, Beancroft Rd
Junction, MARSTON MORETAINE ☎ 08700 850 950
54 en suite

Mowsbury Cleat Hill, Kimbolton Rd, Ravensden
MK41 8DQ
☎ 01234 771041 & 216374 (pro) 🖹 01234 771041
e-mail: mgc@freenet.co.uk
18 holes, 6451yds, Par 72, SSS 71, Course record 66.
Course Designer Hawtree **Location** 2m N of town centre
on B660
Telephone for further details

. . . .

Hotel 🏠 Innkeeper's Lodge Bedford, 403 Goldington Rd,
BEDFORD ☎ 0870 243 0500 & 01234 272707
🖹 01234 343926 47 en suite

CHALGRAVE   Map 04 TL02

Chalgrave Manor Dunstable Rd LU5 6JN
☎ 01525 876556 & 876554 🖹 01525 876556
e-mail: chalgravegolf@onetel.net.uk
Undulating course constructed in 1994, offering a good
test of golf for all standards of golfer. Feature holes include
the short 10th (150 yards) that requires an accurate shot
across water to a splendid sloping green, and the par 4
11th which incorporates an elevated tee, a ditch, several
bunkers, a pond and perilously close out of bounds.
18 holes, 6382yds, Par 72, SSS 70, Course record 69.
Club membership 550.
Visitors welcome, dress code smart casual, after 1pm at
weekends. **Societies** apply in writing or telephone, in
advance. **Green Fees** £20 per round (£30 weekends &
bank holidays). **Cards** 🖶 ▭ 🖬 💷 **Prof** Geoff Swain
Course Designer M Palmer **Facilities** ⊗ 🏌 ♣ ♀ △ 🏠
🚗 ♂ **Conf** fac available Corporate Hospitality Days
available **Location** M1 junct 12 take A5120 through
Toddington, entrance about 1m out, well signposted

. . . .

Hotel ★★★ 65% Hanover International Hotel, Church St,
DUNSTABLE ☎ 01582 662201 68 en suite

COLMWORTH   Map 04 TL15

Colmworth & North Bedfordshire New Rd
MK44 2NN ☎ 01234 378181 🖹 01234 376678
e-mail: colmworth@btopenworld.com
An easy walking course with well-bunkered greens,
opened in 1991. The course is often windy and plays
longer than the yardage suggests. Water comes into
play on 3 holes.

Continued

Colmworth & North Bedfordshire Golf Club
18 holes, 6435yds, Par 72, SSS 71, Course record 69.
Club membership 200.
Visitors advisable to book in advance, may only play at weekends after 9.30am. **Societies** telephone in advance. **Cards** 🏧 💳 ▦ 🏧 🔲 **Prof** Graham Bithrey **Course Designer** John Glasgow **Facilities** ⊗ ⅏ by prior arrangement 🏌 💪 ♀ ⚲ 🏠 🍴 🚩 🚜 ⚑ ⚷ **Leisure** fishing, par 3 course. **Conf** Corporate Hospitality Days available **Location** off A1 between Bedford and St Neots
....
Hotel ★★★ 67% Corus hotel Bedford, Cardington Rd, BEDFORD ☎ 0870 609 6108 48 en suite

Dunstable Downs Whipsnade Rd LU6 2NB
☎ 01582 604472 🖷 01582 478700
e-mail: ddgc@btconnect.com
A fine downland course set on two levels with far-reaching views and frequent sightings of graceful gliders. The 9th hole is one of the best short holes in the country.
18 holes, 6251yds, Par 70, SSS 70, Course record 64.
Club membership 600.
Visitors welcome Mon, Tue, Thur and Fri, weekends with member only. Handicap certificate required. **Societies** apply in advance. **Green Fees** £30 per round. **Prof** Michael Weldon **Course Designer** James Braid **Facilities** ⊗ ⅏ 🏌 💪 ♀ ⚲ 🏠 🚜 ⚷ **Conf** Corporate Hospitality Days available **Location** 2m S off B4541
....
Hotel ★★★ 65% Hanover International Hotel, Church St, DUNSTABLE ☎ 01582 662201 68 en suite

Griffin Chaul End Rd, Caddington LU1 4AX
☎ 01582 415573 🖷 01582 415314
e-mail: griffin@griffingolfclub.fsbusiness.co.uk
A challenging 18-hole course with ponds and lakes on top of Blows Downs.

18 holes, 6240yds, Par 71, SSS 70.
Club membership 470.
Visitors welcome Mon-Fri & after 2pm weekends no need to book. **Societies** welcome midweek and Sat/Sun pm summer. Book by telephone. **Green Fees** £14 per round Mon-Thu (£17 Fri, £20 weekends). **Facilities** ⊗ 🏌 💪 ♀ ⚲ 🏠 🚜 **Conf** Corporate Hospitality Days available **Location** M1 junct 11, after 0.5m exit left at Tesco rdbt, towards Dunstable
....
Hotel ★★★ 65% Hanover International Hotel, Church St, DUNSTABLE ☎ 01582 662201 68 en suite

Leighton Buzzard Plantation Rd LU7 3JF
☎ 01525 244800 (Office) 🖷 01525 244801
e-mail: lbgc.secretary1@btopenworld.com
Parkland course with easy walking. The 17th and 18th holes are challenging tree-lined finishing holes with tight fairways. The par 3 11th is signature hole.

18 holes, 6101yds, Par 71, SSS 70, Course record 64.
Club membership 700.
Visitors may play yellow tees, may not play Tue (Ladies Day). May only play with member weekends and bank holidays. Handicap certificate required unless playing with member. **Societies** prior booking required. **Green Fees** £36 per day; £34 per round, £17 per 9 holes. **Prof** Maurice Campbell **Facilities** ⊗ ⅏ 🏌 💪 ♀ ⚲ 🏠 🚩 🚜 ⚷ **Conf** fac available Corporate Hospitality Days available **Location** 1.5m N of town centre off A4146
....
Hotel ★★★ 65% Hanover International Hotel, Church St, DUNSTABLE ☎ 01582 662201 68 en suite

Mount Pleasant Station Rd SG16 6JL
☎ 01462 850999
e-mail: davidsimsmpgolf@aol.com
A 9-hole course, which when played over 18 totals some 6003yds. The course is undulating meadowland with mature hedges and trees and also 10,000 new trees. Two small ponds are crossed and there is a significant ditch in play on several holes. The 5th, 11th and 14th holes are all 400yds and play long into the prevailing west wind. Visitors consider the greens some of the best conditioned in the area and with good drainage the course rarely has to close. Course improvements and alterations came into play from May 2004, adding 180 yards of length to the course and including a new green and a large pond.
9 holes, 6003yds, Par 70, SSS 69, Course record 68.
Club membership 300.

Continued   *Continued*

Visitors no restrictions, book 2 days in advance, booking advisable weekends & evenings May-Sep. **Societies** telephone or apply in writing. **Green Fees** terms on application. **Cards** ⊟ ▦ ▦ ▦ ▦ ▧ **Prof** Mike Roberts **Course Designer** Derek Young **Facilities** ⊗ ⊬ ♨ ■ ♥ ♁ ♤ ♨ ♦ ✓ **Conf** Corporate Hospitality Days available **Location** 0.75m W of A600, 4m N of Hitchin

....

Hotel ★★★ Menzies Flitwick Manor, Church Rd, FLITWICK ☎ 01525 712242 17 en suite

LUTON   Map 04 TL02

South Beds Warden Hill Rd LU2 7AE
☎ 01582 591500 ▤ 01582 495381
e-mail: office@southbedsgolfclub.co.uk
18- and 9-hole downland courses, slightly undulating.
Galley Hill Course: 18 holes, 6438yds, Par 71, SSS 71, Course record 64.
Warden Hill Course: 9 holes, 2425yds, Par 32, SSS 32.
Club membership 1000.
Visitors must contact in advance and have a handicap certificate for Galley Hill Course. **Societies** telephone for details. **Green Fees** telephone for details. **Cards** ⊟ ▦ ▦ ▧ **Prof** Eddie Cogle **Facilities** ⊗ ⊬ ♨ ■ ♥ ♁ ♤ ♨ ✓ **Conf** Corporate Hospitality Days available **Location** 3m N of Luton on A6

....

Hotel ★★★ 59% The Chiltern Hotel, Waller Av, LUTON ☎ 0870 609 6120 91 en suite

Stockwood Park London Rd LU1 4LX
☎ 01582 413704 (pro shop)
Well laid out municipal parkland course with established trees and several challenging holes.
18 holes, 6049yds, Par 69, SSS 69, Course record 67.
Club membership 600.
Visitors no restrictions. **Societies** Mon, Tue & Thu only, telephone for application. **Green Fees** telephone for details. **Cards** ⊟ ▦ **Prof** Glyn McCarthy **Facilities** ⊗ ⊬ ♨ ■ ♥ ♁ ♤ ♨ ✓ **Location** 1m S

....

Hotel ★★★ 59% The Chiltern Hotel, Waller Av, LUTON ☎ 0870 609 6120 91 en suite

MILLBROOK   Map 04 TL03

Millbrook Millbrook Village MK45 2JB
☎ 01525 840252 ▤ 01525 406249
e-mail: info@themillbrook.com
Long parkland course, on rolling countryside high above the Bedfordshire plains. Laid out on well-drained sandy soil with many fairways lined with silver birch, pine and larch.
The Millbrook: 18 holes, 7021yds, Par 74, SSS 73, Course record 68.
Club membership 470.
Visitors must contact in advance, may not play after 11am on Thu or after 11.30am at weekends. **Societies** telephone for details on 01525 402269. **Green Fees** telephone for details. **Prof** Geraint Dixon **Course Designer** William Sutherland **Facilities** ⊗ ⊬ ♨ ■ ♥ ♁ ♤ ♨ ♦ **Conf** fac available Corporate Hospitality Days available **Location** M1 junct 12 & 13, then take A507 Woburn to Ampthill road

....

Hotel ★★★ Menzies Flitwick Manor, Church Rd, FLITWICK ☎ 01525 712242 17 en suite

PAVENHAM   Map 04 SP95

Pavenham Park MK43 7PE
☎ 01234 822202 ▤ 01234 826602
e-mail: kolvengolf@ukonline.co.uk
Mature, undulating parkland course with fast contoured greens.
18 holes, 6400yds, Par 72, SSS 71, Course record 63.
Club membership 790.
Visitors welcome weekdays, weekends as members guests only. **Societies** telephone in advance. **Green Fees** £25 per round (£40 weekends & bank holidays). **Cards** ⊟ ▦ ▧ **Prof** Zac Thompson **Course Designer** Zac Thompson **Facilities** ⊗ ⊬ ♨ ■ ♥ ♁ ♤ ♨ ♦ **Conf** fac available Corporate Hospitality Days available **Location** 1.5m from A6, N of Bedford

....

Hotel ⌂ Travelodge Bedford South West, Beancroft Rd Junction, MARSTON MORETAINE ☎ 08700 850 950 54 en suite

SANDY   Map 04 TL14

John O'Gaunt Sutton Park SG19 2LY
☎ 01767 260360 ▤ 01767 262834
e-mail: admin@johnogauntgolfclub.co.uk
Two magnificent parkland courses – John O'Gaunt and Carthagena – covering a gently undulating and tree-lined terrain. The John O'Gaunt course makes the most of numerous natural features, notably a river which crosses the fairways of four holes. The Carthagena course has larger greens, longer tees and from the back tees is a challenging course. Fine clubhouse.
John O'Gaunt Course: 18 holes, 6513yds, Par 71, SSS 71, Course record 64.
Carthagena Course: 18 holes, 5869yds, Par 69, SSS 69.
Club membership 1500.
Visitors must contact in advance. **Societies** must pre-book. **Green Fees** £50 per day/round (£60 weekends & bank holidays). **Prof** Lee Scarbrow **Course Designer** Hawtrees **Facilities** ⊗ ⊬ ♨ ■ ♥ ♁ ♤ ♨ ♦ ✓ **Conf** Corporate Hospitality Days available **Location** 3m NE of Biggleswade on B1040

....

Hotel ★★ 63% Abbotsley Golf Hotel & Country Club, Potton Rd, Eynesbury Hardwicke, ST NEOTS ☎ 01480 474000 42 annexe en suite

SHEFFORD   Map 04 TL13

Beadlow Manor Hotel & Golf & Country Club SG17 5PH
☎ 01525 860800 ▤ 01525 861345
e-mail: beadlowmanor@talk21 co.uk
Baroness Course: 18 holes, 6072yds, Par 71, SSS 69, Course record 67.
Baron Course: 18 holes, 6619yds, Par 73, SSS 72, Course record 67.
Location On A507
Telephone for further details

....

Hotel ★★★ Menzies Flitwick Manor, Church Rd, FLITWICK ☎ 01525 712242 17 en suite

TILSWORTH   Map 04 SP92

Tilsworth Dunstable Rd LU7 9PU
☎ 01525 210721/2 ▤ 01525 210465
e-mail: nick@tilsworthgolf.co.uk

Continued

The golf course is in first class condition and, although not a long course, is particularly demanding and challenging where the key is straight driving. The course has its own 'Amen Corner' between the 14th and 16th holes, which will challenge all golfers. Panoramic views of 3 counties from the 6th tee.
18 holes, 5306yds, Par 69, SSS 66, Course record 64. Club membership 400.
Visitors may book up to 7 days in advance. May not play before 10am Sundays. **Societies** welcome weekdays, apply in advance to W Payne **Green Fees** £16 for 18 holes (£18 weekends and bank holidays). **Cards** 🖶 🖅 🛂 🔄 🐾 **Prof** Nick Webb **Facilities** ⊗ ⅢⅢ ᕫᕽ ▼ ♀ ᕿ ᕩ ⚐ ⚑ **Conf** Corporate Hospitality Days available **Location** 0.5m NE off A5, N of Dunstable

....
Hotel ★★★ 65% Hanover International Hotel, Church St, DUNSTABLE ☎ 01582 662201 68 en suite

WYBOSTON   Map 04 TL15

Wyboston Lakes MK44 3AL
☎ 01480 212625 📄 01480 223000
e-mail: venue@wybostonlakes.co.uk
Parkland course, with narrow fairways, small greens, set around four lakes and a river which provide the biggest challenge on this very scenic course.

18 holes, 5955yds, Par 70, SSS 69, Course record 65. Club membership 300.
Visitors a booking system is in operation at weekends, book no more than 8 days in advance. **Societies** telephone in advance. **Green Fees** telephone for details. **Cards** 🖶 🖅 **Prof** Paul Ashwell **Course Designer** N Oakden **Facilities** ⊗ Ⅲ ᕫᕽ ▼ ♀ ᕿ ᕩ ⚐ ⚑ 🐾 ⚐ ⚑ **Leisure** heated indoor swimming pool, fishing, sauna, solarium, gymnasium, watersports. **Conf** fac available Corporate Hospitality Days available **Location** 1m S of St Neots off A1/A428

....
Hotel ★★★ 67% Corus hotel Bedford, Cardington Rd, BEDFORD ☎ 0870 609 6108 48 en suite

BERKSHIRE

ASCOT   Map 04 SU96

Berkshire Swinley Rd SL5 8AY
☎ 01344 621495 📄 01344 623328
Two heathland courses with splendid tree-lined fairways. The Red Course, on slightly higher ground, is a little longer than the Blue. It has an unusual assortment of holes, six par 3s, six par 4s and six par 5s, the short holes, particularly the 10th and 16th, being the most intimidating. The Blue Course starts with a
Continued

par 3 and shares with the 16th the reputation of being the finest holes of the 18.
Red Course: 18 holes, 6379yds, Par 72, SSS 71.
Blue Course: 18 holes, 6260yds, Par 71, SSS 71.
Visitors by prior arrangement **Societies** applications in writing only and must be registered. **Green Fees** £75 per round, £100 per day. **Cards** 🖶 🖅 🛂 **Prof** P Anderson **Course Designer** H Fowler **Facilities** ⊗ ᕫᕽ ▼ ♀ ᕿ ⚐ ⚑ 🐾 🐾 ⚐ ⚑ **Location** 2.5m NW of M3 jct 3 on A332

....
Hotel ★★★★ 66% The Berystede, Bagshot Rd, Sunninghill, ASCOT ☎ 0870 400 8111 90 en suite

Lavender Park Swinley Rd SL5 8BD
☎ 01344 893344
e-mail: lavenderpark@yahoo.com
Public parkland course, ideal for the short game featuring challenging narrow fairways. Driving range with 9-hole par 3 course, floodlit until 10pm.
9 holes, 1102yds, Par 27, SSS 28.
Visitors no restrictions. **Societies** welcome, notice preferred. **Green Fees** telephone for details. **Cards** 🖶 🖅 🖅 🔄 🛂 **Prof** David Johnson **Facilities** ▼ ♀ ᕿ ⚐ ⚑ **Leisure** snooker. **Location** 1.5m W of Ascot, off the A329 on the B3017

....
Hotel ★★★★ 66% The Berystede, Bagshot Rd, Sunninghill, ASCOT ☎ 0870 400 8111 90 en suite

Mill Ride Mill Ride SL5 8LT
☎ 01344 886777 📄 01344 886820
e-mail: archie@millride.com

18 holes, 6807yds, Par 72, SSS 72, Course record 64.
Course Designer Donald Steel **Location** 2m W of Ascot **Telephone for further details**

....
Hotel ★★★★ 66% The Berystede, Bagshot Rd, Sunninghill, ASCOT ☎ 0870 400 8111 90 en suite

Royal Ascot Winkfield Rd SL5 7LJ
☎ 01344 625175 📄 01344 872330
e-mail: golf@royalascotgc.fsnet.co.uk
Heathland course inside Ascot racecourse and exposed to weather.
18 holes, 5716yds, Par 68, SSS 68, Course record 65. Club membership 620.
Visitors must be guest of member **Societies** telephone for provisional booking. **Green Fees** £15 per round (£18.50 weekends) with member only. **Prof** Alistair White **Course Designer** J H Taylor **Facilities** ⊗ Ⅲ ▼ ♀ ᕿ ⚐ **Location** 0.5m N on A330

....
Hotel ★★★★ 66% The Berystede, Bagshot Rd, Sunninghill, ASCOT ☎ 0870 400 8111 90 en suite

Swinley Forest Coronation Rd SL5 9LE

☎ 01344 874979 (Secretary) 📠 01344 874733
e-mail: swinleyfgc@aol.com

An attractive and immaculate course of heather and pine situated in the heart of Swinley Forest. The 17th is as good a short hole as will be found, with a bunkered plateau green, and the 12th hole is one of the most challenging par 4s.

18 holes, 6100yds, Par 69, SSS 70, Course record 62. Club membership 350.

Visitors on introduction of a member or by invitation only. **Societies** must contact in writing. **Green Fees** £100 per day. **Cards** 🔲 🔲 🔲 🔲 **Prof** Stuart Hill **Course Designer** Harry Colt **Facilities** ⊗ ᴸ 🍴 ♀ 🏌 ⌂ ᵀ 🏌 🛒 ⛳ **Leisure** Video studio. **Conf** Corporate Hospitality Days available **Location** 2m S of Ascot, off 4330

Hotel ★★★★ 66% The Berystede, Bagshot Rd, Sunninghill, ASCOT ☎ 0870 400 8111 90 en suite

---

BINFIELD   Map 04 SU87

Blue Mountain Golf Centre Wood Ln RG42 4EX

☎ 01344 300200 📠 01344 360960
e-mail: bluemountain@americangolf.uk.com

An 18-hole Pay and Play course with many testing holes with water hazards. Greens are large, undulating and strategically placed bunkers provide a fair challenge.

18 holes, 6097yds, Par 70, SSS 70, Course record 63. Club membership 400.

Visitors tee times bookable in advance by phoning 01344 300220, **Societies** must contact in advance. **Green Fees** not confirmed. **Cards** 🔲 🔲 🔲 🔲 🔲 🔲 **Prof** Iain Looms **Facilities** ⊗ 🕸 ᴸ 🍴 ♀ 🏌 ⌂ ᵀ 🏌 ⛳ ⌂ **Conf** fac available Corporate Hospitality Days available **Location** From M4 junct 10, take A329(M) signed Bracknell. 1st exit signed B3408 Binfield. Straight over roundabout and traffic lights to next roundabout. 2nd exit, first left into Wood Lane.

Hotel ★★★★ 72% Coppid Beech, John Nike Way, BRACKNELL ☎ 01344 303333 205 en suite

---

CHADDLEWORTH   Map 04 SU47

West Berkshire RG20 7DU

☎ 01488 638574 📠 01488 638781

Challenging and interesting downland course with views of the Berkshire Downs. The course is bordered by ancient woodland and golfers will find manicured fairways with well constructed greens and strategically placed hazards. The testing 627yd 5th hole is one of the longest par 5s in southern England. Bunkers are well placed from tees and around the greens to catch any wayward shots.

18 holes, 7001yds, Par 73, SSS 74. Club membership 650.

Visitors must contact in advance, may play weekends pm only. **Societies** telephone in advance. **Green Fees** £20 per round (£30 per round weekends & bank holidays - pm only). **Cards** 🔲 🔲 🔲 **Prof** Paul Simpson **Facilities** ⊗ ᴸ 🍴 ♀ 🏌 ⌂ 🛒 ⛳ ⌂ **Conf** Corporate Hospitality Days available **Location** 1m S of village off A338

Hotel ★★★ 65% The Chequers Hotel, 6-8 Oxford St, NEWBURY ☎ 01635 38000 46 en suite
11 annexe en suite

COOKHAM   Map 04 SU88

Winter Hill Grange Ln SL6 9RP

☎ 01628 527613 (Secretary) 📠 01628 527479

Parkland course set in a curve of the Thames with wonderful views across the river to Cliveden.

18 holes, 6408yds, Par 72, SSS 71, Course record 63. Club membership 770.

Visitors phone in advance, weekends after 12pm. **Societies** welcome Wed & Fri, telephone initially. **Green Fees** £31 per day. **Cards** 🔲 🔲 🔲 🔲 **Prof** Roger Frost **Course Designer** Charles Lawrie **Facilities** ⊗ ᴸ 🍴 ♀ 🏌 ⌂ 🛒 ⛳ **Conf** fac available Corporate Hospitality Days available **Location** 1m NW off B4447

Hotel ★★★★ 67% The Compleat Angler, Marlow Bridge, MARLOW ☎ 0870 400 8100 64 en suite

---

CROWTHORNE   Map 04 SU86

East Berkshire Ravenswood Ave RG45 6BD

☎ 01344 772041 📠 01344 777378
e-mail: thesecretary@eastberksgc.fsnet.co.uk

An attractive heathland course with an abundance of heather and pine trees. Walking is easy and the greens are exceptionally good. Some fairways become tight where the heather encroaches on the line of play. The course is testing and demands great accuracy.

18 holes, 6236yds, Par 69, SSS 70. Club membership 766.

Visitors must contact in advance and have a handicap certificate; must play with member at weekends & bank holidays. **Societies** telephone for availability. **Green Fees** £45 per day. **Prof** Jason Brant **Course Designer** P Paxton **Facilities** ⊗ ᴸ 🍴 ♀ 🏌 ⌂ ᵀ ⛳ **Location** W side of town centre off B3348

Hotel ★★★★★ Pennyhill Park Hotel & The Spa, London Rd, BAGSHOT ☎ 01276 471774 26 en suite
97 annexe en suite

DATCHET   Map 04 SU97

Datchet Buccleuch Rd SL3 9BP

☎ 01753 543887 & 541872 📠 01753 541872
e-mail: secretary@datchetgolfclub.co.uk

Meadowland course, easy walking.

9 holes, 6087yds, Par 70, SSS 69, Course record 63. Club membership 430.

Visitors may play weekdays. **Societies** Tue only. (Other times by prior arrangement). Mon-Fri. (Telephone in advance) **Green Fees** £20 per 18 holes. **Prof** Ian Godelman **Facilities** ⊗ 🕸 ᴸ 🍴 ♀ 🏌 ⌂ **Location** NW side of Datchet off B470

Continued

Hotel ★★★ 74% The Castle Hotel, 18 High St, WINDSOR ☎ 0870 400 8300 41 en suite 70 annexe en suite

MAIDENHEAD   Map 04 SU88

Bird Hills Drift Rd, Hawthorn Hill SL6 3ST
☎ 01628 771030 🖷 01628 631023
e-mail: info@birdhills.co.uk

A gently undulating course with easy walking and many water hazards. Some challenging holes are the par 5 6th dog-leg, par 39th surrounded by water and bunkers, and the 16th which is a long uphill par 4 and a two-tier green.

18 holes, 6176yds, Par 72, SSS 69, Course record 65. Club membership 400.
Visitors to book ring 7 days in advance, no 2 balls before noon weekends or bank holidays. **Societies** write or telephone in advance **Green Fees** seasonal charges - ring for details. **Cards** 🖸 🖸 🖸 🖸 🖸 **Prof** Nick Slimming **Facilities** ⊗ ℳ ℔ ⚑ ♀ ⚲ 🖿 ⛾ ♂ ℓ **Leisure** pool tables. **Conf** fac available Corporate Hospitality Days available **Location** 4m S of M4 junct 8/9 on A330

Hotel ★★★ 71% Stirrups Country House, Maidens Green, BRACKNELL ☎ 01344 882284 30 en suite

Maidenhead Shoppenhangers Rd SL6 2PZ
☎ 01628 624693 🖷 01628 624693

A pleasant parkland course with excellent greens and some challenging holes. The long par 4 4th and short par 3 13th are only two of the many outstanding aspects of this course.
18 holes, 6364yds, Par 70, SSS 70. Club membership 650.
Visitors may not play after noon on Fri or at weekends. Must contact in advance and have a handicap certificate. **Societies** must contact in writing. **Green Fees** not confirmed. **Cards** 🖸 **Prof** Steve Geary **Course Designer** Alex Simpson **Facilities** ⊗ ℳ ℔ ⚑ ♀ ⚲ 🖿 ⛾ ♂ **Conf** fac available **Location** S side of town centre off A308

Hotel ★★★★ Fredrick's Hotel, Shoppenhangers Rd, MAIDENHEAD ☎ 01628 581000 37 en suite

Temple Henley Rd, Hurley SL6 5LH
☎ 01628 824795 🖷 01628 828119
e-mail: templegolfclub@btconnect.com

An open parkland course offering extensive views over the Thames Valley. Firm, relatively fast greens, natural slopes and subtle contours provide a challenging test to golfers of all abilities. Excellent drainage assures play during inclement weather.

Continued

Temple Golf Club

18 holes, 5826yds, Par 69, SSS 68. Club membership 480.
Visitors must contact in advance, limited weekend access. **Societies** contact Secretary for details. **Green Fees** £50 per day; £40 per round (£60 per day, £50 per round weekends). **Cards** 🖸 🖸 🖸 **Prof** James Whiteley **Course Designer** Willie Park (Jnr) **Facilities** ⊗ ℔ ⚑ ♀ ⚲ 🖿 ⛾ ♂ **Conf** Corporate Hospitality Days available **Location** Exit M4 jct 8/9 take A404M then A4130,or M40 exit jct 4 take A404 then A4130, signposted Henley

Hotel ★★★★ 67% The Compleat Angler, Marlow Bridge, MARLOW ☎ 0870 400 8100 64 en suite

MORTIMER   Map 04 SU66

Wokefield Park Wokefield Park RG7 3AE
☎ 0118 9334018 🖷 0118 9334162

18 holes, 6577yds, Par 72, SSS 72, Course record 65.
Course Designer Jonathan Gaunt **Location** M4 junct 11, A33 towards Basingstoke. 1st rdbt, 3rd exit towards Grazeley and Mortimer. After 2.5m and sharp right bend club on right
Telephone for further details

Hotel ★★★ 72% Romans Country House Hotel, Little London Rd, SILCHESTER ☎ 0118 970 0421 11 en suite 14 annexe en suite

NEWBURY   Map 04 SU46

Donnington Valley Snelsmore House, Snelsmore Common RG14 3BG ☎ 01635 568140 🖷 01635 568141
e-mail: golf@donningtonvalley.co.uk

Undulating, testing course with mature trees and elevated greens, some protected by water.

18 holes, 6353yds, Par 71, SSS 71, Course record 71. Club membership 520.

Continued

Visitors booking system up to 7 days in advance, members have priority weekends. **Societies** write or telephone in advance. **Green Fees** not confirmed. **Cards** 🔲 🔲 🔲 **Prof** Martin Balfour **Course Designer** Mike Smith **Facilities** ⊗ ⅷ ⅃ ♥ ♀ ♨ 🏠 ↑ 🏴 ↘ 🚵 ✆ **Conf** fac available **Location** 2m N of Newbury

....

Hotel ★★★★ 76% Donnington Valley Hotel & Golf Course, Old Oxford Rd, Donnington, NEWBURY ☎ 01635 551199 58 en suite

Newbury & Crookham Bury's Bank Rd,

Greenham RG19 8BZ ☎ 01635 40035 📠 01635 40045 e-mail: steve.myers@newburygolf.co.uk

A well laid out, attractive course running mostly through woodland, and giving more of a challenge than its length suggests.

18 holes, 5949yds, Par 69, SSS 68, Course record 63. Club membership 800.

Visitors must play with member on weekends & bank holidays. Handicap certificate required. **Societies** must contact in advance. **Green Fees** £38 per day; £35 per round. **Cards** 🔲 🔲 🔲 **Prof** David Harris **Course Designer** J H Turner **Facilities** ⊗ ⅷ ⅃ ♥ ♀ ♨ 🏠 ✆ **Conf** Corporate Hospitality Days available **Location** 2m SE off A34

....

Hotel ★★★ 65% The Chequers Hotel, 6-8 Oxford St, NEWBURY ☎ 01635 38000 46 en suite 11 annexe en suite

READING   Map 04 SU77

Calcot Park Bath Rd, Calcot RG31 7RN

☎ 0118 942 7124 📠 0118 945 3373 e-mail: info@calcotpark.com

A delightfully sporting, slightly undulating parkland course just outside the town. Hazards include streams, a lake and many trees. The 6th is a 503-yard par 5, with the tee-shot hit downhill over cross-bunkers to a well-guarded green; the 7th (156 yards) is played over the lake to an elevated green and the 13th (also 156 yards) requires a carry across a valley to a plateau green.

18 holes, 6216yds, Par 70, SSS 70, Course record 63. Club membership 730.

Visitors must have handicap certificate or letter of introduction from club. May play weekdays only, excluding bank holidays. **Societies** must apply in writing. **Green Fees** £40 per day/round. **Prof** Ian Campbell **Course Designer** H S Colt **Facilities** ⊗ ⅷ ⅃ ♥ ♀ ♨ 🏠 ✆ **Leisure** fishing. **Conf** Corporate Hospitality Days available **Location** 1.5m from M4 junct 12 on A4 towards Reading

....

Hotel ★★★ 75% The Copper Inn Hotel & Restaurant, PANGBOURNE ☎ 0118 984 2244 14 en suite 8 annexe en suite

Hennerton Crazies Hill Rd, Wargrave RG10 8LT

☎ 0118 940 1000 📠 0118 940 1042

Overlooking the Thames Valley, this par 68 course has many existing natural features and a good number of hazards such as bunkers, mature trees and two small lakes. The most memorable hole is probably the 7th which is a par 3, 183 yards crossing a sharp valley to the green from which there are spectacular views of the course.

9 holes, 5460yds, Par 68, SSS 67, Course record 62. Club membership 450.

Visitors book 48 hours in advance, play weekends after 10am. **Societies** telephone or write for information. **Green Fees** £20 per 18 holes; £14 per 9 holes (£25/£16 weekends and bank holidays). **Cards** 🔲 🔲 🔲 🔲 💳 **Prof** William Farrow **Course Designer** Col D Beard **Facilities** ⊗ ⅃ ♥ ♀ ♨ 🏠 ✆ ⚑ **Location** Follow signs from A321 Wargrave High Street

....

Hotel ★★★ 71% Red Lion Hotel, Hart St, HENLEY-ON-THAMES ☎ 01491 572161 26 en suite

Mapledurham Chazey Heath, Mapledurham

RG4 7UD ☎ 0118 946 3353 📠 0118 946 3363

18-hole course designed by Bob Sandow. Flanked by hedgerows and mature woods, it is testing for players of all levels.

Mapledurham Golf & Health Club: 18 holes, 5635yds, Par 69, SSS 68, Course record 66. Club membership 1000.

Visitors advanced booking required. No play before noon 2pm at weekends. **Societies** must contact in advance. **Green Fees** £19 (£25 weekends). **Cards** 🔲 🔲 🔲 🔲 💳 **Prof** David Boyce **Course Designer** Robert Sandow **Facilities** ⊗ ⅷ ⅃ ♥ ♀ ♨ 🏠 ↘ ✆ ⚑ **Leisure** heated indoor swimming pool, sauna, solarium, gymnasium. **Conf** Corporate Hospitality Days available **Location** On A4074 to Oxford

....

Hotel ★★★ 78% The French Horn, SONNING ON THAMES ☎ 0118 969 2204 13 en suite 8 annexe en suite

Reading 17 Kidmore End Rd, Emmer Green RG4 8SG

☎ 0118 947 2909 (Secretary) 📠 0118 946 4468 e-mail: secretary@readinggolfclub.com

Pleasant tree-lined parkland course, part hilly and part flat with interesting views and several challenging par 3s. After the opening holes the course moves across the valley. The par 4 5th is played from an elevated tee and although relatively short, the well-placed bunkers and trees come into play. The 470yd par 4 12th is a great hole. It has a slight dog-leg and requires an accurate second shot to hit a well-guarded green. The finishing hole requires two great shots to have any chance of reaching par.

18 holes, 6212yds, Par 70, SSS 70, Course record 65. Club membership 600.

Visitors contact the professional. Welcome weekdays, with member only Fri & weekends. **Societies** apply by telephone, Tues-Thu only. **Green Fees** £48 per day, £30 per round. **Cards** 🔲 🔲 🔲 🔲 💳 **Prof** Scott Fotheringham **Course Designer** James Braid **Facilities** ⊗ ⅷ ⅃ ♥ ♀ ♨ 🏠 ✆ **Leisure** indoor nets. **Location** 2m N off B481

....

Hotel ★★★ 78% The French Horn, SONNING ON THAMES ☎ 0118 969 2204 13 en suite 8 annexe en suite

SINDLESHAM   Map 04 SU76

Bearwood Mole Rd RG41 5DB ☎ 0118 976 0060

e-mail: barrytustin@bearwoodgolf.fsnet.co.uk

Flat parkland course with one water hazard, the 40-acre lake which features on the challenging 6th and 7th holes. Also driving range.

9 holes, 5610yds, Par 70, SSS 68, Course record 66. Club membership 500.

Visitors welcome weekdays and weekend afternoons (contact in advance for pm weekend bookings) **Societies** apply in writing. **Green Fees** terms on application. **Cards**

Continued

Continued

Sunningdale

Map 04 SU96

Sunningdale

☎ **01344 621681** 📄 **01344 6241154**

The Old Course, founded in 1900, was designed by Willie Park. It is a classic course at just 6308 yards long, with gorse and pine trees, silver birch, heather and immaculate turf. The New Course is no less a challenge, created by HS Holt in 1922 at 6443 yards. There is a long wait for anyone wishing to become a member of this prestigious club; its location within easy reach of London is an attraction in itself. Visitors playing two rounds will be asked to alternate onto the other course in the afternoon. Short rounds may be played by finishing at the 10th or 13th green on the Old Course, and the 10th or 11th green on the New Course. On Monday one course is designated the two ball course until 3.00pm; check when booking a tee time.

Visitors May not play Fri, Sat, Sun or public holidays. Must contact in advance, and have a handicap certificate and letter of introduction

Societies Tue, Wed, Thu by arrangement

Green Fees Old Course £135 per round; 36 holes £175 New course £105

Facilities ⊗ 🏌 🍺 🖤 ♀ 🏖 🎏 🍴 🏌

Professional Keith Maxwell

Location Ridgemount Rd, Sunningdale, Ascot SL5 9RR (1m S of Sunningdale, off A30)

Holes/Par/Course record 36 holes.
Old Course: 18 holes, 6308 yds, Par 70, SSS 70
New Course: 18 holes, 6443 yds, Par 71, SSS 72

WHERE TO STAY AND EAT NEARBY

Hotels
ASCOT

★★★★🏵 70% The Royal Berkshire
Rauada Plaza, SL5 OPP.
☎ 01344 623322. 63 en suite

★★★★🏵 66% The Berystede, SLS 9JH.
☎ 0870 400 8111.
90 en suite

★★69% Highclere, 19 Kings Rd,
Sunninghill. ☎ 01344 625220. 11en suite

BAGSHOT

★★★★★★🏵 🏵 🏵
Pennyhill Park,
GU19 5EU. ☎ 01276 471774.
26 en suite 97 annexe en suite

Restaurants
BRAY

🏵 🏵 🏵 🏵 🏵 Fat Duck,
High Street.
☎ 01628 580333.

🏵 🏵 🏵 🏵 Waterside Inn, Ferry Rd.
☎ 01628 620691.

🏵 🏵 Riverside Brasserie (Bray Marina).
SL6 2EB
☎ 01628 780553.

Championship Course

🔲 🔲 🔲 🔲 🔲 **Prof** Barry Tustin **Course Designer**
Barry Tustin **Facilities** ⊗ 🔲 🔲 🔲 🔲 🔲 🔲 🔲 🔲
Location 1m SW on B3030

Hotel ★★★ 65% Edward Court Hotel, Wellington Rd,
WOKINGHAM ☎ 0118 977 5886 27 en suite

SONNING   Map 04 SU77

Sonning Duffield Rd RG4 6GJ
☎ 0118 969 3332 🖨 0118 944 8409
e-mail: secretary@sonning-golf-club.co.uk
**A quality parkland course and the scene of many
county championships. Wide fairways, not over-
bunkered, and very good greens. Holes of changing
character through wooded belts.**
18 holes, 6366yds, Par 70, SSS 70, Course record 65.
Club membership 750.
Visitors weekdays only. Handicap certificate or proof of
membership of another club required. **Societies** must apply
in writing. Wed only, min 16. **Green Fees** £40.50 before
10.30am or £30.50 after 10.30am. **Prof** R McDougall
Course Designer Hawtree **Facilities** ⊗ 🔲 🔲 🔲 🔲 🔲 🔲
🔲 **Conf** fac available Corporate Hospitality Days
available **Location** 1m S off A4

Hotel ★★★ 78% The French Horn, SONNING ON
THAMES ☎ 0118 969 2204 13 en suite 8 annexe en suite

STREATLEY   Map 04 SU58

Goring & Streatley RG8 9QA
☎ 01491 873229 🖨 01491 875224
e-mail: secretary@goringgc.org
**A parkland/moorland course that requires
'negotiating'. Four well-known first holes lead up to the
heights of the 5th tee, to which there is a 300ft climb.
Wide fairways, not over-bunkered, with nice rewards
on the way home down the last few holes. A delightful
course that commands magnificent views of the
Ridgeway and the River Thames.**
18 holes, 6355yds, Par 71, SSS 70, Course record 65.
Club membership 740.
Visitors must contact in advance, with member only at
weekends. Handicap certificate required. **Societies**
telephone in advance. **Green Fees** telephone for details.
Cards 🔲 🔲 🔲 🔲 🔲 **Prof** Jason Hadland **Course Designer**
Tom Morris **Facilities** ⊗ 🔲 🔲 🔲 🔲 🔲 🔲 🔲 **Location** N
of village off A417

Hotel ★★★★ 69% The Swan at Streatley, High St,
Streatley on Thames, STREATLEY ☎ 01491 878800
46 en suite

SUNNINGDALE   See page 25

SUNNINGDALE   Map 04 SU96

Sunningdale Ladies Cross Rd SL5 9RX
☎ 01344 620507
e-mail: ladiesgolf@lineone.net
**A short 18-hole course with a typical Surrey heathland
layout. A very tight course, making for a challenging
game.**
18 holes, 3616yds, Par 60, SSS 60, Course record 51.
Club membership 400.

Continued

Finchampstead Rd
Wokingham RG40 3RQ
Telephone: 0118 9792711   Fax 0118 9770282
email: info@sandmartins.com

A Golf Jewel in the Heart of Berkshire

Sand Martins offers a challenging 6,212 yard par
70 course, maintained to the very highest
standards. The course comprises two contrasting
nines; the front nine is set in parkland with lakes
and water hazards, the back nine is designed in
a stunning links style with an abundance of sand
banks and broom. The Club is proud of its
clubhouse catering and excellent half way house.

Visitors telephone in advance. **Societies** apply in writing
or by telephone. **Green Fees** not confirmed. **Facilities** ⊗
🔲 🔲 🔲 🔲 🔲 **Leisure** Practice net. **Location** 1m S off
A30

Hotel ★★★★ 66% The Berystede, Bagshot Rd,
Sunninghill, ASCOT ☎ 0870 400 8111 90 en suite

WOKINGHAM   Map 04 SU86

Downshire Wayne Owers RG40 3DH
☎ 01344 302030 🖨 01344 301020
e-mail: paul.stanwick@bracknell-forest.gov.uk
**Beautiful municipal parkland course with mature trees.
Water hazards come into play on the 14th and 18th
holes, and especially on the short 7th, a testing downhill
169 yards over the lake. Pleasant easy walking.
Challenging holes: 7th (par 4), 15th (par 4), 16th
(par 3).**
18 holes, 6416yds, Par 73, SSS 71.
Club membership 1000.
Visitors must book up to 10 days in advance. **Societies**
must telephone in advance. **Green Fees** not confirmed.
Cards 🔲 🔲 🔲 🔲 🔲 **Prof** Wayne Owers **Facilities** ⊗
🔲 🔲 🔲 🔲 🔲 🔲 🔲 🔲 **Leisure** 9 hole pitch & putt.
Location 3m SW of Bracknell, M4 junct 10 follow signs
for Crowthorne

Hotel ★★★★ 72% Coppid Beech, John Nike Way,
BRACKNELL ☎ 01344 303333 205 en suite

Booking a tee time is always advisable.

Sand Martins Finchampstead Rd RG40 3RQ
☎ 0118 9792711 🖹 0118 977 0282
e-mail: info@sandmartins.com
Two different 9-hole loops: the front nine is mostly tree-lined with ponds and the back nine is similar to a links course.

18 holes, 6212yds, Par 70, SSS 70, Course record 65. Club membership 800.
Visitors must telephone in advance. With member only at weekends. **Societies** prior arrangement by telephone. **Green Fees** terms on application. **Cards** 💳 ▦ ▨ 💳 🔳 🔲 **Prof** Andrew Hall **Course Designer** Edward Fox **Facilities** ⊗ ⋔ ⅃ 🖪 ⬤ ♀ △ 🖼 🚜 🍴 ⋔ **Conf** fac available **Location** 1m S of Wokingham

Hotel ★★★ 65% Edward Court Hotel, Wellington Rd, WOKINGHAM ☎ 0118 977 5886 27 en suite

---

BRISTOL

BRISTOL   Map 03 ST57

Bristol and Clifton Beggar Bush Ln, Failand
BS8 3TH ☎ 01275 393474 🖹 01275 394611
e-mail: mansec@bristolgolf.co.uk
A downland course with splendid turf and fine tree-lined fairways. The 222-yard (par 3) 13th with the green well below, and the par 4 16th, with its second shot across an old quarry, are outstanding. There are splendid views over the Bristol Channel towards Wales.
18 holes, 6316yds, Par 70, SSS 70, Course record 63. Club membership 850.
Visitors must have a handicap certificate. Weekends restricted. **Societies** telephone to enquire. **Green Fees** £38 per day (£45 weekends). **Cards** 💳 ▦ 🔳 **Prof** Paul Mitchell **Facilities** ⊗ ⋔ ⅃ 🖪 ⬤ ♀ △ 🖼 🍴 🏹 ⋔ **Leisure** chipping green, practice bunkers. **Conf** fac available Corporate Hospitality Days available **Location** M5 junct19, follow A369 for 4m, then take B3129. Club 1m on right

Hotel ★★★ 67% Redwood Lodge Hotel & Country Club, Beggar Bush Ln, Failand, BRISTOL ☎ 0870 609 6144 112 en suite

Filton Golf Course Ln, Filton BS34 7QS
☎ 0117 969 4169 🖹 0117 931 4359
e-mail: thesecretary@filtongolfclub.co.uk
Challenging parkland course situated on high ground in a pleasant suburb to the north of the city. Extensive views can be enjoyed from the course, especially from the second tee and the clubhouse, where on a clear day the Cotswold Hills and the Brecon Beacons can be seen.
Continued

18 holes, 6173yds, Par 70, SSS 70, Course record 61. Club membership 750.
Visitors advisable to contact in advance for availability, may not play at weekends unless with member. Must have a handicap certificate. **Societies** apply in writing/phone for details. **Green Fees** £27 per day; £22 per round. **Cards** 💳 ▦ 🔲 **Prof** D Robinson **Facilities** ⊗ ⋔ ⅃ 🖪 ⬤ ♀ △ 🖼 🍴 **Conf** Corporate Hospitality Days available **Location** 5m NW off A38

Hotel Ⓤ Holiday Inn Bristol Filton, Filton Rd, Hambrook, BRISTOL ☎ 0870 400 9014 198 en suite

---

Henbury Henbury Hill, Westbury-on-Trym BS10 7QB
☎ 0117 950 0044 & 950 2121 (Prof) 🖹 0117 959 1928
e-mail: thesecretary@henburygolfclub.co.uk
18 holes, 6007yds, Par 69, SSS 70, Course record 65.
Location 3m NW of city centre on B4055 off A4018
Telephone for further details

Hotel ★★★ 67% Henbury Lodge Hotel, Station Rd, Henbury, BRISTOL ☎ 0117 950 2615 12 en suite 9 annexe en suite

---

Knowle West Town Ln, Brislington BS4 5DF
☎ 0117 977 0660 🖹 0117 972 0615
A parkland course with nice turf. The first five holes climb up and down hill but the remainder are on a more even plane.
18 holes, 6006yds, Par 69, SSS 69, Course record 61. Club membership 700.
Visitors must have handicap certificate, must telephone professional 0117 977 9193 for weekends. **Societies** Thu only, apply in writing or telephone. **Green Fees** £35 per day, £28 per round (£40/£33 weekends). **Prof** Robert Hayward **Course Designer** Hawtree/J H Taylor **Facilities** ⊗ ⋔ ⅃ 🖪 ⬤ ♀ △ 🖼 🍴 🚜 **Location** 3m SE of city centre off A37

Hotel ★★★ ♨ 79% Hunstrete House Hotel, HUNSTRETE ☎ 01761 490490 25 en suite

---

Mangotsfield Carsons Rd, Mangotsfield BS17 3LW
☎ 0117 956 5501
18 holes, 5337yds, Par 68, SSS 66, Course record 61.
Course Designer John Day **Location** 6m NE of city centre off B4465
Telephone for further details

Hotel Ⓤ Holiday Inn Bristol Filton, Filton Rd, Hambrook, BRISTOL ☎ 0870 400 9014 198 en suite

Shirehampton Park Park Hill, Shirehampton
BS11 0UL ☎ 0117 982 2083 🖹 0117 982 5280
e-mail: info@shirehamptonparkgolfclub.co.uk
A lovely parkland course with views across the Avon Gorge.
18 holes, 5430yds, Par 67, SSS 66, Course record 63. Club membership 600.
Visitors with member only at weekends. Must have a handicap certificate. **Societies** weekdays (book through Secretary) **Green Fees** telephone for details. **Cards** 💳 ▦ ▨ 🔳 **Prof** Brent Ellis **Facilities** ⊗ ⋔ ⅃ 🖪 ⬤ ♀ △ 🖼 🍴 **Location** 2m E of junct 18 M5 on B4054

Continued

Hotel ★★★ 67% Redwood Lodge Hotel & Country Club, Beggar Bush Ln, Failand, BRISTOL ☎ 0870 609 6144 112 en suite

Woodlands Trench Ln, Almondsbury BS32 4JZ
☎ 01454 619319 🖹 01454 619397
e-mail: info@woodlands-golf.com
Situated on the edge of the Severn Valley, bordered by Hortham Brook and Shepherds Wood, this interesting parkland course features five testing par 3s set around the course's five lakes, notably the 206 yd 5th hole which extends over water.
18 holes, 6068yds, Par 70, SSS 69.
Club membership 45.
Visitors no restrictions. Societies Phone or write in advance. Green Fees £13 per round (£15 weekends & bank holidays). Cards 🖼 🖼 ⛿ Prof L Riddiford Facilities ⊗ 🏵 🎿 💁 ♀ 🎿 🏠 ⛳ 🦽 ⛳ Leisure fishing. Conf fac available Corporate Hospitality Days available Location M5 junct 16 left onto A38 towards Bradley Store

Hotel 🅤 Holiday Inn Bristol Filton, Filton Rd, Hambrook, BRISTOL ☎ 0870 400 9014 198 en suite

BUCKINGHAMSHIRE

AYLESBURY   Map 04 SP81

Aylesbury Golf Centre Hulcott Ln, Bierton HP22 5GA ☎ 01296 393644
A parkland course with magnificent views to the Chiltern Hills. A good test of golf with out of bounds coming into play on nine of the holes, plus a number of water hazards and bunkers.
18 holes, 5965yds, Par 71, SSS 69.
Club membership 200.
Visitors no restrictions, but booking advisable. Societies telephone for details. Green Fees not confirmed. Cards 🖼 🖼 Prof Richard Wooster Course Designer T S Benwell Facilities ⊗ 🏵 🎿 💁 ♀ 🎿 🏠 ⛳ 🦽 ⛳ Location 1m N of Aylesbury on A418

Hotel 🅤 Holiday Inn Aylesbury, Aston Clinton Rd, AYLESBURY ☎ 0870 400 9002 140 en suite

Aylesbury Park Andrews Way, Off Coldharbour Way, Oxford Rd HP17 8QQ
☎ 01296 399196 🖹 01296 336830
Parkland course with mature trees, located just south-west of Aylesbury.
18 holes, 6148yds, Par 70, SSS 69, Course record 65.
Club membership 360.
Visitors may book up to 1 week in advance. Societies telephone for Society Pack Green Fees £16 (£21 weekends). Cards 🖼 🖼 🖼 🖼 🖼 ⛿ Course Designer M Hawtree Facilities ⊗ 🏵 🎿 💁 ♀ 🎿 🏠 ⛳ 🦽 ⛳ Leisure new 9 hole par 3 course. Location 0.5m SW of Aylesbury, on the A418

Hotel 🅤 Holiday Inn Aylesbury, Aston Clinton Rd, AYLESBURY ☎ 0870 400 9002 140 en suite

Chiltern Forest Aston Hill, Halton HP22 5NQ
☎ 01296 631267 🖹 01296 632709
e-mail: secretary@chilternforest.co.uk
This very hilly wooded parkland course is on two levels. It is a true test of skill to the low handicap golfer, as

well as being a fair challenge to higher handicap golfers. The surrounding woodland makes the course very scenic.
18 holes, 5765yds, Par 70, SSS 69, Course record 65.
Club membership 650.
Visitors welcome weekdays, must play with member at weekends. Societies telephone in advance. Green Fees £35 per day, £30 per round. Cards 🖼 🖼 🖼 🖼 ⛿ Prof A Lavers Facilities ⊗ 🏵 🎿 💁 ♀ 🎿 🏠 ⛳ 🦽 ⛳ Location off A41 between Tring and Wendover

Hotel 🅤 Holiday Inn Aylesbury, Aston Clinton Rd, AYLESBURY ☎ 0870 400 9002 140 en suite

Ellesborough Butlers Cross HP17 0TZ
☎ 01296 622114 🖹 01296 622114
18 holes, 6360yds, Par 71, SSS 71, Course record 64.
Course Designer James Braid Location 1m E of Ellesborough on B4010
Telephone for further details

Hotel 🅤 Holiday Inn Aylesbury, Aston Clinton Rd, AYLESBURY ☎ 0870 400 9002 140 en suite

BEACONSFIELD   Map 04 SU99

Beaconsfield Seer Green HP9 2UR
☎ 01494 676545 🖹 01494 681148
e-mail: secretary@beaconsfieldgolfclub.co.uk
An interesting and, at times, testing tree-lined and parkland course which frequently plays longer than appears on the card! Each hole differs to a considerable degree and here lies the charm. Walking is easy, except perhaps to the 6th and 8th. Well bunkered.
18 holes, 6493yds, Par 72, SSS 71, Course record 63.
Club membership 850.
Visitors must contact in advance and have a handicap certificate. May not play weekends. Societies phone for details Green Fees £50 per day; £36 per round (with member only at weekend & bank holidays). Prof Michael Brothers Course Designer H S Colt Facilities ⊗ 🎿 💁 ♀ 🎿 🏠 ⛳ 🦽 ⛳ Conf Corporate Hospitality Days available Location Exit M40 junct 2, adjacent to Seer Green railway station

Hotel ★★★★ 68% De Vere Bellhouse, Oxford Rd, BEACONSFIELD ☎ 01753 887211 136 en suite

BLETCHLEY   Map 04 SP83

Windmill Hill Tattenhoe Ln MK3 7RB
☎ 01908 631113 & 366457 (Sec) 🖹 01908 630034
Long, open-parkland course, the first championship course designed by Henry Cotton, opened in 1972. Proprietary Pay & Play. No winter greens.

Continued
Continued

Windmill Hill Golf Course
18 holes, 6720yds, Par 73, SSS 72, Course record 68.
Club membership 400.
Visitors booking system in operation up to 7 days in advance. **Societies** packages available, contact for details. **Green Fees** £11.50 (£16 weekends). **Cards** ⬚ ⬚ ⬚ ⬚ 🅿 **Prof** Colin Clingan **Course Designer** Henry Cotton **Facilities** ⊗ 𝕏 ╟ ⬚ ⚲ ☖ ⛳ ⚐ 🚜 ⚘ ⛏ **Leisure** pool table. **Conf** fac available Corporate Hospitality Days available **Location** W side of town centre on A421

Hotel 🅄 Holiday Inn Milton Keynes, 500 Saxon Gate West, MILTON KEYNES ☎ 0870 400 9057 157 en suite

BUCKINGHAM   Map 04 SP63

Buckingham Tingewick Rd MK18 4AE
☎ 01280 815566 ▤ 01280 821812
Undulating parkland course with a stream and river affecting 8 holes.
18 holes, 6082yds, Par 70, SSS 69, Course record 67.
Club membership 690.
Visitors welcome Mon-Fri, with member only at weekends. **Societies** by prior arrangement. **Green Fees** telephone for details. **Prof** Greg Hannah **Facilities** ⊗ 𝕏 ╟ ⬚ ⚲ ☖ ⛳ ⚐ ⚘ **Leisure** snooker room. **Location** 1.5m W on A421

Hotel ★★★ 66% Buckingham Beales Best Western Hotel, Buckingham Ring Rd, BUCKINGHAM ☎ 01280 822622 70 en suite

BURNHAM   Map 04 SU98

Burnham Beeches Green Ln SL1 8EG
☎ 01628 661448 ▤ 01628 668968
e-mail: enquiries@bbgc.co.uk
A wooded parkland course on the edge of the historic Burnham Beeches Forest with a good variety of holes.
18 holes, 6449yds, Par 70, SSS 71, Course record 66.
Club membership 670.
Visitors must contact in advance. May play only play weekends as guest of member. Handicap certificate required. **Societies** welcome Apr-Oct, write or telephone for information. **Green Fees** £40 per round. **Prof** Ronnie Bolton **Facilities** ⊗ 𝕏 ╟ ⬚ ⚲ ☖ ⛳ ⚐ 🚜 ⚘ **Location** 0.5m NE of Burnham

Hotel ★★★ 64% Burnham Beeches Hotel, Grove Rd, BURNHAM ☎ 0870 609 6124 82 en suite

Lambourne Dropmore Rd SL1 8NF
☎ 01628 666755 ▤ 01628 663301
A championship standard 18-hole parkland course. Undulating terrain with many trees and several lakes,
Continued

notably on the tricky 7th hole which has a tightly guarded green reached via a shot over a lake. Seven par 4s over 400yds with six picturesque lakes, excellent drainage and full irrigation.
18 holes, 6771yds, Par 72, SSS 73, Course record 67.
Club membership 650.
Visitors must contact in advance & have a handicap certificate. May not play at weekends. **Societies** subject to prior application **Green Fees** £60 per round (weekdays). **Cards** ⬚ ⬚ ⬚ ⬚ ⬚ 🅿 **Prof** David Hart **Course Designer** Donald Steel **Facilities** ⊗ 𝕏 ╟ ⬚ ⚲ ☖ ⛳ ⚐ 🚜 ⚘ ⛏ **Leisure** sauna. **Location** Access via M4 junct 7 towards Burnham or M40 junct 2 towards Slough/Burnham

Hotel ★★★ 64% Burnham Beeches Hotel, Grove Rd, BURNHAM ☎ 0870 609 6124 82 en suite

CHALFONT ST GILES   Map 04 SU99

Harewood Downs Cokes Ln HP8 4TA
☎ 01494 762184 ▤ 01494 766869
e-mail: secretary@hdgc.co.uk
A testing undulating parkland course with sloping greens and plenty of trees.
18 holes, 5958yds, Par 69, SSS 69, Course record 64.
Club membership 600.
Visitors must contact in advance. **Societies** apply in writing or telephone. **Green Fees** £33 per round (/£38 weekends). **Prof** G C Morris **Facilities** ⊗ 𝕏 ╟ ⬚ ⚲ ☖ ⛳ ⚐ 🚜 ⚘ **Conf** Corporate Hospitality Days available **Location** 2m E of Amersham on A413

Hotel ★★★★ 68% De Vere Bellhouse, Oxford Rd, BEACONSFIELD ☎ 01753 887211 136 en suite

Oakland Park Threehouseholds HP8 4LW
☎ 01494 871277 & 877333 (pro) ▤ 01494 874692
e-mail: info@oaklandparkgolf.co.uk
Parkland with mature trees, hedgerows and water features, designed to respect the natural features of the land and lakes whilst providing a good challenge for players at all levels.
18 holes, 5246yds, Par 67, SSS 66.
Club membership 750.
Visitors weekdays only unless with a member. Advisable to contact in advance. **Societies** Mon, Wed & Fri. Must apply in writing. **Green Fees** £25. **Cards** ⬚ ⬚ ⬚ ⬚ ⬚ 🅿 **Prof** Allistair Thatcher **Course Designer** Johnathan Gaunt **Facilities** ⊗ 𝕏 ╟ ⬚ ⚲ ☖ ⛳ ⚐ 🚜 ⚘ ⛏ **Location** 3m N of M40 junct 3

Hotel ★★★★ 68% De Vere Bellhouse, Oxford Rd, BEACONSFIELD ☎ 01753 887211 136 en suite

CHARTRIDGE   Map 04 SP90

Chartridge Park HP5 2TF ☎ 01494 791772
e-mail: petergibbins@tinyworld.co.uk
A family run, easy walking parkland course set high in the beautiful Chiltern Hills, affording breathtaking views.
18 holes, 5516yds, Par 69, SSS 67, Course record 65.
Club membership 700.
Visitors may not play before 10.30am weekends. **Societies** must telephone in advance. **Green Fees** telephone for details. **Cards** ⬚ ⬚ ⬚ ⬚ ⬚ ⬚ 🅿 **Prof** Peter Gibbins **Course Designer** John Jacobs **Facilities** ⊗ 𝕏 ╟ ⬚ ⚲ ☖ ⛳ ⚐ ⚘ **Location** 3m NW of Chesham

Hotel ★★★ 69% The Crown, High St, AMERSHAM ☎ 0870 400 8103 19 en suite 18 annexe en suite

CHESHAM   Map 04 SP90

Chesham & Ley Hill Ley Hill Common HP5 1UZ
☎ 01494 784541 📠 01494 785506
e-mail: the.secretary@clhgolfclub.co.uk
Wooded parkland course on hilltop with easy walking.
9 holes, 5296yds, Par 66, SSS 65, Course record 62.
Club membership 400.
Visitors may play Mon & Thu all day, Wed after noon, Fri
up to 4pm. **Societies** subject to approval, Thu & Fri only.
Green Fees £15 weekdays. **Facilities** ⊗ ⊪ ⅃ 🖤 ♀ ⚐
Leisure practice net. **Conf** fac available **Location** 2m E of
Chesham, off A41 on B4504 to Ley Hill.

Hotel ★★★ 69% The Crown, High St, AMERSHAM
☎ 0870 400 8103 19 en suite 18 annexe en suite

DAGNALL   Map 04 SP91

Whipsnade Park Studham Ln HP4 1RH
☎ 01442 842330 📠 01442 842090
e-mail: whipsnadeparkgolfc@btopenworld.com
Parkland course situated on downs overlooking the
Chilterns adjoining Whipsnade Zoo. Easy walking,
good views.
18 holes, 6800yds, Par 73, SSS 72, Course record 66.
Club membership 600.
Visitors welcome weekdays, with member only at
weekends. Must contact in advance. **Societies** by prior
arrangement. **Green Fees** £40 per day; £29 per round.
Cards 🖭 🖭 🖭 **Prof** Darren Turner **Facilities** ⊗ ⊪ ⅃ 🖤
♀ ⚐ 🏠 ⚐ ⚐ ⚒ ⚐ **Location** 1m E off B4506 between
villages of Dagnall & Studham

Hotel ★★★ 65% Hanover International Hotel, Church St,
DUNSTABLE ☎ 01582 662201 68 en suite

DENHAM   Map 04 TQ08

Buckinghamshire Denham Court Dr UB9 5BG
☎ 01895 835777 📠 01895 835210
e-mail: enquiries@buckinghamshiregc.co.uk
A John Jacobs designed championship-standard course.
Visitors only welcome as guests of members to this
beautiful course in 269 acres of lovely grounds
including mature trees, five lakes and two rivers. The
testing 7th hole requires a 185yd carry over a stream,
followed by a second shot over a river to a green
guarded by a lake.
18 holes, 6880yds, Par 72, SSS 73, Course record 70.
Club membership 600.
Visitors contact 48 hours in advance, subject to
availability. **Societies** must contact in advance. **Green Fees**
£80 per 18 holes (£90 weekends). **Cards** 🖭 🖭
🖭 **Prof** John O'Leary **Course Designer** John Jacobs
Facilities ⊗ ⊪ ⅃ 🖤 ♀ ⚐ 🏠 ⚐ ⚒ **Conf** fac available
Corporate Hospitality Days available **Location** M25 junct
16 signposted Uxbridge

Hotel ★★★★ 68% De Vere Bellhouse, Oxford Rd,
BEACONSFIELD ☎ 01753 887211 136 en suite

Denham Tilehouse Ln UB9 5DE
☎ 01895 832022 📠 01895 835340
e-mail: club.secretary@denhamgolfclub.co.uk
A beautifully maintained parkland/heathland course,
home of many county champions. Slightly hilly and
calling for good judgement of distance in the wooded
areas.
Continued

18 holes, 6462yds, Par 70, SSS 71, Course record 66.
Club membership 790.
Visitors must contact in advance & have handicap
certificate. Must play with member Fri-Sun. **Societies** Tue-
Thu. Must book in advance. **Green Fees** not confirmed.
Prof Stuart Campbell **Course Designer** H S Colt **Facilities**
⊗ ⊪ ⅃ 🖤 ♀ ⚐ 🏠 ⚐ ⚐ ⚐ **Conf** Corporate Hospitality
Days available **Location** 0.5m N of North Orbital Road,
2m from Uxbridge

Hotel ★★★★ 68% De Vere Bellhouse, Oxford Rd,
BEACONSFIELD ☎ 01753 887211 136 en suite

FLACKWELL HEATH   Map 04 SU89

Flackwell Heath Treadaway Rd, High Wycombe
HP10 9PE ☎ 01628 520929 📠 01628 530040
e-mail: secretary@flackwellheathgolfclub.co.uk
Open sloping heath and tree-lined course on hills
overlooking the Chilterns. Some good challenging par
3s and several testing small greens.
18 holes, 6211yds, Par 71, SSS 70, Course record 63.
Club membership 700.
Visitors with member only at weekends. Must contact in
advance and hold a handicap certificate. **Societies** Wed &
Thu only, by prior booking. **Green Fees** not confirmed.
Prof Paul Watson **Course Designer** J H Taylor **Facilities**
⊗ ⊪ ⅃ 🖤 ♀ ⚐ 🏠 ⚐ **Conf** Corporate Hospitality
Days available **Location** E side of High Wycombe, NE side
of town centre

Hotel ★★★★ 68% De Vere Bellhouse, Oxford Rd,
BEACONSFIELD ☎ 01753 887211 136 en suite

GERRARDS CROSS   Map 04 TQ08

Gerrards Cross Chalfont Park SL9 0QA
☎ 01753 883263 (Sec) & 885300 (Pro) 📠 01753 883593
e-mail: secretary@gxgolf.co.uk
A wooded parkland course which has been modernised
in recent years and is now a very pleasant circuit with
infinite variety. The best part lies on the plateau above
the clubhouse where there are some testing holes.
18 holes, 6295yds, Par 69, SSS 70, Course record 64.
Club membership 787.
Visitors must contact professional in advance, a handicap
certificate is required, may not play Tues, weekends or
public holidays. **Societies** booking well in advance
necessary, handicap certificates required, packages to suit.
Green Fees £53 per day, £40 per round. **Cards** 🖭 🖭 🖭
📇 **Prof** Matthew Barr **Course Designer** Bill Pedlar
Facilities ⊗ ⊪ ⅃ 🖤 ♀ ⚐ 🏠 ⚐ **Location** NE side of
town centre off A413

Hotel ★★★★ 68% De Vere Bellhouse, Oxford Rd,
BEACONSFIELD ☎ 01753 887211 136 en suite

HIGH WYCOMBE   Map 04 SU89

Hazlemere Penn Rd, Hazlemere HP15 7LR
☎ 01494 719300 📠 01494 713914
e-mail: enquiries@hazlemeregolfclub.co.uk
Undulating parkland course in beautiful countryside
with water hazards in play on some holes. Two long par
5s, one long par 3 and a fine par 4 closing hole.
18 holes, 5810yds, Par 70, SSS 67, Course record 61.
Club membership 600.
Continued

Visitors weekdays all day. Weekends by prior arrangement through Pro. shop telephone 01494 719306 **Societies** by prior telephone arrangement. **Green Fees** telephone for details. **Cards** 💳 💳 💳 💳 **Prof** Gavin Cousins/Paul Harrison **Course Designer** Terry Murray **Facilities** ⊗ ⑂ 🏌 🏌 🍴 ♀ ♂ ⛳ ✈ ♨ ✎ **Conf** fac available **Location** On B474 between Beaconsfield and Hazlemere. 2m NE of High Wycombe, A404 towards Amersham

Hotel ★★★ 69% The Crown, High St, AMERSHAM ☎ 0870 400 8103 19 en suite 18 annexe en suite

IVER   Map 04 TQ08

Iver Hollow Hill Ln, Langley Park Rd SL0 0JJ ☎ 01753 655615 📠 01753 654225 *9 holes, 6288yds, Par 72, SSS 72, Course record 66.* **Location** M4 junct 5, 1.5m SW off B470 **Telephone for further details**

Hotel ★★★★ 70% Slough/Windsor Marriott Hotel, Ditton Rd, Langley, SLOUGH ☎ 0870 400 7244 382 en suite

Richings Park Golf & Country Club North Park SL0 9DL
☎ 01753 655370 & 655352(pro shop) 📠 01753 655409 e-mail: info@richingspark.co.uk
Set amongst mature trees and attractive lakes, this testing par 70 parkland course provides a suitable challenge to golfers of all abilities. Well irrigated greens and abundant wildlife. There is an academy course with five short holes and teaching facilities on the driving range.
18 holes, 6144yds, Par 70, SSS 69.
Club membership 594.
Visitors welcome but may not play until after 12 noon at weekends. **Societies** apply in writing or telephone. **Green Fees** terms on application. **Cards** 💳 💳 💳 💳 💳 💳 **Prof** Robert Mullane **Course Designer** Alan Higgins **Facilities** ⊗ ⑂ 🏌 🏌 ♀ ♂ 🍴 ♨ ✈ ✎ ♟ **Location** Junct 5 on M4, A4 towards Colnbrook, left at lights, Sutton Lane, right at next lights North Park

Hotel ★★★ 69% Courtyard by Marriott Slough/Windsor, Church St, SLOUGH ☎ 0870 400 7215 150 en suite

Thorney Park Thorney Mill Rd SL0 9AL
☎ 01895 422095 📠 01895 431307 e-mail: sales@thorneypark.com
An 18-hole parkland course which will test both the beginner and established golfer. Fairway irrigation ensures lush green fairways and smooth putting surfaces. Many interesting holes including the testing par 4 9th which needs a long drive to the water's edge and a well-hit iron onto the bunker-guarded green. The back 9 finishes with two water holes, the 17th, a near island green and the shot of 150yds makes this a picturesque hole. The 18th has more water than grass!
18 holes, 5731yds, Par 69, SSS 68.
Club membership 300.
Visitors must telephone in advance. Weekends after 11am. May not play bank holidays. **Societies** must telephone in advance. **Green Fees** £30 per day, £19.50 per 18 holes (£22 per round weekends). **Cards** 💳 💳 💳 💳 💳 **Prof** Andrew Killing **Course Designer** David Walker **Facilities** ⊗ ⑂ 🏌 🏌 ♀ ♂ 🍴 ✈ ✎ **Conf** fac available Corporate Hospitality Days available **Location** From M4 junct 5 left onto A4. Left into Sutton Lane and right for Thorney Mill Road

Continued

Hotel ★★★★ 70% Slough/Windsor Marriott Hotel, Ditton Rd, Langley, SLOUGH ☎ 0870 400 7244 382 en suite

LITTLE BRICKHILL   See page 33

LITTLE CHALFONT   Map 04 SU99

Little Chalfont Lodge Ln HP8 4AJ
☎ 01494 764877 📠 01494 762860
Gently undulating parkland course surrounded by mature trees.
9 holes, 5852yds, Par 70, SSS 68, Course record 66.
Club membership 300.
Visitors no restrictions, please phone to ensure there are no competitions in progress. Must contact for weekend play. **Societies** please telephone in advance. **Green Fees** terms on application. **Cards** 💳 💳 💳 💳 💳 **Prof** M Dunne **Course Designer** J M Dunne **Facilities** ⊗ ⑂ 🏌 🏌 ♀ ♂ 🍴 ♨ ✎ **Leisure** one motorised cart for hire by arrangement. **Conf** fac available Corporate Hospitality Days available **Location** Between Little Chalfont & Chorleywood 3m on A404 from M25 junct 18

Hotel ★★★ 69% The Crown, High St, AMERSHAM ☎ 0870 400 8103 19 en suite 18 annexe en suite

LOUDWATER   Map 04 SU89

Wycombe Heights Golf Centre Rayners Ave
HP10 9SZ ☎ 01494 816686 📠 01494 816728

High Course: 18 holes, 6265yds, Par 70, SSS 71, Course record 64.
Course Designer John Jacobs **Location** M40 junct 3, A40 towards High Wycombe. After 0.5m right into Rayners Avenue at traffic lights
Telephone for further details

Hotel 🅷 Holiday Inn High Wycombe, Handy Cross, HIGH WYCOMBE ☎ 0870 400 9042 109 en suite

MARLOW   Map 04 SU88

Harleyford Harleyford Estate, Henley Rd SL7 2SP
☎ 01628 816161 📠 01628 816160 e-mail: info@harleyfordgolf.co.uk
Set in 160 acres, this Donald Steel designed course, founded in 1996, makes the most of the natural rolling contours of the beautiful parkland of the historic Harleyford Estate. A challenging course to golfers of all handicaps. Stunning views across the Thames Valley.

Continued

Harleyford Golf Club

18 holes, 6587yds, Par 72, SSS 72, Course record 68.
Club membership 700.
Visitors Soft spikes only. Must contact in advance. Can play after 10am weekdays and 11.30am weekends. **Societies** Telephone groups co-ordinator on 01628 816172 **Green Fees** £45 per round (£65 weekends). **Cards** **Prof** Lee Jackson **Course Designer** Donald Steel **Facilities** **Conf** fac available Corporate Hospitality Days available **Location** S side A4156 Marlow/Henley road, close to A404 Marlow bypass linking junct 4 M40/junct 8/9 M4

Hotel ★★★★ 76% Danesfield House Hotel & Spa, Henley Rd, MARLOW-ON-THAMES ☎ 01628 891010 87 en suite

MENTMORE Map 04 SP91

Mentmore Golf & Country Club LU7 0UA
☎ 01296 662020 📠 01296 662592
Rosebery Course: 18 holes, 6777yds, Par 72, SSS 72, Course record 68.
Rothschild Course: 18 holes, 6700yds, Par 72, SSS 72.
Course Designer Bob Sandow **Location** 4m S of Leighton Buzzard
Telephone for further details

Hotel Holiday Inn Aylesbury, Aston Clinton Rd, AYLESBURY ☎ 0870 400 9002 140 en suite

MILTON KEYNES Map 04 SP83

Abbey Hill Monks Way, Two Mile Ash MK8 8AA
☎ 01908 562408
e-mail: steve.tompkins@ukonline.co.uk

18 holes, 6122yds, Par 71, SSS 69, Course record 71.
Location 2m W of new town centre off A5
Telephone for further details

Hotel ★★★ 65% Quality Hotel & Suites Milton Keynes, Monks Way, Two Mile Ash, MILTON KEYNES ☎ 01908 561666 88 en suite

Three Locks Great Brickhill MK17 9BH
☎ 01525 270470 & 270050 📠 01525 270470
Parkland course offering a challenge to beginners and experienced golfers, with water coming into play on ten holes. Magnificent views.
18 holes, 6036yds, Par 70, SSS 69, Course record 60.
Club membership 300.
Visitors telephone 01525 270050 to book tee times. **Societies** write or telephone for details. **Green Fees** not confirmed. **Cards** **Prof** G Harding **Course Designer** MRM Sandown **Facilities** **Leisure** fishing. **Location** A4146 between Leighton Buzzard/Bletchley

Hotel Holiday Inn Milton Keynes, 500 Saxon Gate West, MILTON KEYNES ☎ 0870 400 9057 157 en suite

PRINCES RISBOROUGH Map 04 SP80

Whiteleaf Upper Icknield Way, Whiteleaf HP27 0LY
☎ 01844 274058 📠 01844 275551
e-mail: whiteleafgc@tiscali.co.uk
A picturesque 9-hole course on the edge of the Chilterns. Good views over the Vale of Aylesbury. A short challenging course requiring great accuracy.
9 holes, 5391yds, Par 66, SSS 66, Course record 64.
Club membership 300.
Visitors advisable to contact in advance, with member only at weekends. **Societies** on Thu only, must contact the secretary in advance. **Green Fees** £20 per 18 holes. **Prof** Ken Ward **Facilities** **Location** 1m NE off A4010

Hotel ★★ 63% Rose & Crown Hotel, Wycombe Rd, SAUNDERTON ☎ 01844 345299 15 en suite

STOKE POGES Map 04 SU98

Farnham Park Park Rd SL2 4PJ
☎ 01753 643332 & 647065 📠 01753 643332 & 647065
e-mail: farnhamparkgolfclub@btopenworld.com
Fine, public parkland course in a pleasing setting.
18 holes, 6172yds, Par 71, SSS 70, Course record 68.
Club membership 400.
Visitors telephone in advance for tee times. **Societies** apply in writing. **Green Fees** £13 per round (£18 weekends). **Cards** **Prof** Paul Warner **Course Designer** Hawtree **Facilities** **Location** W side of village off B416

Hotel ★★★★ 70% Slough/Windsor Marriott Hotel, Ditton Rd, Langley, SLOUGH ☎ 0870 400 7244 382 en suite

Stoke Poges Stoke Park, Park Rd SL2 4PG
☎ 01753 717171 📠 01753 717181
e-mail: info@stokeparkclub.com
Judgement of the distance from the tee is all important on this first-class parkland course. Fairways are wide and the challenge seemingly innocuous. The 7th hole is the model for the well known 12th hole at Augusta. Stoke Poges is a 27-hole course and is considered the best traditional course in the British Isles.
Course 1: 18 holes, 6721yds, Par 71, SSS 72.
Course 2: 18 holes, 6551yds, Par 72, SSS 73.
Course 3: 18 holes, 6318yds, Par 71, SSS 70.
Club membership 2500.
Visitors must contact in advance. **Societies** telephone in advance. **Green Fees** £125 per 18 holes (£200 weekends).

Continued

Woburn

Map 04 SP93 Little Brickhill

☎ 01908 370756 📄 01908 378436

Conveniently accessible from the M1, Woburn is famed not only for its golf courses, but also for the magnificent stately home and wildlife park. If you are unable to play the courses yourself these are well worth a visit. Charles Lawrie of Cotton Pennink designed two great golf courses here amongst the trees and beautiful countryside. From the back tees, they are rather long for the weekend amateur golfer. The Duke's course is a tough challenge for golfers at all levels. The Duchess course, although relatively easier, still demands a high level of skill to negotiate the fairways guarded by towering pines. The Duke's has become the home of the increasingly popular Weetabix Women's British Open, held here since 1990. The town of Woburn and the abbey are both within Bedfordshire, while the golf and county club are over the border in Buckinghamshire.

e-mail: enquiries@woburngolf.com

Visitors Midweek by arrangement

Societies Must contact in advance

Green Fees Telephone for details

Facilities ⊗ 🍴 ⚲ 🏖 🏠 🎯 🐾 🛺 ⛳

Conf Facilities available; corporate hospitality days available.

Professional Luther Blacklock

Location Little Brickhill, Milton Keynes MK17 9LJ 4m W of J13 M1, off A5130)

Holes/Par/Course record 54 holes

Duke's Course: 18 holes 6973 yds, Par 72, SS 74 Course record 62. Duchess Course: 18 holes, 6651 yds, Par 72, SSS 72 Marquess Course 18 holes, 7214 yds, Par 72, SSS 74

Championship Course

WHERE TO STAY AND EAT NEARBY

Hotels
FLITWICK

★★★ 🏵 🏵 Menzies Flitwick Manor, MK45 JAE ☎ 01525 712242. 17 en suite

WOBURN

★★★ 🏵 73% The Inn at Woburn, MK17 9PX. ☎ 01525 290441. 57 en suite

Restaurant
WOBURN

🏵 🏵 Paris House Restaurant, MK17 9QP. ☎ 01525 290692

Cards 🔲 🔲 🔲 🔲 🔲 🔲 **Prof** Stuart Collier **Course Designer** Harry Shapland Colt **Facilities** ⊗ ⦙⦙⦙ 🏐 💆 ♀ 🏊 🏌 🛴 🛒 ⚙ (**Leisure** hard and grass tennis courts, heated indoor swimming pool, fishing, sauna, gymnasium, indoor tennis courts. **Conf** Corporate Hospitality Days available **Location** Turn off A4 at Slough into Stoke Poges Lane B416, club is 1.5m on left

Hotel ★★★★ 70% Slough/Windsor Marriott Hotel, Ditton Rd, Langley, SLOUGH ☎ 0870 400 7244 382 en suite

STOWE   Map 04 SP63

Silverstone Silverstone Rd MK18 5LH
☎ 01280 850005 🖨 01280 850156
e-mail: proshop@silverstonegolfclub.co.uk
Set in the rolling North Buckinghamshire countryside, the course offers an interesting challenge for both experienced players and those with a higher handicap. Three new holes were opened in 2002, extending the course to over 6500 yards and making a major contribution to providing championship standards for play.
18 holes, 6558yards, Par 72, SSS 71, Course record 65. Club membership 432.
Visitors no restrictions. **Societies** may play weekdays/weekends after noon. Telephone to book. **Green Fees** terms on application. **Cards** 🔲 🔲 🔲 🔲 ⚙ **Prof** Rodney Holt **Course Designer** David Snell **Facilities** ⊗ ⦙⦙⦙ 🏐 💆 ♀ 🏊 🏌 🛴 🛒 ⚙ (**Conf** fac available Corporate Hospitality Days available **Location** from Silverstone village follow signs to the Grand Prix track. Golf club 1m past the entrance on right

Hotel ★★★★ 69% Villiers Hotel, 3 Castle St, BUCKINGHAM ☎ 01280 822444 46 en suite

WAVENDON   Map 04 SP93

Wavendon Golf Centre Lower End Rd MK17 8DA
☎ 01908 281811 🖨 01908 281257
e-mail: wavendon@jack-barker.co.uk

18 holes, 5570yds, Par 69, SSS 68.
Course Designer J Drake/N Elmer **Location** Just off A421, 8 mins from M1 junct 13
Telephone for further details

Hotel ★★★ 69% Moore Place Hotel, The Square, ASPLEY GUISE ☎ 01908 282000 39 en suite 27 annexe en suite

WESTON TURVILLE   Map 04 SP81

Weston Turville Golf New Rd HP22 5QT
☎ 01296 424084 🖨 01296 395376
e-mail: westonturvillegc@btconnect.com
Parkland course situated at the foot of the Chiltern Hills and providing an excellent challenge for the accomplished golfer, yet not too daunting for the higher handicap player. Flat easy walking with water hazards and many interesting holes, notably the testing dog-leg 5th (418yds).
18 holes, 6008yds, Par 69, SSS 69, Course record 68. Club membership 600.
Visitors advance booking advised **Societies** must contact in advance. **Green Fees** £20 per round (£25 weekends & bank holidays). **Cards** 🔲 🔲 🔲 ⚙ **Prof** Gary George **Facilities** ⊗ ⦙⦙⦙ by prior arrangement 🏐 💆 ♀ 🏊 🏌 🛒 🛴 ⚙ **Conf** fac available Corporate Hospitality Days available **Location** 2m SE of Aylesbury, off A41

Hotel Ⓤ Holiday Inn Aylesbury, Aston Clinton Rd, AYLESBURY ☎ 0870 400 9002 140 en suite

WEXHAM STREET   Map 04 SU98

Wexham Park SL3 6ND
☎ 01753 663271 🖨 01753 663318
e-mail: wexhamgolf@freenetname.co.uk
Gently undulating parkland course. Three courses. One 18-hole, one challenging 9-hole and another 9-hole suitable for beginners.
Blue: 18 holes, 5346yds, Par 68, SSS 66.
Red: 9 holes, 2822yds, Par 34.
Green: 9 holes, 2233yds, Par 32.
Club membership 850.
Visitors no restrictions **Societies** must contact in advance. **Green Fees** £14 for 18 holes, £8.50 for 9 holes (£18/£10 weekends). **Cards** 🔲 🔲 🔲 🔲 ⚙ **Prof** John Kennedy **Course Designer** E Lawrence/D Morgan **Facilities** ⊗ 🏐 💆 ♀ 🏊 🏌 🛒 🛴 🛴 ⚙ (**Location** 0.5m S

Hotel ★★★★ 70% Slough/Windsor Marriott Hotel, Ditton Rd, Langley, SLOUGH ☎ 0870 400 7244 382 en suite

WING   Map 04 SP82

Aylesbury Vale Stewkley Rd LU7 0UJ
☎ 01525 240196 🖨 01525 240848
e-mail: info@avgc.co.uk
This gently undulating course is set amid tranquil countryside. There are five ponds to pose the golfer problems, notably on the par 4 420yd 13th - unlucky for some - where the second shot is all downhill with an inviting pond spanning the approach to the green. In addition there is a 10-bay driving range and practice putting green.
18 holes, 6612yds, Par 72, SSS 72, Course record 67. Club membership 515.
Visitors must adhere to dress regulations. Must contact in advance. **Societies** telephone to book in advance. **Green Fees** £17 per day (£25 weekends, £17 after 11am). **Cards** 🔲 🔲 🔲 ⚙ **Prof** Terry Bunyan **Course Designer** D Wright **Facilities** ⊗ ⦙⦙⦙ 🏐 💆 ♀ 🏊 🏌 🛒 🛴 🛴 ⚙ (**Conf** fac available Corporate Hospitality Days available **Location** 2m NW of Leighton Buzzard on unclassified Stewkley road, between Wing/Stewkley

Hotel Ⓤ Holiday Inn Aylesbury, Aston Clinton Rd, AYLESBURY ☎ 0870 400 9002 140 en suite

CAMBRIDGESHIRE

BAR HILL
Map 05 TL36

Cambridgeshire Moat House Moat House Hotel, Bar Hill CB3 8EU
☎ 01954 780098 & 249971 📠 01954 780010
18 holes, 6734yds, Par 72, SSS 73, Course record 68.
Location M11/A14, then B1050 (Bar Hill)
Telephone for further details
....
Hotel 🏰 Holiday Inn Cambridge, Lakeview, Bridge Rd, Impington, CAMBRIDGE ☎ 0870 400 9015 165 en suite

BOURN
Map 05 TL35

Bourn Toft Rd CB3 7TT
☎ 01954 718958 📠 01954 718908
Meadow/parkland golf course with many water features and some very challenging holes.
18 holes, 6417yards, SSS 71.
Visitors welcome. **Societies** apply for booking form.
Green Fees terms on application. **Prof** Craig Watson
Course Designer J Hull **Facilities** ⊗ �🍽 🝙 🝙 🛒 ♀ 🝙 🝙
🝙 🝙 ⌀ **Leisure** heated indoor swimming pool, sauna, solarium, gymnasium.
....
Hotel 🏰 Travelodge, Huntingdon Rd, LOLWORTH
☎ 08700 850 950 36 en suite

BRAMPTON
Map 04 TL27

Brampton Park Buckden Rd PE28 4NF
☎ 01480 434700 📠 01480 411145
e-mail: admin@bramptonparkgc.co.uk
Set in truly attractive countryside, bounded by the River Great Ouse and bisected by the River Lane. Great variety with mature trees, lakes and water hazards. One of the most difficult holes is the 4th, a par 3 island green, 175 yards in length.
18 holes, 6300yds, Par 71, SSS 72, Course record 62.
Club membership 650.
Visitors must contact in advance. **Societies** apply in advance. **Green Fees** terms on application. **Cards** 💳 💳 💳 💳 🝙 **Prof** Alisdair Currie **Course Designer** Simon Gidman **Facilities** ⊗ �🍽 🝙 🝙 🛒 ♀ 🝙 🝙 🝙 ⌀ 🝙 **Conf** fac available Corporate Hospitality Days available
Location Follow signs from A1 or A14 to RAF Brampton
....
Hotel ★★★★ 71% Huntingdon Marriott Hotel, Kingfisher Way, Hinchingbrooke Business Park, HUNTINGDON ☎ 01480 446000 150 en suite

CAMBRIDGE
Map 05 TL45

Gog Magog Shelford Bottom CB2 4AB
☎ 01223 247626 📠 01223 414990
e-mail: secretary@gogmagog.co.uk
Situated just outside the centre of the university town, Gog Magog, established in 1901, is known as the nursery of Cambridge undergraduate golf. The courses are on high ground, and it is said that if you stand on the highest point and could see far enough to the east the next highest ground would be the Ural Mountains! The courses are open but there are enough trees and other hazards to provide plenty of problems. Views from the high parts are superb. The nature of the ground ensures good winter golf. The area has been designated a Site of Special Scientific Interest (SSSI).
Continued

Old Course: 18 holes, 6398yds, Par 70, SSS 70, Course record 62.
Wandlebury: 18 holes, 6735yds, Par 72, SSS 72, Course record 67.
Club membership 1400.
Visitors Must contact in advance. Mon-Fri only. Weekends and bank holidays by special arrangement with secretary. **Societies** Tue & Thu by reservation. **Green Fees** £44 per day, £37 per round (£60 per round weekends and bank holidays). **Prof** Ian Bamborough **Course Designer** Hawtree Ltd **Facilities** ⊗ �🍽 🝙 🝙 🛒 ♀ 🝙 🝙 🝙 🝙 ⌀ 🝙 **Conf** Corporate Hospitality Days available **Location** 3m SE on A1307
....
Hotel ★★★ 71% Gonville Hotel, Gonville Place, CAMBRIDGE ☎ 01223 366611 & 221111
📠 01223 315470 78 en suite

ELY
Map 05 TL58

Ely City 107 Cambridge Rd CB7 4HX
☎ 01353 662751 (Office) 📠 01353 668636
e-mail: elygolf@lineone.net
Parkland course slightly undulating with water hazards formed by lakes and natural dykes. Demanding par 4 5th hole (467yds), often into a headwind, and a testing par 3 2nd hole (160yds) played over two ponds. Magnificent views of cathedral.
18 holes, 6627yds, Par 72, SSS 72, Course record 65.
Club membership 800.
Visitors advisable to contact the club in advance, handicap certificate required. **Societies** Tue to Fri, advisable to contact club well in advance. **Green Fees** £32 per day (£38 weekends). **Prof** Andrew George **Course Designer** Sir Henry Cotton **Facilities** ⊗ �🍽 🝙 🝙 🛒 ♀ 🝙 🝙 🝙 ⌀ **Leisure** snooker. **Conf** Corporate Hospitality Days available
Location S of city on A10
....
Hotel ★★★ 66% Lamb Hotel, 2 Lynn Rd, ELY
☎ 01353 663574 32 en suite

GIRTON
Map 05 TL46

Girton Dodford Ln CB3 0QE
☎ 01223 276169 📠 01223 277150
e-mail: secretary@girtongolfclub.sagehost.co.uk
Flat, open parkland course with many trees and ditches. Easy walking.
18 holes, 6012yds, Par 69, SSS 69, Course record 66.
Club membership 800.
Visitors with member only at weekends. Contact professional in advance (01223 276991). **Societies** apply in writing. **Green Fees** £15. **Prof** Scott Thomson **Course Designer** Allan Gow **Facilities** ⊗ �🍽 🝙 🝙 🛒 ♀ 🝙 🝙 🝙 ⌀
Location 3m from Cambridge. Just off junct 31 of A14
....
Hotel 🏰 Holiday Inn Cambridge, Lakeview, Bridge Rd, Impington, CAMBRIDGE ☎ 0870 400 9015 165 en suite

HEMINGFORD ABBOTS
Map 04 TL27

Hemingford Abbots Cambridge Rd PE28 9HQ
☎ 01480 495000 & 493900 📠 01480 4960000
Interesting 9-hole course featuring a par 5 dog-leg 6th with a testing tapering fairway, two ponds at the entrance to the 8th green and an island green on the 9th.
9 holes, 5468yds, Par 68, SSS 68, Course record 69. Club membership 170.
Continued

Visitors advisable to phone in advance, particularly for weekends. **Societies** advise in writing or telephone. **Green Fees** terms on application. **Course Designer** Ray Paton **Facilities** ⊗ ⓑ 🝙 ♀ △ 🏠 ⛟ ♂ ⛿ **Conf** fac available **Location** A14 Hemingford Abbots turning, midway between St Ives and Huntingdon

Hotel ★★★ 78% The Old Bridge Hotel, 1 High St, HUNTINGDON ☎ 01480 424300 24 en suite

LONGSTANTON   Map 05 TL36

Cambridge Station Rd CB4 5DR ☎ 01954 789388
An undulating parkland course with bunkers and ponds.
18 holes, 6736yds, Par 72, SSS 73.
Club membership 300.
Visitors must telephone in advance to book. **Societies** must telephone in advance. **Green Fees** terms on application. **Cards** 🖃 🖩 🖦 🖽 🖿 **Prof** Geoff Huggett/A Engelman **Facilities** ⊗ 🝙 ⓑ 🝙 ♀ △ ⛟ 🝙 🏌 ♂ **Leisure** fishing, hot air ballons.

Hotel Ⓤ Holiday Inn Cambridge, Lakeview, Bridge Rd, Impington, CAMBRIDGE ☎ 0870 400 9015 165 en suite

MARCH   Map 05 TL49

March Frogs Abbey, Grange Rd PE15 0YH
☎ 01354 652364 📄 01354 658142
Nine hole parkland course with a particularly challenging par 3 9th hole, with out of bounds on the right and high hedges to the left.
9 holes, 6204yds, Par 70, SSS 70, Course record 65.
Club membership 346.
Visitors contact in advance, with member only at weekends. **Societies** must contact in advance. **Green Fees** terms on application. **Cards** 🖃 🖦 🖿 **Prof** Mark Pond **Facilities** 🝙 ♀ △ 🏠 ♂ **Location** 0.5m off A141, March bypass

Hotel ★★ 63% Olde Griffin Hotel, High St, MARCH ☎ 01354 652517 21 rms (20 en suite)

MELDRETH   Map 05 TL34

Malton Malton Rd, Malton SG8 6PE
☎ 01763 262200 📄 01763 262209
e-mail: desk@maltongolf.co.uk
18 holes, 6708yards, Par 72, SSS 72, Course record 67.
Location on unclassified road between Orwell and Meldreth
Telephone for further details

Hotel ★★★ 74% Duxford Lodge Hotel, Ickleton Rd, DUXFORD ☎ 01223 836444 11 en suite 4 annexe en suite

PETERBOROUGH   Map 04 TL19

Elton Furze Bullock Rd, Haddon PE7 3TT
☎ 01832 280189 & 280614 (Pro shop) 📄 01832 280299
e-mail: secretary@eltonfurzegolfclub.co.uk
Wooded parkland 18-hole course in lovely surroundings.
18 holes, 6279yds, Par 70, SSS 71, Course record 66.
Club membership 620.
Visitors welcome, preferably Mon-Fri, weekends only with prior permission (phone in advance). **Societies** by prior arrangement telephone for details. **Green Fees** not confirmed. **Cards** 🖃 🖦 **Prof** Glyn Krause **Course**

Designer Roger Fitton **Facilities** ⊗ 🝙 ⓑ 🝙 ♀ △ 🏠 🏌 ♂ ⛿ **Conf** Corporate Hospitality Days available **Location** 4m SW of Peterborough, off A605/A1

Hotel ★★★★ 67% Peterborough Marriott Hotel, Peterborough Business Park, Lynchwood, PETERBOROUGH ☎ 01733 371111 157 en suite

Orton Meadows Ham Ln, Orton Waterville PE2 5UU
☎ 01733 237478 📄 01733 332774
18 holes, 5269yds, Par 67, SSS 68, Course record 64.
Course Designer D & R Fitton **Location** 3m W of town on A605
Telephone for further details

Hotel ★★★ 67% Orton Hall Hotel, Orton Longueville, PETERBOROUGH ☎ 01733 391111 65 en suite

Peterborough Milton Milton Ferry PE6 7AG
☎ 01733 380489 & 380793 (Pro) 📄 01733 380489
e-mail: miltongolfclub@aol.com
Designed by James Braid, this well-bunkered parkland course is set in the grounds of the Milton Estate, many of the holes being played in full view of Milton Hall. Challenging holes are the difficult dog-leg 10th and 15th. Easy walking.
18 holes, 6479yds, Par 71, SSS 72, Course record 62.
Club membership 800.
Visitors contact in advance. Handicap certificate required. **Societies** bookings by email or telephone to secretary. **Green Fees** £40 per 36 holes; £30 per 18 holes. **Cards** 🖃 🖦 🖿 **Prof** Mike Gallagher **Course Designer** James Braid **Facilities** ⊗ 🝙 ⓑ 🝙 ♀ △ ♂ **Conf** fac available Corporate Hospitality Days available **Location** 2m W of Peterborough on A47,near the villages of Castor & Ailsworth

Hotel ⛫ Travelodge Peterborough, Crowlands Rd, PETERBOROUGH ☎ 08700 850 950 42 en suite

Thorpe Wood Thorpe Wood, Nene Parkway PE3 6SE
☎ 01733 267701 📄 01733 332774
e-mail: enquiries@thorpewoodgolfcourse.co.uk
Gently undulating, parkland course designed by Peter Alliss and Dave Thomas. Challenging holes include the 5th, the longest hole, usually played with prevailing wind, and the 14th, which has a difficult approach shot over water to a two-tier green.
18 holes, 7086yds, Par 73, SSS 74, Course record 68.
Club membership 750.
Visitors phone for reservations 7 days in advance. **Societies** must telephone in advance, society bookings taken up to year ahead. **Green Fees** £11.90 per round (£15.70 weekends & bank holidays). **Cards** 🖃 🖦 🖿 **Prof** Roger Fitton **Course Designer** Peter Allis/Dave Thomas **Facilities** ⊗ 🝙 ⓑ 🝙 ♀ △ 🏠 🏌 ♂ **Location** 3m W of city centre on A47

Hotel ★★★ 67% Orton Hall Hotel, Orton Longueville, PETERBOROUGH ☎ 01733 391111 65 en suite

PIDLEY   Map 05 TL37

Lakeside Lodge Fen Rd PE28 3DF
☎ 01487 740540 📄 01487 740852
e-mail: info@lakeside-lodge.co.uk
A well designed, spacious course incorporating eight lakes, 12,000 trees and a modern clubhouse. The 9th and 18th holes both finish dramatically alongside a lake

Continued   *Continued*

in front of the clubhouse. Also **9** hole par 3, and **25-bay** driving range. **The Manor** provides an interesting contrast with its undulating fairways and angular greens.

Lodge Course: 18 holes, 6885yds, Par 72, SSS 73.
The Manor: 9 holes, 2601yds, Par 34, SSS 33.
The Church: 12 holes, 3290yds, Par 44.
Club membership 1200.

Visitors advance tee time booking recommended. **Societies** must telephone in advance. **Green Fees** £14 per 18 holes (£22 weekends & bank holidays); £7.50 per 9/12 holes (£11 week ends & bank holidays). **Cards** 🖾 🖾 **Prof** Scott Waterman **Course Designer** A W Headley **Facilities** ⊗ �𝍢 ⅃ 🖤 ♀ ♨ 🏢 ⌁ ⌀ 𝄞 **Leisure** solarium, ten pin bowling, smart golf simulator. **Conf** fac available Corporate Hospitality Days available **Location** A141 from Huntingdon

....

Hotel ★★★ 69% Slepe Hall Hotel, Ramsey Rd, ST IVES ☎ 01480 463122 16 en suite

RAMSEY   Map 04 TL28

Old Nene Golf & Country Club Muchwood Ln,
Bodsey PE26 2XQ ☎ 01487 815622 🖺 01487 813610
e-mail: info@oldnene.freeserve.co.uk

An easy walking, well-drained course, with water hazards and tree-lined fairways. There are excellent greens and many challenging holes across water in either a head wind or cross wind.

9 holes, 5605yds, Par 68, SSS 68, Course record 64.
Club membership 170.

Visitors book in advance especially evenings & weekends. Dress code must be adhered to. **Societies** arrange in advance with Secretary. **Green Fees** £13 per 18 holes, £8.50 per holes (£17/£11 weekends and bank holidays). **Cards** 🖾 🖾 🖾 **Prof** Neil Grant **Course Designer** R Edrich **Facilities** ⊗ �𝍢 ⅃ 🖤 ♀ ♨ ⌀ 𝄞 **Leisure** fishing, practice area. **Conf** Corporate Hospitality Days available **Location** 0.75m N of Ramsey towards Ramsey Mereside

....

Hotel ★★★ 78% The Old Bridge Hotel, 1 High St, HUNTINGDON ☎ 01480 424300 24 en suite

Ramsey 4 Abbey Ter PE26 1DD
☎ 01487 812600 🖺 01487 815746
e-mail: admin@ramseyclub.co.uk

Flat, parkland course with water hazards and well-irrigated greens, mature tees and fairways, assuring a good surface whatever the conditions. It gives the impression of wide-open spaces, but the wayward shot is soon punished.

18 holes, 5830yds, Par 71, SSS 68, Course record 64.
Club membership 600.

Visitors contact professional in advance 01487 813022, may only play with member at weekends & bank holidays. **Societies** apply in writing. **Green Fees** £25 per 18 holes. **Prof** Stuart Scott **Course Designer** J Hamilton Stutt **Facilities** ⊗ by prior arrangement �𝍢 by prior arrangement ⅃ 🖤 ♀ ♨ 🏢 ⌁ ⌀ 𝄞 **Leisure** snooker tables, bowls rinks. **Location** 12m SE of Peterborough on B1040

....

Hotel ★★★ 78% The Old Bridge Hotel, 1 High St, HUNTINGDON ☎ 01480 424300 24 en suite

---

ST IVES   Map 04 TL37

St Ives (Cambs) Westwood Rd PE27 6DH
☎ 01480 468392 🖺 01480 468392
e-mail: stivesgolfclub@zoom.co.uk

Picturesque parkland course.

9 holes, 6180yds, Par 70, SSS 70, Course record 68.
Club membership 500.

Visitors may not play weekends. **Societies** welcome Wed & Fri. **Green Fees** not confirmed. **Prof** Darren Glasby **Facilities** ⊗ �𝍢 ⅃ 🖤 ♀ ♨ 🏢 ⌁ ⌀ **Location** W side of town centre off A1123

....

Hotel ★★★ 69% Slepe Hall Hotel, Ramsey Rd, ST IVES ☎ 01480 463122 16 en suite

ST NEOTS   Map 04 TL16

Abbotsley Golf & Squash Club Eynesbury
Hardwicke PE19 6XN ☎ 01480 474000 🖺 01480 403280
e-mail: abbotsley@americangolf.uk.com

Set in 250 acres of idyllic countryside, with two 18-hole courses and a 9-hole par 3. The Cromwell course is the less challenging of the two, offering a contrast to the renowned Abbotsley course with its holes meandering through woods and streams. One of the most memorable holes is the Abbotsley second hole known as the Mousehole, which requires an accurate tee shot to a green that is protected by a stream and shaded by the many trees that surround it.

Abbotsley Course: 18 holes, 6311yds, Par 73, SSS 72,
Course record 69.
Cromwell Course: 18 holes, 6087yds, Par 70, SSS 69,
Course record 66.
Club membership 550.

Visitors welcome all times. Necessary to book weekends. **Societies** prior booking essential. **Green Fees** Abbotsley:£20 per 18 holes (£30 weekends & bank holidays) Cromwell:£14 per 18 holes (£20 weekends & bank holidays). Reduced winter rates. **Cards** 🖾 🖾 🖾 🖾 **Prof** Denise Hastings/Steve Connolly **Course Designer** D Young/V Saunders **Facilities** ⊗ ⟅ ⅃ 🖤 ♀ ♨ 🏢 ⌁ ⌀ 🏸 🐾 ♨ 𝄞 **Leisure** squash, solarium, gymnasium, holistic health & beauty salon. **Conf** fac available Corporate Hospitality Days available **Location** 10 mins from A1 & A428

....

Hotel ★★ 63% Abbotsley Golf Hotel & Country Club, Potton Rd, Eynesbury Hardwicke, ST NEOTS ☎ 01480 474000 42 annexe en suite

St Neots Crosshall Rd PE19 7GE
☎ 01480 472363 🖺 01480 472363
e-mail: office@stneots-golfclub.co.uk

Undulating and very picturesque parkland course with lake and water hazards and exceptional greens, close to the Kym and Great Ouse rivers. Easy, level walking.

18 holes, 6033yds, Par 69, SSS 69, Course record 64.
Club membership 630.

Visitors must book in advance. With member only at weekends. **Societies** must contact in advance. **Green Fees** £40 per day; £30 per round. **Cards** 🖾 🖾 🖾 🖾 **Prof** Jason Boast **Course Designer** H Vardon **Facilities** ⊗ ⟅ ⅃ 🖤 ♀ ♨ 🏢 🐾 ⌀ 𝄞 **Conf** Corporate Hospitality Days available **Location** Just off A1 at junct B1048 heading into St Neots

....

Hotel ★★ 63% Abbotsley Golf Hotel & Country Club, Potton Rd, Eynesbury Hardwicke, ST NEOTS ☎ 01480 474000 42 annexe en suite

Looking to try a new course? Always telephone ahead to confirm visitor arrangements.

THORNEY   Map 04 TF20

Thorney English Drove, Thorney PE6 0TJ
☎ 01733 270570 🖷 01733 270842
The 18-hole Fen course is ideal for the beginner, while the Lakes course has a challenging links-style layout with eight holes around water.
Fen Course: 18 holes, 6104yds, Par 70, SSS 69, Course record 66.
Lakes Course: 18 holes, 6402yds, Par 71, SSS 70, Course record 65.
Club membership 500.
Visitors book in advance for Fen course, limited weekend play Lakes course. **Societies** contact in advance. **Green Fees** terms on application. **Cards** 🖭 💳 💳 🖭 🖭 **Prof** Mark Templeman **Course Designer** A Dow **Facilities** ⊗ 🍴 🖪 🖢 ♀ 🛆 🖨 🏤 🚡 ⚙ 🏌 **Leisure** gymnasium, par 3 course. **Location** Off A47, 7m NE of Peterborough

Hotel ⭐ Travelodge Peterborough, Crowlands Rd, PETERBOROUGH ☎ 08700 850 950 42 en suite

TOFT   Map 05 TL35

Cambridge National Comberton Rd CB3 7RY
☎ 01223 264700 🖷 01223 264701
e-mail: meridian@golfsocieties.com
Set in 207 acres to a Peter Allis/Clive Clark design with sweeping fairways, lakes and well bunkered greens. The 4th hole has bunker complexes, a sharp dog-leg and a river with the green heavily guarded by bunkers. The 9th and 10th holes challenge the golfer with river crossings.

Cambridge National: 18 holes, 6651yds, Par 73, SSS 72, Course record 72.
Club membership 400.
Visitors must contact in advance. **Societies** telephone for provisional booking **Green Fees** £16 per 18 holes (£25 weekends). **Cards** 🖭 💳 💳 🖭 🖭 **Prof** Jamie Donaldson **Course Designer** Peter Alliss/Clive Clark **Facilities** ⊗ 🍴 🖪 🖢 ♀ 🛆 🖨 🏤 🚡 ⚙ **Conf** fac available **Location** 3m W of Cambridge, on B1046

Hotel ⭐⭐ 63% Abbotsley Golf Hotel & Country Club, Potton Rd, Eynesbury Hardwicke, ST NEOTS ☎ 01480 474000 42 annexe en suite

CHESHIRE

ALDERLEY EDGE   Map 07 SJ87

Alderley Edge Brook Ln SK9 7RU ☎ 01625 584493
e-mail: honsecretary@aegc.co.uk
Well-wooded, undulating pastureland course. A stream crosses 7 of the 9 holes.

Continued

9 holes, 5823yds, Par 68, SSS 68, Course record 62.
Club membership 400.
Visitors by arrangement on Thu. Not Sat/Tue Mar-Oct. **Societies** Thu only, apply in writing or telephone. **Green Fees** terms on application. **Cards** 🖭 💳 💳 🖭 🖭 **Prof** Peter Bowring **Facilities** ⊗ 🍴 🖪 🖢 ♀ 🛆 🖨 ⚙ **Location** 1m NW on B5085

Hotel ⭐⭐⭐ 77% Alderley Edge Hotel, Macclesfield Rd, ALDERLEY EDGE ☎ 01625 583033 52 en suite

ALDERSEY GREEN   Map 07 SJ45

Aldersey Green CH3 9EH ☎ 01829 782157
e-mail: bradburygolf@aol.com
Exciting, tricky, beautiful parkland course set in 200 acres of countryside. With tree-lined fairways and 14 lakes.
18 holes, 6145, Par 70, SSS 69, Course record 72.
Club membership 350.
Visitors advisable to book **Societies** by prior arrangement **Green Fees** £25 per day, £15 per round (£30/£20 weekends). **Prof** Stephen Bradbury **Facilities** ⊗ 🍴 🖪 🖢 ♀ 🛆 🖨 ⚙ **Location** On A41 Whitchurch Rd, 6m S of Chester

Hotel ⭐⭐⭐⭐ 74% De Vere Carden Park, Carden Park, BROXTON ☎ 01829 731000 113 en suite 79 annexe en suite

ALSAGER   Map 07 SJ75

Alsager Golf & Country Club Audley Rd ST7 2UR ☎ 01270 875700 🖷 01270 882207
e-mail: business@alsagergolfclub.com
An 18-hole parkland course situated in rolling Cheshire countryside and offering a challenge to all golfers whatever their standard. Clubhouse is well appointed with good facilities and a friendly atmosphere.
18 holes, 6225yds, Par 70, SSS 70, Course record 67.
Club membership 640.
Visitors must contact in advance, may not play Fri afternoon, can only play with member at weekends. **Societies** must contact in advance. **Green Fees** terms on application. **Prof** Richard Brown **Facilities** 🖪 🖢 ♀ 🛆 🖨 ⚙ **Leisure** bowling green. **Conf** fac available **Location** 2m NE of M6 junct 16

Hotel ⭐⭐⭐ 69% Manor House Hotel, Audley Rd, ALSAGER ☎ 01270 884000 57 en suite

ANTROBUS   Map 07 SJ68

Antrobus Foggs Ln CW9 6JQ
☎ 01925 730890 🖷 01925 730100
e-mail: info@antrobusgolfclub.co.uk
Challenging parkland course where water is the main feature with streams and ponds in play on most holes. Large undulating greens.
18 holes, 6220yards, Par 71, SSS 71, Course record 65.
Club membership 500.
Visitors must contact in advance, may not play Sat. **Societies** telephone in advance/apply in writing. May play weekdays/Sun after 11am, not Sat. **Green Fees** £22 per day (£25 Sun). **Cards** 🖭 💳 💳 🖭 🖭 **Prof** Paul Farrance **Course Designer** Mike Slater **Facilities** ⊗ 🍴 🖪 🖢 ♀ 🛆 🖨 🏤 ⚙ 🏌 **Leisure** fishing. **Conf** fac available **Location** M56 Junct 10, take A559 towards Northwich, 2nd left after Birch & Bottle pub onto Knutsford Rd, 1st left into Foggs Lane

Hotel ⭐⭐⭐ 65% Quality Hotel Northwich, London Rd, NORTHWICH ☎ 01606 44443 60 en suite

CHESTER
Map 07 SJ46

Chester Curzon Park CH4 8AR
☎ 01244 677760 📠 01244 676667
e-mail: vfcwood@chestergolfclub.co.uk
Meadowland course on two levels contained within a loop of the River Dee. The car park overlooks the racecourse across the river.
18 holes, 6508yds, Par 72, SSS 71, Course record 66.
Club membership 820.
Visitors must contact in advance. **Societies** must telephone or write in advance. **Green Fees** £30 per day (£35 weekends). **Prof** George Parton **Facilities** ⊗ ⅏ ⅃ ⅃ ⅀ ⅃ 🏠 🏌 ∅ **Location** 1m W of city centre

Hotel ★★★ 71% Grosvenor Pulford Hotel, Wrexham Rd, Pulford, CHESTER ☎ 01244 570560 73 en suite

De Vere Carden Park Hotel Carden Park
CH3 9DQ ☎ 01829 731000 📠 01829 731032
e-mail: reservations.carden@devere-hotels.com
A superb golf resort set in 750 acres of beautiful Cheshire countryside. Facilities include the mature parkland Cheshire Course, the Nicklaus Course, the 9-hole par 3 Azalea Course, Golf School and a luxurious clubhouse.

Cheshire: 18 holes, 6891yds, Par 72, SSS 71, Course record 64.
Nicklaus: 18 holes, 7094yds, Par 72, SSS 72, Course record 64.
Club membership 250.
Visitors must contact in advance, handicap certificate required for the Nicklaus Course. To help maintain the highest quality, metal spikes cannot be worn. **Societies** contact for details, tel: 01829 731594. **Green Fees** terms on application. **Cards** 🟦 🟥 🟩 🟨 **Prof** Paul Hodgson **Course Designer** Jack Nicklaus **Facilities** ⊗ ⅏ ⅃ ⅀ ⅀ ⅃ 🏠 🏌 🏓 🏌 ∅ 🏌 **Leisure** hard tennis courts, heated indoor swimming pool, sauna, solarium, gymnasium, residential golf school, snooker room, dance studio. **Conf** fac available **Location** S of City on A41, right at Broxton rdbt onto A534 signed Wrexham. Situated 1.5m on left

Hotel ★★★★ 74% De Vere Carden Park, Carden Park, BROXTON ☎ 01829 731000 113 en suite 79 annexe en suite

Eaton Guy Ln, Waverton CH3 7PH
☎ 01244 335885 📠 01244 335782
e-mail: office@eatongolfclub.co.uk
A parkland course with a liberal covering of both mature trees and new planting enhanced by natural water hazards.

18 holes, 6562yds, Par 72, SSS 71, Course record 68.
Club membership 550.
Visitors must contact in advance particularly for weekends. **Societies** must contact in advance. May not play weekends (am) or Wednesdays. **Green Fees** £30 per round (£35 weekends & BH). Winter rates £20/£25. **Prof** William Tye **Course Designer** Donald Steel **Facilities** ⊗ ⅏ ⅃ ⅀ ⅀ ⅃ 🏠 🏌 🏓 ∅ 🏌 **Location** 3m SE of Chester off A41

Hotel ★★★★★ The Chester Grosvenor & Grosvenor Spa, Eastgate, CHESTER ☎ 01244 324024 80 en suite

Upton-by-Chester Upton Ln, Upton-by-Chester
CH2 1EE ☎ 01244 381183 📠 01244 376955
Pleasant, tree-lined, parkland course. Not easy for low-handicap players to score well. Testing holes are 2nd (par 4), 14th (par 4) and 15th (par 3).
18 holes, 5808yds, Par 69, SSS 68, Course record 63.
Club membership 750.
Visitors must contact in advance. **Societies** apply in writing. **Green Fees** terms on application. **Cards** 🟦 🟥 🟩 **Prof** Stephen Dewhurst **Course Designer** Bill Davies **Facilities** ⊗ ⅏ ⅃ ⅀ ⅀ ⅃ 🏠 🏓 ∅ **Conf** Corporate Hospitality Days available **Location** N side off A5116

Hotel ★★★★ 70% Mollington Banastre Hotel, Parkgate Rd, CHESTER ☎ 01244 851471 63 en suite

Vicars Cross Tarvin Rd, Great Barrow CH3 7HN
☎ 01244 335595 📠 01244 335686
e-mail: secretary@vcgc.fsnet.co.uk
Tree-lined parkland course, with undulating terrain.
18 holes, 6446yds, Par 72, SSS 71, Course record 64.
Club membership 750.
Visitors advisable to contact in advance, visitors may not play competition days or Wed. **Societies** Tue & Thu only. Must book in advance. **Green Fees** £30 per day. **Prof** J A Forsythe **Course Designer** J Richardson **Facilities** ⊗ ⅏ ⅃ ⅀ ⅀ ⅃ 🏠 🏓 ∅ 🏌 **Conf** fac available **Location** 4m E on A51

Hotel ★★★ 73% Rowton Hall Country House Hotel, Whitchurch Rd, Rowton, CHESTER ☎ 01244 335262 38 en suite

CONGLETON
Map 07 SJ86

Astbury Peel Ln, Astbury CW12 4RE
☎ 01260 272772 📠 01260 276420
e-mail: admin@astburygolfclub.com
Parkland course in open countryside, bisected by a canal. The testing 12th hole involves a long carry over a tree-filled ravine. Large practice area.
18 holes, 6296yds, Par 71, SSS 70, Course record 61.
Club membership 720.
Visitors must be a member of a recognised golf club and possess official handicap. May only play weekdays Apr-Nov. **Societies** contact for details. **Green Fees** terms on application. **Prof** Ashley Salt **Facilities** ⊗ ⅏ by prior arrangement ⅀ ⅃ 🏠 **Location** 1.5m S between A34 and A527

Inn ♦♦♦ Egerton Arms Hotel, Astbury Village, CONGLETON ☎ 01260 273946 6 rms (2 en suite)

Congleton Biddulph Rd CW12 3LZ ☎ 01260 273540
Superbly-manicured parkland course with views over three counties from the balcony of the clubhouse.
9 holes, 5103yds, Par 68, SSS 65.
Club membership 400.

Continued

Continued

Visitors may not play during competitions. Must contact in advance. **Societies** must apply in writing to Secretary. **Green Fees** not confirmed. **Prof** John Colclough **Facilities** ⓑ ⓦ by prior arrangement ⓢ ⓐ ⓔ **Location** 1.5m SE on A527

....

Inn ♦♦♦ Egerton Arms Hotel, Astbury Village, CONGLETON ☎ 01260 273946 6 rms (2 en suite)

CREWE   Map 07 SJ75

Crewe Fields Rd, Haslington CW1 5TB
☎ 01270 584099 🗎 01270 256482
e-mail: secretary@crewsgolfclub.co.uk
Undulating parkland course.
18 holes, 6424yds, Par 71, SSS 71, Course record 63.
Club membership 674.
Visitors may not play at weekends, contact professional for details. **Societies** Tue only, prior arrangement with the secretary. **Green Fees** £24 per round. **Prof** David Wheeler **Course Designer** James Braid **Facilities** ⊗ ⓂⒾ by prior arrangement ⓑ ⓦ ⓈⒶ ⓔ ⓕ **Location** 2.25m NE off A534

....

Hotel ★★★ 71% Hunters Lodge Hotel, Sydney Rd, Sydney, CREWE ☎ 01270 583440 57 en suite

Queen's Park Queen's Park Dr CW2 7SB
☎ 01270 666724 🗎 01270 569902
e-mail: crewe@americangolf.co.uk
A short but testing municipal course, the 9 holes are highlighted by the tight dog-leg 4th hole and 450yrd par 4 7th hole. There is a testing par 4 on the final hole with a bomb crater on left and out of bounds on the right.
9 holes, 4920yds, Par 68, SSS 64, Course record 67.
Club membership 400.
Visitors booking for weekends, cannot play Wed or Sun before 11am. **Societies** must book at least 2 weeks in advance. **Green Fees** not confirmed. **Cards** ⬛⬛⬛ ⬛⬛⬛ **Prof** Graeme Hill **Facilities** ⊗ ⓑ ⓦ ⓈⒶ ⓔ ⓕ ⓕ **Leisure** hard tennis courts, Bowling green. **Conf** Corporate Hospitality Days available **Location** Located behind Queen's Park. Well signposted

....

Hotel ★★★ 71% Hunters Lodge Hotel, Sydney Rd, Sydney, CREWE ☎ 01270 583440 57 en suite

DELAMERE   Map 07 SJ56

Delamere Forest Station Rd CW8 2JE
☎ 01606 883264 (Office) 🗎 01606 889444
e-mail: info@delameregolf.co.uk
Played mostly on undulating open heath there is great charm in the way this course drops down into the occasional pine sheltered valley. Six of the first testing nine hole are between 420 and 455 yards in length.

Continued

---

18 holes, 6328yds, Par 72, SSS 70, Course record 63.
Club membership 500.
Visitors must contact in advance. **Societies** apply in writing or by telephone. **Green Fees** £50 per day; £35 per round weekdays. **Prof** Ellis B Jones **Course Designer** H Fowler **Facilities** ⊗ ⓂⒾ by prior arrangement ⓑ ⓦ ⓈⒶ ⓔ ⓕ ⓕ ⓕ ⓕ **Conf** Corporate Hospitality Days available **Location** 1.5m NE, off B5152

....

Hotel ★★ 62% Hartford Hall, School Ln, Hartford, NORTHWICH ☎ 01606 780320 20 en suite

DISLEY   Map 07 SJ98

Disley Stanley Hall Ln SK12 2JX
☎ 01663 762071 & 764001 (Sec) 🗎 01663 762678

18 holes, 6015yds, Par 71, SSS 69, Course record 63.
Location NW side of village off A6
Telephone for further details

....

Hotel ★★★ 61% The County Hotel, Bramhall Ln South, BRAMHALL ☎ 0870 609 6148 65 en suite

ELLESMERE PORT   Map 07 SJ47

Ellesmere Port Chester Rd, Childer Thornton CH66 1QF ☎ 0151 339 7689 🗎 0151 339 7502
18 holes, 6432yds, Par 71, SSS 70.
Course Designer Cotton, Pennick & Lawrie **Location** NW side of town centre. M53 junct 5, take A41 for Chester, club 2m on left
Telephone for further details

....

Hotel ★★★ 69% Quality Hotel Chester, Berwick Rd, Little Sutton, ELLESMERE PORT ☎ 0151 339 5121 53 en suite

FRODSHAM   Map 07 SJ57

Frodsham Simons Ln WA6 6HE
☎ 01928 732159 🗎 01928 734070
e-mail: office@frodshamgolfclub.co.uk
Undulating parkland course with pleasant views from all parts. Emphasis on accuracy over the whole course, the long and difficult par 5 18th necessitating a drive across water to the green. Crossed by two footpaths so extreme care needed.
18 holes, 6328yds, Par 70, SSS 70, Course record 63.
Club membership 700.
Visitors must contact in advance. Members' guests only at weekends. **Societies** telephone for bookings. **Green Fees** £36 per round (weekdays only). **Cards** ⬛⬛⬛ ⬛⬛⬛ ⬛⬛⬛ **Prof** Graham Tonge **Course Designer** John Day **Facilities** ⊗ ⓂⒾ ⓑ ⓦ ⓈⒶ ⓔ ⓕ ⓕ **Leisure** snooker. **Location** 1.5m SW, M56 junct 12, follow signs for Forest Hills Hotel, Golf Club 1st left on Simons Lane   *Continued*

Hotel ★★★ 70% Forest Hills Hotel & Leisure Complex, Overton Hill, FRODSHAM ☎ 01928 735255 58 en suite

HELSBY
Map 07 SJ47

Helsby Towers Ln WA6 0JB
☎ 01928 722021 ▤ 01928 725384
e-mail: secathgc@aol.com
Beautifully located parkland course with several tree plantations and natural pits as water hazards. Total of 41 bunkers. A fine test of golf for all levels of player.
18 holes, 6221yds, Par 70, SSS 70, Course record 69.
Club membership 640.
Visitors must contact in advance. Weekends and bank holidays with member only. **Societies** Tue & Thu, booking through Hon Secretary. Other days possible by arrangement. **Green Fees** £27.50 per round. **Prof** Matthew Jones **Course Designer** James Braid (part) **Facilities** ⊗ ⅷ ⭌ ♨ ♀ ⚐ ♙ ⚑ ✎ **Conf** Corporate Hospitality Days available **Location** 6 miles from Chester,1 mile from M56 junct 14

Hotel ★★★★★ The Chester Grosvenor & Grosvenor Spa, Eastgate, CHESTER ☎ 01244 324024 80 en suite

KNUTSFORD
Map 07 SJ77

Heyrose Budworth Rd, Tabley WA16 0HZ
☎ 01565 733664 ▤ 01565 734578
e-mail: info@heyrosegolfclub.com
An 18-hole course in wooded and gently undulating terrain. The par 3 16th (237yds), bounded by a small river in a wooded valley, is an interesting and testing hole - one of the toughest par 3s in Cheshire. Several water hazards. Both the course and the comfortable clubhouse have attractive views.
18 holes, 6499yds, Par 73, SSS 71, Course record 66.
Club membership 600.
Visitors contact Pro shop for available times 01565 734267 **Societies** must contact in advance. **Green Fees** £25 per round weekdays and bank holidays (£30 weekends). **Cards** ▦ ▦ ▦ ▨ ▨ **Prof** Paul Affleck **Course Designer** C N Bridge **Facilities** ⊗ ⅷ by prior arrangement ⭌ ♨ ♀ ⚐ ♙ ⚑ ✎ **Conf** Corporate Hospitality Days available **Location** 1m from M6 junct 19 follow tourist signs

Hotel ★★★★ 71% Cottons Hotel & Spa, Manchester Rd, KNUTSFORD ☎ 01565 650333 109 en suite

High Legh Park Warrington Rd, Mere & High Legh
WA16 0WA ☎ 01565 830888 ▤ 01565 830999
Gentle parkland set in 200 acres of a former Anglo-Saxon deer park with 20 lakes and streams. USGA greens for all year play.
Championship: 18 holes, 6715yds, Par 72.
South: 18 holes, 6281yds, Par 70.
North: 18 holes, 6472yds, Par 70.
Club membership 700.
Visitors telephone for details **Societies** telephone for details **Green Fees** terms on application. **Cards** ▦ ▦ ▨ ▨ **Prof** Andrew McKenzie **Facilities** ⊗ by prior arrangement ⅷ by prior arrangement ⭌ by prior arrangement ♀ ♨ ⚐ ✎ **Leisure** sauna. **Conf** Corporate Hospitality Days available **Location** M6 junct 20, follow A50 to High Legh

Knutsford Mereheath Ln WA16 6HS ☎ 01565 633355
9 holes, 6288yds, Par 70, SSS 70.
Location N side of town centre off A50
Telephone for further details

Hotel ★★★★ 71% Cottons Hotel & Spa, Manchester Rd, KNUTSFORD ☎ 01565 650333 109 en suite

Mere Golf & Country Club Chester Rd, Mere
WA16 6LJ ☎ 01565 830155 ▤ 01565 830713
e-mail: enquiries@meregolf.co.uk
A gracious parkland championship course designed by James Braid in the Cheshire sand belt, with several holes close to a lake. The round has a tight finish with four testing holes.

18 holes, 6817yds, Par 71, SSS 73, Course record 64.
Club membership 550.
Visitors by prior arrangement only, not able to play Wed, Fri, Sat & Sun. **Societies** apply by telephone to Karen Gallagher. **Green Fees** £70 per day (£50 Oct-Mar). **Cards** ▦ ▦ ▦ ▨ ▨ **Prof** Peter Eyre **Course Designer** James Braid/George Duncan **Facilities** ⊗ ⅷ ⭌ ♨ ♀ ⚐ ♙ ⚑ ➤ ⚒ ✎ ♟ **Leisure** hard tennis courts, heated indoor swimming pool, squash, sauna, solarium, gymnasium. **Conf** fac available Corporate Hospitality Days available **Location** 1m E of M6 junct 19, 1m W of M56 junct 7

Hotel ★★★★ 71% Cottons Hotel & Spa, Manchester Rd, KNUTSFORD ☎ 01565 650333 109 en suite

Peover Plumley Moor Rd, Lower Peover WA16 9SE
☎ 01565 723337 ▤ 01565 723311
e-mail: mail@peovergolfclub.co.uk
Tees and greens have been positioned to maximise the benefits of the natural contours of the land. An excellent mix of holes varying in design and character, with many dog-legs and water hazards, with a river which three of the fairways cross, including the first.
18 holes, 6702yds, Par 72, SSS 72, Course record 69.
Club membership 400.
Visitors full golfing attire required. Please book for tee times. **Societies** apply in writing/telephone in advance **Green Fees** terms on application. **Cards** ▦ ▦ ▦ ▨ ▨ ▨ **Prof** Mark Twiss **Course Designer** P A Naylor **Facilities** ⊗ ⅷ ⭌ ♨ ♀ ⚐ ♙ ➤ ⚒ ✎ **Conf** fac available Corporate Hospitality Days available **Location** M6 junct19/A556 onto Plumley Moor Rd

Hotel ★★ 75% The Longview Hotel & Restaurant, 55 Manchester Rd, KNUTSFORD ☎ 01565 632119 13 en suite 13 annexe en suite

LYMM — Map 07 SJ68

Lymm Whitbarrow Rd WA13 9AN
☎ 01925 755020 📠 01925 755020
e-mail: mail@lymmgolfclub.fsnet.co.uk
First ten holes are gently undulating with the Manchester Ship Canal running alongside the 6th hole. The remaining holes are comparatively flat.
18 holes, 6341yds, Par 71, SSS 70.
Club membership 800.
Visitors may not play at weekends except with member.
Societies Wed only, must contact in advance. **Green Fees** terms on application. **Prof** Steve McCarthy **Facilities** ⊗ ⵘ ⅃ ♥ ♀ ⚲ 🏠 ⚑ **Location** 0.5m N off A6144

Hotel ★★★ 68% Lymm Hotel, Whitbarrow Rd, LYMM
☎ 01925 752233 18 rms (15 en suite) 48 annexe en suite

MACCLESFIELD — Map 07 SJ97

Macclesfield The Hollins SK11 7EA
☎ 01625 616952 (Pro) 📠 01625 260061
e-mail: secretary@maccgolfclub.co.uk
Hillside heathland course situated on the edge of the Pennines with excellent views across the Cheshire Plain. A pleasant course providing a good test for players of all abilities.
18 holes, 5714yds, Par 70, SSS 68, Course record 63.
Club membership 620.
Visitors apply in advance and have a handicap certificate.
Societies telephone initially. **Green Fees** £30 (£40 weekends and bank holidays). **Prof** Tony Taylor **Course Designer** Hawtree & Son **Facilities** ⊗ ⵘ ⅃ ♥ ♀ ⚲ 🏠 ⚑ **Conf** Corporate Hospitality Days available **Location** SE side of town centre off A523

Hotel ★★★ 70% Best Western Hollin Hall, Jackson Ln, Kerridge, Bollington, MACCLESFIELD ☎ 01625 573246 54 en suite

Shrigley Hall Hotel Shrigley Park, Pott Shrigley
SK10 5SB ☎ 01625 575626 📠 01625 575437
e-mail: shrigleyhall@paramount-hotels.co.uk
Parkland course set in 262-acre estate with breathtaking views over the Peak District and Cheshire Plain. Designed by Donald Steel, this championship standard course provides a real sporting challenge while the magnificent hotel provides a wealth of sporting facilities as well as accommodation and food.

18 holes, 6281yds, Par 71, SSS 71, Course record 68.
Club membership 500.
Visitors must contact in advance by telephone. **Societies** contact in advance. **Green Fees** terms on application.
Cards 🔲🔲 📖 **Prof** Tony Stevens **Course Designer** Donald Steel **Facilities** ⊗ ⵘ ⅃ ♥ ♀ ⚲ 🏠 ⚑ ⚑ 🚗 ⚑

Continued

⚑ **Leisure** hard tennis courts, heated indoor swimming pool, squash, fishing, sauna, solarium, gymnasium.
Location Off A523 Macclesfield to Stockport road

Hotel ★★★★ 68% Shrigley Hall Hotel Golf & Country Club, Shrigley Park, Pott Shrigley, MACCLESFIELD
☎ 01625 575757 150 en suite

Tytherington Dorchester Way, Tytherington
SK10 2JP ☎ 01625 506000 📠 01625 506040
e-mail: tytherington.events@clubhaus.com
Modern championship course in beautiful, mature parkland setting with eight water features and over 100 bunkers. Testing holes, notably the signature 12th hole (par 5), played from an elevated tee with adjacent snaking ditch and a lake guarding the green.
18 holes, 6765yds, Par 72, SSS 74.
Club membership 4800.
Visitors subject to availability and may not play weekends am. **Societies** telephone and apply in writing. **Green Fees** terms on application. **Cards** 🔲🔲 🔲🔲 🔲🔲 🔲🔲 **Prof** Gavin Beddon **Course Designer** Dave Thomas/Patrick Dawson **Facilities** ⊗ ⵘ ⅃ ♥ ♀ ⚲ 🏠 ⚑ 🚗 ⚑ ⚑
Leisure hard tennis courts, heated indoor swimming pool, squash, sauna, solarium, gymnasium. **Location** 1m N of Macclesfield off A523

Hotel ★★★★ 68% Shrigley Hall Hotel Golf & Country Club, Shrigley Park, Pott Shrigley, MACCLESFIELD
☎ 01625 575757 150 en suite

NANTWICH — Map 07 SJ65

Reaseheath Reaseheath College CW5 6DF
☎ 01270 625131
The course here is attached to Reaseheath College, which is one of the major centres of greenkeeper training in the UK. It is a short 9-hole with challenging narrow fairways. Good test of golf.
9 holes, 1882yds, Par 62, SSS 58, Course record 55.
Club membership 600.
Visitors must book in advance. **Societies** by prior arrangement, apply in writing. **Green Fees** £7 per day.
Course Designer D Mortram **Facilities** ⚲ **Conf** fac available **Location** 1.5m NE of Nantwich, off A51

Hotel ★★★ ♣♣ Rookery Hall, Main Rd, Worleston, NANTWICH ☎ 01270 610016 30 en suite 16 annexe en suite

OSCROFT — Map 07 SJ56

Pryors Hayes Willington Rd CH3 8NL
☎ 01829 741250 & 740140 📠 01829 749077
e-mail: info@pryors-hayes.co.uk
Picturesque 18-hole parkland course set in the heart of Cheshire. Gently undulating fairways demand accurate drives, and numerous trees and water hazards make the course a challenging test of golf.
18 holes, 6054yds, Par 69, SSS 69.
Club membership 530.
Visitors no restrictions. **Societies** apply for application form. **Green Fees** £20 (£30 weekends). **Cards** 🔲🔲 🔲🔲 🔲🔲 **Prof** Martin Redrup **Course Designer** John Day **Facilities** ⊗ ⵘ ⅃ ♥ ♀ ⚲ 🏠 ⚑ ⚑ ⚑ **Location** Between A54 & A51 roads, approx 6m E of Chester, village of Oscroft near Tarvin

Hotel ★★★ 66% Blossoms Hotel, St John St, CHESTER
☎ 0870 400 8108 64 en suite

POYNTON
Map 07 SJ98

Davenport Worth Hall, Middlewood Rd SK12 1TS
☎ 01625 876951 📄 01625 877489
Undulating parkland course. Extensive view over Cheshire Plain from elevated 5th tee. Testing 17th hole, par 4.
18 holes, 6027yds, Par 69, SSS 69, Course record 64. Club membership 700.
Visitors contact professional in advance, 01625 858387. May not play Wed or Sat. **Societies** Tue and Thu only. Must apply in advance. **Green Fees** terms on application. **Prof** Gary Norcott **Facilities** ⊗ ⫛ 𝄪 ⏛ ☕ ♟ 🏌 ⚐ ⛳
Leisure snooker. **Location** 1m E off A523

Hotel ★★★ 61% The County Hotel, Bramhall Ln South, BRAMHALL ☎ 0870 609 6148 65 en suite

PRESTBURY
Map 07 SJ97

Prestbury Macclesfield Rd SK10 4BJ
☎ 01625 828241 📄 01625 828241
e-mail: office@prestburygolfclub.com
Undulating parkland course, with many plateau greens. The 9th hole has a challenging uphill 3-tier green and the 17th is over a valley. Host to county and inter-county championships, including hosting an Open qualifying event in July 2004.

18 holes, 6359yds, Par 71, SSS 71, Course record 64. Club membership 702.
Visitors must contact in advance and have an introduction from own club, with member only at weekends. **Societies** apply in writing, Thu only. **Green Fees** £45 per round. **Cards** 💳 💳 💳 **Prof** Nick Summerfield **Course Designer** Harry S Colt **Facilities** ⊗ ⫛ 𝄪 ⏛ ☕ ♟ 🏌 ⚐
Conf Corporate Hospitality Days available **Location** S side of village off A538

Hotel ★★★★ 69% De Vere Mottram Hall, Wilmslow Rd, Mottram St Andrew, Prestbury, ☎ 01625 828135 132 en suite

RUNCORN
Map 07 SJ58

Runcorn Clifton Rd WA7 4SU
☎ 01928 574214 📄 01928 574214
e-mail: secretary@runcorngolfclub.ltd.uk
Parkland course with tree-lined fairways and easy walking. Fine views over Mersey and Weaver valleys. Testing holes: 7th par 5; 14th par 5; 17th par 4.
18 holes, 6048yds, Par 69, SSS 69, Course record 63. Club membership 570.
Visitors weekends restricted to playing with member only, Tuesday Ladies Day. **Societies** telephone in advance.

Green Fees terms on application. **Prof** David Ingman **Facilities** ⊗ ⫛ by prior arrangement 𝄪 ⏛ ☕ ♟ 🏌 ⚐
Location 1.25m S of Runcorn Station

Hotel 🅄 Holiday Inn Runcorn, Wood Ln, Beechwood, RUNCORN ☎ 0870 400 9070 150 en suite

SANDBACH
Map 07 SJ76

Malkins Bank Betchton Rd, Malkins Bank
CW11 4XN ☎ 01270 765931 📄 01270 764730
e-mail: davron.hackney@congleton.gov.uk
Parkland course. Tight 13th hole with stream running through.
18 holes, 6005yds, Par 70, SSS 69, Course record 65. Club membership 500.
Visitors no restrictions. Advisable to book in advance. **Societies** apply for booking form to course professional
Green Fees £9.30 per 18 holes, £6.40 per 9 holes (£10.80/£7.40 weekends). Reduced winter rates. **Cards** 💳 💳 💳 💳 **Prof** D Hackney **Course Designer** Hawtree **Facilities** ⊗ ⫛ 𝄪 ⏛ ☕ ♟ 🏌 🍴 ⚐ **Location** 1.5m SE off A533

Hotel ★★★ 65% The Chimney House Hotel, Congleton Rd, SANDBACH ☎ 0870 609 6164 48 en suite

SANDIWAY
Map 07 SJ67

Sandiway Chester Rd CW8 2DJ
☎ 01606 883247 (Secretary) 📄 01606 888542
e-mail: info@sandiwaygolf.fsnet.co.uk
Delightful undulating wood and heathland course with long hills up to the 8th, 16th and 17th holes. Many dog-legged and tree-lined holes give opportunities for the deliberate fade or draw. True championship test and one of the finest inland courses in north-west England.
18 holes, 6404yds, Par 70, SSS 71, Course record 65. Club membership 750.
Visitors book through secretary, members have reserved tees 8.30-9.30 and 12.30-1.30 (11.30-12.30 winter). Handicap certificate required **Societies** book in advance through Secretary/Manager. **Green Fees** terms on application. **Prof** William Laird **Course Designer** Ted Ray **Facilities** ⊗ ⫛ 𝄪 ⏛ ☕ ♟ 🏌 🍴 ⚐ **Location** 2m W of Northwich on A556

Hotel ★★ 62% Hartford Hall, School Ln, Hartford, NORTHWICH ☎ 01606 780320 20 en suite

SUTTON WEAVER
Map 07 SJ57

Sutton Hall Aston Ln WA7 3ED
☎ 01928 790747 📄 01928 759174
Undulating parkland course on south facing slopes of the Weaver Valley. Providing a challenge to all levels of play.
18 holes, 6608yards, Par 72, SSS 72, Course record 69. Club membership 750.
Visitors contact in advance to book tee-time. **Societies** write/telephone in advance. **Green Fees** terms on application. **Cards** 💳 💳 💳 💳 💳 **Prof** Jamie Hope **Course Designer** Ace Golf Associates **Facilities** ⊗ ⫛ 𝄪 ☕ ♟ 🏌 🍴 🛒 ⚐ **Location** M56 junct 12, follow signs for A56 to Warrington, on entering Sutton Weaver take 1st turn right

Hotel 🅄 Holiday Inn Runcorn, Wood Ln, Beechwood, RUNCORN ☎ 0870 400 9070 150 en suite

Continued

TARPORLEY   Map 07 SJ56

Portal Golf & Country Club Cobbler's Cross Ln
CW6 0DJ ☎ 01829 733933 🖷 01829 733928
e-mail: portalgolf@aol.com

*Championship Course: 18 holes, 7037yds, Par 73, SSS 74,
Course record 64.*
*Premier Course: 18 holes, 6508yds, Par 71, SSS 72,
Course record 64.*
Arderne Course: 9 holes, 1724yds, Par 30.
Course Designer Donald Steel **Location** Off A49
Telephone for further details
....
Hotel ★★★ 68% The Wild Boar, Whitchurch Rd,
Beeston, TARPORLEY ☎ 01829 260309 37 en suite

WARRINGTON   Map 07 SJ68

Birchwood Kelvin Close, Science Park North,
Birchwood WA3 7PB
☎ 01925 818819 (Club) & 816574 (Pro) 🖷 01925 822403
e-mail: birchwoodgolfclub.com@lineone.net
**Very testing parkland course with many natural water
hazards and the prevailing wind creating a problem on
each hole. The 11th hole is particularly challenging.**
*Pilgrims: 18 holes, 6727yds, Par 71, SSS 73, Course
record 66.*
Progress: 18 holes, 6359yds, Par 71, SSS 72.
*Mayflower (ladies course): 18 holes, 5849yds, Par 74, SSS
74.*
Club membership 745.
Visitors advisable to check with the professional to
determine if course is fully booked. **Societies** Mon, Wed &
Thu. Apply in writing, or telephone. **Green Fees** £26 per
day; £20 per round (£34 per day weekends & bank
holidays). **Cards** 🖃 🖃 **Prof** Paul McEwan **Course
Designer** T J A Macauley **Facilities** ⊗ ⅢⅢ ⓛ 🖤 🖢 🛦 🖻
🖤 **Conf** fac available Corporate Hospitality Days
available **Location** Junct 11 on M62, follow signs for
Science Park North, 2m from the junct
....
Hotel ⓤ Holiday Inn Haydock, Lodge Ln, HAYDOCK
☎ 0870 400 9039 138 en suite

Leigh Kenyon Hall, Broseley Ln, Culcheth WA3 4BG
☎ 01925 762943 (Secretary) 🖷 01925 765097
e-mail: golf@leighgolf.fsnet.co.uk
**A pleasant, well-wooded parkland course. Any
discrepancy in length is compensated by the wide
variety of golf offered here. The course is well
maintained and there is a comfortable clubhouse.**
18 holes, 5853yds, Par 69, SSS 69, Course record 64.
Club membership 850.
Visitors contact professional for details. **Societies** Mon (ex
bank holidays), Tue & Fri, apply by telephone. *Continued*

Green Fees Summer: £32 (£40 weekends) Winter: £20
(£27 weekends). **Prof** Andrew Baguley **Course Designer**
Harold Hilton **Facilities** ⊗ ⅢⅢ ⓛ 🖤 🖢 🛦 🖻 🖤 **Conf**
Corporate Hospitality Days available **Location** 5m NE off
A579
....
Hotel ★★★ 72% Fir Grove Hotel, Knutsford Old Rd,
WARRINGTON ☎ 01925 267471 52 en suite

Poulton Park Dig Ln, Cinnamon Brow, Padgate
WA2 0SH ☎ 01925 822802 & 825220 🖷 01925 822802
e-mail: secretary@poultonparkgolfclub.com
**Tight, flat parkland course with good greens and many
trees. A straight drive off each tee is important. The
4/13th has a fairway curving to the left with water and
out-of-bounds on left and trees on right.**
9 holes, 5179yds, Par 68, SSS 66, Course record 66.
Club membership 350.
Visitors midweek only. Contact professional for details
01925 825220. **Societies** apply in advance. **Green Fees** not
confirmed. **Prof** Ian Orrell **Facilities** ⊗ ⅢⅢ ⓛ 🖤 🖢 🛦 🖻
Location 3m from Warrington on A574
....
Hotel ★★★ 72% Fir Grove Hotel, Knutsford Old Rd,
WARRINGTON ☎ 01925 267471 52 en suite

Walton Hall Warrington Rd, Higher Walton
WA4 5LU ☎ 01925 263061 (bookings)
**A quiet, wooded, municipal parkland course on Walton
Hall estate.**
18 holes, 6647yds, Par 72, SSS 73, Course record 70.
Club membership 250.
Visitors must book 6 days in advance. **Societies** must
contact in writing. **Green Fees** terms on application. **Prof**
John Jackson **Course Designer** Peter Allisss/Dave Thomas
Facilities ⊗ 🖤 🖢 🛦 🖻 🖞 🛦 **Location** 2m from junct
11 of M56
....
Hotel ★★★★ 75% De Vere Daresbury Park, Chester Rd,
Daresbury, WARRINGTON ☎ 01925 267331
181 en suite

Warrington Hill Warren, London Rd, Appleton
WA4 5HR ☎ 01925 261775 (Secretary) 🖷 01925 265933
e-mail: secretary@warrington-golf-club.co.uk
**Meadowland, with varied terrain and natural hazards.
Major work has recently been carried out on both the
clubhouse and the course to ensure high standards. The
course is a constant challenge with ponds, trees and
bunkers threatening the errant shot!**

18 holes, 6305yds, Par 72, SSS 70, Course record 61.
Club membership 840.
Visitors contact in advance. **Societies** by prior arrangement
Continued

with Secretary. **Green Fees** £27 per day (£32 weekends & bank holidays). **Prof** Reay Mackay **Course Designer** James Braid **Facilities** ⊗ ⅷ ⅃ 및 ♥ ♀ ♨ 🛈 ⚐ ⚘ **Conf** Corporate Hospitality Days available **Location** 1.5m N of junct 10 of M56 on A49

....

Hotel ★★★★ 72% Hanover International Hotel & Club, Stretton Rd, Stretton, WARRINGTON ☎ 01925 730706 142 en suite

WIDNES   Map 07 SJ58

Mersey Valley Warrington Rd, Bold Heath WA8 3XL
☎ 0151 4246060 📄 0151 2579097
Parkland course, very easy walking.
18 holes, 6374yards, Par 72, SSS 71, Course record 70.
Club membership 500.
Visitors 6 day booking system available. **Societies** telephone in advance. Deposit required. **Green Fees** £30 per day, £20 per round (£40/£25 weekends and bank holidays). **Cards** 🖭 💳 💳 💳 📇 **Prof** Andy Stevenson **Course Designer** R Bush **Facilities** ⊗ ⅷ by prior arrangement ⅃ 및 ♀ ♨ 🛈 ⚐ ⚘ ✿ **Leisure** fishing. **Location** M62 junct , follow A57 towards Warrington. Club 2m on left

....

Hotel ★★★ 62% The Hillcrest Hotel, 75 Cronton Ln, WIDNES ☎ 0151 424 1616 50 en suite

St Michael Jubilee Dundalk Rd WA8 8BS
☎ 0151 424 6230 📄 0151 495 2124
e-mail: dchapmam@aol.com
18 holes, 5925yds, Par 69, SSS 67.
Location W side of town centre off A562
Telephone for further details

....

Hotel ⌂ Travelodge, Fiddlers Ferry Rd, WIDNES ☎ 08700 850 950 32 en suite

Widnes Highfield Rd WA8 7DT
☎ 0151 424 2440 & 424 2995 📄 0151 495 2849
e-mail: email@widnes-golfclub.co.uk
Parkland course, easy walking, challenging in parts.

18 holes, 5719yds, Par 69, SSS 68, Course record 64.
Club membership 700.
Visitors may play after 9am & after 4pm on competition days. Must contact in advance. **Societies** must contact the secretary in writing. **Green Fees** £19 per 18 holes (£24 weekends). **Prof** J O'Brien **Facilities** ⊗ ⅷ ⅃ 및 ♀ ♨ 🛈 **Location** M62 junct 7,A57 to Warrington, right at lights into Wilmere lane, right at T junct. 1st left at rdbt into Birchfield road, immediately right after 3rd pelican crossing to Highfield road, right before traffic lights.

....

Hotel ⌂ Travelodge, Fiddlers Ferry Rd, WIDNES ☎ 08700 850 950 32 en suite

WILMSLOW   Map 07 SJ88

De Vere Mottram Hall Wilmslow Rd, Mottram St Andrew SK10 4QT ☎ 01625 828135 📄 01625 828950
e-mail: dmh.sales@devere-hotels.com
Championship standard course - flat meadowland on the front nine and undulating woodland on the back nine, with well guarded greens. The course is unusual as each half opens and closes with par 5s. The hotel offers many leisure facilities.
Mottram Hall: 18 holes, 7006yds, Par 72, SSS 74, Course record 63.
Club membership 500.
Visitors may book up to 2 week in advance. May not play weekends. Handicap certificate required. **Societies** must contact Golf Co-ordinator in advance. **Green Fees** £50 per round. **Cards** 🖭 💳 💳 💳 📇 **Prof** Dave Thomas **Facilities** ⊗ ⅷ ⅃ 및 ♀ ♨ 🛈 ⚐ ⚘ ✿ ⚘ ✿ **Leisure** hard tennis courts, heated indoor swimming pool, squash, sauna, solarium, gymnasium, day store & drying room. **Conf** fac available Corporate Hospitality Days available **Location** On A538 between Wilmslow and Presbury

....

Hotel ★★★★ 69% De Vere Mottram Hall, Wilmslow Rd, Mottram St Andrew, Prestbury, ☎ 01625 828135 132 en suite

Styal Station Rd, Styal SK9 4JN
☎ 01625 531359 📄 01625 416373
e-mail: gtraynor@styalgolf.co.uk
Well designed flat parkland course. Challenging and enjoyable test for all standards of golfer.
18 holes, 6194yds, Par 70, SSS 70, Course record 63.
Club membership 800.
Visitors contact to reserve tee time. **Societies** telephone in advance. **Green Fees** £21 per round (£26 weekends). **Cards** 🖭 💳 💳 💳 📇 **Prof** Simon Forrest **Course Designer** Tony Holmes **Facilities** ⊗ ⅷ ⅃ 및 ♀ ♨ 🛈 ⚐ ⚘ ✿ **Leisure** par 3 9 hole course. **Conf** fac available Corporate Hospitality Days available **Location** M56 junct 5, 5min drive from Wilmslow/Manchester Airport

....

Hotel ★★★ 66% Belfry House Hotel, Stanley Rd, HANDFORTH ☎ 0161 437 0511 81 en suite

Wilmslow Great Warford, Mobberley WA16 7AY
☎ 01565 872148 📄 01565 872172
e-mail: wilmslowgolfclub@ukf.net
Peaceful parkland course, in the heart of the mid-Cheshire countryside, offering golf at all levels.
18 holes, 6607yds, Par 72, SSS 72, Course record 62.
Club membership 850.
Visitors must contact in advance. **Societies** Tue & Thu only application in writing. **Green Fees** £55 per day; £45 per round (£65/£55 weekends & bank holidays). **Cards** 🖭 💳 💳 💳 📇 **Prof** John Nowicki **Facilities** ⊗ ⅷ ⅃ 및 ♀ ♨ 🛈 ⚐ ⚘ ✿ **Conf** Corporate Hospitality Days available **Location** 2m SW off B5058

....

Hotel ★★★ 77% Alderley Edge Hotel, Macclesfield Rd, ALDERLEY EDGE ☎ 01625 583033 52 en suite

---

In the hotel entries, the percentage figure refers to the AA's most recent Quality Assessment Score.

WINSFORD   Map 07 SJ66

Knights Grange Grange Ln CW7 2PT
☎ 01606 552780
e-mail: knightsgrangewinsford@valeroyal.gov.uk
An 18-hole golf course set in the beautiful Cheshire countryside on the town outskirts. The front nine are mainly flat but players have to negotiate water, ditches and other hazards along the way. The back nine take the player deep into the countryside, with many of the tees offering panoramic views. A lake known as the Ocean is a feature of many holes - a particular hazard for slicers of the ball. There are also many mature woodland areas to catch the wayward drive.
18 holes, 6010yds, Par 71, SSS 70.
Visitors 24 hr booking system for weekly play, after 10am Wed for weekend bookings. **Societies** apply in writing.
Green Fees £8.40 for 18 holes (£10.50 weekends). **Cards** 🖾 🖾 🖾 🖾 🗳 **Prof** Graham Moore **Course Designer** Steve Dawson **Facilities** 🖳 ⌂ 🛆 ⌂ ⅋ ⚡ **Leisure** hard and grass tennis courts. **Location** N side of town off A54

Hotel ⇧ Travelodge, M6 Junction 18, A54, MIDDLEWICH ☎ 08700 850 950 32 en suite

WINWICK   Map 07 SJ69

Alder Root Alder Root Ln WA2 8R2
☎ 01925 291919 📄 01925 291961
A woodland course, flat in nature but with many undulations. Several holes have water hazards. One of the most testing nine-hole courses in the north west.
9 holes, 5837yds, Par 69, SSS 68, Course record 67.
Club membership 400.
Visitors telephone for details of dress code. **Societies** must telephone in advance. **Green Fees** terms on application.
Cards 🖾 🖾 🗳 **Prof** C McKevitt **Course Designer** Mr Lander/Mr Millington **Facilities** ⊗ 🛅 🖳 ⚡ 🛆 ⌂ 🗞 🛶 ⚡ **Location** From M62 junct 9 take A49 N for 800mtrs then left at lights and 1st right into Alder Root Lane

Hotel ★★ 68% Paddington House Hotel, 514 Old Manchester Rd, WARRINGTON ☎ 01925 816767 37 en suite

CORNWALL & ISLES OF SCILLY

BODMIN   Map 02 SX06

Lanhydrock Lostwithiel Rd PL30 5AQ
☎ 01208 73600 📄 01208 77325
e-mail: golfing@lanhydrock-golf.co.uk
An acclaimed parkland/moorland course adjacent to the National Trust property of Lanhydrock House. Nestling in a picturesque wooded valley of oak and birch, this undulating course provides an exciting and enjoyable challenge.

18 holes, 6100yds, Par 70, SSS 70, Course record 66.
Club membership 300.
Visitors tee time reservation in advance advised. **Societies** please telephone in advance. **Green Fees** £42 per day, £33 per round. **Cards** 🖾 🖾 🖾 🖾 🗳 **Prof** Phil Brookes **Course Designer** Hamilton Stutt **Facilities** ⊗ 🛅 🖳 🖳 ⚡ 🛆 ⌂ ⌂ 🛶 ⚡ ⚡ **Conf** fac available **Location** 1m S of Bodmin from B3268 via A30/A38

Hotel ★★★ 69% Restormel Lodge Hotel, Hillside Gardens, LOSTWITHIEL ☎ 01208 872223 21 en suite 12 annexe en suite

BUDE   Map 02 SS20

Bude & North Cornwall Burn View EX23 8DA
☎ 01288 352006 📄 01288 356855
Seaside links course with natural sand bunkers, superb greens and breathtaking views. Club established in 1893.
18 holes, 6057yds, Par 71, SSS 70.
Club membership 800.
Visitors book by telephone 6 days in advance for starting time - or before 6 days with a deposit. Limited tee times at weekends. **Societies** apply in writing or by telephone/fax. **Green Fees** £27 per day (£27 per round weekends & bank holidays). **Cards** 🖾 🖾 🗳 **Prof** John Yeo **Course Designer** Tom Dunn **Facilities** ⊗ 🛅 🖳 🖳 ⚡ 🛆 ⌂ ⌂ 🛶 ⚡ **Leisure** snooker room. **Conf** fac available **Location** N side of town

Hotel ★★★ 68% Camelot Hotel, Downs View, BUDE ☎ 01288 352361 24 en suite

BUDOCK VEAN   Map 02 SW73

Budock Vean Hotel on the River Mawnan Smith
TR11 5LG ☎ 01326 250288 (hotel) & 252102 (shop)
📄 01326 250892
e-mail: relax@budockvean.co.uk
Set in 65 acres of mature grounds with a private foreshore to the Helford River, this 18-tee undulating parkland course has a tough par 4 5th hole (456yds) which dog-legs at halfway around an oak tree. The 16th hole measures 572yds, par 5.
9 holes, 5255yds, Par 68, SSS 65, Course record 61.
Club membership 140.
Visitors must contact in advance. **Societies** apply in writing or telephone in advance. **Green Fees** not confirmed. **Cards** 🖾 🖾 🖾 🖾 🗳 **Prof** Tony Ramsden **Course Designer** James Braid **Facilities** ⊗ 🛅 🖳 🖳 ⚡ 🛆 ⌂ ⌂ 🛶 🗞 🛶 ⚡ **Leisure** hard tennis courts, heated indoor swimming pool, fishing, boating facilities. **Location** 1.5m SW of Mawnan Smith

Continued

Continued

Hotel ★★★★ ⚐ 73% Budock Vean-The Hotel on the River, MAWNAN SMITH
☎ 01326 252100 & 0800 833927 ▤ 01326 250892
57 en suite

CAMBORNE   Map 02 SW64

Tehidy Park TR14 0HH
☎ 01209 842208 ▤ 01209 843680
18 holes, 6241yds, Par 71, SSS 71, Course record 62.
Location On Portreath/Pool road, 2m S of Camborne
Telephone for further details

Hotel ★★★ 70% Penventon Park Hotel, REDRUTH
☎ 01209 203000 69 en suite

CAMELFORD   Map 02 SX18

Bowood Park Lanteglos PL32 9RF
☎ 01840 213017 ▤ 01840 212622
e-mail: golf@bowoodpark.com
A testing parkland course situated in Bowood Park, formerly the largest deer park in Cornwall. The first nine holes are designed around rolling hills; the back nine being played through the River Allen Valley. Plenty of wildlife, water and trees.

18 holes, 6692yds, Par 72, SSS 72, Course record 68.
Club membership 250.
Visitors booking system in operation, contact in advance. **Societies** contact for details. **Green Fees** £30 per round (£35 weekends). **Cards** ▨ ▨ Barclays ▨ ▨ **Prof** John Phillips **Course Designer** Sandow **Facilities** ⊗ 川 ⅃ ♥ ♀ ⚐ 🏠 ⌂ ⚐ ❥ ♣ ⚐ ₵ **Leisure** fishing, masseur available. **Conf** fac available Corporate Hospitality Days available **Location** Through Camelford, 0.5m turn right Tintagel/Boscastle B3266, 1st left at garage

Hotel ★★★ 65% Bowood Park Hotel & Golf Course, Lanteglos, CAMELFORD ☎ 01840 213017 31 en suite

CARLYON BAY   Map 02 SX05

Carlyon Bay Hotel Sea Rd PL25 3RD
☎ 01726 814250 ▤ 01726 814250
e-mail: golf@carlyonbay.co.uk
Championship-length, cliff-top parkland course running east to west and back again and also uphill and down a fair bit. The fairways stay in excellent condition all year as they have since the course was laid down in 1925. Magnificent views from the course across St Austell Bay; particularly from the ninth green, where an approach shot remotely to the right will plummet over the cliff edge.

Continued

18 holes, 6597yds, Par 72, SSS 71, Course record 63.
Club membership 500.
Visitors must contact in advance. **Societies** must contact in advance. **Green Fees** from £25-£39 per round depending on season. **Cards** ▨ ▨ ▨ ▨ ▨ **Prof** Mark Rowe
Course Designer Hamilton Stutt **Facilities** ⅃ ♥ ♀ ⚐ 🏠 🏠 ⚐ ❥ ♣ ⚐ ₵ **Leisure** hard tennis courts, outdoor and indoor heated swimming pools, sauna, solarium. **Conf** Corporate Hospitality Days available **Location** 3m SE of St Austell

Hotel ★★★★ 74% Carlyon Bay Hotel, Sea Rd, Carlyon Bay, ST AUSTELL ☎ 01726 812304 87 en suite

CONSTANTINE BAY   Map 02 SW87

Trevose PL28 8JB ☎ 01841 520208 ▤ 01841 521057
e-mail: info@trevose-gc.co.uk
Well known links course with early holes close to the sea on excellent springy turf. A championship course affording varying degrees of difficulty appealing to both the professional and higher handicap player. It is a good test with well-positioned bunkers, and a meandering stream, and the wind playing a decisive role in preventing low scoring. Self-catering accommodation is available at the club.

Championship Course: 18 holes, 6608yds, Par 71, SSS 71, Course record 66.
New Course: 9 holes, 3031yds, Par 35.
Short Course: 9 holes, 1360yds, Par 29.
Club membership 1650.
Visitors subject to reservations, handicap certificate required for championship course. Advisable to contact in advance. **Societies** telephone or write to the secretary.
Green Fees terms on application. **Cards** ▨ ▨ ▨ ▨ ▨
Prof Gary Alliss **Course Designer** H S Colt **Facilities** ⊗ 川 ⅃ ♀ 🏠 ⚐ ❥ ♣ ⚐ ₵ **Leisure** hard tennis courts, heated outdoor swimming pool, snooker & games room. **Location** 4m W of Padstow on B3276, to St Merryn, proceed 500yds past crossroads and take right turn, signposted

Hotel ★★★ 79% Treglos Hotel, CONSTANTINE BAY ☎ 01841 520727 42 en suite

FALMOUTH   Map 02 SW83

Falmouth Swanpool Rd TR11 5BQ
☎ 01326 314296 ▤ 01326 317783
e-mail: falmouthgc@onetel.net.uk
Seaside/parkland course with outstanding coastal views. Sufficiently bunkered to punish any inaccurate shots. Five acres of practice grounds.

Continued

18 holes, 6037yds, Par 71, SSS 70.
Club membership 500.
Visitors please book for tee time. **Societies** must contact in advance. **Green Fees** not confirmed. **Cards** **Prof** Bryan Patterson **Facilities** **Location** SW side of town centre

Hotel ★★★★ 70% Royal Duchy Hotel, Cliff Rd, FALMOUTH ☎ 01326 313042 43 en suite

HOLYWELL BAY Map 02 SW75

Holywell Bay TR8 5PW

☎ 01637 830095 01637 831000
e-mail: golf@trevornick.co.uk
Situated beside a family fun park with many amenities. The course is an 18-hole par 3 with excellent sea views. Fresh Atlantic winds make the course hard to play and there are several tricky holes, particularly the 18th over the trout pond. The site also has an excellent 18-hole Pitch and Putt course for the whole family.

18 holes, 2784yds, Par 61, Course record 58.
Club membership 100.
Visitors no restrictions. **Societies** telephone in advance. **Green Fees** not confirmed. **Course Designer** Hartley **Facilities** **Leisure** heated outdoor swimming pool, fishing, touring & camping facilities. **Location** Off A3075 Newquay/Perranporth road

Hotel ★★★ 67% Barrowfield Hotel, Hilgrove Rd, NEWQUAY ☎ 01637 878878 81 en suite 2 annexe en suite

LAUNCESTON Map 02 SX38

Launceston St Stephens PL15 8HF

☎ 01566 773442 01566 777506
e-mail: charleshicks@tesco.net
Highly rated golf course with magnificent views over the historic lawn and moors. Dominated by the 'The Hill' up which the 8th and 11th fairways rise, and on which the 8th, 9th, 11th and 12th greens sit.
18 holes, 6407yds, Par 70, SSS 71, Course record 65.
Club membership 800.
Visitors must contact in advance, may not play weekends Apr-Oct. **Societies** telephone in first instance. **Green Fees** not confirmed. **Prof** John Tozer **Course Designer** Hamilton Stutt **Facilities** **Conf** Corporate Hospitality Days available **Location** NW side of town centre on B3254

Hotel ★★ 65% Eagle House Hotel, Castle St, LAUNCESTON ☎ 01566 772036 14 en suite

Trethorne Kennards House PL15 8QE

☎ 01566 86903 01566 86929
e-mail: mark@trethornegolfclub.com
Rolling parkland course with well maintained fairways and computer irrigated greens. Plenty of trees and natural water hazards make this well respected course a good challenge.
18 holes, 6178yds, Par 71, SSS 71, Course record 69.
Club membership 500.
Visitors must contact in advance on 01566 86903. **Societies** write or telephone Mark Boundy. **Green Fees** not confirmed. **Cards** **Prof** Mark Boundy **Course Designer** Frank Frayne **Facilities** **Leisure** leisure farm and tenpin bowling. **Conf** fac available Corporate Hospitality Days available **Location** Off A30, 3m W of Launceston, on junct with A395, Camelford

Hotel ★★ 65% Eagle House Hotel, Castle St, LAUNCESTON ☎ 01566 772036 14 en suite

LELANT Map 02 SW53

West Cornwall TR26 3DZ

☎ 01736 753401 01736 753401
e-mail: ian@westcornwallgolfclub.fsnet.co.uk
A seaside links with sandhills and lovely turf adjacent to the Hayle estuary and St Ives Bay. A real test of the player's skill, especially 'Calamity Corner' starting at the 5th on the lower land by the River Hayle.

18 holes, 5884yds, Par 69, SSS 69, Course record 63.
Club membership 813.
Visitors must prove handicap certificate, be a member of a club affiliated to the EGU, advisable to contact in advance. **Societies** must apply in writing/telephone in advance. **Green Fees** £25 per day (£30 weekends). **Cards** **Prof** Jason Broadway **Course Designer** Reverend Tyack **Facilities** **Leisure** snooker. **Location** N side of village off A3074

Hotel ★★ 72% Pedn-Olva Hotel, West Porthminster Beach, ST IVES ☎ 01736 796222 30 en suite

LOOE Map 02 SX25

Looe Bindown PL13 1PX

☎ 01503 240239 01503 240864
Designed by Harry Vardon in 1935, this downland/parkland course commands panoramic views over south-east Cornwall and the coast. Easy walking.
18 holes, 5940yds, Par 70, SSS 69, Course record 64.
Club membership 420.
Visitors handicap certificate preferred, booking in advance recommended, no limitations subject to availability.

Continued

Societies telephone in advance, booking to be confirmed in writing. **Green Fees** £24 per 18 holes. **Cards** ⊞ ▭ ▭ ▤ **Prof** Jason Bowen **Course Designer** Harry Vardon **Facilities** ⊗ 🏌 ▱ ☕ ♀ ⛳ 🏠 ⛳ 🦌 🏌 ✓ **Conf** Corporate Hospitality Days available **Location** 3.5m NE off B3253

....

Hotel ★★★ 66% Hannafore Point Hotel, Marine Dr, West Looe, LOOE ☎ 01503 263273 37 en suite

Lostwithiel Hotel, Golf & Country Club

Visitors must contact in advance. **Societies** contact in advance. **Green Fees** £29 per day (£33 weekends). Reductions during winter months. **Cards** ⊞ ▭ ▭ ▤ ▭ ▱ ▤ **Prof** Tony Nash **Course Designer** S Wood **Facilities** ⊗ 🏌 ▱ ☕ ♀ ⛳ 🏠 ⛳ 🦌 ✓ ℓ **Leisure** hard tennis courts, heated indoor swimming pool, fishing, gymnasium. **Conf** fac available **Location** 1m outside Lostwithiel off A390

....

Hotel ★★★ 62% Lostwithiel Hotel Golf & Country Club, Lower Polscoe, LOSTWITHIEL ☎ 01208 873550 21 en suite

LOSTWITHIEL　　　　　　　　Map 02 SX15

Lostwithiel Hotel, Golf & Country Club

Lower Polscoe PL22 0HQ
☎ 01208 873550 📠 01208 87479
e-mail: reception@golf-hotel.co.uk
An undulating, parkland course with water hazards. Overlooked by Restormel Castle and the River Fowey flows alongside the course. Driving range.
18 holes, 5984yds, Par 72, SSS 71, Course record 67. Club membership 500.

Continued

MAWGAN PORTH　　　　　　　Map 02 SW86

Merlin TR8 4DN ☎ 01841 540222 📠 01841 541031
A heathland course with fine views of the coast and countryside. Fairly easy walking. The most challenging hole is the par 4 18th with out of bounds on the left and ponds on either side of the green.

Continued

18 holes, 6210yds, Par 71, SSS 71.
Club membership 350.
Visitors no restrictions, except during club competitions, must contact in advance. **Societies** telephone in advance. **Green Fees** not confirmed. **Cards** ⊞ ▨ ▨ ▨ **Course Designer** Ross Oliver **Facilities** ⊗ ⋈ 🍴 ▪ ♥ ♀ 𓏢 🍴 🏌 ⚒ 🏌 ⚑ **Conf** fac available Corporate Hospitality Days available **Location** On the coast rd Newquay/Padstow. After Mawgan Porth follow signs for St Eval, golf course on right

. . . .
Hotel ★★ 72% Tredragon Hotel, MAWGAN PORTH
☎ 01637 860213 26 en suite

MAWNAN SMITH
See **Budock Vean**

MULLION   Map 02 SW61

Mullion Cury TR12 7BP
☎ 01326 240685 & 241176(pro) 🖹 01326 240685
18 holes, 6037yds, Par 70, SSS 70.
Course Designer W Sich **Location** 1.5m NW of Mullion, off A3083
Telephone for further details
. . . .
Hotel ★★★ 71% Polurrian Hotel, MULLION ☎ 01326 240421 39 en suite

NEWQUAY   Map 02 SW86

Newquay Tower Rd TR7 1LT
☎ 01637 874354 🖹 01637 874066
e-mail: info@newquay-golf-club.co.uk
One of Cornwall's finest seaside links with magnificent views over the Atlantic Ocean. Open to the unpredictable nature of the elements and possessing some very demanding greenside bunkers, the prerequisite for good scoring at Newquay is accuracy.
18 holes, 6150yds, Par 69, SSS 69, Course record 63.
Club membership 600.
Visitors please telephone in advance. **Societies** apply in writing or telephone. **Green Fees** £30 per day; £25 per round. **Cards** ⊞ ▨ ▨ ▨ 🔲 **Prof** Mark Bevan **Course Designer** H Colt **Facilities** ⊗ ⋈ 🍴 ▪ ♥ ♀ 𓏢 🍴 🏌 ⚒ **Leisure** Snooker. **Conf** Corporate Hospitality Days available **Location** W side of town

. . . .
Hotel ★★★ 70% Hotel Bristol, Narrowcliff, NEWQUAY
☎ 01637 875181 74 en suite

Treloy TR8 4JN ☎ 01637 878554 🖹 01637 871710
e-mail: paull@treloy.freeserve.co.uk
9 holes, 2143yds, Par 32, SSS 31, Course record 63.
Course Designer M R M Sandow **Location** On A3059 Newquay to St Columb Major Road
Telephone for further details   *Continued*

. . . .
Hotel ★★ 71% Whipsiderry Hotel, Trevelgue Rd, Porth, NEWQUAY ☎ 01637 874777 20 rms (19 en suite)

PADSTOW
See **Constantine Bay**

PERRANPORTH   Map 02 SW75

Perranporth Budnic Hill TR6 0AB
☎ 01872 573701 🖹 01872 573701
e-mail: perranporth@golfclub92.fsnet.co.uk
There are three testing par 5 holes on the links course (2nd, 5th, 11th). This seaside links course has magnificent views of the North Cornwall coastline, and excellent greens. The drainage of the course, being sand-based, is also exceptional.

18 holes, 6228yds, Par 72, SSS 72, Course record 62.
Club membership 600.
Visitors must contact in advance, no reserved tee times. **Societies** by prior arrangement. **Green Fees** £25 per day (£30 per round weekends and bank holidays). **Cards** ⊞ ▨ ▨ 🔲 **Prof** D Michell **Course Designer** James Braid **Facilities** ⊗ ⋈ 🍴 ▪ ♥ ♀ 𓏢 🍴 🏌 ⚒ 🏌 **Conf** Corporate Hospitality Days available **Location** 0.75m NE on B3285

. . . .
Hotel ★★ 70% Rosemundy House Hotel, Rosemundy Hill, ST AGNES ☎ 01872 552101 46 en suite

PRAA SANDS   Map 02 SW52

Praa Sands Germoe Cross Roads TR20 9TQ
☎ 01736 763445 🖹 01736 763399
e-mail: praasandsgolf@aol.com

9 holes, 4122yds, Par 62, SSS 60, Course record 59.
Course Designer R Hamilton **Location** A394 midway between Penzance/Helston
Telephone for further details
. . . .
Inn ◆◆◆◆ Harbour Inn, Commercal Rd, PORTHLEVEN
☎ 01326 573876 10 en suite

St Mellion

Map 02 SX36   **St Mellion**

☎ **01579 351351**   📄 **01579 350537**

S et amongst 450 acres of glorious undulating Cornish countryside, St Mellion International is heralded as the premier Golf and Country Club in the southwest. St Mellion boasts two outstanding golf courses, the first being the interesting yet demanding Old Course, which is perfect for golfers of all abilities. Complete with ideally sited bunkers, strategically tiered greens and difficult water features, the Old Course is definitely one not to be overlooked. However, if you really want to test your game, look no further than the renowned Nicklaus Course, designed by the great man himself. On its opening in 1998 Jack quoted "St Mellion is potentially the finest golf course in Europe". An inspiration to all golfers, the Nicklaus Course offers spectacularly sculptured fairways and carpet-like greens to all who take up its challenge.

e-mail: st-mellion@americangolf.uk.com

Visitors Telephone in advance 01579 352002

Societies Apply in writing or telephone in advance

Green Fees Nicklaus Course: £50 per round. Old Course: £35 per round. £70 per day

Facilities ⊗ ⚒ 🏌 🖥 💆 🍵 ♀ 🏖 ♿ 🏵 🍴
🐎 🛒 ✎ ♞

Professional David Moon

Leisure Tennis, swimming, sauna, solarium, gym

Location Saltash PL12 6SD (A38 to Saltash then A388 to Callington)

Holes/Par/Course record 36 holes.
Nicklaus Course: 18 holes, 6592 yds,
Par 72, SSS 74, Course record 63
The Old Course: 18 holes, 5782 yds,
Par 68, SSS 68 Course record 60

WHERE TO STAY NEARBY

Hotels
ST MELLION
★★★ 68% St Mellion International
PL12 6SD ☎ 01579 351351.
39 annexe en suite

LISKEARD
★★ ⊛ ⊛ ⊛ ♨ Well House, PL14 4RN
☎ 01579 342001. 9 en suite

SALTASH
★★★ 67% China Fleet Country Club,
PL12 6LJ. ☎ 01752 848668. 40 en suite

Championship Course

ROCK
Map 02 SW97

St Enodoc PL27 6LD
☎ 01208 863216 📠 01208 862976
e-mail: stenodocgolfclub@aol.com

Classic links course with huge sand hills and rolling fairways. James Braid laid out the original 18 holes in 1907 and changes were made in 1922 and 1935. On the Church, the 10th is the toughest par 4 on the course and on the 6th is a truly enormous sand hill known as the Himalayas. The Holywell is not as exacting as the Church; it is less demanding on stamina but still a real test of skill for golfers of any handicap.

Church Course: 18 holes, 6243yds, Par 69, SSS 70, Course record 64.
Holywell Course: 18 holes, 4142yds, Par 63, SSS 61.
Club membership 1300.

Visitors may not play on bank holidays. Must have a handicap certificate of 24 or below for Church Course. Must contact in advance. **Societies** must contact in writing/telephone. **Green Fees** Church Course: £60 per day, £40 per round (£50 per round weekends). Holywell Course: £25 per day, £16 per round. **Cards** 💳 💳 💳 💳 💳 **Prof** Nick Williams **Course Designer** James Braid **Facilities** ⊗ ⠇⠇ ⓛ ⠇ ♥ ⍩ ⚘ 🏠 ⚐ ⚘ ⚒ ⚑ **Location** W side of village

Hotel ★★ 66% The Molesworth Arms Hotel, Molesworth St, WADEBRIDGE ☎ 01208 812055 16 rms (14 en suite)

ST AUSTELL
Map 02 SX05

Porthpean Porthpean PL26 6AY
☎ 01726 64613 📠 01726 71643
18 holes, 5210yds, Par 67, SSS 66.
Location 1.5m from St Austell by-pass
Telephone for further details

Hotel ★★ 72% The Pier House, Harbour Front, Charlestown, ST AUSTELL ☎ 01726 67955 26 en suite

St Austell Tregongeeves Ln PL26 7DS
☎ 01726 74756 📠 01726 71978

Very interesting inland parkland course designed by James Braid and offering glorious views of the surrounding countryside. Undulating, well-covered with tree plantations and well-bunkered. Notable holes are 8th (par 4) and 16th (par 3).

18 holes, 6089yds, Par 69, SSS 69, Course record 64.
Club membership 700.

Visitors advisable to contact in advance, weekend play is limited. Must be a member of a recognised golf club and hold a handicap certificate. **Societies** must apply in writing. **Green Fees** not confirmed. **Prof** Tony Pitts **Facilities** ⊗ ⓛ ♥ ⍩ ⚘ 🏠 ⚐ ⚒ **Location** 1m W of St Austell on A390

Hotel ★★★ 72% Porth Avallen Hotel, Sea Rd, Carlyon Bay, ST AUSTELL ☎ 01726 812802 27 en suite

ST IVES
Map 02 SW54

Tregenna Castle Hotel, Golf & Country Club TR26 2DE ☎ 01736 797381 📠 01736 796066
e-mail: tregennabusiness@hotmail.com

Parkland course surrounding a castellated hotel and overlooking St Ives Bay and harbour.

18 holes, 3260yds, Par 60, SSS 58.
Club membership 140.

Visitors no booking needed. Dress code in operation. **Societies** telephone for details. **Green Fees** £5 per round. **Cards** 💳 💳 💳 💳 💳 💳 **Course Designer** Abercrombie **Facilities** ⊗ ⠇⠇ ⓛ ♥ ⍩ 🏠 ⚐ ⚘ **Leisure** hard tennis courts, outdoor and indoor heated swimming pools, squash, sauna, solarium, gymnasium. **Location** From A30 Penzance road turn off just past Hayle onto A3074

Hotel ★★★ 64% Tregenna Castle Hotel, ST IVES ☎ 01736 795254 83 en suite

ST JUST (NEAR LAND'S END)
Map 02 SW33

Cape Cornwall Golf & Country Club Cape Cornwall TR19 7NL ☎ 01736 788611 📠 01736 788611
e-mail: info@capecornwall.com

Coastal parkland, walled course. The walls are an integral part of its design. Britain's first and last 18-hole golf course overlooking the only cape in England, with views of the North Cornish coast and old fishing coves. Features a flat front nine followed by a challenging back nine. Extremely scenic views.

18 holes, 5632yds, Par 69, SSS 68, Course record 64.
Club membership 750.

Visitors must book tee time and wear appropiate clothing including golf shoes. **Societies** must contact in advance. **Green Fees** £20 per day/round holes (£25 Fri-Sun). **Cards** 💳 💳 💳 💳 💳 💳 **Prof** Jonathan Lamb **Course Designer** Bob Hamilton **Facilities** ⊗ ⠇⠇ ⓛ ♥ ⍩ ⚘ 🏠 ⚐ ⚘ **Leisure** heated indoor swimming pool, sauna, solarium, gymnasium. **Conf** fac available Corporate Hospitality Days available **Location** 1m W of St Just

Hotel ★★ 67% The Old Success Inn, Sennen Cove, SENNEN ☎ 01736 871232 12 en suite

ST MELLION
See page 51

ST MINVER
Map 02 SW97

Roserrow Golf & Country Club Roserrow PL27 6QT ☎ 01208 863000 📠 01208 863002
e-mail: mail@roserrow.co.uk

Challenging par 72 course in an undulating wooded valley. Stunning views over the Cornish countryside and out to Hayle Bay. Accommodation and numerous facilities on site.

18 holes, 6551yds, Par 72, SSS 72.
Club membership 450.

Visitors by arrangement weekdays or weekends, must pre book tee times. **Societies** apply in writing or telephone in advance. **Green Fees** terms on application. **Cards** 💳 💳 💳 💳 💳 **Prof** Nigel Sears **Facilities** ⊗ ⠇⠇ ⓛ ♥ ⍩ ⚘ 🏠 ⚐ ⚘ ⚒ **Leisure** hard tennis courts, heated indoor

Continued *Continued*

swimming pool, sauna, solarium, gymnasium, outdoor bowling green. **Location** Between Wadebridge and Polzeath off the B3314

....

Hotel ★★ 66% The Molesworth Arms Hotel, Molesworth St, WADEBRIDGE ☎ 01208 812055 16 rms (14 en suite)

SALTASH   Map 02 SX45

China Fleet Country Club PL12 6LJ
☎ 01752 848668 📠 01752 848456
e-mail: sales@china-fleet.co.uk
A parkland course with river views. The 14th tee shot has to carry a lake of approximately 150 yards.
18 holes, 6551yds, Par 72, SSS 72, Course record 69. Club membership 600.
Visitors may play anytime and can book up to 7 days in advance. **Societies** telephone 01752 854664 for provisional booking. **Green Fees** terms on application. **Cards** 💳 💳 💳 🖫 **Prof** Nick Cook **Course Designer** Hawtree **Facilities** ⊗ ⤬ ⢂ 🖫 💺 🖳 🛆 🖆 🍴 🛵 🚲 ♂ ⼀ **Leisure** hard tennis courts, heated indoor swimming pool, squash, sauna, solarium, gymnasium, Beauty & hairdresser. **Location** 1m from the Tamar Bridge

....

Hotel ⌂ Travelodge, Callington Rd, Carkeel, SALTASH ☎ 08700 850 950 53 en suite

TORPOINT   Map 02 SX45

Whitsand Bay Hotel Golf & Country Club
Portwrinkle PL11 3BU
☎ 01503 230276 📠 01503 230329
e-mail: golf@whitsandbayhotel.co.uk
Testing seaside course laid out on cliffs overlooking Whitsand Bay. Easy walking after first hole. The par 3 3rd hole is acknowledged as one of the most attractive holes in Cornwall.
18 holes, 6030yds, Par 69, SSS 68, Course record 62. Club membership 400.
Visitors visitors welcome. **Societies** must contact in advance. **Green Fees** not confirmed. **Cards** 💳 💳 💳 🖫 🖫 **Prof** Stephen Poole **Course Designer** Fernie **Facilities** ⊗ ⤬ ⢂ 🖫 💺 🖳 🛆 🖆 🍴 🐾 🚲 ♂ **Leisure** heated indoor swimming pool, sauna, solarium, gymnasium. **Location** 5m from Torpoint off A374

....

Hotel ★★ 69% Whitsand Bay Hotel & Golf Club, Portwrinkle, Nr TORPOINT ☎ 01503 230276 32 en suite

TRURO   Map 02 SW84

Killiow Park Kea TR3 6AG
☎ 01872 270246 📠 01872 240915
e-mail: killiowsec@yahoo.co.uk
Picturesque parkland course with mature oaks and woodland and five holes played across or around water hazards. Floodlit, all-weather driving range and practice facilities.
18 holes, 5274yds, Par 69, SSS 68, Course record 64. Club membership 500.
Visitors must telephone in advance to check on course availability. **Societies** apply in writing/telephone **Green Fees** from £18.50 per 18 holes. **Cards** 💳 💳 💳 🖫 🖫 **Course Designer** Ross Oliver **Facilities** ⊗ ⤬ ⢂ 🖳 🛆 ♂ ⼀ **Location** 3m SW of Truro, off A39

....

Hotel ★★★ 73% Alverton Manor, Tregolls Rd, TRURO ☎ 01872 276633 32 en suite

Truro Treliske TR1 3LG
☎ 01872 278684 (manager) 📠 01872 278684
e-mail: trurogolfclub@tiscali.co.uk
Picturesque and gently undulating parkland course with lovely views over the cathedral city of Truro and the surrounding countryside. The 5300yd course offers a great challenge to golfers of all standards and ages. The many trees and shrubs offer open invitations for wayward balls, and with many fairways boasting out of bounds markers, play needs to be safe and sensible. Fairways are tight and the greens small and full of character, making it difficult to play to one's handicap.
18 holes, 5306yds, Par 66, SSS 66, Course record 59. Club membership 1000.
Visitors must have handicap certificate, advisable to ring for availability although casual fees welcome. **Societies** telephone for details. **Green Fees** £25 per day (£30 weekends & bank holidays). **Prof** Nigel Bicknell **Course Designer** Colt, Alison & Morrison **Facilities** ⊗ ⤬ ⢂ 🖫 💺 🖳 🛆 🖆 🚲 ♂ **Location** 1.5m W on A390 towards Redruth, adjacent to Treliske Hospital

....

Hotel ★★★ 73% Alverton Manor, Tregolls Rd, TRURO ☎ 01872 276633 32 en suite

WADEBRIDGE   Map 02 SW97

St Kew St Kew Highway PL30 3EF
☎ 01208 841500 📠 01208 841500
e-mail: fjb@stkewgolfclub.fsnet.co.uk
An interesting, well laid out 9-hole parkland course with 6 holes with water and 15 bunkers. In a picturesque setting there are 10 par 4s and 8 par 3s. No handicap certificate required but some experience of the game is essential. Nine extra tees have now been provided allowing a different teeing area for the back nine.
9 holes, 4550yds, Par 64, SSS 62, Course record 63. Club membership 350.
Visitors no restrictions. Start time system in operation allowing prebooking. **Societies** apply in writing, telephone or fax **Green Fees** £15 for 18 holes, £10 for 9 holes. **Cards** 💳 💳 🖫 **Prof** Nick Rogers **Course Designer** David Derry **Facilities** ⊗ ⤬ ⢂ 🖫 💺 🖳 🛆 🖆 🍴 🐾 🚲 ♂ ⼀ **Leisure** fishing. **Location** 2m N,of Wadebridge main A39

....

Hotel ★★ 66% The Molesworth Arms Hotel, Molesworth St, WADEBRIDGE ☎ 01208 812055 16 rms (14 en suite)

CUMBRIA

ALSTON   Map 12 NY74

Alston Moor The Hermitage, Middleton in Teesdale Rd CA9 3DB
☎ 01434 381675 & 381354 (Sec) 📠 01434 381675
10 holes, 5518yds, Par 68, SSS 66, Course record 67.
 Location 1 S of Alston on B6277
Telephone for further details

....

Hotel ★★ 71% Lowbyer Manor Country House Hotel, ALSTON ☎ 01434 381230 9 en suite 2 annexe en suite

---

Prices may change during the currency of the Guide, please check when booking.

APPLEBY-IN-WESTMORLAND   Map 12 NY62

Appleby Brackenber Moor CA16 6LP
☎ 017683 51432 📠 017683 52773
This remotely situated heather and moorland course offers interesting golf with the rewarding bonus of several long par 4 holes that will be remembered. There are superb views of the Pennines and the Lakeland hills. Renowned for the excellent greens.
18 holes, 5901yds, Par 68, SSS 68, Course record 62.
Club membership 800.
Visitors phone for details. May not play before 3pm weekends/competition days. **Societies** must contact in advance by letter. **Green Fees** £22 per day; £20 per round (£27/£24 weekends and bank holidays). **Prof** James Taylor **Course Designer** Willie Fernie **Facilities** ⊗ 🍴 🏌 💺 ♀ ♨ 🛢 🛒 🏌 ♂ **Conf** Corporate Hospitality Days available
Location 2m E of Appleby 0.5m off A66

Hotel ★★★ 78% Appleby Manor Country House Hotel, Roman Rd, APPLEBY-IN-WESTMORLAND
☎ 017683 51571 23 en suite 7 annexe en suite

ASKAM-IN-FURNESS   Map 07 SD27

Dunnerholme Duddon Rd LA16 7AW
☎ 01229 462675 & 467421 📠 01229 462675
e-mail: meg@dunnerholme.co.uk
Unique 10-hole (18-tee) links course with view of the Cumbrian mountains and Morecambe Bay. Two streams run through and around the course, providing water hazards on the 1st, 2nd, 3rd and 9th holes. The par 3 6th is the feature hole on the course, playing to an elevated green on Dunnerholme Rock, an imposing limestone outcrop jutting out into the estuary.
10 holes, 6138yds, Par 72, SSS 69.
Club membership 400.
Visitors restricted times on Sun. **Societies** apply in writing to the secretary. **Green Fees** £15 per day. **Facilities** 💺 ♀ ♨ **Location** 1m N on A595

Hotel ★★ 64% Lisdoonie Hotel, 307/309 Abbey Rd, BARROW-IN-FURNESS ☎ 01229 827312 12 en suite

BARROW-IN-FURNESS   Map 07 SD26

Barrow Rakesmoor Ln, Hawcoat LA14 4QB
☎ 01229 825444 & 832121 (Pro)
e-mail: barrowgolf@supanet.com
Pleasant course laid out on two levels of meadowland, with extensive views of the nearby Lakeland fells. Upper level is affected by easterly winds.
18 holes, 6184yds, Par 71, SSS 70, Course record 66.
Club membership 700.
Visitors must be a member of a recognised golf club or hold a handicap certificate, advisable to contact the professional regarding tee time.small groups ring administratorl for details, groups over 12 apply to the secretary in advance. **Green Fees** not confirmed. **Prof** Andy Whitehall **Facilities** ⊗ 🍴 🏌 💺 ♀ ♨ 🛢 **Location** 2m from Barrow off A590

Hotel ★★ 64% Lisdoonie Hotel, 307/309 Abbey Rd, BARROW-IN-FURNESS ☎ 01229 827312 12 en suite

Furness Central Dr LA14 3LN ☎ 01229 471232
Links golf with a fairly flat first half but a much sterner second nine played across subtle sloping ground. There are good views of the Lakes, North Wales and the Isle of Man. *Continued*

18 holes, 6363yds, Par 71, SSS 71, Course record 65.
Club membership 630.
Visitors must contact the secretary in advance. **Societies** apply in writing, must be member of recognised club with handicap certificate. **Green Fees** not confirmed. **Facilities** ⊗ 🍴 🏌 💺 ♀ ♨ 🛢 ♂ **Location** 1.75 W of town centre off A590 to Walney Island

Hotel ★★ 64% Lisdoonie Hotel, 307/309 Abbey Rd, BARROW-IN-FURNESS ☎ 01229 827312 12 en suite

BOWNESS-ON-WINDERMERE   Map 07 SD49

Windermere Clearbarrow LA23 3NB
☎ 015394 43123 📠 015394 43123
e-mail: windermeregc@btconnect.com
Enjoyable holiday golf on a short, slightly hilly but sporting course in this delightful area of the Lake District National Park, with superb views of the mountains as the backdrop to the lake and the course.
18 holes, 5122yds, Par 67, SSS 65, Course record 58.
Club membership 890.
Visitors contact pro shop 7 days before day of play, 10-12 & 1.30-4.30 or before 9am by arrangement. **Societies** by arrangement contact the secretary. **Green Fees** £28 per round (£32 weekends & bank holidays). **Cards** 💳 💳 💳 **Prof** W S M Rooke **Course Designer** G Lowe **Facilities** ⊗ 🍴 🏌 💺 ♀ ♨ 🛢 🛒 🏌 ♂ **Leisure** snooker. **Conf** Corporate Hospitality Days available **Location** B5284 1.5m from Bowness

Hotel ★★★ 68% Famous Wild Boar Hotel, Crook, WINDERMERE ☎ 015394 45225 36 en suite

BRAMPTON   Map 12 NY56

Brampton Talkin Tarn CA8 1HN
☎ 016977 2255 📠 016977 41487
e-mail: secretary@bramptongolfclub.com
Challenging golf across glorious rolling fell country demanding solid driving and many long second shots. A number of particularly fine holes, the pick of which may arguably be the 3rd and 11th. The course offers unrivalled panoramic views from a number of vantage points.

18 holes, 6407yds, Par 72, SSS 71, Course record 68.
Club membership 800.
Visitors visitors intending to play at weekends are recommended to telephone in advance. **Societies** apply in writing to I J Meldrum (Secretary), 17 Helvellyn Close, Cockermouth, Cumbria CA13 9BJ or telephone 01900 827985. **Green Fees** £22 per day/round (£30 weekends & bank holidays). **Cards** 💳 💳 💳 💳 💳 **Prof** Stewart Wilkinson **Course Designer** James Braid **Facilities** ⊗ 🍴 🏌 💺 ♀ ♨ 🛢 🛒 🏌 ♂ **Leisure** games room. **Conf** Corporate Hospitality Days available
Location 1.5m SE of Brampton on B6413 *Continued*

··

Hotel ★★ 67% The Tarn End House Hotel, Talkin Tarn,
BRAMPTON ☎ 016977 2340 Fax 016977 2089 7 en suite

●●

Hotel ★★★ ♨ Farlam Hall Hotel, BRAMPTON
☎ 016977 46234 Fax 016977 46683 11 en suite
1 annexe en suite

CARLISLE   Map 11 NY35

Carlisle Aglionby CA4 8AG
☎ 01228 513029 (secretary) 🖺 01228 513303
e-mail: secretary@carlislegolfclub.org
**Majestic looking, long established parkland course with
great appeal. A complete but not too severe test of golf, with
fine turf, natural hazards, a stream and many beautiful
trees. A qualifying course for the Open Championship.**
*18 holes, 6263yds, Par 71, SSS 70, Course record 63.
Club membership 800.*
Visitors may not play before 9am and between 12-1.30 and
when tee is reserved. Very limited play Sunday and with
member only Saturday and Tuesday. **Societies** Mon, Wed
& Fri, contact secretary in advance for details on 01228
513029. **Green Fees** £40 per day; £30 per round (£45
weekends). **Prof** Graeme Lisle **Course Designer**
Mackenzie Ross **Facilities** ⊗ ⅏ ⅊ ♥ ♀ ⚲ 🏌 🛒 ⚑ ⚒ ♂
Conf fac available **Location** On A69 0.5m E of M6 junc 43
··
Hotel ★★★ 71% Crown Hotel, Wetheral, CARLISLE
☎ 01228 561888 49 en suite 2 annexe en suite

Stony Holme Municipal St Aidans Rd CA1 1LS
☎ 01228 625511

18 holes, 5783yds, Par 69, SSS 68, Course record 68.
Location 2m W of M6 (junct 43) and A69
Telephone for further details. See advert on p56
··
Hotel 🆄 Holiday Inn Carlisle, Parkhouse Rd, CARLISLE
☎ 0870 400 9018 127 en suite

COCKERMOUTH   Map 11 NY13

Cockermouth Embleton CA13 9SG
☎ 017687 76223 & 76941 🖺 017687 76941
e-mail: secretary@cockermouthgolf.co.uk
**Fell-land course, fenced, with exceptional views of
Lakeland hills and valleys and the Solway Firth. A hard
climb on the 3rd and 11th holes. Testing holes: 10th and
16th (rearranged by James Braid).**

Continued

Stony Holme Golf Course Carlisle Where Great Golfing Costs Less

With the magnificent back drop of the Lakeland fells, this mature flat easy walking parkland course with abundant water hazards is a challenge to any golfer. Delicious food is served in The Riverside Restaurant & Bar. A fully stocked shop & golf professional is available. Tailored golf packages for visiting groups and a pay as you play system is also in operation.

St. Aidans Road, Carlisle, Cumbria.
Tel: 01228 625511   BBC   GOLF MAGAZINE RECOMMENDED

---

18 holes, 5496yds, Par 69, SSS 67, Course record 62.
Club membership 600.
Visitors restricted Wed, Sat & Sun. **Societies** apply in writing to the secretary. **Green Fees** £20 per day (£25 weekends and bank holidays). **Course Designer** J Braid **Facilities** ⌚ ♨ ♀ ⚘ ⚑ **Conf** Corporate Hospitality Days available **Location** 3m E off A66

....

Hotel ★★★ 74% The Trout Hotel, Crown St, COCKERMOUTH ☎ 01900 823591 43 en suite

Eden CA6 4RA
☎ 01228 573003 & 573013 📠 01228 818435
e-mail: alistair.wannop@virgin.net
Open, championship-length parkland course following the River Eden. A large number of water hazards, including the river on certain holes, demands accuracy, as do the well designed raised greens. Flood-lit driving range and excellent clubhouse facilities.

Continued

---

18 holes, 6410yds, Par 72, SSS 72, Course record 64.
Club membership 700.
Visitors must contact in advance. **Societies** telephone to check availability. **Green Fees** not confirmed. **Cards** 💳 💳 💳 **Prof** Steve Harrison **Facilities** ⊗ ♨ ⌚ ♨ ♀ ⚘ 🏠 ⚑ ⚘ ⚑ **Leisure** hard tennis courts. **Conf** Corporate Hospitality Days available **Location** 5m from M6 junc 44,on A689 towards Brampton & Newcastle-Upon-Tyne

....

Hotel ⌂ Travelodge (Carlisle North), A74 Southbound, Todhills, CARLISLE ☎ 08700 850 950 40 en suite

Grange Fell Fell Rd LA11 6HB ☎ 015395 32536
Hillside course with magnificent views over Morecambe Bay and the surrounding Lakeland mountains.
9 holes, 5292yds, Par 70, SSS 66, Course record 65.
Club membership 300.
Visitors may normally play Mon-Sat. **Green Fees** £15 per day (£20 weekends & bank holidays). **Facilities** ⌚ ♀ ⚘ **Location** 1m W on Grange-Over-Sands/Cartmel

....

Hotel ★★★ 73% Netherwood Hotel, Lindale Rd, GRANGE-OVER-SANDS ☎ 015395 32552 32 en suite

---

Grange-over-Sands Meathop Rd LA11 6QX
☎ 015395 33180 or 33754 📠 015395 33754
e-mail: dwright@ktdinternet.com
Interesting parkland course with well sited tree plantations, ditches and water features. The four par 3s are considered to be some of the best in the area.
18 holes, 5958yds, Par 70, SSS 69, Course record 68.
Club membership 650.
Visitors must be a member of golf club or recognised golf society, advisable to contact in advance for play at weekends. **Societies** apply in writing. **Green Fees** £30 per day; £25 per round (£35/£30 weekends & bank holidays). **Cards** 💳 💳 💳 **Prof** Andrew Pickering **Course Designer** Mackenzie (part) **Facilities** ⊗ ♨ ⌚ ♨ ♀ ⚘ 🏠 ⚑ ⚘ **Conf** Corporate Hospitality Days available **Location** NE of town centre off B5277

....

Hotel ★★★ 65% Graythwaite Manor Hotel, Fernhill Rd, GRANGE-OVER-SANDS ☎ 015395 32001 & 33755 📠 015395 35549 21 en suite

Carus Green Burneside Rd LA9 6EB
☎ 01539 721097 📠 01539 721097
Flat 18-hole course surrounded by the rivers Kent and Mint with an open view of the Kentmere and Howgill fells. The course is a mixture of relatively easy and difficult holes. These rivers come into play on five holes and there are also a number of ponds and bunkers.
Carus Green Golf Course: 18 holes, 5691yds, Par 70, SSS 68, Course record 65.
Club membership 600.
Visitors no restrictions except during club competitions at weekend, check by phone. **Societies** telephone for details. **Green Fees** £21 per day, £16 per round (£25/20 weekends & bank holidays). **Prof** D Turner **Course Designer** W Adamson **Facilities** ⌚ ♨ ♀ ⚘ 🏠 ⚑ ⚘ ⚑ **Conf** Corporate Hospitality Days available **Location** 1m from Kendal town centre

....

Hotel ★★★ 64% Riverside Hotel, Stramongate Bridge, KENDAL ☎ 01539 734861 47 en suite

Kendal The Heights LA9 4PQ

☎ 01539 723499 (pro) 🖺 01539 733708

Elevated parkland/fell course affording breathtaking views of Lakeland fells and surrounding district.
18 holes, 5796yds, Par 70, SSS 68, Course record 65. Club membership 737.
Visitors must have a handicap certificate, weekends subject to availability. Telephone to reserve tee-off time. **Societies** must contact in advance. **Green Fees** £26 per day, £22 per round (£32.50/£27.50 weekends). **Cards** 💳 💳 💳 💳 💳 **Prof** Peter Scott **Facilities** ⊗ ⊪ ⅃ ⍙ 🍴 ♀ ⚲ 🛆 🔝 🕯 🚵 ♨ ⚸ **Leisure** Golf clinic with computer analysis. **Location** 1m W of town centre, turn left at town hall and follow signposts

....

Hotel ★★★ 75% The Castle Green Hotel in Kendal, KENDAL ☎ 01539 734000 100 en suite

KESWICK   Map 11 NY22

Keswick Threlkeld Hall, Threlkeld CA12 4SX

☎ 017687 79324 🖺 017687 79861
e-mail: secretary@keswickgolf.com
Varied fell and tree-lined course with commanding views of Lakeland scenery.
18 holes, 6225yds, Par 71, SSS 72, Course record 68. Club membership 586.
Visitors booking up to 7 days in advance 017687 79010. Restricted on competition days. **Societies** apply in writing to secretary. **Green Fees** not confirmed. **Prof** Gary Watson **Course Designer** Eric Brown **Facilities** ⊗ ⊪ ⅃ ⍙ 🍴 ♀ 🛆 🔝 🕯 ⚸ **Leisure** fishing. **Location** 4m E of Keswick, off A66

....

Hotel ★★★ 69% Keswick Country House Hotel, Station Rd, KESWICK ☎ 0845 458 4333 74 en suite

KIRKBY LONSDALE   Map 07 SD67

Kirkby Lonsdale Scaleber Ln, Barbon LA6 2LJ

☎ 015242 76365 🖺 015242 76503
e-mail: KLGolf@Dial.Pipex.com/
Parkland course on the east bank of the River Lune and crossed by Barbon Beck. Mainly following the lie of the land, the gently undulating course uses the beck to provide water hazards.
18 holes, 6538yds, Par 72, SSS 72, Course record 67. Club membership 600.
Visitors restricted on Sunday, must telephone in advance or call in at pro shop. **Societies** apply in writing for society package. **Green Fees** £26 per day (£32 weekends & bank holidays). **Prof** Chris Barrett **Course Designer** Bill Squires **Facilities** ⊗ ⊪ ⅃ ⍙ 🍴 ♀ 🛆 🔝 🕯 ⚸ **Conf** Corporate Hospitality Days available **Location** 3m NE of Kirkby Lonsdale on A683

....

Hotel ★★ 67% The Whoop Hall, Burrow with Burrow, KIRKBY LONSDALE ☎ 015242 71284 22 en suite

MARYPORT   Map 11 NY03

Maryport Bankend CA15 6PA

☎ 01900 812605 🖺 815626
18 holes, 6088yds, Par 70, SSS 69, Course record 65.
Location 1m N on B5300
Telephone for further details

Continued

Maryport Golf Club
....
Hotel ★★★ 82% Washington Central Hotel, Washington St, WORKINGTON ☎ 01900 65772 46 en suite

PENRITH   Map 12 NY53

Penrith Salkeld Rd CA11 8SG

☎ 01768 891919 🖺 01768 891919
A beautiful and well-balanced course, always changing direction, and demanding good length from the tee. It is set on rolling moorland with occasional pine trees and some fine views.
18 holes, 6047yds, Par 69, SSS 69, Course record 63. Club membership 850.
Visitors contact in advance. Handicap certificate required. **Societies** telephone in advance. **Green Fees** £31 per day; £26 per round (£36/£31 weekends). **Prof** Garry Key **Facilities** ⊗ ⊪ ⅃ ⍙ 🍴 ♀ 🛆 🔝 🕯 ⚸ 🍺 **Conf** fac available **Location** M6 junct 41, follow A6 to Penrith, left after 30mph sign and follow signs for golf club

....

Hotel ★★ 67% Brantwood Country Hotel, Stainton, PENRITH ☎ 01768 862748 7 en suite

ST BEES   Map 11 NX91

St Bees Peckmill, Beach Rd CA27 0EJ ☎ 01946 824300

Links course, down hill and dale, with sea views.
10 holes, 5306yds, Par 66, SSS 66, Course record 64. Club membership 400.
Visitors no allowed after 4pm Wednesday and before 3pm weekends. **Societies** apply in writing in advance to club secretary. **Green Fees** £12 per day. **Facilities** 🍴 ♀ 🛆 **Location** 0.5m W of village off B5345

....

Hotel ★★★ 76% Ennerdale Country House Hotel, CLEATOR ☎ 01946 813907 30 en suite

SEASCALE   Map 06 NY00

Seascale The Banks CA20 1QL

☎ 019467 28202 🖺 019467 28202
e-mail: seascalegolfclub@aol.com
A tough links requiring length and control. The natural terrain is used to give a variety of holes and considerable character. Undulating greens add to the challenge. Fine views over the Western Fells, the Irish Sea and Isle of Man.
18 holes, 6416yds, Par 71, SSS 71, Course record 64. Club membership 650.
Visitors no restrictions, but advisable to contact for tee reservation times. **Societies** telephone to make provisional booking. **Green Fees** £29 per day; £24 per round (£32/£27 weekends & bank holidays). **Prof** Sean Rudd **Course**

Continued

Designer Willie Campbell **Facilities** ⊗ ⋗Ⅲ ᴸ ♥ ♀ ♧ 🏠 ⛳
♂ ⌇ **Conf** fac available Corporate Hospitality Days
available **Location** NW side of village off B5344

Hotel ★★ 72% Westlakes Hotel, GOSFORTH
☎ 01947 725221 6 en suite 3 annexe en suite

SEDBERGH
Map 07 SD69

Sedbergh Dent Rd LA10 5SS
☎ 015396 21551 (Club) 🖷 015396 21551
e-mail: sedberghgc@btinternet.com
A tree-lined grassland course with superb scenery in
the Yorkshire Dales National Park. Feature hole is the
par 3 2nd (110yds) where the River Dee separates the
tee from the green.
9 holes, 5624yds, Par 70, SSS 68, Course record 66.
Club membership 250.
Visitors advance booking advised May-Sep. No visitors on
Sun before 11.30am **Societies** must contact in advance.
Green Fees £18 per 18 holes, £12 per 9 holes (£20/£14
weekends). **Course Designer** W G Squires **Facilities** ⊗ ⋗Ⅲ
ᴸ ♥ ♀ ♧ 🏠 ⛳ ♂ **Leisure** fishing. **Conf** fac available
Corporate Hospitality Days available **Location** 1m S off
A683, 5m junct 37 M6

Hotel ⚑ Travel Inn, Killington Lake, Motorway Service
Area, Killington, KENDAL ☎ 08701 977145 36 en suite

SILECROFT
Map 06 SD18

Silecroft Silecroft, Millom LA18 4NX
☎ 01229 774342 (sec) 🖷 01229 774342
Seaside links course parallel to the coast of the Irish
Sea. Often windy. Easy walking. Spectacular views
inland of Lakeland hills.
9 holes, 5896yds, Par 68, SSS 68, Course record 66.
Club membership 275.
Visitors May be restricted competition days & bank
holidays contact secretary in advance. **Societies** must
contact in writing in advance. **Green Fees** not confirmed.
Facilities ♥ ♀ ♧ **Location** 3m W of Millom

SILLOTH
Map 11 NY15

Silloth on Solway The Clubhouse CA7 4BL
☎ 016973 31304 🖷 016973 31782
e-mail: sillothgolfclub@lineone.net
Billowing dunes, narrow fairways, heather and gorse
and the constant subtle problems of tactics and
judgement make these superb links on the Solway an
exhilarating and searching test. The 13th is a good long
hole. Superb views.
18 holes, 6070yds, Par 72, SSS 73.
Club membership 700.
Visitors must contact in advance. **Societies** telephone for
times available. **Green Fees** £32 per day (£43 per round
weekends). **Cards** 🖶 🖩 🖩 🖩 **Prof** J Graham
Course Designer David Grant/Willie Park Jnr **Facilities**
⊗ ⋗Ⅲ ᴸ ♥ ♀ ♧ 🏠 ♂ **Conf** fac available **Location** S side
of village off B5300

Hotel ★★ 64% Golf Hotel, Criffel St, SILLOTH
☎ 016973 31438 22 en suite

ULVERSTON
Map 07 SD27

Ulverston Bardsea Park LA12 9QJ
☎ 01229 582824 🖷 01229 588910
Inland golf with many medium length holes on
Continued

undulating parkland. The 17th is a testing par 4.
Overlooking Morecambe Bay the course offers
extensive views to the Lakeland Fells.
18 holes, 6201yds, Par 71, SSS 70, Course record 64.
Club membership 750.
Visitors must contact in advance, be a member of an
accredited golf club with a handicap certificate. May not
play on Sat, competition days & restricted on Tue- Ladies
day. **Societies** by arrangement in writing. **Green Fees** not
confirmed. **Prof** M R Smith **Course Designer**
A Herd/H S Colt **Facilities** ⊗ ⋗Ⅲ ᴸ ♥ ♀ ♧ 🏠 ⛳ ♂
Conf Corporate Hospitality Days available **Location** 2m S
off A5087

Hotel ★★★ 67% Whitewater Hotel, The Lakeland
Village, NEWBY BRIDGE ☎ 015395 31133
35 en suite

WINDERMERE
See **Bowness-on-Windermere**

WORKINGTON
Map 11 NY02

Workington Branthwaite Rd CA14 4SS
☎ 01900 67828 🖷 01900 607123
e-mail: golf@workingtongolfclub.freeserve.co.uk

18 holes, 6217yds, Par 72, SSS 70, Course record 65.
Course Designer James Braid **Location** 1.75m E off A596
Telephone for further details

Hotel ★★★ 82% Washington Central Hotel, Washington
St, WORKINGTON ☎ 01900 65772 46 en suite

DERBYSHIRE

ALFRETON
Map 08 SK45

Alfreton Wingfield Rd, Oakerthorpe DE55 7LH
☎ 01773 832070
A small well established parkland course with tight
fairways and many natural hazards.
11 holes, 5393yds, Par 67, SSS 66, Course record 67.
Club membership 350.
Visitors advisable to contact first. Weekends by
arrangement only. **Societies** apply in writing or telephone
in advance. **Green Fees** £25 per day ; £18 per round. **Prof**
Peter Buttifant **Facilities** ⊗ ⋗Ⅲ by prior arrangement ᴸ ♥
♀ ♧ 🏠 **Location** 1m W on A615

Hotel ★★★★ 70% Renaissance Derby/Nottingham
Hotel, Carter Ln East, SOUTH NORMANTON
☎ 01773 812000 158 en suite

ASHBOURNE
Map 07 SK14

Ashbourne Wyaston Rd DE6 1NB
☎ 01335 342078 & 347960(pro shop) 📠 01335 347937
e-mail: sec@ashbournegc.fsnet.co.uk
**With fine views over surrounding countryside, the
course uses natural contours and water features.**
18 holes, 6402yds, Par 71, SSS 71.
Club membership 650.
Visitors must contact professional in advance, may not
play on competition days. **Societies** apply in
writing/telephone in advance. **Green Fees** £40 per 36
holes, £25 per 18 holes (£30 per 18 holes weekends and
bank holidays). Reduced winter rates. **Prof** Andrew Smith
Course Designer D Hemstock **Facilities** ⊗ ⫟ ⑤ ⛫ 💻 ♀ 🏊
🍴 🎿 ⚙ **Leisure** snooker table. **Location** Off Wyaston
Road

Hotel ★★★ ⚓ 74% Callow Hall, Mappleton Rd,
ASHBOURNE ☎ 01335 300900 16 en suite

BAKEWELL
Map 08 SK26

Bakewell Station Rd DE45 1GB ☎ 01629 812307
**Parkland course, hilly, with plenty of natural hazards
to test the golfer. Magnificent views across the Wye
Valley.**
9 holes, 5240yds, Par 68, SSS 66, Course record 70.
Club membership 340.
Visitors limited at weekends due to competitions. Ladies
day Thursday. **Societies** apply in writing. **Green Fees**
terms on application. **Facilities** ⊗ ⫟ ⑤ ⛫ 💻 ♀ ⚙ **Conf**
Corporate Hospitality Days available **Location** E side of
town off A6

Hotel ★★ 73% Croft Country House Hotel, Great
Longstone, BAKEWELL ☎ 01629 640278 9 en suite

BAMFORD
Map 08 SK28

Sickleholme Saltergate Ln S33 0BN
☎ 01433 651306 📠 01433 659498
e-mail: sickleholme.gc@btconnect.com@.
18 holes, 6064yds, Par 69, SSS 69, Course record 62.
Location 0.75m S on A6013
Telephone for further details

Hotel ★★ 72% Yorkshire Bridge Inn, Ashopton Rd, Hope
Valley, BAMFORD ☎ 01433 651361 14 en suite

BREADSALL
Map 08 SK33

Marriot Breadsall Priory Hotel & Country
Club Moor Rd, Morley DE7 6DL
☎ 01332 832235 📠 01332 833509
**Set in 200 acres of mature parkland, the Priory Course
is built on the site of a 13th-century priory. Full use has
been made of natural features and fine old trees. In
contrast the Moorland course, designed by Donald Steel
and built by Brian Piersen, features Derbyshire stone
walls and open moors heavily affected by winds. Open
when most other clubs are closed in winter.**
*Priory Course: 18 holes, 6100yds, Par 72, SSS 69, Course
record 63.*
Moorland Course: 18 holes, 6028yds, Par 70, SSS 69.
Club membership 900.
Visitors must contact in advance, 10 day booking service.
Societies telephone in advance. **Green Fees** from £25.
Cards 🟦 🟦 🟦 🟦 🟦 🟦 **Prof** Darren Steels **Course
Designer** D Steel **Facilities** ⊗ ⫟ ⑤ ⛫ 💻 ♀ 🏊 🍴 🎿 🏌 🚡

⚙ **Leisure** hard tennis courts, heated indoor
swimming pool, sauna, solarium, gymnasium. **Conf** fac
available Corporate Hospitality Days available **Location**
0.75m W

Hotel ★★★★ 65% Marriott Breadsall Priory Hotel&
Country Club, Moor Rd, MORLEY ☎ 01332 832235
12 en suite 100 annexe en suite

BUXTON
Map 07 SK07

Buxton & High Peak Waterswallows Rd SK17
7EN ☎ 01298 26263 & 23453 📠 26333
e-mail: admin@bhpgc.co.uk
**Bracing, well-drained meadowland course; the highest
in Derbyshire. Challenging course where wind direction
is a major factor on some holes; others require blind
shots to sloping greens.**
18 holes, 5966yds, Par 69, SSS 69.
Club membership 650.
Visitors By prior arrangment only. **Societies** Prior
arrangement only. Phone or write to Jane Dobson. **Green
Fees** £30 per day, £24 per round (£36/£30 weekends &
bank holidays). **Cards** 🟦 🟦 🟦 🟦 🟦 **Prof** Gary Brown
Course Designer J Morris **Facilities** ⊗ ⑤ 💻 ♀ 🎿 🍴 🏌
🍴 🎿 ⚙ **Conf** fac available Corporate Hospitality Days
available **Location** 1m NE off A6

Hotel ★★★★ 66% Palace Hotel, Palace Rd, BUXTON
☎ 01298 22001 122 en suite

Cavendish Gadley Ln SK17 6XD
☎ 01298 79708 📠 01298 79708
e-mail: admin@cavendishgolfcourse.com
**This parkland/moorland course with its comfortable
clubhouse nestles below the rising hills. Generally open
to the prevailing west wind, it is noted for its excellent
surfaced greens which contain many deceptive
subtleties. Designed by Dr Alastair McKenzie, good
holes include the 8th, 9th and 18th.**

18 holes, 5721yds, Par 68, SSS 68, Course record 61.
Club membership 650.
Visitors must contact in advance, weekends are restricted
by competitions. Ladies day Thu **Societies** telephone
professional on 01298 25052. **Green Fees** terms on
application. **Cards** 🟦 **Prof** Paul Hunstone **Course
Designer** Dr Mackenzie **Facilities** ⊗ ⑤ 💻 ♀ 🎿 🍴 🏌 ⚙
⚙ **Location** 0.75m W of town centre off A53

Hotel ★★★ 77% Best Western Lee Wood Hotel, The
Park, BUXTON ☎ 01298 23002 35 en suite
5 annexe en suite

Continued

CHAPEL-EN-LE-FRITH   Map 07 SK08

Chapel-en-le-Frith The Cockyard, Manchester Rd
SK23 9UH
☎ 01298 812118 & 813943 (sec) 🖹 01298 814990
e-mail: info@chapelgolf.co.uk
**A scenic parkland course surrounded by spectacular
mountainous views. A new longer and challenging front
9, a testing short par 4 14th and possibly the best last
three-hole finish in Derbyshire.**
18 holes, 6434yds, Par 72, SSS 71, Course record 71.
Club membership 676.
Visitors must contact professional or secretary in advance.
Societies apply in advance to Secretary. **Green Fees** terms
on application. **Cards** 🖭 🖭 🖭 **Prof** David J Cullen
Course Designer David Williams **Facilities** ⊗ ⊪ 🝔 ▣ ♇
🝔 🖴 🎢 ℓ **Location** On B5470
....
Hotel ★★★ 77% Best Western Lee Wood Hotel,
The Park, BUXTON ☎ 01298 23002 35 en suite
5 annexe en suite

CHESTERFIELD   Map 08 SK37

Chesterfield Walton S42 7LA
☎ 01246 279256 🖹 01246 276622
**A varied and interesting, undulating parkland course
with trees picturesquely adding to the holes and the
outlook alike. Stream hazard on back nine.**
18 holes, 6281yds, Par 71, SSS 70, Course record 65.
Club membership 600.
Visitors must contact in advance, must play with member
on Sat & bank holidays, may play on Sun after 1.30. A
handicap certificate is generally required. **Societies** apply
in writing. **Green Fees** £36 per day; £28 per round (£36
per round weekends). **Prof** Mike McLean **Facilities** ⊗ ⊪
🝔 ▣ ♇ 🝔 🖴 **Location** 2m SW off A632
....
Hotel ★★ 71% Abbeydale Hotel, Cross St,
CHESTERFIELD ☎ 01246 277849 11 en suite

Grassmoor Golf Centre North Wingfield Rd,
Grassmoor S42 5EA ☎ 01246 856044 🖹 01246 853486
e-mail: enquiries@grassmoorgolf.co.uk
**An 18-hole heathland course with interesting and
challenging water features. 26-bay floodlit driving
range, practice bunkers and putting area.**
18 holes, 5723yds, Par 69, SSS 69, Course record 67.
Club membership 450.
Visitors contact Manager in advance. Smart dress code.
Societies telephone Manager in advance. **Green Fees** £12
per 18 holes (£15 weekend & BH). **Cards** 🖭 🖭 🖭 🖭
🖭 **Prof** Gary Hagues **Course Designer** Hawtree **Facilities**
⊗ ⊪ 🝔 ▣ ♇ 🝔 🖴 🎢 🝔 ℓ ⎰ **Conf** Corporate
Hospitality Days available **Location** 4m from M1 junct 29,
between Chesterfield & Grassmoor, off B6038
....
Hotel ★★ 71% Abbeydale Hotel, Cross St,
CHESTERFIELD ☎ 01246 277849 11 en suite

Stanedge Walton Hay Farm, Stonedge, Ashover
S45 0LW ☎ 01246 566156
e-mail: chrisshaw56@tiscali.co.uk/stanedge
**Moorland course in hilly situation open to strong winds.
Some tricky short holes with narrow fairways, so
accuracy is paramount. Magnificent views over four
counties. Extended course now open.**
9 holes, 5786yds, Par 69, SSS 68, Course record 68.
Club membership 310.

Visitors with member only Sat & Sun, and tee off before
2pm weekdays. **Societies** apply in writing. **Green Fees** £15
per round. **Facilities** ▣ ♇ 🝔 **Location** 5m SW off B5057
nr Red Lion public house
....
Hotel ★★ 71% Abbeydale Hotel, Cross St,
CHESTERFIELD ☎ 01246 277849 11 en suite

Tapton Park Tapton Park, Tapton S41 0EQ
☎ 01246 239500 & 273887 🖹 01246 558024
**Municipal parkland course with some fairly hard
walking. The 625yd (par 5) 5th is a testing hole.**
Tapton Main: 18 holes, 6065yds, Par 71, SSS 69.
Dobbin Clough: 9 holes, 2613yds, Par 34, SSS 34.
Club membership 400.
Visitors must contact in advance. No caddies allowed.
Societies apply in writing/telephone in advance. **Green
Fees** £8.50 per 18 holes, £4.50 per 9 holes (£10/£5.70
weekends). **Prof** Andrew Carnall **Facilities** ⊗ ⊪ 🝔 ▣
🝔 🖴 🎢 🝔 ℓ **Conf** fac available Corporate Hospitality
Days available **Location** 0.5m E of Chesterfield Station
....
Hotel ★★ 71% Abbeydale Hotel, Cross St,
CHESTERFIELD ☎ 01246 277849 11 en suite

CODNOR   Map 08 SK44

Ormonde Fields Golf & Country Club
Nottingham Rd DE5 9RG
☎ 01773 570043 (Secretary) 🖹 01773 742987
**Parkland course with undulating fairways and natural
hazards. There is a practice area.**
18 holes, 6502yds, Par 71, SSS 72, Course record 68.
Club membership 500.
Visitors must contact in advance. May play at weekends
after 3pm. **Societies** telephone in advance. **Green Fees** £20
per 18 holes (£25 weekend & bank holidays). **Cards** 🖭
Prof Matthew Myford **Course Designer** John Fearn
Facilities ⊗ ⊪ 🝔 ▣ ♇ 🝔 🖴 🎢 ℓ **Conf** fac available
Corporate Hospitality Days available **Location** 1m SE on
A610
....
Hotel ★★★ 71% Makeney Hall Hotel, Makeney, Milford,
BELPER ☎ 0870 609 6136 27 en suite 18 annexe en suite

DERBY   Map 08 SK33

Allestree Park Allestree Hall, Duffield Rd, Allestree
DE22 2EU ☎ 01332 550616 🖹 01332 541195
**Public course, picturesque and undulating, set in 300-
acre park with views across Derbyshire.**
18 holes, 5806yds, Par 68, SSS 68.
Visitors start times may be booked in advance by
telephone, visitors welcome any day. **Societies** apply in
writing or by telephone in advance. **Green Fees** not
confirmed. **Cards** 🖭 🖭 🖭 🖭 **Prof** Leigh Woodward
Facilities ⊗ ⊪ 🝔 ▣ ♇ 🝔 🖴 🎢 ℓ **Leisure** fishing.
Location N of Derby, from A38 take A6 towards N,
Course in 1.5m on left
....
Hotel ★★★★ 65% Marriott Breadsall Priory Hotel&
Country Club, Moor Rd, MORLEY ☎ 01332 832235
12 en suite 100 annexe en suite

Mickleover Uttoxeter Rd, Mickleover DE3 9AD
☎ 01332 518662 🖹 01332 512092
**Undulating parkland course of two loops of nine holes,
in a pleasant setting and affording splendid country
views. There is a premium in hitting tee shots in the
right place for approaches to greens, some of which are**

Continued   *Continued*

on elevated plateaux. Some attractive par 3s which are considered to be very exacting.
18 holes, 5702yds, Par 68, SSS 68, Course record 64.
Club membership 800.
Visitors must contact Professional in advance. **Societies** apply in writing/telephone. **Green Fees** not confirmed.
Cards 🈁 **Prof** Tim Coxon **Course Designer** J Pennink **Facilities** ⊗ ⅛ ㊇ 📐 🖤 ♀ ⚒ 🏠 ⚐ ⚙ **Conf** Corporate Hospitality Days available **Location** 3m W of Derby on A516/B5020

Hotel ★★★★ 73% Menzies Mickleover Court, Etwall Rd, Mickleover, DERBY ☎ 01332 521234 99 en suite

Sinfin Wilmore Rd, Sinfin DE24 9HD
☎ 01332 766462 📠 01332 769004
Municipal parkland course with tree-lined fairways; an excellent test of golf. Generally a flat course, it is suitable for golfers of all ages.
18 holes, 6163yds, Par 70, SSS 69.
Club membership 400.
Visitors starting time must be booked in advance by telephone, visitors welcome any day. **Societies** apply in writing or by telephone in advance. **Green Fees** terms on application. **Cards** 🈁 🈁 🈁 🈁 📧 **Prof** Steve Astle **Facilities** ⊗ ⅛ ㊇ 📐 🖤 ♀ ⚒ 🏠 ⚐ ⚙ **Location** 2.5m S of city centre

Hotel ★★★ 63% International Hotel, 288 Burton Rd, DERBY ☎ 01332 369321 41 en suite 21 annexe en suite

DRONFIELD   Map 08 SK37

Hallowes Hallowes Ln S18 1UR
☎ 01246 411196 📠 01246 411196
Attractive moorland/parkland course set in the Derbyshire hills. Several testing par 4s and splendid views.
18 holes, 6342yds, Par 71, SSS 71, Course record 64.
Club membership 630.
Visitors may only play with member at weekends. Must contact in advance. **Societies** contact in advance, various packages. **Green Fees** £35 per day; £30 per round. **Prof** Philip Dunn **Facilities** ⊗ ⅛ ㊇ 📐 🖤 ♀ ⚒ 🏠 ⚙ **Leisure** snooker. **Location** S side of town. From Sheffield follow old A61(not bypass

Hotel ★★★ 64% Sandpiper Hotel, Sheffield Rd, Sheepbridge, CHESTERFIELD ☎ 01246 450550 46 en suite

DUFFIELD   Map 08 SK34

Chevin Golf Ln DE56 4EE
☎ 01332 841864 📠 01332 844028
e-mail: secretary@chevingolf.fsnet.co.uk
A mixture of parkland and moorland, this course is rather hilly which makes for some hard walking, but with most rewarding views of the surrounding countryside. The 8th hole, aptly named "Tribulation", requires an accurate tee shot, and is one of the most difficult holes in the country.
18 holes, 6057yds, Par 69, SSS 69, Course record 64.
Club membership 750.
Visitors not before 9.30am or off first tee between 12.30 and 2pm. Proof of handicap required. **Societies** contact in advance. **Green Fees** terms on application. **Prof** Willie Bird **Course Designer** J Braid **Facilities** ⊗ ⅛ ㊇ 📐 🖤 ♀ ⚒ 🏠 ⚐ ⚙ **Conf** fac available Corporate Hospitality Days available **Location** N side of town off A6

Continued

Hotel ★★★ 71% Makeney Hall Hotel, Makeney, Milford, BELPER ☎ 0870 609 6136 27 en suite 18 annexe en suite

GLOSSOP   Map 07 SK09

Glossop and District Hurst Ln, off Sheffield Rd
SK13 7PU ☎ 01457 865247(club house)
Moorland course in good position, excellent natural hazards. Difficult closing hole (9th & 18th).
11 holes, 5800yds, Par 68, SSS 68, Course record 64.
Club membership 350.
Visitors may not play Saturdays, Sundays by appointment/reservation. **Societies** must apply in writing to professional, steward or secretary. **Green Fees** terms on application. **Prof** Daniel Marsh **Facilities** ⊗ ⅛ ㊇ 📐 🖤 ♀ ⚒ 🏠 ⚐ ⚙ **Conf** Corporate Hospitality Days available **Location** 1m E off A57 from town centre

HORSLEY   Map 08 SK34

Horsley Lodge Smalley Mill Rd DE21 5BL
☎ 01332 780838 📠 01332 781118
e-mail: enquiries@horsleylodge.co.uk.
This lush meadowland course set in 180 acres of Derbyshire countryside, has some challenging holes. Also floodlit driving range. USGA world class greens designed by former World Champion Peter McEvoy.

18 holes, 6400yds, Par 71, SSS 71, Course record 65.
Club membership 650.
Visitors must contact professional in advance and have handicap. May not play weekends before noon. **Societies** must telephone in advance. **Green Fees** terms on application. **Cards** 🈁 🈁 🈁 🈁 📧 **Prof** G Lyall **Course Designer** Bill White **Facilities** ⊗ ⅛ ㊇ 📐 🖤 ♀ ⚒ 🏠 ⚐ 🚗 🐎 ⚒ ⚙ ♺ **Leisure** fishing. **Conf** fac available Corporate Hospitality Days available **Location** 4m NE of Derby, off A38 at Belper then follow tourist signs

Hotel ★★★★ 65% Marriott Breadsall Priory Hotel& Country Club, Moor Rd, MORLEY ☎ 01332 832235 12 en suite 100 annexe en suite

KEDLESTON   Map 08 SK34

Kedleston Park DE22 5JD
☎ 01332 840035 📠 01332 840035
e-mail: secretary@kedlestonpark.sagehost.co.uk
The course is laid out in flat mature parkland with fine trees and background views of historic Kedleston Hall (National Trust). Many testing holes are included in each nine and there is an excellent modern clubhouse.
18 holes, 6675yds, Par 72, SSS 72, Course record 66.
Club membership 743.
Visitors must contact in advance. **Societies** weekdays only, apply in writing. **Green Fees** £50 per day; £40

Continued

per round. **Cards** ⊞ ▦ ▤ ▣ ▦ ▨ ▢ **Prof** Paul Wesselingh **Course Designer** James Braid **Facilities** ⊗ ⅲ 🖫 ▬ ♀ ⚲ 🏠 ⛳ ⚘ 🚜 ✓ **Leisure** sauna. **Conf** Corporate Hospitality Days available **Location** Signposted Kedleston Hall from A38

Hotel ★★★ 63% International Hotel, 288 Burton Rd, DERBY ☎ 01332 369321 41 en suite 21 annexe en suite

LONG EATON   Map 08 SK43

Trent Lock Golf Centre Lock Ln, Sawley
NG10 2FY ☎ 0115 946 4398 📠 0115 946 1183
Main Course: 18 holes, 5717yds, Par 69, SSS 68, Course record 73.
9 hole: 9 holes, 2911yds, Par 36.
Course Designer E McCausland
Telephone for further details

Hotel ★★★ 66% Novotel Nottingham/Derby, Bostock Ln, LONG EATON ☎ 0115 946 5111 108 en suite

MATLOCK   Map 08 SK36

Matlock Chesterfield Rd, Matlock Moor DE4 5LZ
☎ 01629 582191 📠 01629 582135
Moorland course with fine views of the beautiful Peak District.
18 holes, 5996yds, Par 70, SSS 69, Course record 63.
Club membership 700.
Visitors with member only weekends & bank holidays. Members only weekdays 12.30-1.30pm. **Societies** prior arrangement with Secretary. **Green Fees** terms on application. **Prof** M A Whithorn **Course Designer** Tom Williamson **Facilities** ⊗ ⅲ 🖫 ▬ ♀ ⚲ 🏠 ✓ **Location** 1.5m NE of Matlock on A632

Hotel ★★★ 69% New Bath Hotel, New Bath Rd, MATLOCK BATH ☎ 0870 400 8119 55 en suite

MICKLEOVER   Map 08 SK33

Pastures Social Centre, Hospital Ln DE3 5DQ
☎ 01332 521074
9 holes, 5095yds, Par 64, SSS 65, Course record 67.
Course Designer J F Pennik **Location** 1m SW off A516
Telephone for further details

Hotel ★★★ 63% International Hotel, 288 Burton Rd, DERBY ☎ 01332 369321 41 en suite 21 annexe en suite

MORLEY   Map 08 SK34

Morley Hayes Main Rd DE7 6DG
☎ 01332 780480 782000 (shop) 📠 01332 781094
e-mail: golf@morleyhayes.com
Peaceful pay and play course set in a splendid valley and incorporating charming water features and woodland. Floodlit driving range. Challenging 9-hole short course (Tower Course).
Manor Course: 18 holes, 6726yds, Par 72, SSS 72, Course record 63.
Tower Course: 9 holes, 1614yds, Par 30.
Visitors welcome. **Societies** booking essential telephone for details. **Green Fees** Manor course: £33 per day, £18 per round (£42/£24 weekends) Tower course £15 for 18 holes, £8.50 for 9 holes (£20/£10.50 weekends). **Cards** ⊞ ▦ ▤ ▣ ▨ ▢ **Prof** Mark Marriott **Facilities** ⊗ ⅲ 🖫 ▬ ♀ ⚲ 🏠 ⛳ 🚜 ✓ ♺ **Conf** fac available Corporate Hospitality Days available **Location** 4m N of Derby between Derby and Heanor on A608

Continued

Morley Hayes Golf Course

Hotel ★★★★ 65% Marriott Breadsall Priory Hotel & Country Club, Moor Rd, MORLEY ☎ 01332 832235 12 en suite 100 annexe en suite

NEW MILLS   Map 07 SK08

New Mills Shaw Marsh SK22 4QE
☎ 01663 743485 📠 01663 743485
Moorland course with panoramic views and first-class greens.
18 holes, 5604yds, Par 69, SSS 67, Course record 62.
Club membership 483.
Visitors contact secretary/professional in advance, cannot play during competitions. **Societies** must contact secretary or professional in advance. **Green Fees** terms on application. **Prof** Carl Cross **Course Designer** Williams **Facilities** ⊗ ⅲ 🖫 ▬ ♀ ⚲ 🏠 ⛳ 🚜 ✓ ♺ **Conf** Corporate Hospitality Days available **Location** 0.5m N off B6101

RENISHAW   Map 08 SK47

Renishaw Park Club House, Mill Ln S21 3UZ
☎ 01246 432044 & 435484 📠 01246 432116
Part parkland and part meadowland with easy walking.
18 holes, 6107yds, Par 71, SSS 70, Course record 64.
Club membership 750.
Visitors Visitors not allowed on competition days. Contact professional on 01246 435484 for other days. **Societies** Telephone Secretarys office to arrange. **Green Fees** terms on application. **Prof** John Oates **Course Designer** Sir George Sitwell **Facilities** ⊗ ⅲ 🖫 ▬ ♀ ⚲ 🏠 ✓ **Location** 1.5m W of junct 30 M1

Hotel ★★★ 65% Sitwell Arms Hotel, Station Rd, RENISHAW ☎ 01246 435226 29 en suite

RISLEY   Map 08 SK43

Maywood Rushy Ln DE72 3ST
☎ 0115 939 2306 & 9490043 (pro)
Wooded parkland course with numerous water hazards.
18 holes, 6424yds, Par 72, SSS 71, Course record 70.
Club membership 450.
Visitors advisable to contact in advance during summer, may not play during competitions. Standard dress code applies. **Societies** by prior arrangement. **Green Fees** £15 per day (£20 weekends). **Prof** Simon Purcell-Jackson **Course Designer** P Moon **Facilities** ⊗ ⅲ 🖫 ▬ ♀ ⚲ 🏠 🚜 ✓ **Location** Near junct 25 on M1

Hotel ★★★ 73% Risley Hall Hotel, Derby Rd, RISLEY ☎ 0115 939 9000 16 en suite 18 annexe en suite

SHIRLAND Map 08 SK45

Shirland Lower Delves DE55 6AU
01773 834935 01773 832515
Rolling parkland and tree-lined course with extensive views of Derbyshire countryside.

18 holes, 6072yds, Par 71, SSS 70, Course record 67.
Club membership 250.
Visitors contact professional in advance. **Societies** contact Professional. **Green Fees** not confirmed. **Cards** **Prof** Neville Hallam **Facilities** **Conf** fac available Corporate Hospitality Days available **Location** S side of village off A61

Hotel ★★★★ 70% Renaissance Derby/Nottingham Hotel, Carter Ln East, SOUTH NORMANTON
01773 812000 158 en suite

STANTON BY DALE Map 08 SK43

Erewash Valley DE7 4QR
0115 932 3258 0115 944 0061
e-mail: secretary@erewashvalley.co.uk
Parkland/meadowland course overlooking valley and M1. Unique 4th and 5th in Victorian quarry bottom; 5th testing par 3.
18 holes, 6557yds, Par 72, SSS 71, Course record 67.
Club membership 750.
Visitors no restrictions except when club events in progress. **Societies** contact in advance. **Green Fees** £40 per day, £30 per round (£40 per round weekends). **Prof** M J Ronan **Course Designer** Hawtree **Facilities** **Location** 1m W, 2m from junct 25 on M1

Hotel ★★★ 73% Risley Hall Hotel, Derby Rd, RISLEY
0115 939 9000 16 en suite 18 annexe en suite

UNSTONE Map 08 SK37

Birch Hall Sheffield Rd S18 4DB
01246 291979 01246 412912
18 holes, 6379yds, Par 73, SSS 71, Course record 72.
Course Designer D Tucker **Location** Turn off A61 between Sheffield and Chesterfield, outskirts of Unstone village
Telephone for further details

Hotel ★★★ 64% Sandpiper Hotel, Sheffield Rd, Sheepbridge, CHESTERFIELD 01246 450550
46 en suite

Where to stay, where to eat?
Visit www.theAA.com

DEVON

AXMOUTH Map 03 SY29

Axe Cliff Squires Ln EX12 4AB
01297 21754 & 24371
Undulating links course with coastal views.
18 holes, 6000yds, Par 70, SSS 70, Course record 64.
Club membership 400.
Visitors must contact in advance. **Societies** must contact in advance. **Green Fees** terms on application. **Cards** **Prof** Mark Dack **Facilities** **Location** 0.75m S on B3172

Hotel ★★ 77% Swallows Eaves, COLYFORD
01297 553184 8 en suite

BIGBURY-ON-SEA Map 03 SX64

Bigbury TQ7 4BB
01548 810557 (Secretary) 01548 810207
Clifftop pasture and parkland course with easy walking. Exposed to winds, but with fine views over the sea and River Avon. The 7th hole is particularly tricky.
18 holes, 6061yds, Par 70, SSS 69, Course record 65.
Club membership 850.
Visitors handicap certificate preferred. Must contact Pro shop in advance. **Societies** please telephone or contact in advance. **Green Fees** £30 (£35 weekends). **Prof** Simon Lloyd **Course Designer** J H Taylor **Facilities** by prior arrangement **Conf** Corporate Hospitality Days available **Location** 1m S on B3392 between Bigbury and Bigbury-on-Sea

Hotel ★★★★ 72% Thurlestone Hotel, THURLESTONE
01548 560382 64 en suite

BLACKAWTON Map 03 SX85

Dartmouth Golf & Country Club TQ9 7DE
01803 712686 01803 712628
e-mail: info@dgcc.co.uk
The 9-hole Club course and the 18-hole Championship course are both worth a visit and not just for the beautiful views. The Championship is one of the most challenging courses in the West Country with 12 water hazards and a daunting par 5 4th hole that visitors will always remember. The spectacular final hole, looking downhill and over a water hazard to the green, can be difficult to judge and has been described as one of the most picturesque finishing holes in the country.
Championship Course: 18 holes, 6663yds, Par 72, SSS 72, Course record 68.
Dartmouth Course: 9 holes, 4791yds, Par 66, SSS 64.
Club membership 600.
Visitors must contact in advance, visitors welcome subject to availability. Normal dress standards apply on both courses.Tee times must be pre booked for both courses. **Societies** telephone in advance. **Green Fees** Championship: £30 (£40 weekends). Dartmouth: £13 (£14 weekends). **Cards** **Prof** Steve Dougan **Course Designer** Jeremy Pern **Facilities** **Leisure** heated indoor swimming pool, sauna, solarium, gymnasium, Physiotheraphy. **Conf** fac available Corporate Hospitality Days available **Location** On A3122 Totnes/Dartmouth road, 4m from Dartmouth

Hotel ★★★ 68% Stoke Lodge Hotel, Stoke Fleming, DARTMOUTH 01803 770523 25 en suite

BUDLEIGH SALTERTON   Map 03 SY08

East Devon Links Rd EX9 6DG
☎ 01395 443370 ▧ 01395 445547
e-mail: secretary@edge.co.uk
An interesting course with downland turf, much
heather and gorse, and superb views over the bay. The
early holes climb to the cliff edge. The downhill 17th
has a heather section in the fairway, leaving a good
second to the green.
18 holes, 6231yds, Par 70, SSS 70, Course record 61.
Club membership 850.
Visitors advisable to contact in advance, no visitors before
9am. Visitors must be member of a recognised club and
must produce proof of handicap. Societies Thu only, must
contact in advance. Green Fees £45 per 27/36 holes; £34
per 18 holes. Cards ▨▨ ▨▨ 🖭 ▨▨ ▨ Prof Trevor
Underwood Facilities ⊗ ⒫ ⒧ ▧ ♟ ♨ ⚒ ⛳ ✧ Conf
Corporate Hospitality Days available Location W side of
town centre
....
Hotel ★★ 73% Barn Hotel, Foxholes Hill, Marine Dr,
EXMOUTH ☎ 01395 224411 11 en suite

CHITTLEHAMHOLT   Map 03 SS62

Highbullen Hotel EX37 9HD
☎ 01769 540561 ▧ 01769 540492
e-mail: info@highbullen.co.uk
Mature parkland course with water hazards and
outstanding scenic views to Exmoor and Dartmoor.
Excellent facilities offered by the hotel.
Highbullen Hotel Golf Course: 18 holes, 5755yds, Par 68,
SSS 67.
Club membership 150.
Visitors to book tee time telephone 01769 540530
daytime, 01769 540561 evenings. Societies must contact in
advance. Green Fees £20 (£24 weekends & BH). Cards
▨▨ ▨▨ ▨ Prof Paul Weston Course Designer M Neil/ J
Hamilton Facilities ⊗ ⒫ ⒧ ▧ ♟ ♨ ⚒ ✧ ⚒ ⛳ ✧
Leisure hard and grass tennis courts, outdoor and indoor
heated swimming pools, squash, fishing, sauna, solarium,
gymnasium, golf simulator. Conf fac available Corporate
Hospitality Days available Location 0.5m S of village
....
Hotel ★★★ ⚑ 67% Highbullen Hotel,
CHITTLEHAMHOLT ☎ 01769 540561 12 en suite
25 annexe en suite

CHRISTOW   Map 03 SX88

Teign Valley EX6 7PA
☎ 01647 253026 ▧ 01647 253026
e-mail: welcome@teignvalleygolf.co.uk
A scenically spectacular 18-hole course set beside the
River Teign in the Dartmoor National Park. Offering a
good challenge to both low and high handicap golfers, it
features two lakeside holes, rolling fairways and fine
views.
18 holes, 5913yds, Par 70, SSS 68.
Club membership 300.
Visitors no restrictions, but need to book by telephone.
Societies write or telephone for bookings. Green Fees £20
per round (£28 weekends and bank holidays). Cards ▨▨
▨▨ ▨▨ ▨ Prof Scott Amiet Course Designer P Nicholson
Facilities ⊗ ⒫ ⒧ ▧ ♟ ♨ ⚒ ⛳ ✧ ♥ ⚒ ✧ Conf fac
available Location Take Teignvalley exit off A38,
Exeter/Plymouth Expressway and follow GC signs up
valley on B3193

Teign Valley Golf Club
....
Hotel ⎁ Bovey Castle, MORETONHAMPSTEAD
☎ 01647 445000 61 en suite 19 annexe en suite

CHULMLEIGH   Map 03 SS61

Chulmleigh Leigh Rd EX18 7BL
☎ 01769 580519 ▧ 01769 580519
e-mail: chulmleighgolf@aol.com
Summer Course: 18 holes, 1450yds, Par 54, SSS 54,
Course record 49.
Winter Course: 9 holes, 2310yds, Par 54, SSS 54, Course
record 54.
Course Designer John Goodban Location SW side of
village just off A377
Telephone for further details
....
Hotel ★★★ Northcote Manor, BURRINGTON
☎ 01769 560501 11 en suite

CHURSTON FERRERS   Map 03 SX95

Churston Dartmouth Rd TQ5 0LA
☎ 01803 842751 & 842218 ▧ 01803 845738
e-mail: manager@churstongc.freeserve.co.uk
A cliff-top downland course with splendid views over
Brixham harbour and Tor Bay. There is some gorse
with a wooded area inland. A variety of shots is called
for, with particularly testing holes at the 3rd, 9th and
15th, all par 4. Conference facilities and a well-
equipped shop are also available.
18 holes, 6219yds, Par 70, SSS 70, Course record 64.
Club membership 700.
Visitors must telephone in advance and be a member of
recognised golf club with a handicap certificate. Societies
apply in writing or telephone. Green Fees not confirmed.
Cards ▨▨ Prof Neil Holman Facilities ⊗ ⒫ ⒧ ▧ ♟ ♨ ⚒
⛳ ✧ ⚒ ✧ Location NW side of village on A379
....
Hotel ★★★ 68% Berryhead Hotel, Berryhead Rd,
BRIXHAM ☎ 01803 853225 32 en suite

CREDITON   Map 03 SS80

Downes Crediton Hookway EX17 3PT
☎ 01363 773025 & 774346 ▧ 01363 775060
e-mail: secretary@downescreditongc.co.uk
Parkland course with water features. Flat front nine.
Hilly and wooded back nine.
18 holes, 5954yds, Par 70, SSS 69.
Club membership 700.
Visitors handicap certificate required, must contact in
advance, restricted at weekends. Societies must contact in
advance. Green Fees £25 per day (£28 weekends). Cards

Continued   Continued

⬛ ⬛ ⬛ ⬛ ⬛ **Prof** Scott Macaskill **Facilities** ⊗)Ⅲ ⬛
⬛ ⬛ ⬛ ⬛ ⬛ ⬛ **Conf** Corporate Hospitality Days
available **Location** 1.5m SE off A377

· ·

Hotel ★★★ 73% Barton Cross Hotel & Restaurant,
Huxham, Stoke Canon, EXETER ☎ 01392 841245
9 en suite

CULLOMPTON   Map 03 ST00

Padbrook Park EX15 1RU
☎ 01884 38286 🖹 01884 34359
e-mail: padbrookpark@fsmail.net
**A 9-hole, 18-tee parkland course with many water and
woodland hazards and spectacular views. The dog-leg
2nd and pulpit 7th are particularly challenging to
golfers of all standards.**

*9 holes, 6108yds, Par 70, SSS 70, Course record 67.
Club membership 250.*

Continued

Visitors welcome at all times but preferable to book in
advance. **Societies** apply in writing or telephone. **Green
Fees** not confirmed. **Cards** ⬛ ⬛ ⬛ **Prof** Stewart
Adwick **Course Designer** Bob Sandow **Facilities** ⊗ ⬛ ⬛
⬛ ⬛ ⬛ ⬛ ⬛ ⬛ **Leisure** fishing, solarium,
gymnasium, indoor bowling centre, health suite. **Location**
M5 junct 28, 1m on S edge of town

· ·

Hotel ★★★ 68% The Tiverton Hotel, Blundells Rd,
TIVERTON ☎ 01884 256120 70 en suite

DAWLISH WARREN   Map 03 SX97

Warren EX7 0NF
☎ 01626 862255 & 864002 🖹 01626 888005
e-mail: secretary@dwgc.co.uk
**Typical flat, genuine links course lying on spit between
sea and Exe estuary. Picturesque scenery, a few trees
but much gorse. Testing in windy conditions. The 7th
hole provides the opportunity to go for the green across
a bay on the estuary.**

Continued

18 holes, 5912yds, Par 69, SSS 68, Course record 65.
Club membership 600.
Visitors must contact in advance and be member of a bona
fide golf club **Societies** prior arrangement essential. **Green
Fees** £25 per day (£28 weekends & bank holidays). Rates
exclusive of £1 players' insurance. **Cards** 🃏 💳 💳 💳
🃏 📠 ⑨ **Prof** Darren Prowse **Course Designer** James
Braid **Facilities** ⊗ ⅢⅢ ᴸᴸ 🍺 ♀ ☌ 🏠 ⚐ ✔ **Location** E side
of village

....

Hotel ★★★ 70% Langstone Cliff Hotel, Dawlish Warren,
DAWLISH ☎ 01626 868000 61 en suite
4 annexe en suite

Down St Mary   Map 03 SS70

Waterbridge EX17 5LG ☎ 01363 85111

A testing course of 9 holes set in a gently sloping valley.
The par of 32 will not be easily gained, with one par 5,
three par 4s and five par 3s, although the course record
holder has par 29! The 3rd hole which is a raised green
is surrounded by water and the 4th (439yds) is
demanding for beginners.
9 holes, 3910yds, Par 64, SSS 64.
Club membership 85.
Visitors no restrictions. **Societies** no restrictions. **Green
Fees** £11.50 per 18 holes; £7 per 9 holes (£13.50/£8
weekends & bank holidays). **Cards** 🃏 💳 💳 🃏 ⑨ **Prof**
David Ridyard **Course Designer** D Taylor **Facilities** ⊗ ᴸᴸ
♀ ☌ 🏠 ⚐ ✔ **Conf** Corporate Hospitality Days
available **Location** From Exeter on A377 towards
Barnstaple.1 mile past Copplestone

....

Hotel ★★★ Northcote Manor, BURRINGTON
☎ 01769 560501 11 en suite

Exeter   Map 03 SX99

Exeter Golf & Country Club Topsham Rd,
Countess Wear EX2 7AE
☎ 01392 874139 📄 01392 874914
e-mail: info@exetergcc.fsnet.co.uk
A sheltered parkland course with some very old trees
and known as the flattest course in Devon. The 15th
and 17th are testing par 4 holes. Small, well guarded
greens.
18 holes, 5980yds, Par 69, SSS 69, Course record 62.
Club membership 800.
Visitors welcome but may not play during match or
competitions, very busy pre booking needed up to 1 week
in advance. Must have handicap certificate. Ring starter in
advance on 01392 876303 **Societies** welcome Thu only,
booking available by telephone to manager tel 01392
874639. **Green Fees** £38 per day; £30 per round (£43/£35
weekends). **Cards** 🃏 💳 🃏 ⑨ **Prof** Mike Rowett
Course Designer J Braid **Facilities** ⊗ ⅢⅢ ᴸᴸ 🍺 ♀ ☌ 🏠
🏌 ✔ **Leisure** hard tennis courts, outdoor and indoor
heated swimming pools, squash, sauna, solarium,
gymnasium, jacuzzi. **Conf** fac available Corporate
Hospitality Days available **Location** SE side of city centre
off A379

....

Hotel ★★★ 64% Buckerell Lodge Hotel, Topsham Rd,
EXETER ☎ 01392 221111 53 en suite

Woodbury Park Hotel, Golf & Country
Club Woodbury Castle, Woodbury EX5 1JJ
☎ 01395 233500 📄 01395 233384
e-mail: golfbookings@woodburypark.co.uk

Irrigated 18-hole Oaks Championship course and
excellent 9-hole Acorns course set in 500 acres of
wooded parkland with stunning views.

Woodbury Park Hotel, Golf & Country Club
Oaks: 18 holes, 6905yds, Par 72, SSS 72, Course record 66.
Acorn: 9 holes, 2297yds, Par 32, SSS 32.
Club membership 750.
Visitors welcome, please reserve tee times in advance.
Societies contact in advance on 01395 233500 **Green Fees**
Oaks £40 per 18 holes (£50 weekends). Acorns £13 per 9
holes. **Cards** 🃏 💳 💳 💳 🃏 ⑨ **Prof** Alan Richards
Course Designer J Hamilton-Stutt **Facilities** ⊗ ⅢⅢ ᴸᴸ 🍺 ♀
☌ 🏠 ⚐ ✔ 🏌 ✔ **Leisure** hard tennis courts,
heated indoor swimming pool, squash, fishing, sauna,
gymnasium, health spa. **Conf** fac available Corporate
Hospitality Days available **Location** M5 junct 30 then
A3052

....

Hotel ★★★★ 67% Woodbury Park Hotel Golf &
Country Club, Woodbury Castle, WOODBURY
☎ 01395 233382 57 en suite

High Bickington   Map 02 SS52

Libbaton EX37 9BS
☎ 01769 560269 & 560167 📄 01769 560342
e-mail: gerald.hemiman@tesco.net
Parkland course on undulating land with no steep
slopes. Water comes into play on 11 of the 18 holes, as
well as a quarry, ditches, trees and eight raised greens.
Not a heavily bunkered course, but those present are
well positioned and the sharp sand they contain makes
them tricky. Five par 5s could easily get you thinking
this course is only for big hitters but as with many good
courses, sound course management is the key to success.
18 holes, 6494yds, Par 73, SSS 72, Course record 72.
Club membership 500.
Visitors book in advance. No jeans, trainers or collarless
shirts. **Societies** 6 persons or more. Telephone to book in
advance. **Green Fees** £20 per 18 holes (£24 weekends).
Cards 🃏 💳 🃏 ⑨ **Prof** Andrew Norman
Course Designer Col Badham **Facilities** ⊗ ⅢⅢ ᴸᴸ 🍺 ♀ ☌
🏠 ⚐ ✔ 🏌 ✔ **Conf** fac available Corporate Hospitality
Days available **Location** B3217,1m of High Bickington,
off A377

....

Hotel ★★★ ♨ 67% Highbullen Hotel,
CHITTLEHAMHOLT ☎ 01769 540561 12 en suite
25 annexe en suite

Holsworthy   Map 02 SS30

Holsworthy Killatree EX22 6LP
☎ 01409 253177 📄 01409 253177
e-mail: hgcsecretary@aol.com

Continued   *Continued*

Pleasant parkland course with gentle slopes, numerous trees and a few strategic sand bunkers.

18 holes, 6100yds, Par 70, SSS 69, Course record 64.
Club membership 500.
Visitors book with professional on 01409 254177.
Societies by arrangement with secretary or professional.
Green Fees terms on application. **Cards** 〓 ▬ 〓 ▣ 〓
Prof Graham Webb **Facilities** ⊗ ⟒ ⓑ ♥ ♀ ♨ ☎ ♈ ♦
🏌 ♂ ⌂ **Location** 1.5m W on A3072 towards Bude

·······································

Hotel ★★★ 70% Falcon Hotel, Breakwater Rd, BUDE
☎ 01288 352005 29 en suite

HONITON   Map 03 ST10

Honiton Middlehills EX14 9TR
☎ 01404 44422 & 42943 📄 01404 46383
Founded in 1896, this level parkland course is situated on a plateau 850ft above sea level. Easy walking and good views. The 4th hole is a testing par 3. The 17th and 18th provide a challenging finish.
18 holes, 5902yds, Par 69, SSS 68, Course record 65.
Club membership 800.
Visitors must contact in advance. Handicap certificate necessary. **Societies** society bookings on Thursdays. **Green Fees** £26 per day (£34 weekends & bank holidays). **Prof** Adrian Cave **Facilities** ⊗ ⟒ ⓑ ♥ ♀ ♨ ☎ ♈
Leisure hardstanding for touring caravans with services.
Conf Corporate Hospitality Days available **Location** 1.25m SE of Honiton, turn towards Farway at Tower Cross on A35

·······································

Hotel ★★ 69% Home Farm Hotel & Restaurant, Wilmington, HONITON ☎ 01404 831278 8 en suite 5 annexe en suite

ILFRACOMBE   Map 02 SS54

Ilfracombe Hele Bay EX34 9RT
☎ 01271 862176 & 863328 📄 01271 867731
e-mail: ilfracombe.golfclub@virgin.net
A sporting, clifftop, heathland course with views over the Bristol Channel and moors from every tee and green.
18 holes, 5893yds, Par 69, SSS 69, Course record 66.
Club membership 520.
Visitors recommended to make tee reservation prior to visit, member only before 10am on weekends. **Societies** telephone in advance. **Green Fees** not confirmed. **Cards** 〓 ▬ 〓 〓 ▣ **Prof** Mark Davies **Course Designer** T K Weir **Facilities** ⊗ ⓑ ♥ ♀ ♨ ☎ ♈ 🏌 ♂ ⌂ **Location** 1.5m E off A399

·······································

Hotel ★★ 71% Elmfield Hotel, Torrs Park, ILFRACOMBE ☎ 01271 863377 11 en suite 2 annexe en suite

IPPLEPEN   Map 03 SX86

Dainton Park Totnes Rd, Ipplepen TQ12 5TN
☎ 01803 815000
e-mail: dpgolf@globalnet.co.uk
A challenging parkland course in typical Devon countryside, with gentle contours, tree-lined fairways and raised tees. Water hazards make the two opening holes particularly testing. The 8th, a dramatic 180-yard drop hole totally surrounded by sand, is one of four tough par 3s on the course.
18 holes, 6302yds, Par 71, SSS 70, Course record 70.
Club membership 650.

Visitors prior booking by phone advisable to guarantee start time. **Societies** must contact in advance. **Green Fees** £22 per round (£25 weekends). **Cards** 〓 ▬ ▣ **Prof** Martin Tyson **Course Designer** Adrian Stiff **Facilities** ⊗ ⟒ ⓑ ♥ ♀ ♨ ☎ ♈ ♦ ♂ ⌂ **Leisure** gymnasium. **Conf** Corporate Hospitality Days available **Location** 2m S of Newton Abbot on A381

·······································

Hotel ★★ 68% Queens Hotel, Queen St, NEWTON ABBOT ☎ 01626 363133 20 en suite

IVYBRIDGE   Map 02 SX65

Dinnaton Fitness & Golf Blachford Rd PL21 9HU
☎ 01752 690020 & 892512 📄 01752 698334
e-mail: golf@dinnaton.co.uk
9 holes, 4089yds, Par 64, SSS 60.
Course Designer Cotton & Pink **Location** Leave A38 at Ivybridge junct and continue towards town centre. At first rdbt follow signs for club approx 1m
Telephone for further details

·······································

Hotel ★★ 73% Glazebrook House Hotel & Restaurant, SOUTH BRENT ☎ 01364 73322 10 en suite

MORETONHAMPSTEAD   Map 03 SX78

Bovey Castle TQ13 8RE
☎ 01647 445000 📄 01647 440961
e-mail: richard.lewis@boveycastle.com
This enjoyable parkland course has enough hazards to make any golfer think. Most hazards are natural such as the Rivers Bowden and Bovey which meander through the first eight holes.
18 holes, 6251yds, Par 70, SSS 70, Course record 63.
Club membership 130.
Visitors must contact in advance and pre-arrange starting times. **Societies** must telephone for reservation in advance. **Green Fees** £100 per round any time. **Cards** 〓 ▬ ▣ 〓 ▬ ▣ **Prof** Richard Lewis **Course Designer** J Abercrombie **Facilities** ⊗ ⟒ ⓑ ♥ ♀ ♨ ☎ ♈ ♦ ♂ ⌂ **Leisure** hard and grass tennis courts, heated indoor plus outdoor swimming pool, fishing, sauna, solarium, gymnasium. **Conf** fac available Corporate Hospitality Days available **Location** 2m W of Moretonhampstead, off B3212

·······································

Hotel Ⓤ Bovey Castle, MORETONHAMPSTEAD ☎ 01647 445000 61 en suite 19 annexe en suite

MORTEHOE   Map 02 SS44

Mortehoe & Woolacombe EX34 7EH
☎ 01271 870667 & 870566
e-mail: malcolm_wilkinson@northdevon.gov.uk
Attached to a camping and caravan site, this 9-hole course has 2 par 3s and 7 par 4s. The gently sloping clifftop course has spectacular views across Morte Bay.
Easewell: 9 holes, 4690yds, Par 66, SSS 63, Course record 66.
Club membership 245.
Visitors no restrictions **Societies** must telephone or write in advance. **Green Fees** not confirmed. **Course Designer** D Hoare **Facilities** ⊗ ⟒ ⓑ ♥ ♀ ♨ ☎ ♈ ♂ **Leisure** heated indoor swimming pool, indoor bowls. **Conf** Corporate Hospitality Days available **Location** 0.25m before Mortehoe on station road

·······································

Hotel ★★★ 77% Watersmeet Hotel, Mortehoe, WOOLACOMBE ☎ 01271 870333 25 en suite

Continued

Newton Abbot (Stover) Bovey Rd TQ12 6QQ

☎ 01626 352460 (Secretary) 🖷 01626 330210
e-mail: stovergolfclub@aol.com
Mature wooded parkland course with water coming into play on eight holes.
18 holes, 5764yds, Par 69, SSS 68, Course record 63.
Club membership 800.
Visitors must have proof of membership of recognised club or current handicap certificate. Advised to contact in advance. **Societies** by arrangement on Thu only. **Green Fees** £32 per round/day. **Cards** 🖦 🖦 **Prof** Malcolm Craig **Course Designer** James Braid **Facilities** ⊗ ⫼ ⅃ 🖲 🖵 ♀ 🛆 🖻 ⚷ **Conf** Corporate Hospitality Days available **Location** 3m N of Newton Abbot on A382. Bovey Tracey exit on A38.

....
Hotel ★★ 68% Queens Hotel, Queen St, NEWTON ABBOT ☎ 01626 363133 20 en suite

Ashbury Higher Maddaford EX20 4NL

☎ 01837 55453 🖷 01837 55468
Ashbury Beeches, Pines Willows: 27 holes, 8100yds.
Ashbury Oakwood: 18 holes, 5343yds, Par 68, SSS 66.
Ashbury Acorns: 18 holes, 2018yds, Par 54.
Course Designer David Fensom **Location** Off A3079 Okehampton-Holsworthy
Telephone for further details
....
Hotel ★★ 67% White Hart Hotel, Fore St, OKEHAMPTON ☎ 01837 52730 & 54514 🖷 01837 53979 19 en suite

Okehampton Tors Rd EX20 1EF

☎ 01837 52113 🖷 01837 52734
e-mail: okehamptongc@btconnect.com
A good combination of moorland, woodland and river makes this one of the prettiest, yet testing courses in Devon.
18 holes, 5268yds, Par 68, SSS 66, Course record 66.
Club membership 600.
Visitors advance booking recommended, limited times available at weekends. Saturdays by prior arrangement only **Societies** by prior arrangement. **Green Fees** £20 per day; £17 per round (£25 weekends). **Cards** 🖦 🖦 🖦 🖳 🛒 **Prof** Ashley Moon **Course Designer** J F Taylor **Facilities** ⊗ ⫼ 🖲 ♀ 🛆 🖻 ⅋ ⚷ **Location** 1m S off A30, signposted from town centre
....
Hotel ★★ 67% Oxenham Arms, SOUTH ZEAL ☎ 01837 840244 & 840577 🖷 01837 840791 8 rms (7 en suite)

Elfordleigh Colebrook, Plympton PL7 5EB

☎ 01752 336428 (hotel) & 348425 (golf shop)
🖷 01752 344581
e-mail: elfordleigh@btinternet.com
18 holes, 5664yds, Par 69, SSS 67, Course record 66.
Course Designer J H Taylor **Location** 2m NE off A374, follow signs from Plympton town centre
Telephone for further details
....
Hotel ★★★ 70% Elfordleigh Hotel Golf Leisure, Colebrook, Plympton, PLYMOUTH ☎ 01752 336428 34 en suite

Staddon Heights Plymstock PL9 9SP

☎ 01752 402475 🖷 01752 401998
e-mail: golfclub@btopenworld
Seaside course affording spectacular views across Plymouth Sound, Dartmoor and Bodmin Moor. Testing holes include the par 3 17th with its green cut into a hillside and the par 4 14th across a road. Easy walking.
18 holes, 5804yds, Par 68, SSS 68, Course record 66.
Club membership 750.
Visitors must have handicap certificate and contact the pro or secretary in advance. **Societies** apply by telephone in advance. **Green Fees** not confirmed. **Prof** Ian Marshall **Course Designer** Hamilton Stutt **Facilities** ⊗ ⫼ 🖲 🖵 ♀ 🛆 🖻 ⅋ **Location** 5m SW of city centre
....
Hotel 🅄 Holiday Inn Plymouth, Cliff Rd, The Hoe, PLYMOUTH ☎ 0870 400 9064 112 en suite

Saunton EX33 1LG

☎ 01271 812436 🖷 01271 814241
e-mail: info@sauntongolf.co.uk
Two traditional championship links courses. Windy, with natural hazards.

East Course: 18 holes, 6373yds, Par 71, SSS 71, Course record 64.
West Course: 18 holes, 6138yds, Par 71, SSS 70, Course record 63.
Club membership 1450.
Visitors prior booking recommended and must have handicap certificate. **Societies** must apply in advance, handicap certificates required. **Green Fees** £75 per day; £55 per round. **Cards** 🖦 🖦 🖳 **Prof** A T MacKenzie **Course Designer** F Pennick/W H Fowler **Facilities** ⊗ ⫼ 🖲 🖵 ♀ 🛆 🖻 ⅋ ⚷ ⅃ **Conf** Corporate Hospitality Days available **Location** S side of village off B3231
....
Hotel ★★★★ 70% Saunton Sands Hotel, SAUNTON ☎ 01271 890212 92 en suite

Sidmouth Cotmaton Rd, Peak Hill EX10 8SX

☎ 01395 513451 & 516407 🖷 01395 514661
18 holes, 5100yds, Par 66, SSS 65, Course record 59.
Course Designer J H Taylor **Location** W side of town centre
Telephone for further details
....
Hotel ★★★★ 75% Victoria Hotel, The Esplanade, SIDMOUTH ☎ 01395 512651 61 en suite

SOUTH BRENT
Map 03 SX66

Wrangaton (S Devon) Golf Links Rd, Wrangaton
TQ10 9HJ ☎ 01364 73229 📧 01364 73229
Unique 18-hole course with 9 holes on moorland and 9 holes on parkland. The course lies within Dartmoor National Park. Spectacular views towards sea and rugged terrain. Natural fairways and hazards include bracken, sheep and ponies.
18 holes, 6083yds, Par 70, SSS 69, Course record 66.
Club membership 680.
Visitors contact in advance. **Societies** write or telephone. **Green Fees** terms on application. **Cards** 🖃 🔳 💳 **Prof** Glenn Richards **Course Designer** D M A Steel **Facilities** ⊗ �🃏 ⅃ ⚐ 🖢 ⚐ ℗ ⚐ 🏌 🏆 🚶 ⚑ **Location** 2.25 m SW off A38, between South Brent & Ivybridge

Hotel ★★ 73% Glazebrook House Hotel & Restaurant, SOUTH BRENT ☎ 01364 73322 10 en suite

SPARKWELL
Map 02 SX55

Welbeck Manor & Sparkwell Golf Course
Blacklands PL7 5DF ☎ 01752 837219 📧 01752 837219
9 holes, 2886yds, Par 68, SSS 68, Course record 68.
Course Designer John Gabb **Location** 1m N of A38 Plymouth/Ivybridge road
Telephone for further details

Hotel ★★ 63% The Moorland Hotel, Wotter, Shaugh Prior, PLYMOUTH ☎ 01752 839228 18 en suite

TAVISTOCK
Map 02 SX47

Hurdwick Tavistock Hamlets PL19 0LL
☎ 01822 612746 📧 01822 612746
An executive parkland course with many bunkers and fine views. Executive golf originated in America and the concept is that a round should take no longer than 3 hours whilst offering solid challenge.
18 holes, 5302yds, Par 68, SSS 67, Course record 67.
Club membership 110.
Visitors no restrictions. **Societies** must contact in advance. **Green Fees** £16 per day. **Course Designer** Hawtree **Facilities** 🖢 ⚐ ℗ ⚐ 🏌 🚶 ⚑ **Location** 1m N of Tavistock on the Brentor Road

Hotel ★★★ 70% Bedford Hotel, 1 Plymouth Rd, TAVISTOCK ☎ 01822 613221 30 en suite

Tavistock Down Rd PL19 9AQ
☎ 01822 612344 📧 01822 612344
e-mail: tavygolf@freeserve.net
18 holes, 6495yds, Par 71, SSS 71, Course record 60.
Course Designer H Fowler **Location** 1m SE of town centre, on Whitchurch Down
Telephone for further details

Hotel ★★★ 70% Bedford Hotel, 1 Plymouth Rd, TAVISTOCK ☎ 01822 613221 30 en suite

TEDBURN ST MARY
Map 03 SX89

Fingle Glen EX6 6AF
☎ 01647 61817 📧 01647 61135
e-mail: fingle.glen@btinternet.com
A 9-hole course containing six par 4s and three par 3s set in 52 acres of rolling countryside. Testing 4th, 5th and 9th holes. 12-bay floodlit driving range.

Continued

9 holes, 4818yds, Par 66, SSS 63, Course record 63.
Club membership 750.
Visitors must contact in advance. **Societies** write or telephone in advance. **Green Fees** not confirmed. **Cards** 🖃 🔳 💳 🔵 **Prof** Stephen Gould **Course Designer** Bill Pile **Facilities** ⊗ �🃏 🖢 ⚐ ℗ ⅃ ⚐ 🏌 🚶 🏆 ⚑ **Location** 5m W of Exeter, off A30

Hotel ★★★ 72% St Olaves Hotel & Restaurant, Mary Arches St, EXETER ☎ 01392 217736 15 en suite

TEIGNMOUTH
Map 03 SX97

Teignmouth Haldon Moor TQ14 9NY
☎ 01626 777070 📧 01626 777304
e-mail: tgc@btconnect.com
This fairly flat heathland course is high up with fine panoramic views of sea, moors and river valley. Good springy turf with some heather and an interesting layout makes for very enjoyable holiday golf. Designed by Dr Alister MacKenzie, the world famous architect who also designed Augusta GC USA.
18 holes, 6200yds, Par 71, SSS 70, Course record 64.
Club membership 900.
Visitors handicap certificate required. **Societies** Thu only, telephone in advance and confirm in writing. **Green Fees** £27 (£29.50 weekends). **Prof** Rob Selley **Course Designer** Dr Alister Mackenzie **Facilities** ⊗ �🃏 🖢 ⚐ ℗ ⅃ ⚐ ⚑ **Conf** Corporate Hospitality Days available **Location** 2m NW off B3192

Hotel ★★★ 70% Ness House Hotel, Ness Dr, Shaldon, TEIGNMOUTH ☎ 01626 873480 7 en suite 5 annexe en suite

THURLESTONE
Map 03 SX64

Thurlestone TQ7 3NZ
☎ 01548 560405 📧 01548 562149
e-mail: info@thurlestonegc.co.uk
Situated on the edge of the cliffs with typical downland turf and good greens. The course, after an interesting opening hole, rises to higher land with fine sea views, and finishes with an excellent 502-yard downhill hole to the clubhouse.
18 holes, 6340yds, Par 71, SSS 70, Course record 65.
Club membership 770.
Visitors must contact in advance & have handicap certificate from a recognised club. **Green Fees** terms on application. **Cards** 🖃 🔳 🔵 🔵 **Prof** Peter Laugher **Course Designer** Harry S Colt **Facilities** ⊗ �🃏 by prior arrangement 🖢 ⚐ ℗ ⅃ ⚐ 🏌 ⚑ **Leisure** hard and grass tennis courts. **Location** S side of village

Hotel ★★★★ 72% Thurlestone Hotel, THURLESTONE ☎ 01548 560382 64 en suite

TIVERTON
Map 03 SS91

Tiverton Post Hill EX16 4NE
☎ 01884 252187 📧 01884 251607
e-mail: tivertongolfclub@lineone.net
A parkland course where the many different species of tree are a feature and where the lush pastures ensure some of the finest fairways in the south-west. There are a number of interesting holes which visitors will find a real challenge.
18 holes, 6236yds, Par 71, SSS 71,
Course record 65. Club membership 850.

Continued

Visitors must contact in advance & have a current handicap certificate. Societies apply in writing or telephone. Green Fees £30 per 18 holes. Prof Michael Hawton Course Designer Braid Facilities ⊗ ≋ by prior arrangement ⮜ 🍺 ♀ ⛳ 🏠 ⚐ Conf Corporate Hospitality Days available Location 3m E of Tiverton, M5 Junct 27, proceed through Sampford Peverell and Halberton

Hotel ★★★ 75% Midland Hotel, Midland Rd, DERBY
☎ 01332 345894 100 en suite

TORQUAY
Map 03 SX96

Torquay 30 Petitor Rd, St Marychurch TQ1 4QF
☎ 01803 314591 📠 01803 316116
e-mail: torquaygolfclub@skynow.net
Unusual combination of cliff and parkland golf, with wonderful views over the sea and Dartmoor.
18 holes, 6175yds, Par 69, SSS 69, Course record 63.
Club membership 700.
Visitors must contact in advance. Societies must apply in writing. Green Fees not confirmed. Prof Martin Ruth Facilities ⊗ ≋ ⮜ 🍺 ♀ ⛳ 🏠 ✴ 🎏 ⚐ Location 1.25m N

Hotel ★★ 64% Norcliffe Hotel, 7 Babbacombe Downs Rd, Babbacombe, TORQUAY ☎ 01803 328456 27 en suite

TORRINGTON (GREAT)
Map 02 SS41

Torrington Weare Trees, Great Torrington EX38 7EZ
☎ 01805 622229 & 623878 📠 01805 623878
e-mail: theoffice@torringtongolf.fsnet.co.uk
Attractive and challenging 9-hole course. Free draining to allow play all year round. Excellent greens and outstanding views.
9 holes, 4423yds, Par 64, SSS 62, Course record 58.
Club membership 420.
Visitors contact in advance. May not play Tues, Wed, Sat, Sun or bank holidays before noon. Societies by arrangement. Facilities ⊗ ≋ ⮜ 🍺 ♀ ⛳ 🎏 ⚐ Location 1m W of Torringdon

Hotel ★★★ 69% Royal Hotel, Barnstaple St, BIDEFORD
☎ 01237 472005 32 en suite

WESTWARD HO!
Map 02 SS42

Royal North Devon Golf Links Rd EX39 1HD
☎ 01237 473817 📠 01237 423456
e-mail: info@royalnorthdevongolfclub.co.uk
Oldest links course in England with traditional links features and a museum in the clubhouse.
18 holes, 6716yds, Par 72, SSS 72, Course record 65.
Club membership 1150.
Visitors advisable to telephone and book tee time, handicap certificate preferred or letter of introduction from club. Societies apply in writing or telephone. Green Fees £40 per day; £34 per round (£46/£40 weekends & bank holidays). Cards 💳 💳 💳 Prof Richard Herring Course Designer Old Tom Morris Facilities ⊗ ⮜ 🍺 ♀ ⛳ 🏠 🎏 ⚐ Leisure Museum of Golf Memorabilia, snooker. Location N side of village off B3236

Guesthouse ♦♦♦♦ Culloden House, Fosketh Hill, WESTWARD HO! ☎ 01237 479421 5 en suite

Culloden House

WOOLSERY
Map 02 SS32

Hartland Forest EX39 5RA
☎ 01237 431442 📠 01237 431734
e-mail: castleacre@btconnect.com
Exceptionally varied course with many water hazards.
18 holes, 5900yds, Par 70, SSS 68.
Club membership 60.
Visitors no restrictions. Societies telephone in advance or apply in writing. Green Fees not confirmed. Cards 💳 💳 💳 🌐 Course Designer A Cartwright Facilities ⊗ by prior arrangement ≋ by prior arrangement ⮜ by prior arrangement 🍺 ♀ ⛳ 🎏 🏠 🎏 ⚐ Leisure hard tennis courts, heated indoor swimming pool, fishing, sauna. Location 1.7m E of A39, 4 miles south of Clovelly Cross on A39

Hotel ★★★ 72% Penhaven Country House, Rectory Ln, PARKHAM ☎ 01237 451388 & 451711 📠 01237 451878 12 en suite

YELVERTON
Map 02 SX56

Yelverton Golf Links Rd PL20 6BN
☎ 01822 852824 📠 01822 854869
e-mail: secretary@yelvertongc.co.uk
An excellent course on Dartmoor with plenty of gorse and heather. Tight lies in the fairways, fast greens and challenging hazards. Boasts three of the best holes in Devon (12th, 13th and 16th). Outstanding views.

18 holes, 6351yds, Par 71, SSS 71, Course record 64.
Club membership 650.
Visitors must have handicap certificate and subject to availability, contact in advance. No visitors on Sun. Societies must be booked in advance, by telephone initially. Green Fees £30 per day. Prof Tim McSherry Course Designer Herbert Fowler Facilities ⊗ ≋ ⮜ 🍺 ♀ ⛳ 🏠 🎏 ⚐ Leisure indoor golf academy. Conf fac available Corporate Hospitality Days available Location 1m S of Yelverton, off A386

Continued

Hotel ★★★ 72% Moorland Links Hotel, YELVERTON
☎ 01822 852245 45 en suite

DORSET

ASHLEY HEATH
Map 04 SU10

Moors Valley Horton Rd BH24 2ET
☎ 01425 479776 📠 01425 471656
e-mail: golf@eastdorset.gov.uk
Skilfully designed by Hawtree, this mature heathland/
woodland course is scenically set within a wildlife
conservation area, exuding peace and tranquillity. Each
hole has its own character, the back 7 being in particular
very special. The course is renowned for its greens.
18 holes, 5813yds, Par 69, SSS 68.
Club membership 380.
Visitors must contact in advance. **Societies** telephone for
availability. **Green Fees** £19 per round. **Cards** 🖼 💳 💳
🖼 **Prof** James Daniels **Course Designer** Hawtree & Son
Facilities ⊗ ℍ ⓑ ♥ ♀ ♧ ☎ ⛳ ⛵ **Leisure** fishing, 4 hole
game improvement course, bike hire, aerial assault course.
Location Signposted from A31 Ashley Heath roundabout

Hotel ⛟ Travelodge, St Leonards, RINGWOOD
☎ 08700 850 950

BEAMINSTER
Map 03 ST40

Chedington Court South Perrott DT8 3HU
☎ 01935 891413 📠 01935 891217
e-mail: admincgc@tiscali.co.uk
This beautiful 18-hole parkland course is set on the
Dorset-Somerset borders with mature trees and
interesting water hazards. A challenge from the first
hole, par 5, blind drive to the elevated tee on the 15th,
and the closing holes can be tricky.
18 holes, 5924yds, Par 70, SSS 70, Course record 68.
Club membership 450.
Visitors must book tee time in advance at weekends.
Societies apply in writing or telephone. **Green Fees** terms
on application. **Cards** 🖼 💳 💳 💳 🖼 **Prof** J Lawrence
Course Designer David Hemstock/Donald Steel **Facilities**
⊗ ℍ ⓑ ♥ ♀ ♧ ☎ ⛳ ⛵ ☎ **Conf** Corporate
Hospitality Days available **Location** 5m NE of Beaminster
on A356 Dorchester-Crewkerne

Hotel ★★★ 71% Bridge House Hotel, 3 Prout Bridge,
BEAMINSTER ☎ 01308 862200 9 en suite
5 annexe en suite

BELCHALWELL
Map 03 ST70

Dorset Heights DT11 0EG
☎ 01258 860900 📠 01258 860900
18 holes, 6138yds, Par 70, SSS 70, Course record 74.
Course Designer David Astill
Telephone for further details

Hotel ★★ 70% Crown Hotel, West St, BLANDFORD
FORUM ☎ 01258 456626 32 en suite

BERE REGIS
Map 03 SY89

Dorset Golf & Country Club BH20 7NT
☎ 01929 472244 📠 01929 471294
e-mail: admin@dorsetgolfresort.com
Lakeland is the longest course in Dorset. Designed by

Martin Hawtree with numerous inter-connected water
features, carefully planned bunkers and sculptured
greens. A player who completes a round with his
handicap has every reason to celebrate! The Woodland
course, although shorter, is equally outstanding with
rhododendron and tree-lined fairways.
*Lakeland Course: 18 holes, 6580yds, Par 72, SSS 73,
Course record 69.*
Woodland Course: 9 holes, 5032yards, Par 66, SSS 64.
Club membership 600.
Visitors must book in advance **Societies** apply in advance.
Green Fees Lakeland: £35 (£39 weekends). Woodland:
£24 (£28 weekends). **Cards** 🖼 💳 💳 🖼 🖼 **Prof** Scott
Porter **Course Designer** Martin Hawtree **Facilities** ⊗ ℍ ⓑ
♥ ♀ ♧ ☎ ⛳ ⛵ **Leisure** fishing. **Conf** fac
available Corporate Hospitality Days available **Location**
5m from Bere Regis on Wool Road

Hotel ★★★ 66% Grosvenor Hotel, Bath Rd, East Cliff,
BOURNEMOUTH ☎ 01202 558858 39 en suite

BLANDFORD FORUM
Map 03 ST80

Ashley Wood Wimborne Rd DT11 9HN
☎ 01258 452253 📠 01258 450590
e-mail: ashleywoodgolfclub@hotmail.com
Undulating and well-drained downland course with
superb views over the Tarrant and Stour Valleys.
Provides a good test of golf for golfers of all abilities.
18 holes, 6276yds, Par 70, SSS 70, Course record 65.
Club membership 500.
Visitors phone in advance. Handicap certificate required
weekends unless with member. **Societies** apply to
Secretary. **Green Fees** £40 per day, £25 per 18 holes after
10am (£30 per 18 holes after noon). **Prof** Jon Shimmons
Course Designer P Tallack **Facilities** ⊗ ℍ ⓑ ♥ ♀ ♧ ☎
♧ ⛳ ⛵ **Location** 2m E on B3082

Hotel ★★ 70% Crown Hotel, West St, BLANDFORD
FORUM ☎ 01258 456626 32 en suite

BOURNEMOUTH
Map 04 SZ09

The Club at Meyrick Park Central Dr, Meyrick
Park BH2 6LH ☎ 01202 786000 📠 01202 786020
e-mail: meyrickpark.lodge@clubhaus.com
Picturesque municipal parkland course founded in
1890.
18 holes, 5600yds, Par 69, SSS 69.
Visitors book up to 7 days in advance. **Societies** telephone
in advance. **Green Fees** from £17 Mon-Fri per round (£21
weekends and bank holidays). **Cards** 🖼 💳 💳 💳 🖼
Prof David Miles **Facilities** ⊗ ℍ ⓑ ♥ ♀ ♧ ☎ ⛳ ⛵ ⛵
Leisure heated indoor swimming pool, sauna, solarium,
gymnasium, spa and steam room. **Conf** fac available

Hotel ★★★ 63% Burley Court Hotel, Bath Rd,
BOURNEMOUTH ☎ 01202 552824 & 556704
📠 01202 298514 38 en suite

Knighton Heath Francis Av, West Howe BH11 8NX
☎ 01202 572633 📠 01202 590774
e-mail: khgc@btinternet.com
Undulating heathland course on high ground inland
from Poole.
18 holes, 6084yds, Par 70, SSS 69.
Club membership 700.

Continued

Continued

Visitors may not play weekend. Phone for availability. **Societies** must book in advance. **Green Fees** £30 per day, £25 per round. **Prof** Paul Brown **Facilities** ⊗ ⅃ ⚐ ♀ ⚒ **Location** N side of Poole, junct of A348/A3409 signposted at rdbt

Guesthouse ♦♦♦♦ Ashton Lodge, 10 Oakley Hill, WIMBORNE ☎ 01202 883423 5 rms (3 en suite)

Open Golf Centres
Riverside Av, off Castle Ln East BH7 7ES ☎ 01202 436436 📄 01202 436400
e-mail: info@opengolfcentres.co.uk
A well drained meadowland course beside the river Stour with many mature trees and lakes on five holes. Enjoyable for intermediates and beginners off yellow or white tees and a test for any golfer off the back blue tees. Greens are superb and need careful reading.
Lakes Course: 18 holes, 6277yards, Par 72, SSS 69.
Club membership 600.
Visitors may play any time. Advisable to book in advance for weekends. **Societies** telephone in advance **Green Fees** not confirmed. **Cards** 💳 💳 💳 💳 🅿 **Prof** Lawrence Moxon/Andie Anderson **Course Designer** John Jacobs Golf Associates **Facilities** ⊗ ⅃ ⅃ ⚐ ♀ ⚒ ⚐ ♈ ⚒ ⚒ ⚒ **Leisure** 9 hole par 3 course. **Conf** fac available Corporate Hospitality Days available **Location** off A338 Bournemouth to Southampton road, approx 2m from town centre. At Cooper Dean roundabout take A3060 towards Christchurch, over mini roundabout then turn left into Riverside Avenue. Entrance 500 yds on right

Hotel ⌂ Innkeeper's Lodge Bournemouth, Cooper Dean Roundabout, Castle Ln East, BOURNEMOUTH ☎ 01202 390837 28 en suite

Queen's Park
Queens Park Dr West BH8 9BY ☎ 01202 396198 📄 01202 302611
e-mail: dgibb@qpbgc.fsnet.co.uk
Undulating parkland course of pine and heather, with narrow, tree-lined fairways. Public course played by Boscombe Golf Club and Bournemouth Artisans Golf Club.
18 holes, 6090yds, Par 71, SSS 69, Course record 69.
Club membership 370.
Visitors Not open for play Sun pm. **Societies** Must book in advance. **Green Fees** not confirmed. **Cards** 💳 💳 💳 💳 🅿 **Prof** Richard Hill **Facilities** ⊗ ⅃ ⅃ ⚐ ♀ ⚒ ⚐ **Conf** fac available **Location** 2m NE of Bournemouth town centre off A338

Hotel ★★★ 69% Queens Hotel, Meyrick Rd, East Cliff, BOURNEMOUTH ☎ 01202 554415 109 en suite

BRIDPORT   Map 03 SY49

Bridport & West Dorset
Burton Rd DT6 4PS ☎ 01308 421491 & 421095 📄 01308 421095
e-mail: B_Wdgc@btinternet.com
Seaside links course on the top of the east cliff, with fine views over Lyme Bay and surrounding countryside. A popular feature is the pretty and deceptive 6th hole, its sunken green lying 90 feet below the tee and guarded by natural hazards and bunkers.
18 holes, 5729yds, Par 70, SSS 67.
Club membership 600.
Visitors must contact in advance. **Societies** must contact in writing in advance. **Green Fees** £22 per day; £16 after noon, £10 after 5pm. **Prof** David Parsons **Course Designer** Hawtree **Facilities** ⊗ ⅃ ⅃ ⚐ ♀ ⚒ ⚐ ♈ ⚒

Continued

Leisure pitch & putt (holiday season). **Conf** Corporate Hospitality Days available **Location** 1m E of Bridport on B3157

Hotel ★★★ 65% Haddon House Hotel, West Bay, BRIDPORT ☎ 01308 423626 & 425323 📄 01308 427348 12 en suite

BROADSTONE   Map 03 SZ09

Broadstone (Dorset)
Wentworth Dr BH18 8DQ ☎ 01202 692595 📄 01202 642520
e-mail: admin@broadstonegolfclub.com
Undulating and demanding heathland course with the 2nd, 7th, 13th and 16th being particularly challenging holes.

18 holes, 6315yds, Par 70, SSS 70, Course record 65.
Club membership 620.
Visitors restricted at weekends & bank holidays. Must contact in advance. Handicap certificate required. **Societies** contact in advance. **Green Fees** £60 per 27/36 holes, £40 per round (£45 per round weekends & bank holidays). **Cards** 💳 💳 💳 💳 🅿 **Prof** Nigel Tokely **Course Designer** Colt/Dunn **Facilities** ⊗ ⅃ ⅃ ⚐ ♀ ⚒ ⚐ ♈ ⚒ **Conf** Corporate Hospitality Days available **Location** N side of village off B3074

Guesthouse ♦♦♦♦ Ashton Lodge, 10 Oakley Hill, WIMBORNE ☎ 01202 883423 5 rms (3 en suite)

CHRISTCHURCH   Map 04 SZ19

Dudmoor Farm
Dudmoor Farm Rd, Off Fairmile Rd BH23 6AQ ☎ 01202 483980 📄 01202 480207
A testing par 3 and 4 woodland course in an area of outstanding natural beauty.
9 holes, 1428mtrs, Par 31.
Visitors no restrictions. **Societies** telephone in advance. **Green Fees** £7.50 per 9/18 holes. **Facilities** ⅃ ⚒ ♈ ⚒ **Leisure** squash, fishing, adjoining riding stables. **Location** Located on a private road off B3073 Christchurch to Hurn road

Hotel ★★★ 74% Waterford Lodge Hotel, 87 Bure Ln, Friars Cliff, CHRISTCHURCH ☎ 01425 272948 & 278801 📄 01425 279130 18 en suite

DORCHESTER   Map 03 SY69

Came Down
Came Down DT2 8NR ☎ 01305 813494 (manager) 📄 01305 813494
e-mail: camedown@dorchester39.freeserve.co.uk
Scene of the West of England Championships on several occasions, this fine course lies on a high plateau commanding glorious views over Portland. Three par 5

Continued

holes add interest to a round. The turf is of the springy, downland type.
18 holes, 6244yds, Par 70, SSS 71.
Club membership 750.
Visitors advisable to phone in advance, must have handicap certificate. May play after 9am weekdays & after noon Sun. **Societies** by arrangement **Green Fees** £26 per day weekdays (£29.50 weekends). **Cards** ▨ ▨ ▨ ▨ ▨ ▨ ▨ **Prof** Nick Rodgers **Course Designer** J H Taylor/H S Colt **Facilities** ⊗ ﹀ ⊫ ▪ ♀ ☖ ☞ ☞ ℐ
Location 2m S off A354

Guesthouse ◆◆◆◆◆ Yalbury Cottage Hotel & Restaurant, Lower Bockhampton, DORCHESTER
☎ 01305 262382 8 en suite

FERNDOWN   Map 04 SU00

Dudsbury 64 Christchurch Rd BH22 8ST
☎ 01202 593499 ▤ 01202 594555
e-mail: glegg@dudsbury.demon.co.uk
Set in 160 acres of beautiful Dorset countryside rolling down to the River Stour. Wide variety of interesting and challenging hazards, notably water which comes into play on 14 holes. The well-drained greens are protected by large bunkers and water hazards. A feature hole is the 16th where the green is over two lakes; the more aggressive the drive the greater the reward.
Championship Course: 18 holes, 6904yds, Par 71, SSS 73, Course record 64.
Club membership 650.
Visitors welcome by arrangement with secretary or golf professional. **Societies** telephone in advance. **Green Fees** £45 per 36 holes; £35 per 18 holes (£50/£40 weekend and bank holidays). **Cards** ▨ ▨ ▨ ▨ ▨ **Prof** Kevin Spurgeon **Course Designer** Donald Steel **Facilities** ⊗ ﹀ ⊫ ▪ ♀ ☖ ☞ ☞ ☞ ℐ ℓ **Leisure** fishing, 6 Hole Par 3 Academy Course. **Conf** fac available Corporate Hospitality Days available **Location** 3m N of Bournemouth on B3073, between Parley and Longham

Hotel ★★★★ 73% De Vere Dormy, New Rd, FERNDOWN ☎ 01202 872121 114 en suite

Ferndown 119 Golf Links Rd BH22 8BU
☎ 01202 874602 ▤ 01202 873926
e-mail: ferndowngc@lineone.net
Fairways are gently undulating amongst heather, gorse and pine trees, giving the course a most attractive appearance. There are a number of dog-leg holes.
Championship Course: 18 holes, 6490yds, Par 71, SSS 71, Course record 65.
Presidents Course: 9 holes, 5604yds, Par 70, SSS 68.
Club membership 600.
Visitors must contact in advance & have handicap certificate, no visitors on Thursdays except on Presidents course, numbers restricted at weekends. **Societies** welcome Tue & Fri only, telephone in advance. **Green Fees** Championship: £65 per day, £50 per round (.£80/£60 weekends). **Cards** ▨ ▨ ▨ ▨ ▨ **Prof** Neil PIke **Course Designer** Harold Hilton **Facilities** ⊗ ﹀ ⊫ ▪ ♀ ☖ ☞ **Conf** Corporate Hospitality Days available **Location** S side of town centre off A347

Hotel ★★★★ 73% De Vere Dormy, New Rd, FERNDOWN ☎ 01202 872121 114 en suite

Ferndown Forest Forest Links Rd BH22 9QE
☎ 01202 876096 ▤ 01202 894095
e-mail: golf@ferndownforestgolf.co.uk
Flat parkland course dotted with mature oak trees, several interesting water features, and some tight fairways.
18 holes, 5068yds, Par 68, SSS 65, Course record 69.
Club membership 400.
Visitors advisable to contact in advance. **Societies** apply in writing. **Green Fees** £13 weekdays (£15 weekends and bank holidays). **Cards** ▨ ▨ ▨ ▨ **Prof** Mike Dodd **Course Designer** Guy Hunt/Richard Graham **Facilities** ⊗ ﹀ ⊫ ▪ ♀ ☖ ☞ ☞ ℐ ℓ **Conf** fac available Corporate Hospitality Days available **Location** From London M3 then A31, then A31 on to dual carriageway Dolmans Crossing rdbt right exit Forest Links Rd. Signposted towards Dorset police station

Hotel ★★★★ 73% De Vere Dormy, New Rd, FERNDOWN ☎ 01202 872121 114 en suite

---

HALSTOCK   Map 03 ST50

Halstock Common Ln BA22 9SF
☎ 01935 891689 & 891968 (pro shop) ▤ 01935 891839
e-mail: halstock.golf@feeuk.com
Halstock is a short tight course, but presents an interesting challenge to players of all abilities. The terrain is gently undulating in places and there are plenty of trees and water hazards.
18 holes, 4481yds, Par 66, SSS 63, Course record 63.
Club membership 200.
Visitors must telephone in advance. Restricted until 10.30am on Sundays. **Societies** telephone in advance. **Green Fees** not confirmed. **Cards** ▨ ▨ ▨ ▨ **Prof** Robert Harris **Facilities** ⊗ ﹀ ⊫ ▪ ♀ ☖ ☞ ℐ ℓ **Location** 6m S of Yeovil

Hotel ★★★ ♨ Summer Lodge, EVERSHOT
☎ 01935 83424 10 en suite 7 annexe en suite

HIGHCLIFFE   Map 04 SZ29

Highcliffe Castle 107 Lymington Rd BH23 4LA
☎ 01425 272210 ▤ 01425 272953
Picturesque parkland course with easy walking.
18 holes, 4776yds, Par 64, SSS 63, Course record 58.
Club membership 500.
Visitors must have handicap certificate and be a member of recognised club. Telephone in advance. **Societies** write or telephone in advance. **Green Fees** £25.50 per day (£35.50 weekends am). **Facilities** ⊗ ﹀ ⊫ ▪ ♀ ☖ **Conf** Corporate Hospitality Days available **Location** SW side of town on A337

Hotel ★★★ 74% Waterford Lodge Hotel, 87 Bure Ln, Friars Cliff, CHRISTCHURCH
☎ 01425 272948 & 278801 ▤ 01425 279130 18 en suite

HURN   Map 04 SZ19

Parley Parley Green Ln BH23 6BB
☎ 01202 591600 ▤ 01202 579043
e-mail: info@parleygolf.co.uk
Flat testing parkland course with few hazards and only two par 5s. One hole runs parallel to River Stour. Tiered greens in some places.
9 holes, 4938yds, Par 68, SSS 64, Course record 69.
Club membership 200.

Continued

Visitors good standard of dress expected. **Societies** write or telephone. **Green Fees** £9 for 18 holes, £6.50 for 9 holes (£10/£7.50 weekends). **Cards** **Course Designer** P Goodfellow **Facilities** by prior arrangement **Conf** Corporate Hospitality Days available **Location** Opposite Bournemouth airport

Hotel ★★★★ 73% De Vere Dormy, New Rd, FERNDOWN ☎ 01202 872121 114 en suite

LYME REGIS Map 03 SY39

Lyme Regis Timber Hill DT7 3HQ
☎ 01297 442963 01297 442963
e-mail: secretarylyme regis@hotmail.com
Undulating cliff-top course with magnificent views of Golden Cap and Lyme Bay.

18 holes, 6283yds, Par 71, SSS 70, Course record 65.
Club membership 575.
Visitors must contact in advance & have handicap certificate or be a member of recognised golf club. No play on Thu & Sun mornings. **Societies** Tue, Wed & Fri; must contact in writing. **Green Fees** £35 per day, £30 per 18 holes before 2pm, £25 after 2pm. **Prof** Duncan Driver **Course Designer** Donald Steel **Facilities** **Location** W end of Charmouth bypass (A5), take A3052 to Lyme Regis. 1.5m from A3052/A35 rdbt

Hotel ★★★ 71% Alexandra Hotel, Pound St, LYME REGIS ☎ 01297 442010 25 en suite 1 annexe en suite

LYTCHETT MATRAVERS Map 03 SY99

Bulbury Woods Bulbury Ln BH16 6HR
☎ 01929 459574 01929 459000
e-mail: general@bulbury-woods.co.uk
Parkland course with a mixture of American and traditional style greens and extensive views over the Purbecks and Poole Harbour. A comprehensive programme of tree planting coupled with ancient woodland ensures a round that is picturesque as well as providing interest and challenge.
18 holes, 6002yds, Par 71, SSS 69.
Club membership 450.
Visitors visitors may book 7 days in advance and subject to availability. **Societies** must contact in advance. **Green Fees** terms on application. **Cards** **Prof** David Adams **Facilities** **Conf** fac available Corporate Hospitality Days available **Location** A35 Poole to Dorchester, 3m from Poole centre

Hotel ★★★ 68% Springfield Country Hotel & Leisure Club, Grange Rd, WAREHAM ☎ 01929 552177 48 en suite

POOLE Map 04 SZ09

Parkstone Links Rd, Parkstone BH14 9QS
☎ 01202 707138 01202 706027
e-mail: admin@parkstonegolfclub.co.uk
Very scenic heathland course with views of Poole Bay. Designed in 1909 by Willie Park Jnr and enlarged in 1932 by James Braid. The result of this highly imaginative reconstruction was an intriguing and varied test of golf set among pines and heather fringed fairways where every hole presents a different challenge.
18 holes, 6250yds, Par 72, SSS 70, Course record 63.
Club membership 700.
Visitors must contact in advance and have handicap certificate. **Societies** apply in writing/telephone in advance. Handicap certificates must be provided. **Green Fees** £70 per day; £45 per round (£80/£55 weekends & bank holidays). **Cards** **Prof** Martyn Thompson **Course Designer** Willie Park Jnr **Facilities** **Conf** Corporate Hospitality Days available **Location** E side of town centre off A35

Hotel ★★★ 64% Salterns Harbourside Hotel, 38 Salterns Way, Lilliput, POOLE ☎ 01202 707321 20 en suite

SHERBORNE Map 03 ST61

Sherborne Higher Clatcombe DT9 4RN
☎ 01935 814431 01935 814218
e-mail: sherbornegc@btconnect.com
Beautiful mature parkland course to the north of Sherborne on the Dorset/Somerset border with extensive views. Recently extended to 6415 yds.
18 holes, 6414yds, Par 72, SSS 71, Course record 62.
Club membership 600.
Visitors must contact in advance & have handicap certificate. **Societies** prior booking (Tue & Wed only). **Green Fees** £30 per day, £25 per round (£36 per round weekends). **Prof** Alistair Tresidder **Course Designer** James Braid (part) **Facilities** **Location** 2m N off B3145

Hotel ★★★ 72% Eastbury Hotel, Long St, SHERBORNE ☎ 01935 813131 22 en suite

STURMINSTER MARSHALL Map 03 ST90

Sturminster Marshall Moor Ln BH21 4AH
☎ 01258 858444 01258 858262
9 holes, 4882yds, Par 68, SSS 64.
Course Designer John Sharkey/David Holdsworth
Location On A350. Signposted from village
Telephone for further details

Hotel ★★ 70% Crown Hotel, West St, BLANDFORD FORUM ☎ 01258 456626 32 en suite

SWANAGE Map 04 SZ07

Isle of Purbeck BH19 3AB
☎ 01929 450361 & 450354 01929 450501
e-mail: enquiries@purbeckgolf.co.uk
A heathland course sited on the Purbeck Hills with grand views across Swanage, the Channel and Poole Harbour. Holes of note include the 5th, 8th, 14th, 15th, and 16th where trees, gorse and heather assert themselves. The very attractive clubhouse is built of the local stone.

Continued

Isle of Purbeck Golf Course

Purbeck Course: 18 holes, 6295yds, Par 70, SSS 70, Course record 66.
Dene Course: 9 holes, 4014yds, Par 60.
Club membership 500.
Visitors advisable to telephone. **Societies** must contact in advance. **Green Fees** terms on application. **Cards** ⊞ ▦ ▦ ▢ **Prof** Ian Brake **Course Designer** H Colt **Facilities** ⊗ ℳ by prior arrangement ⓛ ♨ ♀ ♤ 🏠 ⚑ ➥ 🛒 ♂
Location 2.5m N on B3351

· ·

Hotel ★★★ 67% The Pines Hotel, Burlington Rd, SWANAGE ☎ 01929 425211 49 en suite

VERWOOD   Map 04 SU00

Crane Valley The Club House BH31 7LE
☎ 01202 814088 📠 01202 813407
e-mail: general@crane-valley.co.uk
Two secluded parkland courses set amid rolling Dorset countryside and mature woodland - a 9-hole Pay and Play and an 18-hole Valley course for golfers holding a handicap certificate. The 6th nestles in the bend of the River Crane and there are four long par 5s ranging from 499 to 545 yards.
Valley: 18 holes, 6445yds, Par 72, SSS 71, Course record 66.
Woodland: 9 holes, 2060yds, Par 33, SSS 30.
Club membership 700.
Visitors must have handicap certificate for Valley course. Woodland course is pay and play. **Societies** telephone in advance. **Green Fees** Valley: £25 per round (£35 weekends and bank holidays) Woodland: £10 for 18 holes, £5.50 for 9 holes (£12/£6.50 weekends). **Cards** ⊞ ▦ ▦ 📠 ▢ **Prof** Darrel Ranson **Course Designer** Donald Steel **Facilities** ⊗ ℳ ⓛ ♨ ♀ ♤ 🏠 ⚑ ➥ 🛒 ♂ ♟ **Location** 6m W of Ringwood on B3081

· ·

Hotel ★★★★ 73% De Vere Dormy, New Rd, FERNDOWN ☎ 01202 872121 114 en suite

WAREHAM   Map 03 SY98

Wareham Sandford Rd BH20 4DH
☎ 01929 554147 📠 01929 557993
e-mail: admin@warehamgolfclub.com
At the entrance to the Purbecks with splendid views over Poole Harbour and Wareham Forest. A mixture of undulating parkland and heathland fairways. A challenge for golfers of all abilities.
18 holes, 5753yds, Par 69, SSS 68, Course record 66.
Club membership 500.
Visitors Handicap preferred. Course available after 09.30 weekdays and after 1pm weekends **Societies** weekdays only. **Green Fees** £28 per day; £22 per round (£25 per

Continued

round weekends). **Facilities** ⊗ ℳ ⓛ ♨ ♀ ♤ ➥ 🛒 ♂
Location 0.5 mile N of Wareham on A351

· ·

Hotel ★★★ 68% Springfield Country Hotel & Leisure Club, Grange Rd, WAREHAM ☎ 01929 552177 48 en suite

WEYMOUTH   Map 03 SY67

Weymouth Links Rd DT4 0PF
☎ 01305 773981 (Secretary) & 773997 (Prof)
📠 01305 788029
e-mail: weymouthgolfclub@aol.com
Seaside parkland course. The 5th is played off an elevated tee over copse.
18 holes, 5981yds, Par 70, SSS 69, Course record 63.
Club membership 750.
Visitors advisable to contact in advance. EGU or LGU handicap required. **Societies** apply in writing/telephone/e-mail/fax **Green Fees** terms on application. **Prof** Des Lochrie **Course Designer** James Braid **Facilities** ⊗ ℳ ⓛ ♨ ♀ ♤ 🏠 ⚑ ♂ **Conf** Corporate Hospitality Days available **Location** N side of town centre off B3157

· ·

Hotel ★★★ 64% Hotel Rex, 29 The Esplanade, WEYMOUTH ☎ 01305 760400 31 en suite

WIMBORNE   Map 03 SZ09

Canford Magna Knighton Ln BH21 3AS
☎ 01202 592552 📠 01202 592550
e-mail: admin@canfordmagnagc.co.uk
Lying in 350 acres of Dorset countryside, the Canford Magna Golf Club provides 45 holes of challenging golf for the discerning player. The 18-hole Parkland and Riverside courses are quite different and the new 9-hole Knighton course demands the same level of playing skill. For those wishing to improve their handicap, the Golf Academy offers a covered driving range, pitching greens, a chipping green and bunkers, together with a 6-hole par 3 academy course.
Parkland: 18 holes, 6495yds, Par 71, SSS 71, Course record 66.
Riverside: 18 holes, 6214yds, Par 70, SSS 70, Course record 68.
Knighton: 9 holes, 1377yds, Par 27, Course record 26.
Club membership 1000.
Visitors are advised to contact in advance. **Societies** must telephone in advance. **Green Fees** terms on application. **Cards** ⊞ ▦ ▦ 📠 ▢ **Prof** Martin Cummins **Course Designer** Howard Swan **Facilities** ⊗ ℳ ⓛ ♨ ♀ ♤ 🏠 ⚑ 🛒 ♂ ♟ **Leisure** Golf lessons. **Conf** fac available Corporate Hospitality Days available **Location** On A341

· ·

Guesthouse ◆◆◆◆ Ashton Lodge, 10 Oakley Hill, WIMBORNE ☎ 01202 883423 5 rms (3 en suite)

CO DURHAM

BARNARD CASTLE
Map 12 NZ01

Barnard Castle Harmire Rd DL12 8QN
☎ 01833 638355 ▤ 01833 695551
e-mail: sec@barnardcastlegolfclub.org.uk
Perched high on the steep bank of the River Tees, the extensive remains of Barnard Castle with its splendid round tower dates back to the 12th and 13th centuries. The parkland course is flat and lies in open countryside.

18 holes, 6406yds, Par 73, SSS 71, Course record 63.
Club membership 650.
Visitors must contact in advance, restricted at weekends. Handicap certificate required. **Societies** apply in writing.
Green Fees £22 per round (£32 weekends and bank holidays).
Prof Darren Pearce **Course Designer** A Watson **Facilities** ⊗
℠ ⅃ ⬛ ♀ ⌂ ⛟ ⬌ ✔ **Conf** Corporate Hospitality Days available **Location** 1m N of town centre on B6278

Hotel ★★ Rose & Crown Hotel, ROMALDKIRK
☎ 01833 650213 7 en suite 5 annexe en suite

BEAMISH
Map 12 NZ25

Beamish Park DH9 0RH
☎ 0191 370 1382 ▤ 0191 370 2937
e-mail: bpgc@beamishparkgc.fsbusiness.co.uk
Parkland course. Designed by Henry Cotton and W Woodend.

18 holes, 6183yds, Par 71, SSS 70, Course record 64.
Club membership 630.
Visitors must contact in advance and may only play weekdays. **Societies** telephone in advance. Weekdays only
Green Fees £28 per day, £22 per round. **Prof** Chris Cole
Course Designer H Cotton **Facilities** ⊗ ℠ ⅃ ⬛ ♀ ⌂ ⌂
⬌ ⬌ ✔ **Location** 1m NW off A693

Hotel ★★★ 69% Beamish Park Hotel, Beamish Burn Rd, MARLEY HILL ☎ 01207 230666 47 en suite

BILLINGHAM
Map 08 NZ42

Billingham Sandy Ln TS22 5NA
☎ 01642 533816 & 557060 (Pro) ▤ 01642 533816
e-mail: billinghamgc@onetel.net.uk
Undulating parkland course with water hazards.
18 holes, 6346yds, Par 71, SSS 70, Course record 62.
Club membership 1050.
Visitors contact professional in advance on 01642 557060 a handicap certificate may be requested. **Societies** apply in writing to Secretary/Manager, by telephone or e-mail.
Green Fees £25 per day. **Prof** Michael Ure **Course Designer** F Pennick **Facilities** ⊗ ℠ ⅃ ⬛ ♀ ⌂ ⛟ ⬌
✔ **Conf** Corporate Hospitality Days available **Location** 1m W of town centre E of A19

Hotel ★★★ 71% Parkmore Hotel & Leisure Park, 636 Yarm Rd, Eaglescliffe, STOCKTON-ON-TEES
☎ 01642 786815 55 en suite

Wynyard Wellington Dr, Wynyard Park TS22 5QJ
☎ 01740 644399 ▤ 01740 644599
e-mail: chris@wynyardgolfclub.co.uk
Built against the delightful backdrop of the Wynyard state, the Wellington Course combines a fine blend of rolling parkland and mature woodland. It represents the ultimate in challenge and excitement for both the novice and the highly experienced player.
Wellington: 18 holes, 6851yds, Par 72, SSS 72, Course record 63.
Club membership 350.
Visitors must contact in advance for availability. **Societies** telephone in advance **Green Fees** £50 per 18 holes. **Cards** ▦ ▦ ▦ ▦ ▩ **Prof** Chris Mounter **Course Designer** Hawtree **Facilities** ⊗ ℠ ⅃ ⬛ ♀ ⌂ ⛟ ⬌ ✔ ⛟ **Conf** fac available Corporate Hospitality Days available
Location off A689 between A19 & A1

BISHOP AUCKLAND
Map 08 NZ22

Bishop Auckland High Plains, Durham Rd
DL14 8DL ☎ 01388 661618 ▤ 01388 607005
e-mail: enquiries@bagc.co.uk
A rather hilly parkland course with many well-established trees offering a challenging round. A small ravine adds interest to several holes including the short 7th, from a raised tee to a green surrounded by a stream, gorse and bushes. Pleasant views down the Wear Valley and over the residence of the Bishop of Durham. Has the distinction of having three consecutive par 5 holes and two consecutive par 3s.
18 holes, 6420yds, Par 72, SSS 70, Course record 63.
Club membership 950.
Visitors parties must contact in advance. Handicap certificate advisable. Dress rules apply. **Societies** weekdays only; must contact in advance. **Green Fees** £24 per round (£30 per round weekends). **Cards** ▦ ▦ ▦ ▦ ▩ **Prof** David Skiffington **Course Designer** James Kay **Facilities** ⊗ ℠ ⅃ ⬛ ♀ ⌂ ⛟ ✔ **Leisure** snooker. **Location** 1m NE on A689

Hotel ★★★ 74% Whitworth Hall Country Park Hotel, Stanners Ln, SPENNYMOOR ☎ 01388 811772 29 en suite

Booking a tee time is always advisable.

BURNOPFIELD Map 12 NZ15

Hobson Municipal Hobson NE16 6BZ
☎ 01207 271605 Fax 01207 271069
e-mail: s_fox@derwentside.org.uk
18 holes, 6403yds, Par 69, SSS 68, Course record 65.
Location 0.75m S on A692
Telephone for further details

Hotel ★★★ 64% Raven Country Hotel, Broomhill, Ebchester, CONSETT ☎ 01207 562562 28 en suite 1 annexe en suite

CHESTER-LE-STREET Map 12 NZ25

Chester-le-Street Lumley Park DH3 4NS
☎ 0191 388 3218 (Secretary) Fax 0191 388 1220
e-mail: clsgc@ukonline.co.uk
Parkland course in castle grounds, good views, easy walking.
18 holes, 6437yds, Par 71, SSS 71, Course record 71.
Club membership 650.
Visitors must contact in advance and have an introduction from own club or handicap certificate. **Societies** must apply in writing or by telephone/e-mail. **Green Fees** not confirmed. **Prof** David Fletcher **Course Designer** J H Taylor **Facilities** **Location** 0.5m E off B1284

Hotel ★★★ 71% Ramside Hall Hotel, Carrville, DURHAM ☎ 0191 386 5282 80 en suite

Roseberry Grange Grange Villa DH2 3NF
☎ 0191 3700670 Fax 0191 3700224
Parkland course providing a good test of golf for all abilities. Fine panoramic views of County Durham.
18 holes, 6152yds, Par 71, SSS 69.
Club membership 620.
Visitors after 11.30am Sun & 10.30am Sat in summer, pay and play Mon-Fri. **Societies** booking form available on request. **Green Fees** terms on application. **Cards** **Prof** Chris Jones **Course Designer** Durham County Council **Facilities** **Location** 5m W of Chester-le-Street, take A694 and turn left into West Pelton village. Follow signs

Hotel ★★★ 66% George Washington Golf & Country Club, Stone Cellar Rd, High Usworth, WASHINGTON ☎ 0191 402 9988 103 en suite

CONSETT Map 12 NZ15

Consett & District Elmfield Rd DH8 5NN
☎ 01207 502186 Fax 01207 505060
Undulating parkland/moorland course with views across the Derwent Valley to the Cheviot Hills.
18 holes, 6080yds, Par 71, SSS 69, Course record 63.
Club membership 650.
Visitors advised to contact Secretary in advance on 01207 505060 **Societies** apply in writing. **Green Fees** £18 per day (£26 weekends). **Course Designer** Harry Vardon **Facilities** **Leisure** snooker room. **Location** N side of town on A691

Hotel ★★ 69% Lord Crewe Arms Hotel, BLANCHLAND ☎ 01434 675251 9 en suite 10 annexe en suite

CROOK Map 12 NZ13

Crook Low Jobs Hill DL15 9AA
☎ 01388 762429 Fax 01388 762429
Meadowland/parkland course in elevated position with natural hazards, varied holes and terrain. Panoramic views over Durham and Cleveland Hills.
18 holes, 6102yds, Par 70, SSS 69, Course record 64.
Club membership 550.
Visitors weekends by arrangement. **Societies** apply in writing to Secretary or contact professional (01388 768145) **Green Fees** terms on application. **Prof** Craig Dilley **Facilities** **Conf** fac available **Location** 0.5m E off A690

Hotel ★★★ 66% Helme Park Hall Hotel, FIR TREE ☎ 01388 730970 13 en suite

DARLINGTON Map 08 NZ21

Blackwell Grange Briar Close, Blackwell DL3 8QX
☎ 01325 464458 Fax 01325 464458
e-mail: secretary@blackwellgrangegolf.com
Pleasant parkland course with good views, easy walking.
18 holes, 5621yds, Par 68, SSS 67, Course record 63.
Club membership 1000.
Visitors restricted Wed & weekends. **Societies** welcome weekdays except Wed (Ladies Day). **Green Fees** £25 per day; £20 per round (£30 per round weekends and bank holidays). **Prof** Joanne Furby **Course Designer** F Pennink **Facilities** **Conf** Corporate Hospitality Days available **Location** 1m SW off A66, turn into Blackwell, signposted

Hotel ★★★ 66% The Blackwell Grange Hotel, Blackwell Grange, DARLINGTON ☎ 0870 609 6121 99 en suite 11 annexe en suite

Darlington Haughton Grange DL1 3JD
☎ 01325 355324 Fax 01325 488126
e-mail: darlington.golfclub@virgin.net
Fairly flat parkland course with tree-lined fairways, and large first-class greens.
18 holes, 6181yds, Par 70, SSS 69, Course record 65.
Club membership 850.
Visitors may not play weekends unless accompanied by member. **Societies** by prior arrangement with the Secretary but not at weekends. **Green Fees** not confirmed. **Prof** Craig Dilley **Course Designer** Dr Alistair McKenzie **Facilities** **Conf** Corporate Hospitality Days available **Location** N side of town centre off A1150

Hotel ★★★ 73% Headlam Hall Hotel, Headlam, Gainford, DARLINGTON ☎ 01325 730238 19 en suite 17 annexe en suite

Hall Garth Golf & Country Club Hotel
Coatham Mundeville DL1 3LU
☎ 01325 320246 📄 01325 310083

9 holes, 6621yds, Par 72, SSS 72.
Course Designer Brian Moore **Location** 0.5m from
A1(M), junct 59 off A167
Telephone for further details

Hotel ★★★ 74% Hall Garth Golf and Country Club
Hotel, Coatham Mundeville, DARLINGTON
☎ 01325 300400 40 en suite 11 annexe en suite

Stressholme Snipe Ln DL2 2SA
☎ 01325 461002 📄 01325 461002
**Picturesque municipal parkland course, long but wide,
with 98 bunkers and a par 3 hole played over a river.**
18 holes, 6431yds, Par 71, SSS 70, Course record 69.
Club membership 350.
Visitors must book 7 days in advance. **Societies** phone to
book **Green Fees** £20 per day (£25 weekends); £12.50 per
round (£14.50 weekends). **Cards** 🖅 🖅 🖅 🖅 📄 **Prof**
Ralph Givens **Facilities** ⊗ ⫲ ⊫ ⬛ ♀ ⚘ 🖿 ⊓ ⋎ ⚹ (
Conf fac available Corporate Hospitality Days available
Location SW side of town centre on A67

Hotel ★★★ 66% The Blackwell Grange Hotel, Blackwell
Grange, DARLINGTON ☎ 0870 609 6121 99 en suite
11 annexe en suite

DURHAM   Map 12 NZ24

Brancepeth Castle Brancepeth Village DH7 8EA
☎ 0191 378 0075 📄 0191 378 3835
e-mail: brancepethcastle@btclick.com
**Parkland course overlooked at the 9th hole by beautiful
Brancepeth Castle.**
18 holes, 6234yds, Par 70, SSS 70, Course record 64.
Club membership 780.
Visitors must contact in advance, restricted weekends.
Societies must contact in advance. **Green Fees** terms on
application. **Cards** 🖅 🖅 🖅 📄 **Prof** David Howdon
Course Designer H S Colt **Facilities** ⊗ ⫲ ⊫ ⬛ ♀ ⚘ 🖿
⊓ ⚹ **Location** 4m from Durham A690 towards Crook, left
at crossroads in Brancepath, left turn at Castle Gates,
400yds

Hotel ★★★★ 72% Durham Marriott Hotel, Royal
County, Old Elvet, DURHAM ☎ 0191 386 6821
142 en suite 8 annexe en suite

Durham City Littleburn, Langley Moor DH7 8HL
☎ 0191 378 0069 📄 0191 378 4265
e-mail: durhamcitygolf@lineone.net
**Undulating parkland course bordered on several holes
by the River Browney.**

18 holes, 6326yds, Par 71, SSS 70, Course record 67.
Club membership 750.
Visitors restricted on competition days, preferential to
contact in advance. Club competitors have priority.
Societies apply in writing or telephone the club
professional on 0191 378 0029 **Green Fees** not confirmed.
Prof Steve Corbally **Course Designer** C Stanton **Facilities**
⊗ ⫲ ⊫ ⬛ ♀ ⚘ 🖿 ⚞ ⚹ **Conf** Corporate Hospitality
Days available **Location** 2m W of Durham City, turn left
off A690 into Littleburn Ind Est

Hotel ★★★ 60% Bowburn Hall Hotel, Bowburn,
DURHAM ☎ 0191 377 0311 19 en suite

Mount Oswald South Rd DH1 3TQ
☎ 0191 386 7527 📄 0191 386 0975
e-mail: information@mountoswald.co.uk
Gently rolling course providing a test for all golfers.
18 holes, 5984yds, Par 71, SSS 69.
Club membership 200.
Visitors must contact in advance for weekends but may not
play before 10am on Sun, please ring for available tee
times. **Societies** must telephone in advance. **Green Fees**
£12.50 Mon-Thu (£15 Fri-Sun & bank holidays). Reduced
winter rates. **Cards** 🖅 🖅 🖅 🖅 📄 **Prof** Chris Calder
Facilities ⊗ ⫲ ⊫ ⬛ ♀ ⚘ 🖿 ⚞ ⋎ ⚹ (**Conf** fac
available Corporate Hospitality Days available **Location**
On A177, 1m SW of city centre

Hotel ★★★ 71% Ramside Hall Hotel, Carrville,
DURHAM ☎ 0191 386 5282 80 en suite

Ramside Hall Carrville DH1 1TD
☎ 0191 386 9514 📄 0191 386 9519
e-mail: golf@ramsidegolfclub.fsnet.co.uk
**Three recently constructed 9-hole parkland courses -
Princes, Bishops, Cathedral - with 14 lakes and
panoramic views surrounding an impressive hotel.
Excellent golf academy and driving range.**

Princes: 9 holes, 3235yds, Par 36, SSS 36.
Bishops: 9 holes, 3285yds, Par 36.
Cathedral: 9 holes, 2874yds, Par 34.
Club membership 450.
Visitors open at all times subject to tee availability.
Societies telephone in advance. **Green Fees** £35 per 18
holes (£40 weekends). **Cards** 🖅 🖅 🖅 📄 🖅 🖅 🖅
Prof Robert Lister **Course Designer** Jonathan Gaunt
Facilities ⊗ ⫲ ⊫ ⬛ ♀ ⚘ 🖿 ⚞ ⋎ ⚹ ⋎ ⚹ (**Leisure**
sauna, steam room. **Conf** fac available Corporate
Hospitality Days available **Location** 500mtrs from
A1/A690 interchange

Hotel ★★★ 71% Ramside Hall Hotel, Carrville,
DURHAM ☎ 0191 386 5282 80 en suite

Continued

EAGLESCLIFFE
Map 08 NZ41

Eaglescliffe and District Yarm Rd TS16 0DQ
☎ 01642 780238 (office) 🗎 01642 780238
e-mail: eaglescliffegcsec@tiscali.co.uk
This hilly course offers both pleasant and interesting golf to all classes of player. It lies in a delightful setting on a rolling plateau, shelving to the River Tees. There are fine views to the Cleveland Hills.
18 holes, 6275yds, Par 72, SSS 70, Course record 64. Club membership 970.
Visitors restricted Tue, Thu, Fri & weekends. **Societies** must contact in advance, apply to Secretary on 01642 780238 **Green Fees** £40 per day; £30 per round (£50/£36 weekends). **Prof** Graeme Bell **Course Designer** J Braid/H Cotton **Facilities** ⊗ �🝙 ⅃ ⬛ 🛢 ♀ ⌂ 🛢 ⌖ ⅄ 🛢 ♂
Location On eastern side of A135 between Yarm and Stockton-on-Tees

Hotel ★★★ 71% Parkmore Hotel & Leisure Park, 636 Yarm Rd, Eaglescliffe, STOCKTON-ON-TEES ☎ 01642 786815 55 en suite

HARTLEPOOL
Map 08 NZ53

Castle Eden Castle Eden TS27 4SS
☎ 01429 836510 🗎 01429 836510
e-mail: derek.livingston@btinternet.com
Beautiful parkland course alongside a nature reserve. Hard walking but trees provide wind shelter.
Castle Eden & Peterlee Golf Club: 18 holes, 6262yds, Par 70, SSS 70, Course record 64. Club membership 750.
Visitors with member only at certain times, must contact pro in advance 01429 836689. Visitors play off yellow tees. **Societies** must contact in advance tel: 01429 836510. **Green Fees** not confirmed. **Prof** Peter Jackson **Course Designer** Henry Cotton **Facilities** ⊗ �🝙 ⅃ ⬛ 🛢 ♀ ⌂ 🛢 ⌖ ⅄ 🛢 ♂ **Leisure** snooker. **Location** 2m S of Peterlee on B1281 off A19

Hotel ★★ 69% Hardwicke Hall Manor Hotel, Hesleden, PETERLEE ☎ 01429 836326 15 en suite

Hartlepool Hart Warren TS24 9QF
☎ 01429 274398 🗎 01429 274129
A seaside course, half links, overlooking the North Sea. A good test and equally enjoyable to all handicap players. The 10th, par 4, demands a precise second shot over a ridge and between sand dunes to a green down near the edge of the beach, alongside which several holes are played.
18 holes, 6200yds, Par 70, SSS 70, Course record 62. Club membership 700.
Visitors with member only on Sun. **Societies** must apply in writing in advance. **Green Fees** not confirmed. **Cards** 🔳 🔳 🔳 🔳 **Prof** Graham Laidlaw **Course Designer** Partly Braid **Facilities** ⊗ �🝙 ⅃ ⬛ 🛢 ♀ ⌂ 🛢 ⌖ ♂ **Location** N of Hartlepool, off A1086

Hotel ⏱ Travel Inn, Maritme Av, Hartlepool Marina, HARTLEPOOL ☎ 08701 977127 40 en suite

MIDDLETON ST GEORGE
Map 08 NZ31

Dinsdale Spa Neasham Rd DL2 1DW
☎ 01325 332297 🗎 01325 332297
A mainly flat, parkland course on high land
Continued

above the River Tees with views of the Cleveland Hills. Water hazards in front of 10th tee and green; the prevailing west wind affects the later holes. There is a practice area by the clubhouse.
18 holes, 6099yds, Par 71, SSS 69, Course record 65. Club membership 870.
Visitors welcome Mon & Wed-Fri, contact for further details. **Societies** bookings through office, no weekends or Tue. Apply in writing or telephone. **Green Fees** £25 per day. **Prof** Neil Metcalfe **Facilities** ⊗ �🝙 ⅃ ⬛ 🛢 ♀ ⌂ 🛢 ♂
Location 1.5m SW

Hotel ★★★ 64% The St George, Middleton St George, Darlington, TEES-SIDE AIRPORT ☎ 01325 332631 59 en suite

NEWTON AYCLIFFE
Map 08 NZ22

Oakleaf Golf Complex School Aycliffe Ln
DL5 6QZ ☎ 01325 310820
A parkland course in a country setting with established trees, streams and lakes. Excellent views.
18 holes, 5818yds, Par 69, SSS 68, Course record 67. Club membership 450.
Visitors dress code enforced and must contact in advance for weekends. **Societies** apply in writing or telephone. **Green Fees** terms on application. **Cards** 🔳 🔳 🔳 🔳 **Prof** Ernie Wilson **Facilities** ⊗ �🝙 ⅃ ⬛ 🛢 ♀ ⌂ 🛢 🛢 ♂ ⅃ **Leisure** squash, fishing. **Location** 6m N of Darlington, off A6072

Hotel ★★★★ 73% Redworth Hall Hotel, REDWORTH ☎ 01388 770600 100 en suite

Woodham Golf & Country Club Burnhill Way
DL5 4PN ☎ 01325 320574 (Office) 315257 (Pro Shop)
🗎 01325 315254
The golf course was originally opened in 1981 and the excellent design was by James Hamilton Scott. It is laid out in 229 acres of parkland with the two loops of nine holes starting and finishing at the clubhouse. Mature woodland with large trees and numerous lakes.
18 holes, 6688yds, Par 73, SSS 72, Course record 66. Club membership 694.
Visitors must book 1 week in advance for weekends. **Societies** telephone or write in advance. **Green Fees** terms on application. **Cards** 🔳 🔳 🔳 🔳 🔳 **Prof** Peter Kelly **Course Designer** James Hamilton Stutt **Facilities** ⊗ ⅃ ⬛ 🛢 ♀ ⌂ 🛢 ⌖ 🛢 ♂ **Location** From A1 take A689 towards Bishop Auckland 0.5m from Rushford village

Hotel ⏱ Travel Inn Durham (Newton Aycliffe), Great North Rd, NEWTON AYCLIFFE ☎ 08701 977085 44 en suite

SEAHAM
Map 12 NZ44

Seaham Dawdon SR7 7RD ☎ 0191 581 2354
Heathland links course with several holes affected by strong prevailing winds.
18 holes, 6017yds, Par 70, SSS 69, Course record 64. Club membership 600.
Visitors contact professional at all times, with member only weekends until 3.30pm. **Societies** must apply in advance. **Green Fees** £20 per day (£25 weekends). **Prof** Glyn Jones **Facilities** ⊗ ⅃ by prior arrangement ⅃ ⬛ 🛢 ♀ ⌂ 🛢 ⌖ ♂ **Location** 3m E of A19, exit for Seaham
Continued

Hotel ★★★★ 67% Sunderland Marriott Hotel, Queen's Pde, Seaburn, SUNDERLAND ☎ 0191 529 2041 82 en suite

SEATON CAREW | Map 08 NZ52

Seaton Carew Tees Rd TS25 1DE
☎ 01429 261040 🖺 01429 267952
e-mail: seatongc@btinternet.com
A championship links course taking full advantage of its dunes, bents, whins and gorse. Renowned for its par 4 17th; just enough fairway for an accurate drive followed by another precise shot to a pear-shaped, sloping green that is severely trapped.
The Old Course: 18 holes, 6622yds, Par 72, SSS 72.
Brabazon Course: 18 holes, 6857yds, Par 73, SSS 73.
Club membership 761.
Visitors restricted until after 10am at weekends & bank holidays,and after 09.30am midweek. **Societies** must apply in writing/elephone in advance. **Green Fees** terms on application. **Prof** Mark Rogers **Course Designer** McKenzie **Facilities** ⊗ ⅲ ⅃ ⅊ ⅊ ♥ **Leisure** **Location** SE side of village off A178

Hotel ⇧ Travel Inn, Maritme Av, Hartlepool Marina, HARTLEPOOL ☎ 08701 977127 40 en suite

SEDGEFIELD | Map 08 NZ32

Knotty Hill Golf Centre TS21 2BB
☎ 01740 620320 🖺 01740 622227
e-mail: khgc21@btopenworld.com
The 18-hole Princes course is set in rolling parkland with many holes routed through shallow valleys. Several holes are set wholly or partially within woodland and water hazards abound. Bishops Course is a developing 18-hole course with varied water features on attractive terrain. Several holes are routed through mature woodland.
Princes Course: 18 holes, 6433yds, Par 72, SSS 71.
Bishops Course: 18 holes, 5886yds, Par 70.
Visitors restricted weekends. **Societies** package available on request. **Green Fees** £12 per round (£13 weekends & bank holidays). **Course Designer** C Stanton **Facilities** ⊗ ⅲ ⅃ ⅊ ⅀ ⅃ 🏠 ⊓ ♥ ♣ ♂ ⅄ **Leisure** gymnasium, tuition range. **Conf** fac available **Location** 1m N of Sedgefield on A177, 2m from junct 60 on A1(M)

Hotel ★★★ 67% Hardwick Hall Hotel, SEDGEFIELD ☎ 01740 620253 52 en suite

STANLEY | Map 12 NZ15

South Moor The Middles, Craghead DH9 6AG
☎ 01207 232848 🖺 01207 284616
e-mail: bryandavison@southmoorgc.freeserve.co.uk
Moorland course with natural hazards, designed by Dr Alistair McKenzie in 1926 and still one of the most challenging of its type in north east England. Out of bounds features on 11 holes from the tee, and the testing par 5 12th hole is uphill and usually against a strong headwind.
18 holes, 6271yds, Par 72, SSS 70, Course record 66.
Club membership 550.
Visitors welcome except Sun, must contact in advance. Handicap certificate preferred **Societies** apply in writing to Secretary. **Green Fees** £25 per day; £15 per round (£30/20 weekends & bank holidays). **Prof** Shaun Cowell **Course**

Designer Dr Alistair Mackenzie **Facilities** ⊗ ⅲ ⅃ ⅊ ⅊ ⅄ 🏠 ⊓ ♥ ♣ ♂ **Conf** Corporate Hospitality Days available **Location** 1.5m SE on B6313

Hotel ★★★ 69% Beamish Park Hotel, Beamish Burn Rd, MARLEY HILL ☎ 01207 230666 47 en suite

STOCKTON-ON-TEES | Map 08 NZ41

Norton Norton TS20 1SU
☎ 01642 676385 🖺 01642 608467
An interesting parkland course with long drives from the 7th and 17th tees. Several water hazards.
18 holes, 5855yds, Par 70.
Visitors no visiting party tee times booked on weekends. **Societies** apply in advance. Weekdays only. **Green Fees** £11.50 per 18 holes (£13.50 weekends and bank holidays). **Cards** 🖃 🖃 🖃 🖃 🖃 **Course Designer** T Harper **Facilities** ⊗ ⅲ ⅃ ⅊ ⅀ ♂ **Leisure** bowling green. **Conf** Corporate Hospitality Days available **Location** At Norton 2m N off A19

Hotel ★★★ 71% Parkmore Hotel & Leisure Park, 636 Yarm Rd, Eaglescliffe, STOCKTON-ON-TEES ☎ 01642 786815 55 en suite

Teesside Acklam Rd, Thornaby TS17 7JS
☎ 01642 616516 & 673822 (pro) 🖺 01642 676252
e-mail: teesidegolfclub@btconnect.com
Flat parkland course, easy walking.
18 holes, 6535yds, Par 72, SSS 71, Course record 64.
Club membership 700.
Visitors with member only weekdays after 4.30pm, weekends after 11am. **Societies** must contact in writing. **Green Fees** terms on application. **Prof** Ken Hall **Course Designer** Makepiece & Dr Somerville **Facilities** ⊗ ⅲ ⅃ ⅊ ⅀ ⅄ 🏠 ⊓ ♂ **Location** 1.5m SE on A1130, off A19 at Mandale interchange

Hotel 🅄 Holiday Inn Middlesbrough/Teesside, Low Ln, Stainton Village, Thornaby, STOCKTON-ON-TEES ☎ 0870 400 9081 136 en suite

ESSEX

ABRIDGE | Map 05 TQ49

Abridge Golf and Country Club Epping Ln, Stapleford Tawney RM4 1ST
☎ 01708 688396 🖺 01708 688550
e-mail: info@abridgegolf.com
A parkland course with easy walking. The quick drying course is by no means easy to play. This has been the venue of several professional tournaments. Abridge is a Golf and Country Club and has all the attendant facilities.
18 holes, 6680yds, Par 72, SSS 72, Course record 67.
Club membership 600.
Visitors must have current handicap certificate, contact in advance. May play weekends after 2pm. **Societies** telephone in advance. May play Mon, Wed and Fri. **Green Fees** £35 per 18 holes (£45 weekends). **Cards** 🖃 🖃 🖃 🖃 **Prof** Stuart Layton **Course Designer** Henry Cotton **Facilities** ⊗ ⅃ ⅊ ⅀ ⅄ 🏠 ⊓ ♥ ♣ ♂ ⅄ **Leisure** heated outdoor swimming pool, sauna. **Location** 1.75m NE

Hotel ⇧ Premier Lodge (Romford), Whalebone Ln North, Chadwell Heath, ROMFORD ☎ 0870 9906450 40 en suite

Continued

BASILDON   Map 05 TQ78

Basildon Clay Hill Ln, Kingswood SS16 5JP
☎ 01268 533297 ▤ 01268 284163
e-mail: basildongc@onetel.net.uk
Undulating municipal parkland course. Testing 13th hole (par 4).
18 holes, 6236yds, Par 72, SSS 70.
Club membership 350.
Visitors contact professional in advance 01268 533532.
Societies may contact for details. **Green Fees** terms on application. **Prof** M Oliver **Course Designer** A Cotton **Facilities** ⊗ ℐ ⅃ ℞ ♣ ♀ ☖ ☜ ⚒ ♂ **Location** 1m S off A176

Hotel 🅄 Holiday Inn Basildon - Rayleigh, Cranes Farm Rd, BASILDON ☎ 0870 400 9003 149 en suite

BENFLEET   Map 05 TQ78

Boyce Hill Vicarage Hill, South Benfleet SS7 1PD
☎ 01268 793625 & 752565 ▤ 01268 750497
e-mail: secretary@boycehillgolfclub.co.uk
Hilly parkland course with good views.
18 holes, 6003yds, Par 68, SSS 69, Course record 61.
Club membership 700.
Visitors must have a handicap certificate, must contact 24hrs in advance, may not play at weekends. **Societies** Thu only, book well in advance by telephone. **Green Fees** £45 per 27/36 holes, £35 per 18 holes. **Prof** Graham Burroughs **Course Designer** James Braid **Facilities** ⊗ ℐ ⅃ ℞ ♣ ♀ ☖ ♣ ⚒ ♂ **Location** 0.75m NE of Benfleet Station

Hotel 🅄 Holiday Inn Basildon - Rayleigh, Cranes Farm Rd, BASILDON ☎ 0870 400 9003 149 en suite

BILLERICAY   Map 05 TQ69

The Burstead Tye Common Rd, Little Burstead CM12 9SS ☎ 01277 631171 ▤ 01277 632766
The Burstead Golf Course: 18 holes, 6275yds, Par 71, SSS 70, Course record 69.
Course Designer Patrick Tallack **Location** M25 onto A127, located off A176.
Telephone for further details

Hotel ★★★ 67% Chichester Hotel, Old London Rd, Wickford, BASILDON ☎ 01268 560555 2 en suite 32 annexe en suite

Stock Brook Golf & Country Club Queens
Park Av, Stock CM12 0SP
☎ 01277 653616 & 650400 ▤ 01277 633063
e-mail: events@stockbrook.com
Set in 250 acres of picturesque countryside the 27 holes comprise three undulating 9s, offering the challenge of water on a large number of holes. Any combination can be played, but the Stock and Brook courses make the 18-hole, 6750 yard championship course. There are extensive clubhouse facilities.
Stock & Brook Courses: 18 holes, 6728yds, Par 72, SSS 72, Course record 66.
Manor Course: 9 holes, 2997yds, Par 35.
Visitors handicap certificate required, must contact 24hrs in advance. **Societies** apply in writing or telephone. **Green Fees** terms on application. **Cards** ▦ ▬ ▦ 🖭 **Prof** Craig Lawrence **Course Designer** Martin Gillet **Facilities** ⊗ ℐ ⅃ ℞ ♣ ♀ ☖ ☜ ♣ ⚒ ♂ ☖ **Leisure** hard tennis courts, outdoor and indoor heated swimming pools, sauna, gymnasium, bowls.

Continued

Hotel ★★★★ 72% Marygreen Manor Hotel, London Rd, BRENTWOOD ☎ 01277 225252 4 en suite 40 annexe en suite

BRAINTREE   Map 05 TL72

Braintree Kings Ln, Stisted CM77 8DD
☎ 01376 346079 ▤ 01376 348677
e-mail: manager@braintreegolfclub.freeserve.co.uk
Parkland course with many unique mature trees. Good par 3s with the 14th - Devils Lair - regarded as one of the best in the county.
18 holes, 6228yds, Par 70, SSS 70, Course record 64.
Club membership 750.
Visitors contact the pro shop in advance 01376 343465. No visitors Sun before noon. **Societies** society days Wed & Thu. Telephone in advance, early booking advised. **Green Fees** £36 per day, £28 per round (£42 per round weekends and bank holidays). **Prof** Tony Parcell **Course Designer** Hawtree **Facilities** ⊗ ℐ ⅃ ℞ ♣ ♀ ☖ ☖ ♣ ⚒ ♂ **Conf** Corporate Hospitality Days available **Location** 1m E, off A120

Hotel ★★★ 65% White Hart Hotel, Bocking End, BRAINTREE ☎ 01376 321401 31 en suite

Towerlands Panfield Rd CM7 5BJ
☎ 01376 326802 ▤ 01376 552487
Undulating, grassland course. 9 holes with 18 tees.
9 holes, 5559yds, Par 68.
Club membership 250.
Visitors must not play before 12.30pm weekends or after 5pm Wed. Correct dress at all times. Must contact in advance. **Societies** must contact in advance by telephone. **Green Fees** terms on application. **Cards** ▦ ▬ ▦ 🖭 **Course Designer** G Shiels **Facilities** ⊗ ℐ ⅃ ℞ ♣ ♀ ☖ ☜ **Leisure** squash, gymnasium. **Location** On B1053

Hotel ★★★ 65% White Hart Hotel, Bocking End, BRAINTREE ☎ 01376 321401 31 en suite

BRENTWOOD   Map 05 TQ59

Bentley Ongar Rd CM15 9SS
☎ 01277 373179 ▤ 01277 375097
Parkland course with water hazards.
18 holes, 6709yds, Par 72, SSS 72.
Club membership 600.
Visitors should contact in advance, may not play at weekends. **Societies** must write or telephone in advance. **Green Fees** not confirmed. **Cards** ▦ ▬ ▦ 🖭 **Prof** Nick Garrett **Course Designer** Alec Swann **Facilities** ⅃ ℞ ♀ ☖ ☖ ♣ ⚒ ♂ **Conf** Corporate Hospitality Days available **Location** 3m NW on A128

Hotel 🅄 Holiday Inn Brentwood, Brook St, BRENTWOOD ☎ 0870 400 9012 150 en suite

Hartswood King George's Playing Fields, Ingrave Rd CM14 5AE ☎ 01277 218850 ▤ 01277 218850
Municipal parkland course, easy walking.
18 holes, 6192yds, Par 70, SSS 69, Course record 68.
Club membership 300.
Visitors pre-book by telephone up to five days ahead on 01277 214830 **Societies** weekdays only, must contact in advance. **Green Fees** £11.50 (£16.50 weekends & bank holidays). **Cards** ▦ ▬ ▦ 🖭 **Prof** Stephen Cole **Course Designer** H Cotton **Facilities** ℞ ♀ ☖ ☖ ☜ ♂ **Location** 0.75m SE of Brentwood town centre on A128 from A127

Hotel 🅄 Holiday Inn Brentwood, Brook St, BRENTWOOD ☎ 0870 400 9012 150 en suite

Warley Park Magpie Ln, Little Warley CM13 3DX
☎ 01277 224891 📠 01277 200679
e-mail: enquiries@warleyparkgc.co.uk
Parkland course with reasonable walking. Numerous water hazards. There is also a golf practice ground.
1st & 2nd: 18 holes, 5967yds, Par 69, SSS 67, Course record 66.
1st & 3rd: 18 holes, 5925yds, Par 71, SSS 69, Course record 65.
2nd & 3rd: 18 holes, 5917yds, Par 70, SSS 69, Course record 65.
Club membership 800.
Visitors must have handicap certificate and contact in advance. May not play at weekends. **Societies** telephone in advance for provisional booking. **Green Fees** £40 per day, £30 per round. **Cards** 💳 💳 🆔 **Prof** Kevin Smith **Course Designer** Reg Plumbridge **Facilities** ⊗ ⊪ by prior arrangement ㋡ ⬛ ♀ △ 🏠 ♦ ♨ 🏌 ⛳ **Conf** fac available Corporate Hospitality Days available **Location** 0.5m N off junct 29 of M25/A127

Hotel 🅤 Holiday Inn Brentwood, Brook St, BRENTWOOD ☎ 0870 400 9012 150 en suite

Weald Park Coxtie Green Rd, South Weald CM14 5RJ
☎ 01277 375101 📠 01277 374888
e-mail: wealdpark@americangolf.uk.com
18 holes, 6285yds, Par 71, SSS 70, Course record 65.
Course Designer Reg Plumbridge **Location** 3m from M25
Telephone for further details

Hotel ★★★★ 72% Marygreen Manor Hotel, London Rd, BRENTWOOD ☎ 01277 225252 4 en suite 40 annexe en suite

BULPHAN   Map 05 TQ68

Langdon Hills Lower Dunton Rd RM14 3TY
☎ 01268 548444 📠 01268 490084
e-mail: info@golflangdon.co.uk
Well situated with the Langdon Hills on one side and dramatic views across London on the other, the centre offers an interchangeable 27-hole course, a floodlit 22-bay driving range and three academy holes.
Langdon & Bulphan Course: 18 holes, 6760yds, Par 72, SSS 72, Course record 67.
Bulphan & Horndon Course: 18 holes, 6537yds, Par 73, SSS 72.
Horndon & Langdon Course: 18 holes, 6279yds, Par 71, SSS 71.
Club membership 800.
Visitors preference given to members on weekend mornings and visitors may not play Langdon course before noon. Cannot book more than 5 days in advance. **Societies** apply in writing or telephone. **Green Fees** £20 per 18 holes, £12.50 per 9 holes (£30/£17.50 weekends). **Cards** 💳 💳 💳 🔲 **Prof** Terry Moncur **Course Designer** Howard Swan **Facilities** ⊗ ⊪ ㋡ ⬛ ♀ △ 🏠 ♦ ♨ 🏌 ⛳ **Conf** Corporate Hospitality Days available **Location** Between A13 & A127 N of A128 S of Basildon

Hotel ★★★★ 72% Marygreen Manor Hotel, London Rd, BRENTWOOD ☎ 01277 225252 4 en suite 40 annexe en suite

> **Use the maps at the back of the guide to help locate a golf course.**

Burnham-on-Crouch Ferry Rd, Creeksea
CM0 8PQ ☎ 01621 782282 📠 01621 784489
e-mail: burnhamgolf@hotmail.com
Undulating meadowland riverside course, easy walking.
18 holes, 6056yds, Par 70, SSS 69, Course record 66.
Club membership 550.
Visitors welcome weekdays. Must play with member at weekends. **Societies** apply in writing or telephone. **Green Fees** £26 weekdays. **Prof** Steven Cardy **Course Designer** Swan **Facilities** ⊗ ⊪ ㋡ ⬛ ♀ △ ♦ ♨ ⛳ **Location** 1.25m W off B1010

Ballards Gore Gore Rd SS4 2DA
☎ 01702 258917 📠 01702 258571
A parkland course with several lakes.
18 holes, 6874yds, Par 73, SSS 73, Course record 69.
Club membership 500.
Visitors must contact in advance. May play weekdays and Sun after 2pm. **Societies** apply in advance. **Green Fees** terms on application. **Cards** 💳 💳 💳 💳 💳 💳 🔲 **Prof** Richard Emery **Course Designer** D & J J Caton **Facilities** ⊗ ⊪ ㋡ ⬛ ♀ △ ♦ ⛳ **Leisure** snooker room. **Location** 2m NE of Rochford

Guesthouse ♦♦♦♦ Ilfracombe House Hotel, 9-13 Wilson Rd, SOUTHEND-ON-SEA ☎ 01702 351000 20 en suite

Castle Point Somnes Av SS8 9FG
☎ 01268 696298 (Secretary) & 510830 (Pro)
e-mail: sec@castlepointgolfclub.freeserve.co.uk
18 holes, 6176yds, Par 71, SSS 69, Course record 69.
Location SE of Basildon, A130 to Canvey Island
Telephone for further details

Hotel ★★★ 67% Chichester Hotel, Old London Rd, Wickford, BASILDON ☎ 01268 560555 2 en suite 32 annexe en suite

Channels Belstead Farm Ln, Little Waltham CM3 3PT
☎ 01245 440005 📠 01245 442032
e-mail: info@channelsgolf.co.uk
The Channels course is built on land from reclaimed gravel pits, 18 very exciting holes with plenty of lakes providing an excellent test of golf. Belsteads, a nine-hole course, is mainly flat but has 3 holes where water has to be negotiated.

Channels Course: 18 holes, 6402yds, Par 71, SSS 71, Course record 65.

Continued

Belsteads: 9 holes, 2467yds, Par 34, SSS 32.
Club membership 650.
Visitors Channels Course: must contact in advance and may only play with member at weekends. Belsteads Course: available anytime. **Societies** telephone starter on 01245 443311. **Green Fees** terms on application.
Cards 🖃 📠 💳 🖩 📇 🖂 **Prof** Ian Sinclair **Course Designer** Cotton & Swan **Facilities** ⊗ ⋔ 🏌 🏐 💪 ♀ 🖧 🏠 🏹 🕳 🏌 🛤 **Leisure** fishing, 9 hole pitch & putt course.
Conf fac available **Location** 2m NE on A130

Hotel ★★★ 70% County Hotel, Rainsford Rd, CHELMSFORD ☎ 01245 455700 53 en suite 8 annexe en suite

Chelmsford Widford Rd CM2 9AP
☎ 01245 256483 📠 01245 256483
e-mail: office@chelmsfordgc.co.uk
An undulating parkland course, hilly in parts, with three holes in woods and four difficult par 4s. From the reconstructed clubhouse there are fine views over the course and the wooded hills beyond.
18 holes, 5981yds, Par 68, SSS 69, Course record 63.
Club membership 650.
Visitors must contact in advance. Society days Wed/Thu, Ladies Day Tue. With member only at weekends. **Societies** must contact in advance. **Green Fees** £37 per round. **Prof** Mark Welch **Course Designer** Tom Dunn **Facilities** ⊗ 🏌 💪 ♀ 🖧 🏠 🏹 🛤 🕳 **Location** 1.5m S of town centre off A12

Hotel ★★★ 72% Pontlands Park Country Hotel, West Hanningfield Rd, Great Baddow, CHELMSFORD ☎ 01245 476444 36 en suite

Regiment Way Back Ln, Little Waltham CM3 3PR
☎ 01245 362210 & 361100 📠 01245 442032
e-mail: info@channelsgolf.co.uk
A 9-hole course with alternate tee positions, offering a par 64 18-hole course. Fully automatic tee and green irrigation plus excellent drainage ensure play at most times of the year. The course is challenging but at the same time can be forgiving.

9 holes, 4887yds, Par 65, SSS 64.
Club membership 265.
Visitors no restrictions **Societies** Minimum 8 players, telephone for details. **Green Fees** £11 per 18 holes, £8 per 9 holes (£12/£9 weekends). **Prof** David March **Course Designer** R Stubbings/R Clark **Facilities** ⊗ ⋔ 🏌 💪 ♀ 🖧 🏠 🛤 🕳 **Conf** fac available Corporate Hospitality Days available **Location** off A130 N of Chelmsford

Hotel ⛫ Premier Lodge (Chelmsford), Main Rd, Borham, CHELMSFORD ☎ 0870 9906394 78 en suite

CHIGWELL Map 05 TQ49

Chigwell High Rd IG7 5BH
☎ 020 8500 2059 📠 020 8501 3410
e-mail: info@chigwellgolfclub.co.uk
A course of high quality, mixing meadowland with parkland. For those who believe 'all Essex is flat' the undulating nature of Chigwell will be a refreshing surprise. The greens are excellent and the fairways tight with mature trees.
18 holes, 6279yds, Par 71, SSS 70, Course record 66.
Club membership 800.
Visitors must contact in advance & have handicap certificate, but must be accompanied by member at weekends. **Societies** recognised societies welcome by prior arrangement. **Green Fees** not confirmed. **Prof** Ray Beard **Course Designer** Hawtree/Taylor **Facilities** ⊗ 🏌 💪 ♀ 🖧 🏠 🏹 🕳 **Conf** Corporate Hospitality Days available **Location** 0.5m S on A113

CHIGWELL ROW Map 05 TQ49

Hainault Forest Romford Rd, Chigwell Row
IG7 4QW ☎ 020 8500 2131 📠 020 8501 5196
e-mail: info@essexgolfcentres.com
Two championship courses with spectacular views of Essex and Home Counties. Parkland style courses with modern driving range.
No 1 Course: 18 holes, 5687yds, Par 70, SSS 67, Course record 65.
No 2 Course: 18 holes, 6238yds, Par 71, SSS 71.
Club membership 250.
Visitors booking recommended. No restrictions except dress code, no jeans, football shorts/shirts or track suit bottoms and collared shorts. **Societies** please telephone,write or email. **Green Fees** £16 (£21 weekends & bank holidays). **Cards** 🖃 📠 💳 🖩 📇 **Prof** C Hope, B Preston, A Shearn **Course Designer** Taylor & Hawtree **Facilities** ⊗ ⋔ 🏌 💪 ♀ 🖧 🏠 🏹 🛤 🕳 🏌 **Conf** fac available Corporate Hospitality Days available **Location** 0.5m S on A1112

Hotel ★★★ 59% The County Hotel, 30 Oak Hill, WOODFORD GREEN ☎ 0870 609 6156 99 en suite

CLACTON-ON-SEA Map 05 TM11

Clacton West Rd CO15 1AJ
☎ 01255 421919 📠 01255 424602
e-mail: clactongolfclub@btclick.com
Windy, seaside course.
18 holes, 6532yds, Par 71, SSS 71.
Club membership 650.
Visitors must contact in advance. **Societies** apply in writing/ telephone. **Green Fees** £30 per day, £20 per round (£40/£25 weekends and bank holidays). **Prof** S J Levermore **Course Designer** Jack White **Facilities** ⊗ ⋔ 🏌 💪 ♀ 🖧 🏠 🛤 🕳 **Location** 1.25m SW of town centre

Hotel ★★ 67% Esplanade Hotel, 27-29 Marine Pde East, CLACTON-ON-SEA ☎ 01255 220450 29 en suite

COLCHESTER Map 05 TL92

Birch Grove Layer Rd, Kingsford CO2 0HS
☎ 01206 734276
A pretty, undulating course surrounded by woodland - small but challenging with excellent greens.

Continued

Challenging 6th hole cut through woodland with water hazards and out of bounds.
9 holes, 4532yds, Par 66, SSS 63.
Club membership 250.
Visitors restricted Sun mornings. **Societies** apply in writing or telephone. **Green Fees** £13 for 18 holes; £9 for 10 holes. **Course Designer** L A Marston **Facilities** ⊗ ⅢⅢ ㄴ ♥ ♀ ♌ ☎ ✐ **Conf** fac available Corporate Hospitality Days available **Location** 2.5m S on B1026
....
Hotel ★★★ 73% George Hotel, 116 High St, COLCHESTER ☎ 01206 578494 47 en suite

Colchester Braiswick CO4 5AU
☎ 01206 853396 📠 01206 852698
e-mail: colchester.golf@btinternet.com
A fairly flat, yet scenic, parkland course with tree-lined fairways and small copses. Mainly level walking.
18 holes, 6347yds, Par 70, SSS 70, Course record 63.
Club membership 700.
Visitors by prior arrangement, must contact in advance and may not play weekends. **Societies** apply in writing or by telephone, Mon, Thu & Fri only. **Green Fees** terms on application. **Prof** Mark Angel **Course Designer** James Braid **Facilities** ⊗ ♥ ♀ ♌ ☎ ✐ ◖ **Location** 1.5m NW of town centre on B1508 (West Bergholt Rd)
....
Hotel ★★★ 73% George Hotel, 116 High St, COLCHESTER ☎ 01206 578494 47 en suite

Lexden Wood Bakers Ln CO3 4AU
☎ 01206 843333 📠 01206 854775
New 18-hole course within easy reach of the town centre. Also a 9-hole pitch and putt course, and a floodlit driving range.
18 holes, 5500yds, Par 67, Course record 63.
Club membership 500.
Visitors welcome. **Societies** telephone for details. **Green Fees** terms on application. **Cards** 🖅 🖅 🖅 🖅 **Prof** Phil Grice **Course Designer** J Johnson **Facilities** ⊗ ⅢⅢ ㄴ ♥ ♀ ♌ ☎ ✐ 🛒 ✐ ◖ **Leisure** 9 hole par 3. **Location** Adjacent to A12. Take Colchester Central from A12 and then follow tourist signs
....
Hotel Ⓤ Holiday Inn Colchester, Abbotts Ln, Eight Ash Green, COLCHESTER ☎ 0870 400 9020 110 en suite

Stoke-by-Nayland Keepers Ln, Leavenheath
CO6 4PZ ☎ 01206 262836 📠 01206 263356
e-mail: info@golf-club.co.uk
Two 18-hole Championship courses, 'The Gainsborough' and 'The Constable'. Created in the 1970s, both courses are well established and feature mature woodland, undulating fairways and picturesque water features which include 4 large natural lakes. The 18th hole on both courses presents a challenging and spectacular finish with tee-offs over the largest of the lakes to a green resting in front of the clubhouse. The courses are best between March and October but are open all year round and offer winter buggy paths on the Gainsborough course.
Gainsborough Course: 18 holes, 6498yds, Par 72, SSS 71, Course record 66.
Constable Course: 18 holes, 6544yds, Par 72, SSS 71, Course record 67.
Club membership 1300.

Stoke-by-Nayland

Visitors must contact in advance. May not play weekend and bank holidays before noon. Handicap certificate needed at weekends. **Societies** write or telephone for brochures and booking forms. **Green Fees** not confirmed. **Cards** 🖅 🖅 🖅 🖅 🖅 **Prof** Kevin Lovelock **Course Designer** Howard Swan **Facilities** ⊗ ⅢⅢ ㄴ ♥ ♀ ♌ ☎ ✐ 🛒 🦆 🛒 ✐ ◖ **Leisure** heated indoor swimming pool, fishing, sauna, solarium, gymnasium. **Conf** fac available Corporate Hospitality Days available **Location** 1.5m NW of Stoke-by-Nayland on B1068
....
Hotel ★★★ 🍴 Maison Talbooth, Stratford Rd, DEDHAM ☎ 01206 322367 10 en suite

EARLS COLNE   Map 05 TL82

Colne Valley Station Rd CO6 2LT
☎ 01787 224343 & 220770 📠 01787 224126
e-mail: info@colnevalleygolfclub.co.uk
Opened in 1991, this surprisingly mature parkland course belies its tender years. Natural water hazards, and well-defined bunkers, along with USGA standard greens offer year round playability, and a stimulating test for golfers of all abilities.
18 holes, 6301yds, Par 70, SSS 70, Course record 68.
Club membership 450.
Visitors only after 11.00am at weekends, must dress correctly, no sharing of clubs. Must contact in advance. **Societies** apply in writing or telephone, minimum of 12 persons. **Green Fees** terms on application. **Cards** 🖅 🖅 🖅 🖅 🖅 **Prof** Peter Garlick **Course Designer** Howard Swan **Facilities** ⊗ ㄴ ♥ ♀ ♌ ☎ ✐ 🛒 🦆 ✐ **Leisure** fishing. **Conf** fac available Corporate Hospitality Days available **Location** Off A1124
....
Hotel ★★★ 70% White Hart Hotel, Market End, COGGESHALL ☎ 01376 561654 18 en suite

Essex Golf & Country Club CO6 2NS
☎ 01787 224466 📠 01787 224410
e-mail: essex.retail@clubhaus.com
Created on the site of a World War II airfield, this challenging course contains ten lakes and strategically placed bunkering. Also a 9-hole course and a variety of leisure facilities.
County Course: 18 holes, 7019yds, Par 73, SSS 73, Course record 67.
Garden Course: 9 holes, 2190yds, Par 34, SSS 34.
Club membership 700.
Visitors contact golf reception for bookings up to 7 days in advance. **Societies** apply in writing to the Functions Manager or telephone for details. **Green Fees** Country Course: £25 per round (£30 weekends). **Cards** 🖅 🖅 🖅 🖅 **Prof** Lee Cocker **Course Designer** Reg Plumbridge

Continued   *Continued*

Facilities ⊗ 〗Ⅲ ╚ ▆ ♀ ╩ ⌂ ⫟ 🛏 ⬞ 🛒 ♂ ⌇
Leisure hard tennis courts, heated indoor swimming pool,
fishing, sauna, solarium, gymnasium, video golf tuition
studio. **Conf** fac available **Location** Signposted off the
A120 onto the B1024

....

Hotel ★★★ 70% White Hart Hotel, Market End,
COGGESHALL ☎ 01376 561654 18 en suite

EPPING   Map 05 TL40

Epping Fluxs Ln CM16 7PE
☎ 01992 572282 📠 01992 575512
e-mail: neilsjoberg@hotmail.com
**Undulating parkland course with extensive views over
Essex countryside. Incorporates many water features
designed to use every club in the bag. Some driveable
par 4s, and the spectacular 18th 'Happy Valley' is
rarely birdied. A new clubhouse is open, with bar and
restaurant.**
18 holes, 5405yds, Par 68, SSS 65, Course record 67.
Club membership 350.
Visitors welcome at all times. **Societies** telephone in
advance. **Green Fees** £14 per day; £9 per round (£18/£12
weekends & bank holidays). **Course Designer** Sjoberg
Facilities ⊗ 〗Ⅲ by prior arrangement ╚ ▆ ♀ ╩ ⫟ 🛏
⬞ ⌇ ⌇ **Leisure** Petanque. **Conf** fac available Corporate
Hospitality Days available **Location** M11 junct 7, 2.5m on
B1393, left in Epping High Rd towards station

....

Hotel ⛫ Travelodge Harlow East (Stansted), A414
Eastbound, Tylers Green, North Weald, HARLOW
☎ 08700 850 950 60 en suite

Nazeing Middle St, Nazeing EN9 2LW
☎ 01992 893798 📠 01992 893882
**Parkland course built with American sand-based
greens and tees and five strategically placed lakes. One
of the most notable holes is the difficult par 3 13th with
out of bounds and a large lake coming into play.**
18 holes, 6617yds, Par 72, SSS 72, Course record 68.
Club membership 400.
Visitors contact for weekend and bank holidays, may only
play pm. No restrictions weekdays. **Societies** prior
arrangement required in writing. **Green Fees** Mon £16 per
round; Tue-Fri £20 (£28 weekends pm). **Cards** 💳 💳 💳
💳 **Prof** Robert Green **Course Designer** M Gillete
Facilities ⊗ 〗Ⅲ ╚ ▆ ♀ ╩ 🛏 ⬞ ⌇ ⌇ **Conf** fac
available Corporate Hospitality Days available **Location**
Just outside Waltham Abbey

....

Hotel ★★★★ 69% Waltham Abbey Marriott Hotel, Old
Shire Ln, WALTHAM ABBEY ☎ 01992 717170
162 en suite

FRINTON-ON-SEA   Map 05 TM22

Frinton 1 The Esplanade CO13 9EP
☎ 01255 674618 📠 01255 682450
e-mail: frintongolf@lineone.net
**Deceptive, flat seaside links course providing fast, firm
and undulating greens that will test the best putters,
and tidal ditches that cross many of the fairways,
requiring careful placement of shots. Its open character
means that every shot has to be evaluated with both
wind strength and direction in mind. Easy walking.**
*Long Course: 18 holes, 6265yds, Par 71, SSS 70, Course
record 63.*
Short Course: 9 holes, 2834yds, Par 60, SSS 60.
Club membership 850.

Continued

Frinton

Visitors must contact in advance, weekends available by
arrangement. **Societies** by arrangement, apply in writing to
the secretary, Wed, Thu and some Fri. **Green Fees** Main
course: £32 (£38 weekends). Short course £8/£10. **Cards**
💳 💳 💳 💳 **Prof** Peter Taggart **Course Designer**
Willy Park Jnr **Facilities** ⊗ 〗Ⅲ by prior arrangement ╚ ▆
♀ ╩ ⌂ ⫟ 🛏 ⬞ ⌇ **Conf** fac available Corporate
Hospitality Days available **Location** SW side of town
centre,17m East of Colchester

....

Hotel ⛫ Travel Inn, Crown Green Roundabout,
Colchester Rd, Weeley, CLACTON-ON-SEA
☎ 08701 977064 40 en suite

GOSFIELD   Map 05 TL72

Gosfield Lake The Manor House, Hall Dr CO9 1RZ
☎ 01787 474747 📠 01787 476044
e-mail: gosfieldlakegc@btconnect.com
**Parkland course with bunkers, lakes and water
hazards. Designed by Sir Henry Cotton/Howard Swan.
Also 9-hole course; ideal for beginners and improvers.**
*Lakes Course: 18 holes, 6615yds, Par 72, SSS 72, Course
record 68.*
Meadows Course: 9 holes, 4180yds, Par 64, SSS 61.
Club membership 650.
Visitors Lakes Course: must contact in advance. Sat & Sun
from 3.30 only. Meadows Course: Booking advisable.
Societies by prior arrangement. **Green Fees** terms on
application. **Prof** Richard Wheeler **Course Designer**
Henry Cotton/Howard Swan **Facilities** ⊗ 〗Ⅲ ╚ ▆ ♀ ╩
⌂ 🛏 ⬞ ⌇ **Leisure** sauna. **Conf** Corporate Hospitality
Days available **Location** 1m W of Gosfield off B1017

....

Hotel ★★★ 65% White Hart Hotel, Bocking End,
BRAINTREE ☎ 01376 321401 31 en suite

HARLOW   Map 05 TL41

Canons Brook Elizabeth Way CM19 5BE
☎ 01279 421482 📠 01279 626393
**Challenging parkland course designed by Henry
Cotton. Accuracy is the key requiring straight driving
from the tees, especially on the par 5 11th to fly a gap
with out of bounds left and right before setting up the
shot to the green.**
18 holes, 6800yds, Par 73, SSS 72, Course record 65.
Club membership 850.
Visitors may not play at weekends. **Societies** welcome
Mon, Wed and Fri, must book in advance by telephone.
Green Fees not confirmed. **Cards** 💳 💳 💳 💳 **Prof**
Alan McGinn **Course Designer** Henry Cotton **Facilities**
╩ ⌂ ⫟ 🛏 ⌇ **Location** 3m NW of junct 7 on M11

....

Hotel ★★★ 65% The Green Man Hotel, Mulberry Green,
Old Harlow, HARLOW ☎ 0870 609 6146. 55 annexe en suite

North Weald Rayley Ln, North Weald CM16 6AR
☎ 01992 522118 ▤ 01992 522881
e-mail: pat.hillier@virgin.net
Although only opened in November 1995, the blend of lakes and meadowland give this testing course an air of maturity.
*18 holes, 6377yds, Par 71, SSS 70, Course record 66.
Club membership 500.*
Visitors must contact in advance weekday,limited at weekends after 11am. **Societies** contact in advance. **Green Fees** not confirmed. **Cards** 🖭 🖭 **Prof** David Rawlings **Course Designer** David Williams **Facilities** ⊗ ⟯║ ⅃ ⊾ 🐴 ♥ ♀ ⌲ 🏠 ◦ 🏌 ⌐ 🚜 ⌀ ℓ **Leisure** gymnasium. **Conf** fac available Corporate Hospitality Days available **Location** 2m from M11 exit 7, take A414 towards Chipping Ongar & Chelmsford

....

Hotel ⥙ Travelodge Harlow East (Stansted), A414 Eastbound, Tylers Green, North Weald, HARLOW ☎ 08700 850 950 60 en suite

Harwich & Dovercourt Station Rd, Parkeston
CO12 4NZ ☎ 01255 503616 ▤ 01255 503323
Flat parkland course with easy walking.
*9 holes, 5900yds, Par 70, SSS 69, Course record 59.
Club membership 420.*
Visitors visitors with handicap certificate may play by prior arrangement, with member only at weekends. **Societies** prior arrangement essential. **Green Fees** £20 per 18 holes; £10 per 9 holes. **Facilities** ⊗ ⟯║ ⅃ ♥ ♀ ⊾ 🏠 ⌀ **Location** Off A120 near Ferry Terminal

....

Hotel ★★★ 74% The Pier at Harwich, The Quay, HARWICH ☎ 01255 241212 7 en suite
7 annexe en suite

Thorndon Park CM13 3RH
☎ 01277 810345 ▤ 01277 810645
e-mail: tpgc@btclick.com
Course built on clay substructure and playable even at the wettest time of the year. Holes stand on their own surrounded by mature oaks, some of which are more than 700 years old. The lake in the centre of the course provides both a challenge and a sense of peace and tranquillity. The Palladian magnificence of Thorndon Hall, site of the old clubhouse, is the backdrop to the closing hole.
*18 holes, 6492yds, Par 71, SSS 71, Course record 68.
Club membership 600.*
Visitors must contact in advance, at weekends with member only except after 1pm Suns. **Societies** welcome Mon, Tue and Fri but must apply in writing. **Green Fees** terms on application. **Prof** Brian White **Course Designer** Colt/Alison **Facilities** ⊗ ⟯║ by prior arrangement ⅃ ♥ ♀ ⊾ 🏠 ◦ ⌀ **Location** W side of village off A128

....

Hotel ⛿ Holiday Inn Brentwood, Brook St, BRENTWOOD ☎ 0870 400 9012 150 en suite

High Beech Wellington Hill IG10 4AH
☎ 020 8508 7323
Short 9-hole course set in Epping Forest.
9 holes, 1477, Par 27, Course record 25.

Visitors welcome. **Green Fees** terms on application. **Prof** Clark Baker **Facilities** ♥ 🏠 ◦ ⌀ **Location** Close to M25 Waltham Abbey junct

Loughton Clays Ln, Debden Green IG10 2RZ
☎ 020 8502 2923
9-hole parkland course on the edge of Epping Forest. A good test of golf.
*9 holes, 4652yds, Par 66, SSS 63, Course record 71.
Club membership 150.*
Visitors must contact in advance for weekend play. **Societies** telephone in advance. **Green Fees** £11.50 per 18 holes; £7 per 9 holes (£13.50/£8 weekends & bank holidays). **Facilities** ⅃ ♥ ♀ ⊾ 🏠 ◦ ⌀ **Location** 1.5m SE of Theydon Bois

....

Hotel ★★★★ 69% Waltham Abbey Marriott Hotel, Old Shire Ln, WALTHAM ABBEY ☎ 01992 717170 162 en suite

Forrester Park Beckingham Rd, Great Totham
CM9 8EA ☎ 01621 891406 ▤ 01621 891406
Set in undulating parkland in the Essex countryside and commanding some beautiful views across the River Blackwater. Accuracy is more important than distance and judgement more important than strength on this traditional 'club' course. There is a separate 10-acre practice ground.
*18 holes, 6073yds, Par 71, SSS 69, Course record 69.
Club membership 1000.*
Visitors must contact in advance but may not play before noon weekends & bank holidays. **Societies** must apply in advance. **Green Fees** terms on application. **Cards** 🖭 🖭 🖭 🖾 **Prof** Gary Pike **Course Designer** T R Forrester-Muir **Facilities** ⊗ ⅃ ♥ ♀ ⊾ 🏠 🚜 ⌀ ℓ **Leisure** hard tennis courts. **Conf** Corporate Hospitality Days available **Location** 3m NE of Maldon off B1022

....

Hotel ★★★ 72% Pontlands Park Country Hotel, West Hanningfield Rd, Great Baddow, CHELMSFORD ☎ 01245 476444 36 en suite

Maldon Beeleigh, Langford CM9 6LL
☎ 01621 853212 ▤ 01621 855232
e-mail: maldon.golf@virgin.net
Flat, parkland course in a triangle of land bounded by the River Chelmer and the Blackwater Canal. Alternate tees on second nine holes. Testing par 3 14th (166yds) demanding particular accuracy to narrow green guarded by bunkers and large trees.
*9 holes, 6253yds, Par 71, SSS 70, Course record 66.
Club membership 380.*
Visitors telephone to check availability, may only play with member at weekends. Handicap certificate required. **Societies** intially telephone then confirm in writing. **Green Fees** £20 per day; £15 per round. **Prof** John Edgington **Course Designer** Thompson of Felixstowe **Facilities** ⊗ ⟯║ by prior arrangement ⅃ ♥ ♀ ⊾ 🏠 **Location** 1m NW off B1019

....

Hotel ★★★ 72% Pontlands Park Country Hotel, West Hanningfield Rd, Great Baddow, CHELMSFORD ☎ 01245 476444 36 en suite

> **Looking for a driving range? Refer to the listing of driving ranges at the back of this guide.**

Continued

ORSETT
Map 05 TQ68

Orsett Brentwood Rd RM16 3DS
☎ 01375 891352 🖹 01375 892471
e-mail: orsettgc@aol.com
**A very good test of golf - this heathland course with its
sandy soil is quick drying and provides easy walking.
Close to the Thames estuary it is seldom calm and the
main hazards are the prevailing wind and thick gorse.
Any slight deviation can be exaggerated by the wind
and result in a ball lost in the gorse. The clubhouse has
been modernised to very high standards.**
*18 holes, 6614yds, Par 72, SSS 72, Course record 65.
Club membership 750.*
Visitors weekdays only. Must contact in advance and have
a handicap certificate. **Societies** must contact in advance.
Green Fees £30 per round. **Prof** Paul Joiner **Course
Designer** James Braid **Facilities** ⊗ ⅷ ⅃ ⬛ ♀ ⚘ 🏠 ⚑
⚘ ♐ **Leisure** coaching. **Conf** Corporate Hospitality Days
available **Location** At junct of A13 off A128, towards
Chadwell St Mary

Hotel 🅤 Holiday Inn Basildon - Rayleigh, Cranes Farm
Rd, BASILDON ☎ 0870 400 9003 149 en suite

PURLEIGH
Map 05 TL80

Three Rivers Stow Rd, Cold Norton CM3 6RR
☎ 01621 828631 🖹 01621 828060
e-mail: devers@clubhaus.com
*Kings Course: 18 holes, 6449yds, Par 72, SSS 71.
Jubilee Course: 18 holes, 4501yds, Par 64, SSS 62.*
Course Designer Hawtree **Location** 2.5m from South
Woodham Ferrers
Telephone for further details

Hotel ★★★ 72% Pontlands Park Country Hotel, West
Hanningfield Rd, Great Baddow, CHELMSFORD
☎ 01245 476444 36 en suite

ROCHFORD
Map 05 TQ89

Rochford Hundred Hall Rd SS4 1NW
☎ 01702 544302 🖹 01702 541343
e-mail: rochfordhundred@rhgc.sagehost.co.uk
**Parkland course with ponds and ditches as natural
hazards.**
*18 holes, 6292yds, Par 72, SSS 71, Course record 64.
Club membership 800.*
Visitors must have handicap certificate. Visitors may not
play Tue morning (Ladies) or Sun without a member.
Societies must contact in writing. **Green Fees** £45 per day,
£35 per round. **Prof** Graham Hill **Course Designer** James
Braid **Facilities** ⊗ ⅷ ⅃ ⬛ ♀ ⚘ 🏠 ♐ **Location** W on
B1013

Guesthouse ◆◆◆◆ Ilfracombe House Hotel, 9-13 Wilson
Rd, SOUTHEND-ON-SEA ☎ 01702 351000 20 en suite

SAFFRON WALDEN
Map 05 TL53

Saffron Walden Windmill Hill CB10 1BX
☎ 01799 522786 🖹 01799 520313
e-mail: office@swgc.com
Undulating parkland course, beautiful views.
*18 holes, 6606yds, Par 72, SSS 72, Course record 63.
Club membership 950.*
Visitors must contact in advance and have a handicap
certificate. With member only at weekends. **Societies** must

contact in advance. **Green Fees** terms on application.
Cards 🖸 🔲 🔲 💳 🖸 **Prof** Philip Davis **Facilities** ⊗ ⅷ
⅃ ⬛ ♀ ⚘ 🏠 ⚑ ⚘ ♐ ♐ **Location** N side of town centre
off B184

Hotel ★★★ 67% The Crown House, GREAT
CHESTERFORD ☎ 01799 530515 8 en suite
10 annexe en suite

SOUTHEND-ON-SEA
Map 05 TQ88

Belfairs Eastwood Rd North, Leigh on Sea SS9 4LR
☎ 01702 525345 & 520202
18 holes, 5840yds, Par 70, SSS 68, Course record 68.
Course Designer H S Colt **Location** Off A127
Telephone for further details

Hotel ★★ 70% Balmoral Hotel, 34 Valkyrie Rd,
Westcliff-on-Sea, SOUTHEND-ON-SEA
☎ 01702 342947 29 en suite

Thorpe Hall Thorpe Hall Av, Thorpe Bay SS1 3AT
☎ 01702 582205 🖹 01702 584498
e-mail: sec@thorpehallgc.co.uk
**Tree-lined parkland course with narrow fairways
where placement rather than length is essential.**
*18 holes, 6319yds, Par 71, SSS 71, Course record 62.
Club membership 995.*
Visitors must contact in advance and have handicap
certificate. With member only weekends & bank holidays.
Societies Fri only. Apply in writing, only a certain number
a year. **Green Fees** £40 per day/round, weekdays only.
Prof Bill McColl **Course Designer** Various **Facilities** ⊗
ⅷ ⅃ ⬛ ♀ ⚘ 🏠 ⚑ ⚘ ♐ **Leisure** squash, sauna, snooker
room. **Conf** fac available **Location** 2m E off A13

Hotel ★★ 70% Balmoral Hotel, 34 Valkyrie Rd,
Westcliff-on-Sea, SOUTHEND-ON-SEA
☎ 01702 342947 29 en suite

SOUTH OCKENDON
Map 05 TQ58

Belhus Park Belhus Park RM15 4QR
☎ 01708 854260 🖹 01708 854260
**A well established 18-hole course set in beautiful
parkland.**
*18 holes, 5589yds, Par 69, SSS 68, Course record 67.
Club membership 200.*
Visitors no restrictions. Must have proper golf shoes and
shirts to be worn at all times. Booking advisable at
weekends. **Societies** contact in writing or telephone **Green
Fees** terms on application. **Prof** Gary Lunn **Course
Designer** Capability Brown **Facilities** ⅃ ⬛ ♀ ⚘ 🏠 ♐ ♐
♐ **Leisure** heated indoor swimming pool, solarium,
gymnasium. **Location** Off the B1335, follow brown tourist
signs to course

Hotel ⬧ Hotel Ibis Thurrock, Weston Av, WEST
THURROCK ☎ 01708 686000 102 en suite

Top Meadow Fen Ln, North Ockendon RM14 3PR
☎ 01708 852239
e-mail: info@topmeadow.co.uk
**Set in the Essex countryside with a panoramic view of
the area. Excellent test of golf for all standards.**
*18 holes, 6348yds, Par 72, SSS 71, Course record 68.
Club membership 600.*
Visitors welcome Mon-Fri. **Societies** telephone in
advance. **Green Fees** not confirmed. **Cards** 🖸 🔲 🔲 🔲
💳 **Prof** Roy Porter **Course Designer** Burns/Stock

Continued

Continued

Facilities ⊗ 🏌 ▸ ⚏ 🛋 ♨ 🏕 🏐 💈 🛒 ⚑ 🏐 **Leisure** fishing. **Conf** Corporate Hospitality Days available **Location** M25 junct 29, A127 towards Southend, B186 towards Ockendon, Fen Lane

....

Hotel ⬦ Travelodge Brentwood, EAST HORNDON ☎ 08700 850 950 45 en suite

STANFORD LE HOPE   Map 05 TQ68

St Clere's Hall London Rd SS17 0LX
☎ 01375 361565 📠 01375 361565
18 holes, 6474yds, Par 72, SSS 71, Course record 71.
Course Designer A Stiff **Location** 5m from M25 E of London on A13, take Stanford turn off in direction Linford, St Clere on the left
Telephone for further details

....

Hotel 🅤 Holiday Inn Basildon - Rayleigh, Cranes Farm Rd, BASILDON ☎ 0870 400 9003 149 en suite

STAPLEFORD ABBOTTS   Map 05 TQ59

Stapleford Abbotts Horsemanside, Tysea Hill
RM4 1JU ☎ 01708 381108 📠 01708 386345
e-mail: staplefordabbotts@americangolf.uk.com
Abbotts course provides a challenging test for players of all abilities as mature trees, large greenside bunkers and many lakes are all brought into play. The Priors course with its links-type layout gives a fresh challenge on each hole.
Abbotts Course: 18 holes, 6501yds, Par 72, SSS 71.
Priors Course: 18 holes, 5735yds, Par 70, SSS 69.
Friars Course: 9 holes, 1140yds, Par 27, SSS 27.
Club membership 700.
Visitors Visitors may not play weekend mornings. Must book in advance. **Societies** must be pre booked. **Green Fees** terms on application. **Cards** 🔗 💳 🔲 🔳 📇 **Prof** Dean Vickerman **Course Designer** Henry Cotton/Howard Swan **Facilities** ⊗ 🏌 ▸ ⚏ 🛋 △ 🏐 🛒 ⚑ 💈 **Leisure** sauna. **Location** 1m E of Stapleford Abbotts, off B175

....

Hotel ★★★★ 72% Marygreen Manor Hotel, London Rd, BRENTWOOD ☎ 01277 225252 4 en suite 40 annexe en suite

STOCK   Map 05 TQ69

Crondon Park Stock Rd CM4 9DP
☎ 01277 841115 📠 01277 841356
e-mail: paul@crondon.com
Undulating parkland course with many water hazards, set in the Crondon Valley.
18 holes, 6585yards, Par 72, SSS 71, Course record 67.
Club membership 700.
Visitors Contact in advance. May play at weekends after mid-day. **Societies** telephone in advance. **Green Fees** Terms on application. **Cards** 🔗 💳 🔲 **Prof** Paul Barham/Freddie Sunderland **Course Designer** Mr M Gillet **Facilities** ⊗ 🏌 ▸ ⚏ 🛋 △ 📇 🛒 💈 🏐 **Conf** fac available Corporate Hospitality Days available **Location** On B1007, between Stock village and A12

....

Hotel ★★★★ 72% Marygreen Manor Hotel, London Rd, BRENTWOOD ☎ 01277 225252 4 en suite 40 annexe en suite

THEYDON BOIS   Map 05 TQ49

Theydon Bois Theydon Rd CM16 4EH
☎ 01992 812460 & 813054 📠 01992 813054
e-mail: theydongolf@hotmail.com
The course was originally nine holes built into Epping Forest. It was later extended to 18 holes which were well-planned and well-bunkered but in keeping with the 'Forest' tradition. The old nine in the Forest are short and have two bunkers between them, but even so a wayward shot can be among the trees. The autumn colours here are truly magnificent.

18 holes, 5490yds, Par 68, SSS 67, Course record 64.
Club membership 600.
Visitors may not play Wed, Thu, Sat & Sun mornings, ring 01992 812460 in advance to be sure tee is available. **Societies** book through the secretary. **Green Fees** £26 per round. **Cards** 🔗 💳 🔲 🔳 **Prof** R Hall **Course Designer** James Braid **Facilities** ⊗ 🏌 ▸ ⚏ 🛋 △ 📇 🛒 ⚑ 💈 **Location** 2m from junct 26 on M25

....

Hotel ⬦ Travelodge Harlow East (Stansted), A414 Eastbound, Tylers Green, North Weald, HARLOW ☎ 08700 850 950 60 en suite

TOLLESHUNT KNIGHTS   Map 05 TL91

Five Lakes Hotel, Golf, Country Club & Spa Colchester Rd CM9 8HX
☎ 01621 868888 & 862426 📠 869696
e-mail: resort@fivelakes.co.uk
Set in 320 acres, the two 18-hole courses both offer their own particular challenges. The Lakes, a PGA championship course, offers generous fairways with water features. The Links has narrow fairways and strategically placed bunkers.

Links Course: 18 holes, 6181yds, Par 71, SSS 70, Course record 67.
Lakes Course: 18 holes, 6751yds, Par 72, SSS 72, Course record 63.

Continued

Club membership 430.
Visitors must book in advance. **Societies** must contact in advance. **Green Fees** terms on application. **Cards** 🔲 🔲 🔲 🔲 **Prof** Gary Carter **Course Designer** Neil Coles **Facilities** ⊗ ⅷ ᛐ 🍴 ♀ ⚒ 🏌 🛒 🎯 🏌 🏌 ✦ ᛐ
Leisure hard tennis courts, heated indoor swimming pool, squash, sauna, solarium, gymnasium, snooker, badminton. **Conf** fac available Corporate Hospitality Days available **Location** 1.75m NE on B1026, 15 minutes from A12 Kelvedon exit. Signposted by brown tourist signs
....
Hotel ★★★★ 73% Five Lakes Resort, Colchester Rd, TOLLESHUNT KNIGHTS ☎ 01621 868888 114 en suite 80 annexe en suite

TOOT HILL
Map 05 TL50

Toot Hill School Rd CM5 9PU
☎ 01277 365523 📠 01277 364509
18 holes, 6053yds, Par 70, SSS 69, Course record 65.
Course Designer Martin Gillett **Location** 7m SE of Harlow, off A414
Telephone for further details
....
Hotel ★★★ 65% The Green Man Hotel, Mulberry Green, Old Harlow, HARLOW ☎ 0870 609 6146
55 annexe en suite

WITHAM
Map 05 TL81

Benton Hall Wickham Hill CM8 3LH
☎ 01376 502454 📠 01376 521050
e-mail: s.clark@clubhaus.com
Set in rolling countryside surrounded by dense woodland, this challenging course provides a severe test even to the best golfers. The River Blackwater dominates the front nine and natural lakes come into play on five other holes.

18 holes, 6574yds, Par 72, SSS 72, Course record 64.
The Bishops: 1074yds, Par 27, SSS 27, Course record 24.
Club membership 580.
Visitors visitors can book 7 days in advance **Societies** telephone in advance. **Green Fees** not confirmed. **Cards** 🔲 🔲 🔲 🔲 🔲 🔲 **Prof** Colin Fairweather **Course Designer** Alan Walker/Charles Cox **Facilities** ⊗ ⅷ ᛐ 🍴 ♀ ⚒ 🏌 🛒 🎯 ✦ ᛐ **Location** Witham turn off on A12, signposted
....
Hotel ★★★ 65% White Hart Hotel, Bocking End, BRAINTREE ☎ 01376 321401 31 en suite

Braxted Park Braxted Park Estate CM8 3EN
☎ 01376 572372 📠 01621 892840
e-mail: estate-office@braxted-park.demon.co.uk
9 holes, 2940yds, Par 35, SSS 34.

Course Designer Sir Allen Clark **Location** 2m from A12 near Kelvedon/Witham, at Gt Braxted
Telephone for further details
....
Hotel ★★★ 65% White Hart Hotel, Bocking End, BRAINTREE ☎ 01376 321401 31 en suite

WOODHAM WALTER
Map 05 TL80

Bunsay Downs Little Baddow Rd CM9 6RU
☎ 01245 222648 📠 01245 223989
9 holes, 2932yds, Par 70, SSS 68.
Badgers: 1319yds, Par 54.
Course Designer John Durham **Location** 2m signposted from Danbury on A414
Telephone for further details
....
Hotel ★★★ 70% County Hotel, Rainsford Rd, CHELMSFORD ☎ 01245 455700 53 en suite
8 annexe en suite

Warren CM9 6RW ☎ 01245 223258 📠 01245 223989
Attractive parkland course with natural hazards and good views.
18 holes, 6229yds, Par 70, SSS 70, Course record 65.
Club membership 765.
Visitors contact in advance, weekend pm only, Wed pm only. **Societies** arrange by telephone, confirm in writing, weekdays ex Wed. **Green Fees** not confirmed. **Prof** David Brooks **Facilities** ⚒ 🏌 🎯 ✦ ᛐ **Location** 0.5m SW
....
Hotel ★★★ 70% County Hotel, Rainsford Rd, CHELMSFORD ☎ 01245 455700 53 en suite
8 annexe en suite

GLOUCESTERSHIRE

ALMONDSBURY
Map 03 ST68

Bristol St Swithins Park, Blackhorse Hill BS10 7TP
☎ 01454 620000 📠 01454 202700
e-mail: enquiries@bristolgolfclub.co.uk
An undulating parkland course set in 200 acres of parkland with magnificent views over the Severn estuary and surrounding countryside.
The Bristol Golf Club: 18 holes, 6109yds, Par 70, SSS 69, Course record 65.
Club membership 600.
Visitors must book in advance. **Societies** must contact in advance by telephone/writing **Green Fees** terms on application. **Cards** 🔲 🔲 🔲 🔲 **Prof** Richard Berry **Course Designer** Pierson **Facilities** ⊗ ⅷ ᛐ 🍴 ♀ ⚒ 🏌 🛒 🎯 ✦ ᛐ **Leisure** par 3 academy course. **Conf** fac available Corporate Hospitality Days available **Location** 100yds off M5 junct17
....
Hotel ★★★ 67% Henbury Lodge Hotel, Station Rd, Henbury, BRISTOL ☎ 0117 950 2615 12 en suite
9 annexe en suite

CHELTENHAM
Map 03 SO92

Cotswold Hills Ullenwood GL53 9QT
☎ 01242 515264 📠 01242 515317
e-mail: golf@chgc.freeserve.co.uk
A gently undulating course with open aspects and views of the Cotswolds.
18 holes, 6565yds, Par 72, SSS 71, Course record 67.
Club membership 750.

Continued

Continued

Visitors telephone in advance, handicap certificate preferred. May play at weekend if no competitions. **Societies** must apply in writing or telephone. **Green Fees** £33 per day (£38 weekends & bank holidays). **Cards** 💳 💳 💳 💳 ⑨ **Prof** James Latham **Course Designer** M D Little **Facilities** ⊗ ⑪ ⅃ ⅃ ♀ ⚐ 🏌 ⛳ **Conf** Corporate Hospitality Days available **Location** 3m SE on A435 and A436

Hotel 🅄 Holiday Inn Gloucester, Crest Way, Barnwood, GLOUCESTER ☎ 0870 400 9034 122 en suite

Lilley Brook
Cirencester Rd, Charlton Kings GL53 8EG ☎ 01242 526785 📠 01242 256880 e-mail: secretary@lilleybrookgc.fsnet.co.uk
Undulating parkland course. Magnificent views over Cheltenham and surrounding countryside.
18 holes, 6212yds, Par 69, SSS 70, Course record 61. Club membership 900.
Visitors advisable to enquire of availability. Handicap certificate required. May not play Sat or Sun morning **Societies** apply in writing. **Green Fees** terms on application. **Cards** 💳 💳 **Prof** Karl Hayler **Course Designer** Mackenzie **Facilities** ⊗ ⑪ ⅃ ♀ ⅃ ⚐ 🏌 ⛳ **Conf** fac available Corporate Hospitality Days available **Location** 2m S of Cheltenham on A435

Hotel ★★★★ 65% Cheltenham Park Hotel, Cirencester Rd, Charlton Kings, CHELTENHAM ☎ 01242 222021 33 en suite 110 annexe en suite

Shipton
Shipton Oliffe, Andoverford GL54 4HT ☎ 01242 890237 📠 01242 820336
Deceptive, easy walking course situated in the heart of the Cotswolds giving a fair challenge and panoramic views.
9 holes, 2516yds, Par 35, SSS 63, Course record 33.
Visitors pay & play course no bookings taken. **Societies** welcome. **Green Fees** £9 per 18 holes, £6 per 9 holes (£12/£8 weekends & bank holidays). **Prof** Noel Boland **Facilities** ♀ ⅃ ⚐ 🏌 ⛳ **Location** On A436, south of junct with A40

Hotel ★★★ 69% Charlton Kings Hotel, London Rd, Charlton Kings, CHELTENHAM ☎ 01242 231061 13 en suite

Chipping Sodbury
BS37 6PU ☎ 01454 319042 📠 01454 320052 e-mail: info@chippingsodburygolfclub.co.uk
Parkland courses of championship proportions on the edge of the Cotswolds. The old course may be seen from the large opening tee by the clubhouse at the top of the hill. Two huge drainage dykes cut through the course, forming a distinctive hazard on eleven holes. The 527yd par 5 18th provides a fitting finale.
New Course: 18 holes, 6912yds, Par 73, SSS 73, Course record 65. Club membership 800.
Visitors must have a handicap certificate and may only play until after noon at weekends. **Societies** must contact in writing. **Green Fees** not confirmed. **Prof** Mike Watts **Course Designer** Hawtree **Facilities** ⊗ ⑪ ⅃ ♀ ⅃ ⚐ 🏌 🏌 ⛳ **Location** 0.5m N

Hotel ★★ 71% Compass Inn, TORMARTON ☎ 01454 218242 & 218577 📠 01454 218741 26 en suite

Cirencester
Cheltenham Rd, Bagendon GL7 7BH ☎ 01285 653939 & 652465 📠 01285 650665 e-mail: info@cirencestergolfclub.co.uk
Undulating open Cotswold course with excellent views.
18 holes, 6055yds, Par 70, SSS 69, Course record 65. Club membership 800.
Visitors restricted availability at weekends, contact professional shop in advance on 01285 656124. **Societies** telephone Secretary/Manager. **Green Fees** not confirmed. **Cards** 💳 💳 💳 💳 **Prof** Peter Garratt **Course Designer** J Braid **Facilities** ⊗ ⑪ ⅃ ♀ ⅃ ⚐ 🏌 ⛳ **ℓ Leisure** 6 hole par 3 Academy course. **Conf** fac available Corporate Hospitality Days available **Location** 2m N of Cirencester on A435

Hotel ★★★ 69% Stratton House Hotel, Gloucester Rd, CIRENCESTER ☎ 01285 651761 41 en suite

Cleeve Hill
GL52 3PW ☎ 01242 672025 📠 01242 67444
Undulating and open heathland course affected by crosswinds. Fine views over Cheltenham racecourse, Malvern Hills and the Bristol Channel.
18 holes, 6411yds, Par 72, SSS 71, Course record 69. Club membership 600.
Visitors bookings taken 7 days in advance. Limited play weekends. **Societies** telephone pro shop in advance (01242 672592) **Green Fees** £15 per round (£18 weekends). **Cards** 💳 💳 💳 💳 ⑨ **Prof** Dave Finch **Facilities** ⊗ ⑪ ⅃ ♀ ⅃ ⚐ 🏌 ⛳ **Conf** Corporate Hospitality Days available **Location** 1m NE on B4632

Hotel ★★★ 64% The Prestbury House Hotel & Oaks Restaurant, The Burgage, Prestbury, CHELTENHAM ☎ 01242 529533 7 en suite 8 annexe en suite

The Kendleshire
Henfield Rd BS36 2UY ☎ 0117 956 7007 📠 0117 957 3433 e-mail: info@kendleshire.co.uk
Opened in 1997 to much acclaim, this course is high on the priority list of many players. With water coming into play on ten of the holes, the course is never short of interest and the greens have been built to USGA specification. The most difficult holes are probably the 11th, a short hole with an island green set in a three-acre lake and the 16th, with the second shot played over water.
18 holes, 6550, Par 71, SSS 71, Course record 63. Club membership 900.
Visitors must contact in advance and wear soft spikes. **Societies** telephone in advance **Green Fees** not confirmed. **Cards** 💳 💳 💳 💳 ⑨ **Prof** Mike Bessell **Course Designer** A Stiff/P McEvoy **Facilities** ⊗ ⑪ ⅃ ♀ ⅃ ⚐ 🏌 🏌 ⛳ **Conf** fac available Corporate Hospitality Days available **Location** off M32 junct 1 on Avon Ring Road.

Hotel ★★★★ 64% Jurys Bristol Hotel, Prince St, BRISTOL ☎ 0117 923 0333 191 en suite

COLEFORD   Map 03 SO51

Forest Hills Mile End Rd GL16 7BY
☎ 01594 810620 📠 01594 810823
e-mail: rchrdbllrd@aol.com
18 holes, 6740yds, Par 72, SSS 68, Course record 64.
Course Designer A Stiff
Telephone for further details
· ·
Hotel ★★★ 67% The Speech House, COLEFORD
☎ 01594 822607 16 en suite 17 annexe rms (16 en suite)

Forest of Dean Golf Club & Bells Hotel Lords
Hill GL16 8BE ☎ 01594 832583 📠 01594 832584
e-mail: enquiries@bells-hotel.co.uk
18 holes, 6033yds, Par 70, SSS 69, Course record 63.
Course Designer John Day **Location** 0.25m from
Coleford town centre on B4431 Coleford to Parkend road
Telephone for further details
· ·
Hotel ★★★ 67% The Speech House, COLEFORD
☎ 01594 822607 16 en suite 17 annexe rms (16 en suite)

DURSLEY   Map 03 ST79

Stinchcombe Hill Stinchcombe Hill GL11 6AQ
☎ 01453 542015 📠 01453 549545
e-mail: stinchcombehill@golfers.net
**High on the hill with splendid views of the Cotswolds,
the River Severn and the Welsh hills. A downland
course with good turf, some trees and an interesting
variety of greens. Protected greens make this a
challenging course in windy conditions.**
18 holes, 5734yds, Par 68, SSS 68, Course record 63.
Club membership 550.
Visitors restricted at weekends. Must contact professional
in advance 01453 543878. **Societies** must apply in
advance. **Green Fees** £25 per 18 holes (£35 weekends).
Prof Paul Bushell **Course Designer** Arthur Hoare
Facilities ⊗ ⊮ ⅃ 🖳 ♀ ⚘ 🖃 ⌀ **Conf**
Hospitality Days available **Location** 1m W off A4135
· ·
Hotel ★★★ 65% Prince of Wales Hotel, Berkeley Rd,
BERKELEY ☎ 01453 810474 43 en suite

GLOUCESTER   Map 03 SO81

Brickhampton Court Cheltenham Rd, Churchdown
GL2 9QF ☎ 01452 859444 📠 01452 859333
e-mail: info@brickhampton.co.uk
**Rolling parkland courses featuring lakes, streams,
strategic white sand bunkers, tree plantations and no
steep hills.**

'EXCITING
STIMULATING
CHALLENGING
GOLF'

Spa: 18 holes, 6449yds, Par 71, SSS 71, Course record 65.
Glevum: 9 holes, 1859yds, Par 31.

Continued

Club membership 860.
Visitors advance booking recommended, recognised golfing
attire to be worn and evidence of golfing ability preferred.
Societies contact for information and booking form. **Green
Fees** Spa: £21 per round (£23 Fri, £27.50 weekends & bank
holidays). Glevum: £7.50 per 9 holes (£9.50 weekends &
bank holidays). **Cards** 🖃 🖃 🖃 🖃 🖃 **Prof** Bruce Wilson,
Chris Gillick **Course Designer** Simon Gidman **Facilities** ⊗
⊮ ⅃ 🖳 ♀ ⚘ 🖃 🖃 ⌀ ⌀ **Conf** fac available Corporate
Hospitality Days available **Location** Junct 11 M5, A40
towards Gloucester, at Elmbridge Court rdbt B4063 signed
Churchdown, approx 2m
· ·
Hotel ★★★ 62% Hatherley Manor Hotel, Down
Hatherley Ln, GLOUCESTER ☎ 01452 730217
52 en suite

Ramada Jarvis Gloucester Hotel &
Country Club Matson Ln, Robinswood Hill GL4 6EA
☎ 01452 411331 📠 01452 307212
**Undulating, wooded course, built around a hill with
superb views over Gloucester and the Cotswolds. The 12th
is a drive straight up a hill, nicknamed 'Coronary Hill'.**
*Jarvis Gloucester Hotel & Country Club: 18 holes,
6170yds, Par 70, SSS 69, Course record 65.*
Club membership 600.
Visitors can book up to 7 days in advance. **Societies**
telephone in advance. **Green Fees** terms on application.
Cards 🖃 🖃 🖃 🖃 **Prof** John Whiddon **Facilities** ⊗ ⊮ ⅃
🖳 ♀ ⚘ 🖃 🖃 🖃 🖃 ⌀ ⌀ **Leisure** hard tennis courts,
heated indoor swimming pool, squash, sauna, solarium,
gymnasium. **Location** 2.5m SE of Gloucester, off B4073
· ·
Hotel ★★★ 72% Hatton Court, Upton Hill, Upton St
Leonards, GLOUCESTER ☎ 01452 617412 17 en suite
28 annexe en suite

Rodway Hill Newent Rd, Highnam GL2 8DN
☎ 01452 384222 📠 01452 313814
e-mail: jrawl98589@aol.com
**A challenging 18-hole course with superb panoramic
views. Testing front five holes and the par 3 13th and
par 5 16th affected by strong crosswinds off the River
Severn.**
18 holes, 6070yds, Par 70, SSS 69, Course record 71.
Club membership 400.
Visitors no restrictions. **Societies** telephone in advance.
Green Fees terms on application. **Cards** 🖃 🖃 🖃 🖃
🖃 🖃 **Prof** Chris Murphy **Course Designer** John Gabb
Facilities ⊗ ⊮ ⅃ 🖳 ♀ ⚘ 🖃 🖃 🖃 🖃 ⌀ **Conf**
Corporate Hospitality Days available **Location** 2m outside
Gloucester on B4215
· ·
Hotel ★★★ 62% Hatherley Manor Hotel, Down Hatherley
Ln, GLOUCESTER ☎ 01452 730217 52 en suite

LYDNEY   Map 03 SO60

Lydney Lakeside Av GL15 5QA ☎ 01594 841186
**Flat parkland/meadowland course with prevailing wind
along fairways.**
9 holes, 5298yds, Par 66, SSS 66, Course record 63.
Club membership 350.
Visitors with member only at weekends & bank holidays.
Societies apply to Secretary. **Green Fees** terms on application.
Facilities ⅃ ♀ ⚘ **Location** SE side of town centre
· ·
Hotel ★★★ 67% The Speech House, COLEFORD
☎ 01594 822607 16 en suite 17 annexe rms (16 en suite)

MINCHINHAMPTON   Map 03 SO80

Minchinhampton (New Course) New Course
GL6 9BE ☎ 01453 833866 ▤ 01453 837360
e-mail: sec@mgcnew.co.uk

The Cherington course, a South West Regional
qualifying course for the Open Championship, is set in
undulating upland. Large contoured greens, pot
bunkers, and, at times, a stiff breeze present a very fair
test of skill. The Avening course has a variety of holes
including water on the 10th and 13th.
*Avening: 18 holes, 6263yds, Par 70, SSS 70, Course record
61.*
Cherington: 18 holes, 6430yds, Par 71, SSS 71.
Club membership 1200.
Visitors must contact in advance. **Societies** must contact
by telephone. **Green Fees** £42 per day £32 per round
(£50/£38 weekends & bank holidays). **Cards** ▭ ▭ ▤ ▥
Prof Chris Steele **Course Designer** Hawtree & Son
Facilities ⊗ ⅋ ⅃ ⅂ ♀ ⅄ ☇ ↑ ⅌ ⌀ ⌇ **Conf** Corporate
Hospitality Days available **Location** From Nailsworth take
B4014 to Avening/Tetbury. In Avening village left at
Cross pub, towards Minchinhampton. Club 0.25m on right

Hotel ★★ 70% Egypt Mill Hotel, NAILSWORTH
☎ 01453 833449 8 en suite 10 annexe en suite

Hotel ★★★ 70% Hare & Hounds Hotel, Westonbirt,
☎ 01666 880233 & 881000 Fax 01666 880241 24 en suite
7 annexe en suite

Minchinhampton (Old Course) Old Course
GL6 9AQ ☎ 01453 832642 & 836382 ▤ 01453 832642
e-mail: mail@minchcholdcourse.co.uk

An open grassland course 600 feet above sea level. The
numerous humps and hollows around the greens test
the golfer's ability to play a variety of shots - often in
difficult windy conditions. Panoramic Cotswold views.
Two of the par 3s, the 8th and the 16th, often require an
accurate long iron or wood depending on the strength
and direction of the wind.
18 holes, 6019yds, Par 71, SSS 69.
Club membership 650.
Visitors must contact in advance. **Societies** must contact in
advance. **Green Fees** terms on application. **Cards** ▭ ▭
▥ **Facilities** ⊗ ⅃ ♀ ⅄ ☇ ↑ ⌀ **Location** 1m NW

Hotel ★★ 70% Egypt Mill Hotel, NAILSWORTH
☎ 01453 833449 8 en suite 10 annexe en suite

NAUNTON   Map 04 SP12

Naunton Downs GL54 3AE
☎ 01451 850090 ▤ 01451 850091
e-mail: admin@nauntondowns.co.uk

Naunton Downs course plays over beautiful Cotswold
countryside. A valley running through the
course is one of the main features, creating one par 3
hole that crosses over it. The prevailing wind adds extra
challenge to the par 5s (which play into the wind),
combined with small undulating greens.
18 holes, 6161yds, Par 71, SSS 69, Course record 67.
Club membership 750.
Visitors must contact in advance. **Societies** telephone for
details. **Green Fees** £19 (£27.50 weekends). **Cards** ▭ ▭
▭ ▥ ▥ **Prof** Nick Ellis **Course Designer** J Pott
Facilities ⊗ ⅋ ⅃ ♀ ⅄ ☇ ↑ ⌀ **Leisure** hard
tennis courts. **Conf** fac available **Location** B4068
Stow/Cheltenham

Hotel ★★★ ♨ Lords of the Manor, UPPER
SLAUGHTER ☎ 01451 820243 27 en suite

PAINSWICK   Map 03 SO80

Painswick GL6 6TL ☎ 01452 812180
Downland course set on Cotswold Hills at
Painswick Beacon, with fine views. Short course more
than compensated by natural hazards and tight
fairways.
18 holes, 4895yds, Par 67, SSS 63, Course record 61.
Club membership 480.
Visitors member only on Sat pm & Sun. **Societies** must
apply in advance. **Green Fees** not confirmed. **Cards** ▭
▭ ▥ **Facilities** ⊗ ⅋ ⅃ ♀ ⅄ ☇ ↑ ⌀ **Conf** Corporate
Hospitality Days available **Location** 1m N on A46

Hotel ★★★ 77% Painswick Hotel and Restaurant, Kemps
Ln, PAINSWICK ☎ 01452 812160 19 en suite

Continued

TEWKESBURY Map 03 SO83

Hilton Puckrup Hall Puckrup GL20 6EL
☎ 01684 271591 📠 01684 271550
e-mail: golfprophgc70@onetel.net.uk
Set in 140 acres of undulating parkland with lakes, existing trees and marvellous views of the Malvern hills. There are water hazards at the 5th, and a cluster of bunkers on the long 14th, before the challenging tee shot across the water to the par 3 18th.
Puckrup Hall Hotel & Golf Club: 18 holes, 6189yds, Par 70, SSS 70, Course record 63.
Club membership 430.
Visitors must be a regular golfer familiar with rules and etiquette, must book a tee time, may book up to 5 days in advance. **Societies** telephone in advance. **Green Fees** not confirmed. **Cards** **Course Designer** Simon Gidman **Facilities** **Leisure** heated indoor swimming pool, sauna, solarium, gymnasium. **Location** 4m N, of Tewkesbury on A38 or junct 1 M50

Hotel ★★ 65% Bell Hotel, 57 Church St, TEWKESBURY ☎ 01684 293293 24 en suite

Tewkesbury Park Hotel Golf & Country Club Lincoln Green Ln GL20 7DN
☎ 01684 295405 📠 01684 292386
e-mail: tewkesburypark@corushotels.com
A parkland course overlooking the Abbey and rivers Avon and Severn. The par 3 5th is an exciting hole calling for accurate distance judgement. The hotel and country club offer many sports and club facilities including a well-equipped gym with cardio theatre.

18 holes, 6533yds, Par 73, SSS 72, Course record 66.
Club membership 550.
Visitors must book in advance via pro shop/hotel reservations. **Societies** telephone initially. **Green Fees** terms on application. **Cards** **Prof** Charlie Boast **Course Designer** Frank Pennick **Facilities** **Leisure** hard tennis courts, heated indoor swimming pool, squash, sauna, solarium, gymnasium. **Conf** fac available Corporate Hospitality Days available **Location** 1m SW off A38

Hotel ★★★ 69% The Tewkesbury Park Hotel Golf & Country Club, Lincoln Green Ln, TEWKESBURY ☎ 0870 609 6101 80 en suite

Booking a tee time is always advisable.

THORNBURY Map 03 ST69

Thornbury Golf Centre Bristol Rd BS35 3XL
☎ 01454 281144 📠 01454 281177
e-mail: info@thornburygc.co.uk
Two 18-hole pay and play courses designed by Hawtree and set in undulating terrain with extensive views towards the Severn estuary. The Low 18 is a par 3 with holes ranging from 80 to 207 yards and is ideal for beginners. The High course puts to test the more experienced golfer. Excellent 25 bay floodlit driving range.

High Course: 18 holes, 6308yds, Par 71, SSS 69.
Low Course: 18 holes, 2195yds, Par 54.
Club membership 540.
Visitors welcome at all times, telephone to reserve. **Societies** apply in writing/telephone in advance. **Green Fees** terms on application. **Cards** **Prof** Simon Hubbard **Course Designer** Hawtree **Facilities** **Conf** fac available Corporate Hospitality Days available **Location** Off A38

Hotel ★★ 66% Thornbury Golf Lodge, Bristol Rd, THORNBURY ☎ 01454 281144 11 en suite

WESTONBIRT Map 03 ST88

Westonbirt Westonbirt School GL8 8QG
☎ 01666 880242 881338 📠 01666 880385
A parkland course with good views.

9 holes, 4504yds, Par 64, SSS 64.
Club membership 225.
Visitors no restrictions. **Societies** no reserved tees. **Green Fees** not confirmed. **Facilities** **Location** E side of village off A433

Hotel ★★★ 70% Hare & Hounds Hotel, Westonbirt, TETBURY ☎ 01666 880233 & 881000 📠 01666 880241 24 en suite 7 annexe en suite

See photo on page 94

Hare & Hounds Hotel

WICK Map 03 ST77

Tracy Park Tracy Park Estate, Bath Rd BS30 5RN
☎ 0117 937 2251 📠 0117 937 4288
e-mail: golf@thegloucestershire.com
Two 18-hole championship courses on the south-western escarpment of the Cotswolds, affording fine views. Both courses present a challenge to all levels of player, with water playing a part on a number of occasions. The clubhouse dates back to 1600 and is a building of great beauty and elegance, set in the 221-acre estate of this golf and country club.
Crown Course: 18 holes, 6252yds, Par 69, SSS 70.
Cromwell Course: 18 holes, 6246yds, Par 71, SSS 70.
Club membership 600.
Visitors no restrictions, must book tee time(0117 9372251) **Societies** must telephone/write to Robert Ford **Green Fees** terms on application. **Cards** 🌐 💳 🏧 💳 💷 **Prof** David Morgan **Facilities** ⊗ 🏌 ▶ 🍴 ♀ 🛎 🏪 🏸 🛒 🐎 🚜 ♂ ℓ **Conf** fac available Corporate Hospitality Days available **Location** S side of village off A420

Hotel ★★★ The Queensberry Hotel, Russel St, BATH
☎ 01225 447928 29 en suite

WOTTON-UNDER-EDGE Map 03 ST79

Cotswold Edge Upper Rushmire GL12 7PT
☎ 01453 844167 📠 01453 845120
e-mail: nnewman@cotswoldedgegolfclub.org.uk
Meadowland course situated in a quiet Cotswold valley with magnificent views. First half flat and open, second half more varied.
18 holes, 6170yds, Par 71, SSS 71.
Club membership 800.
Visitors preferable to contact in advance, at weekends may only play with member. **Societies** must contact in writing or telephone in advance. **Green Fees** terms on application. **Prof** Rod HIbbitt **Facilities** ⊗ 🏌 ▶ 🍴 ♀ 🛎 🏪 🏸 🛒 🐎 ♂ **Location** N of town on B4058 Wotton-Tetbury road

Hotel ★★ 70% Egypt Mill Hotel, NAILSWORTH
☎ 01453 833449 8 en suite 10 annexe en suite

GREATER LONDON

Those courses which fall within the confines of the London Postal District area (i.e. have London postcodes - W1, SW1 etc) are listed under the county heading of **London** in the gazetteer (see page 170).

GREATER LONDON

ADDINGTON Map 05 TQ36

The Addington 205 Shirley Church Rd CR0 5AB
☎ 020 8777 1055 📠 020 8777 6661
e-mail: addingtogolf@btconnect.com
This heather and woodland course is possibly one of the best laid out courses in Southern England with the world famous 13th, par 3 at 230 yds. A good test of golfing ability.
18 holes, 6338yds, Par 68, SSS 71, Course record 66.
Visitors handicap certificate required. **Societies** weekdays only, telephone for prior arrangement. **Green Fees** £50 (£77.50 weekends after 10.30am). **Cards** 🌐 💳 🏧 💳 💷 **Course Designer** J F Abercromby **Facilities** ⊗ 🏌 ▶ 🍴 ♀ 🛎 ♂ ℓ **Conf** Corporate Hospitality Days available **Location** 3m from Centre of Croydon off M25 junct 4/7

Hotel ★★★★ 69% Le Meridien Selsdon Park & Golf Course, Addington Rd, Sanderstead, CROYDON
☎ 020 8657 8811 204 en suite

Addington Court Featherbed Ln CR0 9AA
☎ 020 8657 0281 (booking) & 8651 5270 (admin)
📠 020 8651 0282
e-mail: addington@americangolf.uk.com
Challenging, well-drained courses designed by F. Hawtree. Two 18-hole courses, 9-hole course and an 18-hole par 3 course designed to suit all standards.
Championship Course: 18 holes, 5577yds, Par 68, SSS 67, Course record 60.
Falconwood: 18 holes, 5472yds, Par 68, SSS 67.
9 Hole: 9 holes, 1804yds, Par 31.
Club membership 587.
Visitors no restrictions. Advisable to phone in advance to play on Championship Course. **Societies** must telephone in advance. **Green Fees** not confirmed. **Cards** 🌐 💳 🏧 💳 💷 **Prof** Tom O'Keefe **Course Designer** Hawtree Snr **Facilities** ⊗ 🏌 ▶ 🍴 ♀ 🛎 🏪 🏸 🛒 🐎 🚜 ♂ ℓ **Conf** fac available Corporate Hospitality Days available **Location** 1m S off A2022

Hotel ★★★★ 69% Le Meridien Selsdon Park & Golf Course, Addington Rd, Sanderstead, CROYDON
☎ 020 8657 8811 204 en suite

Addington Palace Addington Park, Gravel Hill CR0 5BB ☎ 020 8654 3061 📠 020 8655 3632
18 holes, 6286yds, Par 71, SSS 71, Course record 63.
Course Designer J H Taylor **Location** 2miles SE of Croydon station on A212
Telephone for further details

Hotel ★★★★ 69% Le Meridien Selsdon Park & Golf Course, Addington Rd, Sanderstead, CROYDON
☎ 020 8657 8811 204 en suite

BARNEHURST Map 05 TQ57

Barnehurst Mayplace Rd East DA7 6JU
☎ 01322 523746 📠 01322 523860
Public parkland course with well matured greens. Easy walking.
9 holes, 4796yds, Par 70, SSS 67.
Club membership 180.
Visitors Reasonable standard of dress required. No jeans. **Societies** telephone in advance. **Green Fees** not confirmed.

Continued

Cards ▭ ▭ ◻ **Course Designer** James Braid **Facilities** ⊗ ⅲ ᴸ ◗♀♁🛆🖿 🕈 ◊ **Conf** Corporate Hospitality Days available **Location** 0.75m NW of Crayford off A2000

....

Hotel Ⓤ Holiday Inn Bexley, Black Prince Interchange, Southwold Rd, BEXLEY ☏ 0870 400 9006 108 en suite

BARNET   Map 04 TQ29

Arkley Rowley Green Rd EN5 3HL
☏ 020 8449 0394 ▤ 020 8440 5214
e-mail: secretary@arkleygolfclub.co.uk
Wooded parkland course situated on highest spot in Hertfordshire with fine views.
9 holes, 6046yds, Par 69, SSS 69.
Club membership 450.
Visitors may play weekdays only unless accompanied by member. **Societies** must contact in advance. **Green Fees** £32 per day, £25 per round. **Prof** Martin Porter **Course Designer** Braid **Facilities** ⊗ ⅲ ᴸ ◗♀♁🛆 ◊ **Conf** Corporate Hospitality Days available **Location** Off A1 at Arkley sign

....

Hotel ★★★ 72% Edgwarebury Hotel, Barnet Ln, ELSTREE ☏ 0870 609 6151 47 en suite

Dyrham Park Country Club Galley Ln EN5 4RA
☏ 020 8440 3361 ▤ 020 8441 9836
18 holes, 6369yds, Par 71, SSS 70, Course record 65.
Location 3m NW off A1081
Telephone for further details

....

Hotel Ⓤ Holiday Inn South Mimms, SOUTH MIMMS ☏ 0870 400 9072 144 en suite

Old Fold Manor Old Fold Ln, Hadley Green
EN5 4QN ☏ 020 8440 9185 ▤ 020 8441 4863
e-mail: manager@oldfoldmanor.co.uk
Superb heathland course with some of the finest greens in Hertfordshire, breathtaking views and a challenge for all levels of golfer. Slightly undulating in parts, the course meanders around a historic battle site.
18 holes, 6447yds, Par 71, SSS 71, Course record 66.
Club membership 560.
Visitors with member only weekends & bank holidays. **Societies** must apply in writing/telephone in advance. **Green Fees** £38 per 36 holes, £36 per 27 holes, £30 per 18 holes. **Cards** ▭ ▭ ▬ ▬ ◻ **Prof** Peter McEvoy **Facilities** ⊗ ⅲ by prior arrangement ᴸ ◗♀🛆🖿 🕈 ◊ **Conf** Corporate Hospitality Days available **Location** Off A1000 between Barnet/Potters Bar

....

Hotel ★★★★ ⚐ 73% West Lodge Park Hotel, Cockfosters Rd, HADLEY WOOD ☏ 020 8216 3900 46 en suite 13 annexe en suite

BECKENHAM   Map 05 TQ36

Beckenham Place Park The Mansion, Beckenham
Place Park BR3 2BP ☏ 020 8650 2292 ▤ 020 8663 1201
Picturesque course in the grounds of a public park. The course varies from open to tight surroundings with the back nine providing a challenge for both the novice and low handicapper. A water-filled ditch comes into play on several holes.
18 holes, 5722yds, Par 68, SSS 69.
Visitors weekends, dawn-13.30 booked tee times operate contact for details. **Societies** apply in writing or telephone

---

for Society pack. **Green Fees** not confirmed. **Cards** ▭ ▬ ▬ ◻ **Prof** John Denham/Carl Denham **Facilities** ⊗ ᴸ ◗♀🛆🖿 🕈 ▶ 🛆 ◊ **Leisure** hard tennis courts. **Location** Main Catford/Beckenham road, just off A21

....

Hotel ★★★ 73% Bromley Court Hotel, Bromley Hill, BROMLEY ☏ 020 8461 8600 114 en suite

Langley Park Barnfield Wood Rd BR3 6SZ
☏ 020 8658 6849 ▤ 020 8658 6310
e-mail: manager@langleyparkgolf.co.uk
This is a pleasant, but difficult, well-wooded, parkland course with natural hazards including a lake at the 18th hole.
18 holes, 6488yds, Par 69, SSS 71, Course record 65.
Club membership 700.
Visitors must contact in advance and may not play weekends. **Societies** Wed & Thu only, telephone to book. **Green Fees** £40 per day, £30 per round. **Cards** ▭ ▬ ◻ ▭ ▬ **Prof** Colin Staff **Course Designer** J H Taylor **Facilities** ⊗ ⅲ ᴸ ◗♀🛆🖿 🕈 ◊ **Conf** Corporate Hospitality Days available **Location** 0.5 N of Beckenham on B2015

....

Hotel ★★★ 73% Bromley Court Hotel, Bromley Hill, BROMLEY ☏ 020 8461 8600 114 en suite

BEXLEYHEATH   Map 05 TQ47

Bexleyheath Mount Rd DA6 8JS ☏ 020 8303 6951
Undulating course.
9 holes, 5162yds, Par 66, SSS 66, Course record 65.
Club membership 330.
Visitors must contact Secretary in advance, may not play weekends. **Societies** telephone in advance. **Green Fees** terms on application. **Facilities** ⊗ ⅲ ᴸ ◗♀🛆 **Location** 1m SW

....

Hotel Ⓤ Holiday Inn Bexley, Black Prince Interchange, Southwold Rd, BEXLEY ☏ 0870 400 9006 108 en suite

BIGGIN HILL   Map 05 TQ45

Cherry Lodge Jail Ln TN16 3AX
☏ 01959 572250 ▤ 01959 540672
e-mail: info@cherrylodgegc.co.uk
Undulating parkland course set 600 feet above sea level with panoramic views of the surrounding Kent countryside. An enjoyable test of golf for all standards. The 14th is 434 yards across a valley and uphill, requiring two good shots to reach the green.

18 holes, 6652yds, Par 72, SSS 73, Course record 66.
Club membership 700.

Continued   *Continued*

Visitors must contact pro shop for weekday reservation. May only play with member at weekends. **Societies** must telephone in advance. **Green Fees** £35 per 18 holes. **Cards** 🖅 🖃 **Prof** Nigel Child **Course Designer** John Day **Facilities** ⊗ ⅃ 🖳 ⅄ ⚘ 🖼 🚄 ∅ ₹ **Location** 1m E

Hotel ★★★ 71% Donnington Manor, London Rd, Dunton Green, SEVENOAKS ☎ 01732 462681 60 en suite

BROMLEY
Map 05 TQ46

Bromley Magpie Hall Ln BR2 8JF
☎ 020 8462 7014 🗎 020 8462 6916
e-mail: bromley.gov.uk
9 holes, 2745yds, Par 70, SSS 67.
Location 2m SE off A21
Telephone for further details

Hotel ★★★ 73% Bromley Court Hotel, Bromley Hill, BROMLEY ☎ 020 8461 8600 114 en suite

Sundridge Park Garden Rd BR1 3NE
☎ 020 8460 0278 🗎 020 8289 3050
e-mail: gm@spgc.co.uk
The East course is longer than the West but many think the shorter of the two courses is the more difficult. The East is surrounded by trees while the West is more hilly, with good views. Both are certainly a good test of golf. An Open qualifying course with year round irrigation of fairways.
East Course: 18 holes, 6516yds, Par 71, SSS 71, Course record 63.
West Course: 18 holes, 6019yds, Par 69, SSS 69, Course record 65.
Club membership 1200.
Visitors may only play on weekdays. Must contact in advance and must have a handicap certificate. No advance booking necessary. **Societies** must contact well in advance. **Green Fees** £55 per day, weekdays only. **Cards** 🖅 🖃 🖾 **Prof** Stuart Dowsett **Course Designer** Willie Park **Facilities** ⊗ ⅃ ⅃ 🖳 ⅄ ⊿ 🖼 ⚘ 🚄 🖼 ∅ **Leisure** hard tennis courts, heated indoor swimming pool, squash, sauna, solarium, gymnasium. **Conf** fac available Corporate Hospitality Days available **Location** N side of town centre off A2212

Hotel ★★★ 73% Bromley Court Hotel, Bromley Hill, BROMLEY ☎ 020 8461 8600 114 en suite

CARSHALTON
Map 04 TQ26

Oaks Sports Centre Woodmansterne Rd SM5 4AN
☎ 020 8643 8363 🗎 020 8770 7303
e-mail: golf@oaks.sagehost.co.uk
Public parkland course with floodlit, covered driving range.

18 Holes: 18 holes, 6025yds, Par 70, SSS 69, Course record 65.
9 Holes: 9 holes, 1443yds, Par 28, SSS 28.
Club membership 477.
Visitors no restrictions weekdays. May not play at weekends. **Societies** must apply in writing. **Green Fees** £17.40 for 18 holes, £8.70 for 9 holes (£21/£10.50 weekends). **Prof** Horley/Russell/Pilkington **Facilities** 🎿 ⅃ 🖳 ⅄ ⚘ 🖼 ∅ ₹ **Leisure** squash. **Conf** fac available **Location** 0.5m S on B278

Hotel ★★★ 69% Aerodrome Hotel, Purley Way, CROYDON ☎ 020 8710 9000 84 en suite

CHESSINGTON
Map 04 TQ16

Chessington Garrison Ln KT9 2LW
☎ 020 8391 0948 🗎 020 8397 2068
e-mail: info@chessingtongolf.co.uk
Tree-lined parkland course designed by Patrick Tallack, with panoramic views over the Surrey countryside.
9 holes, 1679yds, Par 30, SSS 28.
Club membership 90.
Visitors may not play before 10am on Sun. **Societies** Telephone in advance. **Green Fees** £8.50 per round (£10 weekendsand bank holidays). **Cards** 🖅 🖃 🖾 🖾 🖾 **Prof** Mark Janes **Course Designer** Patrick Tallack **Facilities** ⊗ ⅃ 🖳 ⅄ 🖼 🖼 ∅ ₹ **Leisure** animated ball teeing facility on driving range. **Location** M25 junct 9, 3m N on A243

Hotel ⬨ Travel Inn, Leatherhead Rd, CHESSINGTON ☎ 08701 977057 42 en suite

CHISLEHURST
Map 05 TQ47

Chislehurst Camden Park Rd BR7 5HJ
☎ 020 8467 6798 🗎 020 8295 0874
e-mail: thesecretary@chislehurstgolfclub.co.uk
Pleasantly wooded undulating parkland/heathland course. Magnificent clubhouse with historical associations.
18 holes, 5080yds, Par 66, SSS 65, Course record 62.
Club membership 760.
Visitors with member only weekends, handicap certificate required during the week. **Societies** weekdays only, booked in advance. **Green Fees** £30 per round weekdays only. **Prof** Jonathan Bird **Course Designer** Park **Facilities** ⊗ 🎿 ⅃ 🖳 ⅄ ⚘ 🖼 ∅ **Leisure** snooker room.

★★★ 73% Bromley Court Hotel, Bromley Hill, BROMLEY ☎ 020 8461 8600 114 en suite

COULSDON
Map 04 TQ25

Coulsdon Manor Hotel Coulsdon Court Rd
CR5 2LL ☎ 020 8668 0414 🗎 020 8668 3118
e-mail: coulsdonmanor@marstonhotels.com
Designed by Harry S Colt and set in its own 140 acres of landscaped parkland.

Continued

Coulsdon Manor

18 holes, 6037yds, Par 70, SSS 68.
Visitors telephone for tee times **Societies** telephone to book **Green Fees** £19.95 per round. **Cards** ▭▭▭▭▭ ▭▭ 🔲 **Prof** James Leaver **Course Designer** Harry Colt **Facilities** ⊗ ⅧⅢ ᴸ 🍺 ♀ 🎿 🏠 🍴 𝄐 **Leisure** hard tennis courts, squash, sauna, solarium, gymnasium. **Conf** fac available Corporate Hospitality Days available **Location** 0.75m E off A23 on B2030

Hotel ★★★★ 77% Coulsdon Manor, Coulsdon Court Rd, Coulsdon, CROYDON ☎ 020 8668 0414 35 en suite

---

COULSDON MANOR
AA ★★★★ RAC

Coulsdon Court Road Coulsdon
Nr Croydon Surrey CR5 2LL
www.marstonhotels.com

GOLF SOCIETIES WELCOME

A relaxing but challenging par 70 golf course, designed by H S Colt, with lush fairways and quality greens, stretching over 6,000 yards through 140 acres of beautiful, natural parkland. Signature hole is the picturesque par 3 sixth with an elevated tee.

Golf Tuition ★ Special Winter Rates ★ Professional Shop

TEL: 020 8668 0414 FAX: 020 8668 3118

MARSTON HOTELS 𝓂

HOTEL & GOLF CENTRE

Woodcote Park Meadow Hill, Bridle Way CR5 2QQ
☎ 020 8668 2788 📋 020 8660 0918
e-mail: info@woodcotepgc.com
Slightly undulating parkland course.
18 holes, 6680yds, Par 71, SSS 72, Course record 66.
Club membership 650.
Visitors handicap certificate required, contact professional for details. Visitors may not play weekends. **Societies** must contact Secretary in advance.

Continued

Green Fees £40 per day/round. **Prof** Wraith Grant **Course Designer** H S Colt **Facilities** ⊗ ⅧⅢ by prior arrangement ᴸ 🍺 ♀ 🎿 🏠 🍴 🔜 𝄐 **Location** 1m N of town centre off A237

Hotel ★★★ 69% Aerodrome Hotel, Purley Way, CROYDON ☎ 020 8710 9000 84 en suite

CROYDON   Map 04 TQ36

Croham Hurst Croham Rd CR2 7HJ
☎ 020 8657 5581 📋 020 8657 3229
e-mail: secretary@chgc.co.uk
Parkland course with tree-lined fairways and bounded by wooded hills. Easy walking.
18 holes, 6290yds, Par 70, SSS 70.
Club membership 800.
Visitors must contact in advance & have handicap certificate. With member only weekends & bank holidays. **Societies** Apply in writing/telephone in advance **Green Fees** £40 (£50 weekends). **Prof** Matthew Paget **Course Designer** Hawtree/Braid **Facilities** ⊗ ⅧⅢ ᴸ 🍺 ♀ 🎿 🏠 🍴 𝄐 **Conf** Corporate Hospitality Days available **Location** 1.5m SE,of Croydon between South Croydon & Selsdon on B269

Hotel ★★★★ 69% Le Meridien Selsdon Park & Golf Course, Addington Rd, Sanderstead, CROYDON ☎ 020 8657 8811 204 en suite

Le Meridien Selsdon Park Addington Rd,
Sanderstead CR2 8YA ☎ 020 8657 8811 📋 020 8651 6171
Parkland course. Full use of hotel's sporting facilities by residents.
18 holes, 6473yds, Par 73, SSS 71, Course record 63.
Visitors welcome, booking advisable, booking 1 week in advance for weekends. **Societies** telephone in advance. **Green Fees** terms on application. **Cards** ▭▭▭ ▭▭ ▭▭ 🔲 **Prof** Malcolm Churchill **Course Designer** J H Taylor **Facilities** ⊗ ⅧⅢ ᴸ 🍺 ♀ 🎿 🏠 🍴 🔜 𝄐 🍷 **Leisure** hard and grass tennis courts, outdoor and indoor heated swimming pools, squash, sauna, solarium, gymnasium. **Conf** fac available **Location** 3m S on A2022

Hotel ★★★★ 69% Le Meridien Selsdon Park & Golf Course, Addington Rd, Sanderstead, CROYDON ☎ 020 8657 8811 204 en suite

Shirley Park 194 Addiscombe Rd CR0 7LB
☎ 020 8654 1143 📋 020 8654 6733
e-mail: secretary@shirleyparkgolfclub.co.uk
This parkland course lies amid fine woodland with good views of Shirley Hills. The more testing holes come in the middle section of the course. The remarkable 7th hole calls for a 187-yard iron or wood shot diagonally across a narrow valley to a shelved green set right-handed into a ridge. The 13th hole, 160yds, is considered to be one of the finest short holes in the county.
18 holes, 6210yds, Par 71, SSS 70, Course record 64.
Club membership 600.
Visitors should contact in advance. With member only on Saturdays. **Societies** by arrangement. **Green Fees** £38 weekday (£45 Sun). Reduced winter rates. **Cards** ▭▭ ▭▭ 🔲 🌐 ▭▭ 🔲 **Prof** Michael Taylor **Course Designer** Tom Simpson/Herbert Fowler **Facilities** ⊗ ⅧⅢ ᴸ 🍺 ♀ 🎿 🏠 🍴 𝄐 **Location** E side of town centre on A232

Hotel ★★★★ 69% Le Meridien Selsdon Park & Golf Course, Addington Rd, Sanderstead, CROYDON ☎ 020 8657 8811 204 en suite

DOWNE
Map 05 TQ46

High Elms High Elms Rd BR6 7JL
☎ 01689 853232 & 858175 bookings ▤ 01689 856326
Municipal parkland course. Very tight 13th, 221 yds (par 3).
18 holes, 6210yds, Par 71, SSS 70, Course record 68.
Club membership 450.
Visitors should phone to book/enquire about availability
Societies telephone to book. Tel 01689 861813. **Green Fees** not confirmed. **Prof** Peter Remy **Course Designer** Hawthorn **Facilities** ⊗ ⫼ ⫶ ⫶ ⫶ ⫶ ⫶ ⫶ ⫶ ⫶ ⫶ ⫶ ⫶
Location 2m E of A21

Hotel ★★★ 73% Bromley Court Hotel, Bromley Hill, BROMLEY ☎ 020 8461 8600 114 en suite

West Kent West Hill BR6 7JJ
☎ 01689 851323 ▤ 01689 858693
e-mail: golf@wkgc.co.uk
Undulating woodland course.
18 holes, 6385yds, Par 70, SSS 70, Course record 62.
Club membership 700.
Visitors with member only at weekends. Must contact in advance. **Societies** must apply in writing. **Green Fees** £50 per day; £35 per round. **Cards** ⫶ ⫶ ⫶ **Prof** Chris Forsyth **Course Designer** W Fowler & J Abercrombie
Facilities ⊗ ⫼ ⫶ ⫶ ⫶ ⫶ ⫶ ⫶ **Location** M25 junct 4, take A21 towards Bromley, turn left at sign for Downe, proceed through village on Luxted road 0.5m, West Hill located on right

Hotel ★★★ 73% Bromley Court Hotel, Bromley Hill, BROMLEY ☎ 020 8461 8600 114 en suite

ENFIELD
Map 04 TQ39

Crews Hill Cattlegate Rd, Crews Hill EN2 8AZ
☎ 020 8363 6674 ▤ 020 8363 2343
e-mail: gmchgc@aol.com
Parkland course in country surroundings.
18 holes, 6273yds, Par 70, SSS 70, Course record 65.
Club membership 600.
Visitors all day Mon, 7-9.30am Tue-Fri and after 2pm Wed & Fri are public timings. Handicap certificate required.Not permitted to use club house facilities.
Societies Wed-Fri; must apply in writing. **Green Fees** terms on application. **Cards** ⫶ ⫶ ⫶ ⫶ ⫶ **Prof** Neil Wichelow **Course Designer** Harry Colt **Facilities** ⊗ ⫼ ⫶ ⫶ ⫶ ⫶ ⫶ ⫶ ⫶ **Conf** fac available Corporate Hospitality Days available **Location** M25 junct 24, take A1005 for Enfield and follow signs

Enfield Old Park Rd South EN2 7DA
☎ 020 8363 3970 ▤ 020 8342 0381
Parkland course. Salmons Brook crosses seven holes.
18 holes, 6154yds, Par 72, SSS 70, Course record 61.
Club membership 700.
Visitors must contact the Professional in advance,weekends and bank holidays by arrangement only.
Societies must contact the secretary in advance. **Green Fees** terms on application. **Cards** ⫶ ⫶ ⫶ ⫶ ⫶ ⫶ **Prof** Lee Fickling **Course Designer** James Braid **Facilities** ⊗ ⫼ ⫶ ⫶ ⫶ ⫶ ⫶ **Location** M25 jnct 24, A1005 to Enfield to rdbt with church on left, right down Slades Hill, 1st left to end

Whitewebbs Park Whitewebbs Ln EN2 9HH
☎ 020 8363 4454 ▤ 020 8366 2257
Gently undulating wooded parkland course with an attractive brook running through four holes.
18 holes, 5782yds, Par 68, SSS 68, Course record 67.
Club membership 350.
Visitors can play all times, can book in advance **Societies** must apply in writing or by phone to Course Manager.
Green Fees terms on applcation. **Cards** ⫶ ⫶ ⫶ ⫶ ⫶
Prof Gary Sherriff **Facilities** ⊗ ⫼ ⫶ ⫶ ⫶ ⫶ ⫶ ⫶
Location N side of town centre

GREENFORD
Map 04 TQ18

C & L Golf & Country Club Westend Rd,
Northolt UB5 6RD ☎ 020 8841 5662 ☎ 020 8841 5515
18 holes, 4458yds, Par 67, SSS 62, Course record 58.
Course Designer Patrick Tallack **Location** Junct Westend Road/A40
Telephone for further details

Hotel ★★★ 67% The Bridge Hotel, Western Av, GREENFORD ☎ 020 8566 6246 68 en suite

Ealing Perivale Ln UB6 8SS
☎ 020 8997 0937 ▤ 020 8998 0756
The home of English and European champions. Inland parkland course with River Brent providing natural hazards across several holes.
18 holes, 6216yds, Par 70, SSS 70, Course record 62.
Club membership 650.
Visitors Mon-Fri only on application to pro shop. **Societies** Mon, Wed & Thu only by arrangement. **Green Fees** terms on application. **Cards** ⫶ ⫶ ⫶ **Prof** David Barton **Course Designer** H S Colt **Facilities** ⊗ ⫼ by prior arrangement ⫶ ⫶ ⫶ ⫶ ⫶ ⫶ **Conf** Corporate Hospitality Days available **Location** Off A40 travelling W from London

Hotel ★★★ 67% The Bridge Hotel, Western Av, GREENFORD ☎ 020 8566 6246 68 en suite

Horsenden Hill Whitton Av, Woodland Rise
UB6 0RD ☎ 020 8902 4555 ▤ 020 8902 4555
A well-kept, tree-lined short course.
9 holes, 1632yds, Par 28, SSS 28.
Club membership 135.
Visitors no restrictions. **Societies** telephone for details.
Green Fees terms on application. **Cards** ⫶ ⫶ ⫶ ⫶ ⫶
Prof Jeff Quarshie **Facilities** ⊗ ⫼ ⫶ ⫶ ⫶ ⫶ ⫶ ⫶ ⫶
Location 3m NE on A4090

Hotel ★★★ 67% The Bridge Hotel, Western Av, GREENFORD ☎ 020 8566 6246 68 en suite

Lime Trees Park Ruislip Rd, Northolt UB5 6QZ
☎ 020 8842 0442 ▤ 0208 8420542
9 holes, 5836yds, Par 71, SSS 69.
Location 300yds off A40 at Polish War Memorial/A4180 towards Hayes
Telephone for further details

Hotel ★★★ 67% The Bridge Hotel, Western Av, GREENFORD ☎ 020 8566 6246 68 en suite

Perivale Park Stockdove Way UB6 8TJ
☎ 020 8575 7116
9 holes, 2667yds, Par 68, SSS 67.
Location E side of town centre, off A40
Telephone for further details

Continued

Hotel ★★★ 69% Best Western Cumberland Hotel, 1 St Johns Rd, HARROW ☎ 020 8863 4111 31 en suite 53 annexe en suite

HADLEY WOOD — Map 04 TQ29

Hadley Wood Beech Hill EN4 0JJ
☎ 020 8449 4328 & 4486 📠 020 8364 8633
e-mail: gen.mgr@hadleywoodgc.com
A parkland course on the northwest edge of London. The gently undulating fairways have a friendly width inviting the player to open his shoulders, though the thick rough can be very punishing to the unwary. The course is pleasantly wooded and there are some admirable views.

18 holes, 6514yds, Par 72, SSS 71, Course record 67. Club membership 600.
Visitors handicap certificate required, may not play Tue mornings & weekends.Must contact in advance. **Societies** must contact in advance. **Green Fees** terms on application.
Prof Peter Jones **Course Designer** Alistair Mackenzie
Facilities ⊗ ⅏ ⮜ ⬛ ⬜ ♀ ⅄ 🖿 ⛳ 🚬 ⛳ ⌇ **Location** E side of village

Hotel ★★★★ ♨ 73% West Lodge Park Hotel, Cockfosters Rd, HADLEY WOOD ☎ 020 8216 3900 46 en suite 13 annexe en suite

HAMPTON — Map 04 TQ17

Fulwell Wellington Rd, Hampton Hill TW12 1JY
☎ 020 8977 3844 & 020 8977 2733 📠 020 8977 7732
18 holes, 6544yds, Par 71, SSS 71.
Location 1.5m N on A311
Telephone for further details

Hotel ★★★ 68% The Richmond Hill Hotel, Richmond Hill, RICHMOND UPON THAMES ☎ 020 8940 2247 138 en suite

HAMPTON WICK — Map 04 TQ16

Hampton Court Palace Home Park KT1 4AD
☎ 020 8977 2423 📠 020 8977 5938
e-mail: hamptoncourtpalace@americangolf.uk.com
Flat, parkland course with easy walking.
18 holes, 6584yds, Par 71, SSS 71.
Club membership 550.
Visitors welcome all week subject to club competitions and after 1.30pm weekends. **Societies** telephone Society Organiser (020 8977 2423) **Green Fees** not confirmed.
Cards 🖪 🖪 ⬛ 🖪 🖪 🖪 **Prof** Ashley Weller **Course Designer** Willie Park **Facilities** ⊗ ⅏ ⮜ ⬛ ♀ ⅄ 🖿 🛶 ⌇ **Conf** fac available Corporate Hospitality Days available **Location** Off A308 on W side of Kingston Bridge

Hotel ★★★ 68% The Richmond Hill Hotel, Richmond Hill, RICHMOND UPON THAMES ☎ 020 8940 2247 138 en suite

HILLINGDON — Map 04 TQ08

Hillingdon 18 Dorset Way UB10 0JR
☎ 01895 233956 & 239810 📠 01895 233956
9 holes, 5490yds, Par 68, SSS 67.
Location W side of town off A4020
Telephone for further details

Hotel ★★★ 69% Novotel London Heathrow, Junction 4 M4, Cherry Ln, WEST DRAYTON ☎ 01895 431431 178 en suite

HOUNSLOW — Map 04 TQ17

Airlinks Southall Ln TW5 9PE
☎ 020 8561 1418 📠 88136284
Meadowland/parkland course. Four water holes.
18 holes, 6000yds, Par 71, SSS 69, Course record 63. Club membership 550.
Visitors welcome all times. Must contact in advance **Societies** telephone in advance. **Green Fees** terms on application. **Cards** 🖪 ⬛ 🖪 🖪 🖪 **Prof** Tony Martin **Course Designer** P Alliss/D Thomas **Facilities** ⊗ ⅏ ⮜ ⬛ ♀ ⅄ 🖿 ⛳ 🚬 ⌇ ⌇ **Leisure** hard tennis courts, outdoor and indoor heated swimming pools, squash, sauna, solarium, gymnasium. **Location** W of Hounslow off M4 junc 3

Hotel ★★★ 66% Best Western Master Robert Hotel, 366 Great West Rd, HOUNSLOW ☎ 020 8570 6261 96 annexe en suite

Hounslow Heath Municipal Staines Rd TW4 5DS
☎ 020 8570 5271 📠 020 8570 5205
18 holes, 5901yds, Par 69, SSS 68, Course record 62.
Course Designer Fraser M Middleton **Location** On A315 towards Bedfont
Telephone for further details

Hotel Ⓤ Holiday Inn London Heathrow, Sipson Rd, WEST DRAYTON ☎ 020 8759 2323 610 en suite

ILFORD — Map 05 TQ48

Ilford Wanstead Park Rd IG1 3TR
☎ 020 8554 2930 📠 020 8554 0822
e-mail: info@ilfordgolfclub.co.uk
Fairly flat parkland course with the River Roding running through it. The river borders four holes, and is crossed by three holes. While not a particularly long course, the small greens, and many holes requiring brains rather than brawn, provide a challenging test to all.
18 holes, 5299yds, Par 67, SSS 66, Course record 61. Club membership 500.
Visitors must contact in advance, book with pro on 020 8554 0094. **Societies** telephone for provisional date and booking form. **Green Fees** terms on application. **Cards** 🖪 ⬛ 🖪 🖪 🖪 **Prof** S Jackson **Course Designer** Whitehead **Facilities** ⊗ ⅏ ⮜ ⬛ ♀ ⅄ 🖿 ⌇ **Conf** fac available Corporate Hospitality Days available **Location** NW side of town centre off A12

Hotel ★★★ 59% The County Hotel, 30 Oak Hill, WOODFORD GREEN ☎ 0870 609 6156 99 en suite

Continued

ISLEWORTH — Map 04 TQ17

Wyke Green Syon Ln TW7 5PT
☎ 020 8847 0685 (Prof) & 8560 8777 (Sec)
📠 020 8569 8392
e-mail: office@wykegreengolfclub.co.uk
Fairly flat parkland course. Seven par 4 holes over 420 yards.
18 holes, 6182yds, Par 69, SSS 70, Course record 64.
Club membership 650.
Visitors may not play before 4pm weekends and bank holidays **Societies** must apply in writing or telephone in advance. **Green Fees** £28 per round; (£30 weekends). **Prof** Neil Smith **Course Designer** Hawtree **Facilities** ⊗ ⅢⅢ ⓑ 🍴 ♀ 🏌 🛺 ⚘ **Location** 0.5m N on B454 off A4 at Gillette Corner

Hotel ★★★ 66% Best Western Master Robert Hotel, 366 Great West Rd, HOUNSLOW ☎ 020 8570 6261 96 annexe en suite

KINGSTON UPON THAMES — Map 04 TQ16

Coombe Hill Golf Club Dr, Coombe Ln West
KT2 7DF ☎ 020 8336 7600 📠 020 8336 7601
e-mail: thesecretary@coombehillgolf.demon.co.uk
A splendid course in wooded terrain. The undulations and trees make it an especially interesting course of great charm. And there is a lovely display of rhododendrons in May and June.
18 holes, 6293yds, Par 71, SSS 71, Course record 67.
Club membership 550.
Visitors must contact in advance. With member only at weekends. **Societies** must book in advance. **Green Fees** Weekdays only: £80 per 18 holes(£50 Nov-Mar). **Cards** 💳 💳 **Prof** Craig Defoy **Course Designer** J F Abercromby **Facilities** ⊗ ⅢⅢ ⓑ 🍴 ♀ 🏌 🛺 🍴 🛺 ⚘ **Leisure** sauna. **Conf** Corporate Hospitality Days available **Location** 1.75m E on A238

Coombe Wood George Rd, Kingston Hill KT2 7NS
☎ 020 8942 0388 📠 020 8942 5665
e-mail: cwoodgc@ukonline.co.uk
Mature parkland course with seven varied and challenging par 3s.
18 holes, 5299yds, Par 66, SSS 66, Course record 59.
Club membership 660.
Visitors may not play weekends before 3pm. **Societies** Wed, Thu & Fri; must contact in advance. **Green Fees** £25 per round (£35 per round weekends). **Cards** 💳 💳 **Prof** Phil Wright **Course Designer** Tom Williamson **Facilities** ⊗ ⅢⅢ by prior arrangement ⓑ 🍴 ♀ 🏌 🛺 ⚘ **Conf** Corporate Hospitality Days available **Location** 1.25m NE on A308

MITCHAM — Map 04 TQ26

Mitcham Carshalton Rd CR4 4HN
☎ 020 8648 4280 📠 020 8647 4197
e-mail: mitchdtch@aol.com
A wooded heathland course on a gravel base.
18 holes, 5935yds, Par 69, SSS 68, Course record 65.
Club membership 500.
Visitors must telephone & book in advance, restricted play at weekends. **Societies** must phone in advance. **Green Fees** £15 (£20 weekends and bank holidays). **Cards** 💳 💳 🌐 💳 🔵 💳 **Prof** Jeff Godfrey **Course Designer** T Scott/T Morris **Facilities** ⊗ ⓑ 🍴 ♀ 🏌 🛺 ⚘ **Location** 1m S

Continued

Hotel ★★★ 69% Aerodrome Hotel, Purley Way, CROYDON ☎ 020 8710 9000 84 en suite

NEW MALDEN — Map 04 TQ26

Malden Traps Ln KT3 4RS
☎ 020 8942 0654 📠 020 8336 2219
e-mail: maldengc@lwcdial.net
Parkland course with the hazard of the Beverley Brook which affects 4 holes (3rd, 7th, 8th and 12th).
18 holes, 6295yds, Par 71, SSS 70.
Club membership 800.
Visitors restricted weekends and bank holidays. Advisable to telephone. **Societies** must apply in writing. **Green Fees** not confirmed. **Prof** Robert Hunter **Facilities** ⊗ ⓑ 🍴 ♀ 🏌 🛺 🍴 ⚘ **Location** N side of town centre off B283

NORTHWOOD — Map 04 TQ09

Haste Hill The Drive HA6 1HN ☎ 01923 825224
Parkland course with stream running through. Excellent views.

18 holes, 5787yds, Par 68, SSS 68, Course record 63.
Club membership 250.
Visitors advised to book in advance 01923 825224 **Societies** must apply in advance. **Green Fees** £13.50 (£19.50 weekends). **Cards** 💳 💳 💳 💳 💳 💳 **Prof** Cameron Smilie **Facilities** ⊗ ⅢⅢ **Facilities** ⓑ 🍴 ♀ 🏌 🛺 🍴 🛺 ⚘ **Location** 0.5m S off A404

Hotel ★★★ 68% Quality Harrow Hotel, 12-22 Pinner Rd, HARROW ☎ 020 8427 3435 79 en suite 23 annexe en suite

Northwood Rickmansworth Rd HA6 2QW
☎ 01923 821384 📠 01923 840150
e-mail: secretary@northwoodgolf.co.uk
A high quality parkland course in the heart of Middlesex. The course provides a good test of golf to the experienced golfer and can hold many surprises for the unsuspecting. The par 4 10th hole, 'Death or Glory', has wrecked many good cards in the past, while the long par 4 5th hole requires two very good shots to make par.
18 holes, 6535yds, Par 71, SSS 71, Course record 67.
Club membership 650.
Visitors must contact in advance. May not play weekends. **Societies** must apply in writing or by phone. **Green Fees** £50 per day, £36 per round. **Cards** 💳 💳 💳 💳 💳 💳 **Prof** C J Holdsworth **Course Designer** James Braid **Facilities** ⊗ ⅢⅢ ⓑ 🍴 ♀ 🏌 🛺 🍴 ⚘ **Conf** Corporate Hospitality Days available **Location** On main A404

Continued

Hotel ★★★ 68% Quality Harrow Hotel, 12-22 Pinner Rd, HARROW ☎ 020 8427 3435 79 en suite 23 annexe en suite

Sandy Lodge Sandy Lodge Ln HA6 2JD
☎ 01923 825429 ▤ 01923 824319
e-mail: info@sandylodge.co.uk
A links-type, very sandy, heathland course.
18 holes, 6347yds, Par 71, SSS 71, Course record 64.
Club membership 780.
Visitors must contact in advance, may not play at weekends. Handicap certificate required. **Societies** must telephone in advance. **Green Fees** £35 per round. **Cards** ▤▤ ▤▤ ▣ **Prof** Jeff Pinsent **Course Designer** H Vardon **Facilities** ⊗ ⅱ ▥ ▬ ♀ ♨ ▵ ᐃ ⚲ ⚲ { **Conf** Corporate Hospitality Days available **Location** N side of town centre off A4125 close to M1 & M25

Hotel ★★★ 67% The White House, Upton Rd, WATFORD ☎ 01923 237316 57 en suite

ORPINGTON   Map 05 TQ46

Chelsfield Lakes Golf Centre Court Rd BR6 9BX
☎ 01689 896266 ▤ 01689 824577
18 holes, 6077yds, Par 71, SSS 69, Course record 64.
Warren: 9 holes, 1188yds, Par 27.
Course Designer M Sandow **Location** Exit M25 junct 4, on A224 Court Rd
Telephone for further details

Hotel ★★★ 73% Bromley Court Hotel, Bromley Hill, BROMLEY ☎ 020 8461 8600 114 en suite

GRIM'S DYKE GOLF CLUB
Oxhey Lane, Hatch End, Pinner, Middlesex HA5 4AL
Tel: 020 8428 4539   Fax: 020 8421 5494

One of the joys of Grim's Dyke Golf Club is the friendly atmosphere that exists. Only rarely can members turn up to play and not find anyone to accompany them for a game. The picturesque parkland course is only 5600 yards in length, with a par of 69 (SSS 67) but with its tight fairways and tricky greens it is a very good test of golf.
Professional Golf Shop: 020 8428 7484

Cray Valley Sandy Ln, St Paul's Cray BR5 3HY
☎ 01689 837909 & 871490 ▤ 01689 891428
18 hole: 18 holes, 5669yds, Par 70, SSS 67.
9 holes: 9 holes, 2140yds, Par 32.
Location 1m off A20, Critley's Corner junction
Telephone for further details

Hotel ★★★ 73% Bromley Court Hotel, Bromley Hill, BROMLEY ☎ 020 8461 8600 114 en suite

Lullingstone Park Parkgate Rd, Chelsfield BR6 7PX
☎ 01959 533793 & 533794 ▤ 01959 533795
Main Course: 18 holes, 6778yds, Par 72, SSS 72, Course record 71.
9 hole course: 9 holes, 2432yds, Par 33, SSS 31.
Location Leave M25 junct 4 and take Well Hill turn
Telephone for further details

Hotel ★★★ 73% Bromley Court Hotel, Bromley Hill, BROMLEY ☎ 020 8461 8600 114 en suite

Ruxley Park Golf Centre Sandy Ln, St Paul's Cray
BR5 3HY ☎ 01689 871490 ▤ 01689 891428
18 holes, 5703yds, Par 70, SSS 68, Course record 63.
Location 2m NE on A223
Telephone for further details

Hotel ★★★ 73% Bromley Court Hotel, Bromley Hill, BROMLEY ☎ 020 8461 8600 114 en suite

PINNER   Map 04 TQ18

Grims Dyke Oxhey Ln, Hatch End HA5 4AL
☎ 020 8428 4539 ▤ 020 8421 5494
e-mail: grimsdykegolfclub@hotmail.com
Pleasant, undulating parkland course.

18 holes, 5596yds, Par 69, SSS 67, Course record 61.
Club membership 500.
Visitors May not play weekends except as guest of a member. **Societies** Apply in writing or by phone. Deposit required. **Green Fees** £35 per day, £30 per round. **Cards** ▤▤ ▤▤ ▤▤ ▣ ▧ ▨ **Prof** Lee Curling **Course Designer** James Baird **Facilities** ⊗ ▥ ▬ ♀ ▵ ᐃ ⚲ ♨ ⚲ **Conf** fac available Corporate Hospitality Days available **Location** 3m N of Harrow on A4008

Hotel ★★★ 69% Best Western Cumberland Hotel, 1 St Johns Rd, HARROW ☎ 020 8863 4111 31 en suite 53 annexe en suite

Pinner Hill Southview Rd, Pinner Hill HA5 3YA
☎ 020 8866 0963 ▤ 020 8868 4817
e-mail: pinnerhillgc@uk2.net
On the top of Pinner Hill surrounded by rolling parkland and mature woods, this peaceful atmosphere

Continued

will make you feel a million miles from North West London's suburbia. Two nine-hole loops of mature fairways and undulating greens will lift and challenge your game.
18 holes, 6392yds, Par 71, SSS 71.
Club membership 710.
Visitors are required to have handicap certificate on Mon, Tue & Fri. Public days Wed & Thu. Contact in advance. **Societies** Mon, Tue & Fri only, by arrangement. **Green Fees** not confirmed. **Cards** 🔲 🔲 🔲 🔲 **Prof** Mark Grieve **Course Designer** J H Taylor **Facilities** ⊗ ⅢⅡ 🖳 🖳 ♀ 🏖 🍴 🏌 ⚑ 🚶 🏌 **Conf** Corporate Hospitality Days available **Location** 2m NW off A404

Hotel ★★★ 68% Quality Harrow Hotel, 12-22 Pinner Rd, HARROW ☎ 020 8427 3435 79 en suite
23 annexe en suite

PURLEY   Map 05 TQ36

Purley Downs 106 Purley Downs Rd CR2 0RB
☎ 020 8657 8347 🖷 020 8651 5044
e-mail: info@purleydowns.co.uk
Hilly downland course which is a good test for golfers.
18 holes, 6262yds, Par 70, SSS 70, Course record 64.
Club membership 750.
Visitors must contact in advance & play on weekends only with member. **Societies** must contact in advance. **Green Fees** terms on application. **Cards** 🔲 🔲 🔲 🔲 🔲 🔲 🔲 **Prof** Graham Wilson **Course Designer** J Taylor/H S Colt **Facilities** ⊗ 🖳 ♀ 🏖 🍴 ⚑ 🏌 **Location** E side of town centre off A235

Hotel ★★★ 69% Aerodrome Hotel, Purley Way, CROYDON ☎ 020 8710 9000 84 en suite

RICHMOND (UPON THAMES)   Map 04 TQ17

Richmond Sudbrook Park, Petersham TW10 7AS
☎ 020 8940 4351 (office) & 8940 7792 (shop)
🖷 8940 8332/7914
e-mail: hilkka_rgc@lineone.net
A beautiful and historic wooded, parkland course on the edge of Richmond Park, with six par 3 holes. The 4th is often described as the best short hole in the south. Low scores are uncommon because cunningly sited trees call for great accuracy. The clubhouse is one of the most distinguished small Georgian mansions in England.
18 holes, 6100yds, Par 70, SSS 70, Course record 66.
Club membership 650.
Visitors may not play weekends before 3.30pm. **Societies** must apply in writing. **Green Fees** £40/£45. **Cards** 🔲 🔲 🔲 🔲 🔲 **Facilities** ⊗ 🖳 by prior arrangement 🖳 🖳 ♀ 🏖 🍴 ⚑ 🏌 ⚑ 🍴 **Location** 1.5m S off A307

Hotel ★★★ 68% The Richmond Hill Hotel, Richmond Hill, RICHMOND UPON THAMES ☎ 020 8940 2247 138 en suite

Royal Mid-Surrey Old Deer Park TW9 2SB
☎ 020 8940 1894 🖷 020 8939 0150
e-mail: secretary@rmsgc.co.uk
A long playing parkland course. The flat fairways are cleverly bunkered. The 1st hole at 245 yards from the medal tees is a tough par 3 opening hole. The 18th provides an exceptionally good par 4 finish with a huge bunker before the green to catch the not quite perfect long second. The Inner course, while shorter *Continued*

than the Outer, offers a fair challenge to all golfers. Again the 18th offers a strong par 4 finish with bunkers threatening from the tee. A long second to a sloping, well bunkered green will reward the accurate player.
Outer Course: 18 holes, 6343yds, Par 69, SSS 70, Course record 63.
Inner Course: 18 holes, 5544yds, Par 68, SSS 67.
Club membership 1400.
Visitors may not play at weekends. Must contact in advance and bring a handicap certificate. **Societies** must apply in writing. **Green Fees** terms on application. **Cards** 🔲 🔲 🔲 🔲 **Prof** Philip Talbot **Course Designer** J H Taylor **Facilities** ⊗ 🖳 🖳 🖳 ♀ 🏖 🍴 ⚑ 🏌 🚶 🏌 **Conf** fac available Corporate Hospitality Days available **Location** 0.5m N of Richmond upon Thames off A316

Hotel ★★★ 68% The Richmond Hill Hotel, Richmond Hill, RICHMOND UPON THAMES ☎ 020 8940 2247 138 en suite

ROMFORD   Map 05 TQ58

Maylands Golf Club & Country Park
Colchester Rd, Harold Park RM3 0AZ
☎ 01708 346466 🖷 01708 373080
18 holes, 6361yds, Par 71, SSS 70, Course record 65.
Course Designer H S Colt **Location** Junct 28 off M25, 0.5m down A12 towards London, club on right hand side
Telephone for further details

Hotel Ⓤ Holiday Inn Brentwood, Brook St, BRENTWOOD ☎ 0870 400 9012 150 en suite

Risebridge Golf Centre Risebridge Chase, Lower
Bedfords Rd RM1 4DG
☎ 01708 741429 🖷 01708 741429
e-mail: pa.jennings@virgin.net
18 holes, 6000yds, Par 71, SSS 70, Course record 66.
Course Designer Hawtree **Location** Between Colier Row and Harold Hill
Telephone for further details

Hotel Ⓤ Holiday Inn Brentwood, Brook St, BRENTWOOD ☎ 0870 400 9012 150 en suite

Romford Heath Dr, Gidea Park RM2 5QB
☎ 01708 740986 🖷 01708 752157
A many-bunkered parkland course with easy walking. It is said there are as many bunkers as there are days in the year. The ground is quick drying making a good course for winter play when other courses might be too wet.
18 holes, 6410yds, Par 72, SSS 70, Course record 64.
Club membership 693.
Visitors with member only weekends & bank holidays. Must contact professional in advance & have handicap certificate. **Societies** must telephone in advance. **Green Fees** £40 per 36 holes, £30 per 18 holes. **Prof** Chris Goddard **Course Designer** H Colt **Facilities** ⊗ 🖳 🖳 🖳 ♀ 🏖 🍴 **Location** 1m NE on A118

Hotel Ⓤ Holiday Inn Brentwood, Brook St, BRENTWOOD ☎ 0870 400 9012 150 en suite

> **Looking for a driving range? Refer to the listing of driving ranges at the back of this guide.**

RUISLIP   Map 04 TQ08

Ruislip Ickenham Rd HA4 7DQ
☎ 01895 638081 & 638835 ▤ 01895 635780
Municipal parkland course. Many trees.

18 holes, 5700yds, Par 69, SSS 68, Course record 65.
Club membership 300.
Societies must contact in advance. **Green Fees** not
confirmed. **Cards** ▨ ▨ ▨ ▨ ▨ ▨ **Prof** Paul Glozier
Course Designer Sand Herd **Facilities** ⊗ ⊪ ⅃ ☞ ⌁ ▨
▨ ⌁ ⌁ ⌁ ⌁ **Location** 0.5m SW on B466

....
Hotel ★★★ 68% Quality Harrow Hotel, 12-22 Pinner Rd,
HARROW ☎ 020 8427 3435 79 en suite
23 annexe en suite

SIDCUP   Map 05 TQ47

Sidcup 7 Hurst Rd DA15 9AE
☎ 020 8300 2150 ▤ 0208 3002150
e-mail: sidcupgolfclub@tiscali.co.uk
**Easy walking parkland course with natural water
hazards.**
9 holes, 5722yds, Par 68, SSS 68.
Club membership 370.
Visitors contact in advance and may not play weekends or
bank holidays. **Societies** must contact in advance. **Green
Fees** terms on application. **Course Designer** James Braid
Facilities ⊗ ⊪ ⅃ ☞ ⌁ ⌁ ▨ **Location** N side of town
centre off A222

....
Hotel ★★★★ 66% Bexleyheath Marriott Hotel,
1 Broadway, BEXLEYHEATH ☎ 020 8298 1000
142 en suite

SOUTHALL   Map 04 TQ17

West Middlesex Greenford Rd UB1 3EE
☎ 020 8574 3450 ▤ 020 8574 2383
e-mail: westmid.gc@virgin.net
**Gently undulating parkland course founded in 1891,
the oldest private course in Middlesex designed by
James Braid.**
18 holes, 6119yds, Par 69, SSS 69, Course record 64.
Club membership 600.
Visitors must contact in advance and may only play at
weekends after 3pm **Societies** must apply in advance.
Green Fees Mon: £13 per round; Wed: £15; Tue/Thu-Fri:
£24; Sat-Sun £30. **Cards** ▨ ▨ ▨ ▨ ▨ **Prof** T
Talbot **Course Designer** James Braid **Facilities** ⊗ ⊪ ⅃
☞ ⌁ ⌁ ▨ ⌁ **Conf** fac available **Location** W side of
town centre on A4127 off A4020

....
Hotel ★★★ 66% Best Western Master Robert Hotel,
366 Great West Rd, HOUNSLOW ☎ 020 8570 6261
96 annexe en suite

STANMORE   Map 04 TQ19

Stanmore 29 Gordon Av HA7 2RL
☎ 020 8954 2599 ▤ 020 8954 2599
e-mail: secretary@stanmoregolfclub.co.uk
**A fine mix of heathland, parkland and woodland with
many holes entirely secluded. Undulating landscapes
and incredible views.**

18 holes, 5885yds, Par 68, SSS 68, Course record 61.
Club membership 500.
Visitors Contact professional: 020 8954 2599 **Societies**
phone in advance for booking sheet. **Green Fees** Mon &
Fri: £15 ; Tue-Thu: £22, £30 per day weekends after
12.30pm. **Prof** J Reynolds **Course Designer** Dr A
Mackenzie **Facilities** ⊗ ⊪ ⅃ ☞ ⌁ ⌁ ▨ ⌁ **Conf**
Corporate Hospitality Days available **Location** S side of
town centre, between Stanmore & Belmont

....
Hotel ★★★ 68% Quality Harrow Hotel, 12-22 Pinner Rd,
HARROW ☎ 020 8427 3435 79 en suite
23 annexe en suite

SURBITON   Map 04 TQ16

Surbiton Woodstock Ln KT9 1UG
☎ 020 8398 3101 (Sec) ▤ 020 8339 0992
e-mail: surbitongolfclub@hotmail.com
Parkland course with easy walking.
18 holes, 6055yds, Par 70, SSS 69, Course record 63.
Club membership 700.
Visitors must call in advance, handicap certificate
required. With member only at weekends & bank holidays.
No visitors Tue am (Ladies Day). **Societies** Mon & Fri
only. **Green Fees** not confirmed. **Prof** Paul Milton **Course
Designer** Tom Dunn **Facilities** ⊗ ⅃ ☞ ⌁ ⌁ ▨ ⌁ ⌁
Location 2m S off A3, take A309 from Hook junct of A3,
turn left into Woodstock Lane

....
Hotel ⌂ Travel Inn, Leatherhead Rd, CHESSINGTON
☎ 08701 977057 42 en suite

TWICKENHAM   Map 04 TQ17

Strawberry Hill Wellesley Rd, Strawberry Hill
TW2 5SD ☎ 020 8894 0165 ▤ 020 8898 0786
e-mail: shgc@posthost.com
Parkland course with easy walking.
9 holes, 4762yds, Par 64, SSS 63, Course record 59.
Club membership 300.
Visitors must contact in advance, with member only at
weekends. **Societies** must apply in writing. **Green Fees**
£25/£18 per day, £18/£11 per 18 holes, £14/£8 per 9 holes.
Cards ▨ ▨ **Prof** Peter Buchan **Course Designer** J H Taylor
Facilities ⊗ ⊪ ⅃ ☞ ⌁ ⌁ ▨ ⌁ **Location** S side of town
centre off A316

Continued

Hotel ★★★ 68% The Richmond Hill Hotel, Richmond Hill, RICHMOND UPON THAMES ☎ 020 8940 2247 138 en suite

Twickenham Staines Rd TW2 5JD
☎ 0845 2309 111 ▤ 020 8783 9475
Interesting tree lined parkland course with water feature.
Twickenham Golf Centre: 9 holes, 3180yds, Par 36, SSS 69.
Visitors must book in advance for weekends & bank holidays. **Societies** apply in advance **Green Fees** £6.50 per 9 holes(£7.50 weekends). **Cards** 🏧 🏧 🏧 🏧 ▨ **Prof** Suzy Watt **Facilities** ⊗ ⛳ ▯ 🍽 ♀ 🕾 🍸 ♒ **Conf** fac available Corporate Hospitality Days available **Location** 2m W on A305

Hotel ★★★ 68% The Richmond Hill Hotel, Richmond Hill, RICHMOND UPON THAMES ☎ 020 8940 2247 138 en suite

UPMINSTER Map 05 TQ58

Upminster 114 Hall Ln RM14 1AU
☎ 01708 222788 (Secretary) ▤ 01708 222484
e-mail: thesecretary@upminstergolfclub.com
The meandering River Ingrebourne features on several holes of this partly undulating parkland course situated on one side of the river valley. It provides a challenge for golfers of all abilities. The clubhouse is a beautiful Grade II listed building.
18 holes, 6076yds, Par 69, SSS 69, Course record 64. Club membership 1000.
Visitors contact in advance, may not play at weekends. **Societies** telephone initially. **Green Fees** terms on application. **Prof** Steve Cipa **Course Designer** W G Key **Facilities** ⊗ ⛳ ▯ 🍽 ♀ 🗻 🕾 🍸 ♒ ♒ **Location** 2m W from A127 junct with M25

Hotel ⇧ Travel Inn, Mercury Gardens, ROMFORD ☎ 08701 977220 40 en suite

UXBRIDGE Map 04 TQ08

Stockley Park Stockley Park UB11 1AQ
☎ 020 8813 5700 ▤ 020 8813 5655
e-mail: c.kennedy@stockleyparkgolf.com
Hilly and challenging parkland championship course designed by Trent Jones in 1993 and situated within two miles of Heathrow Airport.
18 holes, 6548yds, Par 72, SSS 71.
Visitors 6 day in advance reservation facility. **Societies** please telephone for details. **Green Fees** not confirmed. **Cards** 🏧 🏧 🏧 🏧 ▨ **Prof** Alex Knox, Martin Hulse **Course Designer** Robert Trent Jones Snr **Facilities** ⊗ ⛳ 🍽 ♀ 🕾 🍸 ♒ ♒ **Conf** Corporate Hospitality Days available **Location** 1m N of junct4 M4, off A408

Hotel ★★★★ 76% Crowne Plaza London - Heathrow, Stockley Rd, WEST DRAYTON ☎ 0870 400 9140 458 en suite

If you have a comment or suggestion concerning the AA Golf Course Guide 2005, you can e-mail us at

lifestyleguides@theAA.com

Uxbridge The Drive, Harefield Place UB10 8AQ
☎ 01895 237287 ▤ 01895 813539
e-mail: higolf@btinternet.com

18 holes, 5750yds, Par 68, SSS 68, Course record 66.
Location 2m N off B467
Telephone for further details

Hotel ★★★★ 76% Crowne Plaza London - Heathrow, Stockley Rd, WEST DRAYTON ☎ 0870 400 9140 458 en suite

WEMBLEY Map 04 TQ18

Sudbury Bridgewater Rd HA0 1AL
☎ 020 8902 3713 ▤ 020 8903 2966
e-mail: enquiries@sudburygolfclubltd.co.uk
Undulating parkland course very near centre of London.

18 holes, 6282yds, Par 69, SSS 70. Club membership 650.
Visitors must have handicap certificate. With member only at weekends. **Societies** must apply in writing. **Green Fees** £25 per 18 holes. **Cards** 🏧 🏧 ▨ **Prof** Neil Jordan **Course Designer** Colt **Facilities** ⊗ ⛳ ▯ 🍽 ♀ 🗻 🕾 ♒ ♒ **Conf** fac available **Location** SW side of town centre on A4090

Hotel ★★★ 67% The Bridge Hotel, Western Av, GREENFORD ☎ 020 8566 6246 68 en suite

WEST DRAYTON Map 04 TQ07

Heathpark Stockley Rd UB7 9NA
☎ 01895 444232 ▤ 01895 444232
9 holes, 2032yds, Par 64, SSS 60, Course record 64.
Course Designer Neal Coles **Location** 1m SE off A408 via junct 4 on M4
Telephone for further details

Hotel ★★★★ 76% Crowne Plaza London - Heathrow, Stockley Rd, WEST DRAYTON ☎ 0870 400 9140 458 en suite

WOODFORD GREEN
Map 05 TQ49

Woodford Sunset Av IG8 0ST
☎ 020 8504 3330 & 8504 0553 📠 020 8559 0504
e-mail: office@woodfordgolfclub.fsnet.co.uk
Forest land course on the edge of Epping Forest. Views over the Lea Valley to the London skyline.
9 holes, 5806yds, Par 70, SSS 68, Course record 66.
Club membership 350.
Visitors advisable to contact in advance. May not play Sat or Sun morning, must wear major item of red. **Societies** telephone for details. **Green Fees** £15 per 18 holes; £9 per 9 holes. **Prof** Richard Layton **Course Designer** Tom Dunn **Facilities** ⊗ ⋙ ♀ ⅃ 📁 **Conf** Corporate Hospitality Days available **Location** NW side of town centre off A104

Hotel ★★★ 59% The County Hotel, 30 Oak Hill, WOODFORD GREEN ☎ 0870 609 6156 99 en suite

GREATER MANCHESTER

ALTRINCHAM
Map 07 SJ78

Altrincham Stockport Rd WA15 7LP
☎ 0161 928 0761 📠 0161 928 8542
e-mail: scott-partington@hotmail.com
Municipal parkland course with easy walking, water on many holes, rolling contours and many trees. Driving range in grounds.
18 holes, 6162yds, Par 71, SSS 69.
Club membership 350.
Visitors must book in advance via course office. **Societies** by prior arrangement. **Green Fees** not confirmed. **Cards** 🟫 🟥 🟦 **Prof** Scott Partington **Facilities** ⊗ ⋙ ♀ ⅃ 📁 🛈 ⚐ ⚑ **Location** 0.75 E of Altrincham on A560

Hotel ★★★ 67% Cresta Court Hotel, Church St, ALTRINCHAM ☎ 0161 927 7272 136 en suite

Dunham Forest Oldfield Ln WA14 4TY
☎ 0161 928 2605 📠 0161 929 8975
e-mail: email@dunhamforestgolfclub.com
Attractive parkland course cut through magnificent beech woods.
18 holes, 6636yds, Par 72, SSS 72.
Club membership 680.
Visitors by prior arrangement. May not play weekends & bank holidays. **Societies** apply in writing or telephone in advance. **Green Fees** not confirmed. **Cards** 🟫 🟥 🟦 **Prof** Ian Wrigley **Course Designer** Dave Thomas **Facilities** ⊗ ⋙ by prior arrangement ⅃ ♀ ⅃ 📁 ⚐ ⚑ ⚓ ⅃ **Leisure** hard tennis courts. **Location** 1.5m W off A56

Hotel ★★★ 66% Quality Hotel Altrincham, Langham Rd, Bowdon, ALTRINCHAM ☎ 0161 928 7121 91 en suite

Ringway Hale Mount, Hale Barns WA15 8SW
☎ 0161 980 8432 (pro) & 0161 980 2630
📠 0160 980 4414
e-mail: enquiries@ringwaygolfclub.co.uk
Parkland course, with interesting natural hazards. Easy walking, good views.
18 holes, 6482yds, Par 71, SSS 71, Course record 67.
Club membership 700.
Visitors must have handicap certificate and contact in advance, may not play before 9.30am or between 1-2pm, play restricted Tue, Fri & Sat. **Societies** *Continued*

telephone for availability **Green Fees** £35 (£45 weekends).
Cards 🟫 🟥 **Prof** Nick Ryan **Course Designer** Colt **Facilities** ⊗ ⋙ ⅃ ♀ ⅃ 📁 ⚐ ⚑ ⅃ **Conf** Corporate Hospitality Days available **Location** M56 junct 6, take A538 for 1m, signposted Hale & Altrincham, turn right into Shay Lane

Hotel ★★★ 67% Cresta Court Hotel, Church St, ALTRINCHAM ☎ 0161 927 7272 136 en suite

ASHTON-IN-MAKERFIELD
Map 07 SJ59

Ashton-in-Makerfield Garswood Park, Liverpool Rd WN4 0YT ☎ 01942 719330 📠 01942 719330
Well-wooded parkland course. Easy walking.
18 holes, 6250yds, Par 70, SSS 70, Course record 63.
Club membership 800.
Visitors with member only weekends & bank holidays. No visitors Wed. **Societies** apply in writing. **Green Fees** not confirmed. **Prof** Peter Allan **Facilities** ⊗ ⋙ ⅃ ♀ ⅃ 📁 ⚐ ⅃ **Location** 0.5m W of M6 (junc 24) on A58

Hotel 🆄 Holiday Inn Haydock, Lodge Ln, HAYDOCK ☎ 0870 400 9039 138 en suite

ASHTON-UNDER-LYNE
Map 07 SJ99

Ashton-under-Lyne Gorsey Way, Higher Hurst OL6 9HT ☎ 0161 330 1537 📠 0161 330 6673
18 holes, 5754yds, Par 69, SSS 68, Course record 64.
Location N off B6194
Telephone for further details

Hotel ★★★★ 66% Menzies Avant Hotel, Windsor Rd, Manchester St, OLDHAM ☎ 0161 627 5500 103 en suite

Dukinfield Lyne Edge, Yew Tree Ln SK16 5DF
☎ 0161 338 2340 📠 0161 303 0205
e-mail: dgc@telinco.co.uk
Recently extended, tricky hillside course with several challenging par 3s and a very long par 5.
18 holes, 5338yds, Par 67, SSS 66.
Club membership 400.
Visitors may not play on Wed afternoons & must play with member at weekends, advisable to contact in advance. Visitors must play from yellow blocks. **Societies** apply in writing or telephone. **Green Fees** £20 per day. **Prof** Andrew Jarrett **Facilities** ⊗ ⋙ ⅃ ♀ ⅃ 📁 ⅃ **Conf** Corporate Hospitality Days available **Location** S off B6175

Hotel 🏠 Premier Lodge (Manchester East), Stockport Rd, Mottram, HYDE ☎ 0870 9906334 83 en suite

BOLTON
Map 07 SD70

Bolton Lostock Park, Chorley New Rd BL6 4AJ
☎ 01204 843067 & 843278 📠 01204 843067
e-mail: boltongolf@lostockpark.fsbusiness.co.uk
This well maintained heathland course is always a pleasure to visit. The 12th hole should be treated with respect and so too should the final four holes which have ruined many a card.
18 holes, 6237yds, Par 70, SSS 70, Course record 64.
Club membership 612.
Visitors not able to play Tue before 4pm or on competition days or before 10am and between 12-2pm. **Societies** write or telephone in advance, not accepted Tue, Sat or Sun.
Green Fees not confirmed. **Prof** R Longworth **Facilities** ⊗ ⋙ ⅃ ♀ ⅃ 📁 ⅃ **Conf** fac available Corporate
Continued

Hospitality Days available **Location** 3m W of Bolton, on A673

....

Hotel ⛿ Travel Inn, 991 Chorley New Rd, Horwich, BOLTON ☎ 08701 977282 40 en suite

---

Breightmet Red Bridge, Ainsworth BL2 5PA
☎ 01204 527381
9 holes, 6416yds, Par 72, SSS 71, Course record 68.
Location E side of town centre off A58
Telephone for further details

....

Hotel ⛿ Express by Holiday Inn Bolton, Arena Approach 3, Horwich, BOLTON ☎ 01204 469111 74 en suite

Deane Broadford Rd, Deane BL3 4NS
☎ 01204 61944 (professional) 651808(secretary)
18 holes, 5652yds, Par 68, SSS 67, Course record 64.
Location 1m from exit 5 on M61 towards Bolton
Telephone for further details

....

Hotel ⛿ Travel Inn, 991 Chorley New Rd, Horwich, BOLTON ☎ 08701 977282 40 en suite

Dunscar Longworth Ln, Bromley Cross BL7 9QY
☎ 01204 303321 📠 01204 303321
e-mail: secretary@dunscargolfclub.fsnet.co.uk
18 holes, 6085yds, Par 71, SSS 69, Course record 63.
Location 2m N off A666
Telephone for further details

....

Hotel ⛿ Travelodge Bolton West, Bolton West Service Area, Horwich, BOLTON ☎ 08700 850 950 32 en suite

Great Lever & Farnworth Plodder Ln, Farnworth BL4 0LQ ☎ 01204 656137 📠 01204 656137
18 holes, 6064yds, Par 70, SSS 69, Course record 67.
Location 1m junct 4 M61
Telephone for further details

....

Hotel ⛿ Express by Holiday Inn Bolton, Arena Approach 3, Horwich, BOLTON ☎ 01204 469111 74 en suite

Harwood Roading Brook Rd, Harwood BL2 4JD
☎ 01204 522878 & 524233 📠 01204 524233
e-mail: secretary@harwoodgolfclub.co.uk
Mainly flat parkland course.
18 holes, 5783yds, Par 68, SSS 65.
Club membership 590.
Visitors must be members of a golf club and hold a current handicap certificate. May not play at weekends except with member. **Societies** contact the Secretary by telephone or in writing. **Green Fees** not confirmed. **Prof** P Slater **Course Designer** G Shuttleworth **Facilities** ⊗ �🍴 🏌 ☕ 🏑 ⛳ 🏠
Location 2.5m NE off B6196

....

Hotel ⛿ Travel Inn, 991 Chorley New Rd, Horwich, BOLTON ☎ 08701 977282 40 en suite

Old Links Chorley Old Rd, Montserrat BL1 5SU
☎ 01204 842307 📠 01204 842307 ext 25
e-mail: mail@boltonoldlinks.co.uk
Championship moorland course.
18 holes, 6406yds, Par 72, SSS 72.
Club membership 600.
Visitors must contact in advance and may only play weekends with member. **Societies** apply by letter or telephone. **Green Fees** not confirmed. **Prof** Paul Horridge

Course Designer Dr Alistair MacKenzie **Facilities** ⊗ �🍴 🏌 ☕ 🏑 🏠 🏑 ⛳ **Conf** fac available **Location** NW of town centre on B6226

....

Hotel ⛿ Travelodge Bolton West, Bolton West Service Area, Horwich, BOLTON ☎ 08700 850 950 32 en suite

Regent Park Links Rd, Chorley New Rd BL2 9XX
☎ 01204 844170
18 holes, 6130yds, Par 70, SSS 69, Course record 67.
Location 3.5m W off A673
Telephone for further details

....

Hotel ⛿ Travelodge Bolton West, Bolton West Service Area, Horwich, BOLTON ☎ 08700 850 950 32 en suite

Turton Wood End Farm, Chapeltown Rd, Bromley Cross BL7 9QH ☎ 01204 852235
Moorland course with panoramic views. A wide variety of holes which challenge any golfer's technique.
18 holes, 6124yds, Par 70, SSS 69, Course record 68.
Club membership 450.
Visitors avoid 10.30-12.30; 1.30-3.00pm on Ladies Day (Wed). Sat tee available after last competition. Sun after 11.00am. **Societies** must contact in writing. **Green Fees** not confirmed. **Course Designer** Alex Herd **Facilities** ⊗ 🏌 ☕ 🏑 **Location** 3m N off A666, follow signs for 'Last Drop Village'

....

Hotel ⛿ Express by Holiday Inn Bolton, Arena Approach 3, Horwich, BOLTON ☎ 01204 469111 74 en suite

BRAMHALL   Map 07 SJ88

Bramall Park 20 Manor Rd SK7 3LY
☎ 0161 485 7101 📠 0161 485 7101
e-mail: secbpgc@hotmail.com
Well-wooded parkland course with splendid views of the Pennines.
18 holes, 6214yds, Par 70, SSS 70, Course record 63.
Club membership 829.
Visitors must contact resident professional or club secretary. **Societies** apply in writing/telephone in advance. **Green Fees** £30 per day/round (£40 weekends & bank holidays). **Prof** M Proffitt **Course Designer** James Braid **Facilities** ⊗ 🍴 🏌 ☕ 🏑 ⛳ **Conf** Corporate Hospitality Days available **Location** NW side of town centre off B5149

....

Hotel ★★★ 61% The County Hotel, Bramhall Ln South, BRAMHALL ☎ 0870 609 6148 65 en suite

Bramhall Ladythorn Rd SK7 2EY
☎ 0161 439 6092 📠 0161 439 0264
e-mail: office@bramhallgolfclub.com
Undulating parkland course, easy walking.
18 holes, 6340yds, Par 70, SSS 70.
Club membership 700.
Visitors must contact in advance. **Societies** apply in writing. **Green Fees** terms on application. **Prof** Richard Green **Facilities** ⊗ 🍴 by prior arrangement 🏌 ☕ 🏑 🏠 ⚑ ⛳ **Conf** Corporate Hospitality Days available **Location** E side of town centre off A5102

....

Hotel ★★★ 61% The County Hotel, Bramhall Ln South, BRAMHALL ☎ 0870 609 6148 65 en suite

---

Booking a tee time is always advisable.

Continued

BURY
Map 07 SD81

Bury Unsworth Hall, Blackford Bridge, Manchester Rd
BL9 9TJ ☎ 0161 766 4897 📄 0161 796 3480
**Moorland course, difficult in part. Tight and good test
of golf.**
18 holes, 5961yds, Par 69, SSS 69, Course record 64.
Club membership 650.
Visitors may not normally play at weekends. Must contact
in advance. **Societies** telephone 0161 766 4897. **Green
Fees** not confirmed. **Cards** 💳 **Course Designer**
Mackenzie **Facilities** ⛏ 🏠 🏌 **Conf** fac available
Corporate Hospitality Days available **Location** 2m S on
A56

. . . .

Hotel ★★★ 66% Bolholt Country Park Hotel, Walshaw
Rd, BURY ☎ 0161 762 4000 65 en suite

Lowes Park Hilltop, Lowes Rd BL9 6SU
☎ 0161 764 1231 📄 0161 763 9503
**Moorland course, with easy walking. Exposed outlook
with good views.**
9 holes, 6009yds, Par 70, SSS 69, Course record 65.
Club membership 350.
Visitors may not play Wed & Sat, by appointment Sun.
Must contact in advance. **Societies** apply in writing. **Green
Fees** not confirmed. **Facilities** ⊗ ⏶ ⛏ 🏆 ♀ ⛳ **Conf** fac
available **Location** N side of town centre off A56

. . . .

Hotel ★★★ 66% Bolholt Country Park Hotel, Walshaw
Rd, BURY ☎ 0161 762 4000 65 en suite

Walmersley Garretts Close, Walmersley BL9 6TE
☎ 0161 764 1429 & 0161 764 7770 📄 0161 764 7770
**Moorland hillside course, with wide fairways, large
greens and extensive views. Testing holes: 2nd (484 yds)
par 5; 5th par 4 with severe dog leg and various
hazards.**
18 holes, 5341yds, Par 69, SSS 66.
Club membership 475.
Visitors welcome by arrangement with Secretary. May
only play with member at weekend, **Societies** must apply
in writing. **Green Fees** not confirmed. **Prof** P Thorpe
Course Designer S Marnoch **Facilities** ⊗ ⏶ ⛏ 🏆 ♀ ⛏
🏠 🏌 **Location** 2m N off A56

. . . .

Hotel ★★★ 66% Bolholt Country Park Hotel, Walshaw
Rd, BURY ☎ 0161 762 4000 65 en suite

CHEADLE
Map 07 SJ88

Cheadle Cheadle Rd SK8 1HW ☎ 0161 491 4452
e-mail: cheadlegolfclub@msn.com
**Parkland course with hazards on every hole, from sand
bunkers and copses to a stream across six of the
fairways.**
9 holes, 5006yds, Par 64, SSS 65.
Club membership 425.
Visitors may not play Tue & Sat, & restricted Sun. Must
contact in advance and have a handicap certificate and be
member of a bona-fide golf club. **Societies** apply in writing
to secretary **Green Fees** £25 (£28 weekends). **Prof** S
Booth **Course Designer** T Renouf **Facilities** ⊗ ⏶ ⛏ 🏆 ♀
⛏ 🏠 🏌 **Location** S side of village off A5149

. . . .

Hotel ★★ 69% The Wycliffe Hotel, 74 Edgeley Rd,
Edgeley, STOCKPORT ☎ 0161 477 5395 18 en suite

DENTON
Map 07 SJ99

Denton Manchester Rd M34 2GG
☎ 0161 336 3218 📄 0161 336 4751
**Easy, flat parkland course with brook running through.
Notable hole is one called 'Death and Glory'.**
18 holes, 6541yds, Par 72, SSS 71, Course record 66.
Club membership 740.
Visitors must contact in advance & may not play summer
weekends. **Societies** apply in advance. **Green Fees** terms
on application. **Prof** M Hollingworth **Course Designer** R
McCauley **Facilities** ⊗ ⏶ ⛏ 🏆 ♀ ⛏ 🏠 🏌 **Location** 1.5m
W on A57, M60 junc 24

. . . .

Hotel ★★★ 65% Old Rectory Hotel, Meadow Ln,
Haughton Green, Denton, MANCHESTER ☎ 0161 336
7516 30 en suite 6 annexe en suite

FAILSWORTH
Map 07 SD80

Brookdale Medlock Rd M35 9WQ
☎ 0161 681 2655 📄 0161 688 6872
e-mail: info@brookdalegolfclub.co.uk
**Challenging parkland course in the Medlock valley
with great Pennine views.**
18 holes, 5841yds, Par 68, SSS 68, Course record 64.
Club membership 700.
Visitors advisable to contact in advance. **Societies** must
contact in advance. **Green Fees** terms on application. **Prof**
Tony Cuppello **Facilities** ⊗ ⏶ 🏆 ♀ ⛏ 🏌 🍴 ✂ 🏌
Location M60/A62, exit for Oldham. and proceed towards
Manchester. Turn left at Nat West bank, follow road to
end, turn left and immediately right. Turn right at mini
rdbt. Course 1/2 mile on left.

. . . .

Hotel ★★★★ 66% Menzies Avant Hotel, Windsor Rd,
Manchester St, OLDHAM ☎ 0161 627 5500 103 en suite

FLIXTON
Map 07 SJ79

William Wroe Municipal Pennybridge Ln, Flixton
Rd M41 5DX ☎ 0161 748 8680
Parkland course, with easy walking.
18 holes, 4395yds, Par 64, SSS 65.
Visitors must book in advance. **Societies** contact for
details. **Green Fees** not confirmed. **Cards** 💳 🏧 💳 🏧
📱 **Prof** Scott Partington **Facilities** 🏆 ♀ ⛏ 🏠 🏌
Location E side of village off B5158, 3m from Manchester
city centre

. . . .

Hotel ⇪ Travel Inn Manchester South, Carrington Ln,
Ashton-Upon-Mersey, SALE ☎ 08701 977179 40 en suite

GATLEY
Map 07 SJ88

Gatley Waterfall Farm, Styal Rd, Heald Green
SK8 3TW ☎ 0161 437 2091
e-mail: enquiries@gatleygolfclub.com
Parkland course. Moderately testing.
9 holes, 5934yds, Par 68, SSS 68, Course record 67.
Club membership 400.
Visitors may not play Tue & Sat. Handicap certificate
required. **Societies** apply in writing or telephone pro shop.
Green Fees £20 per 18 holes. **Cards** 🏧 💳 🏧 💳 🏧
Prof James Matterson **Facilities** ⊗ ⏶ ⛏ 🏆 ♀ ⛏ 🏠 🏌
Conf Corporate Hospitality Days available **Location** S
side of village off B5166

. . . .

Hotel ★★★ 66% Belfry House Hotel, Stanley Rd,
HANDFORTH ☎ 0161 437 0511 81 en suite

HALE
Map 07 SJ78

Hale Rappax Rd WA15 0NU ☎ 0161 980 4225
9 holes, 5780yds, Par 70, SSS 68, Course record 65.
Location Off Bankhall Lane close to Altrincham Priory Hospital
Telephone for further details

Hotel ★★★ 66% Quality Hotel Altrincham, Langham Rd, Bowdon, ALTRINCHAM ☎ 0161 928 7121 91 en suite

HAZEL GROVE
Map 07 SJ98

Hazel Grove Buxton Rd SK7 6LU
☎ 0161 483 3978
Testing parkland course with tricky greens and water hazards coming into play on several holes. Year round play on the greens.
18 holes, 6310yds, Par 71, SSS 70, Course record 62.
Club membership 600.
Visitors must contact in advance tel: 0161 483 7272.
Societies must apply in writing, Mon Thu & Fri. **Green Fees** terms on application. **Prof** J Hopley **Course Designer** McKenzie **Facilities** ⊗ ⅷ ⤵ ⤴ ♥ ♀ ♣ 🏠 ⛳ ♂ **Conf** fac available Corporate Hospitality Days available **Location** 1m E off A6

Hotel ★★★ 61% The County Hotel, Bramhall Ln South, BRAMHALL ☎ 0870 609 6148 65 en suite

HINDLEY
Map 07 SD60

Hindley Hall Hall Ln WN2 2SQ
☎ 01942 255131 📠 01942 253871
18 holes, 5913yds, Par 69, SSS 68, Course record 64.
Location 1m N off A58, 3 miles from M61 junct 6
Telephone for further details

Hotel ★★★ 66% Quality Hotel Wigan, Riverway, WIGAN ☎ 01942 826888 88 en suite

HYDE
Map 07 SJ99

Werneth Low Werneth Low Rd, Gee Cross SK14 3AF
☎ 0161 368 2503 336 9496(secretary) 📠 0161 320 0053
e-mail: david-kmh@btconnect.com
Hard walking but good views from this undulating moorland course. Exposed to wind with small greens. A good test of golfing skill.
11 holes, 6113yds, Par 70, SSS 70, Course record 66.
Club membership 375.
Visitors may not play Tue mornings, Thu afternoons or Sun and by prior arrangement on Sat. **Societies** must contact at least 14 days in advance. **Green Fees** terms on application. **Cards** 🌐 💳 📇 💷 **Prof** Tony Bacchus **Facilities** ⊗ ⅷ ⤵ ♥ ♀ ♣ 🏠 🚜 ♂ **Conf** Corporate Hospitality Days available **Location** 2m S of town centre

Hotel ★★ 78% Wind in the Willows Hotel, Derbyshire Level, GLOSSOP ☎ 01457 868001 12 en suite

KEARSLEY
Map 07 SD70

Manor Moss Ln BL4 8SF
☎ 01204 701027 📠 01204 796914
Parkland course with water features. Tree-lined fairways including evergreen and deciduous trees. Suitable for players of all levels.
18 holes, 5010yds, Par 66, SSS 64, Course record 65.
Club membership 500.

Continued

Visitors book in advance. Must observe dress code.
Societies contact in advance for details. **Green Fees** not confirmed. **Cards** 🌐 💳 **Course Designer** Jeff Yates **Facilities** ⊗ ⅷ ⤵ ♥ ♀ ♣ 🏠 ⛳ ♂ **Leisure** fishing, 5 aside football pitches. **Conf** fac available Corporate Hospitality Days available **Location** Off A666, Manchester Rd

Hotel ★★★ 63% Novotel Manchester West, Worsley Brow, WORSLEY ☎ 0161 799 3535 119 en suite

LITTLEBOROUGH
Map 07 SD91

Whittaker Whittaker Ln OL15 0LH ☎ 01706 378310
Moorland 9-hole course with outstanding views of Hollingworth Lake Countryside Park and the Pennine Hills.
9 holes, 5632yds, Par 68, SSS 67, Course record 61.
Club membership 240.
Visitors welcome except for Tue pm and Sun. **Societies** apply to Secretary. **Green Fees** £14 per 18 holes (£18 weekend and bank holidays). Reduced winter rates.
Facilities ♀ ♣ **Location** 1.5m out of Littleborough off A58

Hotel ★★★★ 62% Norton Grange Hotel, Manchester Rd, Castleton, ROCHDALE ☎ 01706 630788 51 en suite

MANCHESTER
Map 07 SJ89

Blackley Victoria Ave East, Blackley M9 7HW
☎ 0161 643 2980 & 654 7770 📠 0161 653 8300
Parkland course crossed by a footpath. The course has recently been redesigned giving greater challenge and interest including water features.
18 holes, 6237yds, Par 70, SSS 70.
Club membership 800.
Visitors with member only Thu, weekends and bank holidays. **Societies** apply in advance. **Green Fees** not confirmed. **Prof** Craig Gould **Facilities** ⊗ ⅷ ⤵ ♥ ♀ ♣ 🏠 🐾 🚜 ♂ ♩ **Conf** Corporate Hospitality Days available **Location** 4m N of city centre, on Rochdale Rd

Hotel ★★★ 77% Malmaison, Piccadilly, MANCHESTER ☎ 0161 278 1000 167 en suite

Chorlton-cum-Hardy Barlow Hall, Barlow Hall Rd, Chorlton-cum-Hardy M21 7JJ
☎ 0161 881 5830 📠 0161 881 4532
e-mail: chorltongolf@hotmail.com
Meadowland course with trees, stream and several ditches.

18 holes, 5980yds, Par 70, SSS 69, Course record 61.
Club membership 780.
Visitors handicap certificate required. **Societies** on Thu & Fri only by prior booking. **Green Fees** not confirmed.

Continued

Prof David Valentine **Facilities** **Conf** Corporate Hospitality Days available **Location** 4m S of Manchester A5103/A5145

Hotel ★★★ 68% Willow Bank Hotel, 340-342 Wilmslow Rd, Fallowfield, MANCHESTER ☎ 0161 224 0461 117 en suite

Davyhulme Park Gleneagles Rd, Davyhulme M41 8SA ☎ 0161 748 2260 📠 0161 747 4067
e-mail: davyhulmeparkgolfclub@email.com
Parkland course.
18 holes, 6237yds, Par 72, SSS 70, Course record 64.
Club membership 700.
Visitors may play Mon, Tue & Thu. **Societies** telephone in advance. **Green Fees** not confirmed. **Prof** Dean Butler **Facilities** **Leisure** snooker. **Conf** Corporate Hospitality Days available **Location** Adj to Trafford General Hospital

Hotel Travel Inn Manchester South, Carrington Ln, Ashton-Upon-Mersey, SALE ☎ 08701 977179 40 en suite

Didsbury Ford Ln, Northenden M22 4NQ
☎ 0161 998 9278 📠 0161 902 3060
e-mail: golf@didsburygolfclub.com
Parkland course.
18 holes, 6273yds, Par 70, SSS 70, Course record 60.
Club membership 750.
Visitors advised to check dates/times with manager or professional. **Societies** Thu & Fri, must contact in advance. **Green Fees** not confirmed. **Cards** **Prof** Peter Barber **Facilities** **Conf** fac available Corporate Hospitality Days available **Location** 6m S of city centre off A5145

Hotel Travelodge Manchester South, Kingsway, DIDSBURY ☎ 08700 850 950 62 en suite

Fairfield "Boothdale", Booth Rd, Audenshaw M34 5QA ☎ 0161 301 4528 📠 0161 301 4254
e-mail: secretary@fairfieldgolf.co.uk
Parkland course set around a reservoir. Course demands particularly accurate placing of shots.
18 holes, 4956yds, Par 68, SSS 66, Course record 63.
Club membership 450.
Visitors may not play mornings at weekends & may be restricted on Wed & Thu. **Societies** prior booking through Secretary. **Green Fees** terms on application. **Prof** Stephen Pownell **Facilities** **Location** 5m E of Manchester, off A635

Hotel ★★★ 65% Old Rectory Hotel, Meadow Ln, Haughton Green, Denton, MANCHESTER ☎ 0161 336 7516 30 en suite 6 annexe en suite

Marriott Worsley Park Hotel & Country Club Worsley Park, Worsley M28 2QT
☎ 0161 975 2043 📠 0161 975 2058
Set in 200 acres of parkland with a range of tee positions, eight lakes and 70 strategically placed bunkers and providing an exciting challenge to golfers of all abilities, very often requiring brains rather than brawn to make a successful score.
Marriott Worsley Park Hotel & Country Club: 18 holes, 6611yds, Par 71, SSS 72, Course record 61.
Club membership 400.
Visitors must have a handicap certificate. Must contact in advance. **Societies** weekdays only. Telephone in advance.

Continued

Green Fees terms on application. **Cards** **Prof** David Screeton **Course Designer** Ross McMurray **Facilities** **Leisure** heated indoor swimming pool, sauna, solarium, gymnasium, Short game area. **Conf** fac available **Location** M60 junct 13, follow A585 for 0.5m, course on left

Hotel ★★★★ 69% Marriott Worsley Park Hotel & Country Club, Worsley Park, Worsley, MANCHESTER ☎ 0161 975 2000 158 en suite

Northenden Palatine Rd, Northenden M22 4FR
☎ 0161 998 4738 📠 0161 998 5592

18 holes, 6503yds, Par 72, SSS 71, Course record 64.
Course Designer Renouf **Location** 6.5m S of city centre on B1567 off A5103
Telephone for further details

Hotel Travelodge Manchester South, Kingsway, DIDSBURY ☎ 08700 850 950 62 en suite

Withington 243 Palatine Rd, West Didsbury M20 2UE
☎ 0161 445 9544 📠 0161 445 5210
18 holes, 6410yds, Par 71, SSS 71.
Location 4m SW of city centre off B5167
Telephone for further details

Hotel Travelodge Manchester South, Kingsway, DIDSBURY ☎ 08700 850 950 62 en suite

Worsley Stableford Av, Worsley M30 8AP
☎ 0161 789 4202 📠 0161 789 3200
18 holes, 6252yds, Par 71, SSS 70, Course record 65.
Course Designer James Braid **Location** 6.5m NW of city centre off A572
Telephone for further details

Hotel ★★★ 63% Novotel Manchester West, Worsley Brow, WORSLEY ☎ 0161 799 3535 119 en suite

MELLOR Map 07 SJ98

Mellor & Townscliffe Gibb Ln, Tarden SK6 5NA
☎ 0161 427 2208 (secretary)
Scenic parkland and moorland course, undulating with some hard walking. Good views. Testing 200yd 9th hole, par 3.
18 holes, 5925yds, Par 70, SSS 69.
Club membership 650.
Visitors with member only weekends & bank holidays. **Societies** apply by letter or telephone. **Green Fees** £22 per day (£30 weekends and bank holidays). **Prof** Gary R Broadley **Facilities** **Location** 7m SE of Stockport off A626

MIDDLETON   Map 07 SD80

Manchester Hopwood Cottage, Rochdale Rd
M24 6QP ☎ 0161 643 3202 ▤ 0161 643 9174
e-mail: mgc@zen.co.uk
**Moorland golf of unique character over a spaciously
laid out course with generous fairways sweeping along
to large greens. A wide variety of holes will challenge
the golfer's technique, particularly the testing last three
holes.**
18 holes, 6519yds, Par 72, SSS 72, Course record 63.
Club membership 650.
Visitors must contact in advance, limited play weekends
and Wed. **Societies** telephone in advance. **Green Fees** £35
per day, £25 per round (£45 per round weekends and bank
holidays). **Cards** ▦ ▦ ▢ **Prof** Brian Connor **Course
Designer** Shapland Colt **Facilities** ⊗ ⅏ ⅃ ⬤ ♀ ♠ ⛳ ♦
⬥ ♂ 𝄞 **Leisure** snooker. **Conf** fac available Corporate
Hospitality Days available **Location** 2.5m N off A664.
M62 junct 20
....
Hotel ★★★★ 62% Norton Grange Hotel, Manchester Rd,
Castleton, ROCHDALE ☎ 01706 630788 51 en suite

New North Manchester Rhodes House,
Manchester Old Rd M24 4PE
☎ 0161 643 9033 ▤ 0161 643 7775
e-mail: secretary@nmgc.co.uk
**A delightful moorland/parkland course with several
water features. Challenging but fair for the
accomplished golfer.**
18 holes, 6527yds, Par 72, SSS 72, Course record 66.
Club membership 640.
Visitors contact Pro Shop on 0161 643 7094 for
availability. May not play Saturdays. **Societies** telephone in
advance. **Green Fees** £30 per day, £28 per round (£35
Sun). **Prof** Jason Peel **Course Designer** J Braid **Facilities**
⊗ ⅏ ⅃ ⬤ ♀ ♠ 𝄞 **Leisure** 2 full size snooker tables.
Location W side of town centre off A576
....
Hotel ★★★★ 66% Menzies Avant Hotel, Windsor Rd,
Manchester St, OLDHAM ☎ 0161 627 5500 103 en suite

MILNROW   Map 07 SD91

Tunshill Kiln Ln OL16 3TS ☎ 01706 342095
**Testing moorland course with two demanding par 5s
and out of bounds features on 8 of the 9 holes.**
9 holes, 5743yds, Par 70, SSS 68, Course record 64.
Club membership 300.
Visitors must contact in advance, not weekends unless
with member and arranged in advance. **Societies** apply in
writing. **Green Fees** £12 weekdays only. **Facilities** ⊗ ⅏
⅃ ⬤ by prior arrangement ♀ ♠ **Location** 1m NE M62
exit junct 21 off B6225
....
Hotel ★★★★ 62% Norton Grange Hotel, Manchester Rd,
Castleton, ROCHDALE ☎ 01706 630788 51 en suite

OLDHAM   Map 07 SD90

Crompton & Royton Highbarn, Royton OL2 6RW
☎ 0161 624 0986 ▤ 0161 652 4711
e-mail: secretary@cromptonandroytongolfclub.co.uk
Undulating moorland course.
18 holes, 6214yds, Par 70, SSS 70, Course record 62.
Club membership 700.

Continued

Visitors must contact in advance and may not play Tue or
Sat, limited play Sun pm and Wed. **Societies** apply in
advance **Green Fees** £25 per round (£35 weekends and
bank holidays). **Prof** David Melling **Facilities** ⊗ ⅏ ⅃ ⬤ ♥
♀ ♠ ⛳ 𝄞 **Leisure** practice nets. **Location** 0.5m NE of
Royton
....
Hotel ★★★★ 66% Menzies Avant Hotel, Windsor Rd,
Manchester St, OLDHAM ☎ 0161 627 5500 103 en suite

Oldham Lees New Rd OL4 5PN ☎ 0161 624 4986
Moorland course, with hard walking.
18 holes, 5122yds, Par 66, SSS 65, Course record 62.
Club membership 320.
Visitors no restrictions. **Societies** must contact in advance.
Green Fees £18 (£24 weekends & bank holidays). **Prof** R
Heginbotham **Facilities** ⊗ ⅏ ⅃ ⬤ ♀ ♠ ⛳ ♥ 𝄞
Location 2.5m E off A669
....
Hotel ★★★★ 66% Menzies Avant Hotel, Windsor Rd,
Manchester St, OLDHAM ☎ 0161 627 5500 103 en suite

Werneth Green Ln, Garden Suburb OL8 3AZ
☎ 0161 624 1190
**Semi-moorland course, with a deep gully and stream
crossing eight fairways. Testing hole: 3rd (par 3).**
18 holes, 5363yds, Par 68, SSS 66, Course record 61.
Club membership 420.
Visitors may not play on Tue or Thu. Weekends by
arrangement. Must contact in advance. **Societies** must
contact in advance. **Green Fees** £16 per day. **Prof** Roy
Penney **Course Designer** Sandy Herd **Facilities** ⊗ ⅏ ⅃
⬤ ♀ ♠ ⛳ 𝄞 **Conf** Corporate Hospitality Days available
Location S side of town centre off A627
....
Hotel ★★★★ 66% Menzies Avant Hotel, Windsor Rd,
Manchester St, OLDHAM ☎ 0161 627 5500 103 en suite

PRESTWICH   Map 07 SD80

Heaton Park Municipal Heaton Park, Middleton
Rd M25 2SW ☎ 0161 654 9899 ▤ 0161 653 2003
**A parkland-style course in historic Heaton Park, with
rolling hills and lakes, designed by five times Open
Champion, J H Taylor. It boasts some spectacular holes
and is a good test of skill for golfers of all abilities.**
Championship: 18 holes, 5755yds, Par 70, SSS 68.
Visitors no restrictions **Societies** apply in writing or by
telephone to the centre manager. **Green Fees** £10 (£12.50
weekends). **Cards** ▦ ▦ ▦ ▢ **Course Designer** J H
Taylor **Facilities** ⊗ ⅏ ⅃ ⬤ ♀ ♠ ⛳ ♥ 𝄞 **Leisure**
fishing, 18 hole par 3 course. **Conf** Corporate Hospitality
Days available **Location** N of Manchester near junct 19 of
M60
....
Hotel ⌂ Premier Lodge (Manchester West), East Lancs
Rd, SWINTON ☎ 0870 9906480 27 en suite

Prestwich Hilton Ln M25 9XB
☎ 0161 773 1404 ▤ 0161 772 0700
**Well manicured tree-lined parkland course, near to
Manchester city centre. A testing course with small
greens.**
18 holes, 4846yds, Par 65, SSS 65, Course record 60.
Club membership 565.
Visitors weekdays by arrangement. Restricted at
weekends, ladies day Tue. **Societies** apply in writing or
telephone. **Green Fees** £20 per round. **Prof** Simon
Wakefield **Facilities** ⊗ ⅏ ⅃ ⬤ ♀ ♠ ⛳ ⸙ 𝄞 **Location**
N side of town centre on A6044

Continued

Hotel ★★★ 63% Novotel Manchester West, Worsley Brow, WORSLEY ☎ 0161 799 3535 119 en suite

ROCHDALE — Map 07 SD81

Castle Hawk Chadwick Ln, Castleton OL11 3BY
☎ 01706 640841 ▤ 01706 860587
e-mail: teeoff@castlehawk.co.uk
New Course: 9 holes, 2699yds, Par 34, SSS 34, Course record 30.
Old Course: 18 holes, 3189yds, Par 55, SSS 55.
Course Designer T Wilson **Location** S of Rochdale, nr junc 20 (M62)
Telephone for further details

Hotel ★★★★ 62% Norton Grange Hotel, Manchester Rd, Castleton, ROCHDALE ☎ 01706 630788 51 en suite

Marland Park Springfield Park, Bolton Rd OL11 4RE ☎ 01706 656401 (weekends)
Parkland and moorland course in a valley. The River Roch adds an extra hazard to the course.
18 holes, 5237yds, Par 67, SSS 66, Course record 64.
Club membership 300.
Visitors must contact professional in advance. **Societies** telephone in advance. **Green Fees** £8 per round (£11 weekends and bank holidays). **Cards** ⊞ ▬ ▬ **Prof** David Wills **Facilities** 🖼 ⛳ ✎ **Location** 1.5m SW off A58

Hotel ★★★★ 62% Norton Grange Hotel, Manchester Rd, Castleton, ROCHDALE ☎ 01706 630788 51 en suite

Rochdale Edenfield Rd OL11 5YR
☎ 01706 643818 ▤ 01706 861113
e-mail: office@rochdalegolfclub.fsnet.net
Parkland course with enjoyable golf and easy walking.
18 holes, 6050yds, Par 71, SSS 69, Course record 65.
Club membership 750.
Visitors must telephone in advance. **Societies** apply in writing or telephone **Green Fees** £20 per day/round (£25 weekends and bank holidays). **Prof** Andrew Laverty **Course Designer** George Lowe **Facilities** ⊗ ⊪ ⅃ ⛳ ✎ ⛳ ✎ **Location** 1.75m W on A680

Hotel ★★★★ 62% Norton Grange Hotel, Manchester Rd, Castleton, ROCHDALE ☎ 01706 630788 51 en suite

ROMILEY — Map 07 SJ99

Romiley Goose House Green SK6 4LJ
☎ 0161 430 2392 ▤ 0161 430 7258
e-mail: office@romileygolfclub.org
Semi-parkland course on the edge of the Derbyshire Hills, providing a good test of golf with a number of outstanding holes, notably the 6th, 9th, 14th and 16th. The latter enjoys magnificent views from the tee.

18 holes, 6454yds, Par 70, SSS 71, Course record 66.
Club membership 700.
Visitors are advised to contact in advance, may not play Thu or Sat before 4pm. **Societies** Tue & Wed, must book in advance. **Green Fees** terms on application. **Prof** Lee Paul Sullivan **Facilities** ⊗ ⊪ ⅃ ⛳ ✎ ⛳ ✎ **Location** E side of town centre off B6104

Hotel ★★ 69% The Wycliffe Hotel, 74 Edgeley Rd, Edgeley, STOCKPORT ☎ 0161 477 5395 18 en suite

SALE — Map 07 SJ79

Ashton on Mersey Church Ln M33 5QQ
☎ 0161 976 4390 & 962 3727 ▤ 0161 976 4390
e-mail: golf@aomgc.fsnet.co.uk
Parkland course with easy walking alongside the River Mersey.
9 holes, 6146yds, Par 71, SSS 69, Course record 66.
Club membership 485.
Visitors with member only Sun & bank holidays, not Sat or Tue. **Societies** Apply in writing. May not play Tue and weekends. **Green Fees** £20.50. **Prof** Mike Williams **Facilities** ⊗ ⊪ ⅃ ⛳ ✎ ⛳ ✎ **Leisure** sauna. **Location** 1m W of M60 junct 7, off Glebelands Road

Hotel ★★★ 67% Cresta Court Hotel, Church St, ALTRINCHAM ☎ 0161 927 7272 136 en suite

Sale Golf Rd M33 2XU
☎ 0161 973 1638 (Office) & 973 1730 (Pro)
▤ 0161 962 4217
e-mail: mail@salegolfclub.com
Tree-lined parkland course. Feature holes are the 13th - Watery Gap - and the new par 3 3rd hole of 210 yards over water.
18 holes, 6122yds, Par 70, SSS 69, Course record 63.
Club membership 700.
Visitors contact professional in advance. **Societies** apply by letter. **Green Fees** £28 per day (£33 weekends). **Prof** Mike Stewart **Facilities** ⊗ ⊪ ⅃ ⛳ ✎ ⛳ ✎ **Conf** Corporate Hospitality Days available **Location** 0.5m from M60 junct 6, NW side of town centre off A6144

Hotel ★★★ 67% Cresta Court Hotel, Church St, ALTRINCHAM ☎ 0161 927 7272 136 en suite

SHEVINGTON — Map 07 SD50

Gathurst 62 Miles Ln WN6 8EW
☎ 01257 255235 (Secretary) ▤ 01257 255953
Testing parkland course, slightly hilly.
18 holes, 6016yds, Par 70, SSS 69, Course record 64.
Club membership 630.
Visitors may play anytime except competition days, with members only at weekends. **Societies** welcome Mon, Tue, Thu & Fri. Apply in writing to Secretary. **Green Fees** not confirmed. **Prof** David Clarke **Course Designer** N Pearson **Facilities** ⊗ ⊪ ⅃ ⛳ ✎ ⛳ ✎ **Location** W side of village B5375,1m S off junct 27 of M6

Hotel ★★★★ 62% Kilhey Court Hotel, Chorley Rd, Standish, WIGAN ☎ 01257 472100 62 en suite

STALYBRIDGE — Map 07 SJ99

Stamford Oakfield House, Huddersfield Rd SK15 3PY
☎ 01457 832126
e-mail: stamford.golfclub@totalise.co.uk
Undulating moorland course.

Continued

Continued

18 holes, 5701yds, Par 70, SSS 68, Course record 62.
Club membership 600.
Visitors limited play at weekends after 3pm. **Societies**
apply in writing or telephone 0161 633 5721 **Green Fees**
£20 per day (£25 weekends after 3pm). **Cards** 🏧 💳 💳
📇 🏧 💳 🅿 **Prof** Brian Badger **Facilities** ⊗ ⅢⅬ ⅬⅬ 💆 ⅬⅬ
🏊 🖼 🖥 ♂ **Conf** fac available Corporate Hospitality Days
available **Location** 2m NE off A635

Guesthouse ◆◆◆◆ Mallons Restaurant with Guest
Rooms, 792-794 Huddersfield Rd, Austerlands, OLDHAM
☎ 0161 622 1234 5 rms (4 en suite)

STANDISH   Map 07 SD51

Standish Court Rectory Ln WN6 0XD
☎ 01257 425777 📠 01257 425888
e-mail: info@standishgolf.co.uk
Undulating 18-hole parkland course, not overly long
but provides a good test for all levels of players. Front
nine more open with room for errors, back nine very
scenic through woodland, a number of tight driving
holes. Greens in excellent condition.
18 holes, 4860yds, Par 68, SSS 64.
Club membership 375.
Visitors can play anytime, phone up to a week in advance
for tee time, standard golfing dress required. **Societies**
telephone in advance. **Green Fees** not confirmed. **Cards**
🏧 💳 💳 🏧 💳 🅿 **Prof** Blake Toone **Course Designer** P
Dawson **Facilities** ⊗ ⅢⅬ ⅬⅬ 💆 Ⅼ 🏊 🖼 🖥 ♂ **Conf** fac
available Corporate Hospitality Days available **Location**
Off M61, junct 6, follow signs to Aspull/Haigh. M6 junct
27, 0.5m through Standish town centre

Hotel ★★★★ 62% Kilhey Court Hotel, Chorley Rd,
Standish, WIGAN ☎ 01257 472100 62 en suite

STOCKPORT   Map 07 SJ89

Heaton Moor Heaton Mersey SK4 3NX
☎ 0161 432 2134 📠 0161 432 2134
e-mail: hmgc@ukgateway.net
Conveniently located for motorway access. Pleasantly
situated in a gently undulating parkland course with
two separate 9 holes starting from the clubhouse.
18 holes, 5968, Par 70, SSS 69, Course record 66.
Club membership 450.
Visitors restricted Tue, bank holidays & Sat (summer).
Societies apply in writing. **Green Fees** terms on
application. **Cards** 🏧 💳 💳 🏧 💳 🅿 **Prof** Simon Marsh
Facilities ⊗ ⅢⅬ ⅬⅬ 💆 Ⅼ 🏊 🖼 ♂ **Location** N of town
centre off B5169

Hotel ★★★ 69% Bredbury Hall Hotel & Country Club,
Goyt Valley, BREDBURY ☎ 0161 430 7421 150 en suite

Houldsworth Houldsworth Park, Reddish SK5 6BN
☎ 0161 442 1712 📠 0161 947 9678
Flat parkland course, tree-lined and with water
hazards. Testing holes 9th (par 5) and 13th (par 5).
18 holes, 6209yds, Par 71, SSS 70, Course record 65.
Club membership 680.
Visitors may not play weekends & bank holidays unless by
prior arrangement with professional. **Societies** by prior
arrangement, telephone Secretary. Welcome on Mon, Thu
& Fri **Green Fees** terms on application. **Prof** David Naylor
Course Designer Dave Thomas **Facilities** ⊗ ⅢⅬ ⅬⅬ 💆 Ⅼ
🏊 🖼 🖥 ♂ **Location** 4m SE of city centre off A6

Hotel ★★★ 68% Willow Bank Hotel, 340-342 Wilmslow
Rd, Fallowfield, MANCHESTER ☎ 0161 224 0461
117 en suite

Marple Barnsfold Rd, Hawk Green, Marple SK6 7EL
☎ 0161 427 2311 📠 0161 427 2311
e-mail: marple.golf.club@ukgateway-net
Parkland course.
18 holes, 5552yds, Par 68, SSS 67, Course record 66.
Club membership 640.
Visitors restricted Thu afternoon & weekend competition
days. **Societies** apply in writing to professional. **Green**
Fees terms on application. **Prof** David Myers **Facilities** ⊗
ⅢⅬ ⅬⅬ 💆 Ⅼ 🏊 🖼 ♂ **Leisure** snooker. **Conf** Corporate
Hospitality Days available **Location** S side of town centre

Hotel ★★★ 69% Bredbury Hall Hotel & Country Club,
Goyt Valley, BREDBURY ☎ 0161 430 7421 150 en suite

Reddish Vale Southcliffe Rd, Reddish SK5 7EE
☎ 0161 480 2359 📠 0161 477 8242
e-mail: admin@reddishvalegolfclub.co.uk
Undulating heathland course designed by Dr. A
Mackenzie and situated in the River Tame Valley.

18 holes, 6100yds, Par 69, SSS 69, Course record 64.
Club membership 550.
Visitors must play with member at weekends. No societies
at weekends. **Societies** must contact in writing. **Green Fees**
£25-£40. **Prof** Bob Freeman **Course Designer** Dr A
Mackenzie **Facilities** ⊗ ⅢⅬ ⅬⅬ 💆 Ⅼ 🏊 🖼 ♂ **Conf**
Corporate Hospitality Days available **Location** Off
Reddish Road, M6 junct 1/27

Hotel ★★ 69% The Wycliffe Hotel, 74 Edgeley Rd,
Edgeley, STOCKPORT ☎ 0161 477 5395 18 en suite

Stockport Offerton Rd, Offerton SK2 5HL
☎ 0161 427 8369 (Secretary) & 427 2421 (Pro)
📠 0161 449 8293
e-mail: info@stockportgolf.co.uk
A beautifully situated course in wide open countryside
with views of the Cheshire and Derbyshire hills. It is
not too long but requires that the player plays all the
shots, to excellent greens. Demanding holes include the
dog-leg 3rd, 12th and 18th and the 440-yard opening
hole is among the toughest in Cheshire. Regional
qualifying course for Open Championship.
18 holes, 6326yds, Par 71, SSS 71, Course record 64.
Club membership 500.
Visitors must contact professional in advance, limited play
weekends. **Societies** Wed & Thu only, apply in writing to
Secretary. **Green Fees** £50 per day, £40 per 18 holes
(£55/£45 weekends). **Prof** Mike Peel **Course Designer** P
Barrie/A Herd **Facilities** ⊗ ⅢⅬ ⅬⅬ 💆 Ⅼ 🏊 🖼 🖥 ♂ **Conf**

Continued   *Continued*

Corporate Hospitality Days available **Location** 4m SE on A627

Hotel ★★★ 69% Bredbury Hall Hotel & Country Club, Goyt Valley, BREDBURY ☎ 0161 430 7421 150 en suite

SWINTON
Map 07 SD70

Swinton Park East Lancashire Rd M27 5LX
☎ 0161 794 0861 📠 0161 281 0698
e-mail: info@spgolf.com
One of Lancashire's longest inland courses. Designed and laid out in 1926 by James Braid.
18 holes, 6472yds, Par 73, SSS 71.
Club membership 600.
Visitors may not play weekends or Thu. Must contact in advance and have handicap certificate. **Societies** apply by letter. **Green Fees** not confirmed. **Prof** James Wilson **Course Designer** James Braid **Facilities** ⊗ ⊪ ⓑ ☕ ♀ ♣ 🍴 ✓ **Conf** fac available **Location** 1m W off A580

Hotel ★★★ 63% Novotel Manchester West, Worsley Brow, WORSLEY ☎ 0161 799 3535 119 en suite

UPPERMILL
Map 07 SD90

Saddleworth Mountain Ash OL3 6LT
☎ 01457 873653 📠 01457 820647
e-mail: secretary@saddleworthgolfclub.org.uk
Moorland course, with superb views of Pennines.
18 holes, 6118yds, Par 71, SSS 69, Course record 61.
Club membership 800.
Visitors must contact in advance, restricted at weekends. **Societies** contact in advance. **Green Fees** £25 (£35 weekends). **Prof** Robert Johnson **Course Designer** George Lowe/Dr McKenzie **Facilities** ⊗ ⊪ ⓑ ☕ ♀ ♣ 🍴 ⛳ ✓ **Location** E side of town centre off A670

Hotel ★★★ 73% Hotel Smokies Park, Ashton Rd, Bardsley, OLDHAM ☎ 0161 785 5000 73 en suite

URMSTON
Map 07 SJ79

Flixton Church Rd, Flixton M41 6EP
☎ 0161 748 2116 📠 0161 748 2116
Meadowland course bounded by River Mersey.
9 holes, 6410yds, Par 71, SSS 71.
Club membership 430.
Visitors contact professional in advance, with member only weekends & bank holidays. **Societies** apply in writing. **Green Fees** £22 (£32 weekends). **Cards** 💳 🖅 🖾 💳 **Prof** Gary Coope **Facilities** ⊗ ⊪ ⓑ ☕ ♀ ♣ 🍴 ✓ **Location** S side of town centre on B5213

Hotel ★★★★ 68% Copthorne Hotel Manchester, Clippers Quay, Salford Quays, MANCHESTER ☎ 0161 873 7321 166 en suite

WALKDEN
Map 07 SD70

Brackley Municipal M38 9TR ☎ 0161 790 6076
Mostly flat course.
9 holes, 3003yds, Par 35, SSS 69.
Club membership 65.
Visitors no restrictions. **Green Fees** terms on application. **Facilities** ☕ ♣ **Location** 2m NW on A6

Hotel ★★★ 63% Novotel Manchester West, Worsley Brow, WORSLEY ☎ 0161 799 3535 119 en suite

WESTHOUGHTON
Map 07 SD60

Hart Common Wigan Rd BL5 2BX
☎ 01942 813195 📠 01942 840775
e-mail: hartcommon@ukgolfer.org
18 holes, 5719yards, Par 71, SSS 68.
Course Designer Mike Shattock **Location** situated on A58 between Bolton (M61 junct 5) and Hindley/Wigan
Telephone for further details

Hotel Ⓤ Holiday Inn Bolton, Beaumont Rd, BOLTON ☎ 0870 400 9011 96 en suite

Westhoughton Long Island, School St BL5 2BR
☎ 01942 811085 & 608958 📠 01942 811085
Compact downland course.
9 holes, 2886yds, Par 70, SSS 68, Course record 64.
Club membership 280.
Visitors with member only at weekends. **Societies** telephone in advance or apply in writing. **Green Fees** not confirmed. **Prof** Kevin Duffy **Facilities** ⊗ ⊪ ⓑ ☕ ♀ ♣ 🍴 **Location** 0.5m NW off A58

Hotel Ⓤ Holiday Inn Bolton, Beaumont Rd, BOLTON ☎ 0870 400 9011 96 en suite

WHITEFIELD
Map 07 SD80

Stand The Dales, Ashbourne Grove M45 7NL
☎ 0161 766 3197 📠 0161 796 3234
A semi-parkland course with five moorland holes. A fine test of golf with a very demanding finish.
18 holes, 6411yds, Par 72, SSS 71, Course record 66.
Club membership 500.
Visitors must contact professional in advance. **Societies** Wed & Fri, apply by telephone. **Green Fees** £30. **Cards** 💳 🖾 **Prof** Mark Dance **Course Designer** G Lowe/A Herd **Facilities** ⊗ ⊪ ⓑ ☕ ♀ ♣ 🍴 ✓ **Conf** Corporate Hospitality Days available **Location** 1m W off A667

Hotel ★★★ 66% Bolholt Country Park Hotel, Walshaw Rd, BURY ☎ 0161 762 4000 65 en suite

Whitefield Higher Ln M45 7EZ
☎ 0161 351 2700 📠 0161 351 2712
e-mail: enquiries@whitefieldgolfclub.com
Fine sporting parkland course with well-watered greens.
18 holes, 6063yds, Par 69, SSS 69, Course record 64.
Club membership 540.
Visitors play restricted Tue & Sun. Booking essential weekends and bank holidays, contact the professional shop on 0161 766 3096. **Societies** must contact in advance. **Green Fees** terms on application. **Cards** 💳 🖅 🖾 💳 🖾 💳 **Prof** Paul Reeves **Facilities** ⊗ ⊪ ☕ ♀ ♣ 🍴 ✓ **Leisure** hard tennis courts, snooker room. **Conf** Corporate Hospitality Days available **Location** N side of town centre on A665

Hotel ★★★ 77% Malmaison, Piccadilly, MANCHESTER ☎ 0161 278 1000 167 en suite

WIGAN
Map 07 SD50

Haigh Hall Golf Complex Copperas Ln, Haigh WN2 1PE ☎ 01942 831107 📠 01942 831417
e-mail: hhgen@wiganmgc.gov.uk
Balcarres Course: 18 holes, 6300yards, Par 70, SSS 71.
Crawford Course: 9 holes, 1446yards, Par 28.
Course Designer Steve Marnoch **Location** M6 junct 27/M61 junct 5 or 6, follow Haigh Hall direction signs
Telephone for further details

Continued

113

Hotel ★★ 65% Bel-Air Hotel, 236 Wigan Ln, WIGAN ☎ 01942 241410 11 en suite

Wigan Arley Hall, Haigh WN1 2UH ☎ 01257 421360
Among the best of Lancashire's 18-hole courses. The fine old clubhouse is the original Arley Hall, and is surrounded by a 12th-century moat.
18 holes, 6009yds, Par 70, SSS 69.
Club membership 200.
Visitors must contact in advance. May not play Tue or Sat. **Societies** apply by telephone. **Green Fees** not confirmed. **Course Designer** Gaunt & Marnoch **Facilities** ⊗ ⅏ ⅃ ☻ ♀ ♨ **Conf** fac available **Location** M6 junct 27, 3m NE off B5238

Hotel ★★★ 66% Quality Hotel Wigan, Riverway, WIGAN ☎ 01942 826888 88 en suite

WORSLEY   Map 07 SD70

Ellesmere Old Clough Ln M28 7HZ
☎ 0161 799 0554 (office) ▤ 0161 790 7322
e-mail: honsec@ellesmeregolf.fsnet.co.uk
Parkland course with natural hazards. Testing holes: 3rd (par 5), 9th (par 3), 15th (par 5). Hard walking.
18 holes, 6248yds, Par 70, SSS 70, Course record 67.
Club membership 700.
Visitors welcome except club competition days & bank holidays. **Societies** apply in advance. **Green Fees** £30 per day and weekends, £25 per round. **Prof** Terry Morley **Facilities** ⊗ ⅏ ⅃ ☻ ♀ ♨ ☻ ✔ **Location** N side of village off A580

Hotel ★★★ 63% Novotel Manchester West, Worsley Brow, WORSLEY ☎ 0161 799 3535 119 en suite

HAMPSHIRE

ALDERSHOT   Map 04 SU85

Army Laffans Rd GU11 2HF
☎ 01252 337272 ▤ 01252 337562
e-mail: agc@ic24.net
The second oldest course in Hampshire. Picturesque heathland course with three par 3s over 200 yds.
18 holes, 6550yds, Par 71, SSS 71, Course record 66.
Club membership 750.
Visitors may not play weekends. **Societies** telephone or apply in writing **Green Fees** £36 for 36 holes, £30 for 18 holes. **Cards** ▦ ▤ ▨ ⚏ **Prof** Graham Cowley **Facilities** ⊗ ⅏ ⅃ ☻ ♀ ♨ ☻ ✔ **Location** 1.5m N of town centre off A323/A325

Hotel ★★★ 67% Potters International Hotel, 1 Fleet Rd, ALDERSHOT ☎ 01252 344000 100 en suite

ALTON   Map 04 SU73

Alton Old Odiham Rd GU34 4BU ☎ 01420 82042
Undulating meadowland course.
9 holes, 5744yds, Par 68, SSS 68, Course record 62.
Club membership 350.
Visitors must contact in advance and must have a handicap certificate to play at weekends. Correct golf attire must be worn. **Societies** must contact in advance. **Green Fees** terms on application. **Prof** Richard Keeling **Course Designer** James Braid **Facilities** ⊗ ⅃ ☻ ♀ ♨ ☻ ✔ **Location** 2m N of Alton off B3349 at Golden Pot

Hotel ★★★ 66% Alton House Hotel, Normandy St, ALTON ☎ 01420 80033 39 en suite

Worldham Park Cakers Ln, East Worldham GU34 3BF ☎ 01420 543151 ▤ 01420 84124
The course is in a picturesque parkland setting with an abundance of challenging holes (dog-legs, water and sand). Suitable for all golfing standards.
18 holes, 6209yds, Par 71, SSS 70.
Club membership 500.
Visitors are advised to book in advance at weekends. **Societies** must contact in advance. **Green Fees** £12 per 18 holes (£15 weekends). **Cards** ▦ ▨ ▨ ⚏ **Prof** Jon Le Roux **Course Designer** F J Whidborne **Facilities** ⊗ ⅏ ⅃ ☻ ♀ ♨ ☻ ✔ **Conf** Corporate Hospitality Days available **Location** B3004, 2mins from Alton

Hotel ★★★ 70% Alton Grange Hotel, London Rd, ALTON ☎ 01420 86565 26 en suite 4 annexe en suite

AMPFIELD   Map 04 SU42

Ampfield Par Three Winchester Rd SO51 9BQ
☎ 01794 368480
18 holes, 2478yds, Par 54, SSS 53, Course record 49.
Course Designer Henry Cotton **Location** 4m NE of Romsey on A31
Telephone for further details

Hotel ★★★ 66% The Potters Heron Hotel, Winchester Rd, Ampfield, ROMSEY ☎ 0870 609 6155 54 en suite

ANDOVER   Map 04 SU34

Andover 51 Winchester Rd SP10 2EF
☎ 01264 358040 ▤ 01264 358040
e-mail: secretary@andovergolfclub.co.uk
Undulating downland course combining a good test of golf for all abilities with breathtaking views across Hampshire countryside. Well-guarded greens and a notable par 3 9th (225yds) with the tee perched on top of a hill, 100ft above the green.
9 holes, 6096yds, Par 70, SSS 69, Course record 64.
Club membership 450.
Visitors must contact professional in advance tel: 01264 324151. **Societies** telephone in advance or apply in writing **Green Fees** £20 per 18 holes (£25 weekends). **Prof** D Lawrence **Course Designer** J H Taylor **Facilities** ⊗ ⅏ ⅃ ☻ ♀ ♨ ☻ **Conf** fac available Corporate Hospitality Days available **Location** 0.5m S on A3057

Hotel ★★★ 62% Quality Hotel Andover, Micheldever Rd, ANDOVER ☎ 01264 369111 13 en suite
36 annexe en suite

Hampshire Winchester Rd SP11 7TB
☎ 01264 357555 (pro shop) & 356462 (office)
▤ 01264 356606
e-mail: enquiry@thehampshiregolfclub.co.uk
A pleasant undulating parkland course, based on chalk which provides very good drainage, with a superb finishing hole.
18 holes, 6359yds, Par 72, SSS 70, Course record 67.
Club membership 650.
Visitors advisable to book 3 days in advance. **Societies** apply by phone to Jan Miles (01264 356462) **Green Fees** not confirmed. **Cards** ▦ ▨ ▨ ⚏ **Prof** Stewart Cronin **Facilities** ⊗ ⅃ ☻ ♀ ♨ ☻ ✔ ⛾ ✔ **Leisure** 9 hole par 3 course. **Conf** Corporate Hospitality Days available

Continued *Continued*

Location located 1.5m S of Andover on A3057 Winchester road

Hampshire Golf Club

Hotel ★★★ 62% Quality Hotel Andover, Micheldever Rd, ANDOVER ☎ 01264 369111 13 en suite 36 annexe en suite

BARTON-ON-SEA   Map 04 SZ29

Barton-on-Sea Milford Rd BH25 5PP
☎ 01425 615308 🖹 01425 621457
Though not strictly a links course, it is situated on a coastal cliff with views over the Solent to the Isle of Wight. With 27 holes (three loops of nine), sea breezes often add to the test.
9 holes, 3012yds, Par 36.
Needles: 9 holes, 3078yds, Par 35.
Stroller: 9 holes, 2989yds, Par 36.
Club membership 940.
Visitors must contact in advance. Must contact in advance. **Societies** must telephone in advance. **Green Fees** £38 per day (£42 weekends & bank holidays). **Cards** 💳 💳 💳 💳 💳 **Prof** Peter Rodgers **Course Designer** Hamilton Stutt **Facilities** ⊗ ⅷ by prior arrangement ⅊ 💁 ♀ ♨ ⛳ 🏌 🐎 ♂ **Leisure** snooker tables. **Conf** Corporate Hospitality Days available **Location** B3058 SE side of town

Hotel ★★★★★ ♨ Chewton Glen Hotel, Christchurch Rd, NEW MILTON ☎ 01425 275341 58 en suite

BASINGSTOKE   Map 04 SU65

Basingstoke Kempshott Park RG23 7LL
☎ 01256 465990 🖹 01256 331793
e-mail: enquiries@basingstokegolfclub.co.uk
A well-maintained parkland course with wide and inviting fairways. You are inclined to expect longer drives than are actually achieved - partly on account of the trees. There are many two-hundred-year-old beech trees, since the course was built on an old deer park.
18 holes, 6350yds, Par 70, SSS 70, Course record 66.
Club membership 700.
Visitors must contact in advance and play Mon-Fri only (ex bank holidays). **Societies** must contact in advance. **Green Fees** £46 per day; £36 per round (Mon-Fri only). **Cards** 💳 💳 💳 **Prof** Guy Shoesmith **Course Designer** James Braid **Facilities** ⊗ ⅷ ⅊ 💁 ♀ ♨ ⛳ 🏌 🐎 ♂ **Conf** fac available Corporate Hospitality Days available **Location** 3.5m SW on A30 M3 exit 7

Hotel 🅄 Holiday Inn Basingstoke, Grove Rd, BASINGSTOKE ☎ 0870 400 9004 86 en suite

Dummer Dummer RG25 2AR
☎ 01256 397888 🖹 01256 397889
e-mail: golf@dummergc.co.uk
Designed by Peter Alliss/Clive Clark, this course is set in 180 acres of countryside with panoramic views. It provides a challenge for all playing categories and is open all year round.
18 holes, 6403yds, Par 72, SSS 71, Course record 64.
Club membership 600.
Visitors must contact in advance, adhere to dress code, handicap required, limited at weekends. **Societies** contact in advance. **Green Fees** terms on application. **Cards** 💳 💳 💳 💳 💳 **Prof** A Fannon/S Watson **Course Designer** Peter Alliss/Clive Clark **Facilities** ⊗ ⅷ ⅊ 💁 ♀ ♨ ⛳ 🐎 ♂ **Leisure** sauna. **Location** Off junc 7 of M3 towards Dummer village

Weybrook Park Rooksdown Ln RG24 9NT
☎ 01256 320347 🖹 01256 812973
e-mail: weybrookpark@aol.com
A course designed to be enjoyable for all standards of player. Easy walking with fabulous views.
18 holes, 6468yds, Par 71, SSS 71.
Club membership 600.
Visitors telephone for availability. **Societies** telephone in advance for availability and confirm in writing. **Green Fees** terms on application. **Cards** 💳 💳 **Prof** Anthony Dillon **Facilities** ⊗ ⅷ ⅊ 💁 ♀ ♨ ⛳ 🐎 ♂ **Conf** fac available **Location** 2m W of town centre, entrance via A339

Hotel ★★★★ 69% Apollo Hotel, Aldermaston Roundabout, BASINGSTOKE ☎ 01256 796700 125 en suite

BORDON   Map 04 SU73

Blackmoor Firgrove Rd, Whitehill GU35 9EH
☎ 01420 472775 🖹 01420 487666
e-mail: admin@blackmoorgolf.co.uk
A first-class moorland course with a great variety of holes. Fine greens and wide pine tree-lined fairways are a distinguishing feature. The ground is mainly flat and walking easy.
18 holes, 6164yds, Par 69, SSS 69, Course record 63.
Club membership 750.
Visitors must contact in advance, must have handicap certificate and may not play at weekends. **Societies** must telephone in advance. **Green Fees** £47 per 36 holes; £35 per 18 holes (weekdays only). **Cards** 💳 💳 💳 💳 **Prof** Stephen Clay **Course Designer** H S Colt **Facilities** ⊗ by prior arrangement ⅷ by prior arrangement ⅊ 💁 ♀ ♨ ⛳ ♂ **Conf** Corporate Hospitality Days available **Location** Travelling S on A325, 6m beyond Farnham, pass through Whitehill and turn right at roundabout

Hotel ★★★ 66% Alton House Hotel, Normandy St, ALTON ☎ 01420 80033 39 en suite

BOTLEY   Map 04 SU51

Botley Park Hotel, Golf & Country Club
Winchester Rd, Boorley Green SO32 2UA
☎ 01489 780888 🖹 01489 789242
e-mail: info@botleypark.macdonald.hotels.co.uk
18 holes, 6341yds, Par 70, SSS 70, Course record 67.
Course Designer Ewan Murray **Location** 1m NW of Botley on B3354
Telephone for further details

Hotel ★★★★ 68% Botley Park Hotel Golf & Country Club, Winchester Rd, Boorley Green, BOTLEY ☎ 01489 780888 100 en suite

BROCKENHURST — Map 04 SU20

Brockenhurst Manor Sway Rd SO42 7SG
☎ 01590 623332 (Secretary) 🖷 01590 624140
e-mail: secretary@brokenhurst-manor.org.uk
**An attractive forest course set in the New Forest, with
the unusual feature of three loops of six holes each to
complete the round. Fascinating holes include the short
5th and 12th, and the 4th and 17th, both dog-legged. A
stream also features on seven of the holes.**
18 holes, 6222yds, Par 70, SSS 70, Course record 63.
Club membership 700.
Visitors must contact in advance, numbers limited. Must
have a handicap certificate & be a current member of
recognised club, max handicap 24 men 36 ladies. **Societies**
Thu only, apply in writing. **Green Fees** £58 per day; £48
per round (£73/£58 weekends and bank holidays). **Cards**
💳 💳 💳 💳 🔘 **Prof** Bruce Parker **Course Designer** H S
Colt **Facilities** ⊗ ⵣ ⬛ ☕ ♀ ⚒ 🏠 ⚷ **Location** 1m S on
B3055

....

Hotel ★★ 67% Watersplash Hotel, The Rise,
BROCKENHURST ☎ 01590 622344 23 en suite

BURLEY — Map 04 SU20

Burley Cott Ln BH24 4BB
☎ 01425 402431 & 403737 🖷 01425 404168
e-mail: secretary@burleygolfclub.fsnet.co.uk
**Undulating heather and gorseland. The 7th requires an
accurately placed tee shot to obtain par 4. Played off
different tees on second nine.**
9 holes, 6149yds, Par 71, SSS 69, Course record 68.
Club membership 520.
Visitors must contact in advance & preferably have a
handicap certificate or be a member of a recognised golf
club. May not play before 4pm Sat or 8am Sun. **Societies**
telephone in advance, parties up to 14 only. **Green Fees**
terms on application. **Facilities** ⬛ ☕ ♀ ⚒ ⚷ **Location** E
side of village

....

Hotel ★★★ 66% Moorhill House, BURLEY
☎ 01425 403285 31 en suite

CORHAMPTON — Map 04 SU62

Corhampton Shepherds Farm Ln SO32 3GZ
☎ 01489 877279 🖷 01489 877680
e-mail: secretary@corhamptongc.co.uk
**Free draining downland course situated in the heart of
the picturesque Meon Valley.**
18 holes, 6444yds, Par 71, SSS 71.
Club membership 800.

Visitors weekdays only and must contact in advance.
Societies Mon & Thu only, contact in writing or telephone.
Green Fees £40 per 36 holes, £30 per 18 holes. **Prof** Ian
Roper **Facilities** ⊗ ⵣ ⬛ ☕ ♀ ⚒ 🏠 🍴 ⚷ **Location** 1m
W of Corhampton, off B3035

....

Hotel ★★ 70% Old House Hotel, The Square,
WICKHAM ☎ 01329 833049 8 en suite

CRONDALL — Map 04 SU74

Oak Park Heath Ln GU10 5PB
☎ 01252 850850 🖷 01252 850851
e-mail: oakpark@americangolf.uk.com
**Village is a gently undulating parkland course
overlooking pretty village. 16-bay floodlit driving
range, practice green and practice bunker. Woodland is
undulating on holes 10 to 13. Panoramic views, mature
trees, very challenging.**
Woodland: 18 holes, 6352yds, Par 70, SSS 70.
Village: 9 holes, 3279yds, Par 36.
Club membership 550.
Visitors restricted to members 7.30-noon. All tee times
bookable in advance. **Societies** must telephone and book in
advance,min 12 persons. **Green Fees** terms on application.
Cards 💳 💳 💳 💳 💳 🔘 **Prof** Gary Murton
Course Designer Patrick Dawson **Facilities** ⊗ ⵣ ⬛ ☕ ♀
⚒ 🏠 🍴 🏌 ⚷ 🍷 **Leisure** gymnasium. **Conf** fac available
Corporate Hospitality Days available **Location** 0.5m E of
village off A287 Farnham-Odiham

....

Hotel ★★★ ♨♨ 61% Farnham House Hotel, Alton Rd,
FARNHAM ☎ 01252 716908 25 en suite

Continued

DENMEAD — Map 04 SU61

Furzeley Furzeley Rd PO7 6TX ☎ 023 92231180
A well laid parkland course with many features including several strategically placed lakes which provide a good test set in beautiful scenery. Straight hitting and club selection on the short holes is the key to manufacturing a low score.
18 holes, 4454yds, Par 62, SSS 61, Course record 56.
Club membership 250.
Visitors may book 2 days in advance. **Societies** must telephone in advance and confirm in writing. **Green Fees** terms on application. **Prof** Derek Brown **Course Designer** Mark Sale/Robert Brown **Facilities** ⊗ ⊁ by prior arrangement ⓑ ■ ♀ ♨ ⌂ ⌐ ♂ **Location** From Waterlooville take Hambledon Road NW and follow golf course signs

Hotel ★★★★ 65% Portsmouth Marriott Hotel, Southampton Rd, PORTSMOUTH ☎ 0870 400 7285 174 en suite

DIBDEN — Map 04 SU40

Dibden Main Rd SO45 5TB
☎ 023 8020 7508 & 8084 5596
Municipal parkland course with views over Southampton Water. A pond guards the green at the par 5 3rd hole. Twenty bay driving range.
Course 1: 18 holes, 5931yds, Par 70, SSS 69, Course record 64.
Course 2: 9 holes, 1520yds, Par 29.
Club membership 600.
Visitors must book in advance. 9 hole is pay & play. **Societies** must contact in advance. **Green Fees** not confirmed. **Cards** ⊞ ▦ ⊞ ⊠ ☑ **Prof** Paul Smith & John Slade **Course Designer** Hamilton Stutt **Facilities** ⊗ ⊁ ⓑ ■ ♀ ♨ ⌂ ⌐ ♂ ⌕ **Location** 2m NW of Dibden Purlieu, off A326 to Hythe

Hotel ★★★ 65% Forest Lodge Hotel, Pikes Hill, Romsey Rd, LYNDHURST ☎ 023 8028 3677 28 en suite

EASTLEIGH — Map 04 SU41

Fleming Park Passfield Av SO50 9NL
☎ 023 80612797 ▤ 023 80651686
e-mail: ianwarwick@flemingparkgolfcourse.co.uk
Parkland course with stream, Monks Brook, running through.
18 holes, 4436yds, Par 65, SSS 62, Course record 62.
Club membership 390.
Visitors must contact in advance, no restrictions. **Societies** must contact in advance. **Green Fees** terms on application. **Cards** ⊞ ▦ ⊞ ⊠ ☑ **Prof** Ian Warwick **Course Designer** David Miller **Facilities** ⊗ ⊁ ⓑ ■ ♀ ♨ ⌂ ⌐ ♂ **Leisure** hard and grass tennis courts, heated indoor plus outdoor swimming pool, squash, sauna, solarium, gymnasium. **Location** E side of town centre

Hotel Ⓤ Holiday Inn Eastleigh, Leigh Rd, EASTLEIGH ☎ 0870 400 9075 120 en suite

EAST WELLOW — Map 04 SU32

Wellow Ryedown Ln SO51 6BD
☎ 01794 323833 & 322872 ▤ 01794 323832
Three 9-hole courses set in 217 acres of parkland surrounding Embley Park, former home of Florence Nightingale.
Continued

Ryedown & Embley: 18 holes, 5966yds, Par 70, SSS 69, Course record 65.
Embley & Blackwater: 18 holes, 6295yds, Par 72, SSS 70.
Blackwater & Ryedown: 18 holes, 5819yds, Par 70, SSS 68.
Club membership 600.
Visitors advisable to contact in advance weekdays only. **Societies** telephone in advance, Mon-Fri not bank holidays. **Green Fees** £18 per 18 holes (£22 weekends & bank holidays). **Cards** ⊞ ▦ ⊞ ⊠ ☑ **Prof** Neil Bratley **Course Designer** W Wiltshire **Facilities** ⊗ ⊁ ⓑ ■ ♀ ♨ ⌂ ⌐ ♂ **Leisure** gymnasium. **Conf** fac available **Location** M27 exit 2, then A36 to Salisbury then 1m right

Hotel ★★★ 64% The White Horse, Market Place, ROMSEY ☎ 0870 400 8123 26 en suite 7 annexe en suite

FAREHAM — Map 04 SU50

Cams Hall Cams Hall Estate PO16 8UP
☎ 01329 827222 ▤ 01329 827111
e-mail: camshall@americangolf.uk.com
Two Peter Alliss/Clive Clark designed golf courses. The Creek Course is coastal and has salt and fresh water lakes and the fairways are lined with undulating hills. The Park Course is designed in the grounds of Cams Hall.
Creek Course: 18 holes, 6244yds, Par 71, SSS 70, Course record 69.
Park Course: 9 holes, 3247yds, Par 36, SSS 36.
Club membership 950.
Visitors must contact in advance, tee times available any time. **Societies** telephone for details and society golf day pack. **Green Fees** not confirmed. **Cards** ⊞ ▦ ⊞ ☑ **Prof** Jason Neve **Course Designer** Peter Alliss **Facilities** ⊗ ⊁ ⓑ ■ ♀ ♨ ⌂ ⌐ ♂ ⌕ **Leisure** sauna. **Conf** fac available **Location** M27 exit 11 to A27

Hotel ★★★ 66% Lysses House Hotel, 51 High St, FAREHAM ☎ 01329 822622 21 en suite

FARNBOROUGH — Map 04 SU85

Southwood Ively Rd, Cove GU14 0LJ
☎ 01252 548700 ▤ 01252 549091
Municipal parkland golf course.
18 holes, 5738yds, Par 69, SSS 68, Course record 61.
Club membership 650.
Visitors 14 day advance tee time booking available. **Societies** must contact in advance. **Green Fees** not confirmed. **Cards** ⊞ ▦ ⊞ ⊠ ☑ **Prof** James Willmott **Course Designer** Hawtree & Son **Facilities** ⊗ ⊁ ♨ ⌂ ⌐ ♂ **Conf** fac available Corporate Hospitality Days available **Location** 0.5m W

Hotel Ⓤ Holiday Inn Farnborough, Lynchford Rd, FARNBOROUGH ☎ 0870 400 9029 143 en suite

FLEET — Map 04 SU85

North Hants Minley Rd GU51 1RF
☎ 01252 616443 ▤ 01252 811627
e-mail: secretary@north-hants-fleetgc.co.uk
Picturesque tree-lined course with much heather and gorse close to the fairways. A comparatively easy par 4 first hole may lull the golfer into a false sense of security, only to be rudely awakened at the testing holes which follow. The ground is rather undulating and, though not tiring, does offer some excellent 'blind' shots, and more than a few surprises in judging distance.
Continued

North Hants Golf Club
18 holes, 6519yds, Par 70, SSS 72, Course record 69.
Club membership 600.
Visitors must contact at least 48 hours in advance. Must play with member at weekends. **Societies** Tue & Wed only. Subject to pre-booking. **Green Fees** terms on application. **Prof** Steve Porter **Course Designer** James Braid **Facilities** ⊗ ⊪ ⅃ ▬ ♀ ♨ 🖬 ♂ **Conf** Corporate Hospitality Days available **Location** 0.25m N of Fleet station on B3013

Hotel ★★★ 65% Falcon Hotel, 68 Farnborough Rd, FARNBOROUGH ☎ 01252 545378 30 en suite

GOSPORT   Map 04 SZ69

Gosport & Stokes Bay Off Fort Rd, Haslar
PO12 2AT ☎ 023 92527941 🖷 023 92527941
9 holes, 5999yds, Par 70, SSS 69, Course record 65.
Location A32 S from Fareham, E on Fort rd to Haslar
Telephone for further details

Hotel ★★★ 66% Lysses House Hotel, 51 High St, FAREHAM ☎ 01329 822622 21 en suite

HARTLEY WINTNEY   Map 04 SU75

Hartley Wintney London Rd RG27 8PT
☎ 01252 844211 (Sec/Gen Mgr) 🖷 01252 844211
e-mail: office@hartleywintneygolfclub.com
Easy walking, parkland course in pleasant countryside. Provides a good test for golfers of all abilities.

18 holes, 6240yds, Par 71, SSS 71, Course record 63.
Club membership 750.
Visitors must contact in advance, restricted at weekends. **Societies** Mon, Tue, Thu & Fri only by prior arrangement. **Green Fees** £45 per day, £30 per 18 holes (£50/£35 weekends and bank holidays). **Prof** Martin Smith **Facilities** ⊗ ⅃ ▬ ♀ ♨ 🖬 ♨ ♂ **Conf** fac available Corporate Hospitality Days available **Location** NE side of village on A30

Continued

Hotel ★★★ 67% Wellington Arms, STRATFIELD TURGIS ☎ 01256 882214 35 en suite

HAYLING ISLAND   Map 04 SU70

Hayling Links Ln PO11 0BX
☎ 023 92464446 🖷 023 92461119
e-mail: hgcltd@aol.com
A delightful links course among the dunes offering fine sea-scapes and views across to the Isle of Wight. Varying sea breezes and sometimes strong winds ensure that the course seldom plays the same two days running. Testing holes at the 12th and 13th, both par 4. Club selection is important.
18 holes, 6531yds, Par 71, SSS 71, Course record 65.
Club membership 1000.
Visitors must contact in advance by telephone or in writing and have a handicap certificate, no jeans, denims or collarless shirts allowed. **Societies** welcome Tue & Wed, or half days Mon & Thu, apply in writing or telephone. **Green Fees** £48 per day; £40 per round (£50 per round weekends). **Cards** 💳 💳 💳 🅿 **Prof** Raymond Gadd **Course Designer** Taylor 1905, Simpson 1933 **Facilities** ⊗ ⅃ ⅃ ⅃ ♀ ♨ 🖬 ♨ ♂ **Conf** Corporate Hospitality Days available **Location** SW side of island at West Town

Hotel ★★★ 69% Brookfield Hotel, Havant Rd, EMSWORTH ☎ 01243 373363 40 en suite

KINGSCLERE   Map 04 SU55

Sandford Springs Wolverton RG26 5RT
☎ 01635 296800 & 296808 (Pro Shop) 🖷 01635 296801
e-mail: garye@leaderboardgolf.co.uk
The course has unique variety in beautiful surroundings and offers three distinctive loops of 9 holes. There are water hazards, woodlands and gradients to negotiate, providing a challenge for all playing categories.

The Park: 9 holes, 2963yds, Par 34.
The Lakes: 9 holes, 3042yds, Par 35.
The Wood: 9 holes, 3180yds, Par 36.
Club membership 650.
Visitors must contact in advance. Restricted at weekends. **Societies** must contact in advance. **Green Fees** not confirmed. **Cards** 💳 💳 💳 🅿 **Prof** Gary Edmunds **Course Designer** Hawtree & Son **Facilities** ⊗ ⅃ ⅃ ⅃ ♀ ♀ ♨ 🖬 ♨ ♨ ♂ 🍴 **Conf** fac available Corporate Hospitality Days available **Location** On A339 between Basingstoke and Newbury

Hotel ★★★ 65% The Chequers Hotel, 6-8 Oxford St, NEWBURY ☎ 01635 38000 46 en suite
11 annexe en suite

KINGSLEY   Map 04 SU73

Dean Farm GU35 9NG ☎ 01420 489478
Undulating downland course.
9 holes, 1500yds, Par 29.
Visitors no restrictions. **Societies** telephone to book.
Green Fees not confirmed. **Cards** 🖃 **Facilities** ⊗ ⊮ 🖳 🖳
🍴 🖀 🌱 🖋 **Leisure** hard tennis courts. **Location** W side of
village off B3004

⋯⋯⋯⋯⋯⋯⋯⋯⋯⋯⋯⋯⋯

Hotel ★★★ 70% Alton Grange Hotel, London Rd,
ALTON ☎ 01420 86565 26 en suite   4 annexe en suite

LECKFORD   Map 04 SU33

Leckford SO20 6JF ☎ 01264 810320 🖹 01264 811122
e-mail: golf@leckfordestate.co.uk
A testing downland course with good views.
Old Course: 9 holes, 6394yds, Par 72, SSS 71.
New Course: 9 holes, 4562yds, Par 66, SSS 62.
Club membership 200.
Visitors no restrictions **Societies** phone Secretary/Manager
Green Fees not confirmed. **Prof** Tony Ashton **Facilities**
🖳 △ 🖋 **Location** 1m SW off A3057

LEE-ON-THE-SOLENT   Map 04 SU50

Lee-on-the-Solent Brune Ln PO13 9PB
☎ 023 9255 1170 🖹 023 9255 4233
e-mail: enquiries@leeonthesolentgolfclub.co.uk
**A parkland/heathland course that is deceptively
challenging and, in its par 3 13th, possesses an
outstanding signature hole. A further four short holes
all demand a high degree of accuracy, while the final six
represent a particularly demanding end to the round.**
18 holes, 5962yds, Par 69, SSS 69, Course record 63.
Club membership 725.
Visitors Handicap certificate required. Must contact in
advance. **Societies** must contact in advance. **Green Fees**
£34 per day/round (£39 weekends). **Cards** 🖮 🖃 🖃 🖃 🖃
🖃 **Prof** Rob Edwards **Facilities** ⊗ ⊮ 🖳 🖳 🍴 △ 🖋
Conf fac available   Corporate Hospitality Days available
Location 3m S of Fareham

⋯⋯⋯⋯⋯⋯⋯⋯⋯⋯⋯⋯⋯

Hotel ★★★ 66% Lysses House Hotel, 51 High St,
FAREHAM ☎ 01329 822622 21 en suite

LIPHOOK   Map 04 SU83

Liphook Wheatsheaf Enclosure GU30 7EH
☎ 01428 723271 & 723785 🖹 01428 724853
e-mail: liphookgolfclub@btconnect.com
Heathland course with easy walking and fine views.
18 holes, 6167yds, Par 70, SSS 69, Course record 67.
Club membership 800.
Visitors must contact in advance; may not play Tue,
competition days etc. Handicap certificate required.
Societies Wed-Fri only. Must contact in advance. **Green
Fees** £45 per day, £39 per round (£55/£45 Sat, £55 Sun &
bank holidays pm only). **Prof** Ian Mowbray **Course
Designer** A C Croome **Facilities** ⊗ ⊮ 🖳 🖳 🍴 △ 🖀 🌱 ⚲
🖦 🖋 **Location** 1m S on B2070 (old A3)

⋯⋯⋯⋯⋯⋯⋯⋯⋯⋯⋯⋯⋯

Hotel ★★★★ 71% Lythe Hill Hotel & Spa, Petworth Rd,
HASLEMERE ☎ 01428 651251 41 en suite

Old Thorns Hotel, Golf & Country Club
Griggs Green GU30 7PE
☎ 01428 724555 🖹 01428 725036
e-mail: info@oldthorns.com
**A challenging 18-hole championship course with rolling
hills, undulating greens, demanding water features and
magnificent views. A challenge to any level of golfer.**

18 holes, 6581yds, Par 72, SSS 71, Course record 66.
Club membership 250.
Visitors subject to availability. **Societies** must telephone in
advance. **Green Fees** £60 per day, £40 per round (£90/£60
weekends and bank holidays). **Cards** 🖃 🖃 🖃 🖃 🖃
🖳 🖃 **Prof** Roger Hyder **Course Designer** Peter
Alliss/Dave Thomas **Facilities** ⊗ ⊮ ⊮ 🖳 🖳 🍴 △ 🖀 🌱 🖦
🖦 🖋 ⚲ **Leisure** hard tennis courts, heated indoor
swimming pool, sauna, solarium, gymnasium. **Location**
Leave A3 at Griggs Green, S of Liphook, signposted 'Old
Thorns'

⋯⋯⋯⋯⋯⋯⋯⋯⋯⋯⋯⋯⋯

Hotel ★★★ 75% Old Thorns Hotel Golf & Country Club,
Griggs Green, LIPHOOK ☎ 01428 724555 29 en suite
4 annexe rms (3 en suite)

LYNDHURST   Map 04 SU20

Bramshaw Brook SO43 7HE
☎ 023 8081 3433 🖹 023 8081 3460
e-mail: golf@bramshaw.co.uk
**Two 18-hole courses. The Manor Course is landscaped
parkland with excellent greens, and features mature
trees and streams. The Forest course is set amidst
beautiful open forest. Easy walking.**
*Manor Course: 18 holes, 6517yds, Par 71, SSS 71, Course
record 65.*
*Forest Course: 18 holes, 5774yds, Par 69, SSS 68, Course
record 65.*
Club membership 950.
Visitors limited availability weekends and bank holidays
unless accompanied by member or resident of Bell Inn.
Phone in advance. **Societies** apply in writing or telephone
in advance. **Green Fees** Manor course £33; Forest course
£28 (£36/£32 weekends). Both courses £49 per day.
Reduced winter rates. **Prof** Clive Bonner **Facilities** ⊗ ⊮
🖳 🖳 🍴 △ 🖀 🌱 🖦 🖦 ⚲ 🖋 **Conf** Corporate Hospitality
Days available **Location** On B3079 1m W of M27 junc 1

⋯⋯⋯⋯⋯⋯⋯⋯⋯⋯⋯⋯⋯

Hotel ★★★ 67% Bell Inn, BROOK ☎ 023 8081 2214
25 en suite

Continued

⋯⋯⋯⋯⋯⋯⋯⋯⋯⋯⋯⋯⋯⋯⋯⋯⋯⋯⋯⋯⋯⋯⋯⋯

Bell Inn, Brook

New Forest Southampton Rd SO43 7BU
☎ 023 8028 2752 📠 023 8028 2484
e-mail: barbara@nfgc.sagehost.co.uk
This picturesque heathland course is laid out in a typical stretch of the New Forest on high ground a little above the village of Lyndhurst. Natural hazards include the inevitable forest ponies. The first two holes are somewhat teasing, as is the 485-yard (par 5) 9th. Walking is easy.
18 holes, 5742yds, Par 69, SSS 68.
Club membership 520.
Visitors must contact in advance, dress code applies.
Societies must contact in advance. **Green Fees** £12 per 18 holes (£15 weekends). **Cards** 💳 🏧 💳 💳 **Prof** Colin Murray **Facilities** ⊗ ⅃ ⅄ 🍴 🏠 ♂ **Conf** Corporate Hospitality Days available **Location** 0.5m NE off A35)

Hotel ★★★ 70% Crown Hotel, High St, LYNDHURST
☎ 023 8028 2922 39 en suite

NEW ALRESFORD   Map 04 SU53

Alresford Cheriton Rd, Tichborne Down SO24 0PN
☎ 01962 733746 📠 01962 736040
e-mail: secretary@alresford-golf.demon.co.uk
A testing downland course on well drained chalk. Expanded to 18 holes, incorporating the original twelve, but changing direction of play to give two starting points and two closing greens near the clubhouse.
18 holes, 5905yds, Par 69, SSS 68, Course record 63.
Club membership 600.
Visitors must contact in advance. **Societies** must telephone in advance. **Green Fees** not confirmed. **Cards** 💳 🏧 💳 💳 **Prof** Malcolm Scott **Course Designer** Scott Webb Young **Facilities** ⊗ ⅃⅄ 🍴 💼 ⅄ 🏠 ♂ **Location** 1m S on B3046

Hotel ★★ 61% Swan Hotel, 11 West St, ALRESFORD
☎ 01962 732302 & 734427 📠 01962 735274
11 rms (10 en suite) 12 annexe en suite

NEW MILTON   Map 04 SZ29

Chewton Glen Hotel Christchurch Rd BH25 6QS
☎ 01425 275341 📠 01425 272310
e-mail: reservations@chewtonglen.com
A 9-hole, par 3 course with the hotel grounds plus a practice area. Please note - only open to residents of the hotel or as a guest of a member of the club.
9 holes, 854yds, Par 27.
Club membership 150.

Continued

Chewton Glen

Visitors day country club membership. **Societies** must contact in advance. **Green Fees** terms on application.
Cards 💳 🏧 💳 💳 💳 **Facilities** ⊗ by prior arrangement ⅢⅢ by prior arrangement 💼 ⅄ 🍴 🏠 ♂
Leisure hard tennis courts, outdoor and indoor heated swimming pools, sauna, gymnasium, Spa & health club.
Conf fac available Corporate Hospitality Days available
Location M27 to A31. Through Emmery Down to A35, right on A35 toward Christchurch. In Hinton left at staggered junct, through Walkford. Golf course on left

Hotel ★★★★★ Chewton Glen Hotel, Christchurch Rd, NEW MILTON ☎ 01425 275341 58 en suite

---

OVERTON   Map 04 SU54

Test Valley Micheldever Rd RG25 3DS
☎ 01256 771737 📠 01256 771285
e-mail: info@testvalleygolf.com
A downland course with excellent drainage, fine year-round greens and prominent water and

Continued

bunker features. On undulating terrain with lovely views over the Hampshire countryside. Has hosted the Hampshire Open and the PGA Lombard Trophy.
18 holes, 6165yds, Par 72, SSS 69.
Club membership 500.
Visitors must phone in advance. Must play after 11.30am weekends & bank holidays. **Societies** apply in writing or telephone in advance. **Green Fees** terms on application.
Cards 🃏 🎴 🃏 🂠 **Prof** Alastair Briggs **Course Designer** Don Wright **Facilities** ⊗ ⅲ ⅃ ⿈ ⾕ ⼂ ⾕ ⼈ ⼂ 🀫 ⾕ ⼂ **Conf** fac available Corporate Hospitality Days available **Location** 1.5m N of A303 on road to Overton

Hotel ★★★★ 73% The Hampshire Centrecourt Hotel, Centre Dr, Chineham, BASINGSTOKE ☎ 01256 816664 90 en suite

OWER   Map 04 SU31

Paultons Golf Centre Old Salisbury Rd SO51 6AN
☎ 023 80813992 🗎 023 8081 3993
e-mail: paultons@americangolf.uk.com
A Pay and Play parkland/woodland 18-hole course built within the original Paultons parkland which was laid out by 'Capability' Brown. The water features on four of the holes and the tree-lined fairways challenge the ability of all golfers. There is also a 9-hole academy course, ideal for beginners or players wishing to improve their short games as well as a 24-bay floodlit driving range.
18 holes, 6238yds, Par 71, SSS 70, Course record 67.
Club membership 500.
Visitors can book up to 7 days in advance. **Societies** telephone for details. **Green Fees** £16 per 18 holes Mon-Thu, £18 Fri (£22 weekends and bank holidays). **Cards** 🃏 🎴 🃏 🂠 **Prof** Mark Williamson/Mark Patience **Course Designer** J R Smith **Facilities** ⊗ ⅲ ⅃ ⿈ ⾕ ⼂ ⾕ ⼂ 🀫 ⾕ ⼂ **Leisure** 9 hole academy course. **Conf** fac available Corporate Hospitality Days available **Location** M27 junct 2, A36 towards Salisbury, at 1st rdbt 1st exit, then 1st right at Vine public house

Hotel ★★★ 66% Bartley Lodge, Lyndhurst Rd, CADNAM ☎ 023 8081 2248 31 en suite

PETERSFIELD   Map 04 SU72

Petersfield (New Course) Tankerdale Ln, Liss
GU33 7QY ☎ 01730 895165 (office) 🗎 01730 894713
e-mail: richard@petersfieldgolfclub.co.uk
Gently undulating course with mature trees and hedgerows. All the advantages of a course recently built to USGA specifications.
18 holes, 6387yds, Par 72, SSS 71, Course record 68.
Club membership 725.
Visitors start times required at weekends, may play only after 12pm weekends **Societies** booking forms and deposit required. **Green Fees** terms on application. **Prof** Greg Hughes **Course Designer** M Hawtree **Facilities** ⊗ ⅲ ⅃ ⾕ ⼂ 🀫 ⾕ ⼂ **Location** Off the A3(M), between the Liss/Petersfield exits southbound

Hotel ★★★ 🏌 68% Southdowns Country Hotel, Dumpford Ln, Trotton, MIDHURST ☎ 01730 821521 22 en suite

Petersfield (Old Course) Sussex Rd GU31 4EJ
☎ 01730 267732 🗎 01730 894713
Parkland course on level ground in an area of outstanding natural beauty. Numerous trees and water

features. Part of Petersfield Golf Club although 1.5m away from the 18-hole New Course.
9 holes, 3005yds, Par 72, SSS 69.
Visitors starting times required, pay & play at all times.
Societies booking form must be completed & deposit paid. **Green Fees** terms on application. **Prof** Greg Hughes **Facilities** ⾕ ⼂ ⿈ ⾕ ⼂ **Location** Off Sussex Road , B214

Hotel ★★★ 🏌 68% Southdowns Country Hotel, Dumpford Ln, Trotton, MIDHURST ☎ 01730 821521 22 en suite

PORTSMOUTH   Map 04 SU60

Great Salterns Public Course Burrfields Rd
PO3 5HH ☎ 023 9266 4549 🗎 023 9265 0525
Easy walking, seaside course with open fairways and testing shots onto well-guarded, small greens. Testing 13th hole, par 4, requiring 130yd shot across a lake.
Great Salterns Golf Course: 18 holes, 5575yds, Par 70, SSS 67, Course record 64.
Club membership 700.
Visitors book up to 1 week in advance. **Societies** must contact in advance. **Green Fees** terms on application.
Cards 🃏 🎴 🃏 🂠 **Prof** Terry Healy **Facilities** ⊗ ⅲ ⅃ ⾕ ⼂ 🀫 ⾕ ⼂ **Location** NE of town centre on A2030

Hotel ★★★★ 65% Portsmouth Marriott Hotel, Southampton Rd, PORTSMOUTH ☎ 0870 400 7285 174 en suite

Southsea The Clubhouse, Burrfields Rd PO3 5JJ
☎ 023 92664549 🗎 023 92668667
Municipal meadowland course.
Great Salterns: 18 holes, 5800yds, Par 71, SSS 68, Course record 64.
Club membership 400.
Visitors no restrictions. Booking advisable via pro shop.
Societies must contact in advance. **Green Fees** £13 per 18 holes. **Cards** 🃏 🎴 🃏 🂠 **Prof** Terry Healy **Facilities** 🀫 ⾕ ⼂ **Location** 0.5m off M27

Hotel ★★★★ 65% Portsmouth Marriott Hotel, Southampton Rd, PORTSMOUTH ☎ 0870 400 7285 174 en suite

ROMSEY   Map 04 SU32

Dunwood Manor Danes Rd, Awbridge SO51 0GF
☎ 01794 340549 🗎 01794 341215
e-mail: admin@dunwood-golf.co.uk
Undulating parkland course with fine views. Fine holes running through mature woodland.
18 holes, 5767yds, Par 69, SSS 68, Course record 65.
Club membership 620.
Visitors always welcome advisable to contact in advance; essential for weekends after 11am. **Societies** must contact in advance. **Green Fees** £28 per round. **Prof** Heath Teschner **Facilities** ⊗ ⅲ ⅃ ⾕ ⼂ ⿈ ⾕ ⼂ 🀫 ⾕ ⼂ **Location** 4m NW of Romsey off A27

Hotel ★★★ 67% Bell Inn, BROOK ☎ 023 8081 2214 25 en suite

Romsey Romsey Rd, Nursling SO16 0XW
☎ 023 80734637 🗎 023 80741036
e-mail: mike@romseygolf.co.uk
Parkland/woodland course with narrow tree-lined fairways. Six holes are undulating, the rest are sloping.

Continued

Continued

There are superb views over the Test valley. **Excellent test of golf for all standards.**
18 holes, 5718yds, Par 69, SSS 68, Course record 64.
Club membership 800.
Visitors welcome Mon-Fri, must play with member weekends and bank holidays. **Societies** Mon, Tue & Thu, must contact in advance. **Green Fees** £34 per day, £28 per round. **Prof** Mark Desmond **Facilities** ⊗ ⫲⫲⫲ ⛭ 🍴 ♀ ⚲ 🏠 ⚷ **Conf** fac available **Location** 3m S on A3057 or 1m N off M27 junct 3

Hotel ★★★ 64% The White Horse, Market Place, ROMSEY ☎ 0870 400 8123 26 en suite 7 annexe en suite

ROTHERWICK   Map 04 SU75

Tylney Park RG27 9AY
☎ 01256 762079 🖷 01256 763079
e-mail: martinkimberley@msn.com
A very scenic parkland course with many trees and a practice area.
18 holes, 6109yds, Par 70, SSS 69, Course record 66.
Club membership 730.
Visitors must contact in advance at weekends. **Societies** must apply by phone in advance. **Green Fees** £28 (£35 weekends). **Cards** 🚰 🚃 💳 💷 **Prof** Chris de Bruin **Course Designer** W Wiltshire **Facilities** ⊗ ⫲⫲⫲ by prior arrangement ⛭ 🍴 ♀ ⚲ 🏠 🚵 ⚷ **Conf** Corporate Hospitality Days available **Location** 0.5m SW of Rotherwick, 2m NW of Hook, 2.5m from M3 junct 5 via Newnham

Hotel ★★★★ 🞔 Tylney Hall Hotel, ROTHERWICK
☎ 01256 764881 35 en suite 77 annexe en suite

ROWLANDS CASTLE   Map 04 SU71

Rowlands Castle 31 Links Ln PO9 6AE
☎ 023 92412784 🖷 023 92413649
e-mail: manager@rowlandscastlegolfclub.co.uk
Reasonably dry in winter, the flat parkland course is a testing one with a number of tricky dog-legs and bunkers much in evidence. The par 4 13th is a signature hole necessitating a drive to a narrow fairway and a second shot to a two-tiered green. The 7th, at 522yds, is the longest hole on the course and leads to a well-guarded armchair green.
18 holes, 6612yds, Par 72, SSS 72, Course record 68.
Club membership 800.
Visitors may not play Sat; must contact in advance and hold a handicap certificate. **Societies** Tue & Thu only; must contact in writing. **Green Fees** not confirmed. **Prof** Peter Klepacz **Course Designer** Colt **Facilities** ⊗ ⫲⫲⫲ ⛭ 🍴 ♀ ⚲ 🏠 🚵 ⚷ **Conf** Corporate Hospitality Days available **Location** W side of village off B2149

Hotel ★★★ 69% Brookfield Hotel, Havant Rd, EMSWORTH ☎ 01243 373363 40 en suite

SHEDFIELD   Map 04 SU51

Marriott Meon Valley Hotel & Country Club Sandy Ln SO32 2HQ
☎ 01329 833455 🖷 01329 834411
It has been said that a golf course architect is as good as the ground on which he has to work. Here Hamilton Stutt had magnificent terrain at his disposal and a very good and lovely parkland course is the result. There are three holes over water. The hotel provides many sports facilities.
Meon Course: 18 holes, 6520yds, Par 71,
SSS 71, Course record 66.   *Continued*

Valley Course: 9 holes, 2721yds, Par 35, SSS 33.
Club membership 700.
Visitors may book up to seven days in advance. **Societies** telephone in advance, written confirmation. **Green Fees** terms on application. **Cards** 🚰 🚃 💳 💷 **Prof** Rod Cameron **Course Designer** Hamilton Stutt **Facilities** ⊗ ⫲⫲⫲ ⛭ 🍴 ♀ ⚲ 🏠 🍴 🛥 🎣 🏌 🚵 ⚷ 🏇 **Leisure** hard tennis courts, heated indoor swimming pool, sauna, solarium, gymnasium. **Location** Off A334 between Botley and Wickham. Access via junct 7 M27

Hotel ★★★★ 67% Marriott Meon Valley Hotel & Country Club, Sandy Ln, SHEDFIELD ☎ 01329 833455 113 en suite

SOUTHAMPTON   Map 04 SU41

Chilworth Main Rd, Chilworth SO16 7JP
☎ 023 8074 0544 🖷 023 8073 3166
A course with two loops of nine holes, with a booking system to allow undisturbed play. The front nine are fairly long and undulating and include water hazards. The back nine are tighter and quite a challenge.
Manor Golf Course: 18 holes, 5837yds, Par 69, SSS 69, Course record 68.
Club membership 600.
Visitors no restrictions. **Societies** telephone in advance and complete booking form, various packages available. **Green Fees** terms on application. **Cards** 🚰 🚃 💳 💷 **Course Designer** J Garner **Facilities** ⊗ ⫲⫲⫲ ⛭ 🍴 ♀ ⚲ 🏠 ⚷ 🏇 **Location** A27 between Chilworth and Romsey

Hotel ★★★ 65% Chilworth Manor, CHILWORTH
☎ 023 8076 7333 95 en suite

Southampton Golf Course Rd, Bassett SO16 7LE
☎ 023 80760478 & 80760546 (booking) 🖷 023 80760472
e-mail: golf.course@southampton.gov.uk
18 holes, 6103yds, Par 69, SSS 70.
9 holes, 2395yds, Par 33.
Course Designer Halmree/A P Taylor **Location** 4m N of city centre off A33
Telephone for further details

Hotel ★★ 68% The Elizabeth House Hotel, 42-44 The Avenue, SOUTHAMPTON ☎ 023 8022 4327 20 en suite 7 annexe en suite

Stoneham Monks Wood Close, Bassett SO16 3TT
☎ 023 8076 9272 🖷 023 8076 6320
e-mail: richard.penley-martin@stonehamgolfclub.org.uk
A hilly, heather course with sand or peat sub-soil; the fairways are separated by belts of woodland and heather to present a varied terrain. The interesting 4th is a difficult par 4 and the fine 11th has cross-bunkers about 150 yards from the tee.
18 holes, 6387yds, Par 72, SSS 70, Course record 63.
Club membership 800.
Visitors advisable to contact in advance, handicap certificate required. **Societies** Mon, Thu & Fri only. Must telephone in advance or apply in writing. **Green Fees** £40 per day; £35 per round (£57/£45 weekends & bank holidays). **Cards** 🚰 🚃 💳 💷 **Prof** Ian Young **Course Designer** Willie Park **Facilities** ⊗ ⫲⫲⫲ ⛭ 🍴 ♀ ⚲ 🏠 🍴 ⚷ **Conf** Corporate Hospitality Days available **Location** 4m N of city centre off A27

Hotel ★★★ 65% Chilworth Manor, CHILWORTH
☎ 023 8076 7333 95 en suite

SOUTHWICK   Map 04 SU60

Southwick Park Naval Recreation Centre
Pinsley Dr PO17 6EL
☎ 023 923 80131 📄 023 9221 0289
Set in 100 acres of parkland.
18 holes, 5884yds, Par 69, SSS 69, Course record 64.
Club membership 700.
Visitors contact in advance, welcome weekends after 2pm
Societies Tue only, telephone in advance. **Green Fees**
terms on application. **Prof** John Green **Course Designer**
C Lawrie **Facilities** ⊗ ⅛ ⅃ ♿ ♀ ⚐ ☎ ┬ ✆
Location 0.5m SE off B2177

Hotel ★★ 70% Old House Hotel, The Square,
WICKHAM ☎ 01329 833049 8 en suite

TADLEY   Map 04 SU66

Bishopswood Bishopswood Ln RG26 4AT
☎ 0118 9812200 📄 0118 9408606
e-mail: bishopswood@hampshiregolf.u-net.com
**Wooded parkland course. Tight fairways with natural
water hazards.**
9 holes, 6474yds, Par 72, SSS 71, Course record 66.
Club membership 400.
Visitors must contact in advance. No play weekends or
bank holidays. **Societies** must contact by telephone. **Green
Fees** £18 per 18 holes, £12 per 9 holes. **Cards** 🌐 💳 💳
💳 💳 **Prof** Steve Ward **Course Designer** M W Phillips/G
Blake **Facilities** ⊗ ⅛ ⅃ ♿ ♀ ⚐ ✆ ┬ **Conf** Corporate
Hospitality Days available **Location** 6m N of Basingstoke
off the A340

Hotel ★★★ 72% Romans Country House Hotel, Little
London Rd, SILCHESTER ☎ 0118 970 0421 11 en suite
14 annexe en suite

WATERLOOVILLE   Map 04 SU60

Portsmouth Crookhorn Ln, Purbrook PO7 5QL
☎ 023 92372210 📄 023 92200766
e-mail: info@portsmouthgc.com
**Hilly, challenging course with good views of
Portsmouth Harbour. Rarely free from the wind and
the picturesque 6th, 17th and 18th holes can test the
best.**
18 holes, 6139yds, Par 69, SSS 70, Course record 64.
Club membership 600.
Visitors must book in advance. **Societies** must book in
advance, in writing or by telephone. **Green Fees** terms on
application. **Cards** 🌐 💳 💳 💳 💳 **Prof** James
Green **Course Designer** Hawtree **Facilities** ⊗ ⅛ ⅃ ♿ ♀
♿ ⚐ ┬ **Conf** fac available **Location** 2m S, off A3

Hotel ★★★★ 65% Portsmouth Marriott Hotel,
Southampton Rd, PORTSMOUTH ☎ 0870 400 7285 174
en suite

Waterlooville Cherry Tree Av, Cowplain PO8 8AP
☎ 023 92263388 📄 023 92242980
e-mail: secretary@waterloovillegolfclub.co.uk
**Parkland course, easy walking. Challenging course with
five par 5s over 500yds and featuring four ponds and a
stream running through.**
18 holes, 6602yds, Par 72, SSS 72, Course record 64.
Club membership 800.
Visitors must contact in advance & may only play on
weekdays. Handicap certificate required. **Societies** Thu

Continued

only; apply by letter or telephone. **Green Fees** £40 per day,
£30 per round. **Prof** John Hay **Course Designer** Henry
Cotton **Facilities** ⊗ ⅛ ⅃ ♿ ♀ ⚐ ♿ ✆ **Conf** Corporate
Hospitality Days available **Location** NE side of town
centre off A3

Hotel ★★★ 69% Brookfield Hotel, Havant Rd,
EMSWORTH ☎ 01243 373363 40 en suite

WICKHAM   Map 04 SU51

Wickham Park Titchfield Ln PO17 5PJ
☎ 01329 833342 📄 01329 834798
e-mail: wpgc@crown-golf.co.uk
**An attractive 18-hole parkland course set in the Meon
Valley. Ideal for beginners and established golfers alike.
The course is not overly demanding but is challenging
enough to provide an enjoyable round of golf.**
18 holes, 5898yards, Par 69, SSS 68, Course record 69.
Club membership 600.
Visitors may book up to 7 days in advance. May play after
9.30am at weekends. **Societies** weekdays only. **Green Fees**
terms on application. **Cards** 🌐 💳 💳 💳 💳 **Prof** Scott
Edwards **Facilities** ⊗ ⅛ ⅃ ♿ ♀ ⚐ ┬ ♿ ✆ ┆
Leisure driving net, chipping area. **Conf** fac available
Location M27 junct 9/10

Hotel ★★ 70% Old House Hotel, The Square,
WICKHAM ☎ 01329 833049 8 en suite

WINCHESTER   Map 04 SU42

Hockley Twyford SO21 1PL
☎ 01962 713165 📄 01962 713612
e-mail: secretary@hockleygolfclub.com
Downland course with good views.
18 holes, 6336yds, Par 71, SSS 70, Course record 64.
Club membership 750.
Visitors are advised to phone in advance. Restricted times
at weekends. Handicap certificate required. **Societies** must
telephone in advance and confirm in writing with deposit.
Green Fees £45 per day, £35 per round (£50 weekends).
Prof Gary Stubbington **Course Designer** James Braid
Facilities ⊗ ⅛ ⅃ ♿ ♀ ⚐ ♿ ✆ ┆ **Conf** Corporate
Hospitality Days available **Location** Jct 11 M3, follow
sign to Twyford

Hotel ★★★★ 63% The Wessex, Paternoster Row,
WINCHESTER ☎ 0870 400 8126 94 en suite

Royal Winchester Sarum Rd SO22 5QE
☎ 01962 852462 📄 01962 865048
e-mail: manager@royalwinchestergolfclub.com
**The Royal Winchester course is a sporting downland
course centred on a rolling valley, so the course is hilly
in places. Royal Winchester must be included in any list
of notable clubs, because of its age (it dates from 1888)
and also because the club was involved in one of the
very first professional matches.**
18 holes, 6216yds, Par 71, SSS 70, Course record 65.
Club membership 800.
Visitors must play with member at weekends. Must
contact in advance and have a handicap certificate.
Societies must contact in writing or by telephone. **Green
Fees** terms on application. **Prof** Steven Hunter **Course
Designer** J H Taylor **Facilities** ⊗ ⅛ ⅃ ♿ ♀ ⚐ ✆
Conf Corporate Hospitality Days available **Location** 1.5m
W off A3090

Hotel ★★★★ ♨ Lainston House Hotel, Sparsholt,
WINCHESTER ☎ 01962 863588 50 en suite

South Winchester Romsey Rd SO22 5QW
☎ 01962 877800 📄 01962 877900
e-mail: w.sheffield@crownsportsplc.com
This Dave Thomas designed course incorporates downland, meadows and seven lakes. Home of the Hampshire PGA and the venue for European Ladies Tour Pro-Ams.
18 holes, 7086yds, Par 72, SSS 74, Course record 68.
Club membership 750.
Visitors guests only by arrangement. **Societies** must contact in advance. **Green Fees** not confirmed. **Cards** 📧 📧 📧 📧 📧 **Prof** Richard Adams **Course Designer** Dave Thomas **Facilities** ⊗ ℳ 🕭 ♨ ♀ ♁ 🏌 ❀ ❅ 🏌 ∥ {
Location M3 junct 11,on A3090 Romsey road

....

Hotel ★★★ 73% The Winchester Royal, Saint Peter St, WINCHESTER ☎ 01962 840840 75 en suite

HEREFORDSHIRE

CLIFFORD   Map 03 SO24

Summerhill HR3 5EW ☎ 01497 820451
9 holes, 2929yds, Par 70, SSS 67, Course record 72.
Course Designer Bob Sandow **Location** 0.5 mile from Hay-on-Wye into Herefordshire on right hand side of B4350
Telephone for further details

....

Inn ◆◆◆◆◆ The Talkhouse, Pontdolgoch, CAERSWS ☎01686 688919 3 en suite

HEREFORD   Map 03 SO53

Belmont Lodge Belmont HR2 9SA
☎ 01432 352666 📄 01432 358090
e-mail: info@belmont-hereford.co.uk
Parkland course designed in two loops of nine. The first nine take the higher ground, offering magnificent views over Herefordshire. The second nine run alongside the River Wye with five holes in play against the river.

Belmont Lodge & Golf Course: 18 holes, 6511yds, Par 72, SSS 71, Course record 66.
Club membership 450.
Visitors advised to contact in advance at weekends. Tel: 01432 352666 or 352717. **Societies** must telephone in advance. **Green Fees** £39.95 per day, £16.95 per 18 holes. Reduced winter rates. **Cards** 📧 📧 📧 📧 📧 📧
Prof Mike Welsh **Course Designer** Bob Sandow **Facilities** ⊗ ℳ 🕭 ♨ ♀ ♁ 🏌 ❀ ❅ 🏌 ∥ **Leisure** hard tennis courts, fishing. **Conf** fac available Corporate Hospitality Days available **Location** 2m S off A465

....

Hotel ★★★ 69% Belmont Lodge & Golf, Belmont, HEREFORD ☎ 01432 352666 30 en suite

Burghill Valley Tillington Rd, Burghill HR4 7RW
☎ 01432 760456 📄 01432 761654
e-mail: golf@bvgc.co.uk
The course is situated in typically beautiful Herefordshire countryside. The walking is easy on gently rolling fairways with a background of hills and woods and in the distance, the Welsh mountains. Some holes are played through mature cider orchards and there are two lakes to negotiate. A fair but interesting test for players of all abilities.
18 holes, 6239yds, Par 71, SSS 70, Course record 66.
Club membership 700.
Visitors contact in advance. **Societies** apply in writing or telephone in advance. **Green Fees** terms on application.
Cards 📧 📧 📧 📧 📧 📧 **Prof** Keith Preece/Andy Cameron
Course Designer M Barnett **Facilities** ⊗ ℳ 🕭 ♨ ♀ ♁ 🏌 ❀ ❅ 🏌 ∥ **Leisure** chipping practice area. **Location** 4m NW of Hereford

....

Hotel ★★★ 61% The Green Dragon, Broad St, HEREFORD ☎ 0870 400 8113 83 en suite

Hereford Municipal Hereford Leisure Centre, Holmer Rd HR4 9UD ☎ 01432 344376 📄 01432 266281
This municipal parkland course is more challenging than first appearance. The well-drained greens are open all year round with good drainage for excellent winter golf.
9 holes, 3060yds, Par 35, SSS 69.
Club membership 195.
Visitors restrictions on race days. **Societies** telephone in advance. **Green Fees** not confirmed. **Cards** 📧 📧 📧 📧
📧 **Prof** Gary Morgan **Course Designer** J Leek **Facilities** ⊗ ℳ 🕭 ♨ ♀ ♁ 🏌 ❀ 🏌 ∥ **Leisure** squash, gymnasium, Leisure centre. **Location** Located with race course on Holmer Rd,on A49 Hereford to Leominster

....

Hotel ★★★ 61% The Green Dragon, Broad St, HEREFORD ☎ 0870 400 8113 83 en suite

KINGTON   Map 03 SO25

Kington Bradnor Hill HR5 3RE
☎ 01544 230340 (club) & 231320 (pro shop)
📄 01544 230340 /231320 (pro)
The highest 18-hole course in England, with magnificent views over seven counties. A natural heathland course with easy walking on mountain turf cropped by sheep. There is bracken to catch any really bad shots but no sand traps. The greens play true and fast and are generally acknowledged as some of the best in the West Midlands.
18 holes, 5980yds, Par 70, SSS 68, Course record 63.
Club membership 510.
Visitors contact the professional, particularly at weekends by phoning 01544 231320. **Societies** must book in advance through the Professional. **Green Fees** terms on application.
Prof Andy Gealy **Course Designer** Major C K Hutchison
Facilities ⊗ ℳ 🕭 ♨ ♀ ♁ 🏌 ❀ ❅ 🏌 ∥ { **Location** 0.5m N of Kington, off B4355

....

Hotel ★★★ 65% Talbot Hotel, West St, LEOMINSTER ☎ 01568 616347 20 en suite

Use the maps at the back of the guide to help locate a golf course.

LEOMINSTER
Map 03 SO45

Leominster Ford Bridge HR6 0LE
☎ 01568 610055 📠 01568 610055
e-mail: leominstergolf@freeuk.com
On undulating parkland with the lower holes running alongside the River Lugg and others on the higher part of the course affording fine panoramic views over the surrounding countryside.
18 holes, 6026yds, Par 70, SSS 69.
Club membership 520.
Visitors must contact in advance. **Societies** must telephone in advance. **Green Fees** £19 per day, £15.50 per round (£25/£22 weekends and bank holidays). **Cards** 🔲 🔲 🔲
Prof Andrew Ferriday **Course Designer** Bob Sandow
Facilities ⊗ 〕Ⅱ ▙ 🖤 ♀ 🏊 🍴 ♻ ✐ **Leisure** fishing.
Conf fac available Corporate Hospitality Days available
Location 3m S of Leominster on A49. Clearly signposted from Leominster by-pass

···

Hotel ★★★ 65% Talbot Hotel, West St, LEOMINSTER
☎ 01568 616347 20 en suite

ROSS-ON-WYE
Map 03 SO62

Ross-on-Wye Two Park, Gorsley HR9 7UT
☎ 01989 720267 📠 01989 720212
e-mail: secretary@therossonwyegolfclub.co.uk
The club celebrated its centenary in 2003. This undulating, parkland course has been cut out of a silver birch forest. The fairways are well-screened from each other and tight, the greens good and the bunkers have been restructured.
18 holes, 6451yds, Par 72, SSS 71, Course record 68.
Club membership 760.
Visitors must contact secretary or professional in advance.
Societies apply in writing/telephone in advance. **Green Fees** £48 per 36 holes; £44 per 27 holes; £36 per round.
Cards 🔲 🔲 **Prof** Nick Catchpole **Course Designer** Mr
C K Cotton **Facilities** ⊗ 〕Ⅱ ▙ 🖤 ♀ 🏊 🍴 ♻ 🔧 ✐ ✠
Conf Corporate Hospitality Days available **Location** On
B4221 N side of M50 junct 3

···

Hotel ★★★ 74% Pengethley Manor, Pengethley Park,
ROSS-ON-WYE ☎ 01989 730211 11 en suite
14 annexe en suite

South Herefordshire Twin Lakes HR9 7UA
☎ 01989 780535 📠 01989 740611
e-mail: shgc.golf@clara.co.uk
Impressive 6672-yard parkland course fast maturing into one of Herefordshire's finest. Magnificent panoramic views of the Welsh mountains and countryside. Drains well and is playable in any weather. The landscape has enabled the architect to design 18 individual and varied holes.
Twin Lakes: 18 holes, 6672yds, Par 71, SSS 72, Course record 71.
Club membership 300.
Visitors must contact in advance. **Societies** phone in advance. **Green Fees** £20 per day, £15 per round (£25/£20 weekends). **Cards** 🔲 🔲 🔲 🔲 **Prof** Edward Litchfield
Course Designer John Day **Facilities** ⊗ 〕Ⅱ ▙ 🖤 ♀ 🏊 🍴
✠ 🔧 ✐ ꝭ **Conf** Corporate Hospitality Days available
Location J4 M50 to Upton Bishop, right to B4224,
1m left

···

Hotel ★★★ 68% Pencraig Court Country House Hotel,
Pencraig, ROSS-ON-WYE ☎ 01989 770306
10 en suite

UPPER SAPEY
Map 03 SO66

Sapey WR6 6XT
☎ 01886 853288 & 853567 📠 01886 853485
e-mail: anybody@sapeygolf.co.uk

Continued

Parkland course with views of the Malvern Hills. Trees, lakes and water hazards. Not too strenuous a walk.
The Rowan: 18 holes, 5935yds, Par 69, SSS 68, Course record 63.
The Oaks: 9 holes, 1203, Par 27, SSS 27.
Club membership 450.
Visitors must contact in advance. **Societies** telephone in advance. **Green Fees** Rowan: £20 per round (£25 weekends). Oaks: £6 (£7 weekends). **Cards** 🖃 💳 📇 💳 📇 **Prof** Chris Knowles **Course Designer** R McMurray **Facilities** ⊗ ⅛ ⅃ ⅃ 🎿 🛆 🏠 🍴 ⅃ 🚲 🛺 ⅃ Conf Corporate Hospitality Days available **Location** B4203 Bromyard/Stourport Rd

Hotel ★★★ 65% Talbot Hotel, West St, LEOMINSTER ☎ 01568 616347 20 en suite

Herefordshire Ravens Causeway HR4 8LY
☎ 01432 830219 & 830465 (pro) 📠 01432 830095
e-mail: herefordshire.golf@breath.com
Undulating parkland course with expansive views of the Clee Hills to the east and the Black Mountains to the west. Peaceful and relaxing situation.
18 holes, 6078yds, Par 70, SSS 69, Course record 61.
Club membership 750.
Visitors must contact in advance, possibility of weekend play if no competitions are taking place. **Societies** must apply in advance. **Green Fees** £20 (£25 weekends and bank holidays). **Cards** 🖃 💳 📇 💳 **Prof** Richard Hemming **Course Designer** James Braid **Facilities** ⊗ ⅛ ⅃ ⅃ 🎿 🛆 🏠 🍴 ⅃ 🚲 🛺 ⅃ Conf Corporate Hospitality Days available **Location** 7m nw of Hereford on A 'B'road to Weobley

Hotel ★★★ 61% The Green Dragon, Broad St, HEREFORD ☎ 0870 400 8113 83 en suite

HERTFORDSHIRE

Stocks Hotel & Golf Club Stocks Rd HP23 5RX
☎ 01442 851341 & 851491 (pro) 📠 01442 861253
e-mail: info@stockshotel.co.uk
This gently undulating course sits in the shadow of the Ashridge Forest and commands attractive views of the Chiltern Hills. It is ideally suited to golfers of all standards, representing a true test of golf.
18 holes, 6804yds, Par 72, SSS 73, Course record 66.
Club membership 630.
Visitors can book upto 5 days in advance. May not play before 12pm at weekends and bank holidays. **Societies** please telephone Golf Club Manager, Robin Darling on 01442 852504 **Green Fees** £35 per round (£45 weekends). **Cards** 🖃 💳 📇 📇 💳 📇 **Prof** Peter Lane **Course Designer** Mike Billcliffe **Facilities** ⊗ ⅛ ⅃ ⅃ 🎿 🛆 🏠 🍴 ⅃ 🚲 🛺 ⅃ **Leisure** chipping green, practice bunker.
Conf fac available **Location** 2m from A41 at Tring, towards Tring station

Hotel ★★★★ 66% Pendley Manor, Cow Ln, TRING ☎ 01442 891891 74 en suite

Aldenham Golf and Country Club Church Ln
WD25 8NN ☎ 01923 853929 📠 01923 858472
e-mail: info@aldenhamgolfclub.co.uk
Undulating parkland course with many specimen trees. Beautiful views across countryside.

Old Course: 18 holes, 6480yds, Par 70, SSS 71.
White Course: 9 holes, 2350yds, Par 33, SSS 32.
Club membership 500.
Visitors Old Course restricted weekends before 1pm. White Course no restrictions. **Societies** must contact in advance. **Green Fees** Old Course: £26 per round (£35 weekends). White Course £10 (£12 weekends). **Cards** 🖃 💳 📇 💳 📇 **Prof** Tim Dunstan **Facilities** ⊗ ⅛ ⅃ ⅃ 🎿 🛆 🏠 🍴 ⅃ 🚲 🛺 ⅃ **Conf** fac available Corporate Hospitality Days available **Location** W side of village, 0.5 miles from M1 junct 5

Hotel ★★★ 67% The White House, Upton Rd, WATFORD ☎ 01923 237316 57 en suite

BERKHAMSTED
Map 04 SP90

Berkhamsted The Common HP4 2QB
☎ 01442 865832 📠 01442 863730
e-mail: barryh@berkhamstedgc.co.uk
There are no sand bunkers on this Championship heathland course but this does not make it any easier to play. The natural hazards will test the skill of the most able players, with a particularly testing hole at the 11th, 568 yards, par 5. Fine greens, long carries and heather and gorse. The clubhouse is very comfortable.
18 holes, 6605yds, Par 71, SSS 72, Course record 65. Club membership 700.
Visitors must contact in advance and be competent golfer. **Societies** must contact in advance. **Green Fees** £50 per day, £37 per 18 holes (£45 per 18 holes weekends after 11am). **Cards** 📧 🖿 📧 💲 **Prof** John Clarke **Course Designer** Colt/Braid **Facilities** ⊗ ❦ 🖢 🖢 🖢 🖢 🖢 🖢 🖢 **Location** 1.5m E

Hotel ★★★★ 66% Pendley Manor, Cow Ln, TRING ☎ 01442 891891 74 en suite

BISHOP'S STORTFORD
Map 05 TL42

Bishop's Stortford Dunmow Rd CM23 5HP
☎ 01279 654715 📠 01279 655215
e-mail: office@bsgc.co.uk
Well established parkland course, fairly flat, but undulating, with easy walking.

18 holes, 6404yds, Par 71, SSS 71, Course record 64. Club membership 900.
Visitors must have a valid handicap certificate, must play with member at weekends. Ladies day Tue. **Societies** must contact in writing. **Green Fees** £39 per day; £30 per 18 holes. **Cards** 📧 🖿 📧 💲 **Prof** Stephen M Bryan **Course Designer** James Braid **Facilities** ⊗ ❦ 🖢 🖢 🖢 🖢 🖢 🖢 🖢 🖢 **Leisure** snooker tables. **Conf** fac available Corporate Hospitality Days available **Location** 0.5m W of M11 junc 8 on A1250

Great Hadham Golf & Country Club
Great Hadham Rd, Much Hadham SG10 6JE
☎ 01279 843558 📠 01279 842122
e-mail: info@ghgcc.co.uk
An undulating open meadowland/links course offering excellent country views and a challenge with its ever present breeze.
18 holes, 6854yds, Par 72, SSS 73, Course record 67. Club membership 800.
Visitors welcome all times except am Mon, Wed, Sat & Sun. **Societies** weekdays only, by advance booking in writing. **Green Fees** £20 per 18 holes, £12 per 9 holes

(£27/£15 weekends after noon). **Cards** 📧 🖿 📧 **Prof** Kevin Lunt **Course Designer** Iain Roberts **Facilities** ⊗ ❦ 🖢 🖢 🖢 🖢 🖢 🖢 🖢 **Conf** fac available **Location** On the B1004, 3m SW of Bishop's Stortford

BRICKENDON
Map 05 TL30

Brickendon Grange Pembridge Ln SG13 8PD
☎ 01992 511258 📠 01992 511411
e-mail: play@brickendongrangegc.co.uk
Undulating parkland course with some fine par 4s. 17th hole reputed to be best in the county.
18 holes, 6420yds, Par 71, SSS 71, Course record 67. Club membership 680.
Visitors must have handicap certificate. With member only at weekends & bank holidays. **Societies** by arrangement. **Green Fees** £45 per day; £33 per round. **Prof** Graham Tippett **Course Designer** C K Cotton **Facilities** ⊗ ❦ 🖢 🖢 🖢 🖢 🖢 🖢 🖢 🖢 **Location** W side of village

Hotel ★★★ 64% The White Horse, Hertingfordbury, HERTFORD ☎ 01992 586791 42 en suite

BROOKMANS PARK
Map 04 TL20

Brookmans Park Golf Club Rd AL9 7AT
☎ 01707 652487 📠 01707 661851
e-mail: clubbp@aol.com
Brookman's Park is an undulating parkland course, with several cleverly constructed holes. But it is a fair course, although it can play long. The 11th, par 3, is a testing hole which plays across a lake.
18 holes, 6473yds, Par 71, SSS 71, Course record 65. Club membership 750.
Visitors must contact professional in advance 01707 652468 and have a handicap certificate; must play with member at weekends & bank holidays. **Societies** must telephone or write in advance. **Green Fees** £40 per day; £32 per round. **Prof** Ian Jelley **Course Designer** Hawtree/Taylor **Facilities** ⊗ ❦ 🖢 🖢 🖢 🖢 🖢 🖢 🖢 🖢 **Location** N side of village off A1000

Hotel ★★★ 70% Bush Hall, Mill Green, HATFIELD ☎ 01707 271251 25 en suite

BROXBOURNE
Map 05 TL30

Hertfordshire Broxbournebury Mansion, White Stubbs Ln
☎ 01992 466666 & 441268 (pro shop) 📠 01992 470326
e-mail: hertfordshire@americangolf.uk.com
18 holes, 6314yds, Par 70, SSS 70, Course record 62.
Course Designer Jack Nicklaus II **Location** on A10 take Broxbourne exit and follow signs for Paradise Wildlife Park. Turn left at Bell Lane and follow road over A10, course on right.
Telephone for further details

Hotel ★★★ 64% The White Horse, Hertingfordbury, HERTFORD ☎ 01992 586791 42 en suite

BUNTINGFORD
Map 05 TL32

East Herts Hamels Park SG9 9NA
☎ 01920 821922 (Pro) 📠 01920 823700
e-mail: secretary@ehgc.fsnet.co.uk
An attractive undulating parkland course with magnificent specimen trees.

Continued

Continued

18 holes, 6456yds, Par 71, SSS 71.
Club membership 750.
Visitors must contact in advance & have handicap certificate, but may not play on Wed & weekends.
Societies apply in writing. **Green Fees** terms on application. **Prof** G Culmer **Facilities** ⊗ ⓑ ♥ ♀ ⚲ ⚑ ⛨ ♣ ♣ ♂ **Conf** Corporate Hospitality Days available **Location** 1m N of Puckeridge off A10, opposite Pearce's Farm Shop

Hotel ★★★ 66% Novotel Stevenage, Knebworth Park, STEVENAGE ☎ 01438 346100 100 en suite

BUSHEY   Map 04 TQ19

Bushey Golf & Country Club High St WD23 1TT
☎ 020 8950 2215(pro shop) 🗏 020 8386 1181
e-mail: info@busheycountryclub.com
Undulating parkland with challenging 2nd and 9th holes. The latter has a sweeping dog-leg left, playing to a green in front of the club house. For the rather too enthusiastic golfer, Bushey offers its own physiotherapist!

9 holes, 6120yds, Par 70, SSS 69, Course record 67.
Club membership 475.
Visitors must contact in advance. May not play Wed/Thu/Sat/Sun mornings. **Societies** apply in writing or by telephone. **Green Fees** not confirmed. **Prof** Grahame Atkinson **Course Designer** Donald Steele **Facilities** ⊗ ⓜ ⓑ ♥ ♀ ⚑ ♣ ♂ **Leisure** sauna, solarium, gymnasium, health & fitness club. **Conf** Corporate Hospitality Days available

Hotel ★★★ 72% Edgwarebury Hotel, Barnet Ln, ELSTREE ☎ 0870 609 6151 47 en suite

Bushey Hall Bushey Hall Dr WD23 2EP
☎ 01923 222253 🗏 01923 229759
e-mail: info@golfclubuk.co.uk
Tree-lined parkland course.
18 holes, 6099yds, Par 69, SSS 69, Course record 62.
Club membership 500.
Visitors may book 14 days in advance and may only play after 11am weekends. **Societies** must contact in writing.
Green Fees £26 per round (£33 weekends & bank holidays). **Cards** 🖭 🖭 🖭 🖭 💳 **Prof** Ken Wickham
Course Designer J Braid **Facilities** ⊗ ⓜ by prior arrangement ⓑ ♥ ♀ ⚲ ⚑ ⛨ ♣ ♂ **Conf** Corporate Hospitality Days available **Location** Leave M1 junct 5 take A41 to Harrow then B462 to Bushey, at rdbt take 4th exit, Bushey Hall Golf Club is 150yds on left

Hotel ★★★ 72% Edgwarebury Hotel, Barnet Ln, ELSTREE ☎ 0870 609 6151 47 en suite

Hartsbourne Golf & Country Club Hartsbourne
Ave WD2 1JW ☎ 020 8950 1133
18 holes, 6305yds, Par 71, SSS 70, Course record 62.
Location 5m SE of Watford
Telephone for further details

Hotel ★★★ 72% Edgwarebury Hotel, Barnet Ln, ELSTREE ☎ 0870 609 6151 47 en suite

CHESHUNT   Map 05 TL30

Cheshunt Park Cheshunt Park, Park Ln EN7 6QD
☎ 01992 624009 🗏 01992 636403
e-mail: brox.golf@lineone.net
Municipal parkland course, well-bunkered with ponds, easy walking.
Cheshunt Golf Club: 18 holes, 6692yds, Par 72, SSS 71.
Club membership 350.
Visitors must book Tee-times through Reception. Must contact in advance. **Societies** phone for details **Green Fees** terms on application. **Cards** 🖭 🖭 🖭 🖭 💳 **Prof** David Banks **Course Designer** P Wawtry **Facilities** ⊗ ⓜ ⓑ ♥ ♀ ⚲ ⚑ ⛨ ♣ ♂ **Leisure** Club repair service. **Location** 1.5m NW off B156, 3m N of M25 junc 25

Hotel ★★★ 64% The White Horse, Hertingfordbury, HERTFORD ☎ 01992 586791 42 en suite

CHORLEYWOOD   Map 04 TQ09

Chorleywood Common Rd WD3 5LN
☎ 01923 282009 🗏 01923 286739
e-mail: chorleywood.gc@btclick.com
Very attractive mix of woodland and heathland with natural hazards and good views.
9 holes, 5686yds, Par 68, SSS 67.
Club membership 300.
Visitors must contact in advance, restricted weekends & Tues. **Societies** initial contact by telephone. **Green Fees** £20 per round; £15 for 9 holes (£25/15 weekends).
Facilities ⊗ ⓜ by prior arrangement ⓑ ♥ ♀ ⚲ **Location** M25 junct 18,E side of village off A404

Hotel ★★★ 71% The Bedford Arms, CHENIES ☎ 01923 283301 10 en suite

ELSTREE   Map 04 TQ19

Elstree Watling St WD6 3AA
☎ 020 8953 6115 or 8238 6941 🗏 020 8207 6390
e-mail: admin@elstree-golf.co.uk
Parkland course incorporating ponds and streams.
Elstree Golf Club: 18 holes, 6556yds, Par 73, SSS 72.
Club membership 400.
Visitors advisable to contact in advance, no restrictions weekdays, may not play until after 11am, weekends & bank holidays. Dress code applie. **Societies** information pack available from club secretary. **Green Fees** £30 weekdays (£35 weekends). 2 for 1 offers available. **Cards** 🖭 🖭 🖭 🖭 💳 **Prof** Marc Warwick/Mark Wood **Course Designer** Donald Steel **Facilities** ⊗ ⓜ by prior arrangement ⓑ ♥ ♀ ⚲ ⚑ ⛨ ♣ ♂ **Leisure** snooker. **Conf** fac available Corporate Hospitality Days available **Location** A5183 between Radlett and Elstree, next to Wagon & Horses public house

Hotel ★★★ 72% Edgwarebury Hotel, Barnet Ln, ELSTREE ☎ 0870 609 6151 47 en suite

ESSENDON   Map 04 TL20

Hatfield London Country Club Bedwell Park
AL9 6HN ☎ 01707 260360 🗎 01707 278475
e-mail: info@hlccgolf.co.uk
**Parkland course with many varied hazards, including
ponds, a stream and a ditch. 19th-century manor
clubhouse. 9-hole pitch and putt.**
Old Course: 18 holes, 6808yds, Par 72, SSS 72.
New Course: 18 holes, 6938yds, Par 72, SSS 73.
Club membership 250.
Visitors must contact in advance. **Societies** must contact in
advance. **Green Fees** terms on application. **Cards** 🖃 🖃
🖃 🖾 🖾 **Prof** Norman Greer **Course Designer** Fred
Hawtry **Facilities** ⊗ ⍟ 🖳 ⬛ ♀ 🛆 🖨 ⸯ 🚵 ✧ **Leisure** 9
hole pitch and putt, Japanese bath. **Conf** Corporate
Hospitality Days available **Location** On B158 1m S

Hotel ★★★ 65% Quality Hotel Hatfield, Roehyde Way,
HATFIELD ☎ 01707 275701 76 en suite

GRAVELEY   Map 04 TL22

Chesfield Downs Jack's Hill SG4 7EQ
☎ 01462 482929 🗎 01462 482930
18 holes, 6648yds, Par 71, SSS 72.
Course Designer J Gaunt **Location** Jct 8 of A1, B197 to
Graveley
Telephone for further details

Hotel ⛪ Hotel Ibis Stevenage, Danestrete, STEVENAGE
☎ 01438 779955 98 en suite

HARPENDEN   Map 04 TL11

Aldwickbury Park Piggottshill Ln AL5 1AB
☎ 01582 760112 🗎 01582 760113
e-mail: enquiries@aldwickburyparkgolfclub.com
**Attractive parkland course with large areas of mature
woodland and good views across the Lee Valley.**
18 holes, 6352yds, Par 71, SSS 70, Course record 66.
Club membership 700.
Visitors may book up to 3 days in advance by telephone.
May only play after 1pm weekends. **Societies** telephone for
brochure, various packages available. **Green Fees** £27 per
18 holes (£33 Fri-Sun). **Cards** 🖃 🖃 🖾 🖾 **Prof**
Robin Turley **Course Designer** Ken Brown/Martin Gillett
Facilities ⊗ ⍟ 🖳 ⬛ ♀ 🛆 🖨 ⸯ ✦ 🚵 ✧ **Leisure**
gymnasium, 9 hole par 3 course. **Conf** fac available
Corporate Hospitality Days available **Location** Located
just off Wheathampstead Road, between Harpenden/
Wheathampstead, 10mins from junct 9 of M1

Hotel ★★★ 69% Harpenden House, 18 Southdown Rd,
HARPENDEN ☎ 01582 449955 17 en suite
59 annexe en suite

Harpenden Hammonds End, Redbourn Ln AL5 2AX
☎ 01582 712580 🗎 01582 712725
e-mail: office@harpendengolfclub.co.uk
Gently undulating parkland course, easy walking.
18 holes, 6381yds, Par 70, SSS 70, Course record 65.
Club membership 800.
Visitors must contact in advance. May play Thu &
weekends by arrangement only. **Societies** must apply in
writing. **Green Fees** £40 per day, £30 per round (£40 per
round weekends and bank holidays). **Cards** 🖃 🖃 🖾
🖾 **Prof** Peter Cherry **Course Designer** Hawtree & Taylor
Facilities ⊗ ⍟ 🖳 ⬛ ♀ 🛆 🖨 ⸯ ✧ ✦ **Location** 1m S
on B487

Hotel ★★★ 69% Harpenden House, 18 Southdown Rd,
HARPENDEN ☎ 01582 449955 17 en suite
59 annexe en suite

Harpenden Common Cravells Rd, East Common
AL5 1BL ☎ 01582 711328 (pro shop) 🗎 01582 711321
Flat, easy walking, good greens, typical common course.
18 holes, 6214yds, Par 70, SSS 70, Course record 64.
Club membership 710.
Visitors must contact in advance. **Societies** telephone for
availability **Green Fees** £32 per 36 holes, £28 per 27 holes,
£24 per round. 2 for 1 £30, Mon-Fri only. **Prof** Danny
Fitzsimmons **Course Designer** K Brown **Facilities** ⊗ ⍟ 🖳
⬛ ♀ 🛆 🖨 ⸯ ✧ **Location** On A1081, 0.5m S of Harpenden

Hotel ★★★ 66% Glen Eagle Hotel, 1 Luton Rd,
HARPENDEN ☎ 01582 760271 60 en suite

HEMEL HEMPSTEAD   Map 04 TL00

Boxmoor 18 Box Ln, Boxmoor HP3 0DJ
☎ 01442 242434
**The second oldest course in Hertfordshire. Challenging,
hilly, moorland course with sloping fairways divided by
trees. Fine views. Testing holes: 3rd (par 3), 4th (par 4).
The 3rd has not been holed in one since the course was
founded in 1890 and the par for the course (64) has only
been broken once.**
9 holes, 4812yds, Par 64, SSS 63, Course record 62.
Club membership 280.
Visitors may play Sun after 9.30am **Societies** must contact
in advance. **Green Fees** £10 per round. **Facilities** ⊗ 🖳 ⬛
♀ 🛆 **Location** 2m SW on B4505

Hotel ★★ 72% The Two Brewers, The Common,
CHIPPERFIELD ☎ 01923 265266 20 en suite

Little Hay Box Ln, Bovingdon HP3 0DQ
☎ 01442 833798 🗎 01442 831399
e-mail: chris.gordon@dacorum.gov.uk
Semi-parkland, inland links.
18 holes, 6300yds, Par 72, SSS 72.
Visitors advisable to contact in advance. **Societies**
telephone for details. **Green Fees** terms on application.
Cards 🖃 🖃 🖾 🖾 **Prof** N Allen/M Perry **Course
Designer** Hawtree **Facilities** ⊗ ⍟ 🖳 ⬛ ♀ 🛆 🖨 ⸯ 🚵 ✧
✦ **Location** 1.5m SW on B4505 off A41

Hotel 🅄 Holiday Inn Hemel Hempstead, Breakspear Way,
HEMEL HEMPSTEAD ☎ 0870 400 9041 145 en suite

Shendish Manor London Rd, Apsley HP3 0AA
☎ 01442 251806 🗎 01442 230683
e-mail: tconcannon@shendish.fsnet.co.uk
**A hilly course with plenty of trees and good greens. A
tough course for any golfer.**

Continued   *Continued*

18 holes, 5660yds, Par 70, SSS 67.
Club membership 200.
Visitors no restrictions but advisable to book in advance
Societies must contact in advance. **Green Fees** not
confirmed. **Cards** ▭ ▬ **Course Designer** D Steel
Facilities ⊗ ⅷ by prior arrangement ⓑ 🔲 ♀ ♨ ⛳ ⛵ 🚜
♂ **Leisure** sauna, solarium, gymnasium. **Location** Just off
A4251

Hotel ★★★★ 66% Pendley Manor, Cow Ln, TRING
☎ 01442 891891 74 en suite

KNEBWORTH   Map 04 TL22

Knebworth Deards End Ln SG3 6NL
☎ 01438 812752 📄 01438 815216
e-mail: knebworth.golf@virgin.net
Parkland course, easy walking.
18 holes, 6492yds, Par 71, SSS 71, Course record 66.
Club membership 900.
Visitors must have handicap certificate, must play with
member at weekends. **Societies** Mon, Tue & Thu. Must
contact in advance. **Green Fees** £35 per day/round.
(weekdays only). **Cards** ▭ ▬ ▬ 🅅 **Prof** Garry
Parker **Course Designer** W Park (Jun) **Facilities** ⊗ ⅷ ⓑ
🔲 ♀ ♨ ⛳ 🚜 ♂ **Location** N side of village off B197

Hotel ★★★ 65% The Roebuck Inn, London Rd,
Broadwater, STEVENAGE ☎ 0870 011 9076 54 en suite

LETCHWORTH   Map 04 TL23

Letchworth Letchworth Ln SG6 3NQ
☎ 01462 683203 📄 01462 484567
e-mail: letchworthgolfclub@uk2.net
**Planned more than 50 years ago by Harry Vardon, this
adventurous, parkland course is set in a peaceful corner
of 'Norman' England. To its variety of natural and
artificial hazards is added an unpredictable wind.**
18 holes, 6450yds, Par 71, SSS 71.
Club membership 750.
Visitors may not play Tue and with member only at
weekends. Must contact in advance and have a handicap
certificate. **Societies** Wed, Thu & Fri only, must telephone
in advance. **Prof** Karl
Teschner **Course Designer** Harry Vardon **Facilities** ⊗ ⅷ
ⓑ 🔲 ♀ ♨ ⛳ ♂ 🥂 **Leisure** 9 hole par 3 course. **Conf**
Corporate Hospitality Days available **Location** S side of
town centre off A505

Hotel ★★★ 65% The Cromwell Hotel, High St, Old
Town, STEVENAGE ☎ 01438 779954 76 en suite

LITTLE GADDESDEN   Map 04 SP91

Ashridge HP4 1LY ☎ 01442 842244 📄 01442 843770
e-mail: info@ashridgegolfclub.ltd.uk
**Good parkland course, challenging but fair. Good
clubhouse facilities.**
18 holes, 6580yds, Par 72, SSS 71, Course record 63.
Club membership 720.
Visitors must contact in advance, be a member of a
recognised club & have handicap certificate, may not play
weekends/bank holidays. **Societies** must apply in writing
and complete booking form. **Green Fees** terms on
application. **Cards** ▭ ▬ ▬ ▩ 🅅 **Prof** Andrew
Ainsworth **Course Designer** Sir G Campbell/C
Hutchinson/N V Hotchkin **Facilities** ⊗ ⅷ ⓑ 🔲 ♀ ♨ ⛳
⛵ ♂ ⚑ **Location** 5m N of Berkhamsted on the B4506

Hotel ★★★ 69% Harpenden House, 18 Southdown Rd,
HARPENDEN ☎ 01582 449955 17 en suite
59 annexe en suite

MUCH HADHAM   Map 05 TL41

Ash Valley Little Hadham Rd SG10 6HD
☎ 01279 843253 📄 01279 842389
**Naturally undulating course with good views extending
to Canary Wharf in London on a clear day. Tough
enough for lower handicapped players but forgiving for
the beginner and higher handicapped player.**
*Ash Valley Golf Course: 18 holes, 6586yds, Par 72, SSS
71, Course record 64.*
Visitors must contact in advance for weekends **Societies**
telephone in advance. **Green Fees** not confirmed. **Course
Designer** Martin Gillett **Facilities** ⊗ ⓑ 🔲 ♀ ♨ ⛳ 🚜 ♂
Leisure par 3 pitch and putt. **Location** Between Little
Hadham and Much Hadham, 1.5m S of A120 from Little
Hadham traffic lights

Hotel ★★★ 66% Roebuck Hotel, Baldock St, WARE
☎ 01920 409955 50 en suite

POTTERS BAR   Map 04 TL20

Potters Bar Darkes Ln EN6 1DE
☎ 01707 652020 📄 01707 655051
e-mail: info@pottersbargolfclub.com
Undulating parkland course.
18 holes, 6279yds, Par 71, SSS 70.
Club membership 560.
Visitors with member only at weekends, Ladies Day Wed
morning. **Societies** Mon-Fri & Wed (pm only) by
arrangement with Secretary. **Green Fees** £26 for 18 holes.
Prof Gary A'Ris/Julian Harding **Course Designer** James
Braid **Facilities** ⊗ ⓑ 🔲 ♀ ♨ ⛳ ⛵ 🥂 🚜 ♂ **Location**
1m N of M25 junct 24

Hotel 🅤 Holiday Inn South Mimms, SOUTH MIMMS
☎ 0870 400 9072 144 en suite

RADLETT   Map 04 TL10

Porters Park Shenley Hill WD7 7AZ
☎ 01923 854127 📄 01923 855475
e-mail: info@porterspark.fsnet.co.uk
18 holes, 6313yds, Par 70, SSS 70, Course record 64.
Course Designer Braid **Location** NE side of village off
A5183
Telephone for further details

Hotel 🅤 Holiday Inn South Mimms, SOUTH MIMMS
☎ 0870 400 9072 144 en suite

REDBOURN   Map 04 TL11

Redbourn Kinsbourne Green Ln AL3 7QA
☎ 01582 793493 📄 01582 794362
e-mail: enquiries@redbourngolfclub.com
**A mature parkland course offering a fair test of golf to
all standards. Water comes into play on a number of
holes.**
*Ver Course: 18 holes, 6506yds, Par 70, SSS 71, Course
record 67.*
Kingsbourne Course: 9 holes, 1361yds, Par 27.
Club membership 800.
Visitors must contact up to 3 days in advance for Ver
Course. No restrictions for Par 3. **Societies** must telephone

Continued   *Continued*

in advance. **Green Fees** £26 per 18 holes Mon-Thu, £32 Fri-Sun. **Cards** 🔄 💳 📇 📶 💷 **Prof** Stephen Hunter **Facilities** ⊗)Ⓜ️ ⅃ 📶 ♀ ♨ 🏠 ⛟ ᵀ ❧ ⊕ ♂ ᒥ **Conf** Corporate Hospitality Days available **Location** 1m N off A5183

....

Hotel ★★★ 69% Harpenden House, 18 Southdown Rd, HARPENDEN ☎ 01582 449955 17 en suite 59 annexe en suite

---

RICKMANSWORTH   Map 04 TQ09

Moor Park WD3 1QN
☎ 01923 773146 🖶 01923 777109
e-mail: enquiries@moorparkgc.co.uk
Two parkland courses - High Course is challenging and will test the best golfer and West Course demands a high degree of accuracy.
High Golf Course: 18 holes, 6713yds, Par 72, SSS 72, Course record 63.
West Golf Course: 18 holes, 5815yds, Par 69, SSS 68, Course record 60.
Club membership 1700.
Visitors must contact in advance but may not play at weekends, bank holidays or before 1pm on Tue & Thu. **Societies** must contact in advance. **Green Fees** not confirmed. **Cards** 🔄 💳 📇 📶 💷 **Prof** Lawrence Farmer **Course Designer** H S Colt **Facilities** ⊗ ⅃ 📶 ♀ ♨ 🏠 ⛟ ᵀ ❧ ⊕ ♂ ᒥ **Leisure** hard and grass tennis courts, chipping green snooker room. **Conf** fac available Corporate Hospitality Days available **Location** Off A404 to Northwood,close to junct 17 & 18 on M25

Hotel ★★★ 71% The Bedford Arms, CHENIES
☎ 01923 283301 10 en suite

Rickmansworth Public Course Moor Ln
WD3 1QL ☎ 01923 775278
Undulating, municipal parkland course, short but tests skills to the full.
18 holes, 4656yds, Par 65, SSS 63.
Club membership 240.
Visitors must contact the club in advance, 7 day booking. Set of clubs per person. **Societies** must contact in advance. **Green Fees** not confirmed. **Cards** 🔄 💳 📇 📶 **Prof** Alan Dobbins **Course Designer** Colt **Facilities** ⊗)Ⓜ️ ⅃ 📶 ♀ ♨ 🏠 ⛟ ♂ **Conf** fac available Corporate Hospitality Days available **Location** 2m S of town off A4145

....

Hotel ★★★ 71% The Bedford Arms, CHENIES
☎ 01923 283301 10 en suite

ROYSTON   Map 05 TL34

Barkway Park Nuthampstead Rd, Barkway SG8 8EN
☎ 01763 849070
An undulating course criss-crossed by ditches which come into play on several holes. The challenging par 3 7th features a long, narrow green with out of bounds close to the right edge of the green.
18 holes, 6997yds, Par 74, SSS 74.
Club membership 380.
Visitors must contact in advance, telephone for tee times. **Societies** apply for booking form. **Green Fees** terms on application. **Cards** 🔄 💳 📇 📶 💷 **Prof** Jamie Bates **Course Designer** Vivien Saunders **Facilities** ⊗)Ⓜ️ ⅃ 📶 ♀ ♨ 🏠 ⛟ ♂ **Location** Off B1368 from A10

....

Hotel ★★★ 74% Duxford Lodge Hotel, Ickleton Rd, DUXFORD ☎ 01223 836444 11 en suite 4 annexe en suite

Heydon Grange Golf & Country Club
Heydon SG8 7NS ☎ 01763 208988 🖶 01763 208926
e-mail: enquiries@heydon-grange.co.uk
Three 9-hole parkland courses - the Essex, Cambridgeshire and Hertfordshire - situated in gently rolling countryside. Courses are playable all year round.
Essex: 9 holes, 2891yds, Par 36, SSS 35, Course record 66.
Cambridgeshire: 9 holes, 3057yds, Par 36, SSS 36.
Hertfordshire: 9 holes, 2937yds, Par 36, SSS 36.
Club membership 250.
Visitors must contact to book tee times for weekends, visitors welcome at all times. **Societies** telephone in advance for booking form. **Green Fees** terms on application. **Cards** 🔄 💳 📇 📶 💷 **Prof** John O'Leary **Course Designer** Cameron Sinclair **Facilities** ⊗)Ⓜ️ ⅃ 📶 ♀ ♨ 🏠 ⛟ ᵀ ❧ ⊕ ᒥ **Conf** Corporate Hospitality Days available **Location** A505 between Royston/Duxford, off junct 10 on M11

....

Hotel ★★★ 74% Duxford Lodge Hotel, Ickleton Rd, DUXFORD ☎ 01223 836444 11 en suite 4 annexe en suite

Kingsway Cambridge Rd, Melbourn SG8 6EY
☎ 01763 262727 🖶 01763 263298
The Melbourn course is short and deceptively tricky. This 9-hole course provides a good test for both beginners and experienced golfers. Out of bounds and strategically placed bunkers come into play on several holes, particularly the tough par 3 7th. The Orchard course is a cleverly designed par 3 course set amongst trees. Ideal for sharpening the 'short game' or as a family introduction to golf.
Melbourn Course: 9 holes, 2455yds, Par 33, SSS 32.
Orchard Course: 9 holes, 727yds, Par 27, SSS 27.
Club membership 150.
Visitors welcome. **Societies** telephone for details. **Green Fees** terms on application. **Cards** 🔄 💳 📇 📶 💷 **Prof** S Brown/D Hastings/M Sturgess **Facilities** ⊗ ⅃ 📶 ♀ ♨ 🏠 ⛟ ♂ ᒥ **Location** Off the A10

....

Hotel ★★★ 74% Duxford Lodge Hotel, Ickleton Rd, DUXFORD ☎ 01223 836444 11 en suite 4 annexe en suite

Royston Baldock Rd SG8 5BG
☎ 01763 242696 🖶 01763 246910
e-mail: roystongolf@btconnect.com
Heathland course on undulating terrain and fine fairways. The 8th, 10th and 15th are the most notable holes on this all weather course.
18 holes, 6052yds, Par 70, SSS 70, Course record 65.
Club membership 850.
Visitors Mon-Fri only subject to availability. Must contact in advance. **Societies** by arrangement Mon-Fri. **Green Fees** terms on application. **Cards** 🔄 💳 📇 📶 💷 **Prof** Sean Clark **Course Designer** Harry Vardon **Facilities** ⊗ ⅃ 📶 ♀ ♨ 🏠 ⛟ ♂ **Conf** fac available **Location** 0.5m W of town centre

....

Hotel ★★★ 74% Duxford Lodge Hotel, Ickleton Rd, DUXFORD ☎ 01223 836444 11 en suite 4 annexe en suite

Continued

St Albans
Map 04 TL10

Abbey View
Westminster Lodge Leisure Ctr, Holywell Hill AL1 2DL ☎ 01727 868227 📄 01727 848508
e-mail: abbey.view@leisureconnection.co.uk
Abbey View is a picturesque public golf course in the centre of the city, designed for beginners, but sufficiently challenging for experienced golfers. Tees have recently been replaced and the 3rd hole lengthened, providing more of a challenge.
9 holes, 1408yds, Par 29, Course record 27.
Club membership 140.
Visitors welcome but no sharing clubs, suitable footwear & wide wheel trolleys. **Societies** telephone or write in advance. **Green Fees** £5.80 (£6.80 weekends). **Prof** Nigel Lawrence **Facilities** ⛱ 🏪 🍴 🏌 **Leisure** hard and grass tennis courts, heated indoor swimming pool, sauna, solarium, gymnasium, crazy golf. **Conf** Corporate Hospitality Days available **Location** Centre of St Albans, off Holywell Hill, in Verulamium Park

Hotel ★★★ 78% St Michael's Manor, Fishpool St, ST ALBANS ☎ 01727 864444 22 en suite

Batchwood Hall
Batchwood Dr AL3 5XA
☎ 01727 844250 📄 01727 858506
e-mail: batchwood@leisureconnection.co.uk
Municipal parkland course designed by J H Taylor and opened in 1935.
18 holes, 6487yds, Par 71, SSS 71.
Club membership 350.
Visitors can contact/book over the telephone up to 7 days in advance. **Societies** contact the events manager by phone or e-mail. **Green Fees** terms on application. **Cards** 🖃 🖃 🖃 🗺 🗐 **Prof** Mark Flitton **Course Designer** J H Taylor **Facilities** ⊗ 🎍 🏪 🍽 🏌 🍴 🏌 **Leisure** hard tennis courts, squash, gymnasium, Indoor tennis courts. **Conf** Corporate Hospitality Days available **Location** 1m NW off A5183

Hotel ★★★ 78% St Michael's Manor, Fishpool St, ST ALBANS ☎ 01727 864444 22 en suite

Verulam
London Rd AL1 1JG
☎ 01727 853327 📄 01727 812201
e-mail: genman@verulamgolf.co.uk
Easy walking parkland course with fourteen holes having out-of-bounds. Water affects the 12th, 13th and 14th holes. Samuel Ryder was captain here in 1927 when he began the now celebrated Ryder Cup competition.
18 holes, 6448yds, Par 72, SSS 71, Course record 67.
Club membership 720.
Visitors must contact pro shop in advance. With member only at weekends. **Societies** must contact advance. **Green Fees** Mon: £30 per day, £22 per round, Tue-Fri: £40/£28. **Cards** 🖃 🖃 🖃 🗺 🗐 **Prof** Nick Burch **Course Designer** Braid **Facilities** ⊗ 🎍 by prior arrangement 🏪 🍽 🏌 🍴 🍴 **Conf** fac available Corporate Hospitality Days available **Location** 0.5m from St albans town centre on London Rd A1081, signposted by railway bridge

Sawbridgeworth
Map 05 TL41

Manor of Groves Golf & Country Club
High Wych CM21 0JU ☎ 01279 603543 📄 01279 726972
e-mail: golf@manorofgroves.co.uk
The course is set out over 150 acres of established parkland and rolling countryside and is a true test of golf for the club golfer.

18 holes, 6228yds, Par 71, SSS 70, Course record 63.
Club membership 550.
Visitors telephone bookings preferred, restrictions on Tue, Thu and weekends. **Societies** Mon-Fri by prior arrangement, telephone in advance. **Green Fees** not confirmed. **Cards** 🖃 🖃 🖃 🗺 🗐 **Prof** Russell Hurd **Course Designer** S Sharer **Facilities** ⊗ 🎍 🏪 🍽 🏌 🍴 🏌 🍴 ⛳ 🏌 **Leisure** heated indoor swimming pool, sauna, solarium, gymnasium. **Conf** fac available Corporate Hospitality Days available **Location** 1.5m on west side of town

Hotel ★★★ 62% Briggens House Hotel, Stanstead Rd, STANSTEAD ABBOTTS ☎ 01279 829955 54 en suite

Stanstead Abbotts
Map 05 TL31

Briggens House Hotel
Briggens Park, Stanstead Rd SG12 8LD ☎ 01279 793742 📄 01279 793685
An attractive 9-hole course set in the grounds of a hotel which was once a stately house in 80 acres of countryside.
9 holes, 2793yds, Par 36, SSS 69, Course record 31.
Club membership 230.
Visitors may not play Thu 5-6pm and Sun am. No jeans. Must have own clubs and golf shoes (hire available). **Societies** must contact in advance. **Green Fees** £15 per 18 holes (£17 weekends & bank holidays). **Cards** 🖃 🖃 🖃 🗺 🗐 **Prof** Alan McGinn **Facilities** ⊗ 🎍 🏪 🍽 🏌 🍴 🏌 🍴 ⛳ 🏌 **Leisure** hard tennis courts, heated outdoor swimming pool, fishing. **Conf** fac available Corporate Hospitality Days available **Location** Off Stanstead road A414

Hotel ★★★ 62% Briggens House Hotel, Stanstead Rd, STANSTEAD ABBOTTS ☎ 01279 829955 54 en suite

Stevenage
Map 04 TL22

Stevenage Golf Centre
6 Aston Ln, Aston SG2 7EL
☎ 01438 880223 & 880424 (pro shop) 📄 01438 880040
Municipal course designed by John Jacobs, with natural water hazards and some wooded areas.
Bragbury Course: 18 holes, 6451yds, Par 72, SSS 71, Course record 63.
Aston Course: 9 holes, 880yds, Par 27, SSS 27.
Club membership 600.
Visitors no restrictions. **Societies** must contact 1 week in advance. Deposit required. **Green Fees** terms on application. **Cards** 🖃 🖃 🖃 🗺 🗐 **Prof** Steve Barker **Course Designer** John Jacobs **Facilities** ⊗ 🎍 🏪 🍽 🏌 🍴 🏌 🍴 **Leisure** Par 3 course. **Conf** fac available Corporate Hospitality Days available **Location** 4m SE off B5169

Hotel ★★★ 65% The Roebuck Inn, London Rd, Broadwater, STEVENAGE ☎ 0870 011 9076 54 en suite

Continued

Marriott Hanbury Manor

Map 05 TL31   Ware

☎ 01920 487722   📄 01920 487692

There can be few golfing venues that combine so successfully the old and the new. The 'old' is the site itself, dominated since the 19th century by the historic Hanbury Manor, a Jacobean-style mansion; and the wonderful grounds, which included a 9-hole parkland course designed by the legendary Harry Vardon. The 'new' is the conversion of the estate into the golf and country club; the manor now offers a five-star country house hotel, while the grounds have been redesigned by Jack Nicklaus II for an 18-hole course. The American-style design took the best of Vardon's original and added meadowland to produce a course that looks beautiful and plays superbly. Hanbury Manor has hosted a number of professional events, including the Women's European Open in 1996, and the Men's European Tour's English Open from 1997 to 1999, won respectively by Per Ulrik Johannson, Lee Westwood and Darren Clarke.

e-mail: golf.hanburymanor@marriotthotels.co.uk

Visitors Must contact in advance

Societies Must be booked in advance. Mon-Thu only

Green Fees £50-£85 per round as hotel guest according to time of year

Facilities ⊗ ⽻ 🝤 ⽥ 🖝 ♋ 🅿 △ 🝢 🝣 ↑ 🝤 🝥 ♂ ✓

Professional Brian Alderson

Leisure Tennis, swimming, sauna, solarium, gymnasium

Location Ware SG12 0SD (12 miles N of M25 on A10)

Holes/Par/Course record 18 holes, 7016 yds, Par 72, SSS 74, Course record 61

WHERE TO STAY AND EAT NEARBY

Hotel
WARE
★★★★★ ⓖ ⓖ 71%
Marriott Hanbury Manor Hotel & Country Club, SG12 0SD
☎ 01920 487722. 134 en suite 27 annexe en suite

★★★ 66% Roebuck Hotel, SG12 9DR
☎ 01920 409955, 50 en suite

Championship Course

WARE See page 133

WARE Map 05 TL31

Chadwell Springs Hertford Rd SG12 9LE
☎ 01920 461447 📄 01920 466596
9 holes, 6418yds, Par 72, SSS 71, Course record 68.
Location 0.75m W on A119
Telephone for further details

....
Hotel ★★★ 66% Roebuck Hotel, Baldock St, WARE
☎ 01920 409955 50 en suite

Whitehill Dane End SG12 0JS
☎ 01920 438495 📄 01920 438891
e-mail: whitehillgolfcentre@btinternet.com
18 holes, 6618yds, Par 72, SSS 72.
Telephone for further details

....
Hotel ★★★ 66% Roebuck Hotel, Baldock St, WARE
☎ 01920 409955 50 en suite

WATFORD Map 04 TQ19

West Herts Cassiobury Park WD3 3GG
☎ 01923 236484 📄 01923 222300
Another of the many clubs that were inaugurated in the 1890s when the game was being given a tremendous boost by the performances of the first star professionals, Braid, Vardon and Taylor. The West Herts course is close to Watford but its tree-lined setting is beautiful and tranquil. Set out on a plateau the course is exceedingly dry. It also has a very severe finish with the 17th, a hole of 378 yards, the toughest on the course. The last hole measures over 480 yards.
18 holes, 6528yds, Par 72, SSS 71, Course record 65.
Club membership 700.
Visitors must contact in advance. **Societies** must telephone in advance and confirm in writing. **Green Fees** £38 per 18 holes (£48 weekends). **Cards** 🔲 🔳 📄 **Prof** Charles Gough **Course Designer** Tom Morris **Facilities** ⊗ 🏳 🏌
🏌♀♨🏖️ 🏌 **Leisure** indoor teaching facility.
Location W side of town centre off A412

....
Hotel ★★★ 67% The White House, Upton Rd,
WATFORD ☎ 01923 237316 57 en suite

WELWYN GARDEN CITY Map 04 TL21

Mill Green Gypsy Ln AL6 4TY
☎ 01707 276900 & 270542 (Pro shop) 📄 01707 276898
e-mail: millgreen@americangolf.uk.com
The course plays over the second 9 holes around the lakes and sweeps back through the woods. The first 9 holes are subject to the prevailing winds. The par 3 9-hole gives a good test for improving the short game.
18 holes, 6615yds, Par 72, SSS 72, Course record 64.
Club membership 850.
Visitors must contact in advance by telephone. 3 day booking arrangement. **Societies** apply in writing for details.
Green Fees not confirmed. **Cards** 🔲 🔳 🔳 🔲 🔳
📄 **Prof** Ian Parker **Course Designer** Alliss & Clark
Facilities ⊗ 🏳 🏌 🏌♀♨🏖️🏌♀♨ 🏌 **Leisure** 9 hole par 3 course. **Location** Exit 4 of A1(M), A414 to Mill Green

....
Hotel ★★★ 61% Quality Hotel Welwyn, The Link,
WELWYN ☎ 01438 716911 96 en suite

Panshanger Golf & Squash Complex Old
Herns Ln AL7 2ED
☎ 01707 333350 & 333312 📄 01707 390010
e-mail: r.preece@welhat.gov.uk
Picturesque, mature course overlooking Mimram Valley.
18 holes, 6347yds, Par 72, SSS 70, Course record 65.
Club membership 400.
Visitors advisable to book 1 week in advance by telephone. Dress code in force. **Societies** telephone for details. **Green Fees** not confirmed. **Cards** 🔲 🔳 🔳
📄 **Prof** Bryan Lewis/Mick Corlass **Course Designer** Peter Kirkham **Facilities** ⊗ 🏳 🏌♀♨🏌♀♨🏖️ 🏌 **Leisure** squash. **Conf** Corporate Hospitality Days available
Location N side of town centre signposted off B1000 1m from Welwyn Garden City

....
Hotel ★★★ 61% Quality Hotel Welwyn, The Link,
WELWYN ☎ 01438 716911 96 en suite

Welwyn Garden City Mannicotts, High Oaks Rd
AL8 7BP ☎ 01707 325243 📄 01707 393213
e-mail: secretary@welwyngardencitygolfclub.co.uk
Undulating parkland course with a ravine. A former course record holder is Nick Faldo.
18 holes, 6074yds, Par 70, SSS 69, Course record 63.
Club membership 930.
Visitors must contact in advance but may not play Sun am.
Societies must contact in advance. **Green Fees** terms on application. **Cards** 🔲 🔳 🔳 📄 **Prof** Richard May
Facilities ⊗ 🏳 🏌 🏌♀♨🏖️🏌♀♨ 🏌 **Location** W side of city, exit 6 off A1

....
Hotel ★★★ 61% Quality Hotel Welwyn, The Link,
WELWYN ☎ 01438 716911 96 en suite

WHEATHAMPSTEAD Map 04 TL11

Mid Herts Lamer Ln, Gustard Wood AL4 8RS
☎ 01582 832242 📄 01582 834834
e-mail: secretary@mid-hertsgolfclub.co.uk
Commonland, wooded with heather and gorse-lined fairways.
18 holes, 6060yds, Par 69, SSS 69, Course record 61.
Club membership 760.
Visitors may not play Tue, Wed afternoons & weekends.
Societies must contact in writing/telephone **Green Fees** terms on application. **Prof** Barney Puttick **Facilities** ⊗ 🏳
🏌♀♨🏖️ 🏌 **Conf** fac available **Location** 1m N on B651

....
Hotel ★★★ 69% Harpenden House, 18 Southdown Rd,
HARPENDEN ☎ 01582 449955 17 en suite
59 annexe en suite

KENT

ADDINGTON Map 05 TQ65

West Malling London Rd ME19 5AR
☎ 01732 844785 📄 01732 844795
e-mail: mike@westmallinggolf.com
Two 18-hole parkland courses.
Spitfire Course: 18 holes, 6142yds, Par 70, SSS 70, Course record 67.
Hurricane Course: 18 holes, 6281yds, Par 70, SSS 70, Course record 68.
Visitors must contact in advance, may not play weekends until 12 noon. **Societies** prior booking required. **Green**

Continued

Fees terms on application. **Cards** 🖃 💳 💳 💳 🅿 **Prof**
Duncan Lambert **Course Designer** Max Falkner **Facilities**
⊗ ⅢⅬ ⬛ ♥ ♨ 🏠 ➤ 🏌 🏌 (**Leisure** gymnasium,
jaccuzi & steam room. **Conf** fac available Corporate
Hospitality Days available **Location** 1m S off A20
· ·
Hotel ★★★ 67% Larkfield Priory Hotel, London Rd,
Larkfield, MAIDSTONE ☎ 01732 846858 52 en suite

ASH   Map 05 TQ66

The London South Ash Manor Estate TN15 7EN
☎ 01474 879899 📠 01474 879912
e-mail: golf@londongolf.co.uk
Visitors may only play the courses at LGC as guests of
members or prospective members by invitation. The
courses were designed by Jack Nicklaus: both include a
number of lakes, generous fairways framed with native
grasses and many challenging holes. A state-of-the-art
drainage system ensures continuous play.
Heritage Course: 18 holes, 7208yds, Par 72, SSS 75,
Course record 67.
International Course: 18 holes, 7005yds, Par 72, SSS 74.
Club membership 500.
Visitors guest of member & prospective members invited
by the membership office only. **Societies** must write in
advance **Green Fees** not confirmed. **Cards** 🖃 💳 💳 💳
🅿 **Prof** Andrew Brooks **Course Designer** Jack Nicklaus
Facilities ⊗ ⅢⅬ ⬛ ♥ ♨ 🏠 ➤ 🏌 🏌 (**Leisure**
sauna, spa bath. **Conf** fac available Corporate Hospitality
Days available **Location** A20, 2m from Brands Hatch
· ·
Hotel ★★★ 67% Larkfield Priory Hotel, London Rd,
Larkfield, MAIDSTONE ☎ 01732 846858 52 en suite

ASHFORD   Map 05 TR04

Ashford Sandyhurst Ln TN25 4NT
☎ 01233 622655 📠 01233 622655
Parkland course with good views and easy walking.
Narrow fairways and tightly bunkered greens ensure a
challenging game.
18 holes, 6263yds, Par 71, SSS 70, Course record 65.
Club membership 650.
Visitors must contact in advance & have handicap certificate.
Societies Tue & Thu only, by arrangement. **Green Fees**
on application. **Prof** Hugh Sherman **Course Designer** Cotton
Facilities ⊗ Ⅲ by prior arrangement Ⅼ ⬛ ♥ ♨ 🏠 🏌 ⟋
Location 1.5m NW off A20
· ·
Hotel ★★★★ 65% Ashford International, Simone Weil
Av, ASHFORD ☎ 01233 219988 200 en suite

Homelands Bettergolf Centre Ashford Rd,
Kingsnorth TN26 1NJ ☎ 01233 661620 📠 01233 720553
e-mail: isj@bettergolf.co.uk
Challenging 9-hole course designed by Donald Steel to
provide a stern test for experienced golfers and for
others to develop their game. With 4 par 3s and 5 par
4s it demands accuracy rather than length. Floodlit
driving range.
9 holes, 2205yds, Par 32, SSS 31, Course record 32.
Club membership 400.
Visitors no restrictions, but booking essential for weekend
and summer evenings. **Societies** prior arrangements are
essential. **Green Fees** terms on application. **Cards** 🖃 💳
🅿 **Prof** Tony Bowers **Course Designer** Donald Steel
Facilities Ⅼ ⬛ ♥ ♨ 🏠 🏌 ➤ 🏌 ⟋ (**Location** Take exit 10
off M20, follow A2070, course signposted from 2nd rdbt to
Kingsnorth

Continued

· ·
Hotel ⭐ Travel Inn (Ashford Central), Hall Av, Orbital
Park, Sevington, ASHFORD ☎ 08701 977305 60 en suite

BARHAM   Map 05 TR25

Broome Park The Broome Park Estate CT4 6QX
☎ 01227 830728 📠 01227 832591
e-mail: broomepark@o2.co.uk
Championship standard parkland course in a valley,
with a 350-year-old mansion clubhouse.
18 holes, 6580yds, Par 72, SSS 71, Course record 66.
Club membership 700.
Visitors advisable to contact in advance, must have
handicap certificate, but may not play Sat/Sun mornings.
Societies Mon-Fri and Sat-Sun after 1pm, apply in writing
or by telephone. **Green Fees** £40 per round (£50
weekends). **Cards** 🖃 💳 💳 💳 🅿 **Prof** Tienne Britz
Course Designer Donald Steel **Facilities** ⊗ ⅢⅬ ⬛ ♥ ♨
🏠 ➤ 🏌 ⟋ (**Leisure** hard tennis courts. **Conf** fac
available **Location** 1.5m SE on A260

BEARSTED   Map 05 TQ85

Bearsted Ware St ME14 4PQ
☎ 01622 738198 📠 01622 735608
Parkland course with fine views of the North Downs.
18 holes, 6437yds, Par 72, SSS 71.
Club membership 780.
Visitors must have handicap certificate and may not play
weekends unless with member. Must contact in advance.
Societies write for reservation forms. **Green Fees** £42 per
36 holes; £32 per 18 holes. **Prof** Tim Simpson **Facilities** ⊗
ⅢⅬ ⬛ ♥ ♨ 🏠 ⟋ **Location** M20 junct 7, right at
roundabout, left at mini-roundabout, left at 2nd mini-
roundabout. Follow road passing Bell pub on right, under
bridge and golf club on left.
· ·
Hotel ★★★★ 70% Marriott Tudor Park Hotel & Country
Club, Ashford Rd, Bearsted, MAIDSTONE
☎ 01622 734334 120 en suite

BIDDENDEN   Map 05 TQ83

Chart Hills Weeks Ln TN27 8JX
☎ 01580 292222 📠 01580 292233
e-mail: info@charthills.co.uk
Created by Nick Faldo, he has truly left his mark on
this course. Signature features include the 200-yard
long snake-like anaconda bunker on the 5th and the
island green at the short 17th.

18 holes, 7107yds, Par 72, SSS 74, Course record 61.
Club membership 500.
Visitors contact for details. May play Tue, Thu, Fri &
limited availability weekends. **Societies** telephone for
details, welcome Tue, Thu, Fri and limited availability at

Continued

weekends. **Green Fees** not confirmed. **Cards**  ■■ ■■ ■■ ■■ ■■ 🗒 **Course Designer** Nick Faldo **Facilities** ⊗ ⦂⦂⦂ 🅱 💺♀⚐🐾🏌⛳ ⚸♪ **Leisure** fishing, sauna, solarium, gymnasium, teaching academy. **Conf** Corporate Hospitality Days available **Location** 1m N of Biddenden off A274

· ·

Hotel ★★★ 75% London Beach Hotel & Golf Club, Ashford Rd, TENTERDEN ☎ 01580 766279 26 en suite

BOROUGH GREEN   Map 05 TQ65

Wrotham Heath Seven Mile Ln TN15 8QZ
☎ 01732 884800 🗒 01732 887370
Heathland woodland course with magnificent views of North Downs.
18 holes, 5954yds, Par 70, SSS 69, Course record 66. Club membership 550.
Visitors weekends with member only. **Societies** Fri only, by arrangement. **Green Fees** £30 per round. **Cards** ■■ **Prof** Harry Dearden **Course Designer** Donald Steel (part) **Facilities** ⊗ ⦂⦂⦂ 🅱 💺♀⚐🏌 **Location** 2.25m E on B2016

· ·

Hotel 🆄 Holiday Inn Maidstone, London Rd, Wrotham Heath, WROTHAM ☎ 0870 400 9054 106 en suite

BRENCHLEY   Map 05 TQ64

Moatlands Watermans Ln TN12 6ND
☎ 01892 724400 🗒 01892 723300
e-mail: moatlandsgolf@btinternet.com
A rolling parkland course with dramatic views over the Weald of Kent. The challenging holes are the par 4 8th with its tough dog-leg, the 10th where there is a wooded copse with a Victorian bath-house to be avoided, and the 14th where the approach to the green is guarded by oak trees.
18 holes, 6693yds, Par 72, SSS 72, Course record 63. Club membership 620.
Visitors must book in advance. **Societies** apply in writing or telephone. **Green Fees** not confirmed. **Cards** ■■ ■■ ■■ 🗒 **Prof** James Eldridge **Course Designer** T Saito **Facilities** ⊗ ⦂⦂⦂ 🅱 💺♀⚐🏌🐾 ⚸♪ **Leisure** hard tennis courts. **Location** 3m N of Brenchley off B2160

· ·

Hotel ★★ 65% Russell Hotel, 80 London Rd, TUNBRIDGE WELLS ☎ 01892 544833 19 en suite 5 annexe en suite

BROADSTAIRS   Map 05 TR36

North Foreland Convent Rd, Kingsgate CT10 3PU
☎ 01843 862140 🗒 01843 862663
e-mail: office@northforeland.co.uk
A picturesque cliff top course situated where the Thames Estuary widens towards the sea. One of the few courses where the sea can be seen from every hole. Walking is easy and the wind is deceptive. The 8th and 17th, both par 4, are testing holes. There is also an 18-hole approach and putting course.
18 holes, 6430yds, Par 71, SSS 71, Course record 63. Club membership 1100.
Visitors for Main course required to book in advance & have handicap certificate. May play afternoons only Mon and Tue, weekends restricted and no visitors Sun morning. Northcliffe course has no restrictions. **Societies** Wed & Fri only, by arrangement. **Green Fees** £50 per day; £35 per round (£75/50 weekends and bank holidays). *Continued*

Cards  ■■ ■■ ■■ 🗒 **Prof** Darren Parris **Course Designer** Fowler & Simpson **Facilities** ⊗ ⦂⦂⦂ 🅱 💺♀⚐🏌🐾 ⚸♪ **Leisure** hard tennis courts, 18 hole par 3 course. **Location** 1.5m N off B2052

· ·

Hotel ★★★ 65% Royal Albion Hotel, Albion St, BROADSTAIRS ☎ 01843 868071 19 en suite

CANTERBURY   Map 05 TR15

Canterbury Scotland Hills, Littlebourne Rd CT1 1TW
☎ 01227 453532 🗒 01227 784277
e-mail: cgc@freeola.com
Undulating parkland course, densely wooded in places, with elevated tees and challenging drives on several holes.

18 holes, 6272yds, Par 71, SSS 70, Course record 64. Club membership 700.
Visitors may play after 9.30am except when competitions being held. Restricted times weekends and bank holidays. Must have handicap certificate. **Societies** by arrangement. **Green Fees** £40 per day; £34 per round; (£44 weekends). **Cards** ■■ ■■ ■■ ■■ 🗒 **Prof** Paul Everard **Course Designer** Harry Colt **Facilities** ⊗ ⦂⦂⦂ 🅱 💺♀⚐🏌🐾 ⚸ **Conf** fac available Corporate Hospitality Days available **Location** 1.5m E on A257

CHART SUTTON   Map 05 TQ84

The Ridge Chartway St, East Sutton ME17 3DL
☎ 01622 844382
18 holes, 6254yds, Par 71, SSS 70, Course record 68.
Course Designer Tyton Design **Location** 5m S of Bearsted, off A274
Telephone for further details

· ·

Hotel ★★★★ 70% Marriott Tudor Park Hotel & Country Club, Ashford Rd, Bearsted, MAIDSTONE ☎ 01622 734334 120 en suite

CRANBROOK   Map 05 TQ73

Hemsted Forest Golford Rd TN17 4AL
☎ 01580 712833 🗒 01580 714274
e-mail: golf@hemstedforest.co.uk
Scenic, parkland course with easy terrain, backed by Hemstead Forest and close to Sissinghurst Castle and Bodiam Castle. The course has been transformed over recent years with the introduction of over 5,000 mature pine trees. Keeping the ball straight is paramount, a challenging test of golf for all levels.
18 holes, 6305yds, Par 70, SSS 71, Course record 64. Club membership 1600.
Visitors welcome weekdays after 8am, weekends after *Continued*

11am. Tee reservations may be booked up to one calendar month in advance. **Societies** telephone to book. **Green Fees** £25 per round (£40 weekends). **Cards** 🔳 🔳 🔳 🔳 🔳 **Prof** Karl Steptoe **Course Designer** Commander J Harris **Facilities** ⊗ ⅷ 🔳 🔳 🔳 🔳 🔳 🔳 **Conf** fac available **Location** 2m E

....

Hotel ★★★ 75% London Beach Hotel & Golf Club, Ashford Rd, TENTERDEN ☎ 01580 766279 26 en suite

DARTFORD   Map 05 TQ57

Birchwood Park Birchwood Rd, Wilmington
DA2 7HJ ☎ 01322 662038 & 660554 🖹 01322 667283
e-mail: info@birchwoodparkgc.co.uk
The main course offers highly challenging play and will test golfers of all abilities. Beginners and those requiring a quick game or golfers wishing to improve their short game will appreciate the Orchard course where holes range from 96 to 258yds.
18 holes, 6364yds, Par 71, SSS 70, Course record 64.
Orchard: 9 holes, 1349yds, Par 29.
Club membership 500.
Visitors must contact in advance for Main Course.
Societies telephone for details. **Green Fees** terms on application. **Cards** 🔳 🔳 🔳 🔳 🔳 **Course Designer** Howard Swann **Facilities** ⊗ ⅷ 🔳 🔳 🔳 🔳 🔳 🔳 🔳 🔳 🔳 **Leisure** sauna, solarium, gymnasium. **Location** B258 between Dartford & Swanley

....

Hotel ★★★★ 66% Bexleyheath Marriott Hotel, 1 Broadway, BEXLEYHEATH ☎ 020 8298 1000 142 en suite

Dartford Heath Ln (Upper), Dartford Heath DA1 2TN
☎ 01322 226455
e-mail: dartfordgolf@hotmail.com
Heathland course.
18 holes, 5909yds, Par 69, SSS 69, Course record 61.
Club membership 700.
Visitors may not play at weekends. Must have a handicap certificate. **Societies** Mon & Fri only by prior arrangement with Secretary. **Green Fees** £23 per 18 holes. **Prof** John Gregory **Course Designer** James Braid **Facilities** ⊗ ⅷ 🔳 🔳 🔳 🔳 🔳 🔳 **Conf** Corporate Hospitality Days available **Location** 2m from Dartford town centre, just off the A2

....

Hotel 🅄 Holiday Inn Bexley, Black Prince Interchange, Southwold Rd, BEXLEY ☎ 0870 400 9006 108 en suite

DEAL   Map 05 TR35

Royal Cinque Ports Golf Rd CT14 6RF
☎ 01304 374007 🖹 01304 379530
e-mail: rcpgcsec@aol.com
Famous championship seaside links, windy but with easy walking. Outward nine is generally considered the easier, inward nine is longer and includes the renowned 16th, perhaps the most difficult hole. On a fine day there are wonderful views across the Channel.
18 holes, 6899yds, Par 72, SSS 73.
Club membership 950.
Visitors restricted Wed mornings, weekends & bank holidays. Must contact in advance and have a handicap certificate. Men max 20 handicap; Ladies max 30 handicap. **Societies** must contact in advance. **Green Fees** £90 per day, £75 per round (£100/£80 weekends). **Cards**

Continued

🔳 🔳 **Prof** Andrew Reynolds **Course Designer** James Braid **Facilities** ⊗ ⅷ by prior arrangement 🔳 🔳 🔳 🔳 🔳 🔳 🔳 🔳 🔳 **Conf** Corporate Hospitality Days available **Location** Along seafront at N end of Deal

Hotel ★★★ 75% Wallett's Court Country House Hotel & Spa, West Cliffe, St Margarets-at-Cliffe, DOVER ☎ 01304 852424 & 0800 0351628 🖹 01304 853430 3 en suite 13 annexe en suite

EDENBRIDGE   Map 05 TQ44

Sweetwoods Park Cowden TN8 7JN
☎ 01342 850729 (Pro shop) 🖹 01342 850866
e-mail: danhowe@sweetwoodspark.com
An undulating and mature parkland course with very high quality greens, testing water hazards and fine views across the Weald from four holes. A good challenge off the back tees. Signature holes include the 2nd, 4th and 14th.
18 holes, 6617yds, Par 72, SSS 72, Course record 63.
Club membership 700.
Visitors no restrictions. **Societies** Mon-Fri after 9am & Sat pm. Contact for details. **Green Fees** £28 per round (£34 weekends). 2 for 1 Mon and Wed pm. **Cards** 🔳 🔳 🔳 🔳 🔳 🔳 **Prof** Paul Lyons **Course Designer** P Strand **Facilities** ⊗ ⅷ 🔳 🔳 🔳 🔳 🔳 🔳 🔳 🔳 🔳 **Conf** fac available Corporate Hospitality Days available **Location** 5m E of East Grinstead on the A264

....

Hotel ★★★ 🔺 Gravetye Manor Hotel, EAST GRINSTEAD ☎ 01342 810567 18 en suite

EYNSFORD   Map 05 TQ56

Austin Lodge Upper Austin Lodge Rd DA4 0HU
☎ 01322 863000 🖹 01322 862406
e-mail: greg@pentlandgolf.co.uk
A well drained course designed to lie naturally in three secluded valleys in rolling countryside. Over 7000 yds from the medal tees. Practice ground, nets and a putting green add to the features.
18 holes, 6600yds, Par 73, SSS 71, Course record 68.
Club membership 400.
Visitors must contact in advance, may not play until after 12pm on weekends. Soft spikes only. **Societies** telephone for bookings (0800 2585018). **Green Fees** £19 weekdays (£25 weekends and bank holidays). **Cards** 🔳 🔳 🔳 🔳 **Prof** Greg Haenen **Course Designer** P Bevan **Facilities** ⊗ ⅷ 🔳 🔳 🔳 🔳 🔳 🔳 🔳 🔳 🔳 **Location** 6m S of Dartford

....

Hotel ★★★★ 74% Brandshatch Place, Brands Hatch Rd, Fawkham, BRANDS HATCH ☎ 01474 875000 26 en suite 12 annexe en suite

FAVERSHAM   Map 05 TR06

Boughton Brickfield Ln, Boughton ME13 9AJ
☎ 01227 752277 📠 01227 752361
e-mail: greg@pentlandgolf.co.uk
Rolling parkland/downland course set in 160 acres of Kent countryside, providing a good test of golf, even for the more accomplished players.
18 holes, 6469yds, Par 72, SSS 71, Course record 68.
Club membership 350.
Visitors Must phone in advance. **Societies** telephone for details (freephone 0800 2585018) **Green Fees** £19 per 18 holes (£25 weekends and bank holidays). **Cards** ⊞ ▦ 🔫 🖵 **Prof** Trevor Dungate **Course Designer** P Sparks **Facilities** ⊗ 𝍠 ⅃ 🖢 🍴 👤 👜 ⛳ 🔧 🛒 🥤 ⛳ ✆ **Location** Off junct 7 of M2 - Brenley Corner

Hotel ★★★★ 🏨 Eastwell Manor, Eastwell Park, Boughton Lees, ASHFORD ☎ 01233 213000 23 en suite 39 annexe en suite

Faversham Belmont Park ME13 0HB
☎ 01795 890561 📠 01795 890760
e-mail: themanager@favershamgolf.co.uk
A beautiful inland course laid out over part of a large estate with pheasants walking the fairways quite tamely. Play follows two heavily wooded valleys but the trees affect only the loose shots going out of bounds. Fine views.

18 holes, 5965yds, Par 70, SSS 69, Course record 62.
Club membership 800.
Visitors must have handicap certificate. With member only at weekends. Contacting the club in advance is advisable. **Societies** must contact in advance. **Green Fees** £30 per round. **Prof** Stuart Rokes **Facilities** ⊗ 𝍠 ⅃ 🖢 🍴 👤 👜 🛒 ✆ **Conf** Corporate Hospitality Days available **Location** 3.5m S on road to Belmont

Hotel ★★★★ 🏨 Eastwell Manor, Eastwell Park, Boughton Lees, ASHFORD ☎ 01233 213000 23 en suite 39 annexe en suite

FOLKESTONE   Map 05 TR23

Etchinghill Canterbury Rd, Etchinghill CT18 8FA
☎ 01303 863863 📠 01303 863210
e-mail: jill@pentlandgolf.co.uk
A varied course incorporating parkland on the outward 9 holes and an interesting downland landscape with many challenging holes on the back 9.
27 holes, 6101yds, Par 70, SSS 69, Course record 67.
Club membership 600.
Visitors advisable to reserve tee time in advance. **Societies** telephone or write, packages available. **Green Fees** terms

· *Continued*

on application. **Cards** ⊞ ▦ 🔫 ▦ 🔫 🖵 **Prof** Chris Hodgson **Course Designer** John Sturdy **Facilities** ⊗ 𝍠 🖢 🖢 ⅃ 👤 👜 🍴 👤 🛒 🥤 ⛳ ✆ **Leisure** 9 hole par3. **Conf** fac available **Location** N of M20, access from junct 11 or 12

Hotel ★★★ 70% Clifton Hotel, The Leas, FOLKESTONE ☎ 01303 851231 80 en suite

GILLINGHAM   Map 05 TQ76

Gillingham Woodlands Rd ME7 2AP
☎ 01634 853017 (office) 📠 01634 574749
e-mail: golf@gillinghamgolf.idps.co.uk
Mature parkland course with views of the estuary.
18 holes, 5495yds, Par 69, SSS 66, Course record 64.
Club membership 800.
Visitors contact in advance, weekends only with member, must have handicap certificate. **Societies** booked in advance, weekdays only. **Green Fees** £28 per day, £20 per round. **Prof** Steven Green **Course Designer** James Braid/Steel **Facilities** ⊗ 𝍠 🖢 🖢 ⅃ 👤 👜 ✆ **Leisure** small practice area. **Conf** Corporate Hospitality Days available **Location** 1.5m SE on A2

Hotel 🆄 Holiday Inn Rochester, Maidstone Rd, ROCHESTER ☎ 0870 400 9069 150 en suite

GRAVESEND   Map 05 TQ67

Mid Kent Singlewell Rd DA11 7RB
☎ 01474 568035 📠 01474 564218
A well-maintained downland course with some easy walking and some excellent greens. The first hole is short, but nonetheless a real challenge. The slightest hook and the ball is out of bounds or lost.
18 holes, 6106yds, Par 70, SSS 69, Course record 60.
Club membership 900.
Visitors must contact in advance & have handicap certificate. May not play weekends. **Societies** Tue only, apply in writing. **Green Fees** £35 per day; £25 per round. **Prof** Mark Foreman **Course Designer** Frank Pennick **Facilities** ⊗ 𝍠 by prior arrangement 🖢 🖢 ⅃ 👤 👜 🍴 ✆ **Location** S side of town centre off A227

Hotel ⛨ Travel Inn, Wrotham Rd, GRAVESEND ☎ 08701 977118 36 en suite

Southern Valley Thong Ln, Shorne DA12 4LF
☎ 01474 568568 📠 01474 360366
e-mail: info@southernvalley.co.uk
All year playing conditions on a course landscaped with gorse, bracken and thorn and designed to enhance the views across the Thames Estuary. The course features undulating greens, large trees and rolling fairways with both the 9th and 18th holes located close to the clubhouse.
18 holes, 6200yds, Par 69, SSS 69.
Club membership 450.
Visitors no restrictions. **Societies** must telephone in advance. **Green Fees** £16.50 (£20 weekends and bank holidays). **Cards** ⊞ ▦ 🔫 ▦ 🔫 🖵 **Prof** Larry Batchelor **Course Designer** Richardson **Facilities** ⊗ 𝍠 🖢 🖢 ⅃ 👤 👜 🍴 👤 🛒 🥤 ✆ **Conf** Corporate Hospitality Days available **Location** From A2 junct 4 at top of slip-road turn left into Thong Lane and continue for 1m

Hotel ★★★ 72% Manor Hotel, Hever Court Rd, GRAVESEND ☎ 01474 353100 52 en suite

HALSTEAD
Map 05 TQ46

Broke Hill Sevenoaks Rd TN14 7HR
☎ 01959 533225 📠 01959 532680
e-mail: bhgc@crown-golf.co.uk
A challenging game awaits all golfers. The fairways have strategically placed bunkers, some of which come into play off the tee. Five holes have water hazards, the most significant being the 18th where a lake has to be carried to get onto the green.

18 holes, 6454yds, Par 72, SSS 71, Course record 65. Club membership 650.
Visitors weekdays only. Must book in advance. **Societies** telephone for details. **Green Fees** £40 per round midweek only. **Cards** 🎴 💳 💳 📷 🖳 **Prof** Cameron McKillop **Course Designer** David Williams **Facilities** ⊗ ⅢL ⅃ 🖳 ⅃ ⅃ 👭 ♦ ♂ **Leisure** sauna. **Conf** fac available Corporate Hospitality Days available **Location** Off junct 4 of M25, opposite Knockholt railway station

Hotel ★★★ 71% Donnington Manor, London Rd, Dunton Green, SEVENOAKS ☎ 01732 462681 60 en suite

HAWKHURST
Map 05 TQ73

Hawkhurst High St TN18 4JS
☎ 01580 754074 & 752396 📠 01580 754074
e-mail: hawkhurstgolfclub@tiscali.co.uk
Undulating parkland course.
9 holes, 5751yds, Par 70, SSS 68, Course record 69. Club membership 450.
Visitors may play weekdays, weekends after 12 noon. **Societies** must apply in advance. **Green Fees** £26 per day, £20 per round (£24 per round weekdays). **Cards** 🎴 💳 📷 🖳 **Prof** James Walpole **Course Designer** W A Baldock **Facilities** ⊗ Ⅲ by prior arrangement L ⅃ 🖳 ⅃ 👭 ♦ **Leisure** squash. **Conf** fac available **Location** W side of village off A268

Hotel ★★★ 75% London Beach Hotel & Golf Club, Ashford Rd, TENTERDEN ☎ 01580 766279 26 en suite

HEADCORN
Map 05 TQ84

Weald of Kent Maidstone Rd TN27 9PT
☎ 01622 890866 📠 01622 890866
e-mail: weald-of-kent@aol.com
Enjoying delightful views over the Weald of Kent, this pay and play course features a range of natural hazards, including lakes, trees, ditches and undulating fairways. A good test to golfers of every standard.
18 holes, 6240yds, Par 70, SSS 70, Course record 64. Club membership 450.
Visitors can book 3 days in advance, smart casual dress no jeans. **Societies** apply in writing or by telephone.

Green Fees terms on application. **Cards** 🎴 💳 📷 🖳 **Prof** Paul Fosten **Course Designer** John Millen **Facilities** ⊗ ⅢL 🖳 ⅃ ⅃ 👭 ♦ ⅃ **Leisure** training academy. **Conf** fac available Corporate Hospitality Days available **Location** From M20 Leeds castle junct, through Leeds village take A274 towards Headcorn, golf course on left

Hotel ★★★★ 70% Marriott Tudor Park Hotel & Country Club, Ashford Rd, Bearsted, MAIDSTONE ☎ 01622 734334 120 en suite

HERNE BAY
Map 05 TR16

Herne Bay Eddington CT6 7PG ☎ 01227 374727
18 holes, 5567yds, Par 68, SSS 68.
Course Designer James Braid **Location** On A299 at Herne Bay/Canterbury junct
Telephone for further details

Hotel ★★★ 67% The Falstaff Hotel, 8-10 St Dunstan's St, CANTERBURY ☎ 0870 609 6102 25 en suite 22 annexe en suite

HEVER
Map 05 TQ44

Hever Castle Hever Rd, Edenbridge TN8 7NP
☎ 01732 700771 📠 01732 700775
e-mail: mail@hevercastlegolfclub.co.uk
Originally part of the Hever Castle estate, set in 250 acres of Kentish countryside, the Kings and Queens Championship course has matured well and, with the addition of the Princes' 9 holes opened in June 1998, offers a stunning array of holes fit to challenge all golfers. Water plays a prominent part in the design of the course, particularly around Amen Corner, holes 11 through 13. The golfer is then met with the lengthy stretch home, especially up the 17th, a daunting 644 yard par 5, one of Europe's longest.

Kings & Queens Course: 18 holes, 6761yds, Par 72, SSS 73, Course record 69.
Princes Course: 9 holes, 2784yds, Par 35.
Club membership 450.
Visitors must contact in advance. Visitors may not play Kings & Queens course before 11am. **Societies** Apply in writing or by phone. **Green Fees** £40 for 18 holes (£60 weekends). **Cards** 🎴 💳 💳 📷 🖳 **Prof** Peter Parks **Course Designer** Dr Nicholas **Facilities** ⊗ ⅢL 🖳 ⅃ ⅃ 🖳 ⅃ 👭 ♦ ⅃ **Leisure** hard tennis courts. **Conf** fac available Corporate Hospitality Days available **Location** off B269 between Oxted and Tonbridge, 0.5m from Hever Castle.

Hotel ★★★ 78% The Spa Hotel, Mount Ephraim, TUNBRIDGE WELLS ☎ 01892 520331 69 en suite

Continued

HILDENBOROUGH Map 05 TQ54

Nizels Nizels Ln TN11 9LU
☎ 01732 838926 (Bookings) 🖷 01732 833764
e-mail: nizels.retail@clubhaus.com
Woodland course with many mature trees, wildlife and lakes that come into play on several holes. The 2nd hole is a 553yd par 5, the green being guarded by bunkers hidden by a range of hillocks. The par 4 7th has water on both sides of the fairway and a pitch over water to the green. The 10th is 539-yard par 5 with a sharp dog-leg to the right, followed by a very narrow entry between trees for the second shot.
18 holes, 6408yds, Par 72, SSS 71, Course record 65.
Club membership 650.
Visitors telephone professional shop for tee reservation 01732 838926 at least 4 days in advance. **Societies** weekdays only, telephone initially. **Green Fees** terms on application. **Cards** 🖶 📠 📭 📇 🔜 ⬜ **Prof** Ally Mellor/David Brench **Course Designer** Donaldson/Edwards Partnership **Facilities** ⊗ ⫚ ⬛ 🖤 ⬜ ⬜ ♨ △ 🖝 ⬚ 🌤 ⬡ **Leisure** heated indoor swimming pool, sauna, solarium, gymnasium. **Location** Off B245

Hotel ★★★ 66% Rose & Crown Hotel, 125 High St, TONBRIDGE ☎ 01732 357966 54 en suite

HOO Map 05 TQ77

Deangate Ridge Dux Court Rd ME3 8RZ
☎ 01634 251180 🖷 01634 250537
Parkland, municipal course designed by Fred Hawtree. 18-hole pitch and putt.
18 holes, 6300yds, Par 71, SSS 70, Course record 65.
Club membership 500.
Visitors no restrictions. **Societies** please telephone 01634 254481 **Green Fees** terms on application. **Cards** 🖶 📠 🔜 ⬜ **Prof** Richard Fox **Course Designer** Hawtree **Facilities** ⊗ ⫚ ⬛ 🖤 ⬜ ⬜ △ ⬚ 🖝 🌤 ♨ ⬡ ⬚ **Leisure** hard tennis courts, gymnasium. **Location** 4m NE of Rochester off A228

Hotel 🅄 Holiday Inn Rochester, Maidstone Rd, ROCHESTER ☎ 0870 400 9069 150 en suite

HYTHE Map 05 TR13

Hythe Imperial Princes Pde CT21 6AE
☎ 01303 267441 🖷 01303 264610
e-mail: hytheimperial@marstonhotels.com
A 9-hole 18-tee links course bounded by the Royal Military Canal and the English Channel. Although the course is relatively flat, its aspect offers an interesting and challenging round to a wide range of golfers.
9 holes, 5560yds, Par 68, SSS 66, Course record 62.
Club membership 300.
Visitors course closed some Sun until 11am for competitions. **Societies** advisable to telephone. **Green Fees** terms on application. **Cards** 🖶 📠 📭 ② 📇 🔜 ⬜ **Prof** Gordon Ritchie **Facilities** ⊗ ⫚ ⬛ 🖤 ⬜ ⬜ △ 🖝 🖤 ⬡ **Leisure** hard and grass tennis courts, heated indoor swimming pool, squash, sauna, solarium, gymnasium, snooker. **Location** Exit M20 junct 11. Follow into Hythe towards the town centre. Turn right into Twiss Road. Golf course is in grounds of the Hythe Imperial

Hotel ★★★★ 76% The Hythe Imperial, Princes Pde, HYTHE ☎ 01303 267441 100 en suite

Additional Hotel ★★★ 70% Stade Court, West Pde, HYTHE ☎ 01303 268263 Fax 01303 261803 42 en suite

Sene Valley Sene CT18 8BL
☎ 01303 268513 (Manager) 🖷 01303 237513
e-mail: svgc@svgc.freeserve.co.uk
A two-level downland course which provides interesting golf over an undulating landscape with sea views.
18 holes, 6196yds, Par 71, SSS 70, Course record 61.
Club membership 600.
Visitors must contact professional in advance. **Societies** telephone in advance. **Green Fees** terms on application. **Cards** 🖶 📭 ⬜ **Prof** Nick Watson **Course Designer** Henry Cotton **Facilities** ⊗ ⫚ by prior arrangement ⬛ 🖤 ⬜ △ ⬚ 🌤 ⬡ **Conf** Corporate Hospitality Days available **Location** M20 junct 12, A20 towards Ashford for 3m, turn left at rdbt, follow Hythe Road for 1m

Hotel ★★★★ 76% The Hythe Imperial, Princes Pde, HYTHE ☎ 01303 267441 100 en suite

KINGSDOWN Map 05 TR34

Walmer & Kingsdown The Leas CT14 8EP
☎ 01304 373256 🖷 01304 382336
e-mail: kingsdown.golf@gtwiz.co.uk
This beautiful downland site is situated near Deal and offers breathtaking views of the channel from every hole. The course is famous as being the one on which, in 1964, Assistant Professional Roger Game became the first golfer in Britain to hole in one at two successive holes; the 7th and 8th. The course is situated on top of the cliffs, with fine views.

18 holes, 6444yds, Par 72, SSS 71, Course record 66.
Club membership 680.
Visitors must contact in advance. Not before 9.30am weekdays and noon weekends & bank holidays. **Societies** apply in advance. **Green Fees** not confirmed. **Cards** 🖶 📭 ⬜ **Prof** Matthew Paget **Course Designer** James Braid **Facilities** ⊗ ⫚ ⬛ 🖤 ⬜ ⬜ △ ⬚ 🖝 🌤 ⬡ **Conf** Corporate Hospitality Days available **Location** 1.5m E of Ringwould off A258 Dover-Deal road

Hotel ★★★ 71% Dunkerleys Hotel & Restaurant, 19 Beach St, DEAL ☎ 01304 375016 16 en suite

LAMBERHURST Map 05 TQ63

Lamberhurst Church Rd TN3 8DT
☎ 01892 890591 🖷 01892 891140
e-mail: secretary@lamberhurstgolfclub.com
Parkland course crossing the river twice. Fine views.
18 holes, 6345yds, Par 72, SSS 70, Course record 65.
Club membership 650.
Visitors may only play after noon weekends unless with member, handicap certificate required. Advisable to contact in advance. **Societies** Tue, Wed & Thu only from Apr-Oct, by arrangement. **Green Fees** £36 per

Continued

day, £26 per round (£41 per day/round after noon). **Cards** **Prof** Brian Impett **Facilities** **Conf** Corporate Hospitality Days available **Location** N side of village on B2162

Hotel ★★★ 78% The Spa Hotel, Mount Ephraim, TUNBRIDGE WELLS ☎ 01892 520331 69 en suite

LITTLESTONE Map 05 TR02

Littlestone St Andrew's Rd TN28 8RB
☎ 01797 363355 📠 01797 362740
e-mail: secretary@littlestonegolfclub.org.uk
Located in the Romney Marshes, this fairly flat seaside links course calls for every variety of shot. The 8th, 15th, 16th and 17th are regarded as classics by international golfers. Easy going for all ages.
18 holes, 6486yds, Par 71, SSS 72, Course record 66. Club membership 550.
Visitors must contact in advance, no visitors before 11am weekends and bank holidays. **Societies** must apply in advance. **Green Fees** £60 per day; £39 per round (£70/£55 weekends & bank holidays). **Cards** **Prof** Andrew Jones **Course Designer** Laidlaw Purves **Facilities** **Leisure** hard tennis courts. **Conf** Corporate Hospitality Days available **Location** 1m from New Romney off Littlestone road B2070

Hotel ★★★★ 76% The Hythe Imperial, Princes Pde, HYTHE ☎ 01303 267441 100 en suite

Romney Warren St Andrews Rd TN28 8RB
☎ 01797 362231 📠 01797 363511
e-mail: info@romneywarrengolfclub.org.uk
A links style course, normally very dry. Flat providing easy walking and play challenged by sea breezes.
18 holes, 5126yds, Par 67, SSS 65, Course record 63. Club membership 300.
Visitors contact professional in advance. **Societies** contact in advance. **Green Fees** terms on application. **Cards** **Prof** Andrew Jones **Facilities** **Location** N side of Littlestone

Hotel ★★★★ 76% The Hythe Imperial, Princes Pde, HYTHE ☎ 01303 267441 100 en suite

LYDD Map 05 TR02

Lydd Romney Rd TN29 9LS
☎ 01797 320808 📠 01797 321482
e-mail: info@lyddgolfclub.co.uk
A links-type course on marshland, offering some interesting challenges, including a number of eye-catching water hazards, wide fairways and plenty of semi-rough. A good test for experienced golfers and appealing to the complete novice.

Continued

18 holes, 6517yds, Par 71, SSS 71, Course record 65. Club membership 490.
Visitors contact in advance, may play weekends subject to availability. **Societies** telephone in advance. **Green Fees** £17 (£25 weekends). **Cards** **Prof** Richard J Perkins **Course Designer** Mike Smith **Facilities** **Leisure** 6 hole Academy course. **Conf** Corporate Hospitality Days available **Location** Off A259 onto B2075 by Lydd Airport

Hotel ★★★ 63% The George, High St, RYE ☎ 01797 222114 22 en suite

MAIDSTONE Map 05 TQ75

Cobtree Manor Park Chatham Rd, Sandling ME14 3AZ ☎ 01622 753276 📠 01634 262003
An undulating parkland course with some water hazards.
Cobtree Manor Park Golf Club: 18 holes, 5611yds, Par 69, SSS 69, Course record 66. Club membership 400.
Visitors no restrictions but advisable to telephone 4 days in advance. **Societies** Mon-Fri & weekend afternoon only, by arrangement tel: 01622 751881. **Green Fees** terms on application. **Cards** **Prof** Paul Foston **Facilities** **Conf** fac available **Location** On A229 0.25m N of M20 junc 6

Hotel ★★★ 69% Russell Hotel, 136 Boxley Rd, MAIDSTONE ☎ 01622 692221 42 en suite

Leeds Castle Ashford Rd ME17 1PL
☎ 01622 767828 & 880467 📠 01622 735616
e-mail: golf@leeds-castle.co.uk
Situated around Leeds Castle, this is one of the most picturesque courses in Britain. Redesigned in the 1980s by Neil Coles, it is a challenging 9-hole course with the added hazard of the castle moat.

9 holes, 2681yds, Par 33, SSS 33, Course record 30.
Visitors bookings taken from 6 days in advance. **Societies** must telephone in advance. **Green Fees** not confirmed. **Cards** **Prof** Steve Purves **Course Designer** Neil Coles **Facilities** **Leisure** Green fees include admission to Leeds Castle's Gardens & Attractions. **Location** On A20 towards Lenham, 4m E of Maidstone via M20 junct 8

Hotel ★★★★ 70% Marriott Tudor Park Hotel & Country Club, Ashford Rd, Bearsted, MAIDSTONE ☎ 01622 734334 120 en suite

Looking to try a new course? Always telephone ahead to confirm visitor arrangements.

Marriott Tudor Park Hotel & Country Club
Ashford Rd, Bearsted ME14 4NQ
☎ 01622 734334 🖹 01622 735360
e-mail: salesadmin.tudorpark@marriotthotels.co.uk

The course is set in a 220-acre former deer park with the pleasant undulating Kent countryside as a backdrop. The natural features of the land have been incorporated into this picturesque course to form a challenge for those of both high and intermediate standard. The par 5 14th is particularly interesting. It can alter your score dramatically should you gamble with a drive to a narrow fairway. This hole has to be carefully thought out from tee to green depending on the wind direction.

Milgate Course: 18 holes, 6041yds, Par 70, SSS 69, Course record 64.
Club membership 750.

Visitors may not play Sat & Sun before noon. Contact pro shop 01622 739412 for bookings. Societies please telephone Golf Events Green Fees terms on application. Cards 🖭 🖃 🖃 🖳 🖳 🖳 Prof Nick McNally Course Designer Donald Steel Facilities ⊗ ℍ Ꮭ 🖳 ♀ ♨ 🖾 🍴 🛋 🦶 🚣 ⚷ 🏌 Leisure hard tennis courts, heated indoor swimming pool, sauna, solarium, gymnasium, steam room & spa bath, golf academy. Conf fac available Corporate Hospitality Days available Location On A20, 1.25m W of M20 junct 8

· ·

Hotel ★★★★ 70% Marriott Tudor Park Hotel & Country Club, Ashford Rd, Bearsted, MAIDSTONE ☎ 01622 734334 120 en suite

NEW ASH GREEN   Map 05 TQ66

Redlibbets
Manor Ln, West Yoke TN15 7HT
☎ 01474 879190 🖹 01474 879290
e-mail: redlibbets@golfandsport.co.uk

Delightful rolling Kentish course cut through an attractive wooded valley.

18 holes, 6639yds, Par 72, SSS 72, Course record 67.
Club membership 500.

Visitors may play weekdays only Societies Mon, Tue & Thu, apply by phone. Green Fees £40. Cards 🖭 🖃 🖳 🖳 🖳 🖳 Prof Ross Taylor Course Designer Jonathan Gaunt Facilities ⊗ ℍ Ꮭ 🖳 ♀ ♨ 🖾 🍴 🦶 🚣 ⚷ 🏌 Conf Corporate Hospitality Days available Location off A20, close to Brand's Hatch

RAMSGATE   Map 05 TR36

St Augustine's
Cottington Rd, Cliffsend CT12 5JN
☎ 01843 590333 🖹 01843 590444
e-mail: sagc@ic24.net

18 holes, 5254yds, Par 69, SSS 66, Course record 61.
Course Designer Tom Vardon Location Off A256 Ramsgate/Sandwich
Telephone for further details

· ·

Hotel ★★★ 65% Royal Albion Hotel, Albion St, BROADSTAIRS ☎ 01843 868071 19 en suite

ROCHESTER   Map 05 TQ76

Rochester & Cobham Park
Park Pale ME2 3UL
☎ 01474 823411 🖹 01474 824446
e-mail: rcpgc@talk21.com

A first-rate course of challenging dimensions in undulating parkland. All holes differ and each requires accurate drive placing to derive the best   *Continued*

---

advantage. The clubhouse and course are situated a mile from the western end of the M2.

18 holes, 6597yds, Par 71, SSS 72, Course record 64.
Club membership 640.

Visitors must contact in advance & have handicap certificate. No visitors weekends. Societies apply in advance. Green Fees £45 per day, £35 per round. Prof Iain Higgins Course Designer Donald Steel Facilities ⊗ ℍ Ꮭ 🖳 ♀ ♨ 🖾 🦶 🚣 ⚷ 🏌 Conf Corporate Hospitality Days available Location 2.5m W on A2

· ·

Hotel ★★★★ 75% Bridgewood Manor Hotel, Bridgewood Roundabout, Walderslade Woods, CHATHAM ☎ 01634 201333 100 en suite

SANDWICH See page 143

SANDWICH   Map 05 TR35

Prince's
Prince's Dr, Sandwich Bay CT13 9QB
☎ 01304 611118 🖹 01304 612000
e-mail: golf@princes-leisure.co.uk

With 27 championship holes, Prince's Golf Club enjoys a world wide reputation as a traditional links of the finest quality and is a venue that provides all that is best in modern links golf. The purpose built clubhouse, located at the centre of the three loops of nine, can seat 200 diners and offers panoramic views over Sandwich Bay and the course.

Dunes: 9 holes, 3343yds, Par 36, SSS 36.
Himalayas: 9 holes, 3163yds, Par 35, SSS 35.
Shore: 9 holes, 3347yds, Par 36, SSS 36.
Club membership 250.

Visitors available all week, must contact in advance. Societies welcome all week, please contact in advance. Green Fees terms on application. Cards 🖭 🖃 🖳 🖳 🖳 Prof Derek Barbour Course Designer (1951 Sir Guy Campbell & J S F Morrison) Facilities ⊗ ℍ Ꮭ 🖳 ♀ ♨ 🖾 🍴 🦶 🚣 ⚷ 🏌 Leisure private beach area. Conf Corporate Hospitality Days available Location 2m E via toll road, follow signs from Sandwich

· ·

Hotel ★★★ 71% Dunkerleys Hotel & Restaurant, 19 Beach St, DEAL ☎ 01304 375016 16 en suite

SEVENOAKS   Map 05 TQ55

Knole Park
Seal Hollow Rd TN15 0HJ
☎ 01732 452150 🖹 01732 463159
e-mail: secretary@knolepark.fsnet.co.uk

The course is set in a majestic park with many fine trees and deer running loose. It has a wiry turf seemingly impervious to rain. Certainly a pleasure to
Continued on page 144

Royal St George's

| Map 05 TR35 | Sandwich |

☎ **01304 613090** 📄 **01304 611245**

Consistently ranked among the leading golf courses in the world, Royal St George's occupies a unique place in the history of golf, playing host in 1894 to the first Open Championship played outside Scotland. Set among the dunes of Sandwich Bay, the links provide a severe test for the greatest of golfers. Only two Open winners (Bill Rogers in 1981 and Greg Norman in 1993) have managed to under par after 72 holes. The undulations on the fairways, the borrows on the greens, the strategically placed bunkers and the prevailing winds which blow on all but the rarest of occasions – these soon reveal any weakness; there are few over the years who have mastered all the vagaries in one round. It hosted its thirteenth Open Championship in 2003, dramatically won by outsider Ben Curtis.

e-mail: secretary@royalstgeorges.com

Visitors Must contact in advance and have a handicap certificate of 18 or under. Three and four ball golf on Tuesday only. May not play at weekends

Societies Mon-Fri, must apply in writing

Green Fees 18 holes £95; 36 holes £130

Facilities ⊗ ⫫ ⛗ ▦ ⚑ ♀ ⛳ ⛴ 🏌 ⚴ ⚑
Conf Corporate hospitality days available

Professional A. Brooks

Location Sandwich CT13 9PB
(1.5m E of Sandwich, signed from town)

Holes/Par/Course record 18 holes,
7102 yds, Par 70, SSS 74, Course record 67

WHERE TO STAY AND EAT NEARBY

Hotels
CANTERBURY

★★★ 67% Falstaff, CT2 8AF.
☎ 0870 6096102. 25 en suite
22 annexe en suite

★★ 75% Ebury Hotel, CT1 3DX.
☎ 01227 768433. 15 en suite

DOVER

★★★ 🏵 🏵 75% Wallett's Court,
West Cliffe, CT15 6EW.
☎ 01304 852424. 3 en suite
13 annexe en suite

★★★ 71% Best Western Churchill Hotel & Health
Club, CT17 9BP.
☎ 01304 203633. 66 en suite

SANDWICH

★★ 67% Blazing Donkey Country Hotel & Inn,
CT14 0ED.
☎ 01304 617362. 19 en suite
3 annexe en suite

Restaurants
CANTERBURY

🏵 🏵 Dove Inn ME13 9HB
☎ 01227 751360
🏵 Augustine's CT1 1PE
☎ 01227 453063

Play a Piece of History
at
PRINCE'S GOLF CLUB

With 27 championship holes Prince's Golf Club enjoys a worldwide reputation as a traditional links of the finest quality. Individual golfers, societies and corporate golf days are warmly welcomed 7 days a week throughout the year.
Residential golf break packages with the RAC 3 star Bell Hotel, Sandwich, are available at competitive rates.
Scene of Gene Sarazen's famous Open victory in 1932, Prince's has over the years played host to:
• *Open Championship* • *Open Championship Final Qualifier 2003* • *Curtis Cup* • *British Ladies Strokeplay* • *English Ladies' Open* • *PGA Mastercard Tour* • *PGA Club Pro Championship*
"Britain's Finest Course"
Gene Sarazen, first professional Grand Slammer
Prince's Golf Club, Sandwich Bay, Kent CT13 9QB
Tel: 01304 611118 Fax: 01304 612000
www.princesgolfclub.co.uk
e-mail: office@princesgolfclub.co.uk

---

play on. Excellent views of Knole House and the North Downs. Outstanding greens.
18 holes, 6266yds, Par 70, SSS 70, Course record 62.
Club membership 750.
Visitors must have a handicap certificate and contact the secretary in advance, may not play at weekends or bank holidays. **Societies** telephone initially. **Green Fees** £45 per day, £35 per round. **Cards** ⊞ ▦ ▧ ◪ ▨ **Prof** Phil Sykes **Course Designer** J A Abercromby **Facilities** ⊗ ⅲ ⅃ ⚑ ♀ ⚘ 🏠 ⚸ **Leisure** squash. **Location** NE side of town centre off B2019

Hotel ★★★ 71% Donnington Manor, London Rd, Dunton Green, SEVENOAKS ☎ 01732 462681 60 en suite

---

Sheerness Power Station Rd ME12 3AE
☎ 01795 662585 🖷 01795 668100
e-mail: thesecretary@sheernessgc.freeserve.co.uk
Semi-links, marshland course, few bunkers, but many ditches and water hazards.
18 holes, 6460yds, Par 72, SSS 71, Course record 66.
Club membership 650.
Visitors with member only at weekends. **Societies** weekdays only, book in advance. **Green Fees** £28 per day, £20 per 18 holes. **Prof** L Stanford **Facilities** ⊗ ⅲ by prior arrangement ⅃ ▦ ♀ ⚘ 🏠 ⚘ ⚸ **Location** 1.5m E off A249

Hotel ★★★★ 75% Bridgewood Manor Hotel, Bridgewood Roundabout, Walderslade Woods, CHATHAM ☎ 01634 201333 100 en suite

---

Darenth Valley Station Rd TN14 7SA
☎ 01959 522944 🖷 01959 525089
e-mail: darenthvalleygolfcourse@shoreham2000.fsbusiness.co.uk
Gently undulating picturesque parkland course in a beautiful Kentish valley, with excellent well-drained greens. The course has matured and developed to become a challenge to both high and low handicap golfers.

18 holes, 6258yds, Par 72, SSS 71, Course record 64.
Visitors advisable to book in advance. **Societies** contact in advance. **Green Fees** £30 per 36 holes, £18.75 per 18 holes (£45/£25 weekends and bank holidays). **Cards** ⊞ ▦ ▧ ◪ **Prof** David J Copsey **Facilities** ⊗ ⅲ ⅃ ▦ ♀ ♀ 🏠 ⚑ ⚘ **Conf** fac available Corporate Hospitality Days available **Location** 3m N of Sevenoaks, off A225 between Otford and Eynsford

Hotel ★★★ 71% Donnington Manor, London Rd, Dunton Green, SEVENOAKS ☎ 01732 462681 60 en suite

---

The Oast Golf Centre Church Rd, Tonge
ME9 9AR ☎ 01795 473527
e-mail: rmail@oastgolf.co.uk
A par 3 approach course of 9 holes with 18 tees augmented by a 17-bay floodlit driving range and a putting green.
9 holes, 1664yds, Par 54, SSS 54.
Visitors no restrictions. **Societies** telephone in advance. **Green Fees** £7 for 18 holes, £5 for 9 holes. **Prof** D Chambers **Course Designer** D Chambers **Facilities** ⅃ ♀ ♀ 🏠 ⚑ ⚘ ⚸ **Location** 2m NE, A2 between Bapchild/Teynham

Hotel ★★★★ 75% Bridgewood Manor Hotel, Bridgewood Roundabout, Walderslade Woods, CHATHAM ☎ 01634 201333 100 en suite

Sittingbourne & Milton Regis Wormdale,
Newington ME9 7PX ☎ 01795 842261 🖷 01795 844117
e-mail: sittingbourne@golfclub.totalserve.co.uk
A downland course with pleasant vistas. There are a few uphill climbs, but the course is far from difficult. The new back nine holes are very testing.
18 holes, 6291yds, Par 71, SSS 70, Course record 63.
Club membership 715.
Visitors by prior arrangement or letter of introduction. Must contact in advance, may not play at weekends. **Societies** Tue & Thu, apply in advance. **Green Fees** £40 per 36 holes, £30 per 18 holes. **Cards** ⊞ ▦ ▧ ◪

Continued

Prof John Hearn **Course Designer** Donald Steel **Facilities**
⊗ ⅏ ⅃ ♥ ♀ ⅄ ⌂ ⅏ ⅏ ✓ **Conf** Corporate Hospitality
Days available **Location** Turn off Chestnut Street (old
A249) at Danaway

·····················

Hotel ★★★★ 75% Bridgewood Manor Hotel,
Bridgewood Roundabout, Walderslade Woods,
CHATHAM ☎ 01634 201333 100 en suite

Upchurch River Valley Golf Centre Oak Ln,
Upchurch ME9 7AY ☎ 01634 379592 📠 01634 387784
18 holes, 6237yds, Par 70, SSS 70.
Course Designer David Smart **Location** A2 between
Rainham and Newington
Telephone for further details

·····················

Hotel ★★★ 69% Russell Hotel, 136 Boxley Rd,
MAIDSTONE ☎ 01622 692221 42 en suite

SNODLAND   Map 05 TQ76

Oastpark Malling Rd ME6 5LG
☎ 01634 242661 📠 01634 240744
18 holes, 6173yds, Par 69, SSS 69, Course record 71.
Course Designer J D Banks **Location** Access via junct 4
on M20
Telephone for further details

·····················

Hotel ★★★ 67% Larkfield Priory Hotel, London Rd,
Larkfield, MAIDSTONE ☎ 01732 846858 52 en suite

TENTERDEN   Map 05 TQ83

London Beach Hotel & Golf Club Ashford Rd
TN30 6SP ☎ 01580 766279 📠 01580 763884
e-mail: enquiries@londonbeach.com
**Located in a mature parkland setting close to
Tenterden.**
9 holes, 5860yds, Par 70, SSS 69, Course record 66.
Club membership 250.
Visitors must contact in advance and book. **Societies** apply
in writing **Green Fees** not confirmed. **Cards** 💳 💳 💳
💳 💳 💳 💳 **Prof** Mark Chilcott **Course Designer** Golf
Landscapes **Facilities** ⊗ ⅏ ⅃ ♥ ♀ ⅄ ⌂ ⅏ ⅏ ✓
⅄ **Leisure** fishing, pitch & putt clay pigeon shooting. **Conf**
fac available Corporate Hospitality Days available
Location M20 Junct 9 at Ashford and follow A28 towards
Tenterden. Hotel on right hand side, 1m before Tenterden

·····················

Hotel ★★★ 75% London Beach Hotel & Golf Club,
Ashford Rd, TENTERDEN ☎ 01580 766279 26 en suite

Tenterden Woodchurch Rd TN30 7DR
☎ 01580 763987 (sec) & 762409 (shop) 📠 01580 763987
e-mail: enquiries@tenterdengolfclub.co.uk
**Set in tranquil undulating parkland with beautiful
views, the course is challenging with several difficult
holes.**
18 holes, 6071yds, Par 70, SSS 69, Course record 61.
Club membership 600.
Visitors contact secretary. May only play with member
weekends and bank holidays. Handicap certificate required.
Societies contact secretary, full details on request. **Green
Fees** not confirmed. **Cards** 💳 💳 💳 **Prof** Kyle Kelsall
Facilities ⊗ ⅏ ⅃ ♥ ♀ ⅄ ⌂ ⅏ ⅏ ✓ **Location** 0.75m E
on B2067

·····················

Hotel ★★★ 75% London Beach Hotel & Golf Club,
Ashford Rd, TENTERDEN ☎ 01580 766279 26 en suite

TONBRIDGE   Map 05 TQ54

Poultwood Higham Ln TN11 9QR
☎ 01732 364039 & 366180 📠 01732 353781
**There are two public 'pay and play' parkland courses
in an idyllic woodland setting. The courses are
ecologically designed, over predominantly flat land
offering challenging hazards and interesting playing
conditions for all standards of golfer.**
18 holes, 5524yds, Par 68, SSS 66.
9 holes, 2562yds, Par 28.
Visitors non-registered golfers may book up to 5 days in
advance for 18 hole course or take available tee times. Pay
and play system on 9 hole course. **Societies** apply in
advance to the clubhouse manager tel 01732 366180.
Green Fees 18 hole course: £13.50 (£19 weekends and
bank holidays). 9 hole course:£5.20/£6.80. **Cards** 💳 💳
💳 💳 💳 **Prof** Bill Hodkin **Course Designer** Hawtree
Facilities ⊗ ⅏ ⅃ ♥ ♀ ⅄ ⌂ ⅏ ✓ **Leisure** squash. **Conf**
fac available Corporate Hospitality Days available
Location Off A227, 3m N of Tonbridge

·····················

Hotel ★★★ 66% Rose & Crown Hotel, 125 High St,
TONBRIDGE ☎ 01732 357966 54 en suite

TUNBRIDGE WELLS (ROYAL)   Map 05 TQ53

Nevill Benhall Mill Rd TN2 5JW
☎ 01892 525818 📠 01892 517861
e-mail: manager@nevillgolfclub.co.uk
**The county boundaries of Kent and Sussex run along
the northern perimeter of the course. Open undulating
ground, well-wooded with some heather and gorse for
the first half. The second nine holes slope away from
the clubhouse to a valley where a narrow stream
hazards two holes.**
18 holes, 6349yds, Par 71, SSS 70, Course record 64.
Club membership 800.
Visitors must contact 48 hours in advance, handicap
certificate required, permission from secretary for
weekends play. **Societies** must apply in writing one month
in advance. **Green Fees** £45 per day; £30 per round
(£50/£40 weekends). **Prof** Paul Huggett **Course Designer**
Henry Cotton **Facilities** ⊗ ⅏ ⅃ ♥ ♀ ⅄ ⌂ ✓ **Location**
S of Tunbridge Wells, off forest road

·····················

Hotel ★★★ 78% The Spa Hotel, Mount Ephraim,
TUNBRIDGE WELLS ☎ 01892 520331 69 en suite

Tunbridge Wells Langton Rd TN4 8XH
☎ 01892 523034 📠 01892 536918
e-mail: info@tunbridgewellsgolfclub.co.uk
**Somewhat hilly, well-bunkered parkland course with
lake; trees form natural hazards.**
9 holes, 4725yds, Par 65, SSS 62, Course record 59.
Club membership 470.
Visitors must contact in advance, limited availability
weekends. **Societies** weekdays, apply in advance. Subject
to availability **Green Fees** £14 per 18 holes; £10 per 9
holes (£20 per 18 holes; £15 per 9 holes weekends). **Cards**
💳 💳 💳 💳 **Prof** Mike Barton **Facilities** ⊗ ⅏ by prior
arrangement ⅃ ♥ ♀ ⅄ ⌂ ⅏ ✓ **Location** 1m W on
A264

·····················

Hotel ★★★ 78% The Spa Hotel, Mount Ephraim,
TUNBRIDGE WELLS ☎ 01892 520331 69 en suite

WESTERHAM Map 05 TQ45

Park Wood Chestnut Av, Tatsfield TN16 2EG
☎ 01959 577744 & 577177 (pro-shop) 🖷 01959 572702
e-mail: mail@parkwoodgolf.co.uk
Situated in an area of natural beauty, flanked by an ancient woodland with superb views across Kent and Surrey. An undulating course, tree lined and with some interesting water features. Playable in all weather conditions.

Parkwood Golf Club: 18 holes, 6835yds, Par 72, SSS 72, Course record 66.
Club membership 500.
Visitors telephone in advance. May not play bank holidays. **Societies** apply in writing/telephone in advance. **Green Fees** terms on application. **Cards** 🖃 🖃 ⬛ 🖳 **Prof** Nick Terry **Facilities** ⊗ ⅷ ⅃ ⬛ 🖳 ♀ ⅄ 🖻 ➍ 🛒 ⌀ **Conf** fac available Corporate Hospitality Days available **Location** A25 onto B2024 Croydon Rd which becomes Clarks Lane. At Church Hill junct join Chestnut Av

Hotel ★★★ 71% Donnington Manor, London Rd, Dunton Green, SEVENOAKS ☎ 01732 462681 60 en suite

Westerham Valence Park, Brasted Rd TN16 1LJ
☎ 01959 567100 🖷 01959 567101
e-mail: jon.wittenberg@westerhamgc.co.uk
Originally completely wooded forestry land with thousands of mature pines. The storms of 1987 created natural fairways and the mature landscape makes the course both demanding and spectacular. A clubhouse with first-class facilities and magnificent views.

18 holes, 6272yds, Par 72, SSS 72.
Club membership 700.
Visitors welcome but may not play Sat & Sun am. **Societies** telephone events office for details. **Green Fees** £29 Mon-Thu, Fri £32, £36 weekends and bank holidays. **Cards** 🖃 🖃 🖳 🖃 ⬛ 🖳 **Prof** J Marshal **Course Designer** D Williams **Facilities** ⊗ ⅷ ⅃ ⬛ 🖳 ♀ ⅄ 🖻 ➍ 🛒 ⌀ ⅂ **Leisure** short game practice area. **Conf** fac available

Continued

Corporate Hospitality Days available **Location** A25 between Westerham and Brasted

Hotel ★★★ 71% Donnington Manor, London Rd, Dunton Green, SEVENOAKS ☎ 01732 462681 60 en suite

WESTGATE ON SEA Map 05 TR37

Westgate and Birchington 176 Canterbury Rd CT8 8LT ☎ 01843 831115
e-mail: wandbgc@btopenworld.com
A fine blend of inland and seaside holes which provide a good test of the golfer despite the apparently simple appearance of the course.
18 holes, 4926yds, Par 64, SSS 64, Course record 60.
Club membership 350.
Visitors Mon-Sat after 10am, Sun and bank holidays after 11am. **Societies** must contact the secretary. **Green Fees** £17 per day (£20 weekends and bank holidays). **Prof** Roger Game **Facilities** ⊗ by prior arrangement ⅷ by prior arrangement ⅃ ⬛ ♀ ⅄ 🖻 ⌀ **Conf** Corporate Hospitality Days available **Location** E side of town centre off A28

Hotel ★★★ 65% Royal Albion Hotel, Albion St, BROADSTAIRS ☎ 01843 868071 19 en suite

WEST KINGSDOWN Map 05 TQ56

Woodlands Manor Tinkerpot Ln, Otford TN15 6AB
☎ 01959 523806 🖷 01959 524398
e-mail: woodlandsgolf@aol.com
Two distinct nine hole layouts with views over an area of outstanding natural beauty. The course is challenging but fair with varied and memorable holes of which the 7th, 10th and 18th stand out. Good playing conditions all year round.
18 holes, 6015yds, Par 69, SSS 69.
Club membership 600.
Visitors by prior arrangement. May not play weekends before 1pm, or Tue am. **Societies** apply in advance. **Green Fees** £24 per round (£30 per round weekends). **Cards** 🖃 🖃 🖃 ⬛ 🖳 **Prof** Philip Womack **Course Designer** Lyons/Coles **Facilities** ⊗ ⅷ ⅃ ⬛ 🖳 ♀ ⅄ 🖻 ➍ ⌀ ⅂ **Location** Through West Kingsdown on A20, turn right opposite Portbello Inn into School Lane. Continue into Tinkerpot lane, club house left.

Hotel 🄴 Holiday Inn Maidstone, London Rd, Wrotham Heath, WROTHAM ☎ 0870 400 9054 106 en suite

WEST MALLING Map 05 TQ65

Kings Hill Fortune Way, Discovery Dr, Kings Hill ME19 4AG ☎ 01732 875040 🖷 01732 875019
e-mail: khatkhgolf@aol.com
18 holes, 6622yards, Par 72, SSS 72.
Course Designer David Williams Partnership **Location** M20 junct 4, take A228 towards Tonbridge
Telephone for further details

Hotel 🄴 Travel Inn Maidstone (Leybourne), Castle Way, LEYBOURNE ☎ 08701 977170 40 en suite

WHITSTABLE Map 05 TR16

Chestfield (Whitstable) 103 Chestfield Rd, Chestfield CT5 3LU
☎ 01227 794411 & 792243 🖷 01227 794454
e-mail: secretary@chestfield-golfclub.co.uk
Gently undulating parkland course with sea views. The par 3 3rd is generally played into the wind and the 4th has a difficult left-hand dog-leg.

Continued

18 holes, 6200yds, Par 70, SSS 70, Course record 66.
Club membership 650.
Visitors contact for times, not Sun am. **Societies** must apply in writing/telephone. **Green Fees** not confirmed. **Cards** 🖃 ▭ ▭ 🖃 🖃 **Prof** John Brotherton **Course Designer** D Steel/James Braid **Facilities** ⊗ ⅏ 🍴 🍺 ♀ 🏌
🏠 ⅏ 🏌 ♂ **Location** 0.5m S by Chestfield Railway Station, off A2990

Whitstable & Seasalter Collingwood Rd CT5 1EB
☎ 01227 272020 📠 01227 280822
Links course.
9 holes, 5357yds, Par 66, SSS 63, Course record 62.
Club membership 350.
Visitors weekend play by prior arrangement. **Green Fees** not confirmed. **Facilities** ⊗ 🍴 🍺 ♀ 🏌 **Location** W side of town centre off B2205

LANCASHIRE

ACCRINGTON
Map 07 SD72

Accrington & District Devon Av, Oswaldtwistle
BB5 4LS ☎ 01254 381614 📠 01254 233273
e-mail: info@accrington-golf-club.fsnet.co.uk
Moorland course with pleasant views of the Pennines and surrounding areas. The course is a real test for even the best amateur golfers and has hosted many county matches and championships over its 100 plus years of history.
18 holes, 6060yds, Par 70, SSS 69, Course record 63.
Club membership 600.
Visitors must contact in advance, handicap certificate required. **Societies** contact in advance. **Green Fees** £24 daily Mon-Thu, £30 Fri-Sun. **Prof** Bill Harling **Course Designer** J Braid **Facilities** ⊗ ⅏ 🍴 🍺 ♀ 🏌 🏠 ♂ **Location** Mid way between Accrington & Blackburn

Hotel ★★★★ 62% Dunkenhalgh Hotel, Blackburn Rd, Clayton-le-Moors, ACCRINGTON ☎ 01254 398021 53 en suite 69 annexe en suite

Baxenden & District Top o' th' Meadow,
Baxenden BB5 2EA ☎ 01254 234555
e-mail: baxgolf@hotmail.com
Moorland course with a long par 3 to start.
9 holes, 5740yds, Par 70, SSS 68, Course record 65.
Club membership 340.
Visitors may not play Sat, Sun and bank holidays except with member. **Societies** must contact in advance. **Green Fees** terms on application. **Facilities** ⊗ ⅏ 🍴 🍺 ♀ 🏌
Conf fac available Corporate Hospitality Days available **Location** 1.5m SE off A680

Hotel ★★★★ 62% Dunkenhalgh Hotel, Blackburn Rd, Clayton-le-Moors, ACCRINGTON ☎ 01254 398021 53 en suite 69 annexe en suite

Green Haworth Green Haworth BB5 3SL
☎ 01254 237580 & 382510 📠 01254 396176
e-mail: golf@greenhaworth.freeserve.co.uk
9 holes, 5522yds, Par 68, SSS 67, Course record 66.
Location 2m S off A680
Telephone for further details

Hotel ★★★★ 62% Dunkenhalgh Hotel, Blackburn Rd, Clayton-le-Moors, ACCRINGTON ☎ 01254 398021 53 en suite 69 annexe en suite

BACUP
Map 07 SD82

Bacup Maden Rd OL13 8HY
☎ 01706 873170 📠 01706 877726
Moorland course, predominantly flat except climbs to 1st and 10th holes.
9 holes, 6008yds, Par 70, SSS 69.
Club membership 350.
Visitors no restrictions. Club competitions in season on Sat & some Sun, advisable to contact in advance. **Societies** must contact in writing. **Green Fees** not confirmed. **Facilities** 🏌 **Location** W side of town off A671

Hotel ★★★ 68% Rosehill House Hotel, Rosehill Av, BURNLEY ☎ 01282 453931 30 en suite

BARNOLDSWICK
Map 07 SD84

Ghyll Skipton Rd BB18 6JH ☎ 01282 842466
e-mail: secretary@ghyllgc.freeserve.com
Excellent parkland course with outstanding views, especially from the 8th tee where you can see the Three Peaks. Testing 8th hole is an uphill par 4. Eleven holes in total, nine in Yorkshire and two in Lancashire.
11 holes, 5790yds, Par 68, SSS 66, Course record 62.
Club membership 345.
Visitors may not play Tue, Fri after 4.30pm & Sun. **Societies** must contact in writing. **Green Fees** £15 per day (£18 weekends & bank holidays). **Facilities** 🍺 ♀ 🏌 **Location** M65 to Colne (end of motorway). A56 toward Skipton. Turn left after Earby on B6252

BICKERSTAFFE
Map 07 SD40

Mossock Hall Liverpool Rd L39 0EE
☎ 01695 421717 📠 01695 424961
Relatively flat parkland course with scenic views. USGA greens and water features on four holes.
18 holes, 6492yards, Par 71, SSS 70, Course record 68.
Club membership 580.
Visitors must contact in advance. **Societies** write/telephone in advance. **Green Fees** £30 per 18 holes (£35 weekends & bank holidays). **Prof** Phil Atkiss **Course Designer** Steve Marnoch **Facilities** ⊗ ⅏ 🍴 🍺 ♀ 🏌 🏠 ♂ **Location** off M58 junct 3

Hotel ★★★ 64% Quality Hotel Skelmersdale, Prescott Rd, UPHOLLAND ☎ 01695 720401 55 en suite

BLACKBURN
Map 07 SD62

Blackburn Beardwood Brow BB2 7AX
☎ 01254 51122 📠 01254 665578
e-mail: sec@blackburngolfclub.com
Parkland course on a high plateau with stream and hills. Superb views of Lancashire coast and the Pennines.
18 holes, 6144yds, Par 71, SSS 70, Course record 62.
Club membership 550.
Visitors must contact professional in advance. **Societies** must contact in advance. **Green Fees** £26 per day (£30 weekends). **Prof** Alan Rodwell **Facilities** ⊗ ⅏ 🍴 🍺 ♀ 🏌 🏠 ⅏ ♂ **Conf** fac available **Location** 1.25m NW of town centre off A677

Hotel ★★ 77% Millstone Hotel, Church Ln, Mellor, BLACKBURN ☎ 01254 813333 18 en suite 6 annexe en suite

BLACKPOOL   Map 07 SD33

Blackpool North Shore Devonshire Rd FY2 0RD
☎ 01253 352054 ▤ 01253 591240
e-mail: office@blackpoolnorthshoregolfclub.com
Undulating parkland course.

18 holes, 6432yds, Par 71, SSS 71, Course record 65.
Club membership 900.
Visitors may not play Thu & Sat. Advisable to contact in
advance. **Societies** must contact in advance. **Green Fees**
£32 per day, £25 per round (£38/£30 weekends & bank
holidays). **Cards** ▨ ▨ ▨ ▨ **Prof** Brendan Ward
Course Designer H S Colt **Facilities** ⊗ ⅲ ┗ ♥ ♀ ⚑ ⚐
⚑ ♂ **Leisure**. **Location** on A587 N of town centre

Hotel ★★★ 63% Savoy Hotel, Queens Promenade, North
Shore, BLACKPOOL ☎ 01253 352561 131 en suite

Blackpool Park North Park Dr FY3 8LS
☎ 01253 397916 ▤ 01253 397916
e-mail: secretary@bpgc.org.uk
The golf course, situated in Stanley Park, is municipal.
The golf club (Blackpool Park) is private but golfers
may use the clubhouse facilities if playing the course.
An abundance of grassy pits, ponds and open dykes.
18 holes, 6087yds, Par 70, SSS 69, Course record 64.
Club membership 650.
Visitors may not play Saturday. Must apply to Mrs A
Hirst, Town Hall, Talbot Square, Blackpool. **Societies**
telephone 01253 478478 for details. **Green Fees** terms on
application. **Prof** Brian Purdie **Course Designer**
A.McKenzie **Facilities** ⊗ ⅲ ┗ ♥ ♀ ⚑ ⚐ ⚑ ♂
Location 1m E of Blackpool Tower

Hotel ★★★ 63% Savoy Hotel, Queens Promenade, North
Shore, BLACKPOOL ☎ 01253 352561 131 en suite

De Vere Herons Reach East Park Blackpool
FY3 8LL ☎ 01253 766156 & 838866 ▤ 01253 798800
e-mail: dot.kilbride@devere-hotels.com
The course was designed by Peter Alliss and Clive
Clarke. There are 10 man-made lakes and several
existing ponds. Built to a links design, well mounded
but fairly easy walking. Water comes into play on 9
holes, better players can go for the carry or shorter
hitters can take the safe route. Extensive plantation and
landscaping have been carried out as the course
matures. The course provides an excellent and
interesting challenge for golfers of all standards.
18 holes, 6628yds, Par 72, SSS 71, Course record 64.
Club membership 450.

De Vere Herons Reach
Visitors may book up to 2 weeks in advance tel 01253
766156, (hotel guest/visiting society no limit to how far in
advance bookings can be made). Handicap essential,
etiquette and dress rules must be adhered to **Societies**
telephone or write to golf sales office 01253 838866.
Green Fees £45 per round (£40 low season). **Cards** ▨
▨ ▨ ▨ ▨ **Prof** Richard Bowman **Course**
Designer Peter Alliss/Clive Clark **Facilities** ⊗ ⅲ ┗ ♥ ♀
⚑ ⚐ ⚑ ⚐ ⚑ ♂ **Leisure** hard tennis courts, heated
indoor swimming pool, squash, sauna, solarium,
gymnasium, health and beauty facilities. **Conf** fac available
Corporate Hospitality Days available **Location** Off A587
adjacent to Stanley Park & Zoo

Hotel ★★★★ 67% De Vere Herons' Reach, East Park
Dr, BLACKPOOL ☎ 01253 838866 172 en suite

BURNLEY   Map 07 SD83

Burnley Glen View BB11 3RW
☎ 01282 421045 & 451281 ▤ 01282 451281
e-mail: burnleygolfclub@onthegreen.co.uk
Challenging moorland course with exceptional views.
18 holes, 5939yds, Par 69, SSS 69, Course record 62.
Club membership 700.
Visitors suggest contact in advance. Restricted play on Sat
during summer. **Societies** must apply in writing. Telephone
first for details. **Green Fees** £20 per day (£25 weekends &
bank holidays). **Prof** Paul McEvoy **Facilities** ⊗ ⅲ ┗ ♥ ♀
⚑ ⚐ ♂ **Leisure** snooker table. **Conf** fac available
Corporate Hospitality Days available **Location** eastbound
M65 junct 9, follow Halifax signs for 3m to Glen View Rd.
Westbound M65 junct 10/11 to Burnley town centre, take
Manchester Rd for 1m and turn left into Glen View Rd

Hotel ★★★ 68% Rosehill House Hotel, Rosehill Av,
BURNLEY ☎ 01282 453931 30 en suite

Towneley Towneley Park, Todmorden Rd BB11 3ED
☎ 01282 438473
18 holes, 5811yds, Par 70, SSS 68, Course record 67.
Location 1m SE of town centre on A671
Telephone for further details

Hotel ★★★ 74% Oaks Hotel, Colne Rd, Reedley,
BURNLEY ☎ 01282 414141 50 en suite

CHORLEY   Map 07 SD51

Charnock Richard Preston Rd, Charnock Richard
PR7 5LE ☎ 01257 470707 ▤ 01257 794343
Flat parkland course with plenty of Americanised
water hazards. Signature hole the 6th par 5 with an
island green.

Continued   *Continued*

*18 holes, 6239yds, Par 71, SSS 70, Course record 68.
Club membership 550.*
Visitors strict full dress code, members time 8.30-9.30pm and 12.00-1.00pm weekdays, telephone for weekend play. **Societies** contact club secretary in writing. **Green Fees** not confirmed. **Cards** ⊞ ▦ ▧ ▨ **Prof** Lee Taylor/Alan Lunt **Course Designer** Chris Court/Martin Turner **Facilities** ⊗ ⊨ ▥ ▤ ♥ ♀ △ 酓 ⛾ ☞ ⬟ ⚲ **Conf** Corporate Hospitality Days available **Location** On the main A49, 0.25m from Camelot Theme Park

Hotel ★★★ 69% Park Hall Hotel, Park Hall Rd, Charnock Richard, CHORLEY ☎ 01257 452090 455000 ▤ 01257 451838 54 en suite 84 annexe en suite

Chorley Hall o' th' Hill, Heath Charnock PR6 9HX
☎ 01257 480263 ▤ 01257 480722
e-mail: secretary@chorleygolfclub.freeserve.co.uk
A splendid moorland course with plenty of fresh air. The well-sited clubhouse affords some good views of the Lancashire coast and of Angelzarke, a local beauty spot. Beware of the short 3rd hole with its menacing out-of-bounds.
*18 holes, 6269yds, Par 71, SSS 70, Course record 62.
Club membership 550.*
Visitors must contact in advance, must play from yellow tees and may not play weekends or bank holidays. **Societies** must contact in advance. Tue-Fri only. **Green Fees** not confirmed. **Prof** Mark Bradley **Course Designer** J A Steer **Facilities** ⊗ ⊨ ▥ ♥ ♀ △ 酓 ⚲ **Location** 2.5m SE on A673

Hotel ★★★ 70% Pines Hotel, 570 Preston Rd, Clayton-Le-Woods, CHORLEY ☎ 01772 338551 37 en suite

Duxbury Jubilee Park Duxbury Hall Rd PR7 4AT
☎ 01257 265380 ▤ 01257 274500
18 holes, 6390yds, Par 71, SSS 70.
Course Designer Hawtree & Sons **Location** 2.5m S off A6
Telephone for further details

Hotel ⛿ Welcome Lodge, Welcome Break Service Area, CHORLEY ☎ 01257 791746 100 en suite

Shaw Hill Hotel Golf & Country Club Preston Rd, Whittle-Le-Woods PR6 7PP
☎ 01257 269221 ▤ 01257 261223
e-mail: info@shaw-hill.co.uk
A fine heavily wooded parkland course designed by one of Europe's most prominent golf architects and offering a considerable challenge as well as tranquillity and scenic charm. Six holes are protected by water and signature holes are the 8th and the closing 18th played slightly up hill to the imposing Club House.
*18 holes, 6246yds, Par 72, SSS 70, Course record 65.
Club membership 500.*
Visitors Mon-Fri only, must contact in advance, denims and trainers not allowed on course or in clubhouse. **Societies** must telephone in advance. **Green Fees** not confirmed. **Cards** ⊞ ▦ ▧ ▨ ▩ **Prof** David Clark **Course Designer** Harry Vardon **Facilities** ⊗ ⊨ ▥ ▤ ♥ ♀ △ 酓 ⛾ ☞ ⬟ ⚲ **Leisure** heated indoor swimming pool, sauna, solarium, gymnasium. **Location** On A6 1.5m N

CLITHEROE Map 07 SD74

Clitheroe Whalley Rd, Pendleton BB7 1PP
☎ 01200 422292 ▤ 01200 422292
e-mail: secretary@clitheroegolfclub.com
One of the best inland courses in the country. Clitheroe is a parkland-type course with water hazards and good scenic views, particularly towards Longridge, and Pendle Hill.
*18 holes, 6326yds, Par 71, SSS 71, Course record 66.
Club membership 750.*
Visitors must contact in advance. **Societies** must contact in advance. **Green Fees** £32-£45. **Prof** John Twissell **Course Designer** James Braid **Facilities** ⊗ ⊨ ▥ ▤ ♥ ♀ △ 酓 ⛾ ☞ **Conf** Corporate Hospitality Days available **Location** 2m S of Clitheroe on Whalley Road

Hotel ★★ 69% Shireburn Arms Hotel, Whalley Rd, Hurst Green, CLITHEROE ☎ 01254 826518 18 en suite

COLNE Map 07 SD84

Colne Law Farm, Skipton Old Rd BB8 7EB
☎ 01282 863391
9 holes, 5961yds, Par 70, SSS 69, Course record 63.
Location 1m E off A56
Telephone for further details

DARWEN Map 07 SD62

Darwen Winter Hill BB3 0LB
☎ 01254 701287 (club) & 704367 (office)
▤ 01254 773833
e-mail: admin@darwengolfclub.com
First 9 holes on parkland, the second 9 on moorland.
*18 holes, 5863yds, Par 69, SSS 68, Course record 63.
Club membership 600.*
Visitors may not play on Tue or Sat. **Societies** must contact in advance. **Green Fees** not confirmed. **Prof** Wayne Lennon **Facilities** ⊗ ⊪ ⊨ ▥ ▤ ♥ ♀ △ 酓 **Conf** fac available Corporate Hospitality Days available **Location** 1m NW

Hotel ⛿ Travelodge Blackburn, Darwen Motorway services, DARWEN ☎ 08700 850 950

FLEETWOOD Map 07 SD34

Fleetwood Princes Way FY7 8AF
☎ 01253 873661 & 773573 ▤ 01253 773573
e-mail: fleetwoodgc@aol.com
Championship length, flat seaside links where the player must always be alert to changes of direction or strength of the wind.

*18 holes, 6723yds, Par 72, SSS 72.
Club membership 600.*   *Continued*

Visitors may not play on competition days or Tue. **Societies** must contact in advance. A deposit of £5 per player is required. **Green Fees** terms on application. **Prof** S McLaughlin **Course Designer** J A Steer **Facilities** ⊗ ⅢⅢ ⅃ ⊑ ♥ ♀ ⋏ 🏠 ✓ **Location** W side of town centre

Hotel ⇧ Travel Inn Blackpool Bispham, Devonshire Rd, Bispham, BLACKPOOL ☎ 08701 977033 39 en suite

GARSTANG   Map 07 SD44

Garstang Country Hotel & Golf Club Garstang Rd, Bowgreave PR3 1YE
☎ 01995 600100 ▤ 01995 600950
e-mail: reception@garstanghotelandgolf.co.uk
Fairly flat parkland course following the contours of the Rivers Wyre and Calder and providing a steady test of ability, especially over the longer back nine. Exceptional drainage makes the course playable all year round.

18 holes, 6050yds, Par 68, SSS 68.
Visitors tee times bookable 6 days in advance. **Societies** telephone for availability and confirm in writing. **Green Fees** not confirmed. **Cards** ▦ 🖃 🖃 🖃 ⅀ **Prof** Robert Head **Course Designer** Richard Bradbeer **Facilities** ⊗ ⅢⅢ ⅃ ⊑ ♥ ♀ ⋏ 🏠 ⛳ 🏟 🖸 ✓ ⅃ **Conf** fac available Corporate Hospitality Days available **Location** Situated on B6430 1m S of Garstang

Hotel ★★★ 67% Garstang Country Hotel & Golf Club, Garstang Rd, Bowgreave, GARSTANG ☎ 01995 600100 32 en suite

GREAT HARWOOD   Map 07 SD73

Great Harwood Harwood Bar, Whalley Rd BB6 7TE
☎ 01254 884391
Flat parkland course with fine views of the Pendle region.
9 holes, 6404yds, Par 73, SSS 71, Course record 68.
Club membership 400.
Visitors must contact in advance. **Societies** welcome mid-week only, apply in writing. **Green Fees** £16 per day (£22 weekends & bank holidays). **Facilities** ⅃ ⊑ ♥ ♀ ⋏
Location E side of town centre on A680

Hotel ★★★★ 62% Dunkenhalgh Hotel, Blackburn Rd, Clayton-le-Moors, ACCRINGTON ☎ 01254 398021 53 en suite 69 annexe en suite

> **Use the maps at the back of the guide to help locate a golf course.**

Between Royal Birkdale And Royal Lytham

… is the oasis of the Garstang Country Hotel & Golf Club. Our superb golf course offers a rewarding challenge for all standards players, with interesting water hazards and well maintained greens. Hone your skills here and then play some of the great courses of the world nearby. We specialise in looking after golfers. We know what you need – and provide it.

Call 01995 600100 for details of our breaks

Bowgreave, Garstang, Lancashire, PR3 1YE

www.garstanghotelandgolf.co.uk

HASLINGDEN   Map 07 SD72

Rossendale Ewood Ln Head BB4 6LH
☎ 01706 831339 (Secretary) & 213616 (Pro)
▤ 01706 228669
e-mail: rgc@golfers.net
Surprisingly flat parkland course, situated on a plateau with panoramic views and renowned for excellent greens.
18 holes, 6293yds, Par 72, Course record 64.
Club membership 700.
Visitors must contact in advance. Must play with member on Sat. **Societies** must telephone in advance & confirm in writing. **Green Fees** £25.50 (£30.50 Sun). **Prof** Stephen Nicholls **Facilities** ⊗ ⅢⅢ ⅃ ⊑ ♥ ♀ (ex Mon) ⋏ 🏠 ✓ **Conf** Corporate Hospitality Days available **Location** 0.5m S off A56

Hotel ★★ 77% Millstone Hotel, Church Ln, Mellor, BLACKBURN ☎ 01254 813333 18 en suite 6 annexe en suite

HEYSHAM   Map 07 SD46

Heysham Trumacar Park, Middleton Rd LA3 3JH
☎ 01524 851011 (Sec) & 852000 (Pro) ▤ 01524 853030
e-mail: secretary@heyshamgolf.freeserve.co.uk
Seaside parkland course, partly wooded. The 15th is a 459-yard par 4 hole nearly always played into the prevailing south west wind.
18 holes, 5999yds, Par 68, SSS 69.
Club membership 930.
Visitors book in advance via the professional, restricted at weekends. **Societies** must contact in advance.

Continued

Green Fees £30 per day; £25 per round (£40 weekends & bank holidays). Cards 🏧 💳 💳 💳 🖃 Prof Ryan Done Course Designer Alex Herd Facilities ⊗ ⊪ ⓑ 🖤 ♀ ☖ 🏠 ⚲ 🛒 ♂ ⓕ Leisure snooker. Location 0.75m S off A589

Hotel ★★★ 65% Clarendon Hotel, 76 Marine Rd West, West End Promenade, MORECAMBE ☎ 01524 410180 29 en suite

KNOTT END-ON-SEA   Map 07 SD34

Knott End Wyreside FY6 0AA
☎ 01253 810576 🖷 01253 813446
Pleasant, undulating parkland course on banks of River Wyre. Open to sea breezes.
18 holes, 5849yds, Par 69, SSS 68, Course record 63.
Club membership 500.
Visitors book via professional up to 7 days in advance. Societies must contact in advance. Green Fees £31 per day, £28 per round (£41/£36 weekends). Cards 🏧 💳 💳 🖃 Prof Paul Walker Course Designer Braid Facilities ⊗ ⊪ ⓑ 🖤 ♀ ☖ 🏠 ♂ Location W side of village off B5377

Hotel ⬆ Travelodge Lancaster Forton, White Carr Ln, Bay Horse, FORTON ☎ 08700 850 950 53 en suite

LANCASTER   Map 07 SD46

Lancaster Golf Club Ashton Hall, Ashton-with-Stodday LA2 0AJ ☎ 01524 751247 🖷 01524 752742
This course is unusual for parkland golf as it is exposed to the winds coming off the Irish Sea. It is situated on the Lune estuary and has some natural hazards and easy walking. There are several fine holes among woods near the old clubhouse.
18 holes, 6282yds, Par 71, SSS 71, Course record 66.
Club membership 925.
Visitors must play with member or resident weekends. Must contact in advance and have a handicap certificate. Societies Mon-Fri only. Must contact in advance. Handicap certificate required. Green Fees terms on application. Cards 🏧 💳 💳 🖃 Prof David Sutcliffe Course Designer James Braid Facilities ⊗ ⊪ ⓑ 🖤 ♀ ☖ 🏠 🛒 ♂ Conf Corporate Hospitality Days available Location 3m S on A588

Hotel ★★★★ 71% Lancaster House Hotel, Green Ln, Ellel, LANCASTER ☎ 01524 844822 80 en suite

Lansil Caton Rd LA1 3PE ☎ 01524 61233
e-mail: lansilsportsgolfclub@onetel.net
Challenging parkland course.
9 holes, 5540yds, Par 70, SSS 67, Course record 68.
Club membership 375.
Visitors may not play before 1pm on Sun. Contact in advance. Societies weekdays only; must contact in writing. Green Fees not confirmed. Facilities ⊗ by prior arrangement ⊪ by prior arrangement ⓑ 🖤 ♀ Location N side of town centre on A683

Hotel 🅄 Holiday Inn Lancaster, Waterside Park, Caton Rd, LANCASTER ☎ 0870 400 9047 157 en suite

LANGHO   Map 07 SD73

Mytton Fold Hotel & Golf Complex
Whalley Rd BB6 8AB ☎ 01254 245392 🖷 01254 248119
The course has panoramic views across the Ribble
Continued

Valley and Pendle Hill. Tight fairways and water hazards are designed to make this a challenging course for any golfer.
18 holes, 6082yds, Par 72, SSS 70, Course record 69.
Club membership 350.
Visitors weekends restricted must contact in advance. Societies telephone in advance. Green Fees not confirmed. Cards 🏧 💳 💳 💳 🖃 Prof Gary P Coope Course Designer Frank Hargreaves Facilities ⊗ ⊪ ⓑ 🖤 ♀ ☖ 🏠 ⚲ 🛒 ♂ Conf Corporate Hospitality Days available Location On A59 between Langho and Whalley

Hotel 🏠 Northcote Manor, Northcote Rd, LANGHO ☎ 01254 240555 14 en suite

LEYLAND   Map 07 SD52

Leyland Wigan Rd PR25 2UD
☎ 01772 436457 🖷 01772 435605
e-mail: manager@leylandgolfclub.com
Parkland course, fairly flat and usually breezy.

Continued

18 holes, 6256yds, Par 70, SSS 70, Course record 64.
Club membership 750.
Visitors must contact in advance. Welcome weekdays, with member only at weekends. **Societies** must contact in advance and have official handicap. **Green Fees** £27 per day. **Cards** ▆▆ ▆▆ ▆▆ ▆ **Prof** Colin Burgess **Facilities** ⊗ ⊞ ⣿ ⛾ ♨ ⚑ ♟ ⚑ **Conf** fac available Corporate Hospitality Days available **Location** 0.75m from M6 junct 28

· ·

Hotel ★★★ 70% Pines Hotel, 570 Preston Rd, Clayton-Le-Woods, CHORLEY ☎ 01772 338551 37 en suite

LONGRIDGE   Map 07 SD63

Longridge Fell Barn, Jeffrey Hill PR3 2TU
☎ 01772 783291 🖺 01772 783022
e-mail: secretary@longridgegolfclub.fsnet.co.uk
One of the oldest clubs in England, which celebrated its 125th anniversary in 2002. A moorland course with panoramic views of the Trough of Bowland, the Fylde coast and Welsh mountains.

18 holes, 5975yds, Par 70, SSS 69, Course record 65.
Club membership 600.
Visitors Must contact in advance. Limited play at weekends Jul-Aug. **Societies** welcome by prior arrangement. **Green Fees** £27 per day including bar meal (£21 per round weekends). 2 for 1 by arrangement. **Cards** ▆▆ ▆▆ ▆▆ ▆ **Prof** Stephen Taylor **Facilities** ⊗ ⣿ ⛾ ⚑ ♨ ♟ ⚑ **Conf** fac available Corporate Hospitality Days available **Location** 8m NE of Preston off B6243

· ·

Hotel ★★ 69% Shireburn Arms Hotel, Whalley Rd, Hurst Green, CLITHEROE ☎ 01254 826518 18 en suite

LYTHAM ST ANNES See page 153

Chadwick Hotel, South Promenade, LYTHAM ST ANNES, FY8 1NP ☎ 01253 720061

The Chadwick Hotel
South Promenade
Lytham St Annes, FY8 1NP
AA ★★★

Tel: (01253) 720061
Email: sales@thechadwickhotel.com
www.thechadwickhotel.com

A modern family run hotel and leisure complex close to all the Fylde Coast Golf Courses and only 1/2 mile from the famous Royal Lytham. Renowned for its good food, friendly personal service, comfortable en suite bedrooms and a Bar which boasts over 100 Malt Whiskys. After your Golf you can relax in the Health complex which features an indoor pool, sauna, Turkish bath, jacuzzi, solarium and Gymnasium. An ideal Hotel to stay for your golfing break with prices starting from only £41.50 per person per night for Dinner, Bed and Breakfast.

LYTHAM ST ANNES   Map 07 SD32

Fairhaven Lytham Hall Park, Ansdell FY8 4JU
☎ 01253 736741 (Secretary) 🖺 01253 731461
A flat, but interesting parkland links course of good standard. There are natural hazards as well as numerous bunkers, and players need to produce particularly accurate second shots. An excellent test of golf for all abilities.
18 holes, 6883yds, Par 74, SSS 73, Course record 64.
Club membership 750.
Visitors telephone professional in advance. **Societies** must contact in advance. **Green Fees** not confirmed. **Cards** ▆▆ ▆▆ ▆▆ ▆ **Prof** Brian Plucknett **Course Designer** J A Steer **Facilities** ⊗ ⣿ ⛾ ♨ ⚑ ♟ ⚑ **Location** E side of town centre off B5261

· ·

Hotel ★★★ 69% Bedford Hotel, 307-311 Clifton Dr South, LYTHAM ST ANNES ☎ 01253 724636 46 en suite

Lytham Green Drive Ballam Rd FY8 4LE
☎ 01253 737390 🖺 01253 731350
e-mail: sec@greendrive.fsnet.co.uk
Green Drive provides a stern but fair challenge for even the most accomplished golfer. Tight fairways, strategically placed hazards and small tricky greens are the trademark of this testing course which meanders through pleasant countryside and is flanked by woods, pastures and meadows. The course demands accuracy in spite of the relatively flat terrain.
18 holes, 6194yds, Par 70, SSS 70, Course record 64.
Visitors must contact in advance, weekend play by arrangement only. **Societies** telephone to book in advance.

Continued

Royal Lytham & St Annes

Map 07 SD32   **Lytham St Annes**

☎ **01253 724206**   📄 **01256 780946**

Founded in 1886, this huge links course can be difficult, especially in windy conditions.

Unusually for a championship course it starts with a par 3, the nearby railway line and red brick houses creating distractions which only add to the challenge. The course has hosted ten Open Championships with some memorable victories: amateur Bobby Jones famously won the first here in 1926; Bobby Charles of New Zealand became the only left-hander to win the title; in 1969 Tony Jacklin helped to revive British golf with his win; and the most recent in 2001 was won by David Duval.

e-mail: bookings@royallytham.org

Visitors Mon and Thu only (unless guest at Dormy House). Must contact in advance and have a handicap certificate (21 max gentlemen, 30 max ladies)

Societies Must apply to Secretary
(large groups Mon & Thu only)

Green Fees 18 holes £110 weekdays, £165 Sundays

Facilities ⊗ ⊠ 🍴 🍔 🍺 ♀ 🏌 ⛳ 🏌 ✎ ⌇

Professional Eddie Birchenough

Location Links Gate, Lytham FY8 3LQ
(0.5m E of St Annes town)

Holes/Par/Course record 54 holes,
Championship Course: 18 holes 6882 yds, Par 71, SSS 74.
Course record 64.
Members Course: 18 holes, 6630 yds, Par 71, SSS 73.
Visitors Course: 18 holes, 6360 yds, Par 71 SSS 72

WHERE TO STAY AND EAT NEARBY

Hotels
LYTHAM ST ANNES
★★★★ ◉ 67% Clifton
Arms, FY8 5QJ
☎ 01253 739898. 48 en suite

★★★ 67% Chadwick, FY8 1NP
☎ 01253 720061. 75 en suite

★★★ 69% Bedford, FY8 1HN.
☎ 01253 724636.
46 en suite

★★★ 64% Best Western
Glendower, FY8 2NQ
☎ 01253 723241. 60 en suite

★★ 69% Lindum Hotel,
FY8 1LZ
☎ 01253 721534.
76 en suite

Restaurant
LYTHAM ST ANNES

◉ Chicory, FY8 5LE
☎ 01253 737111

◉ Green's Bistro, FY8 1SX
☎ 01253 789990

Championship Course

Green Fees £40 per day; £33 per round. **Cards** ⊞ ▣ 🗉
Prof Andrew Lancaster **Course Designer** Steer **Facilities**
⊗ ⅷ ⅃ ▯ ♀ ⌂ 🛈 ⚸ **Conf** Corporate Hospitality
Days available **Location** E side of town centre off B5259

Hotel ★★★★ 67% Clifton Arms, West Beach, Lytham,
LYTHAM ST ANNES ☎ 01253 739898 48 en suite

St Annes Old Links Highbury Rd East FY8 2LD
☎ 01253 723597 📄 01253 781506
e-mail: secretary@coastalgolf.co.uk
**Seaside links, qualifying course for Open
Championship; compact and of very high standard,
particularly greens. Windy, very long 5th, 17th and
18th holes. Famous hole: 9th (171 yds), par 3. Excellent
club facilities.**

*St Annes Old Links Golf Club: 18 holes, 6616yds, Par 72,
SSS 72, Course record 63.*
Club membership 750.
Visitors may not play on Sat or before 9.30am & between
noon-1.30pm weekdays. Sundays by telephoning on the
day. Handicap certificate requested. **Societies** must contact
in advance. **Green Fees** not confirmed. **Cards** ⊞ ▣ 🗎
🗉 **Prof** D J Webster **Course Designer** George Lowe
Facilities ⊗ ⅷ ⅃ ▯ ♀ ⌂ 🛈 ⚸ ⚸ **Leisure** snooker
room. **Conf** Corporate Hospitality Days available **Location**
N side of town centre

Hotel ★★★ 69% Bedford Hotel, 307-311 Clifton Dr
South, LYTHAM ST ANNES ☎ 01253 724636
46 en suite

MORECAMBE
Map 07 SD46

Morecambe Bare LA4 6AJ
☎ 01524 412841 📄 01524 400088
e-mail: secretary@morecambegolfclub.com
**Holiday golf at its most enjoyable. The well-maintained,
wind-affected seaside parkland course is not long but
full of character. Even so the panoramic views across
Morecambe Bay and to the Lake District and Pennines
make concentration difficult. The 4th is a testing hole.**
18 holes, 5750yds, Par 67, SSS 69, Course record 69.
Club membership 850.
Visitors may play from yellow tees, must contact in
advance. **Societies** must contact in advance. **Green Fees**
terms on application. **Cards** ⊞ ▣ ⊟ 🗉 **Prof** Simon
Fletcher **Course Designer** Dr Alister Mackenzie **Facilities**
⊗ ⅷ ⅃ ▯ ♀ ⌂ 🛈 ⚸ **Location** N side of town centre on
A5105

Hotel ★★★ 62% Elms Hotel, Bare Village,
MORECAMBE ☎ 01524 411501 39 en suite

NELSON
Map 07 SD83

Marsden Park Townhouse Rd BB9 8DG
☎ 01282 661912
18 holes, 5813yds, Par 70, SSS 68, Course record 66.
Location E side of town centre off A56
Telephone for further details

Hotel ★★★ 74% Oaks Hotel, Colne Rd, Reedley,
BURNLEY ☎ 01282 414141 50 en suite

Nelson King's Causeway, Brierfield BB9 0EU
☎ 01282 611834 & 617000 📄 01282 606226
e-mail: nelsongc@onetel.net.uk
**Moorland course. The late Dr. MacKenzie, who laid out
the course, managed a design which does not include
any wearisome climbing and created many interesting
holes with wonderful panoramic views of the
surrounding Pendle area.**
18 holes, 6007yds, Par 70, SSS 69, Course record 64.
Club membership 580.
Visitors must telephone 01282 617000/611834 in advance,
may not play before 9.30am or between 12.30-1.30pm.
Societies must contact in advance. **Green Fees** £30 per day
(£35 weekends & bank holidays). **Prof** Neil Reeves
Course Designer Dr Mackenzie **Facilities** ⊗ ⅷ ⅃ ▯ ♀
⌂ 🛈 ⚸ **Location** M65 junct 12, then take A682 to
Brierfield, left at traffic lights into Halifax Road which
becomes Kings Causeway

Hotel ★★★ 74% Oaks Hotel, Colne Rd, Reedley,
BURNLEY ☎ 01282 414141 50 en suite

ORMSKIRK
Map 07 SD40

Hurlston Hall Hurlston Ln, Southport Rd, Scarisbrick
L40 8HB
☎ 01704 840400 & 841120 (pro shop) 📄 01704 841404
e-mail: hurlston_hall@btinternet.com
**Designed by Donald Steel, this gently undulating course
offers fine views across the Pennines and Bowland Fells.
With generous fairways, large tees and greens, two
streams and seven lakes, it provides a good test of golf
for players of all standards. Luxurious colonial-style
clubhouse.**
18 holes, 6746yds, Par 72, SSS 72, Course record 66.
Club membership 650.
Visitors contact in advance **Societies** registered Golf
Societies and others approved by club, write or telephone
for details. **Green Fees** £35 per 18 holes (£40 weekends).
Cards ⊞ ▤ ▣ ⊟ 🗎 🗉 **Prof** Jon Esclapez **Course
Designer** Donald Steel **Facilities** ⊗ ⅷ ⅃ ▯ ♀ ⌂ 🛈
⚸ ⚸ **Leisure** fishing. **Conf** fac available Corporate
Hospitality Days available **Location** Situated 6m from
Southport and 2m from Ormskirk along A570

Hotel ★★★ 67% Beaufort Hotel, High Ln, Burscough,
ORMSKIRK ☎ 01704 892655 20 en suite

Ormskirk Cranes Ln, Lathom L40 5UJ
☎ 01695 572227 🖷 01695 572227
e-mail: ormskirk@ukgolfer.org
A pleasantly secluded, fairly flat, parkland course with much heath and silver birch. Accuracy from the tees will provide an interesting variety of second shots.
18 holes, 6358yds, Par 70, SSS 71, Course record 63.
Club membership 300.
Visitors restricted Saturdays. **Societies** must telephone or contact in writing. **Green Fees** terms on application. **Prof** Jack Hammond **Course Designer** Harold Hilton **Facilities** ⊗ ⫼ ⯊ ⬥ ♀ ♋ 🖻 ♂ **Conf** Corporate Hospitality Days available **Location** 1.5m NE

Hotel ★★★ 67% Beaufort Hotel, High Ln, Burscough, ORMSKIRK ☎ 01704 892655 20 en suite

---

PLEASINGTON Map 07 SD62

Pleasington BB2 5JF
☎ 01254 202177 🖷 01254 201028
e-mail: secretary.manager@pleasington-golf.co.uk
Plunging and rising across lovely parkland and heathland turf, this course tests judgement of distance through the air to greens of widely differing levels. The 11th and 4th are testing holes.
18 holes, 6417yds, Par 70, SSS 70.
Club membership 700.
Visitors may play Mon & Wed-Fri only. **Societies** must contact in advance. **Green Fees** £44 per day, £38 per round. **Prof** Ged Furey **Course Designer** George Lowe **Facilities** ⊗ ⫼ ⯊ ⬥ ♀ ♋ 🖻 ♂ ℄ **Conf** fac available **Location** M65 junct 3, follow sign for Blackburn

Hotel ★★ 77% Millstone Hotel, Church Ln, Mellor, BLACKBURN ☎ 01254 813333 18 en suite
6 annexe en suite

POULTON-LE-FYLDE Map 07 SD33

Poulton-le-Fylde Breck Rd FY6 7HJ
☎ 01253 892444 & 893150 🖷 01253 892444
9 holes, 4454yds, Par 71, SSS 68.
Course Designer E Astbury **Location** From M55 junct 3 follow A585 to Poulton, club is then signposted
Telephone for further details

Hotel ★★ 70% Hotel Sheraton, 54-62 Queens Promenade, BLACKPOOL ☎ 01253 352723 104 en suite

---

PRESTON Map 07 SD52

Ashton & Lea Tudor Av, Lea PR4 0XA
☎ 01772 735282 🖷 01772 735762
e-mail: ashtonleagolf@supanet.com
Fairly flat, well maintained parkland course with natural water hazards, offering pleasant walks and some testing holes for golfers of all standards. Water comes into play on seven of the last nine holes. The course has three challenging par 3s.
18 holes, 6334yds, Par 71, SSS 70, Course record 65.
Club membership 650.
Visitors must contact professional on 01772 720374 or secretary on 01772 735282. **Societies** must contact in writing or by telephone. **Green Fees** £26 per 18 holes (£30 weekends & bank holidays). **Prof** M Greenough **Course Designer** J Steer **Facilities** ⊗ ⫼ ⯊ ⬥ ♀ ♋ 🖻 ♂

Continued

Leisure snooker table. **Conf** fac available Corporate Hospitality Days available **Location** 3m W of Preston on A5085

Ashton & Lea Golf Club

Hotel Ⓤ Holiday Inn Preston, Ringway, PRESTON ☎ 0870 400 9066 129 en suite

Fishwick Hall Glenluce Dr, Farringdon Park PR1 5TD ☎ 01772 798300 🖷 01772 704600
e-mail: fishwickhallgolfclub@supanet.com
Meadowland course overlooking River Ribble. Natural hazards.
18 holes, 6045yds, Par 70, SSS 69, Course record 66.
Club membership 750.
Visitors advisable to contact in advance. **Societies** must contact in advance. **Green Fees** terms on application. **Prof** Martin Watson **Facilities** ⊗ ⫼ ⯊ ⬥ ♀ ♋ 🖻 ♂ **Conf** Corporate Hospitality Days available **Location** Off M6 junct 31

Hotel Ⓤ Holiday Inn Preston, Ringway, PRESTON ☎ 0870 400 9066 129 en suite

Ingol Tanterton Hall Rd, Ingol PR2 7BY
☎ 01772 734556 🖷 01772 729815
e-mail: ingol@golfers.net
Championship designed course with natural water hazards, set in 250 acres of beautiful parkland. A good test for any calibre of golfer.

18 holes, 6294yds, Par 72, SSS 70, Course record 68.
Club membership 650.
Visitors must contact booking office in advance. **Societies** must contact. **Green Fees** terms on application. **Cards** 🖃 🖃 🖃 🖃 **Prof** Ryan Grimshaw **Course Designer** Henry Cotton **Facilities** ⊗ ⫼ ⯊ ⬥ ♀ ♋ 🖻 ♣ ♂
Leisure squash, Snooker & Pool. **Conf** fac available **Location** Junct 32 off M6, take slip road to Garstang & Preston A6, then follow signs to Ingol

Hotel Ⓤ Holiday Inn Preston, Ringway, PRESTON ☎ 0870 400 9066 129 en suite

Ashton & Lea Golf Club

Down Tudor Avenue, off Blackpool Road,
Lea, Preston, Lancashire PR4 0XA
Tel: 01772 726480 Sec: 01772 735282
Pro: 01772 720374 Fax: 01772 725762

The golf club is conveniently situated on the western
edge of Preston at Lea, affording easy access to all the
Fylde area and the M55 Motorway link to the M6 and
the rest of the motorway network. This well
maintained parkland course with natural water
hazards, length 6334 yards, Par 71, SSS 70 enjoys the
reputation of presenting a fair challenge to all classes
of golfer. The tastefully extended clubhouse offers
comfortable hospitality to suit all needs.
• GOLF PACKAGES • CONFERENCES
• SOCIAL FUNCTIONS
Catering as required, prices for all facilities on request

Penwortham Blundell Ln, Penwortham PR1 0AX
☎ 01772 744630 📠 01772 740172
e-mail: penworthamgolfclub@supanet.com
**A progressive golf club set close to the banks of the
River Ribble. The course has tree-lined fairways,
excellent greens, and provides easy walking. Testing
holes include the 175 yd, par 3 third, the 483 yd, par 5
sixth, and the 385 yd par 4 sixteenth.**

*18 holes, 5877yds, Par 69, SSS 69, Course record 65.
Club membership 1100.*
Visitors must contact in advance, restricted Tue &
weekends. **Societies** must apply in writing/telephone in
advance. **Green Fees** £30 per day; £25 per round (£33 per
day weekends & bank holidays). **Prof** Darren Hopwood
Facilities ⊗ ⊞ 🕭 💺 ♀ ♨ 🖥 𝄐 **Conf** Corporate
Hospitality Days available **Location** 1.5m W of town
centre off A59
....
Hotel ★★★ 66% Tickled Trout, Preston New Rd,
Samlesbury, PRESTON ☎ 01772 877671 102 en suite

Preston Fulwood Hall Ln, Fulwood PR2 8DD
☎ 01772 700011 📠 01772 794234
e-mail: secretary@prestongolfclub.com
**Pleasant inland golf at this course set in very agreeable
parkland. There is a well-balanced selection of holes,
undulating amongst groups of trees, and not requiring
great length.**
*18 holes, 6312yds, Par 71, SSS 71, Course record 68.
Club membership 800.*
Visitors may play midweek only. Must contact in advance
and have a handicap certificate. **Societies** must contact in
writing/telephone. **Green Fees** £40 per day; £36 per round.
Prof Andrew Greenbank **Course Designer** James Braid
Facilities ⊗ ⊞ 🕭 💺 ♀ ♨ 🖥 𝄐 **Conf** fac available
Location 1m N of city centre on A6, right at traffic lights
into Watling St, left into Fulwood Hall Lane. Course
300yds on left
....
Hotel ★★★★ 66% Preston Marriott Hotel, Garstang Rd,
Broughton, PRESTON ☎ 01772 864087 150 en suite

RISHTON · · · · · · · · · · · · · · Map 07 SD73

Rishton Eachill Links, Hawthorn Dr BB1 4HG
☎ 01254 884442 📠 01254 887701
Undulating moorland course.
*9 holes, 6097yds, Par 70, SSS 69, Course record 68.
Club membership 270.*
Visitors must play with member on weekends and bank
holidays. **Societies** must contact in writing. **Green Fees**
£17 weekdays only. **Course Designer** Peter Alliss/Dave
Thomas **Facilities** ⊗ ⊞ 🕭 💺 ♀ by arrangement ♨ **Conf**
Corporate Hospitality Days available **Location** M65 junct
6/7, club 1m from junct. Signed from Station Road in
Rishton
....
Hotel ★★★★ 62% Dunkenhalgh Hotel, Blackburn Rd,
Clayton-le-Moors, ACCRINGTON ☎ 01254 398021
53 en suite 69 annexe en suite

SILVERDALE · · · · · · · · · · · · Map 07 SD47

Silverdale Redbridge Ln LA5 0SP
☎ 01524 701300 📠 01524 702074
e-mail: silverdalegolfclub@ecosse.net
**Challenging heathland course with rock outcrops, set in
an area of outstanding natural beauty with spectacular
views of the Lake District hills and Morecambe Bay.
The 13th hole was recently described as one of Britain's
100 extraordinary golf holes.**
*18 holes, 5535yds, Par 70, SSS 68, Course record 68.
Club membership 500.*
Visitors telephone 01524 701300 to book tee. Sun not
available Apr-Sep inclusive. **Societies** must contact in
writing. **Green Fees** £25 per day; £20 per round (£30/£25
weekends). **Facilities** ⊗ ⊞ 🕭 💺 ♀ ♨ 🖥 **Location**
Opposite Silverdale Station
....
Hotel ★★ 65% Royal Station Hotel, Market St,
CARNFORTH ☎ 01524 732033 & 733636
📠 01524 720267 13 en suite

UPHOLLAND · · · · · · · · · · · · Map 07 SD50

Beacon Park Beacon Ln WN8 7RU
☎ 01695 622700 📠 01695 633066
18 holes, 6000yds, Par 72, SSS 69, Course record 68.
Course Designer Donald Steel **Location** S of Ashurst
Beacon Hill
Telephone for further details

Continued

Hotel ★★★ 67% Beaufort Hotel, High Ln, Burscough, ORMSKIRK ☎ 01704 892655 20 en suite

Dean Wood Lafford Ln WN8 0QZ
☎ 01695 622219 📠 01695 622245
e-mail: office@dwgc.fsnet.co.uk
This parkland course has a varied terrain - flat front nine, undulating back nine. Beware the par 4 11th and 17th holes, which have ruined many a card. If there were a prize for the best maintained course in Lancashire, Dean Wood would be a strong contender.
18 holes, 6179yds, Par 71, SSS 71, Course record 66.
Club membership 800.
Visitors must play with member Tue, Wed. Societies must contact in advance. Green Fees not confirmed. Prof Stuart Danchin Course Designer James Braid Facilities ⊗ ⍢ ⅃ ♥ ♀ ♣ ☈ ⚑ ⚐ Conf Corporate Hospitality Days available Location 1m from junct 26 of M6

Hotel ★★★ 64% Quality Hotel Skelmersdale, Prescott Rd, UPHOLLAND ☎ 01695 720401 55 en suite

WHALLEY
Map 07 SD73

Whalley Long Leese Barn, Clerk Hill Rd BB7 9DR
☎ 01254 822236
Parkland course near Pendle Hill, overlooking the Ribble Valley. Superb views. Ninth hole over pond.
9 holes, 6258yds, Par 72, SSS 71, Course record 69.
Club membership 450.
Visitors must telephone 01254 822236 in advance.
Societies must apply in writing. Green Fees £25 per day (£30 weekends and bank holidays). Prof Jamie Hunt Facilities ⊗ ⍢ ⅃ ♥ ♀ ♣ ⚐ Conf Corporate Hospitality Days available Location 1m SE off A671

Hotel ★★★★ 65% Clarion Hotel & Suites Foxfields, Whalley Rd, Billington, CLITHEROE ☎ 01254 822556 44 en suite

WHITWORTH
Map 07 SD81

Lobden Lobden Moor OL12 8XJ
☎ 01706 343228 & 345598 📠 01706 343228
Moorland course, with hard walking. Windy with superb views of surrounding hills.
9 holes, 5697yds, Par 70, SSS 68, Course record 63.
Club membership 250.
Visitors May not play Sat. Societies must apply in writing to Secretary. Green Fees terms on application. Facilities ⊗ ⍢ ⅃ ♥ ♀ ⅃ Location E side of town centre off A671

Hotel ★★★★ 62% Norton Grange Hotel, Manchester Rd, Castleton, ROCHDALE ☎ 01706 630788 51 en suite

WILPSHIRE
Map 07 SD63

Wilpshire Whalley Rd BB1 9LF
☎ 01254 248260 📠 01254 248260
18 holes, 5971yds, Par 69, SSS 69, Course record 65.
Course Designer James Braid Location 2m NE of Blackburn, on A666 towards Clitheroe
Telephone for further details

Hotel ★★★ 66% Sparth House Hotel, Whalley Rd, Clayton Le Moors, ACCRINGTON ☎ 01254 872263 16 en suite

LEICESTERSHIRE

ASHBY-DE-LA-ZOUCH
Map 08 SK31

Willesley Park Measham Rd LE65 2PF
☎ 01530 414596 📠 01530 564169
e-mail: info@willesleypark.com
Undulating heathland and parkland course with quick draining sandy sub-soil.
18 holes, 6304yds, Par 70, SSS 70, Course record 63.
Club membership 600.
Visitors must contact in advance. Restricted weekends. Handicap certificate required. Societies Wed-Fri only. Must apply in writing. Green Fees £30 per day/round (£35 weekends and bank holidays). Prof Ben Hill Course Designer J Braid Facilities ⊗ ⍢ ⅃ ♥ ♀ ♣ ☈ ⚐ Location SW side of town centre on B5006

BIRSTALL
Map 04 SK50

Birstall Station Rd LE4 3BB
☎ 0116 267 4322 📠 0116 267 4322
Parkland course with trees, shrubs, ponds and ditches, adjacent to Great Central Railway Steam Train line.
18 holes, 6213yds, Par 70, SSS 70.
Club membership 650.
Visitors available weekdays by arrangement. Contact professiona; for weekends. Societies apply in writing. Green Fees £30 per day; £25 per round. Prof David Clark Facilities ⊗ ⍢ ⅃ ♥ ♀ ♣ ☈ ⚐ Leisure billiard room. Conf Corporate Hospitality Days available Location 3m N of Leicester on A6

Hotel ★★★ 64% Rothley Court, Westfield Ln, ROTHLEY ☎ 0116 237 4141 13 en suite 21 annexe en suite

BOTCHESTON
Map 04 SK40

Forest Hill Markfield Ln LE9 9FJ
☎ 01455 824800 📠 01455 828522
18 holes, 6039yds, Par 72, SSS 69.
Telephone for further details

COSBY
Map 04 SP59

Cosby Chapel Ln, Broughton Rd LE9 1RG
☎ 0116 286 4759 📠 0116 286 4484
e-mail: secretary@cosby-golf-club.co.uk
Undulating parkland course with a number of tricky, tight driving holes. Challenging holes include the par 4 1st with an unseen meandering brook, the deceptively long par 4 3rd, the 12th from an elevated tee and the hogs-back shaped par 3 14th, both affected by the prevailing wind.
18 holes, 6410yds, Par 71, SSS 71, Course record 65.
Club membership 750.
Visitors welcome weekdays before 4pm. May not play at weekends. Recommended to telephone in advance. Handicap certificate required. Societies Mon-Fri only, book with secretary in advance. Green Fees £35 per day; £25 per round. Prof Martin Wing Course Designer Hawtree Facilities ⊗ ⍢ ⅃ ♥ ♀ ♣ ⚑ ⚐ Conf fac available Location 3m from M1 junct 21, follow B4114 until L turn at BP petrol station, signposted Cosby

Hotel 🅄 Holiday Inn Leicester - West, Braunstone Ln East, LEICESTER ☎ 0870 400 9051 172 en suite

East Goscote   Map 08 SK61

Beedles Lake 170 Broome Ln LE7 3WQ
☎ 0116 260 4414 📠 0116 260 4414
e-mail: les@jelson.co.uk
Fairly flat parkland course, founded in 1992, with an adjoining lake and well maintained tees and greens that are playable all year. Various new ponds give a better test of golf.
18 holes, 6641yds, Par 72, SSS 72, Course record 71. Club membership 364.
Visitors telephone booking required for weekends by prior Thu **Societies** welcome Mon-Fri **Green Fees** £12 (£16 weekends & bank holidays). **Cards** 📇 💳 💳 💳 📇 Prof Sean Byrne **Course Designer** D Tucker **Facilities** ⊗ ⽊ 🏌 🏌 ♀ ⛳ 🏊 🎯 🏆 ⛳ **Leisure** fishing. **Conf** fac available Corporate Hospitality Days available **Location** Off A46, just N of Leicester through village of Ratcliffe on the Wreake

Hotel ★★★ 64% Rothley Court, Westfield Ln, ROTHLEY ☎ 0116 237 4141 13 en suite 21 annexe en suite

Enderby   Map 04 SP59

Enderby Mill Ln LE19 4LX
☎ 0116 284 9388 📠 0116 284 9388
A gently undulating 9-hole course at which beginners are especially welcome. The longest hole is the 2nd at 407 yards and there are 5 par 3s.
9 holes, 2856yds, Par 72, SSS 71, Course record 71. Club membership 150.
Visitors no restrictions. **Societies** must telephone in advance. **Green Fees** terms on application. **Prof** Chris D'Araujo **Course Designer** David Lowe **Facilities** ⊗ ⽊ 🏌 🏌 ♀ ⛳ 🏊 🎯 🏆 ⛳ **Leisure** heated indoor swimming pool, squash, sauna, solarium, gymnasium, indoor bowls snooker badminton. **Location** 2m S, M1 junct 21 on Narborough road. Right turn off rdbt at Toby Carvery, 0.5m on left

Hinckley   Map 04 SP49

Hinckley Leicester Rd LE10 3DR
☎ 01455 615124 & 615014
📠 01455 890841 & 01455 615014
e-mail: proshop@hinckleygolfclub.com
18 holes, 6467yds, Par 71, SSS 71, Course record 65.
Course Designer Southern Golf Ltd **Location** 1.5m NE on B4668
Telephone for further details

Hotel ★★★ 65% Weston Hall Hotel, Weston Ln, Bulkington, NUNEATON ☎ 024 7631 2989 40 en suite

Kibworth   Map 04 SP69

Kibworth Weir Rd, Beauchamp LE8 0LP
☎ 0116 279 2301 📠 0116 279 6434
e-mail: secretary@kibworthgolfclub.freeserve.co.uk
Parkland course with easy walking. A brook affects a number of fairways
18 holes, 6352yds, Par 71, SSS 71, Course record 64. Club membership 700.
Visitors must contact in advance. With member only weekends. **Societies** must contact in advance. **Green Fees** £30 per day; £25 per round. **Prof** Mike Herbert **Facilities** ⊗ ⽊ 🏌 🏌 ♀ ⛳ 🏊 🎯 🏆 ⛳ **Location** S side of village off A6

Hotel ★★★ 70% Three Swans Hotel, 21 High St, MARKET HARBOROUGH ☎ 01858 466644 18 en suite 43 annexe en suite

Kirby Muxloe   Map 04 SK50

Kirby Muxloe Station Rd LE9 2EP
☎ 0116 239 3457 📠 0116 239 3457
e-mail: kirbymuxloegolf@btconnect.com
Pleasant parkland course with a lake in front of the 17th green and a short 18th.
18 holes, 6351yds, Par 70, SSS 70, Course record 65. Club membership 870.
Visitors must contact in advance and a handicap certificate is required. No visitors on Tue or at weekends. **Societies** must contact in advance. **Green Fees** £35 per day, £30 per round. **Prof** Bruce Whipham **Facilities** ⊗ ⽊ 🏌 🏌 ♀ ⛳ 🏊 🎯 🏆 ⛳ **Conf** Corporate Hospitality Days available **Location** S side of village off B5380

Hotel Ⓤ Holiday Inn Leicester - West, Braunstone East, LEICESTER ☎ 0870 400 9051 172 en suite

Leicester   Map 04 SK50

Humberstone Heights Gypsy Ln LE5 0TB
☎ 0116 276 3680 & 299 5570 (pro) 📠 0116 299 5569
Municipal parkland course with 9 hole pitch and putt and 30 bay driving range.
18 holes, 6343yds, Par 70, SSS 70, Course record 66. Club membership 400.
Visitors must telephone in advance at weekends. **Societies** must telephone in advance. **Green Fees** terms on application. **Cards** 📇 **Prof** Phil Highfield **Course Designer** Hawtry & Sons **Facilities** ⊗ 🏌 🏌 ♀ ⛳ 🏊 🎯 🏆 ⛳ **Location** 2.5m NE of city centre

Hotel ★★★ 74% Belmont House Hotel, De Montfort St, LEICESTER ☎ 0116 254 4773 77 en suite

Leicestershire Evington Ln LE5 6DJ
☎ 0116 273 8825 📠 0116 273 1900
e-mail: theleicestershiregolfclub@hotmail.com
Pleasantly undulating parkland course.
18 holes, 6134yds, Par 68, SSS 70. Club membership 800.
Visitors must contact in advance. May not play Sat. Must hold a handicap certificate. **Societies** must contact in advance. **Green Fees** not confirmed. **Prof** Darren Jones **Course Designer** Hawtree **Facilities** ⊗ ⽊ 🏌 🏌 ♀ ⛳ 🏊 🎯 ⛳ **Conf** Corporate Hospitality Days available **Location** 2m E of city off A6030

Hotel ★★★ 68% Regency Hotel, 360 London Rd, LEICESTER ☎ 0116 270 9634 32 en suite

Western Scudamore Rd, Braunstone Frith LE3 1UQ
☎ 0116 299 5566 📠 0116 299 5568
18 holes, 6518yds, Par 72, SSS 71.
Location 1.5m W of city centre off A47
Telephone for further details

Hotel Ⓤ Holiday Inn Leicester - West, Braunstone East, LEICESTER ☎ 0870 400 9051 172 en suite

> **In the hotel entries, the percentage figure refers to the AA's most recent Quality Assessment Score.**

Continued

LOUGHBOROUGH — Map 08 SK51

Longcliffe Snell's Nook Ln, Nanpantan LE11 3YA
☎ 01509 239129 Fax 01509 231286
e-mail: longcliffegolf@btconnect.com
Course of natural heathland, tree lined fairways with water in play on the 14th and 15th holes. This course is recognised by the English Golf Championship.

18 holes, 6625yds, Par 72, SSS 72, Course record 65.
Club membership 660.
Visitors must contact in advance. With member only at weekends.Handicap certificate required. **Societies** telephone in advance for availability, handicap certificate required. **Green Fees** terms on application. **Cards** **Prof** David Mee **Course Designer** Williamson **Facilities** **Conf** Corporate Hospitality Days available **Location** 1.5m from M1 junct 23 off A512

Hotel ★★★ 65% Quality Hotel Loughborough, New Ashby Rd, LOUGHBOROUGH ☎ 01509 211800 94 en suite

LUTTERWORTH — Map 04 SP58

Kilworth Springs South Kilworth Rd, North Kilworth LE17 6HJ ☎ 01858 575082 Fax 01858 575078
e-mail: kilworthsprings@ukonline.co.uk
An 18-hole course of two loops of 9: the front 9 are links style while the back 9 are in parkland with four lakes. On a windy day it is a very challenging course and the 6th hole well deserves its nickname 'the Devil's Toenail'.
Kilworth Springs Golf Course: 18 holes, 6543yds, Par 72, SSS 71, Course record 66.
Club membership 800.
Visitors welcome subject to availability. May only play after noon at weekends. **Societies** contact in advance. **Green Fees** not confirmed. **Cards** **Prof** Anders Mankert **Course Designer** Ray Baldwin **Facilities** **Conf** Corporate Hospitality Days available **Location** 4m E of M1 junc 20, A4304 to Mkt Harborough

Hotel ★★ 72% The Sun Inn, Main St, MARSTON TRUSSELL ☎ 01858 465531 20 en suite

Lutterworth Rugby Rd LE17 4HN
☎ 01455 552532 Fax 01455 553586
Hilly course with River Swift running through.
18 holes, 6226yds, Par 70, SSS 70.
Club membership 700.
Visitors must play with member at weekends. **Societies** must contact in advance. **Green Fees** £30 per day; £22 per 18 holes. **Prof** Roland Tisdall **Facilities** **Conf** Corporate Hospitality Days available
Location 0.25m from M1 junct 20

Hotel ★★★ 67% Brownsover Hall Hotel, Brownsover Ln, Old Brownsover, RUGBY ☎ 0870 609 6104 27 en suite 20 annexe en suite

MARKET HARBOROUGH — Map 04 SP78

Market Harborough Oxendon Rd LE16 8NF
☎ 01858 463684 Fax 01858 432906
A parkland course close to the town. There are wide-ranging views over the surrounding countryside. Lakes feature on four holes; challenging last three holes.
18 holes, 6070yds, Par 70, SSS 69, Course record 61.
Club membership 650.
Visitors must play with member at weekends. **Societies** must apply in writing. **Green Fees** £25 per round. **Prof** Frazer Baxter **Course Designer** H Swan **Facilities** **Conf** Corporate Hospitality Days available **Location** 1m S on A508

Hotel ★★★ 70% Three Swans Hotel, 21 High St, MARKET HARBOROUGH ☎ 01858 466644 18 en suite 43 annexe en suite

Stoke Albany Ashley Rd, Stoke Albany LE16 8PL
☎ 01858 535208 Fax 01858 535505
e-mail: info@stokealbanygolfclub.co.uk
Parkland course in the picturesque Welland Valley. Affording good views, the course should appeal to the mid-handicap golfer, and provide an interesting test to the more experienced player.
18 holes, 6132yds, Par 71, SSS 69.
Club membership 500.
Visitors welcome at all times. **Societies** please telephone secretary. **Green Fees** £17 per 18 holes (£20 weekends). **Cards** **Prof** Adrian Clifford **Course Designer** Hawtree **Facilities** **Conf** fac available Corporate Hospitality Days available **Location** Located N off A427 Market Harborough/Corby Road, follow Stoke Albany 500m towards Ashley village

Hotel ★★★ 70% Three Swans Hotel, 21 High St, MARKET HARBOROUGH ☎ 01858 466644 18 en suite 43 annexe en suite

MELTON MOWBRAY — Map 08 SK71

Melton Mowbray Waltham Rd, Thorpe Arnold LE14 4SD ☎ 01664 562118 Fax 01664 562118
e-mail: mmgc@le144sd.fsbusiness.co.uk
Easy walking heathland course.

18 holes, 6222yds, Par 70, SSS 70, Course record 61.
Club membership 650.

Continued

Visitors must contact professional on 01664 569629.
Societies must contact in advance. **Green Fees** £45 per
day, £30 per round (£35 per round weekends and bank
holidays). **Prof** Neil Curtis **Facilities** ⊗ ⅢⅢ ㏑ 🍺 ♀ 🏖 🏡
⛳ 🏌 𝄢 ▮ **Location** 2m NE of Melton Mowbray on A607
· ·

Hotel ★★★ 73% Sysonby Knoll Hotel, Asfordby Rd,
MELTON MOWBRAY ☎ 01664 563563 23 en suite
7 annexe en suite

OADBY   Map 04 SK60

Glen Gorse Glen Rd LE2 4RF
☎ 0116 271 4159 🖷 0116 271 4159
e-mail: secretary@gggc.co.uk
**Fairly flat 18-hole parkland course with some
strategically placed mature trees, new saplings and
ponds affecting play on six holes. Ridge and furrow is a
feature of five holes.**
18 holes, 6648yds, Par 72, SSS 72, Course record 64.
Club membership 630.
Visitors must contact in advance. Must play with member
at weekends. **Societies** must telephone secretary in
advance. **Green Fees** terms on application. **Prof** Dominic
Fitzpatrick **Facilities** ⊗ ⅢⅢ ㏑ 🍺 ♀ 🏖 🚑 🏌 **Leisure**
snooker room. **Location** On A6 trunk road between
Oadby/Great Glen, 5m S of Leicester city centre
· ·

Hotel ★★★ 68% Regency Hotel, 360 London Rd,
LEICESTER ☎ 0116 270 9634 32 en suite

Park Hill Golf Club
Park Hill, Seagrave, Leicestershire, LE12 7NG
Tel 01509 815454   Fax 01509 816062
E-mail: mail@parkhillgolf.co.uk
www.parkhillgolf.co.uk

Nestled in the heart of Leicestershire, overlooking
the Charnwood Forest and beyond, Park Hill
boasts an 18 hole, Championship length course,
that utilises the lands natural features to ensure
that no two holes are the same, the combination
of water features and precisely positioned
bunkers provide for a challenging course and
excellent playing conditions all year round.
Our fully licensed Clubhouse is open daily
for meals and refreshments.
DRIVING RANGE NOW OPEN

Oadby Leicester Rd LE2 4AJ ☎ 0116 270 9052
Municipal parkland course.
18 holes, 6376yds, Par 72, SSS 70, Course record 69.
Club membership 300.
Visitors no restrictions. **Societies** by arrangement contact
pro shop. **Green Fees** £11 (£14 weekends). **Prof** Andrew
Wells **Facilities** ⊗ ⅢⅢ ㏑ 🍺 ♀ 🏖 🏡 ⛳ 🏌 **Leisure**
squash, sauna, gymnasium, snooker. **Location** West of
Oadby, off A6
· ·

Hotel ★★★ 68% Regency Hotel, 360 London Rd,
LEICESTER ☎ 0116 270 9634 32 en suite

ROTHLEY   Map 08 SK51

Rothley Park Westfield Ln LE7 7LH
☎ 0116 230 2809 🖷 0116 230 2809
e-mail: secretary@rothleypark.co.uk
Parkland course in picturesque situation.
18 holes, 6477yds, Par 71, SSS 71, Course record 67.
Club membership 600.
Visitors must contact professional on 0116 230 3023. Not
Tue. Weekends and bank holidays with member only.
Societies apply in writing to secretary. **Green Fees** terms
on application. **Prof** D Spillane **Facilities** ⊗ ⅢⅢ ㏑ 🍺 ♀ 🏖
🏡 🏌 **Conf** Corporate Hospitality Days available
Location W of A6, N of Leicester
· ·

Hotel ★★★ 64% Rothley Court, Westfield Ln,
ROTHLEY ☎ 0116 237 4141 13 en suite
21 annexe en suite

SCRAPTOFT   Map 04 SK60

Scraptoft Beeby Rd LE7 9SJ
☎ 0116 241 9000 🖷 0116 241 9000
e-mail: info@scraptoft-golf.co.uk
18 holes, 6166yds, Par 70, SSS 70.
Location 1m NE
Telephone for further details
· ·

Hotel ★★★ 74% Belmont House Hotel, De Montfort St,
LEICESTER ☎ 0116 254 4773 77 en suite

SEAGRAVE   Map 08 SK61

Park Hill Park Hill LE12 7NG
☎ 01509 815454 🖷 01509 816062
e-mail: mail@parkhillgolf.co.uk
**Overlooking the Charnwood Forest and beyond, Park
Hill Golf Club boasts an 18-hole championship length
course that utilises the land's natural features to ensure
that no two holes are the same. A challenging, enjoyable
course, with excellent playing conditions all year round.**

18 holes, 7219yds, Par 73, SSS 75, Course record 71.
Club membership 500.

Continued

Visitors play after 9am weekends. **Societies** apply in advance. **Green Fees** not confirmed. **Cards** 🖻 🖻 🖾 🖾 🖾 **Prof** Matthew Ulyett **Facilities** ⊗)Ⅲ ৬ 🖾 ♀ 🕹 ➾ 🏌 🚚 ♂ 🕻 **Conf** fac available Corporate Hospitality Days available **Location** 3m N of Leicester off A46 northbound, follow signs to Seagrave. 8m from M1 J21A northbound

Hotel ★★★ 65% Quality Hotel Loughborough, New Ashby Rd, LOUGHBOROUGH ☎ 01509 211800 94 en suite

ULLESTHORPE   Map 04 SP58

Ullesthorpe Frosworth Rd LE17 5BZ
☎ 01455 209023 🗋 01455 202537
e-mail: bookings@ullesthorpecourt.co.uk
Set in 130 acres of parkland surrounding a 17th-century manor house, this championship length course can be very demanding and offers a challenge to both beginners and professionals. Excellent leisure facilities. Water plays a part on three holes.

18 holes, 6662yds, Par 72, SSS 72, Course record 67.
Club membership 650.
Visitors must contact in advance. With member only Sat, no play on Sun. **Societies** contact well in advance. **Green Fees** not confirmed. **Cards** 🖻 🖻 🖾 🖾 🖾 🖾 🖾 **Prof** David Bowring **Facilities** ⊗)Ⅲ ৬ 🖾 ♀ 🕹 ➾ 🏌 🚚 ♂ **Leisure** hard tennis courts, heated indoor swimming pool, sauna, solarium, gymnasium. **Conf** fac available Corporate Hospitality Days available **Location** 5m Lutterworth junct 20 M1

Hotel ★★★ 68% Ullesthorpe Court Country Hotel & Golf Club, Frosworth Rd, ULLESTHORPE ☎ 01455 209023 38 en suite

WHETSTONE   Map 04 SP59

Whetstone Cambridge Rd, Cosby LE9 1SJ
☎ 0116 286 1424 🗋 0116 286 1424
Easy to walk, parkland course where accuracy rather than length is required.
18 holes, 5795yds, Par 68, SSS 68, Course record 63.
Club membership 500.
Visitors must contact in advance, limited times at weekends. **Societies** must contact in advance. **Green Fees** not confirmed. **Cards** 🖻 🖻 🖾 🖾 🖾 🖾 **Prof** David Raitt **Course Designer** E Calloway **Facilities** ⊗)Ⅲ ৬ 🖾 ♀ 🕹 ➾ 🏌 🚚 ♂ 🕻 **Location** 1m S of village

Hotel ★★★ 68% Corus hotel Leicester, Enderby Rd, Blaby, LEICESTER ☎ 0116 278 7898 0870 609 6106 🗋 0116 278 1974 48 en suite

> **Booking a tee time is always advisable.**

WILSON   Map 08 SK42

Breedon Priory Green Ln DE73 1AT
☎ 01332 863081 🗋 01332 865319
18 holes, 5777yds, Par 69, SSS 68, Course record 67.
Course Designer David Snell **Location** 4m W of A42/M1 junct 24
Telephone for further details

Hotel ★★★★ 74% The Priest House on the River, Kings Mills, Castle Donington, ☎ 01332 810649 24 en suite 18 annexe en suite

WOODHOUSE EAVES   Map 08 SK51

Charnwood Forest Breakback Ln LE12 8TA
☎ 01509 890259 🗋 01509 890925
e-mail: secretary@charnwoodforestgc.co.uk
Hilly heathland course with hard walking, but no bunkers. Play is round volcanic rock giving panoramic views over the Charnwood Forest area.
9 holes, 5960yds, Par 69, SSS 69, Course record 64.
Club membership 350.
Visitors must contact in advance, weekends restricted. **Societies** Wed & Thu only. Must contact in advance. Mon & Fri by special arrangement. **Green Fees** £20 (£25 weekends). **Course Designer** James Braid **Facilities** ⊗)Ⅲ ৬ 🖾 ♀ 🕹 **Conf** fac available Corporate Hospitality Days available **Location** 3m from junct 22 or 23 of M1

Hotel ★★★★ 68% Quorn Country Hotel, Charnwood House, 66 Leicester Rd, QUORN ☎ 01509 415050 30 en suite

Lingdale Joe Moore's Ln LE12 8TF
☎ 01509 890703 🗋 01509 890703
Parkland course located in Charnwood Forest with some hard walking at some holes. The par 3 3rd and par 5 8th are testing holes. Several holes have water hazards.
18 holes, 6545yds, Par 71, SSS 71, Course record 68.
Club membership 659.
Visitors must telephone professional in advance for play. **Societies** must contact in advance. **Green Fees** terms on application. **Prof** Peter Sellears **Course Designer** David Tucker **Facilities** ⊗)Ⅲ ৬ 🖾 ♀ 🕹 ➾ ♂ **Location** 1.5m S off B5330

Hotel ★★★★ 68% Quorn Country Hotel, Charnwood House, 66 Leicester Rd, QUORN ☎ 01509 415050 30 en suite

> ## LINCOLNSHIRE

BELTON   Map 08 SK93

De Vere Belton Woods Hotel NG32 2LN
☎ 01476 593200 🗋 01476 574547
e-mail: belton.woods@devere-hotels.com
Two challenging 18-hole courses, a 9-hole par 3 and a driving range. The Lakes Course has thirteen lakes, while The Woodside boasts the third longest hole in Europe at 613 yards. Many leisure facilities.
The Lakes Course: 18 holes, 6831yds, Par 72, SSS 73,
Course record 66.
The Woodside Course: 18 holes, 6623yds, Par 73, SSS 72,
Course record 67.
Spitfire Course: 9 holes, 1010yds, Par 27, SSS 27.
Club membership 600.
Continued

De Vere Belton Woods Hotel

Visitors book tee times in advance with exception of the Red Arrows. Dress code in operation. **Societies** welcome all week, reservations to be made by telephone or letter. **Green Fees** Lakes: £40 per round, Woodside:£30, Red Arrows £6. **Cards** 🏧 💳 💳 💳 💳 💳 💳 **Prof** Steve Sayers **Facilities** ⊗ ⊪ ⓑ ▦ ♀ ♨ ☂ ⌂ ✦ 🛵 ⚷ 🏌 **Leisure** hard tennis courts, heated indoor swimming pool, squash, fishing, sauna, solarium, gymnasium. **Conf** fac available Corporate Hospitality Days available **Location** On A607, 2m N of Grantham

Hotel ★★★★ 75% De Vere Belton Woods, BELTON ☎ 01476 593200 136 en suite

BLANKNEY   Map 08 TF06

Blankney LN4 3AZ
☎ 01526 320202 🖨 01526 322521
Parkland course in pleasant surroundings with mature trees and testing greens offering a challenging test of golf. Set in the Blankney estate and 2004 was the centenary year.
18 holes, 6634yds, Par 72, SSS 73, Course record 69.
Club membership 700.
Visitors must contact in advance, may not play Wed mornings, restricted at weekends. **Societies** not Wed mornings, booking required. **Green Fees** terms on application. **Prof** Graham Bradley **Course Designer** C Sinclair **Facilities** ⊗ ⊪ ⓑ ▦ ♀ ☂ ⌂ ☂ 🛵 ⚷ **Leisure** snooker. **Conf** fac available Corporate Hospitality Days available **Location** 10m SW on B1188

Hotel ★★★ 71% Branston Hall Hotel, Branston Park, Branston, LINCOLN ☎ 01522 793305 43 en suite 7 annexe en suite

BOSTON   Map 08 TF34

Boston Cowbridge, Horncastle Rd PE22 7EL
☎ 01205 350589 🖨 01205 367526
e-mail: steveshaw@bostongc.co.uk
Parkland course, many water hazards in play on ten holes.
18 holes, 6490yds, Par 72, SSS 71, Course record 69.
Club membership 650.
Visitors evidence of handicap may be requested, contact in advance for tee time. **Societies** apply in writing/telephone. **Green Fees** £30 per day; £22.50 per round (£30/£27.50 weekends & bank holidays). **Prof** Nick Hiom **Facilities** ⊗ ⊪ ⓑ ▦ ♀ ☂ ⌂ ☂ 🛵 ⚷ **Conf** Corporate Hospitality Days available **Location** 2m N of Boston on B1183

Hotel ★★★ 62% New England Hotel, 49 Wide Bargate, BOSTON ☎ 01205 365255 27 en suite

Kirton Holme Holme Rd, Kirton Holme PE20 1SY
☎ 01205 290669
A young parkland course designed for mid to high handicappers. It is flat but has 2500 young trees, two natural water courses plus water hazards. The 2nd is a challenging, 386 yard par 4 dog-leg.
9 holes, 5778yds, Par 70, SSS 68, Course record 68.
Club membership 320.
Visitors no restrictions but booking advisable for weekends & summer evenings. **Societies** by prior arrangement. **Green Fees** not confirmed. **Course Designer** D W Welberry **Facilities** ⊗ ⊪ ▦ ♀ ☂ ☂ 🛵 ⚷ **Conf** Corporate Hospitality Days available **Location** 4m W of Boston off A52

Hotel ★★ 65% Comfort Inn, Donnington Rd, Bicker Bar Roundabout, BOSTON ☎ 01205 820118 55 en suite

BOURNE   Map 08 TF02

Toft Hotel Toft PE10 0JT
☎ 01778 590616 🖨 01778 590264

18 holes, 6486yds, Par 72, SSS 71, Course record 63.
Course Designer Roger Fitton **Location** On A6121 Bourne/Stamford road
Telephone for further details

Hotel ★★★ 78% The George of Stamford, 71 St Martins, STAMFORD ☎ 01780 750750 & 750700 (Res) 🖨 01780 750701 47 en suite

CLEETHORPES   Map 08 TA30

Cleethorpes Kings Rd DN35 0PN
☎ 01472 816110 🖨 01472 814060
e-mail: secretary@cleethorpesgolfclub.co.uk
A mature coastal course founded in 1894. Slight undulations give variety but the flat landscape makes for easy walking. The course provides a challenge to all levels of player.

18 holes, 6351yds, Par 70, SSS 70, Course record 65.
Club membership 650.

                    Continued

Visitors may not play after 12.30 Wed; handicap certificate preferred, must be a member of a golf club. **Societies** Mon, Thu, Fri, Sun only. Must telephone in advance. **Green Fees** £20 per day (£25 weekends). **Prof** Paul Davies **Course Designer** Harry Vardon **Facilities** ⊗ ⅀Ⅲ ⅃ ⅃ ♀ ♉ ♌ ♎ **Location** 2m SE of Cleethorpes, A180/A46 from W, A16 from S

Hotel ★★★ 69% Kingsway Hotel, Kingsway, CLEETHORPES ☎ 01472 601122 49 en suite

Tetney Station Rd, Tetney DN36 5HY
☎ 01472 211644 📄 01472 211644
18-hole parkland course set at the foot of the Lincolnshire Wolds. Noted for its challenging water features.
18 holes, 6245yds, Par 71, SSS 69, Course record 65.
Club membership 300.
Visitors must contact for start time. **Societies** apply in writing. **Green Fees** terms on application. **Cards** 🎫 📇 📇 🏧 📇 **Prof** Jason Abrams **Course Designer** J S Grant **Facilities** ⊗ ⅀Ⅲ ⅃ ⅃ ♀ ♉ ♌ ⟟ ♍ ♎ ♈ **Conf** fac available **Location** 1m off A16 Louth/Grimsby road

Hotel ★★★ 69% Kingsway Hotel, Kingsway, CLEETHORPES ☎ 01472 601122 49 en suite

CROWLE   Map 08 SE71

The Lincolnshire DN17 4BU
☎ 01724 711619 📄 01724 711619
Traditional flat parkland course. Generous sized greens with discreet use of water and bunkers. Redeveloped greatly in the last few years offering a good test to all standards of golfer.
18 holes, 6283yds, Par 71, SSS 70.
Club membership 420.
Visitors no restrictions. **Societies** welcome any time. **Green Fees** £13 per day (£18 weekends). **Cards** 🎫 📇 📇 📇 **Course Designer** Stubley/Byrne **Facilities** ⊗ ⅀Ⅲ ⅃ ⅃ ♀ ♉ ♌ ♎ **Conf** Corporate Hospitality Days available **Location** M180 junct 2, 0.5m on Crowle road

Hotel ★★★ 64% Belmont Hotel, Horsefair Green, THORNE ☎ 01405 812320 23 en suite

ELSHAM   Map 08 TA01

Elsham Barton Rd DN20 0LS
☎ 01652 680291(Sec) 📄 01652 680308
e-mail: elshamgolfclub@lineone.net
Mature parkland course in a rural setting with a variety of wildlife including many pheasants. Very secluded with easy walking and a reservoir to maintain irrigation.

Elsham Golf Club

18 holes, 6426yds, Par 71, SSS 71, Course record 67.
Club membership 600.

Continued

Visitors with member only weekends & bank holidays. Preferable to contact in advance. **Societies** must apply in writing/telephone in advance **Green Fees** £30 per 36 holes; £24 per 18 holes. **Prof** Stuart Brewer **Course Designer** Various **Facilities** ⊗ ⅀Ⅲ ⅃ ⅃ ♀ ♉ ♌ ♎ **Conf** fac available Corporate Hospitality Days available **Location** 2m NE of Brigg on B1206. M180 junct 5, take exit sign posted Elsham. Through village to T-junct, turn left, 1m on left

Hotel ★★★ 67% Wortley House Hotel, Rowland Rd, SCUNTHORPE ☎ 01724 842223 38 en suite

GAINSBOROUGH   Map 08 SK88

Gainsborough Thonock DN21 1PZ
☎ 01427 613088 📄 01427 810172
e-mail: gainsboroughgc.co.uk
Thonock Park: 18 holes, 6266yds, Par 70, SSS 70, Course record 63.
Karsten Lakes: 18 holes, 6721yds, Par 72, SSS 72, Course record 65.
Course Designer Neil Coles **Location** 1m N off A159. Signposted off A631
Telephone for further details

Hotel ★★★ 65% The West Retford Hotel, 24 North Rd, RETFORD ☎ 0870 609 6162 62 annexe en suite

GEDNEY HILL   Map 08 TF31

Gedney Hill West Drove PE12 0NT
☎ 01406 330922 📄 01406 330323
e-mail: d.t.h@fsddail.co.uk
18 holes, 5493yds, Par 70, SSS 66, Course record 67.
Course Designer Monkwise Ltd **Location** 5m SE of Spalding
Telephone for further details

Hotel ★★ 66% Rose & Crown Hotel, 23/24 Market Place, WISBECH ☎ 01945 589800 29 en suite

GRANTHAM   Map 08 SK93

Belton Park Belton Ln, Londonthorpe Rd NG31 9SH
☎ 01476 567399 📄 01476 592078
e-mail: greatgolf@beltonpark
Three 9-hole courses set in classic mature parkland of Lord Brownlow's country seat, Belton House. Gently undulating with streams, ponds, plenty of trees and beautiful scenery, including a deer park. Famous holes: 5th, 12th, 16th and 18th. Combine any of the three courses for a testing 18-hole round.
Brownlow: 18 holes, 6472yds, Par 71, SSS 71, Course record 64.
Ancaster: 18 holes, 6325yds, Par 70, SSS 70.
Belmont: 18 holes, 6075yds, Par 69, SSS 69.
Club membership 850.
Visitors contact professional for suitable tee times. No green fees on Tuesday before 3pm. **Societies** apply in advance. **Green Fees** £36 per day; £30 per round (£42/36 weekends). **Cards** 🎫 📇 **Prof** Brian McKee **Course Designer** Williamson/Allis **Facilities** ⊗ ⅀Ⅲ ⅃ ⅃ ♀ ♉ ♌ ⟟ ♍ ♎ **Conf** fac available Corporate Hospitality Days available **Location** 1.5m NE of Grantham

Hotel ★★★ 71% Kings Hotel, North Pde, GRANTHAM ☎ 01476 590800 21 en suite

Booking a tee time is always advisable.

163

Sudbrook Moor Charity St, Carlton Scroop
NG32 3AT ☎ 01400 250796
A testing 9-hole parkland/meadowland course in a
picturesque valley setting with easy walking.
9 holes, 4811yds, Par 66, SSS 64, Course record 64.
Club membership 600.
Visitors advisable to telephone in advance. **Green Fees**
£7-£9 (£9-£12 weekends and bank holidays). **Cards** 🌑
🌑 🌑 🌑 🌑 🌑 **Prof** Tim Hutton **Course Designer** Tim
Hutton **Facilities** 🏋 ⚑ △ 🏠 ⚐ ⚒ ✓ **Location** 6m NE of
Grantham on A607

···

Hotel ★★★ 71% Kings Hotel, North Pde, GRANTHAM
☎ 01476 590800 21 en suite

Grimsby Littlecoates Rd DN34 4LU
☎ 01472 342630 📠 01472 342630
e-mail: secretary@grimsby.fsnet.co.uk
Undulating parkland course.
18 holes, 6057yds, Par 70, SSS 69, Course record 65.
Club membership 730.
Visitors contact in advance. **Societies** Mon and Fri by prior
arrangement with secretary. **Green Fees** £22 (£28
weekends and bank holidays). **Prof** Richard Smith **Course**
Designer Colt **Facilities** ⊗ 〗 🏋 ⚑ ♀ △ 🏠 ❧ 🏎 ✓
Conf Corporate Hospitality Days available **Location** 1m
from A180 & 1m from A46

···

Hotel ★★★ 66% Hotel Elizabeth Grimsby, Littlecoates
Rd, GRIMSBY ☎ 01472 240024 52 en suite

Waltham Windmill Cheapside, Waltham
DN37 0HT ☎ 01472 824109 📠 01472 828391
Nestling in 125 acres of Lincolnshire countryside, the
natural springs have been used to great effect giving
individuality and challenge to every shot. The course
has a mixture of long par 5s and water comes into play
on 9 holes.
18 holes, 6442yds, Par 71, SSS 71.
Club membership 620.
Visitors prebooking advisable **Societies** weekdays
prebooked. **Green Fees** £20 (£30 weekends). Reduced
winter rates. **Cards** 🌑 🌑 **Prof** Nigel Burkitt **Course**
Designer J Payne **Facilities** ⊗ 〗 🏋 ⚑ ♀ △ 🏠 ❧ 🏎 ✓
⚐ **Conf** fac available Corporate Hospitality Days available
Location 1m off A16

···

Hotel ★★★ 66% Beeches Hotel, 42 Waltham Rd,
Scartho, GRIMSBY ☎ 01472 278830 18 en suite

Horncastle West Ashby LN9 5PP ☎ 01507 526800
18 holes, 5717yds, Par 70, SSS 68, Course record 71.
Course Designer E C Wright **Location** Off A158
Lincoln/Skegness road at Edlington, off A153 at West
Ashby
Telephone for further details

···

Hotel ★★ 71% Admiral Rodney Hotel, North St,
HORNCASTLE ☎ 01507 523131 31 en suite

Boston West Golf Centre PE20 3QX
☎ 01205 290670 📠 01205 290725
e-mail: info@bostonwestgolfclub.co.uk
A challenging course with water featuring on 8 of the 18
holes. Greens on the front nine are quite undulating,
whereas the more mature trees on the back nine can be
tricky. A well-drained course allowing motorised
buggies and carts nearly all year.

Continued

18 holes, 6333yards, Par 72, SSS 70, Course record 68. Club membership 650.
Visitors advisable to book up to 7 days in advance - booking line 01205 290770. Dress code must be observed. **Societies** telephone for details. **Green Fees** £16 (£18 weekends). **Cards** 🏧 📠 📇 🔳 📇 **Prof** Simon Collingwood **Course Designer** Michael Zara **Facilities** ⊗ 🏊 🎱 🍽 ♀ 👤 🏡 🏌 🐾 ♨ ✓ **Leisure** 6 hole academy course. **Conf** fac available Corporate Hospitality Days available **Location** 2m W of Boston on crossroads of A1121/B1192

Hotel ★★★ 63% Golf Hotel, The Broadway, WOODHALL SPA ☎ 01526 353535 50 en suite

IMMINGHAM   Map 08 TA11

Immingham St Andrews Ln, off Church Ln
DN40 2EU ☎ 01469 575298 📠 01469 577636
e-mail: admin@immgc.com
An excellent, flat parkland course. The natural exaggerated undulations on the fairways form one of the best local examples of medieval strip farming methods. They are a natural phenomenon to the course together with the Lincolnshire drainage channel, which meanders through the course and comes into play on at least half of the holes.
18 holes, 6215yds, Par 71, SSS 70, Course record 69. Club membership 700.
Visitors telephone in advance. **Societies** telephone to arrange date. **Green Fees** terms on application. **Prof** Nick Harding **Course Designer** Hawtree & Son **Facilities** ⊗ 🏊 🎱 🍽 ♀ 👤 🏡 🏌 ✓ **Conf** fac available Corporate Hospitality Days available **Location** 7m NW off Grimsby

Hotel ★★★ 66% Hotel Elizabeth Grimsby, Littlecoates Rd, GRIMSBY ☎ 01472 240024 52 en suite

LACEBY   Map 08 TA20

Manor Barton St, Laceby Manor DN37 7EA
☎ 01472 873468 (shop) 📠 01472 276706
e-mail: judith@manorgolf.com
The first seven holes played as a parkland course lined with mature trees. The second nine are more open fairways with water courses running alongside and through the holes. The 16th hole green is surrounded by water. Holes 17 and 18 are tree-lined like the first seven holes.
18 holes, 6354yds, Par 71, SSS 70.
Club membership 550.
Visitors booked tee system at all times, visitors may book 6 days in advance. **Societies** telephone in advance. **Green Fees** £18 per round (£20 weekends). **Cards** 🏧 📠 📇 🔳 📇 **Prof** Neil Laybourne **Facilities** ⊗ 🏊 🎱 🍽 ♀ 👤 🏡 🐾 ✓ **Leisure** fishing. **Conf** fac available Corporate Hospitality Days available **Location** A18 Barton St - Laceby/Louth

Hotel ★★★ 66% Hotel Elizabeth Grimsby, Littlecoates Rd, GRIMSBY ☎ 01472 240024 52 en suite

LINCOLN   Map 08 SK97

Canwick Park Canwick Park, Washingborough Rd
LN4 1EF ☎ 01522 542912 📠 01522 526997
e-mail: manager@canwickpark.co.uk
Parkland course 2 miles east of the city centre with panoramic views of Lincoln Cathedral. The 5th and 13th holes are testing par 3's both nearly 200 yards in length.

18 holes, 6160yds, Par 70, SSS 69, Course record 65. Club membership 650.
Visitors weekdays/weekends subject to availability. Contact club professional 01522 536870 **Societies** weekdays only by prior arrangement. **Green Fees** £17 (£25 weekends). **Prof** S Williamson **Course Designer** Hawtree & Sons **Facilities** ⊗ 🏊 🎱 🍽 ♀ 👤 🏡 🐾 ✓ **Conf** Corporate Hospitality Days available **Location** 1m E of Lincoln

Hotel ★★★ 68% The Lincoln Hotel, Eastgate, LINCOLN ☎ 0871 220 6070 71 en suite

Carholme Carholme Rd LN1 1SE
☎ 01522 523725 📠 01522 533733
e-mail: info@carholme-golf-club.co.uk
Parkland course with prevailing west winds. Good views. First hole out of bounds left and right of fairway, pond in front of bunkered green at 5th, lateral water hazards across several fairways.
18 holes, 6215yds, Par 71, SSS 70, Course record 67. Club membership 625.
Visitors must contact in advance. Weekends may not play before 2.30pm. **Societies** apply in writing/telephone in advance. **Green Fees** £22 per day; £18 per round. **Course Designer** Willie Park Jnr **Facilities** ⊗ 🏊 🎱 🍽 ♀ 👤 🏡 🏌 ✓ **Conf** Corporate Hospitality Days available **Location** 1m W of city centre on A57

LOUTH   Map 08 TF38

Louth Crowtree Ln LN11 9LJ
☎ 01507 603681 📠 01507 608501
e-mail: enquiries@louthgolfclub.com
Undulating parkland course, fine views in an area of outstanding natural beauty.
18 holes, 6430yds, Par 72, SSS 71, Course record 64. Club membership 700.
Visitors must contact in advance to make sure tee is not reserved for competition. **Societies** a booking form will be sent on request. **Green Fees** £20 per round (£30 weekends & bank holidays). **Cards** 🏧 📠 📇 🔳 📇 **Prof** A Blundell **Facilities** ⊗ 🏊 🎱 🍽 ♀ 👤 🏡 🐾 🏌 ✓ **Leisure** squash. **Conf** fac available Corporate Hospitality Days available **Location** W of Louth between A157/A153

Hotel ★★★ 69% Beaumont Hotel, 66 Victoria Rd, LOUTH ☎ 01507 605005 16 en suite

MARKET RASEN   Map 08 TF18

Market Rasen & District Legsby Rd LN8 3DZ
☎ 01673 842319
Picturesque, well-wooded heathland course, easy walking, breezy with becks forming natural hazards. Good views of Lincolnshire Wolds.

Continued

Continued

18 holes, 6209yds, Par 71, SSS 70, Course record 65. Club membership 600.

Visitors must play with member at weekends and must contact in advance. **Societies** Tue & Fri only; must contact in advance. **Green Fees** £30 per day, £20 per round. **Prof** A M Chester **Course Designer** Hawtree Ltd **Facilities** ⊗ ⋔ ⤶ ⊒ ♀ ⚏ ⌂ ⤶ ⤷ ⌀ **Location** 1m E, off A46 onto A631

Hotel ★★★ 69% Beaumont Hotel, 66 Victoria Rd, LOUTH ☎ 01507 605005 16 en suite

Market Rasen Race Course (Golf Course)

Legsby Rd LN8 3EA ☎ 01673 843434 🖹 01673 844532 e-mail: marketrasen@rht.net
9 holes, 2532yds, Par 32.
Course Designer Edward Stenton **Location** 1m E of Market Rasen
Telephone for further details

Hotel ★★★ 69% Beaumont Hotel, 66 Victoria Rd, LOUTH ☎ 01507 605005 16 en suite

NORMANBY
Map 08 SE81

Normanby Hall Normanby Park DN15 9HU
☎ 01724 720226 (Pro shop)
Well maintained course set in secluded mature parkland. A challenge to golfers of all abilities.
18 holes, 6561yds, Par 72, SSS 71, Course record 66. Club membership 500.
Visitors book in advance by contacting professional. **Societies** must contact professional in advance. **Green Fees** terms on application. **Cards** ⊞ 🔲 🔲 **Prof** Christopher Mann **Course Designer** Hawtree & Son **Facilities** ⊗ ⋔ ⤶ ⊒ ♀ ⚏ ⌂ ⤶ ⌀ **Location** 3m N of Scunthorpe adj to Normanby Hall on B1130

Hotel ★★★ 67% Wortley House Hotel, Rowland Rd, SCUNTHORPE ☎ 01724 842223 38 en suite

SCUNTHORPE
Map 08 SE81

Ashby Decoy Burringham Rd DN17 2AB
☎ 01724 866561 🖹 01724 271708
e-mail: ashby.decoy@btclick.com
Pleasant, flat parkland course to satisfy all tastes, yet test the experienced golfer.
18 holes, 6281yds, Par 71, SSS 71, Course record 66. Club membership 650.
Visitors may not play Tue until 2pm, weekends or bank holidays. Handicap cerificate required. **Societies** apply in advance. **Green Fees** £23 per day; £18 per round. **Prof** A Miller **Facilities** ⊗ ⋔ ⤶ ⊒ ♀ ⚏ ⌂ ⤷ ⌀ **Conf** fac available Corporate Hospitality Days available **Location** 2.5m SW on B1450 near Asda Superstore

Hotel ★★★ 67% Wortley House Hotel, Rowland Rd, SCUNTHORPE ☎ 01724 842223 38 en suite

Forest Pines - Briggate Lodge Inn Hotel
Ermine St, Broughton DN20 0AQ
☎ 01652 650770 🖹 01652 650495
e-mail: enquiries@forestpines.co.uk
Set in 185 acres of mature parkland and open heathland and constructed in a similar design to that of Wentworth or Sunningdale, Forest Pines offers three challenging 9-hole courses - Forest, Pines and Beeches. Any combination can be played. Facilities include a 17-bay driving range and a spacious clubhouse.

Forest Course: 9 holes, 3291yds, Par 36, SSS 36.
Pines Course: 9 holes, 3568yds, Par 37, SSS 37.
Beeches: 9 holes, 3291yds, Par 36, SSS 36.
Club membership 330.
Visitors soft spikes only on all courses. **Societies** telephone in advance. **Green Fees** not confirmed. **Cards** ⊞ 🔲 🔲 🔲 🔲 **Prof** David Edwards **Course Designer** John Morgan **Facilities** ⊗ ⋔ ⤶ ⊒ ♀ ⚏ ⌂ ⤷ ⤶ ⤵ ⤴ ⌀ **Leisure** heated indoor swimming pool, sauna, solarium, gymnasium. **Conf** fac available Corporate Hospitality Days available **Location** 200yds from junct 4 M180

Hotel ★★★★ 72% Forest Pines Hotel, Ermine St, Broughton, SCUNTHORPE ☎ 01652 650770 114 en suite

Holme Hall Holme Ln, Bottesford DN16 3RF
☎ 01724 862078 🖹 01724 862078
e-mail: tracey.curtis@btconnect.com
Heathland course with sandy subsoil. Easy walking. This course is a regular venue of both the Lincolnshire Open and amateur championships.
18 holes, 6404yds, Par 71, SSS 71, Course record 65. Club membership 746.
Visitors must play with member at weekends & bank holidays. Must contact in advance. **Societies** must contact in advance. **Green Fees** not confirmed. **Prof** Richard McKiernan **Facilities** ⊗ ⋔ ⤶ ⊒ ♀ ⚏ ⌂ ⤷ ⤶ ⤵ ⌀ **Conf** Corporate Hospitality Days available **Location** 4m SE of Scunthorpe. M180 junct 4

Hotel ★★★ 67% Wortley House Hotel, Rowland Rd, SCUNTHORPE ☎ 01724 842223 38 en suite

Kingsway Kingsway DN15 7ER ☎ 01724 840945
9 holes, 1915yds, Par 29, SSS 28.
Location W side of town centre off A18
Telephone for further details

Hotel ★★★ 67% Wortley House Hotel, Rowland Rd, SCUNTHORPE ☎ 01724 842223 38 en suite

SKEGNESS
Map 09 TF56

North Shore Hotel & Golf Club North Shore
Rd PE25 1DN ☎ 01754 763298 🖹 01754 761902
e-mail: golf@north-shore.co.uk
Part links, part parkland, with two of the 9 holes situated next to the sea. A challenging course with both greens in front of the main bar.

18 holes, 6200yds, Par 71, SSS 71, Course record 68. Club membership 450.
Visitors tee times must be booked if possible. **Societies** write or telephone in advance. **Green Fees** £40 per day; £27 per round (£48/£33 weekends). **Cards** ⊞ 🔲 🔲 🔲

Continued

Continued

🔲 **Prof** J Cornelius **Course Designer** James Braid **Facilities** ⊗ ⋔ ⮾ 🍺 ☕ ♀ ⚲ 🏠 🛏 🚂 *∂* **Leisure** snooker. **Conf** fac available Corporate Hospitality Days available **Location** 1m N of town centre off A52, right opposite North Shore Holiday Centre into North Shore Road

....

Hotel ★★ 67% North Shore Hotel & Golf Course, North Shore Rd, SKEGNESS ☎ 01754 763298 33 en suite 3 annexe en suite

---

Seacroft Drummond Rd, Seacroft PE25 3AU
☎ 01754 763020 📠 01754 763020
e-mail: richard@seacroft-golfclub.co.uk
A championship seaside links traditionally laid out with tight undulations and hogsback fairways. Adjacent to Gibraltar Point Nature Reserve.

18 holes, 6479yds, Par 71, SSS 71, Course record 65. Club membership 590.
Visitors must be a member of an affiliated golf club/society. **Societies** contact in advance. **Green Fees** terms on application. **Cards** 🔁 💳 💳 🔁 🔲 **Prof** Robin Lawie **Course Designer** Tom Dunn/Willie Fernie **Facilities** ⊗ ⋔ ⮾ 🍺 ☕ ♀ ⚲ 🏠 🚂 *∂* **Conf** Corporate Hospitality Days available **Location** S side of town centre, towards Gibralter Point nature reserve

....

Hotel ★★★ 64% Crown Hotel, Drummond Rd, Seacroft, SKEGNESS ☎ 01754 610760 30 en suite

---

SLEAFORD   Map 08 TF04

Sleaford Willoughby Rd, South Rauceby NG34 8PL
☎ 01529 488273 📠 01529 488326
e-mail: sleafordgolfclub@btinternet.com
Inland links-type course, moderately wooded and fairly flat with a stream to provide additional hazards on several holes.
18 holes, 6503yds, Par 72, SSS 71, Course record 64. Club membership 630.
Visitors contact in advance, may not play Sun in winter. **Societies** telephone enquiry to professional. Written confirmation required. **Green Fees** not confirmed. **Prof** James Wilson **Course Designer** T Williamson **Facilities** ⊗ ⋔ ⮾ 🍺 ☕ ♀ ⚲ 🏠 🚂 *∂* **Conf** fac available Corporate Hospitality Days available **Location** 2m W of Sleaford, off A153

....

Hotel ★★★ 71% Kings Hotel, North Pde, GRANTHAM ☎ 01476 590800 21 en suite

---

> **Use the maps at the back of the guide to help locate a golf course.**

SOUTH KYME   Map 08 TF14

South Kyme Skinners Ln LN4 4AT
☎ 01526 861113 📠 01526 861113
e-mail: southkymegc@hotmail.com
A challenging fenland course described as an 'inland links' with water hazards, trees and fairway hazards.
18 holes, 6568yds, Par 72, SSS 71, Course record 67. Club membership 470.
Visitors advisable to telephone in advance for course availability. **Societies** telephone for booking form. **Green Fees** terms on application. **Cards** 🔁 💳 💳 🔁 🔲 **Prof** Peter Chamberlain **Facilities** ⊗ ⋔ ⮾ 🍺 ☕ ♀ ⚲ 🏠 🚂 *∂* **Leisure** 6 hole short course. **Conf** Corporate Hospitality Days available **Location** Off B1395 in South Kyme village

....

Hotel ⬦ Travelodge, Holdingham, SLEAFORD ☎ 08700 850 950 40 en suite

---

SPALDING   Map 08 TF22

Spalding Surfleet PE11 4EA
☎ 01775 680386 (office) & 680474 (pro)
📠 01775 680988
A pretty, well laid-out course in a fenland area. The River Glen runs beside the 1st, 2nd and 4th holes, and ponds and lakes are very much in play on the 9th, 10th and 11th holes. Challenging holes include the river dominated 2nd and the 10th which involves a tight drive and dog-leg left to reach a raised three-tier green.

18 holes, 6478yds, Par 72, SSS 71, Course record 62. Club membership 750.
Visitors must contact in advance. Handicap certificate required. **Societies** write to the secretary, Societies on Thu all day and Tue pm. **Green Fees** £30 per day; £25 per round (£30 per day weekends & bank holidays). **Prof** John Spencer/Chris Huggins **Course Designer** Price/Spencer/Ward **Facilities** ⊗ ⋔ ⮾ 🍺 ☕ ♀ ⚲ 🏠 🚂 *∂* ♩ **Conf** Corporate Hospitality Days available **Location** 4m N of Spalding adjacent to A16

....

Hotel ★★ 70% Cley Hall Hotel, 22 High St, SPALDING ☎ 01775 725157 4 en suite 8 annexe en suite

---

STAMFORD   Map 04 TF00

Burghley Park St Martins PE9 3JX
☎ 01780 762100 (pro) & 753789 (Sec) 📠 01780 753789
e-mail: burghley.golf@lineone.net
Open parkland course with superb greens, many trees, ponds and bunkers. Situated in the grounds of Burghley House.
18 holes, 6236yds, Par 70, SSS 70, Course record 65. Club membership 775.

Continued

Visitors with member only weekends. Must contact in advance & have handicap certificate. **Societies** prior arrangement in writing, preferably by 1st Dec previous year. **Green Fees** £28 per day; £18 twilight (noon winter, 5pm summer). **Prof** Glenn Davies **Course Designer** Rev J Day (1938) **Facilities** ⊗ ⅏ ⅃ ⅃ ♥ ♣ ⌂ ☂ ♠ ⚲ ⚐ **Location** 1m S of town on B1081

Hotel ★★★ 78% The George of Stamford, 71 St Martins, STAMFORD ☎ 01780 750750 & 750700 (Res) 🖹 01780 750701 47 en suite

STOKE ROCHFORD — Map 08 SK92

Stoke Rochford NG33 5EW
☎ 01476 530275 🖹 01476 530237
Parkland course designed by C. Turner and extended in 1936 to 18 holes by Major Hotchkin.
18 holes, 6252yds, Par 70, SSS 70, Course record 65.
Club membership 525.
Visitors must contact Professional in advance. No visitors before 9am weekdays, weekends by prior arrangement. **Societies** contact one year in advance, in writing. **Green Fees** terms on application. **Cards** ▭▭ ▭▭ ▱ **Prof** Angus Dow **Course Designer** Major Hotchkin **Facilities** ⊗ ⅏ ⅃ ⅃ ♥ ♣ ⌂ ♠ ⚲ ⚐ **Location** Off A1 5m S of Grantham, right off A1 southbound signposted Stoke Rochford, do U turn onto a1 northbound carriageway enter golf club via BP service station

Hotel ★★★ 71% Kings Hotel, North Pde, GRANTHAM ☎ 01476 590800 21 en suite

SUTTON BRIDGE — Map 09 TF42

Sutton Bridge New Rd PE12 9RQ ☎ 01406 350323
Established in 1914 as a golf course, the nine holes are played along, over and in a Victorian dock basin which was abandoned as a dock in 1881. The original walls of the dock are still intact and help to make the course one of the most interesting courses in the region. The greens are recognised as among the best in Lincolnshire.
9 holes, 5724yds, Par 70, SSS 68, Course record 64.
Club membership 350.
Visitors may not play weekends except with a member, must contact in advance. Must have handicap certificate. **Societies** write or telephone in advance. **Green Fees** Apr-Sep: £20 per day; Oct-Mar: £15. **Prof** Simon Dicksee **Facilities** ⊗ ⅏ ⅃ ⅃ ♥ ♣ ⌂ ♠ ⚐ **Conf** Corporate Hospitality Days available **Location** E side of village off A17

Hotel ★★★ 62% The Duke's Head Hotel, Tuesday Market Place, KING'S LYNN ☎ 01553 774996 71 en suite

SUTTON ON SEA — Map 09 TF58

Sandilands Roman Bank LN12 2RJ
☎ 01507 441432 🖹 01507 441617
Well manicured links course next to the sea. Renowned for the standard of its greens.
18 holes, 6173yds, Par 70, SSS 68, Course record 64.
Club membership 200.
Visitors no restrictions. **Societies** telephone in advance. **Green Fees** £25 per day; £18 per round (£30/£20 weekends) Reduced winter rates. **Cards** ▭▭ ▭▭ **Prof** Simon Sherratt **Facilities** ⊗ ⅏ ⅃ ⅃ ♥ ♣ ⌂ ♠ ⚲ ⚐ **Leisure** hard and grass tennis courts, gymnasium. **Conf** fac available **Location** 1.5m S off A52

Continued

Hotel ★★★ 69% Grange & Links Hotel, Sea Ln, Sandilands, MABLETHORPE ☎ 01507 441334 23 en suite

TORKSEY — Map 08 SK87

Lincoln LN1 2EG ☎ 01522 718721 🖹 718721
e-mail: info@lincolngc.co.uk
A mature championship standard course offering a variety of holes, links style to parkland.
18 holes, 6438yds, Par 71, SSS 71, Course record 65.
Club membership 750.
Visitors no restrictions, may play at any time. **Societies** Book in advance. **Green Fees** not confirmed. **Prof** Ashley Carter **Course Designer** J H Taylor **Facilities** ⊗ ⅏ ⅃ ⅃ ♥ ♣ ⌂ ♠ ⚲ ⚐ **Leisure** 3 hole practice course. **Conf** Corporate Hospitality Days available **Location** NE side of village, off A156 midway between Lincoln & Gainsborough

Hotel ★★★ 67% The White Hart, Bailgate, LINCOLN ☎ 0870 400 8117 48 en suite

Millfield Laughterton LN1 2LB
☎ 01427 718255 🖹 01427 718473
e-mail: secretary@millfieldgolfclub.fsnet.co.uk
This golf complex offers a range of facilities to suit every golfer. The Millfield is designed to suit the more experienced golfer and follows the natural contours of the landscape. The Grenville Green is designed for more casual golfers and the par 3 is suitable for beginners, family games or for warm-up and practice play.
The Millfield: 18 holes, 6004yds, Par 72, SSS 69, Course record 68.
The Grenville Green: 18 holes, 4485yds, Par 65.
Visitors Millfield: shoes must be worn, no jeans etc. Grenville Green no restrictions. Par 3 9 hole no restrictions. **Societies** telephone in advance. **Green Fees** terms on application. **Prof** Brian Cummings **Course Designer** C W Watson **Facilities** ⊗ ⅃ ⅃ ♥ ♣ ⌂ ♠ ⚲ ⚐ **Leisure** grass tennis courts. **Location** On A1133 1m N of A57

Hotel ★★★ 67% The White Hart, Bailgate, LINCOLN ☎ 0870 400 8117 48 en suite

WOODHALL SPA — See page 169

WOODTHORPE — Map 09 TF48

Woodthorpe Hall LN13 0DD
☎ 01507 450000 🖹 01507 450000
e-mail: secretary@woodthorpehallgolfclub.fsnet.co.uk
Parkland course.
18 holes, 5140yds, Par 67, SSS 65, Course record 68.
Club membership 300.
Visitors contact in advance . **Societies** Mon-Fri, apply to the secretary at least one month prior to visit. **Green Fees** not confirmed. **Facilities** ⊗ ⅏ ⅃ ⅃ ♥ ♣ ⚲ ⚐ **Leisure** fishing. **Conf** fac available **Location** 3m NNW of Alford on B1373

Hotel ★★★ 69% Grange & Links Hotel, Sea Ln, Sandilands, MABLETHORPE ☎ 01507 441334 23 en suite

Booking a tee time is always advisable.

Woodhall Spa

Map 8 TF16   **Woodhall Spa**

☎ **01526 351835**   📄 **01526 352778**

The Championship Course at Woodhall Spa, now known as the Hotchkin, is arguably the best inland course in Britain. It is a classic British heartland course with cavernous bunkers and heather-lined fairways. Golf has been played here for over 100 years and the Hotchkin has hosted most of the top national and international amateur events. The English Golf Union acquired Woodhall Spa in 1995 to create a centre of excellence. A second course, the Bracken, has been built, together with extensive practice facilities including one of Europe's finest short game practice areas. The English Golf Union actively encourages visitors throughout the year to the National Golf Centre to experience these facilities and to enjoy the unique ambience.

e-mail: munderwood@englishgolfunion.org

Visitors Must contact in advance. Handicap certificate must be produced

Societies Must apply by telephone initially

Green Fees Telephone for details

Facilities ⊗ ⤨ ⥄ 🖳 ♀ ⤧ ⩩ 🖚 🖝 ⚸ 𝄈
Conf Facilities Available

Professional S Williams

Location The Broadway LN10 6PU
(NE side of village off B1191)

Holes/Par/Course record 36 holes.
Hotchkin: 18 holes, 7080 yds, Par 73, SSS 73, Course record 67
Bracken: 18 holes, 6735 yds, Par 72, SSS 74, Course record 68

Championship Course

WHERE TO STAY AND EAT NEARBY

Hotels
WOODHALL SPA

★★★ 68% Petwood Hotel, LN10 6QF.
☎ 01526 352411. 53 en suite

★★★ 63% Golf Hotel, LN10 6SG.
☎ 01526 353535. 50 en suite

★★ 65% Eagle Lodge, LN10 6ST.
☎ 01526 353231. 23 en suite

Restaurant
HORNCASTLE

◎ ◎ Magpies, LN9 6AA.
☎ 01507 527004.

LONDON

Courses within the London Postal District area (ie those that have London Postcodes - W1, SW1 etc) are listed here in postal district order commencing East then North, South and West. Courses outside the London Postal area, but within Greater London are to be found listed under the county of **Greater London** in the gazetteer (see page 94).

LONDON

E4 CHINGFORD

Royal Epping Forest Forest Approach, Chingford
E4 7AZ ☎ 020 8529 2195 📄 020 8559 4664
e-mail: office@refgc.co.uk
Woodland course. Red garments must be worn.
18 holes, 6342yds, Par 71, SSS 70, Course record 64.
Club membership 400.
Visitors booking system in operation,telephone 020 8529 5708 **Societies** must contact secretary in advance. **Green Fees** £12 (£16.50 weekends). **Cards** 🌐 💳 💳 💳 💳 💳 🔲 **Prof** A Traynor **Course Designer** J G Gibson **Facilities** ⊗ by prior arrangement ⅏ by prior arrangement 🏐 by prior arrangement 💟 ♀ 🏖 🛗 ⛵ 🚜 ⛳ **Conf** fac available
Location 300 yds E of Chingford station on Chingford Plain

Hotel ★★★ 59% The County Hotel, 30 Oak Hill, WOODFORD GREEN ☎ 0870 609 6156 99 en suite

West Essex Bury Rd, Sewardstonebury, Chingford
E4 7QL ☎ 020 8529 7558 📄 020 8524 7870
e-mail: sec@westessexgolfclub.co.uk
Testing parkland course within Epping Forest with spectacular views over Essex and Middlesex. Created by James Braid in 1900 and designed to make full use of the landscape's natural attributes. The front nine is the shorter of the two and provides a test of accuracy with tree lined fairways that meander through the undulating countryside. The back nine is equally challenging although slightly longer and requiring more long iron play.
18 holes, 6289yds, Par 71, SSS 70, Course record 63.
Club membership 710.
Visitors must have handicap certificate but may not play on Tue morning & weekends. **Societies** must contact in advance. **Green Fees** £35. **Prof** Robert Joyce **Course Designer** James Braid **Facilities** ⊗ ⅏ 🏐 💟 ♀ 🏖 🏖 ⛵ 🏌 **Conf** Corporate Hospitality Days available **Location** 1.5m N of Chingford station. Access via M25 junct 26

E11 LEYTONSTONE & WANSTEAD

Wanstead Overton Dr, Wanstead E11 2LW
☎ 020 8989 3938 📄 020 8532 9138
e-mail: wgclub@aol.com
A flat, picturesque parkland course with many trees and shrubs and providing easy walking. The par 3 16th involves driving across a lake.
18 holes, 6015yds, Par 69, SSS 69, Course record 62.
Club membership 600.
Visitors must contact in advance and may only play Mon, Tue & Fri. **Societies** by prior arrangement. **Green Fees** £30 per day. **Cards** 🌐 💳 💳 🔲 **Prof** David Hawkins **Course Designer** James Braid **Facilities** ⊗ ⅏ 🏐 💟 ♀ 🏖 🏖 ⛵ ⛳ **Leisure** fishing. **Conf** fac available Corporate Hospitality Days available **Location** From central London A12 NE to Wanstead

Continued

Hotel ★★★ 59% The County Hotel, 30 Oak Hill, WOODFORD GREEN ☎ 0870 609 6156 99 en suite

N2 EAST FINCHLEY

Hampstead Winnington Rd N2 0TU
☎ 020 8455 0203 📄 020 8731 6194
Undulating parkland course with many mature trees.
9 holes, 5822yds, Par 68, SSS 68, Course record 64.
Club membership 526.
Visitors restricted Tue and weekends. Contact Professional in advance on 020 8455 7089. Handicap certificate required. **Green Fees** £30 per 18 holes (£35 weekends). **Prof** Peter Brown **Course Designer** Tom Dunn **Facilities** ⊗ 🏐 💟 ♀ 🏖 🛗 ⛵ ⛳ **Location** Off Hampstead Lane

Hotel 🅄 Holiday Inn Hampstead, 215 Haverstock Hill, LONDON ☎ 0870 400 9037 140 en suite

N6 HIGHGATE

Highgate Denewood Rd N6 4AH
☎ 020 8340 3745 📄 020 8348 9152
e-mail: secretary@highgategolfclub.freeserve.co.uk
Parkland course.
18 holes, 5985yds, Par 69, SSS 69, Course record 66.
Club membership 700.
Visitors may not play Wed, weekends & bank holidays. **Societies** by arrangement. **Green Fees** not confirmed. **Prof** Robin Turner **Course Designer** Cuthbert Butchart **Facilities** ⊗ ⅏ 🏐 💟 ♀ 🏖 🛗 ⛵ ⛳ **Conf** fac available Corporate Hospitality Days available **Location** A1,Bishops Avenue,Hampstead lane,Sheldon Avenue

Hotel ★★★★ 73% London Marriott Hotel Regents Park, 128 King Henry's Rd, LONDON ☎ 0870 400 7240 303 en suite

N9 LOWER EDMONTON

Lee Valley Leisure Lee Valley Leisure Centre, Meridian Way, Edmonton N9 0AS ☎ 020 8803 3611
Tricky municipal parkland course with some narrow fairways and the River Lea providing a natural hazard.
18 holes, 4974yds, Par 66, SSS 64, Course record 66.
Club membership 200.
Visitors may telephone for advance bookings. **Societies** must telephone in advance. **Green Fees** not confirmed. **Prof** R Gerken **Facilities** 🏐 💟 ♀ 🏖 🛗 ⛵ ⛳ 🎿

N14 SOUTHGATE

Trent Park Bramley Rd, Oakwood N14 4XS
☎ 020 8367 4653 📄 0208 366 4581
e-mail: trentpark@americangolf.uk.com
18 holes, 6381yds, Par 70, SSS 69, Course record 64.
Course Designer D McGibbon **Location** Opposite Oakwood underground station
Telephone for further details

Hotel ★★★★ 🅭 73% West Lodge Park Hotel, Cockfosters Rd, HADLEY WOOD ☎ 020 8216 3900 46 en suite 13 annexe en suite

N20 WHETSTONE

North Middlesex The Manor House, Friern Barnet Ln, Whetstone N20 0NL
☎ 020 8445 1604 & 020 8445 3060 📄 020 8445 5023
e-mail: office@northmiddlesexgc.co.uk
Short parkland course renowned for its tricky greens.

Continued

18 holes, 5594yds, Par 69, SSS 67, Course record 64.
Club membership 520.
Visitors advisable to contact in advance. **Societies** bookings in advance, winter offers & summer packages by prior arrangement. **Green Fees** terms on application. **Cards**  **Prof** Freddy George **Course Designer** Willie Park Jnr **Facilities** ⊗ ⅷ ⅃ ⅃ ☑ ♀ ☖ 🏠 ♂ **Conf** fac available Corporate Hospitality Days available **Location** 5m S M25 junct 23

Hotel ★★★ 72% Edgwarebury Hotel, Barnet Ln, ELSTREE ☎ 0870 609 6151 47 en suite

---

South Herts Links Dr, Totteridge N20 8QU
☎ 020 8445 2035 🖹 020 8445 7569
e-mail: secretary@southherts.co.uk
18 holes, 6432yds, Par 72, SSS 71, Course record 63.
Course Designer Harry Vardon **Location** 2m E of A1 at Apex Corner
Telephone for further details

Hotel 🅤 Holiday Inn South Mimms, SOUTH MIMMS ☎ 0870 400 9072 144 en suite

---

N21 WINCHMORE HILL

Bush Hill Park Bush Hill, Winchmore Hill N21 2BU
☎ 020 8360 5738 🖹 020 8360 5583
Pleasant parkland course surrounded by trees. Contains a large number of both fairway sand traps and green side bunkers. Undulating, but not too harsh.
18 holes, 5809yds, Par 70, SSS 68.
Club membership 700.
Visitors may not play Wed mornings or weekends & bank holidays. Handicap certificate required. Prior tee booking. **Societies** by arrangement. **Green Fees** not confirmed. **Prof** Adrian Andrews **Course Designer** Braid **Facilities** ⊗ ⅃ ☑ ♀ ☖ 🏠 ♂ **Conf** Corporate Hospitality Days available **Location** M25 junct 24,1m S of Enfield, off London road N21

N22 WOOD GREEN

Muswell Hill Rhodes Av, Wood Green N22 7UT
☎ 020 8888 1764 🖹 020 8889 9380
e-mail: muswellhillgc@msn.com
Undulating parkland course with a brook running through the centre, set in 87 acres.
18 holes, 6438yds, Par 71, SSS 71, Course record 65.
Club membership 560.
Visitors must contact in advance, restricted weekends. **Societies** apply in writing or telephone. **Green Fees** terms on application. **Prof** David Wilton **Course Designer** Braid/Wilson **Facilities** ⊗ ⅷ by prior arrangement ⅃ ☑ ♀ ☖ 🏠 ♂ **Location** Off N Circular Rd at Bounds Green

Hotel ★★★ 68% Days Inn, Welcome Break Service Area, LONDON ☎ 020 8906 7000 200 en suite

NW4 HENDON   Map 04 TQ28

The Metro Golf Centre Barnet Copthall Sports Centre, Gt North Way NW4 1PS
☎ 020 8202 1202 🖹 020 8203 1203
e-mail: golf@metrogolf.btinternet.com
Located just seven miles from London's West End, the Metro Golf Centre represents a new generation of golf facility dedicated to the development of all standards of golfer. Facilities include a 48 bay two-tiered driving

Continued

---

range, a testing 9-hole par 3 course with water hazards, pot bunkers and postage stamp greens, a short game practice area, and a Golf Academy offering unique teaching methods.
9 holes, 898yds, Par 27, SSS 27, Course record 24.
Club membership 1600.
Visitors welcome any time between 8am-10pm all week for lessons, to play on the course or use driving range. **Societies** telephone in advance. **Green Fees** not confirmed. **Cards**  **Prof** David Morton **Course Designer** Cousells **Facilities** ⊗ ⅷ ⅃ ☑ ♀ ☖ 🏠 ♂ 🍴 **Conf** Corporate Hospitality Days available **Location** Just off A41 and A1 at junct 2 of the M1, within the Barnet Copthall Sporting Complex

Hotel ★★★★ 73% London Marriott Hotel Regents Park, 128 King Henry's Rd, LONDON ☎ 0870 400 7240 303 en suite

NW7 MILL HILL

Finchley Nether Court, Frith Ln, Mill Hill NW7 1PU
☎ 020 8346 2436 🖹 020 8343 4205
e-mail: secretary@finchleygolfclub.co.uk
Easy walking on wooded parkland course.

18 holes, 6411yds, Par 72, SSS 71.
Club membership 500.
Visitors must contact in advance. **Societies** must apply in writing. **Green Fees** £37 per day, £30 per 18 holes (£41/£39 weekends and bank holidays). **Cards**  **Prof** David Brown **Course Designer** James Braid **Facilities** ⊗ ⅷ ⅃ ☑ ♀ ☖ 🏠 🍴 🏌 ♂ **Conf** fac available Corporate Hospitality Days available **Location** Near Mill Hill East Tube Station

Hotel ★★★ 72% Edgwarebury Hotel, Barnet Ln, ELSTREE ☎ 0870 609 6151 47 en suite

Hendon Ashley Walk, Devonshire Rd, Mill Hill NW7 1DG ☎ 020 8346 6023 🖹 020 8343 1974
e-mail: hendongolfclub@globalnet.co.uk
Easy walking, parkland course with a good variety of trees, and providing testing golf.
18 holes, 6289yds, Par 70, SSS 70, Course record 63.
Club membership 560.
Visitors Restricted weekends & bank holidays. Must contact professional in advance on 020 8346 8990 **Societies** Tue-Fri. Must contact in advance. **Green Fees** £35 per day, £30 per round (£35 per round weekends). **Cards**  **Prof** Matt Deal **Course Designer** H S Colt **Facilities** ⊗ ⅷ ⅃ ☑ ♀ ☖ 🏠 🍴 🏌 ♂ **Conf** fac available Corporate Hospitality Days available **Location** 10 mins from junc 2 of M1 southbound

Hotel ★★★ 72% Edgwarebury Hotel, Barnet Ln, ELSTREE ☎ 0870 609 6151 47 en suite

Mill Hill 100 Barnet Way, Mill Hill NW7 3AL
☎ 020 8959 2339 📠 020 8906 0731
e-mail: davidbeal@dbeal.freeserve.co.uk
Parkland course with tree and shrub lined fairways, water features strongly on holes 2, 9, 10 and 17.

18 holes, 6247yds, Par 70, SSS 70, Course record 68.
Club membership 550.
Visitors restricted weekends & bank holidays. Must contact in advance. **Societies** must contact in advance. **Green Fees** £25 per round (£30 weekends). **Cards** 💳 💳
Prof David Beal **Course Designer** J F Abercrombie/H S Colt **Facilities** ⊗ ⊾ 🍴 ♀ ⚲ ⚑ 🏌 ⛳ 🏌 🚜 ⚙ **Leisure** snooker. **Conf** fac available Corporate Hospitality Days available **Location** On A1 S bound carriageway

Hotel ★★★ 72% Edgwarebury Hotel, Barnet Ln, ELSTREE ☎ 0870 609 6151 47 en suite

SE9 ELTHAM

Eltham Warren Bexley Rd, Eltham SE9 2PE
☎ 020 8850 4477
e-mail: secretary@elthamwarren.idps.co.uk
Parkland course with narrow fairways and small greens. The course is bounded by the A210 on one side and Eltham Park on the other.
9 holes, 5874yds, Par 69, SSS 68, Course record 62.
Club membership 440.
Visitors may not play at weekends. Must contact in advance and have a handicap certificate. **Societies** Thu only. Must book in advance. Deposit required. **Green Fees** £28 per day. **Prof** Gary Brett **Course Designer** James Braid **Facilities** ⊗ ⊾ 🍴 ♀ ⚲ ⚑ ⚙ **Leisure** snooker. **Location** 0.5m from Eltham station on A210

Hotel ★★★ 73% Bromley Court Hotel, Bromley Hill, BROMLEY ☎ 020 8461 8600 114 en suite

Royal Blackheath Court Rd SE9 5AF
☎ 020 8850 1795 📠 020 8859 0150
e-mail: info@rbgc.com
A pleasant, parkland course of great character as befits the antiquity of the Club; the clubhouse dates from the 17th century. Many great trees survive and there are two ponds. The 18th requires a pitch to the green over a thick clipped hedge, which also crosses the front of the 1st tee. You may wish to visit the club's fine museum of golf.
18 holes, 6219yds, Par 70, SSS 70, Course record 65.
Club membership 720.
Visitors must contact in advance but may play mid-week only, handicap certificate is required. **Societies** must apply in writing. **Green Fees** £60 per day; £45 per round. **Cards** 💳 💳 📇 **Prof** Richard Harrison **Course Designer** James Braid **Facilities** ⊗ 🍴 ⊾ 🍴 ♀ ⚲ ⚑ 🏌 🚜 ⚙ *Continued*

Leisure golf museum. **Conf** Corporate Hospitality Days available **Location** M25 junct 3 take A20 towards London. Turn right at 2nd traffic lights to club 500yds on right

Hotel ★★★ 73% Bromley Court Hotel, Bromley Hill, BROMLEY ☎ 020 8461 8600 114 en suite

SE18 WOOLWICH

Shooters Hill Eaglesfield Rd, Shooters Hill SE18 3DA
☎ 020 8854 6368 📠 020 8854 0469
e-mail: shgcltd@aol.com
Hilly and wooded parkland course with good view and natural hazards.
18 holes, 5721yds, Par 69, SSS 68, Course record 63.
Club membership 900.
Visitors must have handicap certificate and be a member of a recognised golf club but may not play at weekends, unless with member. **Societies** Tue & Thu only, by arrangement. **Green Fees** £30 per day, £25 per round. **Prof** David Brotherton **Course Designer** Willie Park **Facilities** ⊗ 🍴 ⊾ 🍴 ♀ ⚲ ⚑ 🏌 🚜 ⚙ **Conf** fac available Corporate Hospitality Days available **Location** Shooters Hill Rd from Blackheath

Hotel 🅄 Holiday Inn Bexley, Black Prince Interchange, Southwold Rd, BEXLEY ☎ 0870 400 9006 108 en suite

SE21 DULWICH

Dulwich & Sydenham Hill Grange Ln, College Rd
SE21 7LH ☎ 020 8693 3961 📠 020 8693 2481
e-mail: secretary@dulwichgolf.co.uk
Parkland course overlooking London. Hilly with narrow fairways.
18 holes, 6008yds, Par 69, SSS 69, Course record 63.
Club membership 850.
Visitors must contact in advance and have a handicap certificate. May not play weekends or bank holidays. **Societies** must telephone in advance & confirm in writing. **Green Fees** not confirmed. **Course Designer** H Colt **Facilities** ⊗ ⊾ 🍴 ♀ ⚲ ⚑ 🏌 🚜 ⚙ **Conf** Corporate Hospitality Days available

Hotel ★★★ 73% Bromley Court Hotel, Bromley Hill, BROMLEY ☎ 020 8461 8600 114 en suite

SE22 EAST DULWICH

Aquarius Marmora Rd, Honor Oak, Off Forest Hill Rd
SE22 0RY ☎ 020 8693 1626
e-mail: jim.halliday@btinternet.com
9 holes, 5246yds, Par 66, SSS 66, Course record 66.
Telephone for further details

Hotel ★★★ 73% Bromley Court Hotel, Bromley Hill, BROMLEY ☎ 020 8461 8600 114 en suite

SE28 WOOLWICH

Thamesview Fairway Dr, Summerton Way,
Thamesmead SE28 8PP ☎ 020 8310 7975
e-mail: enquiries@thamesview-golf.fsnet.co.uk
9 holes, 5462yds, Par 70, SSS 66.
Course Designer Heffernan **Location** Off A2 near Woolwich ferry
Telephone for further details

Hotel ★★ 70% Hamilton House Hotel, 14 West Grove, Greenwich, LONDON ☎ 020 8694 9899 9 en suite

SW15 PUTNEY

Richmond Park Roehampton Gate, Priory Ln
SW15 5JR ☎ 020 8876 1795 📄 020 8878 1354
e-mail: info@gcm.com
Two public parkland courses.
Princes Course: 18 holes, 5868yds, Par 69, SSS 67.
Dukes Course: 18 holes, 6036yds, Par 69, SSS 68.
Visitors must contact in advance for weekends. **Societies**
must contact in advance. **Green Fees** £18 per 18 holes;
(£21 weekends). **Cards** 📧 📧 📧 📧 💷 **Prof** Stuart Hill
& David Bown **Course Designer** Fred Hawtree **Facilities**
⊗ 🏌 💻 🏌 🏠 🍴 ➤ 🚜 ⫞ 🏌 **Conf** Corporate
Hospitality Days available **Location** Inside Richmond Park
Roehampton gate

Hotel ★★★ 68% The Richmond Hill Hotel, Richmond
Hill, RICHMOND UPON THAMES ☎ 020 8940 2247
138 en suite

SW17 WANDSWORTH

Central London Golf Centre Burntwood Ln,
Wandsworth SW17 0AT
☎ 020 8871 2468 📄 020 8874 7447
e-mail: clgc@aol.com
9 holes, 2277yds, Par 62, SSS 62.
Course Designer Patrick Tallock **Location** Between
Garatt Lane and Trinity Road
Telephone for further details

SW19 WIMBLEDON

London Scottish Windmill Enclosure, Wimbledon
Common SW19 5NQ
☎ 020 8788 0135 & 8789 1207 📄 020 8789 7517
e-mail: secretary.lsgc@virgin.net
**Heathland course. The original course was 7 holes
around the windmill, laid out by 'Old' Willie Dunn of
Musselburgh. His son, Tom Dunn, was the first
professional to the club and laid out the 18-hole course.**
18 holes, 5458yds, Par 68, SSS 66.
Visitors pillar box red tops must be worn. May not play
weekends/bank holidays. **Societies** preferable to contact in
advance. **Green Fees** Mon: £17 per day, £10 per round.
Tue-Fri £22/£15. **Prof** Steve Barr **Course Designer** Tom
Dunn **Facilities** ⊗ 🏌 🏌 💻 🏌 🏠 🍴 ⫞

Royal Wimbledon 29 Camp Rd SW19 4UW
☎ 020 8946 2125 📄 020 8944 8652
e-mail: secretary@rwgc.co.uk
**Third oldest club in England, established in 1865 and
steeped in the history and traditions of the game.
Mainly heathland with trees and heather, a good test of
golf with many fine holes, the 12th being rated as the
best.**
18 holes, 6350yds, Par 70, SSS 70, Course record 66.
Club membership 1050.
Visitors must be guests of current club member or contact
club in advance, weekdays only. Maximum handicap 18
and must be member of recognised club. **Societies**
welcome Wed-Thu. Must apply in writing. **Green Fees**
£85 per day, £60 per round. **Prof** David Jones **Course
Designer** H Colt **Facilities** ⊗ 🏌 🏌 💻 🏌 🏠 🍴 ⫞
Conf Corporate Hospitality Days available **Location** 1m
from Tibbatt's Corner roundabout on Wimbledon Rd

Wimbledon Common 19 Camp Rd SW19 4UW
☎ 020 8946 0294 (Pro shop) 📄 020 8947 8697
e-mail: secretary@wcgc.co.uk
**Quick-drying course on Wimbledon Common. Well
wooded, with tight fairways, challenging short holes but
no bunkers. The course is also played over by London
Scottish Golf Club. All players must wear plain red
upper garments.**
18 holes, 5438yds, Par 68, SSS 66, Course record 63.
Club membership 290.
Visitors with member only at weekends and bank holidays.
Societies must telephone in advance, confirm in writing.
25% deposit. **Green Fees** £24 per day, £16 per round. **Prof**
J S Jukes **Course Designer** Tom & Willie Dunn **Facilities**
⊗ 🏌 🏌 🏌 💻 🏌 🏠 🍴 ⫞ **Leisure** snooker room. **Conf** fac
available Corporate Hospitality Days available **Location**
0.5m N of Wimbledon Village

Wimbledon Park Home Park Rd, Wimbledon
SW19 7HR ☎ 020 8946 1250 📄 020 8944 8688
e-mail: secretary@wpgc.co.uk
**Easy walking on parkland course. Sheltered lake
provides hazard on three holes.**
18 holes, 5465yds, Par 66, SSS 66.
Club membership 700.
Visitors restricted weekends & bank holidays. Must
contact in advance and have handicap certificate or letter of
introduction. **Societies** must apply in writing. **Green Fees**
£50 per round. **Cards** 📧 📧 📧 💷 **Prof** Dean Wingrove
Course Designer Willie Park Jnr **Facilities** ⊗ 🏌 🏌 💻 🏌
🏠 🍴 ⫞ **Conf** fac available Corporate Hospitality Days
available **Location** 400 yds from Wimbledon Park Station

Hotel ★★★ 68% The Richmond Hill Hotel, Richmond
Hill, RICHMOND UPON THAMES ☎ 020 8940 2247
138 en suite

W7 HANWELL

Brent Valley 138 Church Rd, Hanwell W7 3BE
☎ 020 8567 1287
18 holes, 5426yds, Par 67, SSS 66.
Telephone for further details

Hotel ★★★ 66% Best Western Master Robert Hotel,
366 Great West Rd, HOUNSLOW ☎ 020 8570 6261
96 annexe en suite

MERSEYSIDE

BEBINGTON
Map 07 SJ38

Brackenwood Brackenwood Golf Course, Bracken Ln
CH63 2LY ☎ 0151 608 3093
**Municipal parkland course with easy walking, a very
testing but fair course in a fine rural setting, usually in
very good condition.**
18 holes, 6285yds, Par 70, SSS 70, Course record 66.
Club membership 320.
Visitors must book for weekends one week in advance.
Societies must telephone in advance. **Green Fees** £9 per
round. **Prof** Ken Lamb **Facilities** 💻 🏠 🍴 ⫞ **Location**
0.75m N of M53 junc 4 on B5151

Hotel ★★★★ 68% Thornton Hall Hotel, Neston Rd,
THORNTON HOUGH ☎ 0151 336 3938 63 en suite

BIRKENHEAD · · · · · · · · · · · · Map 07 SJ38

Arrowe Park Woodchurch CH49 5LW
☎ 0151 677 1527
Pleasant municipal parkland course.
18 holes, 6435yds, Par 72, SSS 71, Course record 66.
Club membership 220.
Visitors no restrictions, Booking at weekends 1wk in advance. **Societies** must telephone in advance. **Green Fees** not confirmed. **Cards** 🖾 🖾 **Prof** Colin Disbury
Facilities ⊗ ⅊ ⅃ 🖤 ♀ 🖾 ⚐ 🕹 ∂ **Leisure** tennis courts, pitch & putt. **Location** 1m from M53 junc 3 on A551

Prenton Golf Links Rd, Prenton CH42 8LW
☎ 0151 609 3426 📋 0151 609 3421
e-mail: info@prentongolfclub.co.uk
Parkland course with easy walking and views of the Welsh Hills.
18 holes, 6429yds, Par 71, SSS 71.
Club membership 610.
Visitors no restrictions. **Societies** must telephone in advance and confirm in writing. **Green Fees** terms on application. **Prof** Robin Thompson **Course Designer** James Braid **Facilities** ⊗ ⅊ ⅃ 🖤 ♀ 🖾 🖾 ∂ **Location** M53 junct 3 off A552 towards Birkenhead

Hotel ★★★ 67% Riverhill Hotel, Talbot Rd, Prenton, BIRKENHEAD ☎ 0151 653 3773 15 en suite

Wirral Ladies 93 Bidston Rd CH43 6TS
☎ 0151 652 1255 📋 0151 653 4323
e-mail: sue.headford@virgin.net
Heathland course with heather and birch.
18 holes, 5185yds, Par 68, SSS 65.
Club membership 590.
Visitors may not play before 11am weekends or over Christmas and Easter holidays. **Societies** must telephone in advance. Weekdays only. **Green Fees** £25.50 per day. **Prof** Angus Law **Facilities** ⊗ ⅊ ⅃ 🖤 ♀ 🖾 ∂ **Leisure** indoor training suite. **Location** W side of town centre on B5151

BLUNDELLSANDS · · · · · · · · · · Map 07 SJ39

West Lancashire Hall Rd West L23 8SZ
☎ 0151 924 1076 📋 0151 931 4448
e-mail: golf@westlancashiregolf.co.uk
Challenging, traditional links with sandy subsoil overlooking the Mersey Estuary. The course provides excellent golf throughout the year. The four short holes are very fine.
18 holes, 6763yds, Par 72, SSS 73, Course record 66.
Club membership 650.
Visitors May not play before 9.30am Mon-Fri. No play Tue. **Societies** must contact in advance. **Green Fees** £75 per day; £60 per round (£85/70 weekends). **Cards** 🖾 🖾 🖾 🖾 **Prof** Gary Eoge **Course Designer** C K Cotton
Facilities ⊗ ⅊ ⅃ 🖤 ♀ 🖾 ∂ ₹ **Conf** Corporate Hospitality Days available **Location** N side of village, adjacent to Hall Rd station

Hotel ★★★ 63% Tree Tops Country House Restaurant & Hotel, Southport Old Rd, FORMBY ☎ 01704 572430 11 annexe en suite

BOOTLE · · · · · · · · · · · · · · · Map 07 SJ39

Bootle 2 Dunnings Bridge Rd L30 2PP
☎ 0151 928 1371 📋 0151 949 1815
e-mail: bootlegolfcourse@btconnect.com
Municipal seaside course, with prevailing north-westerly wind. Testing holes: 5th (200 yds) par 3; 7th (415 yds) par 4.
18 holes, 6362yds, Par 70, SSS 70, Course record 64.
Club membership 380.
Visitors must contact Golf Shop on 0151 928 1371 not between 9-9.45am Sat and 7.45-12 Sun. **Societies** contact Miss C Yates **Green Fees** not confirmed. **Cards** 🖾 🖾 🖾 🖾 **Prof** Alan Bradshaw **Facilities** ⊗ ⅃ 🖤 ♀ 🖾 🖾 ⚐ **Leisure** fishing. **Location** 2m NE on A5036

Hotel ⌂ Travel Inn Liverpool North, Northern Perimiter Rd, Bootle, LIVERPOOL ☎ 08701 977158 63 en suite

BROMBOROUGH · · · · · · · · · · Map 07 SJ38

Bromborough Raby Hall Rd CH63 0NW
☎ 0151 334 2155 📋 0151 334 7300
e-mail: sec@bromborough-golf-club.freeserve.co.uk
Parkland course.
18 holes, 6650yds, Par 72, SSS 72, Course record 65.
Club membership 800.
Visitors are advised to contact professional on 0151 334 4499 in advance. **Societies** normal society day Wed ; must apply in advance. **Green Fees** terms on application. **Prof** Geoff Berry **Course Designer** J Hassall **Facilities** ⊗ ⅊ ⅃ 🖤 ♀ 🖾 🕹 ∂ **Conf** Corporate Hospitality Days available **Location** 0.5m W of Station

CALDY · · · · · · · · · · · · · · · · Map 07 SJ28

Caldy Links Hey Rd CH48 1NB
☎ 0151 625 5660 📋 0151 6257394
e-mail: gail@caldygolfclub.fsnet.co.uk
A heathland/cliff top links course situated on the estuary of the River Dee with many of the fairways running parallel to the river. Of championship length, the course offers excellent golf all year, but is subject to variable winds that noticeably alter the day-to-day playing of each hole. There are excellent views of North Wales and Snowdonia.
18 holes, 6651yds, Par 72, SSS 72, Course record 65.
Club membership 800.
Visitors may play on weekdays only by prior arrangement. Not before 3.30pm Tue or after 12.30pm Wed. **Societies** must telephone in advance. **Green Fees** £45 per day, £40 per round. **Prof** K Jones **Course Designer** J Braid **Facilities** ⊗ ⅊ ⅃ 🖤 ♀ 🖾 🕹 ∂ **Conf** Corporate Hospitality Days available **Location** SE side of village, from Caldy rdbt on A540 follow signs to Caldy and golf club

Hotel ★★★★ 68% Thornton Hall Hotel, Neston Rd, THORNTON HOUGH ☎ 0151 336 3938 63 en suite

EASTHAM · · · · · · · · · · · · · · Map 07 SJ38

Eastham Lodge 117 Ferry Rd CH62 0AP
☎ 0151 327 3003 📋 0151 327 7574
e-mail: easthamlodge@ukgolfer.org
A parkland course with many mature trees, recently upgraded to 18 holes. Most holes have a subtle dog-leg to left or right. The 1st hole requires an accurate drive to open up the green which is guarded on the right by a stand of pine trees.

Continued

18 holes, 5436yds, Par 68, SSS 68.
Club membership 800.
Visitors advisable to telephone in advance to check availability, tel 0151 327 3008 professionals shop, start times available up to 2 weeks in advance, with member only at weekends. **Societies** welcome Tue. Must apply in writing. Other days by arrangement. **Green Fees** £23.50 per day/round weekdays. **Prof** N Sargent **Course Designer** Hawtree/D Hemstock **Facilities** ⊗ ⅷ ⮜ ⌷ ☕ ♀ ⛁ 🏠 ⛳ ⚐ **Leisure** snooker. **Conf** Corporate Hospitality Days available **Location** 1.5m N, off A41 to Wirral Metropolitan College & Eastham Country Park

Hotel ★★★ 69% Quality Hotel Chester, Berwick Rd, Little Sutton, ELLESMERE PORT ☎ 0151 339 5121 53 en suite

FORMBY　　　　　　　　　　　　　　　　　Map 07 SD30

Formby Golf Rd L37 1LQ
☎ 01704 872164 ▤ 01704 833028
e-mail: info@formbygolfclub.co.uk
Championship seaside links through sandhills and pine trees. Partly sheltered from the wind by high dunes it features firm, springy turf, fast seaside greens and natural sandy bunkers. Well drained it plays well throughout the year.

18 holes, 6701yds, Par 72, SSS 72, Course record 65.
Club membership 700.
Visitors must contact in advance, weekends after 3.30pm **Societies** must contact well in advance. **Green Fees** £85 per day/round (weekend £95). **Cards** ▦ ▨ **Prof** Gary Butler **Course Designer** Park/Colt **Facilities** ⊗ ⅷ ⮜ ⌷ ☕ ♀ ⛁ 🏠 ⛳ **Conf** fac available Corporate Hospitality Days available **Location** N side of town, next to Freshfield Railway Station

Hotel ★★★ 63% Tree Tops Country House Restaurant & Hotel, Southport Old Rd, FORMBY ☎ 01704 572430 11 annexe en suite

Formby Ladies Golf Rd L37 1YH
☎ 01704 873493 ▤ 01704 873493
e-mail: secretary@formbyladiesgolfclub.co.uk
Seaside links - one of the few independent ladies' clubs in the country. The course has contrasting hard-hitting holes in flat country and tricky holes in sandhills and woods.
18 holes, 5374yds, Par 71, SSS 71, Course record 60.
Club membership 570.
Visitors must contact in advance and may not play Thu or before 11am Sat & Sun. **Societies** must apply in advance. Handicap certificate required. **Green Fees** £40 per day (£45 weekends). **Prof** Gary Butler **Facilities** ⊗ ⮜ ⌷ ♀ ⛁ 🏠 ⛳ **Location** N side of town

Hotel ★★★ 63% Tree Tops Country House Restaurant & Hotel, Southport Old Rd, FORMBY ☎ 01704 572430 11 annexe en suite

HESWALL　　　　　　　　　　　　　　　　　Map 07 SJ28

Heswall Cottage Ln CH60 8PB
☎ 0151 342 1237 ▤ 0151 342 6140
e-mail: dawn@heswellgolfclub.com
A pleasant parkland course in soft undulating country overlooking the estuary of the River Dee. There are excellent views of the Welsh hills and coastline, and a good test of golf. The clubhouse is modern and well-appointed with good facilities.
18 holes, 6492yds, Par 72, SSS 72, Course record 62.
Club membership 940.
Visitors must contact in advance. **Societies** must apply in advance. **Green Fees** £35 (weekends £40). **Prof** Alan Thompson **Facilities** ⊗ ⅷ ⮜ ⌷ ☕ ♀ ⛁ 🏠 ⛳ **Location** 1m S off A540

Hotel ★★★★ 68% Thornton Hall Hotel, Neston Rd, THORNTON HOUGH ☎ 0151 336 3938 63 en suite

HOYLAKE See page 177

HOYLAKE　　　　　　　　　　　　　　　　　Map 07 SJ28

Hoylake Carr Ln, Municipal Links CH47 4BG
☎ 0151 632 2956
Flat, generally windy semi-links course. Tricky fairways, with some very deep bunkers.
18 holes, 6313yds, Par 70, SSS 70, Course record 67.
Club membership 303.
Visitors tee times booked with professional, weekend bookings one week in advance **Societies** must telephone 0151 632 4883 club steward or 0151 632 2956 club professional. **Green Fees** £8.50 per round. **Cards** ▦ ▨ ▩ **Prof** Simon Hooton **Course Designer** James Braid **Facilities** ⊗ ⅷ ⮜ ⌷ ☕ ♀ ⛁ 🏠 ⛳ ⚐ ⛏ ⚒ ⛳ **Location** SW side of town off A540

Hotel ★★★ 68% Leasowe Castle Hotel, Leasowe Rd, MORETON ☎ 0151 606 9191 47 en suite

HUYTON　　　　　　　　　　　　　　　　　Map 07 SJ49

Bowring Roby Rd L36 4HD
☎ 0151 443 0424 489 1901
e-mail: bowringpark@knowsley.gov.uk
Bowring Golf Club: 18 holes, 6082yds, Par 70.
Location On A5080 adjacent M62 junc 5
Telephone for further details

Hotel ⇧ Premier Lodge (Liverpool South East), Roby Rd, Huyton, LIVERPOOL ☎ 0870 9906596 53 en suite

Huyton & Prescot Hurst Park, Huyton Ln L36 1UA
☎ 0151 489 3948 ▤ 0151 489 0797
An easy walking, parkland course providing excellent golf.
18 holes, 5779yds, Par 68, SSS 68, Course record 65.
Club membership 700.
Visitors must contact in advance and be arranged with secretary, **Societies** must apply in writing. **Green Fees** £25 (£30 weekends & bank holidays). **Prof** John Fisher **Facilities** ⊗ ⅷ ⮜ ⌷ ☕ ♀ ⛁ 🏠 ⛳ **Conf** fac available Corporate Hospitality Days available **Location** 1.5m NE off B5199

Continued　　　　　　　　　　　　　　　*Continued*

Huyton & Prescot Golf Club

Hotel ⭫ Travel Inn Liverpool Tarbock, Wilson Rd, Tarbock, LIVERPOOL ☎ 08701 977159 40 en suite

LIVERPOOL   Map 07 SJ39

Allerton Park Allerton Manor Golf Estate, Allerton Rd L18 3JT ☎ 0151 428 7490 🖥 428 7490
18 holes, 5494yds, Par 67, SSS 66.
Location 5.5m SE of city centre off A562 and B5180
Telephone for further details

Hotel ★★★ 67% The Royal Hotel, Marine Ter, Waterloo, LIVERPOOL ☎ 0151 928 2332 25 en suite

The Childwall Naylors Rd, Gateacre L27 2YB
☎ 0151 487 0654 🖥 0151 487 0882
e-mail: manager@childwallgc.fsnet.co.uk
18 holes, 6425yds, Par 72, SSS 71, Course record 66.
Course Designer James Braid **Location** 7m E of city centre off B5178
Telephone for further details

Hotel ⭫ Premier Lodge (Liverpool South East), Roby Rd, Huyton, LIVERPOOL ☎ 0870 9906596 53 en suite

Kirkby-Liverpool Municipal Ingoe Ln, Kirkby L32 4SS ☎ 0151 546 5435
18 holes, 6704yds, Par 72, SSS 72, Course record 68.
Location 7.5m NE of city centre on A506
Telephone for further details

Hotel ★★★ 67% The Royal Hotel, Marine Ter, Waterloo, LIVERPOOL ☎ 0151 928 2332 25 en suite

Lee Park Childwall Valley Rd L27 3YA
☎ 0151 487 3882 🖥 0151 498 4666
e-mail: lee.park@virgin.net
Testing parkland course with plenty of trees, ponds in places and 9 dog legs. Easy walking requiring good iron play.
18 holes, 6016yds, Par 71, SSS 69, Course record 66.
Club membership 600.
Visitors must dress acceptably. Must contact in advance. **Societies** must contact in advance. **Green Fees** £20 per day (£30 weekends & bank holidays). **Course Designer** G Cotton **Facilities** ⊗ ❬ ⮜ ☕ ♀ ⚲ ⚷ **Leisure** snooker room. **Conf** Corporate Hospitality Days available **Location** 7m E of city centre off B5178

Hotel ⭫ Premier Lodge (Liverpool South East), Roby Rd, Huyton, LIVERPOOL ☎ 0870 9906596 53 en suite

West Derby Yew Tree Ln, West Derby L12 9HQ
☎ 0151 254 1034 🖥 0151 259 0505
e-mail: pmilne@westderbygc.freeserve.co.uk
A parkland course always in first-class condition, and so giving easy walking. The fairways are well-wooded. Care must be taken on the first nine holes to avoid the brook which guards many of the greens. A modern well-designed clubhouse with many amenities overlooks the course.
18 holes, 6277yds, Par 72, SSS 70, Course record 65. Club membership 550.
Visitors may not play before 9.30am. May play weekends by arrangement. **Societies** may not play on Sat, Sun & bank holidays; must contact in advance. **Green Fees** £28.50 per day/round (£37 weekends). **Prof** Andrew Witherup **Facilities** ⊗ ❬ ⮜ ☕ ♀ ⚲ ⚷ **Conf** Corporate Hospitality Days available **Location** 4.5m E of city centre off A57

Hotel ★★★ 67% The Royal Hotel, Marine Ter, Waterloo, LIVERPOOL ☎ 0151 928 2332 25 en suite

Woolton Doe Park, Speke Rd, Woolton L25 7TZ
☎ 0151 486 2298 🖥 0151 486 1664
e-mail: keith@wooltongolf.co.uk
Parkland course providing a good round of golf for all standards. A members' owned course which includes two par 5s and five par 3s.
18 holes, 5717yds, Par 69, SSS 68, Course record 63. Club membership 700.
Visitors must contact in advance. Restricted at weekends. **Societies** must contact in advance. **Green Fees** £26 per 18 holes (£40 weekends). **Prof** Dave Thompson **Facilities** ⊗ ❬ ⮜ ☕ ♀ ⚲ ⚷ ⚹ ⚶ **Leisure** Indoor teaching unit. **Conf** fac available Corporate Hospitality Days available **Location** 7m SE of city centre off A562, 5 mins from Liverpool airport

Hotel ★★★ 67% The Royal Hotel, Marine Ter, Waterloo, LIVERPOOL ☎ 0151 928 2332 25 en suite

NEWTON-LE-WILLOWS   Map 07 SJ59

Haydock Park Newton Ln WA12 0HX
☎ 01925 228525 🖥 01925 224984
A well-wooded parkland course, close to the well-known racecourse, and always in excellent condition. The pleasant undulating fairways offer some very interesting golf and the 6th, 9th, 11th and 13th holes are particularly testing. The clubhouse is very comfortable.
18 holes, 6058yds, Par 70, SSS 69, Course record 65. Club membership 560.
Visitors welcome weekdays except Tue, with member only weekends & bank holidays. Must contact in advance. **Societies** must contact in advance. **Green Fees** £30. **Prof** Peter Kenwright **Course Designer** James Braid **Facilities** ⊗ ❬ ⮜ ☕ ♀ ⚲ ⚷ **Location** 0.75m NE off A49

Hotel 🅄 Holiday Inn Haydock, Lodge Ln, HAYDOCK ☎ 0870 400 9039 138 en suite

RAINHILL   Map 07 SJ49

Blundells Hill Blundells Ln L35 6NA
☎ 0151 4309551 (secretary) & 4300100 (pro)
🖥 0151 4265256
e-mail: information@blundellshill.co.uk

Continued

Royal Liverpool Golf Club

Map 07 ST28   Hoylake

☎ 0151 632 3101   📄 0151 632 6737

Built in 1869 on the site of a former racecourse, this world famous championship course was one of the first seaside courses to be established in England. In 1921 Hoylake was the scene of the first international match between the US and Britain, now known as the Walker Cup. Over the years, golfing enthusiasts have continued to come to Hoylake to witness 18 amateur championships and 10 Open Championships, which the club is set to host again in 2006. Visitors playing on this historic course can expect a challenging match, with crosswinds, deep bunkers and hollows, all set against the backdrop of the stunning Welsh hills. Watch out for the 8th hole, which saw the great Bobby Jones take an 8 on this par 5 on the way to his famous Grand Slam in 1930.

e-mail: sec@royal-liverpool-golf.com

Visitors Must contact in advance and have handicap certificate. Restricted before 9.30am and between 1–2pm. No play Thu am. Limited play weekends (pm only)

Societies Must contact in advance

Green Fees £100–£130 midweek

Facilities ⊗ ⋇ ⊞ ⚑ ♀ ♣ 🛆 🖃 ⛳ ⛽ ♂ ⸗
Conf Corporate hospitality days available

Professional John Heggarty

Location Meols Drive, Hoylake, Wirral CH47 4AL (SW side of town on A540)

Holes/Par/Course record
Royal Liverpool: 18 holes, 6240 yds, Par 72, SSS 71
Medal: 18 holes, 6909 yds, Par 72, SSS 74,
Course record 69
Championship: 18 holes, 7168 yds, Par 72, SSS 75,
Course record 64

Championship Course

WHERE TO STAY AND EAT NEARBY

Hotels
MORETON

★★★ 68% Leasowe Castle Hotel, CH46 3RF
☎ 0151 606 9191. 47 en suite

BIRKENHEAD

★★★ 67% Riverhill Hotel, CH43 2HJ
☎ 0151 653 3773. 15 en suite

HOYLAKE

★★★ 65% Kings Gap Court Hotel, CH47 1HE
☎ 0151 632 2073. 30 en suite

Restaurants
BIRKENHEAD

◉ Beadles L43 5SG, ☎ 0151 653 9010.

◉ Capitol L41 6AE, ☎ 0151 647 9212.

Parkland course, with free-draining sandy soil, which allows play throughout the winter.
18 holes, 6256yds, Par 71, SSS 70, Course record 69.
Club membership 600.
Visitors may not play off white tees. **Societies** telephone for prices and availability. **Green Fees** not confirmed. **Cards** 🏧 💳 💳 💳 **Prof** Richard Burbidge **Course Designer** Steve Marnoch **Facilities** ⊗ ⅏ ⅃ ♥ ♀ ⚘ 🏠 ♦ 🕯 **Leisure** pool/snooker. **Conf** fac available Corporate Hospitality Days available **Location** M62 junct 7, A57 towards Prescot, left after garage. 2nd left into Blundells lane, on left behind trees

Hotel ⬆ Premier Lodge (Liverpool East), 804 Warrington Rd, RAINHILL ☎ 0870 9906446 34 en suite

Eccleston Park Rainhill Rd L35 4PG
☎ 0151 493 0033 📠 0151 493 0044
e-mail: eccleston-sales@crown-golf.co.uk
A tough parkland course designed to test all golfing abilities. Strategically placed water features, bunkers and mounding enhance the beauty and difficulty of this manicured course.
18 holes, 6296yds, Par 70, SSS 72.
Club membership 700.
Visitors booking 7 days in advance. **Societies** telephone in advance. **Green Fees** £15 (£20 weekends & bank holidays). **Cards** 🏧 💳 💳 💳 **Prof** Chris McKinney **Facilities** ⊗ ⅏ ⅃ ♀ ⚘ 🏠 ♦ **Conf** fac available Corporate Hospitality Days available **Location** M62 junct 7, follow A57 to Prescot. At hump back bridge turn right at lights, course 1m on left

Hotel ⬆ Premier Lodge (Liverpool East), 804 Warrington Rd, RAINHILL ☎ 0870 9906446 34 en suite

ST HELENS
Map 07 SJ59

Grange Park Prescot Rd WA10 3AD
☎ 01744 26318 📠 01744 26318
e-mail: gpgc@ic24.net
A course of Championship length set in pleasant country surroundings - playing the course it is hard to believe that industrial St Helens lies so close at hand. The course is a fine test of golf and there are many attractive holes liable to challenge all grades.
18 holes, 6446yds, Par 72, SSS 71, Course record 65.
Club membership 730.
Visitors welcome except Tue, may not play weekends. Advisable to contact professional in advance (01744 28785) **Societies** apply in writing **Green Fees** £28 (weekends £33). **Prof** Paul Roberts **Course Designer** James Braid **Facilities** ⊗ ⅏ ⅃ ♥ ♀ ⚘ 🏠 ♦ **Location** 1.5m SW on A58

Hotel ★★ 66% Kirkfield Hotel, 2/4 Church St, NEWTON LE WILLOWS ☎ 01925 228196 20 en suite

Houghwood Golf Billinge Hill, Crank Rd, Crank
WA11 8RL ☎ 01744 894444 & 894754 📠 01744 894754
e-mail: houghwoodgolf@btinternet.com
In a perfect setting Houghwood has magnificent panoramic views over Lancashire plain and Welsh hills. With large USGA greens this undulating course is a superb test of golf for all abilities.
18 holes, 6268yds, Par 70, SSS 69, Course record 67.
Club membership 680.

Houghwood Golf

Visitors no restrictions but dress code must be adhered to. **Societies** telephone enquiries welcome, deposit secures booking. **Green Fees** £25 per round; (£35 weekends & bank holidays). **Cards** 🏧 💳 💳 💳 **Prof** Paul Dickenson **Course Designer** Neville Pearson **Facilities** ⊗ ⅏ ⅃ ♥ ♀ ⚘ 🏠 ♥ ♦ **Leisure** indoor golf simulator. **Conf** fac available Corporate Hospitality Days available **Location** From M6 junct 23 follow A580 to A571 to Billinge

Hotel ⊍ Holiday Inn Haydock, Lodge Ln, HAYDOCK ☎ 0870 400 9039 138 en suite

Sherdley Park Sherdley Rd WA9 5DE
☎ 01744 813149 📠 01744 817967
Fairly hilly, challenging, pay and play parkland course with ponds in places. Excellent greens.
18 holes, 5974yds, Par 71, SSS 69.
Visitors no restrictions. **Societies** telephone or write for application form. After 1.30pm weekends **Green Fees** £10 per 18 holes (£12 weekends). **Prof** Danny Jones **Course Designer** Peter Parkinson **Facilities** ⊗ ⅏ ⅃ ♥ ♀ ♟ ♦ 🕯 **Location** 2m S off A570, on the M62 linkway

Hotel ★★ 66% Kirkfield Hotel, 2/4 Church St, NEWTON LE WILLOWS ☎ 01925 228196 20 en suite

SOUTHPORT See page 179

SOUTHPORT
Map 07 SD31

The Hesketh Cockle Dick's Ln, off Cambridge Rd
PR9 9QQ ☎ 01704 536897 📠 01704 539250
e-mail: hesketh@ukgolfer.org
The Hesketh is the oldest of the six clubs in Southport, founded in 1885. Used as a final qualifying course for the Open Championship.
18 holes, 6655yds, Par 72, SSS 72, Course record 67.
Club membership 650.
Visitors welcome, with handicap certificate, at all times except Tues am (Ladies), 12.30-2pm daily, after 2.30pm Sat & 10.30am Sun. Must contact in advance. **Societies** please contact Martyn G Senior in advance. **Green Fees** £60 per day; £50 per round (£60 per round weekends & bank holidays). **Cards** 🏧 💳 💳 💳 **Prof** John Donoghue **Course Designer** J F Morris **Facilities** ⊗ ⅏ ⅃ ♥ ♀ ⚘ ♟ ♦ **Conf** Corporate Hospitality Days available **Location** 1m NE of town centre off A565

Hotel ★★★ 69% Stutelea Hotel Leisure Club, Alexandra Rd, SOUTHPORT ☎ 01704 544220 20 en suite

Continued   *Continued*

The Royal Birkdale

Map 07 SD31   Southport

☎ 01704 567920 Fax 01704 562327

Founded in 1889, the Royal Birkdale is considered by many to be the ultimate championship venue having hosted every major event in the game including eight Open Championships, two Ryder Cup matches, the Walker Cup, the Curtis Cup and many major amateur events. The first hole provides an immediate taste of what is to come, requiring a well placed drive to avoid a bunker, water hazard and Out of Bounds to leave a reasonably clear view of the green. The 10th, the first of the inward nine, is unique in that it is the only hole to display the significant fairway undulations one expects from the classic links course. The 12th is the most spectacular of the short holes on the course and is considered by Tom Watson to be one of the best par 3s in the world. Tucked away in the sandhills it will continue to claim its fair share of disasters. The approach on the final hole is arguably the most recognisable in golf, with the distinctive clubhouse designed to appear like an ocean cruise liner rising out of the sandhills. It is a par 5 for mere mortals, but played as a par 4 in the Open and it will provide a memorable finish to any round of golf.

e-mail: secretary@royalbirkdale.com

Visitors Must contact in advance and have a handicap certificate. Not Sat, and restricted on Sun, Tue and Fri

Societies Must contact in advance and have a handicap certificate

Green Fees Telephone for details

Facilities ⊗ ✗ (by prior arrangement) ⬆ ☕ ♀ ⚒ 🏌 🛒 ⚑

Corporate hospitality days available

Professional Brian Hodgkinson

Location Waterloo Rd, Birkdale, Southport PR8 2LX (1.75m S of town centre on A565)

Holes/Par/Course record 18 holes, 6726 yds, Par 72, SSS 73

WHERE TO STAY AND EAT NEARBY

Hotels
SOUTHPORT

★★★ 71% Scarisbrick, PR8 1NZ.
☎ 01704 543000. 88 en suite

★★★ 69% Stutelea Hotel & Leisure Club, PR9 0NB.
☎ 01704 544220. 20 en suite

★★★ 65% Royal Clifton, PR8 1RB.
☎ 01704 533771.
111 en suite

★★ 72% Balmoral Lodge, PR9 9EX.
☎ 01704 544298. 15 en suite

Restaurants
WRIGHTINGTON

◎ ◎ Mulberry Tree, WN6 9SE.
☎ 01257 451400

◎ ◎ Southport Warehouse Brasserie PR8 1QN.
☎ 01704 544662

Championship Course

Stutelea Hotel & Leisure Club

Hillside Hastings Rd, Hillside PR8 2LU
☎ 01704 567169 📠 01704 563192
e-mail: secretary@hillside-golfclub.co.uk
Championship links course with natural hazards open to strong wind.
18 holes, 6850yds, Par 72, SSS 74, Course record 65.
Club membership 700.
Visitors welcome except Sat, restricted on Sun & Tue (Ladies Day), must contact in advance through secretary. **Societies** must apply to secretary in advance. **Green Fees** £75 per day; £60 per round (£75 per round Sun). **Cards** 💳 💳 **Prof** Brian Seddon **Course Designer** Hawtree/Steel **Facilities** ⊗ ⅷ ⅃ 🍺 ♀ ⚘ 🏠 🇹 🛇 ⸰ 🍴 **Conf** Corporate Hospitality Days available **Location** 3m S of town centre on A565

Hotel ★★★ 65% Royal Clifton Hotel, Promenade, SOUTHPORT ☎ 01704 533771 111 en suite

Southport & Ainsdale Bradshaws Ln, Ainsdale
PR8 3LG ☎ 01704 578000 📠 01704 570896
e-mail: secretary@sandagolfclub.co.uk
'S and A', as it is known in the North, is another of the fine Championship courses for which this part of the country is famed. This Club has staged many important events and offers golf of the highest order.
18 holes, 6687yds, Par 72, SSS 73, Course record 62.
Club membership 815.
Visitors welcome except Thu after 1pm, Sat after 3pm & Sun after 12 noon & bank holidays. Must contact club in advance & have handicap certificate. **Societies** must apply in advance. **Green Fees** £60 per 18 holes; £75 per 36 holes (£75 per 18 holes weekends). **Cards** 💳 💳 💳 **Prof** J Payne **Course Designer** James Braid **Facilities** ⊗ ⅷ ⅃ 🍺 ♀ ⚘ 🏠 🇹 ⸰ **Location** 3m S off A565

Hotel ★★★ 65% Royal Clifton Hotel, Promenade, SOUTHPORT ☎ 01704 533771 111 en suite

Southport Municipal Park Rd West PR9 0JR
☎ 01704 535286
18 holes, 6400yds, Par 70, SSS 69, Course record 67.
Location N side of town centre off A565
Telephone for further details

Hotel ★★★ 65% Royal Clifton Hotel, Promenade, SOUTHPORT ☎ 01704 533771 111 en suite

Southport Old Links Moss Ln, Churchtown
PR9 7QS ☎ 01704 228207 📠 01704 505353
e-mail: secretary@solgc.freeserve.co.uk
Seaside course with tree-lined fairways and easy walking. One of the oldest courses in Southport, Henry Vardon won the 'Leeds Cup' here in 1922.
9 holes, 6378yds, Par 72, SSS 71.
Club membership 450.
Visitors advisable to contact in advance, no play Wed/Sun **Societies** apply in writing. **Green Fees** £25 per 18 holes (£30 weekends). **Prof** Gary Copeman **Facilities** ⊗ ⅷ ⅃ 🍺 ♀ ⚘ 🏠 ⸰ **Location** NW side of town centre off A5267

Hotel ★★ 70% Bold Hotel, 585 Lord St, SOUTHPORT ☎ 01704 532578 23 en suite

Bidston Bidston Link Rd CH44 2HR ☎ 0151 638 3412
Parkland course, with westerly winds. Flat easy walking.
18 holes, 6233yds, Par 70, SSS 70.
Club membership 600.
Visitors groups of 4 or more should contact in advance. **Societies** must apply in writing. **Green Fees** not confirmed. **Prof** Mark Eagle **Facilities** ⊗ ⅷ ⅃ 🍺 ♀ ⚘ 🏠 🇹 🛇 **Location** 0.5m W of M53 junc 1 entrance off A551

Hotel ★★★ 68% Leasowe Castle Hotel, Leasowe Rd, MORETON ☎ 0151 606 9191 47 en suite

Leasowe Moreton CH46 3RD
☎ 0151 677 5852 📠 0151 604 1448
A semi-links, seaside course which has recently undergone landscaping on the first five holes, new mounds removing the former rather flat appearance.
18 holes, 6151yds, Par 71, SSS 71.
Club membership 637.

Continued

Visitors telephone professional (0151 678 5460). Handicap certificate required. Not Sat play and not before noon on Sun. **Societies** contact in advance. **Green Fees** not confirmed. **Cards** ☷ ☰ 💷 🏧 📷 🖃 **Prof** Andrew Ayres **Course Designer** John Ball Jnr **Facilities** ⊗ ⅀ 🏌 ⬛ 🍴 ♀ ⚘ 🛆 ⛳ 🍸 ✐ **Conf** Corporate Hospitality Days available **Location** 2m W on A551

Hotel ★★★ 68% Leasowe Castle Hotel, Leasowe Rd, MORETON ☎ 0151 606 9191 47 en suite

Wallasey Bayswater Rd CH45 8LA
☎ 0151 691 1024 📠 0151 638 8988
e-mail: wallaseygc@aol.com
A well-established sporting links, adjacent to the Irish Sea, with huge sandhills and many classic holes where the player's skills are often combined with good fortune. Large, firm greens and fine views but not for the faint-hearted.
18 holes, 6503yds, Par 72, SSS 72, Course record 65. Club membership 650.
Visitors must contact one month in advance. **Societies** must apply in writing or telephone. **Green Fees** £60 per day, £50 per round (£75/£65 weekends & bank holidays). **Cards** 📷 **Prof** Mike Adams **Course Designer** Tom Morris **Facilities** ⊗ ⅀ 🏌 ⬛ ♀ ⚘ 🛆 ⛳ 🍸 ✐ **Location** N side of town centre off A554

Hotel ★★★ 70% Grove House Hotel, Grove Rd, WALLASEY ☎ 0151 639 3947 & 0151 630 4558 📠 0151 639 0028 14 en suite

Warren Grove Rd CH45 0JA ☎ 0151 639 8323
e-mail: golfer@warrengc.freeserve.co.uk
Short, undulating links course with first-class greens and prevailing winds off the sea.
9 holes, 5854yds, Par 72, SSS 68, Course record 68. Club membership 100.
Visitors welcome except Sun 7-11am. **Societies** contact in advance. **Green Fees** terms on application. **Prof** Mark Eagles **Facilities** 🏠 ⛳ ✐ **Location** N side of town centre off A554

Hotel ★★★ 68% Leasowe Castle Hotel, Leasowe Rd, MORETON ☎ 0151 606 9191 47 en suite

NORFOLK

BARNHAM BROOM   Map 05 TG00

Barnham Broom Hotel, Golf, Conference, Leisure Honingham Rd NR9 4DD
☎ 01603 759552 & 759393 📠 01603 758224
e-mail: enquiry@barnhambroomhotel.co.uk
Valley course meanders through the River Yare Valley, parkland and mature trees. Hill course has wide fairways, heavily guarded greens and spectacular views.
Valley Course: 18 holes, 6483yds, Par 72, SSS 71.
Hill Course: 18 holes, 6495yds, Par 71, SSS 71.
Club membership 500.
Visitors must contact in advance on 01603 759552. **Societies** must contact in advance on 01603 759393 or 759552 **Green Fees** £30 for 18 holes (£40 weekends). **Cards** ☷ ☰ ☰ 💷 🏧 📷 🖃 **Prof** A Rudge **Course Designer** Frank Pennink **Facilities** ⊗ ⅀ 🏌 ⬛ ♀ ⚘ 🛆 ⛳ 🍸 📭 ➘ ⚒ ✐ 🍸 **Leisure** hard tennis courts, heated indoor swimming pool, squash, sauna, solarium,
Continued

gymnasium, 3 academy holes. Golf school. Squash tuition. **Conf** fac available Corporate Hospitality Days available **Location** 10m SW of Norwich, off A47 at Honingham or A11 at Wymondham

Hotel ★★★ 75% Barnham Broom Hotel, Golf & Country Club, BARNHAM BROOM ☎ 01603 759393 759522 📠 01603 758224 52 en suite

BAWBURGH   Map 05 TG10

Bawburgh Glen Lodge, Marlingford Rd NR9 3LU
☎ 01603 740404 📠 01603 740403
e-mail: info@bawburgh.com
Undulating course, mixture of parkland and heathland. The main feature is a large glacial swale which meanders its way down to the River Yare creating many interesting tee and green locations. Excellent 18th hole to finish requiring a long accurate second shot to clear the lake in front of the elevated green.
18 holes, 6231yds, Par 70, SSS 70, Course record 64. Club membership 750.
Visitors must contact in advance, limited play at weekends. **Societies** must contact in advance. **Green Fees** terms on application. **Cards** ☷ ☰ 📷 🖃 **Prof** Chris Potter **Course Designer** John Barnard **Facilities** ⊗ 🏌 ⬛ ♀ 🛆 🏠 ➘ ⚒ ✐ 🍸 **Conf** Corporate Hospitality Days available **Location** S of Royal Norfolk Showground, on A47, follow signs to Bamburgh

Hotel ★★★ 74% Park Farm Hotel, HETHERSETT ☎ 01603 810264 5 en suite 42 annexe en suite

BRANCASTER   Map 09 TF74

Royal West Norfolk PE31 8AX
☎ 01485 210223 📠 01485 210087
If you want to see what golf courses were like years ago, then go to the Royal West Norfolk where tradition exudes from both clubhouse and course. Close by the sea, the links are laid out in the grand manner and are characterised by sleepered greens, superb cross-bunkering and salt marshes.
18 holes, 6428yds, Par 71, SSS 71, Course record 66. Club membership 825.
Visitors must contact well in advance. Restrictions at weekends and in Aug. **Societies** must contact Secretary in advance. **Green Fees** terms on applicatiobn. **Cards** ☷ ☰ ☰ 📷 **Prof** S Rayner **Course Designer** Holcombe-Ingleby **Facilities** ⊗ ⅀ 🏌 ⬛ ♀ 🛆 🏠 ⛳ 🍸 ✐ **Location** 7m E of Hunstanton. In Brancaster village turn N at the beach/Broad Lane junct with A149 for 1m

Hotel ★★ 75% The White Horse, BRANCASTER STAITHE ☎ 01485 210262 7 en suite 8 annexe en suite

CROMER   Map 09 TG24

Royal Cromer 145 Overstrand Rd NR27 0JH
☎ 01263 512884 📠 01263 512430
e-mail: general.manager@royal-cromer.com
Seaside course set out on cliff edge, hilly and subject to wind. Challenging upland course with spectacular views out to sea and overlooking town. Strong sea breezes affect the clifftop holes, the most famous being the 14th (the Lighthouse) which has a green in the shadow of the lighthouse.
Continued

18 holes, 6508yds, Par 72, SSS 72, Course record 67. Club membership 700.
Visitors must contact in advance, handicap certificate preferred. **Societies** must contact in advance. **Green Fees** £37 per day (£50 weekends & bank holidays). **Cards** 🏧 💳 📧 🟦 💷 **Prof** Lee Patterson **Course Designer** J H Taylor **Facilities** ⊗ 🎿 ⮾ 💺 ♀ 🔼 🏠 🍴 ↰ 🛒 ⚷

Conf Corporate Hospitality Days available **Location** 1m E on B1159

Hotel ★★ 72% Red Lion, Brook St, CROMER
☎ 01263 514964 12 en suite

DENVER   Map 05 TF60

Ryston Park PE38 0HH
☎ 01366 382133 📄 01366 383834
e-mail: rystonparkgc@fsnet.co.uk
Parkland course with two challenging par 4s to open. Water comes into play on holes 5, 6 and 7. The course is well wooded with an abundance of wild life.
9 holes, 6310yds, Par 70, SSS 70, Course record 66. Club membership 330.
Visitors must contact in advance. May not play weekends or bank holidays. **Societies** must apply in writing. **Green Fees** £30 per day; £20 per round. **Prof** Gary Potter **Course Designer** James Braid **Facilities** ⊗ 🎿 ⮾ 💺 ♀ 🔼 🏠 🍴 ⚷

Conf fac available Corporate Hospitality Days available **Location** 0.5m S on A10

Hotel ★★ 72% Castle Hotel, High St, DOWNHAM MARKET ☎ 01366 384311 12 en suite

DEREHAM   Map 09 TF91

Dereham Quebec Rd NR19 2DS
☎ 01362 695900 📄 01362 695904
e-mail: derehamgolfclub@dgolfclub.freeserve.co.uk
Parkland course.
9 holes, 6194yds, Par 71, SSS 70, Course record 64. Club membership 480.
Visitors must contact in advance. Weekends with member only. **Societies** must apply in writing or telephone in advance. **Green Fees** £22.50 per day; £17.50 per round. **Prof** Neil Allsebrook **Facilities** ⊗ 🎿 ⮾ 💺 ♀ 🔼 🏠 🛒 ⚷

Conf Corporate Hospitality Days available **Location** N side of town centre off B1110

Hotel ★★★ 75% Barnham Broom Hotel, Golf & Country Club, BARNHAM BROOM ☎ 01603 759393 759522
📄 01603 758224 52 en suite

The Norfolk Golf & Country Club Hingham Rd, Reymerston NR9 4QQ
☎ 01362 850297 📄 01362 850614
e-mail: ray.norfolkgolf@ukonline.co.uk
The course meanders through more than 200 acres of rolling Norfolk countryside, including ancient ditches, hedging and woodland. Large greens are built to USGA specification.
18 holes, 6609yds, Par 72, SSS 72, Course record 69. Club membership 500.
Visitors contact Golf reception for advance bookings. **Societies** apply in writing to the Society Organiser. **Green Fees** not confirmed. **Cards** 🏧 💳 💷 🟦 💷 **Prof** Tony Varney **Facilities** ⊗ 🎿 ⮾ 💺 ♀ 🔼 🏠 🍴 ↰ 🛒 ⚷ ↾
Leisure heated indoor swimming pool, sauna, solarium, gymnasium, pitch & putt. **Conf** fac available Corporate Hospitality Days available **Location** 12m W of Norwich, off B1135   *Continued*

Hotel ★★★ 75% Barnham Broom Hotel, Golf & Country Club, BARNHAM BROOM ☎ 01603 759393 759522
📄 01603 758224 52 en suite

FAKENHAM   Map 09 TF92

Fakenham Gallow Sports Centre, The Race Course N21 7NY ☎ 01328 863534
9 holes, 6174yds, Par 71, SSS 70, Course record 65.
Course Designer Cotton(UK)
Telephone for further details

Hotel ★★ 72% Crown Hotel, 6 Market Place, FAKENHAM ☎ 01328 851418 12 en suite

FRITTON   Map 05 TG40

Caldecott Hall Golf & Leisure Caldecott Hall, Beccles Rd NR31 9EY
☎ 01493 488488 📄 01493 488561
e-mail: caldecotthall@supanet
Facilities at Caldecott Hall include an 18-hole course with testing dog-leg fairways, a short par 3 9-hole course, a floodlit driving range, and good practising areas.

Main Course: 18 holes, 6685yards, Par 73, SSS 72. Club membership 500.
Visitors visitors always welcome, subject to availability. **Societies** arrangements in advance. **Green Fees** £20 per day (£26 weekends). **Cards** 🏧 💳 📧 🟦 💷 **Prof** Syer Shulver **Facilities** ⊗ 🎿 ⮾ 💺 ♀ 🔼 🏠 🍴 🛒 ⚷ ↾
Leisure heated indoor swimming pool, fishing, gymnasium, 9 hole par 3 course. **Conf** fac available Corporate Hospitality Days available **Location** On the A143 Beccles/Gt Yarmouth road at Fritton

Hotel ★★★ 72% Caldecott Hall Golf & Leisure, Caldecott Hall, Beccles Rd, FRITTON ☎ 01493 488488 8 en suite

GORLESTON ON SEA   Map 05 TG50

Gorleston Warren Rd NR31 6JT
☎ 01493 661911 📄 01493 661911
e-mail: manager@gorlestongolfclub.co.uk
Cliff top course, the most easterly in the British Isles. One of the outstanding features of the course is the 7th hole, which was rescued from the ravages of cliff erosion about 20 years ago. The green, only eight yards from the cliff edge, is at the mercy of the prevailing winds and club selection is critical.
18 holes, 6391yds, Par 71, SSS 71, Course record 68. Club membership 860.
Visitors advisable to contact in advance, must have handicap. Dress code in operation. **Societies** must apply in   *Continued*

writing. **Green Fees** terms on application. **Prof** Nick Brown **Course Designer** J H Taylor **Facilities** ⊗ ⏻ ⮧ ☕ ♀ ⛏ 🏠 ⚲ ⟋ **Conf** Corporate Hospitality Days available **Location** Between Gt Yarmouth and Lowestoft, signposted on the main A12 road

GREAT YARMOUTH   Map 05 TG50

Great Yarmouth & Caister Beach House,
Caister-on-Sea NR30 5TD
☎ 01493 728699 📠 01493 728831
e-mail: office@caistergolf.co.uk
This great old club, which celebrated its centenary in 1982, has played its part in the development of the game. It is a fine old-fashioned links where not many golfers have bettered the SSS in competitions. The 468 yard 8th (par 4) is a testing hole and the 7th is an extremely fine short hole. A feature of the course is a number of sleepered bunkers, a line of four bisecting the 4th.
18 holes, 6330yds, Par 70, SSS 70, Course record 65.
Club membership 720.
Visitors must contact in advance. Restricted weekends. **Societies** must apply in writing or telephone. **Green Fees** £30 per day; £18 after 2pm (£35/£22 weekends & bank holidays). **Cards** 🖃 💳 💳 🖃 **Prof** Martyn Clarke **Course Designer** H Colt **Facilities** ⊗ ⏻ ⮧ ☕ ♀ ⛏ 🏠 ⚲ **Location** 0.5m N off A149

·······················

Hotel ★★★ 71% Imperial Hotel, North Dr, GREAT YARMOUTH ☎ 01493 842000 39 en suite

HUNSTANTON   Map 09 TF64

Hunstanton Golf Course Rd PE36 6JQ
☎ 01485 532811 📠 01485 532319
e-mail: hunstanton.golf@eidosnet.co.uk
A championship links course set among some of the most natural golfing country in East Anglia. Keep out of the numerous bunkers and master the fast greens to play to your handicap - then you only have the wind to contend with! Good playing conditions all year round.
18 holes, 6759yds, Par 72, SSS 73.
Club membership 675.
Visitors must contact in advance and be a club member with current handicap certificate. Restricted at weekends & may not play bank holiday weekends. Play in two ball format ie singles or foursomes. **Societies** apply in advance. **Green Fees** £60 per day; £35 after 3pm (£70/£45 weekends). **Prof** James Dodds **Course Designer** James Braid **Facilities** ⊗ ⏻ by prior arrangement ⮧ ☕ ♀ ⛏ 🏠 ⚲ **Location** Off A149 in Old Hunstanton Village signposted

·······················

Hotel ★★★ 69% Le Strange Arms Hotel, Golf Course Rd, Old Hunstanton, HUNSTANTON ☎ 01485 534411 36 en suite

Searles Leisure Resort South Beach Rd PE36 5BB
☎ 01485 536010 📠 01485 533815
e-mail: golf@searles.co.uk
This 9 hole par 34 course is designed in a links style and provides generous fairways with good greens. A river runs through the 3rd and 4th holes and the par 5 8th follows the ancient reed bed to finish with the lakesided par 3 9th in front of the clubhouse. Good views of Hunstanton and the surrounding countryside.

9 holes, 2773yds, Par 34.
Club membership 200.
Visitors pay and play course. **Societies** telephone or e-mail in advance. **Green Fees** 18 holes £13.50, 9 holes £8 (£15.50/£9 weekends & bank holidays). **Cards** 🖃 💳 🖃 💳 🖾 **Course Designer** Paul Searle **Facilities** ⊗ ⏻ ⮧ ☕ ♀ ⛏ 🏠 ⚲ 🎿 ⚲ ⟋ ⚲ **Leisure** hard tennis courts, outdoor and indoor heated swimming pools, fishing, sauna, solarium, gymnasium, bowls green. **Conf** fac available Corporate Hospitality Days available **Location** A149 to Hunstanton from King's Lynn, 2nd left at roundabout, straight over mini roundabout, 1st left and follow signs to 'Sports and Country Club'

·······················

Hotel ★★★ 69% Le Strange Arms Hotel, Golf Course Rd, Old Hunstanton, HUNSTANTON ☎ 01485 534411 36 en suite

KING'S LYNN   Map 09 TF62

Eagles 39 School Rd, Tilney All Saints PE34 4RS
☎ 01553 827147 📠 01553 829777
e-mail: shop@eagles-golf-tennis.co.uk
Parkland course with plenty of water hazards and bunkers. Also par 3 course and floodlit, covered driving range.
9 holes, 4284yds, Par 64, SSS 61, Course record 64.
Club membership 200.
Visitors Dress code required. **Societies** must apply in writing. **Green Fees** 18 holes £12.50; 9 holes £8.50 (weekends £15.50/£9.50). **Cards** 🖃 💳 💳 🖃 💳 🖾 **Prof** Nigel Pickerell **Course Designer** D W Horn **Facilities** ⊗ by prior arrangement ⏻ ⮧ ☕ ♀ ⛏ 🏠 ⚲ ⟋ **Leisure** hard tennis courts, par 3 course. **Conf** Corporate Hospitality Days available **Location** Off A47 at roundabout to Tilney All Saints between Kings Lynn and Wisbech

·······················

Hotel ★★★ 62% The Duke's Head Hotel, Tuesday Market Place, KING'S LYNN ☎ 01553 774996 71 en suite

King's Lynn Castle Rising PE31 6BD
☎ 01553 631654 📠 631036
e-mail: klgc@eidosnet.co.uk
The course is set among silver birch and fir woodland and benefits, especially in the winter, from well-drained sandy soil.

18 holes, 6609yds, Par 72, SSS 73, Course record 64.
Club membership 910.
Visitors must contact in advance, handicap certificate required. **Societies** apply in writing or by phone in advance. **Green Fees** £45 per day (£50 weekends). **Prof** John Reynolds **Course Designer** Thomas & Allis **Facilities** ⊗ ⏻ ⮧ ☕ ♀ ⛏ 🏠 ⚲ ⟋ **Leisure** Snooker. **Location** 4m NE off A149

Continued   Continued

Hotel ★★★ 62% The Duke's Head Hotel, Tuesday Market Place, KING'S LYNN ☎ 01553 774996 71 en suite

MATTISHALL   Map 09 TG01

Mattishall South Green NR20 3JZ
☎ 01362 850111
Mattishall has the distinction of having the longest hole in Norfolk at a very demanding 625yds.
9 holes, 3300mtrs, Par 72, SSS 69.
Club membership 120.
Visitors no restrictions. **Societies** welcome. **Green Fees** not confirmed. **Course Designer** B Todd **Facilities** ⚑ ♀ ♨ ⚑ 🛒 🏌 **Location** 0.75m S of Mattishall Church

Hotel ★★★ 75% Barnham Broom Hotel, Golf & Country Club, BARNHAM BROOM ☎ 01603 759393 759522 ▤ 01603 758224 52 en suite

MIDDLETON   Map 09 TF61

Middleton Hall Hall Orchards PE32 1RH
☎ 01553 841800 ▤ 01553 841800
e-mail: middleton-hall@btclick.com
The setting is one of natural undulations and mature specimen trees, offering a most attractive environment for golf. The architecturally designed course provides a challenge for the competent golfer; there is also a covered floodlit driving range and practice putting green.
18 holes, 6004yds, Par 71, SSS 68, Course record 70.
Club membership 600.
Visitors no restrictions. **Societies** must contact in advance. **Green Fees** £30 per day; £25 per round (£35/£30 weekends & bank holidays). **Cards** 💳 💳 💳 💳 **Prof** Steve White **Course Designer** D Scott **Facilities** ⚑ ♨ ♀ ♨ ♀ ♨ 🛒 🏌 **Conf** Corporate Hospitality Days available **Location** 4m from King's Lynn on A47 towards Norwich

Hotel ★★★ Congham Hall Country House Hotel, Lynn Rd, GRIMSTON ☎ 01485 600250 14 en suite

MUNDESLEY   Map 09 TG33

Mundesley Links Rd NR11 8ES
☎ 01263 720279 & 720095 ▤ 01263 720279
9 holes, 5377yds, Par 68, SSS 66, Course record 64.
Location W side of village off B1159
Telephone for further details

Hotel ★★ 72% Red Lion, Brook St, CROMER ☎ 01263 514964 12 en suite

NORWICH   Map 05 TG20

Costessey Park Old Costessey NR8 5AL
☎ 01603 746333 & 747085 ▤ 01603 746185
The course lies in the gently contoured Two River valley, providing players with a number of holes that bring the river and man-made lakes into play.
18 holes, 5900yds, Par 71, SSS 69, Course record 65.
Club membership 600.
Visitors may not play competition days, prior booking required for weekends. **Societies** welcome by prior arrangement. **Green Fees** £30 per day/round. **Cards** 💳 💳 💳 **Prof** Andrew Young **Facilities** ⚑ ♨ ♀ ♨ ♀ ♨ 🛒 🏌

Hotel ★★★ 70% Quality Hotel Norwich, 2 Barnard Rd, Bowthorpe, NORWICH ☎ 01603 741161 80 en suite

De Vere Dunston Hall Hotel Ipswich Rd
NR14 8PQ ☎ 01508 470444 ▤ 01508 470689
e-mail: dhreception@devere-hotels.com
Parkland course with water features at many holes. Varied and challenging woodland setting. Floodlit driving range.
18 holes, 6300yds, Par 71, SSS 70, Course record 70.
Visitors must book in advance. **Societies** apply in writing or telephone for details. **Green Fees** not confirmed. **Cards** 💳 💳 💳 💳 💳 **Prof** Peter Briggs **Course Designer** M Shaw **Facilities** ⚑ ♨ ♀ ♨ ♀ ♨ 🛒 🏌 **Leisure** hard tennis courts, heated indoor swimming pool, sauna, solarium, gymnasium. **Conf** fac available Corporate Hospitality Days available **Location** On A140

Hotel ★★★★ 71% De Vere Dunston Hall, Ipswich Rd, NORWICH ☎ 01508 470444 130 en suite

Eaton Newmarket Rd NR4 6SF
☎ 01603 451686 & 452881 ▤ 01603 451686
e-mail: administrator@eatongc.co.uk
An undulating, tree-lined parkland course with excellent trees. Easy opening par 5 followed by an intimidating par 3 that is well bunkered with deep rough on both sides. The challenging 17th hole is uphill to a small hidden green and always needs more club than expected.

18 holes, 6114yds, Par 70, SSS 70, Course record 64.
Club membership 800.
Visitors restricted before 11.30am weekends. Advised to contact in advance. **Societies** must contact in advance. **Green Fees** £35 (£45 weekends). **Cards** 💳 💳 💳 💳 💳 **Prof** Mark Allen **Facilities** ⚑ ♨ by prior arrangement ♨ ♀ ♨ ♀ 🏌 **Location** 1.5m SW of city centre off A11

Hotel ★★★ 74% Park Farm Hotel, HETHERSETT ☎ 01603 810264 5 en suite 42 annexe en suite

Marriott Sprowston Manor Hotel & Country Club Wroxham Rd NR7 8RP
☎ 01603 254290 ▤ 01603 788884
e-mail: golfsales@marriotthotels.co.uk
Set in 100 acres of parkland, including an impressive collection of oak trees which provide a backdrop to many holes. The facilities include a 27-bay driving range.
18 holes, 6543yds, Par 71, SSS 71, Course record 70.
Club membership 600.
Visitors no restrictions. Advisable to book in advance. **Societies** must contact in advance. **Green Fees** £36 weekdays. **Cards** 💳 💳 💳 💳 💳 💳 **Prof** Guy D Ireson **Course Designer** Ross McMurray **Facilities** ⚑ ♨ ♨ ♀ ♨ ♀ ♨ 🛒 🏌 🏌 **Leisure** heated indoor

Continued

swimming pool, sauna, gymnasium. **Location** 4m NE from city centre on A1151

••••••••••••••••

Hotel ★★★★ 75% Marriott Sprowston Manor Hotel & Country Club, Sprowston Park, Wroxham Rd, Sprowston, NORWICH ☎ 01603 410871 94 en suite

Royal Norwich Drayton High Rd, Hellesdon
NR6 5AH ☎ 01603 429928 ◻ 01603 417945
e-mail: mail@royalnorwichgolf.co.uk
Undulating mature parkland course complimented with gorse. Largely unchanged since the alterations carried out by James Braid in 1924. A challenging test of golf.
18 holes, 6506yds, Par 72, SSS 72, Course record 65.
Club membership 700.
Visitors strongly recommended to contact in advance. Restricted weekends & bank holidays. **Societies** must contact in advance. **Green Fees** £38 per day; £24 per round after 2pm (£46/£30 weekends & bank holidays). **Prof** Dean Futter **Course Designer** James Braid **Facilities** ⊗ Ⅲↄↄ by prior arrangement ⅃ ♥ ♀ ♨ ≙ ♂ **Location** 2.5m NW of city centre on A1067

••••••••••••••••

Hotel ★★★ 70% Quality Hotel Norwich, 2 Barnard Rd, Bowthorpe, NORWICH ☎ 01603 741161 80 en suite

Wensum Valley Hotel, Golf & Country Club
Beech Av, Taverham NR8 6HP
☎ 01603 261012 ◻ 01603 261664
e-mail: enqs@wensumvalley.co.uk
An undulating, picturesque golf course situated on the side of a valley. The greens in particular are very undulating and always give the average golfer a testing time. The 12th hole from a raised tee provides a blind and windy tee shot and a very sloping green.
Valley Course: 18 holes, 6172yds, Par 72, SSS 70, Course record 72.
Wensum Course: 18 holes, Par 71, SSS 69.
Club membership 900.
Visitors no restrictions but advisable to book tee times at weekends. **Societies** apply in writing or by telephone. **Green Fees** not confirmed. **Cards** ▦ ▦ ▦ ▦ ▦ ◻
Prof Peter Whittle **Course Designer** B Todd **Facilities** ⊗
Ⅲↄↄ ♥ ♀ ♨ ≙ ♈ ≖ ♞ ♒ ♂ ℓ **Leisure** heated indoor swimming pool, fishing, sauna, solarium, gymnasium.
Conf Corporate Hospitality Days available **Location** 5m N of Norwich, off A1067

••••••••••••••••

Hotel ★★ 73% Stower Grange, School Rd, Drayton, NORWICH ☎ 01603 860210 11 en suite

SHERINGHAM Map 09 TG14

Sheringham Weybourne Rd NR26 8HG
☎ 01263 826129 ◻ 01263 825189
e-mail: sgc.sec@care4free.net
Splendid cliff-top links with gorse, good 'seaside turf' and plenty of space. Straight driving is essential for a low score. The course is close to the shore and can be very windswept, but offers magnificent views.
18 holes, 6495yds, Par 70, SSS 71, Course record 65.
Club membership 760.
Visitors must contact in advance & have handicap certificate. Restricted weekends. **Societies** bookings may be made in writing or by telephone. **Green Fees** terms on application. **Prof** M W Jubb **Course Designer** Tom Dunn
Facilities ⊗ Ⅲↄↄ ♥ ♀ ♨ ≙ ≖ ♂ **Location** W side of town centre on A149

Continued

Hotel ★★ 70% Beaumaris Hotel, South St, SHERINGHAM ☎ 01263 822370 21 en suite

SWAFFHAM Map 05 TF80

Swaffham Cley Rd PE37 8AE
☎ 01760 721621(secretary) ◻ 01760 721621
e-mail: swaffamgc@supanet.com
Heathland course and designated wildlife site in the heart of breckland country. Excellent drainage.
18 holes, 6544yds, Par 71, SSS 71.
Club membership 500.
Visitors must contact in advance. With member only at weekends & not before mid day. **Societies** must contact in advance. **Green Fees** not confirmed. **Prof** Peter Field
Course Designer Jonathan Gaunt **Facilities** ⊗ Ⅲↄↄ ♥ ♀ ♨ ≙ ♈ ♂ **Conf** fac available Corporate Hospitality Days available **Location** 1.5m SW of Swaffam. Turn off A47 Norwich/Yarmouth road.or A1065 Brandon to Fakenham road

••••••••••••••••

Hotel ★★★ 67% George Hotel, Station Rd, SWAFFHAM ☎ 01760 721238 29 en suite

THETFORD Map 05 TL88

Feltwell Thor Ave, Feltwell IP26 4AY
☎ 01842 827644 ◻ 01842 827644
e-mail: secretary@feltwellgolfclub.f9.co.uk
In spite of being an inland links, this 9-hole course is still open and windy.
9 holes, 6488yds, Par 72, SSS 71, Course record 71.
Club membership 400.
Visitors dress restriction, no jeans,tracksuits or collarless shirts, golf shoes to be worn. **Societies** apply in writing or telephone in advance. **Green Fees** £16 per day (£25 weekends & bank holidays). **Prof** Christian Puttock
Facilities ⊗ Ⅲↄↄ ♥ ♀ ♨ (closed Mon) ≙ ♂ **Conf** Corporate Hospitality Days available **Location** On B1112, next to RAF Feltwell

••••••••••••••••

Hotel ★★ 66% The Thomas Paine Hotel, White Hart St, THETFORD ☎ 01842 755631 13 en suite

Thetford Brandon Rd IP24 3NE
☎ 01842 752169 ◻ 01842 766212
e-mail: sally@thetfordgolfclub.co.uk
This is a course with a good pedigree. It was laid out by a fine golfer, C.H. Mayo, later altered by James Braid and then again altered by another famous course designer, Mackenzie Ross. It is a testing heathland course with a particularly stiff finish.
18 holes, 6849yds, Par 72, SSS 73, Course record 66.
Club membership 750.
Visitors pre booking advisable, may not play weekends or bank holidays except with member. Handicap certificate required. **Societies** must contact in advance, Wed-Fri only.
Green Fees £40 per day/round. **Cards** ▦ ▦ ▦ ▦ ◻
Prof Gary Kitley **Course Designer** James Braid **Facilities** ⊗ Ⅲↄↄ ♥ ♀ ♨ ≙ ♈ ♂ **Location** 2m W of Thetford on B1107

••••••••••••••••

Hotel ★★ 66% The Thomas Paine Hotel, White Hart St, THETFORD ☎ 01842 755631 13 en suite

Booking a tee time is always advisable.

WATTON   Map 05 TF90

Richmond Park Saham Rd IP25 6EA
☎ 01953 881803 📠 01953 881817
e-mail: info@richmondpark.co.uk
Compact parkland course with mature and young trees set around the Little Wissey river and spread over 100 acres of Norfolk countryside. The Little Wissey river and other water hazards create an interesting but not daunting challenge.

18 holes, 6258yds, Par 71, SSS 70, Course record 69. Club membership 600.
Societies must contact in advance. **Green Fees** terms on application. **Cards** 🔲 🔲 🔲 🔲 🔲 🔲 **Prof** Alan Hemsley **Course Designer** D Jessup/D Scott **Facilities** ⊗ 🍴🛒 💪 ♀ ⚒ 🏠 ⛳ 🏌 🐎 🚃 ⚓ ⛳ 🏌 **Leisure** gymnasium. **Conf** Corporate Hospitality Days available **Location** 500yds NW of town centre

Hotel ★★★ 67% George Hotel, Station Rd, SWAFFHAM ☎ 01760 721238 29 en suite

WESTON LONGVILLE   Map 09 TG11

Weston Park NR9 5JW
☎ 01603 872363 📠 01603 873040
e-mail: golf@weston-park.co.uk
Superb, challenging course, set in 200 acres of magnificent, mature woodland and parkland.
18 holes, 6648yds, Par 72, SSS 72, Course record 69. Club membership 450.
Visitors must telephone for tee times on 01603 872998. **Societies** must telephone for prices and tee times. **Green Fees** £32 per 18 holes (£40 weekends). **Cards** 🔲 🔲 🔲 🔲 🔲 **Prof** Michael Few **Course Designer** Golf Technology **Facilities** ⊗ 🍴 💪 ♀ ⚒ 🏠 🐎 🚃 ⚓ **Leisure** hard tennis courts, croquet lawn. **Conf** fac available Corporate Hospitality Days available **Location** Follow brown signs off A1067 or A47. 9m NW of Norwich

Hotel ★★★ 70% Quality Hotel Norwich, 2 Barnard Rd, Bowthorpe, NORWICH ☎ 01603 741161 80 en suite

WEST RUNTON   Map 09 TG14

Links Country Park Hotel & Golf Club
NR27 9QH ☎ 01263 838215 📠 01263 838264
e-mail: sales@links-hotel.co.uk
Parkland course 500 yds from the sea, with superb views overlooking West Runton. The hotel offers extensive leisure facilities.
9 holes, 4842yds, Par 66, SSS 64. Club membership 300.

Visitors restrictions weekends. **Societies** must telephone in advance. **Green Fees** terms on application. **Cards** 🔲 🔲 🔲 🔲 🔲 **Prof** James Tuck **Course Designer** J.H Taylor **Facilities** ⊗ 🍴🛒 💪 ♀ ⚒ 🏠 🐎 🚃 ⚓ ⛳ **Leisure** hard tennis courts, heated indoor swimming pool, sauna, solarium, gymnasium. **Location** S side of village off A149

Hotel ★★ 70% Beaumaris Hotel, South St, SHERINGHAM ☎ 01263 822370 21 en suite

NORTHAMPTONSHIRE

CHACOMBE   Map 04 SP44

Cherwell Edge OX17 2EN
☎ 01295 711591 📠 01295 713674
e-mail: cegc@ukonline.co.uk
Parkland course over chalk giving good drainage. The back nine is short and tight with mature trees. The front nine is longer and more open. The course is well bunkered with 3 holes where water can come into play for the wayward golfer.

18 holes, 6092yds, Par 70, SSS 68, Course record 64. Club membership 500.
Visitors no restrictions but golf shoes to be worn and tidy appearance expected. Some restrictions at weekends. **Societies** must apply in advance. **Green Fees** Mon-Thu £20 per 18 holes (£25 weekends). **Cards** 🔲 🔲 🔲 🔲 **Prof** Jason Newman **Course Designer** R Davies **Facilities** ⊗ 🍴🛒 💪 ♀ ⚒ 🏠 🐎 🚃 ⚓ ⛳ 🏌 **Conf** fac available Corporate Hospitality Days available **Location** M40 junct 11, 0.5m S off B4525, 2m from Banbury

Hotel ★★★ 71% Whately Hall, Banbury Cross, BANBURY ☎ 0870 400 8104 69 en suite

COLD ASHBY   Map 04 SP67

Cold Ashby Stanford Rd NN6 6EP
☎ 01604 740548 📠 01604 740548
e-mail: coldashby.golfclub@virgin.net
Undulating parkland course, nicely matured, with superb views. The 27 holes consist of three loops of nine, which can be interlinked with each other. All three loops have their own challenge and any combination of two loops will give an excellent course. The start of the Elkington loop offers five holes of scenic beauty and testing golf and the 3rd on the Winwick loop is a 200-yard par 3 from a magnificent plateau tee.
Ashby-Elkington: 18 holes, 6308yds, Par 72, SSS 71, Course record 68.
Elkington-Winwick: 18 holes, 6293yds, Par 70, SSS 71, Course record 69.

Continued   *Continued*

Winwick-Ashby: 18 holes, 6047yds, Par 70, SSS 70, Course record 65.
Club membership 600.
Visitors start time must be reserved at weekends. **Societies** must contact in advance. **Green Fees** £16 per round (£18.50 weekends). **Cards** 〓 〓 〓 〓 〓 **Prof** Shane Rose **Course Designer** David Croxton **Facilities** ⊗ ⅷ ⅂ ⚑ ♀ ☖ ⚐ ♈ ⚒ ♿ ∮ (**Conf** fac available Corporate Hospitality Days available **Location** Close to junct 1 A14 & junct 18 M1 midway between Rugby, Leicester & Northampton

Hotel Ⓤ Holiday Inn Rugby/Northampton, CRICK ☎ 0870 400 9059 88 en suite

COLLINGTREE   Map 04 SP75

Collingtree Park Windingbrook Ln NN4 0XN
☎ 01604 700000 & 701202 📠 01604 702600
e-mail: info@collingtreeparkgolf.com

18 holes, 6776yds, Par 72, SSS 72, Course record 66.
Course Designer Johnny Miller **Location** M1-junc 15 on A508 to Northampton
Telephone for further details

Hotel ★★★★ 70% Northampton Marriott Hotel, Eagle Dr, NORTHAMPTON ☎ 01604 768700 120 en suite

CORBY   Map 04 SP88

Corby Public Stamford Rd, Weldon NN17 3JH
☎ 01536 260756 📠 01536 260756
Municipal course laid out on made-up quarry ground and open to prevailing wind. Played over by Priors Hall Club. A hidden treasure and good value for money.
18 holes, 6677yds, Par 72, SSS 72, Course record 68.
Club membership 600.
Visitors are advised to book in advance. **Societies** must contact in advance. **Green Fees** £12 for 18 holes (£15.50 weekends). **Cards** 〓 〓 〓 〓 〓 **Prof** Jeff Bradbrook **Course Designer** F Hawtree **Facilities** ⊗ ⅷ ⅂ ⚑ ♀ ☖ ☗ ♈ ⚒ ♿ ∮ **Location** 4m NE on A43

Inn ♦♦ Raven Hotel, Rockingham Rd, CORBY ☎ 01536 202313 17 rms (5 en suite)

DAVENTRY   Map 04 SP56

Daventry & District Norton Rd NN11 5LS
☎ 01327 702829
A hilly course with splendid views, on the site of an iron age fort and Roman camp.
9 holes, 5812yds, Par 69, SSS 68, Course record 67.
Club membership 350.

Visitors no visitors before 11.30am Sun mornings.
Societies contact the club secretary. **Green Fees** terms on application. **Facilities** ♈ ♀ ☖ 🏠 **Location** 0.5m East

Hotel ★★★★ 62% Hanover International Hotel & Club, Sedgemoor Way, DAVENTRY ☎ 0870 241 7078 138 en suite

FARTHINGSTONE   Map 04 SP65

Farthingstone Hotel & Golf Course
NN12 8HA ☎ 01327 361291 📠 01327 361645
e-mail: interest@farthingstone.co.uk
A mature and challenging course set in picturesque countryside.
18 holes, 6299yds, Par 70, SSS 70, Course record 68.
Club membership 350.
Visitors must contact in advance. **Societies** must contact in advance. **Green Fees** terms on application. **Cards** 〓 〓 〓 〓 〓 **Prof** Luke Brockway **Course Designer** Don Donaldson **Facilities** ⊗ ⅷ ⅂ ♀ ☖ ♈ ⚒ ♿ ∮ **Leisure** squash, Snooker room. **Conf** fac available Corporate Hospitality Days available **Location** W of M1 junct 16 close to the village of Farthingstone.

Hotel ⇧ Premier Lodge (Daventry), High St, WEEDON ☎ 0870 9906364 47 en suite

HELLIDON   Map 04 SP55

Hellidon Lakes Hotel & Country Club
NN11 6GG ☎ 01327 262550 📠 01327 262559
e-mail: hellidon@marstonhotels.com
27 holes of interesting and challenging golf set in rolling countryside, designed by David Snell.

18 holes, 6691yds, Par 72, SSS 72.
Club membership 300.
Visitors 18 hole course; must contact in advance & have handicap certificate at weekends. 9 hole; open to beginners. **Societies** must telephone in advance. **Green Fees** £20 per round (£30 weekends & bank holidays). **Cards** 〓 〓 〓 〓 〓 〓 **Prof** Joe Kingstone **Course Designer** D Snell **Facilities** ⊗ ⅷ ⅂ ♀ ☖ ♈ ⚒ ♿ ∮ **Leisure** hard tennis courts, heated indoor swimming pool, fishing, solarium, gymnasium, golf simulator, ten pin bowling. **Conf** fac available Corporate Hospitality Days available **Location** M1 J16, A45 to Daventry, onto A361 to Banbury, right towards Hellidon, take 2nd right

Hotel ★★★★ 74% Hellidon Lakes Hotel & Country Club, HELLIDON ☎ 01327 262550 110 en suite

> **Looking for a driving range? Refer to the listing of driving ranges at the back of this guide.**

Continued

HELLIDON LAKES
AA ★★★★ RAC

Hellidon Daventry
Northamptonshire NN11 6GG

HOTEL & GOLF CENTRE

www.marstonhotels.com

GOLF SOCIETIES WELCOME

An unbelievable 27 holes of 3 loops of nine holes with seventeen leaks spread evenly across the loops, strategically placed to catch the 'bad shot'. Enjoy the challenging fairways in glorious unspoilt countryside with gently rolling hills and valleys.

Golf Tuition ★ Special Winter Rates ★ Professional Shop

TEL: 01327 262550 FAX: 01327 262559

MARSTON HOTELS 𝑚

KETTERING Map 04 SP87

Kettering Headlands NN15 6XA
☎ 01536 511104 ▤ 01536 511104
e-mail: secretary@kettering-golf.co.uk
A very pleasant, mainly flat meadowland course with easy walking.
18 holes, 6081yds, Par 69, SSS 69, Course record 63.
Club membership 700.
Visitors welcome but with member only weekends & bank holidays. **Societies** Wed & Fri only, apply in writing.
Green Fees £28 per round. **Prof** Kevin Theobald **Course Designer** Tom Morris **Facilities** ⊗ ⅏ ⓑ ⚑ ♀ ⚲ 🕾 ☞ ⌀ **Conf** Corporate Hospitality Days available **Location** S side of town centre
....
Hotel ★★★★ 74% Kettering Park Hotel & Spa, Kettering Parkway, KETTERING ☎ 01536 416666 119 en suite

Pytchley Golf Lodge Kettering Rd, Pytchley
NN14 1EY ☎ 01536 511527 ▤ 01536 519113
Nine hole pay & play course, designed with complete beginner in mind, but still challenging for better handicap players.
9 holes, 2574yards, Par 34, SSS 65, Course record 70.
Club membership 300.
Visitors pay and play **Societies** telephone in advance
Green Fees terms on application. **Prof** Peter Machin
Course Designer Roger Griffiths Associates **Facilities** ⊗ ⓑ ⚑ ♀ ⚲ 🕾 ⌀ ☞ **Location** off junct 9 A14/A509 towards Kettering follow tourist signs
....
Hotel ★★★★ 74% Kettering Park Hotel & Spa, Kettering Parkway, KETTERING ☎ 01536 416666 119 en suite

---

NORTHAMPTON Map 04 SP76

Brampton Heath Sandy Ln, Church Brampton
NN6 8AX ☎ 01604 843939 ▤ 01604 843885
e-mail: slawrence@bhgc.co.uk
Appealing to both the novice and experienced golfer, this beautiful, well drained heathland course affords panoramic views over Northampton. It plays like an inland links in the summer - fast running fairways, true rolling greens with the wind always providing a challenge. Excellent play all year round.
18 holes, 6366yds, Par 71, SSS 70, Course record 66.
Club membership 500.
Visitors advisable to book especially for weekends, may book up to 8 days in advance. **Societies** write or telephone for details. **Green Fees** not confirmed. **Cards** 🖃 🖃 🖃 ⓩ **Prof** Richard Hudson **Course Designer** D Snell
Facilities ⊗ ⅏ ⓑ ⚑ ♀ ⚲ 🕾 ☞ 🤝 ⌀ ☞ **Conf** fac available Corporate Hospitality Days available **Location** Signposted off old A50 Kingsthorpe to Welford road, 2m N of Kingsthorpe
....
Hotel ★★★ 72% Lime Trees Hotel, 8 Langham Place, Barrack Rd, NORTHAMPTON ☎ 01604 632188
27 en suite

Delapre Golf Complex Eagle Dr, Nene Valley
Way NN4 7DU ☎ 01604 764036 ▤ 01604 706378
e-mail: delapre@btinternet.com
Rolling parkland course, part of municipal golf complex, which includes two 9-hole par 3 courses, pitch-and-putt and 40-bay floodlit driving range.
The Oaks: 18 holes, 6269yds, Par 70, SSS 70, Course record 66.
Hardingstone Course: 9 holes, 2109yds, Par 32, SSS 32.
Club membership 500.
Visitors no restrictions but advance booking advised for weekends. **Societies** must book and pay full green fees 2 weeks in advance. **Green Fees** terms on application. **Cards** 🖃 🖃 🖃 🖃 ⓩ **Prof** John Cuddihy **Course Designer** John Jacobs/John Corby **Facilities** ⊗ ⅏ ⓑ ⚑ ♀ ⚲ 🕾 ☞ 🤝 ⌀ ☞ **Conf** Corporate Hospitality Days available **Location** 3m from M1 junct 15 on A508/A45
....
Hotel ★★★ 64% Quality Hotel Northampton, Ashley Way, Weston Favell, NORTHAMPTON ☎ 01604 739955
33 en suite 38 annexe en suite

Kingsthorpe Kingsley Rd NN2 7BU
☎ 01604 710610 ▤ 01604 710610
e-mail: secretary@kingsthorpe-golf.co.uk
A compact, undulating parkland course set within the town boundary. Not a long course but the undulating terrain provides a suitable challenge for golfers of all standards. While not a hilly course, the valley that runs through it ensures plenty of sloping lies. The 18th hole is claimed to be the longest 400yds in the county when played into wind and is amongst the finest finishing holes in the area. New clubhouse recently opened.
18 holes, 5918yds, Par 69, SSS 69, Course record 63.
Club membership 600.
Visitors must contact in advance. With member only weekends. **Societies** must contact in advance. **Green Fees** £25 per day (weekdays only). **Cards** 🖃 🖃 🖃 ⓩ **Prof** Paul Armstrong **Course Designer** Mr Alison/ H Colt
Facilities ⊗ ⅏ ⓑ ⚑ ♀ ⚲ 🕾 ⌀ **Conf** fac available **Location** N side of town centre on A5095 between the Racecourse and Kingsthorpe

Continued

Hotel ★★★ 64% Quality Hotel Northampton, Ashley Way, Weston Favell, NORTHAMPTON ☎ 01604 739955 33 en suite 38 annexe en suite

Northampton Harlestone NN7 4EF

☎ 01604 845155 📄 01604 820262
e-mail: golf@northamptongolfclub.co.uk
Parkland course with water in play on three holes.
18 holes, 6615yds, Par 72, SSS 72, Course record 63.
Club membership 750.
Visitors must contact in advance and have handicap certificate. With member only at weekends, no visitors on Wed. **Societies** must contact in advance. **Green Fees** terms on application. **Cards** 〰️ 🔲 🔲 📶 **Prof** Barry Randall **Course Designer** Sinclair Steel **Facilities** ⛄ 🏠 ✅ **Conf** Corporate Hospitality Days available **Location** NW of town centre on A428

Hotel ★★★ 72% Lime Trees Hotel, 8 Langham Place, Barrack Rd, NORTHAMPTON ☎ 01604 632188 27 en suite

Northamptonshire County Golf Ln, Church

Brampton NN6 8AZ ☎ 01604 843025 📄 01604 843463
e-mail: secretary@countrygolfclub.org.uk
A fine, traditional championship golf course situated on undulating heathland with areas of gorse, heather and extensive coniferous and deciduous woodland. A river and a railway line pass through the course. Visit website for pictorial view of each hole.
18 holes, 6505yds, Par 70, SSS 72, Course record 65.
Club membership 750.
Visitors restricted weekends. May not play on bank holidays. Must contact in advance and have a handicap certificate. **Societies** Wed/Thu only, must contact in advance. **Green Fees** £45 per day. (Winter £30 per day). **Prof** Tim Rouse **Course Designer** H S Colt **Facilities** ⛄ 〰️ 🍽️ 🍺 ⛄ 🏠 🅿️ 🚬 ✅ 🚩 **Conf** Corporate Hospitality Days available **Location** 5m NW of Northampton, off A5199

Hotel ★★★ 64% Quality Hotel Northampton, Ashley Way, Weston Favell, NORTHAMPTON ☎ 01604 739955 33 en suite 38 annexe en suite

Overstone Park Billing Ln NN6 0AP

☎ 01604 647666 📄 01604 642635
e-mail: steph@overstonepark.co.uk
18 holes, 6602yds, Par 72, SSS 72, Course record 69.
Course Designer Donald Steel **Location** Exit M1 junct15, follow A45 to Billing Aquadrome turn off, course is 2m on Gt Billing Way
Telephone for further details

Hotel ★★★ 72% Lime Trees Hotel, 8 Langham Place, Barrack Rd, NORTHAMPTON ☎ 01604 632188 27 en suite

OUNDLE Map 04 TL08

Oundle Benefield Rd PE8 4EZ

☎ 01832 273267 (Gen Manager) 272273 (pro)
📄 01832 273267
e-mail: oundlegc@btopenworld.com
Undulating parkland course set in pleasant countryside. Stream running through course in play on nine holes. Small greens demand careful placement from tees and accurate iron play.

18 holes, 6265yds, Par 72, SSS 70, Course record 63.
Club membership 600.
Visitors may not play before 10.30am weekends unless with member. must contact in advance. Ladies day Tue. **Societies** must apply in advance, weekdays only. **Green Fees** £30 per day; £23 per round (£40 per day/round weekends). **Cards** 〰️ 🔲 🔲 📶 🔲 **Prof** Richard Keys **Facilities** ⛄ 〰️ 🍽️ 🍺 🍺 🏠 🅿️ ✅ **Location** 1m W on A427

Inn ♦♦ Raven Hotel, Rockingham Rd, CORBY
☎ 01536 202313 17 rms (5 en suite)

STAVERTON Map 04 SP56

Staverton Park Staverton Park NN11 6JT

☎ 01327 302000
18 holes, 6661yds, Par 71, SSS 72, Course record 65.
Course Designer Cmdr John Harris **Location** 0.75m NE of Staverton on A425
Telephone for further details

Hotel ★★★★ 62% Hanover International Hotel & Club, Sedgemoor Way, DAVENTRY ☎ 0870 241 7078 138 en suite

WELLINGBOROUGH Map 04 SP86

Rushden Kimbolton Rd, Chelveston NN9 6AN

☎ 01933 418511 📄 01933 418511
Parkland course with brook running through the middle.
10 holes, 6335yds, Par 71, SSS 70, Course record 68.
Club membership 400.
Visitors may not play Wed afternoon. With member only weekends. **Societies** must apply in writing. **Green Fees** terms on application. **Facilities** ⛄ 〰️ 🍽️ 🍺 🍺 ⛄ **Location** 2m E of Higham Ferrers on Kimbolton Rd

Hotel ⬆️ Travelodge Wellingborough, Saunders Lodge, RUSHDEN ☎ 08700 850 950 40 en suite

Wellingborough Great Harrowden Hall NN9 5AD

☎ 01933 677234 📄 01933 679379
e-mail: info@wellingboroughgolfclub.org
An undulating parkland course with many trees. The 514 yd 14th is a testing hole. The clubhouse is a stately home. The 18th is the signature hole.

18 holes, 6651yds, Par 72, SSS 72, Course record 68.
Club membership 820.
Visitors may not play at weekends & bank holidays or Tue between 9am and 2.30pm. **Societies** must apply in writing. **Green Fees** £50 per day; £40 per round. **Prof** David Clifford **Course Designer** Hawtree **Facilities** ⛄ 〰️ 🍽️ 🍺 🍺 ⛄ 🏠 🔲 🔲 ✅ **Leisure** outdoor swimming pool.

Continued   *Continued*

Conf fac available Corporate Hospitality Days available
Location 2m N of Wellingborough on A509

Hotel ⇧ Travelodge Wellingborough, Saunders Lodge,
RUSHDEN ☎ 08700 850 950 40 en suite

WHITTLEBURY   Map 04 SP64

Whittlebury Park Golf & Country Club
NN12 8XW ☎ 01327 858092 📠 01327 858009

Grand Prix: 9 holes, 3339yds, Par 36, SSS 36.
Royal Whittlewood: 9 holes, 3323yds, Par 36, SSS 36.
1905: 9 holes, 3256yds, Par 36, SSS 36.
Course Designer Cameron Sinclair Location A413
Buckingham Road
Telephone for further details

Hotel ★★★ 66% Buckingham Beales Best Western
Hotel, Buckingham Ring Rd, BUCKINGHAM
☎ 01280 822622 70 en suite

NORTHUMBERLAND

ALLENDALE   Map 12 NY85

Allendale High Studdon, Allenheads Rd NE47 9DH
☎ 01434 683926 & 685051 📠 01434 683668
e-mail: nostalgiaplus@supanet.com
Challenging and hilly parkland course set 1000 feet
above sea level with superb views of Tynedale. New
club house.
9 holes, 4541yds, Par 66, SSS 62, Course record 69.
Club membership 270.
Visitors may not play Aug bank holiday until after 3pm or
bank holiday Mon mornings. Welcome Sats. Societies
must apply to Secretary. Green Fees £12 per day (£15
weekends) (half-price after 6pm). Facilities ⊗ by prior
arrangement ☕ ⛳ Conf Corporate Hospitality Days
available Location 1m S of Allendale, on B6295

Hotel ★★★ 67% Beaumont Hotel, Beaumont St,
HEXHAM ☎ 01434 602331 25 en suite

ALNMOUTH   Map 12 NU21

Alnmouth Foxton Hall NE66 3BE
☎ 01665 830231 📠 01665 830922
e-mail: secretary@alnmouthgolfclub.com
Coastal course with pleasant views.
18 holes, 6429yds, Par 71, SSS 71, Course record 64.
Club membership 800.
Visitors Not Fri or Sat Societies Mon-Thu & Sun only.
Green Fees £33 per day; £27.50 per round (£35 per round
weekends). Cards 🎫 💳 💳 🎫 💳 Prof Linzi Hardy
Course Designer H S Colt Facilities ⊗ 》↑ 🏪 ☕ ♀ ⛳ 🏨

Continued

Alnmouth

🛏 ⛳ 🏌 Leisure snooker room. Conf Corporate Hospitality
Days available Location 1m NE. 4m E of Alnwick

Alnmouth Village Marine Rd NE66 2RZ
☎ 01665 830370
e-mail: golf@alnmouth-village.fsnet.co.uk
Seaside course with part coastal view.
9 holes, 6090yds, Par 70, SSS 70, Course record 63.
Club membership 480.
Visitors may not play before 11am on competition days.
Societies must contact in advance. Green Fees 18 holes
£15 (weekends & bank holidays £20). Weekly ticket £50.
Course Designer Mungo Park Facilities ⊗ 》↑ 🏪 ☕ ♀ ⛳
Location E side of village

ALNWICK   Map 12 NU11

Alnwick Swansfield Park NE66 1AB ☎ 01665 602632
e-mail: mail@alnwickgolfclub.co.uk
A mixture of mature parkland, open grassland and
gorse bushes with panoramic views out to sea five miles
away. Offers a fair test of golf.
18 holes, 6284yds, Par 70, SSS 70, Course record 66.
Club membership 400.
Visitors some restrictions on competition days. May play
after 10am weekends Societies must contact secretary in
advance. Green Fees £25 per day; £20 per round. Course
Designer Rochester, Rae Facilities ⊗ 》↑ 🏪 ☕ ♀ ⛳ 🏌
🏌 Leisure small practice area. Location From south left
into Willowburn Av. Over rdbt, 2nd left up Swansfield
Park Rd, continue up hill to park gates bend left. 1st right

BAMBURGH   Map 12 NU13

Bamburgh Castle The Club House, 40 The Wynding
NE69 7DE
☎ 01668 214378 (club) & 214321 (sec) 📠 01668 214607
e-mail: bamburghcastlegolfclub@hotmail.com
Superb coastal course with excellent greens that are
both fast and true, natural hazards of heather and whin
bushes abound. Magnificent views of Farne Islands,
Holy Island, Lindisfarne Castle, Bamburgh Castle and
Cheviot Hills.
18 holes, 5621yds, Par 68, SSS 67, Course record 64.
Club membership 785.
Visitors must contact in advance. Restricted weekends,
bank holidays and competition days. Societies apply in
writing. Green Fees Weekdays & Sun only. Green Fees £40 per day,
£30 per round (£45/£35 weekends). Cards 🎫 💳 💳 🎫
🎫 Course Designer George Rochester Facilities ⊗ 》↑ 🏪
☕ ♀ ⛳ 🏌 🏌 Conf Corporate Hospitality Days available
Location 6m E of A1 via B1341 or B1342

Hotel ★★ 69% The Lord Crewe, Front St, BAMBURGH
☎ 01668 214243 18 rms (17 en suite)

BEDLINGTON
Map 12 NZ28

Bedlingtonshire Acorn Bank NE22 6AA
☎ 01670 822457 📠 01670 823048
Meadowland/parkland course with easy walking. Under certain conditions the wind can be a distinct hazard.
18 holes, 6813yards, Par 73, SSS 73, Course record 64.
Club membership 800.
Visitors may not play before 9am weekdays or before 10am weekends and bank holidays. Book with professional. **Societies** contact the Secretary in writing or telephone. **Green Fees** £30 per day; £20 per round (£34/£26 weekends & bank holidays). **Prof** Marcus Webb **Course Designer** Frank Pennink **Facilities** ⊗ ∭ by prior arrangement 🏌 🍷 🍴 🏌 🚶 🛺 ∅ **Conf** Corporate Hospitality Days available **Location** 1m SW on A1068

BELFORD
Map 12 NU13

Belford South Rd NE70 7DP
☎ 01668 213433 📠 01668 213919
e-mail: belfordgolfclub@tiscali.co.uk
An east coast parkland course. Crosswinds affect the 4th but the compensation is spectacular views over Holy Island.
9 holes, 3152yds, Par 72, SSS 70, Course record 72.
Club membership 200.
Visitors not before 10am Sun. **Societies** must contact in advance. **Green Fees** £18 per day, £15 per 18 holes; £10 per 9 holes (£23/£18/£11 weekends & bank holidays). **Course Designer** Nigel Williams **Facilities** ⊗ ∭ 🏌 🍷 🍴 🍴 **∅** **Conf** Corporate Hospitality Days available **Location** Just off A1, midway between Alnwick & Berwick on Tweed

Hotel ⌂ Purdy Lodge, Adderstone Services, BELFORD
☎ 01668 213000 20 en suite

BELLINGHAM
Map 12 NY88

Bellingham Boggle Hole NE48 2DT
☎ 01434 220530 (Secretary) 📠 01434 220160
e-mail: admin@bellinghamgolfclub.com
This highly regarded 18-hole golf course is situated between Hadrian's Wall and the Scottish border. A rolling parkland course with many natural hazards. There is a mixture of testing par 3s, long par 5s and tricky par 4s.

18 holes, 6093yds, Par 70, SSS 70, Course record 65.
Club membership 500.
Visitors welcome all week, advisable to contact in advance as starting sheet in operation. **Societies** must contact in advance. **Green Fees** £22 per day/round (£27 per day/round weekends). **Cards** 💳 💳 💳 💳 💳 **Course Designer** E Johnson/I Wilson **Facilities** ⊗ by prior arrangement ∭ by prior arrangement 🏌 🍷 🍴 🚶 ∅ **{** **Location** N side of village on B6320

Hotel ★★ 69% Riverdale Hall Hotel, BELLINGHAM
☎ 01434 220254 20 en suite

BERWICK-UPON-TWEED
Map 12 NT95

Berwick-upon-Tweed (Goswick) Goswick
TD15 2RW ☎ 01289 387256 📠 01289 387334
e-mail: goswickgc@btconnect.com
Natural seaside links course, with undulating fairways, elevated tees and good greens.

18 holes, 6686yds, Par 72, SSS 72, Course record 69.
Club membership 700.
Visitors must contact in advance for weekends, advisable at other times. **Societies** must telephone in advance (apply in writing Apr-Sep). **Green Fees** not confirmed. **Cards** 💳 💳 💳 💳 💳 **Prof** Paul Terras **Course Designer** James Braid **Facilities** ⊗ ∭ 🏌 🍷 🍴 🏌 🚶 🛺 ∅ **{** **Location** 6m S of Berwick off A1

Hotel ★★★ 63% The King's Arms, 43 Hide Hill, BERWICK-UPON-TWEED ☎ 01289 307454 35 en suite

Magdalene Fields Magdalene Fields TD15 1NE
☎ 01289 306130 🖹 01289 306384
e-mail: mail@magdalene-fields.co.uk
Seaside course with natural hazards formed by sea bays. All holes open to winds. Testing 8th hole over bay (par 3).
18 holes, 6407yds, Par 72, SSS 71, Course record 65.
Club membership 350.
Visitors must contact in advance for weekend play.
Societies must contact in advance. **Green Fees** £20 per round (£22 weekends). **Cards** 🖃 🖃 🖃 🖃 **Course Designer** Willie Park **Facilities** ⊗ ╫ ╚ 🖤 ♀ ♨ 🖻 ⛳ 🛒
⛳ **Conf** Corporate Hospitality Days available **Location** 0.5m on E side of town centre

Hotel ★★★ 🏌 75% Tillmouth Park Country House Hotel, CORNHILL-ON-TWEED ☎ 01890 882255 12 en suite 2 annexe en suite

Blyth New Delaval, Newsham NE24 4DB
☎ 01670 540110 (sec) & 356514 (pro) 🖹 01670 540134
e-mail: clubmanager@blythgolf.co.uk
Course built over old colliery. Parkland with water hazards. Superb greens.
18 holes, 6456yds, Par 72, SSS 71, Course record 63.
Club membership 860.
Visitors with member only after 4pm & at weekends before 2pm. May book up to 3 days in advance. **Societies** apply in writing/telephone. **Green Fees** £28 per day; £24 per round (£28 per round weekends). **Cards** 🖃 🖃 🖃 🖃 🖃 **Prof** Andrew Brown **Course Designer** Hamilton Stutt **Facilities** ⊗ ╚ ♀ ♨ 🖻 ⛳ **Location** 6m N of Whitley Bay

Hotel ★★★ 72% Windsor Hotel, South Pde, WHITLEY BAY ☎ 0191 251 8888 70 en suite

Arcot Hall NE23 7QP
☎ 0191 236 2794 🖹 0191 217 0370
e-mail: arcothall@tiscali.co.uk
A wooded parkland course, reasonably flat.
18 holes, 6380yds, Par 70, SSS 70, Course record 62.
Club membership 695.
Visitors must contact in advance. May not play weekends. **Societies** must contact in advance. **Green Fees** not confirmed. **Prof** John Metcalfe **Course Designer** James Braid **Facilities** ⊗ ╫ ╚ 🖤 ♀ ♨ 🖻 ⛳ **Conf** fac available **Location** 2m SW off A1

Hotel ⌂ Innkeeper's Lodge Cramlington, Blagdon Ln, CRAMLINGTON ☎ 01670 736111 18 en suite

Dunstanburgh Castle NE66 3XQ
☎ 01665 576562 🖹 01665 576562
e-mail: enquiries@dunstanburgh.com
Rolling links designed by James Braid, adjacent to the beautiful Embleton Bay. Historic Dunstansburgh Castle is at one end of the course and a National Trust lake and bird sanctuary at the other. Superb views.
18 holes, 6298yds, Par 70, SSS 69, Course record 69.
Club membership 385.
Visitors advisable to contact in advance at weekends and holiday periods. **Societies** must contact in advance. **Green Fees** £20 per day (£29 per day; £24 per round weekends &

bank holidays). **Course Designer** James Braid **Facilities** ⊗ ╫ ╚ 🖤 ♀ ♨ 🖻 ⛳ **Conf** fac available Corporate Hospitality Days available **Location** 7m NE of Alnwick off A1

Hotel ★★ 71% Dunstanburgh Castle Hotel, EMBLETON ☎ 01665 576111 20 en suite

Burgham Park NE65 8QP
☎ 01670 787898 (office) & 787978 (pro shop)
🖹 01670 787164
PGA associates designed course, making the most of the gentle rolling landscape with views to the sea and the Northumbrian Hills.
18 holes, 6751yards, Par 72, SSS 72, Course record 67.
Club membership 560.
Visitors no restrictions if tee times available. **Societies** contact secretary for advance booking. **Green Fees** terms on application. **Cards** 🖃 🖃 🖃 **Prof** David Mather **Course Designer** Andrew Mair **Facilities** ⊗ ╫ ╚ 🖤 ♀ ♨ 🖻 ⛳ 🛒 ⛳ **Leisure** par 3 course. **Location** 5m N of Morpeth, 0.5m off A1

Hotel ★★★ 74% Linden Hall Hotel, Health Spa & Golf Course, LONGHORSLEY ☎ 01670 500000 50 en suite

Haltwhistle Wallend Farm CA6 7HN
☎ 016977 47367 🖹 01434 344311
18 holes, 5522yds, Par 69, SSS 67, Course record 70.
Location N on A69 past Haltwhistle on Gilsland Road
Telephone for further details

Hotel ★★★ 🏌 Farlam Hall Hotel, BRAMPTON ☎ 016977 46234 11 en suite 1 annexe en suite

De Vere Slaley Hall, Golf Resort & Spa
Slaley NE47 0BY ☎ 01434 673154 🖹 01434 673152
e-mail: slaley.hall@devere-hotels.com
Measuring 7073yds from the championship tees, this Dave Thomas designed course incorporates forest, parkland and moorland with an abundance of lakes and streams. The challenging par 4 9th (452yds) is played over water through a narrow avenue of towering trees and dense rhododendrons. The Priestman course designed by Neil Coles is of equal length and standard as the Hunting course. Opened in spring 1999, it is situated in 280 acres on the western side of the estate, giving panoramic views over the Tyne Valley.

Hunting Course: 18 holes, 7073yds, Par 72, SSS 74, Course record 65.

Continued   Continued

Priestman Course: 18 holes, 7010yds, Par 72, SSS 72, Course record 67.
Club membership 350.
Visitors must contact in advance, times subject to availability. **Societies** apply in writing to bookings co-ordinator, small groups 8 or less may book by telephone. **Green Fees** terms on application. **Cards** ▭ ▭ ▭ ▭ ▭ ▭ **Prof** Gordon Robinson **Course Designer** Dave Thomas/Neil Coles **Facilities** ⊗ ⴰ ⤢ 🖤 ♀ 🏌 🏠 ⴱ ⴲ ⴳ ⴴ ⴵ **Leisure** heated indoor swimming pool, fishing, sauna, solarium, gymnasium. **Conf** fac available **Location** 8m S of Hexham off A68

Hotel ★★★★ 71% De Vere Slaley Hall, Slaley, HEXHAM ☎ 01434 673350 139 en suite

Hexham Spital Park NE46 3RZ
☎ 01434 603072 📄 01434 601865
e-mail: hexham.golf.club@talk21.com
A very pretty well-drained parkland course with interesting natural contours. Exquisite views from parts of the course, of the Tyne Valley below. As good a parkland course as any in the North of England.
18 holes, 6000yds, Par 70, SSS 68, Course record 64.
Club membership 700.
Visitors advance booking advisable. **Societies** welcome weekdays, contact in advance. **Green Fees** £30 per round (£40 weekends & bank holidays). **Cards** ▭ ▭ ▭ ▭ ▭ **Prof** Martin Forster **Course Designer** Vardon/Caird **Facilities** ⊗ ⴰ ⤢ 🖤 ♀ 🏌 🏠 ⴱ **Leisure** squash. **Conf** fac available Corporate Hospitality Days available **Location** 1m NW on B6531

Hotel ★★★ 67% Beaumont Hotel, Beaumont St, HEXHAM ☎ 01434 602331 25 en suite

LONGHORSLEY Map 12 NZ19

Linden Hall NE65 8XF
☎ 01670 500011 📄 01670 500001
e-mail: golf@lindenhall.co.uk
Set within the picturesque Linden Hall Estate on a mixture of mature woodland and parkland with established lakes and burns providing interesting water features to match the peaceful surroundings. This award-winning golf course is a pleasure to play for all standards of golfer.
18 holes, 6846yds, Par 72, SSS 73.
Club membership 350.
Visitors must book in advance. **Societies** must be of reasonable standard of play, observe dress code & etiquette, preferably have handicap certificate. **Green Fees** £45 per day; £28 per round (£50/£35 weekends). **Cards** ▭ ▭ ▭ ▭ ▭ ▭ **Prof** David Curry **Course Designer** Jonathan Gaunt **Facilities** ⊗ ⴰ ⤢ 🖤 ♀ 🏌 🏠 ⴱ ⴲ ⴳ ⴴ **Leisure** hard tennis courts, heated indoor swimming pool, sauna, solarium, gymnasium. **Conf** fac available Corporate Hospitality Days available **Location** From A1 N/S take A697 to Coldstream, approx 4m to Longhorsley, Linden Hall 0.5m past village

Hotel ★★★ 74% Linden Hall Hotel, Health Spa & Golf Course, LONGHORSLEY ☎ 01670 500000 50 en suite

MATFEN Map 12 NZ07

Matfen Hall NE20 0RH
☎ 01661 886400 📄 01661 886055
e-mail: golf@matfenhall.fsnet.co.uk
An 18-hole parkland course set in beautiful countryside with many natural and man-made hazards. The course is an enjoyable test for players of all abilities but it does incorporate challenging water features in the shape of a large lake and a fast flowing river. The dry stone wall presents a unique obstacle on several holes. The 4th, 9th, 12th and 14th holes are particularly testing par 4s, the dog-legged 16th is the pick of the par 5s but Matfen's signature hole is the long par 3 17th with its narrow green teasingly sited just over the river.
18 holes, 6569yds, Par 72, SSS 71, Course record 64.
Club membership 500.
Visitors contact in advance, restricted on weekends between 8-11am. **Societies** telephone for details. **Green Fees** £45 per 36/27 holes; £35 per 18 holes (weekends £50/£40). **Cards** ▭ ▭ ▭ ▭ ▭ **Prof** John Harrison **Course Designer** Mair/James/Gaunt **Facilities** ⊗ ⴰ ⤢ 🖤 ♀ 🏌 🏠 ⴱ ⴲ ⴳ ⴴ **Leisure** heated indoor swimming pool, gymnasium, 9 hole par 3 course. Leisure complex. **Conf** fac available Corporate Hospitality Days available **Location** Just off B6318 Military road 15m W of Newcastle

Hotel ★★★ 76% Matfen Hall, MATFEN ☎ 01661 886500 31 en suite

MORPETH Map 12 NZ28

Morpeth The Clubhouse NE61 2BT
☎ 01670 504942 📄 01670 504918
18 holes, 6206yds, Par 71, SSS 69, Course record 65.
Course Designer Harry Vardon **Location** S side of town centre on A197
Telephone for further details

Hotel ★★★ 74% Linden Hall Hotel, Health Spa & Golf Course, LONGHORSLEY ☎ 01670 500000 50 en suite

NEWBIGGIN-BY-THE-SEA Map 12 NZ38

Newbiggin-by-the-Sea Prospect Place NE64 6DW
☎ 01670 817344 📄 01670 520236
Seaside-links course.
18 holes, 6452yds, Par 72, SSS 71, Course record 65.
Club membership 590.
Visitors must contact clubhouse staff on arrival and may not play before 10am. **Societies** must apply in writing. **Green Fees** not confirmed. **Course Designer** Willie Park **Facilities** ⊗ ⴰ ⤢ 🖤 ♀ 🏌 🏠 ⴱ ⴲ **Leisure** snooker. **Conf** fac available **Location** N side of town

Hotel ★★★ 74% Linden Hall Hotel, Health Spa & Golf Course, LONGHORSLEY ☎ 01670 500000 50 en suite

PONTELAND Map 12 NZ17

Ponteland 53 Bell Villas NE20 9BD
☎ 01661 822689 📄 01661 860077
e-mail: secretary@thepontelandgolfclub.co.uk
Open parkland course offering testing golf and good views.
18 holes, 6524yds, Par 72, SSS 71, Course record 65.
Club membership 720.
Visitors with member only Fri, weekends & bank holidays. **Societies** welcome Tue & Thu only. Must contact in

Continued

advance. **Green Fees** terms on application. **Cards** 💳 **Prof** Alan Robson-Crosby **Course Designer** Harry Fernie **Facilities** ⊗ ⅷ ⅃ 🏌 ♀ 🍴 🏠 🥪 🚗 ♂ **Conf** Corporate Hospitality Days available **Location** 0.5m E on A696

Hotel ★★★ 67% Novotel Newcastle, Ponteland Rd, Kenton, NEWCASTLE UPON TYNE ☎ 0191 214 0303 126 en suite

PRUDHOE   Map 12 NZ06

Prudhoe Eastwood Park NE42 5DX
☎ 01661 832466 📄 01661 830710
18 holes, 5812yds, Par 69, SSS 69, Course record 60.
Location E side of town centre off A695
Telephone for further details

Hotel ★★★ 69% Gibside Hotel, Front St, WHICKHAM ☎ 0191 488 9292 45 en suite

ROTHBURY   Map 12 NU00

Rothbury Old Race Course NE65 7TR
☎ 01669 621271
Scenic, flat parkland course set alongside the River Coquet and surrounded by Simonside hills and Cragside Hall.
9 holes, 5779yds, Par 68, SSS 67, Course record 65.
Club membership 306.
Visitors weekends by arrangement only. **Societies** must contact secretary, D. Woolley, in advance 01669 630378 **Green Fees** £18 per day; £13 per round (weekends £25/£18). **Course Designer** J Radcliffe **Facilities** ⅃ 🏌 ♀ △ **Location** SW side of town off B6342

Hotel ★★★ 74% Linden Hall Hotel, Health Spa & Golf Course, LONGHORSLEY ☎ 01670 500000 50 en suite

SEAHOUSES   Map 12 NU23

Seahouses Beadnell Rd NE68 7XT
☎ 01665 720794 📄 01665 721994
e-mail: seahousesgolfclub@breathemail.net
Typical links course with many hazards, including the famous 10th, 'Logans Loch', water hole.
18 holes, 5542yds, Par 67, SSS 67, Course record 63.
Club membership 750.
Visitors must contact in advance. **Societies** must contact in advance. May not play Sun. **Green Fees** £25 per day; £18 per round (£30/£25 weekends & bank holidays). **Facilities** ⊗ ⅷ ⅃ 🏌 ♀ △ ♂ **Conf** Corporate Hospitality Days available **Location** S side of village on B1340

Hotel ★★ 70% Bamburgh Castle Hotel, SEAHOUSES ☎ 01665 720283 20 en suite

STOCKSFIELD   Map 12 NZ06

Stocksfield New Ridley Rd NE43 7RE
☎ 01661 843041 📄 01661 843046
e-mail: info@sgcgolf.co.uk
Challenging course: parkland (9 holes), woodland (9 holes). Some elevated greens and water hazards.
18 holes, 5978yds, Par 70, SSS 69, Course record 61.
Club membership 550.
Visitors welcome except Wed am & Sat until 4pm, unless accompanied by a member. **Societies** must contact in advance. **Green Fees** not confirmed. **Prof** David Mather **Course Designer** Pennick **Facilities** ⊗ ⅷ by prior arrangement ⅃ 🏌 ♀ △ 🏠 🍴 ♂ **Leisure** snooker. **Conf** Corporate Hospitality Days available

Continued

Location Hexham to Newcastle A695, 1.5m along New Ridley Rd at Esso Station

Hotel ★★★ 67% Beaumont Hotel, Beaumont St, HEXHAM ☎ 01434 602331 25 en suite

SWARLAND   Map 12 NU10

Swarland Hall Coast View NE65 9JG
☎ 01670 787010
e-mail: info@swarlandgolf
Parkland course set in mature woodland. There are seven par 4 holes in excess of 400 yards.
18 holes, 6335yds, Par 72, SSS 72.
Club membership 400.
Visitors restricted on competition days. Advance booking advisable. **Societies** apply in advance. **Green Fees** terms on application. **Cards** 💳 💳 💳 **Facilities** ⊗ ⅷ ⅃ 🏌 ♀ △ 🍴 🥪 🚗 ♂ ⅃ **Conf** Corporate Hospitality Days available **Location** Approx 1m W of A, 1 8m S of Alnwick

Hotel ★★★ 74% Linden Hall Hotel, Health Spa & Golf Course, LONGHORSLEY ☎ 01670 500000 50 en suite

WARKWORTH   Map 12 NU20

Warkworth The Links NE65 0SW ☎ 01665 711596
Seaside links course, with good views and alternative tees for the back nine. The first hole is a very testing par 3 and skill is required to avoid the out of bounds. The course is not friendly to right-handed 'slicers' with heather and bracken on the eastern side on the way out. The fearsome Killiecrankie Gorge is in play four times during the 18 holes, especially challenging when a north wind is blowing.
9 holes, 5870yds, Par 70, SSS 68, Course record 66.
Club membership 470.
Visitors welcome except Tue & Sat. **Societies** must contact in advance. **Green Fees** £12 per day (£20 weekends & bank holidays). **Course Designer** Tom Morris **Facilities** ⊗ ⅃ 🏌 ♀ △ **Location** 0.5m E of village off A1068

WOOLER   Map 12 NT92

Wooler Dod Law, Doddington NE71 6EA
☎ 01668 282135
Hilltop, moorland course with spectacular views over the Glendale valley. Nine greens played from 18 tees. A very challenging course when windy with one par 5 of 580 yards. The course is much under used during the week so is always available.
9 holes, 6411yds, Par 72, SSS 71, Course record 69.
Club membership 300.
Visitors normally no restrictions. **Societies** by prior arrangement with secretary. **Green Fees** £15 (weekends £20) 9 holes £10. **Facilities** ⊗ ⅷ ⅃ by prior arrangement 🏌 ♀ △ 🥪 🚗 ♂ **Location** At Doddington on B6525 Wooler/Berwick Rd

Hotel ⛾ Purdy Lodge, Adderstone Services, BELFORD ☎ 01668 213000 20 en suite

---

If you have a comment or suggestion concerning the AA Golf Course Guide 2005, you can e-mail us at

lifestyleguides@theAA.com

NOTTINGHAMSHIRE

CALVERTON
Map 08 SK64

Ramsdale Park Golf Centre Oxton Rd
NG14 6NU ☎ 0115 965 5600 📠 0115 965 4105
e-mail: info@ramsdaleparkgc.co.uk
The High course is a challenging and comprehensive test for any standard of golf. A relatively flat front nine is followed by an undulating back nine that is renowned as one of the best in the county. The Low course is an 18-hole par 3 course which is gaining a similar reputation.
High Course: 18 holes, 6546yds, Par 71, SSS 71, Course record 70.
Low Course: 18 holes, 2844yds, Par 54, SSS 54.
Club membership 400.
Visitors may book up to 7 days in advance. **Societies** welcome midweek, apply in writing or telephone. **Green Fees** £18.50 (weekends £24). **Cards** 🎫 💳 💳 🎫 🎫 **Prof** Robert Macey **Course Designer** Hawtree **Facilities** ⊗ ⅷ ⅊ ♥ ⅋ ♙ ☎ ♈ ♠ ♨ ⅋ ⅂ **Leisure** fishing. **Conf** fac available Corporate Hospitality Days available **Location** 8m NE of Nottingham, off B6386

Hotel ★★★ 66% Bestwood Lodge, Bestwood Country Park, Arnold, NOTTINGHAM ☎ 0115 920 3011 39 en suite

Springwater Moor Ln NG14 6FZ
☎ 0115 965 2129 (pro shop) & 965 4946
📠 0115 965 4957
e-mail: springwater@rapidial.co.uk
This attractive golf course set in rolling countryside offers an interesting and challenging game of golf to players of all handicaps. The 18th hole is particularly noteworthy, a 183yd par 3 over two lakes.

18 holes, 6262yds, Par 71, SSS 71, Course record 68.
Club membership 440.
Visitors 5 day advance booking by telephone, booking available all week subject to competitions and

Continued

Society/Corporate reservations. **Societies** apply in writing or telephone for Society Pack. **Green Fees** £20 per round (£25 weekends & bank holidays). **Cards** 🎫 💳 💳 🎫 🎫 **Prof** Paul Drew **Course Designer** Neil Footitty/Paul Wharmsby **Facilities** ⊗ ⅷ ⅊ ♥ ⅋ ♙ ☎ ♈ ♠ ♨ ⅋ ⅂ **Leisure** short game academy. **Conf** fac available Corporate Hospitality Days available **Location** 600yds on left along Moor Lane after turning to Calverton off A6097, 1m S of Oxton roundabout

Hotel ★★★ 67% Westminster Hotel, 312 Mansfield Rd, Carrington, NOTTINGHAM ☎ 0115 955 5000 73 en suite

EAST LEAKE
Map 08 SK52

Rushcliffe Stocking Ln LE12 5RL
☎ 01509 852959 📠 01509 852688
e-mail: secretary.rushcliffegc@btopenworld.com
Hilly, tree-lined and picturesque parkland course.
Rushcliffe Golf Club: 18 holes, 6013yds, Par 70, SSS 69, Course record 63.
Club membership 750.
Visitors welcome but may not play Tue and restricted weekends & bank holidays 9.30-11am & 3-4.30pm.
Societies must apply in advance. **Green Fees** terms on application. **Prof** Chris Hall **Facilities** ⊗ ⅷ ⅊ ♥ ⅋ ♙ ☎ ♠ ♨ ⅋ **Location** Off M1 junct 24

Hotel ★★★ 75% Best Western Yew Lodge Hotel, Packington Hill, Kegworth, ☎ 01509 672518 98 en suite

HUCKNALL
Map 08 SK54

Leen Valley Golf Centre Wigwam Ln NG15 7TA
☎ 0115 964 2037 📠 0115 964 2724
e-mail: leen-jackbarker@btinternet.com
An interesting and challenging parkland course, featuring several lakes, the River Leen and the Baker Brook. Suitable for all standards of golfer.
18 holes, 6233yds, Par 72, SSS 70.
Club membership 400.
Visitors tee times can be booked in advance and this is advisable for Fri, Sat & Sun. **Societies** by arrangement.
Green Fees not confirmed. **Cards** 🎫 💳 💳 🎫 🎫 **Prof** John Lines **Course Designer** Tom Hodgetts **Facilities** ⊗ ⅷ ⅊ ♥ ⅋ ♙ ☎ ♠ ♨ ⅋ **Leisure** 9 hole par 3 course. **Location** 0.5m from Hucknall Town Centre, follow signs for railway station and turn right into Wigwam Lane

Hotel ⛫ Premier Lodge (Nottingham North West), Nottingham Rd, HUCKNALL ☎ 0870 9906518 35 en suite

KEYWORTH
Map 08 SK63

Stanton on the Wolds Golf Rd, Stanton-on-the-Wolds NG12 5BH ☎ 0115 937 4885 📠 0115 937 4885
Parkland course, fairly flat with stream running through four holes.
18 holes, 6369yds, Par 73, SSS 71, Course record 67.
Club membership 705.
Visitors must contact in advance. Must play with member at weekends and may not play Tue. **Societies** must apply in writing. **Green Fees** not confirmed. **Prof** Nick Hernon **Course Designer** Tom Williamson **Facilities** ⊗ ⅷ by prior arrangement ⅊ ♥ ⅋ ♙ ☎ ♨ ⅋ **Location** E side of village, 9m S of Nottingham off A606

Hotel ⛫ Premier Lodge (Nottingham South), Loughborough Rd, Ruddington, NOTTINGHAM ☎ 0870 9906422 42 en suite

KIRKBY IN ASHFIELD   Map 08 SK55

Notts Derby Rd NG17 7QR
☎ 01623 753225 📠 01623 753655
e-mail: nottsgolfclub@hollinwell.fsnet.co.uk
Undulating heathland championship course.
18 holes, 7103yds, Par 72, SSS 75, Course record 64.
Club membership 450.
Visitors must contact in advance & have handicap
certificate. With member only weekends & bank holidays.
Societies must apply in advance. **Green Fees** not
confirmed. **Cards** 🖭 🖭 🖭 🖭 **Prof** Alasdair Thomas
Course Designer Willie Park **Facilities** ⊗ ⅢⱢ ⅃ ⅃ ⅃ ⅃
🏠 ⚑ ⚒ ⚒ ⚒ **Conf** fac available **Location** 2m SE of
Mansfield off A611

....

Hotel ★★★★ 70% Renaissance Derby/Nottingham
Hotel, Carter Ln East, SOUTH NORMANTON
☎ 01773 812000 158 en suite

MANSFIELD   Map 08 SK56

Sherwood Forest Eakring Rd NG18 3EW
☎ 01623 627403 & 627403 📠 01623 420412
e-mail: sherwood@forest43.freeserve.co.uk
**As the name suggests, the Forest is the main feature of
this natural heathland course with its heather, silver
birch and pine trees. The homeward nine holes are
particularly testing. The 11th to the 14th are notable
par 4 holes on this well-bunkered course designed by
the great James Braid.**
18 holes, 6853yds, Par 71, SSS 74, Course record 67.
Club membership 750.
Visitors weekdays only by prior arrangement with the golf
manager. **Societies** by arrangement with the golf manager.
Green Fees £55 per day, £40 per round (weekdays only).
Prof Ken Hall **Course Designer** W S Colt/James Braid
Facilities ⊗ ⅢⱢ Ⱡ 🖤 ⅃ ⅃ 🏠 ⚑ ⚒ ⚒ **Leisure** snooker.
Conf fac available **Location** E of Mansfield

....

Hotel ★★ 68% Pine Lodge Hotel, 281-283 Nottingham
Rd, MANSFIELD ☎ 01623 622308 20 en suite

MANSFIELD WOODHOUSE   Map 08 SK56

Mansfield Woodhouse Leeming Ln North
NG19 9EU ☎ 01623 623521
9 holes, 2446yds, Par 68, SSS 64.
Course Designer A Highfield & F Horfman **Location** N
side of town centre off A60
Telephone for further details

....

Hotel ★★ 68% Pine Lodge Hotel, 281-283 Nottingham
Rd, MANSFIELD ☎ 01623 622308 20 en suite

NEWARK-ON-TRENT   Map 08 SK75

Newark Coddington NG24 2QX
☎ 01636 626282 📠 01636 626497
**Wooded, parkland course in secluded situation with
easy walking.**
18 holes, 6458yds, Par 71, SSS 71, Course record 66.
Club membership 650.
Visitors must contact in advance and have handicap
certificate. May not play Tue (Ladies Day). **Societies** must
contact in advance. **Green Fees** £30 per day, £24 per round
(£30 per round weekend & bank holidays). **Prof** P A
Lockley **Course Designer** T Williamson **Facilities** ⊗ ⅢⱢ Ⱡ

🖤 ⅃ 🏠 ⚒ **Leisure** snooker. **Location** 4m E of
Newark on Sleaford Road(A17)

....

Hotel ★★★ 68% The Grange Hotel, 73 London Rd,
NEWARK ☎ 01636 703399 10 en suite 9 annexe en suite

NOTTINGHAM   Map 08 SK53

Beeston Fields Old Dr, Wollaton Rd, Beeston
NG9 3DD ☎ 0115 925 7062 📠 0115 925 4280
e-mail: beestonfieldsgolfclub@supanet.com
**Parkland course with sandy subsoil and wide, tree-lined
fairways. The par 3 14th has an elevated tee and a small
bunker-guarded green.**

18 holes, 6402yds, Par 71, SSS 71, Course record 64.
Club membership 600.
Visitors must contact professional on 0115 925 7062 for
availability. **Societies** must apply in advance. **Green Fees**
£40 per day, £30 per round (£35 per round weekends).
Prof Alun Wardle **Course Designer** Tom Williamson
Facilities ⊗ ⅢⱢ by prior arrangement Ⱡ 🖤 ⅃ ⅃ 🏠 ⚑ ⚒
Conf fac available Corporate Hospitality Days available
Location 400mtrs SW off A52 Nottingham/Derby road,
3m from M1 J25

....

Hotel Ⓤ Holiday Inn Derby/Nottingham, Bostocks Ln,
SANDIACRE ☎ 0870 400 9062 93 en suite

Bramcote Hills Thoresby Rd, off Derby Rd, Bramcote
NG9 3EP ☎ 0115 928 1880
18 holes, 1500yds, Par 54.
Location Off A52 Derby rd
Telephone for further details

....

Hotel Ⓤ Holiday Inn Nottingham City, St James's St,
NOTTINGHAM ☎ 0870 400 9061 160 rms (158 en suite)

Bulwell Forest Hucknall Rd, Bulwell NG6 9LQ
☎ 0115 976 3172 (pro shop) 📠 0115 976 3172
**Municipal heathland course with many natural
hazards. Very tight fairways and subject to wind. Five
challenging par 3s. Excellent drainage.**
18 holes, 5667yds, Par 68, SSS 67, Course record 62.
Club membership 350.
Visitors restricted weekends. Contact pro shop 24 hours in
advance. **Societies** must apply in advance. **Green Fees** not
confirmed. **Cards** 🖭 🖭 🖭 🖭 🖭 🖭 **Course
Designer** John Doleman **Facilities** ⊗ Ⱡ 🖤 ⅃ ⅃ 🏠 ⚑ ⚒
Leisure hard tennis courts, children's playground.
Location 3m from junct 26 on M1. 4m NW of city centre
on A611

> **Prices may change during the currency of
> the Guide, please check when booking.**

Continued

Chilwell Manor Meadow Ln, Chilwell NG9 5AE
☎ 0115 925 8958 📠 0115 922 0575
e-mail: chilwellmanorgolfclub@barbox.net
Flat parkland course. Including 18 newly designed and reconstructed greens.
18 holes, 6255yds, Par 70, SSS 71, Course record 66.
Club membership 750.
Visitors with member only weekends. Must contact in advance and have a handicap certificate. **Societies** welcome Mon, must apply in advance. **Green Fees** £30 per day, £25 per round (weekends £30 per round). **Cards** ⊞
Prof Paul Wilson **Course Designer** Tom Williamson
Facilities ⊗ ⊞ ⓘ ⓑ ♥ ♀ ⚑ ⚐ ✓ **Location** 4m SW on A6005

Hotel ★★ 60% Europa Hotel, 20-22 Derby Rd, LONG EATON ☎ 0115 972 8481 15 en suite

Edwalton Municipal Wellin Ln, Edwalton
NG12 4AS ☎ 0115 923 4775 📠 0115 923 1647
Gently sloping, 9-hole parkland course. Also 9-hole par 3 and large practice ground.
9 holes, 3336yds, Par 72, SSS 72, Course record 71.
Club membership 400.
Visitors booking system in operation, book up to 7 days in advance **Societies** prior booking necessary. **Green Fees** terms on application. **Cards** ⊞ ⊞ ⊞ ⊞ **Prof** Lee Rawlings **Facilities** ⊗ ⓘ ⓑ ♥ ♀ ⚑ ⚐ ⚐ ⚑ ✓ ⚐
Leisure par 3 course. **Conf** fac available Corporate Hospitality Days available **Location** S of Nottingham, off A606

Hotel ⛨ Premier Lodge (Nottingham South), Loughborough Rd, Ruddington, NOTTINGHAM ☎ 0870 9906422 42 en suite

Mapperley Central Av, Plains Rd, Mapperley
NG3 6RH ☎ 0115 955 6672/3 📠 0115 955 6670
e-mail: info@mapperleygolfclub.org
Hilly meadowland course but with easy walking.
18 holes, 5895yds, Par 71, SSS 70.
Club membership 650.
Visitors must contact in advance. May not play Tue or Sat. **Societies** must telephone in advance. **Green Fees** £25 per day/£20 per round (£30/£25 weekends & bank holidays).
Cards ⊞ ⊞ ⊞ ⊞ ⊞ ⊞ **Prof** Jasen Barker **Course Designer** John Mason **Facilities** ⊗ ⓘ ⓑ ♥ ♀ ⚑ ⚐
⚑ ✓ **Leisure** pool room. **Location** 3m NE of city centre off B684

Hotel ⓤ Holiday Inn Nottingham City, St James's St, NOTTINGHAM ☎ 0870 400 9061 160 rms (158 en suite)

Nottingham City Lawton Dr, Bulwell NG6 8BL
☎ 0115 927 6916 & 927 2767 📠 0115 927 6916
A pleasant municipal parkland course on the city outskirts.
18 holes, 6218yds, Par 69, SSS 70, Course record 63.
Club membership 425.
Visitors restricted Sat 7am-3pm. Contact Professional in advance. **Societies** welcome, contact professional. **Green Fees** not confirmed. **Cards** ⊞ ⊞ ⊞ ⊞ ⊞ **Prof** Cyril Jepson **Course Designer** H Braid **Facilities** ⊗ ⓘ ⓑ
♥ ♀ ⚑ ⚐ ✓ **Conf** fac available Corporate Hospitality Days available **Location** 4m NW of city centre off A6002

Booking a tee time is always advisable.

Wollaton Park Limetree Av, Wollaton Park
NG8 1BT ☎ 0115 978 7574 📠 0115 970 0736
e-mail: wollatonparkgc@aol.com
A championship parkland course on slightly undulating land set in historic deer park. Fine views of 16th-century Wollaton Hall.
18 holes, 6445yds, Par 71, SSS 71, Course record 64.
Club membership 700.
Visitors may not play Wed or competition days. **Societies** must apply in advance. **Green Fees** £48 per day; £35 per round (£55/£40 weekends & bank holidays). **Cards** ⊞ ⊞
⊞ ⊞ ⚐ **Prof** John Lower **Course Designer** T Williamson **Facilities** ⊗ ⓘ ⓑ ♥ ♀ ⚑ ⚐ ⚑ ✓ **Conf** Corporate Hospitality Days available **Location** 2.5m W of city centre off Nottingham ring road at junct with A52

Hotel ★★★ 61% Swans Hotel & Restaurant, 84-90 Radcliffe Rd, West Bridgford, NOTTINGHAM ☎ 0115 981 4042 30 en suite

OLLERTON   Map 08 SK66

Rufford Park Golf & Country Club Rufford
Ln, Rufford NG22 9DG
☎ 01623 825253 📠 01623 825254
e-mail: enquiries@ruffordpark.co.uk
Set in the heart of Sherwood Forest, Rufford Park is noted for its picturesque 18 holes with its especially challenging par 3s. From the unique 175 yard par 3 17th over water to the riverside 641 yard 13th, the course offers everything the golfer needs from beginner to professional.
18 holes, 6286yds, Par 70, SSS 70, Course record 67.
Club membership 650.
Visitors booking recommended. **Societies** society packages on request, need to booked in advance. **Green Fees** £19 per round (weekends £25); Winter £16. **Cards** ⊞ ⊞ ⊞ ⊞ ⚐ **Prof** John Vaughan/James Thompson **Course Designer** David Hemstock/Ken Brown **Facilities** ⊗ ⓘ ⓑ ♥ ♀ ⚑ ⚐ ⚑ ⚐ ⚑ ✓ ⚐ **Conf** fac available Corporate Hospitality Days available **Location** S Of Ollerton off A614. Take the 'Rufford Mill' turn

Hotel ★★★ 65% Clumber Park Hotel, Clumber Park, WORKSOP ☎ 01623 835333 48 en suite

OXTON   Map 08 SK65

Oakmere Park Oaks Ln NG25 0RH
☎ 0115 965 3545 📠 0115 965 5628
e-mail: enquiries@oakmerepark.co.uk
Twenty seven holes set in rolling parkland in the heart of picturesque Robin Hood country. The par 4 16th and par 5 1st are notable. Twenty-bay floodlit driving range.

Continued

197

Admirals: 18 holes, 6617yds, Par 73, SSS 72, Course record 64.
Commanders: 9 holes, 6407yds, Par 72, SSS 72.
Club membership 900.
Visitors correct golf attire required, please book for weekends. **Societies** please apply in writing or telephone. **Green Fees** Admirals: £18 per round (£24 weekends). **Cards** ⊞ ▤ ▤ ▧ ▨ **Prof** Daryl St-John Jones **Course Designer** Frank Pennick **Facilities** ⊗ ⟝ ⮟ ⬛ ⬤ ⬤ ⬤ ⬤ ⬤ **Conf** fac available Corporate Hospitality Days available **Location** 7m NE from Nottingham on A614

Hotel ★★★ 67% Westminster Hotel, 312 Mansfield Rd, Carrington, NOTTINGHAM ☎ 0115 955 5000 73 en suite

RADCLIFFE ON TRENT Map 08 SK63

Cotgrave Place Golf Club Stragglethorpe, Nr Cotgrave Village NG12 3HB
☎ 0115 933 3344 ▤ 0115 933 4567
e-mail: cotgrave@americangolf.com
The course offers 36 holes of championship golf. The front nine of the Open Course are placed around a beautiful lake, man-made ponds and the Grantham Canal. The back nine is set in magnificent parkland with mature trees and wide fairways. Masters has an opening nine set amongst hedgerows and coppices. The huge greens with their interesting shapes are a particularly challenging test of nerve. The par 5 17th hole is one of the toughest in the country.

Open course: 18 holes, 5933yds, Par 70, SSS 68, Course record 66.
Masters course: 18 holes, 6290yds, Par 71, SSS 68, Course record 69.
Club membership 850.
Visitors must contact sales manager in advance **Societies** telephone in advance. **Green Fees** not confirmed. **Cards** ⊞ ▤ ▤ ▧ ▨ **Prof** Robert Smith **Course Designer** Peter Aliss/John Small **Facilities** ⊗ ⟝ ⮟ ⬛ ⬤ ⬤ ⬤ ⬤ ⬤ ⬤ ⬤ **Conf** Corporate Hospitality Days available **Location** Off A52, 6 miles from Nottingham

Hotel ★★★ 🏩 73% Langar Hall, LANGAR ☎ 01949 860559 12 en suite

Radcliffe-on-Trent Dewberry Ln, Cropwell Rd NG12 2JH ☎ 0115 933 3000 ▤ 0115 911 6991
e-mail: les.rotgc@talk21.com
Fairly flat, parkland course with three good finishing holes: 16th (427 yds) par 4; 17th (180 yds) through spinney, par 3; 18th (331 yds) dog-leg par 4. Excellent views.
18 holes, 6381yds, Par 70, SSS 71, Course record 64.
Club membership 700.
Visitors must contact in advance, societies only *Continued*

on Wed. **Societies** welcome Wed. Must contact in advance. **Green Fees** £24 per day (£30 weekends & bank holidays). **Cards** ⊞ ▤ ▤ ▧ ▨ **Prof** Craig George **Course Designer** Tom Williamson **Facilities** ⊗ ⟝ ⮟ ⬛ ⬤ ⬤ ⬤ ⬤ ⬤ ⬤ **Conf** Corporate Hospitality Days available **Location** At A46/A52 junction, take the A52 to Nottingham, turn left at 2nd set of traffic lights, 400yds on left

Hotel ★★★ 61% Swans Hotel & Restaurant, 84-90 Radcliffe Rd, West Bridgford, NOTTINGHAM ☎ 0115 981 4042 30 en suite

RETFORD Map 08 SK78

Retford Brecks Rd, Ordsall DN22 7UA
☎ 01777 711188 (Secretary) ▤ 01777 710412
A wooded, parkland course.
18 holes, 6409yds, Par 72, SSS 72, Course record 67.
Club membership 700.
Visitors advisable to contact in advance, with member only at weekends and holidays. **Societies** apply in writing or telephone. **Green Fees** £30 per day; £22 per round (Weekends £28). **Prof** Craig Morris **Course Designer** Tom Williamson **Facilities** ⊗ ⟝ ⮟ ⬛ ⬤ ⬤ ⬤ ⬤ ⬤ ⬤ ⬤ **Location** 1.5m S A620, between Worksop & Gainsborough

Hotel ★★★ 65% The West Retford Hotel, 24 North Rd, RETFORD ☎ 0870 609 6162 62 annexe en suite

RUDDINGTON Map 08 SK53

Ruddington Grange Wilford Rd NG11 6NB
☎ 0115 984 6141 ▤ 0115 9405165
e-mail: info@ruddingtongrange.com
18 holes, 6543yds, Par 72, SSS 72, Course record 69.
Course Designer E MacAusland **Location** 5m S of Nottingham, A60 to Ruddington
Telephone for further details

Hotel ★★★ 61% Swans Hotel & Restaurant, 84-90 Radcliffe Rd, West Bridgford, NOTTINGHAM ☎ 0115 981 4042 30 en suite

SERLBY Map 08 SK68

Serlby Park DN10 6BA ☎ 01777 818268
11 holes, 5325yds, Par 66, SSS 66, Course record 63.
Course Designer Viscount Galway **Location** E side of village off A638
Telephone for further details

Hotel ★★★ 70% Charnwood Hotel, Sheffield Rd, BLYTH ☎ 01909 591610 34 en suite

SUTTON IN ASHFIELD Map 08 SK45

Coxmoor Coxmoor Rd NG17 5LF
☎ 01623 557359 ▤ 01623 557359
e-mail: coxmoor@freeuk.com
Undulating moorland/heathland course with easy walking and excellent views. The clubhouse is traditional with a well-equipped games room. The course lies adjacent to Forestry Commission land over which there are several footpaths and extensive views.
18 holes, 6589yds, Par 73, SSS 72, Course record 65.
Club membership 700.
Visitors must play with member weekends & bank holidays. Must contact in advance. **Societies** must apply in advance. **Green Fees** £55 per day; £40 per round. *Continued*

Cards ⊞ ▦ ▦ ▦ ▦ ▢ **Prof** David Ridley **Facilities** ⊗ ⑂ ⓑ ♥ ♀ ♤ ⚑ ✓ **Leisure** snooker. **Location** 2m SE off A611. 4m from junct 27 on M1

Hotel ★★★★ 70% Renaissance Derby/Nottingham Hotel, Carter Ln East, SOUTH NORMANTON ☎ 01773 812000 158 en suite

WORSOP
Map 08 SK57

Bondhay Golf & Country Club
Bondhay Ln, Whitwell S80 3EH ☎ 01909 723608 ▤ 01909 720226 e-mail: bondhay@freeserve.com

The wind usually plays quite an active role in making this pleasantly undulating championship course testing. Signature holes are the 10th which requires a second shot over water into a basin of trees; the 11th comes back over the same expanse of water and requires a mid to short iron to a long, narrow green; the 18th is a par 5 with a lake - the dilemma is whether to lay up short or go for the carry. The par 3s are generally island-like in design, requiring accuracy to avoid the many protective bunker features.

Devonshire Course: 18 holes, 6705yds, Par 72, SSS 72, Course record 67.
Club membership 400.

Visitors must contact in advance. **Societies** must telephone in advance. **Green Fees** 18 holes: Mon-Tues £14; Wed-Fri £17; Sat-Sun £22. Par 3 Course £5. **Cards** ⊞ ▦ ▦ ▦ ▢ **Prof** Michael Ramsden **Course Designer** Donald Steel **Facilities** ⊗ ⑂ ⓑ ♥ ♀ ♤ ⚑ ✿ ⚘ ✓ ⛳ **Leisure** fishing, par 3 family course. **Conf** fac available Corporate Hospitality Days available **Location** M1 junct 30, 5m W of Worksop, off A619

Hotel ★★★ 65% Sitwell Arms Hotel, Station Rd, RENISHAW ☎ 01246 435226 29 en suite

College Pines
Worksop College Dr S80 3AP ☎ 01909 501431 ▤ 01909 481227

This course was opened in 1994 and the par 73 layout covers 150 acres of well-drained land with heathland characteristics. It is club policy to remain open on full tees and greens all year round.

18 holes, 6801yards, Par 73, SSS 73, Course record 67.
Club membership 500.

Visitors welcome by appointment. **Societies** write/telephone in advance. Deposit required to secure booking. **Green Fees** £20 per day; £13 per round (£30/£19 weekends & bank holidays). **Prof** Charles Snell **Course Designer** David Snell **Facilities** ⊗ ⑂ ⓑ ♥ ♀ ♤ ⚑ ✿ ⚘ ✓ ⛳ **Conf** Corporate Hospitality Days available **Location** Exit M1 at Junct 30/31, club is S of Worksop, on B6034 Edwinstowe road

Hotel ★★★ 65% Clumber Park Hotel, Clumber Park, WORKSOP ☎ 01623 835333 48 en suite

Kilton Forest
Blyth Rd S81 0TL ☎ 01909 486563

Slightly undulating, parkland course on the north edge of Sherwood Forest. Includes three ponds. Excellent conditions all the year round. A true test of golf.

18 holes, 6424yds, Par 72, SSS 71, Course record 66.
Club membership 320.

Visitors must contact in advance. May not play at weekends before 10am. **Societies** must contact in advance. **Green Fees** terms on application. **Prof** Stuart Betteridge

Continued

Facilities ⊗ ⓑ ♥ ♀ ♤ ⚑ ✿ ✿ ⚘ ✓ **Leisure** bowling. **Location** 1m NE of town centre on B6045

Hotel ★★★ 67% Lion Hotel, 112 Bridge St, WORKSOP ☎ 01909 477925 45 en suite

Lindrick
Lindrick Common S81 8BH ☎ 01909 475282 ▤ 01909 488685 e-mail: lgc@ansbronze.com

Heathland course with some trees and masses of gorse.
18 holes, 6486yds, Par 71, SSS 71, Course record 63.
Club membership 510.

Visitors must contact in advance. Restricted Tue & weekends. Handicap certificate required. **Societies** welcome except Tue (am) & weekends by prior arrangement with the Secretary. **Green Fees** £60 per day, £50 per 18 holes. Reduced winter rate. **Cards** ⊞ ▦ ▦ ▦ ▦ ▢ **Prof** John R King **Facilities** ⊗ ⑂ ⓑ ♥ ♀ ♤ ⚑ ✓ **Leisure** buggies for disabled only. **Conf** Corporate Hospitality Days available **Location** 4m NW of Worksop on A57

Hotel ★★★ 67% Lion Hotel, 112 Bridge St, WORKSOP ☎ 01909 477925 45 en suite

Worksop
Windmill Ln S80 2SQ ☎ 01909 477731 ▤ 01909 477732 e-mail: worksopgolfclub@worksop.co.uk

Adjacent to Clumber Park this course has a heathland-type terrain, with gorse, broom, oak and birch trees. Fast, true greens, dry all year round.

18 holes, 6660yds, Par 72, SSS 73.
Club membership 600.

Visitors by arrangement with professional tel: 01909 477731. **Societies** must apply in advance. **Green Fees** £48 per 36 holes, £35 per 18 holes. **Prof** C Weatherhead **Course Designer** Tom Williamson **Facilities** ⊗ ⑂ ⓑ ♥ ♀ ♤ ⚑ ✿ ⚘ ✓ **Leisure** snooker. **Conf** fac available Corporate Hospitality Days available **Location** Off A57 Ringroad, B6034 to Edwinstowe

Hotel ★★★ 65% Clumber Park Hotel, Clumber Park, WORKSOP ☎ 01623 835333 48 en suite

OXFORDSHIRE

ABINGDON
Map 04 SU49

Drayton Park
Steventon Rd, Drayton OX14 4LA ☎ 01235 550607 (Pro Shop) ▤ 01235 525731

Set in the heart of the Oxfordshire countryside, an 18-hole parkland course designed by Hawtree. Five lakes and sand-based greens.

18 holes, 5700yds, Par 67, SSS 67, Course record 60.
Club membership 500.

Visitors may phone to book, must have golf shoes, no jeans or tracksuits. **Societies** contact in advance. **Green Fees** not confirmed. **Cards** ⊞ ▦ ▦ ▦ ▦ ▢ **Prof** Martin Morbey **Course Designer** Hawtree **Facilities** ⊗ ⑂ ⓑ ♥ ♀ ♤ ⚑ ✿ ⚘ ✓ ⛳ **Leisure** 9 hole par 3 course. **Location** Between Oxford & Newbury, off A34 at Didcot

Hotel ★★★ 68% The Upper Reaches, Thames St, ABINGDON ☎ 0870 400 8101 31 en suite

Booking a tee time is always advisable.

BANBURY See also Chacombe (Northamptonshire)

BANBURY   Map 04 SP44

Banbury Aynho Rd, Adderbury OX17 3NT
☎ 01295 810419 & 812880 📠 01295 810056
e-mail: office@banburygolfcentre.co.uk
**Undulating wooded course with water features and
USGA specification greens.**
Red & Yellow: 18 holes, 6557yds, Par 71, SSS 71.
Yellow & Blue: 18 holes, 6603yds, Par 71, SSS 71.
Red & Blue: 18 holes, 6706yds, Par 72, SSS 72.
Club membership 300.
Visitors no restrictions **Societies** write or telephone in
advance. **Green Fees** £17 per 18 holes (£22 weekends).
Cards 🔲 🔲 **Prof** Stuart Kier **Course Designer**
Reed/Payn **Facilities** ⊗ 〉Ⅲ ⓛ ⬛ ♥ ♣ ⌂ ⛳ 🛒 ⛏ ♨
Conf Corporate Hospitality Days available **Location** off
B4100 between Adderbury and Aynho

Hotel ⬆ Premier Lodge (Banbury), Warwick Rd,
Warmington, BANBURY ☎ 0870 9906512 39 en suite

Rye Hill Milcombe OX15 4RU
☎ 01295 721818 📠 01295 720089
e-mail: tony@pennock20.freeserve.co.uk
**Well drained course features wide fairways, large
undulating greens, water hazards on the 10th, and fine
views of the surrounding countryside.**
18 holes, 6919yds, Par 72, SSS 73, Course record 62.
Club membership 575.
Visitors must book in advance, especially at weekends.
Societies telephone for details of Packages available.
Green Fees £30 per day, £20 per round (£40/£25
weekends). **Cards** 🔲 🔲 🔲 🔲 🔲 **Prof** Tony
Pennock **Facilities** ⊗ 〉Ⅲ ⓛ ⬛ ♥ ♣ ⌂ ⛳ ♨
Leisure fishing, 3 hole par 3 academy. **Conf** fac available
Corporate Hospitality Days available **Location** M40 junct
11, take A361 towards Chipping Norton, signed 1m out of
Bloxham

Hotel ★★★ 71% Banbury House, Oxford Rd,
BANBURY ☎ 01295 259361 63 en suite

BURFORD   Map 04 SP21

Burford Swindon Rd OX18 4JG
☎ 01993 822583 📠 01993 822801
e-mail: robin@burfordgc.com
**Parkland with mature, tree-lined fairways and high
quality greens.**
18 holes, 6432yds, Par 71, SSS 71, Course record 64.
Club membership 770.
Visitors must contact in advance. Restricted Tues, Thurs &
weekends **Societies** apply in writing. **Green Fees** £36 per
day. **Prof** Michael Ridge **Course Designer** John H Turner
Facilities ⊗ 〉Ⅲ ⓛ ⬛ ♥ ♣ ⌂ ⛳ ♨ **Location** 0.5m S off
A361

Hotel ★★ 65% Golden Pheasant Hotel, 91 High St,
BURFORD ☎ 01993 823223 12 rms (11 en suite)

CHESTERTON   Map 04 SP52

Bicester Golf & Country Club OX26 1TE
☎ 01869 242023 📠 01869 240754
e-mail: bicestergolf@ukonline.co.uk
**Recently reconstructed, the course has several lakes
and sculpted greens. The 13th and 18th holes require
shots of a very high standard.**
Continued

18 holes, 6600yds, Par 71, SSS 70, Course record 68.
Club membership 700.
Visitors may pre-book up to 7 days ahead. **Societies** by
appointment and in advance **Green Fees** not confirmed.
Cards 🔲 🔲 🔲 🔲 🔲 🔲 **Prof** J Goodman **Course
Designer** R Stagg **Facilities** ⊗ 〉Ⅲ ⓛ ⬛ ♥ ♣ ⌂ ♨
Location 0.5m W off A4095, 1m E of B430 at Weston-on-
the-Green

Hotel ★★ 70% Jersey Arms Hotel, BICESTER
☎ 01869 343234 6 en suite 14 annexe en suite

CHIPPING NORTON   Map 04 SP32

Chipping Norton Southcombe OX7 5QH
☎ 01608 642383 📠 01608 645422
e-mail: chipping.nortongc@virgin.net
**Downland course situated at 800 feet above sea level, its
undulations providing a good walk. On a limestone
base, the course dries quickly in wet conditions. The
opening few holes provide a good test of golf made more
difficult when the prevailing wind makes the player use
the extremes of the course.**

18 holes, 6241yds, Par 71, SSS 70, Course record 62.
Club membership 900.
Visitors with member only at weekends & bank holidays.
Societies telephone in advance. **Green Fees** £32 per day.
Prof Neil Rowlands **Facilities** ⊗ 〉Ⅲ ⓛ ⬛ ♥ ♣ ⌂ ⛳ 🛒
⛏ ♨ **Location** 1.5m E on A44

Hotel ★★★ 74% The Mill House Hotel & Restaurant,
KINGHAM ☎ 01608 658188 21 en suite 2 annexe en suite

Wychwood Lyneham OX7 6QQ
☎ 01993 831841 📠 01993 831775
e-mail: golf@wychwoodgc.freeserve.co.uk
**Lyneham was designed to use the natural features. It is
set in 170 acres on the fringe of the Costwolds and
blends superbly with its surroundings. Lakes and
streams enhance the challenge of the course with water
coming into play on eight of the 18 holes. All greens are
sand based, built to USGA specification.**
*The Wychwood: 18 holes, 6669yds, Par 72, SSS 72, Course
record 67.*
Club membership 750.
Visitors must contact in advance. **Societies** apply in
advance. **Green Fees** £30 per day, £24 per 18 holes
(£37/£28 weekends). **Cards** 🔲 🔲 🔲 🔲 **Prof** James
Fincher **Course Designer** D G Carpenter **Facilities** ⊗ 〉Ⅲ
ⓛ ⬛ ♥ ♣ ⌂ ⛳ 🛒 ⛏ ♨ ♣ **Conf** fac available
Corporate Hospitality Days available **Location** Off A361,
between Burford/Chipping Norton

Hotel ★★★ 74% The Mill House Hotel & Restaurant,
KINGHAM ☎ 01608 658188 21 en suite
2 annexe en suite

DIDCOT
Map 04 SU59

Hadden Hill
Wallingford Rd OX11 9BJ
☎ 01235 510410 📠 01235 511260
e-mail: info@haddenhillgolf.co.uk

A challenging course on undulating terrain with excellent drainage, so visitors can be sure of playing no matter what the weather conditions have been. Two loops of nine holes. Superb greens and fairways.

18 holes, 6563yds, Par 71, SSS 71, Course record 65.
Club membership 400.

Visitors telephone pro shop up to one week in advance to book tee times. **Societies** telephone to arrange times & dates & receive booking form. **Green Fees** £18 per 18 holes; £11 per 9 holes (£23/£14 weekends). **Cards** 💳 💳 🏧 **Prof** Ian Mitchell **Course Designer** Michael V Morley **Facilities** ⊗ ℳ ⅃ ⓑ ♥ ♀ ⚐ ♙ ☞ ♣ ♣ ♂ ℭ **Leisure** teaching academy. **Conf** Corporate Hospitality Days available **Location** A34 Milton interchange, follow A4130, Course located 1m E of Didcot on Wallingford Road

Hotel ★★★ 66% Abingdon Four Pillars Hotel, Marcham Rd, ABINGDON ☎ 0800 374 692 62 en suite

FARINGDON
Map 04 SU29

Carswell
Carswell SN7 8PU
☎ 01367 870422 📠 01367 870592
e-mail: info@carswellgolfandcountryclub.co.uk

An attractive course set in undulating wooded countryside close to Faringdon. Mature trees, five lakes and well placed bunkers add interest to the course. Floodlit driving range.

18 holes, 6183yds, Par 72, SSS 70.
Club membership 520.

Visitors advisable to book 8 days in advance, no earlier for tee time. **Societies** on weekdays only telephone to check availability, deposit required, **Green Fees** £18 per 18 holes (£25 weekends and bank holidays). **Cards** 💳 💳 🏧 **Prof** Steve Parker **Course Designer** J & E Ely **Facilities** ⊗ ℳ ⅃ ⓑ ♥ ♀ ⚐ ♙ ☞ ♣ ♂ ℭ **Leisure** sauna, solarium, gymnasium. **Location** just off the A420 between Oxford and Swindon

Hotel ★★★ 71% Sudbury House Hotel & Conference Centre, London St, FARINGDON ☎ 01367 241272 49 en suite

FRILFORD
Map 04 SU49

Frilford Heath
OX13 5NW
☎ 01865 390864 📠 01865 390823
e-mail: secretary@frilfordheath.co.uk

54 holes in three distinctive layouts of significantly differing character. The Green course is a fully mature heathland course of some 6000 yards. The Red course is of championship length at 6800 yards with a parkland flavour and a marked degree of challenge. The Blue course is of modern design, and at 6728 yards, it incorporates water hazards and large shallow sand traps.

Red Course: 18 holes, 6884yds, Par 73, SSS 73, Course record 66.
Green Course: 18 holes, 6006yds, Par 69, SSS 69, Course record 67.
Blue Course: 18 holes, 6728yds, Par 72, SSS 72, Course record 63.
Club membership 1300.

Visitors contact in advance. Handicap certificates
Continued

required. **Societies** apply in advance. **Green Fees** £55 per day (£70 weekends). **Cards** 💳 💳 **Prof** Derek Craik **Course Designer** J Taylor/D Cotton/S Gidman **Facilities** ⊗ ℳ ⅃ ⓑ ♥ ♀ ⚐ ☞ ♣ ♣ ♂ **Conf** fac available Corporate Hospitality Days available **Location** 3m W of Abingdon off A338 Oxford-Wantage road

Hotel ★★★ 66% Abingdon Four Pillars Hotel, Marcham Rd, ABINGDON ☎ 0800 374 692 62 en suite

HENLEY-ON-THAMES
Map 04 SU78

Aspect Park
Remenham Hill RG9 3EH
☎ 01491 578306 📠 01491 578306
e-mail: enquiries@aspectgolf.com

Parkland course.

18 holes, 6557yds, Par 72, SSS 72.
Club membership 500.

Visitors must contact in advance, suitable golf attire required on course, no jeans in the clubhouse. **Societies** must contact in advance. **Green Fees** £20 per 18 holes (£25 weekends). **Cards** 💳 💳 💳 💳 **Prof** Terry Notley **Course Designer** Tim Winsland **Facilities** ⊗ ℳ ⅃ ⓑ ♥ ♀ ⚐ ☞ ♣ ♣ ♂ ℭ **Conf** fac available **Location** off A4130 at Remenham Hill between Maidenhead and Henley

Hotel ★★★ 71% Red Lion Hotel, Hart St, HENLEY-ON-THAMES ☎ 01491 572161 26 en suite

Badgemore Park
Badgemore RG9 4NR
☎ 01491 572206 📠 01491 576899
e-mail: info@badgemorepark.com

Well established 18 hole parkland course with attractive specimen trees lining the fairways. The signature hole of this easy walking course is the 13th, a tough par 3 played across a valley to a narrow raised green.

18 holes, 6129yds, Par 69, SSS 69, Course record 64.
Club membership 700.

Visitors check for availability by contacting professional shop on 01491 574175. 48 hrs booking minimum for weekend play. Tue mornings, lady members only. **Societies** contact the Club Secretary to book. **Green Fees** not confirmed. **Cards** 💳 💳 💳 💳 **Prof** Jonathan Dunn **Course Designer** Robert Sandow **Facilities** ⊗ ℳ by prior arrangement ⓑ ♥ ♀ ⚐ ☞ ♣ ♣ ♂ **Conf** fac available Corporate Hospitality Days available **Location** From Henley head north west towards Rotherfield Greys. Golf club 1.5m on right

Hotel ★★★ 71% Red Lion Hotel, Hart St, HENLEY-ON-THAMES ☎ 01491 572161 26 en suite

Henley
Harpsden RG9 4HG
☎ 01491 575742 📠 01491 412179
e-mail: henleygolfclub@btinternet.com

Undulating parkland course, with adjoining woodlands.

18 holes, 6329yds, Par 70, SSS 70, Course record 63.
Club membership 800.

Visitors must contact in advance. Weekend only with a member. **Societies** Wed & Thu, apply in writing. **Green Fees** £45 per day; £35 per round; £25 after 4pm. **Cards** 💳 **Prof** Mark Howell **Course Designer** James Braid **Facilities** ⊗ ℳ ⅃ ⓑ ♥ ♀ ⚐ ☞ ♂ **Location** 1.25m S off A4155

Hotel ★★★ 71% Red Lion Hotel, Hart St, HENLEY-ON-THAMES ☎ 01491 572161 26 en suite

HORTON-CUM-STUDLEY   Map 04 SP51

Studley Wood The Straight Mile OX33 1BF
☎ 01865 351122 & 351144 🖩 01865 351166
e-mail: admin@swgc.co.uk.
Woodland course set in a former deer park with twelve lakes and specimen oak trees providing challenging natural hazards on almost all the holes.
18 holes, 6811yds, Par 73, SSS 72, Course record 65. Club membership 700.
Visitors must play to handicap standard, tee times booked up to 4 days in advance. After noon at weekend. **Societies** contact secretary for details. **Green Fees** £36 per round (£46 per round weekends). **Cards** 💳 💳 💳 💳 **Prof** Tony Williams **Course Designer** Simon Gidman **Facilities** ⊗ ⁏ 📭 🏌 ♍ 🛒 🏕 🕏 🐎 🚜 🏌 🕻 **Conf** fac available Corporate Hospitality Days available **Location** 4m from Oxford, follow signs for Horton-cum-Studley from Headington rdbt on Oxford ring road
....
Hotel ★★★★ 70% The Oxford Hotel, Godstow Rd, Wolvercote Roundabout, OXFORD ☎ 01865 489952 168 en suite

KIRTLINGTON   Map 04 SP41

Kirtlington OX5 3JY
☎ 01869 351133 🖩 01869 351143
e-mail: info@kirtlingtongolfclub.co.uk
An inland links type course with challenging greens. The course incorporates many mature natural features and boasts 102 bunkers and a 'bye-hole', the 110-yard par 3 19th when an extra hole is required to determine a winner. New clubhouse, academy course and covered bays on the driving range have recently opened.
18 holes, 6107yds, Par 70, SSS 69, Course record 68. Academy Course: 9 holes, 1535yds, Par 30, SSS 53. Club membership 400.
Visitors must book for weekends and advisable to book for wekdays. Must contact in advance. **Societies** contact for Society packages. **Green Fees** 18 holes £20 (weekends £25). 9 holes £10 (£12). **Cards** 💳 💳 💳 💳 💳 **Prof** Andy Taylor **Course Designer** Graham Webster **Facilities** ⊗ 📭 🏌 ♍ 🛒 🏕 🕏 🐎 🚜 🏌 🕻 **Leisure** 9 hole academy course. **Conf** fac available Corporate Hospitality Days available **Location** on A4095 just outside village of Kirtlington
....
Hotel ★★★ 70% Weston Manor Hotel, WESTON-ON-THE-GREEN ☎ 01869 350621 15 en suite 20 annexe en suite

MILTON COMMON   Map 04 SP60

The Oxfordshire Rycote Ln OX9 2PU
☎ 01844 278300 🖩 01844 278003
e-mail: info@theoxfordshiregolfclub.com
Designed by Rees Jones, The Oxfordshire is considered to be one of the most exciting courses in the country. The strategically contoured holes blend naturally into the surrounding countryside to provide a challenging game of golf. With four lakes and 135 bunkers, the course makes full use of the terrain and the natural elements to provide characteristics similar to those of a links course.
18 holes, 7192yds, Par 72, SSS 75, Course record 64. Club membership 376.
Visitors After 11am weekends and bank holidays, contact in advance, handicap certificates must be provided

Continued

The Oxfordshire Golf Club

Societies Apply in writing/telephone in advance. **Green Fees** Summer: £80 per 18 holes (£100 weekends); Winter: £50 (£60 weekends). **Cards** 💳 💳 💳 💳 💳 **Prof** Stephen Gibson **Course Designer** Rees Jones **Facilities** ⊗ ⁏ 📭 🏌 ♍ 🛒 🏕 🕏 🐎 🚜 🏌 🕻 **Leisure** Japanese ofuro baths. **Conf** fac available Corporate Hospitality Days available **Location** 1.5m from junct 7, M40 on A329
....
Hotel ★★★ 76% Spread Eagle Hotel, Cornmarket, THAME ☎ 01844 213661 33 en suite

NUFFIELD   Map 04 SU68

Huntercombe RG9 5SL
☎ 01491 641207 🖩 01491 642060
e-mail: office@huntercombegolfclub.co.uk
This heathland/woodland course overlooks the Oxfordshire plain and has many attractive and interesting fairways and greens. Walking is easy after the 3rd which is a notable hole. The course is subject to wind and grass pot bunkers are interesting hazards.

18 holes, 6301yds, Par 70, SSS 70, Course record 63. Club membership 800.
Visitors must contact in advance and have a handicap certificate. **Societies** must contact in advance. **Green Fees** not confirmed. **Cards** 💳 💳 💳 **Prof** David Reffin **Course Designer** Willy Park **Facilities** ⊗ ⁏ 📭 🏌 ♍ 🛒 🏕 🕏 🐎 🚜 🏌 🕻 **Location** 6m W of Henley-on-Thames off A4130 at Nuffield
....
Hotel ★★★ 67% Shillingford Bridge Hotel, Shillingford, WALLINGFORD ☎ 01865 858567 34 en suite 8 annexe en suite

OXFORD   Map 04 SP50

Hinksey Heights South Hinksey OX1 5AB
☎ 01865 327775 🖩 01865 736930
e-mail: play@oxford-golf.co.uk
Set in an area of outstanding natural beauty,

Continued

overlooking the incomparable 'Dreaming Spires' of Oxford and the Thames Valley. The course has been designed and built as a series of interesting and distinctive holes that reward the thoughtful golfer. Several of the holes challenge you to be bold, with the inherent risk of danger, or to play safe. There is also a 9 hole par 3 course for golfers of all ages and abilities.

Hinksey Heights Golf Course

18 holes, 6936yds, Par 74, SSS 73.
Club membership 450.
Visitors advisable to telephone in advance. **Societies** apply in advance. **Green Fees** not confirmed. **Cards** ⊞ ▬▬▬ ▬▬ 🖳 🗺 💲 **Prof** David Bolton **Course Designer** David Heads **Facilities** ⊗ ⫙ 🏌 🕪 💺 🍺 👤 🛎 ⛳ 🏌 🛎 **Conf** Corporate Hospitality Days available **Location** on A34 (Oxford ring road) between Abingdon and Oxford Botley junction

Hotel ★★★ 69% Hawkwell House, Church Way, Iffley Village, OXFORD ☎ 01865 749988 51 en suite

North Oxford Banbury Rd OX2 8EZ
☎ 01865 554924 🗎 01865 515921
e-mail: secretary@nogc.co.uk
Gently undulating parkland course.
18 holes, 5736yds, Par 67, SSS 67, Course record 62.
Club membership 700.
Visitors at weekends & bank holidays may only play after 2pm. **Societies** must contact in advance. **Green Fees** £25 per day; £18 per round. **Cards** ⊞ ▬▬ 🖳 💲 **Prof** Robert Harris **Facilities** ⊗ ⫙ 🏌 🕪 💺 🍺 👤 🛎 ⛳ **Conf** Corporate Hospitality Days available **Location** 3m N of city centre on A4165

Hotel ★★★★ 70% The Oxford Hotel, Godstow Rd, Wolvercote Roundabout, OXFORD ☎ 01865 489952 168 en suite

Southfield Hill Top Rd OX4 1PF
☎ 01865 242158 🗎 01865 728544
e-mail: sgcltd@btopenworld.com
Home of the City, University and Ladies Clubs, and well-known to graduates throughout the world. A challenging course, in a varied parkland setting, providing a real test for players.
18 holes, 6328yds, Par 70, SSS 70, Course record 64.
Club membership 740.
Visitors with member only at weekends. **Societies** must apply in writing. **Green Fees** £35 per day; £25 per round. **Cards** ⊞ ▬▬ 🖳 💲 **Prof** Tony Rees **Course Designer** H S Colt **Facilities** ⊗ ⫙ 🏌 🕪 💺 🍺 👤 🛎 ⛳ 🛎 **Conf** Corporate Hospitality Days available **Location** 1.5m SE of city centre off B480

Hotel ★★★ 65% Eastgate Hotel, 73 High St, OXFORD ☎ 0870 400 8201 64 en suite

Shrivenham Park Penny Hooks Ln SN6 8EX
☎ 01793 783853
A flat, mature parkland course with excellent drainage, providing a good challenge for all standards of golfer.
Shrivenham Park Golf Course: 18 holes, 5769yds, Par 69, SSS 69, Course record 64.
Club membership 150.
Visitors phone in advance. **Societies** phone for details. **Green Fees** Mon-Thu 18 holes £14; 9 holes £8, Fri-Sun & bank holidays £18/£12. **Cards** ⊞ ▬▬ ▬▬ 🗺 💲 **Prof** Tony Pocock **Course Designer** Gordon Cox **Facilities** ⊗ ⫙ 🏌 🍺 👤 🛎 ⛳ **Conf** fac available Corporate Hospitality Days available **Location** 0.5m NE of town centre

Hotel ★★★ 71% Sudbury House Hotel & Conference Centre, London St, FARINGDON ☎ 01367 241272 49 en suite

Tadmarton Heath OX15 5HL
☎ 01608 737278 🗎 01608 730548
e-mail: thgc@btinternet.com
A mixture of heath and sandy land, the course, which is open to strong winds, incorporates the site of an old Roman encampment. The clubhouse is an old farm building with a 'holy well' from which the greens are watered. The 7th is a testing hole over water.
18 holes, 5917yds, Par 69, SSS 69, Course record 63.
Club membership 600.
Visitors weekday by appointment, with member only at weekends. no visitors Thursday mornings **Societies** by arrangement with club office. **Green Fees** £45 per day, £35 after 2.30pm, (weekends £50, £40 after 12pm). **Prof** Tom Jones **Course Designer** Col Hutchinson **Facilities** ⊗ ⫙ 🍺 👤 🛎 ⛳ 🛎 **Leisure** fishing. **Conf** Corporate Hospitality Days available **Location** 1m SW of Lower Tadmarton off B4035, 4m from Banbury

Hotel ★★★ 71% Banbury House, Oxford Rd, BANBURY ☎ 01295 259361 63 en suite

Springs Hotel Wallingford Rd, North Stoke
OX10 6BE ☎ 01491 827310 🗎 01491 827312
e-mail: proshop@thespringshotel.com
133 acres of park land, bordered by the River Thames, within which lie three lakes and challenging wetland areas. The course has traditional features like a double green and sleepered bunker with sleepered lake edges of typical American design.
18 holes, 6470yds, Par 72, SSS 71, Course record 67.
Club membership 580.
Visitors handicap certificate required. Dress code must be adhered to. **Societies** apply in writing, telephone/e-mail. **Green Fees** £37 per day, £29 per 18 holes (£45/£35 weekends & bank holidays). **Cards** ⊞ ▬▬ 🖳 🗺 🗺 💲 **Prof** Pete Ivil **Course Designer** Brian Hugget **Facilities** ⊗ ⫙ 🏌 🍺 👤 🛎 ⛳ 🛎 **Leisure** heated outdoor swimming pool, fishing, sauna, croquet lawn. **Conf** fac available Corporate Hospitality Days available **Location** 15 miles SE of Oxford & 12.5 miles NW of Reading.

Hotel ★★★ 72% Springs Hotel & Golf Club, Wallingford Rd, North Stoke, WALLINGFORD ☎ 01491 836687 31 en suite

WATERSTOCK   Map 04 SP60

Waterstock Thame Rd OX33 1HT
☎ 01844 338093 📠 01844 338036
e-mail: wgc_oxfordgolf@btinternet.com
A 6,500 yard course designed by Donald Steel with USGA greens and tees fully computer irrigated. Four par 3s facing north, south, east and west. A brook and hidden lake affect six holes, with dog-legs being 4th and 10th holes. Five par 5s on the course, making it a challenge for players of all standards.
18 holes, 6535yds, Par 73, SSS 71, Course record 69. Club membership 500.
Visitors no restrictions. **Societies** apply by writing, telephone or e-mail. **Green Fees** not confirmed. **Cards** 💳 💳 💳 💳 **Prof** Paul Bryant **Course Designer** Donald Steel **Facilities** ⊗ 〉Ⅲ ⅃ ♭ 🖤 ♀ 🎗 🏊 🕯 🏌 🛒 ∅ 🎗 **Leisure** fishing. **Conf** fac available   Corporate Hospitality Days available **Location** M40 junct 8/8A east of Oxford near Wheatley.

Hotel ★★★ 76%   Spread Eagle Hotel, Cornmarket, THAME ☎ 01844 213661 33 en suite

WITNEY   Map 04 SP31

Witney Lakes Downs Rd OX29 0SY
☎ 01993 893011 📠 01993 778866
e-mail: golf@witney-lakes.co.uk
A lakeland style course with five large lakes coming into play on eight holes. An excellent test of golf that will use every club in your bag.
18 holes, 6700yds, Par 71, Course record 67. Club membership 450.
Visitors may pre-book 5 days in advance, weekends after 10.30 am **Societies** telephone or write in advance. **Green Fees** £18 per 18 holes (weekends £25). **Cards** 💳 💳 💳 💳 **Prof** Adam Souter **Course Designer** Simon Gidman **Facilities** ⊗ 〉Ⅲ ♭ 🖤 ♀ 🎗 🏊 🕯 🛒 ∅ 🎗 **Leisure** heated indoor swimming pool, sauna, solarium, gymnasium. **Conf** fac available   Corporate Hospitality Days available **Location** 2m W of Witney town centre, off B4047 Witney/Burford road

Hotel ★★★ 69%   Witney Four Pillars Hotel, Ducklington Ln, WITNEY ☎ 0800 374 692 83 en suite

RUTLAND

GREAT CASTERTON   Map 04 TF00

Rutland County PE9 4AQ
☎ 01780 460330 📠 01780 460437
e-mail: info@rutlandcountygolf.co.uk
Inland links-style course with gently rolling fairways, large tees and greens. Playable all year round due to good drainage.
18 holes, 6401yds, Par 71, SSS 71, Course record 64. Club membership 740.
Visitors must book in advance at the shop, tel 01780 460239. **Societies** contact office by phone, must be booked in advance. **Green Fees** terms on application. **Cards** 💳 💳 💳 💳 **Prof** Fred Fearn **Course Designer** Cameron Sinclair **Facilities** ⊗ 〉Ⅲ ♭ 🖤 ♀ 🎗 🕯 🏌 🛒 ∅ 🎗 **Leisure** Par 3 course. **Conf** fac available   Corporate Hospitality Days available **Location** 2m N of Stamford on A1

Continued

Hotel ★★ 69%   The White Horse Inn, Main St, EMPINGHAM ☎ 01780 460221 & 460521
📠 01780 460521 4 en suite   9 annexe en suite

GREETHAM   Map 08 SK91

Greetham Valley Wood Ln LE15 7NP
☎ 01780 460004 📠 01780 460623
e-mail: info@gvgc.co.uk
Set in 260 acres, including mature woodland, undulating natural valley, and water hazards. The complex comprises two 18 hole courses, The Lakes and The Valley, a luxurious clubhouse, 9 hole par 3, floodlit driving range and teaching academy.

Lakes: 18 holes, 6779yds, Par 72, SSS 72, Course record 65.
Valley: 18 holes, 5595yds, Par 68, SSS 67. Club membership 1000.
Visitors must contact in advance. **Societies** must contact in advance. **Green Fees** £48 per day; £32 per round (£54/£36 weekends). **Cards** 💳 💳 💳 💳 **Prof** John Pengelly **Course Designer** F E Hinch/B Stephens **Facilities** ⊗ 〉Ⅲ ♭ 🖤 ♀ 🎗 🏊 🕯 🛒 🏌 🛒 ∅ 🎗 **Leisure** fishing, bowls green, 9 hole par 3. **Conf** fac available   Corporate Hospitality Days available **Location** Take the B668 Oakham road off the A1 and follow signs to the course which are clearly marked

Hotel ★★★ 75%   Barnsdale Lodge Hotel, The Avenue, Rutland Water, North Shore, OAKHAM ☎ 01572 724678 46 en suite

KETTON   Map 04 SK90

Luffenham Heath PE9 3UU
☎ 01780 720205 📠 01780 722146
e-mail: jringleby@theluffenhamheathgc.co.uk
This undulating heathland course with low bushes, much gorse and many trees, lies in a conservation area for flora and fauna. From the higher part of the course there is a magnificent view across the Chater Valley. The course places a premium on accuracy with many demanding driving holes, challenging bunkers and well guarded greens. The course is not long but there are several outstanding holes.
18 holes, 6315yds, Par 70, SSS 70, Course record 64. Club membership 550.
Visitors must contact in advance. Weekends with member only before 2.30pm. **Societies** write or telephone in advance. **Green Fees** terms on application. **Cards** 💳 💳 💳 **Prof** Ian Burnett **Course Designer** James Braid **Facilities** ⊗ 〉Ⅲ ♭ 🖤 ♀ 🎗 🕯 ∅ **Conf** Corporate Hospitality Days available **Location** 1.5m SW of Ketton by Fosters Railway Bridge on A6121

Continued

Hotel ★★★ 78% The George of Stamford, 71 St Martins, STAMFORD ☎ 01780 750750 & 750700 (Res) 🖹 01780 750701 47 en suite

SHROPSHIRE

BRIDGNORTH
Map 07 SO79

Bridgnorth Stanley Ln WV16 4SF
☎ 01746 763315 🖹 01746 761381
A pleasant course laid out on parkland on the bank of the River Severn.
18 holes, 6582yds, Par 73, SSS 72, Course record 72.
Club membership 725.
Visitors must contact in advance but may not play on Wed. Restricted weekends. **Societies** contact in writing or by telephone **Green Fees** £30 per day, £24 per round (£30 per round weekends). **Prof** Paul Hinton **Facilities** ⊗ ⊩ ⬛ 🍷 ♀ ♨ 🖿 🐾 🚜 ♂ **Leisure** fishing. **Conf** Corporate Hospitality Days available **Location** 1m N off B4373, 0.5m from town centre

Hotel ★★ 64% Falcon Hotel, Saint John St, Lowtown, BRIDGNORTH ☎ 01746 763134 12 en suite

CHURCH STRETTON
Map 07 SO49

Church Stretton Trevor Hill SY6 6JH
☎ 01694 722281 🖹 01743 861918
e-mail: secretary@churchstrettongolfclub.co.uk
Hillside course designed by James Braid on the lower slopes of the Long Mynd, with magnificent views and well drained turf. No temporary greens or tees.

18 holes, 5020yds, Par 66, SSS 65, Course record 63.
Club membership 450.
Visitors Tee reserved for members Sat 9-10.30am & 1-2.30pm (summer), 12-1.30pm (winter) Sun prior to 10.30am & 1-2.30pm (summer), 12-1.30pm; (winter). **Societies** must contact in advance. **Green Fees** £20 (£25

weekends & bank holidays). **Cards** 💳 **Prof** J Townsend **Course Designer** James Braid **Facilities** ⊗ ⊩ ⬛ 🍷 ♀ ♨ 🖿 ♂ **Location** W of the town. From Cardington Valley drive up Trevor Hill, a steep, winding road

Hotel ★★ 70% Mynd House Hotel, Ludlow Rd, Little Stretton, CHURCH STRETTON ☎ 01694 722212 7 en suite

CLEOBURY MORTIMER
Map 07 SO67

Cleobury Mortimer Wyre Common DY14 8HQ
☎ 01299 271112 🖹 01299 271468
e-mail: enquiries@cleoburygolfclub.com
Well designed 27-hole parkland course set in undulating countryside with fine views from all holes, and offering an interesting challenge to golfers of all abilities.
Foxes Run: 9 holes, 2980yds, Par 34, SSS 34.
Badgers Sett: 9 holes, 3271yds, Par 36, SSS 36.
Deer Park: 9 holes, 3167yds, Par 35, SSS 35.
Club membership 650.
Visitors advisable to book in advance, handicap certificate may be required at weekends. **Societies** write or telephone in advance. **Green Fees** £30 per day, £20 per 18 holes (weekends £36/£30). **Cards** 💳 💳 💳 💳 **Prof** Jon Jones/Martin Payne **Course Designer** E.G.U **Facilities** ⊗ ⊩ ⬛ 🍷 ♀ ♨ 🖿 🐾 ♂ ♪ **Leisure** fishing, snooker table. **Conf** fac available Corporate Hospitality Days available **Location** 10m W of Kidderminster on A4117 1m N of Cleobury Mortimer, off B4201

Inn ♦♦♦♦ The Crown Inn, Hopton Wafers, CLEOBURY MORTIMER ☎ 01299 270372 7 en suite

HIGHLEY
Map 07 SO78

Severn Meadows WV16 6HZ ☎ 01746 862212
9 holes, 5258yds, Par 68, SSS 67.
Telephone for further details

Hotel ★★★★ 66% Mill Hotel & Restaurant, ALVELEY ☎ 01746 780437 41 en suite

LILLESHALL
Map 07 SJ71

Lilleshall Hall TF10 9AS
☎ 01952 603840 & 604776 🖹 01952 604776
18 holes, 5906yds, Par 68, SSS 68, Course record 65.
Course Designer H S Colt **Location** 3m SE
Telephone for further details

Hotel ★★ 68% White House Hotel, Wellington Rd, Muxton, TELFORD ☎ 01952 604276 & 603603 🖹 01952 670336 31 en suite

LUDLOW
Map 07 SO57

Ludlow Bromfield SY8 2BT
☎ 01584 856366 🖹 01584 856366
e-mail: ludlowgo@barbox.net
A long-established heathland course in the middle of the racecourse. Very flat, quick drying, with broom and gorse-lined fairways.
18 holes, 6277yds, Par 70, SSS 70, Course record 65.
Club membership 700.
Visitors advisable to contact in advance. **Societies** apply in advance. **Green Fees** £25 per round/£30 per day (£25 weekends & bank holidays). **Prof** Russell Price **Facilities** ⊗ ⊩ ⬛ 🍷 ♀ ♨ 🖿 ♂ **Conf** Corporate Hospitality Days available **Location** 1m N of Ludlow, off A49

Continued

Continued

Hotel ★★★ 67% The Feathers Hotel & Ludlow Ltd,
The Bull Ring, LUDLOW ☎ 01584 875261 40 en suite

MARKET DRAYTON   Map 07 SJ63

Market Drayton Sutton Ln TF9 2HX
☎ 01630 652266
e-mail: marketdraytongc@btinternet.com
**Parkland course in quiet, picturesque surroundings
providing a good test of golf. Bungalow on course is
available for golfing holidays.**
*18 holes, 6290yds, Par 71, SSS 71, Course record 69.
Club membership 600.*
Visitors may not play on Sun; must play with member on
Sat. Must contact in advance. **Societies** welcome
Mon,Wed,Thu & Fri, must contact in advance. **Green Fees**
Summer £26 per round; Winter £20. **Prof** Russell Clewes
Facilities ⊗ ⊼ ⅃ ⅃ ⚑ ⨯ ⌂ ⛳ Ȿ **Location** 1m SW

Hotel ★★★ 70% Goldstone Hall, Goldstone, MARKET
DRAYTON ☎ 01630 661202 11 en suite

MEOLE BRACE   Map 07 SJ41

Meole Brace Otely Rd SY2 6QQ ☎ 01743 364050
9 holes, 5830yds, Par 68, SSS 68, Course record 66.
Location NE side of village off A49
Telephone for further details

Hotel ★★★ 63% The Lion Hotel, Wyle Cop,
SHREWSBURY ☎ 0870 609 6167 59 en suite

OSWESTRY   Map 07 SJ22

Mile End Mile End, Old Shrewsbury Rd SY11 4JE
☎ 01691 671246 📠 01691 670580
e-mail: info@mileendgolfclub.co.uk
**A gently undulating parkland-type course boasting
challenging holes for all standards of golfing ability.
Longest hole is par 5 14th at 540yds. A number of water
features need to be negotiated including two large
ponds on the 3rd and 17th. The course is set in 140
acres, ensuring all holes are sufficiently isolated.**
*18 holes, 6292yds, Par 71, SSS 70, Course record 66.
Club membership 700.*
Visitors welcome at all times please telephone in advance
to check availability. **Societies** must contact in advance,
information available. **Green Fees** £16 per round (£25
weekends & bank holidays). **Cards** 🃏 💳 💳 💳 💳 🪙
Prof Scott Carpenter **Course Designer** Price/Gough
Facilities ⊗ ⊼ by prior arrangement ⅃ ⅃ ⅃ ⌂ Ȿ ⌇
Conf Corporate Hospitality Days available **Location** 1m
SE of Oswestry, just off A5

Hotel ★★★ 70% Wynnstay Hotel, Church St,
OSWESTRY ☎ 01691 655261 29 en suite

Oswestry Aston Park SY11 4JJ
☎ 01691 610535 📠 01691 610535
e-mail: secretary@oswestrygolfclub.co.uk
**Gently undulating mature parkland course set in
splendid Shropshire countryside. Free draining soils
make Oswestry an ideal year round test of golf.**
*18 holes, 6024yds, Par 70, SSS 69, Course record 61.
Club membership 960.*
Visitors must contact in advance. Must have a handicap
certificate or play with member. **Societies** must contact in
advance. **Green Fees** £32 per day, £26 per round (Sat
£35/£30). **Prof** David Skelton **Course Designer** James
Braid **Facilities** ⊗ ⊼ ⅃ ⅃ ⅃ ⌂ ⌂ ⛳ Ȿ **Conf**

Corporate Hospitality Days available **Location** 2m SE on
A5

Hotel ★★★ 70% Wynnstay Hotel, Church St,
OSWESTRY ☎ 01691 655261 29 en suite

PANT   Map 07 SJ22

Llanymynech SY10 8LB ☎ 01691 830983 & 830542
**Upland course on the site of an early Iron Age/Roman
hillfort with far-reaching views. With 15 holes in Wales
and three in England, drive off in Wales and putt out in
England on 4th hole.**
*18 holes, 6114yds, Par 70, SSS 69, Course record 64.
Club membership 700.*
Visitors prior contact advised, some weekends restricted.
Societies must contact Secretary. **Green Fees** £25 per
day/£20 per round (£25 weekends & bank holidays). **Prof**
Andrew P Griffiths **Facilities** ⊗ ⊼ ⅃ ⅃ ⅃ ⌂ Ȿ **Conf**
Corporate Hospitality Days available **Location** 6m S of
Oswestry on A483. In village of Pant turn at Cross Guns
Inn

Hotel ★★★ 70% Wynnstay Hotel, Church St,
OSWESTRY ☎ 01691 655261 29 en suite

SHIFNAL   Map 07 SJ70

Shifnal Decker Hill TF11 8QL
☎ 01952 460330 📠 01952 461127
e-mail: secretary@shifnalgolfclub.co.uk
**Well-wooded parkland course. Walking is easy and an
attractive country mansion serves as the clubhouse.**
*18 holes, 6468yds, Par 71, SSS 71, Course record 65.
Club membership 700.*
Visitors must contact in advance, may not play at
weekends or on Thursdays. **Societies** must contact in
advance. **Green Fees** £32 per day, £26 per 18 holes. **Cards**
💳 💳 💳 💳 **Prof** Justin Flanagan **Course Designer** Pennick
Facilities ⊗ ⊼ ⅃ ⅃ ⅃ ⌂ Ȿ **Conf** Corporate
Hospitality Days available **Location** 1m N of Shifnal, off
B4379

Hotel ★★★★ 67% Park House Hotel, Park St, SHIFNAL
☎ 01952 460128 38 en suite 16 annexe en suite

SHREWSBURY   Map 07 SJ41

Arscott Arscott, Pontesbury SY5 0XP
☎ 01743 860114 📠 01743 860881
**At 365 feet above sea level, the views from Arscott Golf
Club of the hills of south Shropshire and Wales are
superb. Arscott is a new course, set in mature parkland
with water features and holes demanding all sorts of
club choice. A challenge to all golfers both high and low
handicap.**
*18 holes, 6178yds, Par 70, SSS 69, Course record 68.
Club membership 550.*
Visitors most times available by prior arrangement.
Societies apply in writing or telephone for tee reservation.
Green Fees £18 per round (£22 weekends & bank
holidays). **Cards** 💳 💳 💳 💳 💳 🪙 **Course Designer**
M Hamer **Facilities** ⊗ ⊼ ⅃ ⅃ ⅃ ⌂ ⛳ Ȿ **Leisure**
fishing, sports injury treatment, massage. **Conf** fac
available **Location** Off A488, S of Shrewsbury 3m from
A5

Hotel ★★★ 63% The Lion Hotel, Wyle Cop,
SHREWSBURY ☎ 0870 609 6167 59 en suite

Continued

Shrewsbury Condover SY5 7BL

☎ 01743 872976 & 872977 (sec) 📠 01743 874647
e-mail: info@shrewsbury-golf-club.co.uk
Parkland course. First nine flat, second undulating with good views of the Long Mynd Range. Several holes with water features. Fast putting surfaces.
18 holes, 6300yds, Par 70, SSS 70.
Club membership 872.
Visitors must contact in advance, weekend restrictions and have a handicap certificate. **Societies** must contact in writing. **Green Fees** terms on application. **Prof** Peter Seal
Facilities ⊗ ⅢⅡ ⅃ ⬛ ♀ ♤ 🏠 ♦ ♂ ♪ **Location** 4m S off A49

Hotel ★★★ 71% Prince Rupert Hotel, Butcher Row, SHREWSBURY ☎ 01743 499955 70 en suite

TELFORD   Map 07 SJ60

Shropshire Golf Centre Granville Park, Muxton

TF2 8PQ ☎ 01952 677800 📠 01952 677622
e-mail: sales@theshropshire.co.uk
This 27 hole course set rolling countryside. The three loops of nine make the most on the land's natural undulations and provide a challenge for golfer of all abilities. Ample stretches of water and bullrush lined ditches, wide countered fairways and rolling greens guarded by mature trees, hummocks and vast bunkers.

Blue: 9 holes, 3286yds, Par 35, SSS 35.
Silver: 9 holes, 3303yds, Par 36, SSS 36.
Gold: 9 holes, 3334yds, Par 36, SSS 36.
Club membership 400.
Visitors recommended to book 7 days in advance.
Societies must book in advance. **Green Fees** 18 holes £18; 9 holes £12 (weekends £24/£14). **Cards** 🪧 🪧 🪧 🪧
🪧 🪧 🪧 **Prof** Rob Grier **Course Designer** Martin Hawtree **Facilities** ⊗ ⅢⅡ ⅃ ⬛ ♀ ♤ 🏠 🏌 🚵 ♂ ♪
Leisure 12 hole pitch and putt course. **Conf** fac available Corporate Hospitality Days available **Location** From M54/A5 take B5060 towards Donnington. Take 3rd exit at Granville rdbt and continue

Hotel ★★★ 64% Telford Golf & Country Club, Great Hay Dr, Sutton Heights, TELFORD ☎ 01952 429977 96 en suite

Telford Golf & Country Club Great Hay Dr,

Sutton Heights TF7 4DT
☎ 01952 429977 📠 01952 586602
18 holes, 6761yds, Par 72, SSS 72, Course record 66.
Course Designer Harris/Griffiths **Location** 4m S of town centre off A442
Telephone for further details

Continued

Hotel ★★★ 64% Telford Golf & Country Club, Great Hay Dr, Sutton Heights, TELFORD ☎ 01952 429977 96 en suite

WELLINGTON   Map 07 SJ61

Wrekin Ercall Woods, Golf Links Ln TF6 5BX

☎ 01952 244032 📠 01952 252906
e-mail: wrekingolfclub@lineone.net
Downland course with some hard walking but superb views.

18 holes, 5570yds, Par 67, SSS 66, Course record 64.
Club membership 675.
Visitors must contact in advance. Limited weekends & bank holidays. **Societies** must apply in writing/telephone.
Green Fees terms on application. **Prof** K Housden
Facilities ⊗ ⅢⅡ ⅃ ⬛ ♀ ♤ 🏠 ♂ **Location** Off junct 7 of M54, 1.25m S off B5061

Hotel ★★★★ 65% Buckatree Hall Hotel, The Wrekin, Wellington, TELFORD ☎ 01952 641821 62 en suite

WESTON-UNDER-REDCASTLE   Map 07 SJ52

Hawkstone Park Hotel SY4 5UY

☎ 01939 200611 📠 01939 200335
e-mail: info@hawkstone.co.uk
The Hawkstone Course plays through the English Heritage designated Grade I landscape of the historic park and follies providing a beautiful, tranquil yet dramatic back drop to a round of golf. The Windmill Course utilises many American style features and extensive water hazards and is a challenging alternative.
Hawkstone Course: 18 holes, 6491yds, Par 72, SSS 71, Course record 65.
Windmill Course: 18 holes, 6476yds, Par 72, SSS 72, Course record 64.
Academy Course: 6 holes, 741yds, Par 18, SSS 18.
Club membership 650.

Continued

Visitors advance bookings recommended. **Societies** must contact in advance by telephone. **Green Fees** £34 per round (£44 weekends). **Cards** ▦ ▦ ▦ ▧ ▦ ▦ ▧ **Prof** Stuart Leech **Course Designer** J Braid **Facilities** ⊗ ⫿⫿ ⬛ ⬛ ⬛ ⬛ ⬛ ⬛ ⬛ ♂ ♀ **Leisure** 6 hole, par 3 course, snooker. **Conf** fac available Corporate Hospitality Days available **Location** Located between Whitchurch and Shrewsbury off the A49/A442

Farmhouse ◆◆◆◆ Soulton Hall, Soulton, WEM
☎ 01939 232786 4 en suite 3 annexe en suite

WHITCHURCH Map 07 SJ54

Hill Valley Terrick Rd SY13 4JZ
☎ 01948 663584 & 667788 🖹 01948 665927
e-mail: info@hillvalley.co.uk
Emerald: 18 holes, 6628yds, Par 73, SSS 72, Course record 64.
Sapphire: 18 holes, 4800yds, Par 66, SSS 64.
Course Designer Peter Alliss/Dave Thomas **Location** 1m N. Follow signs from Bypass
Telephone for further details

Hotel ★★ 70% Crown Hotel & Restaurant, High St, NANTWICH ☎ 01270 625283 18 en suite

WORFIELD Map 07 SO79

Chesterton Valley Chesterton WV15 5NX
☎ 01746 783682
Dry course built on sandy soil giving excellent drainage. No temporary greens and no trolley ban.
18 holes, 5671yards, SSS 67.
Club membership 450.
Societies telephone in advance. **Green Fees** not confirmed. **Prof** Philip Hinton **Course Designer** Len Vanes **Facilities** ⬛ ♀ ⬛ ⬛ ⬛ ⬛ ♂ **Location** on B4176 Dudley/Telford road

Hotel ★★★ Old Vicarage Hotel, Worfield, BRIDGNORTH ☎ 01746 716497 10 en suite 4 annexe en suite

Worfield Roughton WV15 5HE
☎ 01746 716372 🖹 01746 716302
e-mail: enquiries@worfieldgolf.co.uk
Superb views and drainage which allows play on full greens and tees all year. Water comes into play on four holes, including the short par 4 18th where it lies in front of the green.
18 holes, 6545yds, Par 73, SSS 72, Course record 68.
Club membership 600.
Visitors must contact in advance, weekends only after 1pm. **Societies** telephone in advance. **Green Fees** £20 (£20 weekends after 1pm). **Cards** ▦ ▦ ▦ ▦ ▦ ▧ **Prof** Steve Russell **Course Designer** T Williams **Facilities** ⊗ ⫿⫿ ⬛ ⬛ ♀ ⬛ ⬛ ⬛ ⬛ ♂ **Conf** fac available Corporate Hospitality Days available **Location** 3m W of Bridgnorth, off A454

Hotel ★★★ Old Vicarage Hotel, Worfield, BRIDGNORTH ☎ 01746 716497 10 en suite 4 annexe en suite

> In the hotel entries, the percentage figure refers to the AA's most recent Quality Assessment Score.

SOMERSET

BACKWELL Map 03 ST46

Tall Pines Cooks Bridle Path, Downside BS48 3DJ
☎ 01275 472076 🖹 01275 474869
e-mail: tallpinesgc@ukonline.co.uk
Parkland course with views over the Bristol Channel.
18 holes, 6049yds, Par 70, SSS 70, Course record 65.
Club membership 500.
Visitors no green fees before 11am unless by prior arrangement. Must book in advance at weekends and may not play before noon. **Societies** prior arrangement by telephone for details. **Green Fees** £18 per round. **Prof** Alex Murray **Course Designer** T Murray **Facilities** ⊗ ⫿⫿ ⬛ ⬛ ♀ ⬛ ⬛ ⬛ ⬛ ♂ **Location** Adjacent to Bristol Airport, 1m off A38 or A370

Hotel ★★★ 65% Beachlands Hotel, 17 Uphill Rd North, WESTON-SUPER-MARE ☎ 01934 621401 23 en suite

BATH Map 03 ST76

Bath Sham Castle, North Rd BA2 6JG
☎ 01225 463834 🖹 01225 331027
e-mail: enquiries@bathgolfclub.org.uk
Considered to be one of the finest courses in the west, this is the site of Bath's oldest golf club. Situated on high ground overlooking the city and with splendid views over the surrounding countryside. The rocky ground supports good quality turf and there are many good holes. The 17th is a dog-leg right past, or over the corner of an out-of-bounds wall, and then on to an undulating green.
18 holes, 6442yds, Par 71, SSS 71, Course record 66.
Club membership 750.
Visitors advisable to contact in advance. Handicap certificates required. **Societies** Wed & Fri by prior arrangement. **Green Fees** 36 holes £36; 18 holes £30 (weekends & bank holidays £36/£40). **Prof** Peter J Hancox **Course Designer** Colt & others **Facilities** ⊗ ⫿⫿ ⬛ ⬛ ♀ ⬛ ⬛ ⬛ ♂ **Location** 1.5m SE city centre off A36

Hotel ★★★ 70% The Francis, Queen Square, BATH ☎ 0870 400 8223 95 en suite

Entry Hill BA2 5NA ☎ 01225 834248
e-mail: timtapley@aol.com
Opened in 1984, this is a short but interesting 9 hole public pay and play facility within a mile of the city centre. With its picturesque settings and stunning views across Bath, the course provides enjoyment for golfers of all standard.
9 holes, 2065yds, Par 33, SSS 30.
Club membership 250.
Visitors advisable to book in advance, must wear golf shoes or training shoes. **Societies** bookings required in advance. **Green Fees** not confirmed. **Prof** Tim Tapley **Facilities** ⬛ ⬛ ⬛ ⬛ ♂ **Location** Off A367

Lansdown Lansdown BA1 9BT
☎ 01225 422138 🖹 01225 339252
e-mail: admin@lansdowngolfclub.co.uk
A flat parkland course situated 800 feet above sea level, providing a challenge to both low and high handicap golfers.
18 holes, 6316yds, Par 71, SSS 70, Course record 63.
Club membership 700.

Continued

Visitors must contact in advance to ascertain availability and have a handicap certificate. **Societies** apply in writing or telephone in advance. **Green Fees** terms on application. **Cards** 💳 💳 💳 💳 💳 **Prof** Terry Mercer **Course Designer** C A Whitcombe **Facilities** ⊗ 🞅 🖣 🖢 💄 🍴 🍽 🏠 🥂 **Conf** fac available Corporate Hospitality Days available **Location** 6m SW of exit 18 of M4, beside Bath racecourse

Hotel ★★★ 69% Pratt's Hotel, South Pde, BATH ☎ 01225 460441 46 en suite

BRIDGWATER
Map 03 ST23

Cannington Cannington College, Cannington TA5 2LS ☎ 01278 655050 📠 01278 655055
Nine hole golf course with 18 tees of 'links-like' appearance, designed by Martin Hawtree of Oxford. The 4th hole is a challenging 464yard par 4, slightly up hill and into the prevailing wind.
9 holes, 6072yds, Par 68, SSS 70.
Club membership 240.
Visitors pay & play anytime ex Wed evening. **Societies** apply in writing. **Green Fees** 18 holes £12.50; 9 holes £9.50 (weekends £12.50/£18.50). **Prof** Ron Macrow **Course Designer** Martin Hawtree **Facilities** 🖢 💄 🏠 🍴 🥂 🍽 **Leisure** Cycle hire. **Location** 4m NW of Bridgwater of A39

Hotel ★★ 76% Combe House Hotel, HOLFORD ☎ 01278 741382 17 rms (16 en suite)

BURNHAM-ON-SEA
Map 03 ST34

Brean Coast Rd, Brean Sands TA8 2QY ☎ 01278 752111(pro shop) 📠 01278 752111
e-mail: proshop@brean.com
Level and open moorland course with water hazards. Facilities of Brean Leisure Park adjoining.

18 holes, 5715yds, Par 69, SSS 68, Course record 66.
Club membership 350.
Visitors may not play on Sat & Sun before 11.30am. Book in advance through professional. **Societies** contact office or professional in advance. **Green Fees** terms on application. **Cards** 💳 💳 💳 💳 💳 **Prof** David Haines **Course Designer** In House **Facilities** ⊗ 🞅 🖣 🖢 💄 🍴 🏠 🍴 🍽 🥂 🥢 **Leisure** heated indoor plus outdoor swimming pool, fishing. **Conf** fac available Corporate Hospitality Days available **Location** 4m from junct 22 M5 on coast road

Hotel ★★ 🏌 69% Batch Country Hotel, Batch Ln, LYMPSHAM ☎ 01934 750371 10 en suite

> **Booking a tee time is always advisable.**

Burnham & Berrow St Christopher's Way TA8 2PE ☎ 01278 785760 📠 01278 795440
e-mail: secretary@BurnhamandBerrow.golfclub.co.uk
Natural championship links course with panoramic views of the Somerset hills sweeping across the famed reed beds and the Bristol Channel with the islands of Steepholm and Flatholm against the background of the Welsh coast line.
Championship Course: 18 holes, 6606yds, Par 71, SSS 73, Course record 66.
Channel Course: 9 holes, 6120yds, Par 70, SSS 69.
Club membership 900.
Visitors must contact in advance & have handicap certificate (22 or under gentlemen, 30 or under ladies) to play on the Championship course. **Societies** telephone in advance. **Green Fees** Championship Course: £60 per day, £45 per round (£60 per round weekends & bank holidays). **Cards** 💳 💳 💳 💳 **Prof** Mark Crowther-Smith **Facilities** ⊗ 🞅 🖢 💄 🍴 🏠 🍴 🍽 🥢 🥂 **Location** 1m N of town on B3140

Hotel ★★ 72% Woodlands Country House Hotel, Hill Ln, BRENT KNOLL ☎ 01278 760232 9 en suite

CHARD
Map 03 ST30

Windwhistle Cricket St Thomas TA20 4DG ☎ 01460 30231 📠 01460 30055
e-mail: info@windwhistlegolf.co.uk
Parkland course at 735ft above sea level with outstanding views over the Somerset Levels to the Bristol Channel and South Wales.
East/West Course: 18 holes, 6510yds, Par 73, SSS 71, Course record 69.
Club membership 500.
Visitors must contact in advance. **Societies** by prior arrangement. **Green Fees** terms on application. **Cards** 💳 💳 💳 💳 💳 **Prof** Paul Deeprose **Course Designer** Braid & Taylor/Fisher **Facilities** ⊗ 🖢 💄 🍴 🏠 🍴 🍽 🥂 🥢 **Leisure** squash. **Conf** fac available Corporate Hospitality Days available **Location** 3m E of Chard on A30

Hotel ★★★ 67% Shrubbery Hotel, ILMINSTER ☎ 01460 52108 16 en suite

CLEVEDON
Map 03 ST47

Clevedon Castle Rd, Walton St Mary BS21 7AA ☎ 01275 874057 📠 01275 341228
e-mail: secretary@clevedongolfclub.co.uk
Situated on the cliff-top overlooking the Severn estuary and with distant views of the Welsh coast. Excellent parkland course in first-class condition. Magnificent scenery and some tremendous 'drop' holes. *Continued*

18 holes, 6557yds, Par 72, SSS 72, Course record 68.
Club membership 750.
Visitors must contact in advance. No play Wed morning.
Societies not bank holidays, telephone or apply in writing.
Green Fees £28 per day (£40 weekends). **Prof** Robert
Scanlan **Course Designer** S Herd **Facilities** ⊗ ⅏ ⅃ ⅃ ♀
⚐ ⌂ ⍾ ♣ ⌀ **Conf** Corporate Hospitality Days available
Location M5 junct 20, 1m NE of town centre

....

Hotel ★★★ 67% Walton Park Hotel, Wellington Ter,
CLEVEDON ☎ 01275 874253 40 en suite

CONGRESBURY   Map 03 ST46

Mendip Spring Honeyhall Ln BS49 5JT
☎ 01934 852322 ▤ 01934 853021
e-mail: msgc@melhuish9790.fsworld.co.uk
Set in peaceful countryside with the Mendip Hills as a
backdrop, this 18-hole course includes lakes and
numerous water hazards covering some 12 acres of the
course. The 12th is an island green surrounded by
water and there are long drives on the 7th and 13th.
The 9-hole Lakeside course is an easy walking course,
mainly par 4. Floodlit driving range.
Brinsea Course: 18 holes, 6352yds, Par 71, SSS 70,
Course record 64.
Lakeside: 9 holes, 2392yds, Par 34, SSS 66.
Club membership 500.
Visitors must contact in advance for Brinsea course and
handicap certificate required for weekends. Lakeside is
play & pay anytime. **Societies** Booking in advance by
arrangement. **Green Fees** Brinsea: £25 (£34 weekends);
Lakeside: £8.50 (9 holes) (£9 weekends). **Cards** ▦ ▦
▦ ▦ ▨ ▨ **Prof** John Blackburn & Robert Moss
Facilities ⊗ ⅏ ⅃ ⅃ ♀ ♀ ⚐ ⌂ ⍾ ♣ ⌀ ⅃ **Conf** fac
available Corporate Hospitality Days available **Location**
8m E of Weston-Super-Mare between A370 and A38

....

Hotel ★★★ ⚑⚑ 72% Daneswood House Hotel, Cuck Hill,
SHIPHAM ☎ 01934 843145 & 843945 ▤ 01934 843824
14 en suite 3 annexe en suite

ENMORE   Map 03 ST23

Enmore Park TA5 2AN
☎ 01278 671481 (office) & 671519 (pro) ▤ 01278 671740
e-mail: golfclub@enmore.fsnet.co.uk
Hilly, parkland course with water features on foothills
of Quantocks. Wooded countryside and views of
Quantocks and Mendips. 1st and 10th are testing holes.
18 holes, 6406yds, Par 71, SSS 71, Course record 66.
Club membership 750.
Visitors phone professional for details, must have handicap
certificate for weekends. **Societies** must contact in
advance. **Green Fees** £25 per round (£30 per round
weekends). **Cards** ▦ ▦ ▦ ▦ ▨ **Prof** Nigel Wixon
Course Designer Hawtree **Facilities** ⊗ ⅏ ⅃ ⅃ ♀ ⚐ ⌂
⍾ ♣ ⌀ **Conf** Corporate Hospitality Days available
Location A39 to Minehead, at first set of lights turn left to
Spaxton, then 1.5m to reservoir and turn left

....

Hotel ★★★ 72% Walnut Tree Hotel, North Petherton,
BRIDGWATER ☎ 01278 662255 33 en suite

Looking for a driving range? Refer to the listing
of driving ranges at the back of this guide.

FARRINGTON GURNEY   Map 03 ST65

Farrington Golf & Country Club Marsh Ln
BS39 6TS ☎ 01761 451596 ▤ 01761 451021
e-mail: info@farringtongolfclub.net
USGA spec greens on both challenging 9 and 18 hole
courses. Newly completed 18 hole course with
computerised irrigation, six lakes, four tees per hole
and excellent views. Testing holes include the 12th
(282yds) with the green set behind a lake at the base of
a 100ft drop, and the 17th which is played between two
lakes.
Main Course: 18 holes, 6335yds, Par 72, SSS 71, Course
record 66.
Club membership 750.
Visitors must book starting times and have a handicap
certificate to play at weekends. **Societies** welcome except
for weekends & bank holidays, telephone or write in
advance. **Green Fees** £30 per day, £18 per round (£30 per
round weekends). **Cards** ▦ ▦ ▦ ▨ **Prof** Jon Cowgill
Course Designer Peter Thompson **Facilities** ⊗ ⅏ ⅃ ⅃ ♀
⚐ ⌂ ⍾ ♣ ⌀ ⅃ **Leisure** sauna, solarium, gymnasium,
video teaching studio. **Conf** fac available Corporate
Hospitality Days available **Location** Turn off A37 onto
A362 just before the A39 at the traffic lights to Midsomer
Morton. Turn right into Marsh Lane after 0.5m

....

Hotel ★★★ 71% Centurion Hotel, Charlton Ln,
MIDSOMER NORTON ☎ 01761 417711 44 en suite

FROME   Map 03 ST74

Frome Golf Centre Critchill Manor BA11 4LJ
☎ 01373 453410
e-mail: fromegolfclub@yahoo.co.uk
Attractive parkland course, founded in 1992, situated in
a picturesque valley just outside the town, complete
with practice areas and a driving range.
18 holes, 5466yds, Par 69, SSS 67, Course record 64.
Club membership 360.
Visitors tee times essential at weekends and bank holidays.
Societies telephone in advance. **Green Fees** £18 per 18
holes; £13 per 9 holes (£20/£15 weekends and bank
holidays). **Prof** L. Wilkin/T. Isaac **Facilities** ⊗ ⅃ ⅃ ♀ ⚐
⌂ ⍾ ⌀ ⅃ **Location** A361 Frome/Shepton Mallet, at
Nunney Catch rdbt through Nunney, course on left before
Frome

....

Hotel ★★ 65% The George at Nunney, 11 Church St,
NUNNEY ☎ 01373 836458 9 rms (8 en suite)

Orchardleigh BA11 2PH
☎ 01373 454200 & 454206 ▤ 01373 454202
e-mail: trevor@orchardleighgolf.co.uk
18 hole parkland course set amidst the Somerset
countryside designed by former Ryder Cup player,
Brian Huggett, with water coming into play on seven
holes and routed through mature trees.
18 holes, 6831yds, Par 72, SSS 73, Course record 67.
Club membership 550.
Visitors no visitors before 11am at weekends. **Societies**
apply in writing or telephone in advance. **Green Fees** £30
per round (£40 weekends & bank holidays). **Cards** ▦ ▦
▦ ▦ ▨ **Prof** Ian Ridsdale **Course Designer** Brian
Huggett **Facilities** ⊗ ⅏ ⅃ ⅃ ♀ ♀ ⚐ ⌂ ⍾ ♣ ⌀ ⅃
Leisure fishing. **Conf** fac available **Location** 1m W of
Frome on the A362

....

Hotel ★★ 65% The George at Nunney, 11 Church St,
NUNNEY ☎ 01373 836458 9 rms (8 en suite)

GURNEY SLADE
Map 03 ST64

Mendip BA3 4UT
☎ 01749 840570 🖨 01749 841439
e-mail: mendipgolfclub@lineone.net
Undulating downland course offering an interesting test of golf on superb fairways and extensive views over the surrounding countryside.
18 holes, 6383yds, Par 71, SSS 71, Course record 65.
Club membership 900.
Visitors Handicap certificates required for play at weekends and bank holidays. **Societies** by arrangement with secretary. **Green Fees** not confirmed. **Prof** Adrian Marsh **Course Designer** C K Cotton **Facilities** ⊗ ⅏ ⅃ ⬥
♀ 🛆 🏠 ⚑ ⏀ ℓ **Location** 1.5m S off A37

Hotel ★★★ 71% Centurion Hotel, Charlton Ln,
MIDSOMER NORTON ☎ 01761 417711 44 en suite

KEYNSHAM
Map 03 ST66

Stockwood Vale Stockwood Ln BS31 2ER
☎ 0117 986 6505 🖨 0117 986 8974
e-mail: stockwoodvalegc@netscapeonline.co.uk
18 holes, 6031yds, Par 71, SSS 69.
Location Off Hicks Gate on A4 junct with A4174
Telephone for further details

Guesthouse ◆◆◆◆ Grasmere Court Hotel, 22-24 Bath
Rd, KEYNSHAM ☎ 0117 986 2662 16 en suite

LANGPORT
Map 03 ST42

Long Sutton Long Sutton TA10 9JU
☎ 01458 241017 🖨 01458 241022
e-mail: reservations@longsuttongolf.com
Gentle, undulating, Pay and Play course.
18 holes, 6367yds, Par 71, SSS 70, Course record 71.
Club membership 750.
Visitors advisable to phone in advance. **Societies** telephone in advance. **Green Fees** terms on application.
Cards 🖭 🟥 🟦 🟥 📇 **Prof** Andrew Hayes
Course Designer Patrick Dawson **Facilities** ⊗ ⅏ ⅃ ⬥
🛆 🏠 ⚑ 🎋 ⏀ ℓ **Conf** fac available Corporate
Hospitality Days available **Location** 10m NW of Yeovil
off A372

Hotel ★★★ 72% The Hollies, Bower Hinton,
MARTOCK ☎ 01935 822232 33 annexe en suite

LONG ASHTON
Map 03 ST57

Long Ashton The Clubhouse, Clarken Coombe
BS41 9DW ☎ 01275 392229 🖨 01275 394395
e-mail: secretary@longashtongolfclub.co.uk
Wooded parkland course with fine turf, wonderful views of Bristol and surrounding areas and a spacious practice area. Good testing holes, especially the back nine, in prevailing south-west winds. The short second hole (126yds) cut from an old quarry and played over a road can ruin many a card! Good drainage ensures pleasant winter golf. Two extra holes have been added, giving a variety of course.
Ashton Course: 18 holes, 6193yds, Par 70, SSS 70.
Coombe Course: 18 holes, 6381, Par 71, SSS 71.
Club membership 700.
Visitors with recognised handicap certificate. **Societies** must contact the secretary in advance. **Green Fees** £30 per round (£35 weekends). **Cards** 🖭 🟥 🟥 📇 **Prof** Mike
Hart **Course Designer** J H Taylor **Facilities** ⊗ ⅏ ⅃ ⬥ ♀

Continued

🛆 🏠 ⏀ **Conf** Corporate Hospitality Days available
Location 0.5m N on B3128

Long Ashton Golf Course

Hotel ★★★ 67% Redwood Lodge Hotel & Country Club,
Beggar Bush Ln, Failand, BRISTOL ☎ 0870 609 6144
112 en suite

Woodspring Golf & Country Club
Yanley Ln
BS41 9LR ☎ 01275 394378 🖨 01275 394473
e-mail: info@woodspring-golf.com
Set in 245 acres of undulating Somerset countryside featuring superb natural water hazards, protected greens and a rising landscape. Designed by Peter Alliss and Clive Clark and laid out by Donald Steel, the course has three individual 9-hole courses, the Avon, Severn & Brunel. The 9th hole on the Brunel course is a feature hole here, with an elevated tee shot over a natural gorge. In undulating hills south of Bristol, long carries to tight fairways, elevated island tees and challenging approaches to greens make the most of the 27 holes.
Avon Course: 9 holes, 2960yds, Par 35, SSS 34.
Brunel Course: 9 holes, 3320yds, Par 37, SSS 35.
Severn Course: 9 holes, 3267yds, Par 36, SSS 35.
Club membership 550.
Visitors must contact in advance, weekends may be limited to play after midday. Dress codes must be adhered to. **Societies** please contact Dave Watson in advance.
Green Fees £28 per 18 holes (£32 weekends). **Cards** 🖭
🟥 🟦 🟥 📇 **Prof** Kevin Pitts **Course Designer**
Clarke/Alliss/Steel **Facilities** ⊗ ⅏ ⅃ ⬥ ♀ 🛆 🏠 ⚑ 🎋
🎋 ⏀ ℓ **Conf** fac available Corporate Hospitality Days
available **Location** Off A38 Bridgwater Road

Hotel ★★★ 67% Redwood Lodge Hotel & Country Club,
Beggar Bush Ln, Failand, BRISTOL ☎ 0870 609 6144
112 en suite

MIDSOMER NORTON
Map 03 ST65

Fosseway Golf Course Charlton Ln BA3 4BD
☎ 01761 412214 🖨 01761 418357
e-mail: centurion@centurionhotel.co.uk
9 holes, 4565yds, Par 67, SSS 61.
Course Designer C K Cotton/F Pennink **Location** SE of
town centre off A367
Telephone for further details

Hotel ★★★ 71% Centurion Hotel, Charlton Ln,
MIDSOMER NORTON ☎ 01761 417711 44 en suite

> **In the hotel entries, the percentage figure refers to the AA's most recent Quality Assessment Score.**

211

MINEHEAD
Map 03 SS94

Minehead & West Somerset The Warren
TA24 5SJ ☎ 01643 702057 ▯ 01643 705095
e-mail: secretary@mineheadgolf.co.uk
Flat seaside links, very exposed to wind, with good turf
set on a shingle bank. The last five holes adjacent to the
beach are testing. The 215-yard 18th is wedged between
the beach and the club buildings and provides a good
finish.
18 holes, 6228yds, Par 71, SSS 70, Course record 65.
Club membership 620.
Visitors must contact secretary in advance. Societies
telephone in advance. Green Fees £30 per day (£35
weekends). Cards 🖃 ▦ 🖿 🖃 🖻 🖿 🖸 Prof Ian Read
Facilities ⊗ ⋔ ﹢ ⬥ ♡ ⚲ 🛆 ⛳ ⸗ Conf Corporate
Hospitality Days available Location E end of esplanade

Hotel ★★★ 67% Northfield Hotel, Northfield Rd,
MINEHEAD ☎ 01643 705155 28 en suite

SALTFORD
Map 03 ST66

Saltford Golf Club Ln BS31 3AA
☎ 01225 873513 ▯ 01225 873525
Parkland course with easy walking and panoramic
views over the Avon Valley. The par 4 2nd and 13th are
notable.
18 holes, 6081yds, Par 71, SSS 71.
Club membership 800.
Visitors must contact in advance & have handicap
certificate. Societies must telephone in advance. Green
Fees not confirmed. Prof Dudley Millinstead Course
Designer Harry Vardon Facilities ⊗ ⋔ ﹢ ⬥ ♡ ⚲ 🛆 ⛳
🛆 ⸗ Conf fac available Corporate Hospitality Days
available Location S side of village

Hotel ★★★ 79% Hunstrete House Hotel,
HUNSTRETE ☎ 01761 490490 25 en suite

SOMERTON
Map 03 ST42

Wheathill Wheathill TA11 7HG
☎ 01963 240667 ▯ 01963 240230
e-mail: wheathill@wheathill.fsnet.co.uk
A par 68 parkland course with nice views in quiet
countryside. It is flat lying with the 13th hole along the
river. There is an Academy 4-hole course and a massive
practice area.
18 holes, 5362yds, Par 68, SSS 66, Course record 61.
Club membership 500.
Visitors telephone to book Fri, Sat & Sun. Societies
telephone to arrange. Green Fees £15 per round (£20
weekends & bank holidays). Prof A England Course
Designer J Pain Facilities ⊗ ⋔ ﹢ ⬥ ♡ ⚲ 🛆 ⛳ 🛆
⸗ Leisure 8 hole academy course. Conf fac available
Corporate Hospitality Days available Location 5m E of
Somerton off B3153

Hotel ★★★ 64% Wessex Hotel, High St, STREET
☎ 01458 443383 49 en suite

TAUNTON
Map 03 ST22

Oake Manor Oake TA4 1BA
☎ 01823 461993 ▯ 01823 461995
e-mail: russell@oakemanor.com
A parkland/lakeland course situated in breathtaking
Somerset countryside with views of the Quantock,

Continued

Blackdown and Brendon Hills. Ten holes feature water
hazards such as lakes, cascades and a trout stream. The
15th hole (par 5, 476yds) is bounded by water all down
the left with a carry over another lake on to an island
green. The course is challenging yet great fun for all
standards of golfer.

Oake Manor

18 holes, 6109yds, Par 70, SSS 69, Course record 65.
Club membership 600.
Visitors no restrictions but visitors must book start times in
order to avoid disappointment. Phone 01823 461993.
Societies contact Golf Manager Russell Gardner by
telephone. Green Fees £22 per 18 holes (£26 weekends).
Cards 🖃 ▦ 🖿 🖃 🖸 Prof Russell Gardner Course
Designer Adrian Stiff Facilities ⊗ ⋔ ﹢ ⬥ ♡ ⚲ 🛆 ⛳ ⸗
⸗ Leisure 2 hole academy course, short game area. Conf
fac available Corporate Hospitality Days available
Location Exit M5 junct 26, take A38 towards Taunton and
follow signs to Oake

Hotel ★★★ 73% Rumwell Manor Hotel, Rumwell,
TAUNTON ☎ 01823 461902 10 en suite 10 annexe en suite

Taunton & Pickeridge Corfe TA3 7BY
☎ 01823 421537 ▯ 01823 421742
e-mail: sec@taunt-pickgolfclub.sagehost.co.uk
Downland course with extensive views of the Quantock
and Mendip Hills, established in 1892. Renowned for its
excellent greens.
18 holes, 6020yds, Par 69, SSS 69, Course record 63.
Club membership 800.
Visitors must have a handicap certificate Societies must
telephone in advance. Green Fees £28 per day; £24 per
round (£35 weekends). Cards 🖃 ▦ 🖿 🖃 🖸 🖿 🖸
Prof Gary Milne Facilities ⊗ ⋔ ﹢ ⬥ ♡ ⚲ 🛆 ⛳ ⸗ Conf
Corporate Hospitality Days available Location 4m S off
B3170

Hotel ★★★ 73% The Mount Somerset Hotel, Lower
Henlade, TAUNTON ☎ 01823 442500 11 en suite

Taunton Vale Creech Heathfield TA3 5EY
☎ 01823 412220 ▯ 01823 413583
e-mail: tvgc@easynet.co.uk
An 18-hole and a 9-hole golf course in a parkland
complex occupying 156 acres in the Vale of Taunton.
Floodlit driving range.
Charlton Course: 18 holes, 6163yds, Par 70, SSS 69.
Durston Course: 9 holes, 2004yds, Par 32.
Club membership 800.
Visitors telephone booking essential. Must contact
Professional Societies must book in advance. Not morning at
weekends. Green Fees 18 hole course: £20 per round (£25
weekends). 9 hole course: £10 per round (£15 weekends).

Continued

Prof Martin Keitch **Course Designer** John Payne **Facilities** ⊗ by prior arrangement **Conf** fac available Corporate Hospitality Days available **Location** Off A361 between juncts 24 & 25 on M5

Taunton Vale

Hotel ★★★ 73% The Mount Somerset Hotel, Lower Henlade, TAUNTON ☎ 01823 442500 11 en suite

Vivary Park Municipal Fons George TA1 3JU
☎ 01823 333875 🖷 01823 352713
e-mail: vivary.golf.course@tauntondeane.gov.uk
18 holes, 4620yds, Par 63, SSS 63, Course record 59.
Course Designer W H Fowler **Location** S side of town centre off A38
Telephone for further details

WEDMORE Map 03 ST44

Isle of Wedmore Lineage BS28 4QT
☎ 01934 712452 (Pro-Shop) 🖷 01934 713554
e-mail: office@wedmoregc.fsnet.co.uk
Gentle undulating course designed to maintain natural environment. Existing woodland and hedgerow enhanced by new planting. Magnificent panoramic views of Cheddar Valley and Glastonbury Tor. A new par 3 16th hole has a water feature and the signature hole is the par 3 11th with a new elevation to the tee.
18 holes, 5850yds, Par 70, SSS 69, Course record 67. Club membership 680.
Visitors telephone professional in advance. Not before 9.30am weekends. **Societies** weekdays telephone in advance,weekends subject to competitions. **Green Fees** £30 per day, £20 per round. **Cards** **Prof** Graham Coombe **Course Designer** Terry Murray **Facilities** ⊗ **Leisure** indoor teaching studio & custom fitting centre. **Conf** fac available Corporate Hospitality Days available **Location** Exit M5 at Junct 22 and take A38 towards Bristol-turn right at Lower Weare 3.5m from turn off

Hotel ★★★ 72% Swan Hotel, Sadler St, WELLS ☎01749 836300 50 en suite

WELLS Map 03 ST54

Wells (Somerset) East Horrington Rd BA5 3DS
☎ 01749 675005 🖷 01749 683170
e-mail: secretary@wellsgolfclub99.freeserve.co.uk
Beautiful wooded course with wonderful views. The prevailing SW wind complicates the 448yd 3rd.
18 holes, 6053yds, Par 70, SSS 69, Course record 66. Club membership 670.
Visitors must contact in advance & have handicap certificate weekends. Tee times restricted at weekends to after 9.30pm **Societies** must apply in advance. **Green Fees** £24 per 18 holes (£30 weekends & bank holidays). **Cards** **Prof** Adrian Bishop **Facilities** ⊗ **Location** 1.5m E off B3139

Hotel ★★★ 72% Swan Hotel, Sadler St, WELLS ☎ 01749 836300 50 en suite

WESTON-SUPER-MARE Map 03 ST36

Weston-Super-Mare Uphill Rd North BS23 4NQ
☎ 01934 626968 & 633360(pro) 🖷 01934 621360
e-mail: karen@wsmgolfclub.fsnet.co.uk
A compact and interesting layout with the opening hole adjacent to the beach. The sandy, links-type course is slightly undulating and has beautifully maintained turf and greens. The 15th is a testing 455-yard par 4.

18 holes, 6245yds, Par 70, SSS 70, Course record 65. Club membership 750.
Visitors must have handicap certificate to play. **Societies** apply in writing or telephone. **Green Fees** £36 per round (£56 weekends). **Cards** **Prof** Mike Laband **Course Designer** T Dunne/Dr Mackenzie **Facilities** ⊗ **Location** S side of town centre off A370

Hotel ★★★ 65% Beachlands Hotel, 17 Uphill Rd North, WESTON-SUPER-MARE ☎ 01934 621401 23 en suite

Worlebury Monks Hill BS22 9SX
☎ 01934 625789 🖷 01934 621935
e-mail: secretary@worleburygc.co.uk
Situated on the ridge of Worlebury Hill, this seaside course offers fairly easy walking and extensive views of the Severn estuary and Wales. New clubhouse facilities recently finished.
18 holes, 5963yds, Par 70, SSS 69, Course record 66. Club membership 650.
Visitors must be recognised golfers, handicap certificate or proof of club membership may be required. **Societies** apply in writing or telephone in advance. **Green Fees** terms on application. **Prof** Gary Marks **Course Designer** H Vardon **Facilities** ⊗ **Location** 2m NE off A370

Hotel ★★★ 65% Beachlands Hotel, 17 Uphill Rd North, WESTON-SUPER-MARE ☎ 01934 621401 23 en suite

YEOVIL Map 03 ST51

Yeovil Sherborne Rd BA21 5BW
☎ 01935 422965 🖷 01935 411283
e-mail: yeovilgolfclub@yeovilgc.fsnet.co.uk
On the Old Course the opener lies by the River Yeo before the gentle climb to high downs with good views. The outstanding 14th and 15th holes

Continued

present a challenge, being below the player with a deep railway cutting on the left of the green. The 1st on the Newton Course is played over the river which then leads to a challenging but scenic golf course.

Old Course: 18 holes, 6150yds, Par 72, SSS 70, Course record 64.

Newton Course: 9 holes, 4891yds, Par 68, SSS 65, Course record 63.

Club membership 1000.

Visitors must contact in advance. Members only before 9.30am and 12.30-2. Handicap certificate required for Old Course. **Societies** telephone in advance. **Green Fees** Old Course Apr-Oct: £30 (£40 weekends & bank holidays); Nov-Mar: £25 (£30). Newton Course: £18 (£20). **Cards**  **Prof** Geoff Kite **Course Designer** Fowler & Allison **Facilities** ⊗ ⫙ ⓑ 💪 ♀ 👫 🏠 ⛳ ➤ ⚓ ♂ (**Location** 1m E on A30

Hotel ★★★ 74% Yeovil Court Hotel, West Coker Rd, YEOVIL ☎ 01935 863746 18 en suite 12 annexe en suite

STAFFORDSHIRE

BROCTON
Map 07 SJ91

Brocton Hall ST17 0TH
☎ 01785 661901 📄 01785 661591

Parkland course with gentle slopes in places, easy walking.

18 holes, 6064yds, Par 69, SSS 69, Course record 66.

Club membership 665.

Visitors not competition days. Must contact in advance. **Societies** must apply in advance. **Green Fees** £38 per day (£45 weekends & bank holidays). **Cards** 🔲 🔲 🔲 **Prof** Nevil Bland **Course Designer** Harry Vardon **Facilities** ⊗ ⫙ ⓑ 💪 ♀ 👫 🏠 ⛳ ➤ ⚓ ♂ Leisure snooker. **Location** NW side of village off A34

Hotel ★★★ 63% The Garth Hotel, Wolverhampton Rd, Moss Pit, STAFFORD ☎ 0870 609 6169 60 en suite

BURTON UPON TRENT
Map 08 SK22

Branston Burton Rd, Branston DE14 3DP
☎ 01283 512211 📄 01283 566984
e-mail: sales@branston-golf-club.co.uk

Flat semi-parkland course, adjacent to River Trent, on undulating ground with natural water hazards on 13 holes. A new 9 hole course has recently been opened.

18 holes, 6697yds, Par 72, SSS 72, Course record 65.

Club membership 800.

Visitors may not play before 12.30pm or at weekends. Must contact in advance. **Societies** must telephone in advance. **Green Fees** terms on application. **Cards** 🔲 🔲

Continued

🔲 🔲 **Prof** Richard Odell **Course Designer** G Ramshall **Facilities** ⊗ ⫙ ⓑ 💪 ♀ 👫 🏠 ⛳ ➤ ⚓ ♂ (**Leisure** heated indoor swimming pool, sauna, solarium, gymnasium, 9 hole course. **Conf** fac available Corporate Hospitality Days available **Location** 1.5m SW on A5121

Hotel ★★ 72% Riverside Hotel, Riverside Dr, Branston, BURTON UPON TRENT ☎ 01283 511234 22 en suite

Burton-upon-Trent 43 Ashby Rd East DE15 0PS
☎ 01283 544551(sec) & 562240 (pro) 📄 01283 544551
e-mail: thesecretary@burtongolfclub.co.uk

Undulating parkland course with trees a major feature. There are testing par 3s at 10th and 12th. The 18th has a lake on the approach to the green.

18 holes, 6579yds, Par 71, SSS 71, Course record 63.

Club membership 650.

Visitors must contact in advance and have a handicap certificate. **Societies** must contact in advance. **Green Fees** £38 per day; £28 per round (£40/£32 weekends & bank holidays). **Prof** Gary Stafford **Course Designer** H S Colt **Facilities** ⊗ ⫙ ⓑ 💪 ♀ 👫 🏠 ⛳ ♂ **Conf** Corporate Hospitality Days available **Location** 3m E of Burton-on-Trent on A511

Guesthouse ♦♦♦♦ Edgecote Hotel, 179 Ashby Rd, BURTON UPON TRENT ☎ 01283 568966 11 rms (5 en suite)

Craythorne Craythorne Rd, Stretton DE13 0AZ
☎ 01283 564329 📄 01283 511908
e-mail: admin@craythorne.co.uk

A relatively short and challenging parkland course with tight fairways and views of the Trent Valley. Excellent greens. Suits all standards but particularly good for society players. The course is now settled and in good condition after major refurbishments.

18 holes, 5645yds, Par 68, SSS 68, Course record 66.

Club membership 500.

Visitors welcome but may not play before 10.30am and must contact in advance. **Societies** apply in writing or telephone for details. **Green Fees** £34 per day, £28 per round. **Cards** 🔲 🔲 🔲 🔲 **Prof** Steve Hadfield **Course Designer** A A Wright **Facilities** ⊗ ⫙ ⓑ 💪 ♀ 👫 🏠 ⛳ ➤ ⚓ ♂ (**Conf** fac available Corporate Hospitality Days available **Location** Off A38 through Stretton village, follow tourist signs

Guesthouse ♦♦♦♦ Edgecote Hotel, 179 Ashby Rd, BURTON UPON TRENT ☎ 01283 568966 11 rms (5 en suite)

Hoar Cross Hall Health Spa Resort
Hoar Cross DE13 8QS ☎ 01283 575671 📄 01283 575652
e-mail: info@hoarcross.co.uk

Golf academy located in the grounds of a stately home, now a well appointed health spa resort and hotel. Driving range, bunker and practice areas.

Hoar Cross Hall Health Spa Golf Academy: .

Club membership 300.

Visitors day guests & residents. **Societies** golfing societies that are resident only. **Green Fees** terms on application. **Prof** Richard Coy **Course Designer** Geoffrey Collins **Facilities** 👫 🏠 ⛳ 🚪 (**Leisure** hard tennis courts, heated indoor swimming pool, sauna, solarium, gymnasium. **Conf** fac available

🏠 Travelodge, Western Springs Rd, RUGELEY ☎ 08700 850 950 32 en suite

CANNOCK
Map 07 SJ91

Beau Desert
Rugeley Rd, Hazelslade WS12 0PJ
☎ 01543 422626 📠 01543 451137
e-mail: beaudesert@btconnect.com
Heathland course surrounded by a forest, and used as an Open Qualifier venue.
18 holes, 6310yds, Par 70, SSS 71, Course record 64.
Club membership 650.
Visitors are advised to contact professional in advance.
Societies must contact in advance. Green Fees £40 per round (£50 weekends and bank holidays)). Prof Barrie Stevens Course Designer Herbert Fowler Facilities ⊗ ⟩Ⅲ Ⅱ ⚑ ♀ ♨ ♍ ♙ ╏ Conf fac available Corporate Hospitality Days available Location from Cannock take A460 towards Rugeley through Hednesford. 1m from Lichfield take A51 (signposted) towards Stone, leave at Brereton via Coalpit Lane

Hotel ★★★ 63% The Roman Way Hotel, Watling St, Hatherton, CANNOCK ☎ 0870 609 6125 56 en suite

Cannock Park
Stafford Rd WS11 2AL
☎ 01543 578850 📠 01543 578850
e-mail: david.dunk@18global.co.uk
Part of a large leisure centre, this parkland-type course plays alongside Cannock Chase. Good drainage, open all year.
18 holes, 5149yds, Par 67, SSS 65.
Club membership 200.
Visitors telephone pro shop on 01543 578850 to book in advance. Societies please telephone in advance. Green Fees £9 per round (£11 weekends). Prof David Dunk Course Designer John Mainland Facilities ⊗ ⟩Ⅲ Ⅱ ⚑ ♀ ♨ 🖃 ♍ ♙ Leisure hard tennis courts, heated indoor swimming pool, sauna, solarium, gymnasium. Location 0.5m N of town centre on A34

Hotel ★★★ 63% The Roman Way Hotel, Watling St, Hatherton, CANNOCK ☎ 0870 609 6125 56 en suite

ENVILLE
Map 07 SO88

Enville
Highgate Common DY7 5BN
☎ 01384 872074 (Office) 📠 01384 873396
e-mail: secretary@envillegolfclub.com
Easy walking on two fairly flat woodland/heathland courses - the 'Highgate' and the 'Lodge'.
Highgate Course: 18 holes, 6556yds, Par 72, SSS 72, Course record 65.
Lodge Course: 18 holes, 6290yds, Par 70, SSS 70, Course record 66.
Club membership 900.
Visitors must play with member at weekends. Societies phone initially for details. Green Fees £45 per day; £35 per 18 holes. Prof Sean Power Facilities ⊗ ⟩Ⅲ Ⅱ ⚑ ♀ ♨ 🖃 ♍ ♙ Conf Corporate Hospitality Days available Location From Stourbridge take A458 towards Bridgnorth, after 4.5m turn right. Golf club signposted

Hotel ★★★★ 66% Mill Hotel & Restaurant, ALVELEY ☎ 01746 780437 41 en suite

GOLDENHILL
Map 07 SJ85

Goldenhill
Mobberley Rd ST6 5SS
☎ 01782 234200 📠 01782 234303
Rolling parkland course with water features on six of the back nine holes.

18 holes, 5957yds, Par 71, SSS 69.
Club membership 300.
Visitors advisable to contact in advance. Societies must apply in writing or telephone. Green Fees Summer: £7 per round (£7.50 weekends). Winter: £4.50 per round (£5 weekends). Facilities ⊗ ⟩Ⅲ Ⅱ ⚑ ♀ ♨ ♍ ♙ Location On A50, 4m N of Stoke

Hotel ★★★ 69% Manor House Hotel, Audley Rd, ALSAGER ☎ 01270 884000 57 en suite

HIMLEY
Map 07 SO89

Himley Hall Golf Centre
Log Cabin, Himley Hall Park DY3 4DF ☎ 01902 895207
Parkland course set in grounds of Himley Hall Park, with lovely views. Large practice area including a pitch-and-putt.
9 holes, 6215yds, Par 72, SSS 70, Course record 65.
Club membership 200.
Visitors restricted weekends. Societies welcome weekday, apply in writing or telephone in advance. Green Fees Summer: 18 holes £11; 9 holes £7.50 (Winter: £10/£7). Prof Jeremy Nichols Course Designer A Baker Facilities Ⅱ ⚑ 🖃 ♙ Location 0.5m E on B4176

Hotel ★★★ 63% The Himley Country Hotel, School Rd, HIMLEY ☎ 0870 609 6112 73 en suite

LEEK
Map 07 SJ95

Leek
Birchall, Cheddleton Rd ST13 5RE
☎ 01538 384779 & 384767 📠 01538 384535
Undulating, challenging mainly parkland course, reputedly one of the best in the area.
18 holes, 6218yds, Par 70, SSS 70, Course record 63.
Club membership 825.
Visitors must contact Professional in advance, may not play after 3pm without a member. Societies must apply in advance to Hon Secretary. Green Fees £26 per day (£32 weekends). Prof Paul Taylor Facilities ⊗ ⟩Ⅲ Ⅱ ⚑ ♀ ♨ 🖃 ♍ ♙ Conf Corporate Hospitality Days available Location 0.75m S on A520

Hotel ★★ 69% Three Horseshoes Inn & Restaurant, Buxton Rd, Blackshaw Moor, LEEK ☎ 01538 300296 6 en suite

Westwood (Leek)
Newcastle Rd ST13 7AA
☎ 01538 398385 📠 01538 382485
A challenging moorland/parkland course set in beautiful open countryside with an undulating front nine. The back nine are more open and longer with the River Churnet coming into play on several holes.
18 holes, 6207yds, Par 70, SSS 69, Course record 66.
Club membership 700.
Visitors must book in advance. Societies apply by phone or in writing. Green Fees terms on application. Prof Darren Squire Facilities ⊗ ⟩Ⅲ Ⅱ ⚑ ♀ ♨ 🖃 ♦ ♙ Conf Corporate Hospitality Days available Location On A53, S of Leek

Hotel ★★ 69% Three Horseshoes Inn & Restaurant, Buxton Rd, Blackshaw Moor, LEEK ☎ 01538 300296 6 en suite

> **If the name of the club appears in *italics*, details have not been confirmed for this edition of the guide.**

Continued

LICHFIELD   Map 07 SK10

Seedy Mill Elmhurst WS13 8HE
☎ 01543 417333 📄 01543 418098
e-mail: seedymill.sales@clubhaus.com
A 27 hole course in picturesque parkland scenery. Numerous holes crossed by meandering mill streams. Undulating greens defended by hazards lie in wait for the practised approach. Well appointed clubhouse.
Mill Course: 18 holes, 6042yds, Par 72, SSS 70, Course record 67.
Spires Course: 9 holes, 1250yds, Par 27, SSS 27.
Club membership 1200.
Visitors must contact no more than 3 days in advance, weekend time restrictions. **Societies** apply in writing or telephone. **Green Fees** Mill course: £25 per 18 holes (£30 weekends); 9 holes: £6.50. **Cards** 🖩 💳 💳 💳 💳 **Prof** Simon Joyce **Course Designer** Hawtree & Son **Facilities** ⊗ ⫙ ⬐ ⬐ ♥ ⛳ ♣ ⛳ ⛳ ♂ ♫ **Conf** fac available Corporate Hospitality Days available **Location** Off A38 onto A515, right onto B5014, entrance on left

Hotel ★★★ 68% Little Barrow Hotel, 62 Beacon St, LICHFIELD ☎ 01543 414500 24 en suite

Whittington Heath Tamworth Rd WS14 9PW
☎ 01543 432317 📄 01543 433962
e-mail: info@whgcgolf.freeserve.co.uk
18 magnificent holes winding their way through heathland and trees, presenting a good test for the serious golfer. Leaving the fairway can be severely punished. The dog-legs are most tempting, inviting the golfer to chance his arm. Local knowledge is a definite advantage. Clear views of the famous three spires of Lichfield Cathedral.
18 holes, 6490yds, Par 70, SSS 71, Course record 64.
Club membership 660.
Visitors must contact in advance. May not play at weekends. Handicap certificate required. **Societies** welcome Wed & Thu, must apply in writing. **Green Fees** £50 per 36 holes; £42 per 27 holes; £35 per 18 holes. **Cards** 🖩 💳 💳 💳 💳 **Prof** Adrian Sadler **Course Designer** Colt **Facilities** ⊗ ⫙ ⬐ ♥ ♣ ⛳ **Conf** Corporate Hospitality Days available **Location** 2.5m SE on A51 Lichfield-Tamworth road

Hotel ★★★ 68% Little Barrow Hotel, 62 Beacon St, LICHFIELD ☎ 01543 414500 24 en suite

NEWCASTLE-UNDER-LYME   Map 07 SJ84

Keele Golf Centre Newcastle Rd, Keele ST5 5AB
☎ 01782 627596 📄 01782 714555
e-mail: jackbarker_keelegolfcentreltd@hotmail.com
Parkland course with mature trees and great views of Stoke-on-Trent and surrounding area.

Continued

18 holes, 6396yds, Par 71, SSS 70, Course record 64.
Club membership 400.
Visitors must contact in advance, bookings from 7 days in advance. **Societies Green Fees** terms on application. **Cards** 🖩 💳 💳 💳 💳 **Course Designer** Hawtree **Facilities** ⊗ ⫙ ⬐ ♥ ♀ ⬉ ⛳ ⛳ ♥ ⛳ ♂ ♫ **Location** On A525 towards Madeley opposite Keele university

Hotel ⛾ Holiday Inn Stoke-on-Trent, Clayton Rd, NEWCASTLE-UNDER-LYME ☎ 0870 400 9077 119 en suite

Newcastle-Under-Lyme Whitmore Rd ST5 2QB
☎ 01782 617006 📄 01782 617531
e-mail: info@newcastlegolfclub.co.uk
Parkland course.
18 holes, 6404yds, Par 72, SSS 71.
Club membership 600.
Visitors must contact in advance. With member only weekends. **Societies** must contact in advance. **Green Fees** £35 per day/round. **Prof** Paul Symonds **Facilities** ⊗ ⫙ ⬐ ♥ ♀ ⬉ ⛳ ♂ **Conf** fac available Corporate Hospitality Days available **Location** 1m SW on A53

Hotel ★★ 62% Comfort Inn Newcastle under Lyme, Liverpool Rd, Cross Heath, NEWCASTLE-UNDER-LYME ☎ 01782 717000 43 en suite 24 annexe en suite

Wolstanton Dimsdale Old Hall, Hassam Pde, Wolstanton ST5 9DR ☎ 01782 622413 (Sec)
A challenging undulating suburban course incorporating six difficult par 3 holes. The 6th hole (par 3) is 233yds from the Medal Tee.
18 holes, 5807yds, Par 68, SSS 68, Course record 63.
Club membership 700.
Visitors must contact in advance. May not play Tue (Ladies Day). With member only at weekends & bank holidays. **Societies** must contact in advance. **Green Fees** £25 per day. **Cards** 🖩 💳 💳 💳 💳 **Prof** Simon Arnold **Facilities** ⊗ ⫙ ⬐ ♥ ♀ ⬉ ⛳ ♂ **Conf** fac available Corporate Hospitality Days available **Location** 1.5m from town centre. Turn off A34 at MacDonalds

Hotel ⛾ Holiday Inn Stoke-on-Trent, Clayton Rd, NEWCASTLE-UNDER-LYME ☎ 0870 400 9077 119 en suite

ONNELEY   Map 07 SJ74

Onneley CW3 5QF ☎ 01782 750577 & 846759
A parkland course offering panoramic views over Cheshire and Shropshire to the Welsh hills. Planned to extend course to 18 holes in Spring 2005.
13 holes, 5781yds, Par 70, SSS 68.
Club membership 410.
Visitors welcome except during competitions, but may not play on Sun and with member only Sat and bank holidays. **Societies** packages available apply in writing to secretary, or by telephone. **Green Fees** £20 per day. **Course Designer** A Benson/G Marks **Facilities** ⊗ ⫙ by prior arrangement ⬐ ♥ ♀ ⬉ **Location** 2m from Woore on A525

Hotel ⛾ Holiday Inn Stoke-on-Trent, Clayton Rd, NEWCASTLE-UNDER-LYME ☎ 0870 400 9077 119 en suite

Booking a tee time is always advisable.

PATTINGHAM   Map 07 SO89

Patshull Park Hotel Golf & Country Club
WV6 7HR ☎ 01902 700100 🖷 01902 700874
e-mail: sales@patshull-park.co.uk
Picturesque course set in 280 acres of glorious Capability Brown landscaped parkland. Designed by John Jacobs, the course meanders alongside trout fishing lakes. Water comes into play alongside the 3rd hole on a challenging drive over water on the 13th. Wellingtonia and cedar trees prove an obstacle to wayward drives off several holes. The 12th is the toughest hole on the course and the tee shot is vital, anything wayward and the trees block out the second to the green.

Patshull Park: 18 holes, 6400yds, Par 72, SSS 71, Course record 64.
Club membership 360.
Visitors must contact in advance. **Societies** must contact in advance. **Green Fees** £40 per round. **Cards** 🖃 🖃 🖃 🖃 **Prof** Richard Bissell **Course Designer** John Jacobs **Facilities** ⊗ 🏿 🖪 🖢 ♀ ⚲ 🖨 🍴 🥢 👟 ⚷ **Leisure** heated indoor swimming pool, fishing, sauna, solarium, gymnasium. **Conf** fac available Corporate Hospitality Days available **Location** 1.5m W of Pattingham at Pattingham Church take the Patshull Rd, Golf club on right
Hotel ★★★ 68% Patshull Park Hotel Golf & Country Club, Patshull Park, PATTINGHAM ☎ 01902 700100 49 en suite

PERTON   Map 07 SO89

Perton Park Wrottesley Park Rd WV6 7HL
☎ 01902 380103 & 380073 🖷 01902 326219
e-mail: golf@swindonperton.fsbusiness.co.uk
Challenging inland links style course set in the picturesque Staffordshire countryside.
18 holes, 6520yds, Par 72, SSS 72, Course record 61.
Club membership 500.
Visitors must book in advance. **Societies** must telephone in advance. **Green Fees** £15 per round (£20 weekends & bank holidays). **Cards** 🖃 🖃 **Prof** Jeremy Harrold **Facilities** ⊗ 🏿 🖪 🖢 ♀ ⚲ 🖨 🍴 👟 ⚷ 🍴 **Leisure** hard tennis courts, bowling greens. **Location** 6m W of Wolverhampton, off A454
Hotel ★★★ 68% Ely House Hotel, 53 Tettenhall Rd, WOLVERHAMPTON ☎ 01902 311311 18 en suite

> **Looking to try a new course? Always telephone ahead to confirm visitor arrangements.**

RUGELEY   Map 07 SK01

St Thomas's Priory Armitage Ln WS15 1ED
☎ 01543 492096 🖷 01543 492096
e-mail: rohanlonpro@aol.com
Parkland course with undulating fairways. Excellent drainage facilitates golf all year round. A good test of golf for both pro and amateur players.
18 holes, 5969yds, Par 70, SSS 70, Course record 64.
Club membership 400.
Visitors phone in advance. **Societies** telephone in advance. **Green Fees** £25 per round (£30 weekends). **Cards** 🖃 🖃 🖃 🖃 🖃 **Prof** P J Mulholland **Facilities** ⊗ 🏿 🖪 🖢 ♀ ⚲ 🖨 🍴 🥢 👟 ⚷ **Leisure** fishing. **Conf** fac available **Location** off A51 on A513
Hotel ⬙ Travelodge, Western Springs Rd, RUGELEY ☎ 08700 850 950 32 en suite

STAFFORD   Map 07 SJ92

Stafford Castle Newport Rd ST16 1BP
☎ 01785 223821
Parkland type course built around Stafford Castle.
9 holes, 6383yds, Par 71, SSS 70, Course record 68.
Club membership 400.
Visitors must contact in advance. May not play Sun morning. **Societies** must apply in writing or by telephone. **Green Fees** £16 per day (£20 weekends ex Sun am). **Facilities** ⊗ 🏿 🖪 🖢 ♀ ⚲ **Conf** Corporate Hospitality Days available **Location** SW side of town centre off A518
Hotel ★★★ 63% The Garth Hotel, Wolverhampton Rd, Moss Pit, STAFFORD ☎ 0870 609 6169 60 en suite

STOKE-ON-TRENT   Map 07 SJ84

Burslem Wood Farm, High Ln, Tunstall ST6 7JT
☎ 01782 837006
On the outskirts of Tunstall, a moorland course with hard walking.
9 holes, 5354yds, Par 66, SSS 66, Course record 66.
Club membership 250.
Visitors except Sun & with member only Sat & bank holidays. **Societies** must telephone in advance. **Green Fees** terms on application. **Facilities** ⊗ 🏿 🖪 🖢 ♀ ⚲ **Location** 4m N of city centre on B5049
Hotel ★★★ 65% Quality Hotel, 66 Trinity St, Hanley, STOKE-ON-TRENT ☎ 01782 202361 128 en suite 8 annexe en suite

Greenway Hall Stanley Rd, Stockton Brook ST9 9LJ
☎ 01782 503158 🖷 01782 504259
e-mail: greenway@jackbarker.com
Moorland course with fine views of the Pennines.

Continued

18 holes, 5678yds, Par 68, SSS 67, Course record 65.
Club membership 350.
Visitors must conform to dress code **Societies** telephone for information and availability. **Green Fees** not confirmed. **Cards** ⊞ ▦ ▦ ▦ ☒ ☑ **Prof** Mark Armitage **Facilities** ⊗ ⅢⅬ Ⅼ ▆ ♀ ♨ ☎ ☞ ⚓ ♣ ♂ **Conf** Corporate Hospitality Days available **Location** 5m NE off A53
· ·

Hotel ★★★ 65% Quality Hotel, 66 Trinity St, Hanley, STOKE-ON-TRENT ☎ 01782 202361 128 en suite 8 annexe en suite

Trentham
14 Barlaston Old Rd, Trentham ST4 8HB
☎ 01782 658109 📋 01782 644024
e-mail: secretary@trenthamgolf.org
Parkland course. The par 3 4th is a testing hole reached through a copse of trees.

18 holes, 6644yds, Par 72, SSS 72, Course record 67.
Club membership 600.
Visitors must contact in advance. **Societies** must contact in advance. **Green Fees** £40 (weekends & bank holidays £50). **Cards** ⊞ ▆ ☑ **Prof** Sandy Wilson **Course Designer** Colt & Alison **Facilities** ⊗ ⅢⅬ Ⅼ ▆ ♀ ♨ ☎ ☞ ♣ ⚓ ♂ **Leisure** squash. **Location** 1st right off A5035 from Trentham Gardens, A34 junct 3 m South of Newcastle under Lyme
· ·

Hotel ★★★ 66% Haydon House Hotel, Haydon St, Basford, STOKE-ON-TRENT ☎ 01782 711311 17 en suite 6 annexe en suite

Trentham Park
Trentham Park ST4 8AE
☎ 01782 658800 📋 01782 658800
e-mail: trevor-berrisford@barbox.net
Fine woodland course. Set in established parkland with many challenging and interesting holes making excellent use of water features. The greens have recently been redesigned and re-bunkered.
18 holes, 6425yds, Par 71, SSS 71, Course record 67.
Club membership 850.
Visitors must contact in advance. **Societies** Wed & Fri, must apply in advance. **Green Fees** £30 per round (£35 weekends). **Prof** Simon Lynn **Facilities** ⊗ ⅢⅬ ▆ ♀ ♨ ☎ ♣ ⚓ ♂ **Conf** Corporate Hospitality Days available **Location** 1m from M6 junct15, adjacent to Trentham Gardens, off A34 3m S of Newcastle-under-Lyme
· ·

Hotel 🆄 Holiday Inn Stoke-on-Trent, Clayton Rd, NEWCASTLE-UNDER-LYME ☎ 0870 400 9077 119 en suite

---

STONE
Map 07 SJ93

Barlaston
Meaford Rd ST15 8UX
☎ 01782 372795 & 372867 📋 01782 372867
e-mail: barlaston.gc@virgin.net
Picturesque parkland course designed by Peter Alliss. A number of water features come into play on several holes.
18 holes, 5800yds, Par 69, SSS 68.
Club membership 650.
Visitors may not play before 10am or after 4pm Fridays, weekends and bank holidays after 10 am. **Societies** telephone or apply in writing. **Green Fees** terms on application. **Prof** Ian Rogers **Course Designer** Peter Alliss **Facilities** ⊗ ⅢⅬ ▆ ♀ ♨ ☎ ♂ ℓ **Location** 9 miles N junct 14 & 5 miles S junct 15 of M6.
· ·

Hotel ★★★ 68% Stone House Hotel, Stafford Rd, STONE ☎ 0870 609 6140 50 en suite

Izaak Walton
Eccleshall Rd, Cold Norton ST15 0NS
☎ 01785 760900
18 holes, 6281yds, Par 72, SSS 72, Course record 72.
Location On B5026 between Stone & Eccleshall
Telephone for further details
· · · · · · · · · · · · · · · · · ·

Hotel ★★★ 68% Stone House Hotel, Stafford Rd, STONE ☎ 0870 609 6140 50 en suite

Stone
Filleybrooks ST15 0NB ☎ 01785 813103
e-mail: stonegolfc@onetel.net.uk
9-hole parkland course with easy walking and 18 different tees.
9 holes, 6299yds, Par 71, SSS 70, Course record 67.
Club membership 310.
Visitors with member only, weekends & bank holidays. **Societies** must apply in writing. **Green Fees** £20 per day or round. **Facilities** ⊗ ⅢⅬ ▆ ♀ ♨ ♂ **Location** 0.5m W on A34
· ·

Hotel ★★★ 68% Stone House Hotel, Stafford Rd, STONE ☎ 0870 609 6140 50 en suite

---

TAMWORTH
Map 07 SK20

Drayton Park
Drayton Park, Fazeley B78 3TN
☎ 01827 251139 📋 01827 284035
e-mail: draytonparkgc.co.uk
18 holes, 6439yds, Par 71, SSS 71, Course record 62.
Course Designer James Braid **Location** 2m S on A4091, next to Drayton Manor Leisure Park
Telephone for further details
· ·

Hotel ★★★★ 74% The De Vere Belfry, WISHAW ☎ 01675 470301 324 en suite

Tamworth Municipal
Eagle Dr, Amington B77 4EG ☎ 01827 709303 📋 01827 709305
e-mail: david-warburton@tamworth.gov.uk
First-class municipal parkland course and a good test of golf.
Tamworth Municipal Golf Club: 18 holes, 6488yds, Par 73, SSS 72, Course record 63.
Club membership 460.
Visitors must book in advance at weekends. **Societies** must contact in advance. **Green Fees** £13.60 (£14.50 weekends). **Cards** ⊞ ▆ ☑ **Prof** Wayne Alcock **Course Designer** Hawtree & Son **Facilities** ⊗ ⅢⅬ ▆ ♀ ♨ ☎ ☞ ♣ ⚓ ♂ **Conf** fac available Corporate Hospitality Days available **Location** 2.5m E off B5000

Continued

Hotel ★★ 63%   Angel Croft Hotel, Beacon St,
LICHFIELD ☎ 01543 258737 10 rms (8 en suite)
8 annexe en suite

UTTOXETER   Map 07 SK03

Manor Leese Hill, Kingstone ST14 8QT
☎ 01889 563234 ▤ 01889 563234
e-mail: ant-foulds@bigfoot.com
**A short but tough course set in the heart of the
Staffordshire countryside with fine views of the
surrounding area.**
18 holes, 6060yds, Par 71, SSS 69, Course record 67.
Club membership 400.
Visitors must contact in advance. **Societies** must telephone
in advance. **Green Fees** £16 per day (£26.50 weekends).
Cards ▤ ▤ ▤ ▤ ▨ **Course Designer** Various **Facilities**
⊗ ⊪ ⅃ ⍁ ♀ ♁ ➤ ♣ ♂ ⏏ **Leisure** fishing. **Conf**
Corporate Hospitality Days available **Location** 2m from
Uttoxeter on A518 towards Stafford

Hotel ★★★ 68%   Stone House Hotel, Stafford Rd,
STONE ☎ 0870 609 6140 50 en suite

Uttoxeter Wood Ln ST14 8JR
☎ 01889 564884 (Pro) & 566552 (Office)
▤ 01889 567501
**Undulating, challenging course with excellent putting
surfaces, manicured fairways, uniform rough and
extensive views across the Dove Valley to the rolling
hills of Staffordshire and Derbyshire.**
18 holes, 5801yds, Par 70, SSS 69, Course record 64.
Club membership 900.
Visitors restricted weekends and competition days.
Advisable to check availability during peak periods.
Societies must book in advance. **Green Fees** £24 per day
(£30 weekends). **Cards** ▤ ▤ ▨ **Prof** Adam McCandless
Course Designer G Rothera **Facilities** ⊗ ⊪ ⅃ ⍁ ♀ ♁ ➤
⏏ ♣ ♂ **Location** Close to A50, 0.5m beyond main
entrance to racecourse

Hotel ★★★ 68%   Stone House Hotel, Stafford Rd,
STONE ☎ 0870 609 6140 50 en suite

WESTON   Map 07 SJ92

Ingestre Park ST18 0RE
☎ 01889 270845 ▤ 01889 271434
e-mail: ipgc@lineone.net
**Parkland course set in the grounds of Ingestre Hall,
former home of the Earl of Shrewsbury, with mature
trees and pleasant views.**
18 holes, 6352yds, Par 70, SSS 70, Course record 67.
Club membership 750.
Visitors with member only weekends & bank holidays.
Must play before 3.30pm weekdays. Advance booking
preferred. Handicap certificate required. **Societies** must
apply in advance. **Green Fees** £30 per day; £25 per round.
Prof Danny Scullion **Course Designer** Hawtree **Facilities**
⊗ ⊪ ⅃ ⍁ ♀ ♁ ➤ ♣ ♂ **Location** 2m SE off A51

Hotel ★★★ 71%   The Swan Hotel, 46 Greengate St,
STAFFORD ☎ 01785 258142 27 en suite

WHISTON   Map 07 SK04

Whiston Hall Mansion Court Hotel ST10 2HZ
☎ 01538 266260 ▤ 01538 266820
e-mail: enquiries@whistonhall.com
A challenging 18-hole course in scenic countryside,

Continued

**incorporating many natural obstacles and providing a
test for all golfing abilities.**
18 holes, 5742yds, Par 71, SSS 69, Course record 70.
Club membership 400.
Visitors reasonable dress on the course. Must telephone in
advance at weekends. **Societies** phone for details. **Green
Fees** terms on application. **Cards** ▤ ▤ ▤ ▤ ▤ ▤ ▤
Course Designer T Cooper **Facilities** ⊗ ⊪ ⅃ ♀ ♁ ⏏
♣ ♂ **Leisure** fishing, snooker. **Conf** fac available
Location Off A52, between Stoke-on-Trent and
Ashbourne

Guesthouse ◆◆◆◆◆   Bank House, Farley Ln,
OAKAMOOR ☎ 01538 702810 3 en suite

SUFFOLK

ALDEBURGH   Map 05 TM45

Aldeburgh Saxmundham Rd IP15 5PE
☎ 01728 452890 ▤ 01728 452937
e-mail: info@aldeburghgolfclub.co.uk
**Fine heathland golf course providing a varied and
interesting challenge for the handicap golfer.
Additional 9 hole course suitable for golfing holiday
makers.**
*18 holes, 6349yds, Par 68, SSS 71, Course record 65.
River Course: 9 holes, 4228yds, Par 64, SSS 61, Course
record 62.*
Club membership 900.
Visitors must contact in advance and have a handicap
certificate. 2 ball/foursomes only. **Societies** must contact in
advance. **Green Fees** £40 per day; £35 after 12 noon
(weekends £50/£40). **Prof** Keith Preston **Course Designer**
Thompson, Fernie, Taylor, Park. **Facilities** ⊗ ⊪ ⅃ ♀ ♁ ⌂
🏠 ⌐ ♣ ♂ **Location** 1m W of Aldeburgh on A1094

Hotel ★★★ 76%   Wentworth Hotel, Wentworth Rd,
ALDEBURGH ☎ 01728 452312 30 rms (28 en suite)
7 annexe en suite. See ad on page 220.

BECCLES   Map 05 TM48

Beccles The Common NR34 9YN ☎ 01502 712244
**Common course with gorse bushes, no water hazards or
bunkers.**
9 holes, 2779yds, Par 68, SSS 67.
Club membership 175.
Visitors no restrictions. **Societies** must telephone in
advance. **Green Fees** terms on application. **Facilities** ♀ ⌂
🏠 ♂ **Location** NE side of town

Hotel ★★★ 68%   Hotel Hatfield, The Esplanade,
LOWESTOFT ☎ 01502 565337 33 en suite

WENTWORTH
HOTEL ★★★
Aldeburgh, Suffolk
Tel: (01728) 452312 Fax: (01728) 454343
E-mail: stay@wentworth-aldeburgh.co.uk
Website: www.wentworth-aldeburgh.com

The Hotel has the comfort and style of a Country House. Two comfortable lounges, with open fires and antique furniture, provide ample space to relax. Each individually decorated bedroom, many with sea views, is equipped with a colour television, radio, hairdryer and tea making facilities. The Restaurant serves a variety of fresh produce whilst a light lunch can be chosen from the Bar menu, eaten outside in the sunken terrace garden. Aldeburgh is timeless and unhurried. There are quality shops, two excellent golf courses within a short distance from the hotel, long walks and some of the best birdwatching at Minsmere Bird reserve. Music and the Arts can be heard at the Internationally famous Snape Malting Concert hall. Lastly, there are miles of beach to sit upon and watch the sea!

BUNGAY   Map 05 TM38

Bungay & Waveney Valley Outney Common
NR35 1DS ☎ 01986 892337 📠 01986 892222
e-mail: bungaygolf@aol.com
Heathland course, lined with fur and gorse. Excellent greens all-year-round, easy walking.
18 holes, 6044yds, Par 69, SSS 69, Course record 64.
Club membership 730.
Visitors should contact in advance. With member only weekends & bank holidays. **Societies** must contact in advance. **Green Fees** £32 per day/£26 per round. **Prof** Andrew Collison **Course Designer** James Braid **Facilities** ⊗ ⅂ ♖ ♀ ♨ 🏠 ⛴ 🏌 **Location** 0.5m NW on A143

Hotel ★★★ 68% Hotel Hatfield, The Esplanade, LOWESTOFT ☎ 01502 565337 33 en suite

BURY ST EDMUNDS   Map 05 TL86

Bury St Edmunds Tut Hill IP28 6LG
☎ 01284 755979 📠 01284 763288
e-mail: info@burygolf.co.uk
A mature, undulating course, full of character with some challenging holes. The 9 hole pay and play course consists of five par 3s and four par 4s with modern construction greens.
18 holes, 6675yds, Par 72, SSS 72, Course record 65.
9 holes, 2217yds, Par 62, SSS 62.
Club membership 850.
Visitors with member only at weekends for 18 hole course. **Societies** must apply in writing. **Green Fees** 18 hole course: £35 per day. 9 hole course: £13 (£16 weekends).
Cards 💳 💳 💳 💳 🈺 **Prof** Mark Jillings **Course**

Designer Ted Ray **Facilities** ⊗ ⅏ by prior arrangement ⅃ ♖ ♀ ♨ 🏠 ⛴ 🏌 **Conf** Corporate Hospitality Days available **Location** 0.5m NW on B1106 off A14

Hotel ★★★ 77% Angel Hotel, Angel Hill, BURY ST EDMUNDS ☎ 01284 714000 64 en suite

Swallow Suffolk Golf & Country Club
Fornham St Genevieve IP28 6JQ
☎ 01284 706777 📠 01284 706721
e-mail: thelodge@the-suffolk.co.uk
A classic parkland course with the River Lark running through it. Criss-crossed by ponds and streams with rich fairways. Considerable upgrading of the course in recent years and the three finishing holes are particularly challenging.

The Genevieve Course: 18 holes, 6376yds, Par 72, SSS 71, Course record 70.
Club membership 600.
Visitors contact in advance to book tee times. **Societies** telephone for details. **Green Fees** £25 per round (£30 weekends & bank holidays)). **Cards** 💳 💳 **Prof** Steve Hall **Facilities** ⊗ ⅏ ⅃ ♖ ♀ ♨ 🏠 ⛴ 🏌 🏇 ⚓ 🏌
Leisure heated indoor swimming pool, fishing, sauna, solarium, gymnasium. **Conf** fac available Corporate Hospitality Days available **Location** off the A14 at Bury St Edmunds W and take B1106 towards Brandon Club approx 2.5m on right.

Hotel ★★★ ⚑ 75% Ravenwood Hall Hotel, Rougham, BURY ST EDMUNDS ☎ 01359 270345 7 en suite 7 annexe en suite

CRETINGHAM   Map 05 TM26

Cretingham IP13 7BA
☎ 01728 685275 📠 01728 685037
Parkland course, tree-lined with numerous water features, including the River Deben which runs through part of the course.
18 holes, 4968yds, Par 68, SSS 66.
Club membership 350.
Visitors booking required for weekends. **Societies** must contact in advance. **Green Fees** terms on application.
Cards 💳 💳 💳 💳 🈺 **Prof** Neil Jackson **Course Designer** J Austin **Facilities** ⊗ ⅃ ♖ ♀ ♨ 🏠 ⛴ 🏌 🏌 **Leisure** hard tennis courts, outdoor swimming pool, fishing, pitch & putt, 9 hole course. **Conf** Corporate Hospitality Days available **Location** 2m from A1120 at Earl Soham

Hotel ★★ 68% Cedars Hotel, Needham Rd, STOWMARKET ☎ 01449 612668 25 en suite

Continued

The Swallow Suffolk Hotel, Golf & Country Club

- Modern 3★★★ Hotel overlooking golf course
- All rooms en suite with Sat TV & modem ports
- Indoor Pool Spa Sauna & Steam Room • Large air cond. Gymnasium • 18-hole Genevieve Course • Buggy & Trolley hire • Beauty & Hairdressing salons • Preferential green fees for hotel guests • Golf breaks available
- 5 mins. from the A14

Fornham St. Genevieve, Bury St. Edmunds, Suffolk IP28 6JQ

01284-706777

www.the-suffolk.co.uk

e-mail: thelodge@the-suffolk.co.uk

FELIXSTOWE   Map 05 TM33

Felixstowe Ferry Ferry Rd IP11 9RY

☎ 01394 286834 📠 01394 273679

e-mail: secretary@felixstowegolf.co.uk

18-hole seaside links with pleasant views, easy walking. Testing 491-yard 7th hole. 9-hole pay and play course, a good test of golf.

Martello Course: 18 holes, 6166yds, Par 72, SSS 70, Course record 66.

Kingsfleet: 9 holes, 2941yds, Par 35, SSS 35.

Club membership 900.

Visitors may play Martello Course weekends after 2.30pm but must contact in advance and have handicap certificate. Kingsfleet course no restrictions. Societies All weekdays ex bank holidays, telephone in advance. Green Fees Martello £35 per day (£25 after 1pm); £40 weekends and bank holidays. Prof Ian MacPherson Course Designer Henry Cotton Facilities ⊗ ⅷ by prior arrangement ⅂ ♥ ♀ ⚘ ⌂ 🖅 ∅ Conf fac available Corporate Hospitality Days available Location NE side of town centre. Signposted from A14

Hotel ★★★ 72% Elizabeth Orwell Hotel, Hamilton Rd, FELIXSTOWE ☎ 01394 285511 58 en suite

FLEMPTON   Map 05 TL86

Flempton IP28 6EQ ☎ 01284 728291

Breckland course.

9 holes, 6240yds, Par 70, SSS 70, Course record 67.

Club membership 250.

Visitors must contact in advance and produce

Continued

---

handicap certificate. Societies limited to small societies - must apply in writing. Green Fees £35 per day/£30 per round. Prof Chris Aldred Course Designer J H Taylor Facilities ⊗ ⅂ ♥ ♀ ⚘ ⌂ ∅ Location 0.5m W on A1101

Hotel ★★★ 74% The Priory Hotel, Tollgate, BURY ST EDMUNDS ☎ 01284 766181 9 en suite 30 annexe en suite

HALESWORTH   Map 05 TM37

Halesworth Bramfield Rd IP19 9XA

☎ 01986 875567 📠 01986 874565

e-mail: info@halesworthgc.co.uk

A 27-hole professionally designed parkland complex of one 18 hole membership course and a 9 hole pay and play.

18 holes, 6580yds, Par 72, SSS 72, Course record 71.

9 holes, 2398yds, Par 33, SSS 33.

Club membership 300.

Visitors visitors welcome at all times except for Sunday before noon on the 18 hole course. Handicap certificate required for 18 hole course. Societies telephone for booking form. Green Fees £25 per day/£18 per round (weekends & bank holidays £30/£22); 9 hole course: £7/£5 (£8.50/£6). Prof Simon Harrison Course Designer J W Johnson Facilities ⊗ ⅷ ⅂ ♥ ♀ ⚘ ⌂ 🖅 ♥ ⚒ ∅ ⌕ Conf fac available Location 0.75m S of town, signposted on left of A144 road to Bramfield

Hotel ★★★ 74% Swan Hotel, Market Place, SOUTHWOLD ☎ 01502 722186 25 en suite 17 annexe en suite

HAVERHILL   Map 05 TL64

Haverhill Coupals Rd CB9 7UW

☎ 01440 761951 📠 01440 761951

e-mail: haverhillgolf@coupalsroad.fsnet.co.uk

An 18 hole course lying across two valleys in pleasant parkland. The front nine with undulating fairways is complemented by a saucer-shaped back nine, bisected by the River Stour, presenting a challenge to golfers of all standards.

18 holes, 5929yds, Par 70, SSS 69, Course record 67.

Club membership 767.

Visitors telephone to check for club competitions (01440 712628) Societies must contact in advance. Weekdays if available. Green Fees terms on application. Cards 💳 💳 💳 💳 💳 💳 Prof Nick Duc Course Designer P Pilgrem/C Lawrie Facilities ⊗ ⅷ ⅂ ♥ ♀ ⚘ ⌂ ∅ Leisure chipping green. Conf fac available Corporate Hospitality Days available Location 1m SE off A1017

HINTLESHAM   Map 05 TM04

Hintlesham IP8 3NS

☎ 01473 652761 📠 01473 652750

e-mail: office@hintleshamhallgolfclub.com

Magnificent championship length course blending harmoniously with the ancient parkland surrounding this exclusive hotel. The 6630yd parkland course was designed by Hawtree and Son, one of the oldest established firms of golf course architects in the world. The course is fair but challenging for low and high handicappers alike.

18 holes, 6638yds, Par 72, SSS 72, Course record 63.

Club membership 470.

Continued

Hintlesham Golf Club

Visitors must contact 24 hours in advance. **Societies** must telephone in advance. **Green Fees** £36 per round (£44 weekends & bank holidays). **Cards** 🖸 🖸 🖸 🖸 🖸 🖸 **Prof** Alastair Spink **Course Designer** Hawtree & Sons **Facilities** ⊗ ⅏ ⅊ ⅊ ⅊ ⅊ ⅊ ⅊ ⅊ ⅊ ⅊ ⅊ ⅊ ⅊ **Leisure** hard tennis courts, heated outdoor swimming pool, sauna, gymnasium. **Conf** Corporate Hospitality Days available **Location** In village on A1071

Hotel ★★★★ 80% Hintlesham Hall Hotel, George St, HINTLESHAM ☎ 01473 652334 33 en suite

---

IPSWICH   Map 05 TM14

Alnesbourne Priory Priory Park IP10 0JT
☎ 01473 727393 📠 01473 278372
e-mail: golf@priory-park.com
A fabulous outlook facing due south across the River Orwell is one of the many good features of this course set in woodland. All holes run among trees with some fairways requiring straight shots. The 8th green is on saltings by the river.
9 holes, 1700yds, Par 29.
Club membership 30.
Visitors closed on Tuesday. Closed 5 Jan-1 Mar. **Societies** Tue only, telephone in advance. **Green Fees** £10 (£11 Sat; £12 Sun & bank holidays). **Facilities** ⊗ ⅏ ⅊ ⅊ ⅊ ⅊ **Leisure** practice net. **Location** 3m SE, off A14

Hotel ★★★ 71% Courtyard by Marriott Ipswich, The Havens, Ransomes Europark, IPSWICH ☎ 01473 272244 60 en suite

Fynn Valley IP6 9JA
☎ 01473 785267 📠 01473 785632
e-mail: enquiries@fynn-valley.co.uk
Undulating parkland course plus par 3 nine-hole and driving range.
18 holes, 6310yds, Par 70, SSS 71, Course record 65.
Club membership 650.
Visitors members only Sun until 10.30am. Ladies priority Wed am. **Societies** must apply in advance. **Green Fees** £22 per 18 holes (£25 weekends). **Cards** 🖸 🖸 🖸 🖸 🖸 **Prof** P Wilby/ A Lucas/S Dainty **Course Designer** Antonio Primavera **Facilities** ⊗ ⅏ ⅊ ⅊ ⅊ ⅊ ⅊ ⅊ **Leisure** 9 hole par 3 course, practice bunker. **Conf** fac available Corporate Hospitality Days available **Location** 2m N of Ipswich on B1077

Hotel ★★★ 65% Novotel Ipswich, Greyfriars Rd, IPSWICH ☎ 01473 232400 100 en suite

> **Booking a tee time is always advisable.**

Ipswich Purdis Heath IP3 8UQ
☎ 01473 728941 📠 01473 715236
e-mail: mail@ipswichgolfclub.com
Many golfers are surprised when they hear that Ipswich has, at Purdis Heath, a first-class golf course. In some ways it resembles some of Surrey's better courses; a beautiful heathland course with two lakes and easy walking.
Purdis Heath: 18 holes, 6439yds, Par 71, SSS 71, Course record 64 or 9 holes, 1930yds, Par 31.
Club membership 865.
Visitors must contact in advance & have a handicap certificate for 18 hole course. **Societies** must contact in advance. **Green Fees** 18 hole course: £45 per day; £35 per round pm (£50/£40 weekends & bank holidays). 9 hole course: £10 per day (£12.50). **Cards** 🖸 🖸 🖸 🖸 🖸 **Prof** Stephen Whymark **Course Designer** James Braid **Facilities** ⊗ ⅏ ⅊ ⅊ ⅊ ⅊ ⅊ **Location** 3 miles E of town centre off A1156, 1m from St Augustines church on Bucklesham road

Hotel ★★★ 71% Courtyard by Marriott Ipswich, The Havens, Ransomes Europark, IPSWICH ☎ 01473 272244 60 en suite

Rushmere Rushmere Heath IP4 5QQ
☎ 01473 725648 📠 01473 273852
e-mail: rushmeregolfclub@talk21.com
Heathland course with gorse and prevailing winds. A good test of golf.
18 holes, 6262yds, Par 70, SSS 70, Course record 66.
Club membership 700.
Visitors not before 2.30pm weekends & bank holidays. Must have a handicap certificate. Must contact in advance. **Societies** weekdays by arrangement. **Green Fees** £30. **Cards** 🖸 🖸 🖸 🖸 🖸 **Prof** K. Vince **Facilities** ⊗ ⅏ ⅊ ⅊ ⅊ ⅊ **Conf** Corporate Hospitality Days available **Location** On A1214 Woodbridge road, close to hospital, signposted

Hotel ★★★ 65% County Hotel Ipswich, London Rd, Copdock, IPSWICH ☎ 0870 609 6171 76 en suite

---

LOWESTOFT   Map 05 TM59

Rookery Park Beccles Rd, Carlton Colville
NR33 8HJ ☎ 01502 509190 📠 01502 509191
e-mail: office@rookeryparkgolfclub.co.uk
Parkland course with a 9-hole par 3 adjacent.
18 holes, 6714yds, Par 72, SSS 72.
Club membership 1000.
Visitors must have handicap certificate. **Societies** by arrangement. **Green Fees** £25 (£30 weekends & bank holidays). **Cards** 🖸 🖸 🖸 🖸 🖸 **Prof** Martin Elsworthy **Course Designer** C D Lawrie **Facilities** ⊗ ⅏ ⅊ ⅊ ⅊ ⅊ ⅊ **Leisure** 9 hole par 3 course. **Location** 3.5m SW of Lowestoft on A146 Lowestoft-Beccles road

Hotel ★★★ 68% Hotel Hatfield, The Esplanade, LOWESTOFT ☎ 01502 565337 33 en suite

---

MILDENHALL   Map 05 TL77

West Suffolk Golf Centre New Drove, Beck Row
IP28 8DY ☎ 01638 718972 📠 01353 675447
This course has been gradually improved over the last 8 years and provides a unique opportunity to play an inland course in all weather conditions. Situated on the

Continued

edge of the Breckland, the dry nature of the course makes for easy walking with unique flora and fauna.
12 holes, 6461yds, Par 71, SSS 71.
Visitors welcome. no restrictions **Societies** telephone 24hrs in advance. More notice required for catering arrangements. **Green Fees** £10.50 per day (£14 weekends and bank holidays). **Cards** 🖃 🎫 🎫 💳 **Prof** Paul Geen **Facilities** ⊗ ⓑ 🎽 ♀ 🏖 🏠 ⛳ 𝄽 ⓒ **Leisure** fishing, pitch and putt practice course. **Location** from Mildenhall take A1101 to Beck Row. 1st turn left after Beck Row to West Row, 0.5m on right

Hotel ★★★ 68% The Smoke House, Beck Row, MILDENHALL ☎ 01638 713223 94 en suite 2 annexe en suite

NEWMARKET   Map 05 TL66

Links Cambridge Rd CB8 0TG
☎ 01638 663000 🗎 01638 661476
e-mail: secretary@linksgc.fsbusiness.co.uk
Gently undulating parkland.
18 holes, 6582yds, Par 72, SSS 72, Course record 66 or , Par 72.
Club membership 780.
Visitors must have handicap certificate, may not play Sun before 11.30am. **Societies** telephone secretary in advance. **Green Fees** £32 per day (£36 weekends). **Prof** John Sharkey **Course Designer** Col. Hotchkin **Facilities** ⊗ 🎽 ⓑ 🎽 ♀ 🏖 🏠 🦆 𝄽 **Location** 1m SW on A1034

Hotel ★★★ 68% Heath Court Hotel, Moulton Rd, NEWMARKET ☎ 01638 667171 41 en suite

NEWTON   Map 05 TL94

Newton Green Newton Green CO10 0QN
☎ 01787 377217 & 377501 🗎 01787 377549
e-mail: info@newtongreengolfclub.co.uk
Flat 18-hole course with lake. First nine holes are open with bunkers. Second nine holes are tight with ditches and gorse.
18 holes, 5960yds, Par 69, SSS 68.
Club membership 540.
Visitors must contact in advance but may not play on Tue before 12.30 **Societies** apply in advance. **Green Fees** £22 per round (£25 weekends). **Cards** 🖃 🎫 💳 **Prof** Tim Cooper **Facilities** ⊗ 🎽 ⓑ 🎽 💆 ♀ 🏖 🏠 ⛳ 𝄽 **Location** W side of village on A134

Hotel ★★★ 73% The Bull, Hall St, LONG MELFORD ☎ 01787 378494 25 en suite

RAYDON   Map 05 TM03

Brett Vale Noakes Rd IP7 5LR ☎ 01473 310718
e-mail: info@brettvalegolf.com
Brett Vale course takes you through a nature reserve and on lakeside walks, affording views over Dedham Vale. The excellent fairways demand an accurate tee and good approach shots. 1, 2, 3, 8, 10 and 15 are all affected by crosswinds, but once in the valley it is much more sheltered. Although only 5813 yards the course is testing and interesting at all levels of golf.
18 holes, 5813yds, Par 70, SSS 69, Course record 65.
Club membership 600.
Visitors must book tee times and wear appropriate clothing, soft spikes only. **Societies** apply in writing or telephone. **Green Fees** £20 per 18 holes (£25 weekends and bank holidays). **Cards** 🖃 🎫 🎫 🎫 💳
Continued

Prof Robert Taylor **Course Designer** Howard Swan **Facilities** ⊗ 🎽 ⓑ 💆 🎽 ♀ 🏖 🏠 ⛳ 🍴 🦆 𝄽 ⓒ **Leisure** fishing, gymnasium. **Conf** fac available Corporate Hospitality Days available **Location** From A12 take B1070 towards Hadleigh. Turn left at Raydon. Water tower marks spot

Hotel ★★★ ♨ Maison Talbooth, Stratford Rd, DEDHAM ☎ 01206 322367 10 en suite

SOUTHWOLD   Map 05 TM57

Southwold The Common IP18 6TB
☎ 01502 723234
Commonland course with 4 acre practice ground and panoramic views of the sea.
9 holes, 6052yds, Par 70, SSS 69, Course record 67.
Club membership 350.
Visitors restricted on competition days (Ladies-Wed, Gents-Sun). Contact in advance. **Societies** must contact in advance. **Green Fees** £26 per 18 holes; £13 per 9 holes (£28/£14 weekends). **Prof** Brian Allen **Course Designer** J Braid **Facilities** ⊗ 🎽 ⓑ 🎽 ♀ 🏖 🏠 𝄽 **Conf** Corporate Hospitality Days available **Location** From A12 - B1140 to Southwold

Hotel ★★★ 74% Swan Hotel, Market Place, SOUTHWOLD ☎ 01502 722186 25 en suite 17 annexe en suite

STOWMARKET   Map 05 TM05

Stowmarket Lower Rd, Onehouse IP14 3DA
☎ 01449 736473 🗎 01449 736826
e-mail: mail@stowmarketgc.sagehost.co.uk
Parkland course.
18 holes, 6107yds, Par 69, SSS 69, Course record 65.
Club membership 630.
Visitors must contact in advance, not Wed. **Societies** Thu or Fri, by arrangement. **Green Fees** terms on application. **Cards** 🖃 🎫 💳 **Prof** Duncan Burl **Facilities** ⊗ 🎽 ⓑ 💆 ♀ 🏖 🏠 🍴 🦆 𝄽 ⓒ **Conf** Corporate Hospitality Days available **Location** 2.5m SW off B1115

Hotel ★★ 68% Cedars Hotel, Needham Rd, STOWMARKET ☎ 01449 612668 25 en suite

STUSTON   Map 05 TM17

Diss Stuston IP21 4AA
☎ 01379 641025 🗎 01379 644586
e-mail: sec.dissgolf@virgin.net
Commonland course with natural hazards.
18 holes, 6206yds, Par 70, SSS 69.
Club membership 750.
Visitors must contact in advance but may not play weekends & bank holidays. **Societies** by arrangement. **Green Fees** £32 per day; £28 per 18 holes, £14 per 9 holes. **Prof** N J Taylor **Facilities** ⊗ 🎽 ⓑ 💆 🎽 ♀ 🏖 𝄽 ⓒ **Conf** fac available Corporate Hospitality Days available **Location** 1.5m SE on B1118

Hotel ★★ 75% The Old Ram Coaching Inn, Ipswich Rd, TIVETSHALL ST MARY ☎ 01379 676794 11 en suite

> **Looking for a driving range? Refer to the listing of driving ranges at the back of this guide.**

THORPENESS   Map 05 TM45

Thorpeness Golf Club & Hotel Lakeside Av
IP16 4NH ☎ 01728 452176 📠 01728 453868
e-mail: info@thorpeness.co.uk
Thorpeness Golf Club provides a 6271 yard coastal
heathland course, designed in 1923 by James Braid.
The quality of his design combined with modern green
keeping techniques has resulted in an extremely
challenging course for golfers at all levels. It is also one
of the driest courses in the region.

18 holes, 6271yds, Par 69, SSS 71, Course record 66.
Club membership 500.
Visitors contact in advance, handicap certificate required.
Societies telephone in advance, handicap certificate and
deposit required. Green Fees not confirmed. Cards ▭
▭ ▭ ▭ 🄿 Prof Frank Hill Course Designer James
Braid Facilities ⊗ ⅏ ⅃ ♥ ♀ ⚥ 🏠 🚮 🥾 ⚲ Leisure
hard and grass tennis courts, fishing, snooker room. Conf
fac available Corporate Hospitality Days available
Location Take A12 heading N of Ipswich, turn onto
A1094 then turn off to Aldeburgh and follow local
signposting
Hotel ★★★ 76% White Lion Hotel, Market Cross Place,
ALDEBURGH ☎ 01728 452720 38 en suite

WALDRINGFIELD   Map 05 TM24

Waldringfield Heath Newbourne Rd IP12 4PT
☎ 01473 736768 📠 01473 736793
e-mail: patgolf1@aol.com
Easy walking heathland course with long drives on 1st
and 13th (590yds) and some ponds.
18 holes, 6141yds, Par 71, SSS 69, Course record 67.
Club membership 550.
Visitors welcome Mon-Fri, weekends & bank holidays
after noon. Must book tee times in advance Societies by
arrangement. Green Fees 18 holes £22 (weekends £26).
Cards ▭ ▭ ▭ ▭ 🄿 Course Designer Phillip Pilgrem
Facilities ⊗ ⅏ ⅃ ♥ ♀ ⚥ 🏠 🚮 ⚲ Conf fac available
Location 3m NE of Ipswich off old A12

Hotel ★★★ 76% Seckford Hall Hotel,
WOODBRIDGE ☎ 01394 385678 22 en suite
10 annexe en suite

WOODBRIDGE   Map 05 TM24

Seckford Seckford Hall Rd, Great Bealings IP13 6NT
☎ 01394 388000 📠 01394 382818
e-mail: info@seckfordgolf.co.uk
Seckford Golf Course: 18 holes, 5303yds, Par 68, SSS 66,
Course record 62.

Continued

Course Designer J Johnson Location 1m W of
Woodbridge, 0ff A12, next to Seckford Hall hotel
Telephone for further details

Hotel ★★★ 🏌 76% Seckford Hall Hotel,
WOODBRIDGE ☎ 01394 385678 22 en suite
10 annexe en suite

Ufford Park Hotel Golf & Leisure Yarmouth
Rd, Ufford IP12 1QW
☎ 01394 383555 📠 01394 383582
e-mail: mail@uffordpark.co.uk
The 18-hole par 71 course is set in 120 acres of ancient
parkland with 12 water features and voted one of the
best British winter courses. The course enjoys excellent
natural drainage and a large reservoir supplements a
spring feed pond to ensure ample water for irrigation.
The course is host to the Sky Sports PGA Europro Tour.

18 holes, 6485yds, Par 71, SSS 71, Course record 65.
Club membership 350.
Visitors must book tee time from golf shop 01394 382836.
Must adhere to dress code. Handicap certificates required
for Sat/Sun mornings. Societies telephone in advance to
book tee time on 01394 3812836 Green Fees £30 per day
(£40 weekends). Cards ▭ ▭ ▭ 🄿 Prof
Stuart Robertson Course Designer Phil Pilgrim Facilities
⊗ ⅏ ⅃ ♥ ♀ ⚥ 🏠 🚮 🥾 ⚲ ⚲ Leisure heated indoor
swimming pool, sauna, solarium, gymnasium. Conf fac
available Corporate Hospitality Days available Location
Just off A12, on the B1438

Hotel ★★★ 72% Best Western Ufford Park Hotel Golf &
Leisure, Yarmouth Rd, Ufford, IPSWICH /
WOODBRIDGE ☎ 01394 383555 90 en suite

Woodbridge Bromeswell Heath IP12 2PF
☎ 01394 382038 📠 01394 382392
e-mail: woodbridgegc@anglianet.co.uk
A beautiful course, one of the best in East Anglia. It is
situated on high ground and in different seasons
presents golfers with a great variety of colour. Some say
that of the many good holes the 16th is the best.
18 holes, 6299yds, Par 70, SSS 70, Course record 64.
Forest Course: 9 holes, 3191yds, Par 70, SSS 70.
Club membership 700.
Visitors Main Course: must contact in advance, handicap
certificate required, with member only weekends. Forest
Course: open all days and no handicap certificate required.
Societies by prior telephone call or in writing. Green Fees
Main Course: £40 per day. Forest Course: £18 per day.
Prof Campbell Elliot Course Designer Davie Grant
Facilities ⊗ ⅏ ⅃ ♥ ♀ ⚥ 🏠 ⚲ Location 2.5m NE off
A1152

Continued

Hotel ★★★ ♨ 76% Seckford Hall Hotel,
WOODBRIDGE ☎ 01394 385678 22 en suite
10 annexe en suite

WORLINGTON
Map 05 TL67

Royal Worlington & Newmarket IP28 8SD
☎ 01638 712216 & 717787 📠 01638 717787
e-mail: pinkjug@lineone.net
Inland 'links' course, renowned as one of the best 9-hole courses in the world. Well drained, giving excellent winter playing conditions.
9 holes, 3105yds, Par 35, SSS 70, Course record 65.
Club membership 325.
Visitors with member only at weekends. Must contact in advance and have a handicap certificate. Societies must apply in writing. Green Fees £54 per day (reductions after 2 pm). Prof Malcolm Hawkins Course Designer Tom Dunn Facilities ⊗ 🏐 ♥ ♀ ⚒ 🛅 ⛳ ⚲ Location 0.5m SE of Worlington village near Mildenhall

Hotel ★★★ 73% Riverside Hotel, Mill St,
MILDENHALL ☎ 01638 717274 17 en suite
6 annexe en suite

SURREY

ADDLESTONE
Map 04 TQ06

New Zealand Woodham Ln KT15 3QD
☎ 01932 345049 📠 01932 342891
e-mail: roger.marrett@nzgc.org
18 holes, 6073yds, Par 68, SSS 69, Course record 66.
Course Designer Muir Fergusson/Simpson Location 1.5m E of Woking
Telephone for further details

Hotel ★★★ 67% The Ship Hotel, Monument Green,
WEYBRIDGE ☎ 01932 848364 39 en suite

ASHFORD
Map 04 TQ07

Ashford Manor Fordbridge Rd TW15 3RT
☎ 01784 424644 📠 01784 424649
e-mail: secretaryatashfordmanorgolfclub@fsnet.co.uk
Tree lined parkland course, looks easy but is difficult.
18 holes, 6352yds, Par 70, SSS 71, Course record 64.
Club membership 700.
Visitors advisable to telephone in advance, handicap certificate required, with member only at weekends but may not play competition days. Societies welcome weekdays, except Thu am, must contact in advance. Green Fees £40 per day, £35 per round (weekdays only). Cards 💳 💳 💳 💳 💳 Prof Ian Partington Facilities ⊗ 🏐 🏐 ♥ ♀ ⚒ 🛅 ⚲ Conf fac available Location 2m E of Staines via A308 Staines by-pass

Hotel ★★★ 70% The Thames Lodge, Thames St,
STAINES ☎ 0870 400 8121 78 en suite

BAGSHOT
Map 04 SU96

Pennyhill Park Hotel & Country Club London
Rd GU19 5EU ☎ 01276 471774 📠 01276 473217
e-mail: pennyhillpark@msn.com
9 holes, 2095yds, Par 32, SSS 32.

Location Off A30 between Camberley and Bagshot
Telephone for further details

Hotel ★★★★★ Pennyhill Park Hotel & The Spa, London
Rd, BAGSHOT ☎ 01276 471774 26 en suite
97 annexe en suite

Windlesham Grove End GU19 5HY
☎ 01276 452220 📠 01276 452290
18 holes, 6650yds, Par 72, SSS 72, Course record 69.
Course Designer Tommy Horton Location Junct of A30/A322
Telephone for further details

Hotel ★★★★★ Pennyhill Park Hotel & The Spa, London
Rd, BAGSHOT ☎ 01276 471774 26 en suite
97 annexe en suite

BANSTEAD
Map 04 TQ25

Banstead Downs Burdon Ln, Belmont, Sutton
SM2 7DD ☎ 020 8642 2284 📠 020 8642 5252
e-mail: secretary@bansteaddowns.com
A natural downland course set on a site of botanic interest. A challenging 18 holes with narrow fairways and tight lies.
18 holes, 6194yds, Par 69, SSS 69, Course record 64.
Club membership 902.
Visitors must book in advance and have handicap certificate or letter of introduction. With member only weekends. Societies Thu, by prior arrangement Green Fees £40 per day, £35 per 18 holes. Prof Ian Golding Course Designer J H Taylor/James Braid Facilities ⊗ 🏐 by prior arrangement 🏐 ♥ ♀ ⚒ 🛅 ⚲ Conf Corporate Hospitality Days available Location M25 Junct 8, N on A217 for 6 miles

Hotel ★★ 63% Thatched House Hotel, 135 Cheam Rd,
Sutton ☎ 020 8642 3131 32 rms (29 en suite)

Cuddington Banstead Rd SM7 1RD
☎ 020 8393 0952 📠 020 8786 7025
e-mail: ds@cuddingtongc.co.uk
Parkland course with easy walking and good views.
18 holes, 6614yds, Par 71, SSS 71, Course record 64.
Club membership 694.
Visitors must contact in advance and have a handicap certificate or letter of introduction. Societies welcome Thu, must apply in advance. Green Fees £20-45 per 18 holes (£25-55 weekends). Prof Mark Warner Course Designer H S Colt Facilities ⊗ 🏐 🏐 ♥ ♀ ⚒ 🛅 ⚲ Conf fac available Corporate Hospitality Days available Location N of Banstead station on A2022

Hotel ★★ 63% Thatched House Hotel, 135 Cheam Rd,
Sutton ☎ 020 8642 3131 32 rms (29 en suite)

BLETCHINGLEY
Map 05 TQ35

Bletchingley Church Ln RH1 4LP
☎ 01883 744666 📠 01883 744284
e-mail: info@bletchingleygolf.co.uk
Panoramic views create a perfect back drop for this course, constructed on rich sandy loam and playable all year round. The course design has made best use of the interesting and undulating land features with a variety of mixed and mature trees providing essential course definition. A mature stream creates several interesting water features.
18 holes, 6169yds, Par 72, SSS 69.

Continued

Continued

Visitors telephone Pro Shop to book (01883 744848). May only play pm Tue, Thu and weekends **Societies** telephone for details. Mon, Wed & Fri all day. Tue, Thu & weekends pm only. **Green Fees** £30 (£42 weekends). **Cards** 💳 💳 💳 🖼 🖳 **Prof** Alasdair Dyer **Facilities** ⊗ 🏌 🍴 🍷 🏖 ⛳ 🏠 ⛳ 🏌 ⚒ ⛳ ⚑ **Conf** fac available **Location** M25 junct 6, A25 towards Redhill. Church Lane is off A25 in Bletchingley Village, between Redhill and Godstone

....

Hotel ★★★★ 74% Nutfield Priory, Nutfield, REDHILL
☎ 01737 824400 60 en suite

BRAMLEY   Map 04 TQ04

Bramley GU5 0AL ☎ 01483 892696 📠 01483 894673
e-mail: secretary@bramleygolfclub.co.uk
Parkland course, from the high ground picturesque views of the Wey Valley on one side and the Hog's Back. Full on course irrigation system with three reservoirs on the course.
18 holes, 5990yds, Par 69, SSS 69, Course record 63.
Club membership 850.
Visitors may not play Tue am (Ladies Morning) and must play with member at weekends & bank holidays. Must contact secretary on 01483 892696. **Societies** must telephone the secretary in advance. **Green Fees** not confirmed. **Prof** Gary Peddie **Course Designer** James Braid **Facilities** ⊗ 🗐 🏌 🍴 🍷 🏖 🏠 ⛳ 🏌 ⚒ ⛳ ⚑
Location 3m S of Guildford on A281

....

Hotel 🅄 Holiday Inn Guildford, Egerton Rd, GUILDFORD ☎ 0870 400 9036 167 en suite

BROOKWOOD   Map 04 SU95

West Hill Bagshot Rd GU24 0BH
☎ 01483 474365 📠 01483 474252
e-mail: secretary@westhill-golfclub.co.uk
A challenging course with fairways lined with heather and tall pines, one of Surrey's finest courses.
18 holes, 6368yds, Par 69, SSS 70, Course record 62.
Club membership 500.
Visitors must contact in advance & have handicap certificate, may not play weekends & bank holidays. **Societies** weekdays only. Telephone in advance. **Green Fees** £75 per day; £50 per round. **Cards** 💳 💳 💳 🖼 🖳 **Prof** John A Clements **Course Designer** C Butchart/W Parke **Facilities** ⊗ 🗐 by prior arrangement 🏌 🍷 🍴 🏖 🏠 ⛳ 🏌 ⚒ **Conf** fac available Corporate Hospitality Days available **Location** E side of village on A322

....

Hotel ★★★★★ Pennyhill Park Hotel & The Spa, London Rd, BAGSHOT ☎ 01276 471774 26 en suite
97 annexe en suite

CAMBERLEY   Map 04 SU86

Camberley Heath Golf Dr GU15 1JG
☎ 01276 23258 📠 01276 692505
e-mail: info@camberleyheathgolfclub.co.uk
One of the great 'heath and heather' courses so frequently associated with Surrey. Several very good short holes - especially the 8th. The 10th is a difficult and interesting par 4, as is the 17th, where the drive must be held well to the left as trouble lies to the right. A fairway irrigation system has been installed.
18 holes, 6147yds, Par 72, SSS 70, Course record 65.
Club membership 600.

Continued

Camberley Heath

Visitors may not play at weekends. Must contact in advance. **Societies** must apply in advance. **Green Fees** £70 per 36 holes, £55 per 18 holes. **Cards** 💳 💳 💳 💳 🖳 💳 **Prof** Glenn Ralph **Course Designer** Harry S Colt **Facilities** ⊗ 🏌 🍴 🍷 🏖 🏠 ⛳ 🏌 ⚒ ⛳ **Conf** fac available Corporate Hospitality Days available **Location** 1.25m SE of town centre off A325

....

Hotel ★★★★★ Pennyhill Park Hotel & The Spa, London Rd, BAGSHOT ☎ 01276 471774 26 en suite
97 annexe en suite

Pine Ridge Old Bisley Rd, Frimley GU16 9NX
☎ 01276 675444 & 20770 📠 01276 678837
e-mail: enquiry@pineridgegolf.co.uk
Pay and play heathland course cut through a pine forest with challenging par 3s, deceptively demanding par 4s and several birdiable par 5s. Easy walking, but gently undulating. Good corporate or society packages.
18 holes, 6458yds, Par 72, SSS 71, Course record 65.
Club membership 400.
Visitors no jeans or trainers,necessary to book for weekends. **Societies** apply in advance by writing/telephone, packages available to suit. **Green Fees** not confirmed. **Cards** 💳 💳 **Prof** Peter Sefton **Course Designer** Clive D Smith **Facilities** ⊗ 🗐 🏌 🍴 🍷 🏖 🏠 ⛳ 🏌 ⚒ ⛳ **Conf** fac available Corporate Hospitality Days available **Location** Just off B3015, near A30

....

Hotel ★★★ 74% Frimley Hall, Lime Av, CAMBERLEY
☎ 0870 400 8224 86 en suite

CATERHAM   Map 05 TQ35

Surrey National Rook Ln, Chaldon CR3 5AA
☎ 01883 344555 📠 01883 344422
e-mail: caroline@surreynational.co.uk
Opened in May 1999, this American style course is set in beautiful countryside and features fully irrigated greens and fairways. It also has large practice areas plus a superb new clubhouse.

Continued

18 holes, 6612yds, Par 72, SSS 73, Course record 70.
Club membership 750.
Visitors may play weekdays and weekends and can book in advance. **Societies** apply in writing/telephone in advance. **Green Fees** £25 per round (£28 weekends).
Cards ⊞ ▦ ▦ ▦ ▦ **Prof** David Kent/Wayne East
Course Designer David Williams **Facilities** ⊗ ⅀Ⅲ ⅃ ⅃ ♥ ⅄
⅋ ⊡ ⅋ ☈ ⅋ ⅋ ⅋ ♪ { **Conf** fac available Corporate Hospitality Days available **Location** M25 junct 7, M23 junct 6/A22

Hotel ★★★★ 77% Coulsdon Manor, Coulsdon Court Rd, Coulsdon, CROYDON ☎ 020 8668 0414 35 en suite

Laleham Laleham Reach KT16 8RP
☎ 01932 564211 ▤ 01932 564448
e-mail: sec@laleham-golf.co.uk
Well-bunkered parkland/meadowland course.
18 holes, 6204yds, Par 70, SSS 70.
Club membership 600.
Visitors members guests only at weekends. **Societies** must contact in writing/telephone. **Green Fees** £27 per round.
Prof Hogan Stott **Course Designer** Jack White **Facilities** ⊗ ⅀Ⅲ ⅃ ♥ ⅄ ⅂ ⅋ ⊡ ⅋ **Conf** fac available **Location** M25 junct 11/A320 to Thorpe Park, at roundabout take exit to Penton Marina and follow signs to club

Hotel ★★★ 70% The Thames Lodge, Thames St, STAINES ☎ 0870 400 8121 78 en suite

Chiddingfold Petworth Rd GU8 4SL
☎ 01428 685888 ▤ 01428 685939
e-mail: chiddingfoldgolf@btconnect.com
With panoramic views across the Surrey Downs, this challenging course offers a unique combination of lakes, mature woodland and wildlife.
18 holes, 5501yds, Par 70, SSS 67.
Club membership 250.
Visitors telephone bookings up to one week in advance.
Societies prior telephone booking required. **Green Fees** terms on application. **Cards** ⊞ ▦ ▦ ▦ ▦ **Prof** Reece McRae **Course Designer** Jonathan Gaunt **Facilities** ⊗ ⅀Ⅲ
⅃ ♥ ⅄ ⅂ ⊡ ⅋ ♪ ♪ ⅋ { **Conf** fac available
Corporate Hospitality Days available **Location** A283

Hotel ★★★★ 71% Lythe Hill Hotel & Spa, Petworth Rd, HASLEMERE ☎ 01428 651251 41 en suite

Chipstead How Ln CR5 3LN
☎ 01737 555781 ▤ 01737 555404
e-mail: office@chipsteadgolf.freeserve.co.uk
Hilly parkland course, hard walking, good views.
Testing 18th hole.
18 holes, 5504yds, Par 68, SSS 67, Course record 61.
Club membership 475.
Visitors must contact in advance. May not play weekends or Tue mornings. **Societies** must apply in writing. **Green Fees** £40 per day, £30 per round. **Cards** ⊞ ▦ ▦ **Prof** Gary Torbett **Facilities** ⊗ ⅀Ⅲ ⅃ ♥ ⅄ ⅂ ⊡ ⅋ ♪ ⅋
Conf fac available Corporate Hospitality Days available
Location 0.5m N of village

Hotel ★★★★ 69% Le Meridien Selsdon Park & Golf Course, Addington Rd, Sanderstead, CROYDON
☎ 020 8657 8811 204 en suite

Chobham Chobham Rd, Knaphill GU21 2TZ
☎ 01276 855584 ▤ 01276 855663
e-mail: chobhamgolfclub.co.uk
Designed by Peter Allis and Clive Clark, Chobham course sits among mature oaks and tree nurseries offering tree-lined fairways, together with six man-made lakes.
18 holes, 5959yds, Par 69, SSS 69, Course record 67.
Club membership 750.
Visitors booking in advance essential. **Societies** by prior arrangement Mon-Thu. **Green Fees** terms on application.
Cards ⊞ ▦ ▦ ▦ ▦ **Prof** Tim Coombes **Course Designer** Peter Alliss/Clive Clark **Facilities** ⊗ ⅀Ⅲ by prior arrangement ⅃ ♥ ⅄ ⅂ ⊡ ⅋ ♪ ⅋ **Conf** fac available Corporate Hospitality Days available **Location** Between Chobham and Knaphill

Hotel ★★★ 65% Falcon Hotel, 68 Farnborough Rd, FARNBOROUGH ☎ 01252 545378 30 en suite

Silvermere Redhill Rd KT11 1EF
☎ 01932 584300 ▤ 01932 584301
e-mail: sales@silvermere.freeserve.co.uk
Parkland course with many very tight holes through woodland, the 17th has 170yd carry over the lake. 18th is played to a new island green. Driving range.
18 holes, 6430yds, Par 71.
Club membership 740.
Visitors may not play at weekends until 11am. Must contact in advance. **Societies** must contact by telephone.
Green Fees not confirmed. **Cards** ⊞ ▦ ▦ ▦ ▦ ▦
Prof Doug McClelland **Facilities** ⊗ ⅀Ⅲ ⅃ ♥ ⅄ ⅂ ⊡ ⅋
⅋ { **Leisure** fishing. **Conf** fac available Corporate Hospitality Days available **Location** 2.25m NW off A245

Hotel ★★★★ 73% Woodlands Park Hotel, Woodlands Ln, STOKE D'ABERNON ☎ 01372 843933 57 en suite

Cranleigh Golf and Leisure Club Barhatch Ln
GU6 7NG ☎ 01483 268855 ▤ 01483 267251
e-mail: info@cranleighgolfandleisure.co.uk
Scenic woodland/parkland course at the base of the Surrey hills, easy walking. Clubhouse in 400-year-old barn.
18 holes, 5648yds, Par 68, SSS 67, Course record 62.
Club membership 1400.
Visitors welcome weekdays but restricted Thu am. For weekends contact professional shop in advance on 01483 277188 **Societies** telephone in advance. **Green Fees** £38 per day, £30 per round (£33 per round weekends & bank holidays). Reduced winter/twilight rates. **Cards** ⊞ ▦
▦ ▦ ▦ **Prof** Trevor Longmuir **Facilities** ⊗ ⅃ ♥ ⅄ ⅂
⊡ ⅋ ♪ ⅋ ⅋ { **Leisure** hard tennis courts, heated indoor swimming pool, sauna, solarium, gymnasium, steam room, spa bath. **Conf** Corporate Hospitality Days available
Location Off A281 Guildford to Horsham road, signposted Cranleigh

Hotel ★★★ 63% Gatton Manor Hotel Golf & Country Club, Standon Ln, OCKLEY ☎ 01306 627555
18 en suite

Wildwood Country Club Horsham Rd, Alfold
GU6 8JE ☎ 01403 753255 📠 01403 752005
Parkland with stands of old oaks dominating several holes, a stream fed by a natural spring winds through a series of lakes and ponds. The greens are smooth, undulating and large. The 5th and 16th are the most challenging holes.
18 holes, 6655yds, Par 72, SSS 73, Course record 65.
Club membership 500.
Visitors welcome subject to availability & booking.
Societies apply in writing or telephone for enquiries.
Green Fees terms on application. **Cards** 🖶 ▦ ▦ ▦
▦ 🖫 **Prof** Simon Andrews **Course Designer** Hawtree & Sons **Facilities** ⊗ ⊪ ⅙ 🖢 ⅞ ⅄ ☖ ⌐ ⅞ 📌 ⅗ 🕻 **Leisure** gymnasium, Par 3 course. **Location** Off A281, approx 9m S of Guildford

Hotel ★★★ 69% Hurtwood Inn Hotel, Walking Bottom, PEASLAKE ☎ 01306 730851 15 en suite
6 annexe en suite

CROYDON
For other golf courses in the area, please see Greater London.

DORKING   Map 04 TQ14

Betchworth Park Reigate Rd RH4 1NZ
☎ 01306 882052 📠 01306 877462
e-mail: manager@betchworthparkgc.co.uk
Established parkland course with beautiful views, on the southern side of the North Downs near Boxhill.
18 holes, 6285yds, Par 69, SSS 70, Course record 64.
Club membership 725.
Visitors weekend play Sun pm only. Must contact in advance. **Societies** apply in writing/telephone/fax. **Green Fees** £35 per day (weekends £45 per round). **Cards** ▦
Prof Andy Tocher **Course Designer** Harry Colt **Facilities** ⊗ ⊪ ⅙ 🖢 ⅄ ☖ ⌐ ⅗ **Conf** Corporate Hospitality Days available **Location** 1m E on A25

Hotel ★★★ 67% The White Horse, High St, DORKING ☎ 0870 400 8282 37 en suite   41 annexe en suite

Dorking Chart Park, Deepdene Av RH5 4BX
☎ 01306 886917
e-mail: dorkinggolfclub@ukgateway.net
9 holes, 5120yds, Par 66, SSS 65, Course record 62.
Course Designer J Braid/Others **Location** 1m S on A24
Telephone for further details

Hotel ★★★★ 65% The Burford Bridge, Burford Bridge, Box Hill, DORKING ☎ 0870 400 8283 57 en suite

EAST HORSLEY   Map 04 TQ05

Drift The Drift, Off Forest Rd KT24 5HD
☎ 01483 284641 & 284772(shop) 📠 01483 284642
e-mail: info@driftgolfclub.com
Woodland course with secluded fairways and picturesque setting. A challenging course that punishes the wayward shot.
18 holes, 6425yds, Par 73, SSS 72, Course record 65.
Club membership 700.
Visitors book 7 days in advance to the pro shop, Mon-Fri only, except bank holidays. **Societies** Mon-Fri, telephone in advance. **Green Fees** not confirmed. **Cards** 🖶 ▦ ▦
▦ 🖫 **Prof** Mark Smith **Course Designer** Sir Henry Cotton/Robert Sandow **Facilities** ⊗ ⅙ 🖢 ⅄ ☖ ⌐ ⅞

Continued

⊶ ⅗ 🕻 **Conf** fac available Corporate Hospitality Days available **Location** Southbound A3 towards Guildford, exit at Wisley then turn left onto the B2039 towards East Horsley. After 1.5m turn left into Drift Rd

Hotel ★★ 65% Bookham Grange Hotel, Little Bookham Common, Bookham, LEATHERHEAD ☎ 01372 452742
27 en suite

EFFINGHAM   Map 04 TQ15

Effingham Guildford Rd KT24 5PZ
☎ 01372 452203 📠 01372 459959
e-mail: secretary@effinghamgolfclub.com
Easy-walking downland course laid out on 270 acres with tree-lined fairways. It is one of the longest of the Surrey courses with wide subtle greens that provide a provocative but by no means exhausting challenge. Fine views over the London skyline.
18 holes, 6524yds, Par 71, SSS 71, Course record 64.
Club membership 800.
Visitors contact in advance. With member only weekends & bank holidays. **Societies** Wed, Thu & Fri only and must book in advance. **Green Fees** terms on application. **Prof** Steve Hoatson **Course Designer** H S Colt **Facilities** ⊗ ⅙ by prior arrangement ⅙ 🖢 ⅄ ☖ ⌐ ⅞ 📌 ⅗ ⅗ 🕻 **Leisure** hard tennis courts. **Conf** fac available Corporate Hospitality Days available **Location** W side of village on A246

Hotel ★★ 65% Bookham Grange Hotel, Little Bookham Common, Bookham, LEATHERHEAD ☎ 01372 452742
27 en suite

ENTON GREEN   Map 04 SU94

West Surrey GU8 5AF
☎ 01483 421275 📠 01483 41519
e-mail: westsurreygolfclub@btinternet.com
A good parkland-type course in rolling, well-wooded setting. Some fairways are tight with straight driving at a premium. The 17th is a testing hole with a long hill walk.
18 holes, 6520yds, Par 71, SSS 71, Course record 65.
Club membership 600.
Visitors must contact in advance and have a handicap certificate. **Societies** must apply in writing. All players to have a handicap. **Green Fees** not confirmed. **Prof** Alister Tawse **Course Designer** Herbert Fowler **Facilities** ⊗ ⅙ 🖢 ⅄ ☖ ⅗ 🕻 **Leisure** hard tennis courts. **Location** S side of village

Hotel ★★★ 68% The Bush Hotel, The Borough, FARNHAM ☎ 0870 400 8225 83 en suite

EPSOM   Map 04 TQ26

Epsom Longdown Ln South KT17 4JR
☎ 01372 721666 📠 01372 817183
e-mail: secretary@epsomgolfclub.co.uk
Traditional downland course with many mature trees and fast undulating greens. Thought must be given to every shot to play to one's handicap.
18 holes, 5656yds, Par 69, SSS 68, Course record 63.
Club membership 700.
Visitors available any day except Tue, Sat & Sun before noon. **Societies** telephone 01372 721666. **Green Fees** £29 per round (£39 weekends). **Cards** 🖶 ▦ ▦ ▦ 🖫

Continued

Prof Ron Goudie **Course Designer** Willie Dunne
Facilities ⊗ ⫛ ⅃ ᐧ♀⚑🏠⚐ ✂ **Conf** fac available
Corporate Hospitality Days available **Location** SE side of
town centre on B288

....

Hotel ★★★★ 73% Woodlands Park Hotel, Woodlands
Ln, STOKE D'ABERNON ☎ 01372 843933 57 en suite

Horton Park Golf & Country Club Hook Rd
KT19 8QG
☎ 020 8393 8400 & 8394 2626 ▤ 020 8394 1369
e-mail: hortonparkgc@aol.com

Millennium: 18 holes, 6257yds, Par 71, SSS 70.
Course Designer Dr Peter Nicholson
Telephone for further details

....

Hotel ★★★★ 73% Woodlands Park Hotel, Woodlands
Ln, STOKE D'ABERNON ☎ 01372 843933 57 en suite

ESHER   Map 04 TQ16

Moore Place Portsmouth Rd KT10 9LN
☎ 01372 463533
Public course on attractive, undulating parkland, laid
out some 80 years ago by Harry Vardon. Examples of
most of the trees that will thrive in the UK are to be
found on the course. Testing short holes at 8th and 9th.
9 holes, 2078yds, Par 33, SSS 30, Course record 27.
Club membership 150.
Visitors no restrictions. **Societies** must contact in advance.
Green Fees terms on application. **Cards** 💳 ▦ ▬ 💳
▦ 💳 🔲 **Prof** Nick Gadd **Course Designer** H Vardon/D
Allen/N Gadd **Facilities** ⊗ ⫛ ⅃ ᐧ♀⚑🏠⚐ ✂ **Conf**
fac available **Location** 0.5m from town centre on A307

....

Hotel ★★★ 67% The Ship Hotel, Monument Green,
WEYBRIDGE ☎ 01932 848364 39 en suite

Thames Ditton & Esher Portsmouth Rd KT10 9AL
☎ 020 8398 1551
Commonland course with public right of way across the
course. Although the course is not long, accuracy is
essential and wayward shots are normally punished.
18 holes, 5149yds, Par 66, SSS 65, Course record 63.
Club membership 250.
Visitors may not play on Sun mornings. Advisable to
telephone for availability. **Societies** must contact in
advance. **Green Fees** not confirmed. **Cards** 💳 🔲 **Prof**
Rob Jones **Facilities** ⊗ ⫛ ⅃ ᐧ♀⚑🏠 ✂ **Location** 1m
NE on A307, adjacent to Marquis of Granby pub

....

Hotel ⬗ Premier Lodge (Cobham), Portsmouth Rd,
Fairmile, COBHAM ☎ 0870 9906358 48 en suite

FARLEIGH   Map 05 TQ36

Farleigh Court Old Farleigh Rd CR6 9PX
☎ 01883 627711 ▤ 01883 627722
e-mail: fcgc@fbd-uk.u-net.com
The course occupies 350 acres of land and is
surrounded by a bird sanctuary and natural
woodlands. The course designer has instinctively
utilised two valleys to make the course interesting and
challenging.
*Members: 18 holes, 6409yds, Par 72, SSS 71, Course
record 67.*
Pay & Play: 9 holes, 3281yds, Par 36.
Club membership 450.
Visitors must book in advance **Societies** welcome, please
and ask for Society Co ordinator. **Green Fees** not
confirmed. **Cards** 💳 ▦ ▬ 💳 **Prof** S
Graham **Course Designer** John Jacobs **Facilities** ⊗ ⫛ ⅃
ᐧ♀⚑🏠⚐ ⚑ **Leisure** sauna. **Conf** fac available
Corporate Hospitality Days available **Location** 1.5m from
Selsdon

....

Hotel ★★★★ 69% Le Meridien Selsdon Park & Golf
Course, Addington Rd, Sanderstead, CROYDON
☎ 020 8657 8811 204 en suite

FARNHAM   Map 04 SU84

Blacknest Binsted GU34 4QL
☎ 01420 22888 ▤ 01420 22001
Privately-owned pay and play golf centre catering for
all ages and levels of ability. Facilities include a 15-bay
driving range, gymnasium and a challenging 18-hole
course featuring water on 14 holes.
18 holes, 5938yds, Par 69, SSS 69, Course record 64.
Club membership 450.
Visitors welcome at all times but should telephone for tee
times especially weekends. No denims or collarless shirts.
Societies prior arrangements necessary telephone or write.
Green Fees £20 per round (£25 weekends). **Cards** 💳 ▬
💳 ▦ 🔲 **Prof** Darren Burgess **Course Designer** Mr
Nicholson **Facilities** ⊗ ⫛ by prior arrangement ⅃ ᐧ♀
⚑🏠⚐ ⚔ ✂ **Leisure** sauna, solarium, gymnasium.
Conf fac available **Location** 1m S of A31 at Bentley

....

Hotel ★★★ ▲▲ 61% Farnham House Hotel, Alton Rd,
FARNHAM ☎ 01252 716908 25 en suite

Farnham The Sands GU10 1PX
☎ 01252 782109 ▤ 01252 781185
e-mail: info@farnhamgolfclub.com
A mixture of meadowland and heath with quick drying
sandy subsoil. Several of the earlier holes have
interesting features.
18 holes, 6447yds, Par 72, SSS 71, Course record 66.
Club membership 700.
Visitors must contact in advance. Must be member of
recognised club & have handicap certificate. With member
only weekends. **Societies** must apply in writing. **Green
Fees** £45 per day; £40 per round. **Cards** 💳 ▬ 💳 🔲 **Prof**
Grahame Cowlishaw **Course Designer** Donald Steel
Facilities ⊗ ⫛ by prior arrangement ⅃ ᐧ♀⚑🏠 ✂
Conf Corporate Hospitality Days available **Location** 3m E
off A31

....

Hotel ★★★ 68% The Bush Hotel, The Borough,
FARNHAM ☎ 0870 400 8225 83 en suite

Farnham Park Folly Hill, Farnham Park GU9 0AU
☎ 01252 715216
9 holes, 1163yds, Par 27, SSS 48, Course record 48.
Course Designer Henry Cotton **Location** N side of town
centre on A287, adjacent to Farnham Castle
Telephone for further details

Hotel ★★★ 68% The Bush Hotel, The Borough,
FARNHAM ☎ 0870 400 8225 83 en suite

GODALMING   Map 04 SU94

Broadwater Park Guildford Rd, Farncombe
GU7 3BU ☎ 01483 429955 🖺 01483 429955
A par 3 public course with floodlit driving range.
9 holes, 1287yds, Par 54, SSS 50.
Club membership 160.
Visitors must book for weekends & bank holidays.
Societies telephone in advance. **Green Fees** terms on
application. **Cards** 🖂 🖃 🔀 🖳 **Prof** Kevin D
Milton/Nick English **Course Designer** Kevin Milton
Facilities ⊗ ⮭ 🍺 ☍ 🏌 ⚘ ⛳ **Conf** Corporate
Hospitality Days available **Location** 4m SW of Guildford

Hotel ★★★ 68% The Manor, Newlands Corner,
GUILDFORD ☎ 01483 222624 50 en suite

Hurtmore Hurtmore Rd, Hurtmore GU7 2RN
☎ 01483 426492 🖺 01483 426121
**A Peter Alliss/Clive Clark Pay and Play course with
seven lakes and 85 bunkers. The 15th hole is the longest
at 537yds. Played mainly into the wind there are 10
bunkers to negotiate. The 3rd hole at 448yds stroke
Index 1 is a real test. A dog-leg right around a lake and
nine bunkers makes this hole worthy of its stroke index.**
18 holes, 5530yds, Par 70, SSS 67, Course record 65.
Club membership 200.
Visitors book by telephone up to 7 days in advance.
Societies telephone in advance. **Green Fees** £12.50 per 18
holes; £9 per 9 holes (£18/£12 weekends); Twilight £8
(£10 weekends). **Cards** 🖂 🖃 🔣 🖳 **Prof** Maxine
Burton **Course Designer** Peter Alliss/Clive Clark
Facilities ⊗ ⮭ 🍺 ☍ 🏌 ⚘ **Leisure** practice nets.
Location 6m S of Guildford on the A3

Hotel ★★★ 68% The Manor, Newlands Corner,
GUILDFORD ☎ 01483 222624 50 en suite

GUILDFORD   Map 04 SU94

Guildford High Path Rd, Merrow GU1 2HL
☎ 01483 563941 🖺 01483 453228
e-mail: secretary@guildfordgolfclub.co.uk
**The course is on typical Surrey downland bordered by
attractive woodlands. Situated on chalk, it is
acknowledged to be one of the best all-weather courses
in the area, and the oldest course in Surrey. Although
not a long course, the prevailing winds across the open
downs make low scoring difficult. It is possible to see
four counties on a clear day.**
18 holes, 6090yds, Par 69, SSS 70, Course record 64.
Club membership 700.
Visitors must contact in advance. With member only
weekends & bank holidays. **Societies** welcome Mon-Fri.
Must apply in advance. **Green Fees** £48 per day; £38 per
round. **Prof** P G Hollington **Course Designer** J H
Taylor/Hawtree **Facilities** ⊗ ⮭ 🍺 ☍ 🏌 ⚘
Conf fac available Corporate Hospitality Days available
Location E side of town centre off A246

Continued

Hotel ★★★ 68% The Manor, Newlands Corner,
GUILDFORD ☎ 01483 222624 50 en suite

Merrist Wood Coombe Ln, Worplesdon GU3 3PE
☎ 01483 238890 🖺 01483 238896
e-mail: mwgc@merristwood-golfclub.co.uk
**More parkland than heathland, Merrist Wood has a bit
of everything. Water comes into play on five holes, the
bunkering is fierce, the greens slope and the back nine
has plenty of trees. Two holes stand out especially: the
picturesque par 3 11th with a tee shot through the trees
and the dastardly par 4 17th, including a 210yd carry
over a lake and ditches either side of the green.**
18 holes, 6600yds, Par 72, SSS 71, Course record 69.
Club membership 500.
Visitors must contact in advance, at weekends only after
11am, subject to availability. **Societies** apply in writing or
by telephone **Green Fees** £35 per 18 holes. **Cards** 🖂 🖃
🔀 🖳 **Prof** Chris Connell **Course Designer** David
Williams **Facilities** ⊗ ⮭ 🍺 ☍ 🏌 ⚘ ⛳ **Conf**
fac available Corporate Hospitality Days available
Location 3m out of Guildford on A323 to Aldershot

Hotel ★★★ 68% The Manor, Newlands Corner,
GUILDFORD ☎ 01483 222624 50 en suite

Milford Station Ln, Milford GU8 5HS
☎ 01483 419200 🖺 01483 419199
e-mail: milford@americangolf.uk.com
**A Peter Alliss/Clive Clark designed course. The design
has cleverly incorporated a demanding course within
an existing woodland and meadow area.**
18 holes, 5960yds, Par 69, SSS 68, Course record 64.
Club membership 750.
Visitors must contact in advance, tee booking system,
telephone 01483 416291 up to 1 week in advance. May not
play weekends until 12 noon. **Societies** telephone in
advance. **Green Fees** £25 per 18 holes (weekends £30).
Cards 🖂 🖃 🔄 🖳 🔀 🖳 **Prof** Paul Creamer
Course Designer Peter Allis **Facilities** ⊗ ⮭ 🍺 ☍ ⚘
☍ 🏌 ⚘ ⛳ **Conf** fac available Corporate Hospitality
Days available **Location** 6m SW Guildford, leave A3 at
Milford, A3100 to Enton

Hotel ★★★ 68% The Manor, Newlands Corner,
GUILDFORD ☎ 01483 222624 50 en suite

Roker Park Rokers Farm, Aldershot Rd GU3 3PB
☎ 01483 236677 🖺 01483 232324
**A Pay and Play 9-hole parkland course. A challenging
course with two par 5 holes.**
9 holes, 3037yds, Par 36, SSS 72.
Club membership 200.
Visitors no restrictions, pay & play, phone for
reservations. **Societies** prior arrangement with deposit at
least 14 days before, minimum 12 persons. **Green Fees**
terms on application. **Prof** Adrian Carter **Course Designer**
W V Roker **Facilities** ⊗ ⮭ 🍺 ☍ ⚘ 🏌 ⚘ ⛳
Location A323, 3m from Guildford

Hotel ★★★ 68% The Manor, Newlands Corner,
GUILDFORD ☎ 01483 222624 50 en suite

> **Looking to try a new course? Always telephone
> ahead to confirm visitor arrangements.**

HINDHEAD   Map 04 SU83

Hindhead Churt Rd GU26 6HX
☎ 01428 604614 📠 01428 608508
e-mail: secretary@hindhead-golfclub.co.uk
A picturesque example of a Surrey heath-and-heather
course. Players must be prepared for some hard
walking. The first nine fairways follow narrow valleys
requiring straight hitting; the second nine are much less
restricted. The Open Championship pre-qualifying
round is played in July.
18 holes, 6356yds, Par 70, SSS 70, Course record 63.
Club membership 610.
Visitors must contact in advance and have a handicap
certificate. Societies Wed & Thu only, contact in advance
Green Fees £50 per day; £40 per round. Prof Ian Benson
Course Designer J H Taylor Facilities ⊗ 🏌 🛄 🍴 🏖 🏡
🍴 🏌 ℂ Conf Corporate Hospitality Days available
Location 1.5m NW of Hindhead on A287

Hotel ★★★★ 71% Lythe Hill Hotel & Spa, Petworth Rd,
HASLEMERE ☎ 01428 651251 41 en suite

KINGSWOOD   Map 04 TQ25

Kingswood Golf and Country House Sandy
Ln KT20 6NE ☎ 01737 832188 📠 01737 833920
e-mail: sales@kingswood-golf.fsnet.co.uk
Mature parkland course sited on a plateau with
delightful views of Chipstead Valley.
*Kingswood Golf and Country Club: 18 holes, 6904yds, Par
72, SSS 73.*
Club membership 700.
Visitors must contact professional 3 days in advance. May
not play weekends until after 11.00am Societies must
apply in advance. Green Fees terms on application. Cards
🖃 🖩 🚒 🖩 🔀 🔲 Prof Terry Sims Course Designer
James Braid Facilities ⊗ 🏌 🛄 🍴 🏖 🏡 🏌 ℂ
Leisure squash, 3 snooker tables. Conf Corporate
Hospitality Days available Location 0.5m S of village off
A217

Hotel ★★★ 67% Reigate Manor Hotel, Reigate Hill,
REIGATE ☎ 01737 240125 50 en suite

Surrey Downs Outwood Ln KT20 6JS
☎ 01737 839090 📠 01737 839080
e-mail: booking@surreydownsgc.co.uk
A new course on a 200 acre site with spectacular views
over the North Downs and home to rabbits, foxes, deer
and herons.
18 holes, 6303yards, Par 71, SSS 70, Course record 67.
Visitors must contact in advance and reserve time.
Societies apply in advance by telephone Green Fees not
confirmed. Cards 🖃 🚒 🖩 🔀 🔲 Prof Stephen Blacklee
Course Designer Aliss/Clarke Facilities 🏖 🏡 🏌 ℂ
Location M25 junct 8, follow signs for Sutton (A217). At
3rd roundabout take last exit to KIngswood (Bonsor
Drive). Turn right at end into Waterhouse Lane and
continue until it merges into Outwood Lane, Club on right
after Eyhurst Park

Hotel ⛫ Premier Lodge (Epsom South), Brighton Rd,
Burgh Heath, TADWORTH ☎ 0870 9906442 78 en suite

LEATHERHEAD   Map 04 TQ15

Leatherhead Kingston Rd KT22 0EE
☎ 01372 843966 & 843956 📠 01372 842241
e-mail: secretary@lgc-golf.co.uk
Undulating parkland course with tree lined fairways
and strategically placed bunkers. Easy walking.
18 holes, 6203yds, Par 71, SSS 70, Course record 63.
Club membership 630.
Visitors telephone pro shop 01372 843956 up to 21 days in
advance. May not play 12pm weekends. Societies
telephone in advance. Green Fees £37.50 per round.
Cards 🖃 🚒 🖩 🔀 🔲 Prof Simon Norman
Facilities ⊗ 🏌 🛄 🍴 🍴 🏖 🏡 🏌 🚗 ℂ Conf fac available
Location 0.25m from junct 9 of M25, on A243

Hotel ★★★★ 73% Woodlands Park Hotel, Woodlands
Ln, STOKE D'ABERNON ☎ 01372 843933 57 en suite

Pachesham Park Golf Complex Oaklawn Rd
KT22 0BT ☎ 01372 843453
e-mail: enquiries@pacheshamgolf.co.uk
An undulating parkland course starting with five
shorter but tight holes on one side of the road, followed
by four longer more open but testing holes to finish.
9 holes, 2805yds, Par 70, SSS 67, Course record 67.
Club membership 250.
Visitors book 2 days in advance by phone. May play
weekends Societies apply in advance. Green Fees £18 per 18
holes; £10.50 per 9 holes (£21/£12 weekends & bank
holidays). Cards 🖃 🚒 🖩 🔀 🔲 Prof Philip Taylor Course
Designer Phil Taylor Facilities ⊗ 🏌 🛄 🍴 🍴 🏖 🏡 🏌 ℂ
Conf fac available Corporate Hospitality Days available
Location Off A244 or A245, 0.5m from M25 junct 9

Hotel ★★★★ 73% Woodlands Park Hotel, Woodlands
Ln, STOKE D'ABERNON ☎ 01372 843933 57 en suite

Tyrrells Wood The Drive KT22 8QP
☎ 01372 376025 📠 01372 360836
Parkland course with easy walking.
18 holes, 6282yds, Par 71, SSS 70, Course record 65.
Club membership 700.
Visitors must contact in advance. Restricted weekends.
Societies must apply in advance. Green Fees terms on
application. Cards 🖃 🚒 🖩 🔀 🔲 Prof Simon
Defoy Course Designer James Braid Facilities ⊗ 🏌 🛄
🍴 🏖 🏡 🏌 ℂ Conf Corporate Hospitality Days
available Location 2m SE of town, off A24

Hotel ★★★★ 65% The Burford Bridge, Burford Bridge,
Box Hill, DORKING ☎ 0870 400 8283 57 en suite

LIMPSFIELD   Map 05 TQ45

Limpsfield Chart Westerham Rd RH8 0SL
☎ 01883 723405 & 722106
Tight heathland course set in National Trust land, well
wooded.
9 holes, 5718yds, Par 70, SSS 68, Course record 64.
Club membership 300.
Visitors with member only or by appointment weekends &
not before 3.30pm Thu (Ladies Day). Societies must apply
in advance. Green Fees terms on application. Facilities 🛄
🍴 🏖 Leisure putting green, practice area. Location 1m E
on A25 from M25 junct 6

Hotel ★★★ 71% Donnington Manor, London Rd, Dunton
Green, SEVENOAKS ☎ 01732 462681 60 en suite

Where to stay, where to eat?
Visit www.theAA.com

LINGFIELD
Map 05 TQ34

Lingfield Park Lingfield Rd, Racecourse Rd
RH7 6PQ ☎ 01342 832659 📠 01342 836077
e-mail: cmorley@lingfieldpark.co.uk
Difficult and challenging, tree-lined parkland course set in 210 acres of beautiful Surrey countryside with water features and 60 bunkers.
18 holes, 6473yds, Par 71, SSS 72, Course record 65.
Club membership 700.
Visitors must be accompanied by member before noon on Sat & Sun. Advisable to telephone first. **Societies** must telephone in advance. **Green Fees** terms on application.
Cards 🟦🟦🟦🟦🟦🟦 **Prof** Christopher Morley
Facilities ⊗ ⫙ ⫧ ⚑ ▼ ♀ ⚘ ☎ ⛳ ⚑ ⛳ ⛳ **Leisure** squash, sauna, solarium, gymnasium, horse racing. **Conf** Corporate Hospitality Days available **Location** M25 junct 6, follow signs to racecourse

Hotel ☖ Travel Inn, London Rd, Felbridge, EAST GRINSTEAD ☎ 08701 977088 41 en suite

NEWDIGATE
Map 04 TQ14

Rusper Rusper Rd RH5 5BX
☎ 01293 871871 (shop) 📠 01293 871456
e-mail: jill@ruspergolfclub.co.uk
The 18-hole course is set in countryside and offers golfers of all abilities a fair and challenging test. After a gentle start the holes wind through picturesque scenery, mature woodland and natural water hazards.
18 holes, 6724yds, Par 72, SSS 72.
Club membership 304.
Visitors welcome but telephone to reserve time, some restrictions if competitions being played. **Societies** telephone in advance for details. **Green Fees** £16.50 per 18 holes, £11 per 9 holes (£20/£15 weekends and bank holidays). **Cards** 🟦🟦🟦🟦 **Prof** Janice Arnold **Course Designer** A Blunden **Facilities** ⊗ ⫙ ⫧ ⚑ ▼ ♀ ⚘ ☎ ⛳ ⛳ ⛳ **Conf** Corporate Hospitality Days available **Location** Between Newdigate/Rusper, off A24

Hotel ★★★★ 65% The Burford Bridge, Burford Bridge, Box Hill, DORKING ☎ 0870 400 8283 57 en suite

OCKLEY
Map 04 TQ14

Gatton Manor Hotel Golf & Country Club
Standon Ln RH5 5PQ
☎ 01306 627555 📠 01306 627713
e-mail: gattonmanor@enterprise.net
Undulating parkland course through woods and over many challenging water holes.
18 holes, 6629yds, Par 72, SSS 72, Course record 68.
Club membership 300.
Visitors may book up to 10 days in advance. Restricted Sun (am). Tee times to be booked through professional 01306 627557 **Societies** must apply in advance. **Green Fees** terms on application. **Cards** 🟦🟦🟦🟦🟦🟦 **Prof** Rae Sargent **Course Designer** Henry Cotton **Facilities** ⊗ ⫙ ⫧ ⚑ ▼ ♀ ⚘ ☎ ⛳ ⚑ ⛳ ⛳ **Leisure** grass tennis courts, fishing, sauna, solarium, gymnasium. **Conf** fac available Corporate Hospitality Days available **Location** 1.5m SW off A29

Hotel ★★★ 63% Gatton Manor Hotel Golf & Country Club, Standon Ln, OCKLEY ☎ 01306 627555 18 en suite

OTTERSHAW
Map 04 TQ06

Foxhills Club and Resort Stonehill Rd KT16 0EL
☎ 01932 872050 📠 01932 875200
e-mail: events@foxhills.co.uk
A pair of parkland courses designed in the grand manner with three championship courses. One course is tree-lined, the other, as well as trees, has massive bunkers and artificial lakes which contribute to the interest. Both courses offer testing golf and they finish on the same long 'double green'. Par 3 'Manor' course also available.
The Bernard Hunt Course: 18 holes, 6770yds, Par 73, SSS 72, Course record 65.
Longcross Course: 18 holes, 6453yds, Par 72, SSS 71, Course record 70.
Visitors tee times bookable through events office Mon-Fri. Only after midday at weekends **Societies** welcome Mon-Fri, must apply in advance. **Green Fees** terms on application. **Cards** 🟦🟦🟦🟦🟦🟦 **Prof** B Hunt/R Summerscales **Course Designer** F W Hawtree **Facilities** ⊗ ⫙ ⫧ ⚑ ▼ ♀ ⚘ ☎ ⛳ ⛳ ⛳ **Leisure** hard tennis courts, outdoor and indoor heated swimming pools, squash, sauna, solarium, gymnasium, par 3 course. **Conf** fac available Corporate Hospitality Days available **Location** M25 junct 11 follow signs to Woking, 2nd rdbt, 3rd exit into Foxhills road, left at T junct, 100yds on right

Hotel ★★★★ 71% Foxhills, Stonehill Rd, OTTERSHAW, Surrey ☎ 01932 872050 38 en suite

PIRBRIGHT
Map 04 SU95

Goal Farm Gole Rd GU24 0PZ
☎ 01483 473183 📠 01483 473205
Beautiful landscaped parkland 'Pay and Play' course with excellent greens.
9 holes, 1273yds, Par 54, SSS 48, Course record 50.
Club membership 350.
Visitors may not play on Sat before 2pm or Thu before 2pm. **Societies** telephone in advance. **Green Fees** terms on application. **Cards** 🟦🟦🟦🟦🟦🟦 **Prof** Peter Fuller **Course Designer** Bill Cox **Facilities** ⫧ ⚑ ▼ ♀ ☎ ⛳ **Location** 1.5m NW on B3012

Hotel Ⓤ Holiday Inn Farnborough, Lynchford Rd, FARNBOROUGH ☎ 0870 400 9029 143 en suite

PUTTENHAM
Map 04 SU94

Puttenham Heath Rd GU3 1AL
☎ 01483 810498 📠 01483 810988
e-mail: enquiries@puttenhamgolfclub.co.uk
Picturesque tree-lined heathland course offering testing golf, easy walking.
18 holes, 6220yds, Par 71, SSS 70.
Club membership 650.
Visitors weekdays by prior arrangement tel: 01483 810498, with member only weekends & public holidays. **Societies** apply in advance to secretary. **Green Fees** £45 per day; £32 per round. **Cards** 🟦🟦🟦🟦 **Prof** Gary Simmons **Facilities** ⊗ ⫙ by prior arrangement ⫧ ⚑ ▼ ♀ ⚘ ☎ ⛳ ⛳ **Conf** Corporate Hospitality Days available **Location** 1m SE on B3000

Hotel ★★★ 68% The Bush Hotel, The Borough, FARNHAM ☎ 0870 400 8225 83 en suite

REDHILL
Map 04 TQ25

Redhill & Reigate Clarence Rd, Pendelton Rd
RH1 6LB ☎ 01737 244433 🖷 01737 242117
Flat well wooded parkland course.
18 holes, 5272yds, Par 68, SSS 66, Course record 65.
Club membership 600.
Visitors may not play before 11am weekends. Must contact in advance. **Societies** must apply in writing or by telephone. **Green Fees** terms on application. **Cards** 💳 💳 💳 💳 💳 **Prof** Warren Pike **Course Designer** James Braid **Facilities** ⊗ 🏌 ⅄ ♥ ♀ 🛆 🍴 🏐 ♂ **Conf** fac available Corporate Hospitality Days available **Location** 1m S on A23

Hotel ★★★ Reigate Manor Hotel, Reigate Hill, REIGATE ☎ 01737 240125 50 en suite

REIGATE
Map 04 TQ25

Reigate Heath Flanchford Rd RH2 8QR
☎ 01737 242610 & 226793 🖷 01737 249226
e-mail: reigateheath@surreygolf.co.uk
Gorse, heather, pine and birch trees abound on this popular 9-hole heathland course. Sandy soil gives all year round play even in the wettest winters. Clubhouse enjoys panoramic views of the North Downs and Leith Hill.
9 holes, 5658yds, Par 67, SSS 67, Course record 65.
Club membership 550.
Visitors with member only weekends & bank holidays. Must contact in advance. **Societies** must apply in writing. **Green Fees** £25 per round. **Prof** Barry Davies **Facilities** ⊗ 🏌 ⅄ ♥ ♀ 🛆 🍴 ♂ **Conf** Corporate Hospitality Days available **Location** 1.5m W off A25

Hotel ★★★ 67% Reigate Manor Hotel, Reigate Hill, REIGATE ☎ 01737 240125 50 en suite

Reigate Hill Gatton Bottom RH2 0TU
☎ 01737 645577 🖷 01737 642650
18 holes, 6175yds, Par 72, SSS 70, Course record 75.
Course Designer David Williams **Location** 1m from junct 8 of M25
Telephone for further details

Hotel ★★★ 67% Reigate Manor Hotel, Reigate Hill, REIGATE ☎ 01737 240125 50 en suite

SHEPPERTON
Map 04 TQ06

American Golf at Sunbury Charlton Ln
TW17 8QA ☎ 01932 771414 🖷 01932 789300
e-mail: sunbury@americangolf.uk.com
Sunbury Golf Course: *18 holes, 5103yds, Par 68, SSS 65, Course record 60.*
Academy: *9 holes, 2444yds, Par 33, SSS 32.*
Location Off junct 1 of the M3
Telephone for further details

Hotel ★★★ 70% The Thames Lodge, Thames St, STAINES ☎ 0870 400 8121 78 en suite

SUTTON GREEN
Map 04 TQ05

Sutton Green New Ln GU4 7QF
☎ 01483 747898 🖷 01483 750289
e-mail: admin@suttongreengc.co.uk
Set in the Surrey countryside, a challenging course with many water features. Excellent year round

Continued

conditions with fairway watering. Many testing holes with water surrounding greens and fairways, making accuracy a premium.
18 holes, 6350yds, Par 71, SSS 70, Course record 64.
Club membership 600.
Visitors must contact in advance, play after 2pm weekends **Societies** Mon-Fri. Call for details. **Green Fees** terms on application. **Cards** 💳 💳 💳 **Prof** Paul Tedder **Course Designer** David Walker/Laura Davies **Facilities** ⊗ 🏌 ⅄ ♥ ♀ 🛆 🍴 🏐 ♂ **Conf** fac available Corporate Hospitality Days available **Location** Off A320 between Woking & Guildford

Hotel ★★★★★ Pennyhill Park Hotel & The Spa, London Rd, BAGSHOT ☎ 01276 471774 26 en suite 97 annexe en suite

TANDRIDGE
Map 05 TQ35

Tandridge RH8 9NQ
☎ 01883 712274 🖷 01883 730537
e-mail: info@tandridge.fsnet.co.uk
A parkland course with two loops of 9 holes from the clubhouse. The first 9 is relatively flat. The second 9 undulates and reveals several outstanding views of the North Downs and the South.
18 holes, 6250yds, Par 70, SSS 70, Course record 66.
Club membership 750.
Visitors must contact in advance. May play Mon, Wed, Thu **Societies** Mon, Wed & Thu, apply in advance. **Green Fees** not confirmed. **Prof** Chris Evans **Course Designer** H S Colt **Facilities** ⊗ 🏌 ⅄ ♥ ♀ 🛆 🍴 ♂ **Conf** Corporate Hospitality Days available **Location** 2m SE junc 6 M25, 1.5m E of Godstone on A25

Hotel ★★★★ 74% Nutfield Priory, Nutfield, REDHILL ☎ 01737 824400 60 en suite

TILFORD
Map 04 SU84

Hankley Common The Club House GU10 2DD
☎ 01252 792493 🖷 01252 795699
A natural heathland course subject to wind. Greens are first rate. The 18th, a long par 4, is most challenging, the green being beyond a deep chasm which traps any but the perfect second shot. The 7th is a spectacular one-shotter.
18 holes, 6438yds, Par 71, SSS 71, Course record 62.
Club membership 700.
Visitors handicap certificate required, restricted to afternoons at weekends. **Societies** apply in writing. **Green Fees** £55 per round/£70 per day (£70 per round weekends). **Cards** 💳 💳 💳 💳 💳 **Prof** Peter Stow **Facilities** ⊗ 🏌 ⅄ ♥ ♀ 🛆 🍴 🏐 ♂ **Location** 0.75m SE of Tilford

Hotel ★★★ 68% The Bush Hotel, The Borough, FARNHAM ☎ 0870 400 8225 83 en suite

VIRGINIA WATER See page 235

WALTON-ON-THAMES
Map 04 TQ16

Burhill Burwood Rd KT12 4BL
☎ 01932 227345 🖷 01932 267159
e-mail: info@burhillgolf-club.co.uk
The Old Course is a picturesque parkland course that offers a challenge to golfers of all abilities. The New Course is in complete contrast, with the River

Continued

A privately owned hotel set on the banks of the River Thames, just minutes from Wentworth Club. The hotel features, 180 guestrooms, the choice of 2 riverside restaurants, a health & fitness spa with an 18m pool, saunas, steam room, 7 beauty treatment rooms, gymnasium & 5 outdoor tennis courts.
The hotel also has a range of function rooms for meetings & events for up to 300 people.

Runnymede
****hotel&spa

Windsor Road, Egham, Surrey, TW20 0AG
Tel 01784 436171   Fax 01784 436340
www.runnymedehotel.com
email: info@runnymedehotel.com

Mole running through the course and coming into play on several holes, the most dramatic being the par 3 18th leading back to the Mansion House.
Old Course: 18 holes, 6479yds, Par 70, SSS 71, Course record 65.
New Course: 18 holes, 6597yds, Par 72, SSS 71.
Club membership 1100.
Visitors no visitors weekends or bank holidays unless introduced by member. Must contact in advance. **Societies** apply in writing. **Green Fees** £85 per day, £62.50 per 18holes. **Cards** ⌷ ⌷ ⌷ **Course Designer** Willie Park/Simon Gidman **Facilities** ⊗ ⍟ ⓑ 里 里 옷 ♤ 向 ⸙ ⚓ ⟡ ⟡ **Conf** Corporate Hospitality Days available **Location** M25 junct 10 on to A3 towards London, 1st exit (Painshill junct

WALTON-ON-THE-HILL See page 237

WEST BYFLEET Map 04 TQ06

West Byfleet Sheerwater Rd KT14 6AA
☎ 01932 343433 🖹 01932 340667
e-mail: secretary@wbgc.co.uk
An attractive course set against a background of woodland and gorse. The 13th is the famous 'pond' shot with a water hazard and two bunkers fronting the green. No less than six holes of 420 yards or more.
18 holes, 6211yds, Par 70, SSS 70.
Club membership 622.
Visitors must contact professional in advance, only with member at weekends. Restricted Thu (Ladies *Continued*

Day). **Societies** must apply in writing/telephone. **Green Fees** £70 per day, £50 per round. **Cards** ⌷ ⌷ ⌷ ⌷ ⌷ **Prof** David Regan **Course Designer** C S Butchart **Facilities** ⊗ ⍟ ⓑ 里 里 옷 ♤ 向 ⸙ ⚓ ⟡ ⟡ **Conf** Corporate Hospitality Days available **Location** W side of village on A245, from A3 take A245 towards Byfleet and West Byfleet, after going over M25 pass through 2 sets lights, mini rdbt turn right into Sheerwater road club left

Hotel ★★★ 68% The Manor, Newlands Corner, GUILDFORD ☎ 01483 222624 50 en suite

WEST CLANDON Map 04 TQ05

Clandon Regis Epsom Rd GU4 7TT
☎ 01483 224888 🖹 01483 211781
e-mail: office@clandonregis-golfclub.co.uk
High quality parkland course with challenging lake holes on the back nine. European Tour specification tees and greens.
18 holes, 6419yds, Par 72, SSS 71, Course record 66.
Club membership 700.
Visitors contact in advance for weekend play. **Societies** telephone in advance. **Green Fees** £30 per 18 holes (£40 weekends). **Cards** ⌷ ⌷ ⌷ ⌷ ⌷ **Prof** Steve Lloyd **Course Designer** David Williams **Facilities** ⊗ ⍟ ⓑ 里 里 옷 向 ⸙ ⟡ ⟡ **Leisure** sauna. **Conf** fac available Corporate Hospitality Days available **Location** From A246 Leatherhead direction

Hotel ★★★ 68% The Manor, Newlands Corner, GUILDFORD ☎ 01483 222624 50 en suite

WEST END Map 04 SU96

Windlemere Windlesham Rd GU24 9QL
☎ 01276 858727
A parkland course, undulating in parts with natural water hazards. There is also a floodlit driving range.
9 holes, 2673yds, Par 34, SSS 33, Course record 30.
Visitors no restrictions. **Societies** advisable to contact in advance. **Green Fees** £10.50 per 9 holes (£12 weekends). **Cards** ⌷ ⌷ ⌷ ⌷ ⌷ **Prof** David Thomas **Course Designer** Clive Smith **Facilities** ⓑ 里 里 옷 向 ⸙ ⟡ ⟡ **Leisure** pool/snooker tables. **Location** N side of village at junct of A319/A322

Hotel ★★★★★ Pennyhill Park Hotel & The Spa, London Rd, BAGSHOT ☎ 01276 471774 26 en suite 97 annexe en suite

WEYBRIDGE Map 04 TQ06

St George's Hill Golf Club Rd, St George's Hill KT13 0NL ☎ 01932 847758 🖹 01932 821564
e-mail: admin@stgeorgeshillgolfclub.co.uk
Comparable and similar to Wentworth, a feature of this course is the number of long and difficult par 4s. To score well it is necessary to place the drive - and long driving pays handsomely. Walking is hard on this undulating, heavily wooded course with plentiful heather and rhododendrons.
Red & Blue: 18 holes, 6513yds, Par 70, SSS 71, Course record 64.
Green: 9 holes, 2897yds, Par 35.
Club membership 600.
Visitors must contact in advance and have a handicap certificate. Visitors may only play Wed-Fri. **Societies** apply in writing/telephone. **Green Fees** £105 per day; £80 *Continued*

Wentworth Club

Map 04 TQ06 Virginia Water

☎ 01344 842201 🖹 01344 842804

Wentworth Club, the home of the Volvo PGA and Cisco World Match Play Championships, is a very special venue for any sporting, business or social occasion. The West Course (7047 yards) is familiar to millions of television viewers who have followed the championships here. There are two other 18-hole courses, the East Course (6188 yards) and the Edinburgh Course (7004 yards), as well as a 9-hole par 3 executive course. The courses are Surrey heathland with woodland of pine, oak and birch trees. The Club is renowned for its fine English food and the superb new tennis and health facilities, which include a holistic spa. The centre opened in January 1999 and has 13 outdoor tennis courts with four different playing surfaces, a 25m indoor pool and further extensive leisure facilities.

e-mail: reception@wentworthclub.com

Visitors Must contact in advance and have a handicap certificate (gentlemen max 24, ladies max 32). May not play weekends

Societies Contact in advance in writing

Green Fees Telephone for details

Facilities

Conf Facilities Available.

Professional David Rennie

Leisure Tennis and health club, squash, swimming, sauna, solarium, gymnasium

Location Wentworth Drive GU25 4LS (main gate directly opposite turning for A329 on main A30)

Holes/Par/Course record 54 holes.
West Course: 18 holes, 7047 yds, Par 73, SSS 74, Course record 63
East Course: 18 holes, 6201 yds, Par 68, SSS 70, Course record 62.
Edinburgh: 18 holes, 7004 yds, Par 72, SSS 74, Course record 67

Championship Course

WHERE TO STAY AND EAT NEARBY

Hotels

ASCOT

★★★★ ⊛ 70% The Royal Berkshire Ramada Plaza SL5 0PP. ☎ 01344 623322. 63 en suite

★★★★ ⊛ 66% The Berystede, SL5 9JH. ☎ 0870 400 8111. 90 en suite

BAGSHOT

★★★★★ ⊛⊛⊛ Pennyhill Park, GU19 5EU. ☎ 01276 471774. 26 en suite 97 annexe en suite

EGHAM

★★★★73% Runnymede Hotel & Spa TW20 0AG. ☎ 01784 436171. 180 en suite

Restaurants

BRAY

⊛⊛⊛⊛⊛ Fat Duck, High Street. ☎ 01628 580333

⊛⊛⊛⊛ Waterside Inn, SL6 2AT. ☎ 01628 620691

⊛⊛ Riverside Brasserie, SL6 2EB. ☎ 01628 780553

per round. **Prof** A C Rattue **Course Designer** H S Colt
Facilities ⊗ ⓛ 🍺 ♀ ⚖ 🏠 🛈 ℰ **Conf** Corporate
Hospitality Days available **Location** 2m S off B374

Hotel ★★★ 67% The Ship Hotel, Monument Green,
WEYBRIDGE ☎ 01932 848364 39 en suite

WOKING   Map 04 TQ05

Hoebridge Golf Centre Old Woking Rd GU22 8JH
☎ 01483 722611 📠 01483 740369
e-mail: info@hoebridge.co.uk
**Three public courses set in parkland on Surrey sand
belt. The main course is a championship length
challenge course; Shey Copse is a 9-hole course, ideal
for the intermediate golfer; and the Maybury an 18-
hole par 3 course which is suited to beginners and
occasional golfers.**
Main Course: 18 holes, 6536yds, Par 72, SSS 71.
Shey Course: 9 holes, 2294yds, Par 33.
Maybury Course: 18 holes, 2230yds, Par 54.
Club membership 600.
Visitors welcome every day, course and reservation desk
open dawn to dusk. Credit card reservations 6 days in
advance. **Societies** Mon-Fri only, telephone in advance
Green Fees not confirmed. **Cards** 🟨 🟥 🟦 **Prof** Tim
Powell **Course Designer** John Jacobs **Facilities** ⊗ ⓜ ⓛ
🍺 ♀ ⚖ 🏠 🛈 🏌 🛥 ℰ ℓ **Leisure** gymnasium, health &
fitness club. **Conf** fac available Corporate Hospitality
Days available **Location** 10 mins off M25 junct 11, on
B382 Old Woking to West Byfleet road

Hotel ★★★★★ Pennyhill Park Hotel & The Spa, London
Rd, BAGSHOT ☎ 01276 471774 26 en suite
97 annexe en suite

Pyrford Warren Ln, Pyrford GU22 8XR
☎ 01483 723555 📠 01483 729777
e-mail: pyrford@americangolf.uk.com
**This inland links-style course was designed by Peter
Alliss and Clive Clark. Set between Surrey woodlands,
the fairways weave between 23 acres of water courses
while the greens and tees are connected by rustic
bridges. The signature hole is the par 5 9th at 595
yards, with a dog-leg and final approach over water
and a sand shelf. Excellent playing conditions all year
round.**
18 holes, 6256yds, Par 72, SSS 70, Course record 64.
Club membership 650.
Visitors must book in advance. After 12pm weekends
Societies must contact in advance. **Green Fees** £40 per
round. **Cards** 🟨 🟥 🟦 🟦 **Prof** Darren Brewer
Course Designer Peter Allis & Clive Clark **Facilities** ⊗
ⓜ ⓛ 🍺 ♀ ⚖ 🏠 🛈 🛥 ℰ ℓ **Conf** Corporate
Hospitality Days available **Location** off A3 Ripley to
Pyrford. 15 mins from A3 & M25

Hotel ★★★★★ Pennyhill Park Hotel & The Spa, London
Rd, BAGSHOT ☎ 01276 471774 26 en suite
97 annexe en suite

Traditions Pyrford Rd, Pyrford GU22 8UE
☎ 01932 350355 📠 01932 350234
e-mail: traditions@americangolf.uk.com
**Situated in the heart of the Surrey countryside with a
mature setting which includes various woodland and
water features. A course with many challenges which
can be enjoyed by golfers of all levels and experience.**

18 holes, 6304yds, Par 71, SSS 70, Course record 67.
Club membership 400.
Visitors no restrictions. **Societies** telephone in advance.
Green Fees not confirmed. **Cards** 🟨 🟥 🟦 🟦 🟦 🟥
🟦 **Prof** Nick Stoner **Course Designer** Peter Alliss
Facilities ⊗ ⓜ ⓛ 🍺 ♀ ⚖ 🏠 🛈 🛥 🛥 ℰ **Conf** fac
available Corporate Hospitality Days available **Location**
M25 junct 10 onto A3, follow signs to Wisley Gardens, off
A3, through village to end of road, right to Pyford road,
course 0.5 miles

Hotel ★★★★★ Pennyhill Park Hotel & The Spa, London
Rd, BAGSHOT ☎ 01276 471774 26 en suite
97 annexe en suite

Woking Pond Rd, Hook Heath GU22 0JZ
☎ 01483 760053 📠 01483 772441
e-mail: woking.golf@btconnect.com
**An 18-hole course on Surrey heathland with few
changes from the original course designed in 1892 by
Tom Dunn. Bernard Darwin, a past Captain and
President, has written 'the beauty of Woking is that
there is something distinctive about every hole.'**
18 holes, 6340yds, Par 70, SSS 70, Course record 65.
Club membership 600.
Visitors must contact secretary at least 7 days prior to
playing. No visitors weekends & bank holidays. **Societies**
telephone intially then confirm in writing, normally 12
months notice. **Green Fees** terms on application. **Cards**
🟨 🟥 🟦 🟦 **Prof** Carl Bianco **Course Designer** Tom
Dunn **Facilities** ⊗ ⓜ ⓛ 🍺 ♀ ⚖ 🏠 🛈 🛥 🛥 ℰ **Conf**
Corporate Hospitality Days available **Location** W of town
centre in area of St Johns/Hook Heath

Hotel ★★★★★ Pennyhill Park Hotel & The Spa, London
Rd, BAGSHOT ☎ 01276 471774 26 en suite
97 annexe en suite

Worplesdon Heath House Rd GU22 0RA
☎ 01483 472277
e-mail: office@worplesdongc.co.uk
**The scene of the celebrated mixed-foursomes
competition. Accurate driving is essential on this
heathland course. The short 10th across a lake from tee
to green is a notable hole, and the 18th provides a
wonderfully challenging par 4 finish.**
18 holes, 6440yds, Par 71, SSS 71, Course record 64.
Club membership 610.
Visitors must play with member at weekends & bank
holidays. Must contact in advance and have a handicap
certificate. **Societies** must contact in writing. **Green Fees**
£80 per day; £60 per round (Winter £35). **Cards** 🟨 🟥
🟦 🟦 **Prof** J Christine **Facilities** ⊗ ⓛ 🍺 ♀ ⚖ 🏠 🛈
ℰ **Location** 6m N of Guildford, off A322

Hotel ★★★★★ Pennyhill Park Hotel & The Spa, London
Rd, BAGSHOT ☎ 01276 471774 26 en suite
97 annexe en suite

WOLDINGHAM   Map 05 TQ35

North Downs Northdown Rd CR3 7AA
☎ 01883 652057 📠 01883 652832
e-mail: info@northdownsgolfclub.co.uk
**Downland course, 850 ft above sea-level, with several
testing holes and magnificent views.**

Continued   *Continued*

Walton Heath

Map 04 TQ25

Walton-on-the-Hill

☎ **01737 812380**   📄 **01737 814225**

B oasting two extremely challenging courses, Walton Heath is a traditional Members' Club. Enjoying an enviable international reputation, the club was founded in 1903. Walton Heath has played host to over 60 major amateur and professional championships, including the 1981 Ryder Cup and five European Open Tournaments (1991, 1989, 1987, 1980 and 1977). Many prestigious amateur events have been held here, and in 2002 Walton Heath hosted the English Amateur. The Old Course is popular with visitors; however the New Course is very challenging, requiring subtle shots to get the ball near the hole. Straying from the fairway brings its punishment with gorse, bracken and heather to test the most patient golfer.

e-mail: secretary@whgc.co.uk

Visitors Limited play weekends. Must contact in advance and have a handicap certificate or letter of introduction

Societies Must contact in advance

Green Fees From £85-£95 per round

Facilities ⊗ ⅃ 🍺 ♀ ⚒ 🏠 ☎ ⚑ ⚐
Corporate hospitality days available

Professional Ken MacPherson

Location Deans Lane, Tadworth KT20 7TP
(SE side of village, off B2032)

Holes/Par/Course record 36 holes.
Old course: 18 holes, 6836 yds, Par 72, SSS 73,
Course record 65
New course: 18 holes, 6613 yds, Par 72, SSS 72,
Course record 67

WHERE TO STAY AND EAT NEARBY

Hotels

DORKING

★★★★ ⊚ ⊚ 65% The Burford Bridge, RH5 6BX.
☎ 0870 400 8283. 57 en suite

★★★ 67% White Horse, RH4 1BE.
☎ 0870 400 8282. 37 en suite
41 annexe en suite

REIGATE

★★★67% Reigate Manor, RH2 9PF.
☎ 01737 240125. 50 en suite

STOKE D'ABERNON

★★★★ ⊚ ⊚ 73% Woodlands Park, KT11 3QB. ☎ 01372 843933.
57 en suite

Restaurants

TADWORTH

⊚ ⊚ Gemini, KT20 5AH.
☎ 01737 812179

REIGATE

⊚ ⊚ The Dining Room, RH2 9AE
☎ 01737 226650

Championship Course

North Downs Golf Course: 18 holes, 5857yds, Par 69, SSS 68, Course record 65.
Club membership 500.
Visitors must play with member weekend mornings. Must contact in advance. **Societies** must telephone in advance and confirm in writing. **Green Fees** not confirmed. **Prof** M Homewood **Course Designer** Pennink **Facilities** ⊗ ⅊ ⅃ ♨ ☕ ♨ ⚷ **Conf** fac available Corporate Hospitality Days available **Location** 0.75m S of Woldingham village

Hotel ★★★ 71% Donnington Manor, London Rd, Dunton Green, SEVENOAKS ☎ 01732 462681 60 en suite

Woldingham Halliloo Valley Rd CR3 7HA
☎ 01883 653501 ▯ 01883 653502
Located in Halliloo Valley and designed by the American architect Bradford Benz, this pleasant course utilises all the contours and features of the valley.

18 holes, 6393yds, Par 71, SSS 70, Course record 64.
Club membership 695.
Visitors tee times should be booked in advance with pro shop. Weekends available after noon for visitors. **Societies** telephone to book. **Green Fees** not confirmed. **Cards** ▭ ▭ ▭ ▭ ▭ **Prof** Nick Carter **Course Designer** Bradford Benz **Facilities** ⊗ by prior arrangement ⅊ by prior arrangement ⅃ ⅊ ⅊ ☕ ♨ ♨ ⚷ **Conf** fac available Corporate Hospitality Days available **Location** M25 junct 6 take A22 north towards London/Croydon. Proceed for 2 miles, at rdbt take Woldingham Exit, continue under viaduct, bear 2nd left at fork into Halliloo Valley road, entrance left.

Hotel ★★★ 71% Donnington Manor, London Rd, Dunton Green, SEVENOAKS ☎ 01732 462681 60 en suite

SUSSEX, EAST

BEXHILL   Map 05 TQ70

Cooden Beach Cooden Sea Rd TN39 4TR
☎ 01424 842040 & 843938 (Pro Shop) ▯ 01424 842040
e-mail: enquiries@coodenbeachgc.com
The course is close by the sea, but is not real links in character. Despite that, it is dry and plays well throughout the year. There are some excellent holes such as the 4th, played to a built-up green, the short 12th, and three good holes to finish. There are added ponds which make the player think more about tee shots and shots to the green.
18 holes, 6504yds, Par 72, SSS 71, Course record 67.
Club membership 730.

Continued

Cooden Beach

Visitors must have a handicap certificate. Restricted at weekends. Book in advance with professional 01424 843938. **Societies** must contact in advance by telephoning secretary. **Green Fees** £35 per day, £32 per day (£40/£35 weekends). **Cards** ▭ ▭ **Prof** Jeffrey Sim **Course Designer** W Herbert Fowler **Facilities** ⊗ ⅊ ⅃ ♨ ⅊ ⅊ ☕ ☕ ♨ ♨ ⚷ **Leisure** indoor practice facility. **Conf** Corporate Hospitality Days available **Location** 2m W of Bexhill on A259

Hotel ★★★ ♨ 73% Powder Mills Hotel, Powdermill Ln, BATTLE ☎ 01424 775511 30 en suite 10 annexe en suite

Highwoods Ellerslie Ln TN39 4LJ
☎ 01424 212625 ▯ 01424 216866
e-mail: secretary@highwoodsgolfclub.co.uk
Undulating parkland course with water on six holes.
18 holes, 6218yds, Par 70, SSS 70, Course record 63.
Club membership 750.
Visitors must play with member on Sun. Must contact in advance and have an introduction from own club. Handicap required. **Societies** advance notice advised. **Green Fees** £30 per 18 holes (weekends £35). **Prof** Mike Andrews **Course Designer** J H Taylor **Facilities** ⊗ ⅊ ⅃ ♨ ⅊ ☕ ♨ ⚷ **Location** 1.5m NW

Hotel ★★★ 66% Royal Victoria Hotel, Marina, St Leonards-on-Sea, HASTINGS ☎ 01424 445544 50 en suite

BRIGHTON & HOVE   Map 04 TQ30

Brighton & Hove Devils Dyke Rd BN1 8YJ
☎ 01273 556482 ▯ 01273 554247
e-mail: phil@bhgc68.fsnet.co.uk
Testing 9 hole course with glorious views over the Downs and the sea. Famous drop hole par 3.
9 holes, 5704yds, Par 68, SSS 68, Course record 64.
Club membership 350.
Visitors must contact in advance, restricted play Wed, Fri & weekends. **Societies** must contact secretary in advance. **Green Fees** £18 per 18 holes; £12 per 9 holes (£25/£15 weekends). **Cards** ▭ ▭ ▭ ▭ ▭ ▭ ▭ **Prof** Phil Bonsall **Course Designer** James Braid **Facilities** ⊗ ⅊ ⅃ ♨ ⅊ ☕ ♨ ⅊ ♨ ⚷ **Conf** fac available Corporate Hospitality Days available **Location** 4m NW of Brighton, 1m from A27 & A23

Hotel ★★★ 69% The Old Tollgate Restaurant & Hotel, The Street, BRAMBER ☎ 01903 879494 11 en suite 20 annexe en suite

Dyke
Dyke Devils Dyke, Dyke Rd BN1 8YJ
☎ 01273 857296(office) & 857260(pro shop)
▤ 01273 857078
e-mail: secretary@dykegolfclub.org.uk
This downland course has some glorious views both towards the sea and inland. The signature hole on the course is probably the 17th; it is one of those tough par 3s of just over 200 yards, and is played across a gully to a high green.
18 holes, 6627yds, Par 72, SSS 72, Course record 66.
Club membership 800.
Visitors advisable to contact in advance. May not play before noon on Sun. **Societies** apply by telephone or in writing. **Green Fees** £28 per round (weekends £35). **Cards** ▤ ▤ ▤ **Prof** Richard Arnold **Course Designer** Fred Hawtree **Facilities** ⊗ ⪫ ⭢ ⭢ ♀ ⪪ ⪪ ↑ ⭢ ⭢ ↑ **Conf** Corporate Hospitality Days available **Location** 4m N of Brighton, between A23 & A27

Hotel ★★★ 69% The Old Tollgate Restaurant & Hotel, The Street, BRAMBER ☎ 01903 879494 11 en suite 20 annexe en suite

Hollingbury Park
Hollingbury Park Ditchling Rd BN1 7HS
☎ 01273 552010 (sec) 500086 (pro) ▤ 01273 552010/6
e-mail: graemecrompton@sussexgolfcentre.fsnet.co.uk
Municipal course in hilly situation on the Downs, overlooking the sea.
18 holes, 6500yds, Par 72, SSS 71, Course record 65.
Club membership 300.
Visitors must contact in advance. **Societies** telephone the secretary for details. **Green Fees** £14 per 18 holes; £22 per day (weekends £19 per round). **Prof** Graeme Crompton **Facilities** ⊗ ⪫ ⭢ ♀ ⪪ ⪪ ↑ ⭢ ⭢ **Location** 2m N of town centre

Hotel ★★★ 64% Quality Hotel Brighton, West St, BRIGHTON ☎ 01273 220033 138 en suite

Waterhall
Waterhall Saddlescombe Rd BN1 8YN
☎ 01273 508658
18 holes, 5773yds, Par 69, SSS 68, Course record 66.
Location 2m NE from A27
Telephone for further details

Hotel ★★★ 69% The Old Tollgate Restaurant & Hotel, The Street, BRAMBER ☎ 01903 879494 11 en suite 20 annexe en suite

West Hove
West Hove Church Farm, Hangleton BN3 8AN
☎ 01273 419738 & 413494 (pro) ▤ 01273 439988
e-mail: info@westhovegolf.co.uk
A downland course designed by Hawtree & Sons.
18 holes, 6226yds, Par 71, SSS 70, Course record 65.
Club membership 600.
Visitors tee times by arrangement. **Societies** by arrangement, telephone, write or e-mail. **Green Fees** £25 per 18 holes. **Prof** Darren Cook **Course Designer** Hawtree & Sons **Facilities** ⊗ ⪫ by prior arrangement ⪫ ⭢ ♀ ⪪ ⪪ ↑ ⭢ ⭢ ↑ **Conf** fac available **Location** Easy access from A27, N of Brighton

Hotel ★★★ 68% The Courtlands, 15-27 The Drive, HOVE ☎ 01273 731055 60 en suite 7 annexe en suite

Looking for a driving range? Refer to the listing of driving ranges at the back of this guide.

CROWBOROUGH
CROWBOROUGH Map 05 TQ53

Crowborough Beacon
Crowborough Beacon Beacon Rd TN6 1UJ
☎ 01892 661511 ▤ 01892 667339
e-mail: cbgc@eastsx.fsnet.co.uk
Standing some 800 feet above sea level, this is a testing heathland course, with panoramic views of the South Downs, Eastbourne and even the sea on a clear day.

18 holes, 6279yds, Par 71, SSS 70, Course record 66.
Club membership 700.
Visitors must contact in advance & have handicap certificate but may only play at weekends & bank holidays after 2.30pm. **Societies** telephone or apply in writing to secretary. **Green Fees** £46 per day; £36 per round (£44 per round weekends after 2.30pm). **Prof** Mr D C Newnham **Facilities** ⊗ ⪫ ⭢ ♀ ⪪ ⪪ ↑ ⭢ **Location** 1m SW on A26

Hotel ★★★ 78% The Spa Hotel, Mount Ephraim, TUNBRIDGE WELLS ☎ 01892 520331 69 en suite

Dewlands Manor
Dewlands Manor Cottage Hill, Rotherfield TN6 3JN
☎ 01892 852266 ▤ 01892 853015
A beautifully kept compact meadowland course. The short par 4 4th can be played by the brave by launching a driver over the trees; the 7th requires accurate driving on a tight fairway; and the final two holes are sweeping par 5s travelling parallel to each other, a small stream guarding the front of the 9th green.
9 holes, 3186yds, Par 36, SSS 70.
Visitors must telephone in advance. **Societies** telephone for availability. **Green Fees** terms on application. **Cards** ▤ ▤ ▤ ▤ **Prof** Nick Godin **Course Designer** R M & N M Godin **Facilities** ⊗ ⪫ ⭢ ♀ ⪪ ⪪ ↑ ⭢ ⭢ **Leisure** indoor teaching facilities with computer analysis. **Conf** Corporate Hospitality Days available **Location** 0.5m S of Rotherfield

DITCHLING
DITCHLING Map 05 TQ31

Mid Sussex
Mid Sussex Spatham Ln BN6 8XJ
☎ 01273 846567 ▤ 01273 841835
e-mail: admin@midsussexgolfclub.co.uk
Mature parkland course with many trees, water hazards, strategically placed bunkers and superbly contoured greens. The 14th hole, a spectacular par 5, demands accurate shotmaking to avoid the various hazards along its length.
18 holes, 6462yds, Par 71, SSS 71, Course record 65.
Club membership 650.
Visitors telephone in advance to book tee times. After 1pm at weekends. **Societies** advance booking required. **Green Fees** £28 per round (weekends £30). **Cards** ▤ ▤ ▤ ▤

Continued

239

🛇 **Prof** Neil Plimmer **Course Designer** David Williams **Facilities** ⊗ 〗⫟ ⯇ ⯈♀⯀🏠⛳🏌 ➔🚃 ⌀ ♣ **Leisure** snooker table. **Conf** fac available Corporate Hospitality Days available **Location** 1m E of Ditchling village

Hotel ★★★ 75% Shelleys Hotel, High St, LEWES
☎ 01273 472361 19 en suite

EASTBOURNE
Map 05 TV69

Eastbourne Downs East Dean Rd BN20 8ES
☎ 01323 720827 📄 01323 412506
This downland course has spectacular views over the South Downs and Channel. Situated in an area of outstanding natural beauty approximately 1 mile behind Beachy Head.
18 holes, 6145yds, Par 72, SSS 72, Course record 70. Club membership 650.
Visitors a handicap certificate is required for weekends. Visitors may not play before 9.15am weekdays and before 11am weekends except by arrangement. **Societies** contact secretary in advance for details. **Green Fees** £23 per day, £18 per round (£30/£25 weekends and bank holidays).
Cards 🖴 🔤 **Prof** T Marshall **Course Designer** J H Taylor **Facilities** ⊗ 〗⫟ ⯇ ⯈♀⯀🏠⛳🏌 **Location** 0.5m W of town centre on A259

Hotel ★★★ 73% Lansdowne Hotel, King Edward's Pde, EASTBOURNE ☎ 01323 725174 110 en suite

---

13 Courses to choose from!
Any 2 days - 14th January - 31st December 2005
Your break includes 2 days' free golf (up to 36 holes each day on the same course), accommodation, full English breakfast, light lunch at the golf club, with a 4 course Dinner and coffee at the hotel.

All our 101 rooms are en suite with every modern facility inc. Satellite TV. Sky Sports TV in public room.

The cost of your golf break from 14th Jan.–28th Feb. £160.00: 1st–31st Mar £170.00: 1st Apr.-31st May £179.00: 1st Jun–30th Sept. £184.00: 1st Oct.–31st Dec. £172.00.

You may, subject to availability, play at a selection of 13 golf clubs (all 18-hole) in this lovely area.

Please write or telephone for our Golfing Break folder.

Lansdowne Hotel
AA
★★★
King Edward's Parade · Eastbourne BN21 4EE
Tel: (01323) 725174   Fax: (01323) 739721

Prices may change during the currency of the Guide, please check when booking.

Royal Eastbourne Paradise Dr BN20 8BP
☎ 01323 729738 📄 01323 729738
A famous club which celebrated its centenary in 1987. The course plays longer than it measures. Testing holes are the 8th, a par 3 played to a high green and the 16th, a par 5 righthand dog-leg.
Devonshire Course: 18 holes, 6074yds, Par 70, SSS 69, Course record 62.
Hartington Course: 9 holes, 2147yds, Par 64, SSS 61. Club membership 800.
Visitors must contact in advance, may not play weekends except by arrangement. Handicap certificate required for Devonshire course. **Societies** must apply in advance. **Green Fees** not confirmed. **Cards** 🖴 🔤 💳 🔤 🛇 **Prof** Alan Harrison **Course Designer** Arthur Mayhewe **Facilities** ⊗ 〗⫟ by prior arrangement ⫟ ⯇ ⯈♀⯀🏠⛳🏌 ➔🚃 ⌀ **Leisure** snooker table. **Conf** Corporate Hospitality Days available **Location** 0.5m W of town centre

Hotel ★★★ 73% Lansdowne Hotel, King Edward's Pde, EASTBOURNE ☎ 01323 725174 110 en suite

---

Willingdon Southdown Rd, Willingdon BN20 9AA
☎ 01323 410981 📄 01323 411510
e-mail: secretary@willingdongolfclub.co.uk
Unique, hilly downland course set in oyster-shaped amphitheatre.
18 holes, 6118yds, Par 69, SSS 69. Club membership 610.
Visitors no restrictions. **Societies** apply in advance. **Green Fees** £25 per day/£20 per round. **Prof** Troy Moore **Course Designer** J Taylor/Dr Mackenzie **Facilities** ⊗ ⫟ ⯇ ⯈♀⯀ 🏠⛳🏌 ➔🚃 ⌀ **Location** 0.5m N of town centre off A22

Hotel ★★★ 72% Hydro Hotel, Mount Rd, EASTBOURNE ☎ 01323 720643 84 rms (83 en suite)

FOREST ROW
Map 05 TQ43

Ashdown Forest Golf Hotel Chapel Ln RH18 5BB
☎ 01342 822018 📄 01342 824869
e-mail: enquiries@ashgolf.co.uk
West Course: 18 holes, 5606yds, Par 68, SSS 67.
Location 4m S of East Grinstead off A22 & B2110
Telephone for further details

Hotel ★★★★ Ashdown Park Hotel and Country Club, Wych Cross, FOREST ROW ☎ 01342 824988 107 en suite

---

Royal Ashdown Forest Chapel Ln RH18 5LR
☎ 01342 822018 📄 01342 825211
e-mail: ashdownoffice@btopenworld.com
Old Course is on undulating heathland with no
Continued

bunkers. Long carries off the tees and magnificent views over the Forest. Not a course for the high handicapper. West Course on natural heathland with no bunkers. Less demanding than Old Course although accuracy is at a premium.
Old Course: 18 holes, 6477yds, Par 72, SSS 71, Course record 67.
West Course: 18 holes, 5606yds, Par 68, SSS 67.
Club membership 450.
Visitors Old Course; some restrictions at weekends & Tue. Must have a handicap certificate . No restrictions on West Course. **Societies** must contact in advance. **Green Fees** Old Course: £45 per round (£60 weekends). West Course: £32/£22 per round (£38/£26 weekends). **Cards** 🔤 🔤 🔤 **Prof** Martyn Landsborough **Facilities** ⊗ ⅏ ⅃ 🖤 🍴 ☖ 🏴 🏌
🏌 ♐ **Location** SE side of Forest Row village, off B2110

Hotel ★★★★ Ashdown Park Hotel and Country Club, Wych Cross, FOREST ROW ☎ 01342 824988 107 en suite

HAILSHAM Map 05 TQ50

Wellshurst Golf & Country Club North St,
Hellingly BN27 4EE
☎ 01435 813456 (pro shop) 🖹 01435 812444
e-mail: info@wellshurst.com
There are outstanding views of the South Downs and the Weald Valley from this 18-hole, well-manicured, undulating course. There are varied features and some water hazards. A practice sand bunker, putting green and driving range are available to improve your golf. The clubhouse and leisure facilities are open to visitors.
18 holes, 5992yds, Par 70, SSS 68, Course record 64.
Club membership 450.
Visitors no restrictions but advisable to book. **Societies** telephone in advance to book tee times. **Green Fees** £18 per 18 holes (weekends £22). **Cards** 🔤 🔤 🔤 🔤 🔤
Prof Mark Jarvis **Course Designer** The Golf Corporation
Facilities ⊗ ⅏ ⅃ 🖤 🍴 ☖ 🏴 ♐ 🏌 **Leisure** sauna, solarium, gymnasium, spa bath. **Conf** fac available Corporate Hospitality Days available **Location** 2.5m N of Hailsham, on A267

HASTINGS & ST LEONARDS Map 05 TQ80

TEN66 Battle Rd TN37 7BP
☎ 01424 854243 🖹 01424 854244
Played over Hastings Public Course. Undulating parkland with stream and fine views.
Hastings Golf Course: 18 holes, 6248yds, Par 71, SSS 70, Course record 70.
Club membership 400.
Visitors no restrictions, pay and play. **Societies** arrangement by telephone. **Green Fees** not confirmed. **Cards** 🔤 🔤 🔤
🔤 🔤 **Prof** Charles Giddins **Facilities** ⊗ ⅏ ⅃ 🖤 🍴 ☖
🏴 🏌 ♐ 🏌 **Leisure** hard tennis courts, outdoor swimming pool. **Location** 3m N of Hastings on A2100

Hotel ★★★ ♨ 70% Beauport Park Hotel, Battle Rd, HASTINGS ☎ 01424 851222 25 en suite

HEATHFIELD Map 05 TQ52

Horam Park Chiddingly Rd, Horam TN21 0JJ
☎ 01435 813477 🖹 01435 813677
e-mail: angie@horamgolf.freeserve.co.uk

Continued

A pretty, woodland course with lakes and quality fast-running greens.
9 holes, 6128yds, Par 70, SSS 70, Course record 64.
Club membership 350.
Visitors contact for tee times Can book up to 2 months in advance. **Societies** prior booking required. **Green Fees** £16.50 per 18 holes; £11 per 9 holes (£18/£11.50 weekends). Twilight 9.50. **Cards** 🔤 🔤 🔤 🔤 🔤 🔤
Prof Giles Velvick **Course Designer** Glen Johnson
Facilities ⊗ ⅏ ⅃ 🖤 🍴 ☖ 🏴 🏌 ♐ 🏌 **Leisure** pitch & putt, video swingbay on range. **Location** Off A267 Hailsham-Heathfield

Hotel ★★★ 66% Boship Farm Hotel, Lower Dicker, HAILSHAM ☎ 01323 844826 47 annexe en suite

HOLTYE Map 05 TQ43

Holtye TN8 7ED
☎ 01342 850635 & 850576 🖹 01342 850576
e-mail: secretary@holtye.com
Undulating forest/heathland course with tree-lined fairways providing testing golf. Different tees on back nine.
9 holes, 5325yds, Par 66, SSS 66, Course record 62.
Club membership 360.
Visitors may not play mornings Wed-Thu & weekends. **Societies** Tue & Fri by arrangement. **Green Fees** terms on application. **Prof** Kevin Hinton **Facilities** ⅃ 🖤 🍴 ☖ 🏌
Location 4m E of East Grinstead and 6m W of Tunbridge Wells on A264

Hotel ⌂ Travel Inn, London Rd, Felbridge, EAST GRINSTEAD ☎ 08701 977088 41 en suite

LEWES Map 05 TQ41

Lewes Chapel Hill BN7 2BB
☎ 01273 483474 🖹 01273 483474
Downland course. Fine views. Proper greens all-year-round.
18 holes, 5929yds, Par 71, SSS 68.
Club membership 615.
Visitors may not play at weekends before 2pm in summer, before 11am in winter **Societies** must contact in advance. **Green Fees** £30 per round (£38 weekends). **Prof** Paul Dobson **Course Designer** Jack Rowe **Facilities** ⊗ ⅏ ⅃
🖤 🍴 ☖ 🏴 🏌 **Location** E side of town centre

Hotel ★★★ 62% White Hart Hotel, 55 High St, LEWES ☎ 01273 476694 23 en suite 29 annexe en suite

NEWHAVEN Map 05 TQ40

Peacehaven Brighton Rd BN9 9UH
☎ 01273 512571 🖹 01273 512571
e-mail: golf@peacehavengc.freeserve.co.uk
Downland course, sometimes windy. Testing holes: 1st (par 3), 4th (par 4), 9th (par 3), 10th (par 3), 18th (par 3). Attractive views over the Sussex Downs, the River Ouse and Newhaven Harbour.
9 holes, 5488yds, Par 70, SSS 67, Course record 65.
Club membership 270.
Visitors may not play before 11am weekends. **Societies** telephone in advance. **Green Fees** terms on application.
Prof Ian Pearson **Course Designer** James Braid **Facilities**
⅃ 🖤 🍴 ☖ 🏌 **Location** 0.75m W of Newhaven on A259

Hotel ★★★ 69% The Star Inn, ALFRISTON ☎ 01323 870495 37 en suite

RYE
Map 05 TQ92

Rye New Lydd Rd, Camber TN31 7QS
☎ 01797 225241 🖹 01797 225460
e-mail: ryelinks@btclick.com
Unique links course with superb undulating greens set amongst ridges of sand dunes alongside Rye Harbour. Fine views over Romney Marsh and towards Fairlight and Dungeness.
Old Course: 18 holes, 6317yds, Par 68, SSS 71, Course record 64.
Jubilee Course: 9 holes, 3109yds, Par 71, SSS 70.
Club membership 1100.
Visitors must be invited/introduced by a member. **Green Fees** terms on application. **Prof** Michael Lee **Course Designer** H S Colt **Facilities** ⊗ 🏌️ 🍴 ⚒ 🏠 🛜 🐎 🏌️
Location 2.75m SE off A259

Hotel ★★★ 63% The George, High St, RYE
☎ 01797 222114 22 en suite

SEAFORD
Map 05 TV49

Seaford Firle Rd, East Blatchington BN25 2JD
☎ 01323 892442 🖹 01323 894113
e-mail: secretary@seafordgolfclub.co.uk
The great H. Taylor did not perhaps design as many courses as his friend and rival, James Braid, but Seaford's original design was Taylor's. It is a splendid downland course with magnificent views and some fine holes.
18 holes, 6551yds, Par 69, SSS 71.
Club membership 600.
Visitors must contact in advance. **Societies** must contact in advance. **Green Fees** terms on application. **Cards** ▦ ▦ ▦ ▦ 🖪 **Prof** David Mills/Clay Morris **Course Designer** J H Taylor **Facilities** ⊗ 🏌️ 🎩 🏌️ 🍴 ⚒ 🏠 🏠 🐎 🏌️ 🏌️ 🏌️
Conf Corporate Hospitality Days available **Location** Turn inland at war memorial off A259

Hotel ★★★ 69% The Star Inn, ALFRISTON
☎ 01323 870495 37 en suite

Seaford Head Southdown Rd BN25 4JS
☎ 01323 890139 & 894843
18 holes, 5848yds, Par 71, SSS 68, Course record 63.
Telephone for further details

Hotel ★★★ 70% Deans Place, Seaford Rd, ALFRISTON
☎ 01323 870248 36 en suite

SEDLESCOMBE
Map 05 TQ71

Sedlescombe Kent St TN33 0SD
☎ 01424 871700 🖹 01424 871712
e-mail: golf@golfschool.co.uk
Situated in the beautiful Sussex countryside. The natural water and tree line adds to the beauty as well as making it an enjoyable round of golf.
18 holes, 6269yds, Par 72, SSS 70.
Club membership 300.
Visitors please telephone and reserve tee times. No jeans or tracksuits allowed, golf shoes must be worn on the course. Hire shoes available. **Societies** please telephone to reserve tee times. **Green Fees** not confirmed. **Cards** ▦ ▦ ▦ ▦ **Prof** James Andrews **Facilities** ⊗ 🏌️ 🎩 🏌️ 🍴 ⚒ 🏠 🛜 🐎 🏌️ 🏌️ 🏌️ **Leisure** hard tennis courts. **Conf** fac available

Corporate Hospitality Days available **Location** A21, 4m N of Hastings

Hotel ★★★ 68% Brickwall Hotel, The Green, SEDLESCOMBE ☎ 01424 870253 26 en suite

TICEHURST
Map 05 TQ63

Dale Hill Hotel & Golf Club TN5 7DQ
☎ 01580 200112 🖹 01580 201249
e-mail: info@dalehill.co.uk
Dale Hill is set in over 350 acres, high on the Kentish Weald in an Area of Outstanding Natural Beauty. Offering two 18 hole golf courses, one of which has been designed by Ian Woosnam to USGA specifications.

Dale Hill: 18 holes, 6106yds, Par 70, SSS 69.
Ian Woosnam: 18 holes, 6512yds, Par 71, SSS 71, Course record 64.
Club membership 850.
Visitors booking only 7 days in advance **Societies** must contact in advance. **Green Fees** Dale Hill:£30 (£40 weekends). Ian Woosnam £45 (£55 weekends). **Cards** ▦ ▦ ▦ ▦ ▦ 🖪 **Prof** Mark Wood **Course Designer** Ian Woosnam **Facilities** ⊗ 🏌️ 🎩 🏌️ 🍴 ⚒ 🏠 🛜 🐎 🏌️ 🏌️ 🏌️ **Leisure** heated indoor swimming pool, sauna, gymnasium. **Conf** fac available Corporate Hospitality Days available **Location** M25 junct 5,A21, B2087 left after 1 mile

Hotel ★★★★ 72% Dale Hill Hotel & Golf Club, TICEHURST ☎ 01580 200112 35 en suite

UCKFIELD
See page 243

UCKFIELD
Map 05 TQ42

Piltdown Piltdown TN22 3XB
☎ 01825 722033 🖹 01825 724192
e-mail: piltdowngolf@lineone.net
Natural heathland course with much heather and gorse. No bunkers, easy walking, fine views.
18 holes, 6076yds, Par 68, SSS 69, Course record 64.
Club membership 400.
Visitors must telephone pro shop in advance 01825 722389 and have a handicap certificate. Play on Tue, Thu and weekends is restricted. **Societies** must contact in writing. **Green Fees** £42 per day, £32 per round, £25 after 1.30pm, £16 after 4pm. **Prof** Jason Partridge **Facilities** ⊗ 🏌️ 🎩 🏌️ 🍴 ⚒ 🏠 🛜 🐎 🏌️ 🏌️ **Location** Between Newick & Maresfield off A272, club signposted

Hotel ★★★ Horsted Place, Little Horsted, UCKFIELD
☎ 01825 750581 17 en suite 3 annexe en suite

Continued

East Sussex National

Map 05 TQ42 — Uckfield

☎ 01825 880088 📄 01825 880066

East Sussex National offers two huge courses ideal for big-hitting professionals. The European Open has been staged here and it is home to the European Headquarters of the David Leadbetter Golf Academy, with indoor and outdoor video analysis. Bob Cupp designed the courses using 'bent' grass from tee to green, resulting in an American-style course to test everyone. The greens on both the East and West Courses are immaculately maintained. The West Course, with stadium design and chosen for future events, is reserved for members and their guests; visitors are welcome on the East Course, also with stadium design, which was the venue for the 1993 and 1994 European Open. The entrance seems daunting for first-time visitors _unprepared for the vast car park, huge red-brick clubhouse and suspended corridor from the reception area through to the well-stocked professional's shop.

e-mail: golf@eastsussexnational.co.uk

Visitors Must contact in advance
Societies Contact Advance Reservations 01825 880228
Green Fees 18 holes £50

Facilities ⊗ ⅷ 🛒 ♨ ♟ 🏠 ⛳ 🍴
🐾 🥪 ♂ ₹
Conf facilities and corporate hospitality days available
Professional Sarah Maclennan/ Paul Charman.
Golf Academy
Leisure Tennis, sauna, solarium
Location Little Horsted TN22 5ES
(2m S of Uckfield on A22)
Holes/Par/Course record 36 holes.
East Course: 18 holes, 7138 yds, Par 72, SSS 74,
Course record 63
West Course: 18 holes, 7154 yds, Par 72, SSS 73

Championship Course

WHERE TO STAY

Hotels
UCKFIELD
★★★★ ⊚ ⊚ 74% Buxted Park Country House Hotel, TN22 4AY.
☎ 01825 732711. 44 en suite

★★★ ⊚ ⊚ Horsted Place, TN22 5TS. ☎ 01825 750581.
17 en suite 3 annexe en suite

NEWICK
★★★ ⊚ ⊚ Newick Park Country Estate BN8 4SB
☎ 01825 723633. 13 en suite 3 annexe en suite

SUSSEX, WEST

ANGMERING   Map 04 TQ00

Ham Manor BN16 4JE
☎ 01903 783288 📄 01903 850886
e-mail: secretary.ham.manor@tinyonline.co.uk
Two miles from the sea, this parkland course has fine springy turf and provides an interesting test in two loops of nine holes each.
18 holes, 6267yds, Par 70, SSS 70, Course record 64.
Club membership 780.
Visitors must have a handicap certificate. Telephone pro shop in advance 01903 783732. **Societies** telephone for details **Green Fees** not confirmed. **Prof** Simon Buckley **Course Designer** Harry Colt **Facilities** ⛴ 🖻 🖌 **Location** Off A259

Guesthouse ♦♦♦♦ Kenmore Guest House, Claigmar Rd, RUSTINGTON ☎ 01903 784634 7 rms (6 en suite)

ARUNDEL   Map 04 TQ00

Avisford Park Yapton Ln, Walberton BN18 0LS
☎ 01243 554611 📄 01243 555580
18 holes, 5703yds, Par 68, SSS 66.
Location Off A27, towards Yapton
Telephone for further details

Hotel ★★★ 67% Norfolk Arms Hotel, High St, ARUNDEL ☎ 01903 882101 21 en suite
13 annexe en suite

BOGNOR REGIS   Map 04 SZ99

Bognor Regis Downview Rd, Felpham PO22 8JD
☎ 01243 821929 (Secretary) 📄 01243 860719
e-mail: sec@bognorgolfclub.co.uk
This flattish, well tree lined, parkland course has more variety than is to be found on some other South Coast courses. The club is also known far and wide for its enterprise in creating a social atmosphere. The course is open to the prevailing wind and the River Rife and many water ditches need negotiation.
18 holes, 6238yds, Par 70, SSS 70, Course record 64.
Club membership 700.
Visitors handicap certificate required. Must contact in advance (pro shop 01243 865209). **Societies** phone initially. **Green Fees** £25 (£30 weekends). **Prof** Stephen Bassil **Course Designer** James Braid **Facilities** ⊗ 🍴 🖺 🍺 ♀ ⛴ 🖻 🦯 🦮 🦯 **Conf** fac available **Location** 0.5m N at Felpham traffic lights on A259

Hotel ★★ 71% Beachcroft Hotel, Clyde Rd, Felpham Village, BOGNOR REGIS ☎ 01243 827142 34 en suite

BURGESS HILL   Map 04 TQ31

Burgess Hill Cuckfield Rd RH15 8RE
☎ 01444 258585 📄 247318
e-mail: enquiries@burgesshillgolfcentre.co.uk
Opened in May 1998, this academy course is bordered by a tributary of the River Adur. Facilities available for public use include a floodlit driving range and a large sweeping putting green.
9 holes, 1250yds, Par 27.
Visitors no restrictions **Societies** contact in advance. **Green Fees** terms on application. **Cards** 🖽 🖽 🖽 🖽 🖽 🖽 **Prof** Mark Collins **Course Designer** Donald Steel **Facilities** ⊗ 🍴 🖺 🍺 ♀ ⛴ 🖻 🦯 🦯 ⛳ **Leisure** pitching & chipping green. **Conf** Corporate Hospitality Days available **Location** N of town on B2036

Hotel ★★ ⛳ 72% Hilton Park Hotel, Tylers Green, CUCKFIELD ☎ 01444 454555 11 en suite

CHICHESTER   Map 04 SU80

Chichester Hunston Village PO20 6AX
☎ 01243 533833 📄 01243 539922
e-mail: chigolfclub@mistral.co.uk
Tower Course: 18 holes, 6175yds, Par 72, SSS 69, Course record 67.
Cathedral Course: 18 holes, 6461yds, Par 72, SSS 71, Course record 65.
Course Designer Philip Saunders **Location** 3m S of Chichester, on B2145 at Hunston
Telephone for further details

Hotel ★★★ 68% The Ship Hotel, North St, CHICHESTER ☎ 01243 778000 36 en suite

COPTHORNE   Map 05 TQ33

Copthorne Borers Arms Rd RH10 3LL
☎ 01342 712033 & 712508 📄 01342 717682
e-mail: info@copthornegolfclub.co.uk
Despite it having been in existence since 1892, this club remains one of the lesser known Sussex courses. It is hard to know why because it is most attractive with plenty of trees and much variety.
18 holes, 6435yds, Par 71, SSS 71, Course record 67.
Club membership 550.
Visitors advised to contact in advance, may not play weekends. **Societies** must contact in advance. **Green Fees** £34 weekdays. **Cards** 🖽 🖽 🖽 **Prof** Joe Burrell **Course Designer** James Braid **Facilities** ⊗ 🖺 🍺 ♀ ⛴ 🖻 🦯 🦯 **Location** E side of village junc 10 of M23 off A264

Hotel ★★★★ 70% Copthorne Hotel London Gatwick, Copthorne Way, COPTHORNE
☎ 01342 348800 & 348888 📄 01342 348833 227 en suite

Effingham Park The Copthorne Effingham Park, Hotel, West Park Rd RH10 3EU
☎ 01342 716528 📄 0870 8900 215
Parkland course.
9 holes, 1822yds, Par 30, SSS 57, Course record 28.
Club membership 230.
Visitors restricted at weekends before 11am and not after 4pm Tue, Apr-Oct. **Societies** Mon-Fri, and Sat/Sun after 1pm, must write/telephone in advance. **Green Fees** terms on application. **Cards** 🖽 🖽 🖽 🖽 🖽 🖽 **Prof** Mark Root **Course Designer** Francisco Escario **Facilities** ⊗ 🍴 🖺 🍺 ♀ ⛴ 🖻 🦯 🏓 🦯 **Leisure** hard tennis courts, heated

Continued

indoor swimming pool, sauna, solarium, gymnasium. **Conf fac** available Corporate Hospitality Days available **Location** 2m E on B2028

Effingham Park

Hotel ★★★★ 66% Copthorne Hotel and Resort Effingham Park, West Park Rd, COPTHORNE ☎ 01342 714994 122 en suite

CRAWLEY
Map 04 TQ23

Cottesmore Buchan Hill, Pease Pottage RH11 9AT
☎ 01293 528256 (reception) & 535399 (shop)
📠 01293 522819
e-mail: cottesmore@americangolf.uk.com
Founded in 1974, the Griffin Course is a fine test of golfing skill with fairways lined by silver birch, pine, oak and rhododendrons. Four holes have lakes as hazards.

Griffin: 18 holes, 6248yds, Par 71, SSS 70, Course record 67.
Phoenix: 18 holes, 5600yds, Par 69, SSS 67.
Visitors Griffin course not before noon at weekends. Dress code applies. Advisable to contact in advance. **Societies** must telephone in advance. **Green Fees** Mon-Thu £28 (Fri-Sun £32). **Cards** 💳 🖃 🖃 🖃 🖃 💳 **Prof** Calum J Callan **Course Designer** Michael J Rogerson **Facilities** ⊗ ⊪ ⬛ 🍴 ♀ 🏖 🏠 🍴 🍴 🏌 ⬛ **Leisure** hard tennis courts, heated indoor swimming pool, sauna, solarium, gymnasium. **Conf** fac available Corporate Hospitality Days available **Location** 2m W 1m W of M23 junc 11

Hotel ★★★ Alexander House Hotel, East St, TURNERS HILL ☎ 01342 714914 18 en suite

Ifield Golf & Country Club Rusper Rd, Ifield
RH11 0LN ☎ 01293 520222 📠 01293 612973
Parkland course.
18 holes, 6330yds, Par 70, SSS 70, Course record 64.
Club membership 750.
Visitors must contact professional in advance. Must be guest of member at weekends. **Societies** apply in advance. **Green Fees** £45 per day; £32 per round weekdays.

Prof Jonathan Earl **Course Designer** Hawtree & Taylor **Facilities** ⊗ ⊪ ⬛ ⬛ 🍴 ♀ 🏖 🏠 🍴 🏌 **Location** 1m W side of town centre off A23

Hotel ★★★ Alexander House Hotel, East St, TURNERS HILL ☎ 01342 714914 18 en suite

Tilgate Forest Golf Centre Titmus Dr RH10 5EU
☎ 01293 530103 📠 01293 523478
Designed by former Ryder Cup players Neil Coles and Brian Huggett, the course has been carefully cut through a silver birch and pine forest. It is possibly one of the most beautiful public courses in the country. The 17th is a treacherous par 5 demanding an uphill third shot to a green surrounded by rhododendrons.
18 holes, 6359yds, Par 71, SSS 70, Course record 69.
Club membership 200.
Visitors public course, pay & play at all times. **Societies** telephone in advance for details. **Green Fees** not confirmed. **Cards** 💳 🖃 🖃 🖃 💳 **Prof** Sean Trussell **Course Designer** Neil Coles/Brian Huggett **Facilities** ⊗ ⊪ ⬛ ⬛ 🍴 ♀ 🏖 🏠 🍴 🏌 🍴 **Leisure** par 3 nine hole course. **Conf** Corporate Hospitality Days available **Location** 2m E of town centre

Hotel ★★★ Alexander House Hotel, East St, TURNERS HILL ☎ 01342 714914 18 en suite

EAST GRINSTEAD
Map 05 TQ33

Chartham Park Felcourt Rd, Felcourt RH19 2JT
☎ 01342 870340 & 870008 (pro shop) 📠 01342 870719
e-mail: b.smith@clubhaus.com
Mature parkland course.
18 holes, 6680yards, Par 72, SSS 72, Course record 64.
Club membership 740.
Visitors may book up to 7 days in advance. Weekdays anytime, weekends after 2pm. **Societies** weekdays only, telephone for details. **Green Fees** terms on application. **Cards** 💳 🖃 🖃 🖃 💳 **Prof** Ben Knight **Course Designer** Neil Coles **Facilities** ⊗ ⊪ ⬛ ⬛ 🍴 ♀ 🏖 🏠 🍴 🏌 **Conf** Corporate Hospitality Days available **Location** M25 junct 6, take A22 towards East Grinstead, at second set of traffic lights turn left. At mini-roundabout take 1st exit, next mini-roundabout take 2nd exit, club 2m on right.

Hotel ★★★ 🏖 Gravetye Manor Hotel, EAST GRINSTEAD ☎ 01342 810567 18 en suite

GOODWOOD
Map 04 SU80

Marriott Goodwood Park Hotel & Country Club PO18 0QB ☎ 01243 520117 📠 01243 520120
A parkland course set within the 12,000 acre Goodwood estate, home to the Dukes of Richmond for over 300 years. Fairly generous over the opening holes but gets progressively harder as you approach the turn.

Continued

Continued

18 holes, 6579yds, Par 72, SSS 71, Course record 68.
Club membership 700.
Visitors tee times are subject to availability, please book in advance. Golf course dress and etiquette must be adhered to. **Societies** telephone or write. **Green Fees** not confirmed. **Cards** 🖃 ▨▨ ▨▨ 🖳 🖾 ▨ **Prof** Adrian Wratting **Course Designer** Donald Steele **Facilities** ⊗ ⅷ 🏋 🍺 🏆 🏖 🏠 🏌 🚜 🦌 🦌 🗡 🍴 **Leisure** hard tennis courts, heated indoor swimming pool, sauna, solarium, gymnasium. **Conf** Corporate Hospitality Days available **Location** 3m NE of Chichester, in the grounds of Goodwood House

Hotel ★★★★ 74% Marriott Goodwood Park Hotel & Country Club, GOODWOOD ☎ 0870 400 7225 94 en suite

HASSOCKS
Map 04 TQ31

Hassocks London Rd BN6 9NA
☎ 01273 846630 & 846990 🖹 01273 846070
e-mail: hgc@hassocksgolfclub.co.uk
Set against the backdrop of the South Downs, Hassocks is an 18 hole par 70 course designed and contoured to blend naturally with the surrounding countryside. A friendly and relaxed course, appealing to golfers of all ages and abilities.
18 holes, 5698yds, Par 70, SSS 68, Course record 66.
Club membership 400.
Visitors phone pro. shop in advance,01273 846990.
Societies apply in writing or telephone in advance. **Green Fees** £15 per 18 holes (£22 weekends and bank holidays).
Cards 🖃 ▨▨ ▨▨ ▨ **Prof** Charles Ledger **Course Designer** Paul Wright **Facilities** ⊗ 🏋 🍺 🏆 🏖 🏠 🏌 🚜 🗡 🍴 **Conf** Corporate Hospitality Days available **Location** On the A273 between Burgess Hill and Hassocks

Hotel ★★★ 62% The Hickstead Hotel, Jobs Ln, Bolney, HICKSTEAD ☎ 01444 248023 49 en suite

HAYWARDS HEATH
Map 05 TQ32

Haywards Heath High Beech Ln RH16 1SL
☎ 01444 414457 🖹 01444 458319
e-mail: haywardsheath.golfclub@virgin.net
Pleasant parkland course with several challenging par 4s and 3s.
18 holes, 6216yds, Par 71, SSS 70, Course record 66.
Club membership 770.
Visitors must have a handicap certificate. Must contact in advance. **Societies** Wed & Thu only by prior arrangement with the secretary. **Green Fees** £26 per 18 holes (£35 weekends). **Prof** Michael Henning **Facilities** ⊗ ⅷ by prior arrangement 🏋 🍺 🏆 🏖 🏠 🏌 🗡 🍴 **Conf** Corporate Hospitality Days available **Location** 1.25m N of Haywards Heath off B2028

Hotel ★★★ 68% The Birch Hotel, Lewes Rd, HAYWARDS HEATH ☎ 01444 451565 51 en suite

Paxhill Park East Mascalls Ln, Lindfield RH16 2QN
☎ 01444 484467 🖹 01444 482709
e-mail: johnbowen@paxhillpark.fsnet.co.uk
A relatively flat parkland course designed by Patrick Tallack. Water hazards on 5th, 13th and 14th holes.
18 holes, 6117yds, Par 70, SSS 69, Course record 67.
Club membership 320.
Visitors welcome but may not play weekend and some weekday mornings. **Societies** must contact in advance.

Continued

Green Fees terms on application. **Cards** 🖃 ▨▨ ▨▨ ▨ **Prof** APPT Penomg **Course Designer** P Tallack **Facilities** ⊗ 🏋 🍺 🏆 🏖 🏠 🏌 🗡 🍴 **Leisure** snooker. **Conf** fac available **Location** Outside Lindfield village just off B2011.

Hotel ★★★ 68% The Birch Hotel, Lewes Rd, HAYWARDS HEATH ☎ 01444 451565 51 en suite

HORSHAM
Map 04 TQ13

See Slinfold

Horsham Worthing Rd RH13 7AX
☎ 01403 271525 🖹 01403 274528
e-mail: admin@horshamgolfandfitness.co.uk
A short but challenging course, with six par 4s and three par 3s, two of which are played across water. Designed for beginners and intermediates but also challenges better players with a standard scratch of six below par.
9 holes, 4122yds, Par 33, SSS 30, Course record 55.
Club membership 280.
Visitors no restrictions. **Societies** apply in advance. **Green Fees** not confirmed. **Cards** 🖃 ▨▨ ▨▨ 🖳 🖾 ▨ **Prof** Lee Morris **Facilities** ⊗ ⅷ 🏋 🍺 🏆 🏖 🏠 🏌 🗡 🍴 **Leisure** solarium, gymnasium. **Conf** Corporate Hospitality Days available **Location** Off A24 rdbt, between Horsham/Southwater, by garage on B2237

Hotel ★★ 68% Ye Olde King's Head Hotel, Carfax, HORSHAM ☎ 01403 253126 42 rms (41 en suite)

HURSTPIERPOINT
Map 04 TQ21

Singing Hills Albourne BN6 9EB
☎ 01273 835353 🖹 01273 835444
e-mail: info@singinghills.co.uk
Three distinct nines (Lake, River and Valley) can be combined to make a truly varied game. Gently undulating fairways and spectacular waterholes make Singing Hills a test of accurate shotmaking. The opening two holes of the River nine have long drives, while the second hole on the Lake course is an island green where the tee is also protected by two bunkers. The Valley Course demands long, accurate tee shots.
Lake: 9 holes, 3253yds, Par 35, SSS 35.
River: 9 holes, 2861yds, Par 34, SSS 34.
Valley: 9 holes, 3362yds, Par 36, SSS 34.
Club membership 390.
Visitors no restrictions, but strict dress code observed. Must book tee-time in advance. **Societies** apply in advance.
Green Fees terms on application. **Cards** 🖃 ▨▨ ▨▨ 🖳 🖾 ▨ **Prof** Wallace Street **Course Designer** M R M Sandow **Facilities** ⊗ ⅷ 🏋 🍺 🏆 🏖 🏠 🏌 🗡 🍴 **Conf** fac available **Location** Off A23, off B2117

Hotel ★★★ 62% The Hickstead Hotel, Jobs Ln, Bolney, HICKSTEAD ☎ 01444 248023 49 en suite

LITTLEHAMPTON
Map 04 TQ00

Littlehampton 170 Rope Walk, Riverside West BN17 5DL ☎ 01903 717170 🖹 01903 726629
e-mail: lgc@talk21.com
A delightful seaside links in an equally delightful setting - and the only links course in the area.
18 holes, 6226yds, Par 70, SSS 70, Course record 64.
Club membership 600.
Visitors may not book tee times, contact Pro Shop for

Continued

availability on 01903 716369. **Societies** welcome weekdays; weekends some restrictions apply **Green Fees** terms on application. **Prof** Guy McQuitty **Course Designer** Hawtree **Facilities** ⊗ ⵑⵒ ⵑ ⵐ ⵛ ⵑ ⵔ ⵑ ⵎ ⵔ **Conf** fac available Corporate Hospitality Days available **Location** 1m W of Littlehampton off A259

Hotel ⬆ Travelodge Littlehampton, Worthing Rd, RUSTINGTON ☎ 08700 850 950 36 en suite

---

LOWER BEEDING   Map 04 TQ22

Mannings Heath Hotel Winterpit Ln RH13 6LY
☎ 01403 891191 ▯ 01403 891499
A 9 hole, 18 tee golf course with 3 par 4s set in glorious countryside.
9 holes, 1529yds, Par 31.
Club membership 150.
Visitors phone for details. **Societies** telephone in advance. **Green Fees** £10 per 18 holes. **Cards** ▭▭ ▭▭ ▭▭ ▭▭ ▭▭ ▯ **Prof** Jim Debenham **Facilities** ⊗ ⵑⵒ ⵑ ⵐ ⵛ ⵑ ⵔ ⵑ ⵌ ⵔ **Leisure** fishing. **Conf** fac available Corporate Hospitality Days available **Location** Located off the A281 south of Horsham

Hotel ★★★★ ⵗ South Lodge Hotel, Brighton Rd, LOWER BEEDING ☎ 01403 891711 45 en suite

MANNINGS HEATH   Map 04 TQ22

Mannings Heath Fullers, Hammerpond Rd
RH13 6PG ☎ 01403 210228 ▯ 01403 270974
e-mail: enquiries@manningsheath.com
The Waterfall is a downhill, parkland, part heathland,
Continued

championship course with streams and trees in abundance. It boasts three spectacular par 3s but all the holes are memorably unique. The Kingfisher course is a modern design with a lake which comes into play.

Waterfall: 18 holes, 6378yds, Par 70, SSS 70, Course record 67.
Kingfisher: 18 holes, 6217yds, Par 70, SSS 70, Course record 67.
Club membership 700.
Visitors must book in advance. **Societies** must contact in advance. **Green Fees** terms on application. **Cards** ▭▭ ▭▭ ▭▭ ▭▭ ▭▭ ▯ **Prof** Clive Tucker **Course Designer** David Williams **Facilities** ⊗ ⵑⵒ ⵑ ⵐ ⵛ ⵑ ⵔ ⵑ ⵌ ⵔ ⵔ **Leisure** hard tennis courts, fishing, sauna, chipping practice area. **Conf** fac available **Location** M23 junct 11, take A281 from Horsham or Brighton. Club on N side of village

Hotel ★★★★ ⵗ South Lodge Hotel, Brighton Rd, LOWER BEEDING ☎ 01403 891711 45 en suite

MIDHURST   Map 04 SU82

Cowdray Park Petworth Rd GU29 0BB
☎ 01730 813599 📠 01730 815900
e-mail: cowdray-golf@lineone.net
Undulating parkland course with scenic views of surrounding countryside, including Elizabethan ruins. The course is situated in a National Park originally designed by Capability Brown in the 18th century.

18 holes, 6212yds, Par 70, SSS 70, Course record 65.
Club membership 720.
Visitors advised to contact in advance. Handicap certificate preferred. **Societies** apply in writing/telephone/e-mail/fax. **Green Fees** £40 per 18 holes. **Cards** ⊞ 🔲 💳 🔲 **Prof** Richard Gough **Course Designer** Jack White **Facilities** ⊗ ⅏ ⯗ ♥ ♀ ♨ 🏠 🍴 ➶ ⚓ ✆ ₡ **Conf** fac available Corporate Hospitality Days available **Location** 1m E of Midhurst on A272

Hotel ★★★ 73% The Angel Hotel, North St, MIDHURST ☎ 01730 812421 24 en suite 4 annexe en suite

PULBOROUGH   Map 04 TQ01

West Sussex Golf Club Ln, Wiggonholt RH20 2EN
☎ 01798 872563 📠 01798 872033
e-mail: secretary@westsussexgolf.co.uk
An outstanding beautiful heathland course occupying an oasis of sand, heather and pine in the middle of attractive countryside which is predominately clay and marsh. The 6th and 13th holes are particularly notable.
18 holes, 6223yds, Par 68, SSS 70, Course record 61.
Club membership 850.
Visitors must contact in advance, may not play weekends except by prior agreement of the secretary, and on Fri except with a member. **Societies** Wed & Thu only, apply in writing. **Green Fees** £75 per 36 holes, £60 per 18 holes (£80/£65 weekends). **Prof** Tim Packham **Course Designer** Campbell/Hutcheson **Facilities** ⊗ ⯗ ♥ ♀ ♨ 🏠 🍴 ➶ ⚓ ✆ ₡ **Location** 1.5m E of Pulborough off A283

Hotel ★★★ 69% Roundabout Hotel, Monkmead Ln, WEST CHILTINGTON ☎ 01798 813838 23 en suite

PYECOMBE   Map 04 TQ21

Pyecombe Clayton Hill BN45 7FF
☎ 01273 845372 📠 01273 843338
e-mail: pyecombegc@btopenworld.com
Typical downland course on the inland side of the South Downs. Picturesque with magnificent views.
18 holes, 6278yds, Par 71, SSS 70, Course record 67.
Club membership 525.

Visitors must contact in advance and may only play after 9.15am weekdays and after 2.15pm weekends **Societies** telephone secretary in advance. **Green Fees** £25 per round/£30 per day (weekends £30/£35). **Prof** C R White **Course Designer** James Braid **Facilities** ⊗ ⅏ by prior arrangement ⯗ ♥ ♀ ♨ 🏠 🍴 ✆ **Location** E side of village on A273

Hotel ★★★ 68% The Courtlands, 15-27 The Drive, HOVE ☎ 01273 731055 60 en suite 7 annexe en suite

SELSEY   Map 04 SZ89

Selsey Golf Links Ln PO20 9DR
☎ 01243 602203 📠 01243 607101
e-mail: selsey.cc@talk21.com
Fairly difficult seaside course, exposed to wind and has natural ditches.
9 holes, 5834yds, Par 68, SSS 68, Course record 64.
Club membership 360.
Visitors must contact in advance. **Societies** must contact in advance in writing **Green Fees** terms on application. **Prof** Peter Grindley **Course Designer** J H Taylor **Facilities** ⊗ ⅏ ⯗ ♥ ♀ ♨ 🏠 🍴 **Leisure** hard tennis courts. **Location** 1m N off B2145

Hotel ★★★ 68% The Ship Hotel, North St, CHICHESTER ☎ 01243 778000 36 en suite

SLINFOLD   Map 04 TQ13

Slinfold Park Golf & Country Club Stane St
RH13 7RE ☎ 01403 791555 📠 01403 791465
e-mail: info@slinfoldpark.co.uk

Championship Course: 18 holes, 6407yds, Par 72, SSS 71, Course record 64.
Academy Course: 9 holes, 1315yds, Par 28.
Course Designer John Fortune **Location** 4m W on the A29
Telephone for further details

Hotel ★★★ 69% Hurtwood Inn Hotel, Walking Bottom, PEASLAKE ☎ 01306 730851 15 en suite 6 annexe en suite

WEST CHILTINGTON   Map 04 TQ01

West Chiltington Broadford Bridge Rd RH20 2YA
☎ 01798 812115 (bookings) & 813574 📠 01798 812631
e-mail: cottongolf@westchiltington.fsbusiness.co.uk
The Main Course has well-drained greens and offers panoramic views of the Sussex Downs. Three large double greens provide an interesting feature to this course. Also 9-hole short course and 13-bay driving range.
Windmill: 18 holes, 5866yds, SSS 69, Course

Continued   *Continued*

record 66 or 9 holes, 1360yds, Par 28.
Club membership 500.
Visitors book tee times in advance. **Societies** by prior arrangement. **Green Fees** not confirmed. **Cards** ▣ ▦
▦ ▦ ▣ **Prof** Lorraine Cousins **Course Designer** Brian Barnes **Facilities** ⊗ ⓛ 🍴 ♀ ⚒ 🏠 ⛳ 🚗 ⛳ ⓕ **Location** On N side of village

....

Hotel ★★★ 69% Roundabout Hotel, Monkmead Ln, WEST CHILTINGTON ☎ 01798 813838 23 en suite

WORTHING   Map 04 TQ10

Hill Barn Hill Barn Ln BN14 9QF
☎ 01903 237301 🗎 01903 217613
e-mail: info@hillbarngolf.com
Downland course with views of both Isle of Wight and Brighton.
18 holes, 6224yds, Par 70, SSS 70.
Club membership 500.
Visitors no restrictions, but advisable to book tee times, 7 days in advance. **Societies** must telephone in advance.
Green Fees £16 per 18 holes (weekends £18.50). **Cards** ▣ ▦ ▦ ▦ ▣ **Prof** F Morley **Course Designer** Fred Hawtree **Facilities** ⊗ ⑪ ⓛ 🍴 ♀ ⚒ 🏠 ⛳ 🚗 ⓕ **Leisure** croquet. **Conf** fac available Corporate Hospitality Days available **Location** N side of town at junct of A24/A27, 1 mile north of Worthing

....

Hotel ★★★ 62% Findon Manor Hotel, High St, Findon, WORTHING ☎ 01903 872733 11 en suite

---

Worthing Links Rd BN14 9QZ
☎ 01903 260801 🗎 01903 694664
e-mail: worthinggolf@easynet.co.uk
The Upper Course, short and tricky with entrancing views, will provide good entertainment. 'Lower Course' is considered to be one of the best downland courses in the country.
Lower Course: 18 holes, 6505yds, Par 71, SSS 72, Course record 62.
Upper Course: 18 holes, 5211yds, Par 66, SSS 66.
Club membership 1200.
Visitors advisable to contact in advance, not weekends during GMT. **Societies** contact in advance. **Green Fees** terms on application. **Prof** Stephen Rolley **Course Designer** H S Colt **Facilities** ⊗ ⑪ ⓛ 🍴 ♀ ⚒ 🏠 ⛳ 🚗 ⓕ ⓕ **Location** N side of town centre off A27

Hotel ★★★ 71% Ardington Hotel, Steyne Gardens, WORTHING ☎ 01903 230451 45 en suite

---

TYNE & WEAR

BACKWORTH   Map 12 NZ37

Backworth The Hall NE27 0AH ☎ 0191 268 1048
9 holes, 5930yds, Par 71, SSS 69, Course record 63.
Location W side of town on B1322
Telephone for further details

....

Hotel ⇪ Travel Inn Newcastle-upon-Tyne Holystone, Holystone Roundabout, NEWCASTLE ☎ 08701 977189 40 en suite

BIRTLEY   Map 12 NZ25

Birtley Birtley Ln DH3 2LR ☎ 0191 410 2207
A nine hole parkland course. Good test of golf with challenging par 3 and par 4 holes.
9 holes, 5662yds, Par 67, SSS 67, Course record 63.
Club membership 270.
Visitors must play with member at weekends & bank holidays. **Societies** apply in writing, must contact 1 month in advance in summer. **Green Fees** £14 per 18 holes.
Facilities ⓛ by prior arrangement 🍴 ♀ restricted ⚒ ⓕ

....

Hotel Ⓤ Holiday Inn Washington, Emerson District 5, WASHINGTON ☎ 0870 400 9084 138 en suite

BOLDON   Map 12 NZ36

Boldon Dipe Ln, East Boldon NE36 0PQ
☎ 0191 536 5360 & 0191 536 4182 🗎 0191 537 2270
e-mail: info@boldongolfclub.co.uk
18 holes, 6362yds, Par 72, SSS 70, Course record 67.
Course Designer Harry Varden **Location** S side of village off A184
Telephone for further details

....

Hotel ★★★ 68% Quality Hotel Sunderland, Witney Way, Boldon, SUNDERLAND ☎ 0191 519 1999 82 en suite

CHOPWELL   Map 12 NZ15

Garesfield NE17 7AP
☎ 01207 561309 🗎 01207 561309
e-mail: information@garesfieldgc.fsbusiness.co.uk
Undulating parkland course with good views and picturesque woodland surroundings.
18 holes, 6458yds, Par 72, SSS 70, Course record 68.
Club membership 697.
Visitors weekends after 4.30pm only, unless with member. Must contact in advance. **Societies** must contact secretary in advance. May play weekends only and max of 24 players. **Green Fees** terms on application. **Prof** David Race **Course Designer** Harry Fernie **Facilities** ⊗ ⑪ ⓛ 🍴 ♀ ⚒ 🏠 ⛳ 🚗 ⓕ **Conf** Corporate Hospitality Days available **Location** From A1 take A694 to Rowlands Gill. Turn right (signed Ryton) to High Spen. Turn left at Bute Arms for Chopwell

....

Hotel ★★★ 63% Quality Hotel Newcastle upon Tyne, Newgate St, NEWCASTLE UPON TYNE ☎ 0191 232 5025 93 en suite

FELLING   Map 12 NZ26

Heworth Gingling Gate, Heworth NE10 8XY
☎ 0191 469 4424 🗎 0191 469 9898
Fairly flat, parkland course.
18 holes, 6422yds, Par 71, SSS 71.
Club membership 800.
Visitors may not play Sat & before 10am Sun, Apr-Sep. **Societies** must apply in writing. **Green Fees** £20 per day. **Prof** Adrian Marshall **Facilities** ⊗ ⑪ ⓛ 🍴 ♀ ⚒ 🏠 ⛳ 🚗 ⓕ **Conf** fac available Corporate Hospitality Days available **Location** On A195, 0.5m NW of junc with A1(M)

....

Hotel Ⓤ Holiday Inn Washington, Emerson District 5, WASHINGTON ☎ 0870 400 9084 138 en suite

---

Use the maps at the back of the guide to help locate a golf course.

Booking a tee time is always advisable.

GATESHEAD — Map 12 NZ26

Ravensworth Angel View, Longbank, Wrekenton NE9 7NE ☎ 0191 487 6014 ▣ 0191 487 6014
e-mail: ravensworth.golfclub@virgin.net
Moorland/parkland course 600 ft above sea level with fine views. Testing 5th and 7th holes (par 3s).
18 holes, 5966yds, Par 69, SSS 69.
Club membership 700.
Visitors apply in advance. no weekends Apr-Sep. **Societies** apply in writing to secretary. **Green Fees** £22 weekdays. **Prof** Shaun Cowell **Course Designer** J W Fraser **Facilities** ⊗ ☶ 🛍 ♍ ♀ ⚐ ⛳ 🕯 🏌 🏖 ✎ **Conf** Corporate Hospitality Days available **Location** leave A1(M) at Junction for A167 (Angel of the North) take A1295 for 300 yds

....

Hotel ★★ 76% Eslington Villa Hotel, 8 Station Rd, Low Fell, GATESHEAD ☎ 0191 487 6017 & 420 0666
▣ 0191 420 0667 17 en suite

GOSFORTH — Map 12 NZ26

Gosforth Broadway East NE3 5ER
☎ 0191 285 3495 & 285 6710(catering) ▣ 0191 284 6274
e-mail: gosforth.golf@virgin.net
Parkland course with natural water hazards, easy walking.
18 holes, 6024yds, Par 69, SSS 68, Course record 62.
Club membership 500.
Visitors must contact in advance. Restricted play on competition days. **Societies** telephone in advance. **Green Fees** terms on application. **Prof** G Garland **Facilities** ⊗ 🕯
☶ 🛍 ♍ ♀ ⚐ 🏖 ✎ **Conf** Corporate Hospitality Days available **Location** N side of town centre off A6125

....

Hotel ★★★★ 78% Newcastle Marriott Hotel Gosforth Park, High Gosforth Park, Gosforth, NEWCASTLE UPON TYNE ☎ 0191 236 4111 178 en suite

Parklands Gosforth Park Golfing Complex, High Gosforth Park NE3 5HQ
☎ 0191 236 4480 ▣ 0191 236 3322
Parklands course is set in pleasant parkland with challenging shots around and sometimes over attractive water hazards. The first 9 holes are easier but the second 9 test even the most experienced golfer.
18 holes, 6013yds, Par 71, SSS 69, Course record 66.
Club membership 650.
Visitors a daily start sheet operates with bookings taken from 4.30pm the previous day during weekdays, and from 8am Fri & Sat for weekends. **Societies** by prior arrangement with club secretary. **Green Fees** terms on application. **Prof** Brian Rumney **Facilities** ⊗ 🕯 ☶ 🛍 ♍ ♀ ⚐ 🏖 ✎ ⚑ **Conf** Corporate Hospitality Days available **Location** 3m N, at the end A1 Western by Pass

....

Hotel ★★★★ 78% Newcastle Marriott Hotel Gosforth Park, High Gosforth Park, Gosforth, NEWCASTLE UPON TYNE ☎ 0191 236 4111 178 en suite

HOUGHTON-LE-SPRING — Map 12 NZ34

Elemore Elemore Ln, Hetton-le-Hole DH5 0QB
☎ 0191 517 3061 ▣ 0191 517 3054
Elmore course tests a player's ability in all aspects of the game, with drives over water as well as wedges. The greens are firm all year round and there are well positioned bunkers.
18 holes, 5947yds, Par 69, Course record 68.
Club membership 100. *Continued*

Visitors no restrictions. Phone to avoid society days.
Societies apply in writing, telephone enquiries welcome.
Green Fees not confirmed. **Course Designer** J Gaunt
Facilities ⊗ ☶ 🛍 ♍ ♀ ⚐ 🏌 🏖 ✎ **Location** 4m S of Houghton-Le-Spring on the A182

....

Hotel ★★ 66% Chilton Country Pub & Hotel, Black Boy Rd, Chilton Moor, Fencehouses, HOUGHTON-LE-SPRING ☎ 0191 385 2694 25 en suite

Houghton-le-Spring Copt Hill DH5 8LU
☎ 0191 584 1198 & 584 0048
18 holes, 6443yds, Par 72, SSS 71, Course record 64.
Location 0.5m E on B1404
Telephone for further details

....

Hotel ★★ 66% Chilton Country Pub & Hotel, Black Boy Rd, Chilton Moor, Fencehouses, HOUGHTON-LE-SPRING ☎ 0191 385 2694 25 en suite

NEWCASTLE UPON TYNE — Map 12 NZ26

City of Newcastle Three Mile Bridge NE3 2DR
☎ 0191 285 1775 ▣ 0191 2840700
e-mail: info@cityofnewcastlegolfclub.com
A well-manicured parkland course in the Newcastle suburbs.
18 holes, 6528yds, Par 72, SSS 71, Course record 64.
Club membership 600.
Visitors no restrictions but advisable to telephone first.
Societies telephone in advance **Green Fees** £34 per day; £28 per round (£35 weekends). **Prof** Steve McKenna **Course Designer** Harry Vardon **Facilities** ⊗ 🕯 ☶ 🛍 ♍ ♀ ⚐ 🏌 ✎ **Conf** Corporate Hospitality Days available **Location** 3m N on B1318

....

Hotel ★★★ 68% The Caledonian Hotel, Newcastle, 64 Osborne Rd, Jesmond, NEWCASTLE UPON TYNE
☎ 0191 281 7881 89 en suite

Newcastle United Ponteland Rd, Cowgate NE5 3JW
☎ 0191 286 9998
e-mail: info@www.nugc.co.uk
Moorland course with natural hazards.
18 holes, 6617yds, Par 69, SSS 72, Course record 66.
Club membership 650.
Visitors must play with member at weekends. **Societies** must contact in writing or telephone in advance. **Green Fees** not confirmed. **Course Designer** Various **Facilities** ⊗ 🕯 ☶ 🛍 ♍ ♀ ⚐ 🏌 🏖 ✎ **Leisure** Snooker table. **Location** 1.25m NW of city centre off A6127

....

Hotel ★★★ 68% The Caledonian Hotel, Newcastle, 64 Osborne Rd, Jesmond, NEWCASTLE UPON TYNE
☎ 0191 281 7881 89 en suite

Northumberland High Gosforth Park NE3 5HT
☎ 0191 236 2498 ▣ 0191 236 2036
e-mail: gun2446@aol.com
Many golf courses have been sited inside racecourses, although not so many survive today. One which does is the Northumberland Club's course at High Gosforth Park. Naturally the course is flat but there are plenty of mounds and other hazards to make it a fine test of golf. It should be said that not all the holes are within the confines of the racecourse, but both inside and out there are some good holes. This is a Championship course.
18 holes, 6683yds, Par 72, SSS 72, Course record 65.
Club membership 580. *Continued*

Visitors may not play at weekends or competition days. Must contact in advance. **Societies** must apply in writing or telephone. **Green Fees** £50 per day; £40 per round. **Course Designer** Colt/Braid **Facilities** ⊗ ⫼ ⯂ ▣ ♀ ⚲ ♂ **Conf** Corporate Hospitality Days available **Location** 4m N of city centre off A1

Hotel ★★★★ 78% Newcastle Marriott Hotel Gosforth Park, High Gosforth Park, Gosforth, NEWCASTLE UPON TYNE ☎ 0191 236 4111 178 en suite

Westerhope Whorlton Grance, Westerhope NE5 1PP
☎ 0191 286 7636 📄 0191 2146287

Attractive parkland course with tree-lined fairways, and easy walking. Good open views towards the airport.
18 holes, 6444yds, Par 72, SSS 71, Course record 64.
Club membership 778.
Visitors with member only at weekends and bank holidays.Must contact in advance. **Societies** must contact Secretary in advance. **Green Fees** £20 per round. **Cards** ▦ ▤ ▧ **Prof** Nigel Brown **Facilities** ⊗ ⫼ ⯂ ▣ ⚲ ⬛ ♈ ♂ **Location** 4.5m NW of city centre off B6324

Hotel ★★★★ 78% Newcastle Marriott Hotel Gosforth Park, High Gosforth Park, Gosforth, NEWCASTLE UPON TYNE ☎ 0191 236 4111 178 en suite

RYTON   Map 12 NZ16

Ryton Clara Vale NE40 3TD
☎ 0191 413 3737 📄 0191 413 1642
e-mail: secretary@rytongolfclub.co.uk
Parkland course.
18 holes, 5950yds, Par 70, SSS 69, Course record 67.
Club membership 600.
Visitors with member only at weekends. **Societies** apply in advance. **Green Fees** £25 per day; £20 per round (£22 per round weekends). **Facilities** ⊗ ⫼ ⯂ ▣ ♀ ⚲ **Location** NW side of town off A695

Hotel ★★★ 69% Gibside Hotel, Front St, WHICKHAM ☎ 0191 488 9292 45 en suite

Tyneside Westfield Ln NE40 3QE
☎ 0191 413 2742 📄 0191 413 2742
Open parkland course, water hazard, hilly, practice area.
18 holes, 6009yds, Par 70, SSS 69, Course record 65.
Club membership 641.
Visitors must contact in advance to play at weekends (after 5pm Sat, 3pm Sun) **Societies** must apply in advance. **Green Fees** terms on application. **Cards** ▦ ▤ ▧ **Prof** Malcolm Gunn **Course Designer** H S Colt **Facilities** ⊗ ⫼ ⯂ ▣ ♀ ⚲ ⬛ ♈ ♣ ♂ **Conf** Corporate Hospitality Days available **Location** NW side of town off A695

Hotel ★★★ 69% Gibside Hotel, Front St, WHICKHAM ☎ 0191 488 9292 45 en suite

SOUTH SHIELDS   Map 12 NZ36

South Shields Cleadon Hills NE34 8EG
☎ 0191 456 8942 📄 0191 456 8942
e-mail: thesecretary@south-shields-golf.freeserve.co.uk
A slightly undulating downland course on a limestone base ensuring good conditions underfoot. Open to strong winds, the course is testing but fair. There are fine views of the coastline.
18 holes, 6174yds, Par 71, SSS 70, Course record 64.

Club membership 700.
Visitors must contact in advance. **Societies** by arrangement. **Green Fees** £32-37 per day; £22-27 per round. **Prof** Glyn Jones **Course Designer** McKenzie-Braid **Facilities** ⊗ ⫼ ⯂ ▣ ♀ ⚲ ♂ **Conf** fac available **Location** SE side of town centre off A1300

Hotel ★★★ 65% Sea Hotel, Sea Rd, SOUTH SHIELDS ☎ 0191 427 0999 32 en suite

Whitburn Lizard Ln NE34 7AF
☎ 0191 529 4944 (Sec) 📄 0191 529 4944
e-mail: wgsec@ukonline.co.uk
Parkland course with sea views.
18 holes, 5899yds, Par 70, SSS 68, Course record 64.
Club membership 700.
Visitors restricted weekends & Tue. Contact professional in advance. **Societies** must apply in writing to secretary **Green Fees** terms on application. **Prof** David Stephenson **Course Designer** Colt, Alison & Morrison **Facilities** ⊗ ⫼ ⯂ ▣ ♀ ⚲ ♂ **Location** 2.5m SE off A183

Hotel ★★★★ 67% Sunderland Marriott Hotel, Queen's Pde, Seaburn, SUNDERLAND ☎ 0191 529 2041 82 en suite

SUNDERLAND   Map 12 NZ35

Ryhope Leechmore Way, Ryhope SR2 0DH
☎ 0191 523 7333
18 holes, 4601yds, Par 65, SSS 63.
Location 3.5m S of city centre
Telephone for further details

Hotel ★★★★ 67% Sunderland Marriott Hotel, Queen's Pde, Seaburn, SUNDERLAND ☎ 0191 529 2041 82 en suite

Wearside Coxgreen SR4 9JT
☎ 0191 534 2518 📄 0191 5346186

Open, undulating parkland course rolling down to the River Wear and beneath the shadow of the famous Penshaw Monument. Built on the lines of an Athenian temple it is a well-known landmark. Two ravines cross the course presenting a variety of challenging holes.
18 holes, 6373yds, Par 71, SSS 74, Course record 63.
Club membership 648.
Visitors may not play before 9.30am, between 12.30-1.30 or after 4pm. **Societies** must apply in writing. **Green Fees** terms on application. **Prof** Doug Brolls **Facilities** ⊗ ⫼ ⯂ ▣ ♀ ⚲ ♂ **Location** 3.5m W off A183

Hotel ★★★★ 67% Sunderland Marriott Hotel, Queen's Pde, Seaburn, SUNDERLAND ☎ 0191 529 2041 82 en suite

TYNEMOUTH   Map 12 NZ36

Tynemouth Spital Dene NE30 2ER
☎ 0191 257 4578 📄 0191 259 5193
e-mail: secretary@tynemouthgolfclub.com
Well-drained parkland course, not physically demanding but providing a strong challenge to both low and high handicap players.
18 holes, 6359yds, Par 70, SSS 70, Course record 66.
Club membership 800.
Visitors must play with member weekends & bank holidays. **Societies** must contact by telephone **Green Fees** £22.50 per 18 holes; £25 per day. **Cards** ▦ ▤ ▧

Continued   *Continued*

▓▓ ▒▒ ▣ **Prof** J P McKenna **Course Designer** Willie Park
Facilities ⊗ ﹖Ⅲ ┗ ▬ ♀ △ 🗄 ⛳ ⌖ ✦ **Location** 0.5m W

Hotel ★★★ 68% Grand Hotel, Grand Pde,
TYNEMOUTH ☎ 0191 293 6666 40 en suite
4 annexe en suite

WALLSEND   Map 12 NZ26

Wallsend Rheydt Av, Bigges Main NE28 8SU
☎ 0191 262 1973
Parkland course.
18 holes, 6571yds, Par 71, SSS 71, Course record 67.
Club membership 655.
Visitors may not play before 12.30pm weekends. Must
book in advance **Societies** must apply in writing. **Green
Fees** terms on application. **Prof** Ken Phillips **Course
Designer** A Snowball **Facilities** ┗ ▬ ♀ △ 🗄 ⌖ ❧
Location NW side of town centre off A193

Hotel ★★★ 68% The Caledonian Hotel, Newcastle, 64
Osborne Rd, Jesmond, NEWCASTLE UPON TYNE
☎ 0191 281 7881 89 en suite

WASHINGTON   Map 12 NZ25

**George Washington Hotel Golf & Country
Club** Stone Cellar Rd, High Usworth, District 12
NE37 1PH ☎ 0191 4178346 ▤ 0191 4151166
**A championship standard course with tree lined
fairways offering a feeling of seclusion even on busy
days.**
18 holes, 6604yds, Par 73, SSS 72, Course record 68.
Club membership 500.
Visitors all tee times must be reserved. members only
before 10.30 am Sat. **Societies** book in advance. **Green
Fees** £20 (£25 weekends). **Cards** 🔲 🔲 🔲 ▒▒ ▣ **Prof**
David Patterson **Course Designer** Eric Watson **Facilities**
⊗ ﹖Ⅲ ┗ ▬ ♀ △ 🗄 ⛳ 🛒 ♿ ▬ ⌖ ✦ **Leisure** heated
indoor swimming pool, squash, sauna, solarium,
gymnasium, 9 hole par 3 course. **Conf** fac available
Corporate Hospitality Days available **Location** From A195
signed Washington North take last exit on rdbt, then right
at mini-rdbt

Hotel ★★★ 66% George Washington Golf & Country
Club, Stone Cellar Rd, High Usworth, WASHINGTON
☎ 0191 402 9988 103 en suite

WHICKHAM   Map 12 NZ26

Whickham Hollinside Park, Fellside Rd NE16 5BA
☎ 0191 488 1577 ▤ 0191 488 1576
**Undulating parkland course with attractive panoramic
views.**
18 holes, 5878yds, Par 68, SSS 68, Course record 61.
Club membership 660.
Visitors must contact Professional in advance. **Societies** by
arrangement. **Green Fees** terms on application. **Prof**
Andrew Hall **Facilities** ⊗ ﹖Ⅲ by prior arrangement ┗ ▬ ♀
△ 🗄 ♿ ⌖ ✦ **Location** 1.5m S

Hotel ★★★ 69% Gibside Hotel, Front St, WHICKHAM
☎ 0191 488 9292 45 en suite

WHITLEY BAY   Map 12 NZ37

Whitley Bay Claremont Rd NE26 3UF
☎ 0191 252 0180 ▤ 0191 297 0030
e-mail: secretary@whitleybaygolfclub.co.uk
An 18-hole links type course, close to the sea, with a

stream running through the undulating terrain.
18 holes, 6579yds, Par 71, SSS 71, Course record 66.
Club membership 800.
Visitors may not play Sat, telephone for Sun play.
Advisable to contact in advance. **Societies** telephone
initially. **Green Fees** £33 per day; £24 per round (weekend
£35 per round). **Prof** Gary Shipley **Facilities** ⊗ ﹖Ⅲ ┗ ▬ ♀
△ 🗄 ♿ ✦ **Location** NW side of town centre off A1148

Hotel ★★★ 72% Windsor Hotel, South Pde, WHITLEY
BAY ☎ 0191 251 8888 70 en suite

⬛⬛⬛ WARWICKSHIRE ⬛⬛⬛

ATHERSTONE   Map 04 SP39

Atherstone The Outwoods, Coleshill Rd CV9 2RL
☎ 01827 713110 ▤ 01827 715686
**Scenic parkland course, established in 1894 and laid out
on hilly ground.**
*Atherstone Golf Club: 18 holes, 6006yds, Par 72, SSS 70,
Course record 68.*
Club membership 495.
Visitors handicap certificate required. With member only
weekends and bank holidays but not Sun except holders of
handicap certificate by permission of Club Secretary.
Societies contact Secretary in advance (01827 892568).
Green Fees £25 per day/round. **Course Designer** Hawtree
& Gaunt Mornoch **Facilities** ⊗ ﹖Ⅲ ┗ ▬ ♀ △ ⌖ ✦ **Conf**
Corporate Hospitality Days available **Location** 0.5m S off
the A5 onto B4116

Hotel ⬧ Travelodge, Green Ln, TAMWORTH
☎ 08700 850 950 0800 850950 ▤ 01525 878450
62 en suite

BIDFORD-ON-AVON   Map 04 SP15

Bidford Grange Stratford Rd B50 4LY
☎ 01789 490319 ▤ 01789 490998
18 holes, 7233yds, Par 72, SSS 74, Course record 66.
Location 4m W of Stratford upon Avon, B439
Telephone for further details

Hotel ★★★ 74% Salford Hall Hotel, ABBOT'S
SALFORD ☎ 01386 871300 14 en suite
19 annexe en suite

BRANDON   Map 04 SP47

City of Coventry-Brandon Wood Brandon Ln,
Wolston CV8 3GQ ☎ 024 76543141 ▤ 024 76545108
**Municipal parkland course surrounded by fields and
bounded by River Avon on east side. Floodlit driving
range.**
18 holes, 6610yds, Par 72, SSS 71, Course record 68.
Club membership 400.
Visitors telephone for details, advance booking
recommended. **Societies** telephone secretary for details
Green Fees terms on application. **Cards** 🔲 🔲 🔲 ▒▒ ▣
Prof Chris Gledhill **Facilities** ⊗ ┗ ▬ ♀ △ 🗄 ♿ ▬ ✦
❧ **Leisure** Pitching area. **Location** Off A45 southbound

Hotel ★★★ 66% Brandon Hall, Main St, BRANDON
☎ 0870 400 8105 60 en suite

Continued

COLESHILL   Map 04 SP28

Maxstoke Park Castle Ln B46 2RD

☎ 01675 466743 ▤ 01675 466185
e-mail: sec@maxstonepark.fsnet.co.uk
Parkland course with easy walking. Numerous trees and a lake form natural hazards.
18 holes, 6442yds, Par 71, SSS 71, Course record 64.
Club membership 720.
Visitors with member only at weekends & bank holidays.
Societies contact in advance. **Green Fees** £27.50 per 18 holes (weekdays only). **Prof** Neil McEwan **Course Designer** various **Facilities** ⊗ ⋌ ℔ ♥ ♀ ⏚ 🏠 ⛳ ❯ 🚜
⛳ Conf Corporate Hospitality Days available **Location** 3m NE of Coleshill on B4114 turn right for Maxstoke then 1m on right

Hotel ★★★ 66% Grimstock Country House Hotel, Gilson Rd, Gilson, COLESHILL ☎ 01675 462121 & 462161 ▤ 01675 467646 44 en suite

HENLEY-IN-ARDEN   Map 04 SP16

Henley Golf & Country Club Birmingham Rd

B95 5QA ☎ 01564 793715 ▤ 01564 795754
e-mail: enquiries@henleygcc.co.uk
This improving course is maturing well and provides a good golfing challenge for all handicaps. All facilities recently upgraded.
18 holes, 6933yds, Par 73, SSS 73.
Club membership 675.
Visitors may book up to 7 days in advance. **Societies** apply in writing or telephone in advance. **Green Fees** £39 per day, £26 per round (weekends £45/£32). **Cards** 🖭 🖭 🖭 🖭 🖭 🖭 **Prof** Neale Hyde **Course Designer** N Selwyn Smith **Facilities** ⊗ ⋌ ℔ ♥ ♀ ⏚ 🏠 ❯ 🚜 ⛳ ❯
Leisure hard tennis courts, 9 hole par 3 course, beauty salon. **Conf** fac available Corporate Hospitality Days available **Location** On A3400 Birmingham to Stratford road, just N of Henley-in-Arden

Hotel ★★★ 64% Quality Hotel Redditch, Pool Bank, Southcrest, REDDITCH ☎ 01527 541511 73 en suite

KENILWORTH   Map 04 SP27

Kenilworth Crewe Ln CV8 2EA

☎ 01926 858517 ▤ 01926 864453
e-mail: secretary@kenilworthgolfclub.co.uk
Parkland course in open hilly situation. Club founded in 1889.
18 holes, 6400yds, Par 73, SSS 71, Course record 62.
Club membership 755.
Visitors must contact in advance. **Societies** apply in writing. **Green Fees** £35 per day/round (weekends £45).
Cards 🖭 🖭 🖭 🖭 🖭 🖭 **Prof** Steve Yates **Course Designer** Hawtree **Facilities** ⊗ ⋌ ℔ ♥ ♀ ⏚ 🏠 ❯ 🚜
⛳ Leisure Par 3 chipping green. **Conf** fac available Corporate Hospitality Days available **Location** 0.5m NE

LEA MARSTON   Map 04 SP29

Lea Marston Hotel & Leisure Complex

Haunch Ln B76 0BY
☎ 01675 470468 ▤ 01675 470871
e-mail: info@leamarstonhotel.co.ukr
The Marston Lakes course was completed in June 2000 and opened April 2001. The layout includes many water and sand hazards through undulating parkland. While short by modern standards, it is a good test for even low

Continued

handicap players, requiring virtually everything in the bag. Tees and greens have been built to championship course specifications.

Lea Marston Hotel & Leisure Complex

Marston Lakes: 9 holes, 2054yds, Par 31, SSS 30.
Club membership 150.
Visitors book in advance and dress code applies. **Societies** must telephone in advance. **Green Fees** Mon-Thu: £12.50 per 18 holes, £7.50 per 9 holes (£16/£12.50 Fri-Sun and bank holidays). **Cards** 🖭 🖭 🖭 🖭 🖭 🖭 **Prof** Darren Lewis **Course Designer** Contour Golf **Facilities** ⊗ ⋌ ℔ ♥ ♀ ⏚ 🏠 ❯ 🚜 ⛳ ❯ **Leisure** hard tennis courts, heated indoor swimming pool, sauna, solarium, gymnasium, golf simulator. **Conf** fac available Corporate Hospitality Days available **Location** From M42 take the A4097 to Kingsbury. Turn right after 1 mile and golf club is signposted 1.5m on right

Hotel ★★★★ 67% Lea Marston Hotel & Leisure Complex, Haunch Ln, LEA MARSTON ☎ 01675 470468 80 en suite. See advert on page 254

LEAMINGTON SPA   Map 04 SP36

Leamington & County Golf Ln, Whitnash

CV31 2QA ☎ 01926 425961 ▤ 01926 425961
e-mail: secretary@leamingtongolf.co.uk
Undulating parkland course with extensive views.
18 holes, 6418yds, Par 72, SSS 71, Course record 65.
Club membership 854.
Visitors must contact in advance. **Societies** telephone in advance. **Green Fees** £35 per round (£40 per round weekends). **Cards** 🖭 🖭 🖭 **Prof** Julian Mellor **Course Designer** H S Colt **Facilities** ⊗ ⋌ ℔ ♥ ♀ ⏚ 🏠 ❯ 🚜 ⛳
Leisure snooker. **Conf** Corporate Hospitality Days available **Location** 10 mins from M40, S side of town centre

Hotel ★★★ 70% Courtyard by Marriott Leamington Spa, Olympus Av, Tachbrook Park, ROYAL LEAMINGTON SPA ☎ 01926 425522 91 en suite

Newbold Comyn Newbold Ter East CV32 4EW

☎ 01926 421157
Municipal parkland course with hilly front nine. The par 4 9th is a 467-yd testing hole. The back nine holes are rather flat but include two par 5s. Presently undergoing extensive upgrade.
18 holes, 6315yds, Par 70, SSS 70, Course record 69.
Club membership 280.
Visitors no restrictions. **Societies** apply to professional.
Green Fees 18 holes £10.25; 9 holes £6 (weekends £12.70; £9.80). **Cards** 🖭 🖭 🖭 **Prof** Ricky Carvell
Facilities ⊗ ⋌ ℔ ♥ ♀ ⏚ 🏠 ❯ ⛳ **Leisure** heated indoor swimming pool, gymnasium. **Location** 0.75m E of town centre off B4099

Continued

Lea Marston is a superb venue for a relaxing golf break. The Marston Lakes course flows across undulating parkland and features many beautifully designed water and sand hazards, creating an enjoyable test for golfers of all abilities. There is also a magnificent Par 3 Academy course, floodlit driving range, indoor Smart Golf Simulator and a putting green. Guests can also enjoy complimentary use of the health club including indoor pool, sauna and gymnasium.

Haunch Lane, Lea Marston, Sutton Coldfield, Warwickshire B76 0BY
Tel:01675 470468 Fax: 01675 470871
www.leamarstonhotel.co.uk
e-mail: info@leamarstonhotel.co.uk

....
Hotel ★★★ 65% The Best Western Royal Leamington Hotel, 64 Upper Holly Walk, LEAMINGTON SPA ☎ 01926 883777 32 en suite

LEEK WOOTTON   Map 04 SP26

The Warwickshire CV35 7QT
☎ 01926 409409 🖹 01926 408409
e-mail: b.fotheringham@clubhaus.com
Designed by Karl Litten, the 36 holes are laid out as four loops of 9 holes to create 2 championship standard courses. Each 9 has its own character: parkland, woodland, inland links and Americano. The place for golfers of any age or ability.
East South Course: 18 holes, 7000yds, Par 72, SSS 72, Course record 68.
North West Course: 18 holes, 7421yds, Par 74, SSS 73, Course record 70.
Club membership 1500.
Visitors can book up to 7 days in advance. **Societies** apply to sales office for details. **Green Fees** Mon-Thu £39 per 18 holes; Fri-Sun £49 (£23 with member). **Cards** 🌐 📇 📇 🌑 🔄 **Prof** Mark Dulson **Course Designer** Karl Litten **Facilities** ⊗ ⫻ 🏌 🛒 ♈ 🔄 ⛳ ✆ **Location** 1m from Kenilworth on B4115

....
Hotel ★★★★ 63% The Chesford Grange Hotel, Chesford Bridge, KENILWORTH ☎ 01926 859331 210 en suite 9 annexe en suite

> **If the name of the club appears in *italics*, details have not been confirmed for this edition of the guide.**

NUNEATON   Map 04 SP39

Nuneaton Golf Dr, Whitestone CV11 6QF
☎ 024 7634 7810 🖹 024 7632 7563
e-mail: sec.nuneatongc@ukonline.co.uk
Undulating parkland and woodland course with silver birch lining the fairways. Easy walking.
18 holes, 6429yds, Par 71, SSS 71.
Club membership 700.
Visitors must produce evidence of membership of a recognised golf club or society, with member only at weekends. **Societies** apply in writing. **Green Fees** not confirmed. **Prof** Jon Salter **Facilities** ⊗ ⫻ 🏌 🛒 ♈ 🔄 🏠 ⛳ **Location** 2m SE off B4114

....
Hotel ★★★ 65% Weston Hall Hotel, Weston Ln, Bulkington, NUNEATON ☎ 024 7631 2989 40 en suite

Oakridge Arley Ln, Ansley Village CV10 9PH
☎ 01676 541389 & 540542 🖹 01676 542709
e-mail: admin@oakridgegolf.fsnet.co.uk
There are a number of water hazards on the back nine which add to the natural beauty of the countryside. The undulating course is affected by winter cross winds on several holes. Overall it will certainly test golfing skills.
18 holes, 6242yds, Par 71, SSS 70.
Club membership 500.
Visitors contact in advance, with members only at weekends. **Societies** apply in writing or telephone in advance. **Green Fees** £16 per day. **Cards** 🌐 📇 📇 🌑 **Course Designer** Algy Jayes **Facilities** ⊗ ⫻ 🏌 🛒 ♈ 🔄 🏠 ⛳ **Conf** Corporate Hospitality Days available **Location** 4m W

....
Hotel ★★★ 65% Weston Hall Hotel, Weston Ln, Bulkington, NUNEATON ☎ 024 7631 2989 40 en suite

Purley Chase Pipers Ln, Ridge Ln CV10 0RB
☎ 024 7639 3118 🖹 024 7639 8015
e-mail: enquiries@purley-chase.co.uk
Meadowland course with tricky water hazards on eight holes and undulating greens.
18 holes, 6772yds, Par 72, SSS 72, Course record 64.
Club membership 550.
Visitors welcome weekends after 12 noon and Mon-Fri. **Societies** telephone for provisional booking (Mon-Fri only). **Green Fees** terms on application. **Cards** 🌐 📇 📇 🌑 **Prof** Gary Carver **Facilities** ⊗ ⫻ 🏌 🛒 ♈ 🔄 🏠 ⛳ **Conf** fac available Corporate Hospitality Days available **Location** 2m NW off B4114

....
Hotel ★★★ 65% Weston Hall Hotel, Weston Ln, Bulkington, NUNEATON ☎ 024 7631 2989 40 en suite

RUGBY   Map 04 SP57

Rugby Clifton Rd CV21 3RD
☎ 01788 542306 (Sec) & 575134 (Pro) 🖹 01788 542306
e-mail: golf@rugbygc.fsnet.co.uk
Parkland course with brook running through the middle and crossed by a viaduct. Testing course, with emphasis on accuracy over length.
18 holes, 5457yds, Par 68, SSS 67, Course record 60.
Club membership 700.
Visitors weekends & bank holidays with member only. **Societies** apply in writing. **Green Fees** £25 per day, £20 per round. £50 per week. **Prof** Nat Summers **Facilities** ⊗ ⫻ 🏌 🛒 ♈ 🔄 🏠 ⛳ **Location** 1m NE on B5414, on Rugby to Clifton Road

Continued

The De Vere Belfry

Map 07 SP19

Wishaw

☎ **01675 470301** 📄 **01675 470178**

The Belfry is unique as the only venue to have staged the biggest golf event in the world, the Ryder Cup Matches, an unprecedented four times, most recently in 2002. The Brabazon is regarded throughout the world as a great championship course with some of the most demanding holes in golf; world famous holes like the 10th (Ballesteros's Hole) and the 18th with its dangerous lakes and its amphitheatre around the final green. These remained intact during the £2.4 million redevelopment in 1998 which made the course even more testing. Alternatively, you can pit your wits against a new legend in the making, the PGA National Course, which has won plaudits from near and far. The Dave Thomas/Peter Alliss designed course has been used for professional competition and is already established as one of Britain's leading courses. For those who like their golf a little easier or like to get back into the swing gently, the Derby is ideal and can be played by golfers of any standard. The Bel Air nightclub, the De Vere Club leisure centre and the Aqua Spa with its fire and ice bio-thermal treatments offer unique experiences away from the golf course.

e-mail: enquiries@thebelfry.com

Visitors Handicap certificate is required for the Brabazon and PGA courses (24 or better for gentlemen, 32 or better for ladies and juniors).
Reservations 24 hrs in advance for non-residents

Societies Must telephone in advance

Green Fees Prices on application - dependent on season.

Facilities ⊗ 🍴 🏪 ☕ 🍺 🏌 🛏 ⚘ 🏠 🍵 🐴 🚃 ✏ 🏌

Conf Facilities Available.

Professional Simon Wordsworth

Leisure Tennis, squash, swimming, sauna, solarium, gymnasium, PGA National Golf Academy

Location Wishaw B76 9PR
(exit J9 M42, 4m E on A446)

Holes/Par/Course record Brabazon: 18 holes, 6724 yds, Par 72, SSS 71
Derby: 18 holes, 6057 yds, Par 69, SSS 69
PGA: 18 holes, 6639 yds, Par 71, SSS 70

WHERE TO STAY NEARBY

Hotels
WISHAW

★★★★ 🏵 74%
The De Vere Belfry, Lichfield Rd.
☎ 01675 470301. 324 en suite

LEA MARSTON

★★★ 67%
Lea Marston Hotel and Leisure Complex, B76 0BY.
☎ 01675 470468. 80 en suite

SUTTON COLDFIELD

★★★★ 68% Moor Hall Hotel, Four Oaks, B75 6LN
☎ 0121 308 3751.
82 en suite

Championship Course

Hotel ★★★ 64% Grosvenor Hotel Rugby, 81-87 Clifton Rd, RUGBY ☎ 01788 535686 26 en suite

Whitefields Hotel Golf & Country Club

Coventry Rd, Thurlaston CV23 9JR
☎ 01788 815555 & 817777 📄 01788 817777
e-mail: mail@whitefields-hotel.co.uk
Whitefields has superb natural drainage. There are many water features and the 13th has a stunning dog-leg 442yard par 4 with a superb view across Draycote Water. The 16th is completely surrounded by water and is particularly difficult.

18 holes, 6289yds, Par 71, SSS 70, Course record 66. Club membership 400.
Visitors advisable to book unless hotel guest, available 7 days, contact secretary on 01788 815555. **Societies** contact secretary in advance. brochure available **Green Fees** terms on application. **Cards** 🌐 💳 💳 💳 💳 🅾 **Prof** Mario Luca **Course Designer** Reg Mason **Facilities** ⊗ ⏶ 🏌 🍴 ♀ ⚘ 🏠 🍴 🐎 🐾 🚃 ♂ ⚘ **Conf** fac available Corporate Hospitality Days available **Location** Junct of M45 where it meets the A45 Coventry road, near Dunchurch

Hotel ★★ 69% The Golden Lion Inn, Easenhall, RUGBY ☎ 01788 832265 12 en suite

STONELEIGH   Map 04 SP37

Stoneleigh Deer Park

The Clubhouse, The Old Deer Park, Coventry Rd CV8 3DR
☎ 024 76639991 & 76639912 📄 024 76511533
Parkland course in old deer park with many mature trees. The River Avon meanders through the course and comes into play on 4 holes. Also 9-hole course.
Tantara Course: 18 holes, 6023yds, Par 71, SSS 69, Course record 67.
Avon Course: 9 holes, 1251yds, Par 27.
Club membership 800.
Visitors must contact in advance. **Societies** by prior arrangement. **Green Fees** terms on application. **Cards** 🌐 💳 💳 🅾 **Prof** Matt McGuire & Sarah Perkins **Facilities** ⊗ ⏶ 🏌 🍴 ♀ ⚘ 🏠 🍴 🐎 ♂ **Location** 3m NE of Kenilworth

Hotel ★★★★ 62% De Montfort Hotel, Abbey End, KENILWORTH ☎ 01926 855944 108 en suite

STRATFORD-UPON-AVON   Map 04 SP25

Menzies Welcombe Hotel

Warwick Rd CV37 0NR ☎ 01789 295252 📄 01789 414666
e-mail: sales@welcombe.co.uk
Wooded parkland course of great character and boasting superb views of the River Avon, Stratford and

the Cotswolds. Set within the hotel's 157-acre estate, it has two lakes and other water features.
18 holes, 6288yds, Par 70, SSS 69, Course record 64.
Visitors must contact in advance. **Societies** booking via Hotel or golf clubhouse. Write, phone or e-mail in advance, **Green Fees** terms on application. **Cards** 🌐 💳 💳 💳 💳 🅾 **Prof** Matt Nixon **Course Designer** Thomas Macauley **Facilities** ⊗ ⏶ 🏌 🍴 ♀ ⚘ 🏠 🍴 🐎 🐾 🚃 ♂ ⚘ **Leisure** hard tennis courts, fishing, solarium, gymnasium, golf lessons for individual/groups/company days. **Conf** fac available Corporate Hospitality Days available **Location** 1.5m NE off A46, follow signs to Stratford-upon-Avon

Hotel ★★★★ 72% Menzies Welcombe Hotel and Golf Course, Warwick Rd, STRATFORD-UPON-AVON ☎ 01789 295252 65 en suite

Stratford Oaks

Bearley Rd, Snitterfield CV37 0EZ
☎ 01789 731980 📄 01789 731981
e-mail: admin@stratfordoaks.co.uk
American styled, level parkland course with some water features designed by Howard Swan.
18 holes, 6135yds, Par 71, SSS 69, Course record 61. Club membership 700.
Visitors contact in advance. **Societies** telephone in advance. **Green Fees** £23 (£28 weekends). **Cards** 🌐 💳 💳 🅾 **Prof** Andrew Dunbar **Course Designer** H Swann **Facilities** ⊗ ⏶ 🏌 🍴 ♀ ⚘ 🏠 🍴 ♂ ⚘ **Leisure** gymnasium, massage and physiotherapy facility. **Location** 4m N of Stratford-upon-Avon

Hotel ★★★★ 70% Stratford Manor, Warwick Rd, STRATFORD-UPON-AVON ☎ 01789 731173 104 en suite

Continued

Stratford-upon-Avon Tiddington Rd CV37 7BA
☎ 01789 205749 ▤ 414909
e-mail: sec@stratfordgolf.co.uk
Beautiful parkland course. The par 3 16th is tricky and the par 5 17th and 18th provide a tough end.
18 holes, 6311yds, Par 72, SSS 70, Course record 63.
Club membership 750.
Visitors may not play before 11.00am weekends. Phone in advance. **Societies** must apply in advance. Tues & Thurs only. **Green Fees** not confirmed. **Prof** D Sutherland **Course Designer** Taylor **Facilities** ⊗ ⟩ℿ ⮂ ⯑ ♟ ⯑ ♿ 🏌 **Location** 0.75m E on B4086

Hotel ★★★★ 65% The Alveston Manor, Clopton Bridge, STRATFORD-UPON-AVON ☎ 0870 400 8181 113 en suite

TANWORTH IN ARDEN   Map 07 SP17

Ladbrook Park Poolhead Ln B94 5ED
☎ 01564 742264 ▤ 01564 742909
e-mail: secretary@ladbrookparkgolfclub.fsnet.co.uk
Parkland course lined with trees.
18 holes, 6427yds, Par 71, SSS 71, Course record 65.
Club membership 700.
Visitors welcome weekdays, with member at weekends. Must contact in advance & have handicap certificate. **Societies** apply in advance. **Green Fees** £43 per 36 holes, £35 per 28 holes, £28 per 18 holes. **Cards** ▥ ▤ ▨ 🛇 **Prof** Richard Mountford **Course Designer** H S Colt **Facilities** ⊗ ⟩ℿ ⮂ ⯑ ♟ ⯑ 🏌 **Location** 2.5m SE of M42 junct 3

Hotel ★★★ ⛺ Nuthurst Grange Country House Hotel, Nuthurst Grange Ln, HOCKLEY HEATH ☎ 01564 783972 15 en suite

UPPER BRAILES   Map 04 SP33

Brailes Sutton Ln, Lower Brailes OX15 5BB
☎ 01608 685633 ▤ 01608 685205
e-mail: office@brailes-golf-club.co.uk
Undulating meadowland on 105 acres of Cotswold countryside. Sutton Brook passes through the course and must be crossed five times. The par 5 17th offers the most spectacular view of three counties from the tee. Challenging par 3 short holes. Suitable for golfers of all standards.
18 holes, 6304yds, Par 71, SSS 70, Course record 67.
Club membership 600.
Visitors must telephone in advance on 01608 685633. **Societies** telephone or write for information to the General Manager. **Green Fees** £35 per day, £25 per round (£35 per round weekends) Winter: £18/£25 (£25). **Cards** ▥ ▤ ▨ 🛇 **Prof** Alistair Brown **Course Designer** B A Hull **Facilities** ⊗ ⟩ℿ ⮂ ⯑ ♟ ⯑ 🏌 ⚲ **Location** 4m E of Shipston-on-Stour, on B4035, towards Banbury

Inn ♦♦♦♦ The Red Lion Hotel, Main St, Long Compton, SHIPSTON ON STOUR ☎ 01608 684221 5 en suite

WARWICK   Map 04 SP26

Warwick The Racecourse CV34 6HW
☎ 01926 494316
Parkland course with easy walking. Driving range with floodlit bays.
9 holes, 2682yds, Par 34, SSS 66, Course record 67.
Club membership 150.
Visitors must contact in advance. May not play Sun before

Continued

12.30pm **Societies** contact in advance. **Green Fees** terms on application. **Prof** Mario Luca **Course Designer** D G Dunkley **Facilities** ⯑ ♟ ⮂ ⯑ ♿ 🏌 **Location** W side of town centre

Hotel ★★ 63% Warwick Arms Hotel, 17 High St, WARWICK ☎ 01926 492759 35 en suite

WISHAW   See page 255

WISHAW   Map 07 SP19

Wishaw Bulls Ln B76 9QW
☎ 0121 313 2110 ▤ 0121 351 7498
Parkland course with one hill on course at 9th and 18th holes. Course well drained with irrigation on tees and greens.
18 holes, 5729yards, Par 70, SSS 68, Course record 67.
Club membership 338.
Visitors telephone for details **Societies** telephone to book. **Green Fees** terms on application. **Cards** ▥ ▤ ▨ ▩ 🛇 **Prof** Alan Partridge **Course Designer** R. Wallis **Facilities** ⊗ ⟩ℿ ⮂ ⯑ ♟ ⯑ ♿ 🏌 ⚲ **Conf** fac available Corporate Hospitality Days available **Location** M42 J9, take A4097 towards Cordworth, 1m from White Horse Pub

Hotel ★★★★ 67% Lea Marston Hotel & Leisure Complex, Haunch Ln, LEA MARSTON ☎ 01675 470468 80 en suite

WEST MIDLANDS

ALDRIDGE   Map 07 SK00

Druids Heath Stonnall Rd WS9 8JZ
☎ 01922 455595 (Office) ▤ 01922 452887
Testing, undulating heathland course. Large greens.
18 holes, 6661yds, Par 72, SSS 73, Course record 68.
Club membership 660.
Visitors contact in advance recommended. Weekend play permitted after 2pm, not bank holidays. **Societies** phone initially. **Green Fees** £32 per day (£38 weekends after 2pm) (with member £10 & £15). **Prof** Glenn Williams **Facilities** ⊗ ⟩ℿ ⮂ ⯑ ♟ ⮂ 🏌 **Leisure** snooker. **Location** NE side of town centre off A454

Hotel ★★★ 76% The Fairlawns at Aldridge, 178 Little Aston Rd, Aldridge, WALSALL ☎ 01922 455122 50 en suite

BIRMINGHAM   Map 07 SP08

Alison Nicholas Golf Academy Host Centre, Queslett Park, Great Barr B42 2RG
☎ 0121 360 7600 ▤ 0121 360 7603
e-mail: info@ the hostcorporation.com
This golf academy consists of a 9 hole short game improvement course, a covered floodlit driving range and teaching and training facilities.
9 holes, 905yds, Par 27, SSS 27, Course record 21.
Club membership 800.
Visitors no restrictions **Societies** apply in advance by telephone or in writing. **Green Fees** terms on application. **Cards** ▥ ▤ ▨ ▩ 🛇 **Prof** Gary Broadbent **Course Designer** Alison Nicholas/Francis Colella **Facilities** ⊗ ⮂ ⯑ ♟ ⮂ 🏌 **Conf** fac available **Location** off M6 junct 7

Hotel ⛢ Express by Holiday Inn Birmingham North, Birmingham Rd, Great Barr, BIRMINGHAM ☎ 0121 358 4044 32 en suite

Brandhall Heron Rd, Oldbury, Warley B68 8AQ
☎ 0121 552 2195
18 holes, 5734yds, Par 70, SSS 68, Course record 66.
Location 5.5m W of Birmingham city centre off A4123
Telephone for further details

Hotel Ⓤ Holiday Inn Birmingham, Chapel Ln, Great Barr, BIRMINGHAM ☎ 0870 400 9009 192 en suite

Cocks Moors Woods Alcester Rd South, Kings Heath B14 4ER ☎ 0121 464 3584 ▤ 0121 441 1305
18 holes, 5769yds, Par 69, SSS 68.
Location 4m N of M42 junct 3 on A435
Telephone for further details

Hotel Ⓤ Holiday Inn Birmingham City, Smallbrook Queensway, BIRMINGHAM ☎ 0870 400 9008 280 en suite

Edgbaston Church Rd, Edgbaston B15 3TB
☎ 0121 454 1736 ▤ 0121 454 2395
e-mail: secretary@edgbastongc.co.uk
Set in 144 acres of woodland, lake and parkland, two miles from the centre of Birmingham, this delightful course utilises the wealth of natural features to provide a series of testing and adventurous holes set in the traditional double loop that starts directly in front of the clubhouse, an imposing Georgian mansion.
18 holes, 6106yds, Par 69, SSS 69, Course record 63.
Club membership 970.
Visitors recommended to contact in advance through golf reservations, must have handicap certificate. Most weekends pm. **Societies** must apply in writing. **Green Fees** terms on application. **Cards** ▦ ▦ **Prof** Jamie Cundy **Course Designer** H S Colt **Facilities** ⊗ ⫴ ⬧ ♥ ♀ ⚐ ⌂ ↑ ⚲ ⚑ ⚡ **Conf** fac available Corporate Hospitality Days available **Location** 2m S of city centre on B4217 off A38

Hotel ★★★ 64% The Plough & Harrow Hotel, 135 Hagley Rd, EDGBASTON ☎ 0870 609 6118 44 en suite

Great Barr Chapel Ln, Great Barr B43 7BA
☎ 0121 357 5270
Parkland course with easy walking. Pleasant views of Barr Beacon National Park.
18 holes, 6523yds, Par 72, SSS 72, Course record 67.
Club membership 600.
Visitors no visitors at weekends. **Societies** must contact in writing. **Green Fees** terms on application. **Prof** Richard Spragg **Facilities** ⊗ by prior arrangement ⫴ by prior arrangement ⬧ ♥ ♀ ⚐ ⌂ ⚡ **Location** 6m N of city centre off A 34

Hotel Ⓤ Holiday Inn Birmingham, Chapel Ln, Great Barr, BIRMINGHAM ☎ 0870 400 9009 192 en suite

Handsworth 11 Sunningdale Close, Handsworth Wood B20 1NP
☎ 0121 554 0599 & 554 3387 ▤ 0121 554 3387
e-mail: info@handsworthgolfclub.net
Undulating parkland course with some tight fairways and strategic bunkering.
18 holes, 6267yds, Par 70, SSS 71, Course record 64.
Club membership 730.
Visitors restricted weekends, bank holidays & Xmas. Must contact in advance and have a handicap certificate. **Societies** must contact in advance. **Green Fees** £35 per day. **Prof** Lee Bashford **Course Designer** H. S. Colt

Facilities ⊗ ⫴ ⬧ ♥ ♀ ⚐ ⌂ ⚲ ⚡ **Leisure** squash.
Location 3.5m NW of city centre off A4040

Hotel ⓣ Travel Inn, New Gas St, WEST BROMWICH ☎ 08701 977264 40 en suite

Harborne 40 Tennal Rd, Harborne B32 2JE
☎ 0121 427 3058 ▤ 0121 427 4039
e-mail: harborne@hgolf.fsnet.co.uk
Parkland course in hilly situation, with a brook running through.
18 holes, 6230yds, Par 70, SSS 70, Course record 65.
Club membership 600.
Visitors must have handicap certificate, contact in advance, may not play weekends except with member, Ladies have priority Tue. **Societies** Mon, Wed-Fri apply to secretary, by phone or letter. **Green Fees** £30 per 36/18 holes. **Prof** Paul Johnson **Course Designer** Harry Colt **Facilities** ⊗ ⫴ ⬧ ♥ ♀ ⚐ ⌂ ↑ ⚡ **Location** 3.5 m SW of city centre off A4040

Hotel ★★★ 64% The Plough & Harrow Hotel, 135 Hagley Rd, EDGBASTON ☎ 0870 609 6118 44 en suite

Harborne Church Farm Vicarage Rd, Harborne B17 0SN ☎ 0121 427 1204 ▤ 0121 428 3126
Parkland course with water hazards and easy walking. Some holes might prove difficult.
9 holes, 4882yds, Par 66, SSS 64, Course record 62.
Club membership 130.
Visitors must contact in advance. **Societies** must telephone in advance. **Green Fees** £9 per 18 holes; £6 per 9 holes (£10.50/£7 weekends). **Cards** ▦ ▦ ▦ ▦ ▦ ▦ **Prof** Paul Johnson **Facilities** ⊗ ⫴ ⬧ ♥ ♀ ⚐ ⌂ ↑ ⚡ **Leisure** practice net. **Location** 3.5m SW of city centre off A4040

Hotel ★★★ 64% The Plough & Harrow Hotel, 135 Hagley Rd, EDGBASTON ☎ 0870 609 6118 44 en suite

Hatchford Brook Coventry Rd, Sheldon B26 3PY
☎ 0121 743 9821 ▤ 0121 743 3420
e-mail: idt@hbgc.freeserve.co.uk
Fairly flat, municipal parkland course.
Hatchford Brook Golf Club: 18 holes, 6155yds, Par 69, SSS 70.
Club membership 350.
Visitors are restricted early Sat & Sun. **Societies** must contact in advance. **Green Fees** terms on application. **Cards** ▦ ▦ ▦ ▦ ▦ **Prof** Mark Hampton **Facilities** ⊗ ⬧ ♥ ♀ ⚐ ⌂ ↑ ⚡ **Location** 6m E of city centre on A45

Hotel Ⓤ Holiday Inn Birmingham Airport, Coventry Rd, BIRMINGHAM ☎ 0870 400 9007 141 en suite

Hilltop Park Ln, Handsworth B21 8LJ
☎ 0121 554 4463
A good test of golf with interesting layout, undulating fairways and large greens, located in the Sandwell Valley conservation area.
18 holes, 6208yds, Par 71, SSS 70.
Club membership 400.
Visitors no restrictions but booking necessary. **Societies** Mon-Fri, telephone Professional in advance. **Green Fees** 18 holes £9.50; 9 holes £6 (£11/£7 weekends and bank holidays). **Cards** ▦ ▦ ▦ ▦ ▦ ▦ **Prof** Kevin Highfield **Course Designer** Hawtree **Facilities** ⊗ ⫴ ⬧ ♀ ⚐ ⌂ ↑ ⚡ **Conf** fac available Corporate Hospitality Days available **Location** On A41, 1m from junct 1 M5

Continued

Continued

Hotel ⏱ Travel Inn, New Gas St, WEST BROMWICH
☎ 08701 977264 40 en suite

Lickey Hills Rosehill, Rednal B45 8RR
☎ 0121 453 3159 🖹 0121 457 8779
18 holes, 5835yds, Par 68, SSS 68.
Location 10m SW of city centre on B4096
Telephone for further details

Hotel ★★ 68% Norwood Hotel, 87-89 Bunbury Rd,
Northfield, BIRMINGHAM ☎ 0121 411 2202 18 en suite

Moseley Springfield Rd, Kings Heath B14 7DX
☎ 0121 444 2115 🖹 0121 441 4662
e-mail: admin@mosgolf.freeserve.co.uk
**Parkland course with a lake, pond and stream to
provide natural hazards. The par 3 4th goes through a
cutting in woodland to a tree and garden-lined
amphitheatre, and the par 4 5th entails a drive over a
lake to a dog-leg fairway.**

18 holes, 6300yds, Par 70, SSS 71, Course record 63.
Club membership 600.
Visitors may only play by prior arrangement, weekdays
excluding bank holidays. **Societies** by prior arrangement.
on certain Wed and Fri. **Green Fees** £37 per round (£15
with member; £20 Sat/Sun with member). **Prof** Martin
Griffin **Course Designer** H S Colt with others **Facilities** ⊗
𝍇 🌢 🎏 ♀ ♿ 🏠 ♂ **Conf** Corporate Hospitality Days
available **Location** 4m S of city centre on B4146 off A435

Hotel ★★ 68% Norwood Hotel, 87-89 Bunbury Rd,
Northfield, BIRMINGHAM ☎ 0121 411 2202 18 en suite

North Worcestershire Frankley Beeches Rd,
Northfield B31 5LP ☎ 0121 475 1047 🖹 0121 476 8681
**Designed by James Braid and established in 1907, this
is a mature parkland course. Tree plantations rather
than heavy rough are the main hazards.**
18 holes, 5959yds, Par 69, SSS 68, Course record 64.
Club membership 600.
Visitors by prior arrangement with professional. Must play
with member at weekends. All visitors must have an
official CONGU handicap. **Societies** apply in advance in
writing or by telephone to the professional tel: 0121 475
5721. **Green Fees** terms on application. **Prof** Finley Clarke
Course Designer James Braid **Facilities** ⊗ 𝍇 🌢 ♀ ♿
🏠 🎏 ♂ **Location** 7m SW of Birmingham city centre, off
A38

Hotel ★★ 68% Norwood Hotel, 87-89 Bunbury Rd,
Northfield, BIRMINGHAM ☎ 0121 411 2202 18 en suite

> **Looking to try a new course? Always telephone
> ahead to confirm visitor arrangements.**

Warley Woods The Pavilion, Lightswood Hill,
Warley B67 5ED
☎ 0121 429 2440 & 6862619(secretary) 🖹 0121 434 4430
**Municipal parkland course in Warley Woods. New out
of bounds areas and bunkers have tightened the course
considerably with further improvement following tree
planting.**
9 holes, 5346yds, Par 68, SSS 66, Course record 64.
Club membership 200.
Visitors must contact in advance. **Societies** booking
advised, times very limited for large parties. **Green Fees**
terms on application. **Prof** D. Ashington **Facilities** ⊗ 🌢
♥ ♿ 🏠 🎏 ♂ **Leisure** practice nets. **Conf** fac available
Location 4m W of city centre off A456

Hotel ★★★ 64% The Plough & Harrow Hotel, 135
Hagley Rd, EDGBASTON ☎ 0870 609 6118 44 en suite

COVENTRY   Map 04 SP37

Ansty Golf Centre Brinklow Rd, Ansty CV7 9JH
☎ 024 7662 1341 🖹 024 7660 2568
**18-hole Pay and Play parkland course of two 9-hole
loops**
18 holes, 6079yds, Par 71, SSS 68, Course record 66.
Club membership 350.
Visitors no restrictions. **Societies** welcome, telephone in
advance. **Green Fees** £11 per 18 holes (£16 weekends &
bank holidays). Academy £4 (£5.50 weekends and bank
holidays]. **Cards** 🔲 💳 📠 🔳 ⚊ **Prof** Matt Fisher
Course Designer David Morgan **Facilities** ⊗ 𝍇 🌢 ♥ ♀ ♿
🏠 🎏 🌢 ♿ 🏌 ♂ **Leisure** par 3 course. **Conf** fac
available Corporate Hospitality Days available **Location**
1m from M6/M69 junct 2

Hotel ★★★ 64% Novotel Coventry, Wilsons Ln,
COVENTRY ☎ 024 7636 5000 98 en suite

Coventry St Martins Rd, Finham Park CV3 6RJ
☎ 024 76414152 🖹 024 76690131
e-mail: coventrygolfclub@hotmail.com
**The scene of several major professional events, this
undulating parkland course has a great deal of quality.
More than that, it usually plays its length, and thus
scoring is never easy, as many professionals have found
to their cost.**
18 holes, 6601yds, Par 73, SSS 73, Course record 66.
Club membership 500.
Visitors must contact in advance. May not play at
weekends and bank holidays. **Societies** must apply in
writing/telephone. **Green Fees** £35 per day. **Cards** 🔲 💳
📠 ⚊ **Prof** Philip Weaver **Course Designer** Vardon
Bros/Hawtree **Facilities** ⊗ 𝍇 🌢 ♥ ♀ ♿ 🏠 🎏 ♂ **Conf**
Corporate Hospitality Days available **Location** 3m S of
city centre on B4113, 2m from jct of A45/A46

Hotel ★★★ 66% Hylands Hotel, Warwick Rd,
COVENTRY ☎ 024 7650 1600 61 en suite

Coventry Hearsall Beechwood Av CV5 6DF
☎ 024 76713470 🖹 024 76691534
**Parkland course with fairly easy walking. A brook
provides an interesting hazard.**
18 holes, 6005yds, Par 70, SSS 69.
Club membership 650.
Visitors with member only at weekends. **Societies** apply in
writing to secretary. **Green Fees** £30 per day. **Prof** Mike
Tarn **Facilities** ⊗ 𝍇 🌢 ♥ ♀ ♿ 🏠 🎏 ♂ **Leisure** hard

Continued

and grass tennis courts, outdoor and indoor heated swimming pools. **Location** 1.5m SW of city centre off A429

••••••••••••••••••••••••••••••••••

Hotel ★★★ 66% Hylands Hotel, Warwick Rd, COVENTRY ☎ 024 7650 1600 61 en suite

Windmill Village Hotel Golf & Leisure Club

Birmingham Rd, Allesley CV5 9AL
☎ 024 7640 4040 📄 024 7640 4042
e-mail: sales@windmillvillagehotel.co.uk
18 holes, 5213yds, Par 70, SSS 67, Course record 63.
Course Designer Robert Hunter **Location** On A45 W of Coventry
Telephone for further details

••••••••••••••••••••••••••••••••••

Hotel ★★★ 72% Brooklands Grange Hotel & Restaurant, Holyhead Rd, COVENTRY ☎ 024 7660 1601 31 en suite

---

DUDLEY   Map 07 SO99

Dudley Turner's Hill, Rowley Regis, Warley B65 9DP
☎ 01384 233877 📄 01384 233177
18 holes, 5714yds, Par 69, SSS 68.
Location 2m S of town centre off B4171
Telephone for further details

••••••••••••••••••••••••••••••••••

Hotel ★★★ 63% The Himley Country Hotel, School Rd, HIMLEY ☎ 0870 609 6112 73 en suite

Swindon Bridgnorth Rd, Swindon DY3 4PU
☎ 01902 897031 📄 01902 326219
e-mail: golf@swindonperton.fsbusiness.co.uk
Attractive undulating woodland/parkland course, with spectacular views.
Old Course: 18 holes, 6121yds, Par 71, SSS 70.
Club membership 700.
Visitors must contact in advance. **Societies** must apply in writing. **Green Fees** £20 per round (£30 weekends & bank holidays). **Cards** 💳 💳 **Prof** Phil Lester **Facilities** ⊗ ⊞ 🏌 ♥ 🍴 🎯 🍸 ♂ **Leisure** fishing, Par 3 9-hole course. **Location** On B4176, 3m from A449 at Himley

••••••••••••••••••••••••••••••••••

Hotel ★★★ 63% The Himley Country Hotel, School Rd, HIMLEY ☎ 0870 609 6112 73 en suite

---

HALESOWEN   Map 07 SO98

Halesowen The Leasowes, Leasowes Ln B62 8QF
☎ 0121 501 3606 📄 0121 501 3606
e-mail: halesowen-gc@msn.com
Parkland course in convenient position within the only Grade I listed park in the Midlands.
18 holes, 5754yds, Par 69, SSS 69, Course record 66.
Club membership 625.
Visitors welcome weekdays, may only play weekends or bank holidays with member unless previously agreed. **Societies** must apply in writing/telephone. **Green Fees** not confirmed. **Prof** Jon Nicholas **Facilities** ⊗ ⊞ 🏌 ♥ 🍸 ♥ 🍴 🎯 ♂ **Conf** Corporate Hospitality Days available
Location 1m E junct 3 M5, Leasowes Lane off Manor Lane

••••••••••••••••••••••••••••••••••

Hotel ★★★ 64% The Plough & Harrow Hotel, 135 Hagley Rd, EDGBASTON ☎ 0870 609 6118 44 en suite

---

> **In the hotel entries, the percentage figure refers to the AA's most recent Quality Assessment Score.**

KNOWLE   Map 07 SP17

Copt Heath 1220 Warwick Rd B93 9LN
☎ 01564 772650 📄 01564 771022
e-mail: golf@copt-heath.co.uk
Flat heathland/parkland course designed by H. Vardon.
18 holes, 6517yds, Par 71, SSS 71, Course record 64.
Club membership 700.
Visitors must contact in advance and possess official handicap certificate. May play weekends & bank holidays in limited numbers, please contact in advance. **Societies** must contact in advance. **Green Fees** £50 per day, £40 per round (£50 per round weekends). **Prof** Brian J Barton
Course Designer H Vardon **Facilities** ⊗ ⊞ 🏌 ♥ 🍸 🍴 🎯
♥ 🎯 ♂ **Conf** Corporate Hospitality Days available
Location On A4141, 0.50m S of junct 5 of M42

••••••••••••••••••••••••••••••••••

Hotel ★★★★ 70% Renaissance Solihull Hotel, 651 Warwick Rd, SOLIHULL ☎ 0121 711 3000 179 en suite

---

MERIDEN   See page 261

MERIDEN   Map 04 SP28

North Warwickshire Hampton Ln CV7 7LL
☎ 01676 522259 (shop) & 522915 (sec) 📄 01676 523004
Parkland course with easy walking.
9 holes, 6390yds, Par 72, SSS 71, Course record 65.
Club membership 425.
Visitors must contact in advance. Must play with member at weekends. **Societies** must apply in writing to secretary. **Green Fees** £20 per round. **Prof** Andrew Bownes
Facilities ⊗ by prior arrangement ⊞ by prior arrangement 🏌 ♥ 🍸 🍴 🎯 ♂ **Location** 1m SW on B4102

••••••••••••••••••••••••••••••••••

Hotel ★★★ 70% Manor Hotel, Main Rd, MERIDEN ☎ 01676 522735 110 en suite

Stonebridge Golf Centre Somers Rd CV7 7PL

☎ 01676 522442 📄 01676 522447
e-mail: golf.shop@stonebridgegolf.co.uk
A parkland course set in 170 acres of beautiful landscape with towering oak trees, lakes and the river Blythe on its borders.
18 holes, 6240yds, Par 70, SSS 70, Course record 67.
Club membership 400.
Visitors visitors can book up to 7 days in advance in person or by telephone. **Societies** apply in writing or telephone in advance. **Green Fees** £18.50 per 18 holes Mon-Thu, £20 Fri, £25 weekends and bank holidays.
Cards 💳 💳 💳 💳 💳 **Prof** Emma Clifford **Course Designer** Mark Jones **Facilities** ⊗ ⊞ 🏌 ♥ 🍸 🍴 🎯 🍸 ♥
🎯 ♂ 🍴 **Leisure** fishing, golf academy. **Conf** fac available Corporate Hospitality Days available **Location** 3m from M42 junct 6

••••••••••••••••••••••••••••••••••

Hotel ★★★ 70% Manor Hotel, Main Rd, MERIDEN ☎ 01676 522735 110 en suite

---

SEDGLEY   Map 07 SO99

Sedgley Golf Centre Sandyfields Rd DY3 3DL
☎ 01902 880503
e-mail: info@sedgleygolf.co.uk
Public Pay and Play course. Undulating contours and mature trees with extensive views over surrounding countryside.
9 holes, 3147yds, Par 72, SSS 70.
Club membership 100.

Continued

Marriott Forest of Arden

Map 04 SP28 Meriden

☎ 0870 400 7272 🖹 0870 400 7372

This is one of the finest golf destinations in the UK, with a range of facilities to impress every golfer. The jewel in the crown is the Arden championship parkland course, set in 10,000 acres of the Packington estate. Designed by Donald Steel, it presents one of the country's most spectacular challenges and has hosted a succession of international tournaments, including the British Masters and English Open. Beware the 18th hole, which is enough to stretch the nerves of any golfer. The shorter Aylesford course offers a varied and enjoyable challenge which golfers of all abilities will find rewarding. Golf events are a speciality, and there is a Golf Academy as well as extensive leisure facilities.

Visitors Ring to book in advance

Societies By arrangement

Green Fees Telephone for details

Facilities

Conf Facilities available; corporate hospitality days available

Professional Philip Hoye

Leisure Tennis, swimming, fishing, sauna, solarium, gymnasium

Location Maxstoke Lane, Meriden CV7 7HR (1m SW of Meriden on B4102)

Holes/Par/Course record
Arden Course: 18 holes, 6707 yds, Par 72, SSS 73, Course record 63
Aylesford Course: 18 holes, 5801 yds, Par 69, SSS 68

WHERE TO STAY AND EAT NEARBY

Hotels
MERIDEN

★★★★ 73% Marriott Forest of Arden Hotel & Country Club, CV7 7HR.
☎ 0870 400 7272. 214 en suite

★★★ 70% Manor Hotel, CV7 7NH.
☎ 01676 522735.
110 en suite

Championship Course

Visitors booking advisable for weekends. **Societies** must contact in advance. **Green Fees** £7 per 9 holes; £9.50 per 18 holes. **Prof** Garry Mercer **Course Designer** W G Cox **Facilities** ♨ ⚒ ♨ ♨ ♨ ♨ ♨ **Location** 0.5m from town centre off A463

Hotel ★★★ 63% The Himley Country Hotel, School Rd, HIMLEY ☎ 0870 609 6112 73 en suite

SOLIHULL   Map 07 SP17

Olton Mirfield Rd B91 1JH
☎ 0121 704 1936 ▤ 0121 711 2010
e-mail: mailbox@oltongolfclub.fsnet.co.uk
Parkland course with prevailing southwest wind.
18 holes, 6265yds, Par 69, SSS 71, Course record 63.
Club membership 600.
Visitors must contact in advance. No visitors at weekend. **Societies** apply in writing. **Green Fees** not confirmed. **Prof** Charles Haynes **Course Designer** J H Taylor **Facilities** ⊗ ♨ ♨ ♨ ♨ ♨ ♨ ♨ ♨ **Conf** Corporate Hospitality Days available **Location** Exit M42 junct 5 and take A41 for 1.5m

Hotel ★★★★ 70% Renaissance Solihull Hotel, 651 Warwick Rd, SOLIHULL ☎ 0121 711 3000 179 en suite

Robin Hood St Bernards Rd B92 7DJ
☎ 0121 706 0061 ▤ 0121 706 0061
e-mail: robin.hood.golf.club@dial.pipex.com
Pleasant parkland course with easy walking and open to good views. Tree lined fairways and varied holes, culminating in two excellent finishing holes. Modern clubhouse.
18 holes, 6635yds, Par 72, SSS 72, Course record 68.
Club membership 650.
Visitors must contact in advance. With member only at weekends. **Societies** must contact in advance. **Green Fees** £30 per round/£35 for 27 holes. **Prof** Alan Harvey **Course Designer** H S Colt **Facilities** ⊗ ♨ ♨ ♨ ♨ ♨ ♨ ♨ **Conf** Corporate Hospitality Days available **Location** 2m W off B4025

Hotel ★★★★ 70% Renaissance Solihull Hotel, 651 Warwick Rd, SOLIHULL ☎ 0121 711 3000 179 en suite

Shirley Stratford Rd, Monkpath, Shirley B90 4EW
☎ 0121 744 6001 ▤ 0121 745 8220
e-mail: shirleygolfclub@btclick.com
Fairly flat parkland course.
18 holes, 6510yds, Par 72, SSS 71.
Club membership 600.
Visitors may not play bank holidays & with member only at weekends. Handicap certificate is required. **Societies** only on Thu, must contact in advance. **Green Fees** terms on application. **Prof** S Bottrill **Facilities** ⊗ ♨ ♨ ♨ ♨ ♨ ♨ ♨ **Conf** fac available **Location** 0.5m N of junct 4 M42 on A34

Hotel ★★★ 67% The Regency Hotel, Stratford Rd, Shirley, SOLIHULL ☎ 0870 609 6133 111 en suite

West Midlands Marsh House Farm Ln, Barston B92 0LB ☎ 01675 444890 ▤ 01675 444891
e-mail: westmidlandsgc@aol.com
New golf course built to USGA specification with no temporary greens or tees. The 18th hole is a par 3 to an island green.
18 holes, 6624yds, Par 72, SSS 72.

Club membership 750.
Societies telephone for details **Green Fees** £19.95 (£24.95 weekends). **Cards** ☒ ☒ ☒ ☒ ☒ ☒ ☒ **Course Designer** Nigel & Mark Harrhy/David Griffith **Facilities** ⊗ ♨ ♨ ♨ ♨ ♨ ♨ ♨ **Leisure** fishing. **Conf** Corporate Hospitality Days available **Location** from NEC take A45 towards Coventry for 0.5m. Then take A452 towards Leamington and Balsall Common, club on right by car showroom

Hotel ★★★ 68% Arden Hotel & Leisure Club, Coventry Rd, Bickenhill, SOLIHULL ☎ 01675 443221 216 en suite

Widney Manor Saintbury Dr, Widney Manor B91 3SZ ☎ 0121 704 0704 ▤ 0121 704 7999
Parkland course, fairly easy walking. Of medium length, it is ideal for beginners and improvers. Other facilities include a driving range, all weather greens and buggy paths.
18 holes, 5654yards, Par 71, SSS 66.
Club membership 650.
Visitors may book up to 7 days in advance. **Societies** telephone for details **Green Fees** £11.95 weekday & weekend pm (£16.95 weekend am). **Cards** ☒ ☒ ☒ ☒ ☒ ☒ ☒ **Prof** Tim Atkinson **Course Designer** Nigel & Mark Harry **Facilities** ⊗ ♨ ♨ ♨ ♨ ♨ ♨ ♨ **Leisure** heated indoor swimming pool, sauna, solarium, gymnasium. **Conf** Corporate Hospitality Days available **Location** M42 junct 4, follow signs to Monkspath and Widney Manor

Hotel ★★★★ 70% Renaissance Solihull Hotel, 651 Warwick Rd, SOLIHULL ☎ 0121 711 3000 179 en suite

STOURBRIDGE   Map 07 SO88

Hagley Golf & Country Club Wassell Grove Ln, Hagley DY9 9JW
☎ 01562 883701 ▤ 01562 887518
Undulating parkland course set beneath the Clent Hills; there are superb views. Testing 15th, par 5, 557 yards.
18 holes, 6353yds, Par 72, SSS 72, Course record 66.
Club membership 700.
Visitors welcome weekdays but restricted Wed (Ladies Day) & with member only at weekends. **Societies** Mon-Fri only, must apply in writing. **Green Fees** £28 per 18 holes; £33 per day (Mon-Fri). **Cards** ☒ ☒ **Prof** Iain Clark **Course Designer** Garratt & Co **Facilities** ⊗ ♨ ♨ ♨ ♨ ♨ ♨ **Leisure** squash. **Conf** fac available Corporate Hospitality Days available **Location** 1m E of Hagley off A456. 2m from junct 3 on M5

Hotel ⛺ Travel Inn, Birmingham Rd, HAGLEY ☎ 08701 977123 40 en suite

Stourbridge Worcester Ln, Pedmore DY8 2RB
☎ 01384 395566 ▤ 01384 444660
e-mail: secretary@stourbridge-golf-club.co.uk
Parkland course.
18 holes, 6231yds, Par 70, SSS 69, Course record 67.
Club membership 859.
Visitors contact secretary, no casual visitors weekends. Ladies day Wednesday. **Societies** must apply in writing/by e-mail. **Green Fees** £30 per 18 holes; £37.50 per day. **Prof** M Male **Facilities** ⊗ ♨ ♨ ♨ ♨ ♨ ♨ **Location** 2m from town centre

Hotel ⛺ Travel Inn, Birmingham Rd, HAGLEY ☎ 08701 977123 40 en suite

Continued

SUTTON COLDFIELD   Map 07 SP19

Boldmere Monmouth Dr B73 6JL
☎ 0121 354 3379 📖 0121 355 4534
Established municipal course with 10 par 3s and a lake
coming into play on the 16th and 18th holes.
18 holes, 4493yds, Par 63, SSS 62, Course record 57.
Club membership 300.
Visitors must contact in advance. **Societies** midweek only,
apply in writing. **Green Fees** not confirmed. **Cards** ☷
🏧 🚉 📠 📇 **Prof** Trevor Short **Facilities** ⊗ 🍴 🏳
⛳ 🏠 ♟ ℰ **Location** Adjacent to Sutton Park

Hotel ★★★★ 68% Moor Hall Hotel, Moor Hall Dr, Four
Oaks, SUTTON COLDFIELD ☎ 0121 308 3751
82 en suite

Little Aston Streetly B74 3AN
☎ 0121 353 2942 📖 0121 580 8387
e-mail: manager@littleastongolf.co.uk
This parkland course is set in the rolling countryside of
the former Little Aston Hall and there is a wide variety
of mature trees. There are three par 3 holes and three
par 5 holes and although the fairways are not unduly
narrow there are rewards for accuracy - especially
from the tee. The course features two lakes. At the par
5 twelfth the lake cuts into the green and at the par 4
seventeenth the lake is also adjacent to the green.
18 holes, 6670yds, Par 72, SSS 73, Course record 63.
Club membership 350.
Visitors must contact in advance & may not play on
Saturdays. **Societies** must apply in writing. **Green Fees**
£60 per round/£75 per day. **Cards** ☷ 🏧 📠 📇 🚉 **Prof**
Brian Rimmer **Course Designer** H Vardon **Facilities** ⊗ 🍴
🏳 🍺 ♀ ⛳ 🏠 🍃 🏌 ℰ **Location** 3.5m NW of Sutton
Coldfield off A454

Hotel ★★★★ 68% Moor Hall Hotel, Moor Hall Dr, Four
Oaks, SUTTON COLDFIELD ☎ 0121 308 3751
82 en suite

Moor Hall Moor Hall Dr B75 6LN
☎ 0121 308 9560 📖 0121 308 9560
e-mail: manager@moorhallgolfclub.fsnet.co.uk
Outstanding parkland course. The 14th hole is notable
and is part of a challenging finish to the round.
18 holes, 6249yds, Par 70, SSS 70.
Club membership 600.
Visitors must contact in advance. With member only
weekends & bank holidays.Ladies day Thu am. **Societies**
must apply in writing/telephone in advance. **Green Fees**
£50 per day, £38 per round. **Cards** ☷ 🏧 📠 🚉 📇 **Prof**
Cameron Clark **Course Designer** Hawtree & Taylor
Facilities ⊗ 🍴 🏳 🍺 ♀ ⛳ 🏠 ℰ **Conf** Corporate
Hospitality Days available **Location** 2.5m N of town
centre off A453

Hotel ★★★★ 68% Moor Hall Hotel, Moor Hall Dr, Four
Oaks, SUTTON COLDFIELD ☎ 0121 308 3751
82 en suite

Pype Hayes Eachel Hurst Rd, Walmley B76 1EP
☎ 0121 351 1014 📖 0121 313 0206
18 holes, 5927yds, Par 71, SSS 69.
Course Designer Bobby Jones **Location** 2.5m S off B4148
Telephone for further details

Hotel ★★★★ 68% Moor Hall Hotel, Moor Hall Dr, Four
Oaks, SUTTON COLDFIELD ☎ 0121 308 3751
82 en suite

Sutton Coldfield 110 Thornhill Rd, Streetly B74 3ER
☎ 0121 580 7878 📖 0121 353 5503
e-mail: sc.golfclub@virgin.net
A fine natural, all-weather, heathland course, with tight
fairways, gorse, heather and trees. A good challenge for
all standards of golfer.
18 holes, 6541yds, Par 72, SSS 71, Course record 65.
Club membership 600.
Visitors must contact professional in advance. Restricted at
weekends and bank holidays. **Societies** must apply in
writing. **Green Fees** £40 per day; £30 per round (£40 per
round weeekends). **Prof** Jerry Hayes **Course Designer** Dr
A McKenzie **Facilities** ⊗ 🍴 🏳 🍺 ♀ ⛳ 🏠 ℰ **Conf** fac
available Corporate Hospitality Days available **Location**
M6 junct 7, take A34 signposted Birmingham to 1st set of
traffic lights, turn left into A4041(QueslettRd). Continue to
island with petrol station on left and straight on to B4138
(Thornhill Rd). Entrance after 4th turning on left.

Hotel ★★★★ 68% Moor Hall Hotel, Moor Hall Dr, Four
Oaks, SUTTON COLDFIELD ☎ 0121 308 3751
82 en suite

Walmley Brooks Rd, Wylde Green B72 1HR
☎ 0121 373 0029 & 377 7272 📖 0121 377 7272
e-mail: walmleygolfclub@aol.com
Pleasant parkland course with many trees. The hazards
are not difficult.
18 holes, 6585yds, Par 72, SSS 72, Course record 67.
Club membership 700.
Visitors must contact in advance. Weekends may only play
as guest of member. **Societies** must contact in advance.
Green Fees £35 per 18+ holes, £30 per 18 holes. **Cards**
☷ 🏧 📠 🚉 **Prof** C J Wicketts **Facilities** ⊗ 🍴 🏳 🍺 ♀ ⛳
🏠 🏌 ℰ **Conf** Corporate Hospitality Days available
Location 2m S off A5127

Hotel ★★★★ 68% Moor Hall Hotel, Moor Hall Dr, Four
Oaks, SUTTON COLDFIELD ☎ 0121 308 3751
82 en suite

WALSALL   Map 07 SP09

Bloxwich Stafford Rd, Bloxwich WS3 3PQ
☎ 01922 476593 ext 20 📖 01922 493449
e-mail: bloxwich.golf-club@virgin.net
Undulating parkland course with natural hazards and
subject to strong north wind.
18 holes, 6257yds, Par 71, SSS 71, Course record 68.
Club membership 680.
Visitors may not play at weekends unless guest of member
Societies must contact in advance. **Green Fees** terms on
application. **Prof** Richard J Dance **Facilities** ⊗ 🍴 🏳 🍺 ♀
⛳ 🏠 ℰ **Conf** fac available Corporate Hospitality Days
available **Location** 3m N of town centre on A34

Hotel ★★★ 76% The Fairlawns at Aldridge, 178 Little
Aston Rd, Aldridge, WALSALL ☎ 01922 455122
50 en suite

Calderfields Aldridge Rd WS4 2JS
☎ 01922 632243 📖 01922 640540
e-mail: calderfields@bigfoot.com
Parkland course with lake.
18 holes, 6509yds, Par 73, SSS 71.
Club membership 480.
Visitors no restrictions. **Societies** telephone 01922 632243
in advance. **Green Fees** £12 per 18 holes; 36 holes £20.
Cards ☷ 🏧 📠 🚉 📇 **Prof** Ian Roberts

Continued

263

Course Designer Roy Winter **Facilities** ⊗ ∭ ⓛ 💺 ♀ ⚒
🏠 🍴 🐟 🛶 ⚷ ⏻ **Leisure** fishing. **Location** On A454

Hotel ★★★ 76% The Fairlawns at Aldridge, 178 Little
Aston Rd, Aldridge, WALSALL ☎ 01922 455122
50 en suite

Walsall The Broadway WS1 3EY
☎ 01922 613512 📄 01922 616460
18 holes, 6300yds, Par 70, SSS 70, Course record 65.
Course Designer McKenzie **Location** 1m S of town centre
off A34
Telephone for further details
....

Hotel ★★★ 64% Quality Hotel Birmingham North,
Birmingham Rd, WALSALL ☎ 01922 633609 96 en suite

WEST BROMWICH   Map 07 SP09

Dartmouth Vale St B71 4DW ☎ 0121 588 5746
**Meadowland course with undulating but easy walking.
The 617yd par 5 first hole is something of a challenge.**
9 holes, 6036yds, Par 71, SSS 71, Course record 66.
Club membership 250.
Visitors with member only at weekends. May not play bank
holidays or medal weekends until after 2pm contact pro
first. **Societies** must apply in writing/telephone. **Green Fees**
£25 per day/18 holes. **Prof** G. Kilmaster **Facilities** ⊗ ∭ ⓛ
💺 ♀ ⚒ 🏠 **Location** E side of town centre off A4041
....

Hotel ⇧ Express by Holiday Inn Oldbury, Birchley Park,
OLDBURY ☎ 0121 511 0000 109 en suite

Sandwell Park Birmingham Rd B71 4JJ
☎ 0121 553 4637 📄 0121 525 1651
e-mail: secretary@sandwellparkgolfclub.co.uk
**A picturesque golf course wandering over wooded
heathland and utilising natural features. Each hole is
entirely separate, shielded from the others by either
natural banks or lines of trees. A course that demands
careful placing of shots that have been given a great
deal of thought. Natural undulating fairways create
difficult and testing approach shots to the greens.**

18 holes, 6204yds, Par 71, SSS 71.
Club membership 550.
Visitors must contact in advance. May not play at
weekends. **Societies** must contact in advance. **Green Fees**
£42 per 27/36 holes; £36 per 18 holes. **Prof** Nigel Wylie
Course Designer H S Colt **Facilities** ⊗ ∭ ⓛ 💺 ♀ ⚒ 🏠
⚷ **Leisure** practice chipping area. **Conf** fac available
Corporate Hospitality Days available **Location** On A41,
200yds from juct 1 of the M5
....

Hotel ⇧ Express by Holiday Inn Oldbury, Birchley Park,
OLDBURY ☎ 0121 511 0000 109 en suite

WOLVERHAMPTON   Map 07 SO99

Oxley Park Stafford Rd, Bushbury WV10 6DE
☎ 01902 425892 📄 01902 773981
e-mail: secretary@oxleyparkgolfclub.fsnet.co.uk
**Rolling parkland course with trees, bunkers and water
hazards.**
18 holes, 6226yds, Par 71, SSS 71, Course record 66.
Club membership 550.
Visitors must contact in advance. **Societies** must contact in
advance. **Green Fees** £35 per day, £30 per 18 holes. **Cards**
💳 💳 💳 💳 💳 **Prof** Les Burlison **Course Designer** H S
Colt **Facilities** ⊗ ∭ by prior arrangement ⓛ 💺 ♀ ⚒ 🏠
⚷ **Leisure** snooker. **Location** 2m south of M54 Junct 2
....

Hotel ★★★ 68% Ely House Hotel, 53 Tettenhall Rd,
WOLVERHAMPTON ☎ 01902 311311 18 en suite

Penn Penn Common, Penn WV4 5JN
☎ 01902 341142 📄 01902 620504
e-mail: penn-golf.freeserve.co.uk
Heathland course just outside the town.
18 holes, 6487yds, Par 70, SSS 72, Course record 68.
Club membership 650.
Visitors must play with member at weekends. **Societies**
must contact in advance. **Green Fees** £28 per 18 holes/£33
per day. **Prof** B Burlison **Facilities** ⊗ ∭ ⓛ 💺 ♀ ⚒ 🏠 ⚷
Location SW side of town centre off A449
....

Hotel ★★★ 66% Quality Hotel Wolverhampton, Penn
Rd, WOLVERHAMPTON ☎ 01902 429216 66 en suite
26 annexe en suite

South Staffordshire Danescourt Rd, Tettenhall
WV6 9BQ ☎ 01902 751065 📄 01902 741753
18 holes, 6513yds, Par 71, SSS 71, Course record 67.
Course Designer Harry Vardon **Location** 3m NW off A41
Telephone for further details
....

Hotel ★★★ 68% Ely House Hotel, 53 Tettenhall Rd,
WOLVERHAMPTON ☎ 01902 311311 18 en suite

Three Hammers Short Course Old Stafford Rd,
Coven WV10 7PP ☎ 01902 790940
18 holes, 1438yds, Par 54, SSS 54, Course record 43.
Course Designer Henry Cotton **Location** On A449 N of
junct 2 M54
Telephone for further details
....

Hotel ★★★ 63% The Roman Way Hotel, Watling St,
Hatherton, CANNOCK ☎ 0870 609 6125 56 en suite

Wergs Keepers Ln, Tettenhall WV6 8UA
☎ 01902 742225 📄 01902 744748
**Open parkland course with gently undulating fairways,
large greens and all year round tees.**
18 holes, 6949yds, Par 72, SSS 73.
Club membership 150.
Visitors are advised to contact in advance. **Societies** must
contact in advance. **Green Fees** £15 per day/round (£20
weekends & bank holidays). **Cards** 💳 💳 💳 💳 **Prof**
Steve Weir **Course Designer** C W Moseley **Facilities** ⊗
∭ by prior arrangement ⓛ 💺 ♀ ⚒ 🏠 🐟 🛶 ⚷ **Location**
From Wolverhampton take A41 towards Newport for 2.5m
then R for 0.5m then R again
....

Hotel ★★★ 68% Ely House Hotel, 53 Tettenhall Rd,
WOLVERHAMPTON ☎ 01902 311311 18 en suite

WIGHT, ISLE OF

COWES
Map 04 SZ49

Cowes Crossfield Av PO31 8HN
☎ 01983 292303 (secretary) 🖹 01983 292303
Fairly level, tight parkland course with difficult par 3s and Solent views.
9 holes, 5934yds, Par 70, SSS 68, Course record 66.
Club membership 300.
Visitors restricted Thu & Sun mornings. **Societies** Mon-Wed, must contact in advance. **Green Fees** terms on application. **Course Designer** Hamilton-Stutt **Facilities** ⊗ ⓑ ♥ ♀ ⚐ ⌁ ✍ **Location** NW side of town, next to Cowes High School

Hotel ★★★ 68% New Holmwood Hotel, Queens Rd, Egypt Point, COWES ☎ 01983 292508 26 en suite

EAST COWES
Map 04 SZ59

Osborne Osborne House Estate PO32 6JX
☎ 01983 295421
Undulating parkland course in the grounds of Osborne House. Quiet and peaceful situation.
9 holes, 6398yds, Par 70, SSS 70, Course record 69.
Club membership 450.
Visitors may not play Tue before noon, weekends before noon & bank holidays before 11am. **Societies** telephone initially. **Green Fees** £20 (£22 weekends and bank holidays). **Facilities** ⊗ ⫼ ⓑ ♥ ♀ ⚐ ⌁ ✍ **Location** E side of town centre off A3021, in grounds of Osborne House

Hotel ★★★ 68% New Holmwood Hotel, Queens Rd, Egypt Point, COWES ☎ 01983 292508 26 en suite

FRESHWATER
Map 04 SZ38

Freshwater Bay Afton Down PO40 9TZ
☎ 01983 752955 🖹 01983 752955
e-mail: tr.fbgc@btopenworld.com
A downland/seaside links with wide fairways and spectacular coastal views of the Solent and Channel.
18 holes, 5725yds, Par 69, SSS 68.
Club membership 550.
Visitors may play daily after 9.30 ex Thu & Sun (10.30). **Societies** apply to secretary. **Green Fees** not confirmed. **Cards** ⊟ 🟧 📠 🔳 **Course Designer** J H Taylor **Facilities** ⊗ ⫼ ⓑ ♥ ♀ ⚐ ⌁ ✍ **Conf** Corporate Hospitality Days available **Location** 0.5m E of village off A3055

Hotel ★★★ 68% Sentry Mead Hotel, Madeira Rd, TOTLAND BAY ☎ 01983 753212 14 en suite

NEWPORT
Map 04 SZ58

Newport St George's Down, Shide PO30 2JB
☎ 01983 525076
9 holes, 5710yds, Par 68, SSS 68.
Location 1.5m S off A3020
Telephone for further details

Hotel ★★★ 68% New Holmwood Hotel, Queens Rd, Egypt Point, COWES ☎ 01983 292508 26 en suite

RYDE
Map 04 SZ59

Ryde Binstead Rd PO33 3NF
☎ 01983 614809 🖹 01983 567418
e-mail: secretary@rydegolfclub.freeserve.co.uk
Downland course with wide views over the Solent.

Very tight with out of bound areas on most holes and 5 dog-legs.
9 holes, 5772yds, Par 70, SSS 69.
Club membership 575.
Visitors may not play Wed before 2.15pm, weekdays before 10.15am and weekends before 11am **Societies** must contact in writing. **Green Fees** 18 holes £18, 9 holes £12 (with member £10/£7); weekends £20/£14 (£12/£9). **Course Designer** Hamilton-Stutt **Facilities** ⊗ ⫼ by prior arrangement ⓑ ♥ ♀ ⚑ ⌁ ✍ **Location** Right out of Fishbourne ferry terminal, left at lights,1m W on A3054

Hotel ★★ 67% Yelf's Hotel, Union St, RYDE
☎ 01983 564062 30 en suite

SANDOWN
Map 04 SZ58

Shanklin & Sandown The Fairway, Lake
PO36 9PR ☎ 01983 403217 (office) & 404424 (pro) 🖹 01983 403007 (office)/404424 (pro)
An 18 hole county championship course, recognised for its natural heathland beauty, spectacular views and challenging qualities. The course demands respect, with accurate driving and careful club selection the order of the day.
18 holes, 6062yds, Par 70, SSS 69, Course record 63.
Club membership 700.
Visitors must contact in advance & have handicap certificate. May not play before noon Sat or 9.30am Sun. **Societies** telephone 01983 404424 **Green Fees** £27.50 (weekends & bank holidays £35). **Cards** ⊟ 🟧 📠 🔳 **Prof** Peter Hammond **Course Designer** Braid **Facilities** ⊗ ⫼ ⓑ ♥ ♀ ⚐ ⌁ ✍ **Location** From Sandown drive towards Shanklin past Heights Leisure Centre after 200yds right into Fairway for 1m

Hotel ★★ 66% Cygnet Hotel, 58 Carter St, SANDOWN
☎ 01983 402930 46 rms (45 en suite)

VENTNOR
Map 04 SZ57

Ventnor Steephill Down Rd PO38 1BP
☎ 01983 853326 🖹 01983 853326
e-mail: ventnorgolf@lineone.net
12 holes, 5767yds, Par 70, SSS 68, Course record 68.
Location 1m NW off B3327, turning at the chip shop
Telephone for further details

Hotel ★★★★ 71% The Royal Hotel, Belgrave Rd, VENTNOR ☎ 01983 852186 55 en suite

WILTSHIRE

BISHOPS CANNINGS
Map 04 SU06

North Wilts SN10 2LP
☎ 01380 860627 🖹 01380 860877
e-mail: secretary@northwiltsgolfclub.fsnet.co.uk
Established in 1890 and one of the oldest courses in Wiltshire, North Wilts is situated high on the downlands of Wiltshire, with spectacular views over the surrounding countryside. The chalk base allows free draining and the course provides a challenge to golfers of all abilities.
18 holes, 6414yds, Par 71, SSS 71, Course record 65.
Club membership 800.
Visitors a handicap certificate is required at weekends. **Societies** must book in advance. **Green Fees** £30 per day (£35 per round weekends). **Cards** ⊟ 🟧 📠 🔳

Continued

Continued

Prof Graham Laing **Course Designer** H. S. Colt **Facilities**
⊗ ⫟ ⬧ ⬛ ♀ ⚘ 🏠 ⛳ ⚑ ⛴ ♘ *Conf* Corporate
Hospitality Days available **Location** 2m NW of Devizes.
M4 junct 17, follow A4 to Calne between A4 and A361

Hotel ★★★ 64% Bear Hotel, Market Place, DEVIZES
☎ 01380 722444 24 en suite

BRADFORD-ON-AVON — Map 03 ST86

Cumberwell Park BA15 2PQ
☎ 01225 863322 🗎 01225 868160
e-mail: enquiries@cumberwellpark.com
**Cumberwell Park offers a perfect golfing challenge
which at the same time doesn't discourage the
newcomer. The 27-hole course comprises three linked
sets of 9 holes. A new undercover driving range
includes two teaching bays.**
*Parkland: 9 holes, 6405yds, Par 71, SSS 71, Course record
63.*
Woodland: 9 holes, 6356yds, Par 72, SSS 70.
Lakeland: 9 holes, 6509, Par 71, SSS 71.
Club membership 1300.
Societies telephone for details. **Green Fees** £48 per day,
£26 per 18 holes, £16 per 9 holes (£58/£32/£19 weekends
and bank holidays). **Cards** 🔲 🔲 🔲 🔲 🔲 **Prof** John
Jacobs **Course Designer** Adrian Stiff **Facilities** ⊗ ⫟ ⬧
⬛ ♀ ⚘ 🏠 ⛳ ⚑ ⛴ ♘ *Conf* fac available Corporate
Hospitality Days available **Location** on A363, 6m from
Bath

Hotel ★★★ ⚘ 73% Woolley Grange, Woolley Green,
BRADFORD-ON-AVON ☎ 01225 864705 14 en suite
12 annexe en suite

CALNE — Map 03 ST97

Bowood Golf & Country Club Derry Hill
SN11 9PQ ☎ 01249 822228 🗎 01249 822218
e-mail: golfclub@bowood.org
**A championship golf course set in the beautiful
surroundings of 'Capability' Brown's Great Park.**

18 holes, 6890yds, Par 72, SSS 73, Course record 63.
Club membership 500.
Visitors welcome except before noon on Sat and Sun.
Booking essential. **Societies** booking by telephone. **Green
Fees** terms on application. **Cards** 🔲 🔲 🔲 🔲 🔲 🔲
Prof Max Taylor **Course Designer** Dave Thomas
Facilities ⊗ ⫟ ⬧ ⬛ ♀ ⚘ 🏠 ⛳ ⚑ ⛴ ♘ *Leisure*
Bowood House and Gardens. **Conf** fac available **Location**
M4 junct 17 off A4 between Chippenham & Calne

Hotel ★★★ 67% Lansdowne Strand Hotel, The Strand,
CALNE ☎ 01249 812488 20 en suite 5 annexe en suite

CASTLE COMBE — Map 03 ST87

Manor House SN14 7JW
☎ 01249 782206 🗎 01249 782992
e-mail: teereservations@manorhousegolfclub.com
**Set in a wonderful location within the wooded estate of
the 14th-century Manor House, this course includes five
par 5s and some spectacular par 3s. A special feature is
the River Bybrook, which meanders its way through
many holes, the most memorable being the 17th with a
breathtaking drop to the green.**

*The Manor House Golf Club at Castle Combe: 18 holes,
6286yds, Par 72, SSS 71, Course record 67.*
Club membership 450.
Visitors must have a handicap certificate and must contact
in advance. **Societies** contact in advance. **Green Fees**
terms on application. **Cards** 🔲 🔲 🔲 🔲 🔲 **Prof** Peter
Green **Course Designer** Peter Alliss/Clive Clark **Facilities**
⊗ ⫟ ⬧ ⬛ ♀ ⚘ 🏠 ⛳ ⚑ ⛴ ♘ *Leisure* hard tennis
courts, heated outdoor swimming pool, fishing, sauna,
snooker, croquet. **Conf** fac available Corporate Hospitality
Days available **Location** On B4039, 5m NW of
Chippenham

Hotel ★★★★ ⚘ Manor House Hotel and Golf Club,
CASTLE COMBE ☎ 01249 782206 22 en suite
26 annexe en suite

CHAPMANSLADE — Map 03 ST84

Thoulstone Park BA13 4AQ
☎ 01373 832825 🗎 01373 832821
18 holes, 6161yds, Par 70, SSS 70.
Location On A36 between Bath/Warminster
Telephone for further details

Hotel ★★ 68% Woolpack Inn, BECKINGTON
☎ 01373 831244 12 en suite

CHIPPENHAM — Map 03 ST97

Chippenham Malmesbury Rd SN15 5LT
☎ 01249 652040 🗎 01249 446681
e-mail: chippenhamgc@onetel.net.uk
**Easy walking on downland course. Testing holes at 1st
and 15th.**
18 holes, 5570yds, Par 69, SSS 67, Course record 64.
Club membership 650.
Visitors must contact in advance and play from tees of the
day **Societies** must contact in writing, by phone or via e-
mail. **Green Fees** £30 per day, £22 per round (£27 per
round weekends & bank holidays). **Prof** Bill Creamer
Facilities ⊗ ⫟ ⬧ ⬛ ♀ ⚘ 🏠 ⛳ ♘ *Conf* Corporate
Hospitality Days available **Location** M4 junct 17, 1m N of
Chippenham beside A350

Continued

THE MANOR HOUSE GOLF CLUB

Magnificent setting in the rolling Wiltshire Countryside

The Manor House Golf Club's magnificent setting in the rolling Wiltshire countryside is unsurpassed. With an extraordinary number of feature holes include the 17th rated as one of the top ten par 3's in the world, the course is testing yet fair.

- 18 hole par 72 golf course
- tree lined fairways
- putting green
- driving range
- golf shop
- buggie hire
- golf days
- individual membership
- corporate membership

- spectacular waterfalls
- outside terraces
- 365 acres of stunning views
- tennis courts
- brown trout fishing
- swimming pool
- sauna
- gymnasium

- numerous meeting rooms
- private dining
- Woodbury restaurant
- informal bars
- 17th century manor house
- 48 bedrooms
- 20 minutes from Bristol
- 20 minutes from Bath
- 10 minutes from the M4

EXCLUSIVE HOTELS

THE MANOR HOUSE GOLF CLUB
Castle Combe, Nr Bath, Wiltshire SN14 7JW
T: +44 (0) 1249 782982   F: +44 (0) 1249 782 992   E: enquiries@manorhousegolf.club.com

Hotel   The Manor House Hotel, Castle Combe, nr Bath, Wiltshire
T: +44 (0) 1249 782206   48 bedrooms

www.exclusivehotels.co.uk

Hotel ★★★★ 🏵 Manor House Hotel and Golf Club, CASTLE COMBE ☎ 01249 782206 22 en suite 26 annexe en suite

Cricklade Hotel & Country Club Common
Hill SN6 6HA ☎ 01793 750751 📠 01793 751767
e-mail: info@crickladehotel.fsnet.co.uk
A challenging 9-hole course with undulating greens and beautiful views. Par 3 6th (128yds) signature hole from an elevated tee to a green protected by a deep pot bunker.

9 holes, 1830yds, Par 62, SSS 58, Course record 59. Club membership 130.
Visitors may not play weekends or bank holidays unless accompanied by a member. Must contact in advance.
Societies apply in writing. **Green Fees** £25 per day; £18 for 18 holes. **Cards** 🔲🔲🔲🔲🔲🔲 **Prof** Ian Bolt
Course Designer Ian Bolt/Colin Smith **Facilities** ⊗ ⅏ 🏌

💼 🍴 ⚴ ⛳ 🏕 🏌 **Leisure** hard tennis courts, heated indoor swimming pool, solarium, gymnasium, snooker, pool, jacuzzi, tennis. **Conf** fac available **Location** On the B4040 out of Cricklade, towards Malmesbury

Hotel ★★★ 71% Cricklade Hotel, Common Hill, CRICKLADE ☎ 01793 750751 25 en suite 21 annexe en suite

Erlestoke Sands SN10 5UB
☎ 01380 831069 📠 01380 831284
e-mail: info@erlestokesands.co.uk
The course is set on the lower slopes of Salisbury Plain with distant views to the Cotswolds and Marlborough Downs. The 7th plunges from an elevated three-tiered tee, high in the woods, to a large green with a spectacular backdrop of a meandering river and hills. The course was built to suit every standard of golfer from the novice to the very low handicapper and its two tiers offer lakes and rolling downland.
18 holes, 6406yds, Par 73, SSS 71, Course record 66. Club membership 720.
Visitors phone for tee booking in advance 01380 830300. Dress rules apply. **Societies** must book in advance. **Green Fees** £30 per 36 holes, £25 per 18 holes (£40/£30 weekends and bank holidays). **Cards** 🔲🔲🔲 **Prof** Michael Waters **Course Designer** Adrian Stiff **Facilities** ⊗ ⅏ 🏌 💼 ⚴ 🏕 🏌 ⛳ 🏌 **Location** On B3098 Devizes/Westbury road

Hotel ★★★ 64% Bear Hotel, Market Place, DEVIZES ☎ 01380 722444 24 en suite

Continued

GREAT DURNFORD   Map 04 SU13

High Post SP4 6AT
☎ 01722 782356 📠 01722 782674
e-mail: highpostgolfclub@lineone.net
An interesting downland course on Wiltshire chalk with good turf and splendid views over the southern area of Salisbury Plain. The par 3 17th and the two-shot 18th require good judgement. The course is noted for the quality of its greens and year round playability.

18 holes, 6305yds, Par 70, SSS 70, Course record 64. Club membership 625.
Visitors a handicap certificate is required at weekends & bank holidays. Telephone professional in advance 01722 782219. **Societies** apply by telephone to manager. **Green Fees** £40 per day; £32 per round (£50/£42 weekends). **Prof** Tony Isaacs **Course Designer** Hawtree & Ptrs **Facilities** ⊗ 𝄞 🏌 ♥ ♀ ⚑ 🏠 🍴 ⚙ 🏌 **Conf** fac available **Location** Midway between Sailsbury and Amesbury on A345

Hotel ★★★ 64% The Rose & Crown Hotel, Harnham Rd, Harnham, SALISBURY ☎ 0870 6096163 28 en suite

HIGHWORTH   Map 04 SU29

Highworth Community Golf Centre Swindon
Rd SN6 7SJ ☎ 01793 766014 📠 01793 766014
9 holes, 3120yds, Par 35, SSS 35, Course record 29.
Course Designer T Watt/ B Sandry/D Lang **Location** Off A361 Swindon to Lechlade
Telephone for further details

Hotel ★★★ 71% Sudbury House Hotel & Conference Centre, London St, FARINGDON ☎ 01367 241272 49 en suite

Wrag Barn Golf & Country Club Shrivenham
Rd SN6 7QQ ☎ 01793 861327 📠 01793 861325
e-mail: info@wragbarn.com
An outstanding course for golfers of all abilities.
18 holes, 6595yds, Par 72, SSS 71, Course record 65. Club membership 600.
Visitors no restrictions but may not play before noon at weekends. **Societies** contact in advance. **Green Fees** terms on application. **Prof** Barry Loughrey **Course Designer** Hawtree **Facilities** ⊗ 🏋 ♥ ♀ ⚑ 🏠 🍴 ⚑ 🏌 🏌
Location On B4000 Shrivenham Road out of Highworth. Follow signs

Hotel ★★★ 69% Stanton House Hotel, The Avenue, Stanton Fitzwarren, SWINDON ☎ 01793 861777 86 en suite

KINGSDOWN   Map 03 ST86

Kingsdown SN13 8BS
☎ 01225 743472 📠 01225 743472
Fairly flat, open downland course with very sparse tree cover but surrounding wood.
18 holes, 6445yds, Par 72, SSS 71, Course record 64. Club membership 650.
Visitors weekends only with a member. Handicap certificate required weekdays. **Societies** apply by letter. **Green Fees** £28 per day. (weekdays only). **Prof** Andrew Butler **Facilities** ⊗ 𝄞 🏋 ♥ ♀ ⚖ 🏠 🍴 ⚙ 🏌 **Location** W side of village, between Corsham & Bath

Hotel ★★★★ ♨ Lucknam Park, COLERNE ☎ 01225 742777 23 en suite 18 annexe en suite

LANDFORD   Map 04 SU21

Hamptworth Golf & Country Club Hamptworth
Rd, Hamptworth SP5 2DU
☎ 01794 390155 📠 01794 390022
e-mail: info@hamptworthgolf.co.uk
Hamptworth enjoys ancient woodland and an abundance of wildlife in a beautiful setting on the edge of the New Forest. The 14th is one of its most challenging holes with a narrow fairway guarded by established forest oaks. The 2nd is a dog-leg of 543yds and plays differently all year.

18 holes, 6516yds, Par 72, SSS 71, Course record 68. Club membership 450.
Visitors telephone to check availability. **Societies** write or telephone in advance. **Green Fees** not confirmed. **Cards** 💳 💳 💳 💳 💳 **Prof** Phil Stevens **Course Designer** Philip Sanders/Brian Pierson **Facilities** ⊗ 𝄞 🏋 ♥ ♀ ⚑ 🏠 🍴 ⚖ ⚙ 🏌 **Leisure** gymnasium, croquet lawns. **Conf** Corporate Hospitality Days available **Location** Into Lyndhurst Rd at Landford Poacher, then right into Hamptworth Rd. Situated 0.5m on right after Cuckoo Inn

Hotel ★★★ 66% Bartley Lodge, Lyndhurst Rd, CADNAM ☎ 023 8081 2248 31 en suite

MARLBOROUGH   Map 04 SU16

Marlborough The Common SN8 1DU
☎ 01672 512147 📠 01672 513164
e-mail: contactus@marlboroughgolfclub.co.uk
Downland course with extensive views over the Og Valley and Marlborough Downs.
18 holes, 6514yds, Par 72, SSS 71, Course record 61. Club membership 900.
Visitors restricted at certain times. Must have a handicap certificate at weekends. Must contact in advance. **Societies** must contact in advance. **Green Fees** £37 per day; £28 per

Continued

round (£47/£34 weekends). **Cards** 🏧 💳 💳 💳 💳 **Prof**
S Amor **Facilities** ⊗ ⑩ ⓛ 💺 ♀ 🏌 🏚 ♦ 🏌 ♂ **Conf** fac
available Corporate Hospitality Days available **Location**
N side of town centre on A346

•••••••••••••

Hotel ★★★ 66% The Castle & Ball, High St,
MARLBOROUGH ☎ 01672 515201 34 en suite

OAKSEY
Map 03 ST99

Oaksey Park Golf & Leisure SN16 9SB
☎ 01666 577995 🖥 01666 577174
9 holes, 3100yds, Par 70, SSS 69, Course record 66.
Course Designer Chapman & Warren **Location** On B road
connecting A419 & A429, on outskirts of village of
Oaksey. S of Cirencester
Telephone for further details

•••••••••••••

Hotel ★★★ 69% Stratton House Hotel, Gloucester Rd,
CIRENCESTER ☎ 01285 651761 41 en suite

OGBOURNE ST GEORGE
Map 04 SU27

Ogbourne Downs SN8 1TB
☎ 01672 841327 🖥 01672 841101
**Downland turf and magnificent greens. Wind and
slopes make this one of the most challenging courses in
Wiltshire. Extensive views.**
18 holes, 6363yds, Par 71, SSS 70, Course record 65.
Club membership 800.
Visitors phone in advance. Handicap certificate required.
Societies must apply for booking form in advance. **Green
Fees** terms on application. **Cards** 🏧 💳 💳 💳 💳 **Prof**
Andrew Kirk **Course Designer** J H Taylor **Facilities** ⊗ ⓛ
💺 ♀ 🏚 🏌 ♦ 🏌 ♂ **Location** N side of village on A346

•••••••••••••

Hotel ★★★ 66% The Castle & Ball, High St,
MARLBOROUGH ☎ 01672 515201 34 en suite

SALISBURY
Map 04 SU12

Salisbury & South Wilts Netherhampton SP2 8PR
☎ 01722 742645 🖥 01722 742676
e-mail: mail@salisburygolf.co.uk
**Gently undulating and well drained parkland courses
in country setting with panoramic views of the
cathedral and surrounding countryside. Never easy
with six excellent opening holes and four equally testing
closing holes. A joy to play.**
*Main Course: 18 holes, 6485yds, Par 71, SSS 71, Course
record 61.*
Bibury Course: 9 holes, 2837yds, Par 34.
Club membership 1150.
Visitors advisable to telephone in advance. **Societies**
telephone, write or e-mail for information park. **Green
Fees** not confirmed. **Prof** John Cave/Geraldine Teschner
Course Designer J H Taylor/S Gidman **Facilities** ⊗ ⑩ ⓛ
💺 ♀ 🏚 🏌 ♦ 🏌 ♂ **Conf** fac available Corporate
Hospitality Days available **Location** 2m SW of
Salisbury,on A3094

•••••••••••••

Hotel ★★★ 64% The Rose & Crown Hotel, Harnham Rd,
Harnham, SALISBURY ☎ 0870 6096163 28 en suite

SWINDON
Map 04 SU18

Broome Manor Golf Complex Pipers Way
SN3 1RG
☎ 01793 532403 (bookings) 495761 (enquiries)
🖥 01793 433255
Two courses and a 34-bay floodlit driving range.

Continued

Parkland with water hazards, open fairways and short
cut rough. Walking is easy on gentle slopes.
*18 holes, 5989yds, Par 71, SSS 70, Course record 62.
Broom Manor Golf complex: 9 holes, Par 33.
Club membership 800.*
Visitors pre-booking necessary 6 days in advance for 18
hole course. **Societies** must be prebooked. **Green Fees** 18
hole: £19.10; 9 hole: £11.60. **Cards** 🏧 💳 💳 💳 💳 **Prof**
Barry Sandry **Course Designer** Hawtree **Facilities** ⊗ ⑩ ⓛ
💺 ♀ 🏚 🏌 ♦ 🏌 **Leisure** gymnasium. **Conf** fac
available Corporate Hospitality Days available **Location**
1.75m SE of town centre off B4006

•••••••••••••

Hotel ★★★★ 64% Swindon Marriott Hotel, Pipers Way,
SWINDON ☎ 0870 400 7281 156 en suite

TIDWORTH
Map 04 SU24

Tidworth Garrison Bulford Rd SP9 7AF
☎ 01980 842301 🖥 01980 842301
e-mail: tidworth@garrison-golfclub.fsnet.co.uk
**A breezy, dry downland course with lovely turf, fine
trees and views over Salisbury Plain and the
surrounding area. The 4th and 12th holes are notable.
The 565-yard 14th, going down towards the clubhouse,
gives the big hitter a chance to let fly.**
*18 holes, 6320yds, Par 70, SSS 70, Course record 63.
Club membership 800.*
Visitors must contact in advance, weekend & bank holiday
bookings may not be made until Thursday prior, handicap
certificate required. **Societies** Tue & Thu, bookings
required 12-18 months in advance. **Green Fees** £33 per
round/day (with member £14.50 per round/£21 per day).
Prof Terry Gosden **Course Designer** Donald Steel
Facilities ⊗ ⑩ ⓛ 💺 ♀ 🏚 🏌 🏌 ♦ 🏌 **Location** W side
of village off A338

•••••••••••••

Hotel ★★★ 62% Quality Hotel Andover, Micheldever
Rd, ANDOVER ☎ 01264 369111 13 en suite
36 annexe en suite

TOLLARD ROYAL
Map 03 ST91

Rushmore Park Golf Club SP5 5QB
☎ 01725 516326 🖥 01725 516437
e-mail: rushmoregolf@btinternet.com
**Peaceful and testing parkland course situated on
Cranborne Chase with far-reaching views. An
undulating course with avenues of trees and well
drained greens. With water on 7 out of 18 holes, it will
test the most confident of golfers.**
*Rushmore Park Golf Club: 18 holes, 6172yds, Par 71, SSS
69.
Club membership 475.*
Visitors must book in advance. Strict dress code enforced.
Societies welcome by appointment, apply in writing.
Green Fees not confirmed. **Cards** 🏧 💳 💳 💳 💳 **Prof**
Sean McDonagh **Course Designer** David Pottage/John
Jacobs Developments **Facilities** ⊗ ⑩ by prior arrangement
ⓛ 💺 ♀ 🏚 🏌 🏌 ♦ 🏌 **Location** 16m SW of Salisbury,
entrance off the B3081 between Sixpenny Handley and
Tollard Royal

•••••••••••••

Hotel ★★★ 66% Royal Chase Hotel, Royal Chase
Roundabout, SHAFTESBURY ☎ 01747 853355
33 en suite

UPAVON

Map 04 SU15

Upavon Douglas Av SN9 6BQ
☎ 01980 630787 & 635419 ▤ 01980 635419
e-mail: play@upavongolfclub.co.uk
Free-draining course on chalk downland with panoramic views over the Vale of Pewsey and the Alton Barnes White Horse. A fair test of golf with a good mixture of holes including a 602 yard par 5 and an excellent finishing hole, a par 3 of 169 yards across a valley.
18 holes, 6402yds, Par 71, SSS 71, Course record 69.
Club membership 600.
Visitors must contact in advance and may not play before noon at weekends. **Societies** telephone in advance. **Green Fees** £26 per day (£36 weekends). **Cards** 🏧 💳 💳 💳 💳 💳 **Prof** Richard Blake **Course Designer** Richard Blake **Facilities** ⊗ ⑭ by prior arrangement ⓫ ⬤ ♀ ⌂ ⛳ 🛒 ⛳ **Location** 1.5m SE of Upavon on A342 Andover road

Hotel ★★★ 64% Bear Hotel, Market Place, DEVIZES
☎ 01380 722444 24 en suite

WARMINSTER

Map 03 ST84

West Wilts Elm Hill BA12 0AU
☎ 01985 213133 ▤ 01985 219809
e-mail: westwiltsgc@btopenworld.com
A hilltop course among the Wiltshire downs on downland turf. Free draining, short, but a very good test of accurate iron play. Excellent greens and clubhouse facilities.
18 holes, 5754yds, Par 70, SSS 68, Course record 60.
Club membership 570.
Visitors may not play Sat. must contact in advance. Handicap certificate required. **Societies** Wed only. Apply by letter or phone **Green Fees** £30 per day; £25 per round (£40/30 Sun & bank holidays). **Cards** 💳 **Prof** Simon Swales **Course Designer** J H Taylor **Facilities** ⊗ ⑭ ⓫ ⬤ ♀ ⌂ ⛳ ⛳ **Location** N side of town centre off A350

Hotel ★★★★ 74% Bishopstrow House, WARMINSTER
☎ 01985 212312 32 en suite

WOOTTON BASSETT

Map 04 SU08

Brinkworth Longmans Farm, Brinkworth SN15 5DG
☎ 01666 510277
18 holes, 5884yds, Par 70, SSS 70.
Course Designer Jullian Sheppard **Location** Just off B4042 between Malmesbury/Wootton Bassett
Telephone for further details

Hotel ★★★ 71% Marsh Farm Hotel, Coped Hall, WOOTTON BASSETT ☎ 01793 848044 11 en suite
39 annexe en suite

Wiltshire Vastern SN4 7PB
☎ 01793 849999 ▤ 01793 849988
e-mail: tracey@the-wiltshire.co.uk
A Peter Alliss/Clive Clark design set in rolling Wiltshire downland countryside. A number of lakes add a challenge for both low and high handicappers.
The Wiltshire Golf Club: 18 holes, 6519yds, Par 72, SSS 72, Course record 67.
Club membership 800.

Wiltshire Golf Club
Visitors must contact in advance. **Societies** contact in advance. **Green Fees** £25 per 18 holes (£35 weekends and bank holidays). **Cards** 🏧 💳 💳 💳 💳 **Prof** Kevin Pickett **Course Designer** Peter Alliss & Clive Clark **Facilities** ⊗ ⑭ ⓫ ⬤ ♀ ⌂ ⛳ 🛒 ⛳ ⛳ **Leisure** heated indoor swimming pool, sauna, solarium, gymnasium, creche, jacuzzi. **Conf** fac available Corporate Hospitality Days available **Location** Leave M4 at junc 16, on A3102, follow Wootton Bassett. left at 2nd rdbt through town, approx 1.5 miles course left opposite Vastern Manor

Hotel ★★★ 71% Marsh Farm Hotel, Coped Hall, WOOTTON BASSETT ☎ 01793 848044 11 en suite
39 annexe en suite

WORCESTERSHIRE

ALVECHURCH

Map 07 SP07

Kings Norton Brockhill Ln, Weatheroak B48 7ED
☎ 01564 826706 & 826789 ▤ 01564 826955
e-mail: info@kingsnortongolfclub.co.uk
Parkland course with water hazards. A 27 hole Championship venue playing as three combinations of 9 holes.
Weatheroak: 18 holes, 6748yds, Par 72, SSS 72, Course record 65.
Brockhill: 18 holes, 6648yds, Par 72, SSS 72.
Wythall: 18 holes, 6612yds, Par 72, SSS 72.
Club membership 1000.
Visitors must contact in advance. No visitors at weekends. **Societies** must telephone in advance. **Green Fees** terms on application. **Cards** 🏧 💳 💳 💳 💳 **Prof** Kevin Hayward **Course Designer** F Hawtree **Facilities** ⊗ ⑭ ⓫ ⬤ ♀ ⌂ ⛳ 🛒 ⛳ **Leisure** par 3 course. **Conf** fac available Corporate Hospitality Days available **Location** M42 junct3, off A435

Hotel ★★★★ 66% Hanover International Hotel & Club, Kidderminster Rd, BROMSGROVE ☎ 01527 576600
114 en suite

BEWDLEY

Map 07 SO77

Little Lakes Golf and Country Club Lye
Head DY12 2UZ ☎ 01299 266385 ▤ 01299 266398
e-mail: marklaing@littlelakesgc.fsnet.co.uk
A pleasant undulating 18 hole parkland course. A challenging test of golf with stunning views of the Worcestershire countryside. Well acclaimed for the use of natural features.
18 holes, 6278yds, Par 71, SSS 70, Course record 68.
Club membership 475.

Continued

Continued

Little Lakes Golf and Country Club

Visitors advisable to telephone in advance. **Societies** must telephone in advance. **Green Fees** £17 (weekends £22). **Cards** 💳 💳 💳 💳 💳 **Prof** Mark A Laing **Course Designer** M Laing **Facilities** ⊗ by prior arrangement 🍽 by prior arrangement 🍸 by prior arrangement 🍺 by prior arrangement ♬ 🏌 🏠 🛒 🛺 ♟ **Leisure** hard tennis courts, heated outdoor swimming pool, fishing. **Conf** fac available **Location** 2.25m W of Bewdley off A456

....

Hotel ★★ 67% The George Hotel, Load St, BEWDLEY ☎ 01299 402117 11 en suite

Wharton Park Longbank DY12 2QW
☎ 01299 405163 📄 01299 405121
e-mail: enquiries@whartonpark.co.uk
18-hole championship-standard course set in 200 acres of beautiful Worcestershire countryside, with stunning views. Some long par 5s such as the 9th (594yds) as well as superb par 3 holes at 3rd, 10th and 15th make this a very challenging course.

18 holes, 6603yds, Par 72, SSS 71, Course record 66.
Club membership 500.
Visitors must contact in advance. May not play weekend mornings. **Societies** prior booking required. **Green Fees** terms on application. **Cards** 💳 💳 💳 💳 💳 **Prof** Angus Hoare **Course Designer** Howard Swan **Facilities** ⊗ 🍽 🍴 🍸 🏌 🏠 🛒 🛺 ♟ **Conf** fac available Corporate Hospitality Days available **Location** Off A456 Bewdley bypass

....

Hotel ★★ 67% The George Hotel, Load St, BEWDLEY ☎ 01299 402117 11 en suite

BISHAMPTON   Map 03 SO95

Vale Golf Club Hill Furze Rd WR10 2LZ
☎ 01386 462781 📄 01386 462597
e-mail: vale-sales@crown-golf.co.uk
This course offers an American-style layout, with large greens, trees and bunkers and several water hazards. Its

rolling fairways provide a testing round, as well as superb views of the Malvern Hills. Picturesque and peaceful.

Vale Golf Club

International Course: 18 holes, 7174yds, Par 74, SSS 74, Course record 67.
Lenches Course: 9 holes, 5518yds, Par 70, SSS 66.
Club membership 700.
Visitors booking up to one week in advance. Some weekend restrictions on International course. **Societies** must apply in advance. Some weekend restrictions. **Green Fees** International: £25 per round (£35 weekend) Lenchese: 9 holes £10 (£11). **Cards** 💳 💳 💳 💳 💳 **Prof** Paul Edgcombe **Course Designer** Bob Sandow **Facilities** ⊗ 🍽 🍴 🍸 🍺 🏌 🏠 🛒 🛺 ♟ **Conf** fac available Corporate Hospitality Days available **Location** Signposted off A44, between Evesham & Worcester

....

Hotel ★★★ 74% Salford Hall Hotel, ABBOT'S SALFORD ☎ 01386 871300 14 en suite   19 annexe en suite

BROADWAY   Map 04 SP03

Broadway Willersey Hill WR12 7LG
☎ 01386 853683 📄 01386 858643
e-mail: Beta.BroadwayGolfClub@care4free.net
At the edge of the Cotswolds this downland course lies at an altitude of 900 ft above sea level, with extensive views. Natural contours and man made hazards mean that drives have to be placed, approaches carefully judged and the greens expertly read.
18 holes, 5970yds, Par 72, SSS 70, Course record 65.
Club membership 850.
Visitors may not play Sat between Apr-Sep before 3pm. Restricted play Sun. Must contact in advance. **Societies** Wed-Fri, must contact in advance. **Green Fees** £38 per day, £30 per round (£38 weekends & bank holidays). **Cards** 💳 💳 💳 💳 **Prof** Martyn Freeman **Course Designer** James Braid **Facilities** ⊗ 🍽 🍴 🍸 🏌 🏠 🛒 🛺 ♟ **Conf** Corporate Hospitality Days available **Location** 1.5m E on A44

....

Hotel ★★★ 78% Dormy House Hotel, Willersey Hill, BROADWAY ☎ 01386 852711 25 en suite 23 annexe en suite

BROMSGROVE   Map 07 SO97

Blackwell Agmore Rd, Blackwell B60 1PY
☎ 0121 445 1994 📄 0121 445 4911
e-mail: info@blackwellgolfclub.com
Pleasantly undulating parkland with a variety of trees. Laid out in two 9-hole loops.
18 holes, 6080yds, Par 70, SSS 71.
Club membership 355.
Visitors must contact in advance, must have handicap

Continued   *Continued*

certificate, may not play at weekends, **Societies** must contact in advance. **Green Fees** 18 holes £60; 27/36 holes £70. **Prof** Nigel Blake **Course Designer** Herbert Fowler/Tom Simpson **Facilities** ⊗ by prior arrangement ⫚ by prior arrangement ⯐ ♥ ♀ ♨ ♠ ⛟ ⛳ **Conf** Corporate Hospitality Days available **Location** 2m W of Alvechurch. M42 junct 1 westbound, then B4096 or M5 junct.4, then take A38 towards Bromsgrove and B4096 to Burcot, club signed

Hotel ★★★★ 66% Hanover International Hotel & Club, Kidderminster Rd, BROMSGROVE ☎ 01527 576600 114 en suite

Bromsgrove Golf Centre Stratford Rd B60 1LD
☎ 01527 575886 & 570505 🖹 01527 570964
e-mail: enquiries@bromsgrovegolfcentre.com
This gently undulating course with superb views over Worcestershire is not to be underestimated. Creative landscaping and a selection of well defined bunkers ensure that the course delivers a uniquely satisfying experience through a variety of challenging, yet enjoyable, holes.

18 holes, 5969yds, Par 68, SSS 69.
Club membership 900.
Visitors dress restriction, no T-shirts, jeans, tracksuits etc. 7 day booking facilities available. **Societies** packages available, apply in writing or telephone. **Green Fees** 18 holes £16.30; 9 holes £9.50 (£21.50/£13.20 weekends). **Cards** ⊟ ⬛ ⬛ ☑ **Prof** Graeme Long/Danny Wall **Course Designer** Hawtree & Son **Facilities** ⊗ ⫚ ⯐ ♥ ♀ ♨ ♠ ⛟ ⛳ **Conf** fac available Corporate Hospitality Days available **Location** 1m from Bromsgrove town centre at junct of A38/A448

Hotel ★★★★ 66% Hanover International Hotel & Club, Kidderminster Rd, BROMSGROVE ☎ 01527 576600 114 en suite

DROITWICH   Map 03 SO86

Droitwich Ford Ln WR9 0BQ
☎ 01905 774344 🖹 01905 797290
Undulating parkland course.
18 holes, 5976yds, Par 70, SSS 69, Course record 62.
Club membership 732.
Visitors with member only weekends & bank holidays. **Societies** must apply by telephone and letter. **Green Fees** £26 per day, £18 per round. **Prof** C Thompson **Course Designer** J Braid/G Franks **Facilities** ⊗ ⫚ ⯐ ♥ ♀ ♨ ♠ ⛳ **Leisure** snooker. **Conf** Corporate Hospitality Days available **Location** Off A38 Droitwich to Bromsgrove road, midway between Droitwich and M5 junct 5

Hotel ★★★★ 67% Chateau Impney Hotel, DROITWICH SPA ☎ 01905 774411 67 en suite 53 annexe en suite

Gaudet Luce Middle Ln, Hadzor WR9 7DP
☎ 01905 796375 🖹 01905 797245
e-mail: info@gaudet-luce.co.uk
A challenging 18-hole course with two contrasting 9-hole loops. The front nine are long and fairly open, the back nine are tight and compact requiring good positional and approach play. Water features on several holes.
18 holes, 6040yds, Par 70, SSS 68.
Club membership 600.
Visitors welcome, advisable to telephone in advance, proper golfing attire required at all times. **Societies** telephone for details. **Green Fees** not confirmed. **Cards** ⊟ ⬛ ⬛ ⬛ ☑ **Prof** Phil Cundy **Course Designer** M A Laing **Facilities** ⊗ ⫚ ⯐ ♥ ♀ ♨ ♠ ⛳ **Conf** Corporate Hospitality Days available **Location** M5 junct 5, left at Tagwell road into Middle Lane, 1st driveway on left to clubhouse

Hotel ★★★★ 67% Chateau Impney Hotel, DROITWICH SPA ☎ 01905 774411 67 en suite 53 annexe en suite

Ombersley Bishops Wood Rd, Lineholt, Ombersley WR9 0LE ☎ 01905 620747 🖹 01905 620047
e-mail: enquiries@ombersleygolfclub
Undulating course in beautiful countryside high above the edge of the Severn Valley. Covered driving range and putting green.
18 holes, 6139yds, Par 72, SSS 69, Course record 67.
Club membership 750.
Visitors suitable dress expected, no jeans, shirts must have a collar. **Societies** telephone in advance. **Green Fees** terms on application. **Cards** ⊟ ⬛ ⬛ ⬛ ☑ **Prof** G Glenister/N Woodman/D Hall **Course Designer** David Morgan **Facilities** ⊗ ⫚ ⯐ ♥ ♀ ♨ ♠ ⛟ ⛳ **Location** 3m W of Droitwich, off A449. At Mitre Oak pub, take A4025 to Stourport, signposted 400yds on left

Hotel ★★★★ 65% Raven Hotel, Victoria Square, DROITWICH SPA ☎ 01905 772224 72 en suite

FLADBURY   Map 03 SO94

Evesham Craycombe Links, Old Worcester Rd
WR10 2QS ☎ 01386 860395 🖹 861356
e-mail: eveshamgolfclub@talk21.com
Parkland, heavily wooded, with the River Avon running alongside 5th and 14th holes. Good views. Nine greens played from eighteen different tees.
9 holes, 6415yds, Par 72, Course record 65.
Club membership 450.
Visitors must contact in advance, and have a handicap certificate. **Societies** must apply by in advance by phone or writing. **Green Fees** £25 per day (£15 with member). **Prof** Dan Cummins **Facilities** ⊗ ⫚ ⯐ ♥ ♀ ♨ ♠ ⛳ **Location** 0.75m N on A4538

Hotel ★★★ 75% The Evesham Hotel, Coopers Ln, Off Waterside, EVESHAM ☎ 01386 765566 & 0800 716969 (Res) 🖹 01386 765443 39 en suite 1 annexe en suite

HOLLYWOOD   Map 07 SP07

Gay Hill Hollywood Ln B47 5PP
☎ 0121 430 8544 & 474 6001 (pro) 🖹 0121 436 7796
A meadowland course, some 7 miles from Birmingham.
18 holes, 6406yds, Par 72, SSS 72, Course record 64.
Club membership 740.

Continued

Visitors must contact in advance. **Societies** telephone in advance. **Green Fees** £32 per day. **Prof** Andrew Potter **Facilities** ⊗ ⅷ ᴸ ♥ ♀ ᐃ 🏠 ⚲ ⚘ **Location** N side of village

Hotel ★★★ 67% The Regency Hotel, Stratford Rd, Shirley, SOLIHULL ☎ 0870 609 6133 111 en suite

KIDDERMINSTER — Map 07 SO87

Churchill and Blakedown Churchill Ln,
Blakedown DY10 3NB
☎ 01562 700018 & 700200 🖹 01562 700018
Pleasant course on hilltop with extensive views.
9 holes, 6488yds, Par 72, SSS 71.
Club membership 400.
Visitors with member only weekends & bank holidays. Handicap certificate required. Must contact in advance. **Societies** by arrangement through secretary. **Green Fees** £25 weekdays. **Prof** G. Wright **Facilities** ⊗ ⅷ ᴸ ♥ ♀ ᐃ 🏠 ⚘ **Conf** Corporate Hospitality Days available **Location** W side of village off A456

Hotel ★★★★ 68% Stone Manor Hotel, Stone, KIDDERMINSTER ☎ 01562 777555 52 en suite 5 annexe en suite

Habberley Low Trimpley DY11 5RF
☎ 01562 745756 🖹 01562 745756
Very hilly, wooded parkland course.
9 holes, 5401yds, Par 69, Course record 62.
Club membership 152.
Visitors may only play weekends with a member, weekdays by prior arrangement. **Societies** telephone initially. **Green Fees** £15 per day (£10 winter). **Cards** 🖿 🖿 🖿 🖿 🖿 🖿 🖿 **Facilities** ⊗ ⅷ ᴸ ♥ ♀ ᐃ **Location** 2m NW of Kidderminster

Hotel ★★★★ 68% Stone Manor Hotel, Stone, KIDDERMINSTER ☎ 01562 777555 52 en suite 5 annexe en suite

Kidderminster Russell Rd DY10 3HT
☎ 01562 822303 🖹 01562 827866
e-mail: info@kiddigolf.com
Pleasant wooded parkland course, mainly flat, but a good test of golf for all levels of player. Two small lakes add to the challenge.

18 holes, 6422yds, Par 72, SSS 71, Course record 65.
Club membership 860.
Visitors with member only weekends & bank holidays. Must have a handicap certificate. **Societies** weekdays only apply in advance. **Green Fees** £35 per day, £30 per round. **Cards** 🖿 🖿 🖿 **Prof** Nick Underwood **Facilities** ⊗ ⅷ ᴸ ♥ ♀ ᐃ 🏠 ⚲ ⚘ ⚘ **Conf** fac available Corporate

Hospitality Days available **Location** 0.5m SE of town centre, signposted off A449

Hotel ★★★★ 68% Stone Manor Hotel, Stone, KIDDERMINSTER ☎ 01562 777555 52 en suite 5 annexe en suite

Wyre Forest Zortech Av DY11 7EX
☎ 01299 822682 🖹 01299 879433
e-mail: simon@wyreforestgolf.com
Making full use of the existing contours, this interesting and challenging course is bounded by woodland and gives extensive views over the surrounding area. Well drained fairways and greens.
18 holes, 5790yds, Par 70, SSS 68, Course record 68.
Club membership 397.
Visitors must telephone in advance. **Societies** brochure on request, deposit secures date, write or telephone. **Green Fees** not confirmed. **Cards** 🖿 🖿 🖿 🖿 🖿 **Prof** Simon Price **Facilities** ᴸ ♀ ᐃ 🏠 ⚲ ⚘ ⚘ ⚘ 🍴 **Location** Halfway between Kidderminster & Stourport, on A451

Hotel ★★★★ 73% Menzies Stourport Manor, Hartlebury Rd, STOURPORT-ON-SEVERN ☎ 01299 289955 68 en suite

MALVERN WELLS — Map 03 SO74

Worcestershire Wood Farm, Wood Farm Rd
WR14 4PP ☎ 01684 575992 🖹 01684 893334
e-mail: secretary@theworcestershiregolfclub.co.uk
Fairly easy walking on windy downland course with trees, ditches and other natural hazards. Outstanding views of Malvern Hills and Severn Valley. 17th hole (par 5) is approached over small lake.
18 holes, 6500yds, Par 71, SSS 72.
Club membership 750.
Visitors handicap certificate required. Phone for availability **Societies** Apply in advance by telephone. **Green Fees** £35 per day; £28 per round (£40/£34 weekends & bank holidays). **Prof** Richard Lewis **Course Designer** J H Taylor **Facilities** ⊗ ⅷ ᴸ ♥ ♀ ᐃ 🏠 ⚘ **Leisure** indoor teaching facility. **Conf** Corporate Hospitality Days available **Location** 2m S of Gt Malvern on B4209

Hotel ★★★ 74% The Cottage in the Wood Hotel, Holywell Rd, Malvern Wells, MALVERN ☎ 01684 575859 8 en suite 23 annexe en suite

Additional hotel ★★ 74% Holdfast Cottage Hotel, Marlbank Rd, Little Malvern, MALVERN ☎ 01684 310288 Fax 01684 311117 8 en suite

Continued

REDDITCH   Map 07 SP06

Set amidst a beautiful undulating landscape in North Worcestershire, the Abbey course offers a variety of challenges from wooded areas to water early in your round but many holes offer welcome relief with their spacious fairways. Extensive drainage works have ensured the course is playable during all seasons. All guests have complimentary use of the health club, including indoor pool and gymnasium. Packages are available for corporate golf and societies.

Hither Green Lane, Dagnell End Road, Redditch, Worcestershire B98 9BE
Tel: 01527 406600 Fax: 01527 406514
www.theabbeyhotel.co.uk

Abbey Hotel Golf & Country Club Dagnell End Rd, Hither Green Ln B98 9BE
☎ 01527 406600 & 406500 📠 01527 406514
e-mail: info@theabbeyhotel.co.uk
Parkland course with rolling fairways with many trees and lakes on several holes. Recent course improvements have resulted in a course which requires more thought than before. Pure putting surfaces are a worthy reward for some solid iron play, allowing the golfer to make the most of a birdie.

18 holes, 6561yds, Par 72, SSS 72.
Club membership 500.
Visitors must contact in advance, dress code applies. **Societies** must apply in writing/by telephone. **Green Fees** £18 per round (£25 Fri-Sun and bank holidays). **Cards** 🟥 🟥 🟥 🟦 🟥 🟥 **Prof** R Davies **Course Designer** Donald Steele **Facilities** ⊗ 𝄞 🕭 ⬛ 𝅘 🛆 🏠 🚩 🏌 🛒 🛺

Continued

♂ ↆ **Leisure** heated indoor swimming pool, fishing, sauna, solarium, gymnasium. **Conf** fac available Corporate Hospitality Days available **Location** from M42 junct 2 take A441 to Redditch for approx 2m. Turn left at 1st roundabout, after approx 0.75m turn left at traffic lights, signposted Beoley (B4101) and then right into Hither Green Lane.

Hotel ★★★★ 67% The Abbey Hotel Golf & Country Club, Hither Green Ln, Dagnell End Rd, Bordesley, REDDITCH ☎ 01527 406600 72 en suite

Pitcheroak Plymouth Rd B97 4PB
☎ 01527 541054 📠 01527 65216
9 holes, 4561yds, Par 65, SSS 62.
Location SW side of town centre off A448
Telephone for further details

Hotel ★★★ 64% Quality Hotel Redditch, Pool Bank, Southcrest, REDDITCH ☎ 01527 541511 73 en suite

Redditch Lower Grinsty, Green Ln, Callow Hill
B97 5PJ ☎ 01527 543079 (sec) 📠 01527 547413
e-mail: redditchgolfclub@btconnect.com
Parkland course, the hazards including woods, ditches and large ponds. The par 4 14th is a testing hole.
18 holes, 6671yds, Par 72, SSS 72, Course record 68.
Club membership 650.
Visitors with member only weekends & bank holidays, no visitors on competition days, advisable to telephone in advance. **Societies** apply in writing to secretary. **Green Fees** £35 per round/£45 per day (£10 with member). **Prof** David Down **Course Designer** F Pennick **Facilities** ⊗ 𝄞 🕭 ⬛ 𝅘 🛆 🏠 🛒 🛺 ♂ **Location** 2m SW

Hotel ★★★ 64% Quality Hotel Redditch, Pool Bank, Southcrest, REDDITCH ☎ 01527 541511 73 en suite

TENBURY WELLS   Map 07 SO56

Cadmore Lodge Hotel & Country Club St Michaels, Berrington Green WR15 8TQ
☎ 01584 810044 📠 01584 810044
e-mail: info@cadmorelodge.demon.co.uk
A picturesque 9-hole course in a brook valley. Challenging holes include the 1st and 6th over the lake, 8th over the valley and 9th over hedges.
9 holes, 5132yds, Par 68, SSS 65.
Club membership 200.
Visitors no restrictions but check availability. **Societies** telephone in advance. **Green Fees** not confirmed. **Cards** 🟥 🟥 🟥 🟦 🟥 🟥 🟥 **Facilities** ⊗ 𝄞 🕭 ⬛ 𝅘 🛆 🏠 🛒 ♂
Leisure hard tennis courts, heated indoor swimming pool, fishing, sauna, gymnasium, pool table. **Location** From Tenbury take A4112 to Leominster, after approx 2m turn right for Berrington, 0.75 on left

Hotel ★★ 67% Cadmore Lodge Hotel & Country Club, Berrington Green, St Michaels, TENBURY WELLS ☎ 01584 810044 15 rms (14 en suite)

WORCESTER   Map 03 SO85

Bank House Hotel Golf & Country Club
Bransford WR6 5JD
☎ 01886 833545 📠 01886 832461
e-mail: info@bransfordgolfclub.co.uk
The Bransford course is designed as a 'Florida' style course with fairways weaving between water courses, 13 lakes and sculpted mounds with colourful plant

Continued

displays. The 6,204yd course has dog-legs, island greens and tight fairways to challenge all standards of player. The 10th, 16th and 18th (The Devil's Elbow) are particularly tricky.

Bank House Hotel Golf & Country Club
Bransford Course: 18 holes, 6204yds, Par 72, SSS 71, Course record 65.
Club membership 380.
Visitors all tee times must be booked, no play before 9.30am. **Societies** contact the golf secretary, all tee times must be booked in advance. **Green Fees** not confirmed. **Cards** ▦ ▦ ▦ ▦ ▦ ▦ **Prof** Scott Fordyce **Course Designer** Bob Sandow **Facilities** ⊗ ⅷ ▯ ▭ ♀ ♧ ▦ ⌂ ⅋ ⇆ ⛟ ♘ **Leisure** outdoor swimming pool, sauna, solarium, gymnasium, spa pool, vertical sunbed. **Conf** fac available Corporate Hospitality Days available **Location** Exit M5 Junct 7, club is 3m S of Worcester, A4103

Hotel ★★★ 70% Bank House Hotel Golf & Country Club, Bransford, WORCESTER ☎ 01886 833551 68 en suite

Worcester Golf & Country Club Boughton Park WR2 4EZ ☎ 01905 422555 ▤ 01905 749090
Fine parkland course with many trees, a lake, and views of the Malvern Hills.
18 holes, 6251yds, Par 70, SSS 70, Course record 67.
Club membership 1000.
Visitors must contact professional in advance. May not play at weekends. **Societies** telephone in advance. **Green Fees** not confirmed. **Prof** Colin Colenso **Course Designer** Dr A Mackenzie **Facilities** ⊗ by prior arrangement ⅷ by prior arrangement ▯ ▭ ♀ ♧ ▦ ⅋ **Leisure** hard and grass tennis courts, squash. **Location** 1.5m from city centre on A4103

Hotel ★★★ 70% Bank House Hotel Golf & Country Club, Bransford, WORCESTER ☎ 01886 833551 68 en suite

Fulford Heath Tanners Green Ln B47 6BH
☎ 01564 824758 ▤ 01564 822629
e-mail: secretary@fulfordheath.co.uk
A mature parkland course encompassing two classic par threes. The 11th, a mere 149 yards, shoots from an elevated tee through a channel of trees to a well-protected green. The 16th, a 166-yard par 3, elevated green, demands a 140 yard carry over an imposing lake.
18 holes, 6179yds, Par 70, SSS 70, Course record 65.
Club membership 750.
Visitors with member only weekend & bank holidays. Handicap certificate required. **Societies** must apply in

advance. **Green Fees** £35 per day/round. **Prof** Richard Dunbar **Course Designer** Braid/Hawtree **Facilities** ⊗ ⅷ ▯ ▭ ♀ ♧ ▦ ⇆ ⛟ ♘ **Conf** Corporate Hospitality Days available **Location** 1m SE off A435

Hotel ★★★★ 70% Renaissance Solihull Hotel, 651 Warwick Rd, SOLIHULL ☎ 0121 711 3000 179 en suite

Oaks Aughton Common YO42 4PW
☎ 01757 288577 & 288007 ▤ 01757 289029
e-mail: oaksgolfclub@hotmail.com
The Oaks: 18 holes, 6743yds, Par 72, SSS 72.
Course Designer Julian Covey **Location** 1m N of Bubwith on B1228
Telephone for further details

Hotel ★★★ 73% The Parsonage Country House Hotel, York Rd, ESCRICK ☎ 01904 728111 12 en suite 34 annexe en suite

Beverley & East Riding The Westwood
HU17 8RG ☎ 01482 868757 ▤ 01482 868757
Picturesque parkland course with some hard walking and natural hazards - trees and gorse bushes. Also cattle (spring to autumn); horse-riders are an occasional hazard in the early morning.
Westwood: 18 holes, 6127yds, Par 69, SSS 69, Course record 64.
Club membership 530.
Visitors must contact in advance. **Societies** telephone 01482 868757, then written confirmation. **Green Fees** £20 per day; £15 per round (£25/£20 weekends). **Prof** Alex Ashby **Facilities** ⊗ ⅷ ▯ ▭ ♀ ♧ ▦ ⅋ **Location** 1m SW on B1230

Hotel ★★★ 67% The Beverley Arms Hotel, North Bar Within, BEVERLEY ☎ 0870 609 6149 56 en suite

Hainsworth Park Burton Holme YO25 8RT
☎ 01964 542362
A parkland course based on sand and gravel giving excellent drainage. Demands straight driving due to mature trees.
18 holes, 6362yds, Par 71, SSS 71.
Club membership 500.
Visitors contact in advance. **Societies** telephone initially. **Green Fees** £22 per day; £18 per round (£27/£22 weekends). **Cards** ▦ ▦ ▦ ▦ ▦ **Prof** Paul Binnington **Facilities** ⊗ ⅷ ▯ ▭ ♀ ♧ ▦ ⌂ ⅋ ⇆ ♘ ⛟ **Location** SW side of village on A165

Hotel ★★ 68% Burton Lodge Hotel, BRANDESBURTON ☎ 01964 542847 7 en suite 2 annexe en suite

Bridlington Belvedere Rd YO15 3NA
☎ 01262 606367 ▤ 01262 606367
e-mail: enquiries@bridlingtongolfclub.co.uk
Parkland course alongside Bridlington Bay, with tree-lined fairways and six ponds. There are many well

Continued   Continued

positioned fairway and greenside bunkers which
protect excellent putting surfaces.
18 holes, 6638yds, Par 72, SSS 72, Course record 66.
Club membership 600.
Visitors must contact in advance, professional 01262
674721 limited at weekends. **Societies** telephone bookings
in advance. **Green Fees** £30 per day, £24 per round (£37
per 27 holes, £30 per round weekends). **Cards** 🖃 🖭 📇
🔲 **Prof** Anthony Howarth **Course Designer** James Braid
Facilities ⊗ ⫼ ⮣ 💺 ♀ 🛆 🖭 ⛳ ⚒ 🏌 ⬢ **Leisure**
snooker. **Conf** Corporate Hospitality Days available
Location 1m S off A165

···

Hotel ★★★ 70% Revelstoke Hotel, 1-3 Flamborough Rd,
BRIDLINGTON ☎ 01262 672362 26 en suite

Bridlington Links Flamborough Rd, Marton
YO15 1DW ☎ 01262 401584 📄 01262 401702
*Main: 18 holes, 6719yds, Par 72, SSS 72, Course record
70.*
Course Designer Swan **Location** On the B1255 between
Bridlington and Flamborough
Telephone for further details

···

Hotel ★★★ 67% Expanse Hotel, North Marine Dr,
BRIDLINGTON ☎ 01262 675347 48 en suite

BROUGH   Map 08 SE92

Brough Cave Rd HU15 1HB
☎ 01482 667291 📄 01482 669873
e-mail: gt@brough-golfclub.co.uk
**Parkland course, where accurate positioning of the tee
ball is required for good scoring. Testing for the scratch
player without being too difficult for the higher
handicap.**
18 holes, 6067yds, Par 68, SSS 69, Course record 62.
Club membership 700.
Visitors must have handicap certificate and contact in
advance. **Societies** apply by letter. **Green Fees** £45 per
day: £32 per round (£60/£45 weekends and bank holidays).
Prof Gordon Townhill **Facilities** ⊗ ⫼ ⮣ 💺 ♀ 🛆 🖭 ⛳
⚒ **Location** 8m W of Hull off the A63

COTTINGHAM   Map 08 TA03

Cottingham Parks Golf & Country Club
Woodhill Way HU16 5RZ
☎ 01482 846030 📄 01482 845932
e-mail: jane.wiles@cottinghamparks.co.uk
**Gently undulating parkland course incorporating many
natural features, including lateral water hazards, several
ponds on the approach to greens, and rolling fairways.**

18 holes, 6459yds, Par 72, SSS 71, Course record 66.
Club membership 600.

Visitors may book by telephone in advance, times
available weekdays and weekends. **Societies** deposit
required and confirmation in writing. After 2pm weekends.
Green Fees £20 per round (£28 weekends & bank
holidays). **Cards** 🖃 🖭 📇 🔲 **Prof** Chris Gray
Course Designer Terry Litten **Facilities** ⊗ ⫼ ⮣ 💺 ♀ 🛆
🖭 ⛳ ⚒ 🏌 **Leisure** heated indoor swimming pool, sauna,
solarium, gymnasium, Jacuzzi Remedial masseur. **Conf** fac
available **Location** 4m from A63/M62 on A164. Turn off
to Cottingham on B1233, in 100yds turn left into Woodhill
Way

···

Hotel ★★ 68% The Rowley Manor Hotel, Rowley Rd,
LITTLE WEIGHTON ☎ 01482 848248 16 en suite

DRIFFIELD (GREAT)   Map 08 TA05

Driffield Sunderlandwick YO25 9AD
☎ 01377 253116 📄 01377 240599
e-mail: info@driffieldgolfclub.com
**An easy walking, mature parkland course set within the
beautiful Sunderlandwick Estate, including numerous
water features, one of which is a renowned trout
stream.**
18 holes, 6215yds, Par 70, SSS 69, Course record 67.
Club membership 693.
Visitors must book in advance and adhere to club dress
rule. **Societies** apply in writing or telephone. **Green Fees**
£30 per day, £24 per round;(£40/£30 weekends). **Prof**
Kenton Wright **Facilities** ⊗ ⫼ ⮣ 💺 ♀ 🛆 🖭 ⛳ ⚒
Leisure fishing. **Conf** Corporate Hospitality Days
available **Location** 2m S off A164

···

Hotel ★★★ 72% Bell Hotel, 46 Market Place,
DRIFFIELD ☎ 01377 256661 16 en suite

FLAMBOROUGH   Map 08 TA27

Flamborough Head Lighthouse Rd YO15 1AR
☎ 01262 850333 & 850417 & 850683 📄 01262 850279
e-mail: secretary@flamboroughheadgolfclub.co.uk
**Undulating cliff top course on the Flamborough
headland.**
18 holes, 6189yds, Par 71, SSS 69, Course record 71.
Club membership 500.
Visitors welcome but may not play before 1pm Sun, Wed
between 10.30 & 1.30, Sat between 11.30 & 12.30.
Societies must contact in advance. **Green Fees** not
confirmed. **Prof** Paul Harrison **Facilities** ⊗ ⫼ ⮣ 💺 ♀ 🛆
🖭 ⚒ **Location** 2m E off B1259. 5m NE of
Bridlington on the Flamborough headland

···

Hotel ★★ 72% North Star Hotel, North Marine Dr,
FLAMBOROUGH ☎ 01262 850379 7 en suite

HESSLE   Map 08 TA02

Hessle Westfield Rd, Raywell HU16 5YL
☎ 01482 650171 & 650190 (Prof) 📄 01482 652679
e-mail: secretary@hessle-golf-club.co.uk
**Well-wooded downland course with easy walking. The
greens, conforming to USGA specification, are large
and undulating with excellent drainage, enabling play
throughout the year.**
18 holes, 6604yds, Par 72, SSS 72, Course record 65.
Club membership 720.
Visitors not Tue between 9-1 and may not play before
11.30am on Sat & Sun. **Societies** by prior arrangement.
Green Fees £32 per day; £25 per round (£32 per round
weekends). **Cards** 🖃 🖭 📇 🔲 **Prof** Grahame Fieldsend

Continued   *Continued*

Course Designer D Thomas/P Allis **Facilities** ⊗)∭ ⮞ ⛳
♀ ⬟ 🏠 ⚐ **Conf** fac available Corporate Hospitality Days
available **Location** 3m SW of Cottingham

HORNSEA   Map 08 TA14

Hornsea Rolston Rd HU18 1XG
☎ 01964 532020 📋 01964 532080
e-mail: hornseagolfclub@aol.com
**Easy walking parkland course renowned for the quality
of its greens.**
18 holes, 6685yds, Par 72, SSS 72, Course record 66.
Club membership 600.
Visitors with member only at weekends until 3pm Sats,
2pm Sun. Must contact in advance. **Societies** contact
Secretary in advance. **Green Fees** £32 per day; £26 per
round (Sat £34 per round; Sun £26). **Prof** Stretton Wright
Facilities ⊗)∭ by prior arrangement ⮞ ⛳ ♀ ⬟ 🏠 ⛵ ⚐
Conf Corporate Hospitality Days available **Location** 1m S
on B1242, follow signs for Hornsea Freeport

Hotel ★★★ 67% The Beverley Arms Hotel, North Bar
Within, BEVERLEY ☎ 0870 609 6149 56 en suite

HOWDEN   Map 08 SE72

Boothferry Park Spaldington Ln DN14 7NG
☎ 01430 430364 📋 01430 430567
**Pleasant, meadowland course in the Vale of York with
interesting natural dykes, creating challenges on some
holes. The par 5 ninth is a test for any golfer with its
dyke coming into play on the tee shot, second shot and
approach.**
18 holes, 6651yds, Par 73, SSS 72, Course record 64.
Club membership 250.
Visitors must contact in advance, tee times bookable.
Societies must contact for booking form. **Green Fees**
terms on application. **Prof** James Major **Course Designer**
Donald Steel **Facilities** ⊗)∭ ⮞ ⛳ ♀ ⬟ 🏠 ⛵ 🚬 ⚐ ⛿
Conf Corporate Hospitality Days available **Location** M62.
junct 37, 2.5m N of Howden off B1228

Hotel ⇧ Travel Inn, Rawcliffe Rd, Airmyn, GOOLE
☎ 08701 977177 41 en suite

KINGSTON UPON HULL   Map 08 TA02

Ganstead Park Longdales Ln, Coniston HU11 4LB
☎ 01482 817754 📋 01482 817754
e-mail: secretary@gansteadpark.co.uk
Parkland course, easy walking, with water features.
18 holes, 6801yds, Par 72, SSS 73, Course record 62.
Club membership 500.
Visitors contact in advance. **Societies** telephone in
advance. **Green Fees** terms on application. **Prof** Michael J
Smee **Course Designer** P Green **Facilities** ⊗)∭ ⮞ ⛳ ♀
⬟ 🏠 ⛵ 🚬 🚬 ⚐ **Conf** Corporate Hospitality Days
available **Location** Leave Hull on A165, pass village of
Ganstead and immediately turn right along B1238 to
Bilton. Course on right

Hotel ★★★ 67% Quality Hotel Hull, 170 Ferensway,
HULL ☎ 01482 325087 155 en suite

Hull The Hall, 27 Packman Ln HU10 7TJ
☎ 01482 658919 📋 01482 658919
Parkland course.
18 holes, 6242yds, Par 70, SSS 70.
Club membership 768.
Visitors only weekdays. Contact professional 01482

653074. **Societies** Mon Tue Thu & Fri by prior
arrangement. **Green Fees** Dec-Feb £21 per day/round;
Mar-Nov £32 per day/round. **Prof** David Jagger **Course
Designer** James Braid **Facilities** ⊗)∭ ⮞ ⛳ ♀ ⬟ 🏠 ⚐
🚬 ⚐ **Location** 5m W of city centre off A164

Hotel ★★★ 73% Willerby Manor Hotel, Well Ln,
WILLERBY ☎ 01482 652616 51 en suite

Springhead Park Willerby Rd HU5 5JE
☎ 01482 656309
18 holes, 6402yds, Par 71, SSS 71.
Location 5m W off A164
Telephone for further details

Hotel ★★★ 73% Willerby Manor Hotel, Well Ln,
WILLERBY ☎ 01482 652616 51 en suite

Sutton Park Salthouse Rd HU8 9HF
☎ 01482 374242 📋 01482 701428
Municipal parkland course.
18 holes, 6251yds, Par 70, SSS 69, Course record 67.
Club membership 300.
Visitors no restrictions. **Societies** prior arrangement via
club, telephone and confirm in writing. **Green Fees** not
confirmed. **Prof** To be appointed **Facilities** ⊗ by prior
arrangement)∭ by prior arrangement ⮞ ⛳ ♀ ⬟ 🏠 ⛵ ⚐
⚐ **Location** 3m NE on B1237 off A165

Hotel ★★★ 67% Quality Hotel Hull, 170 Ferensway,
HULL ☎ 01482 325087 155 en suite

POCKLINGTON   Map 08 SE84

Kilnwick Percy Kilnwick Percy YO42 1UF
☎ 01759 303090
**Parkland course on the edge of the Wolds above
Pocklington combines a good walk with interesting golf.
Undulating fairways, mature trees, water hazards and
breathtaking views from every hole.**
*Kilnwick Percy Golf Course: 18 holes, 6218yards, Par 70,
SSS 70.*
Club membership 300.
Visitors telephone to book tee. May only play after 10am
weekends/bank holidays **Societies** telephone for details of
society packages. **Green Fees** £25 per day; £18 per 18
holes; £12 per 9 holes (£28/£20/£14 weekends & bank
holidays). **Prof** Joe Townhill **Course Designer** John Day
Facilities ⊗ ⮞ ⛳ ♀ ⬟ 🏠 ⛵ 🚬 ⚐ **Conf** Corporate
Hospitality Days available **Location** 1m E of Pocklington,
off B1246

Hotel ★★ 63% Feathers Hotel, 56 Market Place,
POCKLINGTON ☎ 01759 303155 6 en suite
6 annexe en suite

SOUTH CAVE   Map 08 SE93

Cave Castle Hotel & Country Club
Church Hill, South Cave HU15 2EU
☎ 01430 421286 📋 01430 421118
**An undulating meadow and parkland course at the foot
of the Wolds, with superb views. Golf breaks are
available.**
18 holes, 6500yds, Par 73, SSS 72, Course record 71.
Club membership 450.
Visitors must contact in advance, may not play before
11am weekends/bank holidays. **Societies** by arrangement
with Professional or golf administrator. **Green Fees** terms
on application. **Cards** 🃏 🃏 ⚐ **Prof** Stephen MacKinder

Continued   *Continued*

Course Designer Mrs N Freling **Facilities** ⊗ ⑩ 🍴 ⚑ 🏌 ⛳ 🖪 🍴 ⚑ ↕ 🍴 **Leisure** heated indoor swimming pool, fishing, sauna, solarium, gymnasium. **Conf** fac available Corporate Hospitality Days available **Location** 1m from A63

Withernsea Chesnut Av HU19 2PG
☎ 01964 612078 & 612258 📠 01964 612078
e-mail: golf@withernseagolfclub.fsnet.co.uk
Exposed seaside links with narrow, undulating fairways, bunkers and small greens.
9 holes, 6207yds, Par 72, SSS 69.
Club membership 300.
Visitors with member only at weekends before 3pm.
Societies apply in writing/telephone **Green Fees** £12 per 18 holes/per day. **Facilities** ⊗ ⑩ 🍴 🖪 ↕ ⚑ 🍴 **Leisure** senior/junior coaching. **Conf** fac available Corporate Hospitality Days available **Location** S side of town centre off A1033, sign post in Victoria avenue, through residential estate. Course signposted

······························

Hotel ★★★ 67% Quality Hotel Hull, 170 Ferensway, HULL ☎ 01482 325087 155 en suite

YORKSHIRE, NORTH

Aldwark Manor YO61 1UF
☎ 01347 838353 📠 01347 833991
An easy walking, scenic 18-hole parkland course with holes both sides of the River Ure. The course surrounds the Victorian Aldwark Manor Golf Hotel. A warm welcome to society and corporate days.

18 holes, 6187yds, Par 72, SSS 70, Course record 67.
Club membership 400.
Visitors must contact in advance, restricted weekends.
Societies must telephone in advance. **Green Fees** £35 per day; £25 per round (£40/£30 weekends & bank holiday).
Cards 🖃 🖃 🖃 🖃 🖃 🖃 **Facilities** ⊗ ⑩ 🍴 🖪 ↕ ⚑ 🍴 🖪 ⚑ 🍴 🏌 🏌 **Leisure** heated indoor swimming pool, fishing, sauna, gymnasium. **Conf** Corporate Hospitality Days available **Location** 5m SE of Boroughbridge off A1, 12m NW of York off A19

······························

Hotel ★★★★ 75% Aldwark Manor, ALDWARK ☎ 01347 838146 60 en suite

> **Use the maps at the back of the guide to help locate a golf course.**

Bedale Leyburn Rd DL8 1EZ
☎ 01677 422451 (sec) 📠 01677 427143
e-mail: bedalegolfclub@aol.com
One of North Yorkshire's most picturesque and interesting golf courses. An 18-hole course set in a parkland landscape with mature trees, water hazards and strategically placed bunkers. Easy walking, no heavy climbs.
18 holes, 6610yds, Par 72, SSS 72, Course record 68.
Club membership 600.
Visitors welcome, contact in advance. **Societies** must contact secretary for details. **Green Fees** £28 per day, £23 per round (£35/£30 weekends). **Cards** 🖃 🖃 🖃 **Prof** Tony Johnson **Course Designer** Hawtree **Facilities** ⊗ ⑩ 🍴 🖪 ↕ ⚑ 🍴 🏌 🍴 ⚑ 🏌 🍴 **Conf** Corporate Hospitality Days available **Location** From A1 take A684 at Leeming Bar to Bedale

······························

Hotel ★ 69% Buck Inn, THORNTON WATLASS ☎ 01677 422461 7 rms (5 en suite)

Bentham Robin Ln LA2 7AG ☎ 01524 62455
e-mail: secretary@benthamgolfclub.co.uk
Moorland course with glorious views and excellent greens.
18 holes, 5914yds, Par 72, SSS 69, Course record 69.
Club membership 600.
Visitors no restrictions. **Societies** must apply in advance.
Green Fees £30 per day, £26 per round (£35/£30 weekends). **Prof** Alan Watson **Facilities** ⊗ ⑩ 🍴 🖪 ↕ ⚑ 🍴 🏌

Continued

ALDWARK MANOR
AA ★★★★ RAC
Aldwark Nr. Alne York YO61 1UF

An easy walking scenic 18 hole parkland course, set in 120 acres with holes both sides of the River Ure. Many mature trees and water features. A warm welcome to society and company golf days.

TEL: 01347 838353 FAX: 01347 833991

MARSTON HOTELS 𝓂

HOTEL & GOLF CENTRE

🏨 ⚲ ⛳ ✆ **Conf** Corporate Hospitality Days available
Location N side of High Bentham

Guesthouse ♦♦♦♦ Turnerford Fold, Keasden,
CLAPHAM ☎ 015242 51731 2 en suite

CATTERICK GARRISON Map 08 SE29

Catterick Leyburn Rd DL9 3QE
☎ 01748 833268 📠 01748 833268
e-mail: grant@catterickgolfclub.co.uk
**Scenic parkland/moorland course of Championship
standard, with good views of the Pennines and
Cleveland hills. Testing 1st and 6th holes.**
18 holes, 6329yds, Par 71, SSS 71, Course record 64.
Club membership 700.
Visitors tee reservation system in operation telephone
professional shop 01748 833671. May not play before
10am Tue/Thu/weekends and bank holidays. **Societies** by
arrangement. **Green Fees** £28 per day, £25 per 18 holes
(£35 per 18 holes weekends). **Cards** 💳 🔲 💷 **Prof** Andy
Marshall **Course Designer** Arthur Day **Facilities** ⊗ ⏀ ⅃⌸ ╠
💺 ♀ 🏌 🏨 🏐 ⚲ ⛳ ✆ **Conf** fac available Corporate
Hospitality Days available **Location** 0.5m W of Catterick
Garrison Centre

Hotel ★★★ 66% King's Head Hotel, Market Place,
RICHMOND ☎ 01748 850220 26 en suite
4 annexe en suite

COPMANTHORPE Map 08 SE54

Pike Hills Tadcaster Rd YO23 3UW
☎ 01904 700797 📠 01904 700797
e-mail: thesecretary@pikehills.fsnet.co.uk
**Parkland course surrounding nature reserve. Level
terrain.**
18 holes, 6146yds, Par 71, SSS 70, Course record 63.
Club membership 750.
Visitors welcome weekdays, with member only weekends
& bank holidays. **Societies** must apply in advance. **Green
Fees** terms on application. **Prof** Ian Gradwell **Facilities** ⊗
⏀ ⅃⌸ ╠ 💺 ♀ 🏌 🏨 🏐 ⚲ ⛳ ✆ **Conf** fac available
Corporate Hospitality Days available **Location** 3m SW of
York on A64

Hotel ★★★★ 68% York Marriott Hotel, Tadcaster Rd,
YORK ☎ 01904 701000 108 en suite

EASINGWOLD Map 08 SE56

Easingwold Stillington Rd YO61 3ET
☎ 01347 821964 (Pro) & 822474 (Sec) 📠 01347 822474
e-mail: brian@easingwold-golf-club.fsnet.co.uk
**Parkland course with easy walking. Trees are a major
feature and on six holes water hazards come into play.**
18 holes, 6559yds, Par 74, SSS 72.
Club membership 750.
Visitors prior enquiry essential. **Societies** prior application
in writing essential or by telephone **Green Fees** £35 per
day; £28 per round. **Prof** John Hughes **Course Designer**
Hawtree **Facilities** ⊗ ⏀ ⅃⌸ ╠ 💺 ♀ 🏌 🏨 🏐 ⚲ ⛳ ♦ **Conf**
Corporate Hospitality Days available **Location** 1m S of
Easingwold, 12m N of York

Hotel ★★ 72% George Hotel, Market Place,
EASINGWOLD ☎ 01347 821698 15 en suite

Booking a tee time is always advisable.

FILEY Map 08 TA18

Filey West Av YO14 9BQ
☎ 01723 513293 📠 01723 514952
e-mail: secretary@fileygolfclub.com
**Parkland course with good views. Stream runs through
course. Testing 9th and 13th holes.**
18 holes, 6112yds, Par 70, SSS 69, Course record 64.
Club membership 900.
Visitors must telephone to reserve tee time. **Societies** contact
by telephone. **Green Fees** £25 per day (weekends £35). **Prof**
Gary Hutchinson **Course Designer** Braid **Facilities** ⊗ ⏀ ⅃⌸ ╠
💺 ♀ 🏌 🏨 🏐 ⚲ ⛳ ✆ **Location** 0.5m S of Filey

Hotel ★★ 69% Wrangham House Hotel, 10 Stonegate,
HUNMANBY ☎ 01723 891333 8 en suite
4 annexe en suite

GANTON Map 08 SE97

Ganton YO12 4PA
☎ 01944 710329 📠 01944 710922
e-mail: secretary@gantongolfclub.com
**Championship course, heathland, gorse-lined fairways
and heavily bunkered; variable winds. The opening
holes make full use of the contours of the land and the
approach to the second demands the finest touch. The
fourth is considered one of the best holes on the outward
half with its shot across a valley to a plateau green, the
surrounding gorse punishing anything less than a
perfect shot. Hosted the Walker Cup in September 2003.**
18 holes, 6734yds, Par 72, SSS 73, Course record 65.
Club membership 500.
Visitors by prior arrangement. Restricted play at
weekends. **Societies** prior arrangement in writing. **Green
Fees** £65 per day/round (£75 weekends and bank holidays).
Cards 💳 🔲 🟦 📇 💷 **Prof** Gary Brown **Course
Designer** Dunn/Vardon/Braid/Colt **Facilities** ⊗ ⏀ ⅃⌸ ╠ 💺 ♀
🏌 🏨 🏐 ⚲ ⛳ ✆ **Conf** Corporate Hospitality Days
available **Location** 11m SW of Scarborough on A64

Hotel ★★★ 62% East Ayton Lodge Country House,
Moor Ln, Forge Valley, EAST AYTON ☎ 01723 864227
10 en suite 20 annexe en suite

HARROGATE Map 08 SE35

Harrogate Forest Ln Head, Starbeck HG2 7TF
☎ 01423 862999 📠 01423 860073
e-mail: hon.secretary@harrogate-gc.co.uk
**One of Yorkshire's oldest and best courses was
designed in 1897 by 'Sandy' Herd. A perfect example of
golf architecture, its greens and fairways offer an
interesting but fair challenge. The undulating parkland
course once formed part of the ancient Forest of
Knaresborough. Excellent clubhouse.**
18 holes, 6241yds, Par 69, SSS 70, Course record 63.
Club membership 700.
Visitors advisable to contact professional in advance,
weekend play limited. **Societies** must contact in writing or
intially by telephone. **Green Fees** £36 per round/day
(weekends £40). **Cards** 💳 🔲 🟦 📇 🟥 💷 **Prof** Paul
Johnson **Course Designer** Sandy Herd **Facilities** ⊗ ⏀ ⅃⌸ ╠
💺 ♀ 🏌 🏨 🏐 ⚲ ⛳ ✆ **Leisure** snooker. **Conf** Corporate
Hospitality Days available **Location** 2.25m N on A59

Hotel ★★★ 74% Grants Hotel, 3-13 Swan Rd,
HARROGATE ☎ 01423 560666 42 en suite

Oakdale Oakdale Glen HG1 2LN
☎ 01423 567162 📠 01423 536030
e-mail: sec@oakdale-golfclub.com
A pleasant, undulating parkland course which provides a good test of golf for the low handicap player without intimidating the less proficient. A special feature is an attractive stream which comes in to play on four holes. Excellent views from the clubhouse with good facilities.
18 holes, 6456yds, Par 71, SSS 71, Course record 61.
Club membership 1034.
Visitors no party bookings weekends. **Societies** telephone followed by letter. **Green Fees** £40 for 27 holes, £33 per round (£45 per round weekends and bank holidays). **Prof** Clive Dell **Course Designer** Dr McKenzie **Facilities** ⊗ ⫢ ⯑ ⯑ ♀ ☂ 🏠 ⚑ 🛒 ♿ ⌀ **Conf** Corporate Hospitality Days available **Location** N side of town centre off A61

Hotel ★★★ 74% Grants Hotel, 3-13 Swan Rd, HARROGATE ☎ 01423 560666 42 en suite

Rudding Park Hotel & Golf Rudding Park,
Follifoot HG3 1JH ☎ 01423 872100 📠 01423 873400
e-mail: sales@ruddingpark.com
The course provides panoramic views over the surrounding countryside and all year buggy tracks make it accessible for most of the year.

Rudding Park Hotel& Golf: 18 holes, 6883yds, Par 72, SSS 73, Course record 65.
Club membership 600.
Visitors handicap certificate required, tee reservation available 7 days in advance. **Societies** apply by telephone in advance. **Green Fees** Mon-Thu £40 per day, £27.50 per 18 holes (£50/£33 Fri-Sun). **Cards** ▦ ▤ 🟥 🟦 ▧ 🟥 ♿ **Prof** M & N Moore/Hobkinson/Fountain **Course Designer** Martin Hawtree **Facilities** ⊗ ⫢ ⯑ ⯑ ♀ ☂ 🏠 ⚑ 🛒 ♿ ⌀ ♀ **Conf** fac available Corporate Hospitality Days available **Location** 2m SE of Harrogate town centre, off A658 follow brown tourist signs

Hotel ★★★★ Rudding Park Hotel & Golf, Rudding Park, Follifoot, HARROGATE ☎ 01423 871350 50 en suite

Kirkbymoorside Manor Vale YO62 6EG
☎ 01751 431525 📠 01751 433190
e-mail: enqs@kirkbymoorsidegolf.co.uk
Hilly parkland course with narrow fairways, gorse and hawthorn bushes. Beautiful views.
18 holes, 6207yds, Par 69, SSS 69, Course record 65.
Club membership 500.
Visitors are advised to contact in advance, may not play before 9.30 or between 12.30-1.30. **Societies** must apply in

advance. **Green Fees** £22 per round/£28 per day (weekends £32). **Cards** ▦ ▤ 🟥 ♿ **Prof** John Hinchliffe **Facilities** ⊗ ⫢ ⯑ ⯑ ♀ ☂ 🏠 ⚑ ⌀ **Leisure** gymnasium. **Location** N side of village

Hotel ★★ 66% George & Dragon Hotel, 17 Market Place, KIRKBYMOORSIDE ☎ 01751 433334 11 en suite 7 annexe en suite

Knaresborough Boroughbridge Rd HG5 0QQ
☎ 01423 862690 📠 01423 869345
e-mail: knaresboroughgolfclub@btopenworld.com
Pleasant and well presented parkland course in rural setting with excellent views on the back nine.
18 holes, 6354yds, Par 70, SSS 71, Course record 65.
Club membership 840.
Visitors restricted start times summer weekends. **Societies** apply by telephone, email or letter. **Green Fees** £30 (weekends £35) (50% discount with member). **Prof** Gary J Vickers **Course Designer** Hawtree **Facilities** ⊗ ⫢ ⯑ ⯑ ♀ ☂ 🏠 🛒 ⌀ **Conf** Corporate Hospitality Days available **Location** 1.25 N on A6055

Hotel ★★★ 70% Dower House Hotel, Bond End, KNARESBOROUGH ☎ 01423 863302 28 en suite 3 annexe en suite

Malton & Norton Welham Park, Norton YO17 9QE
☎ 01653 697912 📠 01653 697912
e-mail: maltonandnorton@btconnect.com
Parkland course, consisting of 3 nine hole loops, with

Continued   Continued

panoramic views of the moors. Very testing 1st hole (564 yds dog-leg, left) on the Welham course.
Welham Course: 18 holes, 6456yds, Par 72, SSS 71, Course record 66.
Park Course: 18 holes, 6251yds, Par 72, SSS 70, Course record 67.
Derwent Course: 18 holes, 6295yds, Par 72, SSS 70, Course record 66.
Club membership 880.
Visitors anytime except during competitions, no parties on Saturdays. **Societies** telephone and confirm in writing. **Green Fees** £27 per round/day (£32 weekends & bank holidays). **Cards** **Prof** S Robinson **Facilities** **Conf** Corporate Hospitality Days available **Location** Approx 20m E of York/0.75m of Malton

Hotel ★★★ 72% Burythorpe House Hotel, Burythorpe, MALTON ☎ 01653 658200 11 en suite 5 annexe en suite

MASHAM Map 08 SE28

Masham Burnholme, Swinton Rd HG4 4HT
☎ 01765 688054 01765 688054
9 holes, 6068yds, Par 70, SSS 69, Course record 73.
Location 8m from junction of B6267 off A1 signposted Thirsk/Masham. Then 1m SW off A6108
Telephone for further details

Hotel ★ 69% Buck Inn, THORNTON WATLASS ☎ 01677 422461 7 rms (5 en suite)

MIDDLESBROUGH Map 08 NZ41

Middlesbrough Brass Castle Ln, Marton TS8 9EE
☎ 01642 311515 01642 319607
e-mail: enquiries@middlesbroughgolfclub.co.uk
Undulating wooded parkland course, prevailing winds. Testing 6th, 8th and 12th holes.
18 holes, 6278yds, Par 70, SSS 70, Course record 63.
Club membership 1004.
Visitors restricted Tue & Sat. **Societies** Mon, Wed, Thu & Fri only. Must contact the club in advance. **Green Fees** £37 (£42 weekends). **Prof** Don Jones **Course Designer** Baird **Facilities** **Leisure** snooker table. **Conf** fac available Corporate Hospitality Days available **Location** 4m S off A172

Hotel ★★★ 71% Parkmore Hotel & Leisure Park, 636 Yarm Rd, Eaglescliffe, STOCKTON-ON-TEES ☎ 01642 786815 55 en suite

Middlesbrough Municipal Ladgate Ln TS5 7YZ
☎ 01642 315533 01642 300726
Parkland course with good views. The front nine holes

Continued

have wide fairways and large, often well-guarded greens while the back nine demand shots over tree-lined water hazards and narrow entrances to subtly contoured greens. Driving range.
18 holes, 6333yds, Par 71, SSS 70, Course record 67.
Club membership 630.
Visitors can book up to 7 days in advance weekdays and weekends **Societies** apply in writing giving at least 2 weeks in advance. **Green Fees** not confirmed. **Prof** Alan Hope **Course Designer** Shuttleworth **Facilities** **Location** 2m S of Middlesbrough on the A174

Hotel ★★★ 71% Parkmore Hotel & Leisure Park, 636 Yarm Rd, Eaglescliffe, STOCKTON-ON-TEES ☎ 01642 786815 55 en suite

NORTHALLERTON Map 08 SE39

Romanby Yafforth Rd DL7 0PE
☎ 01609 778855 01609 779084
e-mail: mark@romanby.com
Set in natural undulating terrain with the River Wiske meandering through the course, it offers a testing round of golf for all abilities. In addition to the river, two lakes come into play on the 2nd, 5th and 11th holes. 12-bay floodlit driving range.
18 holes, 6663yds, Par 72, SSS 72, Course record 72.
Club membership 635.
Visitors welcome everyday please book tee time in advance. **Societies** contact Mark Boersma for details, tel 01609 778855. **Green Fees** terms on application. **Cards** **Prof** Tim Jenkins **Course Designer** Will Adamson **Facilities** **Leisure** 6 hole par 3 academy course. **Conf** fac available Corporate Hospitality Days available **Location** On the main Northallerton/Richmond road B6271, 1m W of Northallerton

Hotel ★★ 65% The Golden Lion, High St, NORTHALLERTON ☎ 01609 777411 25 en suite

PANNAL Map 08 SE35

Pannal Follifoot Rd HG3 1ES
☎ 01423 872628 01423 870043
e-mail: secretary@pannalgc.co.uk
Fine championship course. Moorland turf but well-wooded with trees closely involved with play. Excellent views enhance the course.
18 holes, 6622yds, Par 72, SSS 72, Course record 62.
Club membership 780.
Visitors preferable to contact in advance, weekends limited. Not Tue am **Societies** apply in advance. **Green Fees** £60 per day, £45 per round (£60 per round weekends). **Cards** **Prof** David Padgett **Course Designer** Sandy Herd **Facilities** **Leisure** snooker. **Conf** Corporate Hospitality Days available **Location** E side of village off A61

Hotel ★★★ 69% The Yorkshire, Prospect Place, HARROGATE ☎ 01423 565071 80 en suite

RAVENSCAR Map 08 NZ90

Raven Hall Hotel Golf Course YO13 0ET
☎ 01723 870353 01723 870072
e-mail: enquiries@ravenhall.co.uk
Opened by the Earl of Cranbrook in 1898, this 9-hole

Continued

clifftop course is sloping and with good quality small greens. Because of its clifftop position it is subject to strong winds which make it great fun to play, especially the 6th hole.
9 holes, 1894yds, Par 32, SSS 32.
Club membership 120.
Visitors must contact in advance, busy at weekends, spikes essential, no jeans/T shirts. **Societies** telephone in advance. **Green Fees** terms on application. **Cards** **Facilities** **Leisure** hard tennis courts, heated indoor plus outdoor swimming pool, sauna, gymnasium, snooker, croquet, bowls. **Conf** fac available Corporate Hospitality Days available **Location** from Scarborough take A171 to Whitby Rd. Through Cloughton village and right to Ravenscar. Hotel on cliff top overlooking sea.

Hotel ★★★ 67% Raven Hall Country House Hotel & Golf Course, RAVENSCAR 01723 870353 51 en suite

REDCAR Map 08 NZ62

Cleveland Majuba Rd TS10 5BJ
01642 471798 01642 471798
e-mail: secretary@clevelandgolfclub.co.uk
The oldest golf club in Yorkshire playing over the only links championship course in Yorkshire. A true test of traditional golf, especially when windy. Flat seaside links with easy walking.
18 holes, 6696yds, Par 72, SSS 72, Course record 67.
Club membership 920.
Visitors advisable to book in advance. **Societies** initially telephone for details. **Green Fees** £35 per day, £28 per round. **Prof** Craig Donaldson **Course Designer** Donald Steel (new holes) **Facilities** **Conf** Corporate Hospitality Days available **Location** 8m E of Middlesborough, at N end of Redcar

Hotel ★★★ 66% Rushpool Hall Hotel, Saltburn Ln, SALTBURN-BY-THE-SEA 01287 624111 21 en suite

Wilton Wilton TS10 4QY
01642 465265 (Secretary) 01642 465463
e-mail: secretary@wiltongolfclub.co.uk
Parkland course with some fine views.
18 holes, 6176yds, Par 70, SSS 69, Course record 64.
Club membership 730.
Visitors telephone professional 01642 452730 to check availability, no visitors Saturday, Ladies competition have priority Tuesday, tee off 10am or later. **Societies** must telephone secretary in advance. **Green Fees** £24 per day (£28 weekends & bank holidays). **Prof** P D Smillie **Facilities** by prior arrangement **Leisure** snooker. **Conf** Corporate Hospitality Days available **Location** 3m W of Redcar, on A174

Hotel ★★★ 66% Rushpool Hall Hotel, Saltburn Ln, SALTBURN-BY-THE-SEA 01287 624111 21 en suite

RICHMOND Map 07 NZ10

Richmond Bend Hagg DL10 5EX
01748 823231(Secretary) 01748 821709
Undulating parkland course. Ideal to play 27 holes, not too testing but very interesting.
18 holes, 5886yds, Par 70, SSS 68, Course record 63.
Club membership 600.
Visitors may not play before 3.30am on Sun. **Societies** must contact in writing or telephone 01748 822457. **Green Fees** £22 per round/£24 per day (£25/£30 weekends & bank holidays). **Prof** Paul Jackson **Course Designer** P Pennink **Facilities** **Conf** fac available **Location** 0.75m N, 4 miles from Scotch Corner.

Continued

Hotel ★★★ 66% King's Head Hotel, Market Place, RICHMOND 01748 850220 26 en suite 4 annexe en suite

RIPON Map 08 SE37

Ripon City Palace Rd HG4 3HH
01765 603640 01765 692880
e-mail: office@ripongolf.com
Moderate walking on undulating parkland course; two testing par 3s at 5th and 14th.
18 holes, 6084yds, Par 70, SSS 69, Course record 66.
Club membership 750.
Visitors book with professional. No play Saturdays,limited play Sundays. **Societies** contact in writing or telephone. **Green Fees** not confirmed. **Prof** S T Davis **Course Designer** H Varden **Facilities** **Location** 1m NW on A6108

Hotel ★★★ 69% Ripon Spa Hotel, Park St, RIPON 01765 602172 40 en suite

SALTBURN-BY-THE-SEA Map 08 NZ62

Hunley Hall Golf Club & Hotel Ings Ln, Brotton TS12 2QQ
01287 676216 01287 678250
e-mail: enquiries@hunleyhall.co.uk
A picturesque 27 hole coastal course with panoramic views of the countryside and coastline, providing a good test of golf and a rewarding game for all abilities.

Morgans: 18 holes, 6918yds, Par 73, SSS 73, Course record 63.
Millennium: 18 holes, 5948yds, Par 68, SSS 68, Course record 69.
Jubilee: 18 holes, 6292yds, Par 71, SSS 70, Course record 66.
Club membership 600.
Visitors please telephone for information and availability **Societies** telephone for information and availability. **Green Fees** £25 per day (£35 weekends and bank holidays). **Cards** **Prof** Andrew Brook **Course Designer** John Morgan **Facilities** **Conf** fac available Corporate Hospitality Days available **Location** From A174 in Brotton take St Margarets Way, 700yds to club

Hotel ★★ 63% Hunley Hall Golf Club & Hotel, Ings Ln, Brotton, SALTBURN 01287 676216 8 en suite

Saltburn by the Sea Hob Hill, Guisborough Rd
TS12 1NJ ☎ 01287 622812 📠 01287 625988
e-mail: info@saltburngolf.co.uk
**Undulating meadowland course surrounded by
woodland. Particularly attractive in autumn. There are
fine views of the Cleveland Hills and of Tees Bay.**
18 holes, 5846yds, Par 70, SSS 68, Course record 62.
Club membership 900.
Visitors telephone in advance, no visitors on Saturday.
Societies apply in writing. **Green Fees** terms on
application. **Cards** 🖿 🖿 💳 **Prof** Mike Nutter **Course
Designer** J Braid **Facilities** ⊗ ⫼ ⌶ ♥ ♀ 🏌 🏮 ⌀
Location 0.5m out of Saltburn on Guisborough road

Hotel ★★★ 66% Rushpool Hall Hotel, Saltburn Ln,
SALTBURN-BY-THE-SEA ☎ 01287 624111 21 en suite

SCARBOROUGH   Map 08 TA08

Scarborough North Cliff North Cliff Av
YO12 6PP ☎ 01723 360786 📠 01723 362134
**Seaside course beginning on cliff top overlooking North
bay and castle winding inland through parkland with
stunning views of the North Yorkshire Moors.**
18 holes, 6425yds, Par 71, SSS 71, Course record 66.
Club membership 895.
Visitors must be member of a club with handicap
certificate. May not play before 10.30am Sun. **Societies**
prior booking with secretary for parties of 8-40. **Green
Fees** not confirmed. **Prof** Simon N Deller **Course
Designer** James Braid **Facilities** ⊗ ⫼ ⌶ ♥ ♀ 🏌 🏮 ❀
⌀ **Conf** Corporate Hospitality Days available **Location**
2m N of town centre off A165

Hotel ★★★ 66% Esplanade Hotel, Belmont Rd,
SCARBOROUGH ☎ 01723 360382 73 en suite

Scarborough South Cliff Deepdale Av YO11 2UE
☎ 01723 374737 📠 01723 374737
e-mail: secretary@scarboroughgolfclub.co.uk
Parkland/seaside course designed by Dr McKenzie.
18 holes, 6405yds, Par 72, SSS 71, Course record 68.
Club membership 700.
Visitors contact in advance may not play before 9.30am
Mon-Fri, 10am Sat and 10.30am Sun. **Societies** must
contact Secretary in advance. **Green Fees** £30 per day, £25
per round (£35/£30 weekends). **Prof** Tony Skingle **Course
Designer** McKenzie **Facilities** ⊗ ⫼ ⌶ ♥ ♀ 🏌 🏮 ⌀
Location 1m S on A165

Hotel ★★ 65% Bradley Court Hotel, Filey Rd, South
Cliff, SCARBOROUGH ☎ 01723 360476 40 en suite

SELBY   Map 08 SE63

Selby Mill Ln, Brayton YO8 9LD
☎ 01757 228622 📠 01757 228622
e-mail: selbygolfclub@hotmail.com
**Mainly flat, links-type course; prevailing SW wind.
Testing holes including the 3rd, 7th and 16th.**
18 holes, 6374yds, Par 71, SSS 71, Course record 68.
Club membership 840.
Visitors contact professional on 01757 228785, members
and guests only at weekends. **Societies** welcome Mon-Fri,
must apply in advance. **Green Fees** £35 per day, £30 per
round. **Cards** 🖿 🖿 🖿 💳 **Prof** Nick Ludwell **Course
Designer** J Taylor & Hawtree **Facilities** ⊗ ⫼ ⌶ ♥ ♀ 🏌
🏮 ❀ ⌀ 🖤 **Location** off A63 Selby by-pass

Hotel ★★★ 70% Monk Fryston Hall Hotel, MONK
FRYSTON ☎ 01977 682369 29 en suite

SETTLE   Map 07 SD86

Settle Buckhaw Brow, Giggleswick BD24 0DH
☎ 01729 825288 📠 01729 825288
**Picturesque parkland course with stream affecting play
on four holes.**
9 holes, 6200yds, Par 72, SSS 72.
Club membership 380.
Visitors may not play before 2pm on Sun. **Societies** apply
in writing 4 weeks in advance. **Green Fees**
£15 per round. **Course Designer** Tom Vardon **Facilities**
⌂ **Location** 1m W of Settle on Kendal Rd

Inn ◆◆◆◆ Golden Lion, 5 Duke St, SETTLE
☎ 01729 822203 12 rms (10 en suite)

SKIPTON   Map 07 SD95

Skipton Short Lee Ln BD23 3LF
☎ 01756 795657 📠 01756 796665
e-mail: enquiries@skiptongolfclub.co.uk
**Undulating parkland course with some water hazards
and panoramic views.**
18 holes, 6049yds, Par 70, SSS 69, Course record 67.
Club membership 800.
Visitors welcome by prior arrangement **Societies** must
apply by telephone or in writing. **Green Fees** £30 per day,
£24 per 18 holes (£26 per 18 holes). **Prof** Peter Robinson
Facilities ⊗ ⫼ ⌶ ♥ ♀ 🏌 🏮 ❀ ⌀ **Leisure** snooker.
Conf Corporate Hospitality Days available **Location** 1m N
of Skipton on A59

Hotel ★★★ The Devonshire Arms Country House Hotel,
BOLTON ABBEY ☎ 01756 710441 41 en suite

TADCASTER   Map 08 SE44

Cocksford Cocksford, Stutton LS24 9NG
☎ 01937 834253 📠 01937 834253
e-mail: enquiries@cocksfordgolfclub.freeserve.co.uk
*Old Course: 18 holes, 5570yds, Par 71, SSS 69, Course
record 68.*
Location Between York & Leeds, adjacent to the village of
Stutton
Telephone for further details

Hotel ★★★★ ♨ 75% Wood Hall Hotel, Trip Ln, Linton,
WETHERBY ☎ 01937 587271 14 en suite
30 annexe en suite

Scathingwell Scarthingwell LS24 9PF
☎ 01937 557864 (pro) 557878 (club) 📠 01937 557909
**Testing water hazards and well placed bunkers and
trees provide a challenging test of golf for all handicaps
at this scenic parkland course.**
*Scathingwell Golf Club: 18 holes, 6771yds, Par 72, SSS
72.*
Club membership 500.
Visitors dress code must be adhered to.May play anytime
midweek and sundays,after 2.00pm saturdays. **Societies**
golf packages available, book one month in advance.
Green Fees terms on application. **Prof** Steve Footman
Facilities ⊗ ⫼ ⌶ ♥ ♀ 🏌 🏮 ⌀ **Conf** fac available
Location 4m S of Tadcaster on the A162
Tadcaster/Ferrybridge road, approx 2m from the A1

Hotel ★★★ 80% Hazlewood Castle, Paradise Ln,
Hazlewood, TADCASTER ☎ 01937 535353 9 en suite
12 annexe en suite

THIRSK   Map 08 SE48

Thirsk & Northallerton Thornton-le-Street
YO7 4AB ☎ 01845 522170 & 525115 📠 01845 525115
**The course has good views of the nearby Hambleton
Hills to the east and Wensleydale to the west. Testing
course, mainly flat land.**
*18 holes, 6495yds, Par 72, SSS 71, Course record 69.
Club membership 500.*
Visitors must telephone in advance, and have handicap
certificate. No play Sun unless with member. **Societies**
must apply in writing. **Green Fees** not confirmed. **Prof**
Robert Garner **Course Designer** ADAS **Facilities** ⊗ ⋙ 🏌
💺 ♀ 🏌 🏠 ⛳ 🐾 🗮 ✧ **Location** 2m N on A168
....
Hotel ★★ 73% Golden Fleece Hotel, 42 Market Place,
THIRSK ☎ 01845 523108 23 en suite

WHITBY   Map 08 NZ81

Whitby Low Straggleton, Sandsend Rd YO21 3SR
☎ 01947 600660 📠 01947 600660
e-mail: whitby_golf_club@compuserve.com
**Seaside course with 4 holes along cliff tops and over
ravines. Good views and fresh sea breeze.**
*18 holes, 6134yds, Par 71, Course record 66.
Club membership 600.*
Visitors may not play on competition days, parties must
contact in advance. **Societies** must contact in writing.
Green Fees £22 per day (£28 weekends). **Prof** Tony
Mason **Facilities** ⊗ ⋙ 🏌 💺 ♀ 🏠 🏌 ✧ **Location**
1.5m NW on A174
....
Hotel ★★ 67% White House Hotel, Upgang Ln, West
Cliff, WHITBY ☎ 01947 600469 10 en suite

YORK   Map 08 SE65

Forest of Galtres Moorlands Rd, Skelton YO32 2RF
☎ 01904 766198 📠 01904 769400
e-mail: sue@forestofgaltres.co.uk
**Level parkland course in the heart of the ancient Forest
of Galtres with mature oak trees and interesting water
features coming into play on the 6th, 14th and 17th
holes. Views towards York Minster.**
*18 holes, 6412yds, Par 72, SSS 70, Course record 63.
Club membership 450.*
Visitors telephone to book, may play anytime subject to
availability **Societies** not Sat, booking system, telephone
for forms. **Green Fees** £25 per day; £20 per round
(£32/£27 weekends & bank holidays). **Cards** 🖭 🖭 🖭
🖭 🖭 🖭 🖭 **Prof** Phil Bradley **Course Designer** Simon
Gidman **Facilities** ⊗ ⋙ by prior arrangement 🏌 💺 ♀ 🏌
🏠 🏌 ✧ 🐾 **Location** 0.5m from the York ring road B1237,
just off A19 Thirsk road through the village of Skelton
....
Hotel ★★ 70% Beechwood Close Hotel, 19 Shipton Rd,
Clifton, YORK ☎ 01904 658378 14 en suite

Forest Park Stockton-on-the-Forest YO32 9UW
☎ 01904 400425 & 400688 📠 01904 400717
e-mail: admin@forestparkgolfclub.co.uk
**A parkland/meadowland course with natural features
including a stream and mature trees.**
*Old Foss Course: 18 holes, 6600yds, Par 71, SSS 72,
Course record 73.
The West Course: 9 holes, 3186yds, Par 70, SSS 70.
Club membership 600.*
Visitors welcome, subject to tee availability. Advisable to

contact club in advance. **Societies** by prior arrangement.
Green Fees 18 holes £20 (weekends £25); 9 holes £9
(£11). **Cards** 🖭 🖭 🖭 **Prof** Mark Winterburn **Facilities**
⊗ ⋙ 🏌 💺 ♀ 🏠 🏌 🐾 🗮 ✧ 🐾 **Conf** Corporate
Hospitality Days available **Location** 4m NE of York, 1.5m
from end of A64, York bypass
....
Hotel ★★ 67% Jacobean Lodge Hotel, Plainville Ln,
Wigginton, YORK ☎ 01904 762749 8 en suite

Fulford Heslington Ln YO10 5DY
☎ 01904 413579 📠 01904 416918
e-mail: info@fulfordgolfclub.co.uk
**A flat, parkland/heathland course well-known for the
superb quality of its turf, particularly the greens, and
now famous as the venue for some of the best golf
tournaments in the British Isles in past years. In
particular, 19 years of hosting the Benson & Hedges
Trophy.**
*18 holes, 6775yds, Par 72, SSS 72, Course record 62.
Club membership 775.*
Visitors must contact in advance. Not Tue am. Limited
weekends **Societies** not Tue am, book with the manager.
Green Fees £55 per day, £45 per round. **Prof** Martin
Brown **Course Designer** C. MacKenzie **Facilities** ⊗ ⋙ 🏌
💺 ♀ 🏠 🐾 ✧ **Conf** Corporate Hospitality Days
available **Location** 2m S of York off A19
....
Hotel ★★★★ 68% York Marriott Hotel, Tadcaster Rd,
YORK ☎ 01904 701000 108 en suite
....
Additional hotel ★★★ 73% York Pavilion Hotel,
45 Main St, Fulford, YORK ☎ 01904 622099
Fax 01904 626939 57 en suite

Heworth Muncaster House, Muncastergate YO31 9JY
☎ 01904 422389 📠 01904 426156
e-mail: golf@heworth-gc.fsnet.co.uk
**12-hole parkland course, easy walking. Holes 3 to 7 and
9 played twice from different tees.**
*12 holes, 6141yds, Par 70, SSS 69, Course record 68.
Club membership 550.*
Visitors advisable to telephone the professional in
advance, no catering Mondays **Societies** apply in
writing/telephone professional 01904 422389 **Green Fees**
£20 per day; £15 per round (£25/£20 weekends & bank
holidays). **Prof** Stephen Burdett **Course Designer** B Cheal
Facilities ⊗ ⋙ 🏌 💺 ♀ 🏠 🏌 ✧ **Conf** Corporate
Hospitality Days available **Location** 1.5m NE of city
centre on A1036
....
Hotel ★★★ 70% Monkbar Hotel, Monkbar, YORK
☎ 01904 638086 99 en suite

Continued

Swallow Hall Crockey Hill YO19 4SG
☎ 01904 448889 🖹 01904 448219
e-mail: jtscores@hotmail.com
A small 18-hole, par 3 course with 3 par 4s. Attached to a caravan park and holiday cottages.
18 holes, 3600yds, Par 57, SSS 56, Course record 58.
Club membership 100.
Visitors no restrictions. **Societies** must telephone in advance. **Green Fees** £10 per round (£12 weekends).
Cards 🌐 💳 📇 📲 **Course Designer** Brian Henry **Facilities** ⊗ 🎕 🏌 💺 ♂ ♀ ♣ 🛱 🛶 🥨 ♫ ⌄ **Leisure** hard tennis courts, fishing. **Conf** fac available **Corporate Hospitality Days** available **Location** Off A19, signposted to Wheldrake

Hotel ★★★ 73% York Pavilion Hotel, 45 Main St, Fulford, YORK ☎ 01904 622099 57 en suite

York Lords Moor Ln, Strensall YO32 5XF
☎ 01904 491840 (Sec) 490304 (Pro) 🖹 01904 491852
e-mail: secretary@yorkgolfclub.co.uk
A pleasant, well-designed, heathland course with easy walking. The course is of good length but is flat so not too tiring. The course is well bunkered with excellent greens and there are two testing pond holes.
18 holes, 6301yds, Par 70, SSS 70, Course record 66.
Club membership 750.
Visitors with member only Sun, must contact in advance Sat. **Societies** initial enquiry through professional. **Green Fees** £41 for 36 holes, £37 for 27 holes, £33 for 18 holes (weekends £47 for 27 holes, £42 for 18 holes). **Prof** A P Hoyles **Course Designer** J H Taylor **Facilities** ⊗ 🎕 🏌 💺 ♀ ♣ 🛱 ♫ **Location** 6m NE of York, E of Strensall village

Hotel ★★★ 76% Dean Court Hotel, Duncombe Place, YORK ☎ 01904 625082 39 en suite

YORKSHIRE, SOUTH

Barnsley Wakefield Rd, Staincross S75 6JZ
☎ 01226 382856 🖹 01226 382856
Undulating municipal parkland course with easy walking apart from last 4 holes. Testing 8th and 18th holes.
18 holes, 5951yds, Par 69, SSS 69, Course record 64.
Club membership 450.
Visitors booking advisable, telephone professional on 01226 380358. **Societies** by arrangement, contact club professional at on 01226 380358 **Green Fees** 18 holes £10.50 (weekends & bank holidays £12.50). **Prof** Shaun Wyke **Facilities** ⊗ by prior arrangement 🎕 by prior arrangement 🏌 by prior arrangement 💺 ♀ ♣ 🛱 ♫ ⌄ **Location** 3m N on A61

Hotel ★★★ 73% Ardsley House Hotel & Health Club, Doncaster Rd, Ardsley, BARNSLEY ☎ 01226 309955 75 en suite

Sandhill Middlecliffe Ln, Little Houghton S72 0HW
☎ 01226 753444 🖹 01226 753444
The course is reasonably flat with generously wide fairways laid out between and amongst 25 acres of newly planted woodlands. Holes of note are the 4th, a 311 yard par 4 to a horseshoe green around a 9-foot deep bunker; the 7th par 3 to blind reverse Mackenzie

Green; and the 11th 416-yard par 4 dog-leg where the brave can take on the out of bounds.
18 holes, 6257yds, Par 71, SSS 70, Course record 69.
Club membership 420.
Visitors welcome by prior booking. **Societies** telephone for availability, write to confirm. **Green Fees** £12 per round (weekends £16). **Cards** 🌐 💳 📇 📲 🗨 **Course Designer** John Royston **Facilities** ⊗ 🎕 🏌 💺 ♀ ♣ 🛶 🥨 ♫ ⌄ **Location** 5m E of Barnsley, off A635

Hotel ★★★ 73% Ardsley House Hotel & Health Club, Doncaster Rd, Ardsley, BARNSLEY ☎ 01226 309955 75 en suite

Bawtry Cross Ln, Austerfield DN10 6RF
☎ 01302 710841 🖹 01302 711755
Championship moorland course featuring the 618 yard 7th and the Postage Stamp 8th. Well drained and easy walking with attached driving range.
Bawtry Golf & Country Club: 18 holes, 6900yds, Par 73, SSS 73, Course record 67.
Club membership 600.
Visitors phone in advance for weekends. **Societies** must contact in advance. **Green Fees** £15 (£20 weekends and bank holidays). **Cards** 🌐 💳 📇 📲 🗨 **Prof** Darren Roberts **Facilities** ⊗ 🎕 🏌 💺 ♀ ♣ 🛱 🥨 ♫ ⌄ **Conf** Corporate Hospitality Days available **Location** 2m from Bawtry on A614

Hotel ★★★★ 69% Mount Pleasant Hotel, Great North Rd, ROSSINGTON ☎ 01302 868696 & 868219 🖹 01302 865130 45 en suite

Crookhill Park Municipal Carr Ln DN12 2AH
☎ 01709 862979 🖹 01709 866455
18 holes, 5849yds, Par 70, SSS 68, Course record 64.
Location 1.5m SE on B6094
Telephone for further details

Hotel ★★★ 67% Danum Hotel, High St, DONCASTER ☎ 01302 342261 66 en suite

Doncaster 278 Bawtry Rd, Bessacarr DN4 7PD
☎ 01302 865632 🖹 01302 865994
e-mail: doncastergolf@aol.com
Pleasant undulating heathland course with wooded surroundings. Quick drying, ideal all year round course.
18 holes, 6220yds, Par 69, SSS 70, Course record 66.
Club membership 500.
Visitors must contact in advance for both weekdays and weekends. **Societies** must contact in advance. **Green Fees** not confirmed. **Prof** Graham Bailey **Course Designer** Mackenzie/Hawtree **Facilities** ⊗ 🎕 🏌 💺 ♀ ♣ 🛱 🥨 ♫ ⌄ **Conf** Corporate Hospitality Days available **Location** 4m SE on A638

Hotel ★★★★ 69% Mount Pleasant Hotel, Great North Rd, ROSSINGTON ☎ 01302 868696 & 868219 🖹 01302 865130 45 en suite

> **Prices may change during the currency of the Guide, please check when booking.**

Continued

Doncaster Town Moor Bawtry Rd, Belle Vue
DN4 5HU ☎ 01302 535286 (pro shop) & 533167 (bar)
📠 01302 533778
e-mail: dtmgc@btconnect.com
**Easy walking, but testing, heathland course with good
true greens. Friendly club. Notable hole is 11th (par 4),
464 yds. Situated in centre of racecourse.**
*18 holes, 6072yds, Par 69, SSS 69, Course record 63.
Club membership 520.*
Visitors may not play on Sun morning. Contact in
advance. **Societies** must contact in advance. **Green Fees**
£20 per round (weekends £22). **Prof** Steven Shaw
Facilities ⊗ ⫩ ⯑ ☕ ♀ 🛆 🖽 ✔ **Conf** Corporate
Hospitality Days available **Location** 1.5m E, at racecourse,
on A638
....
Hotel ★★★ 67% Danum Hotel, High St, DONCASTER
☎ 01302 342261 66 en suite

Owston Park Owston Ln, Owston DN6 8EF
☎ 01302 330821
e-mail: will@owstonpark.fsnet.co.uk
9 holes, 2866yds, Par 35, SSS 70.
Course Designer M Parker **Location** 5m N of Doncaster
off A19
Telephone for further details
....
Hotel ★★★ 67% Danum Hotel, High St, DONCASTER
☎ 01302 342261 66 en suite

Thornhurst Park Holme Ln, Owston DN5 0LR
☎ 01302 337799 📠 01302 721495
e-mail: info@thornhurst.co.uk
**Surrounded by Owston Wood, this scenic parkland
course has numerous strategically placed bunkers, and
a lake comes into play at the 7th and 8th holes.**
*18 holes, 6490yds, Par 72, SSS 72, Course record 72.
Club membership 160.*
Visitors must wear trousers, shirt with collar and golf
shoes, can contact 2 days in advance. **Societies** telephone
or write in advance. **Green Fees** terms on application.
Cards 💳 ▬ ▬ ▬ 🖳 **Prof** Kevin Pearce **Facilities** ⊗
⫩ ⯑ ☕ ♀ 🛆 🖽 ✔ **Conf** fac available Corporate
Hospitality Days available **Location** On the A19 between
Bentley/Askern, easy access from M62 and A1(M)
....
Hotel ★★★ 67% Danum Hotel, High St, DONCASTER
☎ 01302 342261 66 en suite

Wheatley Armthorpe Rd DN2 5QB
☎ 01302 831655 📠 01302 812736
18 holes, 6405yds, Par 71, SSS 71, Course record 64.
Course Designer George Duncan **Location** NE side of
town centre off A18
Telephone for further details
....
Hotel ★★★ 68% Regent Hotel, Regent Square,
DONCASTER ☎ 01302 364180 52 en suite

HATFIELD   Map 08 SE60

Kings Wood Thorne Rd DN7 6EP ☎ 01405 741343
**A flat course with ditches that come into play on several
holes, especially on the testing back nine. Notable holes
are the 12th par 4, 16th and par 5 18th. Water is a
prominent feature with several large lakes strategically
placed.**
*18 holes, 6002yds, Par 70, SSS 69, Course record 67.
Club membership 100.*

Continued

Visitors visitors are welcome any time. **Societies** or
telephone in advance. **Green Fees** terms on application.
Cards 💳 ▬ ▬ ▬ 🖳 **Prof** Mark Cunningham
Course Designer John Hunt **Facilities** ☕ 🖽 ⫩ 🛒 ✔
Location 2m SW of junct 1 of M180, take A614 to
Thorne, then Thorne road to Hatfield
....
Hotel ★★★ 64% Belmont Hotel, Horsefair Green,
THORNE ☎ 01405 812320 23 en suite

HICKLETON   Map 08 SE40

Hickleton Lidgett Ln DN5 7BE
☎ 01709 896081 📠 01709 896083
e-mail: hickleton@hickletongolfclub.freeserve.co.uk
**Undulating, picturesque parkland course designed by
Neil Coles and Brian Huggett offering a good test of
golf.**
*18 holes, 6434yds, Par 71, SSS 71, Course record 67.
Club membership 625.*
Visitors weekdays after 9am & weekends after 2.30pm.
Must contact in advance. **Societies** must contact in
advance. **Green Fees** £27 per day, £22 per round (£27 per
round weekends & bank holidays). **Prof** Paul J Audsley
Course Designer Huggett/Coles **Facilities** ⊗ ⫩ ⯑ ☕ ♀
🛆 🖽 🛒 ⚒ ✔ **Conf** Corporate Hospitality Days available
Location 3m W from A1(M) junct 37, off A635
....
Hotel ★★★ 67% Danum Hotel, High St, DONCASTER
☎ 01302 342261 66 en suite

HIGH GREEN   Map 08 SK39

Tankersley Park S35 4LG
☎ 0114 246 8247 📠 0114 245 7818
18 holes, 6212yds, Par 69, SSS 70, Course record 64.
Course Designer Hawtree **Location** Off A61/M1 onto
A616, Stocksbridge bypass
Telephone for further details
....
Hotel ★★★★ 71% Tankersley Manor, Church Ln,
TANKERSLEY ☎ 01226 744700 69 en suite

RAWMARSH   Map 08 SK49

Wath Abdy Ln S62 7SJ
☎ 01709 878609 📠 01709 877097
e-mail: wath.golfclub@virgin.net
**Parkland course, not easy in spite of its length. Testing
course with narrow fairways and small greens. The
signature hole is the 15th par 3, 165yds over water.**
*18 holes, 6123yds, Par 70, SSS 69, Course record 65.
Club membership 650.*
Visitors must play with member at weekends. Must
contact in advance and have a handicap certificate.
Societies must contact in writing, may not play at
weekends. **Green Fees** £29 per day; £24 per round. **Prof**
Chris Bassett **Facilities** ⊗ ⫩ ⯑ ☕ ♀ 🛆 🖽 🛒 ⚒ ✔
Conf fac available Corporate Hospitality Days available
Location 2m N of Rotherham on B6089
....
Hotel ★★★ 65% Carlton Park Hotel, 102/104 Moorgate
Rd, ROTHERHAM ☎ 01709 849955 80 en suite

ROTHERHAM   Map 08 SK49

Grange Park Upper Wortley Rd S61 2SJ
☎ 01709 559497
e-mail: crowncourt@bun.com
**Parkland/meadowland course, with panoramic views
especially from the back nine. The golf is testing,**

Continued

particularly at the 1st, 4th and 18th holes (par 4), and 8th, 12th and 15th (par 5).
18 holes, 6421yds, Par 71, SSS 71, Course record 65.
Club membership 214.
Visitors no restrictions. **Societies** apply in writing to professional. **Green Fees** not confirmed. **Prof** Eric Clark **Course Designer** Fred Hawtree **Facilities** ⊗ ⁊ⅢⅢ ⅼ ⅼ ☗ ♀ ⚒
🏠 ⚑ ⚘ Ⅼ **Conf** fac available **Location** 3m NW off A629

Hotel ★★★★ 71% Tankersley Manor, Church Ln, TANKERSLEY ☎ 01226 744700 69 en suite

Phoenix Pavilion Ln, Brinsworth S60 5PA
☎ 01709 363864 & 382624 📠 01709 363788
Undulating meadowland course with variable wind.
18 holes, 6182yds, Par 71, SSS 70, Course record 65.
Club membership 970.
Visitors must contact in advance. **Societies** must apply in writing. **Green Fees** not confirmed. **Prof** M Roberts **Course Designer** C K Cotton **Facilities** ⊗ ⁊ⅢⅢ ⅼ ⅼ ☗ ♀ ⚒
🏠 ⚑ ⚘ Ⅼ **Leisure** hard tennis courts, squash, fishing, gymnasium. **Conf** fac available Corporate Hospitality Days available **Location** E from M1 junct 34 for 0.75m, SW side of town centre off A630

Hotel ★★★ 65% Carlton Park Hotel, 102/104 Moorgate Rd, ROTHERHAM ☎ 01709 849955 80 en suite

Rotherham Golf Club Ltd Thrybergh Park,
Doncaster Rd, Thrybergh S65 4NU
☎ 01709 859500 📠 01709 859517
Parkland course with easy walking along tree-lined fairways.
18 holes, 6324yds, Par 70, SSS 70, Course record 65.
Club membership 500.
Visitors must contact in advance. **Societies** must contact secretary in advance. **Green Fees** £35 per round (weekends £45). **Prof** Simon Thornhill **Facilities** ⊗ ⁊ⅢⅢ ⅼ ☗ ♀ ⚒ 🏠
⚘ ⚘ ⚒ **Location** 3.5m E on A630

Hotel ★★★ 69% Best Western Elton Hotel, Main St, Bramley, ROTHERHAM ☎ 01709 545681 13 en suite 16 annexe en suite

Sitwell Park Shrogswood Rd S60 4BY
☎ 01709 541046 📠 01709 703637
e-mail: secretary@sitwellgolf.co.uk
Undulating parkland course.
18 holes, 5960yds, Par 71, SSS 69.
Club membership 450.
Visitors must contact in advance. May not play on Sat. **Societies** must contact in advance. **Green Fees** £38 per day; £28 per round (£46/£36 Sundays). **Prof** Nic Taylor **Course Designer** A MacKenzie **Facilities** ⊗ ⁊ⅢⅢ ⅼ ☗ ♀
⚒ 🏠 ⚑ ⚘ ⚒ **Conf** Corporate Hospitality Days available **Location** M1 junct33, take 1st exit at roundabout signed Rotherham, then 2nd exit at roundabout. Straight across traffic lights, 3rd exit at roundabout, sign for golf club on right

Hotel ★★★★ 64% Hellaby Hall Hotel, Old Hellaby Ln, Hellaby, ROTHERHAM ☎ 01709 702701 90 en suite

SHEFFIELD   Map 08 SK38

Abbeydale Twentywell Ln, Dore S17 4QA
☎ 0114 236 0763 📠 0114 236 0762
e-mail: abbeygolf@compuserve.com
Undulating parkland course set in the Beauchief Estate.

18 holes, 6261yds, Par 71, SSS 71, Course record 64.
Club membership 696.
Societies larger groups must apply in writing, smaller groups by telephone. **Green Fees** £40 per day; £30 per round (£45 per round weekends £35 after 2.30pm). **Prof** Nigel Perry **Course Designer** Herbert Fowler **Facilities** ⊗
⁊ⅢⅢ ⅼ ☗ ♀ ⚒ ⚑ ⚘ ⚒ **Conf** fac available **Location** 4m SW of city centre off A621

Hotel ★★★ 71% The Beauchief Hotel, 161 Abbeydale Rd South, SHEFFIELD ☎ 0114 262 0500 50 en suite

Beauchief Public Abbey Ln S8 0DB
☎ 0114 236 7274
18 holes, 5469yds, Par 67, SSS 66, Course record 65.
Location 4m SW of city centre off A621
Telephone for further details

Hotel ★★★ 71% The Beauchief Hotel, 161 Abbeydale Rd South, SHEFFIELD ☎ 0114 262 0500 50 en suite

Birley Wood Birley Ln S12 3BP ☎ 0114 264 7262
e-mail: birleysec@hotmail.com
Undulating meadowland course with well-varied features, easy walking and good views. Practice range and putting green.
Fairway course: 18 holes, 5734yds, Par 69, SSS 67, Course record 64.
Birley Course: 18 holes, 5037, Par 66, SSS 65.
Club membership 278.
Visitors apply in advance. **Societies** apply in advance. Telephone 0114 223 3411 **Green Fees** not confirmed. **Cards** 🖃 🖾 **Prof** Peter Ball **Facilities** ⊗ ⁊ⅢⅢ ⅼ ☗ ♀ ⚒
⚑ ⚘ ⚘ ⚒ **Location** 4.5m SE of city centre off A616

Hotel ★★★ 66% Mosborough Hall Hotel, High St, Mosborough, SHEFFIELD ☎ 0114 248 4353 52 en suite

Concord Park Shiregreen Ln S5 6AE
☎ 0114 257 7378
Hilly municipal parkland course with some fairways wood-flanked, good views, often windy. Seven par 3 holes.
18 holes, 4872yds, Par 67, SSS 64, Course record 57.
Club membership 150.
Visitors no restrictions. **Societies** pay & play **Green Fees** terms on application. **Prof** W Allcroft **Facilities** ⊗ ⅼ ☗ ♀
⚒ 🏠 ⚑ ⚘ ⚒ Ⅼ **Leisure** hard tennis courts, heated indoor swimming pool, squash, gymnasium. **Conf** Corporate Hospitality Days available **Location** 3.5m N of city centre on B6086 off A6135

Hotel 🅄 Holiday Inn Sheffield - West, Manchester Rd, Broomhill, SHEFFIELD ☎ 0870 400 9071 138 en suite

Dore & Totley Bradway Rd, Bradway S17 4QR
☎ 0114 2366 844 📠 0114 2366 844
e-mail: dtgc@lineone.net
Flat parkland course.
18 holes, 6265yds, Par 70, SSS 70, Course record 65.
Club membership 580.
Visitors must contact in advance a handicap certificate may be requested, may not play weekends. **Societies** must apply in writing. **Green Fees** not confirmed. **Prof** Gregg Roberts **Facilities** ⊗ ⁊ⅢⅢ ⅼ ☗ ♀ ⚒ 🏠 ⚘ ⚒ **Leisure** snooker. **Conf** fac available Corporate Hospitality Days available **Location** 7m S of city centre on B6054 off A61

Hotel 🅄 Holiday Inn Sheffield - West, Manchester Rd, Broomhill, SHEFFIELD ☎ 0870 400 9071 138 en suite

Continued

Hallamshire Golf Club Ltd Sandygate S10 4LA
☎ 0114 230 2153 📠 0114 230 5413
**Situated on a shelf of land at a height of 850 ft.
Magnificent views to the west. Moorland turf, long
carries over ravine. Good natural drainage.**
*18 holes, 6346yds, Par 71, SSS 71, Course record 65.
Club membership 600.*
Visitors contact professional or secretary in advance. Tees
reserved for members 8-9.30 and noon-1.30. **Societies**
parties of 12+ should book in advance with secretary.
Green Fees £41 per day. **Cards** 🗟 💳 **Prof** G R Tickell
Course Designer Various **Facilities** ⊗ ℳ ⅃ ♥ ♀ ⚐ ♨
🐾 ♂ **Conf** Corporate Hospitality Days available **Location**
Off A57 at Crosspool onto Sandygate Rd, clubhouse 0.75m
on right
....
Hotel 🅄 Holiday Inn Sheffield - West, Manchester Rd,
Broomhill, SHEFFIELD ☎ 0870 400 9071 138 en suite

Hillsborough Worrall Rd S6 4BE
☎ 0114 234 9151 (Sec) 📠 0114 229 4105
e-mail: admin@hillsboroughgolfclub.co.uk
**Beautiful moorland/woodland course 500 ft above sea-
level, reasonable walking. Challenging first four holes
into a prevailing wind and a tight, testing 14th hole.**
*18 holes, 6345yards, Par 71, SSS 70, Course record 63.
Club membership 650.*
Visitors contact professional in advance. May not play Tue
(Ladies Day), Thu and weekends before 2pm without prior
arrangement. **Societies** must apply in writing to secretary.
Green Fees terms on application. **Prof** Lewis Horsman
Facilities ⊗ ℳ ⅃ ♥ ♀ ⚐ ♨ 🐾 ♂ ⚑ **Location** 3m
NW of city centre off A616

Lees Hall Hemsworth Rd, Norton S8 8LL
☎ 0114 250 7868
**Parkland/meadowland course with panoramic view of
city.**
*18 holes, 6171yds, Par 71, SSS 70, Course record 63.
Club membership 695.*
Visitors welcome. **Societies** must apply in writing or by
telephone. **Green Fees** not confirmed. **Prof** S Berry
Facilities ⊗ ℳ ⅃ ♥ ♀ ⚐ ♨ 🐾 ♂ **Conf** Corporate
Hospitality Days available **Location** 3.5m S of city centre
off A6102
....
Hotel 🅄 Holiday Inn Sheffield - West, Manchester Rd,
Broomhill, SHEFFIELD ☎ 0870 400 9071 138 en suite

Rother Valley Golf Centre Mansfield Rd, Wales
Bar S26 5PQ ☎ 0114 247 3000 📠 0114 247 6000
e-mail: rother-jackbarker@btinternet.com
**The challenging Blue Monster parkland course features
a variety of water hazards. Notable holes include the
7th, with its island green fronted by water and
dominated by bunkers to the rear. Lookout for the
water on the par 5 18th.**
*18 holes, 6602yds, Par 72, SSS 72, Course record 70.
Club membership 500.*
Visitors 2 days in advance booking format. **Societies** apply
in writing or telephone in advance. **Green Fees** terms on
application. **Cards** 🗟 💳 🏧 📇 📇 **Prof** Jason Ripley
Course Designer Michael Shattock & Mark Roe **Facilities**
⊗ ℳ ⅃ ♥ ♀ ⚐ ♨ 🐾 ♂ ⚑ **Location** Off junct 31
of the M1, follow signs to Rother Valley Country Park
....
Hotel ★★★ 66% Mosborough Hall Hotel, High St,
Mosborough, SHEFFIELD ☎ 0114 248 4353 52 en suite

Tinsley Park Municipal Golf High Hazels Park,
Darnall S9 4PE ☎ 0114 203 7435
e-mail: tinsleyparkgc@hotmail.com
**Undulating meadowland course with plenty of trees and
rough. A test for all categories of golfer.**
*18 holes, 6064yds, Par 70, SSS 68, Course record 66.
Club membership 150.*
Visitors prior booking essential. **Societies** apply to
professional shop on 0114 203 7435 **Green Fees** not
confirmed. **Cards** 🗟 📇 **Prof** W Yellott **Facilities** ⊗ ℳ ⅃
♥ ♀ ⚐ ♨ 🐾 ♂ **Leisure** hard tennis courts. **Location** 4m
E of city centre off A630
....
Hotel ★★★ 66% Mosborough Hall Hotel, High St,
Mosborough, SHEFFIELD ☎ 0114 248 4353 52 en suite

SILKSTONE   Map 08 SE20

Silkstone Field Head, Elmhirst Ln S75 4LD
☎ 01226 790328 📠 01226 792653
**Parkland/downland course, fine views over the
Pennines. Testing golf.**
*18 holes, 6069yds, Par 70, SSS 70, Course record 64.
Club membership 530.*
Visitors with member only at weekends. **Societies** contact
in advance. **Green Fees** £24 per round/£30 per day (with
member £12). **Prof** Kevin Guy **Facilities** ⊗ ℳ ⅃ ♥ ♀ ⚐ ♨
⚐ ♨ ⚑ ♂ **Conf** Corporate Hospitality Days available
Location 1m E off A628
....
Hotel ★★★ 73% Ardsley House Hotel & Health Club,
Doncaster Rd, Ardsley, BARNSLEY ☎ 01226 309955
75 en suite

STOCKSBRIDGE   Map 08 SK29

Stocksbridge & District Royd Ln, Deepcar
S36 2RZ ☎ 0114 288 2003 (office) 📠 0114 283 1460
e-mail: secretary@stocksbridgeanddistrictgolfclub.com
Hilly moorland course.
*18 holes, 5200yds, Par 65, SSS 65, Course record 60.
Club membership 470.*
Visitors contact the professional. **Societies** apply to
secretary. **Green Fees** 18 holes £17 (weekends £31).
Cards 🗟 💳 📇 **Prof** Roger Broad **Course Designer**
Dave Thomas **Facilities** ⊗ ℳ ⅃ ♥ ♀ ⚐ ♨ ♂ **Location**
S side of town centre
....
Hotel 🅄 Holiday Inn Sheffield - West, Manchester Rd,
Broomhill, SHEFFIELD ☎ 0870 400 9071 138 en suite

THORNE   Map 08 SE61

Thorne Kirton Ln DN8 5RJ
☎ 01405 812084 📠 01405 741899
**Picturesque parkland course with 6000 newly planted
trees. Water hazards on 11th, 14th and 18th holes.**
*18 holes, 5366yds, Par 68, SSS 66, Course record 62.
Club membership 300.*
Visitors no restrictions. **Societies** telephone in advance.
Green Fees terms on application. **Cards** 🗟 💳
Prof Edward Highfield **Course Designer** R D Highfield
Facilities ⊗ ℳ ⅃ ♥ ♀ ⚐ ♨ 🐾 ♂ ⚑ **Conf** fac
available Corporate Hospitality Days available **Location**
M18 junct 5, M180 Junct 1, A614 for 3m then turn onto
Kirton Lane
....
Hotel ★★★ 64% Belmont Hotel, Horsefair Green,
THORNE ☎ 01405 812320 23 en suite

WORTLEY
Map 08 SK39

Wortley Hermit Hill Ln S35 7DF
☎ 0114 288 8469 🖷 0114 288 8469
e-mail: wortley.golfclub@virgin.net
Well-wooded, undulating parkland course sheltered from prevailing wind. Excellent greens in a totally pastoral setting.
18 holes, 6028yds, Par 69, SSS 68, Course record 62.
Club membership 510.
Visitors may not play between 11.30am and 1pm. Must contact professional in advance and hold a handicap certificate. **Societies** telephone in advance and confirm in writing with deposit. **Green Fees** £28 per day (£35 weekends). **Cards** 🖾 🖾 **Prof** Ian Kirk **Facilities** ⊗ ⊓ 🖺 🖳 ♀ ⚐ 🖻 ⛳ ♂ **Conf** Corporate Hospitality Days available **Location** 0.5m NE of village off A629

Hotel 🅄 Holiday Inn Sheffield - West, Manchester Rd, Broomhill, SHEFFIELD ☎ 0870 400 9071 138 en suite

YORKSHIRE, WEST

ADDINGHAM
Map 07 SE04

Bracken Ghyll Skipton Rd LS29 0SL
☎ 01943 831207
e-mail: office@brackenghyll.co.uk
On the edge of the Yorkshire Dales, the course commands superb views over Ilkley Moor and the Wharfe Valley. The demanding 18 hole layout is a test of both golfing ability and sensible course management.
18 holes, 5310yds, SSS 66.
Club membership 350.
Visitors contact in advance. **Societies** telephone for information **Green Fees** terms on application. **Facilities** ⊗ ⊓ 🖺 🖳 ♀ ⚐ 🖻 ♂ ⛳ **Conf** Corporate Hospitality Days available

Hotel ★★★ 76% Rombalds Hotel & Restaurant, 11 West View, Wells Rd, ILKLEY ☎ 01943 603201 18 en suite

ALWOODLEY
Map 08 SE24

Alwoodley Wigton Ln LS17 8SA
☎ 0113 268 1680 🖷 0113 293 9458
A fine heathland course with length, trees and abundant heather. Many attractive situations - together a severe test of golf.
18 holes, 6666yds, Par 72, SSS 72.
Club membership 460.
Visitors must contact Secretary in advance. **Societies** must apply in advance. **Green Fees** £65 per day (£80 weekends). **Cards** 🖾 🖾 🖾 🖾 **Prof** John R Green **Course Designer** Dr Alistair Mackenzie **Facilities** ⊗ ⊓ 🖺 🖳 ♀ ⚐ 🖻 ⛳ ♂ **Conf** Corporate Hospitality Days available **Location** 5m N off A61

Hotel ★★★ 70% The Merrion Hotel, Merrion Centre, LEEDS ☎ 0113 243 9191 109 en suite

BAILDON
Map 07 SE13

Baildon Moorgate BD17 5PP ☎ 01274 584266
e-mail: sec@baildongolfclub.freeserve.co.uk
Moorland course set out in links style with outward front nine looping back to clubhouse. Panoramic views with testing short holes in prevailing winds. The 2nd hole has been described as one of Britain's 'scariest'.
Continued

Baildon Golf Club

18 holes, 6225yds, Par 70, SSS 70, Course record 63.
Club membership 750.
Visitors contact in advance, restricted Tue & weekends. **Societies** large numbers apply in writing, small numbers check with the professional. **Green Fees** 18 holes £20 (£12 with member). Weekends £24 (£12). **Prof** Richard Masters **Course Designer** Tom Morris **Facilities** ⊗ ⊓ 🖺 🖳 ♀ ⚐ 🖻 ⛳ ♂ **Leisure** snooker tables practice net. **Location** 3m N of Bradford, off A6038 at Shipley

Hotel ★★★★ 70% Marriott Hollins Hall Hotel & Country Club, Hollins Hill, Baildon, SHIPLEY ☎ 0870 400 7227 122 en suite

BINGLEY
Map 07 SE13

Bingley St Ives Golf Club House, St Ives Estate, Harden BD16 1AT ☎ 01274 562436 🖷 01274 511788
e-mail: bingleyst-ives@harden.freeserve.co.uk
Parkland/moorland/wooded course.

18 holes, 6485yds, Par 71, SSS 71, Course record 69.
Club membership 450.
Visitors contact professional on 01274 562506, no green fees Sat. **Societies** telephone in advance, the professional 01274 562506. **Green Fees** terms on application. **Cards** 🖾 🖾 🖾 🖾 **Prof** Ray Firth **Course Designer** Alastair Mackenzie **Facilities** ⊗ ⊓ 🖺 🖳 ♀ ⚐ 🖻 🖴 ♂ **Location** 0.75m W off B6429

Hotel ★★ 67% Dalesgate Hotel, 406 Skipton Rd, Utley, KEIGHLEY ☎ 01535 664930 20 en suite

Shipley Beckfoot Ln BD16 1LX
☎ 01274 568652 (Secretary) 🖷 01274 567739
e-mail: office@shipleygc.co.uk
Well established parkland course, founded in 1922, featuring six good par 3s.
18 holes, 6235yds, Par 71, SSS 70, Course record 65.
Club membership 600.
Visitors may play Mon, Wed-Fri & Sun, but Tue only after
Continued

2.30pm & Sat after 4pm. **Societies** initial enquiry by phone to professional 01274 563674 and or by letter. **Green Fees** not confirmed. **Cards** 🖃 ▦ ▦ 🖅 ▨ **Prof** J R Parry **Course Designer** Colt, Allison, Mackenzie, Braid **Facilities** ⊗ ⅢⅢ ฿ 🟤 ♥ ♀ ঌ 🏠 ⛳ ⚒ �’ ⚐ **Location** 6m N of Bradford on A650

Hotel ★★ 67% Dalesgate Hotel, 406 Skipton Rd, Utley, KEIGHLEY ☎ 01535 664930 20 en suite

BRADFORD — Map 07 SE13

Bradford Moor Scarr Hall, Pollard Ln BD2 4RW
☎ 01274 771716 & 771693
Moorland course with tricky undulating greens.
9 holes, 5900yds, Par 70, SSS 68, Course record 65.
Club membership 330.
Visitors no visitors at weekends except with member. **Societies** can book starting times by application in writing. **Green Fees** £10 weekdays only. **Facilities** 🟤 ♀ ঌ **Location** 2m NE of city centre off A658

Clayton Thornton View Rd, Clayton BD14 6JX
☎ 01274 880047
Parkland course, difficult in windy conditions.
9 holes, 6300yds, Par 72, SSS 72.
Club membership 250.
Visitors may not play before 4pm on Sun during summer months **Societies** apply in writing to the Secretary or Captain. **Green Fees** £12 per 18 holes; £6 per 9 holes. **Facilities** ⊗ ⅢⅢ ฿ 🟤 ♀ ঌ **Location** 2.5m SW of city centre on A647

Hotel ★★★ 63% Novotel Bradford, 6 Roydsdale Way, BRADFORD ☎ 01274 683683 119 en suite

East Bierley South View Rd, East Bierley BD4 6PP
☎ 01274 681023 ▯ 01274 683666
e-mail: rjwelch@hotmail.com
Hilly moorland course with narrow fairways. Two par 3 holes over 200 yds.
9 holes, 4700yds, Par 64, SSS 63, Course record 59.
Club membership 300.
Visitors restricted Sat (am), Sun & Mon evening. Must contact in advance. **Societies** must apply in writing. **Green Fees** terms on application. **Prof** J. Whittom **Facilities** ⊗ ฿ 🟤 ♀ ঌ 🏠 **Location** 4m SE of city centre off A650

Hotel ★★★ 63% Novotel Bradford, 6 Roydsdale Way, BRADFORD ☎ 01274 683683 119 en suite

Headley Headley Ln, Thornton BD13 3LX
☎ 01274 833481 ▯ 01274 833481
e-mail: honsec-hgc@yahoo.com
Hilly moorland course, short but very testing, windy, fine views.
9 holes, 4864yds, Par 65, SSS 65, Course record 57.
Club membership 256.
Visitors must contact in advance, restricted weekends. **Societies** must contact in advance. **Green Fees** not confirmed. **Facilities** ⊗ ⅢⅢ ฿ 🟤 ♀ ঌ **Location** 4m W of city centre off B6145 at Thornton

Hotel ★★★ 70% Midland Hotel, Forster Square, BRADFORD ☎ 01274 735735 90 en suite

Queensbury Brighouse Rd, Queensbury BD13 1QF
☎ 01274 882155 & 816864 ▯ 01274 882155
Undulating woodland/parkland course.
9 holes, 5024yds, Par 66, SSS 65, Course record 63.

Club membership 380.
Visitors preferable to telephone in advance, restricted at weekends. **Societies** apply in writing. **Green Fees** terms on application. **Prof** David Delaney **Course Designer** Jonathan Gaunt **Facilities** ⊗ ⅢⅢ ฿ 🟤 ♀ ঌ 🏠 ⚒ ⛳ **Location** 4m from Bradford on A647

Hotel ★★★ 70% Midland Hotel, Forster Square, BRADFORD ☎ 01274 735735 90 en suite

South Bradford Pearson Rd, Odsal BD6 1BH
☎ 01274 673346 (pro shop) & 690643 ▯ 01274 690643
Hilly course with good greens, trees and ditches. Interesting short 2nd hole (par 3) 200 yds, well-bunkered and played from an elevated tee.
9 holes, 6068yds, Par 70, SSS 68, Course record 65.
Club membership 300.
Visitors must contact professional in advance. Weekends contact for availability. Tuesday Ladies Day. **Societies** must apply in writing to the secretary. **Green Fees** terms on appliaction. **Cards** ▦ ▨ **Prof** Paul Cooke **Facilities** ⊗ ⅢⅢ ฿ 🟤 ♀ ঌ ⚒ **Location** 2m S of city centre off A638

Hotel ★★★ 63% Novotel Bradford, 6 Roydsdale Way, BRADFORD ☎ 01274 683683 119 en suite

West Bowling Newall Hall, Rooley Ln BD5 8LB
☎ 01274 393207 (office) & 728036 (pro)
▯ 01274 393207
Undulating, tree-lined parkland course. Testing hole: 'the Coffin' short par 3, very narrow.
18 holes, 5769yds, Par 69, SSS 67, Course record 65.
Club membership 500.
Visitors must apply in writing, very limited at weekends. **Societies** must apply in writing/telephone in advance. **Green Fees** terms on application. **Prof** Ian A Marshall **Facilities** ⊗ ⅢⅢ ฿ 🟤 ♀ ঌ 🏠 ⚒ **Conf** Corporate Hospitality Days available **Location** Corner of M606 & A638 (east)

Hotel ★★★★ 63% Hanover International Hotel & Club, Mayo Av, Off Rooley Ln, BRADFORD ☎ 01274 406606 & 406601 ▯ 01274 406600 131 en suite

West Bradford Chellow Grange Rd, Haworth Rd BD9 6NP ☎ 01274 542767 ▯ 01274 482079
e-mail: westbradfordgc@supanet.com
Parkland course, can be windy (especially 3rd, 4th, 5th and 7th holes). Undulating but easy walking.
18 holes, 5738yds, Par 69, SSS 68, Course record 63.
Club membership 440.
Visitors restricted Sat & Sun. Tue is Ladies day, (can play if times available). Must telephone 01274 542102 to reserve a time. **Societies** must contact in advance. **Green Fees** £21 per day/round (. **Prof** Nigel M Barber **Facilities** ⊗ by prior arrangement ⅢⅢ by prior arrangement ฿ 🟤 ♀ ঌ 🏠 ⚒ **Leisure** snooker room. **Conf** fac available Corporate Hospitality Days available **Location** 3.5 m W of city centre off B6144

Hotel ★★★★ 70% Marriott Hollins Hall Hotel & Country Club, Hollins Hill, Baildon, SHIPLEY ☎ 0870 400 7227 122 en suite

BRIGHOUSE — Map 07 SE12

Willow Valley Golf & Country Club
Highmoor Ln, Clifton HD6 4JB ☎ 01274 878624
e-mail: golf@wvgc.co.uk
A championship length 18-hole course offering a unique

Continued *Continued*

golfing experience, featuring island greens, shaped fairways and bunkers, and multiple teeing areas. The 9-hole course offers an exciting challenge to less experienced golfers.

Willow Valley Golf & Country Club
South: 18 holes, 6496yds, Par 72, SSS 74, Course record 69.
North: 9 holes, 2039yds, Par 62, SSS 60.
Club membership 350.
Visitors tee times may be booked by phone on payment of green fee by credit/debit card. **Societies** telephone in advance for availability and booking form. **Green Fees** Summer: 18 holes Mon-Fri £23 (£28 weekends); 9 holes £7.50 (£9 weekends). Reduced winter rates. **Cards** 💳 🔳 💳 🔳 🔃
Prof Julian Haworth **Course Designer** Jonathan Gaunt **Facilities** ⊗ ⟨⟩ 🖳 🖤 💂 🏌 🏠 🏋 ⚓ 🏌 ⛳ **Leisure** 3 hole floodlit academy course. **Conf** Corporate Hospitality Days available **Location** Junct 25 of M62 follow A644 towards Brighouse, at small rdbt right, A643, course is 2m on right

Hotel ★★★ 64% Healds Hall Hotel, Leeds Rd, Liversedge, DEWSBURY ☎ 01924 409112 24 en suite

CLECKHEATON   Map 08 SE12

Cleckheaton & District Bradford Rd BD19 6BU
☎ 01274 851266 📄 01274 871382
e-mail: info@cleckheatongolf.fsnet.co.uk
Parkland course with gentle hills.
18 holes, 5769yds, Par 71, SSS 68.
Club membership 550.
Visitors parties must arrange in advance, Sun by arrangement. **Societies** weekdays only; must contact in advance, Sun by prior arrangement. **Green Fees** May-Sep £27.50 per round/£33 per day (over 20, £25/£30); Nov-Apr £22 per day (over 20, £20 per day). **Prof** Mike Ingham **Facilities** ⊗ ⟨⟩ 🖳 🖤 💂 🏠 🏋 ⚓ ⛳ **Location** 1.5m NW on A638 junc 26 M62

Hotel ★★★ 73% Gomersal Park Hotel, Moor Ln, GOMERSAL ☎ 01274 869386 100 en suite

DEWSBURY   Map 08 SE22

Hanging Heaton White Cross Rd WF12 7DT
☎ 01924 461606 📄 01924 430100
e-mail: ken.wood@hhgc.org
Arable land course, easy walking, fine views. Testing 4th hole (par 3).
9 holes, 5836yds, Par 69, SSS 68.
Club membership 500.
Visitors must play with member at weekends & bank holidays. Must contact in advance. **Societies** must telephone in advance. **Green Fees** terms on application.
Prof Gareth Moore **Facilities** ⊗ ⟨⟩ 🖳 🖤 💂 🏠 🏋 **Conf** fac available **Location** 0.75m NE off A653

Hotel ★★★ 64% Healds Hall Hotel, Leeds Rd, Liversedge, DEWSBURY ☎ 01924 409112 24 en suite

ELLAND   Map 07 SE12

Elland Hammerstone, Leach Ln HX5 0TA
☎ 01422 372505 & 374886 (pro)
9 hole Parkland course played off 18 tees.
9 holes, 5498yds, Par 66, SSS 67, Course record 66.
Club membership 450.
Visitors welcome. **Societies** must contact in writing.
Green Fees £18 per round/day (£30 weekends & bank holidays). **Prof** N Krzywicki **Facilities** ⊗ ⟨⟩ 🖳 🖤 💂 🏠 🏋 🏠 ⛳ **Location** M62 junct 24, follow signs to Blackley

Hotel ★★ 67% The Rock Inn Hotel, Holywell Green, HALIFAX ☎ 01422 379721 30 en suite

FENAY BRIDGE   Map 08 SE11

Woodsome Hall HD8 0LQ
☎ 01484 602739 📄 01484 608260
A parkland course with good views and an historic clubhouse.
18 holes, 6096yds, Par 70, SSS 69, Course record 67.
Club membership 800.
Visitors must contact in advance. Jacket and tie required in all rooms except casual bar. **Societies** must apply in writing. **Green Fees** terms on application. **Cards** 💳 🔳 🔃
Prof M Higginbottom **Facilities** ⊗ ⟨⟩ 🖳 🖤 💂 🏠 🏋 🏠 ⛳ **Location** 1.5m SW off A629

Hotel ★★★ 67% Bagden Hall, Wakefield Rd, Scissett, HUDDERSFIELD ☎ 01484 865330 16 en suite

GARFORTH   Map 08 SE43

Garforth Long Ln LS25 2DS
☎ 0113 286 2021 📄 0113 286 3308
e-mail: garforthgcltd@lineone.net
Parkland course with fine views, easy walking.
18 holes, 6304yds, Par 70, SSS 70, Course record 64.
Club membership 600.
Visitors must contact in advance and have handicap certificate. With member only weekends & bank holidays. **Societies** must apply in advance. **Green Fees** Mon-Fri £36 per round/£42 per day. **Prof** Ken Findlater **Course Designer** Dr Alister Mackenzie **Facilities** ⊗ ⟨⟩ 🖳 🖤 💂 🏠 🏋 🏠 ⛳ **Conf** Corporate Hospitality Days available **Location** 6m E of Leeds, adjacent to A1/M1 link road

Hotel ★★★ 73% Milford Hotel, A1 Great North Rd, Peckfield, LEEDS ☎ 01977 681800 47 en suite

GUISELEY   Map 08 SE14

Bradford (Hawksworth) Hawksworth Ln
LS20 8NP ☎ 01943 875570 📄 01943 875570
Moorland course with eight par 4 holes of 360 yards or more. The course is a venue for county championship events. Extensive views over Baildon Moor to Ilkley Moor.
Hawksworth: 18 holes, 6066yds, Par 71, SSS 70.
Club membership 650.
Visitors must have a handicap certificate and contact in advance. May not play Sat. **Societies** make prior arrangements with manager. **Green Fees** £33 per round (£40 weekends & bank holidays). **Prof** Sydney Weldon **Course Designer** W H Fowler **Facilities** ⊗ ⟨⟩ 🖳 🖤 💂 🏠 🏋 🏠 ⛳ **Conf** Corporate Hospitality Days available **Location** SW side of town centre off A6038

Continued

Continued

Hotel ★★★★ 70% Marriott Hollins Hall Hotel & Country Club, Hollins Hill, Baildon, SHIPLEY ☎ 0870 400 7227 122 en suite

HALIFAX   Map 07 SE02

Halifax Union Ln, Ogden HX2 8XR
☎ 01422 244171 📠 01422 241459
Moorland course crossed by streams, natural hazards and offering fine views of wildlife and the surroundings. Testing 172-yd 17th (par 3).
18 holes, 6037yds, Par 70, SSS 69, Course record 65. Club membership 700.
Visitors contact professional for tee times, 01422 240047. Limited play weekend. Societies contact secretary for dates. Green Fees £25 per round/£30 per day. Prof Michael Allison Course Designer A Herd/J Braid Facilities ⊗ ⅲ ⓑ ⬛ ♀ ♨ 🏠 🎯 ♂ Conf fac available Corporate Hospitality Days available Location A629 Halifax/Keighley, 4 miles from Halifax

Hotel ★★★ 77% Holdsworth House Hotel, Holdsworth, HALIFAX ☎ 01422 240024 40 en suite

Lightcliffe Knowle Top Rd, Lightcliffe HX3 8SW
☎ 01422 202459 204081
Heathland course.
9 holes, 5388mtrs, Par 68, SSS 68. Club membership 460.
Visitors Must contact in advance. Societies Must apply in writing. Green Fees terms on application. Prof Robert Kershaw Facilities ⊗ ⅲ ⓑ ⬛ ♀ ♨ 🏠 ♂ Location 3.5m E of Halifax on A58

Hotel ★★★ 77% Holdsworth House Hotel, Holdsworth, HALIFAX ☎ 01422 240024 40 en suite

West End Paddock Ln, Highroad Well HX2 0NT
☎ 01422 341878 📠 01422 341878
e-mail: info@westendgc.co.uk
Semi-moorland course. Tree lined. Two ponds.
18 holes, 5951yds, Par 69, SSS 69, Course record 62. Club membership 560.
Visitors contact in advance. visitors may not play on Sat Societies must apply in writing to Secretary. Green Fees £27 per round (£32 Sunday & bank holidays). Prof David Rishworth Facilities ⊗ ⅲ ⓑ ⬛ ♀ ♨ 🏠 ♨ ♂ Conf Corporate Hospitality Days available Location W side of town centre off A646

Hotel ★★★ 77% Holdsworth House Hotel, Holdsworth, HALIFAX ☎ 01422 240024 40 en suite

HEBDEN BRIDGE   Map 07 SD92

Hebden Bridge Mount Skip, Wadsworth HX7 8PH
☎ 01422 842896 & 842732
9 holes, 5242yds, Par 68, SSS 67, Course record 61.
Location 1.5m E off A6033
Telephone for further details

Hotel ★★ 71% Old White Lion Hotel, Main St, HAWORTH ☎ 01535 642313 15 en suite

HOLYWELL GREEN   Map 07 SE01

Halifax Bradley Hall HX4 9AN ☎ 01422 374108
Moorland/parkland course, tightened by tree planting, easy walking.
18 holes, 6138yds, Par 70, SSS 70, Course record 65. Club membership 500.

Continued

Visitors contact in advance. Societies must apply in advance. Green Fees terms on application. Prof Peter Wood Facilities ⊗ ⅲ ⓑ ⬛ ♀ ♨ 🏠 ♂ Location S on A6112

Hotel ★★ 67% The Rock Inn Hotel, Holywell Green, HALIFAX ☎ 01422 379721 30 en suite

HUDDERSFIELD   Map 07 SE11

Bagden Hall Hotel & Golf Course Wakefield Rd, Scissett HD8 9LE
☎ 01484 865330 📠 01484 861001
e-mail: info@bagdenhall.demon.co.uk.
Well maintained tree-lined course set in idyllic surroundings and offering a challenging test of golf for all levels of handicap. Lake guarded greens require pin-point accuracy.
9 holes, 3002yds, Par 56, SSS 55, Course record 60.
Visitors anytime. Societies company day packages available, telephone Director of golf. Green Fees not confirmed. Cards 💳 💳 💳 💳 💳 Course Designer F O'Donnell/R Braithwaite Facilities ⊗ ⅲ ⓑ ♀ ♨ 🏠 ♂ Conf fac available Corporate Hospitality Days available Location A636 Wakefield-Denby Dale

Hotel ★★★ 67% Bagden Hall, Wakefield Rd, Scissett, HUDDERSFIELD ☎ 01484 865330 16 en suite

Bradley Park Off Bradley Rd HD2 1PZ
☎ 01484 223772 📠 01484 451613
e-mail: parnellreilly@tinyworld.co.uk
Parkland course, challenging with good mix of long and short holes. Also 14-bay floodlit driving range and 9-hole par 3 course, ideal for beginners. Superb views.
18 holes, 6284yds, Par 70, SSS 70, Course record 65. Club membership 300.
Visitors may book by phone for weekends and bank holidays from the preceeding Thu. No restrictions on other days. Societies welcome midweek, apply in writing to professional. Green Fees £14 (£16 weekends). Cards 💳 💳 💳 💳 💳 Prof Parnell E Reilly Course Designer Cotton/Pennick/Lowire & Ptnrs Facilities ⊗ ⅲ ⓑ ⬛ ♀ ♨ 🏠 ♨ ♨ ♂ ♂ Leisure 9 hole par 3 course. Conf fac available Corporate Hospitality Days available Location 2.5m from junct 25 of M62

Hotel ★★★★ 63% Cedar Court Hotel, Ainley Top, HUDDERSFIELD ☎ 01422 375431 114 en suite

Crosland Heath Felk Stile Rd, Crosland Heath HD4 7AF ☎ 01484 653216 📠 01484 461079
e-mail: croslandheath@onetel.net.uk
Moorland course with fine views over valley.
18 holes, 6007yds, Par 70, SSS 69. Club membership 650.
Visitors welcome, but advisable to check with professional. May not play Sat. Societies must telephone in advance. Green Fees terms on application. Prof John Eyre Course Designer Dr. McKenzie Facilities ⊗ ⅲ ⓑ ⬛ ♀ ♨ 🏠 ♂ Conf fac available Location SW off A62

Hotel ★★★ 66% Pennine Manor Hotel, Nettleton Hill Rd, Scapegoat Hill, HUDDERSFIELD ☎ 01484 642368 31 en suite

Huddersfield Fixby Hall, Lightridge Rd, Fixby HD2 2EP ☎ 01484 426203 📠 01484 424623
e-mail: secretary@huddersfield-golf.co.uk
A testing heathland course of championship standard laid out in 1891.

Continued

18 holes, 6432yds, Par 71, SSS 71, Course record 63.
Club membership 778.
Visitors must book tee times with professional. **Societies** welcome Mon & Wed-Fri, prior arrangement required.
Green Fees £47 per day, £37 per round (£57/£47 weekends & bank holidays). **Cards** 🎴 🎴 🎴 🎴 ☑ **Prof** Paul Carman **Facilities** ⊗ ⑪ ⅃ 🍺 ♀ 🎍 🏠 🎡 ∂ 〔 **Conf** fac available Corporate Hospitality Days available **Location** 2m N off A641

Hotel ★★★★ 63% Cedar Court Hotel, Ainley Top, HUDDERSFIELD ☎ 01422 375431 114 en suite

Longley Park Maple St, Off Somerset Rd HD5 9AX
☎ 01484 422304
9 holes, 5212yds, Par 66, SSS 66, Course record 61.
Location 0.5m SE of town centre off A629
Telephone for further details

ILKLEY   Map 07 SE14

Ben Rhydding High Wood, Ben Rhydding LS29 8SB
☎ 01943 608759
e-mail: secretary@benrhyddinggc.freeserve.co.uk
Moorland/parkland course with splendid views over the Wharfe valley. A compact but testing course.
9 holes, 4611yds, Par 65, SSS 63, Course record 64.
Club membership 290.
Visitors contact in advance. May only play at weekend as guest of member. **Societies** advance notice in writing. In view of limited resources requests considered by monthly committee meeting. **Green Fees** terms on application.
Course Designer William Dell **Facilities** ♀ 🎍 **Location** SE side of town, up Wheatley lane beyond Wheatley Hotel, fork left at bottom of steep section along Wheatley grove, left into High Wood. Clubhouse drive 50 yds left

Hotel ★★★ 76% Rombalds Hotel & Restaurant, 11 West View, Wells Rd, ILKLEY ☎ 01943 603201 18 en suite

Ilkley Nesfield Rd, Myddleton LS29 0BE
☎ 01943 600214 📄 01943 816130
e-mail: honsec@ilkleygolfclub.co.uk
This beautiful parkland course is situated in Wharfedale and the Wharfe is a hazard on each of the first seven holes. In fact, the 3rd is laid out entirely on an island in the middle of the river.
18 holes, 5953yds, Par 69, SSS 70, Course record 64.
Club membership 450.
Visitors advisable to contact in advance. **Societies** apply in writing. **Green Fees** terms on application. **Cards** 🎴 🎴 🎴 🎴 🎴 ☑ **Prof** John L Hammond **Course Designer** Mackenzie **Facilities** ⊗ ⑪ ⅃ 🍺 ♀ 🎍 🏠 🎡 ∂ **Leisure** fishing. **Conf** Corporate Hospitality Days available **Location** W side of town centre off A65

Hotel ★★★ 76% Rombalds Hotel & Restaurant, 11 West View, Wells Rd, ILKLEY ☎ 01943 603201 18 en suite

KEIGHLEY   Map 07 SE04

Branshaw Branshaw Moor, Oakworth BD22 7ES
☎ 01535 643235 (sec) 📄 01535 648011
e-mail: branshaw@golfclub.fslife.co.uk
Picturesque moorland course with fairly narrow fairways and good greens. Extensive views.
18 holes, 5823yds, Par 69, SSS 68, Course record 64.
Club membership 500.

Visitors welcome most times, restrictions at weekends advisable to ring. **Societies** apply in writing to Professional. **Green Fees** £20 per day (£30 weekends).
Prof Mark Tyler **Course Designer** James Braid **Facilities** ⊗ ⑪ ⅃ 🍺 ♀ 🎍 🏠 ∂ **Conf** Corporate Hospitality Days available **Location** 2m SW on B6149

Hotel ★★ 67% Dalesgate Hotel, 406 Skipton Rd, Utley, KEIGHLEY ☎ 01535 664930 20 en suite

Keighley Howden Park, Utley BD20 6DH
☎ 01535 604778 📄 01535 604833
e-mail: manager@keighleygolfclub.com
Parkland course is good quality and has great views down the Aire Valley. The 17th hole has been described as 'one of the most difficult and dangerous holes in Yorkshire golf'. The club celebrated its centenary in 2004.
18 holes, 6141yds, Par 69, SSS 70, Course record 64.
Club membership 650.
Visitors restricted Sat & Sun. Must contact in advance. Ladies day on Tuesday. **Societies** must apply in advance.
Green Fees £40 per day; £33 per round (£45/£37 weekends & bank holidays). **Cards** 🎴 🎴 🎴 🎴 🎴 🎴 ☑ **Prof** Mike Bradley **Facilities** ⊗ ⑪ ⅃ 🍺 ♀ 🎍 🏠 🎡 ∂ **Leisure** Snooker table. **Conf** Corporate Hospitality Days available **Location** 1m NW of town centre off B6143, turn N at Roebuck pub and follow signs

Hotel ★★ 67% Dalesgate Hotel, 406 Skipton Rd, Utley, KEIGHLEY ☎ 01535 664930 20 en suite

LEEDS   Map 08 SE33

Brandon Holywell Ln, Shadwell LS17 8EZ
☎ 0113 273 7471
18 holes, 4000yds, Par 63.
Course Designer William Binner **Location** From Leeds-Wetherby Rd turn left to Shadwell left again up Main St, right at Red Lion Pub
Telephone for further details

Hotel ★★★★ 74% Haley's Hotel & Restaurant, Shire Oak Rd, Headingley, LEEDS ☎ 0113 278 4446 22 en suite 6 annexe en suite

Cookridge Hall Golf & Country Club
Cookridge Ln LS16 7NL
☎ 0113 2300641 📄 0113 203 0198
e-mail: cookridgehall@americangolf.uk.com
American-style course designed by Karl Litten. Expect plenty of water hazards, tees for all standards. Large bunkers and fairways between mounds and young trees.
Cookridge Hall: 18 holes, 6788yds, Par 72, SSS 72.
Club membership 520.
Visitors must contact in advance. Strict dress code applies.
Societies telephone in advance. **Green Fees** Mon-Thu £23; Fri-Sun & bank holidays £28. **Cards** 🎴 🎴 🎴 🎴 ☑ **Prof** Martin Jackson **Course Designer** Karl Liiten **Facilities** ⊗ ⑪ ⅃ 🍺 ♀ 🎍 🏠 🎡 ∂ 〔 **Leisure** chipping and practice bunker. **Conf** Corporate Hospitality Days available **Location** On Otley Old Road, off A660, 6m NW of Leeds

Hotel ★★★★ 74% Haley's Hotel & Restaurant, Shire Oak Rd, Headingley, LEEDS ☎ 0113 278 4446 22 en suite 6 annexe en suite

Continued

Gotts Park Armley Ridge Rd LS12 2QX
☎ 0113 231 1896 & 2562994
e-mail: maurice.gl@sagainternet.co.uk
Municipal parkland course; hilly and windy with narrow fairways. Some very steep hills to some greens. A challenging course requiring accuracy rather than length from the tees.
18 holes, 4960yds, Par 65, SSS 64, Course record 63.
Club membership 200.
Visitors no restrictions.apply directley to Leeds leisure services. **Green Fees** terms on application. **Facilities** ⊗ ▐ ♀ ⚑ ⛳ **Location** 3m W of city centre off A647

Hotel ★★★★ 68% The Queens Hotel, City Square, LEEDS ☎ 0113 243 1323 199 en suite

Headingley Back Church Ln, Adel LS16 8DW
☎ 0113 267 9573 ▋ 0113 281 7334
e-mail: headingley-golf@talk21.com
An undulating course with a wealth of natural features offering fine views from higher ground. Its most striking hazard is the famous ravine at the 18th. Leeds's oldest course, founded in 1892.
18 holes, 6298yds, Par 69, SSS 70, Course record 64.
Club membership 700.
Visitors must contact in advance, restricted at weekends. **Societies** must telephone in advance and confirm in writing. **Green Fees** not confirmed. **Prof** Neil M Harvey **Course Designer** Dr Mackenzie **Facilities** ⊗ ⅷ ▐ ▐ ♀ ♣ 🏠 ⛳ ⚗ **Conf** Corporate Hospitality Days available **Location** 5.5m N of city centre off A660. Take A660 to Skipton, right at lights junct Farrar lane/Church lane. Follow Eccup signs

Hotel Ⓤ Holiday Inn Leeds Bradford Airport, Leeds Rd, BRAMHOPE ☎ 0113 284 2911 124 en suite

Horsforth Layton Rise, Layton Rd, Horsforth LS18 5EX
☎ 0113 258 6819 ▋ 0113 258 9336
e-mail: secretary@horsforthgolfclubltd.co.uk
Moorland/parkland course combining devilish short holes with some more substantial challenges. Extensive views across Leeds and on a clear day York Minster can be seen from the 14th tee.
18 holes, 6243yds, Par 71, SSS 70, Course record 65.
Club membership 750.
Visitors restricted Sat & Sun. Must contact professional (0113 258 5200) **Societies** must apply in writing/by telephone **Green Fees** £27 per round (£36 weekends & bank holidays). **Prof** Dean Stokes/Simon Booth **Course Designer** Alistair MacKenzie **Facilities** ⊗ ⅷ ▐ ▐ ♀ ♣ 🏠 ⚗ ⚗ **Conf** fac available Corporate Hospitality Days available **Location** 6.5m NW of city centre off A65

Hotel Ⓤ Holiday Inn Leeds Bradford Airport, Leeds Rd, BRAMHOPE ☎ 0113 284 2911 124 en suite

Leeds Elmete Ln LS8 2LJ
☎ 0113 265 8775 ▋ 0113 232 3369
e-mail: leedsgccobble@btconnect.com
Parkland course with pleasant views.
18 holes, 6097yds, Par 69, SSS 69, Course record 63.
Club membership 600.
Visitors with member only weekends. Must book in advance weekdays. **Societies** must apply in writing. **Green Fees** 18 holes £32 (weekends £36). **Prof** Simon Longster **Facilities** ⊗ ⅷ ▐ ▐ ♀ ♣ 🏠 ⛳ ⚗ ⚗ **Location** 5m NE of city centre on A6120 off A58

Hotel ★★★★🏰 74% Haley's Hotel & Restaurant, Shire Oak Rd, Headingley, LEEDS ☎ 0113 278 4446 22 en suite 6 annexe en suite

Leeds Golf Centre Wike Ridge Ln, Shadwell LS17 9JW
☎ 0113 288 6000 ▋ 0113 288 6185
e-mail: info@leedsgolfcentre.com
Two courses - the 18-hole Wike Ridge, a traditional heathland course designed by Donald Steel. The sand-based greens are constructed to USGA specification and there are an excellent variety of holes with some very challenging par 5s. The 12-hole Oaks is complemented by a floodlit driving range and other practice facilities. The course is the home of the Leeds Golf Academy.
Wike Ridge Course: 18 holes, 6482yds, Par 72, SSS 71.
Oaks: 12 holes, 1610yds, Par 36.
Club membership 500.
Visitors no restrictions, telephone booking advisable. **Societies** tee reservation available in advance. **Green Fees** Wike Ridge: £15 (weekends £20); Oaks £6.50 (weekends £7). **Cards** 🔄 ▄ 🔲 🔳 💳 **Prof** Mark Pinkett **Course Designer** Donald Steel **Facilities** ⅷ ▐ ▐ ♀ ♣ 🏠 ⛳ ⚗ ⚗ 🏌 **Conf** fac available Corporate Hospitality Days available **Location** 5m N, take A58 course on N side of Shadwell

Hotel ★★★★🏰 74% Haley's Hotel & Restaurant, Shire Oak Rd, Headingley, LEEDS ☎ 0113 278 4446 22 en suite 6 annexe en suite

Middleton Park Municipal Middleton Park, Middleton LS10 3TN
☎ 0113 270 0449 ▋ 0113 270 0449
e-mail: lynn@ratcliffel.fsnet.co.uk
18 holes, 5263yds, Par 68, SSS 66, Course record 63.
Location 3m S off A653
Telephone for further details

Hotel ★★★★ 68% The Queens Hotel, City Square, LEEDS ☎ 0113 243 1323 199 en suite

Moor Allerton Coal Rd, Wike LS17 9NH
☎ 0113 266 1154 ▋ 0113 237 1124
e-mail: info@moorallerton.demon.co.uk
Lakes Course: 18 holes, 6470yds, Par 71, SSS 72.
Blackmoor Course: 18 holes, 6673yds, Par 71, SSS 73.
High Course: 18 holes, 6841yds, Par 72, SSS 74.
Course Designer Robert Trent Jones **Location** 5.5m N of city centre on A61
Telephone for further details

Hotel ★★★ 70% The Merrion Hotel, Merrion Centre, LEEDS ☎ 0113 243 9191 109 en suite

Moortown Harrogate Rd, Alwoodley LS17 7DB
☎ 0113 268 6521 ▋ 0113 268 0986
e-mail: secretary@moortown-gc.co.uk
Championship course, tough but fair. Springy moorland turf, natural hazards of heather, gorse and streams, cunningly placed bunkers and immaculate greens. Original home of Ryder Cup in 1929.
18 holes, 6782yds, Par 72, SSS 73, Course record 66.
Club membership 568.
Visitors contact in advance. **Societies** apply in writing in advance. **Green Fees** £65 per day/round (£75

Continued

Continued

weekends & bank holidays). **Prof** Martin Heggie **Course Designer** A McKenzie **Facilities** ⊗ ⫙ ⬧ ⬧ ♀ ⚒ ⚐ ⚘ ⚒ ♂ **Conf** Corporate Hospitality Days available **Location** 6m N of city centre on A61

Hotel ★★★ 70% The Merrion Hotel, Merrion Centre, LEEDS ☎ 0113 243 9191 109 en suite

Oulton Park Rothwell LS26 8EX
☎ 0113 282 3152 📋 0113 282 6290
Hall Course: 9 holes, 3286yds, Par 36, SSS 36.
Park Course: 9 holes, 3184yds, Par 35, SSS 35.
Royds Course: 9 holes, 3169yds, Par 35, SSS 35.
Course Designer Dave Thomas **Location** Junc 30 on M62
Telephone for further details

Hotel ★★★★★ 62% De Vere Oulton Hall, Rothwell Ln, Oulton, LEEDS ☎ 0113 282 1000 152 en suite

Roundhay Park Ln LS8 2EJ
☎ 0113 266 2695 & 266 4225
Attractive municipal parkland course, natural hazards, easy walking.
9 holes, 5223yds, Par 70, SSS 65, Course record 61.
Club membership 240.
Visitors must contact professional at all times. **Societies** telephone or write to the professional. **Prof** James Pape **Facilities** ♀ ⚒ ⚐ ⚘ ⚒ **Location** 4m NE of city centre off A58

Hotel ★★★★♨ 74% Haley's Hotel & Restaurant, Shire Oak Rd, Headingley, LEEDS ☎ 0113 278 4446 22 en suite 6 annexe en suite

Sand Moor Alwoodley Ln LS17 7DJ
☎ 0113 268 5180 📋 0113 266 1105
e-mail: sandmoorgolf@btclick.com
A beautiful, inland course situated next to Eccup reservoir on the north side of Leeds. It has been described as the finest example of golfing paradise being created out of a barren moor. With magnificent views of the surrounding countryside, the course has sandy soil and drains exceptionally well.
18 holes, 6414yds, Par 71, SSS 71, Course record 63.
Club membership 600.
Visitors restricted weekends & bank holidays. **Societies** must apply in advance. **Green Fees** £50 per day, £40 per round (£50 per round weekends). **Cards** ▦ ▦ 💳 **Prof** Frank Houlgate **Course Designer** Dr A Mackenzie **Facilities** ⊗ ⫙ ⬧ ⬧ ♀ ⚒ ⚐ ⚘ ⚒ ♂ **Conf** Corporate Hospitality Days available **Location** 5m N of city centre off A61

Hotel 🅤 Holiday Inn Leeds Bradford Airport, Leeds Rd, BRAMHOPE ☎ 0113 284 2911 124 en suite

South Leeds Gipsy Ln, Beeston LS11 5TU
☎ 0113 277 1676 (office)
e-mail: sec@slgc.freeserve.co.uk
Parkland course, windy, hard walking, good views.
18 holes, 5769yds, Par 69, SSS 68, Course record 64.
Club membership 400.
Visitors welcome weekdays except competition time, may not play weekends. **Societies** must apply in advance to professional on 0113 270 2598 **Green Fees** £16 per round/£28 per day (weekends £23/£36). **Prof** Laurie Turner **Facilities** ⊗ ⫙ ⬧ ⬧ ♀ ⚒ ⚐ ⚒ ♂ **Conf** Corporate Hospitality Days available **Location** 3m S of city centre off A653

Hotel ★★★★ 68% The Queens Hotel, City Square, LEEDS ☎ 0113 243 1323 199 en suite

Temple Newsam Temple-Newsam Rd LS15 0LN
☎ 0113 264 5624
Lord Irwin: 18 holes, 6460yds, Par 68, SSS 71, Course record 66.
Lady Dorothy: 18 holes, 6299yds, Par 70, SSS 70, Course record 67.
Location 3.5m E of city centre off A63
Telephone for further details

Hotel ★★★★♨ 74% Haley's Hotel & Restaurant, Shire Oak Rd, Headingley, LEEDS ☎ 0113 278 4446 22 en suite 6 annexe en suite

MARSDEN   Map 07 SE01

Marsden Mount Rd, Hemplow HD7 6NN
☎ 01484 844253
Moorland course with good views, natural hazards, windy.
9 holes, 5702yds, Par 68, SSS 68, Course record 64.
Club membership 280.
Visitors must play with member at weekends but not before 4pm Sat. **Societies** Mon-Fri; must contact in advance. **Green Fees** £15 per round (£20 bank holidays). **Cards** ▦ ▦ **Prof** David Pemberton-Nash **Course Designer** Dr McKenzie **Facilities** ⊗ ⫙ ⬧ ⬧ ⚒ ⚐ **Leisure** hard tennis courts. **Location** S side off A62

Hotel ★★ 65% Old Bridge Hotel, HOLMFIRTH ☎ 01484 681212 20 en suite

MELTHAM   Map 07 SE01

Meltham Thick Hollins Hall HD9 4DQ
☎ 01484 850227 (office) & 851521 (pro)
📋 01484 859051
e-mail: melthamgolf@supanet.com
Parkland course with good views. Testing 548 yard 13th hole (par 5).
18 holes, 6396yds, Par 71, SSS 70, Course record 65.
Club membership 756.
Visitors may not play Sat & Wed (Ladies Day), contact professional in advance. **Societies** apply in writing/telephone. **Green Fees** £30 per day; £25 per round (£35/£30 weekends & bank holidays). **Prof** Paul Davies **Course Designer** Alex Herd **Facilities** ⊗ ⫙ ⬧ ⬧ ♀ ⚒ ⚐ ⚘ ⚒ **Location** From Huddersfield take A616 signed Sheffield, ahead at 3rd set of traffic lights on B6108 to Meltham. Left on B6107, 0.5m up hill, club entrance ahead

Hotel ★★ 69% Hey Green Country House Hotel, Waters Rd, MARSDEN ☎ 01484 844235 12 en suite

MIRFIELD   Map 08 SE21

Dewsbury District Sands Ln WF14 8HJ
☎ 01924 492399 & 496030 📠 01924 492399
e-mail: dewsbury.golf@btconnect.com
**Moorland/parkland terrain with panoramic views.
Ponds in middle of 3rd fairway, left of 5th green and
17th green. A challenging test of golf.**
18 holes, 6360yds, Par 71, SSS 71.
Club membership 700.
Visitors At weekends only after 3pm. Telephone in
advance. **Societies** telephone bookings. **Green Fees** £25
per day; £20 per round (£17.50 weekend after 3pm). **Cards**
🖃 🖃 💳 **Prof** Nigel P Hirst **Course Designer** Old Tom
Morris/ Peter Alliss **Facilities** ⊗ ⅏ by prior arrangement
⅃ 🖳 ♀ ⚘ ⛳ ⚲ **Leisure** snooker tables. **Conf** fac
available Corporate Hospitality Days available **Location**
Off A644, 6m from junct 25 on M62
·······································
Hotel ★★★ 64% Healds Hall Hotel, Leeds Rd,
Liversedge, DEWSBURY ☎ 01924 409112
24 en suite

MORLEY   Map 08 SE22

Howley Hall Scotchman Ln LS27 0NX
☎ 01924 350100 📠 01924 350104
e-mail: office@howleyhall.co.uk
**Parkland course with easy walking and superb views of
the Pennines and Calder Valley.**
18 holes, 6092yds, Par 71, SSS 69.
Club membership 700.
Visitors play from yellow markers. May not play Sat.
Societies contact secretary/manager for details. **Green
Fees** £36 per day; £30 per round (£40 weekends & bank
holidays). **Prof** Gary Watkinson **Course Designer**
MacKenzie **Facilities** ⊗ ⅏ ⅃ 🖳 ♀ ⚘ 🏠 ⚲ **Conf** fac
available Corporate Hospitality Days available **Location**
1.5m S on B6123
··························
Hotel ★★ 70% Alder House Hotel, Towngate Rd, Healey
Ln, BATLEY ☎ 01924 444777 20 en suite

OSSETT   Map 08 SE22

Low Laithes Parkmill Ln, Flushdyke WF5 9AP
☎ 01924 274667 & 266067 📠 01924 266067
Testing parkland course.
18 holes, 6463yds, Par 72, SSS 71, Course record 65.
Club membership 600.
Visitors may not play before 9.30am and 12.30-1.30
weekdays and before 10am and 12-2 weekends/bank
holidays. **Societies** by prior arrangement. **Green Fees** not
confirmed. **Prof** Paul Browning **Course Designer** Dr
Mackenzie **Facilities** ⊗ ⅏ ⅃ 🖳 ♀ ⚘ 🏠 ⚘ ⚲ **Conf**
Corporate Hospitality Days available **Location** Leave M1
at jct 40 then signposted on Dewsbury road 0.5m from
M1
·······································
Hotel ★★★ 66% Heath Cottage Hotel & Restaurant,
Wakefield Rd, DEWSBURY ☎ 01924 465399 23 en suite
6 annexe en suite

OTLEY   Map 08 SE24

Otley Off West Busk Ln LS21 3NG
☎ 01943 465329 📠 01943 850387
e-mail: office@otley-golfclub.co.uk
**An expansive course with magnificent views across
Wharfedale. It is well-wooded with streams**
Continued

crossing the fairway. The 4th is a fine hole which generally
needs two woods to reach the plateau green. The 17th is a
good short hole. A test of golf as opposed to stamina.
18 holes, 6256yds, Par 70, SSS 70, Course record 62.
Club membership 700.
Visitors telephone to check tee time. May not play Tue
morning or Sat. **Societies** telephone enquiries welcome,
bookings in writing. **Green Fees** £37 per day, £30 per
18/27 holes (£44/£37 weekends & bank holidays). **Cards**
🖃 🖃 🖃 💳 📇 🖃 💳 **Prof** Steven Tomkinson
Facilities ⊗ ⅏ ⅃ 🖳 ♀ ⚘ 🏠 ⚲ **Leisure** practice
bunker. **Conf** fac available Corporate Hospitality Days
available **Location** 1m W of Otley off A6038
·······································
Hotel 🆄 Holiday Inn Leeds Bradford Airport, Leeds Rd,
BRAMHOPE ☎ 0113 284 2911 124 en suite

OUTLANE   Map 07 SE01

Outlane Slack Ln, Off New Hey Rd HD3 3FQ
☎ 01422 374762 📠 01422 311789
**18-hole moorland course with undulating fairways.
Four par 3 holes with an 8th hole of 249 yards and a
15th regarded as the hardest par 3 in Yorkshire. The
three par 5s may be reachable on a good day in two
strokes but in adverse conditions will take more than
three. Smaller than average greens on some holes,
which makes for accurate second shots.**
*Outlane Golf Club: 18 holes, 6015yds, Par 71, SSS 69,
Course record 67.*
Club membership 600.
Visitors telephone in advance, must be correctly equipped
and attired. No play Sat, limited Sun morning. **Societies**
apply in writing. **Green Fees** £19 per day (£29 weekends
& bank holidays). **Prof** David Chapman **Facilities** ⊗ ⅏ ⅃
🖳 ♀ ⚘ 🏠 ⚲ 🛒 ⚲ **Location** S side of village off A640,
0.5m from junct 23 of M62
·······································
Hotel ★★★ 67% The Old Golf House Hotel, New Hey
Rd, Outlane, HUDDERSFIELD ☎ 01422 379311
52 en suite

PONTEFRACT   Map 08 SE42

Mid Yorkshire Havercroft Ln, Darrington WF8 3BP
☎ 01977 704522 📠 01977 600823
e-mail: linda_midyorksgc@btconnect.com
**An 18-hole championship-standard course opened in
1993, and widely considered to be one of the finest new
courses in Yorkshire.**

18 holes, 6500yds, Par 72, SSS 71, Course record 68.
Club membership 500.
Visitors tee times bookable by telephone, visitors after 12
noon at weekends. **Societies** apply by telephoning in
Continued

advance to the secretary. **Green Fees** not confirmed.
Cards 🏧 💳 💷 **Prof** Alistair Cobbett **Course Designer**
Steve Marnoch **Facilities** ⊗ ⫘ ⅃ ⅃ ♥ ♀ ⚲ ☎ ⚐ ⚑ ⚶ ♂
⚡ **Conf** fac available **Location** On the A1, 0.5m south
intersection of A1/M62

Hotel ★★★ 74% Wentbridge House Hotel, Wentbridge,
PONTEFRACT ☎ 01977 620444 14 en suite
4 annexe en suite

Pontefract & District Park Ln WF8 4QS
☎ 01977 792241 📋 01977 792241
e-mail: manager@pdgc.co.uk
18 holes, 6227yds, Par 72, SSS 70.
Course Designer A McKenzie **Location** M62 junct 32,
through 1st traffic lights, filter left following B6134 signs
North Featherstone/Aketon. Club 1m on right
Telephone for further details

Hotel ★★★ 74% Wentbridge House Hotel, Wentbridge,
PONTEFRACT ☎ 01977 620444 14 en suite
4 annexe en suite

Calverley Golf Club Woodhall Ln LS28 5QY
☎ 0113 256 9244 📋 0113 256 4362
**Parkland course on gently undulating terrain where
accurate approach shots are rewarded to small greens.**

*Calverley Golf Course: 18 holes, 5590yds, Par 68, SSS 67,
Course record 62.*
Club membership 535.
Visitors advisable to book 18 hole course in advance and
may not play weekend morning. 9 hole course, pay and
play at all times. **Societies** contact in writing or telephone.
Green Fees £13 per round (£16 weekends). **Cards** 🏧 💳
💷 💷 **Prof** Neil Wendel-Jones **Facilities** ⊗ ⫘ ⅃ ♥ ♀ ⚲
☎ ⚐ ⚑ ⚶ ⚡ **Conf** Corporate Hospitality Days available
Location Signposted Calverley from A647 Leeds/Bradford
road

Hotel ⟴ Travelodge Bradford, 1 Mid Point, Dick Ln,
PUDSEY ☎ 08700 850 950 48 en suite

Fulneck LS28 8NT ☎ 0113 256 5191
9 holes, 5456yds, Par 66, SSS 67, Course record 65.
Location Pudsey, between Leeds/Bradford
Telephone for further details

Hotel ★★★ 63% Novotel Bradford, 6 Roydsdale Way,
BRADFORD ☎ 01274 683683 119 en suite

Woodhall Hills Calverley LS28 5UN
☎ 0113 255 4594 📋 0113 255 4594
e-mail: whhgc@tiscali.co.uk
Meadowland course, recently redeveloped with

an improved layout and open ditches around the
course. A challenging opening hole, a good variety of
par 3's and testing holes at the 6th and 11th.
18 holes, 6184yds, Par 71, SSS 70, Course record 64.
Club membership 550.
Visitors any day advise manager/professional in
advance,sat after 4.30; Sun after 9.30am. **Societies**
telephone in advance. **Green Fees** £20.50 per round
(£25.50 weekends). Twilight weekends£12. **Prof** Warren
Lockett **Facilities** ⊗ ⫘ ⅃ ♥ ♀ ⚲ ☎ ⚡ **Conf** fac
available Corporate Hospitality Days available **Location**
1m NW off A647

Hotel ⟴ Travelodge Bradford, 1 Mid Point, Dick Ln,
PUDSEY ☎ 08700 850 950 48 en suite

Rawdon Golf & Lawn Tennis Club
Buckstone Dr LS19 6BD ☎ 0113 250 6040
Undulating parkland course.
9 holes, 5980yds, Par 72, SSS 69, Course record 65.
Club membership 600.
Visitors must contact in advance & have handicap
certificate. With member only. **Societies** must contact in
advance. **Green Fees** £10 for 18 holes (£11 weekends &
bank holidays). **Facilities** ⊗ ⫘ ⅃ ♥ ♀ ⚲ ☎ ⚡ **Leisure**
hard and grass tennis courts. **Conf** fac available Corporate
Hospitality Days available **Location** Nw of Leeds off A65

Hotel ★★★★ 70% Marriott Hollins Hall Hotel &
Country Club, Hollins Hill, Baildon, SHIPLEY
☎ 0870 400 7227 122 en suite

Riddlesden Howden Rough BD20 5QN
☎ 01535 602148
**Undulating moorland course with prevailing west winds
and beautiful views. Nine par 3 holes and spectacular
6th and 15th holes played over old quarry sites.**
18 holes, 4295yds, Par 63, SSS 61.
Club membership 350.
Visitors restricted before 2pm weekends. **Societies** apply
by telephone or in writing. **Green Fees** £16 per day/round
(£21 weekends). **Facilities** ⊗ ⫘ ⅃ ♥ ♀ ⚲ **Conf**
Corporate Hospitality Days available **Location** 1m NW

Hotel ★★ 67% Dalesgate Hotel, 406 Skipton Rd, Utley,
KEIGHLEY ☎ 01535 664930 20 en suite

Scarcroft Syke Ln LS14 3BQ
☎ 0113 289 2311 📋 0113 289 3835
e-mail: sge@cwcomm.net
18 holes, 6426yds, Par 71, SSS 69.
Course Designer Charles Mackenzie **Location** 0.5m N of
village off A58
Telephone for further details

Hotel ★★★ 70% The Merrion Hotel, Merrion Centre,
LEEDS ☎ 0113 243 9191 109 en suite

Marriott Hollins Hall Hotel & Country Club
Hollins Hill, Otley Rd BD17 7QW
☎ 01274 534212 📋 01274 534220
**Set in natural heathland amongst the beautiful
Yorkshire moors and dales. The course is majestic,**

Continued　　　　　　　　　　　　　*Continued*

challenging and classically designed in the spirit of the game.

Marriott Hollins Hall Hotel & Country Club
18 holes, 6671yds, Par 71, SSS 71, Course record 66.
Club membership 350.
Visitors must contact in advance, restrictions at weekend may apply, handicap certificate required weekends, 10 day advanced booking system. **Societies** telephone in advance 01274 530053. **Green Fees** not confirmed. **Cards** 🔲 🔲 🔲 📟 **Prof** G Brand/M Wood **Course Designer** Ross McMurray **Facilities** ⊗ ⅷ ᕞ ⬛ ♀ ⚘ 🏠 ⛵ 🍴 🛥 🔧 ⚷ ⚷ **Leisure** heated indoor swimming pool, sauna, solarium, gymnasium. **Conf** fac available Corporate Hospitality Days available **Location** 3m N on the A6038 Otley road

·······················

Hotel ★★★★ 70% Marriott Hollins Hall Hotel & Country Club, Hollins Hill, Baildon, SHIPLEY
☎ 0870 400 7227 122 en suite

Northcliffe High Bank Ln BD18 4LJ
☎ 01274 596731 📠 01274 584148
e-mail: northcliffe@bigfoot.com
Parkland course with magnificent views of moors. Testing 1st hole, dog-leg left over a ravine. The 18th hole is one of the most picturesque and difficult par 3s in the country, with a green 100 feet below the tee and protected by bunkers, water and trees.
18 holes, 6104yds, Par 71, SSS 70, Course record 64.
Club membership 700.
Visitors limited access at weekend. **Societies** book via secretary in advance, weekdays only. **Green Fees** £30 per day; £25 per round (£30 per round weekends & bank holidays). **Prof** M Hillas **Course Designer** James Braid **Facilities** ⊗ ⅷ ᕞ ⬛ ♀ ⚘ 🏠 ⛵ 🔧 ⚷ **Conf** Corporate Hospitality Days available **Location** 1.25m SW of Shipley, off A650

·······················

Hotel ★★★★ 70% Marriott Hollins Hall Hotel & Country Club, Hollins Hill, Baildon, SHIPLEY
☎ 0870 400 7227 122 en suite

Silsden Brunthwaite Ln, Brunthwaite BD20 0ND
☎ 01535 652998 📠 01535 654273
e-mail: info@silsdengolfclub.co.uk
18 holes, 5259yds, Par 67, SSS 66, Course record 62.
Location entering Silsden from direction of Aire Valley trunk road, turn immediately right after canal bridge
Telephone for further details

·······················

Hotel ★★ 67% Dalesgate Hotel, 406 Skipton Rd, Utley, KEIGHLEY ☎ 01535 664930 20 en suite

Ryburn The Shaw, Norland HX6 3QP
☎ 01422 831355
Moorland course, easy walking. Panoramic views of the Ryburn and Calder valleys.
9 holes, 5127yds, Par 66, SSS 65, Course record 64.
Club membership 300.
Visitors must contact in advance. **Societies** apply in writing. **Green Fees** terms on application. **Facilities** ⊗ ⅷ ᕞ ⬛ ♀ ⚘ **Conf** Corporate Hospitality Days available **Location** 1m S of Sowerby Bridge off A58

·······················

Hotel ★★ 67% The Rock Inn Hotel, Holywell Green, HALIFAX ☎ 01422 379721 30 en suite

Todmorden Rive Rocks, Cross Stone Rd OL14 8RD
☎ 01706 812986 📠 01706 812986
Pleasant moorland course.
9 holes, 5902yds, Par 68, SSS 68, Course record 67.
Club membership 240.
Visitors restricted Thu & weekends. Advisable to contact in advance. **Societies** must apply in writing. **Green Fees** £10 (weekends & bank holidays £20) (50% off with member). **Facilities** ⊗ by prior arrangement ⅷ by prior arrangement ᕞ ⬛ ♀ ⚘ **Location** NE off A646

·······················

Hotel ★★★ 77% Holdsworth House Hotel, Holdsworth, HALIFAX ☎ 01422 240024 40 en suite

City of Wakefield Horbury Rd WF2 8QS
☎ 01924 360282
Mature, level parkland course.
18 holes, 6319yds, Par 72, SSS 70, Course record 64.
Club membership 600.
Visitors restricted weekends. **Societies** must apply in advance to stewardess 01924 367242. **Green Fees** not confirmed. **Cards** 🔲 🔲 🔲 📟 **Prof** Roger Holland **Course Designer** J S F Morrison **Facilities** ⊗ ⅷ ᕞ ⬛ ♀ ⚘ 🏠 ⛵ 🔧 **Location** 1.5m W of city centre on A642

·······················

Hotel 🅷 Holiday Inn Wakefield, Queen's Dr, Ossett, WAKEFIELD ☎ 0870 400 9082 105 en suite

Lofthouse Hill Leeds Rd WF3 3LR
☎ 01924 823703 📠 01924 823703
New parkland course.
18 holes, 5988yds, Par 70, SSS 69.
Visitors must contact in advance **Societies Green Fees** £10 per 18 holes. **Cards** 🔲 🔲 🔲 📟 **Prof** Derek Johnson **Facilities** ⊗ ⅷ ᕞ ⬛ ♀ ⚘ 🏠 ⛵ 🛥 **Location** off A6, 4m from Wakefield

·······················

Hotel 🅷 Holiday Inn Wakefield, Queen's Dr, Ossett, WAKEFIELD ☎ 0870 400 9082 105 en suite

Normanton Hatfield Hall, Aberford Rd WF3 4JP
☎ 01924 377943 📠 01924 200777
A championship course occupying 145 acres of the Hatfield Hall Estate. A blend of parkland and elevations, the course incorporates impressive lakes and benefits from the sympathetic preservation of long established trees and wildlife. The large undulating greens are built to USGA standards and are playable all year.
18 holes, 6205yds, Par 72, SSS 71.

Continued

Club membership 1000.
Visitors may not play weekends. **Societies** weekdays only, apply in writing. **Green Fees** £23 per 18 holes. **Cards** ▨ ▨ ▨ ▨ ▨ **Prof** Gary Pritchard **Facilities** ⊗ ⅷ ⅃ ▉ ♀ ⚘ ⚐ ⛟ ✇ **Conf** fac available **Location** M62 junct 30, take A642 towards Wakefield, 2m on right

Hotel ★★★ 64% Chasley Hotel, Queen St, WAKEFIELD ☎ 01924 372111 64 en suite

Painthorpe House Painthorpe Ln, Painthorpe, Crigglestone WF4 3HE
☎ 01924 254737 & 255083 🖹 01924 252022
Undulating meadowland course, easy walking.
9 holes, 4544yds, Par 62, SSS 62, Course record 63.
Club membership 100.
Visitors pay and play Mon-Sat, after 2.30pm on Sun.
Societies must telephone in advance. **Green Fees** £6 for 18 holes (£7 weekends). **Cards** ▨ ▨ **Facilities** ⊗ ⅷ ⅃ ▉ ♀ ⚘ **Leisure** bowling green. **Location** 2m S off A636, 0.5m from jct 39 M1

Hotel Ⓤ Holiday Inn Wakefield, Queen's Dr, Ossett, WAKEFIELD ☎ 0870 400 9082 105 en suite

Wakefield Woodthorpe Ln, Sandal WF2 6JH
☎ 01924 258778 (sec) 🖹 01924 242752
A well-sheltered meadowland/parkland course with easy walking and good views.
18 holes, 6653yds, Par 72, SSS 72, Course record 67.
Club membership 540.
Visitors contact must be made in advance. Visitors Wed, Thu and Fri only. **Societies** must apply in writing. **Green Fees** £32 per round/£37 per day (weekends £40). **Prof** Ian M Wright **Course Designer** A McKenzie/S Herd **Facilities** ⊗ ⅷ ⅃ ▉ ♀ ⚘ ⛟ ✇ **Conf** Corporate Hospitality Days available **Location** 3m S of Wakefield, off A61

Hotel Ⓤ Holiday Inn Wakefield, Queen's Dr, Ossett, WAKEFIELD ☎ 0870 400 9082 105 en suite

WETHERBY   Map 08 SE44

Wetherby Linton Ln LS22 4JF
☎ 01937 580089 🖹 01937 581915
e-mail: info@wetherbygolfclub.fsnet.co.uk
Parkland course with fine views.
18 holes, 6235yds, Par 71, SSS 70, Course record 63.
Club membership 950.
Visitors may not play Mon & Tues morning. Must contact in advance **Societies** apply in writing,email or telephone in advance. **Green Fees** £30.50 per round/£37.50 per day.
Prof Mark Daubney **Facilities** ⊗ ⅷ ⅃ ▉ ♀ ⚘ ⛟ ✇ **Location** 1m W off A661

Hotel ★★★★ ♨ 75% Wood Hall Hotel, Trip Ln, Linton, WETHERBY ☎ 01937 587271 14 en suite
30 annexe en suite

WIKE   Map 08 SE34

The Village Golf Course Backstone Gill Ln
LS17 9JU ☎ 0113 273 7471
A 9-hole pay and play course in an elevated position enjoying long panoramic views. The holes are par 3, 4 and 5s and include water hazards and shaped large greens. There are now three extra optional holes (no extra charge), all par 3s over water.
12 holes, 5780yds, Par 75, SSS 68, Course record 66.
Visitors smart casual wear **Societies** contact in *Continued*

advance by letter/telephone **Green Fees** 18 holes £10 (weekends £12); 12 holes £7 (£8). **Course Designer** William Binner **Facilities** ⊗ ⅷ ⅃ ▉ ♀ ⛟ ✇ **Leisure** fishing. **Conf** fac available Corporate Hospitality Days available **Location** signposted, 1m off A61, 2m off A58

Hotel ★★ 75% Aragon Hotel, 250 Stainbeck Ln, LEEDS ☎ 0113 275 9306 12 en suite

CHANNEL ISLANDS
ALDERNEY

ALDERNEY   Map 16

Alderney Route des Carrieres GY9 3YD
☎ 01481 822835
9 holes, 5046yds, Par 64, SSS 65, Course record 65.
Location 1m E of St Annes
Telephone for further details

GUERNSEY

L'ANCRESSE VALE   Map 16

Royal Guernsey GY3 5BY
☎ 01481 246523 🖹 01481 243960
e-mail: bobby@rggc.fsnet.co.uk
Not quite as old as its neighbour Royal Jersey, Royal Guernsey is a sporting course which was re-designed after World War II by Mackenzie Ross, who has many fine courses to his credit. It is a pleasant links, well-maintained, and administered by the States of Guernsey in the form of the States Tourist Committee. The 8th hole, a good par 4, requires an accurate second shot to the green set amongst the gorse and thick rough. The 18th, with lively views, needs a strong shot to reach the green well down below. The course is windy, with hard walking. There is a junior section.
18 holes, 6215yds, Par 70, SSS 70, Course record 64.
Club membership 934.
Visitors must have a handicap certificate; may not play on Thu, Sat afternoons & Sun. **Green Fees** £44 per day/round (with member £30). **Prof** Norman Wood **Course Designer** Mackenzie Ross **Facilities** ⊗ ⅷ ⅃ ▉ ♀ ⚘ ⛟ ✇ ⚐ **Location** 3m N of St Peter Port

Hotel ★★★★ 66% St Pierre Park Hotel, Rohais, ST PETER PORT ☎ 01481 728282 131 en suite

CATEL   Map 16

La Grande Mare Vazon Bay GY5 7LL
☎ 01481 253544 🖹 01481 255197
e-mail: lgmgolf@cwgsy.net
This hotel and golf complex is set in over 120 acres of land. The Hawtree designed parkland course opened in 1994 and was originally designed around 14 holes with four double greens. The course was extended to a full 18 holes in 2001. Practice areas are now in place along with a teaching area.
18 holes, 4596yards, Par 64, SSS 63, Course record 65.
Club membership 800.
Visitors may book a tee time up to 2 days in advance.
Societies must book in advance, **Green Fees** £30 per 18 holes (£34 weekends). **Cards** ▨ ▨ ▨ ▨ ▨ ▨ **Prof** Matt Groves **Course Designer** Hawtree *Continued*

Facilities ⊗ ⊼ ⓛ 💺 ♀ ⚲ 🏠 🍴 🚑 ⚷ ℓ **Leisure** hard tennis courts, outdoor and indoor heated swimming pools, fishing, sauna, gymnasium, sports massage. **Conf** Corporate Hospitality Days available

Hotel ★★★ 70% Hotel Hougue du Pommier, Hougue du Pommier Rd, CATEL ☎ 01481 256531 37 en suite 6 annexe en suite

ST PETER PORT   Map 16

St Pierre Park Golf Club Rohais GY1 1FD
☎ 01481 728282 📄 01481 712041
e-mail: stppark@itl.net
Par 3 parkland course with delightful setting, with lakes, streams and many tricky holes.
9 holes, 2610yds, Par 54, SSS 50, Course record 52.
Club membership 200.
Visitors must book tee times. Strict dress code, contact club in advance for datails. **Societies** must contact in advance. **Green Fees** not confirmed. **Cards** 💳 💳 💳 📇 💳 💳 💳 **Prof** Roy Corbet **Course Designer** Jacklin **Facilities** ⊗ ⊼ ⓛ 💺 ♀ ⚲ 🏠 🍴 🚑 ⚷ ℓ **Leisure** hard tennis courts, heated indoor swimming pool, sauna, solarium, gymnasium. **Conf** fac available **Location** 1m W off Rohais Rd

Hotel ★★★★ 66% St Pierre Park Hotel, Rohais, ST PETER PORT ☎ 01481 728282 131 en suite

JERSEY

GROUVILLE   Map 16

Royal Jersey Le Chemin au Greves JE3 9BD
☎ 01534 854416 📄 01534 854684
e-mail: thesecretary@royaljersey.com
A seaside links, historic because of its age: its centenary was celebrated in 1978. It is also famous for the fact that Britain's greatest golfer, Harry Vardon, was born in a little cottage on the edge of the course and learned his golf here.
18 holes, 6100yds, Par 70, SSS 70, Course record 63.
Club membership 1234.
Visitors restricted to 10am-noon & 2pm-4pm Mon-Fri & after 2.30pm weekends & bank holidays. **Societies** welcome Mon-Fri. Must apply in writing. **Green Fees** £50 per round. **Cards** 💳 💳 💳 💳 💳 **Prof** David Morgan **Facilities** ⊗ ⊼ ⓛ 💺 ♀ ⚲ 🏠 🍴 🏌 🚑 ⚷ **Location** 4m E of St Helier off coast rd

Hotel ★★★ 68% Old Court House Hotel, GOREY ☎ 01534 854444 58 en suite

LA MOYE   Map 16

La Moye La Route Orange JE3 8GQ
☎ 01534 743401 📄 01534 747289
Seaside championship links course (venue for the Jersey Seniors Open) situated in an exposed position on the south western corner of the island overlooking St Ouens Bay. Offers spectacular views, two start points, full course all year - no temporary greens.
18 holes, 6664yds, Par 72, SSS 72, Course record 68.
Club membership 1300.
Visitors must contact Course Ranger in advance 01534 747166. Visitors may play after 2.30pm

Continued

weekends and bank holidays. **Societies** apply in writing. **Green Fees** 18 holes £45 (weekends & bank holidays £50). **Cards** 💳 💳 💳 💳 💳 **Prof** Mike Deeley **Course Designer** James Braid **Facilities** ⊗ ⊼ ⓛ 💺 ♀ ⚲ 🏠 🍴 🚑 ⚷ ℓ **Location** W side of village off A13

Hotel ★★★★ The Atlantic Hotel, Le Mont de la Pulente, ST BRELADE ☎ 01534 744101 50 en suite

ST CLEMENT   Map 16

St Clement Jersey Recreation Grounds JE2 6PN
☎ 01534 721938 📄 01534 721012
Very tight moorland course. Impossible to play to scratch. Suitable for middle to high handicaps.
9 holes, 2244yds, Par 30, SSS 31, Course record 30.
Club membership 500.
Visitors may not play Sun am or Tue am. **Green Fees** terms on application. **Cards** 💳 💳 💳 💳 💳 **Prof** Lee Elstone **Facilities** ⊗ ⊼ ⓛ 💺 ♀ ⚲ 🍴 ⚷ **Leisure** hard tennis courts, squash, bowls. **Location** E side of St Helier on A5

Hotel ★★★★ ⚓ Longueville Manor Hotel, ST SAVIOUR ☎ 01534 725501 29 en suite 1 annexe en suite

ST OUEN   Map 16

Les Mielles Golf & Country Club JE3 7FQ
☎ 01534 482787 📄 01534 485414
e-mail: enquiry@lesmielles.co.je
Challenging championship course with bent grass greens, dwarf rye fairways and picturesque ponds situated in the Island's largest conservation area within St Ouen's Bay.

Continued

Les Mielles Golf & Country Club

St Ouens Bay, Jersey, JE3 7FQ

Tel: 01534 482787   Fax: 01534 485414
Web: www.lesmielles.com

Situated 5 minutes from the airport, Les Mielles Golf & Country Club is set in an area of outstanding natural beauty boasting a Championship 18 Hole Course, Europe's First Realistic Miniature Course, Laser Clay Pigeon Shooting, VAT Free Shopping, Driving Range & Rocco's Restaurant with al fresco area.

18 holes, 5261yds, Par 70, SSS 68, Course record 68.
Club membership 1500.
Visitors welcome all times, prior booking recommended.
Societies book in advance to avoid disappointment. **Green
Fees** terms on application. **Cards** 🖼️🖼️🖼️🖼️🖼️🖼️
Prof Wayne Osmand/Lynne Cummins **Course Designer** J
Le Brun/R Whitehead **Facilities** ⊗ ⅢⅢ ⚑ ♣ ♀ ♬
🏌️ ⚷ ¢ **Leisure** Laser clay pigeon shooting, 'Breakers'
realistic golf course. **Conf** fac available Corporate
Hospitality Days available **Location** Centre of St Ouen's
Bay

Hotel ★★★★ 77% Hotel L'Horizon, St Brelade's Bay,
ST BRELADE ☎ 01534 743101 106 en suite

ISLE OF MAN

CASTLETOWN   Map 06 SC26

Castletown Golf Links Fort Island, Derbyhaven
IM9 1UA ☎ 01624 822220 📠 01624 829661
e-mail: 1sttee@manx.net
**Set on the Langness Peninsula, this superb
Championship course is surrounded on three sides by
the sea, and holds many surprises from its
Championship tees.**

18 holes, 6707yds, Par 72, SSS 72, Course record 64.
Club membership 600.
Visitors contact in advance. Sat reserved for hotel
residents and club members, Wed for Ladies, but times
may be available on both days. **Societies** must telephone in
advance. **Green Fees** £35 Mon-Thu (£40 Fri-Sun & bank
holidays). **Cards** 🖼️🖼️🖼️🖼️🖼️ **Prof** Murray
Crowe **Course Designer** McKenzie Ross **Facilities** ⊗ ⅢⅢ
⚑ ♣ ♀ ♬ 🏌️ ⚷ 🏓 ➤ 🏌️ ¢ **Leisure** heated indoor
swimming pool, sauna. **Conf** fac available Corporate
Hospitality Days available

Hotel ★★ 65% Falcon's Nest, The Promenade, PORT
ERIN ☎ 01624 834077 37 en suite

DOUGLAS   Map 06 SC37

Douglas Pulrose Park IM2 1AE ☎ 01624 675952
e-mail: mikevipondgolf@aol.com
**Hilly, parkland and moorland course under the control
of Douglas Corporation.**
18 holes, 5937yds, Par 69, SSS 69, Course record 62.
Club membership 330.
Visitors no restrictions. **Societies** telephone to book tee
time. **Green Fees** not confirmed. **Prof** Mike Vipond
Course Designer Dr A Mackenzie **Facilities** ⊗ ⅢⅢ ⚑ ♣ ♀
♬ 🏌️ 🏓 ➤ 🏌️ ¢ **Location** 1m outside Douglas on the
Castletown Road on the Pulrose Estate

Hotel ★★★ 68% The Empress Hotel, Central Promenade,
DOUGLAS ☎ 01624 661155 102 en suite

Mount Murray Hotel & Country Club
Mount Murray, Santon IM4 2HT
☎ 01624 661111 📠 01624 611116
e-mail: hotel@mountmurray.com
**A challenging course with many natural features, lakes,
streams etc. Six par 5s, five par 3s and the rest par 4.
Fine views over the whole island.**

18 holes, 6664yds, Par 73, SSS 73, Course record 69.
Club membership 378.
Visitors must contact in advance. Visitors may not play
before 9.30am weekends **Societies** telephone in advance.
Green Fees £25 per round (£30 weekends). **Cards** 🖼️🖼️
🖼️🖼️🖼️ **Prof** Andrew Dyson **Course Designer** Bingley
Sports Research **Facilities** ⊗ ⅢⅢ ⚑ ♣ ♀ 🏌️ ⚷ 🏌️ 🏓 ➤ 🏌️
⚷ ¢ **Leisure** hard tennis courts, heated indoor swimming
pool, squash, sauna, solarium, gymnasium. **Conf** fac
available Corporate Hospitality Days available **Location**
Located on main road 5m from Douglas towards airport

Hotel ★★★★ 70% Mount Murray Hotel & Country Club,
Santon, DOUGLAS ☎ 01624 661111 90 en suite

ONCHAN   Map 06 SC47

King Edward Bay Golf & Country Club
Howstrake, Groudle Rd IM3 2JR
☎ 01624 672709 620430
e-mail: mail@kebgc.com
**Club plays over King Edward Bay course. Hilly seaside
links with natural hazards and good views. Though a
short course, it is a fair test of golf.**
18 holes, 5492yds, Par 67, SSS 65, Course record 58.
Club membership 350.
Visitors must have a handicap certificate and contact in
advance. **Societies** must contact in advance. **Green Fees**
terms on application. **Prof** Donald Jones **Course Designer**
Tom Morris **Facilities** ⊗ ⅢⅢ ⚑ ♣ ♀ 🏌️ ⚷ 🏌️ 🏓 ⚷ **Conf**
fac available **Location** E side of town off A11

Continued

Hotel ★★★★ 72% Sefton Hotel, Harris Promenade, DOUGLAS ☎ 01624 645500 100 en suite

PEEL
Map 06 SC28

Peel Rheast Ln IM5 1BG
☎ 01624 842227 & 843456 🖹 01624 843456
e-mail: lcullen@peelgolfclub.idps.co.uk
18 holes, 5850yds, Par 69, SSS 69, Course record 64.
Course Designer James Braide **Location** SE side of town centre on A1
Telephone for further details

Hotel ★★★ 68% The Empress Hotel, Central Promenade, DOUGLAS ☎ 01624 661155 102 en suite

PORT ERIN
Map 06 SC16

Rowany Rowany Dr IM9 6LN
☎ 01624 834108 or 834072 🖹 01624 834072
e-mail: rowany@iommail.net
Undulating seaside course with testing later holes, which cut through gorse and rough. However, those familiar with this course maintain that the 7th and 12th holes are the most challenging.
18 holes, 5840yds, Par 70, SSS 69, Course record 63.
Club membership 550.
Visitors must contact in advance. **Societies** telephone in advance. **Green Fees** terms on application. **Course Designer** G Lowe **Facilities** ⊗ ⫰ by prior arrangement ⓛ
⬛ ♀ △ ⌂ ⌇ ⬅ ⚬ ✂ **Conf** Corporate Hospitality Days available **Location** N side of village off A32

Hotel ★★★ 67% Ocean Castle Hotel, The Promenade, PORT ERIN ☎ 01624 836399 40 en suite

PORT ST MARY
Map 06 SC26

Port St Mary Kallow Point Rd ☎ 01624 834932
Slightly hilly course with beautiful scenic views over Port St Mary and the Irish Sea.
9 holes, 5702yds, Par 68, SSS 68, Course record 62.
Club membership 324.
Visitors anytime except between 8-10.30 am weekends.
Societies contact for details. **Green Fees** terms on application. **Cards** ▦ ▧ ▨ ▩ **Course Designer** George Duncan **Facilities** ⊗ ⫰ ⓛ ⬛ ♀ △ ⌇ ✂ **Leisure** hard tennis courts, Croquet lawn. **Conf** Corporate Hospitality Days available **Location** Signposted on entering Port St Mary. Follow road into one way system, take 2nd left to end and turn right. Then take 1st right

Hotel ★★★ 67% Ocean Castle Hotel, The Promenade, PORT ERIN ☎ 01624 836399 40 en suite

RAMSEY
Map 06 SC49

Ramsey Brookfield IM8 2AH
☎ 01624 812244 🖹 01624 815833
e-mail: ramsey.golfclub@iofm.net
Parkland course, with easy walking. Windy. Good views. Testing holes: 1st, par 5; 18th, par 3.
18 holes, 5960yds, Par 70, SSS 69, Course record 63.
Club membership 1000.
Visitors contact in advance, visitors may not play before 10am weekdays. **Societies** must apply in advance. **Green Fees** £20 per day (£28 weekends & bank holidays). Reduced winter rates. **Cards** ▦ ▨ **Prof** Andrew Dyson **Course Designer** James Braid **Facilities** ⊗ ⫰ by prior arrangement ⓛ ⬛ ♀ △ ⌂ ⌇ ✂ **Conf** Corporate Hospitality Days available **Location** SW side of town

Hotel ★★★ 68% The Empress Hotel, Central Promenade, DOUGLAS ☎ 01624 661155 102 en suite

Scotland

ABERDEEN CITY

ABERDEEN   Map 15 NJ90

Auchmill Bonnyview Rd, West Heatheryfold
AB16 7FQ ☎ 01224 714577 📄 01224 648693
18 holes, 5123metres, Par 70, SSS 67, Course record 67.
Course Designer Neil Coles/Brian Hugget **Location**
Outskirts Aberdeen, A96 Aberdeen/Inverness
Telephone for further details

....

Hotel ★★★ 70% The Craighaar Hotel, Waterton Rd,
Bucksburn, ABERDEEN ☎ 01224 712275 55 en suite

Balnagask St Fitticks Rd AB11 3QT
☎ 01224 876407 📄 01224 648693
Links course. Used by the Nigg Bay Club.
18 holes, 5986yds, Par 70, SSS 69.
Visitors book in person on day of play. **Societies** apply to
council tel 01224 522000. **Green Fees** terms on
application. **Facilities** ⊗ � ⅃ ⬛ ♀ ☂ ⌇ **Leisure** 9 hole
pitch & putt course. **Location** 2m E of city centre

....

Hotel ★★★ 68% Maryculter House Hotel, South Deeside
Rd, Maryculter, ABERDEEN ☎ 01224 732124 23 en suite

Craibstone Golf Centre Craibstone Estate,
Bucksburn AB21 9YA
☎ 01224 716777 711012 📄 01224 711298
e-mail: g.bruce@ab.sac.ac.uk
**Course comprises two halves of quite different
character and appearance in its mixture of heath and
parkland. The wide fairways make drives look tempting
and the 11th to 15th present a trio of holes that would
fit into many of the great parkland courses. The greens
are top quality despite their early years.**
18 holes, 5613yards, Par 69, SSS 68, Course record 66.
Club membership 425.
Visitors seven day booking system. 50% of prime times
for visitors. **Societies** telephone in advance **Green Fees** not
confirmed. **Cards** ⊞ ⊟ ⬛ 🅿 **Prof** David MacCormack
Facilities ⊗ ⅃ ⅃ ⬛ ♀ ⌇ ⌇ ⌇ **Leisure** sauna,
gymnasium, floodlit astroturf sports area. **Conf** fac
available **Location** NW of city off A96 Aberdeen-
Inverness road. Take A96 through Bucksburn village and
out of town past research institute on right. Before the next
roundabout take turning left signed 'Forrit Brae' . At top of
road there is a sign for golf club.

....

Hotel ★★★★ 67% Aberdeen Marriott Hotel, Overton
Circle, Dyce, ABERDEEN ☎ 01224 770011 155 en suite

Deeside Golf Rd, Bieldside AB15 9DL
☎ 01224 869457 📄 01224 869457
e-mail: admin@deesidegolfclub.com
**An interesting riverside course with several tree-lined
fairways. A stream comes into play at nine of the 18
holes on the main course. In recent years major
reconstruction work has taken place to provide a
testing course in which only five of the original holes
are virtually unchanged. These include the 15th (the old
6th) which bears the name of James Braid who advised
the club during previous course alterations. Various
water features are incorporated into the course
including pools at the 4th, 10th and 17th.**
*Deeside Golf Club-Haughton: 18 holes, 6286yds, Par 70,
SSS 71.*
*Deeside Golf Club-Blairs: 9 holes, 5889yds, Par 70, SSS
67.*

Continued

Club membership 1000.
Visitors must contact in advance **Societies** apply in writing.
Green Fees terms on application. **Cards** ⊞ ⬛ ⬛ 🅿 📱
Prof Frank J Coutts **Course Designer** Archie Simpson
Facilities ⊗ ⅃ ⅃ ⬛ ♀ ☂ 🔒 ⌇ **Conf** Corporate Hospitality
Days available **Location** 3m W of city centre off A93

....

Hotel ★★★★ 74% Ardoe House, South Deeside Rd,
Blairs, ABERDEEN ☎ 01224 860600 117 en suite

Hazelhead Public Hazlehead AB1 8BD
☎ 01224 321830 📄 01224 648693
No 1 Course: 18 holes, 6211yds, Par 70, SSS 70.
No 2 Course: 18 holes, 5742yds, Par 67, SSS 67.
Location 4m W of city centre off A944
Telephone for further details

....

Hotel ★★★★ 74% Ardoe House, South Deeside Rd,
Blairs, ABERDEEN ☎ 01224 860600 117 en suite

Kings Links AB24 1RZ
☎ 01224 632269 📄 01224 648693
18 holes, 6384yds, Par 72, SSS 71.
Location 0.75m NE of city centre
Telephone for further details

....

Hotel ★★★ 64% Grampian Hotel, Stirling St,
ABERDEEN ☎ 01224 589101 49 en suite

Murcar Bridge of Don AB23 8BD
☎ 01224 704354 📄 01224 704354
e-mail: golf@murcar.co.uk
**Seaside links course with a prevailing SW wind. Its
main attraction is the challenge of playing round and
between gorse, heather and sand dunes. The additional
hazards of burns and out of bounds give any golfer a
testing round of golf.**
*Murcar: 18 holes, 6314yds, Par 71, SSS 72, Course record
64.*
Strabathie: 9 holes, 2680yds, Par 35, SSS 35.
Club membership 850.
Visitors must contact in advance. **Societies** advance
booking required. **Green Fees** £70 per day, £50 per round
(£80/£60 (weekends & bank holidays)). Strabathie: £25 per
day, £10 per 9 holes (£35/£15 weekends & bank holidays).
Cards ⊞ ⬛ ⬛ 📱 **Prof** Gary Forbes **Course Designer**
Archie Simpson/James Braid **Facilities** ⊗ ⅃ ⅃ ⬛ ♀ ☂
🔒 ⌇ ⌇ **Location** 5m NE of city centre off A90

....

Hotel ★★★ 70% The Craighaar Hotel, Waterton Rd,
Bucksburn, ABERDEEN ☎ 01224 712275 55 en suite

Royal Aberdeen Links Rd, Balgownie, Bridge of
Don AB23 8AT ☎ 01224 702571 📄 01224 826591
e-mail: admin@royalaberdeengolf.com
**Championship links course with undulating dunes.
Windy, easy walking.**
*Balgownie Course: 18 holes, 6504yds, Par 71, SSS 71,
Course record 63.*
Silverburn Course: 18 holes, 4066yds, Par 60, SSS 60.
Club membership 500.
Visitors times for visitors 10-11.30 and 2-3.30pm
weekdays, after 3.30pm weekends. Must contact in advance.
Societies apply in writing. **Green Fees** £75 per round
(weekends £85). **Cards** ⊞ ⬛ **Prof** Ronnie MacAskill
Course Designer Baird & Simpson **Facilities** ⊗ ⅃ ⬛ ♀
☂ 🔒 ⌇ ⌇ **Location** 2.5m N of city centre off A92

....

Hotel ★★★ 64% Grampian Hotel, Stirling St,
ABERDEEN ☎ 01224 589101 49 en suite

Westhill Westhill Heights, Westhill AB32 6RY
☎ 01224 740159 ▤ 01224 749124&01224 740159
e-mail: WGolfclub@aol.com
A relatively new course, it is now maturing and has been altered and improved since its opening.
18 holes, 5921yds, Par 69, SSS 69, Course record 65.
Club membership 808.
Visitors no restrictions **Societies** telephone in advance.
Green Fees £14 per round (£20 weekends). **Prof** George Bruce **Course Designer** Charles Lawrie **Facilities** ⊗ ⅷ ⅃
♥ ♀ ☆ ⚐ ∅ **Conf** fac available Corporate Hospitality Days available **Location** 7m NW of city centre off A944
....
Hotel ★★★ 70% Westhill Hotel, Westhill, ABERDEEN
☎ 01224 740388 38 en suite

Peterculter Oldtown, Burnside Rd AB14 0LN
☎ 01224 734994(shop) & 735245(office) ▤ 01224 735580
e-mail: info@petercultergolfclub.co.uk
Five new holes were brought into play in 2001. Surrounded by wonderful scenery and bordered by the River Dee, a variety of birds, deer and foxes may be seen on the course, which also has superb views up the Dee Valley.
18 holes, 6207yds, Par 71, SSS 70, Course record 64.
Club membership 1035.
Visitors contact 3 days in advance, welcome between 10am-3.15pm weekdays, 11am-6pm weekends. **Societies** contact up to 7 days in advance. **Green Fees** £22 per round/£30 per day (weekend £27/£35). **Cards** 🖃 🖃
🌑 ⊡ **Prof** Dean Vannet **Course Designer** Greens of Scotland **Facilities** ⊗ ⅷ ⅃ ♥ ♀ ☆ ⚐ ⚐ ∅
Location On A93
....
Hotel ★★★ 70% Westhill Hotel, Westhill, ABERDEEN
☎ 01224 740388 38 en suite

ABERDEENSHIRE

Aboyne Formaston Park AB34 5HP
☎ 013398 86328 ▤ 013398 87592
e-mail: aboynegolf@btinternet.com
18 holes, 5975yds, Par 68, SSS 69, Course record 62.
Location E side of village, N of A93
Telephone for further details
....
Hotel ★★ 73% Loch Kinord Hotel, Ballater Rd, Dinnet,
BALLATER ☎ 013398 85229 17 rms (15 en suite)

Alford Montgarrie Rd AB33 8AE
☎ 019755 62178 ▤ 019755 64910
e-mail: info@alford-golf-club.co.uk
A flat parkland course in scenic countryside. Divided into sections by a road, a narrow-gauge railway and a burn.
18 holes, 5483yds, Par 69, SSS 65, Course record 64.
Club membership 800.
Visitors advisable to contact in advance. **Societies** telephone/e-mail/write in advance. **Green Fees** £15 per round/£20 per day (weekends £20/£26). **Cards** 🖃 🖃 ⊡
Facilities ⊗ ⅷ ⅃ ♥ ♀ ☆ ⚐ ⚐ ∅ **Location** In the centre of the village on A944
....
Hotel ★★ 63% Gordon Arms Hotel, The Square,
HUNTLY ☎ 01466 792288 13 en suite

Auchenblae AB30 1WQ ☎ 01561 320002
Picturesque, small, undulating parkland course offering good views, upgraded to allow safer play and longer, more spacious greens and tees.
9 holes, 2217yds, Par 32, SSS 61, Course record 60.
Club membership 450.
Visitors anytime exceptWed & Fri evenings during peak season but telephone to confirm. **Societies** must telephone in advance. **Green Fees** £9 per day (£12 weekends).
Course Designer Robin Hiseman **Facilities** ♥ ☆ ∅
Leisure hard tennis courts. **Location** 5 miles NW of Laurencekirk off A90
....
Hotel ★★ 66% County Hotel & Squash Club, Arduthie Rd, STONEHAVEN ☎ 01569 764386 14 en suite

Ballater Victoria Rd AB35 5QX
☎ 013397 55567 ▤ 013397 55057
e-mail: sec@ballatergolfclub.co.uk
Heather covered course with testing long holes and beautiful scenery.
18 holes, 5638yds, Par 67, SSS 67, Course record 62.
Club membership 750.
Visitors advisable to contact in advance. **Societies** prior booking recommended. **Green Fees** £22 per round (weekend £26). **Cards** 🖃 🖃 🌑 ⊡ **Prof** Bill Yule
Facilities ⊗ ⅷ ⅃ ♥ ♀ ☆ ⚐ ⚐ ⚒ ∅ **Leisure** hard tennis courts, fishing, snooker. **Conf** Corporate Hospitality Days available **Location** W side of town
....
Hotel ★★★ Darroch Learg Hotel, Braemar Rd,
BALLATER ☎ 013397 55443 13 en suite
5 annexe en suite

East Aberdeenshire Golf Centre Millden
AB23 8YY ☎ 01358 742111 ▤ 01358 742123
e-mail: me@eagolf.com
Designed as two loops of 9 holes each, starting and finishing outside the clubhouse. Skilful use of 130 acres of rolling Buchan farmland has resulted in a challenging course of 6276 yards in length. Even in the short history of the course, the par 3 holes have gained the reputation of being equal to any in the north of Scotland.
18 holes, 6276yards, Par 71, SSS 71, Course record 69.
Club membership 400.
Visitors telephone pro shop to book tee time on 01358 742111 ext 21 **Societies** write/telephone to Sandra Watson.
Green Fees not confirmed. **Cards** 🖃 🖃 🌑 ⊡ **Prof** Ian Bratton **Course Designer** Ian Cresswell **Facilities** ⊗ ⅷ ⅃
♥ ♀ ☆ ⚐ ⚐ ⚒ ∅ ⅃
....
Hotel 🅤 Holiday Inn Aberdeen, Claymore Dr, Bridge of Don, ABERDEEN ☎ 0870 400 9046 123 en suite

Banchory Kinneskie Rd AB31 5TA
☎ 01330 822365 ▤ 01330 822491
e-mail: info@banchorygolfclub.co.uk
Sheltered parkland course situated beside the River Dee, with easy walking and woodland scenery. Twelfth and 13th holes are testing.
18 holes, 5781yds, Par 69, SSS 68, Course record 63.

Continued

Club membership 975.
Visitors must contact in advance, telephone for details on 01330 822447 **Societies** must book in advance. **Green Fees** £22 per round/£30 per day. **Cards** ⊞ 🔳 🔳 ⚏ **Prof** David Naylor **Facilities** ⊗ 🍴 ᛒ ⬛ ♀ ♨ ⬛ ↑ ♦ 🏌 ⚘ **Location** A93, 300 yds from W end of High St

·······························
Hotel ★★★ ⚘ 75% Banchory Lodge Hotel, BANCHORY ☎ 01330 822625 22 en suite

Inchmarlo Golf Centre Inchmarlo AB31 4BQ
☎ 01330 822557 📄 01330 822557
e-mail: info@inchmarlo.com
Laird's Course: 18 holes, 6218yards, Par 71, SSS 71.
9 holes, 1996yards, Par 32, SSS 32.
Course Designer Graeme Webster **Location** 0.5m from A93 Aberdeen-Braemar road
Telephone for further details
·······························
Hotel ★★★ 78% Tor-na-Coille Hotel, BANCHORY ☎ 01330 822242 22 en suite

Duff House Royal The Barnyards AB45 3SX
☎ 01261 812062 📄 01261 812224
e-mail: duff-house-royal@btinternet.com
Well-manicured flat parkland, bounded by woodlands and the River Deveron. Well bunkered and renowned for its large, two-tier greens. The river is a hazard for those who wander off the tee at the 7th, 16th and 17th holes.
18 holes, 6161yds, Par 68, SSS 70, Course record 63.
Club membership 1000.
Visitors telephone professional in advance, handicap certificate is preferred. Restrictions at weekends during summer. **Societies** must apply in writing. **Green Fees** £28 per day, £22 per round (£34/£29 weekends). **Cards** ⚏ **Prof** Bob Strachan **Course Designer** Dr McKenzie **Facilities** ⊗ 🍴 ᛒ ⬛ ♀ ♨ ⬛ ⚘ **Conf** fac available **Location** 0.5m S on A98
·······························
Hotel ★★★ 68% Banff Springs Hotel, Golden Knowes Rd, BANFF ☎ 01261 812881 31 en suite

Braemar Cluniebank Rd AB35 5XX
☎ 013397 41618 📄 013397 41400
Flat course, set amid beautiful countryside on Royal Deeside, with River Clunie running through several holes. The 2nd hole is one of the most testing in the area.
18 holes, 5000yds, Par 65, SSS 64, Course record 59.
Club membership 450.
Visitors are advised to book 24 hours in advance to play at weekends. Tee reserved until 12.30 on Sat for members only. **Societies** must contact secretary in advance 013397 41595. **Green Fees** £20 per round/£23 per day (weekend £25/£28). **Course Designer** Joe Anderson **Facilities** ⊗ 🍴 ᛒ ⬛ ♀ ♨ ⬛ ↑ ⚘ **Location** 0.5m S

Cruden Bay Aulton Rd AB42 0NN
☎ 01779 812285 📄 01779 812945
e-mail: cbaygc@aol.com
A typical links course which epitomises the old fashioned style of rugged links golf. The drives require accuracy with bunkers and protecting greens, blind holes and undulating greens. The 10th provides a
Continued

panoramic view of half the back nine down at beach level, and to the east can be seen the outline of the spectacular ruin of Slains Castle featured in Bram Stoker's Dracula. The figure eight design of the course is quite unusual.
Main Course: 18 holes, 6395yds, Par 70, SSS 72, Course record 65.
St Olaf Course: 9 holes, 5106yds, Par 64, SSS 65.
Club membership 1100.
Visitors welcome on weekdays, at weekends only when there are no competitions, must pre-book **Societies** weekdays only telephone in advance. **Green Fees** £55 per round/£75 per day (weekend £65 per round). **Cards** ⚏ 🔳 🔳 🔳 ⚏ **Prof** Robbie Stewart **Course Designer** Thomas Simpson **Facilities** ⊗ 🍴 ᛒ ⬛ ♀ ♨ ⬛ ↑ ⚘ 🏌 **Conf** Corporate Hospitality Days available **Location** SW side of village on A975
·······························
Hotel ★★ 70% Red House Hotel, Aulton Rd, CRUDEN BAY ☎ 01779 812215 6 rms (5 en suite)

McDonald Hospital Rd AB41 9AW
☎ 01358 720576 📄 01358 720001
e-mail: mcdonald.golf@virgin.net
Tight, parkland course with streams.
18 holes, 5986yds, Par 70, SSS 70, Course record 62.
Club membership 710.
Visitors advisable to book in advance **Societies** telephone in advance. **Green Fees** £18 per round/£25 per day (weekend £20/£28). **Cards** ⚏ 🔳 🔳 ⚏ **Prof** Ronnie Urquhart **Facilities** ⊗ 🍴 ᛒ ⬛ ♀ ♨ ⬛ ⚘ **Conf** Corporate Hospitality Days available **Location** 0.25m N on A948
·······························
Hotel ★★ 72% Udny Arms Hotel, Main St, NEWBURGH ☎ 01358 789444 26 en suite

Fraserburgh AB43 8TL
☎ 01346 516616 📄 01346 516616
e-mail: fburghgolf@aol.com
Testing seaside course, natural links. An extremely scenic course, surrounded and protected by substantial sand dunes.
Corbie: 18 holes, 6308yds, Par 70, SSS 71, Course record 63.
Rosehill: 9 holes, 2416yds, Par 66, SSS 63.
Club membership 650.
Visitors no restrictions but advised to check availability. **Societies** must contact in advance. **Green Fees** not confirmed. **Cards** ⚏ 🔳 🔳 ⚏ 🔳 🔳 ⚏ **Course Designer** James Braid **Facilities** ⊗ 🍴 ᛒ ⬛ ♀ ♨ ⬛ ↑ ⚘ **Leisure** Various open competitions throughout the year. **Conf** Corporate Hospitality Days available **Location** 1m SE on B9033

Huntly Cooper Park AB54 4SH
☎ 01466 792643 📄 01466 792643
e-mail: huntlygc@tinyworld.co.uk
A parkland course lying between the Rivers Deveron and Bogie.
18 holes, 5399yds, Par 67, SSS 66.
Club membership 850.
Visitors may not play before 8am. **Societies** must contact the secretary. **Green Fees** terms on application. **Facilities** ⊗ 🍴 ᛒ ⬛ ♀ ♨ ⬛ ⚘ 🏌 **Location** N side of Huntly, turn off A96 at bypass roundabout
Continued

Hotel ★★ 63% Gordon Arms Hotel, The Square,
HUNTLY ☎ 01466 792288 13 en suite

INSCH   Map 15 NJ62

Insch Golf Ter AB52 6JY
☎ 01464 820363 📄 01464 820363
e-mail: inschgolf@tiscali.co.uk
A challenging 18 hole course, a mixture of flat
undulating parkland, with trees, stream and pond. The
most challenging hole of the course is the 9th, a testing
par 5 of 536 yards requiring long and accurate play.
This follows the par 3 8th, a hole which demands a well
positioned tee shot played over a large water hazard to
a long narrow green. Although a relatively short course,
the natural woodland, water hazards and large
contoured greens require accurate play.
18 holes, 5350yds, Par 69, SSS 67.
Club membership 400.
Visitors restricted during club competitions and Tee times,
ie Mon - Ladies night, Tue - Mens night, Wed - juniors,
telephone clubhouse 01464 820363 for information. Pre-
booking is advised. Societies apply in writing or telephone,
bookings accepted. Green Fees terms on application.
Course Designer Greens of Scotland Facilities ⊗ by prior
arrangement ⅏ by prior arrangement ⅃ ⬥ ♀ ⚎ ⚑ ⚒ ⚍
Location A96

Hotel ★★★ 68% Strathburn Hotel, Burghmuir Dr,
INVERURIE ☎ 01467 624422 25 en suite

INVERALLOCHY   Map 15 NK06

Inverallochy Whitelink AB43 8XY ☎ 01346 582000
Seaside links course with natural hazards, tricky par 3s
and easy walking.
18 holes, 5351yds, Par 67, SSS 66, Course record 57.
Club membership 600.
Visitors restricted at weekends and competition days,
contact for availability. Societies apply in
writing/telephone in advance. Green Fees Sun-Fri £14. Sat
£17. Facilities ⊗ ⅏ ⬥ ⚎ ♀ ⚍ ⚑ Location E side of
village off B9107

INVERURIE   Map 15 NJ72

Inverurie Blackhall Rd AB51 5JB
☎ 01467 624080 📄 01467 621051
e-mail: administrator@inveruriegc.co.uk
Parkland course, part of which is through a wooded area.
18 holes, 5711yds, Par 69, SSS 68, Course record 63.
Club membership 750.
Visitors book tee time through shop up to 24 hrs in
advance 01467 620193. Societies telephone administrator.
Green Fees £20 per day; £16 per round (£24/£20
weekends). Cards 💳 💳 📇 📇 Prof John
Logue Facilities ⊗ ⅏ ⬥ ⚎ ♀ ⚍ ⚑ ⚒ Location
Easily accessible from Blackhall rdbt off A96 bypass

Hotel ★★★ 68% Strathburn Hotel, Burghmuir Dr,
INVERURIE ☎ 01467 624422 25 en suite

KEMNAY   Map 15 NJ71

Kemnay Monymusk Rd AB51 5RA
☎ 01467 642225 (shop) 📄 01467 643746
e-mail: administrator@kemnaygolfclub.co.uk
A parkland course with stunning views, incorporating
both tree lined and open fairways and a stream crossing
four holes. The course is not physically demanding but

Continued

a challenge is presented to every level of golfer due to
the diverse characteristics of each hole.
18 holes, 6362yds, Par 71, SSS 71, Course record 67.
Club membership 800.
Visitors telephone shop for booking. Societies must
telephone in advance. Green Fees £26 per day; £20 per
round (£30/£24 weekends). Cards 💳 💳 📇 📇 Prof
Ronnie McDonald Course Designer Greens of Scotland
Facilities ⊗ ⅏ ⬥ ⚎ ♀ ⚍ ⚑ ⚒ ⚒ ⚍ Conf
Corporate Hospitality Days available Location W side of
village on B993

Hotel ★★★ 70% Westhill Hotel, Westhill, ABERDEEN
☎ 01224 740388 38 en suite

KINTORE   Map 15 NJ71

Kintore Balbithan AB51 0UR
☎ 01467 632631 📄 01467 632995
e-mail: kintoregolfclub@lineone.net
The course covers a large area of ground, from the Don
Basin near the clubhouse, to mature woodland at the
far perimeter. The 1st is one of the toughest opening
holes in the North East, and the 7th requires an
accurate drive followed by a second shot over a burn
which runs diagonally across the front of the green. The
11th is the longest hole on the course, made longer by
the fact that it slopes upwards all the way to the green.
The final holes are short, relatively hilly and quite
tricky but offer spectacular views to the Bennachie and
Grampian hills.
18 holes, 6019yds, Par 70, SSS 69, Course record 62.
Club membership 700.
Visitors during season booking system is in operation &
slots for visitors are available. Other times can be booked
24 hours in advance. Societies apply in writing or
telephone. Green Fees terms on application. Cards 💳 💳
📇 Facilities ⊗ ⅏ ⬥ ⚎ ♀ ⚍ ⚒ ⚍ Location 1m from
village centre on B977

MACDUFF   Map 15 NJ76

Royal Tarlair Buchan St AB44 1TA
☎ 01261 832897 📄 01261 833455
e-mail: info@royaltarlair.co.uk
Seaside clifftop course. Testing 13th, 'Clivet' (par 3).
18 holes, 5866yds, Par 71, SSS 68, Course record 62.
Club membership 520.
Visitors no restrictions. Societies apply in writing. Green
Fees £15 per round (£20 per day). Facilities ⊗ ⅏ ⬥ ⚎ ♀
⚍ ⚑ ⚒ ⚍ Conf Corporate Hospitality Days available
Location 0.75m E off A98

Hotel ★★★ 68% Banff Springs Hotel, Golden Knowes
Rd, BANFF ☎ 01261 812881 31 en suite

NEWBURGH   Map 15 NJ92

Newburgh on Ythan Beach Rd AB41 6BE
☎ 01358 789058 📄 01358 788104
e-mail: secretary@newburgh-on-ythan.co.uk
This seaside course was founded in 1888 and is adjacent
to a bird sanctuary. The course was extended in 1996
and the nine new holes, the outward half, are
characterised by undulations and hills, with elevated
tees and greens requiring a range of shot making. The
original inward nine demands accurate golf from tee to
green. Testing 550yd dog-leg (par 5).
18 holes, 6162yds, Par 72, SSS 71, Course record 68.
Club membership 800.

Continued

Visitors must contact in advance, may not play Sat before 1pm. **Societies** apply in advance. **Green Fees** £25 per round/£30 per day (weekend £30/£35). **Cards** ▦ ▬ ▩ 🖭 🗿 **Facilities** ⊗ ⊪ ⅃ 🖤 ♀ ⚲ 🝙 🏌 ⚘ ℓ **Leisure** hard tennis courts. **Conf** Corporate Hospitality Days available **Location** 10 miles North of Aberdeen on A975 (off A90)

Hotel ★★ 72% Udny Arms Hotel, Main St, NEWBURGH ☎ 01358 789444 26 en suite

Newmachar Swailend AB21 7UU
☎ 01651 863002 🗎 01651 863055
e-mail: info@newmachargolfclub.co.uk
Hawkshill is a championship-standard parkland course designed by Dave Thomas. Several lakes affect five of the holes and there are well developed birch and Scots pine trees. Swailend is a parkland course, also designed by Dave Thomas and opened in 1997. It provides a test all of its own with some well positioned bunkering and testing greens.
Hawkshill Course: 18 holes, 6659yds, Par 72, SSS 74, Course record 67.
Swailend Course: 18 holes, 6338yds, Par 72, SSS 71, Course record 67.
Club membership 900.
Visitors contact in advance & must have handicap certificate for Hawkshill course. **Societies** apply in writing. **Green Fees** terms on application. **Cards** ▦ ▬ ▩ 🗿 **Prof** Gordon Simpson **Course Designer** Dave Thomas/Peter Allis **Facilities** ⊗ ⊪ ⅃ 🖤 ♀ ⚲ 🝙 🏌 ⚘ ℓ **Location** 2m N of Dyce, off A947

Hotel ★★★ 68% Strathburn Hotel, Burghmuir Dr, INVERURIE ☎ 01467 624422 25 en suite

Old Meldrum Kirk Brae AB51 0DJ
☎ 01651 872648 🗎 01651 872896
e-mail: admin@oldmeldrumgolf.co.uk
Parkland course with tree-lined fairways and superb views. Challenging 196 yard, par 3 11th over two ponds to a green surrounded by bunkers.
18 holes, 5988yds, Par 70, SSS 69, Course record 66.
Club membership 850.
Visitors may not play during Club competitions. Must contact in advance **Societies** apply in writing to secretary **Green Fees** £20 per round (weekend £26). **Prof** Hamish Love **Course Designer** Various **Facilities** ⊗ ⊪ ⅃ 🖤 ♀ ⚲ 🝙 🏌 ⚘ ℓ **Location** E side of village off A947

Hotel ★★★ 68% Strathburn Hotel, Burghmuir Dr, INVERURIE ☎ 01467 624422 25 en suite

Peterhead Craigewan Links, Riverside Dr AB42 1LT
☎ 01779 472149 & 480725 🗎 01779 480725
e-mail: phdgc@freenetname.co.uk
The Old Course is a natural links course bounded by the sea and the River Ugie. Varying conditions of play depending on wind and weather. The New Course is more of a parkland course.
Old Course: 18 holes, 6173yds, Par 70, SSS 71, Course record 64.
New Course: 9 holes, 2228yds, Par 31.
Club membership 650.
Visitors welcome any day apart from Saturdays, restricted

Continued

times on the Old Course. Telephone for details. **Societies** apply in writing, restricted availability on Saturdays **Green Fees** £26 per round/£36 per day (weekend £32/£40). **Cards** ▬ **Course Designer** W Park/ L Auchterconie/J Braid **Facilities** ⊗ ⊪ ⅃ 🖤 ♀ ⚲ 🏌 ⚘ **Location** N side of town centre off A90

Portlethen Badentoy Rd AB12 4YA
☎ 01224 782575 & 781090 🗎 01224 781090
e-mail: info@portlethengc.fsnet.co.uk
Set in pleasant parkland, this new course features mature trees and a stream which affects a number of holes.
18 holes, 6707yds, Par 72, SSS 72, Course record 63.
Club membership 1000.
Visitors may not play Sat. Contact in advance. **Societies** apply in advance. **Green Fees** not confirmed. **Cards** ▦ ▬ ▩ 🗿 **Course Designer** Cameron Sinclair **Facilities** ⊗ ⊪ ⅃ 🖤 ♀ ⚲ 🝙 🏌 ⚘ **Conf** fac available **Location** Off A90 S of Aberdeen

Hotel ★★ 66% County Hotel & Squash Club, Arduthie Rd, STONEHAVEN ☎ 01569 764386 14 en suite

Stonehaven Cowie AB39 3RH
☎ 01569 762124 🗎 01569 765973
e-mail: stonehaven.golfclub@virgin.net
Challenging meadowland course overlooking sea with three gullies and splendid views.
18 holes, 5103yds, Par 66, SSS 65, Course record 61.
Club membership 850.
Visitors prefer prior booking, may not play before 4pm Sat. **Societies** telephone or fax in advance to W A Donald. **Green Fees** £18 per round/£24 per day (weekend £25/£30). **Cards** ▦ ▬ ▩ 🗿 **Course Designer** C Simpson **Facilities** ⊗ ⊪ ⅃ 🖤 ♀ ⚲ 🝙 🏌 ⚘ **Leisure** snooker. **Location** 1m N off A92

Hotel ★★ 66% County Hotel & Squash Club, Arduthie Rd, STONEHAVEN ☎ 01569 764386 14 en suite

Tarland Aberdeen Rd AB34 4TB
☎ 013398 81000 🗎 013398 81000
Difficult upland course, but easy walking. Some spectacular holes, mainly 4th (par 4) and 5th (par 3) and fine scenery.
9 holes, 5888yds, Par 67, SSS 68, Course record 65.
Club membership 392.
Visitors must contact in advance. **Societies** must telephone in advance. **Green Fees** £15 per day (£20 weekends). **Course Designer** Tom Morris **Facilities** ⊗ ⊪ ⅃ 🖤 ♀ ⚲ ℓ **Location** E side of village off B9119

Hotel ★★ 73% Loch Kinord Hotel, Ballater Rd, Dinnet, BALLATER ☎ 013398 85229 17 rms (15 en suite)

Torphins Bog Rd AB31 4JU
☎ 013398 82115 & 82402 (Sec) 🗎 013398 82402
e-mail: stuart@macgregor5.fsnet.co.uk
Heathland/parkland course built on a hill with views of the Cairngorms.
9 holes, 4800yds, Par 64, SSS 64, Course record 59.
Club membership 380.

Continued

Visitors Restricted on competition days (alternate Sat and Sun).No visitors on Tuesday evenings. **Societies** apply in advance. **Green Fees** £13 per day (£14 weekends). £7 per 9 holes. **Facilities** ⊗ ⓑ ☕ ⌂ **Location** 0.25m W of village off A980

Hotel ★★★ 78% Tor-na-Coille Hotel, BANCHORY
☎ 01330 822242 22 en suite

TURRIFF
Map 15 NJ75

Turriff Rosehall AB53 4HD
☎ 01888 562982 📠 01888 568050
e-mail: grace@turriffgolf.sol.co.uk
A well-maintained parkland course alongside the River Deveron in picturesque surroundings. Sixth and 12th particularly challenging in a testing course.
18 holes, 6107yds, Par 70, SSS 69, Course record 64.
Club membership 860.
Visitors may not play before 10am weekends. Must contact in advance. **Societies** apply in writing to the secretary. **Green Fees** £25 per day, £21 per day (£31/£25 weekends & holidays). **Prof** John Black **Facilities** ⊗ ⫟ ⓑ ☕ ⓨ ⌂ 🖚 🖋 **Location** 1m W off B9024

Hotel ★★★ 68% Banff Springs Hotel, Golden Knowes Rd, BANFF ☎ 01261 812881 31 en suite

ANGUS

ARBROATH
Map 12 NO64

Arbroath Elliot DD11 2PE
☎ 01241 875837 📠 01241 875837
e-mail: golfshop@fsmail.net
This predominantly flat course has wide undulating fairways and controlled rough 'flatters to deceive'. Sea breezes combined with fast greens and difficult approaches catch out the unwary, as will the subtly positioned bunkers.
18 holes, 6185yds, Par 70, SSS 69, Course record 64.
Club membership 550.
Visitors contact professional 01241 875837. **Societies** contact professional 01241 875837. **Green Fees** terms on application. **Cards** ⊞ 🔳 💷 **Prof** Lindsay Ewart **Course Designer** Braid **Facilities** ⊗ ⫟ ⓑ ☕ ⓨ ⌂ 🖚 🖋 **Location** 2m SW on A92

Hotel ★★ 65% Hotel Seaforth, Dundee Rd, ARBROATH
☎ 01241 872232 19 en suite

Letham Grange Colliston DD11 4RL
☎ 01241 890373 & 809377 📠 01241 890725
e-mail: lethamgrange@sol.co.uk
Old Course: 18 holes, 6632yds, Par 73, SSS 73, Course record 68.

Glens Course: 18 holes, 5528yds, Par 68, SSS 68, Course record 63.
Course Designer G K Smith/Donald Steel **Location** 4m N on A933
Telephone for further details

Hotel ★★ 65% Hotel Seaforth, Dundee Rd, ARBROATH
☎ 01241 872232 19 en suite

BARRY
Map 12 NO53

Panmure Burnside Rd DD7 7RT
☎ 01241 855120 📠 01241 859737
e-mail: secretary@panmuregolfclub.co.uk
A nerve-testing, adventurous course set amongst sandhills - its hazards belie the quiet nature of the opening holes. This tight links has been used as a qualifying course for the Open Championship, and features Ben Hogan's favourite hole, the dog-leg 6th, which heralds the toughest stretch, around the turn.

18 holes, 6317yds, Par 70, SSS 71, Course record 62.
Club membership 700.
Visitors may not play Tuesday am, Saturday before 4pm. Parties of 5 or more must contact in advance. **Societies** must contact secretary in advance. **Green Fees** not confirmed. **Cards** ⊞ 🔳 📭 💷 **Prof** Neil Mackintosh **Facilities** ⊗ ⫟ ⓑ ☕ ⓨ ⌂ 🖚 🖋 ⌊ **Conf** Corporate Hospitality Days available **Location** S side of village off A930

Hotel ⏾ Premier Lodge (Dundee East), 115-117 Lawers Dr, Panmurefield Village, BROUGHTY FERRY
☎ 0870 9906324 60 en suite

BRECHIN
Map 15 NO56

Brechin Trinity DD9 7PD
☎ 01356 622383 📠 01356 625270
e-mail: brechingolfclub@btconnect.com
Rolling parkland course, with easy walking and good views of the Grampian Mountains. A good test of golf. Refurbished clubhouse and pro-shop.
18 holes, 6092yds, Par 72, SSS 70, Course record 66.
Club membership 850.
Visitors contact Professional on 01356 625270 in advance. Restricted weekends. **Societies** must contact club steward in advance. **Green Fees** £33 per day, £25 pe round (£40/£30 weekends). **Cards** 🔳 💷 **Prof** Stephen Rennie **Course Designer** James Braid (partly) **Facilities** ⊗ ⫟ ⓑ ☕ ⓨ ⌂ 🖚 🖋 ⚒ 🖋 **Leisure** squash. **Conf** Corporate Hospitality Days available **Location** 1m N on B966

Hotel ★★★ 65% Glenesk Hotel, High St, EDZELL
☎ 01356 648319 24 en suite

Continued

CARNOUSTIE See page 311

EDZELL Map 15 NO66

Edzell High St DD9 7TF
☎ 01356 647283 (Secretary) 🖹 01356 648094
e-mail: secretary@edzellgolfclub.net
This delightful course is situated in the foothills of the Scottish Highlands and provides good golf as well as conveying a feeling of peace and quiet to everyone who plays here. The village of Edzell is one of the most picturesque in Scotland.
18 holes, 6367yds, Par 71, SSS 71, Course record 62.
West Water: 9 holes, 2057yds, Par 32, SSS 31.
Club membership 855.
Visitors may not play 4.45-6.15 weekdays & 7.30-10, 12-2 weekends. Not before 2pm on 1st Sat each month. **Societies** must contact secretary at least 14 days in advance. **Green Fees** £36 per day; £26 per round (£46/£32 weekends). West Water: £15 per 18 holes, £10 per 9 holes. **Cards** 💳 📇 💷 **Prof** A J Webster **Course Designer** Bob Simpson **Facilities** ⊗ 🏯 🍴 💷 🍵 ⛳ 🏌 🛒 🎱 ♨ 🛖 ♨ ⏱ **Location** N of Brechin on A90, take B966 signposted Edzell, continue 3.5 miles

Hotel ★★★ 65% Glenesk Hotel, High St, EDZELL ☎ 01356 648319 24 en suite

FORFAR Map 15 NO45

Forfar Cunninghill, Arbroath Rd DD8 2RL
☎ 01307 463773 🖹 01307 468495
e-mail: forfargolfclub@uku.co.uk
Moorland course with wooded, undulating fairways, excellent greens and fine views.
Continued

---

18 holes, 6066yds, Par 69, SSS 70, Course record 61.
Club membership 850.
Visitors may not play before 2.30pm Sat. Advance booking required. **Societies** must contact in advance. **Green Fees** £30 per day; £24 per round. **Cards** 💳 📇 💷 💶 📠 🎱 **Prof** Peter McNiven **Course Designer** James Braid **Facilities** ⊗ 🏯 🍴 💷 🍵 ⛳ 🍴 🏌 ⏱ **Conf** Corporate Hospitality Days available **Location** 1.5m E of Forfar on A932

Hotel ★★★ ♨ Castleton House Hotel, Castleton of Eassie, GLAMIS ☎ 01307 840340 6 en suite

KIRRIEMUIR Map 15 NO35

Kirriemuir Shielhill Rd, Northmuir DD8 4LN
☎ 01575 573317 🖹 01575 574608
e-mail: kirriemuirgc@aol.com
18 holes, 5553yds, Par 68, SSS 67, Course record 62.
Course Designer James Braid **Location** 1m N off B955
Telephone for further details

Hotel ★★★ ♨ Castleton House Hotel, Castleton of Eassie, GLAMIS ☎ 01307 840340 6 en suite

MONIFIETH Map 12 NO43

Monifieth Princes St DD5 4AW
☎ 01382 532767 (Medal) & 532967 (Ashludie) 🖹 01382 535553
Medal Course: 18 holes, 6655yds, Par 71, SSS 72, Course record 63.
Ashludie Course: 18 holes, 5123yds, Par 68, SSS 66.
Location NE side of town on A930
Telephone for further details

Hotel 🏯 Premier Lodge (Dundee East), 115-117 Lawers Dr, Panmurefield Village, BROUGHTY FERRY ☎ 0870 9906324 60 en suite

MONTROSE Map 15 NO75

Montrose Links Trust Traill Dr DD10 8SW
☎ 01674 672932 🖹 01674 671800
e-mail: secretary@montroselinks.co.uk
The links at Montrose like many others in Scotland are on commonland and are shared by three clubs. The Medal course at Montrose - the fifth oldest in the world - is typical of Scottish seaside links, with narrow, undulating fairways and problems from the first hole to the last. The Broomfield course is flatter and easier.

Medal Course: 18 holes, 6544yds, Par 71, SSS 72, Course record 63.
Broomfield Course: 18 holes, 4830yds, Par 66, SSS 63.
Club membership 1300.
Visitors may not play on the Medal Course on
Continued

Carnoustie Golf Links

Map 12 NO53   **Carnoustie**

☎ **01241 853789**   📄 **01241 852720**

This Championship Course has been voted the top course in Britain by many golfing greats and described as Scotland's ultimate golfing challenge. The course developed from origins in the 1560s; James Braid added new bunkers, greens and tees in the 1920s. The Open Championship first came to the course in 1931 and Carnoustie recently returned to prominence as the host of the Scottish Open in 1995 and 1996 and the venue for the 1999 Open Championship. The Burnside Course (6020 yards) is enclosed on three sides by the Championship Course and has been used for Open Championship qualifying rounds. The Buddon Course (5420 yards) has been extensively remodelled, making it ideal for mid to high handicappers.

e-mail: golf@carnoustiegolflinks.co.uk

Visitors Must contact in advance, Sat after 2pm, Sun after 11.30am. Must have handicap certificate for championship course

Societies Must contact in advance

Green Fees Telephone for details

🔲🔲🔲🔲🔲🔲🔲

Facilities ⊗ 🎽 ♨ ⚑ 🏠 🍴 ☕ 🍺 ⛳
Conf facilities available, corporate hospitality days available.

Professional Lee Vannet

Leisure Swimming, sauna, solarium, gym

Location Links Parade, Carnoustie DD7 7JE
(SW side of town, off A930)

Holes/Par/Course record 54 holes
Championship Course: 18 holes, 6941 yds, Par 72, SSS 75, Course record 64
Burnside Course: 18 holes, 6020 yds, Par 68, SSS 69
Buddon Links: 18 holes, 5420 yds, Par 66, SSS 67

WHERE TO STAY AND EAT NEARBY

Hotels
ARBROATH

★★ 65% Hotel Seaforth, DD11 1QF.
☎ 01241 872232. 19 en suite

BROUGHTY FERRY

★★★ 72% The Woodlands Hotel, DD5 2QL.
☎ 01382 480033. 38 en suite

Restaurant
CARNOUSTIE

🏅 11 Park Avenue.
☎ 01241 853336.

Championship Course

Sat before 2.45pm & before 10am on Sun. Must have a handicap certificate for Medal Course. Contact in advance. No restrictions on Broomfield Course. Must contact in advance. **Societies** must contact secretary in advance. **Green Fees** Medal: £48 per day; £38 per round (£56/£42 weekends). Broomfield: £18 per round (£20 weekends). **Cards** 🔵 💳 💳 💳 💳 **Prof** Jason J Boyd **Course Designer** W Park/Tom Morris **Facilities** ⊗ ⬚ ⓛ 💺 💺 ♀ 🛆 🏠 ⚑ ⚬ **Location** NE side of town off A92

Hotel ★★★ 73% Best Western Links Hotel, Mid Links, MONTROSE ☎ 01674 671000 25 en suite

ARGYLL & BUTE

CARDROSS   Map 10 NS37

Cardross Main Rd G82 5LB
☎ 01389 841754 📄 01389 842162
e-mail: golf@cardross.com
Undulating, testing parkland course with good views.
18 holes, 6469yds, Par 71, SSS 72, Course record 64.
Club membership 800.
Visitors may not play at weekends unless introduced by member. Contact professional in advance 01359 841350. **Societies** must contact in writing. **Green Fees** £30 per round/£45 per day. Reduced winter rates. **Cards** 🔵 💳 💳 **Prof** Robert Farrell **Course Designer** James Braid **Facilities** ⊗ ⬚ ⓛ 💺 💺 ♀ 🛆 🏠 ⚑ ⚬ **Location** In centre of village on A814

Hotel ★★★★★ 68% De Vere Cameron House, BALLOCH ☎ 01389 755565 96 en suite

CARRADALE   Map 10 NR83

Carradale The Arch PA28 6QT ☎ 01583 431321
Pleasant seaside course built on a promontory overlooking the Isle of Arran. Natural terrain and small greens are the most difficult natural hazards. Described as the most sporting 9-hole course in Scotland. Testing 7th hole (240 yds), par 3.
9 holes, 2358yds, Par 65, SSS 64, Course record 62.
Club membership 320.
Visitors no restrictions,advisable to contact at weekends during summer months. **Societies** contact in advance. **Green Fees** £12 per day. **Facilities** 🛆 ⚬ **Location** S side of village, on B842

DALMALLY   Map 10 NN12

Dalmally Old Saw Mill PA33 1AE ☎ 01838 200370
e-mail: golfclub@lock-awe.com
A 9-hole flat parkland course bounded by the River Orchy and surrounded by mountains. Many water hazards and bunkers.
9 holes, 2257yds, Par 64, SSS 63, Course record 64.
Club membership 130.
Visitors no visitors on Sun between 9-10 & 1-2 or Mon 17.45-18.15 **Societies** telephone in advance. **Green Fees** £10 per day/round. **Course Designer** MacFarlane Barrow Co **Facilities** ⊗ by prior arrangement ⓛ by prior arrangement 💺 by prior arrangement ♀ 🛆 ⚑ ⚬ **Location** On A85, 1.5m W of Dalmally

Hotel ★★ 60% Polfearn Hotel, TAYNUILT
☎ 01866 822251 14 en suite

DUNOON   Map 10 NS17

Cowal Ardenslate Rd PA23 8LT
☎ 01369 705673 📄 01369 705673
e-mail: info@cowalgolfclub.co.uk
Moorland course. Panoramic views of Clyde Estuary and surrounding hills.

COWAL GOLF CLUB

18 holes, 6063yds, Par 70, SSS 70, Course record 63.
Club membership 900.
Visitors advisable to book in advance. **Societies** must telephone in advance. **Green Fees** terms on application. **Cards** 🔵 💳 💳 **Prof** Russell Weir **Course Designer** James Braid **Facilities** ⊗ ⬚ ⓛ 💺 💺 ♀ 🛆 🏠 ⚑ ⚬ **Conf** Corporate Hospitality Days available **Location** 1m N

Hotel ★★ 78% Enmore Hotel, Marine Pde, Hunters Quay, DUNOON ☎ 01369 702230 9 en suite

ERISKA   Map 10 NM94

Isle of Eriska PA37 1SD
☎ 01631 720371 📄 01631 720531
e-mail: gc@eriska-hotel.co.uk
This remote and most beautiful 6-hole course, set around the owners' hotel, is gradually being upgraded to a testing 9-hole challenge, complete with stunning views.
6 holes, 1588yds, Par 22.
Club membership 40.
Visitors contact in advance. **Green Fees** £10 per day. **Cards** 🔵 💳 💳 💳 💳 **Course Designer** H Swan **Facilities** ⊗ ⓛ 💺 ♀ 🛆 ⚑ ◖ ⚬ Ⓣ **Leisure** hard tennis courts, heated indoor swimming pool, sauna, gymnasium. **Location** A828 Connel/Fort William, signposted 4m from North of Benderloch village

Hotel ★★★★ ⚘ Isle of Eriska, Eriska, Ledaig, BY OBAN ☎ 01631 720371 17 en suite

GIGHA ISLAND   Map 10 NR64

Isle of Gigha PA41 7AA
☎ 01583 505242 📄 01583 505244
A 9-hole course with scenic views of the Sound of Gigha and Kintyre. Ideal for the keen or occasional golfer.
Isle of Gigha Golf Course: 9 holes, 5042yds, Par 66, SSS 65.
Club membership 40.
Visitors no restrictions. **Societies** telephone for details. **Green Fees** £10 per day/round. **Course Designer** Members **Facilities** 🛆 ⚑ **Location** Short distance from ferry landing

> **Booking a tee time is always advisable.**

HELENSBURGH　Map 10 NS28

Helensburgh 25 East Abercromby St G84 9HZ
☎ 01436 674173 🖹 01436 671170
e-mail: thesecretary@helensburghgolfclub.org.uk
Sporting moorland course with superb views of Loch Lomond and River Clyde.
18 holes, 6104yds, Par 69, SSS 70, Course record 64.
Club membership 880.
Visitors may not play at weekends. **Societies** weekdays only, must contact in writing. **Green Fees** £35 per day; £25 per round. **Prof** David Fotheringham **Course Designer** Old Tom Morris **Facilities** ⊗ ⅷ ᒪ ☑ ♀ ᒧ 🖻 ⌀ **Conf** Corporate Hospitality Days available **Location** NE side of town off B832

Hotel ★★★★★ 68% De Vere Cameron House, BALLOCH ☎ 01389 755565 96 en suite

INNELLAN　Map 10 NS17

Innellan Knockamillie Rd PA23 7SG
☎ 01369 830242 & 702573
Situated above the village of Innellan, this undulating hilltop course has extensive views of the Firth of Clyde.
9 holes, 4683yds, Par 64, SSS 64, Course record 63.
Club membership 199.
Visitors welcome but may not play after 5pm on Mondays. **Societies** telephone initially. **Green Fees** terms on application. **Facilities** ᒪ ☑ ♀ ᶻ **Location** 4m S of Dunoon

Hotel ★★ 73% Royal Marine Hotel, Hunters Quay, DUNOON ☎ 01369 705810 31 en suite
10 annexe en suite

INVERARAY　Map 10 NN00

Inveraray North Cromalt PA32 8XT ☎ 01499 302116
Testing parkland course with beautiful views overlooking Loch Fyne.
9 holes, 5790yds, Par 70, SSS 68, Course record 69.
Club membership 160.
Visitors no restrictions. **Societies** write or telephone to the secretary. **Green Fees** £15 per day. **Facilities** ᐃ ᶻ **Location** 1m S of Inveraray

Hotel ★★★ 68% Loch Fyne Hotel & Leisure Club, INVERARAY ☎ 01499 302148 80 en suite

LOCHGILPHEAD　Map 10 NR88

Lochgilphead Blarbuie Rd PA31 8LE
☎ 01546 602340 510383
A varied and challenging scenic course with a spectacular par 3 finishing hole.

9 holes, 2242yds, Par 64, SSS 63, Course record 58.
Club membership 250.
Visitors restricted during weekend club competitions. **Societies** apply in advance, restricted weekends. **Green Fees** £15 per 18 holes. **Course Designer** Dr I McCamond **Facilities** ᒪ ☑ ♀ ᐃ 🖻 ᶻ ⌀ **Location** Adjacent to the hospital. Signposted from the village.

Hotel ★★ 62% Stag Hotel & Restaurant, Argyll St, LOCHGILPHEAD ☎ 01546 602496 18 en suite

LUSS　Map 10 NS39

Loch Lomond Rossdhu House G83 8NT
☎ 01436 655555 🖹 01436 655500
e-mail: info@lochlomond.com
A stunning and challenging golf course set in the heart of some of the most beautiful Scottish scenery. The exclusive club is strictly for members only. Nick Faldo called it the finest new course in Europe. It was designed by two Americans, Jay Morrish and Tom Weiskopf and was founded in 1993. There is a putting green, practice area and driving range. The clubhouse used to be the home of the chiefs of Clan Colquhoun.
18 holes, 7095yds, Par 71, Course record 62.
Visitors strictly members only. No visitors strictly private. **Green Fees** terms on application. **Prof** Colin Campbell **Course Designer** Tom Weiskopf **Facilities** ᐃ 🖻 ⊨ ⌀ ⌀ **Leisure** fishing. **Location** Off A82 at Luss

Hotel ★★★★★ 68% De Vere Cameron House, BALLOCH ☎ 01389 755565 96 en suite

MACHRIHANISH　Map 10 NR62

Machrihanish PA28 6PT
☎ 01586 810213 🖹 01586 810221
e-mail: secretary@machgolf.com
Magnificent natural links of championship status. The 1st hole is the famous drive across the Atlantic. Sandy soil allows for play all year round. Large greens, easy walking, windy. Fishing.
18 holes, 6225yds, Par 70, SSS 71.
Club membership 1200.
Visitors no restrictions. **Societies** apply in writing. **Green Fees** Sun-Fri £35 per round/£55 per day. Sat £45/£70. (9 hole course £10 per day). **Cards** ⊞ 🟥 🟥 🟥 ⌷ **Prof** Ken Campbell **Course Designer** Tom Morris **Facilities** ⊗ ⅷ ᒪ ☑ ♀ ᐃ ᶻ ♣ ⌀ **Location** 5m W of Campbeltown on B843

OBAN　Map 10 NM83

Glencruitten Glencruitten Rd PA34 4PU
☎ 01631 564604
There is plenty of space and considerable variety of hole on this downland course - popular with holidaymakers. In a beautiful, isolated situation, the course is hilly and testing, particularly the 1st and 12th (par 4s) and 10th and 17th (par 3s).
18 holes, 4452yds, Par 61, SSS 63, Course record 55.
Club membership 500.
Visitors restricted Thu & weekends. **Societies** must contact in writing. **Green Fees** terms on application. **Course Designer** James Braid **Facilities** ⊗ ⅷ ᒪ ☑ ♀ ᐃ 🖻 ᶻ ⌀ **Location** NE side of town centre off A816

Hotel ★★★ 72% Manor House Hotel, Gallanach Rd, OBAN ☎ 01631 562087 11 en suite

Continued

SOUTHEND — Map 10 NR60

Dunaverty PA28 6RW
☎ 01586 830677 📠 01586 830677
e-mail: dunavertygc@aol.com
Undulating, seaside course with spectacular views of Ireland and the Ayrshire coast.
18 holes, 4799yds, Par 66, SSS 63, Course record 58.
Club membership 400.
Visitors limited Sat, contact in advance. **Societies** apply in advance. **Green Fees** £16 per round; £24 per day (£20/£28 weekends). **Facilities** ⊗ 〗⠇ ⠇ 💺 ⌂ ⛳ ⚷ **Leisure** fishing. **Location** 10m S of Campbeltown on B842

TARBERT — Map 10 NR86

Tarbert PA29 6XX ☎ 01546 606896
Beautiful moorland course. Four fairways crossed by streams.
9 holes, 4460yds, Par 66, SSS 63, Course record 62.
Visitors may not play Sat pm. **Societies** apply in writing. **Green Fees** terms on applications. **Location** N1m W on B8024

TIGHNABRUAICH — Map 10 NR97

Kyles of Bute PA212AB
☎ 01700 811603
Moorland course which is hilly and exposed. Fine mountain and sea views.
9 holes, 4778yds, Par 66, SSS 64, Course record 62.
Club membership 150.
Visitors may not play Wed 6pm or Sun am. **Societies** telephone in advance. **Green Fees** £10 per day. **Facilities** ⌂ ⛳ ⚷ **Location** 1.25m S off B8000

Hotel ★★ 79% Royal Hotel, Shore Rd, TIGHNABRUAICH ☎ 01700 811239 11 en suite

CITY OF EDINBURGH

EDINBURGH — See page 317

EDINBURGH — Map 11 NT27

Baberton 50 Baberton Av, Juniper Green EH14 5DU
☎ 0131 453 4911 📠 0131 453 4678
e-mail: babertongolfclub@btinternet.com
Parkland course offering the golfer a variety of interesting and challenging holes. The outward half follows the boundary of the course and presents some demanding par 3 and 4 holes over the undulating terrain. The inward half has some longer, equally challenging holes contained within the course and presents some majestic views of the Pentland Hills and the Edinburgh skyline.
18 holes, 6129yds, Par 69, SSS 70, Course record 64.
Club membership 900.
Visitors may not play at weekdays up to 3.30pm and weekends after 1pm. Contact professional in advance. **Societies** must contact in advance. **Green Fees** £37 per day, £27 per round (£40/£30 weekends). **Cards** 💳 💳
Prof Ken Kelly **Course Designer** Willie Park Jnr **Facilities** ⊗ 〗⠇ ⠇ 💺 ⌂ ⍟ ⌂ ⛳ ⚷ **Conf** Corporate Hospitality Days available **Location** 5m W of city centre off A70

Hotel ★★★★ 69% Edinburgh Marriott Hotel, 111 Glasgow Rd, EDINBURGH ☎ 0131 334 9191 245 en suite

Braid Hills Braid Hills Approach EH10 6JZ
☎ 0131 447 6666 📠 0131 651 2299
e-mail: golf@edinburghleisure.co.uk
Municipal heathland course with superb views of Edinburgh and the Firth of Forth, quite challenging.

Course No 1: 18 holes, 5345yds, Par 70, SSS 66.
Visitors must contact in advance. Braids 1: Mar-Oct, (incl Sun). **Societies** contact in advance **Green Fees** terms on application. **Cards** 💳 💳 💳 💳 **Course Designer** Peter McEwan & Bob Ferguson **Facilities** ⌂ ⛳ ⚷ **Conf** fac available **Location** 2.5m S of city centre off A702

Hotel ★★★ 70% Braid Hills Hotel, 134 Braid Rd, EDINBURGH ☎ 0131 447 8888 67 en suite

Bruntsfield Links Golfing Society 32 Barnton Av EH4 6JH ☎ 0131 336 1479 📠 0131 336 5538
e-mail: secretary@bruntsfield.sol.co.uk
Mature parkland course with magnificent views over

Continued

the Firth of Forth and to the west. Greens and fairways are generally immaculate. Challenging for all categories of handicap.
18 holes, 6407yds, Par 71, SSS 71, Course record 64.
Club membership 1180.
Visitors must telephone in advance. 0131 336 4050 or 0131 336 1479 **Societies** apply in writing. **Green Fees** £60 per day; £45 per round (£65/£50 weekends). **Cards** ▨ ▨ ▨ **Prof** Brian Mackenzie **Course Designer** Willie Park Jr, A Mackenzle, Hawtree **Facilities** ⊗ ⅷ ┗ ▐ ♀ ᐃ 🖰 ⅋ ⚐ **Conf** Corporate Hospitality Days available **Location** 4m NW of city centre off A90

Hotel ★★★★ 70% Menzies Belford Hotel, 69 Belford Rd, EDINBURGH ☎ 0131 332 2545 146 en suite

Carrick Knowe Carrick Knowe, Glendevon Park EH12 5UZ ☎ 0131 337 1096 ▤ 0131 651 2299
e-mail: golf@edinburghleisure.co.uk
Flat parkland course. Played over by two clubs, Carrick Knowe and Carrick Vale.
18 holes, 5697yds, Par 70, SSS 69.
Visitors may be restricted at weekends. Must contact in advance. **Societies** contact in advance **Green Fees** not confirmed. **Cards** ▨ ▨ ▨ ▨ **Facilities** ⊗ ⅷ ┗ ▐ ᐃ ⅋ ⚐ **Location** 3m W of city centre, S of A8

Hotel 🅄 Holiday Inn Edinburgh, Corstorphine Rd, EDINBURGH ☎ 0870 400 9026 303 en suite

Craigentinny Fillyside Rd EH7 6RG
☎ 0131 554 7501 ▤ 0131 651 2299
e-mail: golf@edinburghleisure.co.uk
To the north east of Edinburgh, Craigentinny course is between Leith and Portobello. It is generally flat although there are some hillocks with gentle slopes. The famous Arthur's Seat dominates the southern skyline.
18 holes, 5205yds, Par 67, SSS 65.
Visitors must contact in advance. **Societies** contact in advance **Green Fees** not confirmed. **Cards** ▨ ▨ ▨ ▨ **Facilities** ᐃ ⅋ ⚐ **Location** NE side of city, between Leith & Portobello

Hotel ★★★ 68% Kings Manor, 100 Milton Rd East, EDINBURGH ☎ 0131 669 0444 67 en suite

Craigmillar Park 1 Observatory Rd EH9 3HG
☎ 0131 667 0047 ▤ 0131 662 8091
e-mail: secretary@craigmillarpark.co.uk
Parkland course, with good views.
18 holes, 5851yds, Par 70, SSS 69, Course record 63.
Club membership 750.
Visitors must contact in advance, welcome Monday-Friday and Sunday afternoons after 2.30pm **Societies** must contact in writing. **Green Fees** £30 per day, £20 per round (£30 per round Sun). **Cards** ▨ ▨ ▨ ▨ **Prof** Scott Gourlay **Course Designer** James Braid **Facilities** ⊗ ⅷ ┗ ▐ ♀ ᐃ 🖰 ⅋ ⚐ **Location** 2m S of city centre off A7

Hotel ★★ 70% Allison House Hotel, 15/17 Mayfield Gardens, EDINBURGH ☎ 0131 667 8049 23 rms (21 en suite)

Duddingston Duddingston Rd West EH15 3QD
☎ 0131 661 4301 ▤ 0131 661 4301
e-mail: generalmanager@duddingston-golf-club.com
Parkland course with burn as a natural hazard. Testing 11th hole. Easy walking.
18 holes, 6473yds, Par 72, SSS 72, Course record 63.
Club membership 700.

Visitors limited availability at weekends - booking advised. **Societies** Mon,Tue & Thu. Must contact in advance. **Green Fees** £35 per day/round. **Cards** ▨ ▨ ▨ **Prof** Alastair McLean **Course Designer** Willie Park Jnr **Facilities** ⊗ ⅷ ┗ ▐ ♀ ᐃ 🖰 ⅋ ⚐ **Conf** fac available Corporate Hospitality Days available **Location** 2.5m SE of city centre off A1

Hotel ★★★ 68% Kings Manor, 100 Milton Rd East, EDINBURGH ☎ 0131 669 0444 67 en suite

Kingsknowe 326 Lanark Rd EH14 2JD
☎ 0131 441 1145 (Secretary) ▤ 0131 441 2079
e-mail: kingsknowe.golfclub@virgin.net
Picturesque parkland course set amidst gently rolling hills.

18 holes, 5981yds, Par 69, SSS 69, Course record 63.
Club membership 930.
Visitors contact in advance and subject to availability of tee times. **Societies** apply in writing or telephone secretary. **Green Fees** £30 per day; £23 per round (£35 per round weekends). **Prof** Chris Morris **Course Designer** A Herd/James Braid **Facilities** ⊗ ⅷ ┗ ▐ ♀ ᐃ 🖰 ⅋ ⚐ **Conf** Corporate Hospitality Days available **Location** 4m SW of city centre on A70

Hotel ★★★ 76% Best Western Bruntsfield Hotel, 69/74 Bruntsfield Place, EDINBURGH ☎ 0131 229 1393 75 en suite

Liberton 297 Gilmerton Rd EH16 5UJ
☎ 0131 664 3009 (sec) ▤ 0131 666 0853
e-mail: secretary@libertongc.co.uk
Undulating, wooded parkland course.
18 holes, 5170yds, Par 67, SSS 65, Course record 61.
Club membership 846.
Visitors must contact in advance. **Societies** must contact in writing. **Green Fees** £20 per round/£36 two rounds (weekends £30). **Cards** ▨ **Prof** Iain Seath **Facilities** ⊗ ⅷ ┗ ▐ ♀ ᐃ 🖰 ⚐ **Location** 3m SE of city centre on A7

Hotel ★★★ 75% Dalhousie Castle and Aqueous Spa, Bonnyrigg, EDINBURGH ☎ 01875 820153 27 en suite 5 annexe en suite

Lothianburn 106A Biggar Rd, Fairmilehead EH10 7DU ☎ 0131 445 2288 (pro) & 445 5067 (sec)
▤ 0131 445 7067
e-mail: lothianburngc@golfers.net
Situated to the south west of Edinburgh, on the slopes of the Pentland Hills, the course rises from the clubhouse approximately 300ft to its highest point at the 13th green. There is only one real climb of note, after playing the 2nd shot to the 9th green. The course is noted for its excellent greens, and challenging holes

Continued

Continued

include the 5th, where one drives for position in order to pitch at almost right angles to a plateau green; and the 14th, longest hole on the course, three-quarters of which is downhill with out of bounds on both sides of the fairway.
18 holes, 5662yds, Par 71, SSS 68, Course record 64.
Club membership 850.
Visitors weekends after 3.30pm contact professional, weekdays up to 4pm. Societies apply to the secretary or telephone in the first instance. Green Fees £16.50 per round (weekend £22.50 per round). Prof Kurt Mungall Course Designer J Braid (re-designed 1928) Facilities ⊗ 〣 🏌 🏐 ⚑ ⛳ 🛉 🐟 ℰ Conf Corporate Hospitality Days available Location 4.5m S of city centre on A702

Hotel ★★★ 70% Braid Hills Hotel, 134 Braid Rd, EDINBURGH ☎ 0131 447 8888 67 en suite

Merchants of Edinburgh 10 Craighill Gardens
EH10 5PY ☎ 0131 447 1219 📄 0131 446 9833
e-mail: admin@merchantsgolf.com
Testing hill course with fine views over the city and the surrounding countryside.
18 holes, 4889yds, Par 65, SSS 64, Course record 59.
Club membership 980.
Visitors must contact Secretary in advance. Societies must contact secretary in writing/telephone 48 hours in advance. Green Fees £24 per day, £18 per round. Cards 🖃 🖃 🖃 Prof Neil Colquhoun Course Designer Ben Sayers Facilities ⊗ 〣 🏌 🏐 ♀ 🛉 🐟 ⚑ ℰ Leisure snooker room. Conf fac available Corporate Hospitality Days available Location 2m SW of city centre off A702

Hotel ★★★ 70% Braid Hills Hotel, 134 Braid Rd, EDINBURGH ☎ 0131 447 8888 67 en suite

Mortonhall 231 Braid Rd EH10 6PB
☎ 0131 447 6974 📄 0131 447 8712
e-mail: clubhouse@mortonhallgc.co.uk
Moorland/parkland course with views over Edinburgh.
18 holes, 6502yds, Par 72, SSS 72, Course record 66.
Club membership 525.
Visitors advisable to contact by phone. Societies may not play at weekends. Must contact in writing. Green Fees £35 per round/£45 per day. Cards 🖃 🖃 Prof Malcolm Leighton Course Designer James Braid/F Hawtree Facilities ⊗ 🏌 🏐 ♀ 🛉 ⚑ 🛉 ℰ Location 3m S of city centre off A702

Hotel ★★★ 70% Braid Hills Hotel, 134 Braid Rd, EDINBURGH ☎ 0131 447 8888 67 en suite

Murrayfield 43 Murrayfield Rd EH12 6EU
☎ 0131 337 3478 📄 0131 313 0721
e-mail: marjorie@mfieldgolfclub.giointernet.co.uk
Parkland course on the side of Corstorphine Hill, with fine views.
18 holes, 5725yds, Par 70, SSS 69.
Club membership 815.
Visitors contact in advance, may not play at weekends. Societies apply in writing Green Fees £35 per round/£37 per day. Cards 🖃 🖃 🖉 Prof K. Stevenson Facilities ⊗ 🏌 🏐 ♀ 🛉 ⚑ 🛉 ℰ Location 2m W of city centre off A8

Hotel 🆄 Holiday Inn Edinburgh, Corstorphine Rd, EDINBURGH ☎ 0870 400 9026 303 en suite

Portobello Stanley St EH15 1JJ
☎ 0131 669 4361 & 557 5457(bookings)
📄 0131 557 5170
Public parkland course, easy walking.

Continued

9 holes, 2252yds, Par 32, SSS 32.
Club membership 55.
Visitors advanced booking recommended. Contact Edinburgh Leisure. Societies contact in advance, telephone 0131 557 5457 or write to Edinburgh Leisure, 23 Waterloo Place EH1 3BH. Green Fees terms on application. Cards 🖃 🖃 🖃 🖉 Facilities 🛉 🛉 ⚑ ℰ Location 3m E of city centre off A1

Hotel ★★★ 68% Kings Manor, 100 Milton Rd East, EDINBURGH ☎ 0131 669 0444 67 en suite

Prestonfield 6 Priestfield Rd North EH16 5HS
☎ 0131 667 9665 📄 0131 667 9665
e-mail: prestonfield@btclick.com
Parkland course with beautiful views.
18 holes, 6212yds, Par 70, SSS 70, Course record 66.
Club membership 850.
Visitors contact secretary in advance. May not play Sat before 10.30am or between 12pm-1.30pm & Sun before 11.30am. Societies must contact secretary. Green Fees not confirmed. Cards 🖃 🖉 Prof John Macfarlane Course Designer James Braid Facilities ⊗ 〣 🏌 🏐 ♀ 🛉 ⚑ 🛉 🐟 ℰ Conf Corporate Hospitality Days available Location 1.5m S of city centre off A68

Hotel ★★★ 68% Kings Manor, 100 Milton Rd East, EDINBURGH ☎ 0131 669 0444 67 en suite

Ravelston 24 Ravelston Dykes Rd EH4 3NZ
☎ 0131 315 2486 📄 0131 315 2486
Parkland course on NE side of Corstorphine Hill, overlooking the Firth of Forth.
9 holes, 5230yds, Par 66, SSS 66, Course record 64.
Club membership 610.
Visitors must contact in advance but may not play at weekends & bank holidays. Green Fees terms on application. Course Designer James Braid Facilities 🛉 🏐 🛉 Location 3m W of city centre off A90

Hotel 🆄 Holiday Inn Edinburgh, Corstorphine Rd, EDINBURGH ☎ 0870 400 9026 303 en suite

Royal Burgess 181 Whitehouse Rd, Barnton EH4 6BU
☎ 0131 339 2075 📄 0131 339 3712
e-mail: secretary@royalburgess.co.uk
No mention of golf clubs would be complete without the Royal Burgess, which was instituted in 1735, and is the oldest golfing society in the world. Its course is a pleasant parkland, and one with a great deal of variety. A club which anyone interested in the history of the game should visit.
18 holes, 6111yds, Par 68, SSS 69.
Club membership 620.
Visitors must contact in advance, may not play at weekend. Societies must contact in advance. Green Fees not confirmed. Cards 🖃 🖃 🖃 🖃 🖉 Prof Steven Briar Course Designer Tom Morris Facilities ⊗ 🛉 🏐 ♀ 🛉 ⚑ 🛉 ℰ Conf Corporate Hospitality Days available Location 5m W of city centre off A90

Hotel ★★★★ 70% Menzies Belford Hotel, 69 Belford Rd, EDINBURGH ☎ 0131 332 2545 146 en suite

Silverknowes Silverknowes, Parkway EH4 5ET
☎ 0131 336 3843 📄 0131 651 2299
e-mail: golf@edinburghleisure.co.uk
Public links course on coast overlooking the Firth of Forth with magnificent views.

Continued

Marriott Dalmahoy Hotel

Map 11 NT27   **Kirknewton**

☎ **0131 3358010**   📄 **0131 3353577**

The Championship East Course has hosted many major events including the Solheim Cup, the Scottish Seniors Open Championship and the PGA Championship of Scotland. The greens are large with immaculate putting surfaces and many of the long par 4 holes offer a serious challenge to the golfer. The short holes are well bunkered and the 15th hole in particular, known as the 'Wee Wrecker', will test your nerve and skill. The shorter West Course offers a different test with small greens requiring accuracy from the player's short game. The finishing holes with the Gogar Burn meandering through the fairway create a tough finish.

e-mail: golf.dalmahoy@marriotthotels.co.uk

Visitors Welcome Mon-Fri, weekend by application. Call in advance to book tee times, subject to availability

Societies Mon-Fri only, telephone or write for details

Green Fees Telephone for details

Facilities ⊗ 🍴 🛒 ⚡ 🛋 🍺 ⛳ 🏌

Conf facilities available; corporate hospitality days available

Professional Neal Graham

Leisure Tennis, swimming, sauna, solarium, gymnasium, beauty salon, fitness studio, jogging trail

Location Kirknewton EH27 8EB (7m W of city centre on A71)

Holes/Par/Course record 36 holes.
East Course 18 holes, 6684 yds, Par 72, SSS 72, Course record 62
West Course: 18 holes, 5168 yds, Par 68, SSS 66, Course record 60

WHERE TO STAY AND EAT NEARBY

Hotels
EDINBURGH

★★★★ ◎ ◎ 71%
Marriott Dalmahoy Hotel & Country Club, EH27 8EB.
☎ 0131 333 1845.
43 en suite, 172 annexe en suite

★★★★ 69%
Edinburgh Marriott,
EH12 8NF.
☎ 0131 334 9191.
245 en suite

UPHALL

★★★★ ◎ 68%
Houstoun House, EH52 6JS.
☎ 01506 853831.
24 en suite,
47 annexe en suite

Restaurants
LINLITHGOW

◎ ◎ Champany Inn,
EH49 7LU.
☎ 01506 834532

◎ ◎ Livingston's
Restaurant, EH49 7AE.
☎ 01506 846565

Championship Course

18 holes, 6070yds, Par 71, SSS 70.
Visitors advanced booking recommended in summer
Societies contact in advance **Green Fees** terms on
application. **Cards** 🔁 💳 🔳 📇 **Facilities** ⊗ 〉Ⅲ ℉ ⚑ 🚻 ☖
♈ ✂ **Location** 4m NW of city centre, easy access from
city by-pass

Hotel ★★★★ 70% Menzies Belford Hotel, 69 Belford
Rd, EDINBURGH ☎ 0131 332 2545 146 en suite

Swanston 111 Swanston Rd, Fairmilehead EH10 7DS
☎ 0131 445 2239 📖 0131 445 2239
Hillside course with steep climb at 12th and 13th holes.
18 holes, 5024yds, Par 66, SSS 65, Course record 63.
Club membership 600.
Visitors contact in advance. Weekends restricted. May not
play on competition days. **Societies** must contact in
advance 0131 445 4002. **Green Fees** terms on application.
Prof Stu Pardoe **Course Designer** Herbert More **Facilities**
⊗ 〉Ⅲ ℉ ⚑ 🚻 ☖ ♈ 🎣 ✂ **Conf** Corporate Hospitality
Days available **Location** 4m S of city centre off B701

Hotel ★★★ 70% Braid Hills Hotel, 134 Braid Rd,
EDINBURGH ☎ 0131 447 8888 67 en suite

Torphin Hill Torphin Rd, Colinton EH13 0PG
☎ 0131 441 1100 📖 0131 441 7166
e-mail: info@torphinhillgc.co.uk
Beautiful hillside, heathland course, with fine views of
Edinburgh and the Forth Estuary.
18 holes, 5247yds, Par 68, SSS 67, Course record 64.
Club membership 550.
Visitors must contact in advance, limited access Sat & Sun
(only after 2pm) **Societies** must contact in advance. **Green
Fees** terms on application. **Cards** 🔁 **Prof** Jamie Browne
Facilities ⊗ 〉Ⅲ ℉ ⚑ 🚻 ☖ ♈ **Conf** Corporate
Hospitality Days available **Location** 5m SW of city centre
S of A720

Hotel ★★★ 70% Braid Hills Hotel, 134 Braid Rd,
EDINBURGH ☎ 0131 447 8888 67 en suite

Turnhouse 154 Turnhouse Rd EH12 0AD
☎ 0131 339 1014
e-mail: secretary@turnhousegc.com
Hilly, parkland/heathland course, good views over the
Pentland Hills and Forth Valley.
18 holes, 6171yds, Par 69, SSS 70, Course record 62.
Club membership 800.
Visitors with member only at weekends, and no visitors
Wed or Medal days. Must contact professional in advance.
Societies must contact in writing to secretary. **Green Fees**
£30 per day (£38 per day, £25 per 18 holes weekends).
Prof John Murray **Course Designer** J Braid **Facilities** ⊗
〉Ⅲ ℉ ⚑ 🚻 ☖ ♈ ✂ **Conf** fac available Corporate
Hospitality Days available **Location** 6m W of city centre N
of A8

Hotel ★★★★ 69% Edinburgh Marriott Hotel, 111
Glasgow Rd, EDINBURGH ☎ 0131 334 9191
245 en suite

RATHO   Map 11 NT17

Ratho Park EH28 8NX
☎ 0131 335 0068 & 335 0068 📖 0131 333 1752
e-mail: secretary.rpgc@btconnect.com
Easy walking, parkland course with converted mansion
as the clubhouse.

18 holes, 5960yds, Par 69, SSS 68, Course record 62.
Club membership 850.
Visitors must contact in advance. **Societies** must contact in
writing. Only able to play Tue-Thu **Green Fees** £35 per
day, £25 per round (£35 per round weekends). **Cards** 🔁
💳 🔳 **Prof** Alan Pate **Course Designer** James Braid
Facilities ⊗ 〉Ⅲ ℉ ⚑ 🚻 ☖ ♈ 🎣 ✂ **Location** 0.75m
E, N of A71

Hotel 🄷 Holiday Inn Edinburgh, Corstorphine Rd,
EDINBURGH ☎ 0870 400 9026 303 en suite

SOUTH QUEENSFERRY   Map 11 NT17

Dundas Parks Dundas Estate EH30 9SS
☎ 0131 331 4252
Parkland course situated on the estate of Dundas
Castle, with excellent views. For 18 holes, the 9 are
played twice.
9 holes, 6024yds, Par 70, SSS 69, Course record 64.
Club membership 500.
Visitors must contact in advance. May not play at
weekends. **Societies** must contact in writing. **Green Fees**
£12. **Facilities** ☖ **Location** 0.5m S on A8000

Hotel 🄷 Travel Inn Edinburgh Queensferry, Builyeon Rd,
SOUTH QUEENSFERRY ☎ 08701 977094 46 en suite

CITY OF GLASGOW

GLASGOW   Map 11 NS56

Alexandra Alexandra Park, Alexandra Pde G31 8SE
☎ 0141 556 1294
Parkland course, hilly with some woodland. Many
bunkers and a barrier of trees between 1st and 9th
fairway. Work has been in progress to improve the
fairways.
9 holes, 2800yds, Par 31, Course record 25.
Club membership 85.
Visitors no restrictions. **Societies** telephone 24 hrs in
advance or by writing one week in advance. **Green Fees**
£3.60. **Course Designer** G McArthur **Facilities** ☖ **Leisure**
bowling green. **Location** 2m E of city centre off M8/A8

Hotel ★★★ 71% Holiday Inn, 161 West Nile St,
GLASGOW ☎ 0141 352 8300 113 en suite

Cowglen Barrhead Rd G43 1AU
☎ 0141 632 0556 📖 01505 503000
e-mail: r.jamieson-accountants@rsmail.net
Undulating and challenging parkland course with good
views over the Clyde Valley to the Campsie Hills. Club
and line selection is most important on many holes due
to the strategic placing of copses on the course.
18 holes, 6053yds, Par 70, SSS 69, Course record 64.
Club membership 805.
Visitors play on shorter course. Must contact secretary for
times in advance and have a handicap certificate. No
visitors Tue, Fri and weekends. **Societies** must be booked
in writing through the secretary. **Green Fees** £35 per day;
£27.50 per round. **Prof** Simon Payne **Course Designer**
David Adams/James Braid **Facilities** ⊗ 〉Ⅲ ℉ ⚑ 🚻 ☖ 🚹
♈ 𝔯 **Conf** fac available Corporate Hospitality Days
available **Location** M77 South from Glasgow, take
Pollok/Barrhead slip road, left at lights club 0.5 miles right

Hotel 🄷 Travelodge (Glasgow Paisley Road), 251 Paisley
Rd, GLASGOW ☎ 08700 850 950 75 en suite

Continued

Haggs Castle 70 Dumbreck Rd, Dumbreck G41 4SN
☎ 0141 427 1157 📠 0141 427 1157
e-mail: haggscastlegc@lineone.net
Wooded, parkland course where Scottish National Championships and the Glasgow and Scottish Open have been held. Quite difficult.
18 holes, 6426yds, Par 72, SSS 71, Course record 63.
Club membership 900.
Visitors may not play at weekends. Must contact in advance. **Societies** apply in writing. **Green Fees** £40 per round; £50 per day. **Cards** 💳 💳 💳 💳 💳 **Prof** Campbell Elliott **Course Designer** James Braid **Facilities** ⊗ ℋ ㏑ ♥ ♀ ♧ ⛳ ♈ 🏇 ♂ **Conf** Corporate Hospitality Days available **Location** 2.5m SW of city centre off M77 junct 1

Kirkhill Greenless Rd, Cambuslang G72 8YN
☎ 0141 641 8499 📠 0141 641 8499
Meadowland course designed by James Braid.
18 holes, 6030yds, Par 70, SSS 70, Course record 63.
Club membership 650.
Visitors must play with member at weekends. **Societies** must contact in advance. **Green Fees** terms on application. **Prof** Duncan Williamson **Course Designer** J Braid **Facilities** ⊗ ℋ ㏑ ♥ ♀ ♧ ⛳ 🏇 **Location** 5m SE of city centre off A749

Hotel ★★★ 67% Bothwell Bridge Hotel, 89 Main St, BOTHWELL ☎ 01698 852246 90 en suite

Knightswood Lincoln Av G13 5QZ
☎ 0141 959 6358
Flat parkland course within easy reach of city. Two dog-legs.
9 holes, 5586yds, Par 68, SSS 67.
Club membership 40.
Visitors reserved tee Wed and Fri am bookings 1 day in advance, no other restrictions. **Societies** welcome, must book 1 day in advance. **Green Fees** £3.60 per 9 holes.
Facilities ♧ **Location** 4m W of city centre off A82

Hotel ★★★ 64% Jurys Glasgow Hotel, Great Western Rd, GLASGOW ☎ 0141 334 8161 137 en suite

Lethamhill 1240 Cumbernauld Rd, Millerston G33 1AH ☎ 0141 770 6220 & 0141 770 7135 📠 1041 770 0520
Municipal parkland course.
18 holes, 5859yds, Par 70, SSS 69.
Visitors must contact in advance. **Societies** must contact in advance. **Green Fees** £8 per round. **Cards** 💳 💳 💳 💳 **Prof** Gary Taggart **Facilities** ♧ **Location** 3m NE of city centre on A80

Hotel ★★★★ 71% Millennium Hotel Glasgow, George Square, GLASGOW ☎ 0141 332 6711 117 en suite

Linn Park Simshill Rd G44 5EP ☎ 0141 633 0377
Municipal parkland course with six par 3s in outward half.
18 holes, 4952yds, Par 65, SSS 65, Course record 61.
Visitors must contact in advance. **Societies** advance booking in writing **Green Fees** not confirmed. **Facilities** ♧ **Location** 4m S of city centre off B766

Hotel ★★★ 65% Bruce Hotel, Cornwall St, EAST KILBRIDE ☎ 01355 229771 65 en suite

Pollok 90 Barrhead Rd G43 1BG
☎ 0141 632 4351 📠 0141 649 1398
e-mail: secretary@pollokgolf.com
Parkland course with woods and river.
18 holes, 6254yds, Par 71, SSS 70, Course record 62.
Club membership 620.
Visitors Members only until 2pm weekends. Must contact in advance. Ladies only as part of visiting parties **Societies** must contact in writing for large parties, telephone for up to 4 **Green Fees** £50 per round weekdays. **Cards** 💳 💳 💳 **Course Designer** James Braid **Facilities** ⊗ ℋ by prior arrangement ㏑ ♥ ♀ ♧ ♈ ♂ **Conf** fac available **Location** M77 junct 2 S bound to Barrhead Rd (A762), club 1m E

Hotel ★★★ 66% The Ewington, Balmoral Ter, 132 Queens Dr, Queens Park, GLASGOW ☎ 0141 423 1152 43 en suite

Williamwood Clarkston Rd G44 3YR
☎ 0141 637 1783 📠 0141 571 0166
Undulating parkland course with mature woodlands.
18 holes, 5878yds, Par 68, SSS 69, Course record 61.
Club membership 800.
Visitors apply in writing to secretary, no weekend play. **Societies** midweek bookings only, apply in writing to secretary. **Green Fees** £37 per day; £27 per round. **Cards** 💳 **Prof** Stewart Marshall **Course Designer** James Braid **Facilities** ⊗ ℋ ㏑ ♥ ♀ ♧ ⛳ ♂ **Location** 5m S of city centre on B767

Hotel ★★★ 65% Bruce Hotel, Cornwall St, EAST KILBRIDE ☎ 01355 229771 65 en suite

CLACKMANNANSHIRE

ALLOA   Map 11 NS89

Alloa Schawpark, Sauchie FK10 3AX
☎ 01259 724476 📠 01259 724476
e-mail: bellville51@hotmail.com
Set amongst 150 acres of rolling parkland beneath the Ochil hills, this course will challenge the best golfers whilst offering great enjoyment to the average player. The challenging finishing holes, 15th to 18th, consist of two long par 3s split by two long and demanding par 4s which will test any golfer's ability. Privacy provided by mature tree lined fairways.
18 holes, 6229yds, Par 69, SSS 71, Course record 63.
Club membership 910.
Visitors 7 day booking system through professional. Advised to book especially at weekends. **Societies** apply in writing/telephone. **Green Fees** terms on applications. **Cards** 💳 💳 💳 💳 💳 **Prof** Bill Bennett **Course Designer** James Braid **Facilities** ⊗ ℋ ㏑ ♥ ♀ ♧ ⛳ ♈ ♂ **Location** 1.5m NE on A908

Hotel ★★ 68% Terraces Hotel, 4 Melville Ter, STIRLING ☎ 01786 472268 17 en suite

Braehead Cambus FK10 2NT
☎ 01259 722078 📠 01259 214070
e-mail: braehead.gc@btinternet.com
Attractive parkland course at the foot of the Ochil Hills, and offering spectacular views.
18 holes, 6086yds, Par 70, SSS 69, Course record 64.
Club membership 800.
Visitors advisable to telephone in advance. **Societies** must

Continued

contact the professional in advance on 01259 722078
Green Fees £30 per day, £20 per round (£40/£30
weekends). **Cards** ⊞ ▦ ▬ ▨ ▨ **Prof** Jamie Stevenson
Course Designer Robert Tait **Facilities** ⊗ ⊪ ⊪ ⏛ ♀ ⚲
🖶 🍴 🕈 🚅 𝒥 **Conf** Corporate Hospitality Days available
Location 1m W on A907

....

Hotel ★★ 68% Terraces Hotel, 4 Melville Ter,
STIRLING ☎ 01786 472268 17 en suite

ALVA   Map 11 NS89

Alva Beauclerc St FK12 5LD ☎ 01259 760431
9 holes, 2423yds, Par 66, SSS 64, Course record 63.
Location 7m from Stirling, A91 Stirling/St Andrews rd
Telephone for further details

....

Hotel ★★★ 71% Royal Hotel, Henderson St, BRIDGE
OF ALLAN ☎ 01786 832284 32 en suite

DOLLAR   Map 11 NS99

Dollar Brewlands House FK14 7EA
☎ 01259 742400 📱 01259 743497
e-mail: dollargc@brewlandshousefreeserve.co.uk
**Compact hillside course with magnificent views along
the Ochil Hills.**
18 holes, 5242yds, Par 69, SSS 66, Course record 60.
Club membership 450.
Visitors weekdays course available but restricted Wed
ladies day, weekends advised to contact in advance.
Societies write or telephone in advance. **Green Fees** terms
on application. **Course Designer** Ben Sayers **Facilities** ⊗
⊪ ⊪ ⏛ ♀ ⚲ 🕈 𝒥 **Leisure** snooker table. **Conf**
Corporate Hospitality Days available **Location** 0.5m N off
A91

....

Hotel ★★★ 71% Royal Hotel, Henderson St, BRIDGE
OF ALLAN ☎ 01786 832284 32 en suite

MUCKHART   Map 11 NO00

Muckhart FK14 7JH
☎ 01259 781423 & 781493 📱 01259 781544
e-mail: enquiries@muckhartgolf.com
**Scenic heathland/downland course comprising 27 holes
in three combinations of nine, all of which start and
finish close to the clubhouse. Each of the nine holes
requires a different approach, demanding tactical
awareness and a skilful touch with all the clubs in the
bag. There are superb views from the course's many
vantage points, including the aptly named 5th 'Top of
the World'.**
Cowden: 9 holes, 3251yds, Par 36.
Naemoor Course: 9 holes, 3234yards, SSS 36.
Arndean: 9 holes, 2835yds, Par 35.
Club membership 750.
Visitors telephone to book - 01259 781423 or professional
01259 781493.Correct attire to be worn at all times.
Societies booking by prior arrangement. **Green Fees** terms
on application. **Cards** ⊞ ▬ ▨ **Prof** Keith Salmoni
Facilities ⊗ ⊪ ⊪ ⏛ ♀ ⚲ 🖶 𝒥 **Location** South of
village between A91& A823

....

Hotel ★★ 71% Castle Campbell Hotel, 11 Bridge St,
DOLLAR ☎ 01259 742519 8 en suite

> **Looking for a driving range? Refer to the listing
> of driving ranges at the back of this guide.**

TILLICOULTRY   Map 11 NS99

Tillicoultry Alva Rd FK13 6BL
☎ 01259 750124 📱 01259 750124
e-mail: miket@tillygc.freeserve.co.uk
**Parkland course at foot of the Ochil Hills entailing
some hard walking but affording fine views.**
9 holes, 5004metres, Par 68, SSS 67, Course record 64.
Club membership 400.
Visitors must contact in advance. **Societies** apply to the
secretary. **Green Fees** £12 per 18 holes(£17 weekends and
bank holidays). **Facilities** ⊪ ⏛ ♀ ⚲ **Conf** Corporate
Hospitality Days available **Location** A91, 9m E of Stirling

....

Hotel ★★★ 71% Royal Hotel, Henderson St, BRIDGE
OF ALLAN ☎ 01786 832284 32 en suite

DUMFRIES & GALLOWAY

CASTLE DOUGLAS   Map 11 NX76

Castle Douglas Abercromby Rd DG7 1BB
☎ 01556 502801 & 502877
Parkland course, one severe hill.
9 holes, 2704yds, Par 68, SSS 66, Course record 62.
Club membership 400.
Societies apply by writing to secretary. **Green Fees** £15
per round/day. **Facilities** ⊗ ⊪ ⊪ ⏛ ♀ ⚲ 🖶 🕈 𝒥 **Conf**
Corporate Hospitality Days available **Location** W side of
town

....

Hotel ★★ 67% Imperial Hotel, 35 King St, CASTLE
DOUGLAS ☎ 01556 502086 12 en suite

COLVEND   Map 11 NX85

Colvend Sandyhills DG5 4PY
☎ 01556 630398 📱 01556 630495
e-mail: thesecretary@colvendgolfclub.co.uk
**Picturesque and challenging course on Solway coast.
Superb views.**
18 holes, 5250yds, Par 68, SSS 67, Course record 64.
Club membership 490.
Visitors restricted Apr-Sep on Tue, 1st tee reserved for
weekly Medal 1-1.30 & 4-6pm and some weekends for
open competitions. **Societies** must telephone in advance.
Green Fees not confirmed. **Course Designer** Allis &
Thomas **Facilities** ⊗ ⊪ ⊪ ⏛ ♀ ⚲ 🕈 🚅 𝒥 **Location**
6m from Dalbeattie on A710 Solway Coast Rd

....

Hotel ★★ 69% Clonyard House Hotel, COLVEND
☎ 01556 630372 15 en suite

CUMMERTREES   Map 11 NY16

Powfoot DG12 5QE
☎ 01461 700276 📱 01461 700276
e-mail: bsutherland@powfootgolfclub.fsnet.co.uk
**This British Championship Course is on the Solway
Firth, playing at this delightfully compact semi-links
seaside course is a scenic treat. Lovely holes include the
2nd, the 8th and the 11th, also 9th with World War II
bomb crater.**
18 holes, 6283yds, Par 71, SSS 70, Course record 63.
Club membership 950.
Visitors contact in advance. May not play before 9am
between 11am-1pm and after 3.30pm weekdays, no visitors
Sat or before 1pm Sun. **Societies** must book in advance.

Continued

Green Fees terms on appointment. **Cards** 🔲 💳 **Prof** Stuart Smith **Course Designer** J Braid **Facilities** ⊗ ⌇⊫ 🍴 ♟🏌️🛒 ⚷ **Location** 0.5m off B724

Hotel ★★★ 68% Hetland Hall Hotel, CARRUTHERSTOWN ☎ 01387 840201 14 en suite 15 annexe en suite

---

DALBEATTIE   Map 11 NX86

Dalbeattie 60 Maxwell Park DG5 4LS
☎ 01556 610311 & 611421
e-mail: arthurhowatson@aol.com
This 9 hole course provides an excellent challenge for golfers of all abilities. There are a few gentle slopes to negotiate but compensated by fine views along the Urr Valley. The 363 yard 4th hole is a memorable par 4. A good straight drive is required to the corner of the course where a right angle dog-leg is taken for a pitch to a smallish green.
9 holes, 5710yds, Par 68, SSS 68.
Club membership 300.
Visitors wellcomed any day, effort made to accomodate on club competitions days **Societies** apply in writing to Secretary or telephone 01556 610311 **Green Fees** £16 for 18holes/£20 per day. **Facilities** ⊗ ⊫ ♟ ♀ ⚺ ⚘ 🛒 **Location** Signposted off B794

Hotel ★★ 67% King's Arms Hotel, St Andrew's St, CASTLE DOUGLAS ☎ 01556 502626 10 rms (9 en suite)

DUMFRIES   Map 11 NX97

Dumfries & County Nunfield, Edinburgh Rd DG1 1JX ☎ 01387 253585 📄 01387 253585
e-mail: dumfriesc@aol.com
Parkland course alongside River Nith, with views over the Queensberry Hills. Greens built to USPGA specifications.

Nunfield: 18 holes, 5918yds, Par 69, SSS 69, Course record 61.
Club membership 800.
Visitors must contact in advance but may not play Saturdays and during competitions on Sundays **Societies** telephone professional in advance 01387 268918 **Green Fees** £37 per 36 holes, £33 per 24 holes, £27 per round (£37 per 24/36 hours, £33 per round weekends). **Cards** 🔲 💳 **Prof** Stuart Syme **Course Designer** William Fernie **Facilities** ⊗ ⌇⊫ 🍴 ♀ ⚺ 🍴 ♟🏌️ ⚷ **Conf** Corporate Hospitality Days available **Location** 1m NE of Dumfries on A701

Hotel ★★★ 71% Cairndale Hotel & Leisure Club, English St, DUMFRIES ☎ 01387 254111 91 en suite

Dumfries & Galloway 2 Laurieston Av DG2 7NY
☎ 01387 263848 📄 01387 263848
e-mail: info@dandggc.co.uk
Attractive parkland course, a good test of golf but not physically demanding.
18 holes, 6309yds, Par 70, SSS 71.
Club membership 800.
Visitors may not play on competition days. Must contact in advance. No visitors on Saturdays during season. Some Sundays not available. **Societies** apply in writing. **Green Fees** £25 per round/£27 per day (weekend £30/£33). **Prof** Joe Fergusson **Course Designer** W Fernie **Facilities** ⊗ ⌇⊫ ⊫ 🍴 ♀ ⚺ 🍴 ⚷ **Location** W side of town centre on A75

Hotel ★★★ 69% Station Hotel, 49 Lovers Walk, DUMFRIES ☎ 01387 254316 32 en suite

Pines Golf Centre Lockerbie Rd DG1 3PF
☎ 01387 247444 📄 01387 249600
e-mail: admin@pinesgolf.com
A mixture of parkland and woodland with numerous water features and dog-legs. Excellent greens.
18 holes, 5604yds, Par 68, SSS 67, Course record 66.
Club membership 280.
Visitors visitors welcome at all times. **Societies** telephone in advance. **Green Fees** £18 per day. **Prof** Brian Gemmell/Bruce Gray **Course Designer** Duncan Gray **Facilities** ⊗ ⌇⊫ ⊫ 🍴 ♀ ⚺ 🍴 ♟ 🛒 ⚷ ♟ **Conf** Corporate Hospitality Days available

Hotel ★★★ 71% Cairndale Hotel & Leisure Club, English St, DUMFRIES ☎ 01387 254111 91 en suite

---

GATEHOUSE OF FLEET   Map 11 NX55

Gatehouse Laurieston Rd DG7 2BE
☎ 01644 450260 📄 01644 450260
e-mail: gatehousegolf@sagainternet.co.uk
Set against a background of rolling hills with scenic views of Fleet Bay and the Solway Firth.
9 holes, 2521yds, Par 66, SSS 66, Course record 62.
Club membership 300.
Visitors restricted Sun before 11.30am. **Societies** telephone in advance. **Green Fees** £12 per day. **Course Designer** Tom Fernie **Facilities** ⚺ **Location** 0.25m N of town

Hotel ★★★★ 71% Cally Palace Hotel, GATEHOUSE OF FLEET ☎ 01557 814341 55 en suite

Continued   Continued

Cally Palace Hotel, Gatehouse of Fleet

GLENLUCE   Map 10 NX15

Wigtownshire County Mains of Park DG8 0NN
☎ 01581 300420 📠 01581 300420
e-mail: enquiries@wigtownshirecountygolfclub.com
**Seaside links course on the shores of Luce Bay, easy
walking but affected by winds. The 12th hole, a dog-leg
with out of bounds to the right, is named after the
course's designer, Gordon Cunningham.**
*18 holes, 5843yds, Par 70, SSS 68, Course record 66.
Club membership 450.*
Visitors may play any day by prior arrangement ex
competition days. **Societies** must contact in advance.
Green Fees £28 per day; £22 per round (£30/£24
weekends). **Course Designer** W Gordon Cunningham
Facilities ⊗ ℳ ⮐ 🍴 ♀ ⚐ 🛍 ⛳ 🐾 🏌 ⚒ **Location** 1.5m
W off A75, 200 yds off A75 on shores of Luce Bay

Hotel ★★★★ 68% North West Castle Hotel,
STRANRAER ☎ 01776 704413 70 en suite
2 annexe en suite

GRETNA   Map 11 NY36

Gretna Kirtle View DG16 5HD
☎ 01461 338464 📠 01461 337362
e-mail: georgebirnie@aol.co.uk
9 holes, 3214yds, Par 72, SSS 71, Course record 71.
Course Designer N Williams **Location** 0.5m W of Gretna
on B721,signposted
Telephone for further details

Hotel ★★★ 67% Garden House Hotel, Sarkfoot Rd,
GRETNA ☎ 01461 337621 38 en suite

KIRKCUDBRIGHT   Map 11 NX65

Brighouse Bay Brighouse Bay, Borgue DG6 4TS
☎ 01557 870409 📠 01557 870409
e-mail: leisureclub@brighouse-bay.co.uk
**A beautifully situated scenic maritime course on free
draining coastal grassland and playable all year.
Making use of many natural features - water, gullies
and rocks - it provides a testing challenge to golfers of
all handicaps.**
*18 holes, 6366yds, Par 73, SSS 73.
Club membership 170.*
Visitors pay as you play - payment at adjacent Golf &
Leisure Club. Phoning in advance recommended. **Societies**
prior arrangement necessary. **Green Fees** £26 per day, £22
per round (£30/£26 weekends). **Cards** 💳 💳 💳 💳
Course Designer D Gray **Facilities** ⊗ ℳ ⮐ 🍴 ♀ ⚐ 🛍
🏌 🍴 ⚒ ⛳ 🍴 **Leisure** heated indoor swimming pool,
fishing, sauna, gymnasium, Turkish steam

Continued

room,jacuzzi,pool tables. **Conf** fac available Corporate
Hospitality Days available **Location** 3m S of Borgue off
B727

Hotel ★★★ 71% Selkirk Arms Hotel, Old High St,
KIRKCUDBRIGHT ☎ 01557 330402 13 en suite
3 annexe en suite

Kirkcudbright Stirling Crescent DG6 4EZ
☎ 01557 330314 📠 01557 330314
e-mail: david@kirkcudbrightgolf.co.uk
**Parkland course. Hilly, with good views over the
harbour town of Kirkcudbright and the Dee Estuary.**
*18 holes, 5739yds, Par 69, SSS 69, Course record 63.
Club membership 500.*
Visitors advisable to contact in advance. **Societies** contact
in advance. **Green Fees** £25 per day; £20 per round.
Facilities ⊗ ℳ ⮐ 🍴 ♀ ⚐ 🏌 🐾 ⚒ ⛳ **Location** NE side
of town off A711

Hotel ★★★ 71% Selkirk Arms Hotel, Old High St,
KIRKCUDBRIGHT ☎ 01557 330402 13 en suite
3 annexe en suite

LANGHOLM   Map 11 NY38

Langholm Whiteside DG13 0JR ☎ 013873 81247
e-mail: golf@langholmgolfclub.co.uk
**Hillside course with fine views, easy to medium
walking.**
*9 holes, 6180yds, Par 70, SSS 70, Course record 65.
Club membership 200.*
Visitors restricted Sat & Sun. **Societies** apply in writing to
secretary. **Green Fees** terms on application. **Facilities** ⊗
by prior arrangement ℳ by prior arrangement 🛍 by prior
arrangement ♀ **Location** E side of village off A7

Guesthouse ♦♦♦♦ The Reivers Rest, 81 High St,
LANGHOLM ☎ 01387 381343 5 en suite

LOCHMABEN   Map 11 NY08

Lochmaben Castlehillgate DG11 1NT
☎ 01387 810552
**Attractive parkland course surrounding the Kirk Loch,
excellent views on this well maintained course.**
*18 holes, 5357yds, Par 67, SSS 67, Course record 60.
Club membership 850.*
Visitors advised to contact in advance,01387 810552,
visitors weekdays up to 5pm weekends available **Societies**
must contact in advance, on 01387-810552 **Green Fees**
£25 per day; £20 per round (£30/£25 weekends). **Course
Designer** James Braid **Facilities** ⊗ ℳ ⮐ 🍴 ♀ ⚐ 🏌 ⚒ ⛳
Leisure fishing. **Conf** Corporate Hospitality Days
available **Location** 4m from Lockerbie on A74. S side of
village off A709

Hotel ★★★ 80% The Dryfesdale Country House Hotel,
Dryfebridge, LOCKERBIE ☎ 01576 202427 16 en suite

LOCKERBIE   Map 11 NY18

Lockerbie Corrie Rd DG11 2ND
☎ 01576 203363 📠 01576 203363
18 holes, 5614yds, Par 68, SSS 67, Course record 64.
Course Designer James Braid **Location** E side of town
centre off B7068
Telephone for further details

Hotel ★★★ 80% The Dryfesdale Country House Hotel,
Dryfebridge, LOCKERBIE ☎ 01576 202427 16 en suite

MOFFAT
Map 11 NT00

Moffat Coatshill DG10 9SB
☎ 01683 220020 📠 01683 221802
e-mail: moffatgolfclub@onetel.net.uk
Scenic moorland course overlooking the town, with panoramic views of southern uplands.
18 holes, 5259yds, Par 69, SSS 67, Course record 60.
Club membership 350.
Visitors advised to contact in advance, no visitors after 3pm on Wed. **Societies** apply in writing/telephone the clubmaster. **Green Fees** not confirmed. **Cards** 💳 💳 💳
📶 🖥 **Course Designer** Ben Sayers **Facilities** ⊗ 🍴 🍽 🛒 ⚑
🏌 🅿 ⛳ 🚩 ⚑ **Leisure** snooker. **Conf** Corporate Hospitality Days available **Location** From A74(M) junct 15, take A701 to Moffat, course signposted on left after 30mph limit sign

Hotel ★★★ 71% Moffat House Hotel, High St, MOFFAT
☎ 01683 220039 21 en suite

MONREITH
Map 10 NX34

St Medan DG8 8NJ ☎ 01988 700358
Scotland's most southerly course. This links course nestles in Monreith Bay with panoramic views across to the Isle of Man and, A testing 9 hole course offering a challenge to both high and low handicaps.
9 holes, 4608yds, Par 64, SSS 63, Course record 60.
Club membership 300.
Visitors no restrictions. **Societies** apply in advance by telephone or writing **Green Fees** £22 per day; £15 per 18 holes; £10 per 9 holes. **Course Designer** James Braid **Facilities** ⊗ 🛒 🍽 🅿 🏌 🚩 ⚑ **Location** 1m SE off A747

Hotel ★★ 67% Kelvin House Hotel, 53 Main St, GLENLUCE ☎ 01581 300303 6 rms (5 en suite)

NEW GALLOWAY
Map 11 NX67

New Galloway High St DG7 3RN
☎ 01644 420737 & 450685 📠 01644 450685
Set on the edge of the Galloway Hills and overlooking Loch Ken, the course has excellent tees and first class greens. The course rises through the first two fairways to a plateau with all round views that many think unsurpassed.
9 holes, 5006yds, Par 68, SSS 67, Course record 64.
Club membership 350.
Visitors restricted on Sun (competition days). All visitors play off yellow markers. Contact Secretary in advance. Smart/casual dress. **Societies** contact secretary in advance. **Green Fees** not confirmed. **Course Designer** James Braid **Facilities** 🛒 🍽 🅿 🏌 🚩 ⚑ **Location** S side of town on A762

Hotel ★★ 67% Imperial Hotel, 35 King St, CASTLE DOUGLAS ☎ 01556 502086 12 en suite

NEWTON STEWART
Map 10 NX46

Newton Stewart Kirroughtree Av, Minnigaff DG8 6PF ☎ 01671 402172 📠 01671 402172
Parkland course in picturesque setting. A good test for all standards of golfer with a variety of shots required.
18 holes, 5903yds, Par 69, SSS 70, Course record 66.
Club membership 380.
Visitors must contact in advance. **Societies** must contact in advance. **Green Fees** terms on application. **Facilities** ⊗ 🛒
🍽 🅿 🏌 🚩 🛒 ⚑ **Location** 0.5m N of town centre off A75

PORTPATRICK
Map 10 NX05

Portpatrick Golf Course Rd DG9 8TB
☎ 01776 810273 📠 01776 810811
e-mail: enquiries@portpatrickgolfclub.com
Seaside links-type course, set on cliffs overlooking the Irish Sea, with magnificent views.
Dunskey Course: 18 holes, 5908yds, Par 70, SSS 69, Course record 66.
Dinvin Course: 9 holes, 1504yds, Par 27, SSS 27, Course record 23.
Club membership 750.
Visitors must contact in advance. £5 deposit required **Societies** must contact in advance. **Green Fees** £37 per day; £27 per round (£42/£32 weekends). **Cards** 💳 💳 💳
🖥 **Course Designer** Charles Hunter **Facilities** ⊗ 🍴 🛒 🍽
🅿 🏌 🚩 🛒 🏌 ⚑ **Location** On entering village fork right at War Memorial, 300yds signposted

Hotel ★★★ 74% Fernhill Hotel, Heugh Rd, PORTPATRICK ☎ 01776 810220 27 en suite 9 annexe en suite

SANQUHAR
Map 11 NS70

Sanquhar Euchan Golf Course, Blackaddie Rd DG4 6JZ ☎ 01659 50577
e-mail: tich@rossirence.fsnet.co.uk
Parkland course, fine views, easy walking. A good test for all standards of golfer.
9 holes, 5594yds, Par 70, SSS 68, Course record 66.
Club membership 200.
Visitors no restrictions. **Societies** must pre-book. **Green Fees** £10 per day (£12 weekends). **Course Designer** Willie Fernie **Facilities** 🅿 🏌 🚩 **Leisure** snooker, pool. **Conf** Corporate Hospitality Days available **Location** 0.5m SW off A76

Hotel ★★ 66% Blackaddie House Hotel, Blackaddie Rd, SANQUHAR ☎ 01659 50270 9 en suite

SOUTHERNESS
Map 11 NX95

Southerness DG2 8AZ
☎ 01387 880677 📠 01387 880644
e-mail: admin@southernessgc.sol.co.uk
Natural links, Championship course with panoramic views. Heather and bracken abound.
18 holes, 6566yds, Par 69, SSS 73, Course record 64.
Club membership 830.
Visitors must have handicap certificate and contact in advance. May only play from yellow markers. **Societies** must contact in advance. **Green Fees** £38 per day (£48 weekends & bank holidays). **Cards** 💳 💳 💳 🖥 **Course Designer** McKenzie Ross **Facilities** ⊗ 🍴 🛒 🍽 🅿 🏌 ⚑ **Location** 3.5m S of Kirkbean off A710

Hotel ★★ 69% Clonyard House Hotel, COLVEND ☎ 01556 630372 15 en suite

STRANRAER
Map 10 NX06

Stranraer Creachmore DG9 0LF
☎ 01776 870245 📠 01776 870445
e-mail: stranraergolf@btclick.com
Parkland course with beautiful views overlooking Loch Ryan to Ailsa Craig, Arran and beyond. Several notable holes including the 3rd, where a winding burn is crossed three times to a green set between a large bunker and a steep bank sloping down to the burn; the

Continued

scenic 5th with spectacular views; the 11th requiring a demanding tee shot with trees and out of bounds to the left, then a steep rise to a very fast green. The 15th is a difficult par 3 where accuracy is paramount with ground sloping away either side of the green.
18 holes, 6308yds, Par 70, SSS 72, Course record 66. Club membership 700.
Visitors must contact in advance. Members times reserved throughout year. **Societies** must telephone in advance. **Green Fees** Terms on application. **Cards** ⊞ ▆▆ 💳 **Course Designer** James Braid **Facilities** ⊗ ⫚ ⮂ 🍺 ⛳ 🛒 🏌
🛒 🏌 **Location** 2.5m NW on A718 from Stranraer

Hotel ★★★★ 68% North West Castle Hotel, STRANRAER ☎ 01776 704413 70 en suite
2 annexe en suite

THORNHILL   Map 11 NX89

Thornhill Blacknest DG3 5DW
☎ 01848 331779 & 330546
e-mail: coordinatorthornhillgc@btinternet.com
Moorland/parkland course with fine views over the southern uplands.
18 holes, 6085yds, Par 71, SSS 70, Course record 67. Club membership 600.
Visitors apply in advance, restricted competition days. **Societies** apply in writing. **Green Fees** £19 per round/£27 per day (weekends £23/£32). **Course Designer** Willie Fernie **Facilities** ⊗ ⫚ 🍺 🏌 **Location** 1m E of town off A76

Hotel ★★ 74% Trigony House Hotel, Closeburn, THORNHILL ☎ 01848 331211 8 en suite

---

WIGTOWN   Map 10 NX45

Wigtown & Bladnoch Lightlands Ter DG8 9EF
☎ 01988 403354
Slightly hilly parkland course with fine views over Wigtown Bay to Galloway Hills.
9 holes, 5462yds, Par 68, SSS 67, Course record 62. Club membership 150.
Visitors advisable to contact in advance for weekend play. Course closed to visitors during open competitions. **Societies** contact secretary in advance. **Green Fees** £15 for 18 holes/£10 for 9 holes. **Course Designer** W Muir **Facilities** 🛒 **Location** SW on A714

DUNDEE CITY

DUNDEE   Map 11 NO43

Caird Park Mains Loan DD4 9BX
☎ 01382 438871 📠 01382 433211
e-mail: cp.olympia@dundeecity.gov.uk
18 holes, 6280yds, Par 72, SSS 69, Course record 67.
Location From Kingsway (A90) take Forfar Road, turn left onto Claverhouse Road, 1st left into Caird Park
Telephone for further details

Camperdown Camperdown Park, Coupar Angus Rd DD2 4TF ☎ 01382 432688
18 holes, 6548yds, Par 71, SSS 72.
Location Kingsway (A90), turn off at Coupar Angus Road (A923) then turn left into Camperdown Park
Telephone for further details

Hotel ★★ 73% The Shaftesbury, 1 Hyndford St, DUNDEE ☎ 01382 669216 12 en suite

---

Downfield Turnberry Av DD2 3QP
☎ 01382 825595 📠 01382 813111
e-mail: downfieldgc@aol.com
A 1999 Open Qualifying venue. A course with championship credentials providing an enjoyable test for all golfers.
18 holes, 6803yds, Par 73, SSS 73, Course record 65. Club membership 750.
Visitors must contact in advance, no visitors at weekends. **Societies** must contact in advance. **Green Fees** terms on application. **Cards** ⊞ ▆▆ 🟥 💳 **Prof** Kenny Hutton **Course Designer** James Braid **Facilities** ⊗ ⫚ 🍺 🏌 ♀
🍺 🏌 🛒 🏌 **Leisure** snooker room. **Conf** Corporate Hospitality Days available **Location** N of city centre, signposted on A90 Perth/Aberdeen road at junct with A923

Hotel ★★ 73% The Shaftesbury, 1 Hyndford St, DUNDEE ☎ 01382 669216 12 en suite

---

EAST AYRSHIRE

GALSTON   Map 11 NS53

Loudoun Edinburgh Rd KA4 8PA
☎ 01563 821993 📠 01563 820011
e-mail: secretary@loudowf.sol.co.uk
Pleasant, fairly flat parkland course with many mature trees, located in the Irvine Valley in the rural heart of Ayrshire.
Loudoun Gowf Club: 18 holes, 6005yds, Par 68, SSS 69, Course record 61.
Club membership 700.
Visitors must contact in advance. Weekdays only, must play with member at weekends/public holidays **Societies** telephone in advance. **Green Fees** £35 per day, £25 per 18 holes. **Cards** ⊞ ▆▆ 🟥 💳 **Facilities** ⊗ ⫚ 🍺 ♀ 🛒 ⛳
🛒 🏌 **Conf** Corporate Hospitality Days available **Location** NE side of town on A71

Hotel ★★★ 74% Strathaven Hotel, Hamilton Rd, STRATHAVEN ☎ 01357 521778 22 en suite

---

KILMARNOCK   Map 10 NS43

Annanhill Irvine Rd KA1 2RT
☎ 01563 521644 & 521512
Municipal, tree-lined parkland course.
18 holes, 6269yds, Par 71, SSS 70, Course record 66. Club membership 394.
Visitors must book at starters office,01563-521512. **Societies** apply in writing. **Green Fees** terms on application. **Course Designer** Jack McLean **Facilities** ⊗ by prior arrangement ⫚ by prior arrangement 🍺 by prior arrangement 🍺 by prior arrangement 🛒 ⛳ **Location** 1m N on B7081

Hotel ⭐ Travel Inn, Annadale, KILMARNOCK ☎ 08701 977148 40 en suite

Hotel ★★★ 72% Montgreenan Mansion House Hotel, Montgreenan Estate, KILWINNING ☎ 01294 557733 Fax 01294 850397 21 en suite

Caprington Ayr Rd KA1 4UW
☎ 01563 523702 & 521915 (Gen Enq)
18 holes, 5810yds, Par 68, SSS 68.
Location 1.5m S on B7038
Telephone for further details

Continued

Hotel ⏩ Travelodge, Kilmarnock By Pass,
KILMARNOCK ☎ 08700 850 950 40 en suite

MAUCHLINE   Map 11 NS42

Ballochmyle Catrine Rd KA5 6LE
☎ 01290 550469 📄 01290 553657
e-mail: secretary@ballochmyle.freeserve.co.uk
Wooded parkland course.
18 holes, 5972yds, Par 70, SSS 69, Course record 64.
Club membership 730.
Visitors welcome. May not play Sat. **Societies** apply in
writing/telephone. **Green Fees** £20 18 holes/£30 36 holes
(weekends £25/£35). **Cards** ⊞ ▦ 🖩 **Facilities** ⊗ ⍔ ⓛ
🍽 ♀ ⚲ 🏠 𝄃 **Leisure** snooker. **Location** 1m SE on B705

Hotel ⏩ Travelodge, Kilmarnock By Pass,
KILMARNOCK ☎ 08700 850 950 40 en suite

NEW CUMNOCK   Map 11 NS61

New Cumnock Lochhill, Cumnock Rd KA18 4PN
☎ 01290 338848
9 holes, 5176yds, Par 68, SSS 68, Course record 63.
Course Designer Willie Fernie **Location** 0.75m N on A76
Telephone for further details

Hotel ★★ 66% Blackaddie House Hotel, Blackaddie Rd,
SANQUHAR ☎ 01659 50270 9 en suite

PATNA   Map 10 NS41

Doon Valley Hillside Park KA6 7JT
☎ 01292 531607
**Established parkland course located on an undulating
hillside.**
9 holes, 5886yds, Par 70, SSS 70, Course record 56.
Club membership 100.
Visitors no restrictions mid week, advisable to contact in
advance for weekends. **Societies** telephone to arrange.
Green Fees £10 per 18 holes. **Facilities** ♀ ⚲ **Leisure**
fishing, fitness and games hall nearby. **Location** 10m S of
Ayr on the A713

Hotel ★★ Ladyburn, MAYBOLE ☎ 01655 740585
5 en suite

EAST DUNBARTONSHIRE

BALMORE   Map 11 NS57

Balmore Golf Course Rd G64 4AW
☎ 01360 620284 📄 01360 622742
e-mail: secretary@balmoregolfclub.co.uk
Parkland course with fine views.
18 holes, 5530yds, Par 66, SSS 67, Course record 62.
Club membership 700.
Visitors must contact in advance,may not play at weekends
Societies apply in writing. **Green Fees** not confirmed. **Prof**
Kevin Craggs **Course Designer** Harry Vardon **Facilities**
⊗ ⍔ ⓛ 🍽 ♀ ⚲ 🏠 𝄃 **Location** N off A807

Hotel ⏩ Premier Lodge (Glasgow North), Milngavie Rd,
BEARSDEN ☎ 0870 9906532 61 en suite

BEARSDEN   Map 11 NS57

Bearsden Thorn Rd G61 4BP ☎ 0141 942 2351
**Parkland course, with 16 greens and 11 teeing grounds.
Easy walking and views over city and Campsie Hills.**

9 holes, 6014yds, Par 68, SSS 69, Course record 64.
Club membership 600.
Visitors must be accompanied by and play with member.
Societies apply by writing. **Green Fees** terms on
application. **Facilities** ⊗ ⍔ ⓛ 🍽 ♀ ⚲ **Location** 1m W
off A809

Hotel ⏩ Premier Lodge (Glasgow North), Milngavie Rd,
BEARSDEN ☎ 0870 9906532 61 en suite

Douglas Park Hillfoot G61 2TJ
☎ 0141 942 2220 (Clubhouse) 📄 0141 942 0985
e-mail: secretary@douglasparkgolfclub.net
Parkland course with wide variety of holes.
18 holes, 5962yds, Par 69, SSS 69, Course record 64.
Club membership 900.
Visitors must be accompanied by member or must contact
in advance, Wednesdays and Thursdays for visiting parties
only. **Societies** Wed & Thu. Must telephone in advance.
Green Fees £31 per day; £23 per round. **Prof** David Scott
Course Designer Willie Fernie **Facilities** ⊗ ⍔ ⓛ 🍽 ♀
⚲ 🏠 🛒 𝄃 **Location** E side of town on A81

Hotel ⏩ Premier Lodge (Glasgow North), Milngavie Rd,
BEARSDEN ☎ 0870 9906532 61 en suite

Glasgow Gailes Killermont G61 2TW
☎ 0141 942 2011
Glasgow Golf Club: 18 holes, 5968yds, Par 70, SSS 69.
Location SE side off A81
Telephone for further details

Windyhill Baljaffray Rd G61 4QQ
☎ 0141 942 2349 📄 0141 942 5874
e-mail: secretary@windyhill.co.uk
**Interesting parkland/moorland course with panoramic
views of Glasgow and beyond; testing 12th hole.**
18 holes, 6254yds, Par 71, SSS 70, Course record 64.
Club membership 800.
Visitors may not play at weekends. Must contact
professional in advance. Must have a handicap certificate.
Societies must apply in writing. **Green Fees** £25 per
round/£35 per day. **Cards** ⊞ ▦ 🖩 **Prof** Chris Duffy
Course Designer James Braid **Facilities** ⊗ ⍔ ⓛ 🍽 ♀ ⚲
🏠 🕈 𝄃 **Location** 2m NW off B8050, 1.5m from Bearsden
cross, just off Drymen road

Hotel ⏩ Premier Lodge (Glasgow North), Milngavie Rd,
BEARSDEN ☎ 0870 9906532 61 en suite

BISHOPBRIGGS   Map 11 NS67

Bishopbriggs Brackenbrae Rd G64 2DX
☎ 0141 772 1810 772 8938 📄 7622532
e-mail: secretarybgc@yahoo.co.uk
Parkland course with views to Campsie Hills.
18 holes, 6041yds, Par 69, SSS 69, Course record 63.
Club membership 800.
Visitors Must contact in advance. May not play at
weekends. **Societies** apply in writing in advance. **Green
Fees** £32.50 per day, £22.50 per round. **Course Designer**
James Braid **Facilities** ⊗ ⍔ ⓛ 🍽 ♀ ⚲ 🏠 **Conf** fac
available Corporate Hospitality Days available **Location**
0.5m NW off A803

Hotel ★★★★ 67% Glasgow Marriott Hotel, 500 Argyle
St, Anderston, GLASGOW ☎ 0141 226 5577 300 en suite

Continued

Cawder Cadder Rd G64 3QD
☎ 0141 761 1281 📠 0141 761 1285
e-mail: secretary@cawdergolfclub.org.uk
**Two parkland courses; Cawder Course is hilly, with the
5th, 9th, 10th and 11th testing holes. Keir Course is flat.**
*Cawder Course: 18 holes, 6295yds, Par 70, SSS 71,
Course record 63.*
Keir Course: 18 holes, 5877yds, Par 68, SSS 68.
Club membership 1150.
Visitors must contact in advance & may play on weekdays
only. **Societies** must contact in writing, not on Bank
Holidays **Green Fees** £30 per round/£40 per day. **Cards**
💳 💳 💳 **Prof** Ken Stevely **Course Designer** James
Braid **Facilities** ⊗ ⫼ 🏌 💷 ♀ 🛆 🏠 🍴 ⚷ **Location** 5 m
NE off A803

Hotel ★★★★ 67% Glasgow Marriott Hotel, 500 Argyle
St, Anderston, GLASGOW ☎ 0141 226 5577 300 en suite

Littlehill Auchinairn Rd G64 1UT
☎ 0141 772 1916
18 holes, 6240yds, Par 70, SSS 70.
Location 3m NE of Glasgow city centre on A803
Telephone for further details

Hotel ★★★★ 67% Glasgow Marriott Hotel, 500 Argyle
St, Anderston, GLASGOW ☎ 0141 226 5577 300 en suite

KIRKINTILLOCH   Map 11 NS67

Hayston Campsie Rd G66 1RN
☎ 0141 776 1244 📠 0141 7769030
An undulating, tree-lined course with a sandy subsoil.
18 holes, 6042yds, Par 70, SSS 70, Course record 60.
Club membership 800.
Visitors must apply in advance, may not play weekends.
Societies Tue & Thu, apply in writing **Green Fees** not
confirmed. **Prof** Steven Barnett **Course Designer** James
Braid **Facilities** ⊗ ⫼ 🏌 💷 ♀ 🛆 🏠 ⚷ **Location** 1m NW
off A803

Hotel ★★★★ 69% The Westerwood Hotel, 1 St Andrews
Dr, Westerwood, CUMBERNAULD ☎ 01236 457171
100 en suite

Kirkintilloch Campsie Rd G66 1RN
☎ 0141 776 1256 & 775 2387 📠 0141 775 2424
Parkland course in rural setting.
18 holes, 5860yds, Par 70, SSS 69.
Club membership 650.
Visitors must be introduced by member. **Societies** apply in
writing. **Green Fees** terms on application. **Course
Designer** James Braid **Facilities** ⊗ ⫼ 🏌 💷 ♀ 🛆 🏠
Location 1m NW off A803

Hotel ★★★★ 69% The Westerwood Hotel, 1 St Andrews
Dr, Westerwood, CUMBERNAULD ☎ 01236 457171
100 en suite

LENNOXTOWN   Map 11 NS67

Campsie Crow Rd G66 7HX
☎ 01360 310244 📠 01360 310244
e-mail: campsiegolfclub@aol.com
Scenic hillside course.
18 holes, 5507yds, Par 70, SSS 68, Course record 69.
Club membership 620.
Visitors preferred weekdays. Weekends only by prior
arrangment, contact professional 01360 310920. **Societies**
written application. **Green Fees** £25 per day, £20 per

Continued

round (£25 per round weekends). **Prof** Mark Brennan
Course Designer W Auchterlonie **Facilities** ⊗ ⫼ 🏌 💷 ♀
🛆 🏠 **Conf** Corporate Hospitality Days available
Location 0.5m N on B822

Hotel ★★★★ 69% The Westerwood Hotel, 1 St Andrews
Dr, Westerwood, CUMBERNAULD ☎ 01236 457171
100 en suite

LENZIE   Map 11 NS67

Lenzie 19 Crosshill Rd G66 5DA
☎ 0141 776 1535 & 812 3018
📠 0141 777 7748 or 0141 812 3018
e-mail: scottdavidson@lenziegolfclub.demon.co.uk
**The course is parkland and prominent features include
the old beech trees, which line some of the fairways
together with thorn hedges and shallow ditches.
Extensive larch and fir plantations have also been
created. The course is relatively flat apart from a steep
hill to the green at the 5th hole.**
18 holes, 5984yds, Par 69, SSS 69, Course record 64.
Club membership 890.
Visitors must contact in advance. **Societies** apply in
writing/telephone in advance. **Green Fees** not confirmed.
Prof Jim McCallum **Facilities** ⊗ ⫼ 🏌 💷 ♀ 🛆 🏠 ⚷
Conf fac available **Location** N of Glasgow, approx 15
mins from Glasgow city centre, Kirkintilloch turn off M80

Hotel ★★★★ 69% The Westerwood Hotel, 1 St Andrews
Dr, Westerwood, CUMBERNAULD ☎ 01236 457171
100 en suite

MILNGAVIE   Map 11 NS57

Clober Craigton Rd G62 7HP
☎ 0141 956 1685 📠 0141 955 1416
e-mail: secretary@clober.co.uk
18 holes, 4824yds, Par 66, SSS 65, Course record 61.
Location NW side of town
Telephone for further details

Esporta, Dougalston Strathblane G62 8HJ
☎ 0141 955 2404 & 955 2434 📠 0141 955 2406
e-mail: hilda.everett@esporta.com
**A golf course of tremendous character set in 300 acres of
beautiful woodland dotted with drumlins, lakes and
criss-crossed by streams and ditches. The course makes
excellent use of the natural features to create mature,
tree-lined fairways. The course is currently being
upgraded to improve drainage and introduce three new
holes as well as clearing shrubbery to widen some others.**
18 holes, 6225yds, Par 71, SSS 72, Course record 68.
Club membership 800.
Visitors book tee time 1 week in advance. May play at
weekends after 2pm subject to availability. **Societies**
weekdays only, telephone in advance. **Green Fees** terms
on application. **Cards** 💳 💳 💳 **Prof** Craig Everett
Course Designer Commander Harris **Facilities** ⊗ ⫼ 🏌
💷 ♀ 🛆 🏠 🍴 ⚷ **Leisure** hard tennis courts, heated
indoor swimming pool, sauna, solarium, gymnasium. **Conf**
Corporate Hospitality Days available **Location** NE side of
town on A81

Hotel ⚑ Travel Inn Glasgow North, 103 Main St,
MILNGAVIE ☎ 08701 977112 60 en suite

> **Looking for a driving range? Refer to the listing
> of driving ranges at the back of this guide.**

Hilton Park Auldmarroch Estate, Stockiemuir Rd
G62 7HB ☎ 0141 956 4657 🗎 0141 956 4657
e-mail: info@hiltonparkgolfclub.fsnet.co.uk
Moorland courses set amidst magnificent scenery.
Hilton Course: 18 holes, 6054yds, Par 70, SSS 70, Course record 65.
Allander Course: 18 holes, 5487yards, Par 69, SSS 67, Course record 65.
Club membership 1200.
Visitors must contact in advance but may not play at weekends. **Societies** apply in advance to secretary. **Green Fees** £25 per round/£35 per day. **Prof** W McCondichie **Course Designer** James Braid **Facilities** ⊗ ⅢⅡ ⅃ 🖢 ➥ ⅃ ☖
🖻 ⅎ ▾ 𝄁 **Location** 3m NW of Milngavie, on A809

Hotel ⬫ Travel Inn Glasgow North, 103 Main St, MILNGAVIE ☎ 08701 977112 60 en suite

Milngavie Laighpark G62 8EP
☎ 0141 956 1619 🗎 0141 956 4252
18 holes, 5818yds, Par 68, SSS 68, Course record 59.
Course Designer The Auchterlonie Brothers **Location** 1.25m N
Telephone for further details

Hotel ⬫ Travel Inn Glasgow North, 103 Main St, MILNGAVIE ☎ 08701 977112 60 en suite

EAST LOTHIAN

ABERLADY   Map 12 NT47

Kilspindie EH32 0QD
☎ 01875 870358 🗎 01875 870358
e-mail: kilspindie@btconnect.com
Traditional Scottish seaside links, short but good challenge of golf and well-bunkered. Situated on the shores of the River Forth with panoramic views.
Kilspindie: 18 holes, 5480yds, Par 69, SSS 66, Course record 59.
Club membership 750.
Visitors must contact in advance, prefered days for visitors Mon-Fri, but tee times available at weekends. **Societies** contact secretary in advance. **Green Fees** £45 per day, £28.50 per round (£57.50/£35 weekends). **Cards** 🖷 🖷
🖷 🖷 🗗 **Prof** Graham J Sked **Course Designer** Various **Facilities** ⊗ ⅢⅡ ⅃ 🖢 ➥ ⅃ ☖ ⅎ ▾ 🗗 𝄁 **Conf**
Corporate Hospitality Days available **Location** N side of village off A198, private road access located at eastern end of village of Aberlady

Hotel ★★★ 🏌 Greywalls Hotel, Muirfield, GULLANE ☎ 01620 842144 17 en suite 5 annexe en suite

Luffness New EH32 0QA
☎ 01620 843336 🗎 01620 842933
e-mail: secretary@luffnessnew.com
Links course, national final qualifying course for Open Championship.
18 holes, 6122yds, Par 69, SSS 70, Course record 61.
Club membership 750.
Visitors must contact in advance and may not play at weekends & public holidays. **Societies** telephone for application form. **Green Fees** £66 per day; £46 per round. **Course Designer** Tom Morris **Facilities** ⊗ ⅢⅡ ➥ ⅃ ☖ 🖻
𝄁 **Location** 1m E Aberlady on A198

Hotel ★★★ 🏌 Greywalls Hotel, Muirfield, GULLANE ☎ 01620 842144 17 en suite 5 annexe en suite

DUNBAR   Map 12 NT67

Dunbar East Links EH42 1LL
☎ 01368 862317 🗎 01368 865202
e-mail: secretary@dunbargolf.sol.co.uk
Another of Scotland's old links. It is said that it was some Dunbar members who first took the game of golf to the North of England. A natural links course on a narrow strip of land, following the contours of the sea shore. There is a wall bordering one side and the shore on the other side making this quite a challenging course for all levels of player. The wind, if blowing from the sea, is a problem.
18 holes, 6406yds, Par 71, SSS 71, Course record 64.
Club membership 1000.
Visitors may not play Thu, between 12.30-2 weekdays, 12-2 weekends or before 9.30am any day. **Societies** telephone in advance. **Green Fees** £40 per round/£55 per day (weekend £50/£70). **Cards** 🖷 🖷 🖷 🖷 🖷 🖷 **Prof** Jacky Montgomery **Course Designer** Tom Morris **Facilities** ⊗ ⅢⅡ ⅃ 🖢 ➥ ⅃ ⅃ ☖ ⅎ 𝄁 **Conf** Corporate Hospitality Days available **Location** 0.5m E off A1087

Winterfield North Rd EH42 1AU
☎ 01368 863562 🗎 01368 863562
e-mail: kevinphillips@tiscali.co.uk
Seaside course with superb views.
18 holes, 5155yds, Par 65, SSS 64, Course record 61.
Club membership 350.
Visitors contact in advance. Weekends from 10am-12 noon & 2pm-4pm **Societies** must arrange in advance through professional, telephone or email **Green Fees** terms on application. **Prof** Kevin Phillips **Facilities** ⊗ ⅢⅡ ⅃ 🖢 ➥ ⅃
⅃ ☖ ⅎ ▾ 🗗 𝄁 **Location** W side of town off A1087

GIFFORD   Map 12 NT56

Gifford Edinburgh Rd EH41 4JE
☎ 01620 810267
e-mail: thesecretary@giffordgolfclub.fsnet.co.uk
Parkland course, with easy walking.

9 holes, 6057yds, Par 71, SSS 69.
Club membership 600.
Visitors may not play on the 1st Sun of the month during Apr-Oct. Telephone Starter on 01620 810 591 to book tee times. **Societies** telephone in advance. 01620 810 591 **Green Fees** £25 per day; £15 per 18 holes; £10 per 9 holes. **Course Designer** W Wood **Facilities** ⅃ 🖢 ➥ ⅃ 𝄁 **Location** 1m SW off B6355

> **Prices may change during the currency of the Guide, please check when booking.**

GULLANE
Map 12 NT48

Gullane West Links Rd EH31 2BB
☎ 01620 842255 📠 01620 842327
e-mail: bookings@gullanegolfclub.com
Gullane is a delightful village and one of Scotland's great golf centres. Gullane Golf Club was formed in 1882. There are three Gullane courses of which numbers 1 and 2 are of championship standard. It differs from most Scottish courses in as much as it is of the upland links type and really quite hilly. The first tee is literally in the village. The views from the top of the course are magnificent and stretch far and wide in every direction - in fact, it is said that 14 counties can be seen from the highest spot.
Course No 1: 18 holes, 6466yds, Par 71, SSS 72, Course record 65.
Course No 2: 18 holes, 6244yds, Par 71, SSS 71, Course record 64.
Course No 3: 18 holes, 5252yds, Par 68, SSS 66.
Club membership 1200.
Visitors advance booking recommended. **Societies** advance booking advised. **Green Fees** terms on application. **Cards** 🌐 📧 🔳 📧 🔲 **Prof** Alasdair Good **Course Designer** Various **Facilities** ⊗ ⅷ ⅊ ▦ ▬ ♀ ⚐ 🏠 ⚑ ➷ 🏌 ⚙ 🍴 **Location** At west end of village on A198

Hotel ★★★ ♨ Greywalls Hotel, Muirfield, GULLANE
☎ 01620 842144 17 en suite 5 annexe en suite

GULLANE See page 329

HADDINGTON
Map 12 NT57

Haddington Amisfield Park EH41 4PT
☎ 01620 822727 & 823627 📠 01620 826580
e-mail: info@haddingtongolf.co.uk
Slightly undulating parkland course, within the grounds of a former country estate running alongside the River Tyne. New ponds and bunkers have been constructed to improve the course even more.

18 holes, 6335yds, Par 71, SSS 70, Course record 68.
Club membership 850.
Visitors may not play between 7am-10am & noon-2pm at weekends. Must contact in advance. **Societies** Mon-Fri at all timesmust contact in advance; deposits required. May play weekdays anytime and weekends 10-12 and 2-4 **Green Fees** £33 per day, £24 per round (£43/£34 weekends). **Prof** John Sandilands **Facilities** ⊗ ⅷ ⅊ ▬ ♀ ▦ 🏠 ➷ ⚙ **Leisure** driving net, practice bunker. **Conf** fac available Corporate Hospitality Days available **Location** E side off A613 off A1,17 miles E of Edinburgh

Hotel ★★★ ♨ Greywalls Hotel, Muirfield, GULLANE
☎ 01620 842144 17 en suite 5 annexe en suite

LONGNIDDRY
Map 12 NT47

Longniddry Links Rd EH32 0NL
☎ 01875 852141 📠 01875 853371
e-mail: secretary@longniddrygolfclub.co.uk
Undulating seaside links and partial parkland course with no par 5s. One of the numerous courses which stretch east from Edinburgh right to Dunbar. The inward half is more open than the wooded outward half, but can be difficult in prevailing west wind.
18 holes, 6260yds, Par 68, SSS 70, Course record 63.
Club membership 1140.
Visitors deposit required if booking more than 7 days in advance. May not play on competition days. **Societies** Mon-Thu, apply in writing, handicap certificate required. **Green Fees** £55 per day, £37.50 per round (weekends £48 per round). **Cards** 🌐 📧 🔳 📧 🔲 **Prof** John Gray **Course Designer** H S Colt **Facilities** ⊗ ⅷ ⅊ ▬ ♀ ▦ 🏠 ⚐ ⚑ ➷ ⚙ **Conf** Corporate Hospitality Days available **Location** N side of village off A198

Hotel ★★★ ♨ Greywalls Hotel, Muirfield, GULLANE
☎ 01620 842144 17 en suite 5 annexe en suite

MUSSELBURGH
Map 11 NT37

Musselburgh Monktonhall EH21 6SA
☎ 0131 665 2005 📠 0131 665 4435
e-mail: secretary@themusselburghgolfclub.com
Testing parkland course with natural hazards including trees and a burn; easy walking.
18 holes, 6725yds, Par 71, SSS 73, Course record 65.
Club membership 1000.
Visitors must contact in advance. **Societies** must contact in advance. **Green Fees** £35 per day; £25 per round (£40/£30 weekends). **Prof** Fraser Mann **Course Designer** James Braid **Facilities** ⊗ ⅷ ⅊ ▬ ♀ ▦ 🏠 ⚐ ⚑ ➷ ⚙ **Conf** Corporate Hospitality Days available **Location** 1m S on B6415

Hotel ⬦ Travel Inn Edinburgh Inveresk, Carberry Rd, Inveresk, Musselburgh, EDINBURGH ☎ 08701 977092 40 en suite

Musselburgh Links, The Old Golf Course
10 Balcarres Rd EH21 7SD
☎ 0131 665 5438 (Starter) 665 6981(clubhouse)
📠 0131 665 5438
e-mail: info@musselburgholdlinks.co.uk
A delightful nine hole links course weaving in and out of the famous Musselburgh Race Course. This course is steeped in the history and tradition of golf. Mary Queen of Scots reputedly played golf at the old course in 1567, but documentary evidence dates back to 1672. The 1st hole is a par 3 and the next three holes play eastward from the grandstand at the racecourse. The course turns north west towards the sea then west for the last four holes. Designed by nature and defined over the centuries by generations of golfers, the course boasts many natural features and hazards.
9 holes, 2874yds, Par 34, SSS 34, Course record 29.
Club membership 250.
Visitors must book in advance **Societies** must contact in advancein writing or by telephone. **Green Fees** £9 per 9 holes, £18 per 18 holes. **Cards** 🌐 📧 🔳 📧 **Facilities** ⅊ ⚑ ⚙ **Conf** fac available **Location** 1m E of town off A1

Hotel ⬦ Travel Inn Edinburgh Inveresk, Carberry Rd, Inveresk, Musselburgh, EDINBURGH ☎ 08701 977092 40 en suite

(Honourable Company of Edinburgh Golfers) Muirfield

Map 12 NT48

Gullane

☎ 01620 842123 📄 01620 842977

The course at Muirfield was designed by Old Tom Morris in 1891 and is generally considered to be one of the top ten courses in the world. The club itself has an excellent pedigree - it was founded in 1744, making it just ten years older than the Royal and Ancient but not as old as Royal Blackheath. Muirfield has staged some outstanding Open Championships. Perhaps one of the most memorable was in 1972 when Lee Trevino, the defending champion, seemed to be losing his grip until a spectacular shot brought him back to beat Tony Jacklin, who subsequently never won another Open.

e-mail: hceg@btinternet.com

Visitors Tue and Thu only. Must contact in advance and have a handicap certificate (18 gentlemen, 24 ladies)

Societies Tue and Thu with handicap limits (18 gentlemen, 24 ladies). Must be members of recognised golf course. Up to 12 in a group

Green Fees Telephone for details

Facilities ⊗ 🏆 ♀ 🏌 ⚑ 🏌

Location Muirfield, Gullane EH31 2EG (NE side of village)

Holes/Par/Course record 18 holes, 6801 yds, Par 70, SSS 73, Course record 63

Championship Course

WHERE TO STAY NEARBY

Hotels
DIRLETON
★★★ ◉ 70% The Open Arms, EH39 5EG.
☎ 01620 850241. 10 en suite

GULLANE
★★★ ◉ ◉ 🌲 Greywalls, EH31 2EG.
☎ 01620 842144. 17 en suite
5 annexe en suite

NORTH BERWICK
★★★ 67% The Marine, EH39 4LZ.
☎ 0870 400 8129. 83 en suite

★★ 64% Nether Abbey, EH39 4BQ.
☎ 01620 892802. 13 en suite

NORTH BERWICK   Map 12 NT58

Glen East Links, Tantallon Ter EH39 4LE
☎ 01620 892726 📠 01620 895447
e-mail: secretary@glengolfclub.co.uk
**An interesting course with a good variety of holes
including the famous 13th. The views of the town, the
Firth of Forth and the Bass Rock are breathtaking.**

*18 holes, 6243yds, Par 70, SSS 70, Course record 67.
Club membership 650.*
Visitors booking advisable. **Societies** advance booking
recommended. **Green Fees** £38 per day, £28 per round
(weekends £50/39). **Cards** 💳 💳 💳 💳 💳 **Course Designer**
Ben Sayers/James Braid **Facilities** ⊗ ⊪ ⅃ ⚑ ☿ ⚁ ⚑ ⚑
⚘ **Conf** Corporate Hospitality Days available **Location**
follow A198 off A1 to North Berwick. Turn right at
seabird centre and follow beach road

....

Hotel ★★ 64% Nether Abbey Hotel, 20 Dirleton Av,
NORTH BERWICK ☎ 01620 892802 13 en suite

North Berwick Beach Rd EH39 4BB
☎ 01620 892135 📠 01620 893274
e-mail: secretary@northberwickgolfclub.com
**Another of East Lothian's famous courses, the links at
North Berwick is still popular. A classic championship
links, it has many hazards including the beach, streams,
bunkers, light rough and low walls. The great hole on
the course is the 15th, the famous 'Redan'. Used by
both the Tantallon and Bass Rock Golf Clubs.**
*West Links: 18 holes, 6420yds, Par 71, SSS 72, Course
record 63.*
Club membership 730.
Visitors must contact in advance 01620 892135 (beyond 7
days) or 01620 892666 (within 7 days). **Societies** must
contact in advance. **Green Fees** £75 per day; £50 per round
(£70 weekends). **Cards** 💳 💳 💳 💳 💳 **Prof** D Huish
Facilities ⊗ ⊪ ⅃ ⚑ ☿ ⚁ ⚑ ⚘ **Location** W side of
town on A198

....

Hotel ★★★ 67% The Marine, Cromwell Rd, NORTH
BERWICK ☎ 0870 400 8129 83 en suite

Whitekirk Whitekirk EH39 5PR
☎ 01620 870300 📠 01620 870330
e-mail: countryclub@whitekirk.com
**Scenic coastal course with lush green fairways, gorse
covered rocky banks and stunning views. Natural water
hazards and strong sea breezes make this well designed
course a good test of golf.**
18 holes, 6526yds, Par 72, SSS 72, Course record 64.
Club membership 400.
Visitors no restrictions. **Societies** apply in writing or
telephone. **Green Fees** £25 per round/£35 per

Continued

day (weekend £35/£50). **Cards** 💳 💳 💳 💳 💳 **Prof**
Paul Wardell **Course Designer** Cameron Sinclair
Facilities ⊗ ⊪ ⅃ ⚑ ☿ ⚁ ⚑ ⚑ ⚘ **Location** 3m
off the main A1 Edinburgh/Berwick-upon-Tweed road
A198 North Berwick

....

Hotel ★★ 64% Nether Abbey Hotel, 20 Dirleton Av,
NORTH BERWICK ☎ 01620 892802 13 en suite

PRESTONPANS   Map 11 NT37

Royal Musselburgh Prestongrange House
EH32 9RP ☎ 01875 810276 📠 01875 810276
e-mail: royalmusselburgh@btinternet.com
**Tree-lined parkland course overlooking Firth of Forth.
Well maintained and providing an excellent challenge.
The final third of the course can make or break a score.
The tough four hole stretches from the long par 4 13th
including 'The Gully', a par 3 14th where to be short is
to court disaster, followed by the par 4 15th huddled
tight beside trees to the left. A precision drive is
required to find the rollercoaster fairway and from
there a long iron or fairway wood is played over an
uphill approach to a tilting green.**
18 holes, 6237yds, Par 70, SSS 70, Course record 64.
Club membership 1000.
Visitors must contact professional in advance, restricted
Fri afternoons & weekends. **Societies** should contact in
advance through Management secretary **Green Fees** £35
per day; £25 per round (£35 per round weekends). **Prof**
John Henderson **Course Designer** James Braid **Facilities**
⊗ ⊪ ⅃ ⚑ ☿ ⚁ ⚑ ⚑ ⚘ **Conf** fac available
Corporate Hospitality Days available **Location** W side of
town centre on B1361 Prestonpans to North Berwick rd

....

Hotel ⬆ Travel Inn Edinburgh Inveresk, Carberry Rd,
Inveresk, Musselburgh, EDINBURGH ☎ 08701 977092
40 en suite

EAST RENFREWSHIRE

BARRHEAD   Map 11 NS45

Fereneze Fereneze Av G78 1HJ
☎ 0141 880 7058 📠 0141 881 7149
e-mail: ferenezegc@lineone.net
**Hilly moorland course, with a good view at the end of a
hard climb to the 3rd, then levels out.**
18 holes, 5962yds, Par 71, SSS 69, Course record 66.
Club membership 750.
Visitors must contact in advance but may not play at
weekends. **Societies** apply in writing. **Green Fees** £22 per
round; £25 per day. **Prof** Haldane Lee **Facilities** ⊗ ⊪ ⅃
⚑ ☿ ⚁ ⚑ ⚘ **Location** NW side of town off B774

....

Hotel ★★ 76% Uplawmoor Hotel, Neilston Rd,
UPLAWMOOR ☎ 01505 850565 14 en suite

CLARKSTON   Map 11 NS55

Cathcart Castle Mearns Rd G76 7YL
☎ 0141 638 9449 📠 0141 638 1201
18 holes, 5832yds, Par 68, SSS 68.
Location 0.75m SW off A726
Telephone for further details

....

Hotel ⬆ Premier Lodge (East Kilbride), Eaglesham Rd,
EAST KILBRIDE ☎ 0870 9906542 40 en suite

EAGLESHAM
Map 11 NS55

Bonnyton Kirktonmoor Rd G76 0QA
☎ 01355 302781 🖹 01355 303151
Dramatic moorland course offering spectacular views of beautiful countryside as far as snow-capped Ben Lomond. Tree-lined fairways, plateau greens, natural burns and well situated bunkers and a unique variety of holes offer golfers both challenge and reward.
18 holes, 6255yds, Par 72, SSS 71.
Club membership 960.
Visitors welcome Mon & Thu. Must contact in advance.
Societies must telephone in advance. **Green Fees** £40 per day. **Prof** Kendal McWade **Facilities** ⊗ ⅊⅃ ⅊ ⅃ 🖤 ⅃ ⅃ 🖪
🏴‍ ⅃ **Location** 0.25m SW off B764

....
Hotel ★★★ Bruce Hotel, Cornwall St, EAST KILBRIDE ☎ 01355 229771 65 en suite

NEWTON MEARNS
Map 11 NS55

East Renfrewshire Pilmuir G77 6RT
☎ 01355 500256 🖹 01355 500323
e-mail: david@eastrengolfclub.demon.co.uk
Undulating moorland with loch; prevailing SW wind.
18 holes, 6097yds, Par 70, SSS 70, Course record 63.
Club membership 900.
Visitors must contact professional in advance **Societies** must contact secretary in advance. **Green Fees** £40 per round/£50 per day (weekends £50/£60). **Prof** Stewart Russell **Course Designer** James Braid **Facilities** ⊗ ⅊⅃ ⅊ 🖤 ⅃ ⅃ 🖪 ⅃
Location 3m SW off Newton Mearns on A77

....
Hotel ★★ 76% Uplawmoor Hotel, Neilston Rd, UPLAWMOOR ☎ 01505 850565 14 en suite

Eastwood Muirshield, Loganswell G77 6RX
☎ 01355 500285 500280 🖹 01355 500280
e-mail: secretary@eastwoodgolfclub.demon.co.uk
An undulating moorland course situated in a scenic setting. Or5iginally built in 1937, the course was redesigned in 2003. The greens are now of modern design, built to USGA specification.
18 holes, 6071yds, Par 70, SSS 69.
Club membership 900.
Visitors contact in advance. No visitors at weekends.
Societies must contact in advance. **Green Fees** £30 per day; £24 per round. **Cards** 🖭 🖃 🖪 ⅃ **Prof** Iain J Darroch **Course Designer** Graeme J. Webster **Facilities** ⊗ ⅊⅃ ⅊ 🖤 ⅃ ⅃ 🖪 ⅃ **Location** 2.5m S of Newton Mearns, on A77

....
Hotel ★★ 76% Uplawmoor Hotel, Neilston Rd, UPLAWMOOR ☎ 01505 850565 14 en suite

Whitecraigs 72 Ayr Rd G46 6SW
☎ 0141 639 4530 🖹 0141 616 3648
e-mail: wcraigsgc@aol.com
Beautiful parkland course only twenty minutes from the centre of Glasgow.
18 holes, 6230yds, Par 70, SSS 70, Course record 63.
Club membership 1050.
Visitors must contact professional in advance and have a handicap certificate. **Societies** apply in advance. **Green Fees** £50 per day inc food & drink; £40 per round inc food & drinks. **Cards** 🖭 🖃 🖪 ⅃ **Prof** Alastair Forrow **Course Designer** Fernie **Facilities** ⊗ ⅊⅃ ⅊ 🖤 ⅃ ⅃ 🖪 🏴‍
⅃ **Location** 1.5m NE on A77

....
Hotel ★★ 76% Uplawmoor Hotel, Neilston Rd, UPLAWMOOR ☎ 01505 850565 14 en suite

UPLAWMOOR
Map 10 NS45

Caldwell G78 4AU
☎ 01505 850366 (Secretary) & 850616 (Pro)
🖹 01505 850604
e-mail: caldwellgolfclub@aol.com
Parkland course.
18 holes, 6294yds, Par 71, SSS 70, Course record 62.
Club membership 600.
Visitors must be with member at weekends & bank holidays. Must contact professional in advance. **Societies** writing to Secretary. **Green Fees** £25 per round/£35 per day. **Prof** Stephen Forbes **Course Designer** W. Fernie **Facilities** ⊗ ⅊⅃ ⅊ 🖤 ⅃ ⅃ 🖪 ⅃ **Location** 5m SW of Barrhead on A736 Irvine road

....
Hotel ★★ 76% Uplawmoor Hotel, Neilston Rd, UPLAWMOOR ☎ 01505 850565 14 en suite

FALKIRK

FALKIRK
Map 11 NS88

Falkirk Carmuirs, 136 Stirling Rd, Camelon FK2 7YP
☎ 01324 611061 (club) 🖹 01324 639573 (Sec)
e-mail: carmuirs.fgc@virgin.net
Parkland course with trees, gorse and streams.
18 holes, 6230yds, Par 71, SSS 70, Course record 65.
Club membership 800.
Visitors telephone starter 01324 612219, visiting parties may not play Sat. **Societies** telephone 01324 612219 in advance.
Green Fees £30 per day; £20 per round (£40/£30 Sun). **Cards** 🖭 🖃 🖪 ⅃ **Prof** Stewart Craig **Course Designer** James Braid **Facilities** ⊗ ⅊⅃ ⅊ 🖤 ⅃ ⅃ 🖪 ⅃ **Conf** Corporate Hospitality Days available **Location** 1.5m W on A9

....
Hotel ★★★★ 69% The Inchyra, Grange Rd, POLMONT ☎ 01324 711911 109 en suite

LARBERT
Map 11 NS88

Falkirk Tryst 86 Burnhead Rd FK5 4BD
☎ 01324 562054 🖹 01324 562054
Links-type course, fairly level with trees and broom, well-bunkered. Winds can affect play.
18 holes, 6053yds, Par 70, SSS 69, Course record 62.
Club membership 850.
Visitors must contact in advance no play at weekends.
Societies visitors welcome Mon-Fri must book or telephone. **Green Fees** not confirmed. **Prof** Steven Dunsmore **Facilities** ⊗ ⅃ 🖤 ⅃ ⅃ 🖪 🏴‍ ⅃ **Location** On A88 between A9 and A905

....
Hotel ★★★★ 69% The Inchyra, Grange Rd, POLMONT ☎ 01324 711911 109 en suite

Glenbervie Clubhouse Stirling Rd FK5 4SJ
☎ 01324 562605 🖹 01324 551054
Parkland course with good views.
Glenbervie: 18 holes, 6423yds, Par 71, SSS 71, Course record 64.
Club membership 600.
Visitors Mon to Fri till 4pm, parties Tues & Thurs only
Societies Tue & Thu only. Apply in writing. **Green Fees** not confirmed. **Cards** 🖭 🖃 **Prof** David Ross **Course Designer** James Braid **Facilities** ⊗ ⅃ 🖤 ⅃ ⅃ 🖪 ⅃ **Location** 2m NW on A9

....
Hotel ★★★★ 69% The Inchyra, Grange Rd, POLMONT ☎ 01324 711911 109 en suite

POLMONT   Map 11 NS97

Grangemouth Polmont Hill FK2 0YE
☎ 01324 503840 📠 01324 503841
Windy parkland course. Testing holes: 3rd, 4th (par 4s); 5th (par 5); 7th (par 3) 216 yds over reservoir (elevated green); 8th, 9th, 18th (par 4s).
18 holes, 6314yds, Par 71, SSS 71, Course record 65.
Club membership 800.
Visitors must contact 24 hours in advance.Must have own golf shoes and clubs, sats after 4pm. Societies must contact in writing. Green Fees £15 per round (£19 weekends). Prof Greg McFarlane Facilities ⊗ ⽱ ⓛ ♥ ♀ ♨ 🏠 ♂ Location On unclass rd 0.5m N of M9 junc 4

••••••••••••••••••••••••••••••••
Hotel ★★★★ 69% The Inchyra, Grange Rd, POLMONT
☎ 01324 711911 109 en suite

Polmont Manuelrigg, Maddiston FK2 0LS
☎ 01324 711277 📠 01324 712504
Parkland course, hilly with few bunkers. Views of the River Forth and Ochil Hills.
9 holes, 3073yds, Par 72, SSS 69, Course record 66.
Club membership 300.
Visitors no visitors on Sat from Apr-Sep, Mon-Fri. Societies apply in writing to club secretary. Green Fees terms on applications. Facilities ⊗ ⽱ ⓛ ♥ ♀ Conf fac available Location A805 from Falkirk, 1st right after fire brigade headquarters

••••••••••••••••••••••••••••••••
Hotel ★★★★ 69% The Inchyra, Grange Rd, POLMONT
☎ 01324 711911 109 en suite

FIFE

ABERDOUR   Map 11 NT18

Aberdour Seaside Place KY3 0TX
☎ 01383 860080 📠 01383 860050
e-mail: aberdourgc@aol.com
Parkland course with lovely views over Firth of Forth.

18 holes, 5460yds, Par 67, SSS 66, Course record 63.
Club membership 800.
Visitors must contact in advance, may not play Saturdays. Societies telephone or write to secretary in advance Green Fees not confirmed. Cards ▥ ▨▨ ▨▨ 🅿 Prof David Gemmell Facilities ⊗ ⽱ ⓛ ♥ ♀ ♨ 🏠 ⍑ ♦ ♂ Location S side of village

••••••••••••••••••••••••••••••••
Hotel ★★★ 65% Woodside Hotel, High St, ABERDOUR
☎ 01383 860328 20 en suite

Looking to try a new course? Always telephone ahead to confirm visitor arrangements.

ANSTRUTHER   Map 12 NO50

Anstruther Marsfield, Shore Rd KY10 3DZ
☎ 01333 310956 📠 01333 312283
Seaside links course with some excellent par 3 holes; always in good condition.
9 holes, 2266yds, Par 62, SSS 63, Course record 60.
Club membership 550.
Visitors advised to phone in advance. Societies Must apply in writing for weekend bookings. Green Fees £16 per 18 holes; £10 per 9 holes (£18/£12 weekends). Course Designer Tom Morris Facilities ⊗ ⽱ ⓛ ♥ ♀ ♨ ♂ Location Turn right at Craw's Hotel, SW off A917

••••••••••••••••••••••••••••••••
Hotel ★★ 65% Balcomie Links Hotel, Balcomie Rd, CRAIL ☎ 01333 450237 15 rms (13 en suite)

BURNTISLAND   Map 11 NT28

Burntisland Golf House Club Dodhead, Kirkcaldy Rd KY3 9LQ
☎ 01592 874093 (Manager) 📠 01592 873247
e-mail: wktbghc@aol.com
A lush, testing course offering magnificent views over the Forth Estuary.

18 holes, 5965yds, Par 70, SSS 70, Course record 62.
Club membership 800.
Visitors weekend play may be restricted. Book by telephoning professional or manager. Societies apply in writing to manager. Green Fees £30 per day; £20 per round (£40/£30 weekends). Cards ▥ ▨▨ ▨▨ ▨▨ 🅿 Prof Paul Wytrazek Course Designer Willie Park Jnr Facilities ⊗ ⽱ ⓛ ♥ ♀ ♨ 🏠 ⍑ ⟟ ♦ ♂ ♂ Conf fac available Corporate Hospitality Days available Location 1m E on B923

••••••••••••••••••••••••••••••••
Hotel ★★ 68% Inchview Hotel, 69 Kinghorn Rd, BURNTISLAND ☎ 01592 872239 12 en suite

CARDENDEN   Map 11 NT29

Auchterderran Woodend Rd KY5 0NH
☎ 01592 721579
9 holes, 5250yds, Par 66, SSS 66, Course record 63.
Location N end Cardendon, Kirkcaldy/Glenrothes road Telephone for further details

••••••••••••••••••••••••••••••••
Hotel ★★★ 69% Dean Park Hotel, Chapel Level, KIRKCALDY ☎ 01592 261635 34 en suite 12 annexe en suite

COLINSBURGH   Map 12 NO40

Charleton Charleton KY9 1HG
☎ 01333 340249 📠 01333 340583
e-mail: bonde@charleton.co.uk
Parkland course with wonderful views over the Firth of Forth.

Continued

18 holes, 6216yds, Par 72, SSS 70.
Visitors preferable to contact in advance **Societies**
telephone/e-mail in advance. **Green Fees** £37 per day, £24
per round (£42/£27 weekends and bank holidays). **Cards**
⊞ 🔳 🏧 📇 ⚙ **Prof** George Finlayson **Course Designer**
J Salvesen **Facilities** ⊗ ℍ ⑂ ♥ ♀ ♨ ⚲ 🗡 ⏍ **Location** Off
B942, NW of Colinsburgh

....

Hotel ★★ 74% The Inn at Lathones, Largoward, ST
ANDREWS ☎ 01334 840494 14 annexe en suite

COWDENBEATH   Map 11 NT19

Cowdenbeath Seco Place KY4 8PD ☎ 01383 511918
*Dora Course: 18 holes, 6201yds, Par 70, SSS 70, Course
record 68.*
Location Turn off A92 into Cowdenbeath. Take 2nd right
and follow signs to course.
Telephone for further details

....

Hotel ★★★ 65% Woodside Hotel, High St, ABERDOUR
☎ 01383 860328 20 en suite

CRAIL   Map 12 NO60

Crail Golfing Society Balcomie Clubhouse,
Fifeness KY10 3XN
☎ 01333 450686 & 450960 📄 01333 450416
e-mail: crailgs@hotmail.com
**Perched on the edge of the North Sea, the Crail Golfing
Society's courses at Balcomie are picturesque and
sporting. Crail Golfing Society began its life in 1786 and
the course is highly thought of by students of the game
both for its testing holes and the standard of its greens.
Craighead Links has panoramic seascape and country
views. With wide sweeping fairways and USGA
specification greens it is a testing but fair challenge.**
*Balcomie Links: 18 holes, 5922yds, Par 69, SSS 70, Course
record 62.*
*Craighead Links: 18 holes, 6700yds, Par 72, SSS 74,
Course record 69.*
Club membership 1735.
Visitors must contact in advance, restricted 10am-noon &
2-4.30pm. **Societies** must contact in advance, as much
notice as possible for weekend play. **Green Fees** per day:
Balcomie/Balcomie £60, Craighead/Balcomie £50; per
round £35 (weekends £72/£62/£44). **Cards** ⊞ 🔳
🔳 ⚙ **Prof** Graeme Lennie **Course Designer** Tom Morris
Facilities ⊗ ℍ ⑂ ♥ ♀ ♨ ⚲ 🗡 🕊 ⏍ **Location** 2m
NE off A917

....

Hotel ★★ 65% Balcomie Links Hotel, Balcomie Rd,
CRAIL ☎ 01333 450237 15 rms (13 en suite)

Additional Guesthouse ♦♦♦♦The Spindrift, Pittenweem
Rd, ANSTRUTHER ☎ 01333 310573 Fax 01333 310573
8 en suite

CUPAR   Map 11 NO31

Cupar Hilltarvit KY15 5JT
☎ 01334 653549 📄 01334 653549
e-mail: secretary@cupargolfclub.freeserve.co.uk
**Hilly parkland course with fine views over north-east
Fife. 5th/14th hole is most difficult - uphill and into the
prevailing wind. Said to be the oldest 9 holes club in the
UK.**
9 holes, 5153yds, Par 68, SSS 66, Course record 61.
Club membership 400.
Visitors welcome except Sat. **Societies** must

Continued

contact in advance. **Green Fees** £15 per day. **Course
Designer** Allan Robertson **Facilities** ⊗ ℍ ⑂ ♥ ♀ ♨ 🗡
⏍ **Conf** Corporate Hospitality Days available **Location**
0.75m S off A92

....

Hotel ★★ 60% Eden House Hotel, 2 Pitscottie Rd,
CUPAR ☎ 01334 652510 9 en suite 2 annexe en suite

DUNFERMLINE   Map 11 NT08

Canmore Venturefair Av KY12 0PE
☎ 01383 724969 📄 01383 731649
**Parkland course with excellent turf, moderate in length
but a good test of accuracy demanding a good short
game. Ideal for 36 hole play, and suitable for all ages.**
18 holes, 5376yds, Par 67, SSS 66, Course record 61.
Club membership 710.
Visitors Sat not usually available. Limited Sun. Must
contact Professional in advance. **Societies** apply in writing
to secretary. **Green Fees** £21 per day: £16 per round (£21
per round weekends). **Prof** Gavin Cook **Course Designer**
Ben Sayers & others **Facilities** ⊗ ℍ ⑂ ♥ ♀ ♨ 🗡 ⏍ ⚲
Location 1m N on A823

....

Hotel ★★★ 74% Keavil House Hotel, Crossford,
DUNFERMLINE ☎ 01383 736258 47 en suite

Dunfermline Pitfirrane, Crossford KY12 8QW
☎ 01383 723534 & 729061
e-mail: pitfirrane@aol.com
**Gently undulating parkland course with interesting
contours. Five par 5s, five par 3s. No water hazards.
Centre of the course is a disused walled garden that is a
haven for wildlife.**
18 holes, 6121yds, Par 72, SSS 70, Course record 65.
Club membership 980.
Visitors may not play Saturdays. Contact to check times.
Societies must contact in advance. **Green Fees** £38 per
round, £27 per round (Sun £35 per round). **Prof** Chris
Nugent **Course Designer** J R Stutt **Facilities** ⊗ ℍ ⑂ ♥ ♀
♨ 🗡 🕊 ⏍ ⚲ **Location** 2m W of Dunfermline on
A994

....

Hotel ★★★ 74% Keavil House Hotel, Crossford,
DUNFERMLINE ☎ 01383 736258 47 en suite

Pitreavie Queensferry Rd KY11 8PR
☎ 01383 722591 📄 01383 722591
**Picturesque woodland course with panoramic view of
the River Forth Valley. Testing golf.**
18 holes, 6086yds, Par 70, SSS 69, Course record 64.
Club membership 700.
Visitors welcome except for competition days. **Societies**
must write or telephone in advance. **Green Fees** not
confirmed. **Prof** Paul Brookes **Course Designer** Dr
Alaistair McKenzie **Facilities** ⊗ ℍ ⑂ ♥ ♀ ♨ 🗡 ⚲
Conf Corporate Hospitality Days available **Location** SE
side of town on A823

....

Hotel ★★★ 65% King Malcolm, Queensferry Rd,
DUNFERMLINE ☎ 01383 722611 48 en suite

ELIE   Map 12 NO40

Golf House Club KY9 1AS
☎ 01333 330301 📄 01333 330895
e-mail: sandy@golfhouseclub.freeserve.co.uk
**One of Scotland's most delightful holiday courses with
panoramic views over the Firth of Forth. Some of the
holes out towards the rocky coastline are**

Continued

splendid. This is the course which has produced many good professionals, including the immortal James Braid.
18 holes, 6273yds, Par 70, SSS 70, Course record 62. Club membership 600.
Visitors advisable to contact in advance, limited availability Sat May-Sep and no visitors Sun May-Sep, ballot in operation for tee times during July and August. **Societies** must contact in advance. **Green Fees** £55 per day; £40 per round (£65/£50 weekends). **Cards** 🖃 ▦ 🖃.
▨ **Prof** Robin Wilson **Course Designer** James Braid **Facilities** ⊗ ⅢⅡ ⓛⓛ ⯑ ♀ ⚐ 🖝 📙 ✎ ⚑ **Leisure** hard tennis courts. **Location** W side of village off A917

Hotel ★★ 74% The Inn at Lathones, Largoward, ST ANDREWS ☎ 01334 840494 14 annexe en suite

FALKLAND   Map 11 NO20

Falkland The Myre KY15 7AA ☎ 01337 857404
A flat, well kept course with excellent greens and views of East Lomond Hill and Falkland Palace.
9 holes, 4988yds, Par 67, SSS 65, Course record 62.
Visitors parties must make prior arrangements, please check availability at weekends. **Societies** must contact in advance. **Green Fees** £10 per round/£15 per day/£40 for Mon to Fri ticket (weekend £15). **Facilities** ⊗ by prior arrangement ⓛⓛ ⯑ ♀ 🖝 **Location** N side of town on A912

Hotel ★★ 67% Lomond Hills Hotel, Parliament Square, FREUCHIE ☎ 01337 857329 & 857498 📄 01337 858180 24 en suite

GLENROTHES   Map 11 NO20

Glenrothes Golf Course Rd KY6 2LA
☎ 01592 754561
18 holes, 6444yds, Par 71, SSS 71, Course record 67.
Course Designer J R Stutt **Location** W side of town off B921
Telephone for further details

Hotel ★★★★ 🏌️ Balbirnie House, Balbirnie Park, MARKINCH ☎ 01592 610066 30 en suite

KINCARDINE   Map 11 NS98

Tulliallan Alloa Rd FK10 4BB
☎ 01259 730798 📄 01259 733950
e-mail: enquires@tulliallangc.f9.co.uk
Pleasant parkland course with scenic views of the Ochil hills and the river Forth. A burn meanders throughout the course which, combined with maturing trees, make this a challenging test o golf. There are a number of slopes which are easily negotiable.
18 holes, 5965yds, Par 69, SSS 69, Course record 63. Club membership 700.
Visitors restricted at weekends, must contact professional shop. **Societies** must contact in advance. **Green Fees** £32 per day, £18 per round (£42/£24 weekends). **Cards** 🖃 ▦ ▧ 📙 **Prof** Steven Kelly **Facilities** ⊗ ⅢⅡ ⓛⓛ ⯑ ♀ 🖝 🖝 ✎ **Conf** fac available **Location** 1m NW on A977

Hotel ⎔ Travel Inn Falkirk North, Bowtrees Farm, KINCARDINE BRIDGE ☎ 08701 977099 40 en suite

KINGHORN   Map 11 NT28

Kinghorn Macduff Cres KY3 9RE
☎ 01592 890345 & 890978
Municipal course, 300 ft above sea level with views over

Firth of Forth and North Sea. Undulating and quite testing. Facilities shared by Kinghorn Ladies.
18 holes, 5269yds, Par 65, SSS 67, Course record 62. Club membership 190.
Visitors may not play between 7.30am-10.30am & 12pm-3pm Sat. **Societies** must contact in writing. **Green Fees** £13 per round/£20 per day (weekend £17/£25). **Course Designer** Tom Morris **Facilities** ⊗ ⅢⅡ ⯑ ♀ 🖝 **Location** S side of town on A921

Hotel ★★★ 69% Dean Park Hotel, Chapel Level, KIRKCALDY ☎ 01592 261635 34 en suite 12 annexe en suite

KIRKCALDY   Map 11 NT29

Dunnikier Park Dunnikier Way KY1 3LP
☎ 01592 261599 📄 01592 642541
e-mail: raymondjohnston@blueyonder.co.uk
Parkland, rolling fairways, not heavily bunkered, views of Firth of Forth.
18 holes, 6036metres, Par 72, SSS 72, Course record 65. Club membership 700.
Visitors visitors must contact course starter in person. **Societies** apply in writing. **Green Fees** terms on application. **Prof** Gregor Whyte **Course Designer** R Stutt **Facilities** ⊗ ⅢⅡ ⓛⓛ ⯑ ♀ 🖝 🖝 ✎ **Location** 2m N on B981, take Kirkcaldy West turnoff and follow signs for Kirkaldy High School, club next left

Hotel ★★★ 69% Dean Park Hotel, Chapel Level, KIRKCALDY ☎ 01592 261635 34 en suite 12 annexe en suite

Kirkcaldy Balwearie Rd KY2 5LT
☎ 01592 205240 & 203258 (Pro Shop) 📄 01592 205240
e-mail: enquiries@kirkcaldygolfclub.co.uk
Challenging parkland course in rural setting, with beautiful views. A traditional Scottish burn meanders its way by five holes. The club celebrates its centenary in 2004.
18 holes, 6086yds, Par 71, SSS 69, Course record 65. Club membership 822.
Visitors limited play Sat. Advised to contact pro-shop 01592 203258. **Societies** apply in writing/telephone. **Green Fees** £30 per day, £24 per round (weekends £38/£30). **Cards** 🖃 ▦ ▧ 📙 **Prof** Anthony Caira **Course Designer** Tom Morris **Facilities** ⊗ ⅢⅡ ⓛⓛ ⯑ ♀ 🖝 🖝 📙 🠹 🖝 ✎ **Conf** fac available Corporate Hospitality Days available **Location** SW side of town off A910

Hotel ★★★ 69% Dean Park Hotel, Chapel Level, KIRKCALDY ☎ 01592 261635 34 en suite 12 annexe en suite

LADYBANK   Map 11 NO30

Ladybank Annsmuir KY15 7RA
☎ 01337 830814 📄 01337 831505
e-mail: info@ladybankgolf.co.uk
Picturesque parkland/heathland course of championship status set amongst heather, pine trees and silver birch and comprising two loops of nine holes. The drive at the dog-leg 3rd and 9th holes requires extreme care as do the 15th and 16th on the back nine. The greens are compact and approach shots require precision to find the putting surface. Qualifying course for the British Open.
18 holes, 6601yds, Par 71, SSS 72, Course record 63. Club membership 1000.

Continued   *Continued*

Ladybank

Visitors advance booking weekdays, restricted times at weekends. **Societies** must telephone or write in advance. **Green Fees** £55 per day; £45 per round (£50 per round weekends). **Cards** ☰☰ ▨▨ ▩▩ ▩▩ ▨ **Prof** Sandy Smith **Course Designer** Tom Morris **Facilities** ⊗ ⁊Ⅲ ⅃⚑ ▦ ♥ ♀ ♣ ❤ ⁊ ⚑ ⚑ ᷢ ᷰ **Conf** fac available Corporate Hospitality Days available **Location** Take Kirkcaldy Rd for 0.5miles,at A91/A92 intersection.

....

Hotel ★★★ 61% Fernie Castle, Letham, CUPAR ☎ 01337 810381 20 en suite

Leslie Balsillie Laws KY6 3EZ ☎ 01592 620040
9 holes, 4686yds, Par 63, SSS 64, Course record 63.
Course Designer Tom Morris **Location** N side of town off A911
Telephone for further details

....

Hotel ★★ 77% Rescobie House Hotel & Restaurant, 6 Valley Dr, Leslie, GLENROTHES ☎ 01592 749555 10 en suite

Drumoig Hotel & Golf Course Drumoig

KY16 0BE ☎ 01382 541800 ▤ 01382 542211
e-mail: drumoig@sol.co.uk
A developing but challenging young championship course. Set in a parkland environment, the course is links-like in places. Features include Whinstone Quarries and views over to St Andrews and Carnoustie. Water features are demanding, especially on the 9th where the fairway runs between Drumoig's two mini-lochs.
18 holes, 6835yds, Par 72, SSS 73, Course record 68.
Club membership 350.
Visitors advisable to telephone in advance. **Societies** telephone in advance. **Green Fees** winter £17 per day (weekends £22). summer £31 per day (weekends £36).
Cards ☰☰ ▨▨ ▩▩ ▩ ▩▩ ▨ **Facilities** ⊗ ⁊Ⅲ ⅃⚑ ▦ ♥ ♀ ♣ ᷢ ⚑ ᷰ **Leisure** Scottish National Golf Centre in grounds.
Location On the A914 between St Andrews and Dundee

....

Hotel ★★★ ♨♨ Rufflets Country House & Garden Restaurant, Strathkinness Low Rd, ST ANDREWS ☎ 01334 472594 19 en suite 5 annexe en suite

St Michaels KY16 0DX

☎ 01334 839365 ▤ 01334 838789
e-mail: honsec@stmichaelsgolf.co.uk
Parkland course with open views over Fife and Tayside. The undulating course weaves its way through tree plantations. The short par 4 17th, parallel to the railway and over a pond to a stepped green, poses an interesting challenge. *Continued*

18 holes, 5802yds, Par 70, SSS 68, Course record 67.
Club membership 650.
Visitors may not play on Sun before noon. **Societies** must apply in writing, limited weekends. Special deals midweek **Green Fees** terms on application. **Cards** ☰☰ ▨▨ ▩▩ ▨
Facilities ⊗ ⁊Ⅲ by prior arrangement ⅃⚑ ▦ ♥ ♀ ♣ ᷰ
Location NW side of village on A919

....

Hotel ★★ 60% Eden House Hotel, 2 Pitscottie Rd, CUPAR ☎ 01334 652510 9 en suite 2 annexe en suite

Leven Links The Promenade KY8 4HS

☎ 01333 428859 & 421390 ▤ 01333 428859
e-mail: secretary@leven-links.com
Leven has the classic ingredients which make up a golf links in Scotland; undulating fairways with hills and hollows, out of bounds and a 'burn' or stream. A top class championship links course used for British Open final qualifying stages, it has fine views over Largo Bay.

18 holes, 6436yds, Par 71, SSS 70, Course record 62.
Club membership 1000.
Visitors contact in advance. Limited availability Fri pm & Sat, contact for these times no more than 5 days in advance. **Societies** apply in advance. **Green Fees** £42 per day, £32 per round (weekends £55/£37). **Cards** ☰☰ ▨▨ ▩▩ ▩ **Course Designer** Tom Morris **Facilities** ⊗ ⁊Ⅲ ⅃⚑ ▦ ♥ ♀ ♣ ᷢ ᷰ

....

Hotel ★★★ 78% Old Manor Hotel, Leven Rd, LUNDIN LINKS ☎ 01333 320368 24 en suite

Scoonie North Links KY8 4SP
☎ 01333 423437(Starter) & 307007 (Club)
e-mail: manager@scooniegc.fsnet.co.uk
18 holes, 4979mtrs, Par 67, SSS 65, Course record 63.
Telephone for further details

....

Hotel ★★★ 78% Old Manor Hotel, Leven Rd, LUNDIN LINKS ☎ 01333 320368 24 en suite

Lochgelly Cartmore Rd KY5 9PB ☎ 01592 780174
Parkland course with easy walking and often windy.
18 holes, 5491yds, Par 68, SSS 67, Course record 62.
Club membership 650.
Visitors no restrictions, parties must book in advance by writing. **Societies** must apply in writing. **Green Fees** terms on application. **Prof** Martin Goldie **Course Designer** Ian Marchbanks **Facilities** ⊗ ⁊Ⅲ ⅃⚑ ▦ ♥ ♀ ♣ ᷢ ᷰ **Location** W side of town off A910

....

Hotel ★★★ 69% Dean Park Hotel, Chapel Level, KIRKCALDY ☎ 01592 261635 34 en suite 12 annexe en suite

Lochore Meadows Lochore Meadows Country Park,
Crosshill, Lochgelly KY5 8BA
☎ 01592 414300 📠 01592 414345
e-mail: info@lochore-meadows.co.uk
**Lochside course with natural stream running through,
and woodland nearby. Country park offers many
leisure facilities.**
9 holes, 3207yds, Par 72, SSS 71.
Club membership 240.
Visitors no restrictions. **Societies** must contact in advance.
Green Fees £10 per 18 holes (weekends £13). **Facilities** ⊗
📧 🏠 **Leisure** fishing, outdoor education centre,
childrens play park. **Conf** fac available **Location** 2m N off
B920

Hotel ★★★ 75% Green Hotel, 2 The Muirs, KINROSS
☎ 01577 863467 46 en suite

LUNDIN LINKS Map 12 NO40

Lundin Golf Rd KY8 6BA
☎ 01333 320202 📠 01333 329743
e-mail: secretary@lundingolfclub.co.uk
**The Leven Links and the course of the Lundin Club
adjoin each other. The course is part seaside and part
inland. The holes are excellent but those which can be
described as seaside holes have a very different nature
from the inland style ones. The par 3 14th looks
seawards across the Firth of Forth towards Edinburgh
and the old railway line defines out of bounds at several
holes. A number of burns snake across the fairways.**
18 holes, 6371yds, Par 71, SSS 71, Course record 63.
Club membership 850.
Visitors visitors welcome weekdays 9-3.30 (3pm Fridays)
and Sat after 2.30pm, limited times on Sun. Book well in
advance. **Societies** book well in advance by telephoning
Secretary (mornings). **Green Fees** £50 per day; £40 per
round. (£50 per round weekends). **Cards** 💳 💳 📧 **Prof**
David Webster **Course Designer** James Braid **Facilities** ⊗
📧 🏠 **Location** W side of village off A915

Hotel ★★★ 78% Old Manor Hotel, Leven Rd, LUNDIN
LINKS ☎ 01333 320368 24 en suite

Lundin Ladies Woodielea Rd KY8 6AR
☎ 01333 320832
e-mail: secretary@lundinladies.co.uk
**Short, lowland course with Bronze Age standing stones
on the second fairway, and coastal views.**
9 holes, 2365yds, Par 68, SSS 67, Course record 64.
Club membership 400.
Visitors contact in advance. Competition days Wed and
some weekends. **Societies** telephone secretary. **Green Fees**
£12.50 per 18 holes, £8 per 9 holes (£15/£10 weekend).
Course Designer James Braid **Facilities** 📧 🏠 ✎
Location W side of village off A915

Hotel ★★★ 78% Old Manor Hotel, Leven Rd, LUNDIN
LINKS ☎ 01333 320368 24 en suite

MARKINCH Map 11 NO20

Balbirnie Park Balbirnie Park KY7 6NR
☎ 01592 612095 & 752006 (tee times)
📠 01592 612383/752006
e-mail: craigfdonnelly@aol.com
**Set in the magnificent Balbirnie Park, a fine example of
the best in traditional parkland design, with natural
contours the inspiration behind the layout.** *Continued*

Balbirnie Park

18 holes, 6214yds, Par 71, SSS 70, Course record 62.
Club membership 900.
Visitors must contact in advance. Numbers restricted
weekends and visitors must play from yellow tees, smart
but casual dress code. **Societies** booking forms sent out on
request by professional. **Green Fees** £29 per round/£40 per
day (weekends £35/£50). **Cards** 💳 💳 📧 **Prof** Craig
Donnelly **Course Designer** Fraser Middleton **Facilities** ⊗
📧 🏠 ✎ **Conf** fac available
Location 2m E of Glenrothes, off A92

Hotel ★★★★ ♨ Balbirnie House, Balbirnie Park,
MARKINCH ☎ 01592 610066 30 en suite

ST ANDREWS See also page 337 Map 12 NO51

British Golf Museum
☎ 01334 460046 (situated opposite Royal & Ancient
Golf Club)
The museum which tells the history of golf from its origins
to the present day, is of interest to golfers and non-golfers
alike. Themed galleries and interactive displays explore the
history of the major championships and the lives of the
famous players, and trace the development of golfing
equipment. An audio-visual theatre shows historic golfing
moments. **Open:** Etr-mid Oct, daily 9.30am-5.30pm (mid
Oct-Etr Thu-Mon 11am-3pm, closed Tue & Wed.
Admission: There is a charge. ☎ for details.

Dukes Course Craigtoun KY16 8NS
☎ 01334 474371 📠 01334 479456
e-mail: reservations@oldcoursehotel.co.uk
**Blending the characteristics of a links course with an
inland course, Dukes offers rolling fairways,
undulating greens and a testing woodland section, and
magnificent views over St Andrews Bay towards
Carnoustie.**
18 holes, 6749yds, Par 72, SSS 73, Course record 67.
Club membership 500. *Continued*

St Andrews Links Trust

Map 12 NO51   St Andrews

☎ 01334 466666   📄 01334 479555

G olf was first played here around 1400 and the Old Course is acknowledged worldwide as the home of golf. The Old Course has played host to the greatest golfers in the world and many of golf's most dramatic moments. The New Course (6604 yards) opened in 1895, having been laid out by Old Tom Morris. The Jubilee opened in 1897, and is 6805 yards long from the medal tees. A shorter version of the Jubilee Course is also available, known as the Bronze Course, measuring 5674 yards. There is no handicap limit for the shorter course and it is best for lower/middle handicap golfers. The Eden opened in 1914 and is recommended for middle to high handicap golfers. The Strathyrum has a shorter, less testing layout best for high handicap golfers. The Balgove 9-hole course, upgraded and re-opened in 1993, is best for beginners and children. The extent of facilities and courses here make this the largest golf complex in Europe.

e-mail: linkstrust@standrews.otg.uk

Visitors Must telephone in advance and have handicap certificate for Old Course. Old Course closed Sun. Advance booking two years for Old Course, one month New. 24 hr booking on Jubilee/Eden/Strath. No advance booking Sat

Societies Must book at least a month in advance

Green Fees Old Course £110 ▦ ▬ ▬ 🖳 🖂 ▨

Facilities ⊗ ⅃ ㏑ ♥ ♀ ⚘ 🖙 ▾ 🦅 🐾 🌳 ⚲ ⚲
Corporate hospitality days available on Eden Course

Location Pilmour House, St Andrews KY16 9SF (NW of town, off A91)

Holes/Par/Course record Old Course: 18 holes, 6566 yds, Par 72, SSS 72, Course record 63
New (West Sands Rd): 18 holes, 6604 yds, Par 71, SSS 73
Jubilee (West Sands Rd): 18 holes, 6742 yds, Par 72, SSS 73
Eden (Dundee Rd): 18 holes, 6112 yds, Par 70, SSS 70
Strathyrum: 18 holes, 5094 yds, Par 69, SSS 69

WHERE TO STAY AND EAT NEARBY

Hotels

ST ANDREWS

★★★★★ ◉ ◉ Old Course Hotel Golf Resort and Spa, KY16 9SP.
☎ 01334 474371. 134 en suite

★★★★ ◉ ◉ 74% Rusacks Hotel, KY16 9JQ.
☎ 0870 4008128.
68 en suite

★★★ ◉ ◉ ♣♣ Rufflets Country House & Garden Restaurant, KY16 9TX
☎ 01334 472594.
24 en suite

★★★ ◉ ◉ St Andrews Golf Hotel,
KY16 9AS. ☎ 01334 472611.
21 en suite

★★★ 66% Scores, KY16 9BB
☎ 01334 472451. 30 en suite

Restaurant

CUPAR

◉ ◉ Ostlers Close, KY15 4BU.
☎ 01334 655574

Championship Course

Visitors booking should be in advance to avoid disappointment through the hotel resort reservations team.

Dukes Course

Societies apply in writing or fax in advance. **Green Fees** £75. **Cards** 🌐 💳 💳 🅿️ 💳 🔲 **Prof** Ron Walker **Course Designer** Peter Thomson **Facilities** ⊗ ⦚ ⅃ 🍺 ♚ ♀ 🅰️ 🏠 ⅂ 🍴 🏌️ 🛒 ♂️ ⅃ **Leisure** heated indoor swimming pool, sauna, solarium, gymnasium, computer swing analyses. **Conf** fac available **Location** Follow M90 from Edinburgh onto A91 to Cupar then to St Andrew turning off for Strathkiness

Hotel ★★★★★ The Old Course Hotel, Golf Resort & Spa, ST ANDREWS ☎ 01334 474371 134 en suite

SALINE   Map 11 NT09

Saline Kinneddar Hill KY12 9LT ☎ 01383 852591 e-mail: saline-golf-club@supanet.com **Hillside parkland course with excellent turf and panoramic view of the Forth Valley.** *9 holes, 5302yds, Par 68, SSS 66, Course record 62. Club membership 330.* **Visitors** advisable to contact in advance and may not play Sat, some restrictions Sun. **Societies** contact in advance. **Green Fees** terms on application. **Facilities** ⊗ ⦚ ⅃ 🍺 ♀ 🅰️ ⅃ **Location** Junct 4 of M90, 0.5m E at junct B913/914

Hotel ★★★ 65% King Malcolm, Queensferry Rd, DUNFERMLINE ☎ 01383 722611 48 en suite

TAYPORT   Map 12 NO42

Scotscraig Golf Rd DD6 9DZ ☎ 01382 552515 📠 01382 553130 e-mail: scotscraig@scottishgolf.com **An Open qualifying links course with more trees in evidence than most, giving a heathland feel.** *18 holes, 6550yds, Par 71, SSS 72, Course record 62. Club membership 950.* **Visitors** restricted at weekends **Societies** advance booking. **Green Fees** £54 per day, £44 per round (weekends £60/£50). **Cards** 🌐 💳 🔲 **Prof** John Kelly **Course Designer** James Braid **Facilities** ⊗ ⦚ ⅃ 🍺 ♀ 🅰️ 🏠 🍴 🏌️ 🛒 ♂️ **Conf** Corporate Hospitality Days available **Location** S side of village off B945

Hotel ★★★ 68% Sandford Country House Hotel, Newton Hill, Wormit, DUNDEE ☎ 01382 541802 16 en suite

THORNTON   Map 11 NT29

Thornton Station Rd KY1 4DW ☎ 01592 771111 📠 01592 774955 e-mail: johntgc@ic24.net

Continued

A relatively flat, lightly tree-lined, parkland course bounded on three sides by a river which comes into play at holes 14-16. *18 holes, 6170yds, Par 70, SSS 69, Course record 61. Club membership 700.* **Visitors** restricted at weekends before 10am & between 12.30-2pm, also Tue 1-1.30 & Thu 9-10. Booking in advance recommended. **Societies** apply in advance. **Green Fees** £30 per day; £20 per round (£40/£30 weekends). **Facilities** ⊗ ⦚ ⅃ 🍺 ♀ 🅰️ 🛒 ♂️ ⅃ **Location** 1m E of town off A92

Hotel ★★★★ 🍴 Balbirnie House, Balbirnie Park, MARKINCH ☎ 01592 610066 30 en suite

HIGHLAND

ALNESS   Map 14 NH66

Alness Ardross Rd IV17 0QA ☎ 01349 883877 e-mail: info@alness-golfclub.co.uk **A testing, parkland course with beautiful views over the Cromarty Firth and the Black Isle. It is located on the north west edge of the village of Alness and four holes run parallel to the gorge of the River Averon. Golfers of all abilities will find the course interesting and challenging. A particular test of skill is required at the 14th hole where the tee is located far above the green which lies beside the gorge at a distance of 406 yards.** *18 holes, 4886yds, Par 67, SSS 64, Course record 62. Club membership 300.* **Visitors** telephone in advance for weekend play, parties must telephone for booking **Societies** must contact in advance. **Green Fees** terms on application. **Cards** 🌐 💳 🔲 **Prof** Gary Lister **Facilities** ⊗ ⦚ ⅃ 🍺 ♀ 🅰️ 🏠 🍴 ⅃ **Leisure** fishing. **Conf** fac available Corporate Hospitality Days available **Location** 0.5m N off A9

Hotel ★★★ 74% Morangie House Hotel, Morangie Rd, TAIN ☎ 01862 892281 26 en suite

ARISAIG   Map 13 NM68

Traigh Traigh PH39 4NT ☎ 01687 450337 📠 01678 450293 **According to at least one newspaper Traigh is 'probably the most beautifully sited nine-hole golf course in the world'. Whether that is true or not, Traigh lies by the sea alongside sandy beaches with views to Skye and the Inner Hebrides. The feature of the course is a line of grassy hills, originally sand dunes, that rise to some 60 feet, and provide a challenge to the keenest golfer.** *9 holes, 2456yds, Par 68, SSS 65, Course record 67. Club membership 150.* **Visitors** no restrictions. **Societies** contact in advance. **Green Fees** terms on application. **Course Designer** John Salvesen 1994 **Facilities** 🍺 🏠 🍴 ⅃ **Location** Take the A830 to Arisaig, turn off where signposted on to the B8008, 2 Miles N of Arisaig

Hotel ★★ 72% Arisaig Hotel, ARISAIG ☎ 01687 450210 13 en suite

BOAT OF GARTEN   Map 14 NH91

Boat of Garten PH24 3BQ ☎ 01479 831282 📠 01479 831523 e-mail: boatgolf@enterprise.net **This heathland course was cut out from a silver birch forest though the fairways are adequately**

Continued

wide. There are natural hazards of broom and heather, good views and walking is easy. A round provides great variety.
18 holes, 5876yds, Par 70, SSS 69, Course record 67.
Club membership 650.
Visitors must contact in advance. Handicap certificate required. Play restricted to 10am-4pm weekends & 9.20am-7pm weekdays **Societies** must telephone or emial in advance. **Green Fees** £34 per day; £29 per round (£39/£34 weekends). **Cards** 🌐 💳 📶 🔲 **Course Designer** James Braid **Facilities** ⊗ ⵑ ⵈ 🍺 🍴 ⛾ 🏌 ⛳ 🏴󠁿 ⛳ **Leisure** hard tennis courts. **Conf** Corporate Hospitality Days available **Location** E side of village

Hotel ★★★ 72%   Boat Hotel, BOAT OF GARTEN
☎ 01479 831258 30 en suite

BONAR BRIDGE   Map 14 NH69

Bonar Bridge-Ardgay Migdale Rd IV24 3EJ
☎ 01863 766750 (Sec) & 766199 (Clubhouse)
e-mail: bonarardgaygolf@aol.com
Wooded moorland course with picturesque views of hills and loch.
9 holes, 5162yds, Par 68, SSS 65.
Club membership 250.
Visitors no restrictions. **Societies** apply in writing. **Green Fees** £14 per day. **Course Designer** Various **Facilities** ⵈ 🍺 ⛾ 🏴󠁿 ⛳ **Location** 0.5m E

Guesthouse ♦♦♦ Kyle House, Dornoch Rd, BONAR BRIDGE ☎ 01863 766360 6 rms (3 en suite)

BRORA   Map 14 NC90

Brora Golf Rd KW9 6QS
☎ 01408 621417 📠 01408 622157
e-mail: secretary@broragolf.co.uk
Typical seaside links with little rough and fine views. Some testing holes including the 17th Tarbatness, so called because of the lighthouse which gives the line; the elevated tee is one of the best driving holes in Scotland.
18 holes, 6110yds, Par 69, SSS 69, Course record 61.
Club membership 704.
Visitors advisable to book in advance May-Oct. **Societies** advisable to book in advance. **Green Fees** £28 per round/£35 per day (weekend £33/£40). **Cards** 🌐 💳 **Course Designer** James Braid **Facilities** ⊗ ⵑ ⵈ 🍺 🍴 ⛾ 🏴󠁿 🏌 ⛳ **Location** E side of village. Follow signs to Beach Car Park

Hotel ★★★ 72%   Royal Marine Hotel, Golf Rd, BRORA
☎ 01408 621252 22 en suite

CARRBRIDGE   Map 14 NH92

Carrbridge Inverness Rd PH23 3AU
☎ 01479 841623
e-mail: enquiries@carrbridgegolf
Challenging part-parkland, part-moorland course with magnificent views of the Cairngorms.
9 holes, 5402yds, Par 71, SSS 68, Course record 64.
Club membership 550.
Visitors during May-Sep, course not open most Sunday mornings. **Societies** small parties welcome, apply in writing. **Green Fees** £16 per day; £18 weekends. **Facilities** ⊗ 🍺 ⛾ 🏴󠁿 ⛳ **Location** N side of village

Hotel ★★★ 68%   Dalrachney Lodge Hotel, CARRBRIDGE ☎ 01479 841252 11 en suite

---

DORNOCH   Map 14 NH78

The Carnegie Club Skibo Castle IV25 3RQ
☎ 01862 894600 📠 01862 894601
e-mail: skibo@carnegieclubs.com
18 holes, 6403yds, Par 71, SSS 71.
Course Designer J Sutherland/Donald Steel **Location** Off A9 3m before Dornoch
Telephone for further details

Hotel ★★ 67%   Burghfield House Hotel, DORNOCH
☎ 01862 810212 13 en suite   15 annexe en suite

Royal Dornoch Golf Rd IV25 3LW
☎ 01862 810219 ext.185 📠 01862 810792
e-mail: bookings@royaldornoch.com
The Championship course was recently rated 9th amongst Britain's top courses and is a links of rare subtlety. It appears amicable but proves very challenging in play. The 18 hole Struie links course provides, in a gentler style, an enjoyable test of a golfer's accuracy for players of all abilities.

Championship: 18 holes, 6514yds, Par 70, SSS 73.
Struie Course: 18 holes, 6276yds, Par 72, SSS 70.
Club membership 1700.
Visitors Recommended to contact in advance for Championship course **Societies** must apply in advance. **Green Fees** Championship course: £69 per round (£79 weekends). Struie course: £40 per day; £25 per round. **Cards** 🌐 💳 📶 🔲 **Prof** A Skinner **Course Designer** Tom Morris **Facilities** ⊗ ⵑ ⵈ 🍺 🍴 ⛾ 🏴󠁿 🏌 ⛳ **Leisure** hard tennis courts. **Conf** Corporate Hospitality Days available **Location** E side of town.
See advert on page 340

Hotel ★★★ 71%   Royal Golf Hotel, The 1st Tee, DORNOCH ☎ 01862 810283 25 en suite

---

DURNESS   Map 14 NC46

Durness Balnakeil IV27 4PG
☎ 01971 511364 📠 01971 511321
e-mail: lucy@durnessgolfclub.org
A 9-hole course set in tremendous scenery overlooking Balnakeil Bay. Part links and part inland with water hazards. Off alternative tees for second 9 holes giving surprising variety. Tremendous last hole played across the sea to the green over 100 yards away.
9 holes, 5555yds, Par 70, SSS 67, Course record 69.
Club membership 150.
Visitors restricted 10am-12.30 on Sun during Jun-Sep. **Societies** must telephone in advance 01971 511364 (ex Sun). **Green Fees** £15 per day (£10 after 5pm) (£5 with member).

Continued

The Royal Dornoch Golf Club

Golf Road, Dornoch IV25 3LW

Tel: 01862 810219 ext 185   Fax: 01862 81072
Website: www.royaldornoch.com

The **Championship Course** is consistently rated amongst the world's top twenty courses. It is a classic links providing both pleasure to the eye and challenge to one's skills.

Suitable to all abilities, with its own character, the second 18 hole links, **The Struie**, was extended to 6275 yards in 2003.

Course Designer F Keith **Facilities** ⊗ ⬛ 🏊 ⛳ 🛒 **Leisure** fishing. **Conf** Corporate Hospitality Days available **Location** 1m W of village overlooking Balnakeil Bay

Guesthouse ◆◆◆◆ Port-Na-Con House, Loch Eriboll, LAIRG ☎ 01971 511367 3 en suite

FORT AUGUSTUS   Map 14 NH30

Fort Augustus Markethill PH32 4DP

☎ 01320 366660 & 366758
e-mail: alex.barnett@freeuk.com
Moorland course, with narrow fairways and good views. Bordered by the tree-lined Caledonian Canal to the north and heather clad hills to the south.
9 holes, 5379yds, Par 67, SSS 67, Course record 67.
Club membership 170.
Visitors may not play Sat 1.30-4 & occasional Sun.
Societies telephone in advance. **Green Fees** £15 per day; £12 per round. **Course Designer** Colt **Facilities** ⬛ 🍴 ⛳ 🛒 **Location** 1m SW on A82

FORTROSE   Map 14 NH75

Fortrose & Rosemarkie Ness Rd East IV10 8SE

☎ 01381 620529 📠 01381 621328
e-mail: secretary@fortrosegolfclub.co.uk
Seaside links course, set on a peninsula with sea on three sides. Easy walking, good views. Designed by James Braid; the club was formed in 1888.
18 holes, 5883yds, Par 71, SSS 69, Course record 63.
Club membership 770.
Visitors restricted 8.45-10.15am & 1-2.15, 4.45-6.30pm.
Societies must telephone in advance. **Green Fees** £30 per round/£40 per day (weekends £35/£45). **Cards** 💳 💳

Continued

Course Designer James Braid **Facilities** ⊗ ⬛ 🍴 🍷 🏊 🛒 **Location** N on A9 over Kessock Bridge, follow signs to Munlochy and Fortrose

Fortrose & Rosemarkie

Hotel ★★★★ 71% Inverness Marriott Hotel, Culcabock Rd, INVERNESS ☎ 01463 237166 76 en suite 6 annexe en suite

FORT WILLIAM   Map 14 NN17

Fort William Torlundy PH33 6SN ☎ 01397 704464

Spectacular moorland location looking onto the cliffs of Ben Nevis. Tees and greens are in excellent condition following major drainage improvements to the fairways.
18 holes, 6217yds, Par 72, SSS 71, Course record 67.
Club membership 420.
Visitors no restrictions. **Societies** must contact in writing.
Green Fees £22 per round. **Cards** 💳 💳 💳 💳 💳
Course Designer Hamilton Stutt **Facilities** ⬛ 🍴 🍷 🏊 🛒 **Location** 3m NE on A82

Hotel ★★★ 75% Moorings Hotel, Banavie, FORT WILLIAM ☎ 01397 772797 28 en suite

GAIRLOCH   Map 14 NG87

Gairloch IV21 2BE

☎ 01445 712407 📠 01445 712865
e-mail: secretary@gairlochgc.freeserve.co.uk
Fine seaside links course running along Gairloch Sands with good views over the sea to Skye. In windy conditions each hole is affected. The par 5 eighth hole is described by one of Scotland's teaching professionals as one of the best natural par 5s in the country.
9 holes, 4514yds, Par 63, SSS 64, Course record 64.
Club membership 275.
Visitors must be competent golfer and member of a recognised club. **Societies** apply in writing to secretary. **Green Fees** terms on application. **Cards** 💳 **Course Designer** Capt Burgess **Facilities** ⊗ ⬛ 🍴 🍷 🏊 🛒 🛒 **Conf** Corporate Hospitality Days available **Location** 1m S on A832

Continued

Hotel ★★ 69% Myrtle Bank, Low Rd, GAIRLOCH
☎ 01445 712004 12 en suite

GOLSPIE
Map 14 NH89

Golspie Ferry Rd KW10 6ST
☎ 01408 633266 ▤ 01408 633393
e-mail: info@golspie-golf-club.co.uk
Founded in 1889, Golspie's seaside course offers easy walking and natural hazards including beach heather and whins. Spectacular scenery.
18 holes, 5980yds, Par 68, SSS 68, Course record 64.
Club membership 300.
Visitors contact in advance. Visitors welcome 7 days a week. **Societies** contact in advance. **Green Fees** £35 per day, £25 per round. **Cards** ▨▨ ▨▨ ▨ **Course Designer** James Braid **Facilities** ⊗ ⅲ ▮ ♥ ♀ ♨ ▥ ⚑ ⚬ **Location** 0.5m S off A9

Hotel ★★★ 72% Royal Marine Hotel, Golf Rd, BRORA
☎ 01408 621252 22 en suite

GRANTOWN-ON-SPEY
Map 14 NJ02

Grantown-on-Spey Golf Course Rd PH26 3HY
☎ 01479 872079 ▤ 01479 873725
e-mail: secretary@grantownonspeygolfclub.co.uk
Parkland and woodland course. Part easy walking, remainder hilly. The 7th to 13th holes really sort out the golfers.

18 holes, 5710yds, Par 70, SSS 68, Course record 60.
Club membership 800.
Visitors advisable to contact in advance. No visitors before 10am weekends. **Societies** clubhouse open Apr-Oct, apply in advance to secretary. **Green Fees** terms on application.
Cards ▨▨ ▨▨ ▨ ▨▨ ▨ **Course Designer** A Brown/W Park/J Braid **Facilities** ⊗ ⅲ by prior arrangement ▮ ♥ ♀ ♨ ▥ ⚑ ⚬ **Location** NE side of town centre

Hotel ★★ 77% Culdearn House, Woodlands Ter, GRANTOWN ON SPEY ☎ 01479 872106 7 en suite

HELMSDALE
Map 14 ND01

Helmsdale Golf Rd KW8 6JA ☎ 01431 821063
Sheltered, undulating course following the line of the Helmsdale River.
9 holes, 1860yds, Par 62, SSS 61.
Club membership 58.
Visitors no restrictions. **Societies** apply in writing or telephone in advance. **Green Fees** £10 per 18 holes.
Facilities ♨ **Location** NW side of town on A896

Hotel ★★★ 72% Royal Marine Hotel, Golf Rd, BRORA
☎ 01408 621252 22 en suite

INVERGORDON
Map 14 NH76

Invergordon King George St IV18 0BD
☎ 01349 852715 ▤ 01349 852715
e-mail: info@invergordongolf.com
Fairly easy but windy 18-hole parkland course, with woodland, wide fairways and good views over Cromarty Firth. Very good greens and a fair challenge, especially if the wind is from the west.
18 holes, 6030yds, Par 69, SSS 69, Course record 65.
Club membership 240.
Visitors visitors advised to avoid Tue & Thu 4.30-6, Mon & Wed 5-6 and Sat 8.30-10 & 1-2pm. **Societies** must contact in advance, call 01349 852715. **Green Fees** not confirmed. **Cards** ▨▨ ▨▨ ▨ **Course Designer** A Rae **Facilities** ▮ ♥ ♀ ♨ ⚑ ⚬ **Location** W side of town centre on B817

Hotel ★★★ 74% Morangie House Hotel, Morangie Rd, TAIN ☎ 01862 892281 26 en suite

INVERNESS
Map 14 NH64

Inverness Culcabock IV2 3XQ
☎ 01463 239882 ▤ 01463 239882
e-mail: igc@freeuk.com
Fairly flat parkland course with a burn running through and alongside several of the holes, and also acting as a lateral water hazard and out of bounds at several. Considered short by modern day standards, it is an excellent test of golf rewarding straight drives and accurate iron play to well manicured greens.
18 holes, 6256yds, Par 69, SSS 70, Course record 64.
Club membership 1100.
Visitors prior booking and handicap certificate required. Limited play Sat. Dress code in lounge/dining room. **Societies** must telephone in advance. **Green Fees** £42 per day, £33 per round (£7.50 with member). **Cards** ▨▨ ▨▨ ▨▨ ▨▨ ▨ **Prof** Alistair P Thomson **Course Designer** J Fraser/G Smith **Facilities** ⊗ ⅲ ▮ ♥ ♀ ♨ ⚑ ⚬ **Location** 1 mile from town centre on Culcabock road.

Hotel ★★★★ 71% Inverness Marriott Hotel, Culcabock Rd, INVERNESS ☎ 01463 237166 76 en suite
6 annexe en suite

Loch Ness Fairways Leisure, Castle Heather IV2 6AA
☎ 01463 713335 ▤ 01463 712695
e-mail: info@golflochness.com
Challenging parkland course with superb views over Inverness, the Beauly Firth and the Black Isle. Built on a gentle slope but none of the holes play uphill. With a base of mature farmland, this lush and green course rewards straight and long hitters but its tricky approach play can challenge even those with a skilful short game.
18 holes, 6772yds, Par 73, SSS 72, Course record 67.
Club membership 500.
Visitors no restrictions **Societies** telephone for details. **Green Fees** £25 per day (£30 weekends). **Cards** ▨▨ ▨▨ ▨▨ ▨ **Prof** Martin Piggot **Course Designer** Caddies **Facilities** ⊗ ⅲ ▮ ♥ ♀ ♨ ⚑ ⚑ ⚬ ▥ ⚬ ♦ **Leisure** solarium, indoor bowls,target archery. **Conf** fac available Corporate Hospitality Days available **Location** SW outskirts of Inverness, along new bypass

Hotel ★★★ 63% Loch Ness House Hotel, Glenurquhart Rd, INVERNESS ☎ 01463 231248 21 en suite

Torvean Glenurquhart Rd IV3 8JN
☎ 01463 711434 (Starter) & 225651 (Office)
🖥 01463 711417
e-mail: info@torveangolfclub.com
**Municipal parkland course, easy walking, good views.
Boasts one of the longest par 5s in the North at 565
yards. Three ponds come into play at the 8th, 15th and
17th holes.**
18 holes, 5784yds, Par 69, SSS 68, Course record 64.
Club membership 800.
Visitors Advance booking advisable especially at
weekends. **Societies** advance bookings through starter.
Green Fees £20 per 18 holes (£25 weekends). **Cards** ⊞
▭ 🖸 **Course Designer** Hamilton **Facilities** ⊗ ⊪ ⬚ 🖳 ⛾
⚐ 🖰 ⅌ ∅ **Location** 1.5m SW on A82

Hotel ★★★ 63% Loch Ness House Hotel, Glenurquhart
Rd, INVERNESS ☎ 01463 231248 21 en suite

Kingussie Gynack Rd PH21 1LR
☎ 01540 661600 🖥 01540 662066
e-mail: kinggolf@globalnet.co.uk
**Upland course with natural hazards and magnificent
views. Stands about 1000ft above sea level at its highest
point, and the River Gynack, which runs through the
course, comes into play on five holes.**
18 holes, 5500yds, Par 67, SSS 68, Course record 61.
Club membership 800.
Visitors advisable to book in advance. **Societies** must
contact in advance. **Green Fees** £22 per round/£27 per day
(weekends £24/£30). **Course Designer** Vardon/Herd
Facilities ⬚ 🖳 ⛾ ⚐ 🖰 ⅌ 🖰 ∅ **Location** 0.25m N off
A86

Hotel 🏠 The Cross, Tweed Mill Brae, Ardbroilach Rd,
KINGUSSIE ☎ 01540 661166 8 en suite

Lochcarron IV54 8YU ☎ 01520 766211
**Seaside links course with some parkland with an
interesting 1st hole. A short course but great accuracy
is required.**
9 holes, 3575yds, Par 60, SSS 60, Course record 58.
Club membership 130.
Societies welcome but restricted Sat 2-5pm. **Green Fees**
£12 per day/ £50 per week. **Facilities** 🖳 ⚐ ⅌ **Location**
By A896,1 mile E of Lochcarron village

Lybster Main St KW3 6AE ☎ 01593 721308
9 holes, 1896yds, Par 62, SSS 61, Course record 59.
Location E side of village
Telephone for further details

Hotel ★★ 69% Mackay's Hotel, Union St, WICK
☎ 01955 602323 27 rms (19 en suite)

Muir of Ord Great North Rd IV6 7SX
☎ 01463 870825 🖥 01463 871867
e-mail: muirgolf@supanet.com-email
**Old established (1875) heathland course with tight
fairways and easy walking. Testing par 3 13th, 'Castle
Hill'.**

Muir of Ord
18 holes, 5596yds, Par 68, SSS 68, Course record 61.
Club membership 730.
Visitors may not play during competitions. Booking
required for weekends. **Societies** write to or phone
Secretary **Green Fees** £16 per round/£20 per day (weekends
£20/£25). **Course Designer** James Braid **Facilities** ⊗ by
prior arrangement ⊪ by prior arrangement ⬚ 🖳 ⛾ ⚐ 🖰
🖐 🖰 ∅ **Location** S side of village on A862

Hotel ★★★ 72% Priory Hotel, The Square, BEAULY
☎ 01463 782309 34 en suite

Nairn Seabank Rd IV12 4HB
☎ 01667 453208 🖥 01667 456328
e-mail: secretary@nairngolfclub.co.uk
18 holes, 6430yds, Par 71, SSS 73, Course record 64.
Newton: 9 holes, 3542yds, Par 58, SSS 57.
Course Designer A Simpson/Old Tom Morris/James Braid
Location 16m E of Inverness on A96
Telephone for further details

Hotel ★★★★ 71% Golf View Hotel & Leisure Club, The
Seafront, NAIRN ☎ 01667 452301 42 en suite

Nairn Dunbar Lochloy Rd IV12 5AE
☎ 01667 452741 🖥 01667 456897
e-mail: secretary@nairndunbar.com
**Links course with sea views and testing gorse and whin-
lined fairways. Testing hole: 'Long Peter' (527 yards).**
18 holes, 6765yds, Par 72, SSS 73, Course record 64.
Club membership 1200.
Visitors Weekends restricted, contact in advance through
Secretary's office. **Societies** must contact in advance.
Green Fees not confirmed. **Cards** ⊞ ▭ 🖸 **Prof** David
Torrance **Facilities** ⊗ ⊪ ⬚ 🖳 ⛾ ⚐ 🖰 ⅌ 🖐 🖰 ∅ **Conf**
fac available Corporate Hospitality Days available
Location E side of town off A96

Hotel ★★ 64% Alton Burn Hotel, Alton Burn Rd,
NAIRN ☎ 01667 452051 & 453325 🖥 01667 456697
23 en suite

Abernethy PH25 3EB
☎ 01479 821305 🖥 01479 821 305
e-mail: info@abernethygolfclub.com
**Traditional Highland course built on natural moorland
surrounded by pine trees and offering a great variety of
shot making for the low handicapped or casual visitor.
The 2nd hole, although very short is played across
bogland and a B class road to a two-tiered green. The**

Continued   *Continued*

small and fast greens are the most undulating and tricky in the valley. The Abernethy forest lies on the boundary and from many parts of the course there are splendid views of Strathspey.

9 holes, 2551yds, Par 66, SSS 66.
Club membership 480.
Visitors contact in advance. **Societies** must contact in advance. **Green Fees** terms on application. **Facilities** ⊗ 🏌
💺 ⛳ ⛳ *✓* **Location** N side of village on B970

Hotel ★★★ 71% Muckrach Lodge Hotel, Dulnain Bridge, GRANTOWN-ON-SPEY ☎ 01479 851257
9 en suite 4 annexe en suite

NEWTONMORE　　　　　Map 14 NN79

Newtonmore Golf Course Rd PH20 1AT
☎ 01540 673878 📠 01540 670147
e-mail: secretary@newtonmoregolf.com
Inland course beside the River Spey. Beautiful views and easy walking. Testing 17th hole (par 3).
18 holes, 6031yds, Par 70, SSS 69, Course record 64.
Club membership 420.
Visitors contact in advance. **Societies** apply in writing or by telephone to secretary. **Green Fees** terms on application. **Prof** Robert Henderson **Facilities** ⊗ ⫿ 🏌 💺
⛳ ⛳ ⛳ *✓* **Location** E side of town off A9

Hotel ★★ 71% The Scot House Hotel, Newtonmore Rd, KINGUSSIE ☎ 01540 661351 9 en suite

REAY　　　　　　　　　Map 14 NC96

Reay KW14 7RE ☎ 01847 811288 📠 01847 894189
e-mail: info@reaygolfclub.co.uk
Picturesque seaside links with natural hazards, following the contours of Sandside Bay. Most northerly 18-hole links on the British mainland. The 581-yard par 5 4th hole 'Sahara' requires a solid tee shot and fairway wood to set up an approach to a sheltered green protected by a burn. The 196-yard par 3 7th 'Pilkington' is a beautiful short hole played across Reay burn to a raised green. The two-tiered 18th protected by its greenside bunkers provides a formidable finishing hole. Unique feature in that it opens and closes with a par 3 and the sea is visible from every hole. An excellent natural seaside links.
18 holes, 5831yds, Par 69, SSS 69, Course record 64.
Club membership 350.
Visitors restricted competition days **Societies** apply to the secretary in advance. **Green Fees** £20 per day/round.
Course Designer Braid **Facilities** ⊗ by prior arrangement ⫿ by prior arrangement 🏌 by prior arrangement 💺 ⛳ ⛳
⛳ ⛳ *✓* **Leisure** see web site. **Location** 11m W of Thurso on A836

Hotel ★★★ 60% Royal Hotel, Traill St, THURSO
☎ 01847 893191 102 en suite

STRATHPEFFER　　　　　Map 14 NH45

Strathpeffer Spa IV14 9AS
☎ 01997 421219 & 421011 📠 01997 421011
e-mail: mail@strathpeffergolf.co.uk
Beautiful, testing upland course in this historic village. Many natural hazards mean only three sand bunkers on the course and the course's claim to fame is the 1st hole which features the longest drop from tee to green in Scotland. Stunning views.
18 holes, 4792yds, Par 65, SSS 64, Course record 60.

Club membership 400.
Visitors advisable to contact in advance. **Societies** apply in writing. **Green Fees** £23 per day; £18 per round. **Cards** 💳 💳 💳 💳 **Course Designer** Willie Park/Tom Morris
Facilities 🏌 💺 🍴 ⛳ ⛳ ⛳ ⛳ *✓* **Location** 5m W of Dingwall, 0.25m N of village off A834, signposted

Hotel ★★ 74% Achilty Hotel, CONTIN
☎ 01997 421355 9 en suite 2 annexe en suite

TAIN　　　　　　　　　Map 14 NH78

Tain Chapel Rd IV19 1JE
☎ 01862 892314 📠 01862 892099
e-mail: info@tain-golfclub.co.uk
Heathland/links course with river affecting three holes; easy walking, fine views.

18 holes, 6404yds, Par 70, SSS 71, Course record 68.
Club membership 500.
Visitors weekends after 11.30am. **Societies** must book in advance. **Green Fees** £40 per day. £35 per round before noon, £30 after noon (£50 per day/£40 per round weekends). **Cards** 💳 💳 💳 💳 **Course Designer** Tom Morris **Facilities** ⊗ ⫿ 🏌 💺 ⛳ ⛳ ⛳ ⛳ *✓*
Location E side of town centre off B9174

Hotel ★★★ 74% Morangie House Hotel, Morangie Rd, TAIN ☎ 01862 892281 26 en suite

THURSO　　　　　　　　Map 15 ND16

Thurso Newlands of Geise KW14 7XD
☎ 01847 893807
18 holes, 5853yds, Par 69, SSS 69, Course record 63.
Course Designer W S Stewart **Location** 2m SW of Thurso on B874
Telephone for further details

Hotel ★★★ 60% Royal Hotel, Traill St, THURSO
☎ 01847 893191 102 en suite

WICK　　　　　　　　　Map 15 ND35

Wick Reiss KW1 4RW ☎ 01955 602726
e-mail: wickgolfclub@hotmail.com
Typical seaside links course, fairly flat, easy walking. 9 holes straight out and straight back. Normally breezy.
18 holes, 6123yds, Par 69, SSS 71, Course record 63.
Club membership 352.
Visitors no restrictions. **Societies** apply in writing or telephone in advance. **Green Fees** £20 per day. **Course Designer** James Braid **Facilities** 🏌 💺 ⛳ ⛳ ⛳ *✓*
Location 3.5m N off A9

Hotel ★★ 69% Mackay's Hotel, Union St, WICK
☎ 01955 602323 27 rms (19 en suite)

Continued

INVERCLYDE

GOUROCK   Map 10 NS27

Gourock Cowal View PA19 1HD
☎ 01475 631001 & 636834 (pro) 🖥 01475 638307
e-mail: adt@gourockgolfclub.freeserve.co.uk
18 holes, 6408yds, Par 73, SSS 72, Course record 64.
Course Designer J Braid/H Cotton **Location** SW side of
town off A770
Telephone for further details
....

Hotel ⇧ Express by Holiday Inn Greenock, Cartsburn,
GREENOCK ☎ 01475 786666 71 en suite

GREENOCK   Map 10 NS27

Greenock Forsyth St PA16 8RE
☎ 01475 720793 🖥 01475 791912
**Testing moorland course with panoramic views of
Clyde Estuary.**
18 holes, 5838yds, Par 69, SSS 69.
Club membership 700.
Visitors may not play Sat. Must contact in advance and
have a handicap certificate. **Societies** must telephone in
advance. **Green Fees** not confirmed. **Course Designer**
James Braid **Facilities** ⊗ ⋔ 🖬 💺 🍴 ♙ 🖺 🏌 **Location**
SW side of town off A770
....

Hotel ⇧ Express by Holiday Inn Greenock, Cartsburn,
GREENOCK ☎ 01475 786666 71 en suite

Greenock Whinhill Beith Rd PA16 9LN
☎ 01475 724694 evenings & weekends only
18 holes, 5504yds, Par 68, SSS 68, Course record 64.
Location 1.5m SW off B7054
Telephone for further details
....

Hotel ⇧ Express by Holiday Inn Greenock, Cartsburn,
GREENOCK ☎ 01475 786666 71 en suite

KILMACOLM   Map 10 NS36

Kilmacolm Porterfield Rd PA13 4PD
☎ 01505 872139 🖥 01505 874007
e-mail: secretary@kilmacolmgolf.sagehost.co.uk
18 holes, 5961yds, Par 69, SSS 69, Course record 64.
Course Designer Willie Campbell **Location** SE side of
town off A761
Telephone for further details
....

Hotel ★★★★ ♨ 68% Gleddoch House Hotel,
LANGBANK ☎ 01475 540711 39 en suite

PORT GLASGOW   Map 10 NS37

Port Glasgow Devol Rd PA14 5XE
☎ 01475 704181 & 791214 (Sec)
18 holes, 5712yds, Par 68, SSS 68.
Location 1m S
Telephone for further details
....

Hotel ★★★★ ♨ 68% Gleddoch House Hotel,
LANGBANK ☎ 01475 540711 39 en suite

**If the name of the club appears in *italics*, details
have not been confirmed for this
edition of the guide.**

MIDLOTHIAN

BONNYRIGG   Map 11 NT36

Broomieknowe 36 Golf Course Rd EH19 2HZ
☎ 0131 663 9317 🖥 0131 663 2152
e-mail: administrator@broomieknowe.com
**Easy walking mature parkland course laid out by Ben
Sayers and extended by James Braid. Elevated site with
excellent views.**
18 holes, 6150yds, Par 70, SSS 70, Course record 65.
Visitors must contact in advance. **Societies** contact for
details. **Green Fees** terms on application. **Prof** Mark
Patchett **Course Designer** Ben Sayers/Hawtree **Facilities**
⊗ ⋔ 🖬 💺 🍴 ♙ 🖺 🏌 **Conf** Corporate Hospitality
Days available **Location** 0.5m NE off B704
....

Hotel ★★★ 75% Dalhousie Castle and Aqueous Spa,
Bonnyrigg, EDINBURGH ☎ 01875 820153 27 en suite
5 annexe en suite

DALKEITH   Map 11 NT36

Newbattle Abbey Rd EH22 3AD
☎ 0131 663 2123 & 0131 663 1819 🖥 0131 654 1810
e-mail: newbattlegolf@freeuk.com
**Gently undulating parkland course, dissected by the
river South Esk and surrounded by woods.**
18 holes, 6025yds, Par 69, SSS 70, Course record 61.
Club membership 700.
Visitors Mon-Fri ex public holidays, before 4pm. **Societies**
welcome weekdays ex public holidays, before 4pm. **Green
Fees** £30 per day; £20 per round. **Prof** Scott McDonald
Course Designer S Colt **Facilities** ⊗ ⋔ 🖬 💺 🍴 ♙ 🖺 🏌 🚜
🏌 **Conf** Corporate Hospitality Days available **Location**
SW side of town off A68
....

Hotel ★★★ 75% Dalhousie Castle and Aqueous Spa,
Bonnyrigg, EDINBURGH ☎ 01875 820153 27 en suite
5 annexe en suite

GOREBRIDGE   Map 11 NT36

Vogrie Vogrie Estate Country Park EH23 4NU
☎ 01875 821986
9 holes, 2530yds, Par 33.
Location Off B6372
Telephone for further details

PENICUIK   Map 11 NT25

Glencorse Milton Bridge EH26 0RD
☎ 01968 677189 🖥 01968 674399
**Picturesque parkland course with burn affecting ten
holes. Testing 5th hole (237 yds) par 3.**

Continued

18 holes, 5217yds, Par 64, SSS 66, Course record 60.
Club membership 700.
Visitors contact secretary, unable to play during club competitions **Societies** contact secretary for details. **Green Fees** £32 per day, £25 per round. **Prof** Cliffe Jones **Course Designer** Willie Park **Facilities** ⊗ ⅢⅢ ⅙ ⬛ ♀ ⚤ ⛳ ⛵ ⟶
♂ **Location** 9m S of Edinburgh on A701 Pebbles Road. 1.5m N of Penicuik on A701

Inn ♦♦♦ Olde Original Rosslyn Inn, 4 Main St, ROSLIN ☎ 0131 440 2384 6 en suite

MORAY

BUCKIE
Map 15 NJ46

Buckpool Barhill Rd, Buckpool AB56 1DU
☎ 01542 832236 📱 01542 832236
e-mail: golf@buckpoolgolf.com
Links course with superlative view over Moray Firth, easy walking.
18 holes, 6257yds, Par 70, SSS 70, Course record 64.
Club membership 430.
Visitors parties please apply in advance. **Societies** apply in advance. **Green Fees** £20 per day, £15 per round (weekends £25/£20). **Course Designer** J H Taylor **Facilities** ⊗ ⅢⅢ ⅙ ⬛ ♀ ⚤ ♂ **Leisure** squash, snooker. **Location** Off A98

Hotel ★★★ 65% The Seafield Hotel, Seafield St, CULLEN ☎ 01542 840791 19 en suite

Strathlene Portessie AB56 2DJ
☎ 01542 831798 📱 01542 831798
e-mail: strathgolf@ukonline.co.uk
Raised seaside links course with magnificent view. A special feature of the course is approach shots to raised greens (holes 4, 5, 6 and 13).
18 holes, 5980yds, Par 69, SSS 69, Course record 65.
Club membership 370.
Visitors booking essential at weekends. Contact professional at shop or training facility on arrival or in advance by phone. **Societies** telephone for Mon-Fri & apply in writing for weekends. **Green Fees** £18 per round (weekend £21). **Prof** Brian Slorach **Course Designer** George Smith **Facilities** ⊗ ⅙ ⬛ ♀ ⚤ ⛳ ♂ ✆ ⛵ **Conf** Corporate Hospitality Days available **Location** 2m E of Buckie on A942

Hotel ★★★ 65% The Seafield Hotel, Seafield St, CULLEN ☎ 01542 840791 19 en suite

CULLEN
Map 15 NJ56

Cullen The Links AB56 4WB ☎ 01542 840685
e-mail: cullengolfclub@btinternet.com
Interesting links on two levels with rocks and ravines offering some challenging holes. Spectacular scenery.
18 holes, 4610yds, Par 63, SSS 62, Course record 58.
Club membership 500.
Visitors no restrictions but during summer club medal matches given preference on Mon/Wed/Sat. Book tee times advisable. **Societies** advance applications advisable. **Green Fees** not confirmed. **Course Designer** Tom Morris/Charlie Neaves **Facilities** ⊗ ⅢⅢ ⅙ ⬛ ♀ ⚤ ♂ **Conf** Corporate Hospitality Days available **Location** 0.5m W off A98

Hotel ★★★ 65% The Seafield Hotel, Seafield St, CULLEN ☎ 01542 840791 19 en suite

DUFFTOWN
Map 15 NJ34

Dufftown Tomintoul Rd AB55 4BS
☎ 01340 820325 📱 01340 820325
e-mail: marion_dufftowngolfclub@yahoo.com
A short and undulating inland course with spectacular views. The tee of the highest hole, the 9th, is over 1200 ft above sea level.
18 holes, 5308yds, Par 67, SSS 67, Course record 64.
Club membership 250.
Visitors tee reserved Tue & Wed 4.30-6.30 & Sun 7.30-9 & 12.30-2. Prior booking recommended. **Societies** apply in writing or by telephone **Green Fees** £15 per round/£20 per day. **Course Designer** Members **Facilities** ⊗ by prior arrangement ⅢⅢ by prior arrangement ⅙ by prior arrangement ⬛ by prior arrangement ♀ ⚤ ⛳ ♂ **Conf** fac available Corporate Hospitality Days available **Location** 0.75m SW off B9009

Hotel ★★★ 78% Craigellachie Hotel, CRAIGELLACHIE ☎ 01340 881204 25 en suite

ELGIN
Map 15 NJ26

Elgin Hardhillock, Birnie Rd, New Elgin IV30 8SX
☎ 01343 542338 📱 01343 542341
e-mail: secretary@elgingolfclub.com
Possibly the finest inland course in the north of Scotland, with undulating greens and compact holes that demand the highest accuracy. There are thirteen par 4s and one par 5 hole on its parkland layout, seven of the par 4's being over 400 yards in length.
Hardhillock: 18 holes, 6416yds, Par 68, SSS 69, Course record 63.
Club membership 1000.
Visitors must contact in advance, weekend play only by prior arrangement. **Societies** telephone secretary for details. **Green Fees** £40 per day, £30 per round. **Cards** 🪙 💳 💳 💳 💳 🪙 **Prof** Kevin Stables **Course Designer** John Macpherson **Facilities** ⊗ ⅢⅢ ⅙ ⬛ ♀ ⚤ ⛳ ✆ ⛵ ⟶ ♂ ⛵ **Conf** fac available **Location** 1m S on A941

Hotel ★★★ 74% Mansion House Hotel, The Haugh, ELGIN ☎ 01343 548811 23 en suite

FORRES
Map 14 NJ05

Forres Muiryshade IV36 2RD
☎ 01309 672250 📱 01309 672250
e-mail: sandy@forresgolfclub.fsnet.co.uk
An all-year parkland course laid on light, well-drained soil in wooded countryside. Walking is easy despite some hilly holes. A test for the best golfers.
18 holes, 6240yds, Par 70, SSS 70, Course record 60.
Club membership 1000.
Visitors welcome although club competitions take priority. Weekends may be restricted in summer. **Societies** advised to telephone 2-3 weeks in advance. **Green Fees** £26 per round/£34 per day. **Cards** 🪙 💳 🪙 **Prof** Sandy Aird **Course Designer** James Braid/Willie Park **Facilities** ⊗ ⅢⅢ ⅙ ⬛ ♀ ⚤ ⛳ ✆ ⛵ ♂ **Conf** Corporate Hospitality Days available **Location** SE side of town centre off B9010

Hotel ★★★ 67% Ramnee Hotel, Victoria Rd, FORRES ☎ 01309 672410 20 en suite

---

Booking a tee time is always advisable.

GARMOUTH   Map 15 NJ36

Garmouth & Kingston Spey St IV32 7NJ
☎ 01343 870388 📄 01343 870388
e-mail: garmouthgolfclub@aol.com
Flat seaside course with several parkland holes and
tidal waters. The 8th hole measures only 328 yards
from the medal tee but the fairway is bounded by a
ditch on either side, the left hand one being out of
bounds for the entire length of the hole. The par 5 17th
'Whinny Side' has gorse bordering on both sides of the
fairway which can be intimidating to any level of golfer.
18 holes, 5935yds, Par 69, SSS 69, Course record 62.
Club membership 500.
Visitors must contact in advance. Societies advisable to
phone in advance. Green Fees £25 per day, £20 per round
(£25 weekends). Cards 🌐 ▬ ▬ 💳 Course Designer
George Smith Facilities ⊗ by prior arrangement 🎯 by
prior arrangement 🎽 💷 ♀ ⛳ ⌕ Conf Corporate
Hospitality Days available Location In village on B9015

Hotel ★★★ 74% Mansion House Hotel, The Haugh,
ELGIN ☎ 01343 548811 23 en suite

HOPEMAN   Map 15 NJ16

Hopeman Clubhouse IV30 5YA
☎ 01343 830578 📄 01343 830152
e-mail: hopemangc@aol.com
Links-type course with beautiful views over the Moray
Firth. The 12th hole, called the Priescach, is a short
hole with a drop of 100 feet from tee to green. It can
require anything from a wedge to a wood depending on
the wind.
18 holes, 5590yds, Par 68, SSS 67.
Club membership 700.
Visitors must contact in advance, restricted tee times at
weekend and between 12:45-1:45 weekdays Societies
contact in advance. Green Fees £18 per round (weekend
£23). Cards 🌐 ▬ ▬ 💳 Facilities ⊗ 🎯 🎽 💷 ♀ ⛳ 🏠
🍴 ⌕ Location E side of village off B9040

Hotel ★★★ 74% Mansion House Hotel, The Haugh,
ELGIN ☎ 01343 548811 23 en suite

KEITH   Map 15 NJ45

Keith Fife Park AB55 5DF
☎ 01542 882469 📄 01542 888176
e-mail: secretary@keithgolfclub.org.uk
Parkland course, with natural hazards over first 9
holes. Testing 7th hole, 232 yds, par 3.
18 holes, 5767yds, Par 69, SSS 68, Course record 65.
Club membership 500.
Visitors no restrictions except competitions. Societies by
arrangement with outings secretary (01542 886742) Green
Fees not confirmed. Course Designer Roy Phimister
Facilities 💷 ♀ ⛳ 🍴 ⌕ Location NW side of town centre
off A96, onto B9014 and first right

Hotel ★★★ 78% Craigellachie Hotel,
CRAIGELLACHIE ☎ 01340 881204 25 en suite

LOSSIEMOUTH   Map 15 NJ27

Moray Stotfield Rd IV31 6QS
☎ 01343 812018 📄 01343 815102
e-mail: secretary@moraygolf.co.uk
Two fine Scottish Championship links courses, known
as Old and New (Moray), and situated on the Moray

Continued

Firth where the weather is unusually mild.
*Old Course: 18 holes, 6643yds, Par 71, SSS 73, Course
record 65.*
*New Course: 18 holes, 6004yds, Par 69, SSS 69, Course
record 62.*
Club membership 1550.
Visitors must contact in advance 01343 812018 Secretary.
Societies Contact in advance. Green Fees not confirmed.
Cards 🌐 ▬ ▬ 💳 Prof Alistair Thomson
Course Designer Tom Morris Facilities ⊗ 🎯 🎽 💷 ♀ ⛳ 🏠
🍴 🛒 ⌕ Conf Corporate Hospitality Days available
Location N side of town

Hotel ★★★ 74% Mansion House Hotel, The Haugh,
ELGIN ☎ 01343 548811 23 en suite

ROTHES   Map 15 NJ24

Rothes Blackhall AB38 7AN
☎ 01340 831443 (evenings) 📄 01340 831443
e-mail: rothesgolfclub@netscapeonline.co.uk
9 holes, 4972yds, Par 68, SSS 64.
Course Designer John Souter Location 9m S of Elgin on
A941
Telephone for further details

Hotel ★★★ 78% Craigellachie Hotel,
CRAIGELLACHIE ☎ 01340 881204 25 en suite

SPEY BAY   Map 15 NJ36

Spey Bay IV32 7PJ ☎ 01343 820424 📄 01343 829282
e-mail: info@speybay.com
Championship standard seaside links course over
gently undulating banks and well-drained ground.
Good views along Moray coast. Driving range.

18 holes, 6182yds, Par 70, SSS 70, Course record 65.
Club membership 350.
Visitors telephone for details (especially for Sun) Societies
book by telephone. Green Fees £25 per round (£30
weekends). Cards 🌐 ▬ 💳 Course Designer Ben Sayers
Facilities ⊗ 🎯 🎽 💷 ♀ ⛳ 🍴 🏠 🛒 ⌕ ⌕ Conf fac
available Corporate Hospitality Days available Location
4.5m N of Fochabers on B9104, just off main
Aberdeen/Inverness road A96

NORTH AYRSHIRE

BEITH   Map 10 NS35

Beith Threepwood Rd KA15 2JR
☎ 01505 503166 & 506814 📄 01505 506814
e-mail: bgc-secretary@hotmail.com
Hilly course, with panoramic views over 7 counties.

Continued

Beith

18 holes, 5616yds, Par 68, SSS 68.
Club membership 620.
Visitors contact for details. **Societies** apply in writing to secretary at least 1 month in advance. **Green Fees** £20 per round/£30 per day (weekend £25 per round). **Course Designer** Members **Facilities** ⊗ ⫫ ⅃ ⚑ ⌣ ♨ **Location** 1st left on Beith bypass, Sbound on A737
....
Guesthouse ◆◆◆◆ Whin Park, 16 Douglas St, LARGS ☎ 01475 673437 5 en suite

Gt Cumbrae Island (Millport) Map 10 NS15

Millport Golf Rd KA28 0HB
☎ 01475 530305 (Prof) 🖹 01475 530306
e-mail: secretary@millportgolfclub.co.uk
Pleasantly situated on the west side of Cumbrae looking over Bute to Arran and the Mull of Kintyre. Exposure means conditions may vary according to wind strength and direction. A typical seaside resort course welcoming visitors.
18 holes, 5828yds, Par 68, SSS 69, Course record 64.
Club membership 460.
Visitors advisable to phone and book tee times especially in summer months. **Societies** telephone or write in advance. **Green Fees** terms on application. **Cards** 🔳 🔳 🔳 **Course Designer** James Braid **Facilities** ⊗ ⫫ ⅃ ⚑ ⌣ ⅃ ♨ **Location** Approx 4m from ferry slip
....
Hotel ★★ 69% Willowbank Hotel, 96 Greenock Rd, LARGS ☎ 01475 672311 & 675435 🖹 01475 689027 30 en suite

Irvine Map 10 NS34

Glasgow Gailes KA11 5AE
☎ 0141 942 2011 🖹 0141 942 0770
e-mail: secretary@glasgow-golf.com
A lovely seaside links. The turf of the fairways and all the greens is truly glorious and provides tireless play. Established in 1882, and is a qualifying course for the Open Championship.
Glasgow Gailes: 18 holes, 6535yds, Par 71, SSS 72, Course record 63.
Club membership 1200.
Visitors prior booking through secretary reccomended, no visitors before 2.30pm Sat & Sun. **Societies** initial contact by telephone. **Green Fees** £70 per day, £55 per round (£60 per round weekends). **Cards** 🔳 🔳 🔳 🔳 **Prof** J Steven **Course Designer** W Park Jnr **Facilities** ⊗ ⫫ by prior arrangement ⅃ ⚑ ⅃ ⌣ ♨ ⚐ ♠ ♨ ♨ **Conf** Corporate Hospitality Days available **Location** Off A78 at Newhouse junct, South of Irvine
....
Hotel ★★★ 72% Montgreenan Mansion House Hotel, Montgreenan Estate, KILWINNING ☎ 01294 557733 21 en suite

Irvine Bogside KA12 8SN
☎ 01294 275979 🖹 01294 278209
Testing links course; only two short holes.
18 holes, 6400yds, Par 71, SSS 73, Course record 65.
Club membership 450.
Societies are welcome weekdays and pm weekends, telephone in advance. **Green Fees** terms on application. **Cards** 🔳 🔳 **Prof** Keith Erskine **Course Designer** James Braid **Facilities** ⊗ ⫫ ⅃ ⚑ ⌣ ⅃ ♨ ♨ **Location** N side of town off A737
....
Hotel ★★★ 72% Montgreenan Mansion House Hotel, Montgreenan Estate, KILWINNING ☎ 01294 557733 21 en suite

Irvine Ravenspark 13 Kidsneuk Ln KA12 8SR
☎ 01294 271293
e-mail: secretary@irgc.co.uk
Parkland course.
18 holes, 6457yds, Par 71, SSS 71, Course record 65.
Club membership 600.
Visitors may not play Sat before 2pm. **Societies** not allowed Sat before 3pm, contact club steward in advance. **Green Fees** Mon-Sun £16 per round/£29 per day. **Prof** Peter Bond **Facilities** ⊗ ⫫ ⅃ ⚑ ⌣ ⅃ ♨ **Location** N side of town on A737
....
Hotel ★★★ 72% Montgreenan Mansion House Hotel, Montgreenan Estate, KILWINNING ☎ 01294 557733 21 en suite

Western Gailes Gailes by Irvine KA11 5AE
☎ 01294 311649 🖹 01294 312312
e-mail: enquiries@westerngailes.com
A magnificent seaside links with glorious turf and wonderful greens. The view is open across the Firth of Clyde to the neighbouring islands. It is a well-balanced course crossed by three burns. There are two par 5s, the 6th and 14th, and the 11th is a testing 445-yard par 4 dog-leg.
18 holes, 6639yds, Par 71, SSS 74, Course record 65.
Visitors welcome Mon, Wed, Fri. Must contact in advance. Limited number of times on Sundays pm must reserve in advance **Societies** Mon/Wed/Fri,Sun pm must contact in advance. **Green Fees** £90 per 18 holes, £135 per 36 holes (both including lunch). £90 Sun (no lunch). **Cards** 🔳 🔳 🔳 🔳 **Course Designer** Mr Marress **Facilities** ⊗ ⫫ by prior arrangement ⅃ ⚑ ⌣ ⅃ ♨ **Conf** Corporate Hospitality Days available **Location** 2m S off A737
....
Hotel ★★★ 72% Montgreenan Mansion House Hotel, Montgreenan Estate, KILWINNING ☎ 01294 557733 21 en suite

Kilbirnie Map 10 NS35

Kilbirnie Place Largs Rd KA25 7AT
☎ 01505 684444 & 683398
Easy walking parkland course. The fairways are generally narrow and burns come into play on five holes.
18 holes, 5543yds, Par 69, SSS 67, Course record 65.
Club membership 578.
Visitors must contact in advance, may not play Sat or on competition days. **Societies** telephone in advance **Green Fees** not confirmed. **Facilities** ⊗ ⫫ ⅃ ⚑ ⌣ ⅃ **Location** 1m W from Kilbirnie Cross on A760
....
Hotel ★★ 69% Willowbank Hotel, 96 Greenock Rd, LARGS ☎ 01475 672311 & 675435 🖹 01475 689027 30 en suite

LARGS   Map 10 NS25

Largs Irvine Rd KA30 8EU
☎ 01475 673594 📠 01475 673594
e-mail: secretary@largsgolfclub.co.uk
**A parkland, tree-lined course with views to the Clyde
coast and Arran Isles.**
18 holes, 6115yds, Par 70, SSS 71, Course record 63.
Club membership 850.
Visitors may not play competition days. Other times by
arrangement with secretary. **Societies** apply in writing.
Green Fees terms on application. **Prof** Kenneth Docherty
Course Designer H Stutt **Facilities** ⊗ ⦀ ⅋ ⬤ ♟ ♀ ⌕ 🖾
⚑ ✐ **Location** 1m S of town centre on A78

Hotel ★★ 69% Willowbank Hotel, 96 Greenock Rd,
LARGS ☎ 01475 672311 & 675435 📠 01475 689027
30 en suite

Routenburn Routenburn Rd KA30 8QA
☎ 01475 673230 & 686475
Heathland course with fine views over Firth of Clyde.
18 holes, 5675yds, Par 68, SSS 68, Course record 63.
Club membership 450.
Visitors no restrictions. Visitors may request a tee off time,
contact Professional (01475 687240) **Societies** apply in
writing. **Green Fees** terms on application. **Cards** 💳 **Prof**
J Grieg McQueen **Course Designer** J Braid **Facilities** ⊗
⦀ ⅋ ⬤ ♀ ⌕ 🖾 ✐ **Conf** Corporate Hospitality Days
available **Location** 1m N off A78

Hotel ★★ 69% Willowbank Hotel, 96 Greenock Rd,
LARGS ☎ 01475 672311 & 675435 📠 01475 689027
30 en suite

SKELMORLIE   Map 10 NS16

Skelmorlie Beithglass PA17 5ES
☎ 01475 520152 📠 01475 521902
e-mail: sec@skelmorliegolf.co.uk
**Parkland/moorland course with magnificent views over
Firth of Clyde. Designed by James Braid.**
18 holes, 5030yds, Par 65, SSS 65, Course record 63.
Club membership 450.
Visitors no visitors before 3pm Sat. **Societies** apply by
telephone. **Green Fees** terms on application. **Course
Designer** James Braid **Facilities** ⊗ by prior arrangement
⦀ by prior arrangement ⬤ by prior arrangement ⅋ ♀ ♟
⚑ ✐ **Leisure** fishing. **Location** E side of village off A78

Hotel ★★ 69% Willowbank Hotel, 96 Greenock Rd,
LARGS ☎ 01475 672311 & 675435 📠 01475 689027
30 en suite

STEVENSTON   Map 10 NS24

Ardeer Greenhead KA20 4LB
☎ 01294 464542 & 465316 📠 01294 465316
e-mail: peewee_watson@lineone.net
Parkland course with natural hazards.
18 holes, 6401yds, Par 72, SSS 71, Course record 66.
Club membership 650.
Visitors may not play Sat. Must contact in advance.
Societies must contact in advance. Special rates for parties
of 12 or more. **Green Fees** £35 per day; £22 per round
(£45/£30 Sun). **Course Designer** Stutt **Facilities** ⊗ ⬤ ⅋
♀ ♟ 🖾 🚗 ✐ **Leisure** snooker. **Conf** Corporate
Hospitality Days available **Location** 0.5m N off A78

Continued

Hotel ★★★ 72% Montgreenan Mansion House Hotel,
Montgreenan Estate, KILWINNING ☎ 01294 557733
21 en suite

WEST KILBRIDE   Map 10 NS24

West Kilbride 33-35 Fullerton Dr, Seamill
KA23 9HT ☎ 01294 823911 📠 01294 829573
e-mail: golf@westkilbridegolfclub.com
**Seaside links course on Firth of Clyde, with fine views
of Isle of Arran from every hole.**
18 holes, 5974yds, Par 70, SSS 70, Course record 63.
Club membership 840.
Visitors may not play at weekends or bank holidays, must
contact in advance. **Societies** Tue & Thu only; must
contact in advance. **Green Fees** terms on application. **Prof**
Graham Ross **Course Designer** James Braid **Facilities** ⊗
⦀ ⬤ ⅋ ♀ ⌕ 🖾 ⚑ ✐ **Location** W side of town off A78

Hotel ★★ 69% Willowbank Hotel, 96 Greenock Rd,
LARGS ☎ 01475 672311 & 675435 📠 01475 689027
30 en suite

NORTH LANARKSHIRE

AIRDRIE   Map 11 NS76

Airdrie Rochsoles ML6 0PQ ☎ 01236 762195
18 holes, 6004yds, Par 69, SSS 69, Course record 63.
Course Designer J Braid **Location** 1m N on B802
Telephone for further details

Hotel ★★★★ 69% The Westerwood Hotel, 1 St Andrews
Dr, Westerwood, CUMBERNAULD ☎ 01236 457171
100 en suite

Easter Moffat Mansion House, Station Rd, Plains
ML6 8NP ☎ 01236 842878 📠 01236 842904
e-mail: gordonmiller@emgc.freeserve.co.uk
**A challenging moorland/parkland course which enjoys
good views of the Campsie and Ochil hills. Although
fairways are generous, accurate placement from the tee
is essential on most holes. The signature hole on the
course, the 18th is a truly memorable par 3, played
from an elevated tee, to a receptive green in front of the
club house.**
18 holes, 6221yds, Par 72, SSS 70, Course record 66.
Club membership 500.
Visitors may not play weekends. **Societies** must contact in
advance. **Green Fees** not confirmed. **Prof** Graham King
Facilities ⊗ ⦀ ⬤ ⅋ ♀ ♟ 🖾 ✐ **Location** 2m E of
Airdrie on A89

Hotel ★★★★ 69% The Westerwood Hotel, 1 St Andrews
Dr, Westerwood, CUMBERNAULD ☎ 01236 457171
100 en suite

BELLSHILL   Map 11 NS76

Bellshill Community Rd, Orbiston ML4 2RZ
☎ 01698 745124 📠 01698 292576
**Tree lined 18 holes situated in the heart of Lanarkshire
near Strathclyde Park. First opened for play in 1905
and extended in 1970. The 2nd hole has recently been
redesigned by Mark James and Andrew Mair. The first
five holes are extremely demanding but are followed by
the gentler 'birdie alley' where shots can be recovered.
The signature hole is the 17th, a par 3 which involves a
tricky tee shot from an elevated tee to a small**

Continued

well bunkered green with out of bounds on the right.
18 holes, 6272yds, Par 70, SSS 69.
Club membership 700.
Visitors apply in writing in advance, may not play on
competition Sat & Sun. **Societies** apply in writing in
advance. **Green Fees** terms on application. **Facilities** ⊗ ⊤
⯊ ☗ ♀ ⚲ **Location** 1m SE off A721

Hotel ⏚ Travel Inn Glasgow Bellshill, Belziehill Farm,
New Edinburgh Rd, BELLSHILL ☎ 08701 977106
40 en suite

COATBRIDGE   Map 11 NS76

Drumpellier Drumpellier Av ML5 1RX
☎ 01236 424139 📄 01236 428723
e-mail: administrator@drumpelliergc.freeserve.co.uk
Parkland course.
18 holes, 6227yds, Par 71, SSS 70, Course record 62.
Club membership 827.
Visitors must contact in advance, may not play Sat.
Societies apply in advance. **Green Fees** £40 per day, £30
per round. **Cards** 🗠 🗠 🗠 🗠 🗠 **Prof** Jaimie Carver
Course Designer W Fernie **Facilities** ⊗ ⯊ ⯊ ☗ ♀ ⚲ 🏠
⌇ ⛟ ⚙ ⚷ **Conf** fac available Corporate Hospitality
Days available **Location** 0.75m W off A89

Hotel ★★★ 67% Bothwell Bridge Hotel, 89 Main St,
BOTHWELL ☎ 01698 852246 90 en suite

CUMBERNAULD   Map 11 NS77

Dullatur 1A Glen Douglas Dr G68 0DW
☎ 01236 723230 📄 01236 727271
e-mail: carol.millar@dullaturgolf.com
**Dullatur Carrickstone is a parkland course, with
natural hazards and wind. Dullatur Antonine, designed
by Dave Thomas, is a modern course.**
*Carrickstone: 18 holes, 6204yds, Par 70, SSS 70, Course
record 68.*
Antonine: 18 holes, 5875yds, Par 69, SSS 68.
Club membership 700.
Visitors telephone for availability. **Societies** must apply in
writing to secretary. **Green Fees** not confirmed. **Cards** 🗠
🗠 ⚙ **Prof** Duncan Sinclair **Course Designer** James Braid
Facilities ⊗ ⯊ ⯊ ☗ ♀ ⚲ 🏠 ⛟ ⚙ **Leisure** hard
tennis courts, sauna, solarium, gymnasium, bowling green.
Conf Corporate Hospitality Days available **Location** 1.5m
N of A80 at Cumbernauld

Hotel ★★★★ 69% The Westerwood Hotel, 1 St Andrews
Dr, Westerwood, CUMBERNAULD ☎ 01236 457171
100 en suite

Palacerigg Palacerigg Country Park G67 3HU
☎ 01236 734969 & 721461 📄 01236 721461
e-mail: palacerigg-golfclub@lineone.net
**Well wooded parkland course set in Palacerigg Country
Park with good views to the Campsie Hills.**
18 holes, 6444yds, Par 72, SSS 71, Course record 65.
Club membership 300.
Visitors anytime except club competitions, advance
booking advisable. **Societies** apply in writing to the
Secretary. **Green Fees** £6.50 per round/£9 per day
(weekend £10 per round). **Course Designer** Henry Cotton
Facilities ⊗ ⯊ ⯊ ☗ ♀ ⚲ 🏠 ⚙ **Location** 2m S of
Cumbernauld on Palacerigg road off Lenziemill road B8054

Hotel ★★★★ 69% The Westerwood Hotel, 1 St Andrews
Dr, Westerwood, CUMBERNAULD ☎ 01236 457171
100 en suite

Westerwood Hotel 1 St Andrews Dr, Westerwood
G68 0EW ☎ 01236 457171 📄 01236 738478
e-mail: westerwood@morton-hotels.com
**Undulating parkland/woodland course designed by
Dave Thomas and Seve Ballasteros. Holes meander
through silver birch, firs, heaths and heather, and the
spectacular 15th, 'The Waterfall', has its green set
against a 40ft rockface. Buggie track. Hotel facilities.**

*Westerwood: 18 holes, 6616yds, Par 72, SSS 72, Course
record 65.*
Club membership 1200.
Visitors advised to book 24hrs in advance. **Societies** all
bookings in advance to 01236 725281. **Green Fees** Apr-
Oct £27.50 (£30 weekends), Nov-Mar £15. **Cards** 🗠 🗠
🗠 🗠 ⚙ **Prof** Alan Tait **Course Designer** Seve
Ballesteros/Dave Thomas **Facilities** ⊗ ⯊ ⯊ ☗ ♀ ⚲ 🏠
⌇ ⛟ ⚙ ⚷ **Leisure** hard tennis courts, heated indoor
swimming pool, sauna, gymnasium, Beauty salon. **Conf**
fac available Corporate Hospitality Days available
Location Adjacent to A80, 14m from Glasgow City Centre

Hotel ★★★★ 69% The Westerwood Hotel, 1 St Andrews
Dr, Westerwood, CUMBERNAULD ☎ 01236 457171
100 en suite

GARTCOSH   Map 11 NS66

Mount Ellen Johnston Rd G69 8EY
☎ 01236 872277 📄 01236 872249
**Downland course with 73 bunkers. Testing hole: 10th
('Bedlay'), 156 yds, par 3.**
18 holes, 5525yds, Par 68, SSS 67, Course record 67.
Club membership 500.
Visitors may play Mon-Fri 9am-4pm. Must contact in
advance. **Societies** must contact in advance. **Green Fees**
terms on application. **Prof** Iain Bilsborough **Facilities** ⯊
☗ ♀ ⚲ 🏠 ⛟ ⚙ **Location** 0.75m N off A752

Hotel ★★★★ 71% Millennium Hotel Glasgow, George
Square, GLASGOW ☎ 0141 332 6711 117 en suite

KILSYTH   Map 11 NS77

Kilsyth Lennox Tak Ma Doon Rd G65 0RS
☎ 01236 824115 📄 01236 823089
18 holes, 5912yds, Par 70, SSS 70, Course record 66.
Location N side of town off A803
Telephone for further details

Hotel ★★★★ 69% The Westerwood Hotel, 1 St Andrews
Dr, Westerwood, CUMBERNAULD ☎ 01236 457171
100 en suite

Booking a tee time is always advisable.

MOTHERWELL — Map 11 NS75

Colville Park New Jerviston House, Jerviston Estate, Merry St ML1 4UG
☎ 01698 265779 (pro) ▤ 01698 230418
Parkland course. First nine, tree-lined, second nine, more exposed. Testing 10th hole par 3, 16th hole par 4.
18 holes, 6250yds, Par 71, SSS 70, Course record 63.
Club membership 875.
Visitors must contact in advance in writing. Smart dress code. **Societies** apply in writing. **Green Fees** not confirmed. **Prof** John Curriet **Course Designer** James Braid **Facilities** ⊗ ⅢⓉ ⅃ ⧫ ♀ ⚘ 🏠 **Location** 1.25m NE on A723 from Motherwell town centre

Hotel ★★★ 67% Bothwell Bridge Hotel, 89 Main St, BOTHWELL ☎ 01698 852246 90 en suite

MUIRHEAD — Map 11 NS66

Crow Wood Garnkirk House, Cumbernauld Rd G69 9JF ☎ 0141 779 1943 ▤ 0141 779 9148
e-mail: crowwood@golfclub.fsbusiness.co.uk
Parkland course.
18 holes, 6261yds, Par 71, SSS 71, Course record 62.
Club membership 800.
Visitors must contact in advance but may not play weekends, bank holidays or competition days. **Societies** apply in advance in writing. **Green Fees** terms on application. **Cards** ▧ ▨ **Prof** Brian Moffat **Course Designer** James Braid **Facilities** ⊗ ⅢⓉ ⅃ ⧫ ♀ ⚘ 🏠 ✔ **Leisure** snooker,pool. **Location** 6 miles from Glasgow city centre, off A80 to Stirling, between villages of Stepps and Muirhead

Hotel ★★★ 76% Malmaison, 278 West George St, GLASGOW ☎ 0141 572 1000 72 en suite

SHOTTS — Map 11 NS86

Shotts Blairhead ML7 5BJ
☎ 01501 822658 ▤ 01501 822650
Moorland course with fine panoramic views. A good test for all abilities.
18 holes, 6205yds, Par 70, SSS 70, Course record 63.
Club membership 800.
Visitors visitors by arrangement on Sat/Sun. Any other time by appointment. **Societies** apply in writing. **Green Fees** £16 per round.£25 per day (weekend £18 per round). **Prof** John Strachan **Course Designer** James Braid **Facilities** ⊗ ⅢⓉ ⅃ ⧫ ♀ ⚘ 🏠 ✔ **Location** 2m from M8 off Benhar Road

Hotel ★★★ 67% The Hilcroft Hotel, East Main St, WHITBURN ☎ 01501 740818 31 en suite

WISHAW — Map 11 NS75

Wishaw 55 Cleland Rd ML2 7PH
☎ 01698 372869 (club house) & 357480 (admin)
▤ 01698 357480
e-mail: jwdouglas@btconnect.com
Parkland course with many tree-lined fairways. Bunkers protect 17 of the 18 greens.
18 holes, 5999yds, Par 69, SSS 69, Course record 62.
Club membership 984.
Visitors must contact in advance. May not play Sat but may play alternate Sun. **Societies** apply in writing. **Green Fees** terms on application. **Prof** Stuart Adair **Course Designer** James Braid **Facilities** ⊗ ⅢⓉ ⅃ ⧫ ♀ ⚘ 🏠 ✔ **Location** NW side of town off A721

Hotel ★★★ 71% Popinjay Hotel, Lanark Rd, ROSEBANK ☎ 01555 860441 38 en suite

PERTH & KINROSS

ABERFELDY — Map 14 NN84

Aberfeldy Taybridge Rd PH15 2BH
☎ 01887 820535 ▤ 01887 820535
e-mail: abergc@tiscali.com.uk
Founded in 1895, this flat, parkland course is situated by the River Tay near the famous Wade Bridge and Black Watch Monument, and enjoys some splendid scenery. The new layout will test the keen golfer.
18 holes, 5283yds, Par 68, SSS 66, Course record 67.
Club membership 250.
Visitors are advised to book in advance especially at weekends. **Societies** must contact in advance. **Green Fees** terms on application. **Cards** ▨ ▧ ▩ ▥ **Course Designer** Soutars **Facilities** ⊗ ⅢⓉ ⅃ ⧫ ♀ ⚘ 🏠 ✔ **Location** N side of town centre

Hotel ★★★ 63% Moness House Hotel & Country Club, Crieff Rd, ABERFELDY ☎ 0870 443 1460 12 en suite

ALYTH — Map 15 NO24

Alyth Pitcrocknie PH11 8HF
☎ 01828 632268 ▤ 01828 633491
e-mail: enquiries@alythgolfclub.co.uk
Windy, heathland course with easy walking.
18 holes, 6205yds, Par 71, SSS 71, Course record 64.
Club membership 1000.
Visitors advance booking advisable, handicap certificate required and dress etiquette must be observed. **Societies** must telephone in advance. **Green Fees** terms on application. **Cards** ▨ ▧ ▥ **Prof** Tom Melville **Course Designer** James Braid **Facilities** ⊗ ⅢⓉ ⅃ ⧫ ♀ ⚘ 🏠 ✔ ❀ ✔ **Conf** fac available **Location** 1m E on B954

Hotel ★★★ 62% Angus Hotel, 46 Wellmeadow, BLAIRGOWRIE ☎ 01250 872455 81 en suite

Strathmore Golf Centre Leroch PH11 8NZ
☎ 01828 633322 ▤ 01828 633533
e-mail: enquiries@strathmoregolf.com
The Rannaleroch course is set on rolling parkland and heath with splendid views over Strathmore. The course is laid out in two loops of nine which both start and finish at the clubhouse. It is generous off the tee but beware of the udulating, links-style greens! Among the challenging holes is the 480-yard 5th with a 180-yard carry over water from a high tee position. The nine-hole Leitfie Links has been specially designed with beginners, juniors and older golfers in mind.

Continued | *Continued*

Rannaleroch Course: 18 holes, 6454yds, Par 72, SSS 72, Course record 67.
Leitfie Links: 9 holes, 1719yds, Par 29, SSS 29.
Club membership 537.
Visitors no restrictions, advised to book in advance.
Societies must contact in advance. **Green Fees** £24 per round (weekends £28). Leitfie £9 per round (weekend £11). **Cards** 🖃 🖃 💳 🕭 **Prof** Andy Lamb **Course Designer** John Salvesen **Facilities** ⊗ ⫼ 🕭 💺 🖳 ⛳ 🛋 🚡 ♨ **Location** 2m SE of Alyth, off B954 at Meigle onto A926, clearly signposted from Blairgowrie

Hotel ★★★ 62% Angus Hotel, 46 Wellmeadow, BLAIRGOWRIE ☎ 01250 872455 81 en suite

AUCHTERARDER   Map 11 NN91

Auchterarder Orchil Rd PH3 1LS
☎ 01764 662804 (Sec) 📠 01764 664423(Sec)
e-mail: secretary@auchterardergolf.co.uk
Flat parkland course, part woodland with pine, larch and silver birch. It may be short but tricky with cunning dog-legs and guarded greens that require accuracy rather than sheer power. The 14th 'Punchbowl' hole is perhaps the trickiest. A blind tee shot needs to be hit accurately over the left edge of the cross bunker to a long and narrow green - miss and you face a difficult downhill chip shot from deep rough.
18 holes, 5775yds, Par 69, SSS 68, Course record 61.
Club membership 820.
Visitors must contact professional/secretary in advance.
Societies must contact in advance. **Green Fees** £24 per round/£35 per day (weekends £29/£45). **Prof** Gavin Baxter **Course Designer** Ben Sayers **Facilities** ⊗ ⫼ 🕭 💺 🖳 ♀ 🛋 ⛳ ♨ **Conf** Corporate Hospitality Days available **Location** 0.75m SW on A824

Hotel ★★★★★ The Gleneagles Hotel, AUCHTERARDER ☎ 01764 662231 270 en suite

AUCHTERARDER See page 353

BLAIR ATHOLL   Map 14 NN86

Blair Atholl Invertilt Rd PH18 5TG
☎ 01796 481407 📠 01796 481292
Parkland course, river runs alongside 3 holes, easy walking.
9 holes, 5816yds, Par 70, SSS 68, Course record 65.
Club membership 460.
Visitors apply in advance to avoid competition times.
Societies apply in writing. **Green Fees** not confirmed.
Course Designer Morriss **Facilities** ⊗ ⫼ 🕭 💺 🖳 ♀ 🛋 ⛳ ♨ **Location** 0.5m S off B8079

Hotel ★★ 71% Atholl Arms Hotel, Old North Rd, BLAIR ATHOLL ☎ 01796 481205 30 en suite

BLAIRGOWRIE   Map 15 NO14

Blairgowrie Golf Course Rd, Rosemount PH10 6LG
☎ 01250 872622 📠 01250 875451
e-mail: admin@blairgowrie-golf.co.uk
Two 18-hole heathland courses, also a 9-hole course.
Rosemount Course: 18 holes, 6590yds, Par 72, SSS 73, Course record 64.
Lansdowne Course: 18 holes, 6802yds, Par 72, SSS 73, Course record 67.
Wee Course: 9 holes, 2327yds, Par 32.
Club membership 1550.

Continued

Visitors must contact in advance & have handicap certificate, restricted Wed, Fri & weekends. **Societies** must contact in advance. **Green Fees** not confirmed. **Cards** 🖃 🖃 🖃 🕭 **Prof** Charles Dernie **Course Designer** J Braid/P Allis/D Thomas/Old Tom Morris **Facilities** ⊗ ⫼ 🕭 💺 🖳 ♀ 🛋 ⛳ ♨ **Conf** Corporate Hospitality Days available **Location** Off A93 Rosemount

Hotel ★★★ 62% Angus Hotel, 46 Wellmeadow, BLAIRGOWRIE ☎ 01250 872455 81 en suite

COMRIE   Map 11 NN72

Comrie Laggan Braes PH6 2LR ☎ 01764 670055
e-mail: enquiries@comriegolf.co.uk
Scenic highland course with two tricky par 3 holes.
9 holes, 6040yds, Par 70, SSS 70, Course record 62.
Club membership 350.
Visitors apply in advance (for party bookings) **Societies** must contact in advance. **Green Fees** £20 per day, £16 per 18 holes (£25/£20 weekends and bank holidays). **Course Designer** Col. Williamson **Facilities** ⊗ 🖳 🛋 ⛳ ♨ **Location** E side of village off A85

Hotel ★★★ 70% The Four Seasons Hotel, Loch Earn, ST FILLANS ☎ 01764 685333 12 en suite 6 annexe en suite

CRIEFF   Map 11 NN82

Crieff Ferntower, Perth Rd PH7 3LR
☎ 01764 652909 📠 01764 655096
e-mail: bookings@crieffgolf.co.uk
Set in the dramatic countryside of Perthshire, Crieff Golf Club was established in 1891. The Ferntower championship course has magnificent views over the Strathearn Valley and offers all golfers an enjoyable round. The short 9 hole Dornoch course, which incorporates some of the James Braid designed holes from the original 18 holes, provides an interesting challenge for juniors, beginners and others short of time.

Ferntower Course: 18 holes, 6427yds, Par 71, SSS 72, Course record 64.
Dornoch Course: 9 holes, 2372yds, Par 32.
Club membership 720.
Visitors must contact professional in advance. **Societies** must contact professional in advance. **Green Fees** Ferntower: weekday per round: Mar-Apr £23 May&Oct £26 Jun-Sep £28 (weekends £28/£33/£38). Dornock £9 for 9 holes, £14 for 18 holes. **Cards** 🖃 🖃 🕭 **Prof** David Murchie **Course Designer** James Braid **Facilities** ⊗ ⫼ 🕭 💺 🖳 ♀ 🛋 🚡 ⛳ 🛋 ♨ **Conf** Corporate Hospitality Days available **Location** 0.5m NE on A85

Guesthouse ♦♦♦♦ Gwydir House Hotel, Comrie Rd, CRIEFF ☎ 01764 653277 8 en suite

DUNKELD   Map 11 NO04

Dunkeld & Birnam Fungarth PH8 0HU
☎ 01350 727524 📠 01350 728660
e-mail: richbrrnc@aol.com
Interesting and challenging course with spectacular
views of the surrounding countryside. The original
9-hole heathland course is now augmented by an
additional 9 holes of parkland character close to the
Loch of the Lowes.
18 holes, 5511yds, Par 70, SSS 67, Course record 63.
Club membership 600.
Visitors must contact in advance at weekends, public
holidays, or large parties during the week. Societies apply
in writing/telephone. Green Fees terms on application.
Cards 💳 🃏 💳 🔁 💳 💳 💳 Course Designer D A
Tod Facilities ⊗ ⅷ ⅃ ♥ ♀ ⚲ 🏠 ⛳ ♂ Conf Corporate
Hospitality Days available Location 1m N of village on
A923

Hotel ★★★ ⚕ Kinnaird, Kinnaird Estate, DUNKELD
☎ 01796 482440 9 en suite

DUNNING   Map 11 NO01

Dunning Rollo Park PH2 0QX ☎ 01764 684747
Parkland course with a series of stone built bridges
crossing a burn meandering over a large part of the
course.
9 holes, 4836yds, Par 66, SSS 63, Course record 62.
Club membership 580.
Visitors Gents competitions Saturday, Ladies Tue, no
restrictions otherwise. Societies must contact in advance in
writing. Green Fees £15 per 18 holes (9 holes £10);
weekends £16. Facilities ♥ ⚲ ⛳ ♂ Location 1.5m off
A9, 4m N of Auchterarder on B9146

Hotel ★★★ 69% Lovat Hotel, 90 Glasgow Rd, PERTH
☎ 01738 636555 30 en suite

Whitemoss Whitemoss Rd PH2 0QX
☎ 01738 730300 📠 01738 730490
e-mail: info@whitemossgolf.com
Undulating parkland course situated in the scenic
Strathearn Valley, ten miles from Perth (off the A9).

18 holes, 5595yds, Par 68, SSS 68, Course record 63.
Club membership 600.
Visitors advisable to telephone in advance, visitors
welcome all week, may play 9 holes half price. Societies
please telephone for details. Green Fees not confirmed.
Course Designer Whitemoss Leisure Facilities ⊗ ⅷ ⅃
♥ ♀ ⚲ 🏠 ⛳ ♂ Leisure practice range, chipping
bunkers, practice net. Conf Corporate Hospitality Days
available Location Turn off A9 at Whitemoss Road junct,
3m N of Gleneagles

Continued

Hotel ★★ 76% Cairn Lodge, Orchil Rd,
AUCHTERARDER ☎ 01764 662634 10 en suite

GLENSHEE (SPITTAL OF)   Map 15 NO17

Dalmunzie Dalmunzie Estate PH10 7QG
☎ 01250 885226 📠 01250 885225
e-mail: dalmunzie@aol.com
Well maintained Highland course with difficult
walking. Testing short course with small but good
greens.
9 holes, 2099yds, Par 30, SSS 30.
Club membership 91.
Visitors restricted Sun 10.30-11.30am. Societies advance
contact preferred. Green Fees £12 per day. Course
Designer Alistair Campbell Facilities ⊗ ⅷ ⅃ ♥ ♀ ⛳
🏐 Leisure hard tennis courts, fishing. Conf fac available
Corporate Hospitality Days available Location 2m NW of
Spittal of Glenshee

Hotel ★★ 72% Dalmunzie House Hotel, SPITTAL OF
GLENSHEE ☎ 01250 885224 18 rms (16 en suite)

KENMORE   Map 14 NN74

Kenmore PH15 2HN
☎ 01887 830226 📠 01887 829059
e-mail: golf@taymouth.co.uk
Testing course in mildly undulating natural terrain.
Beautiful views in tranquil setting by Loch Tay. The
par 5 4th is 560 yards and only one of the par 4s, the
2nd, is under 400 yards - hitting from the tee out of a
mound of trees down a snaking banking fairway which
encourages the ball to stay on the fairway. The slightly
elevated green is surrounded by banks to help hold the
ball on the green. The fairways are generous and the
rough short, which tends to encourage an unhindered
round.
9 holes, 6052yds, Par 70, SSS 69, Course record 67.
Club membership 200.
Visitors advance booking advisable. Societies telephone in
advance. Green Fees £20 per day, £16 per 18 holes, £12
per 9 holes (£25/£17/£13 weekends). Cards 💳 💳
Course Designer Robin Menzies Facilities ⊗ ⅷ ⅃ ♥ ♀
⚲ 🏠 ⛳ 🐾 ♂ Leisure fishing. Location On
A827, beside Kenmore Bridge

Hotel ★★★ 64% Kenmore Hotel, The Square,
KENMORE ☎ 01887 830205 27 en suite
13 annexe en suite

Taymouth Castle Taymouth Castle Estate PH15 2NT
☎ 01887 830228 📠 01887 830830
e-mail: taymouth@fishingnet.com
18 holes, 6066yds, Par 69, SSS 69, Course record 62.
Course Designer James Braid Location 1m E on A827,
5m W of Aberfeldy
Telephone for further details

Hotel ★★★ 64% Kenmore Hotel, The Square,
KENMORE ☎ 01887 830205 27 en suite
13 annexe en suite

KINROSS   Map 11 NO10

Green Hotel 2 The Muirs KY13 8AS
☎ 01577 863407 📠 01577 863180
e-mail: golf@green-hotel.com
Two interesting and picturesque parkland courses, with
easy walking. Many of the fairways are bounded by

Continued

The Gleneagles Hotel

Map 11 NN91   Auchterarder

☎ 01764 662231   📄 01764 662134

The PGA Centenary Course, designed by Jack Nicklaus and James Braid, and launched in style in May 1993, boasts an American/Scottish layout with many water hazards, elevated tees and raised contoured greens. It is the selected venue for the Ryder Cup 2014. It boasts a five-tier tee structure, making it both the longest and shortest playable course at the resort, as well as the most accommodating to all standards of golfer. The King's Course with its abundance of heather, gorse, raised greens and plateau tees, is set within the valley of Strathearn with the Grampian mountains spectacularly in view to the north. The shorter Queen's course, with its Scots Pine-lined fairways and water hazards, is set within a softer landscape and is considered an easier test of golf. You can improve your game at the Golf Academy at Gleneagles, where the philosophy is that golf should be fun and fun in golf comes from playing better. A complete corporate golf package is available.

e-mail: resort.sales@gleneagles.com

Visitors Advance booking essential, 8 weeks notice

Societies Contact for details. Full payment in advance is required to secure tee times

Green Fees Contact for details. 📧 🔲 🟰 💳 🔲 🟦 🔲

Facilities ⊗ 🍴 🍺 💺 🟥 🔵 ⛱ 🏔 🍽 🟨 🍴 🔵 ⛳ ♀ 🏌

Conf Facilities available; corporate hospitality days available

Professional Sandy Smith. Golf Academy

Leisure Tennis, squash, swimming, sauna, solarium, gymnasium, riding, shooting, fishing, falconry, off-road driving

Location Auchterarder PH3 1NF (2m SW on A823)

Holes/Par/Course record 63 holes.
Kings: 18 holes, 6471 yds, Par 70, SSS 73, Course record 60
Queens: 18 holes, 5965 yds, Par 68, SSS 70, Course record 62
Centenary: 18 holes, 6551 yds, Par 72, SSS 73, Course record 63

WHERE TO STAY AND EAT NEARBY

Hotels
AUCHTERARDER

★★★★★ 🏨 🏨 🏨 🏨
The Gleneagles Hotel
☎ 01764 662231. 270 en suite

★★ 🏨 🏨 76% Cairn Lodge, PH8 1LX
☎ 01764 662634. 10 en suite

Restaurants
Perth

🏨 🏨 Lets Eat PH1 5EZ
☎ 01738 643377

🏨 🏨 63 Tay Street, PH2 8NN
☎ 01738 441451

Championship Course

trees and plantations. A number of holes, particularly on the Blue Course, have views over Loch Leven to the hills beyond. The 4th is a really challenging par 3. Some holes have burns or ditches to catch the unwary while those playing the 6th on the Red Course have to negotiate a difficult pond.

Red Course: 18 holes, 6256yds, Par 73, SSS 71.
Blue Course: 18 holes, 6438yds, Par 71, SSS 72.
Club membership 600.
Visitors advisable to contact in advance **Societies** must contact in advance. **Green Fees** £35 per day, £22 per round (£45/£33 weekends). **Cards** ▦ ▭ ▨ 🎴 **Prof** Stuart Geraghty **Course Designer** Sir David Montgomery **Facilities** ⊗ ⅷ ⅃ ☕ ♀ ♤ 🏠 ⚐ ⌇ ✈ ♥ ⚙ **Leisure** hard tennis courts, heated indoor swimming pool, squash, fishing, sauna, 4 sheet curling rink. **Conf** fac available Corporate Hospitality Days available **Location** NE side of town on B996

....

Hotel ★★★ 75% Green Hotel, 2 The Muirs, KINROSS ☎ 01577 863467 46 en suite

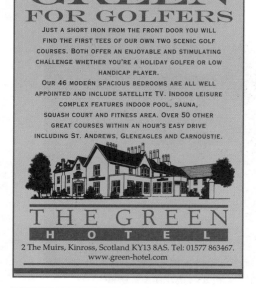

THE IDEAL
GREEN
FOR GOLFERS

JUST A SHORT IRON FROM THE FRONT DOOR YOU WILL FIND THE FIRST TEES OF OUR OWN TWO SCENIC GOLF COURSES. BOTH OFFER AN ENJOYABLE AND STIMULATING CHALLENGE WHETHER YOU'RE A HOLIDAY GOLFER OR LOW HANDICAP PLAYER.

OUR 46 MODERN SPACIOUS BEDROOMS ARE ALL WELL APPOINTED AND INCLUDE SATELLITE TV. INDOOR LEISURE COMPLEX FEATURES INDOOR POOL, SAUNA, SQUASH COURT AND FITNESS AREA. OVER 50 OTHER GREAT COURSES WITHIN AN HOUR'S EASY DRIVE INCLUDING ST. ANDREWS, GLENEAGLES AND CARNOUSTIE.

THE GREEN
H O T E L

2 The Muirs, Kinross, Scotland KY13 8AS. Tel: 01577 863467.
www.green-hotel.com

MILNATHORT   Map 11 NO10

Milnathort South St KY13 9XA ☎ 01577 864069
e-mail: milnathortgolf@ukgateway.net
Undulating inland course with lush fairways and excellent greens for most of the year. Strategically placed copses of trees require accurate tee shots. Different tees and greens for some holes will make for more interesting play.
9 holes, 5969yds, Par 71, SSS 69, Course record 62.
Club membership 575.
Visitors no restrictions. **Societies** advisable to book in advance. **Green Fees** terms on application. **Facilities** ⊗ ⅷ by prior arrangement ▯ ⚏ ♀ ♤ ⚙ **Location** S side of town on A922

....

Hotel ★★★ 75% Green Hotel, 2 The Muirs, KINROSS ☎ 01577 863467 46 en suite

---

MUTHILL   Map 11 NN81

Muthill Peat Rd PH5 2DA
☎ 01764 681523 🖷 01764 681557
e-mail: muthillgolfclub@lineone.net
A 9 hole course which, although short, requires accurate shot making to match the SSS. The three par 3s are all challenging holes with the 9th, a 205 yard shot to a small well bunkered green making a fitting end to 9 holes characterised by great views and springy well maintained fairways.
9 holes, 4700yds, Par 66, SSS 63, Course record 62.
Club membership 370.
Visitors no restrictions telephone in advance. **Societies** book in advance. **Green Fees** £16 per day; £10 per 9 holes (£20 weekends and bank holidays)). **Course Designer** Members **Facilities** ⊗ ▯ ⚏ ♀ ♤ ⚐ ⚙ **Location** W side of village off A822

....

Hotel ★★ 76% Cairn Lodge, Orchil Rd, AUCHTERARDER ☎ 01764 662634 10 en suite

---

PERTH   Map 11 NO12

Craigie Hill Cherrybank PH2 0NE
☎ 01738 622644 (pro) 🖷 01738 620829
e-mail: golf@craigiehill.com
Slightly hilly, heathland course. Panoramic views over Perth and surrounding hills.
18 holes, 5386yds, Par 66, SSS 67, Course record 60.
Club membership 600.
Visitors Restricted access Sat. Telephone up to 3 days in advance. **Societies** must contact in writing. Restricted play on Sats. **Green Fees** £30 per day; £20 per round (£30/£25 weekends). **Prof** Ian Muir **Course Designer** Fernie/Anderson **Facilities** ⊗ ⅷ ▯ ⚏ ♀ ♤ ⚐ ⚙
Conf fac available **Location** 1m SW of city centre off A952

....

Hotel ★★★ 66% Queens Hotel, Leonard St, PERTH ☎ 01738 442222 50 en suite

King James VI Moncreiffe Island PH2 8NR
☎ 01738 445132 (Secretary) & 632460 (Pro)
🖷 01738 445132
e-mail: info@kjvigc.fsnet.co.uk
Parkland course, situated on island in the middle of the River Tay. Easy walking.
18 holes, 6038yds, Par 70, SSS 69, Course record 62.
Club membership 650.

Continued

Visitors visitors restricted on competition days. Must contact professional in advance for bookings. May not play Sat. **Societies** book by telephone. **Green Fees** terms on application. **Prof** Andrew Crerar **Course Designer** Tom Morris **Facilities** ⊗ ⅃ ┗ ▆ ♀ △ ⌂ ┅ ┳ ✓ **Location** SE side of city centre

Hotel ★★★ 66% Queens Hotel, Leonard St, PERTH ☎ 01738 442222 50 en suite

Murrayshall Country House Hotel Murrayshall, Scone PH2 7PH
☎ 01738 552784 & 551171 📋 01738 552595
e-mail: info@murrayshall.com

Murrayshall Course: 18 holes, 6441yds, Par 73, SSS 72. Lyndoch Course: 18 holes, 5800yds, Par 69.
Course Designer Hamilton Stutt **Location** E side of village off A94
Telephone for further details

Hotel ★★★ 74% Murrayshall Country House Hotel & Golf Course, New Scone, PERTH ☎ 01738 551171 27 en suite   14 annexe en suite

North Inch North Inch, off Hay St PH1 5PH
☎ 01738 636481
e-mail: es@pkc.gov.uk
An enjoyable short and often testing course incorporating mature trees, open parkland with fine views and attractive riverside. This ancient course has recently been transformed by a new layout. This has resulted in one or two more challenging holes. Situated beside the Tay, this course offers both links and parkland characteristics.
18 holes, 5442yds, Par 68, SSS 66, Course record 62.
Club membership 459.
Visitors advisable to telephone in advance. **Societies** apply in writing. **Green Fees** £12 per round (weekend £15).
Course Designer Tom Morris **Facilities** ⊗ ⅃ ┗ ▆ ♀ △ ┳ ✓ **Leisure** squash. **Location** N of City

Hotel ★★★ 66% Queens Hotel, Leonard St, PERTH ☎ 01738 442222 50 en suite

PITLOCHRY
Map 14 NN95

Pitlochry Golf Course Rd PH16 5QY
☎ 01796 472792 📋 01796 473947
e-mail: mark.pirie@foremostgolf.com
A varied and interesting heathland course with fine views and posing many problems. Its SSS permits few errors in its achievement.
Pitlochry Golf Course: 18 holes, 5811yds, Par 69, SSS 69, Course record 63.
Club membership 400.
Continued

Visitors Must book times in advance. **Societies** must contact in advance. **Green Fees** £35 per day, £24 per round (£45/£30 weekends). **Cards** 🃏 💳 💳 💳 **Prof** Mark Pirie **Course Designer** Willy Fernie **Facilities** ⊗ ⅃ ┗ ▆ ♀ △ ⌂ ┳ ♦ ✓ **Location** Larchwood road from A924, golf club on left.

Hotel ★★★ 72% Pine Trees Hotel, Strathview Ter, PITLOCHRY ☎ 01796 472121 20 en suite

ST FILLANS
Map 11 NN62

St Fillans South Loch Earn Rd PH6 2NJ
☎ 01764 685312 📋 01764 685312
9 holes, 6054yds, Par 69, SSS 69, Course record 73.
Course Designer W Auchterlonie **Location** E side of village off A85
Telephone for further details

Hotel ★★★ 70% The Four Seasons Hotel, Loch Earn, ST FILLANS ☎ 01764 685333 12 en suite   6 annexe en suite

STRATHTAY
Map 14 NN95

Strathtay Lyon Cottage PH9 0PG ☎ 01887 840211
Very attractive highland golf course in charming location. Steep in places but with fine views of surrounding hills and River Tay valley.
9 holes, 4082yds, Par 63, SSS 63, Course record 61.
Club membership 280.
Visitors welcome, no restrictions **Societies** in
Continued

MURRAYSHALL HOUSE HOTEL AND GOLF COURSE
SCONE, BY PERTH

Set within 300 acres of parkland surrounded by 2 18 hole golf courses, this 4 star, STB highly commended country house hotel has 41 bedrooms. Leisure facilities include sauna, gymnasium, jacuzzi, tennis courts, driving range and indoor golf school.
Special golf packages available
Society welcome groups
Our clubhouse facilities are available
to non members
Pro Shop 01738 552784

writing/telephone Secretary. **Green Fees** £12 per day (£15 weekends and bank holidays). **Facilities** ⛳ **Location** W of Ballinluig on A9. take A827 towards Aberfeldy

Hotel ★★★ 63% Moness House Hotel & Country Club, Crieff Rd, ABERFELDY ☎ 0870 443 1460 12 en suite

RENFREWSHIRE

BISHOPTON   Map 10 NS47

Erskine PA7 5PH ☎ 01505 862108
Parkland course.
18 holes, 6287yds, Par 71, SSS 70.
Club membership 700.
Visitors introduced by member or by prior arrangement.
Societies apply in writing. **Green Fees** £31 per round/£42 per day. **Prof** Peter Thomson **Facilities** ⊗ ∭ ⅃ ♨ ♀ ⛳ 🖪 ⅃ ⚒ ⚘ **Location** 0.75 NE off B815

BRIDGE OF WEIR   Map 10 NS36

Ranfurly Castle The Clubhouse, Golf Rd PA11 3HN
☎ 01505 612609 🖺 01505 610406
e-mail: secranfur@aol.com
A highly challenging, 240 acre, picturesque moorland course.
18 holes, 6284yds, Par 70, SSS 71, Course record 65.
Club membership 825.
Visitors golf club members on weekends only. **Societies** weekdays only, apply in writing/telephone in advance.
Green Fees £25 per round; £35 per day. **Cards** 🖭 ▆▆ 🖭 🖬 **Prof** Tom Eckford **Course Designer** A Kirkcaldy/W Auchterlomie **Facilities** ⊗ ∭ ⅃ ♨ ♀ ⛳ 🖪 ⅃ ⚒ ⚘ **Location** 5m NW of Johnstone

Hotel ⇧ Travel Inn Glasgow Paisley, Phoenix Retail Park, PAISLEY ☎ 08701 977113 40 en suite

JOHNSTONE   Map 10 NS46

Cochrane Castle Scott Av, Craigston PA5 0HF
☎ 01505 320146 🖺 01505 325338
Fairly hilly parkland course, wooded with two small streams running through it.
18 holes, 6194yds, Par 71, SSS 71, Course record 63.
Club membership 721.
Visitors contact professional for booking, may play at weekends if introduced by a member. **Societies** apply in writing. **Green Fees** not confirmed. **Prof** Alan J Logan **Course Designer** J Hunter **Facilities** ⊗ ∭ ⅃ ♨ ♀ ⛳ 🖪 ⚒ **Location** 1m from Johnstone town centre, off Beith Rd

Hotel ★★★ 70% Lynnhurst Hotel, Park Rd, JOHNSTONE ☎ 01505 324331 & 324600 🖺 01505 324219 21 en suite

Elderslie 63 Main Rd, Elderslie PA5 9AZ
☎ 01505 323956 🖺 01505 340346
e-mail: anneanderson@eldersliegolfclub.freeserve.co.uk
Parkland course, undulating, with good views.
18 holes, 6175yds, Par 70, SSS 70, Course record 61.
Club membership 940.
Visitors may not play at weekends & bank holidays. Must contact club in advance and preferably have a handicap certificate. **Societies** must telephone in advance. **Green Fees** £30.50 per round/£40.50 per day. **Prof** Richard Bowman **Course Designer** J Braid **Facilities** ⊗ ∭ ⅃ ♨ ♀ ⛳ 🖪 ⚒ **Location** E side of town on A737

Hotel ★★★ 70% Lynnhurst Hotel, Park Rd, JOHNSTONE ☎ 01505 324331 & 324600 🖺 01505 324219 21 en suite

LANGBANK   Map 10 NS37

Gleddoch Golf and Country Club PA14 6YE
☎ 01475 540304 🖺 01475 540201
e-mail: golf@gleddochhouse.co.uk
Parkland and heathland course with other sporting facilities available to temporary members. Good views over Firth of Clyde.
18 holes, 6330yds, Par 71, SSS 71, Course record 64.
Club membership 600.
Visitors must contact in advance. **Societies** must contact in advance. **Green Fees** not confirmed. **Cards** 🖭 ▆▆ 🖭 🖬 **Prof** Keith Campbell **Course Designer** Hamilton Strutt **Facilities** ⊗ ∭ ⅃ ♨ ♀ ⛳ 🖪 ⅃ ⚒ ⚘ **Leisure** heated indoor swimming pool, sauna, gymnasium. **Conf** Corporate Hospitality Days available **Location** B789-Old Greenock Road

Hotel ⇧ Express by Holiday Inn Greenock, Cartsburn, GREENOCK ☎ 01475 786666 71 en suite

LOCHWINNOCH   Map 10 NS35

Lochwinnoch Burnfoot Rd PA12 4AN
☎ 01505 842153 & 01505 843029 🖺 01505 843668
Well maintained parkland course incorporating natural burns. Throughout the course the majority of fairways are wide with tricky greens, but always in good condition. Very scenic with lots of bunkers.
18 holes, 6243yds, Par 71, SSS 71, Course record 63.
Club membership 650.
Visitors may not play at weekends and bank holidays unless accompanied by member(check with Pro Shop). Restricted during competition days. **Societies** apply in writing to club administrator. **Green Fees** £22 per round/£30 per day. **Prof** Gerry Reilly **Facilities** ⊗ ∭ ⅃ ♨ ♀ ⛳ 🖪 ⅃ ⚒ ⚘ **Conf** fac available Corporate Hospitality Days available **Location** W side of town off A760, between Johnstone & Beith, off A737 on Largs road A760

Guesthouse ◆◆◆◆◆ East Lochhead, Largs Rd, LOCHWINNOCH ☎ 01505 842610 3 en suite

PAISLEY   Map 11 NS46

Barshaw Barshaw Park PA1 3TJ ☎ 0141 889 2908
18 holes, 5703yds, Par 68, SSS 67, Course record 63.
Course Designer J R Stutt **Location** 1m E off A737
Telephone for further details

Hotel ★★★ 70% Glynhill Hotel & Leisure Club, Paisley Rd, RENFREW ☎ 0141 886 5555 & 885 1111 🖺 0141 885 2838 125 en suite

Paisley Braehead PA2 8TZ
☎ 0141 884 3903 884 4114 🖺 0141 884 3903
e-mail: paisleygc@onetel.net.uk
Moorland course with good views which suits all handicaps. The course has been designed in two loops of nine holes. Holes feature trees and gorse.
18 holes, 6466yds, Par 71, SSS 72, Course record 64.
Club membership 850.
Visitors must have handicap certificate. May not play Sat. Contact in advance. **Societies** handicaps certificate essential. Groups over 12 must apply in writing, smaller

Continued

Continued

groups may phone in advance. **Green Fees** £35 per day; £24 per round. **Cards** 🔲 ▨ 📰 💲 **Prof** Gordon Stewart **Course Designer** Stutt **Facilities** ⊗ 米 ╚ ☒ ♀ ⚐ 🏠 ⛳ ❦ ♨ **Location** S side of town off B774

Hotel ★★★ 70% Glynhill Hotel & Leisure Club, Paisley Rd, RENFREW ☎ 0141 886 5555 & 885 1111 📋 0141 885 2838 125 en suite

Ralston Strathmore Av, Ralston PA1 3DT

☎ 0141 882 1349 📋 0141 883 9837
Parkland course.
18 holes, 6071yds, Par 71, SSS 69, Course record 62.
Club membership 750.
Visitors Mon-Fri only and must be accompanied by member, contact in advance. **Societies** written notice required **Green Fees** £28 per day; £18 per round. **Cards** 🔲 ▨ 💲 **Prof** Colin Munro **Course Designer** J Braid **Facilities** ⊗ 米 ╚ ☒ ♀ ⚐ 🏠 ❦ **Conf** fac available **Location** 2m E off A737

RENFREW Map 11 NS46

Renfrew Blythswood Estate, Inchinnan Rd PA4 9EG

☎ 0141 886 6692 📋 0141 886 1808
e-mail: secretary@renfrew.scottishgolf.com
Tree-lined parkland course.
18 holes, 6818yds, Par 72, SSS 73, Course record 65.
Club membership 800.
Visitors restricted to Mon, Tue & Thu, apply in advance. **Societies** apply in writing in advance. **Green Fees** not confirmed. **Course Designer** Commander Harris **Facilities** ⊗ 米 ╚ ☒ ♀ ⚐ 🏠 ❦ **Location** 0.75m W off A8

Hotel ★★★ 70% Glynhill Hotel & Leisure Club, Paisley Rd, RENFREW ☎ 0141 886 5555 & 885 1111 📋 0141 885 2838 125 en suite

SCOTTISH BORDERS

COLDSTREAM Map 12 NT83

Hirsel Kelso Rd TD12 4NJ

☎ 01890 882678 & 882233 📋 01890 882233
e-mail: bookings@hirselgc.co.uk
A beautifully situated parkland course set in the Hirsel Estate, with panoramic views of the Cheviot Hills. Each hole offers a different challenge especially the 7th, a 170yd par 3 demanding accuracy of flight and length from the tee to ensure achieving a par.
18 holes, 6111yds, Par 70, SSS 70, Course record 65.
Club membership 680.
Visitors contact for details, no restrictions. **Societies** write or telephone the secretary in advance. **Green Fees** £26 per day (£32 weekends). **Cards** 🔲 ▨ 📰 💲 **Facilities** ⊗ 米 ╚ ☒ ♀ ⚐ 🏠 ❦ ♨ **Conf** Corporate Hospitality Days available **Location** At W end of Coldstream on A697

Hotel ★★★ 71% Ednam House Hotel, Bridge St, KELSO ☎ 01573 224168 30 en suite

DUNS Map 12 NT75

Duns Hardens Rd TD11 3NR

☎ 01361 882194 📋 01361 883599
e-mail: secretary@dunsgolfclub.com
Interesting upland course, with natural hazards of water and hilly slopes. Views south to the Cheviot Hills. A burn comes into play at 7 of the holes.

18 holes, 6209yds, Par 70, SSS 70, Course record 67.
Club membership 426.
Visitors welcome except competition days and Mon, Tue and Wed after 4pm. Advisable to contact in advance Apr-Oct. **Societies** write or telephone the secretary in advance for booking details. **Green Fees** £26 per day; £22 per round (£30/£25 weekends and bank holidays). **Course Designer** A H Scott **Facilities** ⊗ 米 ╚ ☒ ♀ ⚐ 🏠 ❦ ♨ **Conf** Corporate Hospitality Days available **Location** 1m W off A6105

Hotel ★★★ 70% Marshall Meadows Country House Hotel, BERWICK-UPON-TWEED ☎ 01289 331133 19 en suite

EYEMOUTH Map 12 NT96

Eyemouth Gunsgreen Hill TD14 5SF

☎ 01890 750551 (clubhouse) & 750004 (Pro shop)
e-mail: eyemouth@gxn.co.uk
A superb course set on the coast, containing interesting and challenging holes, in particular the intimidating 6th hole, a formidable par 3 across a vast gully with the waves crashing below and leaving little room for error. The clubhouse overlooks the picturesque fishing village of Eyemouth and provides panoramic views over the course and North Sea.
18 holes, 6520yds, Par 72, SSS 72, Course record 66.
Club membership 400.
Visitors May play at any time by arrangement. Some competition restrictions on Sat & Sun mornings. Telephone pro shop. **Societies** apply in writing, email or telephone. **Green Fees** £30 per day; £22 per 18 holes (£35/£27 weekends). **Cards** 🔲 ▨ 📰 💲 **Prof** Paul Terras, Tony McLeman **Course Designer** J R Bain **Facilities** ⊗ 米 by prior arrangement ╚ ☒ ♀ ⚐ 🏠 ⛳ ❦ ♨ 🚜 **Conf** Corporate Hospitality Days available **Location** E side of town, 8m N of Berwick and 2m off A1

Hotel ★★★ 70% Marshall Meadows Country House Hotel, BERWICK-UPON-TWEED ☎ 01289 331133 19 en suite

GALASHIELS Map 12 NT43

Galashiels Ladhope Recreation Ground TD1 2NJ

☎ 01896 753724
Hillside course, superb views from the top; 10th hole very steep.
18 holes, 5185yds, Par 67, SSS 66, Course record 61.
Club membership 311.
Visitors must contact the secretary in advance especially for weekends. **Societies** arrangements with secretary especially for weekends. **Green Fees** £25 per day; £20 per round (£30/£25 weekends). **Course Designer** James Braid **Facilities** ⊗ 米 ╚ ☒ ♀ ⚐ ❦ **Location** N side of town centre off A7

Hotel ★★★ 67% Kingsknowes Hotel, Selkirk Rd, GALASHIELS ☎ 01896 758375 11 en suite

Torwoodlee Edinburgh Rd TD1 2NE

☎ 01896 752260 📋 01896 752260
e-mail: thesecretary@torwoodleegolfclub.org.uk
Parkland course with natural hazards designed by Willie Park with a new extension by John Garner, provides a good test for all abilities of play.
18 holes, 6021yds, Par 69, SSS 70, Course record 68.
Club membership 550.
Visitors restricted Thu - Ladies day and Sat - Men's

Continued   *Continued*

competitions. **Societies** letter to secretary. **Green Fees** not confirmed. **Cards** ⊞ ▭ ▨ **Course Designer** Willie Park **Facilities** ⊗ ⊪ ⅃ ♚ ♟ ⅄ ⚒ ⚡ **Location** 1.75m NW off A7

Hotel ★★★ 67% Kingsknowes Hotel, Selkirk Rd, GALASHIELS ☎ 01896 758375 11 en suite

HAWICK   Map 12 NT51

Hawick Vertish Hill TD9 0NY ☎ 01450 372293
e-mail: thesecretary@hawickgolfclub.fsnet.co.uk
18 holes, 5929yds, Par 68, SSS 69, Course record 63.
Location SW side of town
Telephone for further details

INNERLEITHEN   Map 11 NT33

Innerleithen Leithen Water, Leithen Rd EH44 6NL
☎ 01896 830951
Moorland course, with easy walking. Burns and rivers are natural hazards. Testing 5th hole (100 yds) par 3.
9 holes, 6066yds, Par 70, SSS 69, Course record 65.
Club membership 280.
Visitors advisable to check for availability for weekends.
Societies by prior booking. **Green Fees** terms on application. **Course Designer** Willie Park **Facilities** ♚ ♟ ⅄ ⅄ **Location** 1.5m N on B709

Hotel ★★★★ 69% Peebles Hotel Hydro, PEEBLES ☎ 01721 720602 128 en suite

JEDBURGH   Map 12 NT62

Jedburgh Dunion Rd TD8 6TA ☎ 01835 863587
Mature, undulating parkland course with great views. Some unusual 'square' greens.
9 holes, 5760yds, Par 68, SSS 67, Course record 62.
Club membership 410.
Visitors weekend restrictions. Weekdays prior to 6pm.
Societies must contact at least one month in advance by writing or telephone. **Green Fees** £18 per day/round.
Course Designer William Park **Facilities** ⊗ ⊪ ♚ ♟ ⅄ ⚒ **Conf** Corporate Hospitality Days available **Location** 1m W on B6358

KELSO   Map 12 NT73

Kelso Racecourse Rd TD5 7SL
☎ 01573 223009 ▤ 01573 228490
18 holes, 6046yds, Par 70, SSS 69, Course record 64.
Course Designer James Braid **Location** N side of town centre off B6461
Telephone for further details

Hotel ★★★ 66% Cross Keys Hotel, 36-37 The Square, KELSO ☎ 01573 223303 27 en suite

Roxburghe Heiton TD5 8JZ
☎ 01573 450333 ▤ 01573 450611
e-mail: golf@roxburghe.net
An exceptional parkland layout designed by Dave Thomas and opened in 1997. Surrounded by natural woodland on the banks of the river Teviot. Owned by the Duke of Roxburghe, this course has numerous bunkers, wide rolling and sloping fairways and strategically placed water features.
Roxburghe Golf Course: 18 holes, 6925yds, Par 72, SSS 74, Course record 66.
Club membership 310.

Continued

Roxburghe Golf Club

Visitors dress code (smart casual, no jeans, no training shoes). Book in advance **Societies** please telephone in advance, a number of packages available. **Green Fees** £80 per day, £60 per round. **Cards** ⊞ ▭ ▬ ▨ ▨ **Prof** Craig Montgomerie **Course Designer** Dave Thomas **Facilities** ⊗ ⊪ ♚ ♟ ⅄ ⅄ ⚑ ♙ ⚒ ⚡ **Leisure** tennis courts, fishing, Clay pigeon shooting, falconry, archery, mountain bikes. **Conf** fac available Corporate Hospitality Days available **Location** 5m E of Jedburgh on A698, 2m W of Kelso on A698

Hotel ★★★ ♨ 76% The Roxburghe Hotel & Golf Course, Heiton, KELSO ☎ 01573 450331 16 en suite 6 annexe en suite

LAUDER   Map 12 NT54

Lauder Galashiels Rd TD2 6RS ☎ 01578 722240
e-mail: laudergc@aol.com
Inland course and practice area on gently sloping hill with stunning views of the Lauderdale district. The 'signature' holes are The Wood, a dog-leg par 4 played round the corner of a wood which is itself out of bounds, and The Quarry, a 150 yard par 3 played over several old quarry holes into a bowl shaped green.
9 holes, 3001yds, Par 72, SSS 69, Course record 66.
Club membership 260.
Visitors restricted Mon, Tues & Wed 4.30-6pm and Sun before noon. **Societies** telephone in advance. **Green Fees** £10 per day/round. **Course Designer** Willie Park Jnr **Facilities** ⅄ **Conf** Corporate Hospitality Days available **Location** On Galashiels Rd, off A68, 0.5m from Lauder

Hotel ★★ 66% Lauderdale Hotel, 1 Edinburgh Rd, LAUDER ☎ 01578 722231 10 en suite

MELROSE   Map 12 NT53

Melrose Dingleton TD6 9HS ☎ 01896 822855
Undulating tree-lined fairways with spendid views. Many bunkers.
9 holes, 5562yds, Par 70, SSS 68, Course record 61.
Club membership 380.
Visitors competitions all Sats and many Suns Apr-Oct, ladies priority Tue, junior priority Wed am in holidays.
Societies apply in writing. **Green Fees** not confirmed.
Course Designer James Braid **Facilities** ⅄ **Location** Off A68, S side of town centre on B6359

Hotel ★★★ 71% Burt's Hotel, Market Square, MELROSE ☎ 01896 822285 20 en suite

Booking a tee time is always advisable.

358

MINTO   Map 12 NT52

Minto TD9 8SH ☏ 01450 870220 🖷 01450 870126
e-mail: pat@mintogolfclub.freeserve.co.uk
Pleasant, undulating parkland course featuring mature trees and panoramic views of Scottish Border country. Short but quite testing.
18 holes, 5542yds, Par 69, SSS 67, Course record 63.
Club membership 600.
Visitors advisable to telephone in advance, and essential for weekends. **Societies** contact in advance. **Green Fees** £30 per day, £25 per round (£38/£30 weekends and bank holidays). **Cards** 🖾 🖾 🖾 🖾 🖃 🖇 **Course Designer** Thomas Telford **Facilities** ⊗ ⅷ ⅊ ⅊ ⅊ ☙ ♨ ⅌ **Conf** Corporate Hospitality Days available **Location** 5m from Hawick, 1.25m off A698 at Denholm

NEWCASTLETON   Map 12 NY48

Newcastleton Holm Hill TD9 0QD
☏ 01387 375608
Hilly course with scenic views over the Liddesdale Valley and Newcastleton.
9 holes, 5491yds, Par 69, SSS 70, Course record 69.
Club membership 100.
Visitors contact the Secretary in advance. **Societies** contact by telephone or in writing in advance. **Green Fees** £10 per day/round. **Course Designer** J Shade **Facilities** ⅊ ⅌ **Leisure** fishing. **Location** W side of village

Hotel ★★★ 67% Garden House Hotel, Sarkfoot Rd, GRETNA ☏ 01461 337621 38 en suite

PEEBLES   Map 11 NT24

Peebles Kirkland St EH45 8EU
☏ 01721 720197 🖷 01721 724441
e-mail: secretary@peeblesgolfclub.co.uk
This parkland course is one of the most picturesque courses in Scotland, shadowed by the rolling border hills and Tweed Valley and set high above the town.
18 holes, 6160yds, Par 70, SSS 70, Course record 63.
Club membership 750.
Visitors advisable to ring for information on availability, no visitors on Sat. **Societies** apply by telephone or in writing in advance. **Green Fees** £34 per round/£48 per day. **Cards** 🖾 🖾 🖇 **Prof** Craig Imlah **Course Designer** H S Colt **Facilities** ⊗ ⅷ ⅊ ⅊ ⅊ ⅊ ☙ ⅌ **Location** W side of town centre off A72

Hotel ★★★★ 69% Peebles Hotel Hydro, PEEBLES ☏ 01721 720602 128 en suite

ST BOSWELLS   Map 12 NT53

St Boswells Braeheads TD6 0DE
☏ 01835 823527
Attractive parkland course by the banks of the River Tweed; easy walking.
9 holes, 5274yds, Par 68, SSS 66.
Club membership 320.
Visitors contact in advance. **Societies** booking by writing to secretary. **Green Fees** £18 per round/day (weekend £20), 9 holes £12. **Course Designer** W Park **Facilities** ⅊ by prior arrangement ⅊ ⅊ ⅊ **Location** 500yds off A68 east end of village

Hotel ★★★ 🏊 73% Dryburgh Abbey Hotel, ST BOSWELLS ☏ 01835 822261 37 en suite
1 annexe en suite

SELKIRK   Map 12 NT42

Selkirk Selkirk Hill TD7 4NW ☏ 01750 20621
Pleasant moorland course set around Selkirk Hill. Unrivalled views.
9 holes, 5620yds, Par 68, SSS 68, Course record 61.
Club membership 349.
Visitors contact in advance, may not play Mon evening, competition/match days. **Societies** must telephone in advance. **Green Fees** £20 per 18 holes. **Facilities** ⊗ by prior arrangement ⅊ by prior arrangement ⅊ by prior arrangement ⅊ ⅊ ⅌ ⅌ **Location** 1m S on A7

Hotel ★★★ 71% Burt's Hotel, Market Square, MELROSE ☏ 01896 822285 20 en suite

WEST LINTON   Map 11 NT15

Rutherford Castle Golf Club EH46 7AS
☏ 01968 661 233 🖷 01968 661 233
e-mail: info@ruth-castlegc.co.uk
Undulating parkland set beneath the Pentland hills. With many challenging holes. A good test for the better player whilst offering great enjoyment to the average player.
18 holes, 6525yds, Par 72, SSS 71.
Club membership 360.
Visitors telephone booking anytime. **Societies** application form forwarded on request. **Green Fees** not confirmed. **Prof** Martin Brown **Course Designer** Bryan Moore **Facilities** ⅊ ⅊ ⅊ ⅊ ⅊ ☙ ⅌ **Leisure** fishing. **Location** S of Edinburgh city bypass (A720) on A702 towards Carlisle

Hotel ★★★★ 69% Peebles Hotel Hydro, PEEBLES ☏ 01721 720602 128 en suite

West Linton EH46 7HN
☏ 01968 660256 & 660970 🖷 01968 660970
e-mail: secretarywlgc@btinternet.com
Moorland course with beautiful views of Pentland Hills. The 14th hole is usually played into the prevailing west wind from an elevated tee and subsequently ranks as one of the toughest holes. The finish could not be more demanding, a 230 yard par 3 which is played uphill to a small elevated green.
18 holes, 6132yds, Par 69, SSS 70, Course record 63.
Club membership 900.
Visitors weekdays anytime, weekends not before 1pm. Contact Professional. **Societies** contact the secretary by telephone. **Green Fees** not confirmed. **Prof** Ian Wright **Course Designer** Millar/Braid/Fraser **Facilities** ⊗ ⅷ ⅊ ⅊ ⅊ ⅊ ☙ ♨ ⅌ **Conf** Corporate Hospitality Days available **Location** NW side of village off A702

Hotel ★★★★ 69% Peebles Hotel Hydro, PEEBLES ☏ 01721 720602 128 en suite

SOUTH AYRSHIRE

AYR   Map 10 NS32

Belleisle Belleisle Park KA7 4DU
☏ 01292 441258 🖷 01292 442632
Belleisle Course: 18 holes, 6431yds, Par 71, SSS 72, Course record 63.
Seafield Course: 18 holes, 5498yds, Par 68, SSS 67.
Course Designer James Braid **Location** 2m S of Ayr on Coastal Road
Telephone for further details

Continued

Hotel ★★★ 72% Savoy Park Hotel, 16 Racecourse Rd, AYR ☎ 01292 266112 15 en suite

Dalmilling Westwood Av KA8 0QY
☎ 01292 263893 📄 01292 610543

Meadowland course, with easy walking. Tributaries of the River Ayr add interest to early holes.

18 holes, 5724yds, Par 69, SSS 68, Course record 61.
Club membership 260.

Visitors must contact in advance. Societies must contact in advance. Green Fees £12 per round/£20 per day (weekends £16/£25). Cards 🖽 🖃 💷 🕁 🔣 ⊘ Prof Philip Cheyney Facilities ⊗ ⟭ ⓑ ☕ 👤 🏠 🎯 ⊘ Location 1.5m E of town centre off A77

Hotel ★★★★ 71% Fairfield House Hotel, 12 Fairfield Rd, AYR ☎ 01292 267461 40 en suite 4 annexe en suite

BARASSIE — Map 10 NS33

Kilmarnock (Barassie) 29 Hillhouse Rd
KA10 6SY ☎ 01292 313920 📄 01292 318300
e-mail: secretarykbgc@lineone.net

The club now has a 27 hole layout. Magnificent seaside links, relatively flat with much heather and small, undulating greens.

18 holes, 6817yds, Par 72, SSS 74, Course record 63.
9 hole course: 9 holes, 2888yds, Par 34.
Club membership 600.

Visitors limited availability Wed & weekends. May not play Fri am. Contact secretary in advance. Societies must telephone in advance and confirm in writing. Green Fees £58 for up to 36 holes. Cards 🖽 🖃 ⊘ Prof Gregor Howie Course Designer Theodore Moone Facilities ⊗ ⟭ ⓑ ☕ 👤 🏠 🌳 ⊘ Location E side of village on B746, 2m N of Troon

Hotel ★★★★ 64% Marine Hotel, Crosbie Rd, TROON ☎ 01292 314444 90 en suite

GIRVAN — Map 10 NX19

Brunston Castle Golf Course Rd, Dailly KA26 9GD
☎ 01465 811471 📄 01465 811545
e-mail: golf@brunstoncastle.co.uk

Sheltered inland parkland course. A championship design by Donald Steel, the course is bisected by the River Girvan and shaped to incorporate all the natural surroundings. Lined with mature trees and incorporating a number of water features in addition to the river.

Burns: 18 holes, 6662yds, Par 72, SSS 72, Course record 63.
Club membership 400.

Visitors reserved for members at weekends 8-10 & 12.30-1.30. Must contact in advance. Societies telephone 01465 811471 to book. Green Fees 18 holes £28; 36 holes £45 (weekends £32; £50). Cards 🖽 🖃 ⊘ Prof Malcolm Harrison Course Designer Donald Steel Facilities ⊗ ⟭ ⓑ ☕ 👤 🏠 🎯 🌳 ⊘ ⓒ Conf fac available Corporate Hospitality Days available Location 6m SE of Turnberry, 5m E of Girvan

Hotel ★★★ 76% Malin Court, TURNBERRY ☎ 01655 331457 18 en suite

Girvan Golf Course Rd KA26 9HW
☎ 01465 714346 📄 01465 714272

18 holes, 5098yds, Par 64, SSS 65, Course record 61.
Course Designer D Kinnell/J Braid Location N side of town off A77
Telephone for further details

Hotel ★★★ 76% Malin Court, TURNBERRY ☎ 01655 331457 18 en suite

MAYBOLE — Map 10 NS20

Maybole Municipal Memorial Park KA19 7DX
☎ 01655 889770

9 holes, 2635yds, Par 33, SSS 65, Course record 64.
Location Off A77 S of town
Telephone for further details

Hotel ★★ Ladyburn, MAYBOLE ☎ 01655 740585 5 en suite

PRESTWICK — Map 10 NS32

Prestwick 2 Links Rd KA9 1QG
☎ 01292 477404 📄 01292 477255
e-mail: bookings@prestwickgc.co.uk

Seaside links with natural hazards, tight fairways and difficult fast undulating greens.

18 holes, 6544yds, Par 71, SSS 73, Course record 67.
Club membership 575.

Visitors restricted Thu and Sun, no play on Sat. Must contact in advance and have a handicap certificate. Societies must contact in writing. Green Fees £95 per round/£135 per day (Sundays £115 per round). Cards 🖽 🖃 🔣 ⊘ Prof F C Rennie Course Designer Tom Morris Facilities ⊗ ⟭ ⓑ ☕ 👤 🏠 🎯 ⊘ Location In town centre off A79

Hotel ★★★ 69% Parkstone Hotel, Esplanade, PRESTWICK ☎ 01292 477286 22 en suite

Prestwick St Cuthbert East Rd KA9 2SX
☎ 01292 477101 📄 01292 671730
e-mail: secretary@stcuthbert.co.uk

Parkland course with easy walking, natural hazards and sometimes windy.

18 holes, 6470yds, Par 71, SSS 71, Course record 64.
Club membership 880.

Visitors must contact in advance but may not play at weekends & bank holidays. Societies Mon-Fri, apply in writing. Green Fees £35 per round/£45 per day. Cards 🖽 🖃 ⊘ Course Designer Stutt & Co Facilities ⊗ ⟭ ⓑ ☕ 👤 ⊘ Conf Corporate Hospitality Days available Location 0.5m E of town centre off A77

Hotel ★★★ 69% Parkstone Hotel, Esplanade, PRESTWICK ☎ 01292 477286 22 en suite

Prestwick St Nicholas Grangemuir Rd KA9 1SN
☎ 01292 477608 📄 01292 473900
e-mail: secretary@prestwickstnicholas.com

Classic seaside links course with views across the Firth of Clyde to the Isle of Arran to the west and Ailsa Craig to the south.

18 holes, 5952yds, Par 69, SSS 69, Course record 63.
Club membership 750.

Visitors no play Sat & Sun am. Must contact in advance. Societies must contact in advance. Green Fees not confirmed. Cards 🖽 🖃 🔣 ⊘ Course Designer Charles

Continued

Royal Troon

Map 10 NS33

Troon

☎ **01292 311555** 📄 **01292 318204**

Troon was founded in 1878 with just five holes on linksland. In its first decade it grew from five holes to six, then 12, and finally 18 holes. It became Royal Troon in 1978 on the occasion of its 100th anniversary. Royal Troon's reputation is based on its combination of rough and sandy hills, bunkers, and a severity of finish that has diminished the championship hopes of many. The most successful players have relied on an equal blend of finesse and power. The British Open Championship has been played at Troon eight times - in 1923, 1950, 1962, 1973, 1982, 1989, 1997 and finally in 2004 when it hosted the 133rd tournament. It has the shortest and longest holes of courses hosting the Open. Ten new bunkers and four new tees were added between the 1997 and 2004 competitions. It is recommended that you apply to the course in advance for full visitor information.

e-mail: booking@royaltroon.com

Visitors Welcome May to Oct: Mon, Tue and Thu only. Must write in advance and have a letter of introduction from own club and a handicap certificate (gentlemen under 20, ladies under 30). Under 18s may play on the Portland

Green Fees £185 per day, 1 round on each course plus lunch

Facilities ⊗ ⓑ 💂 ♀ ♨ 🏠 🦯 ✍ ✆

Corporate hospitality days available

Professional R. B. Anderson

Location Craigend Rd, Troon KA10 6EP (S side of town on B749 5 miles from Prestwick airport)

Holes/Par/Course record 36 holes.
Old Course: 18 holes, 6641 yds, Par 71, SSS 73, Course record 64
Portland: 18 holes, 6289 yds, Par 71, SSS 71, Course record 65

WHERE TO STAY NEARBY

Hotels
TROON

★★★★ ⓖ 64% Marine, KA10 6HE.
☎ 01292 314444.
90 en suite

★★★ ⓖ ⓖ ⓖ ♣
Lochgreen House, KA10 7EN.
☎ 01292 313343.
32 en suite
8 annexe en suite

★★★ 74% Piersland House Hotel, KA10 6HD.
☎ 01292 314747.
9 en suite,
15 annexe en suite

Championship Course

Hunter **Facilities** ⊗ ⫶ ⅃ ↳ ⬛ ♀ ⚐ ⌂ ⛳ ♂ **Location** S side of town off A79

Hotel ★★★ 69% Parkstone Hotel, Esplanade, PRESTWICK ☎ 01292 477286 22 en suite

TROON See page 361

TROON   Map 10 NS33

Troon Municipal Harling Dr KA10 6NE
☎ 01292 312464 ▤ 01292 312578
Three links courses, two of championship standard.
Lochgreen Course: 18 holes, 6820yds, Par 74, SSS 73.
Darley Course: 18 holes, 6360yds, Par 71, SSS 63.
Fullarton Course: 18 holes, 4870yds, Par 66, SSS 64.
Club membership 3000.
Visitors no restrictions. **Societies** apply in writing. **Green Fees** terms on application. **Cards** ▭ ▭ ▭ ▭ **Prof** Gordon McKinlay **Facilities** ⊗ ⫶ ⅃ ↳ ⬛ ♀ ⚐ ⌂ ⛳ ♂ **Location** 100yds from railway station

Hotel ★★★★ 64% Marine Hotel, Crosbie Rd, TROON ☎ 01292 314444 90 en suite

TURNBERRY See page 363

SOUTH LANARKSHIRE

BIGGAR   Map 11 NT03

Biggar The Park, Broughton Rd ML12 6AH
☎ 01899 220618(club) & 220319(course)
Flat parkland course, easy walking and fine views.
18 holes, 5600yds, Par 68, SSS 67, Course record 61.
Club membership 240.
Visitors Must contact in advance. Smart casual wear required. **Societies** must book in advance, observe dress code. **Green Fees** £10.15 per round. **Course Designer** W Park Jnr **Facilities** ⊗ ⫶ ⅃ ↳ ⬛ ♀ ⚐ ♣ ♂ **Leisure** hard tennis courts, boating. **Location** S side of town

Hotel ★★★ 🏅 73% Shieldhill Castle, Quothquan, BIGGAR ☎ 01899 220035 16 en suite

BOTHWELL   Map 11 NS75

Bothwell Castle Blantyre Rd G71 8PJ
☎ 01698 853177 & 852052 ▤ 01698 854052
Flattish tree lined parkland course in residential area.
18 holes, 6200yds, Par 71, SSS 70, Course record 63.
Club membership 1000.
Visitors may only play Mon-Fri 9.30-10.30am & 2-3pm.
Societies (Tues only, apply in writing) **Green Fees** not confirmed. **Prof** Alan McCloskey **Facilities** ⊗ ⫶ ⅃ ↳ ⬛ ♀ ⚐ ⌂ ⛳ ♂ **Conf** Corporate Hospitality Days available **Location** NW of village off B7071

Hotel ★★★ 67% Bothwell Bridge Hotel, 89 Main St, BOTHWELL ☎ 01698 852246 90 en suite

BURNSIDE   Map 11 NS65

Blairbeth Fernbrae Av, Fernhill G73 4SF
☎ 0141 634 3355 & 634 3325 ▤ 0141 634 3325
18 holes, 5518yds, Par 70, SSS 68, Course record 63.
Location 2m S of Rutherglen off Burnside road
Telephone for further details

Hotel ★★★ 65% Bruce Hotel, Cornwall St, EAST KILBRIDE ☎ 01355 229771 65 en suite

Cathkin Braes Cathkin Rd G73 4SE
☎ 0141 634 6605 ▤ 0141 630 9186
e-mail: golf@cathkinbraes.freeserve.co.uk
Moorland course, relatively flat with a prevailing westerly wind and views over Glasgow. A small loch hazard at 5th hole. Very strong finishing holes.
18 holes, 6208yds, Par 71, SSS 71, Course record 64.
Club membership 920.
Visitors must contact in advance & have handicap certificate but may not play at weekends. **Societies** apply in writing. **Green Fees** £28 per round/£38 per day (£39 or £52 incl. food). **Prof** Stephen Bree **Course Designer** James Braid **Facilities** ⊗ ⫶ ⅃ ↳ ⬛ ♀ ⚐ ⌂ ⛳ ♂ **Conf** Corporate Hospitality Days available **Location** 1m S on B759

Hotel ★★★ 65% Bruce Hotel, Cornwall St, EAST KILBRIDE ☎ 01355 229771 65 en suite

CARLUKE   Map 11 NS85

Carluke Mauldslie Rd, Hallcraig ML8 5HG
☎ 01555 770574 & 771070
e-mail: admin.carlukegolf@supanet.com
18 holes, 5853yds, Par 70, SSS 68, Course record 63.
Location 1m W off A73
Telephone for further details

Hotel ★★★ 71% Popinjay Hotel, Lanark Rd, ROSEBANK ☎ 01555 860441 38 en suite

CARNWATH   Map 11 NS94

Carnwath 1 Main St ML11 8JX
☎ 01555 840251 ▤ 01555 841070
Picturesque parkland course slightly hilly, with small greens calling for accuracy. Panoramic views.
18 holes, 5222yds, Par 66, SSS 66, Course record 63.
Club membership 586.
Visitors restricted after 5pm, no visitors Sat. **Societies** apply in writing or telephone. **Green Fees** £28 per day; £18 per round (£34/£24 Sun). **Facilities** ⊗ ⫶ ⅃ ↳ ⬛ ♀ ⚐ ♂ **Location** W side of village on A70

Hotel ★★★ 66% Cartland Bridge Hotel, Glasgow Rd, LANARK ☎ 01555 664426 20 rms (18 en suite)

EAST KILBRIDE   Map 11 NS65

East Kilbride Chapelside Rd, Nerston G74 4PF
☎ 01355 247728
18 holes, 6419yds, Par 71, SSS 71, Course record 64.
Location 0.5m N off A749
Telephone for further details

Hotel ★★★ 65% Bruce Hotel, Cornwall St, EAST KILBRIDE ☎ 01355 229771 65 en suite

Torrance House Calderglen Country Park, Strathaven Rd G75 0QZ
☎ 01355 248638 ▤ 01355 570916
A mature parkland course.
18 holes, 6476yds, Par 72, SSS 69, Course record 71.
Club membership 700.
Visitors welcome, may book up to six days in advance.
Societies Mon-Fri. Apply in writing to, South Lanarkshire Leisure, Hamilton Palace sports grounds-Hamilton **Green Fees** terms on application. **Course Designer** Hawtree & Son **Facilities** ⊗ ⫶ ⅃ ↳ ⬛ ♀ ⚐ ⌂ ⛳ ♂ **Location** 1.5m SE of East Kilbride on A726

Hotel ★★★ 65% Bruce Hotel, Cornwall St, EAST KILBRIDE ☎ 01355 229771 65 en suite

The Westin Turnberry Resort

| Map 10 NS20 | Turnberry |

☎ 01655 331000 📄 01655 331069

For thousands of players of all nationalities, Turnberry is one of the finest of all golf destinations, where some of the most remarkable moments in Open history have taken place. The legendary Ailsa course is complemented by the new highly acclaimed Kintyre course, while the 9-hole Arran Academy Course, created by Donald Steel and Colin Montgomerie, has similar challenges such as undulating greens, tight tee shots, pot bunkers and thick Scottish rough. With the famous hotel on the left and the magnificent Ailsa Craig away to the right, there are few vistas in world golf to match the first tee here. To help you prepare for your game the Colin Montgomerie Links Golf Academy, alongside the luxurious and extensive clubhouse, opened in April 2000; it features 12 driving bays, four short game bays, two dedicated teaching rooms and a group teaching room.

e-mail: turnberry@westin.com

Visitors Residents of hotel have preferential booking

Societies Apply in writing

Green Fees Fees on application

Facilities ⊗ ⅢⅢ ⅃ ⅊ ⅌ ⅋ ☈ ⛟ ▲ ⛫

Conf Facilities available; corporate hospitality days available

Professional Paul Burley. Golf Academy

Leisure Tennis, squash, swimming, sauna, solarium, gymnasium

Location Turnberry KA26 9LT (15m SW of Ayr on A77)

Holes/Par/Course record 36 holes.
Ailsa Course: 18 holes, 6440 yds, Par 69, SSS 72, Course record 63
Kintyre Course: 18 holes, 6481 yds, Par 72, SSS72
Arran Academy Course: 9 holes, 1996 yds, Par 31, SSS31

WHERE TO STAY NEARBY

Hotel
TURNBERRY

★★★★★ ◉ ◉
The Westin Turnberry Resort, KA26 9LT.
☎ 01655 331000.
132 en suite 89 annexe en suite

★★★ ◉ ◉ 76%
Malin Court, KA26 9PB.
☎ 01655 331457. 18 en suite

Championship Course

HAMILTON

Map 11 NS75

Hamilton Carlisle Rd, Ferniegair ML3 7UE
☎ 01698 459537
Beautiful parkland course.
18 holes, 6498yds, Par 70, SSS 70, Course record 62.
Visitors must contact in advance, may not play weekends.
Societies apply in writing. **Green Fees** terms on application.
Prof Derek Wright **Course Designer** James Braid **Facilities** ⊗ ⅷ ⅊ ⚑ ⅊ ⅄ ⟐ ♂ **Location** 1.5m SE on A72

⋯⋯⋯⋯⋯⋯⋯⋯

Hotel ⇧ Express by Holiday Inn, Hamilton Rd,
HAMILTON ☎ 01698 858585 120 en suite

Strathclyde Park Mote Hill ML3 6BY
☎ 01698 429350
**Municipal wooded parkland course with views into the
Strathclyde Park sailing loch. Surrounded by a nature
reserve and Hamilton race course.**
9 holes, 3113yds, Par 36, SSS 70, Course record 68.
Club membership 140.
Visitors telephone, same day booking system in operation.
May book up to 1 week in advance in summer months.
Societies must contact in advance on above telephone
number,for prior booking. **Green Fees** £3.40 per 9 holes.
Prof William Walker **Facilities** ⚑ ⟐ ♂ ⅄ **Location** N
side of town off B7071

⋯⋯⋯⋯⋯⋯⋯⋯

Hotel ⇧ Express by Holiday Inn, Hamilton Rd,
HAMILTON ☎ 01698 858585 120 en suite

LANARK

Map 11 NS84

Lanark The Moor, Whitelees Rd ML11 7RX
☎ 01555 663219 & 661456 ▤ 01555 663219
e-mail: lanarkgolfclub@talk21.com
**The address of the club, 'The Moor', gives some
indication of the kind of golf to be found there. Golf has
been played at Lanark for well over a century and the
club dates from 1851.**
*Old Course: 18 holes, 6306yds, Par 70, SSS 71, Course
record 62.*
Wee Course: 9 holes, 1489yds, Par 28.
Club membership 880.
Visitors booking advisable, no visitors weekends.
Societies apply in advance. **Green Fees** £40 per day; £30
per round. Wee Course; £7 per day. **Prof** Alan White
Course Designer Tom Morris **Facilities** ⊗ ⅷ ⅊ ⚑ ⅊ ⅄
⟐ ⋎ ⚒ ♂ **Conf** Corporate Hospitality Days available
Location E side of town centre off A73

⋯⋯⋯⋯⋯⋯⋯⋯

Hotel ★★★ 66% Cartland Bridge Hotel, Glasgow Rd,
LANARK ☎ 01555 664426 20 rms (18 en suite)

LARKHALL

Map 11 NS75

Larkhall Burnhead Rd ML9 3AA ☎ 01698 889597
Small, inland parkland course.
9 holes, 6234yds, Par 70, SSS 70, Course record 69.
Club membership 250.
Visitors restricted Tue & Sat. **Green Fees** not confirmed.
Facilities ⅊ ⅊ **Location** E side of town on B7019

⋯⋯⋯⋯⋯⋯⋯⋯

Hotel ★★★ 71% Popinjay Hotel, Lanark Rd,
ROSEBANK ☎ 01555 860441 38 en suite

⬛ **Where to stay, where to eat?**
Visit www.theAA.com

LEADHILLS

Map 11 NS81

Leadhills 51 Main St ML12 6XP ☎ 01659 74456
9 holes, 4354yds, Par 66, SSS 64.
Location E side of village off B797
Telephone for further details

⋯⋯⋯⋯⋯⋯⋯⋯

Hotel ★★ 66% Blackaddie House Hotel, Blackaddie Rd,
SANQUHAR ☎ 01659 50270 9 en suite

LESMAHAGOW

Map 11 NS83

Holland Bush Acretophead ML11 0JS
☎ 01555 893484 & 893646 ▤ 01555 893984
e-mail: mail@hollandbushgolfclub.co.uk
**Fairly difficult, tree-lined municipal parkland and
moorland course. 1st half is relatively flat, while 2nd
half is hilly.**
18 holes, 6246yds, Par 71, SSS 70, Course record 63.
Club membership 400.
Visitors contact shop on 01555 893646 for times etc.
Societies contact shop on 01555 893646 in advance.
Green Fees not confirmed. **Course Designer** J Lawson/K
Pate **Facilities** ⊗ ⅷ ⅊ ⚑ ⅊ ⅄ ⟐ ♂ **Location** 2-3m S of
Lesmahagow on the Lesmahagow-Coalburn Road

⋯⋯⋯⋯⋯⋯⋯⋯

Hotel ★★★ 74% Strathaven Hotel, Hamilton Rd,
STRATHAVEN ☎ 01357 521778 22 en suite

RIGSIDE

Map 11 NS83

Douglas Water Ayr Rd ML11 9NP ☎ 01555 880361
9 holes, 5890yds, Par 72, SSS 69, Course record 63.
Location Ayr road A70
Telephone for further details

⋯⋯⋯⋯⋯⋯⋯⋯

Hotel ★★★ 66% Cartland Bridge Hotel, Glasgow Rd,
LANARK ☎ 01555 664426 20 rms (18 en suite)

STRATHAVEN

Map 11 NS74

Strathaven Glasgow Rd ML10 6NL
☎ 01357 520421 ▤ 01357 520539
e-mail: info@strathavengc.com
**Gently undulating, tree-lined, Championship parkland
course with panoramic views over town and Avon valley.**
18 holes, 6250yds, Par 71, SSS 71, Course record 65.
Club membership 1050.
Visitors welcome weekdays up to 4pm only. May not play
at weekends. Must contact in advance. **Societies** apply in
writing to general manager. **Green Fees** £37 per day, £27
per round. **Prof** Stuart Kerr **Course Designer** Willie
Fernie/J Stutt **Facilities** ⊗ ⅷ ⅊ ⚑ ⅊ ⅄ ⟐ ⋎ ⚒ ♂
Location NE side of town on A726

⋯⋯⋯⋯⋯⋯⋯⋯

Hotel ★★★ 74% Strathaven Hotel, Hamilton Rd,
STRATHAVEN ☎ 01357 521778 22 en suite

UDDINGSTON

Map 11 NS66

Calderbraes 57 Roundknowe Rd G71 7TS
☎ 01698 813425
**Parkland course with good view of Clyde Valley.
Testing 4th hole (par 4), hard uphill.**
9 holes, 5046yds, Par 66, SSS 67, Course record 65.
Club membership 230.
Visitors weekdays before 5pm. **Societies** welcome **Green
Fees** £12 per day. **Facilities** ⊗ ⅷ ⅊ ⚑ ⅊ ⅄ **Location**
1.5m NW off A74

⋯⋯⋯⋯⋯⋯⋯⋯

Hotel ★★★ 67% Bothwell Bridge Hotel, 89 Main St,
BOTHWELL ☎ 01698 852246 90 en suite

STIRLING

ABERFOYLE
Map 11 NN50

Aberfoyle Braeval FK8 3UY ☎ 01877 382493
Scenic heathland course with mountain views.
18 holes, 5210yds, Par 66, SSS 66, Course record 64.
Club membership 665.
Visitors weekend restrictions, must contact in advance.
Societies must contact in advance. **Green Fees** not
confirmed. **Facilities** ⊗ ⫟ ⅃ ᖧ ♀ ♨ ☆ ☆ ⓖ **Location** 1m
E on A81

....

Hotel ★★★★ 65% Forest Hills Hotel, Kinlochard,
ABERFOYLE ☎ 01877 387277 54 en suite

BANNOCKBURN
Map 11 NS89

Brucefields Family Golfing Centre Pirnhall Rd
FK7 8EH ☎ 01786 818184 📄 01786 817770
e-mail: brucefields@freenetname.co.uk
**Gently rolling parkland with fine views. Most holes can
be played without too much difficulty with the
exception of the 2nd which is a long and tricky par 4
and the 6th, a par 3 which requires exact club selection
and a straight shot.**
*Main Course: 9 holes, 2513yds, Par 68, SSS 68, Course
record 66.*
Visitors no restrictions **Societies** apply in writing. **Green
Fees** £16 per 18 holes, £9 per 9 holes (£18/£10 weekends).
Cards ⊟ ⚌ ⚌ ⚌ ⓖ **Course Designer** Souters
Sportsturf **Facilities** ⊗ ⫟ ⅃ ᖧ ♀ ♨ ☆ ☆ ♨ ⓖ ᒥ
Leisure golf academy, par 3 9 hole course. **Conf** fac
available **Corporate Hospitality Days available Location**
Exit at interchange of M80/M9 (junct 9), from roundabout
take A91, 1st left at sign for Brucefields

....

Hotel ★★ 68% Terraces Hotel, 4 Melville Ter,
STIRLING ☎ 01786 472268 17 en suite

BRIDGE OF ALLAN
Map 11 NS79

Bridge of Allan Sunnylaw FK9 4LY
☎ 01786 832332
**Parkland course, very hilly with good views of Stirling
Castle and beyond to the Trossachs. Testing par 3 1st
hole, 221 yards uphill, with a 6-ft wall 25 yards before
green.**
9 holes, 4932yds, Par 66, SSS 66, Course record 59.
Club membership 400.
Visitors restricted Mon & Thu evenings, Sat, contact in
advance. **Societies** must contact in advance. **Green Fees**
not confirmed. **Course Designer** Tom Morris **Facilities** ⊗
⅃ ♀ ♀ ♨ ⓖ **Location** 0.5m N off A9

....

Hotel ★★★ 71% Royal Hotel, Henderson St, BRIDGE
OF ALLAN ☎ 01786 832284 32 en suite

CALLANDER
Map 11 NN60

Callander Aveland Rd FK17 8EN
☎ 01877 330090 & 330975 📄 01877 330062
e-mail: callandergc@nextcall.net
**Challenging parkland course with tight fairways and a
number of interesting holes. Designed by Tom Morris
Snr and overlooked by the Trossachs.**
18 holes, 5151yds, Par 66, SSS 65, Course record 61.
Club membership 600.
Visitors prior booking 24-48 hrs is advised in the playing
Continued

season. Handicap certificate Wed/Sun. **Societies** write or
telephone for booking form. **Green Fees** £20 per
round/£28 per day (weekends £30/£40). **Cards** ⊟ ⚌ ⚌
⚌ **Prof** Allan Martin **Course Designer** Morris/Fernie
Facilities ⊗ ⫟ ⅃ ᖧ ♀ ♀ ♨ ☆ ☆ ⓖ **Conf** Corporate
Hospitality Days available **Location** E side of town off
A84

....

Hotel ★★★ Roman Camp Country House Hotel,
CALLANDER ☎ 01877 330003 14 en suite

DRYMEN
Map 11 NS48

Buchanan Castle G63 0HY
☎ 01360 660307 📄 01360 660993
e-mail: buchanancastle@sol.co.uk
**Parkland course, with easy walking and good views.
Owned by the Duke of Montrose.**
18 holes, 6059yds, Par 70, SSS 69.
Club membership 830.
Visitors must contact professional on 01360 660330 in
advance. **Societies** must contact in advance. **Green Fees**
not confirmed. **Cards** ⚌ **Prof** Keith Baxter **Course
Designer** James Braid **Facilities** ⊗ ⫟ ⅃ ᖧ ♀ ♀ ♨ ☆ ☆ ⓖ
Conf fac available **Corporate Hospitality Days available
Location** 1m W

....

Hotel ★★★ 65% Winnock Hotel, The Square, DRYMEN
☎ 01360 660245 48 en suite

Strathendrick G83 8EL
☎ 01360 660690 📄 01389 600567
e-mail: marrisonpe@aol.com
9 holes, 4982yards, Par 66, SSS 64, Course record 60.
Location 0.5m S of Drymen via access lane E of A811
Telephone for further details

....

Hotel ★★★★★ 68% De Vere Cameron House,
BALLOCH ☎ 01389 755565 96 en suite

DUNBLANE
Map 11 NN70

Dunblane New Golf Club Perth Rd FK15 0LJ
☎ 01786 821521 📄 01786 821522
e-mail: secretary@dngc.co.uk
**Well maintained parkland course, with reasonably
hard walking. Testing par 3 holes.**
18 holes, 5930yds, Par 69, SSS 69.
Club membership 1000.
Visitors may play 9.30am-noon & 2.30-4pm Mon-Fri.
Must contact in advance. **Societies** welcome Mon, Wed-
Fri, contact in advance. **Green Fees** £35 per day; £25 per
round. **Prof** Bob Jamieson **Facilities** ⊗ ⫟ ⅃ ᖧ ♀ ♀ ♨ ☆
♨ ⓖ **Conf** Corporate Hospitality Days available **Location**
E side of town on A9

....

Hotel ★★★ ♨♨ Cromlix House Hotel, Kinbuck, Nr
DUNBLANE ☎ 01786 822125 14 en suite

KILLIN
Map 11 NN53

Killin FK21 8TX ☎ 01567 820312 📄 01567 820312
e-mail: info@killingolfclub.co.uk
**Parkland course at West End of Loch Tay with
outstanding views. Challenging 9-hole course with 14
different tees.**
9 holes, 2600yds, Par 66, SSS 65, Course record 61.
Club membership 250.
Visitors may not play competition days, parties must book
in advance. **Societies** Apply in writing or telephone in
Continued

advance. **Green Fees** terms on application. **Cards** 💳 💳 🔲 🔳 🔲 **Course Designer** John Duncan/J Braid **Facilities** ⊗ ⫯ ᛒ ᛒ ♈ ♉ ⚬ ᚱ 🦌 ♗ **Location** 0.5m N of centre of village on A827

....

Guesthouse ♦♦♦♦ Fairview House, Main St, KILLIN ☎ 01567 820667 6 en suite

STIRLING   Map 11 NS79

Stirling Queens Rd FK8 3AA
☎ 01786 464098 ▤ 01786 460090
e-mail: enquiries@stirlinggolfclub.tv
Undulating parkland course with magnificent views of Stirling Castle and the Grampian Mountains. Testing 15th, 'Cotton's Fancy', 384 yards (par 4).
18 holes, 6438yds, Par 72, SSS 71, Course record 64.
Club membership 1100.
Visitors may reserve tee off times mid week 9-4.30pm. At weekends tee off times may be reserved on day of play subject to availability. **Societies** must apply in writing or telephone. **Green Fees** £40 per day; £28 per round. **Cards** 💳 💳 🔲 **Prof** Ian Collins **Course Designer** James Braid/Henry Cotton **Facilities** ⊗ ⫯ ᛒ ᛒ ♈ ♉ ⚬ ᚱ 🦌 ♗ **Conf** Corporate Hospitality Days available **Location** W side of town on B8051

....

Hotel ★★ 68% Terraces Hotel, 4 Melville Ter, STIRLING ☎ 01786 472268 17 en suite

WEST DUNBARTONSHIRE

BONHILL   Map 10 NS37

Vale of Leven North Field Rd G83 9ET
☎ 01389 752351 ▤ 0870 749 8950
e-mail: clubadministrator@valeoflevengolfclub.org.uk
Moorland course, tricky with many natural hazards - gorse, burns, trees. Overlooks Loch Lomond.
18 holes, 5277yds, Par 67, SSS 66, Course record 63.
Club membership 750.
Visitors may not play Sat. **Societies** apply to the secretary in writing or telephone call. **Green Fees** £25 per day, £17 per round (£31/£21 weekends). **Prof** Barry Campbell **Facilities** ⊗ ⫯ ᛒ ᛒ ♈ ♉ ⚬ ♗ **Conf** fac available **Location** E side of town off A813

....

Hotel ★★★★★ 68% De Vere Cameron House, BALLOCH ☎ 01389 755565 96 en suite

CLYDEBANK   Map 11 NS56

Clydebank & District Glasgow Rd, Hardgate G81 5QY ☎ 01389 383831 & 383833 ▤ 01389 383831
An undulating parkland course established in 1905 overlooking Clydebank.
18 holes, 5823yds, Par 68, SSS 68, Course record 64.
Club membership 889.
Visitors round only, weekdays only and no bank holidays. Must tee off before 4.30pm. Apply to professional 01389 383835 **Societies** must apply in writing. **Green Fees** terms on application. **Prof** Paul Jamieson **Course Designer** Members **Facilities** ⊗ ⫯ ᛒ ᛒ ♈ ♉ ⚬ ♗ **Location** 2m E of Erskine Bridge

....

Hotel ⇧ Premier Lodge (Glasgow North), Milngavie Rd, BEARSDEN ☎ 0870 9906532 61 en suite

Clydebank Municipal Overtoun Rd, Dalmuir G81 3RE ☎ 0141 952 6372
Dalmuir Municipal Golf Course: 18 holes, 5349yds, Par 67, SSS 66, Course record 63.
Location 2m NW of town centre
Telephone for further details

DUMBARTON   Map 10 NS37

Dumbarton Broadmeadow G82 2BQ
☎ 01389 732830 & 765995 ▤ 01389 765995
Flat parkland course.
18 holes, 5992yds, Par 71, SSS 69, Course record 64.
Club membership 700.
Visitors may play Mon- Fri only. **Societies** must apply in writing to Secretary. **Green Fees** per day. **Facilities** ⊗ ⫯ ᛒ ᛒ ♈ ♉ ⚬ **Conf** Corporate Hospitality Days available **Location** 0.25m N off A814

....

Guesthouse ♦♦♦♦♦ Kirkton House, Darleith Rd, CARDROSS ☎ 01389 841951 6 en suite

WEST LOTHIAN

BATHGATE   Map 11 NS96

Bathgate Edinburgh Rd EH48 1BA
☎ 01506 630553 & 652232/630505 ▤ 01506 636775
e-mail: bathgate.golfclub@lineone.net
Moorland course. Easy walking. Testing 11th hole, par 3.
18 holes, 6328yds, Par 71, SSS 70, Course record 58.
Club membership 900.
Visitors casual visitors welcome other than on competition days. Handicap certificate advisable. **Societies** apply in writing. **Green Fees** £25 per day; £20 per round (£35/£25 weekends). **Prof** Sandy Strachan **Course Designer** W Park **Facilities** ⊗ ⫯ ᛒ ᛒ ♈ ♉ ⚬ ♗ **Conf** Corporate Hospitality Days available **Location** E side of town off A89

....

Hotel ★★★ 67% The Hilcroft Hotel, East Main St, WHITBURN ☎ 01501 740818 31 en suite

BROXBURN   Map 11 NT07

Niddry Castle Castle Rd, Winchburgh EH52 6RQ
☎ 01506 891097 ▤ 01506 891097
An 18 hole parkland course, requiring accurate golf to score well.
18 holes, 5965yds, Par 70, SSS 69, Course record 63.
Club membership 600.
Visitors advisable to contact at weekends, restricted during competition time. **Societies** must contact in advance. **Green Fees** terms on application. **Course Designer** A Scott **Facilities** ⊗ ⫯ ᛒ ᛒ ♈ ♉ ⚬ **Conf** Corporate Hospitality Days available **Location** 9m W of Edinburgh on B9080

....

Hotel ★★★★ 68% Houstoun House, UPHALL ☎ 01506 853831 24 en suite 47 annexe en suite

FAULDHOUSE   Map 11 NS96

Greenburn 6 Greenburn Rd EH47 9HJ
☎ 01501 770292
e-mail: administrator@greenburngolfclub.freeserve.co.uk
Exposed rolling course with sparse tree cover. Water hazards from a pond and a burn.

Continued

18 holes, 6045yds, Par 71, SSS 70, Course record 65.
Club membership 900.
Visitors contact in advance for details. **Societies** by prior arrangement. **Green Fees** terms on application. **Prof** Scott Catlin **Facilities** ⊗ ⵊⵜ ⵏ ⵕ ♀ ⵣ 🛍 ✓ **Location** 3m SW of Whitburn

Hotel ★★★ 67% The Hilcroft Hotel, East Main St, WHITBURN ☎ 01501 740818 31 en suite

LINLITHGOW   Map 11 NS97

Linlithgow Braehead EH49 6QF
☎ 01506 844356 (Pro) 📖 01506 842764
e-mail: info@linlithgowgolf.co.uk
A short but testing undulating parkland course with panoramic views of the Forth Valley.
18 holes, 5800yds, Par 70, SSS 68, Course record 64.
Club membership 450.
Visitors may not play Weds & Sat. **Societies** must contact in writing. **Green Fees** £25 per day; £20 per round (£30/£25 Sun). **Cards** 🖃 🖼 🖬 **Prof** Steven Rosie **Course Designer** R Simpson of Carnoustie **Facilities** ⊗ ⵊⵜ ⵏ ⵕ ♀ ⵣ 🛍 ❦ ✓ **Location** 1m S off Bathgate Road off A803

Hotel ★★★★ 69% The Inchyra, Grange Rd, POLMONT ☎ 01324 711911 109 en suite

West Lothian Airngath Hill EH49 7RH
☎ 01506 825060 📖 01506 826462
Hilly parkland course with superb views of River Forth.
18 holes, 6249yds, Par 71, SSS 70.
Club membership 800.
Visitors weekends by arrangement. Advisable to contact in high season. **Societies** apply in writing. **Green Fees** £20 per round (weekends £30). **Cards** 🖃 🖼 🖬 **Prof** Ian Taylor **Course Designer** Fraser Middleton **Facilities** ⊗ ⵏ ⵕ ♀ ⵣ 🛍 ⵟ ❦ ✓ **Conf** Corporate Hospitality Days available **Location** 1m N off A706

Hotel ★★★★ 69% The Inchyra, Grange Rd, POLMONT ☎ 01324 711911 109 en suite

LIVINGSTON   Map 11 NT06

Deer Park Golf & Country Club Golf Course
Rd EH54 8AB ☎ 01506 446699 📖 01506 435608
e-mail: deerpark@muir-group.com
Long testing course, fairly flat, championship standard.
18 holes, 6688yds, Par 72, SSS 72, Course record 65.
Visitors proper golfing attire to be worn, must book in advance, Sun after 10am. **Societies** telephone or write **Green Fees** £28 per 18 holes (£38 unlimited weekend play). **Cards** 🖃 🖼 🖼 🖬 **Prof** Brian Dunbar **Course Designer** Alliss/Thomas **Facilities** ⊗ ⵊⵜ ⵏ ⵕ ♀ ⵣ 🛍 ⵟ ❦ 🎱 ✓ **Leisure** heated indoor swimming pool, squash, sauna, solarium, gymnasium, snooker table. **Conf** Corporate Hospitality Days available **Location** N side of town off A809

Hotel ⊡ Travel Inn, Deer Park Av, Knightsridge, LIVINGSTON ☎ 08701 977161 83 en suite

Pumpherston Drumshoreland Rd, Pumpherston
EH53 0LH ☎ 01506 432869 & 433337 (pro)
📖 01506 438250
Undulating, well bunkered parkland course with very testing 2nd & 15th holes. Panoramic views of

Edinburgh and the Pentland Hills from the course.
18 holes, 5233yds, Par 71, SSS 72.
Club membership 731.
Visitors pay and play anytime **Societies** apply in writing to the secretary. **Green Fees** terms on application. **Cards** 🖃 🖼 🖬 **Prof** Richard Fyvie **Course Designer** G Webster **Facilities** ⊗ ⵏ ⵕ ♀ ⵣ 🛍 ✓ **Location** 1m E of Livingston between A71 & A89

Hotel ⊡ Travel Inn, Deer Park Av, Knightsridge, LIVINGSTON ☎ 08701 977161 83 en suite

UPHALL   Map 11 NT07

Uphall EH52 6JT ☎ 01506 856404 📖 01506 855358
e-mail: uphallgolfclub@businessunmetered.com
Windy parkland course, easy walking.
18 holes, 5588yds, Par 69, SSS 67, Course record 61.
Club membership 650.
Visitors must contact in advance, restricted weekends. **Societies** must contact in advance. **Green Fees** terms on application. **Prof** Gordon Law **Facilities** ⊗ ⵊⵜ ⵏ ⵕ ♀ ⵣ 🛍 ✓ **Location** W side of village on A899

Hotel ★★★★ 68% Houstoun House, UPHALL ☎ 01506 853831 24 en suite 47 annexe en suite

WEST CALDER   Map 11 NT06

Harburn EH55 8RS
☎ 01506 871131 & 871256 📖 01506 870286
e-mail: harburn@whsmithnet.co.uk
Moorland, reasonably flat.

18 holes, 5921yds, Par 69, SSS 69, Course record 62.
Club membership 870.
Visitors must contact secretary in advance **Societies** contact by telephone. **Green Fees** £30 per day, £25 per 18 holes (Fri £35/£30, Sat-Sun £40/£35). **Prof** Stephen Mills **Facilities** ⊗ ⵊⵜ ⵏ ⵕ ♀ ⵣ 🛍 ⵟ 🎱 ✓ **Conf** Corporate Hospitality Days available **Location** 2m S of West Calder on B7008

Hotel ★★★ 67% The Hilcroft Hotel, East Main St, WHITBURN ☎ 01501 740818 31 en suite

WHITBURN   Map 11 NS96

Polkemmet Country Park EH47 0AD
☎ 01501 743905 📖 01506 846256
e-mail: mail@beecraigs.com
Public parkland course surrounded by mature woodland and rhododendron bushes. 15-bay floodlit driving range.
9 holes, 2969mtrs, Par 37.
Visitors no restrictions. **Societies** weekdays only, apply in writing. **Green Fees** 9 holes £5.10; 18 holes £8.85

Continued   *Continued*

(weekends and bank holidays £5.95/£10.40). **Facilities** ⊗
𝍫 ᴸ ⬛ ♀ ♂ ℓ **Leisure** bowling green. **Location** 2m W
on B7066

Hotel ★★★ 67% The Hilcroft Hotel, East Main St,
WHITBURN ☎ 01501 740818 31 en suite

ARRAN, ISLE OF

BLACKWATERFOOT   Map 10 NR92

Shiskine Shore Rd KA27 8HA
☎ 01770 860226 ▤ 01770 860205
e-mail: info@shiskinegolf.com
**Unique 12-hole links course with gorgeous outlook to
the Mull of Kintyre. The course is crossed by two burns
and includes the longest par 5 on the island at 509
yards. There are several blind holes at which various
signals indicate when the green is clear and it is safe to
play.**
*12 holes, 2990yds, Par 42, SSS 42, Course record 38.
Club membership 670.*
Visitors must contact in advance. **Societies** must contact in
writing in advance. Jul and Aug no parties. **Green Fees**
£25 per day; £15 per round (£30/£19 weekends and bank
holidays). **Course Designer** Fernie of Troon **Facilities** ⊗
𝍫 by prior arrangement ᴸ ⬛ ⬔ 🏠 ⚑ 🏌 ℓ **Leisure**
hard tennis courts, bowling green, golf practice nets. **Conf**
Corporate Hospitality Days available **Location** W side of
village off A841

Hotel ★★ ≜≜ Kilmichael Country House Hotel, Glen
Cloy, BRODICK ☎ 01770 302219 4 en suite
3 annexe. en suite

BRODICK   Map 10 NS03

Brodick KA27 8DL ☎ 01770 302349 ▤ 01770 302349
e-mail: info@brodickgolfclub.org
**Short seaside course, very flat, incorporating both links
and parkland holes to offer a diverse and scenic round
of golf.**
*18 holes, 4747yds, Par 65, SSS 64, Course record 60.
Club membership 621.*
Visitors parties (6 or more) must contact in advance. No
play at competition times. **Societies** must contact secretary
in writing in advance. **Green Fees** not confirmed. **Prof**
Peter McCalla **Facilities** ⊗ 𝍫 ᴸ ⬛ ♀ ⬔ 🏠 🏌 ℓ **Conf**
fac available **Location** N side of village, 0.5m N of
Brodick Ferry Terminal

Hotel ★★★ 76% Auchrannie Country House Hotel,
BRODICK ☎ 01770 302234 28 en suite

LAMLASH   Map 10 NS03

Lamlash KA27 8JU
☎ 01770 600296 ▤ 01770 600296
**Undulating heathland course with magnificent views of
the mountains and sea.**
*18 holes, 4510yds, Par 64, SSS 64, Course record 59.
Club membership 480.*
Visitors book in advance by letter **Societies** must contact
in writing. **Green Fees** terms on application. **Cards** ▦
Course Designer Auchterlonie **Facilities** ⊗ 𝍫 ᴸ ⬛ ♀ ⬔
🏠 ⚑ ⛏ 🏌 ℓ **Location** 0.75m N of Lamlash on A841.
3m S of Brodick Ferry Terminal

Hotel ★★★ 76% Auchrannie Country House Hotel,
BRODICK ☎ 01770 302234 28 en suite

LOCHRANZA   Map 10 NR95

Lochranza KA27 8HL
☎ 01770 830273 ▤ 01770 830600
e-mail: office@lochgolf.demon.co.uk
18 holes, 5033mtrs, Par 70, SSS 67, Course record 72.
Course Designer re laid 1991 I Robertson **Location** Main
road, Lochranza village.
Telephone for further details

Hotel ★★ ≜≜ Kilmichael Country House Hotel, Glen
Cloy, BRODICK ☎ 01770 302219 4 en suite
3 annexe en suite

MACHRIE   Map 10 NR83

Machrie Bay KA27 8DZ
☎ 01770 840259 ▤ 01770 840266
e-mail: office@dougarie.com
**Fairly flat seaside course. Designed at turn of century
by William Fernie.**
*Machrie Bay Golf Club: 9 holes, 4400yds, Par 66, SSS 62,
Course record 62.
Club membership 315.*
Visitors no restrictions. **Societies** write in advance. **Green
Fees** £12 per day. **Course Designer** W Fernie **Facilities** ⊗
⬛ ⬔ ⚑ ℓ **Leisure** hard tennis courts. **Location** 9m W
of Brodick via String Rd

Hotel ★★ ≜≜ Kilmichael Country House Hotel, Glen
Cloy, BRODICK ☎ 01770 302219 4 en suite
3 annexe en suite

SANNOX   Map 10 NS04

Corrie KA27 8JD ☎ 01770 810223 & 810606
**A heathland course on the coast with beautiful
mountain scenery. An upward climb to 6th hole, then a
descent from the 7th. All these holes are subject to
strong winds in bad weather.**
*9 holes, 1948yds, Par 62, SSS 61, Course record 56.
Club membership 300.*
Visitors welcome except Sat pm and first Thu afternoon of
the month. **Societies** maximum size of party 12, apply in
advance. **Green Fees** £14 per day/round. **Facilities** ⊗ 𝍫
⬛ ⬔ **Location** 6m N of A841

Hotel ★★★ 76% Auchrannie Country House Hotel,
BRODICK ☎ 01770 302234 28 en suite

WHITING BAY   Map 10 NS02

Whiting Bay KA27 8QT ☎ 01770 700487
18 holes, 4405yds, Par 63, SSS 63, Course record 59.
Location NW side of village off A841
Telephone for further details

Hotel ★★ ≜≜ Kilmichael Country House Hotel, Glen
Cloy, BRODICK ☎ 01770 302219 4 en suite
3 annexe en suite

BUTE, ISLE OF

KINGARTH   Map 10 NS05

Bute St Ninians, 32 Marine Place, Ardbeg, Rothesay
PA20 0LF ☎ 01700 502158
e-mail: info@butegolfclub.com
**Flat seaside course with good fenced greens and fine
views.**

Continued

Bute Golf Course: 9 holes, 2361mtrs, Par 68, SSS 64, Course record 61.
Club membership 250.
Visitors restricted Sat until after 11.30am. **Societies** apply in advance. **Green Fees** £10 per round/day. **Facilities** **Location** From Rothesay pier 6m on A845

Hotel ★★ 79% Royal Hotel, Shore Rd, TIGHNABRUAICH ☎ 01700 811239 11 en suite

PORT BANNATYNE — Map 10 NS06

Port Bannatyne Bannatyne Mains Rd PA20 0PH
☎ 01700 505142
e-mail: macleodbute@btopenworld.com
Seaside hill course with panoramic views. Almost unique in having 13 holes, with the first 5 holes being played again before a separate 18th. Difficult hole: 4th (par 3).
13 holes, 5085yds, Par 68, SSS 65, Course record 63.
Club membership 150.
Visitors no restrictions. **Societies** must telephone in advance. **Green Fees** terms on application. **Course Designer** Peter Morrison **Facilities** **Location** W side of village off A886

Hotel ★★ 79% Royal Hotel, Shore Rd, TIGHNABRUAICH ☎ 01700 811239 11 en suite

ROTHESAY — Map 10 NS06

Rothesay Canada Hill PA20 9HN
☎ 01700 503554 Fax 01700 503554
e-mail: thepro@rothesaygolfclub.com
A scenic island course designed by James Braid and Ben Sayers. The course is fairly hilly, with views of the Firth of Clyde, Rothesay Bay or the Kyles of Bute from every hole. Winds are a regular feature which makes the two par 5 holes extremely challenging.
18 holes, 5419yds, Par 69, SSS 66, Course record 62.
Club membership 400.
Visitors pre-booking essential for weekends, telephone professional 01700 503554. **Societies** contact in advance, booking essential at weekends. **Green Fees** terms on application. **Cards** **Prof** James M Dougal **Course Designer** James Braid & Ben Sayers **Facilities** **Conf** Corporate Hospitality Days available **Location** 2 min drive from main ferry terminal

Hotel ★★ 79% Royal Hotel, Shore Rd, TIGHNABRUAICH ☎ 01700 811239 11 en suite

COLONSAY, ISLE OF

SCALASAIG — Map 10 NR39

Colonsay Machrins Farm PA61 7YP
☎ 01951 200364 Fax 01951 200312
e-mail: golf@machrin.free-online.co.uk
18 holes, 4775yds, Par 72, SSS 72.
Location 2m W on A870
Telephone for further details

If you have a comment or suggestion concerning the AA Golf Course Guide 2005, you can e-mail us at
lifestyleguides@theAA.com

ISLAY, ISLE OF

PORT ELLEN — Map 10 NR34

Machrie Hotel Machrie PA42 7AN
☎ 01496 302310 Fax 01496 302404
e-mail: machrie@machrie.com
Championship links course opened in 1891, where golf's first £100 Open Championship was played in 1901. Fine turf and many blind holes. Par 4.
18 holes, 6226yds, Par 71, SSS 71, Course record 65.
Club membership 340.
Visitors no restrictions. **Societies** apply in writing or telephone. **Green Fees** £55 per day, £40 per round. **Cards** **Course Designer** W Campbell **Facilities** **Leisure** fishing, snooker, table tennis. **Location** 4m N off A846

LEWIS, ISLE OF

STORNOWAY — Map 13 NB43

Stornoway Lady Lever Park HS2 0XP
☎ 01851 702240
e-mail: admin@stornowaygolfclub.co.uk
A short but tricky undulating parkland course set in the grounds of Lews Castle with fine views over the Minch to the mainland. The terrain is peat based and there has been substantial investment in drainage works.
18 holes, 5252yds, Par 68, SSS 67, Course record 62.
Club membership 450.
Visitors no golf on Sun. **Societies** apply in writing. **Green Fees** terms on application. **Facilities** **Location** 0.5m from town centre off A857

MULL, ISLE OF

CRAIGNURE — Map 10 NM73

Craignure Scallastle PA65 6BA
☎ 01680 300402 Fax 01680 300402
e-mail: mullair@btinternet.com
A natural links course designed round the estuary of the Scallastle Burn that flows into the Sound of Mull. Continual improvements such as five new tees in 1998 have provided 18 teeing areas for the 9-hole layout.
9 holes, 5357yds, Par 69, SSS 66, Course record 72.
Club membership 104.
Visitors may not play on competition days, contact for fixture list. **Societies** write to the secretary 10 days in advance. **Green Fees** not confirmed. **Facilities** **Location** 1.5m N of Craignure A849

TOBERMORY — Map 13 NM55

Tobermory PA75 6PG
☎ 01688 302338 Fax 01688 302140
e-mail: enquiries@tobermorygolfclub.com
A beautifully maintained hilltop course with superb views over the Sound of Mull. Testing 7th hole (par 3). Often described as the best 9 hole course in Scotland.
9 holes, 4890yds, Par 64, SSS 64, Course record 65.
Club membership 150.
Visitors no restrictions except competition days. **Societies** preferable to contact in advance. **Green Fees** £15 per day.

Continued

half price for less than 18 holes. **Course Designer** David Adams **Facilities** ⓑ 🍺 ♀ ⚐ ⚑ 🏌 🏌 ✪ **Location** 0.5m N off A848

....

Hotel ★★ ♨ 78% Druimard Country House Hotel, DERVAIG ☎ 01688 400345 & 400291 📄 01688 400345 5 en suite 2 annexe en suite

ORKNEY

KIRKWALL   Map 16 HY41

Orkney Grainbank KW15 1RB ☎ 01856 872457
18 holes, 5411yds, Par 70, SSS 67, Course record 64.
Location 0.5m W off A965
Telephone for further details

STROMNESS   Map 16 HY20

Stromness Ness KW16 3DW ☎ 01856 850772
e-mail: sgc@stromnessgc.co.uk
Testing parkland/seaside course with easy walking. Beautiful holiday course with magnificent views of Scapa Flow. New clubhouse opened 1999.
18 holes, 4762yds, Par 65, SSS 64, Course record 61. Club membership 350.
Visitors no restrictions except during major competitions.
Societies no restrictions. **Green Fees** £15 per day.
Facilities ⊗ ⓑ 🍺 ♀ ⚐ 🏌 ✪ **Leisure** hard tennis courts, Bowling. **Conf** fac available **Location** S side of town centre off A965

SHETLAND

LERWICK   Map 16 HU44

Shetland PO Box 18, Dale ZE2 9SB
☎ 01595 840369 📄 840369
e-mail: clubhousemanager@shetlandgolfclub.co.uk
Dale Course: 18 holes, 5776yds, Par 68, SSS 68, Course record 67.
Course Designer Fraser Middleton **Location** 4m N on A970
Telephone for further details
....
Hotel ★★★ 68% Lerwick Hotel, 15 South Rd, LERWICK ☎ 01595 692166 34 en suite

WHALSAY, ISLAND OF   Map 16 HU56

Whalsay Skaw Taing ZE2 9AA
☎ 01806 566450 566705
18 holes, 6009yds, Par 70, SSS 68, Course record 65.
Location Whalsay Island
Telephone for further details
....
Hotel ★★ 64% The Baltasound Hotel, UNST
☎ 01957 711334 8 rms (6 en suite) 17 annexe en suite

SKYE, ISLE OF

SCONSER   Map 13 NG53

Isle of Skye IV48 8TD ☎ 01478 650414
e-mail: isleofskye.golfclub@btinternet.com
Seaside course with spectacular views. 9 holes with 18 tees. Suitable for golfers of all abilities.
18 holes, 4677yds, Par 66, SSS 64, Course record 62. Club membership 270.
Visitors during competition play. **Societies** apply in advance. **Green Fees** £18 per round/day. 9 holes £12.
Cards 🖮 🖦 🖦 🖦 **Facilities** ⊗ ⓑ 🍺 ♀ ⚐ 🏌 🏌 ✪
Location A87 between Broadford and Portree
....
Hotel ★★ 73% Rosedale Hotel, Beaumont Crescent, PORTREE ☎ 01478 613131 18 en suite

SOUTH UIST

ASKERNISH   Map 13 NF72

Askernish Lochboisdale PA81 5SY ☎ 01878 700298
e-mail: askernish.golf.club@cwcom.net
18 holes, 5042yds, Par 68, SSS 67, Course record 64.
Course Designer Tom Morris **Location** 5m NW of Lochboisdale off A865
Telephone for further details

> If the name of the club appears in *italics*, details have not been confirmed for this edition of the guide.

Wales

ANGLESEY, ISLE OF

AMLWCH
Map 06 SH49

Bull Bay LL68 9RY
☎ 01407 830960 📄 01407 832612
e-mail: secretary@bullbaygolf.freeserve.co.uk
Wales's northernmost course, Bull Bay is a pleasant coastal, heathland course with natural rock, gorse and wind hazards. Views from several tees across Irish Sea to Isle of Man, and across Anglesey to Snowdonia.
18 holes, 6217yds, Par 70, SSS 70, Course record 60.
Club membership 700.
Visitors advisable to contact in advance. **Societies** advance booking essential. **Green Fees** £22 per day(£27 weekends & bank holidays). **Cards** 🃏 🃏 🃏 🃏 🃏 📷 **Prof** John Burns **Course Designer** W H Fowler **Facilities** ⊗ ⟨ ⊩ ⊾ ♥ ♀ ⚘ 🏠 ⚑ ⟶ ⚓ ⚒ **Location** 1m W of Amlwch on A5025

BEAUMARIS
Map 06 SH67

Baron Hill LL58 8YW
☎ 01248 810231 📄 01248 810231
e-mail: golf@baronhill.co.uk
Undulating course with natural hazards of rock and gorse. Testing 3rd and 4th holes (par 4s). Hole 5/14 plays into the prevailing wind with an elevated tee across two streams. The hole is between two gorse covered mounds.
9 holes, 5572yds, Par 68, SSS 68, Course record 65.
Club membership 400.
Visitors ladies have priority on Tue am & club competitions Sun, seniors Thurs only. **Societies** apply in writing to secretary. **Green Fees** £15 per day. **Facilities** ⊗ ⊾ ♥ ♀ ⚘ ⚑ ⚒ **Conf** Corporate Hospitality Days available **Location** Take A545 from Menai Bridge to Beaumaris, course signed on approach to town

Hotel ★★ 75% Ye Olde Bulls Head Inn, Castle St, BEAUMARIS ☎ 01248 810329 12 en suite
1 annexe en suite

Princes Henllys Hall LL58 8HU
☎ 01248 811717 📄 01248 811511
e-mail: henllys@hpbsite.com
18 holes, 6062yards.
Course Designer Roger Jones **Location** A545 to Beaumaris and through town. After 1/4 mile, Henllys Hall signed on left
Telephone for further details

Hotel ★★ 75% Ye Olde Bulls Head Inn, Castle St, BEAUMARIS ☎ 01248 810329 12 en suite
1 annexe en suite

HOLYHEAD
Map 06 SH28

Holyhead Lon Garreg Fawr, Trearddur Bay LL65 2YL
☎ 01407 763279 📄 01407 763279
e-mail: mqrsec@aol.com
Treeless, undulating seaside course which provides a varied and testing game, particularly in a south wind. The fairways are bordered by gorse, heather and rugged outcrops of rock. Accuracy from most tees is paramount as there are 43 fairway and greenside bunkers and lakes. Designed by James Braid.
18 holes, 6058yds, Par 70, SSS 70, Course record 64.
Club membership 1350.

Continued

Visitors must contact in advance. **Societies** must contact in advance. **Green Fees** £22 per day (£29 weekends & bank holidays). **Cards** 🃏 🃏 **Prof** Stephen Elliot **Course Designer** James Braid **Facilities** ⊗ ⟨ ⊩ ⊾ ♥ ♀ ⚘ 🏠 ⚑ 🏐 ⚒ **Location** A55 to rdbt at Hollyhead, left on B4545 to Trearddur Bay 1 mile

Hotel ★★★ 72% Trearddur Bay Hotel, TREARDDUR BAY ☎ 01407 860301 36 en suite

LLANGEFNI
Map 06 SH47

Llangefni (Public) Clai Rd LL77 7LJ
☎ 01248 722193 📄 01248 750156
9 holes, 1342yds, Par 28, SSS 28.
Course Designer Hawtree & Sons **Location** 1.5m off A5
Telephone for further details

Hotel ★★ 67% Anglesey Arms, MENAI BRIDGE ☎ 01248 712305 16 en suite

RHOSNEIGR
Map 06 SH37

Anglesey Station Rd LL64 5QX
☎ 01407 811127 📄 01407 810816
e-mail: info@theangleseygolfclub.com
An interesting 18 hole links course set amongst sand dunes and heather, renowned for its excellent greens and numerous streams. The whole course boasts an abundance of wildlife and is an important conservation area.
18 holes, 6300yds, Par 70, SSS 70, Course record 64.
Club membership 500.
Visitors phone in advance, some times are reserved for members. Dress restrictions. **Societies** telephone & confirm in writing. **Green Fees** terms on application. **Cards** 🃏 🃏 🃏 🏐 📷 **Prof** Mr Matthew Parry **Course Designer** H Hilton **Facilities** ⊗ ⟨ ⊩ ⊾ ♥ ♀ ⚘ 🏠 ⚑ ⟶ ⚓ ⚒ **Location** NE side of village on A4080

Hotel ★★★ 72% Trearddur Bay Hotel, TREARDDUR BAY ☎ 01407 860301 36 en suite

BLAENAU GWENT

NANTYGLO
Map 03 SO11

West Monmouthshire Golf Rd, Winchestown NP23 4QT ☎ 01495 310233 📄 01495 310361
18 holes, 6300yds, Par 71, SSS 69, Course record 65.
Course Designer Ben Sayers **Location** 0.25m W off A467
Telephone for further details

Hotel ★★ 69% Llanwenarth Hotel & Riverside Restaurant, Brecon Rd, ABERGAVENNY ☎ 01873 810550 18 en suite

TREDEGAR
Map 03 SO10

Tredegar and Rhymney Cwmtysswg, Rhymney NP2 3BQ ☎ 01685 840743 (club) 07944 843400 (sec)
e-mail: golfclub@tredegarandrhymney.fsnet.co.uk
Mountain course with lovely views. The course has now been developed into an 18 hole course with easy walking.
18 holes, 6250yds, Par 67, SSS 67, Course record 68.
Club membership 194.
Visitors cannot play Sun before 12. **Societies**

Continued

must contact in advance. **Green Fees** £10 per day. **Facilities** by prior arrangement by prior arrangement by prior arrangement by prior arrangement **Location** 1.75m SW on B4256

Hotel ★★ 60% Tregenna Hotel, Park Ter, MERTHYR TYDFIL ☎ 01685 723627 14 en suite 7 annexe en suite

BRIDGEND

BRIDGEND — Map 03 SS97

Coed-Y-Mwstwr The Clubhouse, Coychurch CF35 6AF ☎ 01656 864934 01656 864934
e-mail: secretary@coed-y-mwstwr.co.uk
Challenging holes on this 12-hole course include the par 3 11th(180yds) involving a drive across a lake and the par 4 5th (448yds) which is subject to strong prevailing winds.
12 holes, 6144yds, Par 70, SSS 70, Course record 71.
Club membership 300.
Visitors must have handicap certificate, advisable to contact in advance. May only play Sat if with member. **Societies** by prior application. **Green Fees** £17.50 per 18 holes (£19.50 weekends). **Cards** **Course Designer** Chapman/Warren **Facilities** **Conf** fac available Corporate Hospitality Days available **Location** 1m out of Coychurch, turn at village garage. 2m W of junct 35 on M4

Hotel ★★★★ 76% Coed-Y-Mwstwr Hotel, Coychurch, BRIDGEND ☎ 01656 860621 28 en suite

Southerndown Ewenny CF32 0QP
☎ 01656 880476 01656 880317
e-mail: southerndowngolf@btconnect.com
Downland-links championship course with rolling fairways and fast greens. The par 3 5th is played across a valley and the 18th, with its split level fairway, is a demanding finishing hole. Superb views.
18 holes, 6449yds, Par 70, SSS 72, Course record 64.
Club membership 710.
Visitors must contact in advance & have handicap certificate. **Societies** by arrangement with secretary. **Green Fees** £40 (£60 weekends or 36 holes). **Cards** **Prof** D G McMonagle **Course Designer** W Fernie **Facilities** **Location** 3m SW of Bridgend on B4524

Hotel ★★★ 69% Heronston Hotel, Ewenny Rd, BRIDGEND ☎ 01656 668811 69 en suite 6 annexe en suite

MAESTEG — Map 03 SS89

Maesteg Mount Pleasant, Neath Rd CF34 9PR
☎ 01656 734106 01656 731822
Reasonably flat hill-top course with scenic views.
18 holes, 5929yds, Par 70, SSS 69, Course record 69.
Club membership 789.
Visitors must be a member of a recognised golf club & have a handicap certificate. **Societies** apply in writing. **Green Fees** terms on application. **Cards** **Course Designer** James Braid **Facilities** **Conf** fac available **Location** 0.5m W off B4282

Hotel ★★★ 68% Aberavon Beach Hotel, PORT TALBOT ☎ 01639 884949 52 en suite

PENCOED — Map 03 SS98

St Mary's Hotel Golf & Country Club St Mary Hill CF35 5EA ☎ 01656 868900 01656 863400
A parkland course with many American-style features. The par 3 10th, called 'Alcatraz', has a well deserved reputation.

St Mary's Course: 18 holes, 5291yds, Par 69, SSS 66, Course record 65.
Sevenoaks Course: 12 holes, 3125yds, Par 35.
Club membership 830.
Visitors St. Mary's Course: must contact in advance, handicap certificate not required between 9-4 Mon-Fri, after 1pm weekends. Sevenoaks: no restrictions **Societies** telephone in advance **Green Fees** £20 per round (£25 weekends), Sevenoaks: £6.50 (£7.50 weekends). **Cards** **Prof** John Peters **Course Designer** Peter Johnson **Facilities** **Leisure** tennis courts. **Location** 5m from junct 35 of M4

Hotel ★★★ 73% St Mary's Hotel & Country Club, St Marys Golf Club, PENCOED ☎ 01656 861100 & 860280 01656 863400 24 en suite

PORTHCAWL — Map 03 SS87

Royal Porthcawl Rest Bay CF36 3UW
☎ 01656 782251 01656 771687
e-mail: royalporthcawl@aol. com
One of the great links courses, Royal Porthcawl is unique in that the sea is in full view from every single hole. The course enjoys a substantial reputation with heather, broom, gorse and a challenging wind demanding a player's full skill and attention.
18 holes, 6440yds, Par 72, SSS 73.
Club membership 800.
Visitors must contact in advance & produce handicap certificate limit men 20, ladies 30. Restricted at weekends & bank holidays. **Societies** apply in writing/telephone/email **Green Fees** £90 per day, £70 per round (£100/£80 weekends). **Cards** **Prof** Peter Evans **Course Designer** Ramsey Hunter **Facilities** **Location** M4 J37, proceed to Porthcawl & Rest Bay

Hotel ★★★ 64% Seabank Hotel, The Promenade, PORTHCAWL ☎ 01656 782261 67 en suite

PYLE — Map 03 SS88

Pyle & Kenfig Waun-Y-Mer CF33 4PU
☎ 01656 783093 01656 772822
e-mail: secretary@pyleandkenfiggolfclub.co.uk
Links and downland course, with sand-dunes. Easy walking.

Continued

St. Mary's Hotel, ★ ★ ★
Golf & Country Club

St. Mary's Hill Pencoed, South Glamorgan CF35 5EA.
Hotel Reservation: Tel: (01656) 861100 Fax: (01656) 863400

A luxury country hotel converted from a 17th century farmhouse, we offer elegance and comfort with first class friendly service. Set in picturesque surroundings on a privately owned 150 acre 27 hole golf complex 2 mins from M4, making it the perfect location for business or pleasure.

- 18 hole St Mary's Course
- 12 hole Sevenoaks Course
- 15 bay floodlit driving range
- Bars
- Restaurant

All rooms fitted with:
- Whirlpool baths
- Satellite TV
- Coffee & tea facilities
- Direct dial telephone

Golf, Equestrian and Weekend Breaks available.

Please call us for a brochure and sample for yourselves "The Magic of St. Mary's".

---

18 holes, 6776yds, Par 71, SSS 73, Course record 61. Club membership 1020.
Visitors by arrangement weekdays and Sun **Societies** for large numbers apply in writing, small numbers telephone booking accepted. **Green Fees** £45 per day (£65 Sun). **Cards** 💳 💳 💳 💳 💳 **Prof** Robert Evans **Course Designer** Colt **Facilities** ⊗ ⊪ ⅃ ♥ ♀ ☒ 🖻 ⛳ ✾ 𝄢 ⚐ **Location** S side of Pyle off A4229. Access via junct 37 on M4

Hotel ★★★ 64% Seabank Hotel, The Promenade, PORTHCAWL ☎ 01656 782261 67 en suite

CAERPHILLY

BARGOED   Map 03 ST19

Bargoed Heolddu CF81 9GF
☎ 01443 836179 📠 01143 830608
Mountain parkland course, challenging par 70 course with panoramic views. Easy walking.
18 holes, 6049yds, Par 70, SSS 70, Course record 64. Club membership 600.
Visitors must contact in advance, must play with member at weekends. **Societies** must contact in advance. **Green Fees** £15 per round. **Cards** 💳 💳 💳 💳 **Prof** Craig Easton **Facilities** ⊗ ⊪ ⅃ ♥ ♀ ☒ 🖻 ⛳ ∅ **Conf** fac available Corporate Hospitality Days available **Location** NW side of town

Hotel ★★★ 67% Maes Manor Hotel, BLACKWOOD
☎ 01495 224551 & 220011 📠 01495 228217 8 en suite 14 annexe en suite

BLACKWOOD   Map 03 ST19

Blackwood Cwmgelli NP12 1BR
☎ 01495 222121 (Office) & 223152 (Club)
9 holes, 5332yds, Par 67, Course record 62.
Location 0.25m N of Blackwood, off A4048
Telephone for further details
....
Hotel ★★★ 67% Maes Manor Hotel, BLACKWOOD
☎ 01495 224551 & 220011 📠 01495 228217 8 en suite 14 annexe en suite

CAERPHILLY   Map 03 ST18

Caerphilly Pencapel, Mountain Rd CF83 1HJ
☎ 029 20883481 & 20863441 📠 029 20863441
Undulating mountain course with woodland affording good views especially from 9th hole, 700 ft above sea level.
18 holes, 5732yds, Par 71, SSS 69.
Club membership 650.
Visitors telephone in advance, must produce a current handicap certificate or letter from club secretary, may not play at weekends except with member, no visitors bank holidays. **Societies** apply in writing in advance to the secretary. **Green Fees** not confirmed. **Prof** Joel Hill **Facilities** ⊪ ⅃ ♥ ♀ ☒ 🖻 ∅ **Location** 0.5m S on A469
....
Hotel ★★★ 74% Manor Parc Country Hotel & Restaurant, Thornhill Rd, Thornhill, CARDIFF
☎ 029 2069 3723 12 en suite

Looking to try a new course? Always telephone ahead to confirm visitor arrangements.

Mountain Lakes & Castell Heights

Blaengwynlais CF83 1NG
029 20861128 & 20886666 029 20863243
e-mail: sales@golfclub.co.uk

The 9-hole Castell Heights course within the Mountain Lakes complex was established in 1982 on a 45-acre site. In 1988 a further 18-hole course, Mountain Lakes was designed by Bob Sandow to take advantage of 160 acres of mountain heathland, combining both mountain-top golf and parkland. Most holes are tree-lined and there are 20 'lakes' as hazards. Host to major PGA tournaments.

Mountain Lakes Course: 18 holes, 6046mtrs, Par 74, SSS 73, Course record 69.
Castell Heights Course: 9 holes, 2751mtrs, Par 35, SSS 32, Course record 32.
Club membership 500.

Societies written or telephone notice in advance. **Cards** **Prof** Sion Bebb **Course Designer** Bob Sandow **Facilities** **Conf** fac available Corporate Hospitality Days available **Location** Near Black Cock Inn, Caerphilly Mountain, junct 32 M4

Hotel ★★★ 74% Manor Parc Country Hotel & Restaurant, Thornhill Rd, Thornhill, CARDIFF 029 2069 3723 12 en suite

Virginia Park Golf Club

Virginia Park CF83 3SW
024 20863919 & 20585368
9 holes, 2566yds, Par 33.
Location Off Pontygwindy Rd
Telephone for further details

Hotel ★★★ 74% Manor Parc Country Hotel & Restaurant, Thornhill Rd, Thornhill, CARDIFF 029 2069 3723 12 en suite

MAESYCWMMER — Map 03 ST19

Bryn Meadows Golf & Country Hotel

Mr G Mayo CF82 7FN
01495 225590 or 224103 01495 228272
e-mail: information@brynmeadows.co.uk

A heavily wooded parkland course with panoramic views of the Brecon Beacons.

18 holes, 6132yds, Par 72, SSS 69, Course record 68.
Club membership 540.

Visitors may not play Sun mornings. Must contact in advance. **Societies** Mon-Fri **Green Fees** terms on application. **Cards** **Prof** Bruce Hunter **Course Designer** Mayo/Jeffries **Facilities** **Leisure** heated indoor swimming pool, sauna, solarium, gymnasium. **Conf** fac available Corporate Hospitality Days available **Location** On the A4048 Blackwood to Ystrad Mynach rd

Hotel ★★★ 67% Maes Manor Hotel, BLACKWOOD 01495 224551 & 220011 01495 228217 8 en suite 14 annexe en suite

NELSON — Map 03 ST19

Whitehall

The Pavilion CF46 6ST 01443 740245
e-mail: mark@wilde6755.freeserve.co.uk

Hilltop course. Testing 4th hole (225 yds) par 3, and 6th hole (402 yds) par 4. Pleasant views.

9 holes, 5666yds, Par 69, SSS 68, Course record 63.
Club membership 300.

Continued

Visitors must be a member of a recognised golf club & have a handicap certificate. Must contact in advance to play at weekends. **Societies** must contact in writing 4 weeks in advance. **Green Fees** not confirmed. **Facilities** **Leisure** snooker. **Conf** fac available Corporate Hospitality Days available **Location** Turn off A470 to Nelson and take A4054 S

Hotel ★★★ 70% Llechwen Hall Hotel, Llanfabon, PONTYPRIDD 01443 742050 & 743020 01443 742189 12 en suite 8 annexe en suite

OAKDALE — Map 03 ST19

Oakdale

Llwynon Ln NP12 0NF
01495 220044 220440
9 holes, 1344yds, Par 28, Course record 27.
Course Designer Ian Goodenough **Location** Situated off the B4251 to Portllanfraith Road at Oakdale.
Telephone for further details

Hotel ★★★ 67% Maes Manor Hotel, BLACKWOOD 01495 224551 & 220011 01495 228217 8 en suite 14 annexe en suite

CARDIFF

CARDIFF — Map 03 ST17

Cardiff

Sherborne Av, Cyncoed CF23 6SJ
029 20753320 029 20680011
e-mail: cardiff.golfclub@virgin.net

Parkland course, where trees form natural hazards. Interesting variety of holes, mostly bunkered. A stream flows through course and comes into play on nine separate holes.

18 holes, 6099yds, Par 70, SSS 70, Course record 66.
Club membership 900.

Visitors Must contact in advance, only with member at weekends. **Societies** Fri only, pre-booking essential. **Green Fees** terms on application. **Cards** **Prof** Terry Hanson **Facilities** **Leisure** snooker. **Conf** fac available Corporate Hospitality Days available **Location** 3m N of city centre

Hotel Holiday Inn Cardiff North, Pentwyn Rd, Pentwyn, CARDIFF 0870 400 8141 142 en suite

Cottrell Park

Cottrell Park, St Nicholas CF5 6SJ
01446 781781 01446 781187
e-mail: admin@cottrell-park.co.uk

Two well designed courses, opened in 1996, set in historic parkland which was landscaped 200 years ago and offers spectacular views, especially from the Button course. An enjoyable yet testing game of golf for players of all abilities.

Mackintosh: 18 holes, 6407yds, Par 72, SSS 73, Course record 65.
Button: 18 holes, 6156yds, Par 71, SSS 72.
Club membership 1470.

Visitors should have a valid handicap certificate or be member of golf club. **Societies** contact for details. **Green Fees** not confirmed. **Cards** **Prof** Steve Birch **Course Designer** MRM Sandow **Facilities** **Conf** fac available Corporate Hospitality Days available **Location** M4 junct 33 to Culverhouse Cross A48 to Cowbridge, through St Nicholas on right hand side

Continued

Cottrell Park Golf Club

Hotel ★★★★ 70% Copthorne Hotel Cardiff-Caerdydd, Copthorne Way, Culverhouse Cross, CARDIFF ☎ 029 2059 9100 135 en suite

Llanishen Cwm Lisvane CF4 5UD
☎ 029 20755078 🖹 029 20755078
Sloping course overlooking the Bristol Channel.
18 holes, 5338yds, Par 68, SSS 67, Course record 63.
Club membership 900.
Visitors must play with member at weekends & bank holidays, may not play Wed. Must contact in advance. **Societies** contact in advance. **Green Fees** terms on application. **Prof** Adrian Jones **Facilities** ⊗ ⫟ ⯗ 🖤 ♀ ⚘ ⛳ ⌀ **Conf** fac available **Location** 5m N of city centre off A469

Hotel 🅄 Holiday Inn Cardiff North, Pentwyn Rd, Pentwyn, CARDIFF ☎ 0870 400 8141 142 en suite

Peterstone Peterstone, Wentloog CF3 2TN
☎ 01633 680009 🖹 01633 680563
e-mail: peterstone_lakes@yahoo.com
Peterstone Golf Club: 18 holes, 6555yds, Par 72.
Course Designer Bob Sandow **Location** 3m from Castleton off A48
Telephone for further details

Hotel ★★★ 72% St Mellons Hotel & Country Club, Castleton, CARDIFF ☎ 01633 680355 21 en suite 20 annexe en suite

Radyr The Clubhouse, Drysgol Rd, Radyr CF15 8BS
☎ 029 20842408 🖹 029 20843914
e-mail: manager@radyrgolf.co.uk
Parkland course which celebrated its centenary year in 2002. Good views. Venue for many county and national championships.
18 holes, 6031yds, Par 69, SSS 70, Course record 62.
Club membership 920.
Visitors must play with member at weekends, or by special arrangement with Club Office. **Societies** must contact in advance. **Green Fees** £38.50 per day. **Cards** 🎫 🎫 🎫 🎫 🎫 **Prof** Robert Butterworth **Course Designer** Colt **Facilities** ⊗ ⫟ ⯗ 🖤 ♀ ⚘ 🖀 ⛳ 🎿 ⌀ Ⅼ **Leisure** Table tennis, snooker room. **Conf** fac available Corporate Hospitality Days available **Location** M4 junct32, 4.5m NW of city centre off A4119

Hotel ★★★ 74% Manor Parc Country Hotel & Restaurant, Thornhill Rd, Thornhill, CARDIFF ☎ 029 2069 3723 12 en suite

St Mellons St Mellons CF3 2XS
☎ 01633 680408 🖹 01633 681219
e-mail: stmellons@golf2003.fsnet.co.uk
First opened in 1936, St Mellons is a parkland course on the eastern edge of Cardiff. The course is laid out in the shape of a clover leaf and provides one of the best tests of golf in South Wales. The course comprises 3 par fives, 5 par threes and 10 par fours. The par threes will make or break your card but the two finishing par 4 holes are absolutely superb.
18 holes, 6275yds, Par 70, SSS 70, Course record 63.
Club membership 700.
Visitors must contact in advance. With member only at weekends. **Societies** must contact in advance. **Green Fees** £25 per round, £32 per day. **Cards** 🎫 🎫 🎫 **Prof** Barry Thomas **Course Designer** Colt & Morrison **Facilities** ⊗ ⫟ ⯗ 🖤 ♀ ⚘ 🖀 ⛳ 🎿 ⌀ **Conf** fac available Corporate Hospitality Days available **Location** 2m from Junct 30 M4, 0.5m off A48

Hotel ★★★ 72% St Mellons Hotel & Country Club, Castleton, CARDIFF ☎ 01633 680355 21 en suite 20 annexe en suite

Whitchurch Pantmawr Rd, Whitchurch CF14 7TD
☎ 029 20620985 🖹 029 20529860
e-mail: secretary@whitchurchcardiffgolfclub.com
Undulating parkland course providing an oasis within an urban setting and offering panoramic views of the city. It is an easy walk and always in good condition with excellent drainage and smooth, quick greens.
18 holes, 6258yds, Par 71, SSS 71, Course record 62.
Club membership 750.
Visitors must contact in advance **Societies** Thu only. Must contact in advance. **Green Fees** £35 per day (£40 weekends). **Cards** 🎫 🎫 🎫 🎫 **Prof** Rhys Davies **Course Designer** F Johns **Facilities** ⊗ ⫟ ⯗ 🖤 ♀ ⚘ 🖀 ⛳ ⌀ **Conf** Corporate Hospitality Days available **Location** 4m N of city centre on A470, 600 yds south of junct 32 off M4

Hotel ★★★ 74% Manor Parc Country Hotel & Restaurant, Thornhill Rd, Thornhill, CARDIFF ☎ 029 2069 3723 12 en suite

CREIGIAU (CREIYIAU)
Map 03 ST08

Creigiau Llantwit Rd CF15 9NN
☎ 029 20890263 🖹 029 20890706
e-mail: manager@creigiaugolf.co.uk
Downland course, with small greens and many interesting water hazards.
18 holes, 6063yds, Par 71.
Club membership 700.
Visitors must contact in advance, must be member of a club, not at weekends or bank holidays Must contact in advance. **Societies** Deposit required. Apply by telephone or writing. **Green Fees** £35 per day. **Cards** 🎫 🎫 🎫 🎫 🎫 **Prof** Iain Luntz **Facilities** ⊗ ⫟ ⯗ 🖤 ♀ ⚘ 🖀 ⛳ ⌀ **Location** 6m NW of Cardiff on A4119

Hotel ★★★★ 69% Miskin Manor Hotel & Health Club, Groes Faen, Pontyclun, MISKIN ☎ 01443 224204 33 en suite 9 annexe en suite

> **Booking a tee time is always advisable.**

CARMARTHENSHIRE

AMMANFORD
Map 03 SN61

Glynhir Glynhir Rd, Llandybie SA18 2TF
☎ 01269 851365 🖥 01269 851365
e-mail: glynhir.golfclub@virgin.net
Parkland course with good views, latter holes close to Upper Loughor River. The 14th is a 394-yd dog-leg.
18 holes, 5917yds, Par 69, SSS 70, Course record 66.
Club membership 700.
Visitors no visitors Sun. Contact professional in advance (01269 851010). **Societies** Contact in advance. **Green Fees** Winter £12.50 (£17 weekends), Summer £18 (weekends £24). **Prof** Duncan Prior **Course Designer** F Hawtree **Facilities** ⊗ ⫫ ⊾ ♥ ♀ ♨ 🖕 ✝ 🎣 ⛏ ⚸ **Conf** fac available Corporate Hospitality Days available **Location** 2m N of Ammanford

Hotel ★★ 67% Mill at Glynhir, Glynhir Rd, Llandybie, AMMANFORD ☎ 01269 850672 7 en suite 3 annexe en suite

BURRY PORT
Map 02 SN40

Ashburnham Cliffe Ter SA16 0HN
☎ 01554 832269 & 833846
18 holes, 6916yds, Par 72, SSS 74, Course record 70.
Course Designer J H Taylor **Location** 5m W of Llanelli, A484 road
Telephone for further details

Hotel ★★ 70% Ashburnham Hotel, Ashburnham Rd, Pembrey, LLANELLI ☎ 01554 834343 & 834455 🖥 01554 834483 12 en suite

CARMARTHEN
Map 02 SN42

Carmarthen Blaenycoed Rd SA33 6EH
☎ 01267 281588 🖥 01267 281493
e-mail: john@morgan6279.freeserve.co.uk
Hilltop course with good views.
18 holes, 6245yds, Par 71, SSS 71, Course record 66.
Club membership 600.
Visitors must have a handicap certificate, telephone for times at weekends. **Societies** apply in writing minimum of ten days in advance. **Green Fees** £20 (£25 weekends). **Prof** Pat Gillis **Course Designer** J H Taylor **Facilities** ⊗ ⫫ ⊾ ♥ ♀ ♨ 🖕 ✝ 🎣 ⚸ **Conf** fac available Corporate Hospitality Days available **Location** 4m N of town

Hotel ★★ 70% Falcon Hotel, Lammas St, CARMARTHEN ☎ 01267 234959 & 237152 🖥 01267 221277 14 en suite

Derllys Court Llysonnen Rd SA33 5DT
☎ 01267 211575 🖥 01267 211575
e-mail: derllys@hotmail.com
This course has recently been extended to an 18 hole parkland course. The extra nine holes are of a similar nature to the existing ones although a little longer in length and include water hazards and sand bunkers.
18 holes, 5915yds, Par 70, SSS 68.
Club membership 30.
Visitors welcome at all times. **Societies** telephone in advance. **Green Fees** terms on application. **Cards** 💳 💳 💳 💳 🖥 **Course Designer** Peter Johnson/Stuart Finney **Facilities** ⊗ ⊾ ♨ 🖕 ✝ 🎣 ⚸ **Conf** Corporate Hospitality Days available **Location** Just off A40 between Carmarthen/St Clears

Hotel ★★ 70% Falcon Hotel, Lammas St, CARMARTHEN ☎ 01267 234959 & 237152 🖥 01267 221277 14 en suite

KIDWELLY
Map 02 SN40

Glyn Abbey Trimsaran SA17 4LB
☎ 01554 810278 🖥 01554 810889
e-mail: course-enquiries@glynabbey.co.uk
Beautiful parkland course on the slopes of the Gwendraeth valley, set in 200 acres with mature wooded backdrops.
18 holes, 6173yds, Par 70, SSS 70, Course record 68.
Club membership 320.
Visitors telephone booking advisable. **Societies** must contact in advance. **Green Fees** £15 per round (£20 weekends & holidays). **Cards** 💳 💳 💳 💳 🖥 **Prof** Darren Griffiths **Course Designer** Hawtree **Facilities** ⊗ ⫫ ⊾ ♥ ♀ ♨ 🖕 ✝ 🎣 🏌 ⚒ ⚸ **Leisure** solarium, gymnasium. **Conf** fac available Corporate Hospitality Days available **Location** 4.5m NW of Llanelli, on B4317 between Trimsaran and Carway

Hotel ★★ 70% Ashburnham Hotel, Ashburnham Rd, Pembrey, LLANELLI ☎ 01554 834343 & 834455 🖥 01554 834483 12 en suite

CEREDIGION

ABERYSTWYTH
Map 06 SN58

Aberystwyth Brynmor Rd SY23 2HY
☎ 01970 615104 🖥 01970 626622
e-mail: aberystwythgolf@talk21.com
Undulating meadowland course. Testing holes: 16th (The Loop) par 3; 17th, par 4; 18th, par 3. Good views over Cardigan Bay.
18 holes, 6119yds, Par 70, SSS 69, Course record 66.
Club membership 400.
Visitors must contact in advance. **Societies** write or telephone in advance. **Green Fees** £20 per round £25 per day(£25/£30 weekends & bank holidays). **Course Designer** Harry Vardon **Facilities** ⊗ ⫫ ⊾ ♥ ♀ ♨ 🖕 ⚒ ⚸ **Conf** fac available **Location** N side of town

Hotel ★★★ 66% Belle Vue Royal Hotel, Marine Ter, ABERYSTWYTH ☎ 01970 617558 37 rm (34 en suite)

BORTH
Map 06 SN69

Borth & Ynyslas SY24 5JS
☎ 01970 871202 📠 01970 871202
e-mail: secretary@borthgolf.co.uk
Seaside links, over 100 years old, with strong winds at times although part of the course is sheltered amongst the dunes. Some narrow fairways and plenty of natural hazards.
18 holes, 6116yds, Par 70, SSS 70, Course record 65. Club membership 550.
Visitors must contact in advance, may play weekends ring to check no competitions in progress. **Societies** telephone in advance. **Green Fees** winter £19 per round/summer £28. **Cards** 🌐 💳 💳 💳 💳 **Prof** J G Lewis **Facilities** ⊗ ⅷ by prior arrangement 🍴 ⬛ ♀ ⬥ 🏠 ⛳ 🚬 ⛳ **Conf** Corporate Hospitality Days available **Location** 0.5m N on B4353

Hotel ★★★ ⚘ Ynyshir Hall, EGLWYSFACH
☎ 01654 781209 7 en suite 2 annexe en suite

CARDIGAN
Map 02 SN14

Cardigan Gwbert-on-Sea SA43 1PR
☎ 01239 621775 & 612035 📠 01239 621775
e-mail: golf@cardigan.fsnet.co.uk
A links course, very dry in winter, with wide fairways, light rough and gorse. Every hole overlooks the sea.
18 holes, 6687yds, Par 72, SSS 73, Course record 68. Club membership 600.
Visitors may not play between 1-2pm. Handicap certificate preferred. Contact in advance **Societies** must telephone in advance. **Green Fees** £22 per day (£27.50 weekends & bank holidays). **Cards** 🌐 💳 💳 💳 💳 **Prof** Colin Parsons **Course Designer** Hawtree **Facilities** ⊗ ⅷ 🍴 ⬛ ♀ ⬥ 🏠 ⛳ 🚬 🚬 ⛳ **Leisure** squash. **Location** 3m N off A487

Hotel ★★★ 67% Cliff Hotel, GWBERT-ON-SEA
☎ 01239 613241 72 en suite

GWBERT ON SEA
Map 02 SN15

Cliff Hotel SA43 1PP
☎ 01239 613241 📠 01239 615391
e-mail: cliffhotel@btopenworld.com
This is a short course with two par 4s and the remainder are challenging par 3s. Particularly interesting holes are played across the sea on to a small island.

9 holes, 1545yds, Par 29.
Visitors telephone to book in advance. **Societies** telephone in advance. **Green Fees** not confirmed. **Cards** 🌐 💳 💳 🖼 💳 💳 **Facilities** ⊗ ⅷ 🍴 ⬛ ♀ ⬥ 🏠 ⛳ 🚬 🚬 ⛳

Continued

Leisure heated outdoor swimming pool, fishing, sauna, solarium, gymnasium. **Location** 3 miles from Cardigan

Hotel ★★★ 67% Cliff Hotel, GWBERT-ON-SEA
☎ 01239 613241 72 en suite

LLANDYSSUL
Map 02 SN44

Penwern Saron, Penwern SA44 5EL
☎ 01559 370705
Set in 50 acres of mature parkland with large trees and magnificent Teifi Valley views. Numerous water hazards and bunkers.
Saron Golf Course: 9 holes, 2400yds, Par 32, Course record 34.
Visitors may play at all times no arrangements required. **Societies** telephone for details. **Green Fees** £10 per 18 holes, £7 per 9 holes. **Course Designer** Adas **Facilities** ⬛ 🚬 🏠 ⛳ **Leisure** fishing. **Location** Off A484 at Saron

Hotel ★★ 73% The Penbontbren Farm Hotel, Glynarthen, Llandysul, CARDIGAN ☎ 01239 810248 10 annexe en suite

LLANGYBI
Map 02 SN65

Cilgwyn SA48 8NN ☎ 01570 493286
9 holes, 5309yds, Par 68, SSS 66, Course record 66.
Course Designer Sandor **Location** 5m N of Lampeter on A485
Telephone for further details

Hotel ★★★ 71% Falcondale Mansion, LAMPETER
☎ 01570 422910 20 en suite

LLANRHYSTUD
Map 06 SN56

Penrhos Golf & Country Club SY23 5AY
☎ 01974 202999 📠 01974 202100
e-mail: info@penrhosgolf.co.uk
Beautifully scenic course incorporating lakes and spectacular coastal and inland views. Many leisure facilities.
Penrhos: 18 holes, 6641yds, Par 72, SSS 73, Course record 71.
Academy: 9 holes, 1827yds, Par 31.
Club membership 300.
Visitors must telephone, no jeans allowed on main course. **Societies** must telephone in advance. **Green Fees** Mon-Thu Main £30 Academy £20, Fri £35/£25 (weekends & bank holidays £37/£27.50). **Cards** 🌐 💳 💳 💳 💳 **Prof** Paul Diamond **Course Designer** Jim Walters **Facilities** ⊗ ⅷ 🍴 ⬛ ♀ ⬥ 🏠 ⛳ 🚬 🚬 ⛳ **Leisure** hard tennis courts, heated indoor swimming pool, sauna, solarium, gymnasium, bowling green. **Conf** fac available Corporate Hospitality Days available **Location** Turn off A487 onto B4337 in Llanrhystud. Course 0.25m on left

Hotel ★★★ ⚘ 75% Conrah Hotel, Ffosrhydygaled, Chancery, ABERYSTWYTH ☎ 01970 617941 11 en suite 6 annexe en suite

CONWY

ABERGELE
Map 06 SH97

Abergele Tan-y-Gopa Rd LL22 8DS
☎ 01745 824034 📠 01745 824772
e-mail: secretary@abergelegolfclub.freeserve.co.uk
A beautiful parkland course with views of the Irish Sea and Gwrych Castle. There are splendid finishing holes:

Continued

a testing par 5 16th; a 185-yd 17th to an elevated green; and a superb par 5 18th with out of bounds just behind the green.
18 holes, 6520yds, Par 72, SSS 71, Course record 66.
Club membership 1250.
Visitors must contact in advance. Limited play weekends. **Societies** must contact in advance. **Green Fees** terms on application. **Prof** Iain R Runcie **Course Designer** Hawtree **Facilities** ⊗ 〒 ⓑ ☕ ♀ ⚐ 🛢 🏌 🚜 ⌀ **Location** 0.5m W off A547/A55

Hotel ★★★ 66% Kinmel Manor Hotel, St George's Rd, ABERGELE ☎ 01745 832014 51 en suite

BETWS-Y-COED · · · · · · · · · · · · · · Map 06 SH75

Betws-y-Coed LL24 0AL ☎ 01690 710556
e-mail: betwsycoed.golfclub@tesco.net
Attractive flat meadowland course set between two rivers in Snowdonia National Park, known as the 'Jewel of the Nines'.
9 holes, 4874yds, Par 64, SSS 63, Course record 63.
Club membership 350.
Visitors advisable to contact in advance. **Societies** must telephone in advance. **Green Fees** Summer £16 per 18 holes (£21 weekends). **Facilities** ⊗ 〒 ⓑ ☕ ♀ ⚐ ⌀ **Location** NE side of village off A5

Hotel ★★★ 71% The Royal Oak Hotel, Holyhead Rd, BETWS-Y-COED ☎ 01690 710219 27 en suite

COLWYN BAY · · · · · · · · · · · · · · · · Map 06 SH87

Old Colwyn Woodland Av, Old Colwyn LL29 9NL
☎ 01492 515581
9 holes, 5243yds, Par 68, SSS 66, Course record 63.
Course Designer James Braid **Location** E side of town centre on B5383
Telephone for further details

Hotel ★★★ 68% Hopeside Hotel, 63-67 Prince's Dr, West End, COLWYN BAY ☎ 01492 533244 18 en suite

CONWY · Map 06 SH77

Conwy (Caernarvonshire) Beacons Way, Morfa LL32 8ER ☎ 01492 592423 🖷 01492 593363
e-mail: secretary@conwygolfclub.co.uk
Founded in 1890, Conwy has hosted national and international championships since 1898. Set among sandhills, possessing true links greens and a profusion of gorse on the latter holes, especially the 16th, 17th and 18th. This course provides the visitor with real golfing enjoyment against a background of stunning beauty.
18 holes, 6647yds, Par 72, SSS 72, Course record 64.
Club membership 1050.
Visitors must to contact secretary in advance. Limited play weekends. **Societies** must contact in advance. **Green Fees** £42 per day; £35 per round (£48/£42 weekends & bank holidays). **Prof** Peter Lees **Facilities** ⊗ 〒 ⓑ ☕ ♀ ⚐ 🛢 🏌 🚜 ⌀ **Location** 1m W of town centre on A55

Hotel ★★★ 73% The Groes Inn, Tyn-y-Groes, CONWY ☎ 01492 650545 14 en suite

LLANDUDNO · · · · · · · · · · · · · · · · Map 06 SH78

Llandudno (Maesdu) Hospital Rd LL30 1HU
☎ 01492 876450 🖷 01492 871570
Part links, part parkland, this championship *Continued*

course starts and finishes on one side of the main road, the remaining holes, more seaside in nature, being played on the other side. The holes are pleasantly undulating and present a pretty picture when the gorse is in bloom. Often windy, this varied and testing course is not for beginners.
18 holes, 6545yds, Par 72, SSS 72, Course record 62.
Club membership 1045.
Visitors must book in advance. **Societies** must apply in advance to secretary. **Green Fees** not confirmed. **Prof** Simon Boulden **Facilities** ⊗ 〒 ⓑ ☕ ♀ ⚐ 🛢 🏌 🚜 ⌀ **Leisure** snooker. **Location** S side of town centre on A546

Hotel ★★★ 73% Imperial Hotel, The Promenade, LLANDUDNO ☎ 01492 877466 100 en suite

North Wales 72 Bryniau Rd, West Shore LL30 2DZ
☎ 01492 875325 🖷 01492 873355
e-mail: golf@nwgc.freeserve.co.uk
Challenging seaside links with superb views of Anglesey and Snowdonia. It possesses humpy, hillocky fairways, awkward stances and the occasional blind hole. Heather and gorse lurk beyond the fairways and several of the greens are defended by deep bunkers. The first outstanding hole is the 5th, a par 5 that dog-legs into the wind along a rollercoasting, bottleneck-shaped fairway. Best par 4s include the 8th, played through a narrow valley menaced by a railway line and the beach and the 11th, which runs uphill into the wind and where the beach again threatens. The finest par 3 is the 16th with a bunker to the left of a partially hidden, bowl-shaped green.
18 holes, 6287yds, Par 71, SSS 71, Course record 66.
Club membership 670.
Visitors must contact in advance. **Societies** must contact in advance. **Green Fees** £30 per day, £25 per round (£36/£30 weekends and bank holidays). **Cards** 💳 🃏 💳 🃏 🔋 **Prof** Richard Bradbury **Course Designer** Tancred Cummins **Facilities** ⊗ 〒 ⓑ ☕ ♀ ⚐ 🛢 🏌 🚜 ⌀ **Leisure** snooker. **Location** W side of town on A546

Hotel ★★ St Tudno Hotel and Restaurant, The Promenade, LLANDUDNO ☎ 01492 874411 19 en suite

Rhos-on-Sea Penryhn Bay LL30 3PU
☎ 01492 548115 (Prof) & 549641 (clubhouse)
🖷 01492 549100
Seaside course, with easy walking and panoramic views.
18 holes, 6064yds, Par 69, SSS 69, Course record 68.
Club membership 400.
Visitors advised to telephone beforehand to guarantee tee times. **Societies** booking essential, telephone in advance. **Green Fees** not confirmed. **Prof** Mike Macara **Course Designer** J J Simpson **Facilities** ⊗ 〒 ⓑ ☕ ♀ ⚐ 🛢 ⌀ **Location** 0.5m W of LLandudno, off the A55

Hotel ★★★ 68% Hopeside Hotel, 63-67 Prince's Dr, West End, COLWYN BAY ☎ 01492 533244 18 en suite

LLANFAIRFECHAN · · · · · · · · · · · · Map 06 SH67

Llanfairfechan Llannerch Rd LL33 0ES
☎ 01248 680144 & 680524
Hillside course with panoramic views of coast.
9 holes, 3119yds, Par 54, SSS 57, Course record 53.
Club membership 159.
Visitors contact in advance for weekends and *Continued*

bank holidays **Societies** apply in writing. **Green Fees** £10 per day (£7 with member). **Facilities** ♀ ⚲ **Location** W side of town on A55

....

Hotel ★★ 66% Garden Hotel, 1 High St, BANGOR
☎ 01248 362189 11 rms (10 en suite)

PENMAENMAWR   Map 06 SH77

Penmaenmawr Conway Old Rd LL34 6RD
☎ 01492 623330 🖥 01492 622105
Hilly course with magnificent views across the bay to Llandudno and Anglesey. Dry-stone wall natural hazards.
9 holes, 5350yds, Par 67, SSS 66, Course record 62.
Club membership 600.
Visitors advisable to contact in advance. May not play Sat. **Societies** must contact in advance. **Green Fees** £12 per day (£18 weekends and bank holidays). **Facilities** ⊗ ⅢⅢ ┗ 🖤
♀ ⚲ 🐄 ♂ **Location** 1.5m NE off A55

....

Hotel ★★★ 71% Castle Hotel Conwy, High St, CONWY
☎ 01492 582800 29 en suite

DENBIGHSHIRE

BODELWYDDAN   Map 06 SJ07

Kimnel Park LL18 5SR
☎ 01745 833548 🖥 01745 833544
Flat nine hole pay and play course, ideal for all levels of golfing ability.
Kimnel Park Golf Course: 9 holes, 3100, Par 58, SSS 58.
Visitors no restrictions. **Societies** telephone for details.
Green Fees not confirmed. **Prof** Andrew Barnett **Facilities**
┗ 🖤 ♀ ⚲ 🏠 ⫯ ♂ Ⅰ **Leisure** golf academy. **Conf**
Corporate Hospitality Days available

....

Hotel ★★★ 70% Oriel House Hotel, Upper Denbigh Rd, ST ASAPH ☎ 01745 582716 31 en suite

DENBIGH   Map 06 SJ06

Bryn Morfydd Hotel Llanrhaedr LL16 4NP
☎ 01745 589090 🖥 01745 589093
e-mail: reception@brynmorfyddhotelgolf.co.uk
In a beautiful setting in the Vale of Clwyd, the original 9-hole Duchess course was designed by Peter Alliss in 1982. In 1992, the 18-hole Dukes course was completed: a parkland course designed to encourage use of finesse in play.
Dukes Course: 18 holes, 5650yds, Par 70, SSS 67, Course record 74.
Duchess Course: 9 holes, 2098yds, Par 27.
Club membership 200.
Visitors must book in advance, good standards of dress apply. **Societies** apply in writing. **Green Fees** Dukes £17.50 (£25 weekends). Duchess £4 per 18 holes. **Cards** ⊞ ▤ ▦ ▨ 🄯 **Prof** Richard Hughes **Course Designer** Peter Allis **Facilities** ⊗ ⅢⅢ ┗ 🖤 ♀ ⚲ 🏠 ⫯ ♂ ♂
Conf fac available Corporate Hospitality Days available
Location On A525 between Denbigh and Ruthin

....

Hotel ★★★ 69% Ruthin Castle, RUTHIN
☎ 01824 702664 58 en suite

Denbigh Henllan Rd LL16 5AA
☎ 01745 814159 🖥 814888
e-mail: secretary@denbighgolfclub.fsbusiness.co.uk
Parkland course, giving a testing and varied game. Good views.

Continued

18 holes, 5712yds, Par 69, SSS 68, Course record 64.
Club membership 725.
Visitors must contact in advance. **Societies** apply in writing/telephone. **Prof** Mike Jones **Course Designer** John Stockton **Facilities** ⊗ ⅢⅢ ┗ 🖤 ♀ ⚲ 🏠 ⫯ ♂ **Conf**
Corporate Hospitality Days available **Location** 1.5m NW on B5382

....

Hotel ★★★ 70% Oriel House Hotel, Upper Denbigh Rd, ST ASAPH ☎ 01745 582716 31 en suite

LLANGOLLEN   Map 07 SJ24

Vale of Llangollen Holyhead Rd LL20 7PR
☎ 01978 860906 🖥 01978 860906
Parkland course, set in superb scenery by the River Dee.
18 holes, 6656yds, Par 72, SSS 73, Course record 66.
Club membership 800.
Visitors must contact in advance. Restricted club competition days. Handicap certificate required. **Societies** apply in writing to the secretary. **Green Fees** £30 per round (£35 weekends). **Cards** ⊞ ▤ ▦ ▨ 🄯 **Prof** David Vaughan **Facilities** ⊗ ⅢⅢ ┗ 🖤 ♀ ⚲ 🏠 🐄 ♂
Location 1.5m E on A5

PRESTATYN   Map 06 SJ08

Prestatyn Marine Rd East LL19 7HS
☎ 01745 854320 🖥 01745 854320
e-mail: prestatyngcmanager@freenet.co.uk
Set besides rolling sand dunes and only a few hundred yards from the sea, this course enjoys a temperate climate and its seaside location ensures that golfers can play on superb greens all year round. Some holes of note are the par 5 3rd with out of bounds on the left dog leg followed by the Ridge, a par 4 of 468 yards normally played with the prevailing wind. The pretty 9th is surrounded by a moat where birdies and double bogies are common followed by the challenging par 4 450 yard 10th.

18 holes, 6568yds, Par 72, SSS 72, Course record 65.
Club membership 695.
Visitors welcome except Sat & Tue mornings. Must contact in advance. **Societies** prior booking required.
Green Fees terms on application. **Cards** ⊞ ▤ ▦ 🄯
Prof David Ames **Course Designer** S Collins **Facilities** ⊗ ⅢⅢ ┗ 🖤 ♀ ⚲ 🏠 ⫯ 🐄 ♂ **Leisure** snooker. **Conf**
Corporate Hospitality Days available **Location** 0.5m N off A548

....

Hotel ★★ 67% Traeth Ganol Hotel, 41 Beach Rd West, PRESTATYN ☎ 01745 853594 9 en suite

> **Use the maps at the back of the guide to help locate a golf course.**

Prestatyn Golf Club

Prestatyn Golf course is the most North Easterly Links in Wales. A challenge for all standards of golfers giving a memorable examination of their game. Visitors and Societies are welcome on Sundays and Weekdays except Tuesday am.

To reserve your Golf Day:
Tel/Fax: 01745 854320
E-mail: prestatytngcmanager@freenet.co.uk
Visit our website: www.prestatyngc.co.uk
Additional website: www.ukgolfer.org

St Melyd The Paddock, Meliden Rd LL19 8NB
☎ 01745 854405 🖹 01745 856908
e-mail: info@stmelydgolf.co.uk
Parkland course with good views of mountains and Irish Sea. Testing 1st hole (423 yds) par 4. 18 tees.
9 holes, 5829yds, Par 68, SSS 68, Course record 65.
Club membership 400.
Visitors must contact in advance. **Societies** must telephone in advance. **Green Fees** not confirmed. **Prof** Andrew Carr **Facilities** ⊗ ⅲ ⅄ 🖤 ♀ ⌂ 🏌 Leisure snooker. **Location** 0.5m S on A547

RHUDDLAN   Map 06 SJ07

Rhuddlan Meliden Rd LL18 6LB
☎ 01745 590217 (Sec) & 590898(Pro) 🖹 01745 590472
e-mail: golf@rhuddlangolfclub.fsnet.co.uk
18 holes, 6471yds, Par 71, SSS 71, Course record 66.
Course Designer Hawtree & Son **Location** E side of town on A547
Telephone for further details

Hotel ★★★ 66% Kinmel Manor Hotel, St George's Rd, ABERGELE ☎ 01745 832014 51 en suite

RHYL   Map 06 SJ08

Rhyl Coast Rd LL18 3RE
☎ 01745 353171 🖹 01745 360007
e-mail: rhylgolfclub@hotmail.com
Seaside course.
9 holes, 6220yds, Par 70, SSS 70, Course record 65.
Club membership 600.
Visitors must contact in advance. Limited availability at weekends due to club competitions. **Societies** must contact

Continued

---

in advance/see web site **Green Fees** not confirmed. **Prof** Tim Leah **Course Designer** James Braid **Facilities** ⊗ ⅲ ⅃ 🖤 ♀ ⌂ 🏠 ⼃ ➧ ⚒ ♂ **Conf** Corporate Hospitality Days available **Location** 1m E on A548

Hotel ★★ 67% Traeth Ganol Hotel, 41 Beach Rd West, PRESTATYN ☎ 01745 853594 9 en suite

RUTHIN   Map 06 SJ15

Ruthin-Pwllglas Pwllglas LL15 2PE
☎ 01824 702383
Hilly parkland course in elevated position with panoramic views. Stiff climb to 3rd and 9th holes. At 600 feet above sea level, the 355 yard 5th hole is the highest point at Pwliglas. When the seventh is played the second time - as the 16th - the tee is from a spectacular sheer rock face.
18 holes, 5362yds, Par 66, SSS 66.
Club membership 380.
Visitors welcome except for competition days. **Societies** apply in writing or telephone. **Green Fees** £15 per day (£20 weekends and bank holidays) **Prof** M Jones **Facilities** ⊗ ⅲ ⅃ 🖤 ♀ ⌂ **Leisure** motorised cart available for disabled. **Conf** Corporate Hospitality Days available **Location** 2.5m S off A494

Hotel ★★★ 69% Ruthin Castle, RUTHIN ☎ 01824 702664 58 en suite

ST ASAPH   Map 06 SJ07

Llannerch Park North Wales Golf Range, Llannerch Park LL17 0BD ☎ 01745 730805
Mainly flat parkland course with one dog-leg hole.
9 holes, 1587yds, Par 30.
Visitors pay & play. **Societies** telephone in advance.
Green Fees £3.50 per round. **Course Designer** B Williams **Facilities** 🖤 ⌂ ⼃ ⚒ **Location** 200yds S off A525

Hotel ★★ 67% Plas Elwy Hotel & Restaurant, The Roe, ST ASAPH ☎ 01745 582263 & 582089 🖹 01745 583864 7 en suite 6 annexe en suite

FLINTSHIRE

BRYNFORD   Map 07 SJ17

Holywell Brynford CH8 8LQ
☎ 01352 713937 & 710040 🖹 01352 713937
e-mail: holywell_golf_club@lineone.net
Links type course on well drained mountain turf, with bracken and gorse flanking undulating fairways. 720 ft above sea level.
18 holes, 6100yds, Par 70, SSS 70, Course record 67.
Club membership 505.
Visitors advisable to book in advance particularly for weekends. **Societies** by prior arrangement with the secretary. **Green Fees** terms on application. **Prof** Matt Parsleyr **Facilities** ⊗ ⅲ ⅃ 🖤 ♀ ⌂ 🏠 ➧ ⚒ ♂ **Location** 1.25m SW off B5121

Hotel ★★ 69% Stamford Gate Hotel, Halkyn Rd, HOLYWELL ☎ 01352 712942 12 en suite

FLINT
Map 07 SJ27

Flint Cornist Park CH6 5HJ ☎ 01352 735645
e-mail: paulm@jcarrins.demon.co.uk
Parkland course incorporating woods and streams. Excellent views of Dee estuary and the Welsh hills.
9 holes, 6984yds, Par 70, SSS 69, Course record 65. Club membership 300.
Visitors contact in advance, not Sun. **Societies** apply in writing or telephone,not weekends. **Green Fees** £12 per day, £18 per 18 holes, £5 per 9 holes. **Course Designer** H G Griffith **Facilities** ⊗ ⅏ ▣ ⚑ ⚲ **Location** 1m W, follow signs from A55 for Flint, on entering Flinttown look for signs for Cornist hall & Flint golf club

Hotel ★★★ 59% Mountain Park Hotel, Northop Rd, Flint Mountain, FLINT ☎ 01352 736000 & 730972 ▤ 01352 736010 21 annexe en suite

HAWARDEN
Map 07 SJ36

Hawarden Groomsdale Ln CH5 3EH
☎ 01244 531447 & 520809 ▤ 01244 536901
18 holes, 5842yds, Par 69, SSS 69.
Location W side of town off B5125
Telephone for further details

Hotel ★★★ 66% The Gateway To Wales Hotel, Welsh Rd, Sealand, Deeside, CHESTER ☎ 01244 830332 39 en suite

MOLD
Map 07 SJ26

Old Padeswood Station Ln, Padeswood CH7 4JL
☎ 01244 547401 & 547701 ▤ 01244 545082
Situated in the beautiful Alyn Valley, part bounded by the river Alyn, this challenging course suits all categories of golfers. Major tree planting over the years has resulted in many tree lined fairways, which combined with the natural ditches that meander through the course add to its attraction. A major development is two new greens which came into play in 2002 and it is hoped more greens will be renewed in the near future.
18 holes, 6685yds, Par 72, SSS 72, Course record 66. Club membership 600.
Visitors welcome, subject to tee availability. **Societies** telephone in advance. **Green Fees** not confirmed. **Prof** Tony Davies **Course Designer** Jeffries **Facilities** ⊗ ⅏ ⅃ ▣ ⚑ ⚲ 🏌 ⛳ **Location** 3m SE off A5118

Hotel ★★★ 67% Beaufort Park Hotel, Alltami Rd, New Brighton, MOLD ☎ 01352 758646 106 en suite

Padeswood & Buckley The Caia, Station Ln, Padeswood CH7 4JD
☎ 01244 550537 ▤ 01244 541600
e-mail: admin@padeswoodgolf.plus.com
Gently undulating parkland course, with natural hazards and good views of the Welsh Hills.
18 holes, 5982yds, Par 70, SSS 69. Club membership 800.
Visitors weekdays only, contact secretary in advance. **Societies** apply in writing/telephone. **Green Fees** £22 per round weekdays. **Prof** David Ashton **Course Designer** Williams Partnership **Facilities** ⊗ ⅏ ▣ ⚑ ⚲ ⛳ 🏌 **Leisure** snooker (full size tables). **Conf** Corporate Hospitality Days available **Location** 3m SE off A5118

Hotel ★★★ 67% Beaufort Park Hotel, Alltami Rd, New Brighton, MOLD ☎ 01352 758646 106 en suite

NORTHOP
Map 07 SJ26

Northop Country Park CH7 6WA
☎ 01352 840440 ▤ 01352 840445
Designed by former British Ryder Cup captain, John Jacobs, the parkland course gives the impression of having been established for many years. No two holes are the same and design allows all year play.

18 holes, 6750yds, Par 72, SSS 73, Course record 64. Club membership 500.
Visitors must contact in advance and have own equipment. **Societies** apply in writing or by telephone in advance. **Green Fees** £30 (£35 weekends & bank holidays). **Cards** ▨▨▨ ▨▨ ▨▨ ▨ ▨▨ ▨ **Prof** Neil Sweeney **Course Designer** John Jacobs **Facilities** ⊗ ⅏ ⅃ ▣ ⚑ ⚲ 🏌 ⛳ **Leisure** hard tennis courts, sauna, gymnasium. **Conf** fac available **Location** 150 yds from Connahs Quay turnoff on A55

Hotel ★★★★ 70% De Vere St David's Park, St Davids Park, EWLOE ☎ 01244 520800 145 en suite

PANTYMWYN
Map 07 SJ16

Mold Cilcain Rd CH7 5EH
☎ 01352 741513 ▤ 01352 741517
e-mail: info@moldgolfclub.co.uk
Meadowland course with some hard walking and natural hazards. Fine views.
18 holes, 5512yds, Par 67, SSS 67, Course record 63. Club membership 700.
Visitors contact in advance. Restricted play at weekends **Societies** provisional booking by telephone. **Green Fees** winter: £15 per day (£25 weekends & bank holidays) £20 per round. summer: £20 per day (£30 weekends & bank holidays) £25 per round. **Cards** ▨▨ ▨▨ **Prof** Mark Jordan **Course Designer** Hawtree **Facilities** ⊗ ⅏ ⅃ ▣ ⚑ ⚲ 🏌 ⛳ **Conf** fac available Corporate Hospitality Days available **Location** E side of village

Hotel ★★★ 67% Beaufort Park Hotel, Alltami Rd, New Brighton, MOLD ☎ 01352 758646 106 en suite

GWYNEDD

ABERDYFI
See page 383 and advert on page 384

ABERSOCH
Map 06 SH32

Abersoch LL53 7EY
☎ 01758 712622(shop) 712636(office) ▤ 01758 712777
e-mail: admin@abersochgolf.co.uk
18 holes, 5819yds, Par 69, SSS 68, Course record 66.
Course Designer Harry Vardon **Location** S side of village
Telephone for further details

Continued

Aberdovey

Map 06 SN69   Aberdyfi

☎ **01654 767493** 📄 **01654 767027**

G olf was first played at Aberdovey in 1886, with the club founded six years later. The links has since developed into one of the finest championship courses in Wales. The club has hosted many prestigious events over the years; it is popular with golfing societies and clubs who regularly return here. Golfers can enjoy spectacular views and easy walking, next to the dunes of this characteristically true seaside links. Fine holes include the 3rd, the 11th and a good short hole at the 12th. The late Bernard Darwin, former president and captain of the club, was a golf correspondent for The Times. Many of his writings feature the course, which he referred to as 'the course that my soul loves best of all the courses in the world', and he was a major contributor to its success. Darwin would easily recognise the course if he were to play it today. In 1995 the old clubhouse was destroyed by fire, and rebuilt with the help of a lottery grant. The fine new clubhouse which now graces the course was opened by HRH the Duke of York in 1998.

Visitors Welcome, handicap certificate required, must contact in advance, restrictions at weekends

Societies Prior arrangement essential

Green Fees Weekday £38-£50, weekend £42-£55

Facilities ⊗ ⟩⫿⫿ ⯭ ⯭ ♀ ♀ ⯶ ⬠ ⬠ ⬠ ⬠
Conf Facilities available

Professional John Davies

Location Aberdyfi LL35 0RT (0.5m W on A493)

Holes/Par/Course record 18 holes,
6445 yds, Par 71, SSS 71 Course record 66

WHERE TO STAY NEARBY

Hotels
ABERDYFI

★★★ 74% Trefeddian Hotel LL35 0SB.
☎ 01654 767213. 59 en suite. See advert on page 384

★★ ⊛ 74% Penhelig Arms Hotel & Restaurant, LL35 0LT.
☎ 01654 767215. 10 en suite, 4 annexe en suite

★★ 66% Dovey Inn, LL35 0EF.
☎ 01654 767332. 8 en suite

Championship Course

AA ★★★

74%

TREFEDDIAN HOTEL

En-suite bedrooms, some balcony. Lift, indoor
swimming pool, tennis, snooker. Children's
playroom. Ideal base for touring North/Mid Wales.
½ mile north of Aberdyfi village.
Family owned/managed award-winning three-star
country hotel. Close to sea in Snowdonia National
Park. Views of sand dunes, beaches, Cardigan Bay
and Aberdovey Championship Golf Links.
Telephone for full colour brochure
Aberdyfi (Aberdovey) LL35 0SB Wales
01654 767213
Fax: 01654 767777
www.trefwales.com

Abersoch Golf Club

Hotel ★★ 77% Neigwl Hotel, Lon Sarn Bach,
ABERSOCH ☎ 01758 712363 7 en suite
2 annexe en suite

BALA
Map 06 SH93

Bala Penlan LL23 7YD
☎ 01678 520359 & 521361 📄 01678 521361
Upland course with natural hazards. All holes except
first and last affected by wind. First hole is a most
challenging par 3. Irrigated greens and spectacular
views of surrounding countryside.
10 holes, 4962yds, Par 66, SSS 64, Course record 64.
Club membership 229.
Visitors book in advance at weekends. Parties of more than
4 people contact the secretary in advance. Societies must
contact in advance. Green Fees £20 summer £12 winter.
Prof A R Davies Facilities 🖳 ♀ ⌂ 🏠 ⛳ ✓ Location
0.5m SW off A494

Hotel ★★ 66% Plas Coch Hotel, High St, BALA
☎ 01678 520309 10 en suite

BANGOR
Map 06 SH57

St Deiniol Penybryn LL57 1PX
☎ 01248 353098 📄 01248 370792
e-mail: secretary@stdeiniol.fsbusiness.co.uk
Elevated parkland course with panoramic views of
Snowdonia, Menai Straits, and Anglesey. Designed by
James Braid in 1905 this course is a test test of accuracy
and course management. The 3rd has a narrow driving
area and a shot to an elevated green. The fourth, one of
six par threes, provides a choice of pitching the green or
utilising the contours, making it one of the most
difficult holes on the course. The 13th, a dog leg par 4,
is the last hole of the course' own amen corner with its
out of bounds to the right and left.
18 holes, 5654yds, Par 68, SSS 67, Course record 61.
Club membership 300.
Visitors must contact in advance. Societies must contact in
advance. Green Fees £18 per day (£22 weekends & bank
holidays). Cards 🖩 🟰 📰 📊 💳 Course Designer
James Braid Facilities ⊗ ☰ 🖳 🖳 ♀ ⌂ 🏠 ⛳ ✓ Location
E side of town centre off A5122, off J11 A55

Hotel ★★ 67% Anglesey Arms, MENAI BRIDGE
☎ 01248 712305 16 en suite

CAERNARFON
Map 06 SH46

Caernarfon Llanfaglan LL54 5RP
☎ 01286 673783 & 678359 📄 01286 672535
e-mail: caerngc@talk21.com
Parkland course with gentle gradients.
*Caernarfon Golf Club: 18 holes, 5891yds, Par 69, SSS 68,
Course record 63.*
Club membership 660.
Visitors must contact in advance. Societies must apply in
advance, in writing or by telephone. Green Fees £22 per
18 holes (£30 weekends). Cards 🖩 🟰 📰 📊 💳
Prof Aled Owen Facilities ⊗ ☰ 🖳 🖳 ♀ ⌂ 🏠 🐾 🏌 ✓
Conf Corporate Hospitality Days available Location
1.75m SW

Hotel ★★★ 71% Celtic Royal Hotel, Bangor St,
CAERNARFON ☎ 01286 674477 110 en suite

CRICCIETH
Map 06 SH43

Criccieth Ednyfed Hill LL52 0PH ☎ 01766 522154
18 holes, 5787yds, Par 69, SSS 68.
Location 1m NE
Telephone for further details

Hotel ★★★ ♨ 75% Bron Eifion Country House Hotel,
CRICCIETH ☎ 01766 522385 19 en suite

DOLGELLAU
Map 06 SH71

Dolgellau Hengwrt Estate, Pencefn Rd LL40 2ES
☎ 01341 422603 📄 01341 422603
e-mail: dolgellaugolfclub@hengwrt.fsnet.co.uk
Undulating parkland course set on former hunting
grounds of the last Welsh prince, with ancient oak and
holly trees. Good views of mountains and Mawddach
estuary.
9 holes, 4671yds, Par 66, SSS 63, Course record 62.
Club membership 150.
Visitors no restrictions Societies must contact in advance.

Continued

Continued

Green Fees £15 per day (£18 weekends). **Cards** 🏧 💳 🖥️ 🖨️ 📷 📀 **Course Designer** Jack Jones **Facilities** ⊗ ⅲ ㉿ 🍴 🏌️ 🦵 🎯 ✿ 💬 🏊 ✈ 🚗 🏌️ **Leisure** grass tennis courts, fishing, gymnasium. **Conf** fac available Corporate Hospitality Days available **Location** 0.5m N, near to Town Bridge

Hotel ★★★ 74% Plas Dolmelynllyn, Ganllwyd, DOLGELLAU ☎ 01341 440273 10 en suite

HARLECH   Map 06 SH53

Royal St Davids LL46 2UB
☎ 01766 780361 📄 01766 781110
e-mail: secretary@royalstdavids.co.uk
Championship links, with easy walking and natural hazards.
18 holes, 6427yds, Par 69, SSS 72, Course record 62.
Club membership 800.
Visitors pre booking essential, must hold current handicap certificate. **Societies** contact secretary in advance. Handicap certificates required. **Green Fees** £50 per day, £40 per round after 3pm £25 (£60/£50 weekends & holidays, after 3pm £30) Reduced winter rates. **Cards** 🏧 💳 🖥️ 📀 **Prof** John Barnett **Course Designer** Harold Finch-Hatton **Facilities** ⊗ ⅲ ㉿ 🍴 🦵 🏊 🎯 ✿ **Conf** Corporate Hospitality Days available **Location** W side of town on A496

Hotel ★★ 64% Ty Mawr Hotel, LLANBEDR
☎ 01341 241440 10 en suite

MORFA NEFYN   Map 06 SH24

Nefyn & District LL53 6DA
☎ 01758 720966 📄 01758 720476
e-mail: nefyngolf@tesco.net
A 27-hole course played as two separate 18s, Nefyn is a cliff-top links where you never lose sight of the sea. A well-maintained course which will be a very tough test for the serious golfer, but still user friendly for the casual visitor. Every hole has a different challenge and the old 13th fairway is approximately 30 yards across from sea-to-sea. The course has an added bonus of a pub on the beach roughly halfway round for those whose golf may need some bolstering!
Old Course: 18 holes, 6201yds, Par 71, SSS 71, Course record 67.
New Course: 18 holes, 6317yds, Par 71, SSS 71, Course record 66.
Club membership 800.
Visitors must contact in advance. **Societies** apply by telephone. **Green Fees** £36 per day, £29 per round, Sat £42/£36, Sun £38/£33. **Cards** 🏧 💳 🖥️ 📀 **Prof** John Froom **Course Designer** James Braid **Facilities** ⊗ ⅲ ㉿ 🍴 🦵 🏊 🎯 ✿ 🏌️ 🏊 ✿ **Conf** fac available **Location** 0.75m NW

Hotel ★★★ ♨ 75% Porth Tocyn Hotel, Bwlch Tocyn, ABERSOCH ☎ 01758 713303 17 en suite

PORTHMADOG   Map 06 SH53

Porthmadog Morfa Bychan LL49 9UU
☎ 01766 514124 📄 01766 514638
e-mail: secretary@porthmadog-golf-club.co.uk
Seaside links, very interesting but with easy walking and good views.

---

18 holes, 6363yds, Par 71, SSS 71.
Club membership 1000.
Visitors must contact in advance. Handicap certificate required. **Societies** apply by telephone initially. **Green Fees** £25 per round (£32 per day (weekends £30/£37) **Prof** Peter L Bright **Course Designer** James Braid **Facilities** ⊗ ⅲ ㉿ 🍴 🦵 🏊 🎯 ✿ 🏌️ 🦵 **Leisure** snooker. **Conf** Corporate Hospitality Days available **Location** 1.5m SW

Hotel ★★★ 75% Bron Eifion Country House Hotel, CRICCIETH ☎ ♨ 01766 522385 19 en suite

PWLLHELI   Map 06 SH33

Pwllheli Golf Rd LL53 5PS ☎ 01758 701644
18 holes, 6091yds, Par 69, SSS 69, Course record 66.
Course Designer Tom Morris **Location** 0.5m SW off A497
Telephone for further details

Hotel ★★★ 75% Porth Tocyn Hotel, Bwlch Tocyn, ABERSOCH ☎ 01758 713303 17 en suite

MERTHYR TYDFIL

MERTHYR TYDFIL   Map 03 SO00

Merthyr Tydfil Cilsanws Mountain, Cefn Coed
CF48 2NU ☎ 01685 723308
Mountain-top course in the Brecon Beacons National Park with beautiful views of the surrounding area. The course plays longer than its card length and requires accuracy off the tee.
18 holes, 5625yds, Par 69, SSS 68, Course record 65.
Club membership 160.
Visitors may not play on Sun unitl after 3pm **Societies** by prior arrangement. **Green Fees** £10 per day (£15 weekends & bank holidays). **Course Designer** V Price/R Mathias **Facilities** ⊗ by prior arrangement ⅲ by prior arrangement ㉿ by prior arrangement 🍴 by prior arrangement 🦵 🏊 **Location** Off A470 at Cefn Coed

Hotel ★★★ 75% Nant Ddu Lodge, Bistro & Spa, Cwm Taf, Nant Ddu, MERTHYR TYDFIL ☎ 01685 379111 12 en suite 16 annexe en suite

Morlais Castle Pant, Dowlais CF48 2UY
☎ 01685 722822 📄 01685 388700
e-mail: info@mcgc.fsnet.co.uk
Beautiful moorland course overlooking National Park with excellent views of Brecon Beacons and surrounding countryside. The interesting layout of the course makes for a testing game.
18 holes, 6320yds, Par 71, SSS 71, Course record 64.
Club membership 600.
Visitors contact in advance, especially for weekends. **Societies** apply in writing. **Green Fees** terms on application. **Prof** H Jarrett **Course Designer** James Braid **Facilities** ⊗ ⅲ ㉿ 🍴 🦵 🏊 🎯 ✿ 🏌️ 🦵 **Conf** fac available Corporate Hospitality Days available **Location** 2.5m N off A465. Follow signs for Mountain Railway. Course entrance opposite railway car park

Hotel ★★★ 75% Nant Ddu Lodge, Bistro & Spa, Cwm Taf, Nant Ddu, MERTHYR TYDFIL ☎ 01685 379111 12 en suite 16 annexe en suite

Continued

MONMOUTHSHIRE

ABERGAVENNY   Map 03 SO21

Monmouthshire Gypsy Ln, LLanfoist NP7 9HE
☎ 01873 852606 📠 01873 850470
e-mail: secretary@mgcabergavenny.fsnet.co.uk
**This parkland course is very picturesque, with the
beautifully wooded River Usk running alongside. There
are a number of par 3 holes and a testing par 4 at the 15th.**
18 holes, 5806yds, Par 70, SSS 69, Course record 65.
Club membership 700.
Visitors must play with member at weekends. Must
contact in advance & have handicap certificate. **Societies**
must confirm in writing. **Green Fees** terms on application.
Prof B Edwards **Course Designer** James Braid **Facilities**
⊗ ▥ by prior arrangement ⓑ 🍺 ♀ ⚲ 🏠 🎿 ♂ **Location**
2m S off B4269

....

Hotel ★★ 69% Llanwenarth Hotel & Riverside
Restaurant, Brecon Rd, ABERGAVENNY
☎ 01873 810550 18 en suite

Wernddu Golf Centre Old Ross Rd NP7 8NG
☎ 01873 856223 📠 01873 852177
e-mail: info@wernddu-golf-club.co.uk
**A parkland course with magnificent views, wind
hazards on several holes in certain conditions and water
hazards on four holes. There is a 22 bay floodlit driving
range, practice bunker and chipping area.**
18 holes, 5403yds, Par 68, SSS 67, Course record 64.
Club membership 550.
Visitors advisable to book in advance. **Societies** telephone
in advance. **Green Fees** £15 per 18 holes. **Cards** 🌐 💳
🌐 💳 **Prof** Tina Tetley **Course Designer** G Watkins
Facilities ⊗ ⓑ 🍺 ♀ ⚲ 🏠 🎿 🛺 ♂ ⚑ **Leisure** fishing.
Location 1.5m NE on B4521

....

Hotel ★★★ 70% Llansantffraed Court Hotel,
Llanvihangel Gobion, ABERGAVENNY
☎ 01873 840678 21 en suite

BETTWS NEWYDD   Map 03 SO30

Alice Springs Kemeys Commander NP15 1JY
☎ 01873 880708 📠 01873 881075
e-mail: alice@springs18.fsnet.co.uk
Monow Course: 18 holes, 5544yds, Par 69, SSS 69.
Usk Course: 18 holes, 5934, Par 70, SSS 70.
Course Designer Keith R Morgan **Location** N of Usk on
B4598 towards Abergavenny
Telephone for further details

....

Hotel ★★★ 70% Three Salmons Hotel, Porthycarne St,
USK ☎ 01291 672133 10 en suite   14 annexe en suite

HOTEL & RESTAURANT

The atmospheric Three Salmons Hotel once a 17th
Century Coaching Inn offers the perfect blend of
excellent cuisine and traditional hospitality, in an
environment of warmth, comfort and charm.

Bridge Street, Usk, Monmouthshire.

Bookings and enquiries welcome

(01291) 672133

★★★

CAERWENT   Map 03 ST49

Dewstow NP26 5AH
☎ 01291 430444 📠 01291 425816
e-mail: info@dewstow.com
**Two picturesque parkland courses with easy walking
and spectacular views over the Severn estuary towards
Bristol. Testing holes include the par three 7th, Valley
Course, which is approached over water, some 50 feet
lower than the tee, and the par four 15th, Park Course,
which has a 50ft totem pole in the middle of the
fairway, a unique feature. There is also a 26-bay floodlit
driving range.**
*Valley Course: 18 holes, 6110yds, Par 72, SSS 70, Course
record 64.*
*Park Course: 18 holes, 6226yds, Par 69, SSS 69, Course
record 67 or 18 holes, 6341yds, Par 70, SSS 69, Course
record 66.*
Club membership 950.
Societies apply in writing or telephone for details. **Green
Fees** not confirmed. **Cards** 🌐 💳 💳 🌐 💳 **Prof**
Jonathan Skuse **Facilities** ⊗ ▥ ⓑ 🍺 ♀ ⚲ 🏠 🎿 🛺 ♂
⚑ **Conf** fac available   Corporate Hospitality Days available
Location 0.5m S of A48 at Caerwent

....

Hotel ⌂ Travelodge, Magor Service Area, MAGOR
☎ 08700 850 950 43 en suite

CHEPSTOW   See page 387

Booking a tee time is always advisable.

Marriott St Pierre

Map 03 ST59 Chepstow

☎ 01291 625261 📄 01291 627977

Set in 400 acres of beautiful parkland, Marriott St Pierre offers two 18-hole golf courses. The Old Course is one of the finest golf courses in the country and has played host to many major championships. The par 3 18th is famous for its tee shot over the lake to an elevated green. The Mathern presents its own challenges and is highly enjoyable for golfers of all abilities. The hotel has teaching professionals as well as hire of clubs and equipment. A new 13 bay driving range was added in late 1998.

e-mail: golf.stpierre@marriotthotels.co.uk

Visitors Welcome

Societies Must make advance reservation

Green Fees Telephone for details

Facilities ⊗ ⣿ ⣾ ⣶ ⣷ ⣸ ⣺ ⣻ ⣼ ⣽

Conf facilities Available Corporate Hospitality Days Available

Leisure Tennis, swimming, sauna, solarium, gymnasium, steam room, jacuzzi, health and beauty suite, private fishing.

Location St Pierre Park, Chepstow, NP16 6YA, (leave M4 at - J23 to M48. Leave M48 at J2. A466 towards Chepstow)

Holes/Par/Course record 36 holes.
Old Course: 18 holes, 6733 yds, Par 71, SSS 72, course record 64.
Mathern Course: 18 holes, 5732 yds, Par 68, SSS 67

WHERE TO STAY AND EAT NEARBY

Hotels
CHEPSTOW

★★★★ 71% Marriott St Pierre Hotel & Country Club NP16 6YA
☎ 01291 626261,
148 en suite

★★★ 66% Chepstow Hotel, NP16 5PR ☎ 01291 626261
31 en suite

★★ 66% Castle View, NP6 5EZ.
☎ 01291 620340 9 en suite 4 annexe en suite

★★ 66% Beaufort Hotel, NP16 5EP
☎ 01291 622497 22 en suite

TINTERN PARVA

★★ ⊛ 73% Parva Farmhouse Hotel & Restaurant
☎ 01291 689411 9 en suite

★★★ ⊛ 67% Royal George Hotel NP16 6SF
☎ 01291 689205 2 en suite 14 annexe en suite

WHITEBROOK

🏨 ⊛ ⊛ 71% The Crown at Whitebrook, NP25 4TX
☎ 01600 860254 10 en suite

Restaurant
CHEPSTOW

⊛ ⊛ Wye Knot, NP16 5HH
☎ 01291 622929

Championship Course

CHEPSTOW   Map 03 ST59

Shirenewton Shirenewton NP16 6RL
☎ 01291 641642 📠 01291 641472
18 holes, 6605yds, Par 72, SSS 72.
Location Junct 2 of M48 off A48 at Crick
Telephone for further details

Hotel ★★ 66% Beaufort Hotel, Beaufort Square,
CHEPSTOW ☎ 01291 622497 22 en suite

MONMOUTH   Map 03 SO51

Monmouth Leasebrook Ln NP25 3SN
☎ 01600 712212 (clubhouse) 📠 01600 772399
e-mail: sec.mongc@barbox.net
**Parkland course in scenic setting. High, undulating
land with beautiful views.**

18 holes, 5698yds, Par 69, SSS 69, Course record 68.
Club membership 500.
Visitors advisable to contact in advance, bank holidays only
with member. Not before 11.30am on Sun. **Societies** advance
notice required, write or telephone secretary. **Green Fees**
£20 - £24 weekends. **Cards** 🎫 ▆▆ 🎫 🎫 💳 **Prof** Mike
Waldron **Course Designer** George Walden **Facilities** ⊗ 〗╢
🍴 🍺♀⛅🏌🍴🛒🏌 ⛳ **Conf** fac available Corporate
Hospitality Days available **Location** 1.5m NE off A40, turn
left 100yds past Dixton roundabout on Monmouth to Ross on
Wye road

Hotel ★★ 63% Riverside Hotel, Cinderhill St,
MONMOUTH ☎ 01600 715577 & 713236
📠 01600 712668 17 en suite

Rolls of Monmouth The Hendre NP25 5HG
☎ 01600 715353 📠 01600 713115
e-mail: enquiries@therollsgolfclub.co.uk
**A hilly and challenging parkland course encompassing
several lakes and ponds and surrounded by woodland.
Set within a beautiful private estate complete with listed
mansion and panoramic views towards the Black
Mountains. The short 4th has a lake beyond the green
and both the 17th and 18th holes are magnificent holes
with which to end your round.**
18 holes, 6733yds, Par 72, SSS 73, Course record 69.
Club membership 160.
Visitors must telephone in advance. **Societies** must contact
in advance. **Green Fees** £38 per day (weekends £42) (Mon
special, £33 for round + lunch). **Cards** 🎫 ▆▆ 📖 💳 💳
Facilities ⊗ 〗╢🍺♀⛅🏌 ⛳ **Location** 4m W
on B4233

Hotel ★★ 63% Riverside Hotel, Cinderhill St,
MONMOUTH ☎ 01600 715577 & 713236
📠 01600 712668 17 en suite

RAGLAN   Map 03 SO40

Raglan Parc Parc Lodge, Station Rd NP5 2ER
☎ 01291 690077
18 holes, 6604yds, Par 72, SSS 73, Course record 67.
Location Off junct of A449/A40
Telephone for further details

Hotel ★★★ 70% Llansantffraed Court Hotel,
Llanvihangel Gobion, ABERGAVENNY
☎ 01873 840678 21 en suite

NEATH PORT TALBOT

GLYNNEATH   Map 03 SN80

Glynneath Pen-y-graig, Pontneathvaughan SA11 5UH
☎ 01639 720452 & 720872 📠 01639 720452
18 holes, 5656yds, Par 69, SSS 68, Course record 63.
Course Designer Cotton/Pennick/Lawrie **Location** 2m NE
of Glynneath on B4242
Telephone for further details

Hotel ★★★ 66% Castle Hotel, The Parade, NEATH
☎ 01639 641119 & 643581 📠 01639 641624 29 en suite

MARGAM   Map 03 SS78

Lakeside Water St SA13 2PA ☎ 01639 899959
18 holes, 4550yds, Par 63, SSS 63, Course record 65.
Course Designer Matthew Wootton **Location** Off junct 38
of M4
Telephone for further details

Hotel ★★★ 68% Aberavon Beach Hotel, PORT
TALBOT ☎ 01639 884949 52 en suite

NEATH   Map 03 SS79

Earlswood Jersey Marine SA10 6JP ☎ 01792 321578
**Earlswood is a hillside course offering spectacular
scenic views over Swansea Bay. The terrain is gently
undulating downs with natural hazards and is designed
to appeal to both the new and the experienced golfer.**
18 holes, 5084yds, Par 68, SSS 68.
Visitors no restrictions. **Societies** advisable to contact in
advance. **Green Fees** £9 per round. **Prof** Mike Day
Course Designer Gorvett Estates **Facilities** 🍺 🍴 ⛅ 🏌
🍴 ⛳ **Location** Approx 4m E of Swansea, off A483

Hotel ★★★ 66% Castle Hotel, The Parade, NEATH
☎ 01639 641119 & 643581 📠 01639 641624 29 en suite

Neath Cadoxton SA10 8AH
☎ 01639 643615 (clubhouse) & 632759 (secretary)
18 holes, 6492yds, Par 72, SSS 72, Course record 66.
Course Designer James Braid **Location** 2m NE off A4230
Telephone for further details

Hotel ★★★ 66% Castle Hotel, The Parade, NEATH
☎ 01639 641119 & 643581 📠 01639 641624 29 en suite

Swansea Bay Jersey Marine SA10 6JP
☎ 01792 812198 & 814153
Fairly level seaside links with part sand dunes.
18 holes, 6605yds, Par 72, SSS 71, Course record 69.
Club membership 500.
Visitors advisable to contact in advance. **Societies**
telephone enquiry or letter stating requirements. **Green**

Continued

Fees £17 per round (£24 weekends & bank holidays). **Prof** Mike Day **Facilities** ⊗ 🎍 🛅 💺 🏵 🍴 ⛱ 🏠 🚩 ⛳ **Location** M4 exit 42 onto A483, take 1st right onto B4290 towards Jersey Marine, then 1st right to clubhouse.

Hotel ★★★ 66% Castle Hotel, The Parade, NEATH ☎ 01639 641119 & 643581 📖 01639 641624 29 en suite

Additional hotel ★★★ 68% Aberavon Beach Hotel, PORT TALBOT ☎ 01639 884949 Fax 01639 897885 52 en suite

PONTARDAWE
Map 03 SN70

Pontardawe Cefn Llan SA8 4SH
☎ 01792 863118 📖 01792 830041
e-mail: pontardawe@btopenworld.com
Meadowland course situated on plateau 600 ft above sea-level with good views over Bristol Channel and Brecon Beacons.
18 holes, 6101yds, Par 70, SSS 70, Course record 64.
Club membership 500.
Visitors must contact in advance, but may not play on weekends. **Societies** phone for availability **Green Fees** £18 per day. **Prof** Gary Hopkins **Facilities** ⊗ 🎍 🛅 💺 🏵 ⛱ 🏠 ⛳ **Leisure** snooker & pool rooms. **Location** N side of town centre M4 junc 45 off A4067

Hotel ★★★ 66% Castle Hotel, The Parade, NEATH ☎ 01639 641119 & 643581 📖 01639 641624 29 en suite

PORT TALBOT
Map 03 SS78

British Steel Port Talbot Sports & Social Club, Margam SA13 2NF ☎ 01639 791938
e-mail: tony.edwards@ntlworld.com
9 holes, 4726yds, Par 62, SSS 63, Course record 60.
Location M4 junct 40
Telephone for further details

Hotel ★★★ 68% Aberavon Beach Hotel, PORT TALBOT ☎ 01639 884949 52 en suite

NEWPORT

CAERLEON
Map 03 ST39

Caerleon NP6 1AY ☎ 01633 420342 📖 01633 420342
Parkland course.
9 holes, 2900yds, Par 34, SSS 34, Course record 29.
Club membership 148.
Visitors play is allowed on all days, contact for details.
Societies telephone 01633 420342. **Prof** M Phillips
Course Designer Steel **Facilities** ⊗ 🎍 🛅 💺 🏵 ⛱ 🏠 🚩 ⛳ 🍴 **Location** 3m from M4 turn off for Caerleon, 1st left after Priory hotel, follow road to bottom

Continued

Hotel ★★★★★ 70% The Celtic Manor Resort, Coldra Woods, NEWPORT ☎ 01633 413000 400 en suite

LLANWERN
Map 03 ST38

Llanwern Tennyson Av NP18 2DY
☎ 01633 412029 📖 01633 412029
e-mail: royherbert@btopenworld.com
Parkland course.
18 holes, 6177yds, Par 70, SSS 69, Course record 66.
Club membership 650.
Visitors welcome, but with member only at weekends. **Societies** telephone and confirm in writing. **Green Fees** terms on application. **Prof** Stephen Price **Facilities** ⊗ 🎍 🛅 💺 🏵 ⛱ 🏠 **Location** 0.5m S off A455

Hotel ★★★★★ 70% The Celtic Manor Resort, Coldra Woods, NEWPORT ☎ 01633 413000 400 en suite

NEWPORT See page 391

NEWPORT
Map 03 ST38

Newport Great Oak, Rogerstone NP10 9FX
☎ 01633 892643 📖 01633 896676
e-mail: newportgolfclub.gwent@euphony.net
An undulating parkland course, in an ideal situation on an inland plateau 300ft above sea level with fine views over the surrounding wooded countryside. There are no blind holes but, plenty of natural hazards and bunkers.
18 holes, 6460yds, Par 72, SSS 71, Course record 63.
Club membership 800.
Visitors must contact in advance, handicap certificate required. Not on Sat, limited time Sun. **Societies** must contact in writing or telephone **Green Fees** £35 per day; £30 per round (£40 weekends & bank holidays). **Prof** Paul Mayo **Course Designer** W Fernie **Facilities** ⊗ 🎍 🛅 💺 🏵 ⛱ 🏠 ⛳ **Location** 1m NW of junct 27 on M4 on B4591 just beyond 'Promotive' Garage

Hotel ★★★★★ 70% The Celtic Manor Resort, Coldra Woods, NEWPORT ☎ 01633 413000 400 en suite

Parc Church Ln, Coedkernew NP10 8TU
☎ 01633 680933 📖 01633 681011
A challenging but enjoyable 18-hole course with water hazards and accompanying wildlife. The 38-bay driving range is floodlit until 10pm.
18 holes, 5619yds, Par 70, SSS 68, Course record 66.
Club membership 400.
Visitors must contact in advance 01633 680933. **Societies** telephone in advance. **Green Fees** not confirmed. **Cards** 💳 💳 💳 💳 **Prof** B Thomas/G Edwards **Course Designer** B Thomas/T F Hicks **Facilities** ⊗ 🎍 🛅 💺 🏵 ⛱ 🏠 🚩 ❀ 🍴 ⛳ **Conf** fac available Corporate Hospitality Days available **Location** 3m SW of Newport, off A48

Hotel ★★★ 66% The Kings Hotel, High St, NEWPORT ☎ 01633 842020 61 en suite

Tredegar Park Parc-y-Brain Rd, Rogerstone NP10 9TG ☎ 01633 894433 📖 01633 897152
e-mail: tpgc@btinternet.com
A new course completed in 1999 with two balanced halves, mostly in view from the clubhouse. A rolling, open course with fine scenic views.
18 holes, 6150yds, Par 72, SSS 72.
Club membership 822.

Continued

Visitors must be a member of a golf club affiliated to a national golf union, please contact in advance. **Societies** apply to secretary. **Green Fees** not confirmed. **Cards** 🏧 💳 📇 **Prof** Lee Pagett **Course Designer** R Sandow **Facilities** ⊗ ⏶ ⭢ ⭢ ♨ ⛳ ⛳ ✿ ⛳ **Location** N of M4, Junct 27, B4591, club signposted from here

Hotel ★★★ 66% The Kings Hotel, High St, NEWPORT ☎ 01633 842020 61 en suite

PEMBROKESHIRE

HAVERFORDWEST — Map 02 SM91

Haverfordwest Arnolds Down SA61 2XQ
☎ 01437 764523 & 768409 📄 01437 764143
e-mail: haverwestgolf@lineone.net
Fairly flat parkland course, a good challenge for golfers of all handicaps. Set in attractive surroundings with fine views over the Preseli Hills.
18 holes, 5966yds, Par 70, SSS 69, Course record 63. Club membership 770.
Visitors restricted at weekends. **Societies** apply in writing or telephone for booking form. **Green Fees** terms on application. **Cards** 🏧 💳 📇 **Prof** Alex Pile **Facilities** ⊗ ⏶ ⭢ ♨ ⛳ ✿ ⛳ **Conf** fac available **Location** 1m E on A40

Hotel ★★ 68% Hotel Mariners, Mariners Square, HAVERFORDWEST ☎ 01437 763353 28 en suite

LETTERSTON — Map 02 SM92

Priskilly Forest Castlemorris SA62 5EH
☎ 01348 840276 📄 01348 840276
e-mail: jevans@priskilly-forest.co.uk
Challenging parkland course with panoramic views and a stunning 18th hole.
9 holes, 5874yds, Par 70, SSS 68, Course record 73. Club membership 130.
Visitors advance booking advisable at weekends during summer. **Societies** telephone in advance. **Green Fees** £12 for 9 holes, £18 for 18 holes. **Cards** 🏧 💳 📇 **Prof** S Parsons **Course Designer** J Walters **Facilities** ⊗ ⭢ ♨ ⛳ ✿ ⛳ ⛳ ⛳ **Leisure** fishing. **Location** Off B4331 between Letterston and Mathry

Hotel ★★ 73% Wolfscastle Country Hotel, WOLF'S CASTLE ☎ 01437 741688 & 741225 📄 01437 741383 20 en suite 1 annexe en suite

MILFORD HAVEN — Map 02 SM90

Milford Haven Woodbine House, Hubberston SA73 3RX ☎ 01646 697762 📄 01646 697870
e-mail: enquiries@mhgc.co.uk
Parkland course with excellent greens and views of the Milford Haven waterway.
18 holes, 6030yds, Par 71, SSS 70, Course record 64. Club membership 650.
Visitors no restrictions, advisable to contact in advance. **Societies** telephone to book. **Green Fees** not confirmed. **Cards** 🏧 💳 📇 **Facilities** ⊗ ⭢ ♨ ⛳ ✿ ⛳ **Location** 1.5m W of M.Haven

Hotel ★★★ 67% Cleddau Bridge Hotel, Essex Rd, PEMBROKE DOCK ☎ 01646 685961 & 0800 279 4055 📄 01646 685746 24 en suite

NEWPORT (PEMBROKESHIRE) — Map 02 SN03

Newport (Pemb) The Golf Club SA42 0NR
☎ 01239 820244 📄 01239 820085
e-mail: newportgc@lineone.net
9 holes, 5815yds, Par 70, SSS 68, Course record 64.
Course Designer James Baird **Location** 1.25m N
Telephone for further details

Hotel ★★ 68% Trewern Arms, NEVERN ☎ 01239 820395 10 en suite

PEMBROKE DOCK — Map 02 SM90

South Pembrokeshire Military Rd SA72 6SE
☎ 01646 621453 & 682442 📄 01646 621453
A hillside course located at Pembroke dock on an elevated site overlooking the river Cleddau and the Haven Waterway.
18 holes, 6100yds, Par 71, SSS 70, Course record 65. Club membership 350.
Visitors must contact in advance, especially during season. **Societies** apply in advance. **Green Fees** terms on application. **Cards** 📇 **Prof** Mr Jeremy Tilson **Course Designer** Committee **Facilities** ⊗ ⭢ ♨ ⛳ ✿ ⛳ **Location** SW side of town centre off B4322

Hotel ★★ 65% Old Kings Arms, Main St, PEMBROKE ☎ 01646 683611 18 en suite

ST DAVID'S — Map 02 SM72

St David's City Whitesands Bay SA62 6HR
☎ 01437 720572 & 721751
9 holes, 6117yds, Par 70, SSS 70, Course record 68.
Location 2m W overlooking Whitesands Bay
Telephone for further details

Hotel ★★★ 77% Warpool Court Hotel, ST DAVID'S ☎ 01437 720300 25 en suite

TENBY — Map 02 SN10

Tenby The Burrows SA70 7NP
☎ 01834 844447 842978 📄 01834 844447
e-mail: tenbygolfclub@ukn.co.uk
The oldest club in Wales, this fine old seaside links, with sea views and natural hazards, provides good golf all the year round.
18 holes, 6224yds, Par 69, SSS 71, Course record 65. Club membership 800.
Visitors subject to competition & tee reservation. **Societies** must apply in advance. **Green Fees** terms on application. **Cards** 🏧 💳 📇 **Prof** Mark Hawkey **Course Designer** James Braid **Facilities** ⊗ ⭢ ♨ ⛳ ✿ ⛳ **Conf** Corporate Hospitality Days available **Location** Close to railway station in the town

Hotel ★★★ 75% Atlantic Hotel, The Esplanade, TENBY ☎ 01834 842881 & 844176 📄 01834 842881 ex 256 42 en suite

Trefloyne Trefloyne Park, Penally SA70 7RG
☎ 01834 842165 📄 01834 842165
Idyllic parkland course with backdrop of mature mixed woodlands and distant views of Tenby, Carmarthen Bay and Caldey Island. Opened in 1996, natural features and hazards such as the Old Quarry make for exciting and challenging golf.

Continued

Celtic Manor

Map 03 ST38   Newport

☎ 01633 410255   📄 01633 410269

This relatively new resort has quickly become a world-renowned venue for golf, set in 1,400 acres of beautiful, unspoilt parkland at the gateway to Wales. Boasting three championship courses, Celtic Manor offers a challenge for all levels of play, complemented by a golf school and one of the largest clubhouses in Europe, as well as extensive leisure facilities. The Wentwood Hills (par 72), a favoured course for championships, is home to the Wales Open and due to host the Ryder Cup in 2010. Roman Road is a par 69 and is ideal for golfers of all levels, with a variety of tees, generous fairways and deep greens. For shorter round golfers, Coldra Woods, at par 59, is a challenging test of iron play.

e-mail: rholland@celtic-manor.com

Visitors Welcome. May play subject to availability. Must book in advance.

Societies Telephone with details in advance

Green Fees Telephone for details

Facilities ⊗ 🍴 ♟ ⚒ 🏠 🛎 🐾 🐕 🛺 ⚑
Conf facilities available; corporate hospitality days available

Professional Scott Patience

Leisure Tennis, swimming, sauna, solarium, gym, off roading, walking trails, health spa

Location Coldra Woods, Newport, NP18 1HQ.
(Off M4 J24, take A48 to Newport, R after 300 metres)

Holes/Par/Course record
Roman Road: 18 holes 6495 yds, Par 69, SSS 72, Course record 68
Coldra Woods: 18 holes, 3807 yds, Par 59, SSS 61
Wentworth Hills: 18 holes, 7097 yds, Par 72, SSS 75

Championship Course

WHERE TO STAY AND EAT NEARBY

Hotels
NEWPORT

★★★★★ ◉ ◉ 70% The Celtic Manor Resort, NP18 1HQ
☎ 01633 413000. 400 en suite

★★★ 68% Newport Lodge Hotel, NP20 5QV.
☎ 01633 821818. 27 en suite

★★★ 66% The Kings Hotel, NP20 1QU.
☎ 01633 842020. 61 en suite

Restaurants

◉ ◉ Chandlery, NP20 1EH.
☎ 01633 256622.

◉ Inn at the Elm Tree, NP20 8SQ.
☎ 01633 680225.

18 holes, 6635yds, Par 71, SSS 73.
Club membership 300.
Visitors must contact in advance, must play a reasonable standard of golf and adhere to golf etiiquette and dress code of club. **Societies** must book in advance by telephone or in writing. **Green Fees** not confirmed. **Cards** 🎴 💳 📇 💳 🗓 **Prof** Steven Laidler **Course Designer** F H Gillman **Facilities** ⊗ 🝙 🝙 💂 🏖 🏠 ⛳ 🐾 🏌 ⛳ **Leisure** lessons by PGA Professional. **Location** Within Trefloyne Park, just west of Tenby

Hotel ★★★ 69% Fourcroft Hotel, North Beach, TENBY ☎ 01834 842886 40 en suite

POWYS

BRECON Map 03 SO02

Brecon Newton Park LD3 8PA ☎ 01874 622004
Parkland course, with easy walking. Natural hazards include two rivers on its boundary. Good river and mountain scenery.
9 holes, 5476yds, Par 68, SSS 66, Course record 63.
Club membership 360.
Visitors advisable to contact in advance, limited availability at weekends. **Societies** apply in writing. **Green Fees** £12 per day/per round, £15 weekends & bank holidays. **Course Designer** James Braid **Facilities** ⊗ 🝙 🝙 💂 🏖 🏠 ⛳ ⛳ **Location** 0.75m W of town centre on A40

Hotel ★★ 67% The Castle of Brecon Hotel, Castle Square, BRECON ☎ 01874 624611 31 en suite 12 annexe en suite

Cradoc Penoyre Park, Cradoc LD3 9LP
☎ 01874 623658 📠 01874 611711
e-mail: secretary@cradoc.co.uk
Parkland with wooded areas, ponds and spectacular views over the Brecon Beacons. Challenging golf.

18 holes, 6331yds, Par 72, SSS 72, Course record 65.
Club membership 700.
Visitors must contact secretary in advance. Limited availability on Sundays **Societies** apply in writing or telephone in advance to secretary. **Green Fees** £24 per day (£29 weekends & bank holidays). **Cards** 🎴 💳 🗓 **Prof** Richard Davies **Course Designer** C K Cotton **Facilities** ⊗ 🝙 🝙 💂 🏖 🏠 ⛳ 🐾 🏌 ⛳ ⛳ **Location** 2m N past Catherdral off B4520

Hotel ★★ 67% The Castle of Brecon Hotel, Castle Square, BRECON ☎ 01874 624611 31 en suite 12 annexe en suite

BUILTH WELLS Map 03 SO05

Builth Wells Golf Links Rd LD2 3NF
☎ 01982 553296 📠 01982 551064
e-mail: builthwellsgolfclub1@btinternet.com
Well guarded greens and a stream running through the centre of the course add interest to this 18-hole undulating parkland course. The clubhouse is a converted 16th-century Welsh long house.
18 holes, 5376yds, Par 66, SSS 67, Course record 63.
Club membership 380.
Visitors Handicap certificate perferred. **Societies** by prior arrangement. **Green Fees** £25 per day; £18 per round (£30/£25 weekends & bank holidays). **Prof** Simon Edwards **Facilities** ⊗ 🝙 🝙 💂 🏖 🏠 ⛳ ⛳ **Conf** Corporate Hospitality Days available **Location** N of A483

Hotel ★★★ 🏸 70% Caer Beris Manor Hotel, BUILTH WELLS ☎ 01982 552601 23 en suite

KNIGHTON Map 07 SO27

Knighton Ffrydd Wood LD7 1DG
☎ 01547 528646 & 528046 (Sec)
Upland course with some hard walking. Fine views over the Welsh/English border.
9 holes, 5362yds, Par 68, SSS 66, Course record 65.
Club membership 150.
Visitors may not play on Sun until after 4.30pm. **Societies** telephone in advance **Green Fees** not confirmed. **Course Designer** Harry Vardon **Facilities** ⊗ 🝙 💂 🏖 **Location** 0.5m S off B4355

Hotel ★★ 80% Milebrook House Hotel, Milebrook, KNIGHTON ☎ 01547 528632 10 en suite

LLANDRINDOD WELLS Map 03 SO06

Llandrindod Wells The Clubhouse LD1 5NY
☎ 01597 823873 (sec) 📠 01597 823873
e-mail: secretary@lwgc.co.uk
An upland links course, designed by Harry Vardon, with easy walking and panoramic views. One of the highest courses in Wales (1,100 ft above sea level).
18 holes, 5759yds, Par 69, SSS 69, Course record 65.
Club membership 465.
Visitors no restrictions. **Societies** must telephone in advance. **Green Fees** £20 per round/£28 per day (weekends & bank holidays £25/£32). **Prof** Philip Davies **Course Designer** H Vardon **Facilities** ⊗ 🝙 🝙 💂 🏖 🏠 ⛳ 🐾 🏌 ⛳ 🍴 **Conf** fac available **Location** 1m SE off A483

Hotel ★★★ 71% Hotel Metropole, Temple St, LLANDRINDOD WELLS ☎ 01597 823700 120 en suite

LLANGATTOCK Map 03 SO21

Old Rectory NP8 1PH
☎ 01873 810373 📠 01873 810373
9 holes, 2200yds, Par 54, SSS 59, Course record 53.
Location SW of village
Telephone for further details

Hotel ★★★ 71% Gliffaes Country House Hotel, CRICKHOWELL ☎ 01874 730371 & 0800 146719 (Freephone) 📠 01874 730463 19 en suite 3 annexe en suite

LLANIDLOES
Map 06 SN98

St Idloes Penrallt SY18 6LG ☎ 01686 412559
9 holes, 5540yds, Par 66, SSS 66, Course record 61.
Location 1m N off B4569
Telephone for further details

Guesthouse ♦♦♦♦ Old Vicarage, LLANGURIG
☎ 01686 440280 4 en suite

MACHYNLLETH
Map 06 SH70

Machynlleth Ffordd Drenewydd SY20 8UH
☎ 01654 702000
9 holes, 5726yds, Par 68, SSS 68, Course record 65.
Course Designer James Braid **Location** 0.5m E off A489
Telephone for further details

Hotel ★★ 67% Wynnstay Hotel, Maengwyn St,
MACHYNLLETH ☎ 01654 702941 23 en suite

NEWTOWN
Map 06 SO19

St Giles Pool Rd SY16 3AJ
☎ 01686 625844 ▤ 01686 625844
e-mail: st.giles.newtown@euphony.net
Inland country course with easy walking. Testing 2nd
hole, par 3, and 4th hole, par 4. River Severn skirts four
holes.
9 holes, 6012yds, Par 70, SSS 70, Course record 67.
Club membership 350.
Visitors advisable to contact in advance. **Societies** must
contact in advance. **Green Fees** terms on application. **Prof**
D P Owen **Facilities** ⊗ by prior arrangement ⅷ by prior
arrangement ▤ by prior arrangement ⬤ by prior
arrangement ⚲ ∅ **Location** 0.5m NE on A483

Hotel ★★ 67% Wynnstay Hotel, Maengwyn St,
MACHYNLLETH ☎ 01654 702941 23 en suite

WELSHPOOL
Map 07 SJ20

Welshpool Golfa Hill SY21 9AQ
☎ 01938 850249 ▤ 01938 850249
e-mail: welshpool.golfclub@virgin.net
Undulating, hilly, heathland course with bracing air.
Testing holes are 2nd (par 5), 14th (par 3), 17th (par 3)
and a memorable 18th.
18 holes, 5716yds, Par 71, SSS 68, Course record 68.
Club membership 400.
Visitors must book in advance, restricted some weekends.
Societies must book in advance. **Green Fees** £15.50 per
day (£25.50 weekend & bank holiday) (£15.50 winter
weekends and bank holidays). **Prof** Bob Barlow **Course
Designer** James Braid **Facilities** ⊗ ⅷ ▤ ⬤ ♀ ⚲ 🛍 ↑ ⚑
🛒 ∅ **Conf** Corporate Hospitality Days available
Location 3m W off A458

Hotel ★★★ 68% Royal Oak Hotel, The Cross,
WELSHPOOL ☎ 01938 552217 24 en suite

RHONDDA CYNON TAFF

ABERDARE
Map 03 SO00

Aberdare Abernant CF44 0RY
☎ 01685 872797 ▤ 01685 872797
Mountain course with parkland features overlooking
Brecon Beacons. Tree-lined with many mature oak
trees.

18 holes, 5875yds, Par 69, SSS 69, Course record 64.
Club membership 550.
Visitors must have handicap certificate. May play
weekends by prior arrangment with professional. **Societies**
apply in writing in advance to the secretary. **Green Fees**
£17 (weekends & bank holidays £21). **Prof** A Palmer
Facilities ⊗ ⅷ ▤ ⬤ ♀ ⚲ 🛍 ∅ **Conf** fac available
Location A470 to Abercynon, take A4059 to Aberdare.
Follow sign to hospital, 400 yds on right

Hotel ★★ 60% Tregenna Hotel, Park Ter, MERTHYR
TYDFIL ☎ 01685 723627 14 en suite 7 annexe en suite

MOUNTAIN ASH
Map 03 ST09

Mountain Ash Cefnpennar CF45 4DT
☎ 01443 479459 ▤ 01443 479628
Mountain course on heathland with panoramic views of
the Brecon Beacons.
18 holes, 5553yds, Par 69, SSS 67, Course record 60.
Club membership 600.
Visitors contact in advance for details. **Societies** must
contact in writing. **Green Fees** £20 (£30 weekend). **Cards**
▭▭ ▭▭ 🖃 ▭▭ ▭ 🖂 **Prof** Darren Clark **Facilities** ⊗ ⅷ ▤
⬤ ♀ ⚲ 🛍 ∅ **Conf** fac available **Location** 1m NW off
A4059

Hotel ★★ 60% Tregenna Hotel, Park Ter, MERTHYR
TYDFIL ☎ 01685 723627 14 en suite 7 annexe en suite

PENRHYS
Map 03 ST09

Rhondda Golf Club House CF43 3PW
☎ 01443 441384 ▤ 01443 441384
e-mail: rhondda@btinternet.com
18 holes, 6205yds, Par 70, SSS 71, Course record 67.
Location 0.5m W off B4512
Telephone for further details

Hotel ★★★ 67% Heritage Park Hotel, Coed Cae Rd,
Trehafod, PONTYPRIDD ☎ 01443 687057 44 en suite

PONTYPRIDD
Map 03 ST08

Pontypridd Ty Gwyn Rd CF37 4DJ
☎ 01443 409904 ▤ 01443 491622
Well-wooded mountain course with springy turf. Good
views of the Rhondda Valley and coast.
18 holes, 5721yds, Par 69, SSS 68, Course record 65.
Club membership 850.
Visitors must contact in advance. Must play with member
on weekends & bank holidays. Must have a handicap
certificate. **Societies** weekdays only. Must contact in
advance. **Green Fees** not confirmed. **Prof** Wade Walters
Facilities ⊗ ⅷ ▤ ⚲ 🛍 ⬤ 🛒 ∅ **Location** E side of
town centre off A470

Hotel ★★★ 67% Heritage Park Hotel, Coed Cae Rd,
Trehafod, PONTYPRIDD ☎ 01443 687057 44 en suite

TALBOT GREEN
Map 03 ST08

Llantrisant & Pontyclun Off Ely Valley Rd
CF72 8AL ☎ 01443 228169 ▤ 01443 224601
e-mail: lpgc@barbox.com
A scenic, undulating parkland course, recently
extended to 18 holes.
18 holes, 5328yds, Par 68, SSS 66.
Club membership 600.
Visitors must have handicap certificate, must contact in
advance, not at weekends **Societies** telephone in advance

Continued

Continued

Green Fees £20 per day (weekends £25). **Cards** 🖃 **Prof** Steve Hurley & Matt Vanstone **Facilities** ⊗ ⅷ ఓ ☕ ♀ ⚐ 🖼 🍴 ✂ **Conf** Corporate Hospitality Days available **Location** M4 J34 for A4119 to Llantrisant. over 1st roundabout, left at 2nd set of lights to Talbot Green. Right at mini roundabout, club 50yds on left.

Hotel ★★★★ 69% Miskin Manor Hotel & Health Club, Groes Faen, Pontyclun, MISKIN ☎ 01443 224204 33 en suite 9 annexe en suite

SWANSEA

CLYDACH   Map 03 SN60

Inco SA6 5QR ☎ 01792 842929
Flat meadowland course bordered by meandering River Tawe and the historic Swansea Valley. Recently completed an ambitious development programme.
18 holes, 6064yds, Par 70, SSS 69.
Club membership 450.
Visitors no restrictions. **Societies** must contact in advance. **Green Fees** £18 per round (weekend £23). **Facilities** ⊗ ⅷ ఓ ☕ ♀ ⚐ **Leisure** outdoor bowling green. **Location** Junct 25 on M4 then 1.5m NE on A4067

Hotel ⭥ Travel Inn, Upper Fforest Way, Morriston, SWANSEA ☎ 08701 977246 40 en suite

PONTLLIW   Map 02 SS69

Allt-y-Graban Allt-y-Grabam Rd SA4 1DT
☎ 01792 885757
A challenging parkland course with fine panoramic views, opened in 1993. It is a 9-hole course but with plans for 12 holes. There are 6 par 4 holes and 3 par 3 holes. The 6th is a challenging hole with a blind tee shot into the valley and a dog-leg to the left onto an elevated green.
9 holes, 2210yds, Par 66, SSS 66, Course record 63.
Club membership 158.
Visitors no restrictions. **Societies** telephone in advance. **Green Fees** £7 for 9 holes, £12 for 18 holes. **Course Designer** F G Thomas **Facilities** ఓ ♀ ⚐ ✂ **Location** From junct 47 on M4 take A48 towards Pontardulais. Turn left after Glamorgan Arms

Hotel 🆄 Holiday Inn Swansea, The Kingsway Circle, SWANSEA ☎ 0870 400 9078 106 en suite

SOUTHGATE   Map 02 SS58

Pennard 2 Southgate Rd SA3 2BT
☎ 01792 233131 & 233451 📄 01792 234797
e-mail: pigeon01@globalnet.co.uk
Undulating, cliff-top seaside links with good coastal views.
18 holes, 6265yds, Par 71, SSS 72, Course record 69.
Club membership 1020.
Visitors advisable to contact the office in advance. not Tue **Societies** by prior arrangement, telephone or email in advance. **Green Fees** £30 per 18 holes (£40 weekends & bank holidays). **Cards** 🖃 🖾 💳 📇 📇 🖾 📇 **Prof** M V Bennett **Course Designer** James Braid **Facilities** ⊗ ⅷ ఓ ☕ ♀ ⚐ 🖼 🍴 ✂ **Conf** fac available **Location** 8m W of Swansea by A4067 and B4436

Hotel ★★ Fairyhill, REYNOLDSTON ☎ 01792 390139 8 en suite

SWANSEA   Map 03 SS69

Clyne 120 Owls Lodge Ln, The Mayals, Blackpyl SA35DP ☎ 01792 401989 📄 01792 401078
e-mail: clynegolfclub@supanet.com
Challenging moorland course with excellent greens and scenic views of Swansea Bay and The Gower.
18 holes, 6334yds, Par 70, SSS 72, Course record 64.
Club membership 900.
Visitors must be member of a club with handicap certificate. Groups over 8 advised to book in advance. **Societies** must contact in advance. **Green Fees** £26 per round (£32 weekends). **Prof** Jonathan Clewett **Course Designer** H S Colt & Harries **Facilities** ⊗ ⅷ ఓ ☕ ♀ ⚐ 🖼 🍴 ✂ ┇ **Leisure** chipping green,driving nets,indoor practice net. **Location** 3.5m SW on B4436 off A4067

Hotel ★★★ 65% St Anne's Hotel, Western Ln, MUMBLES ☎ 01792 369147 33 en suite

Additional hotel ★★★ 68% Aberavon Beach Hotel, PORT TALBOT ☎ 01639 884949 Fax 01639 897885 52 en suite

Langland Bay Langland Bay SA3 4QR
☎ 01792 361721 📄 01792 361082
e-mail: golf@langlandbay.sagehost.co.uk
Parkland course overlooking Gower coast. The par 4 6th is an uphill dog-leg open to the wind, and the par 3 16th (151 yards) is aptly named 'Death or Glory'.

18 holes, 5857yds, Par 70, SSS 69.
Club membership 850.
Visitors no restrictions. Tue is Ladies Day. No societies at weekends **Societies** must telephone in advance. **Green Fees** £30. **Prof** Mark Evans **Course Designer** Henry Cotton **Facilities** ⊗ ⅷ ఓ ☕ ♀ ⚐ 🖼 🍴 ✂ **Location** 6m W on A4067

Hotel ★★★ 65% St Anne's Hotel, Western Ln, MUMBLES ☎ 01792 369147 33 en suite

Morriston 160 Clasemont Rd SA6 6AJ
☎ 01792 796528 📄 01792 796528
e-mail: morristongolf@btconnect.com
Pleasant parkland course with a very difficult par 3 15th hole, one of the most challenging short holes in Wales. The 17th is aptly nicknamed 'Temple of Doom'.
18 holes, 5891yds, Par 68, SSS 68, Course record 61.
Club membership 700.
Visitors may not play Sat. Must contact in advance. **Societies** apply in writing. **Green Fees** £18 per day (weekends & bank holidays £30). **Prof** M. Govier **Facilities** ⊗ ⅷ ఓ ☕ ♀ ⚐ 🖼 ✂ **Conf** fac available Corporate Hospitality Days available **Location** 5m N of Swansea on A48. 1m E of junct 46 of M4

Continued

Hotel ⚓ Travel Inn, Upper Fforest Way, Morriston, SWANSEA ☎ 08701 977246 40 en suite

THREE CROSSES — Map 02 SS59

Gower Cefn Goleu SA4 3HS
☎ 01792 872480 (Off) 📠 01792 872480
e-mail: arichards@gowergolf.co.uk
Set in attractive rolling countryside, this Donald Steel designed course provides good strategic hazards, including trees, water and bunkers, outstanding views and a challenging game of golf.
18 holes, 6441yds, Par 71, SSS 72, Course record 67.
Club membership 500.
Visitors tee booking up to 7 days in advance, reservations recommended, some weekend vacancies, dress code and course etiquette must be observed. **Green Fees** Mon-Thu £20 per 18 holes (£25 weekends). **Cards** 🖦 🖦 🖦 🖦 📓 **Prof** Alan Williamson **Course Designer** Donald Steel **Facilities** ⊗ ⅷ ᛒ ⬛ ♀ ⚲ 🖴 ⛳ 🖝 🖟 ♪ **Conf** fac available Corporate Hospitality Days available **Location** Sign posted from the village of Three Crosses, off A4118 from Swansea to Gower

Hotel ★★ 72% Beaumont Hotel, 72-73 Walter Rd, SWANSEA ☎ 01792 643956 16 en suite

UPPER KILLAY — Map 02 SS59

Fairwood Park Blackhills Ln SA2 7JN
☎ 01792 203648 📠 01792 297849
e-mail: admin@fairwoodgolf.co.uk
Parkland championship course on the beautiful Gower Peninsula.
18 holes, 6650yds, Par 73, SSS 73, Course record 68.
Club membership 621.
Visitors welcome except when championship or club matches are being held. Must contact in advance and provide handicap certificate. **Societies** must contact in advance. **Green Fees** terms on application. **Cards** 🖦 **Prof** Gary Hughes **Course Designer** Hawtree **Facilities** ⊗ ⅷ ᛒ ⬛ ♀ ⚲ 🖴 🖝 🖟 ♪ **Conf** Corporate Hospitality Days available **Location** 1.5m S off A4118

Hotel ★★ 71% Windsor Lodge Hotel & Restaurant, Mount Pleasant, SWANSEA ☎ 01792 642158 & 652744 📠 01792 648996 18 en suite

TORFAEN

CWMBRAN — Map 03 ST29

Green Meadow Golf & Country Club
Treherbert Rd, Croesyceiliog NP44 2BZ
☎ 01633 869321 & 862626 📠 01633 868430
Undulating parkland course with panoramic views. Tree lined undulating fairways, water hazards and pot bunkers. The greens are excellent and are playable all year round.
18 holes, 6029yds, Par 70, SSS 70, Course record 66.
Club membership 400.
Visitors by prior arrangement advised especially at weekends, tel 01633 862626. Correct standard of dress compulsory. **Societies** telephone for brochure, Golf Shop 01633 862626. **Green Fees** not confirmed. **Cards** 🖦 🖦 📓 **Prof** Dave Woodman **Course Designer** Peter Richardson **Facilities** ⊗ ⅷ ᛒ ⬛ ♀ ⚲ 🖴 ⛳ 🖟 ♪ 🖟

Continued

Leisure hard tennis courts. **Conf** fac available **Location** 5m N of junct 26 M4, off A4042 from Cardiff

Hotel ★★★★ 66% Parkway Hotel, Cwmbran Dr, CWMBRAN ☎ 01633 871199 70 en suite

Pontnewydd Maesgwyn Farm, Upper Cwmbran
NP44 1AB ☎ 01633 482170 📠 01633 838598
e-mail: ct.phillips@virgin.net
Mountainside course, with hard walking. Good views across the Severn Estuary.
18 holes, 5278yds, Par 68, SSS 67, Course record 61.
Club membership 502.
Visitors must be accompanied by a member weekends & bank holidays. **Green Fees** £15 per round. **Facilities** ⊗ ⅷ ᛒ ⬛ ♀ ⚲ **Location** N side of town centre

Hotel ★★★★ 66% Parkway Hotel, Cwmbran Dr, CWMBRAN ☎ 01633 871199 70 en suite

PONTYPOOL — Map 03 SO20

Pontypool Lasgarn Ln, Trevethin NP4 8TR
☎ 01495 763655 📠 01495 755564
e-mail: pontypoolgolf@btconnect.com
Undulating, mountain course with magnificent views of the Bristol Channel.
18 holes, 6046yds, Par 69, SSS 69, Course record 64.
Club membership 638.
Visitors must have a handicap certificate, restricted availability at weekends, advisable to call in advance. **Societies** apply in writing or by phone, deposit payable. **Green Fees** terms on application. **Prof** James Howard **Facilities** ⊗ ⅷ ᛒ ⬛ ♀ ⚲ 🖴 🖝 🖟 ♪ **Conf** Corporate Hospitality Days available **Location** 1.5m N off A4043

Hotel ★★ 67% Mill at Glynhir, Glynhir Rd, Llandybie, AMMANFORD ☎ 01269 850672 7 en suite
3 annexe en suite

Woodlake Park Golf & Country Club
Glascoed NP4 0TE ☎ 01291 673933 📠 01291 673811
e-mail: golf@woodlake.co.uk
Undulating parkland course with magnificent views over Llandegfedd Reservoir. Superb green constructed to USGA specification. Holes 4, 7 and 16 are par 3s which are particularly challenging. Holes 6 and 17 are long par 4s which can be wind affected.
18 holes, 6278yds, Par 71, SSS 72, Course record 67.
Club membership 500.
Visitors book in advance. **Societies** telephone or write for society package. **Green Fees** £22.50 per 18 holes (£30 weekends and bank holidays). **Cards** 🖦 🖦 **Prof** Leon Lancey **Facilities** ⊗ ⅷ ᛒ ⬛ ♀ ⚲ 🖴 🖝 🖟 ♪ 🖟 **Leisure** fishing. **Conf** fac available Corporate Hospitality Days available **Location** Overlooking Llandegfedd Reservoir

Hotel ★★ 67% Mill at Glynhir, Glynhir Rd, Llandybie, AMMANFORD ☎ 01269 850672 7 en suite
3 annexe en suite

If you have a comment or suggestion concerning the AA Golf Course Guide 2005, you can e-mail us at

lifestyleguides@theAA.com

VALE OF GLAMORGAN

BARRY
Map 03 ST16

Brynhill Port Rd CF62 8PN
☎ 01446 720277 🖹 01446 740422
e-mail: gershenson@lineone.net
Meadowland course with some hard walking. Prevailing west wind.
18 holes, 6336yds, Par 72, SSS 71.
Club membership 750.
Visitors must contact in advance. May not play on Sun.
Societies phone secretary for details. **Green Fees** not confirmed. **Cards** 🌐 **Prof** Mike Herbert **Facilities** ⊗ ⅷ 🍴 ♥ ♀ ⚘ 🏠 ⚑ ✓ **Location** 1.25m N on B4050
....
Hotel ★★★ 69% Mount Sorrel Hotel, Porthkerry Rd, BARRY ☎ 01446 740069 42 en suite

RAF St Athan Clive Rd, St. Athan CF62 4JD
☎ 01446 797186 & 751043 🖹 01446 751862
A parkland course with strong winds blowing straight from the sea. Further interest is added by this being a very tight course with lots of trees. Beware of low flying RAF jets.
9 holes, 6480yds, Par 72, SSS 72.
Club membership 450.
Visitors contact in advance, Sun mornings club competitions only. **Societies** apply in advance. **Green Fees** £15 per day (weekend £20). **Course Designer** the members **Facilities** ⊗ 🍴 ♥ ♀ ⚘ 🏠 **Location** Between Barry & Llantwit Major
....
Hotel ★★★ ♨ 73% Egerton Grey Country House Hotel, Porthkerry, BARRY ☎ 01446 711666 10 en suite

St Andrews Major Argae Ln, Coldbrook Rd East, Cadoxton CF63 1BL ☎ 01446 722227 🖹 01446 748953
e-mail: info@standrewsmajorgolfclub.co.uk
A scenic 18 hole parkland golf course, suitable for all standards of golfer. The greens are designed to US specifications. The course provides excellent challenges to all levels of golfers without being physically exerting.
18 holes, 5300yds, Par 69.
Club membership 400.
Visitors advisable to contact in advance. **Societies** telephone in advance. Min 12 people, £10 deposit payable. **Green Fees** £16 per round (weekends £18). **Cards** 🌐 🌐 🌐 🌐 💲 **Prof** Iestyn Taylor **Course Designer** Richard Hurd **Facilities** ⊗ 🍴 ♥ ♀ ⚘ 🏠 ⚑ ✓ 🏌 ✓ **Conf** fac available Corporate Hospitality Days available **Location** Off Barry new link road, Coldbrook Road East
....
Hotel ★★★ 69% Egerton Grey Country House Hotel, Porthkerry, BARRY ☎ 01446 711666 10 en suite

DINAS POWYS
Map 03 ST17

Dinas Powis High Walls Av CF64 4AJ
☎ 029 2051 2727 🖹 029 2051 2727
18 holes, 5486yds, Par 67, SSS 67, Course record 60.
Location NW side of village
Telephone for further details
....
Hotel ★★★ 69% Mount Sorrel Hotel, Porthkerry Rd, BARRY ☎ 01446 740069 42 en suite

Booking a tee time is always advisable.

PENARTH
Map 03 ST17

Glamorganshire Lavernock Rd CF64 5UP
☎ 029 20701185 🖹 029 20701185
e-mail: glamgolf@btconnect.com
Parkland course, overlooking the Bristol Channel.
18 holes, 6184yds, Par 70, SSS 70, Course record 64.
Club membership 1000.
Visitors contact professional in advance. **Societies** must contact in advance. **Green Fees** £35 per day (£40 weekends and bank holidays). **Cards** 🌐 🌐 🌐 🌐 **Prof** Andrew Kerr-Smith **Course Designer** James Braid **Facilities** ⊗ ⅷ 🍴 ♥ ♀ ⚘ 🏠 ⚑ ✓ 🏌 ✓ **Location** S side of town centre on B4267
....
Hotel ★★★ 69% Mount Sorrel Hotel, Porthkerry Rd, BARRY ☎ 01446 740069 42 en suite

WENVOE
Map 03 ST17

Wenvoe Castle CF5 6BE ☎ 029 20594371
18 holes, 6422yds, Par 72, SSS 71, Course record 64.
Location 1m S off A4050
Telephone for further details
....
Hotel ★★★ ♨ 73% Egerton Grey Country House Hotel, Porthkerry, BARRY ☎ 01446 711666 10 en suite

HENSOL
Map 03 ST07

Vale Hotel Golf & Spa Resort Hensol Park CF72 8JY ☎ 01443 665899 🖹 01443 222220
e-mail: golf@vale-hotel.com
Two championship courses set in 200 acres of glorious countryside with views over Hensol Park lake and castle. The Wales National with greens constructed to USGA standard will prove a stern test for even the very best players. The aptly named Lake course has water coming into play on 12 holes. The signature hole, the 12th, has an island green reached via a stone bridge. The club is also home to the Welsh PGA.
Lake: 18 holes, 6426yds, Par 72, SSS 71.
Hensol: 9 holes, 3115yds, Par 72, SSS 71.
Club membership 1100.
Visitors must have a handicap certificate. May only play with member at weekends on Lake course. **Societies** apply in writing. **Green Fees** terms on application. **Cards** 🌐 🌐 🌐 🌐 🌐 🌐 💲 **Prof** D Llewellyn/P Johnson/C Coombs **Course Designer** Peter Johnson **Facilities** ⊗ ⅷ 🍴 ♥ ♀ ⚘ 🏠 ⚑ 🏌 ✓ ✓ **Leisure** hard tennis courts, heated indoor swimming pool, squash, fishing, sauna, solarium, gymnasium, many facilities in process of being built. **Conf** fac available Corporate Hospitality Days available **Location** 2 mins from junct 34 of M4
....
Hotel ★★★★ 71% Vale Hotel Golf & Country Club, Hensol Park, HENSOL ☎ 01443 667800 29 en suite 114 annexe en suite

WREXHAM

CHIRK
Map 07 SJ23

Chirk Golf Club LL14 5AD
☎ 01691 774407 🖹 01691 773878
e-mail: chirkjackbarker@btinternet.com
Overlooked by the National Trust's Chirk Castle, a championship-standard 18-hole course with a 664-yard

Continued

par 5 at the 9th - one of the longest in Europe. Also a 9-hole course, driving range and golf academy.
Chirk: 18 holes, 7045yds, Par 72, SSS 73, Course record 69.
Club membership 300.
Visitors advisable to contact in advance. **Societies** must telephone in advance **Green Fees** terms on application.
Cards ⬚ ⬚ ⬚ ⬚ 🔲 **Prof** Rhodri Lloyd Jones **Facilities** ⊗ ⁑ ⅃⅃ ⅃ 🍺 ⅃ ⚹ 🏠 ⚘ ⚡ 🔱 **Leisure** 9 hole par 3 course. **Conf** fac available **Location** A483 from Wrexham towards A5 Llangollen for 5m. Near to Chirk Castle.

Hotel ★★★ 66% Moreton Park Lodge, Moreton Park, Gledrid, CHIRK ☎ 01691 776666 46 en suite

EYTON
Map 07 SJ34

Plassey LL13 0SP ☎ 01978 780020 🖹 01978 781397
Picturesque 9 hole course in undulating parkland.
9 holes, 4962yds, Par 66, SSS 64, Course record 62.
Club membership 222.
Visitors must contact in advance to book starting time **Societies** telephone then confirm in writing. **Green Fees** £16 per 18 holes; £9.50 per 9 holes (£17.50/£11 weekends & bank holidays). **Cards** ⬚ ⬚ ⬚ ⬚ 🔲 **Prof** Simon Ward **Course Designer** Welsh Golf Union **Facilities** ⅃ 🍺 ⚹ 🏠 ⚘ ⚡ **Location** 2.5m off A483 Chester/Oswestry, signposted

Hotel ★★★ 68% Cross Lanes Hotel & Restaurant, Cross Lanes, Bangor Rd, Marchwiel, WREXHAM ☎ 01978 780555 16 en suite

RUABON
Map 07 SJ34

Penycae Ruabon Rd, Penycae LL14 1TP ☎ 01978 810108
9 holes, 2140yds, Par 64, SSS 62, Course record 62.
Course Designer John Day **Location** 1m off A5
Telephone for further details

Hotel ★★★ 66% Moreton Park Lodge, Moreton Park, Gledrid, CHIRK ☎ 01691 776666 46 en suite

WREXHAM
Map 07 SJ35

Clays Bryn Estyn Rd, Llan-y-Pwll LL13 9UB
☎ 01978 661406 🖹 01978 661417
e-mail: clays@wrexham.fsnet.co.uk
Gently undulating parkland course in a rural setting with views of the Welsh mountains and noted for the difficulty of its par 3s.
18 holes, 6010yds, Par 69, SSS 69, Course record 63.
Club membership 420.
Visitors must book in advance. **Societies** prior arrangement in writing. **Green Fees** £18 per 18 holes (£24 weekends). **Cards** ⬚ ⬚ ⬚ ⬚ 🔲 **Prof** David Larvin **Course Designer** R D Jones **Facilities** ⊗ ⁑ ⅃ 🍺 ⚹ 🏠 ⚘ 🔱 🦽 ⚡ ⚡ **Conf** Corporate Hospitality Days available **Location** Off A534

Hotel ★★★ 66% Llwyn Onn Hall Hotel, Cefn Rd, WREXHAM ☎ 01978 261225 13 en suite

Wrexham Holt Rd LL13 9SB
☎ 01978 364268 🖹 01978 364268
e-mail: info@wrexhamgolfclub.co.uk
Inland, sandy course with easy walking. Testing dog-legged 7th hole (par 4), and short 14th hole (par 3) with full carry to green.
18 holes, 6233yds, Par 70, SSS 70, Course record 64.
Club membership 600.
Visitors may not play competition days, and are advised to contact in advance. A handicap certificate is required. **Societies** welcome Mon & Wed-Fri. Apply in writing **Green Fees** terms on application. **Prof** Paul Williams **Course Designer** James Braid **Facilities** ⊗ ⁑ ⅃ 🍺 ⚹ ⚘ 🏠 🦽 ⚡ **Location** 2m NE on A534

Hotel ★★★ 66% Llwyn Onn Hall Hotel, Cefn Rd, WREXHAM ☎ 01978 261225 13 en suite

> **Prices may change during the currency of the Guide, please check when booking.**

Ireland

ANTRIM   Map 01 D5

Massereene 51 Lough Rd BT41 4DQ
☎ 028 94428096 📠 028 94487661
18 holes, 6602yds, Par 72, SSS 72, Course record 63.
Course Designer F Hawtree **Location** 1m SW of town
Telephone for further details

Hotel ★★★★ 66% Galgorm Manor, BALLYMENA
☎ 028 2588 1001 24 en suite

BALLYCASTLE   Map 01 D6

Ballycastle Cushendall Rd BT54 6QP
☎ 028 2076 2536 📠 028 2076 9909
e-mail: info@ballycastlegolfclub.com
An unusual mixture of terrain beside the sea, lying at
the foot of one of the nine glens of Antrim, with
magnificent views from all parts. The first five holes are
parkland with natural hazards; the middle holes are
links type and the rest on adjacent upland. Accurate
iron play is essential for good scoring while the
undulating greens will test putting skills.
18 holes, 5927mtrs, Par 71, SSS 70, Course record 64.
Club membership 920.
Visitors are welcome during the week. **Societies** apply in
writing. **Green Fees** £20 per round (£30 weekends & bank
holidays). **Cards** 🌐 💳 🔳 🖭 **Prof** Ian McLaughlin
Facilities ⊗ ⽆ 🟙 🍺 ♀ 🏌 🖺 ✆ **Conf** fac available
Corporate Hospitality Days available **Location** Between
Portrush & Cushendall (A2)

Hotel ★★★ 70% The Royal Court Hotel, 233 Ballybogey
Rd, PORTRUSH ☎ 028 7082 2236 18 en suite

BALLYCLARE   Map 01 D5

Ballyclare 23 Springdale Rd BT39 9JW
☎ 028 9332 2696 📠 028 9332 2696
e-mail: ballyclaregolfclub@supanet
Parkland course with lots of trees and shrubs and water
hazards provided by the river, streams and lakes.
18 holes, 5745mtrs, Par 71, SSS 71, Course record 66.
Club membership 580.
Visitors must contact in advance. **Societies** must contact in
advance. **Green Fees** terms on application. **Prof** Alan
Johnston **Course Designer** T McCauley **Facilities** ⊗ ⽆ 🟙
🍺 ♀ 🏌 🖭 ✆ **Conf** Corporate Hospitality Days
available **Location** 1.5m N of Ballyclare

Hotel ★★★★ 66% Galgorm Manor, BALLYMENA
☎ 028 2588 1001 24 en suite

Greenacres 153 Ballyrobert Rd BT39 9RT
☎ 028 9335 4111 📠 028 9335 4166
Designed and built into the rolling countryside, and
with the addition of lakes at five of the holes, provides a
challenge for both the seasoned golfer and the higher-
handicapped player.
18 holes, 5819yds, Par 71, SSS 69.
Club membership 440.
Visitors may not play Sat mornings. **Societies** apply in
writing. **Green Fees** not confirmed. **Cards** 🌐 💳 🖭 🖭

Prof Roy Skillen **Facilities** ⊗ ⽆ 🟙 🍺 ♀ 🏌 🖭 ✆ **Conf**
Corporate Hospitality Days available **Location** 12m from
Belfast city centre

BALLYGALLY   Map 01 D5

Cairndhu 192 Coast Rd BT40 2QG
☎ 028 2858 3324 📠 028 2858 3324
e-mail: cairndhugc@utvinternet.com
Built on a hilly headland, this course is both testing and
scenic, with wonderful coastal views. The par 3 second
hole can require anything from a 9 to a 3 iron
depending on the wind, while the 3rd has a carry of 180
yards over a headland to the fairway. The 10th, 11th
and 12th holes constitute Cairndhu's 'Amen Corner',
feared and respected by any standard of golfer.
18 holes, 5611mtrs, Par 70, SSS 69, Course record 64.
Club membership 905.
Visitors may not play on Sat. **Societies** must apply in
writing. **Green Fees** £20 per 18 holes (£25 Sun). **Cards**
🌐 💳 **Prof** Robert Walker **Course Designer** Mr
Morrison **Facilities** ⊗ ⽆ 🟙 🍺 ♀ 🏌 🖭 ✆
Conf fac available **Location** 4m N of Larne on coast road

Guesthouse ◆◆◆◆ Manor Guest House, 23 Older Fleet
Rd, Harbour Highway, LARNE ☎ 028 2827 3305
8 en suite

BALLYMENA   Map 01 D5

Ballymena 128 Raceview Rd BT42 4HY
☎ 028 2586 1487 📠 028 2586 1487
Parkland course of level heathland with plenty of
bunkers.
18 holes, 5299mtrs, Par 68, SSS 67, Course record 62.
Club membership 895.
Visitors may not play on Tue or Sat. **Societies** must
contact in advance. **Green Fees** not confirmed. **Prof** Ken
Revie **Facilities** ⊗ ⽆ 🟙 🍺 ♀ 🏌 🖭 ✆ **Location**
2m E on A42

Hotel ★★★★ 66% Galgorm Manor, BALLYMENA
☎ 028 2588 1001 24 en suite

Galgorm Castle Golf & Country Club
Galgorm Rd BT42 1HL
☎ 028 2564 6161 📠 028 2565 1151
e-mail: golf@galgormcastle.co.uk
18 hole USGA championship course set in 220 acres of
mature parkland in the grounds of one of Ireland's
most historic castles. The course is bordered by two
rivers which come into play and includes five lakes. A
course of outstanding beauty offering a challenge to
both the novice and low handicapped golfer.
18 holes, 6736yds, Par 72, SSS 72, Course record 67.
Club membership 450.
Visitors ring to book times. **Societies** telephone in advance
to book tee time. **Green Fees** £30 (weekends £35). **Cards**
🌐 💳 🖭 **Prof** Phil Collins **Course Designer** Simon
Gidman **Facilities** ⊗ ⽆ 🟙 🍺 ♀ 🏌 🖭 ✆
Leisure fishing, PGA staffed Academy. **Conf** fac available
Corporate Hospitality Days available **Location** 1m S of
Ballymena on A42

Hotel ★★★★ 66% Galgorm Manor, BALLYMENA
☎ 028 2588 1001 24 en suite

**Looking for a driving range? Refer to the listing
of driving ranges at the back of this guide.**

Continued

CARRICKFERGUS — Map 01 D5

Carrickfergus 25 North Rd BT38 8LP
☎ 028 9336 3713 🖹 028 9336 3023
e-mail: carrickfergusgc@talk21.com
Parkland course, fairly level but nevertheless demanding, with a notorious water hazard at the 1st. Well-maintained, with an interesting in-course riverway and fine views across Belfast Lough.
18 holes, 5768yds, Par 68, SSS 68.
Club membership 850.
Visitors restrictions at weekends. **Societies** must contact in advance. **Green Fees** terms on application. **Cards** 🌐 💳
🔳 🅿 **Prof** Gary Mercer **Facilities** ⊗ ⍢ 🦆 💺 ♀ ♨ 🏠 🏌
Conf fac available Corporate Hospitality Days available
Location 9m NE of Belfast on A2
....
Hotel ★★ 67% Dobbins Inn Hotel, 6-8 High St,
CARRICKFERGUS ☎ 028 9335 1905 15 en suite

Greenisland 156 Upper Rd, Greenisland BT38 8RW
☎ 028 9086 2236
A parkland course nestling at the foot of Knockagh Hill with scenic views over Belfast Lough.
9 holes, 6045yds, Par 71, SSS 69.
Club membership 660.
Visitors contact club in advance. Play restricted Sat and Thu. **Societies** by prior arrangement. **Green Fees** £12 (£18 weekends). **Facilities** ⊗ ⍢ 🦆 💺 ♀ ♨ **Location** N of Belfast, close to Carrickfergus
....
Hotel ★★ 67% Dobbins Inn Hotel, 6-8 High St,
CARRICKFERGUS ☎ 028 9335 1905 15 en suite

CUSHENDALL — Map 01 D6

Cushendall 21 Shore Rd BT44 0NG
☎ 028 2177 1318
e-mail: cushendallgolfclub@hotmail.com
Scenic course with spectacular views over the Sea of Moyle and Red Bay to the Mull of Kintyre. The River Dall winds through the course, coming into play in seven of the nine holes.
9 holes, 4386mtrs, Par 66, SSS 63, Course record 62.
Club membership 834.
Visitors Ladies day Thu, time sheet at weekends. **Societies** must contact in writing. **Green Fees** £13 per day (£18 weekends and bank holidays). **Course Designer** D Delargy
Facilities 🦆 💺 ♀ ♨ **Location** In village of Cushendall beside beach on main Antrim coast road, halfway between Larne and Bally Castle.
....
Guesthouse ♦♦♦♦ The Villa Farm House, 185 Torr Rd,
CUSHENDUN ☎ 028 2176 1252 3 en suite

LARNE — Map 01 D5

Larne 54 Ferris Bay Rd, Islandmagee BT40 3RT
☎ 028 9338 2228 🖹 028 9338 2088
e-mail: info@larnegolfclub.co.uk
An exposed part links, part heathland course offering a good test, particularly on the last three holes along the sea shore.
9 holes, 6686yds, Par 70, SSS 70, Course record 64.
Club membership 430.
Visitors may not play on Sat, advisable to avoid Fridays. **Societies** apply in writing or telephone in advance.
Green Fees £10 per day (weekends & bank holidays £18).
Course Designer G L Bailie

Continued

Facilities ⊗ ⍢ 🦆 💺 ♀ ♨ **Location** 6m N of Whitehead on Browns Bay rd
....
Guesthouse ♦♦♦♦ Drumkeerin, 201A Torr Rd,
CUSHENDUN ☎ 028 2176 1554 3 en suite

LISBURN — Map 01 D5

Aberdelghy Bell's Ln, Lambeg BT27 4QH
☎ 028 92662738 🖹 028 92603432
e-mail: info@mmsportsgolf.com
This parkland course, extended to 18 holes in 1997, has no bunkers. The hardest hole on the course is the 340m 3rd, a dog-leg through trees to a green guarded by water. The par 3 12th high on the hill and the 14th hole over the dam provide a challenge. The par 4 15th hole is a long dog-leg.
18 holes, 4139mtrs, Par 66, SSS 62, Course record 64.
Club membership 200.
Visitors restricted Sat 7.15am-1pm. Ring in advance for Sun. **Societies** telephone in advance. **Green Fees** £11 per 18 holes (£13.20 weekends & bank holidays). **Cards** 🌐
💳 🔳 🅿 **Prof** Ian Murdoch **Course Designer** Alec Blair **Facilities** 💺 ♨ 🏠 🏌 **Location** 1.5m N of Lisburn off A1
....
Hotel ★★★ 69% White Gables Hotel, 14 Dromore Rd,
HILLSBOROUGH ☎ 028 9268 2755 31 en suite

Lisburn 68 Eglantine Rd BT27 5RQ
☎ 028 9267 7216 🖹 028 9260 3608
e-mail: lisburngolfclub@aol.com
Meadowland course, fairly level, with plenty of trees and shrubs. Challenging last three holes, the par 3 finishing hole is a spectacular downhill hole and reaching par is a bonus.
18 holes, 6647yds, Par 72, SSS 72, Course record 67.
Club membership 1200.
Visitors must play with member on Sun. Must tee off before 3pm weekdays unless with a member. **Societies** must apply in writing. **Green Fees** terms on application.
Prof Stephen Hamill **Course Designer** Hawtree **Facilities** ⊗ ⍢ 🦆 💺 ♀ ♨ 🏠 🏌 ⛳ 🛒 🏌 **Conf** Corporate Hospitality Days available **Location** 2m from town on A1
....
Hotel ★★★ 69% White Gables Hotel, 14 Dromore Rd,
HILLSBOROUGH ☎ 028 9268 2755 31 en suite

MAZE — Map 01 D5

Down Royal Park Dunygarton Rd BT27 5RT
☎ 028 92621339 🖹 028 92621339
The 9-hole Valley course and the 18-hole Down Royal Park are easy walking, undulating heathland courses. Down Royal's 2nd hole is 628yds and thought to be among the best par 5 holes in Ireland.
Down Royal Park Course: 18 holes, 6824yds, Par 72, SSS 72, Course record 69.
Valley Course: 9 holes, 2019, Par 33.
Visitors no restrictions, except dress code. **Societies** reservations in advance. **Green Fees** terms on application.
Cards 🌐 💳 🅿 🅿 **Prof** P Ball **Facilities** ⊗ by prior arrangement ⍢ 🦆 💺 ♀ ♨ 🏠 🏌 🏴 🛒 🏌 ⛳ **Location** Inside Down Royal Race Course
....
Hotel ★★★ 69% White Gables Hotel, 14 Dromore Rd,
HILLSBOROUGH ☎ 028 9268 2755 31 en suite

> **Booking a tee time is always advisable.**

Royal Portrush

Map 01 C6 — Portrush

☎ 028 70822311   📄 028 70823139

This course, designed by Harry S. Colt, is considered among the six best in the UK. Founded in 1888, it was the venue of the first professional golf event held in Ireland, in 1895, where Sandy Herd beat Harry Vardon in the final. It is spectacular and breathtaking, and one of the tightest driving tests known to man. On a clear day, you have a fine view of Islay and the Paps of Jura from the 3rd tee, and the Giant's Causeway from the 5th. While the greens have to be 'read' from the start, there are fairways up and down valleys, and holes called Calamity Corner and Purgatory for good reason. The second hole, Giant's Grave, is 509 yards; there is an even longer hole at the 17th.

e-mail: info@royalportrushgolfclub.com

Visitors Must contact in advance, with a letter of introduction from their own club and a handicap certificate. Restricted Wed and Fri pm, Sat and Sun am on Dunluce Links

Societies Must apply in writing

Green Fees Dunluce IEP £85-£95, Valley £30-£35.

Facilities ⊗ ⚒ ▯ ▆ ♀ ⚚ 🏠 🍴 ✐

Professional Gary McNeill

Location Dunluce Rd, Portrush BT56 8JQ (0.5m from Portrush, on main road to Bushmills)

Holes/Par/Course record 45 holes.
Dunluce Links: 18 holes, 6641 yds, Par 72, SSS 73
Valley Links: 18 holes, 6054 yds, Par 70, SSS 72

WHERE TO STAY AND EAT NEARBY

Hotels
PORTRUSH
★★★ 70% The Royal Court,
BT56 8NF
☎ 028 70822236
18 en suite

Restaurants

PORTRUSH
◉ Ramore Wine Bar, BT56 8BN.
☎ 028 70824313

PORTSTEWART
◉ Smyths BT55 7EF.
☎ 028 70833564

Championship Course

NEWTOWNABBEY   Map 01 D5

Ballyearl Golf & Leisure Centre 585 Doagh Rd,
Mossley BT36 5RZ
☎ 028 9084 8287 📠 028 9084 4896
9 holes, 2520yds, Par 27.
Visitors no restrictions. **Societies** telephone in advance.
Green Fees not confirmed. **Cards** 💳 💳 💳 **Prof** Richard
Johnston **Course Designer** V Lathery **Facilities** 🏌 🏖 🏠
🏌 🍴 **Leisure** squash, solarium, gymnasium, Theatre and
arts centre.

Mallusk Antrim Rd BT36 ☎ 028 90843799
9 holes, 4444yds, Par 62, SSS 62, Course record 62.
Course Designer David Fitzgerald
Telephone for further details

PORTBALLINTRAE   Map 01 C6

Bushfoot 50 Bushfoot Rd, Portballintrae BT57 8RR
☎ 028 2073 1317 📠 028 2073 1852
e-mail: bushfootgolfclub@btinternet.com
A seaside links course with superb views in an area of
outstanding beauty. A challenging par 3 7th is ringed
by bunkers with out-of-bounds beyond, while the 3rd
has a blind approach. Also a putting green and pitch
and putt course.
9 holes, 6075yds, Par 70, SSS 68, Course record 68.
Club membership 850.
Visitors must contact in advance. **Societies** must contact in
advance. **Green Fees** terms on application. **Facilities** ⊗ 🍴
🏖 🏌 🏖 🍴 🏌 **Location** Off Ballaghmore rd

Hotel ★★★ 70% The Royal Court Hotel, 233 Ballybogey
Rd, PORTRUSH ☎ 028 7082 2236 18 en suite

PORTRUSH   See page 401

WHITEHEAD   Map 01 D5

Bentra Municipal Slaughterford Rd BT38 9TG
☎ 028 9337 8996
A well matured course designed with the experienced
golfer and novice in mind with wide fairways and some
particularly long holes.
9 holes, 2885mtrs, Par 37, SSS 35.
Visitors no restrictions. **Societies** contact in advance.
Green Fees £8.25 per round (£11.35 weekends & bank
holidays). **Facilities** 🏌 🏖 🏠 🍴 🏌 **Leisure** restaurant
on site. **Location** 6m from Carrickfergus

Hotel ★★ 67% Dobbins Inn Hotel, 6-8 High St,
CARRICKFERGUS ☎ 028 9335 1905 15 en suite

Whitehead McCrae's Brae BT38 9NZ
☎ 028 93370820 & 93370822 📠 028 93370825
e-mail: robin@whiteheadgc.fsnet.co.uk
18 holes, 6050yds, Par 69, SSS 69, Course record 67.
Course Designer A B Armstrong **Location** 1m from town
Telephone for further details

Hotel ★★ 67% Dobbins Inn Hotel, 6-8 High St,
CARRICKFERGUS ☎ 028 9335 1905 15 en suite

**If the name of the club appears in *italics*, details
have not been confirmed for this
edition of the guide.**

CO ARMAGH

ARMAGH   Map 01 C5

County Armagh The Demesne, Newry Rd BT60 1EN
☎ 028 3752 5861 & 3752 8768 📠 028 3752 5861
e-mail: june@golfarmagh.co.uk
Mature parkland course with excellent views of
Armagh city and its surroundings.
18 holes, 6212yds, Par 70, SSS 69, Course record 63.
Club membership 1300.
Visitors time sheet operates at weekends. Must contact in
advance. **Societies** must contact in advance. **Green Fees**
not confirmed. **Cards** 💳 💳 💳 💳 **Prof** Alan Rankin
Facilities ⊗ 🍴 🏖 🏌 🏖 🏠 🍴 🏌 **Leisure**
snooker. **Conf** Corporate Hospitality Days available
Location On the Newry road

Hotel 🛏 The Cohannon Inn & Autolodge, 212
Ballynakilly Rd, DUNGANNON ☎ 028 8772 4488
42 en suite

CULLYHANNA   Map 01 C5

Ashfield 44 Cregganduff Rd BT35 0JJ
☎ 028 3086 8611
Parkland course with lakes. The course has seen
continuous improvement over the years with thousands
of trees planted from a wide variety of species.
18 holes, 5840yds, Par 69.
Visitors must contact in advance. **Societies** telephone in advance
(028 3086 8180) **Green Fees** £12 (£15 weekends). **Prof**
Paddy Gribben **Course Designer** Frank Ainsworth
Facilities ⊗ 🍴 🏖 🏌 🏖 🏠 🍴 🏌

Hotel ★★ 67% Enniskeen House Hotel, 98 Bryansford
Rd, NEWCASTLE ☎ 028 4372 2392 12 en suite

LURGAN   Map 01 D5

Craigavon Golf & Ski Centre Turmoyra Ln,
Silverwood BT66 6NG
☎ 028 3832 6606 📠 028 3834 7272
e-mail: geoffcoupland@craigavon.gov.uk
Parkland course with a lake and stream providing
water hazards.
18 holes, 6496yds, Par 72, SSS 72.
Club membership 400.
Visitors restricted Sat am. **Societies** telephone in advance.
Green Fees not confirmed. **Cards** 💳 💳 **Facilities** ⊗ 🏌
🏖 🍴 🏌 **Leisure** gymnasium, Ski slope. **Location** 2m N
at Silverwood off M1

Hotel ★★★ 69% White Gables Hotel, 14 Dromore Rd,
HILLSBOROUGH ☎ 028 9268 2755 31 en suite

Lurgan The Demesne BT67 9BN
☎ 028 38322087 📠 028 38316166
e-mail: lurgan@btclick.com
Testing parkland course bordering Lurgan Park Lake
with a need for accurate shots. Drains well in wet
weather and suits a long straight hitter.
18 holes, 6257yds, Par 70, SSS 70, Course record 66.
Club membership 903.
Visitors may not play Sat, contact in advance. **Societies**
must contact in advance, not Sat. **Green Fees** not
confirmed. **Prof** Des Paul **Course Designer** A Pennink
Facilities ⊗ 🍴 🏖 🏌 🏖 🏠 🍴 **Conf** fac available
Corporate Hospitality Days available **Location** 0.5m from
town centre near Lurgan Park

Continued

402

Hotel ★★★ 69% White Gables Hotel, 14 Dromore Rd, HILLSBOROUGH ☎ 028 9268 2755 31 en suite

PORTADOWN
Map 01 D5

Portadown 192 Gilford Rd BT63 5LF
☎ 028 3835 5356 📄 028 3839 1394
Well wooded parkland course on the banks of the River Bann, which features among the water hazards.
18 holes, 6130yds, Par 70, SSS 69, Course record 65.
Club membership 922.
Visitors may not play on Tue & Sat. **Societies** apply in writing. **Green Fees** not confirmed. **Prof** Paul Stevenson **Facilities** ⊗ ⊮ 🏌 ♥ ♀ 🏖 🍴 🍷 ∮ **Leisure** squash. **Conf** fac available Corporate Hospitality Days available **Location** SE via A59

Hotel ⚓ The Cohannon Inn & Autolodge, 212 Ballynakilly Rd, DUNGANNON ☎ 028 8772 4488 42 en suite

TANDRAGEE
Map 01 D5

Tandragee Markethill Rd BT62 2ER
☎ 028 3884 1272 📄 028 3884 0664
e-mail: office@tandragee.co.uk
Pleasant parkland course, the signature hole is the demanding par 4 11th known as 'The Wall Hole'; the real strength of Tandragee is in the short holes.
18 holes, 5747mtrs, Par 71, SSS 70, Course record 65.
Club membership 1256.
Visitors contact in advance. Ladies day Thu, after 3.30pm Sat & Sun. **Societies** must contact in advance. **Green Fees** not confirmed. **Course Designer** Dympna Keenan **Course Designer** John Stone **Facilities** ⊗ ⊮ 🏌 ♥ ♀ 🏖 🍴 🚃 ∮ **Leisure** sauna, gymnasium, snooker. **Conf** fac available **Location** On B3 out of Tandragee towards Markethill

CO BELFAST

BELFAST
Map 01 D5
See also The Royal Belfast, Holywood, Co Down.

Balmoral 518 Lisburn Rd BT9 6GX
☎ 028 9038 1514 📄 028 9066 6759
e-mail: admin@balmoralgolf.com
Parkland course, situated in the suburbs of South Belfast, offering an enjoyable challenge for golfers of all levels.
18 holes, 6276yds, Par 69, SSS 70, Course record 64.
Club membership 912.
Visitors may not play Sat or Sun before 2.30pm. **Societies** Mon & Thu. Must contact in advance. **Green Fees** not confirmed. **Prof** Geoff Bleakley **Facilities** ⊗ ⊮ 🏌 ♥ ♀ 🏖 🍴 🍷 ∮ **Leisure** snooker. **Conf** fac available Corporate Hospitality Days available **Location** 2m S next to Kings Hall

Hotel ★★★ 71% Malone Lodge Hotel, 60 Eglantine Av, BELFAST ☎ 028 9038 8000 51 en suite

Cliftonville 44 Westland Rd BT14 6NH
☎ 028 9074 4158 & 9022 8585
Parkland course with rivers bisecting two fairways.
9 holes, 6242yds, Par 70, SSS 70, Course record 65.
Club membership 430.
Visitors may not play after 5pm unless with member on

Sat or on Sun mornings. **Societies** must contact in writing. **Green Fees** not confirmed. **Prof** R Duckett **Facilities** ⊗ ⊮ 🏌 ♥ ♀ 🏖 🍴 ∮ **Location** Between Cavehill Rd & Cliftonville Circus

Hotel ⚓ Express by Holiday Inn Belfast, 106a University St, BELFAST ☎ 028 9031 1909 114 en suite

Dunmurry 91 Dunmurry Ln, Dunmurry BT17 9JS
☎ 028 9061 0834 📄 028 9060 2540
e-mail: dunmurrygc@hotmail.com
Maturing very nicely, this tricky parkland course has several memorable holes which call for skilful shots.
18 holes, 6096yds, Par 70, SSS 69, Course record 65.
Club membership 900.
Visitors telephone in advance. May not play Sat . **Societies** must contact in writing. **Green Fees** £27 (weekends & bank holidays £37). **Prof** John Dolan **Facilities** ⊗ ⊮ 🏌 ♥ ♀ 🏖 🍴 ∮ **Conf** Corporate Hospitality Days available

Hotel ★★★ 71% Malone Lodge Hotel, 60 Eglantine Av, BELFAST ☎ 028 9038 8000 51 en suite

Fortwilliam Downview Ave BT15 4EZ
☎ 028 90370770 (Office) & 90770980 (Pro)
📄 028 90781891
e-mail: fortwilliamgc@utvinternet.com
18 holes, 5993yds, Par 70, SSS 68, Course record 65.
Location Off Antrim road
Telephone for further details

Hotel ⚓ Express by Holiday Inn Belfast, 106a University St, BELFAST ☎ 028 9031 1909 114 en suite

Malone 240 Upper Malone Rd, Dunmurry BT17 9LB
☎ 028 9061 2758 (Office) & 9061 4917 (Pro)
📄 028 9043 1394
e-mail: manager@malonegolfclub.co.uk
Two parkland courses, extremely attractive with a large lake, mature trees and flowering shrubs and bordered by the River Lagan. Very well maintained and offering a challenging round.

Main Course: 18 holes, 6591yds, Par 71, SSS 71.
Edenderry: 9 holes, 6320yds, Par 72, SSS 70.
Club membership 1450.
Visitors advisable to contact pro-shop in advance. Main Course: Unable to play Sat, before 3pm, Sun morning, Wed after 12 noon; Tue & Fri between 12 and 2pm **Societies** apply in writing or fax to club manager. Large group normally Mon & Thu only. **Green Fees** Main Course: £45 per day (£50 weekends); Edenberry: £20 per day (£22 weekends). **Cards** 💳 💳 💳 💳 **Prof** Michael McGee **Course Designer** C K Cotton **Facilities** ⊗ ⊮ 🏌

Continued

Continued

♟♟⅄🏠🍴🐟🚕 ⅃ **Leisure** fishing, Outdoor bowling green. **Conf** Corporate Hospitality Days available **Location** 4.5m S opposite Lady Dixon Park

Hotel ★★★ 71% Malone Lodge Hotel, 60 Eglantine Av, BELFAST ☎ 028 9038 8000 51 en suite

Mount Ober Golf & Country Club

24 Ballymaconaghy Rd BT8 6SB
☎ 028 9040 1811 & 9079 5666 🗎 028 9070 5862
Inland parkland course which is a great test of golf for all handicaps.
18 holes, 5419yds, Par 67, SSS 66, Course record 67.
Club membership 400.
Visitors must contact in advance at weekends & bank holidays, may play Sat after 3.30pm and Sun after 10.30am. **Societies** book by telephone or fax. **Green Fees** £15 per 18 holes (Sun £17). **Cards** 🖃 🖾 **Prof** Wesley Ramsay/Steve Rourke **Facilities** ⊗ 🍴 🏌 ♟♟⅄🏠🍴⅃ ¶ **Leisure** American billiards. **Conf** fac available Corporate Hospitality Days available **Location** Off Saintfield Road

Ormeau 50 Park Rd BT7 2FX
☎ 028 90640700 🗎 028 90646250
e-mail: ormeau.golfclub@virgin.net
9 holes, 2688yds, Par 68, SSS 66.
Location S of city centre between Ravenhill & Ormeau roads
Telephone for further details

Shandon Park 73 Shandon Park BT5 6NY
☎ 028 90401856
18 holes, 6261yds, Par 70, SSS 70.
Location Off Knock road
Telephone for further details

DUNDONALD · · · · · Map 01 D5

Knock Summerfield BT16 2QX
☎ 028 9048 3251 🗎 028 9048 7277
Parkland course with huge trees, deep bunkers and a river cutting across several fairways. This is a hard but fair course and will test the best of golfers.
18 holes, 6435yds, Par 70, SSS 71, Course record 66.
Club membership 920.
Visitors with member only on Sat, Mon & Thu are Society Days, Tue is Ladies Day, advisable to contact in advance. **Societies** must contact in advance. **Green Fees** not confirmed. **Prof** Gordon Fairweather **Course Designer** Colt, Allison & McKenzie **Facilities** ⊗ 🍴 🏌 ♟♟⅄🏠 🍴🐟🚕 ⅃ **Conf** Corporate Hospitality Days available **Location** 5m E of Belfast

Hotel ★★★ 78% Old Inn, 15 Main St, CRAWFORDSBURN ☎ 028 9185 3255 31 en suite 1 annexe en suite

NEWTOWNBREDA · · · · · Map 01 D5

The Belvoir Park 73 Church Rd BT8 7AN
☎ 028 90491693 🗎 028 90646113
18 holes, 6516yds, Par 71, SSS 71, Course record 65.
Course Designer H Holt **Location** 2m from city centre off Saintfield/Newcastle rd
Telephone for further details

Hotel ★★★ 77% Clandeboye Lodge Hotel, 10 Estate Rd, Clandeboye, BANGOR ☎ 028 9185 2500 43 en suite

CO DOWN

ARDGLASS · · · · · Map 01 D5

Ardglass Castle Place BT30 7TP
☎ 028 44841219 🗎 028 44841841
e-mail: golfclub@ardglass.force9.co.uk
18 holes, 5498mtrs, Par 70, SSS 69, Course record 65.
Course Designer David Jones **Location** 7m from Downpatrick on the B1
Telephone for further details

Hotel ★★ 67% Enniskeen House Hotel, 98 Bryansford Rd, NEWCASTLE ☎ 028 4372 2392 12 en suite

ARDMILLAN · · · · · Map 01 D5

Mahee Island 14 Mahee Island, Comber BT23 6EP
☎ 028 9754 1234
e-mail: mahee_gents@hotmail.com
An undulating parkland course, almost surrounded by water, with magnificent views of Strangford Lough and its islands, with Scrabo Tower in the background. The greens are small and tricky to play. The first professional here was Fred Daly (1933-4) who became British Open Champion in 1947.
9 holes, 5822yds, Par 71, SSS 70, Course record 66.
Club membership 600.
Visitors may not play Sat before 5pm. **Societies** contact in advance. **Green Fees** £10 (weekends & bank holidays £15). **Course Designer** Mr Robinson **Facilities** ⊗ by prior arrangement 🍴 by prior arrangement 🏌 by prior arrangement ♟ by prior arrangement ⅄🏠🍴 ⅃
Location Off Comber/Killyleagh road to the left 0.5m from Comber

Hotel ★★★ 77% Clandeboye Lodge Hotel, 10 Estate Rd, Clandeboye, BANGOR ☎ 028 9185 2500 43 en suite

BALLYNAHINCH · · · · · Map 01 D5

Spa 20 Grove Rd BT24 8PN
☎ 028 97562365 🗎 028 97564158
e-mail: spagolfclub@btconnect.com
Parkland course with tree-lined fairways and scenic views of the Mourne Mountains. A long and demanding course and feature holes include the par 3 2nd and 405 yard par 4 11th.

18 holes, 6003mtrs, Par 72, SSS 72, Course record 66.
Club membership 871.
Visitors must contact in advance. No play on Sat. **Societies** must contact in advance. **Green Fees** £16 per round (£20 Suns & bank holidays). **Cards** 🖃 🖾 🖾 **Course Designer** F Ainsworth **Facilities** ⊗ 🍴 🏌 ♟♟⅄🏠🍴🚕 ⅃ **Leisure** gymnasium, outdoor bowls. **Conf** fac available

Continued

Corporate Hospitality Days available **Location** 1m S on the Grove Rd

Hotel ★★ 67% Enniskeen House Hotel, 98 Bryansford Rd, NEWCASTLE ☎ 028 4372 2392 12 en suite

BANBRIDGE   Map 01 D5

Banbridge 116 Huntly Rd BT32 3UR
☎ 028 40662211 █ 028 40669400
e-mail: info@banbridge-golf.freeserve.co.uk
18 holes, 5003mtrs, Par 69, SSS 67, Course record 61.
Course Designer F Ainsworth **Location** 0.5m along Huntly road
Telephone for further details

Hotel ★★★ 69% White Gables Hotel, 14 Dromore Rd, HILLSBOROUGH ☎ 028 9268 2755 31 en suite

BANGOR   Map 01 D5

Bangor Broadway BT20 4RH
☎ 028 9127 0922 █ 028 9145 3394
Undulating parkland course in the town. It is well maintained and pleasant and offers a challenging round, particularly at the 5th.
18 holes, 6410yds, Par 71, SSS 71, Course record 62.
Club membership 1147.
Visitors may not play Sat & weekdays 1-2 pm. **Societies** must contact in advance, Mon/Wed by telephone, Fri by letter. **Green Fees** terms on application. **Prof** Michael Bannon **Course Designer** James Braid **Facilities** ⊗ ⅀Ⅱ ┗ ┗ ♀ ♨ 🏠 ⌐ 🚜 ✔ **Conf** Corporate Hospitality Days available **Location** 1m from town on Donaghadee Road

Hotel ★★★ 66% Royal Hotel, Seafront, BANGOR ☎ 028 9127 1866 50 en suite

Blackwood Golf Centre 150 Crawfordsburn Rd, Clandeboye BT19 1GB
☎ 028 9185 2706 █ 028 9185 3785
The golf centre is a pay and play development with a computerised booking system for the 18-hole championship-standard Hamilton course. The course is built on mature woodland with man-made lakes that come into play on 5 holes. The Temple course is an 18-hole par 3 course with holes ranging from the 75yd 1st to the 185yd 10th, which has a lake on the right of the green. Banked by gorse with streams crossing throughout, this par 3 course is no pushover.
Hamilton Course: 18 holes, 6392yds, Par 71, SSS 70, Course record 62.
Temple Course: 18 holes, 2492yds, Par 54.
Visitors pay as you play, computerised booking system for the Hamilton Course, bookable 7 days in advance.
Societies telephone in advance. **Green Fees** terms on application. **Cards** ⊟ ▦ ▦ ☑ **Prof** Debbie Hanna **Course Designer** Simon Gidman **Facilities** ⊗ ┗ ♀ ♨ ⌐ ✔ ¥ **Location** 2m from Bangor, off A2 to Belfast

Hotel ★★★ 77% Clandeboye Lodge Hotel, 10 Estate Rd, Clandeboye, BANGOR ☎ 028 9185 2500 43 en suite

Carnalea Station Rd BT19 1EZ
☎ 028 9127 0368 █ 028 9127 3989
A scenic course on the shores of Belfast Lough.
18 holes, 5647yds, Par 69, SSS 67, Course record 63.
Club membership 1354.
Visitors restricted Sat. **Societies** must contact in advance.
Green Fees £17.50 (£22 Sun). **Prof** Tom Loughran

Facilities ⊗ ⅀Ⅱ ┗ ♀ ♨ 🏠 ⌐ ✔ **Location** 2m W adjacent to railway station

Hotel ★★★ 78% Old Inn, 15 Main St, CRAWFORDSBURN ☎ 028 9185 3255 31 en suite 1 annexe en suite

Clandeboye Tower Rd, Conlig, Newtownards BT23 3PN ☎ 028 9127 1767 █ 028 9147 3711
e-mail: contact@cgc-ni.com
Parkland/heathland courses. The Dufferin is the championship course and offers a tough challenge demanding extreme accuracy, with gorse, bracken and strategically placed trees that flank every hole. Errors will be punished. The Ava compliments the Dufferin perfectly. Accuracy is the key on this course with small targets and demanding tee shots. Outstanding panoramic views.
Dufferin Course: 18 holes, 6559yds, Par 71, SSS 71.
Ava Course: 18 holes, 5755yds, Par 70, SSS 68.
Club membership 1450.
Visitors must contact in advance, weekends after 2.30pm. **Societies** Mon-Wed & Fri. Must contact in advance. **Green Fees** Dufferin: £27.50 (£33 weekends); Ava: £22 (£27.50 weekends). **Cards** ⊟ ▦ **Prof** Peter Gregory **Course Designer** Von Limburger **Facilities** ⊗ ⅀Ⅱ ┗ ┗ ♀ ♨ 🏠 ⌐ ✔ 🚜 ✔ **Leisure** snooker, table tennis, indoor bowls.
Conf fac available Corporate Hospitality Days available **Location** 2m S on A1 between Bangor & Newtownards

Hotel ★★★ 66% Royal Hotel, Seafront, BANGOR ☎ 028 9127 1866 50 en suite

Helen's Bay Golf Rd, Helen's Bay BT19 1TL
☎ 028 91852815 & 91852601 █ 028 91852815
e-mail: mail@helensbaygc.com
9 holes, 5161mtrs, Par 68, SSS 67, Course record 67.
Location A2 from Belfast
Telephone for further details

Hotel ★★★ 78% Old Inn, 15 Main St, CRAWFORDSBURN ☎ 028 9185 3255 31 en suite 1 annexe en suite

CARRYDUFF   Map 01 D5

Rockmount 28 Drumalig Rd, Carryduff BT8 8EQ
☎ 028 9081 2279 █ 020 9081 5851
e-mail: rockmountgc@btconnect.com
A demanding 18-hole course set in open parkland with mature trees, several streams, and a tricky lake at the 11th hole. Panoramic views.
18 holes, 6373yds, Par 71, SSS 71, Course record 68.
Club membership 750.
Visitors welcome except for Sat or Wed afternoon.
Societies welcome except for Wed & Sat, book by telephone. **Green Fees** terms on application. **Cards** ⊟ ▦ ▦ ☑ **Course Designer** Robert Patterson **Facilities** ⊗ ⅀Ⅱ ┗ ┗ ♀ ♨ 🏠 ⌐ ✔ **Conf** Corporate Hospitality Days available **Location** 10m S of Belfast

Hotel ★★★ 69% White Gables Hotel, 14 Dromore Rd, HILLSBOROUGH ☎ 028 9268 2755 31 en suite

CLOUGHEY   Map 01 D5

Kirkistown Castle 142 Main Rd, Cloughey
BT22 1JA ☎ 028 4277 1233 █ 028 4277 1699
e-mail: kirkistown@supanet.com
A seaside semi-links, designed by James Braid, popular

Continued   *Continued*

with visiting golfers because of its quiet location. The course is exceptionally dry and remains open when others in the area have to close. The short but treacherous par 4 15th hole was known as 'Braid's Hole'. The 2nd and 10th holes are long par 4s with elevated greens, which are a feature of the course. The 10th is particularly distinctive with a long drive and a slight dog-leg to a raised green with a gorse covered motte waiting for the wayward approach shot. It has the reputation of being one of the hardest par 4s in Ireland.
18 holes, 6167yds, Par 69, SSS 70, Course record 65.
Club membership 1012.
Visitors must contact in advance, restricted weekends. **Societies** contact in writing or by phone. **Green Fees** £20.75 per day (£27.75 weekends). **Prof** Richard Whitford **Course Designer** James Braid **Facilities** ⊗ ⑪ ⓑ ☕ ♥ ♀ ⌂ ☜ ⚲ **Conf** Corporate Hospitality Days available **Location** 16m from Newtownards on the A2

....
Hotel ★★★ 78% Old Inn, 15 Main St, CRAWFORDSBURN ☎ 028 9185 3255 31 en suite 1 annexe en suite

Donaghadee Warren Rd BT21 0PQ
☎ 028 9188 3624 ▤ 028 9188 8891
e-mail: deegolf@freenet.co.uk
Undulating seaside course, part links, part parkland, requiring a certain amount of concentration. Splendid views.
18 holes, 5616mtrs, Par 71, SSS 69, Course record 64.
Club membership 1200.
Visitors contact in advance. **Societies** write/telephone in advance. **Green Fees** £22 (£25 weekends). **Prof** Gordon Drew **Facilities** ⊗ ⑪ ⓑ ☕ ♥ ♀ ⌂ ☜ ⚲ **Conf** Corporate Hospitality Days available **Location** 5m S Bangor on Coast Rd

....
Hotel ★★★ 78% Old Inn, 15 Main St, CRAWFORDSBURN ☎ 028 9185 3255 31 en suite 1 annexe en suite

Bright Castle 14 Coniamstown Rd, Bright BT30 8LU
☎ 028 44841319
18 holes, 7300yds, Par 74, SSS 74, Course record 69.
Course Designer Mr Ennis Snr **Location** 5m S
Telephone for further details

....
Hotel ★★ 67% Enniskeen House Hotel, 98 Bryansford Rd, NEWCASTLE ☎ 028 4372 2392 12 en suite

Downpatrick 43 Saul Rd BT30 6PA
☎ 028 44615947 ▤ 028 44617502
e-mail: info@downpatrickgolfclub.org.com
A classic parkland course with most holes boasting spectacular views of Co Down, Strangford Lough and even the Isle of Man, on a clear day. Undulating fairways, strategically placed sand traps and quick but true greens make the course a testing yet pleasurable challenge to golfers of all abilities.
18 holes, 6100yds, Par 70, SSS 69, Course record 66.
Club membership 960.
Visitors must contact in advance. **Societies** must telephone in advance. **Green Fees** not confirmed. **Cards** ▭ ▬ ▢ **Prof** Robert Hutton **Course Designer** Hawtree & Son **Facilities** ⊗ ⑪ ⓑ ☕ ♥ ♀ ⌂ ☜ ⚲ **Leisure** snooker. **Conf** fac available **Location** 1.5m from town centre

Continued

Hotel ★★ 67% Enniskeen House Hotel, 98 Bryansford Rd, NEWCASTLE ☎ 028 4372 2392 12 en suite

Holywood Nuns Walk, Demesne Rd BT18 9LE
☎ 028 90423135 ▤ 028 90425040
e-mail: mail@holywoodgolfclub.co.uk
18 holes, 5480mtrs, Par 69, SSS 68, Course record 64.
Location Just outside Belfast, off the Bangor dual carriageway, behind the town of Holywood
Telephone for further details

....
Hotel ★★★ 78% Old Inn, 15 Main St, CRAWFORDSBURN ☎ 028 9185 3255 31 en suite 1 annexe en suite

The Royal Belfast Station Rd, Craigavad BT18 0BP
☎ 028 9042 8165 ▤ 028 9042 1404
e-mail: royalbelfastgc@btclick.com
On the shores of Belfast Lough, this attractive course consists of wooded parkland on undulating terrain which provides a pleasant, challenging game.
18 holes, 6185yds, Par 70, SSS 69.
Club membership 1200.
Visitors may not play on Wed or Sat before 4.30pm; must be accompanied by a member or present a letter of introduction from their own golf club. Must contact in advance. **Societies** must contact in writing. **Green Fees** not confirmed. **Cards** ▭ ▬ ▦ ▢ **Prof** Chris Spence **Course Designer** H C Colt **Facilities** ⊗ ⑪ ⓑ ☕ ♥ ♀ ⌂ ☜ ⚲ **Leisure** hard tennis courts, squash. **Conf** Corporate Hospitality Days available **Location** 2m E on A2

....
Hotel ★★★ 78% Old Inn, 15 Main St, CRAWFORDSBURN ☎ 028 9185 3255 31 en suite 1 annexe en suite

Kilkeel Mourne Park BT34 4LB
☎ 028 4176 5095 ▤ 028 4176 5579
e-mail: kilkeelgolfclub@tinyonline.co.uk
Picturesquely situated at the foot of the Mourne Mountains. Eleven holes have tree-lined fairways with the remainder in open parkland. The 13th hole is testing and a well positioned tee shot is essential.
18 holes, 6579yds, Par 72, SSS 72, Course record 67.
Club membership 750.
Visitors contact in advance, especially for weekend play. **Societies** must contact in advance. **Green Fees** terms on application. **Course Designer** Babington/Hackett **Facilities** ⊗ ⑪ ⓑ ☕ ♥ ♀ ⌂ ☜ ⚲ **Conf** Corporate Hospitality Days available **Location** 3m from Kilkeel on Newry road

....
Hotel ★★ 67% Enniskeen House Hotel, 98 Bryansford Rd, NEWCASTLE ☎ 028 4372 2392 12 en suite

Ringdufferin Golf Course 31 Ringdufferin Rd, Toye BT30 9PH ☎ 028 44828812 ▤ 028 44828812
18 holes, 4652mtrs, Par 68, SSS 66.
Course Designer Frank Ainsworth **Location** 2m N of Killyleagh
Telephone for further details

....
Hotel ★★★ 69% Portaferry Hotel, 10 The Strand, PORTAFERRY ☎ 028 4272 8231 14 en suite

Royal County Down

Map 01 D5

Newcastle

☎ 028 43723314 📄 028 43726281

The Championship Course is consistently rated among the world's top ten courses. Laid out beneath the imperious gaze of the Mourne Mountains, the course enjoys a magnificent stage-like setting as it stretches out along the shores of Dundrum Bay. As well as being one of the world's most beautiful courses, it is also one of the most challenging, with great swathes of heather and gorse lining fairways that tumble beneath vast sand hills, and wild tussock-faced bunkers defending small 0subtly contoured greens. The Annesley Links offers a less formidable, yet extremely characterful game played against the same incomparable backcloth. Recently substantially revised under the direction of Donald Steel, the course begins quite benignly before charging headlong into the dunes. Several charming and one or two teasing holes have been carved out amid the gorse, heather and bracken.

e-mail: golf@royalcountydown.org

Visitors Advisable to contact in advance. May not play Championship Course Sat or Wed. May not play Annesley Course Sat.

Societies Telephone for availability and confirm in writing

Green Fees Championship £110 - £125 Sunday

Facilities ⊗ ⅛ 🍺 🍽 ⚲ ⚘ 🏠 🛒 ♂

Professional Kevan Whitson

Location Newcastle BT33 0AN -(30m S of Belfast via A24)

Holes/Par/Course record 36 holes.
Championship Links: 18 holes, 7065 yds, Par 71, SSS 74, Course record 66
Annesley Links: 18 holes, 4681 yds, Par 66, SSS 63

Championship Course

WHERE TO STAY NEARBY

Hotels
NEWCASTLE

★★ 67% Enniskeen Hotel, BT33 0LF.
☎ 028 43722392. 12 en suite

★★★★ 61% Slieve Donald Hotel, Downs Rd.
☎ 028 43723681.
124 en suite

MAGHERALIN   Map 01 D5

Edenmore Edenmore House, 70 Drumnabreeze Rd
BT67 0RH ☎ 028 9261 1310 🖹 028 9261 3310
e-mail: edenmoregc@aol.com
**Set in mature parkland with gently rolling slopes. The
front nine holes provide an interesting contrast to the
back nine with more open play involved. Many new
paths and features have been added. The 13th hole,
Edenmore, is the most memorable hole with a small
lake protecting a contoured green.**
*Edenmore Golf Course: 18 holes, 6244yds, Par 71, SSS 70,
Course record 70.*
Club membership 600.
Visitors telephone in advance essential at weekends, may
not play until after 3pm Sat. **Societies** telephone in
advance. **Green Fees** not confirmed. **Cards** 🖩 💳 📇 🔳 💶
Course Designer F Ainsworth **Facilities** ⊗ 〉Ⅲ ⑤ 🍴 ⚑
📠 ⛳ 🏌 ♨ ⛳ **Leisure** sauna, gymnasium. **Conf** fac
available Corporate Hospitality Days available **Location**
20m SW of Belfast, take Moira exit on M1 from Belfast,
go through Moira towards Lurgan. Take turn off in village
of Magheralin and follow signs for golf club.

Hotel ★★★ 78% Old Inn, 15 Main St,
CRAWFORDSBURN ☎ 028 9185 3255 31 en suite
1 annexe en suite

NEWCASTLE   See page 407

NEWRY   Map 01 D5

Newry 11 Forkhill Rd BT35 8LZ
☎ 028 30263871 🖹 028 30263871
18 holes, 3000mtrs, Par 53, SSS 52, Course record 51.
Course Designer Michael Heaney **Location** 1m from
Newry just off the main Dublin road
Telephone for further details

Hotel ★★ 67% Enniskeen House Hotel, 98 Bryansford
Rd, NEWCASTLE ☎ 028 4372 2392 12 en suite

NEWTOWNARDS   Map 01 D5

Scrabo 233 Scrabo Rd BT23 4SL
☎ 028 9181 2355 🖹 028 9182 2919
e-mail: scrabogc@compuserve.com
**Hilly and picturesque, this course offers a good test of
golf for golfers of all abilities. It benefits from good
drainage and remains dry and playable most of the year.**
18 holes, 5722mtrs, Par 71, SSS 71, Course record 65.
Club membership 1002.
Visitors may not play on Saturdays. Contact in advance.
Societies must contact in advance. **Green Fees** terms on
application. **Prof** Paul McCrystal **Facilities** ⊗ 〉Ⅲ ⑤ 🍴 ♀
⛳ 📠 ⛳ **Location** Borders of Newtownards on the Ards
Peninsula, follow signs for Scrabo Country Park

Hotel ★★★ 77% Clandeboye Lodge Hotel, 10 Estate Rd,
Clandeboye, BANGOR ☎ 028 9185 2500 43 en suite

WARRENPOINT   Map 01 D5

Warrenpoint Lower Dromore Rd BT34 3LN
☎ 028 4175 3695 🖹 028 4175 2918
e-mail: warrenpointgolfclub@talk21.com
**Parkland course with marvellous views and a need for
accurate shots.**
18 holes, 6108yds, Par 71, SSS 70, Course record 61.
Club membership 1460.

Continued

Visitors must contact in advance. **Societies** must contact in
advance. **Green Fees** £25 per 18 holes (£30 weekends &
bank holidays). **Cards** 💳 🖩 **Prof** Nigel Shaw **Course
Designer** Tom Craddock/Pat Ruddy **Facilities** ⊗ 〉Ⅲ 🍴 ⑤
♀ ⛳ 📠 ⛳ ♨ ⛳ **Conf** fac available Corporate
Hospitality Days available **Location** 1m W

Hotel ★★ 67% Enniskeen House Hotel, 98 Bryansford
Rd, NEWCASTLE ☎ 028 4372 2392 12 en suite

CO FERMANAGH

ENNISKILLEN   Map 01 C5

Ashwoods Golf Centre Sligo Rd BT74 7JY
☎ 028 66325321 & 66322908 🖹 028 66329411
14 holes, 1930yds, Par 42. **Course Designer** P Loughran
Location 1.5m W of Enniskillen on main Sligo road
Telephone for further details

Hotel ★★★★ 69% Killyhevlin Hotel, ENNISKILLEN
☎ 028 6632 3481 43 en suite

Castle Hume Castle Hume, Belleek Rd BT93 7ED
☎ 028 6632 7077 🖹 028 6632 7076
e-mail: info@castlehumegolf.com
**Castle Hume is a particularly scenic and challenging
course. Set in undulating parkland with large rolling
greens, rivers, lakes and water hazards all in play on a
championship standard course.**
18 holes, 5770mtrs, Par 72, SSS 70, Course record 69.
Club membership 350.
Visitors may play any time subject to advance
arrangement. **Societies** telephone in advance. **Green Fees**
terms on application. **Cards** 🖩 💳 ⑤ **Prof** Shaun
Donnelly **Course Designer** B Browne **Facilities** ⊗ 〉Ⅲ 🍴
⛳ ♀ ⛳ 📠 ⛳ 🎣 ♨ ⛳ ♭ **Leisure** fishing. **Conf** fac
available Corporate Hospitality Days available **Location**
4m from Enniskillen on the Belleek/Donegal Road A46

Hotel ★★★★ 69% Killyhevlin Hotel, ENNISKILLEN
☎ 028 6632 3481 43 en suite

Enniskillen Castlecoole BT74 6HZ
☎ 028 6632 5250 🖹 028 6632 5250
e-mail: enquiries@enniskillengolfclub.com
**Tree lined parkland course offering panoramic views of
Enniskillen town and the surrounding lakeland area.
Situated beside the National Trust's Castlecoole Estate.**
18 holes, 6230yds, Par 71, SSS 69, Course record 67.
Club membership 550.
Visitors restricted Tue and weekends. Contact Hon
Secretary or bar steward. **Societies** must contact club
steward in advance by telephone or writing. **Green Fees**
not confirmed. **Facilities** ⊗ 〉Ⅲ ⑤ 🍴 ⛳ ♀ 📠 ♨ ⛳ ⛳
Conf Corporate Hospitality Days available **Location** 1m E

Hotel ★★★★ 69% Killyhevlin Hotel, ENNISKILLEN
☎ 028 6632 3481 43 en suite

CO LONDONDERRY

AGHADOWEY   Map 01 C6

Brown Trout Golf & Country Inn 209 Agivey
Rd BT51 4AD ☎ 028 7086 8209 🖹 028 7086 8878
e-mail: bill@browntroutinn.com
A challenging course with two par 5s. During the course
Continued

of the 9 holes, players have to negotiate water 7 times and all the fairways are lined with densely packed fir trees.
9 holes, 5510yds, Par 70, SSS 68, Course record 64.
Club membership 100.
Visitors no restrictions. **Societies** must contact by telephone, restricted tee-off times Sun. **Green Fees** £10 (£15 weekends). **Cards** 🔄 ▦ ▨ 🅿️ 🔄 🄾 **Prof** Ken Revie **Course Designer** Bill O'Hara Snr **Facilities** ⊗ ⅷ 🅱️ ♥ ♀ ♨ ⛟ 🗗 ✐ **Leisure** fishing, gymnasium. **Location** Junct of A54 & B66, 7m S of Coleraine

· ·

Hotel ★★ 70% Brown Trout Golf & Country Inn, 209 Agivey Rd, AGHADOWEY ☎ 028 7086 8209 15 en suite

CASTLEDAWSON   Map 01 C5

Moyola Park 15 Curran Rd BT45 8DG
☎ 028 7946 8468 & 7946 8830 (Prof) 🖹 028 7946 8626
e-mail: moyolapark@btconnect.com
Parkland championship course with some difficult shots, calling for length and accuracy. The Moyola River provides a water hazard at the 8th. Newly designed par 3 17th demands good shot placement to a green on an island in the Moyola river, when players' capabilities will be tested by the undulating green.
18 holes, 6519yds, Par 71, SSS 71, Course record 67.
Club membership 1000.
Visitors contact professional in advance, G.U.I. dress code applies, Ladies day Wednesday, Sat & Sun after 1.30pm, book in advance to avoid dissappointment. **Societies** must contact in advance, preferably in writing **Green Fees** Mon-Thu £20 per round; Fri £25; Sat-Sun £30. **Cards** 🔄 ▦ 🔄 🄾 **Prof** Bob Cockcroft **Course Designer** Don Patterson **Facilities** ⊗ ⅷ 🅱️ ♥ ♀ ♨ 🗗 ⛟ 🚲 ✐ **Conf** fac available Corporate Hospitality Days available **Location** Take sign for Castledawson. Golf Club signposted

· ·

Hotel ★★★★ 66% Galgorm Manor, BALLYMENA
☎ 028 2588 1001 24 en suite

CASTLEROCK   Map 01 C6

Castlerock 65 Circular Rd BT51 4TJ
☎ 028 7084 8314 🖹 028 7084 9440
e-mail: info@castlerockgc.co.uk
A most exhilarating course with three superb par 4s, four testing short holes and five par 5s. After an uphill start, the hazards are many, including the river and a railway, and both judgement and accuracy are called for. A challenge in calm weather, any trouble from the elements will test your golf to the limits.
Mussenden Course: 18 holes, 6499yds, Par 73, SSS 71, Course record 64.
Bann Course: 9 holes, 2938yds, Par 34, SSS 33, Course record 60.
Club membership 1250.
Visitors contact in advance, limited number of places at weekends. Must be members of a recognised club. **Societies** must contact in advance. **Green Fees** £35 per round; £50 per day (£70 per round weekends and bank holidays). **Cards** 🔄 ▦ 🄾 **Prof** Ian Blair **Course Designer** Ben Sayers **Facilities** ⊗ ⅷ 🅱️ ♥ ♀ ♨ 🗗 ✐ **Location** 6m from Coleraine on A2

· ·

Hotel ★★★ 70% The Royal Court Hotel, 233 Ballybogey Rd, PORTRUSH ☎ 028 7082 2236 18 en suite

KILREA   Map 01 C5

Kilrea 47a Lisnagrot Rd BT51 5TB
☎ 028 2954 0044
Inland golf course, winner of an environmental award. Current phase of course development due for completion by Spring 2005 when the par for the course will increase to 70.
9 holes, 5578yds, Par 68, SSS 68, Course record 66.
Club membership 300.
Visitors welcome but restricted Tue pm, Wed pm during summer and Sat all year. **Societies** telephone in advance, avoid Sundays **Green Fees** £12.50 per 18 holes (£15 weekends & bank holidays). **Facilities** ⊗ ⅷ 🅱️ ♥ ♀ ♨

· ·

Hotel ★★ 70% Brown Trout Golf & Country Inn, 209 Agivey Rd, AGHADOWEY ☎ 028 7086 8209 15 en suite

LIMAVADY   Map 01 C6

Benone 53 Benone Ave BT49 0LQ
☎ 028 77750555 🖹 77750919
Benone Golf Course: 9 holes, 1334mtrs, Par 27.
Location Between Coleraine/Limavady on A2
Telephone for further details

Radisson Roe Park Hotel & Golf Resort Roe
Park BT49 9LB ☎ 028 7772 2222 🖹 028 7772 2313
e-mail: sales@radissonroepark.com
A parkland course opened in 1992 on an historic Georgian estate. The course surrounds the original buildings and a driving range has been created in the old walled garden. Final holes 15-18 are particularly memorable with water, trees and out-of-bounds to provide a testing finish.
18 holes, 6318yds, Par 70, SSS 70.
Club membership 500.
Visitors advance booking recommended. Handicap certificate required. May not play before 10.30am at weekends. **Societies** contact in advance. **Green Fees** not confirmed. **Cards** 🔄 ▦ 🔄 🅿️ ▦ 🔄 🄾 **Prof** Seamus Duffy **Course Designer** Frank Ainsworth **Facilities** ⊗ ⅷ 🅱️ ♥ ♀ ♨ 🗗 ⛟ 🎣 ➤ 🚲 ✐ ⛾ **Leisure** heated indoor swimming pool, fishing, sauna, solarium, gymnasium, indoor golf academy. **Conf** fac available Corporate Hospitality Days available **Location** Just outside Limavady on A2 Ballykelly/Londonderry road

· ·

Hotel ★★★★ 70% Radisson SAS Roe Park Resort, LIMAVADY ☎ 028 7772 2222 118 en suite

LONDONDERRY   Map 01 C5

City of Derry 49 Victoria Rd BT47 2PU
☎ 028 71346369 🖹 028 71310008
e-mail: cityofderry@aol.com
Two parkland courses on undulating parkland with good views and lots of trees. The 9-hole course will particularly suit novices.
Prehen Course: 18 holes, 6406yds, Par 71, SSS 71, Course record 68.
Dunhugh Course: 9 holes, 2354yds, Par 66, SSS 66.
Club membership 700.
Visitors must make a booking to play on Prehen Course at weekends or before 4.30pm on weekdays. **Societies** must contact in advance. **Green Fees** £18 per 18 holes (weekends £23). **Cards** ▦ **Prof** Michael Doherty **Facilities** ⊗ ⅷ 🅱️ ♥ ♀ ♨ 🗗 ⛟ ✐ **Conf** fac available **Location** 2m S

Continued

Hotel ★★★ 72% Beech Hill Country House Hotel, 32 Ardmore Rd, LONDONDERRY ☎ 028 7134 9279 17 en suite 10 annexe en suite

Foyle International Golf Centre 12 Alder Rd
BT48 8DB ☎ 028 7135 2222 ▤ 028 7135 3967
e-mail: mail@foylegolf.club24.co.uk
Foyle International boasts a championship course, a 9 hole par 3 course and a driving range. It is a fine test of golf with water coming into play on the 3rd, 10th and 11th holes. The 6th green overlooks the Amelia Earhart centre.
18 holes, 6678yds, Par 72, SSS 71, Course record 70.
Club membership 320.
Visitors welcome any time, no restrictions. **Societies** booking up to 12 months in advance with deposit. **Green Fees** £14 (£17 weekends). **Cards** 🖃 🖃 🖃 Ɗ **Prof** Kieran McLaughlin **Course Designer** Frank Ainsworth **Facilities** ⊗ ⅢⅡ 🃏 🌢 ♥ ♀ ⚐ 🖿 ⓡ ⚐ ℓ **Leisure** 9 hole par 3 course . **Conf** fac available **Location** 1.5m from Foyle Bridge driving torwards Moville

Hotel ★★★ 66% White Horse Hotel, 68 Clooney Rd, Campsie, LONDONDERRY ☎ 028 7186 0606 57 en suite

Portstewart 117 Strand Rd BT55 7PG
☎ 028 70832015 & 70833839 ▤ 028 70834097
e-mail: bill@portstewartgc.co.uk
Strand Course: 18 holes, 6784yds, Par 72, SSS 72, Course record 67.
Old Course: 18 holes, 4733yds, Par 64, SSS 62.
Riverside: 18 holes, 2622yds, Par 32.
Course Designer Des Giffin
Telephone for further details

Hotel ★★★ 70% The Royal Court Hotel, 233 Ballybogey Rd, PORTRUSH ☎ 028 7082 2236 18 en suite

CO TYRONE

Killymoon 200 Killymoon Rd BT80 8TW
☎ 028 8676 3762 & 8676 2254 ▤ 028 8676 3762
Parkland course on elevated, well drained land.
18 holes, 5481mtrs, Par 70, SSS 69, Course record 64.
Club membership 950.
Visitors booking essential through pro shop on 016487 63460. Must contact in advance, have a golf handicap and play after 3.30pm Saturdays. **Societies** must contact in advance. **Green Fees** Mon (except bank holidays) £15 per 18 holes; Tues-Fri £20; Sat-Sun £25. **Prof** Gary Chambers **Facilities** ⊗ ⅢⅡ 🃏 🌢 ♥ ♀ ⚐ 🖿 🌢 ⚐ **Leisure** snooker & pool. **Conf** Corporate Hospitality Days available

Guesthouse ♦♦♦♦♦ Grange Lodge, 7 Grange Rd, DUNGANNON ☎ 028 8778 4212 5 en suite

Dungannon 34 Springfield Ln BT70 1QX
☎ 028 8772 2098 ▤ 028 8772 7338
e-mail: info@dungannongolfclub.com
Parkland course with five par 3s and tree-lined fairways.

18 holes, 6046yds, Par 72, SSS 69, Course record 62.
Club membership 1100.
Visitors contact in advance, may not play before 3.30pm Sat and Sun. Handicap certificate required. Ladies Day (Tue) phone in advance. **Societies** apply in writing to secretary. **Green Fees** not confirmed. **Prof** Vivian Teague **Course Designer** Sam Bacon **Facilities** ⊗ ⅢⅡ 🃏 ♥ ♀ ⚐ 🖿 🌢 ⚙ ℓ **Location** 0.5m outside town on Donaghmore road

Hotel ⇧ The Cohannon Inn & Autolodge, 212 Ballynakilly Rd, DUNGANNON ☎ 028 8772 4488 42 en suite

Fintona Ecclesville Demesne, 1 Kiln St BT78 2BJ
☎ 028 82841480 & 82840777 (office) ▤ 028 82841480
Attractive 9-hole parkland course with a notable water hazard - a trout stream that meanders through the course causing many problems for badly executed shots.
9 holes, 5765mtrs, Par 72, SSS 70.
Club membership 400.
Visitors advised to contact in advance at weekends. **Societies** apply in writing well in advance, weekends not advisable as competitions played. **Green Fees** not confirmed. **Prof** Paul Leonard **Facilities** ⊗ by prior arrangement ⅢⅡ by prior arrangement ♥ ♀ ⚐ **Location** 8m S of Omagh

Hotel ★★ 63% Mahons Hotel, Mill St, IRVINESTOWN ☎ 028 6862 1656 18 en suite

Newtownstewart 38 Golf Course Rd BT78 4HU
☎ 028 8166 1466 ▤ 028 8166 2506
e-mail: newtown.stewart@lineone.net
Parkland course bisected by a stream. Deer and pheasant are present on the course.
18 holes, 5468mtrs, Par 70, SSS 69, Course record 65.
Club membership 700.
Visitors contact golf shop in advance, to obtain tee times. **Societies** must contact secretary in advance. **Green Fees** not confirmed. **Course Designer** Frank Pennick **Facilities** ⊗ ⅢⅡ by prior arrangement 🃏 ♥ ♀ ⚐ 🖿 ⓡ 🌢 🌢 ⚐ **Leisure** snooker. **Conf** fac available **Location** 2m SW on B84

Guesthouse ♦♦♦♦ Hawthorn House, 72 Old Mountfield Rd, OMAGH ☎ 028 8225 2005 5 en suite

Omagh 83a Dublin Rd BT78 1HQ
☎ 028 82243160 ▤ 028 82243160
18 holes, 5683mtrs, Par 71, SSS 70.
Course Designer Dun Patterson **Location** On S outskirts of town
Telephone for further details

Guesthouse ♦♦♦♦ Hawthorn House, 72 Old Mountfield Rd, OMAGH ☎ 028 8225 2005 5 en suite

Strabane Ballycolman Rd BT82 9HY
☎ 028 7138 2271 & 7138 2007 ▤ 028 7188 6514
e-mail: strabanegc@btconnect.com
Testing parkland course with the River Mourne

Continued

Continued

running alongside and creating a water hazard.
18 holes, 5537mtrs, Par 69, SSS 69, Course record 62.
Club membership 650.
Visitors by prior arrangement, may not play Tue & Sat
Societies must telephone in advance. **Green Fees** terms on
application. **Cards** ▩ ▩ **Course Designer** Eddie
Hackett/P Jones **Facilities** ⊗ ⅶ ▮ ▬ ♀ ⚘ ⚒ ✐
Location 1m from Stranbane on the Dublin Road

Guesthouse ♦♦♦♦ Hawthorn House, 72 Old Mountfield
Rd, OMAGH ☎ 028 8225 2005 5 en suite

REPUBLIC OF IRELAND

CO CARLOW

BORRIS
Map 01 C3

Borris Deerpark ☎ 059 9773310 ▤ 059 9773750
e-mail: borrisgolfclub@eircom.net
**Testing parkland course with tree-lined fairways
situated within the McMorrough Kavanagh Estate at
the foot of Mount Leinster. Modern sand based greens.**
9 holes, 5680mtrs, Par 70, SSS 69, Course record 66.
Club membership 718.
Visitors advisable to contact in advance, weekends with
member only. **Societies** applications in writing. **Green
Fees** €25 per 18 holes. **Facilities** ⊗ ⅶ ▮ ▬ ♀ ⚘ ✐

Hotel ★★★★ ⚓ Mount Juliet Conrad Hotel,
THOMASTOWN ☎ 056 777 3000 32 en suite
27 annexe en suite

CARLOW
Map 01 C3

Carlow Deerpark
☎ 059 91 31695 ▤ 059 91 40065
e-mail: carlowgolfclub@eircom.net
**Created in 1922 to a design by Cecil Barcroft, this
testing and enjoyable course is set in a wild deer park,
with beautiful dry terrain and a varied character. With
sandy sub-soil, the course is playable all year round.
There are water hazards at the 2nd, 10th and 11th and
only two par 5s, both offering genuine birdie
opportunities.**
18 holes, 5974mtrs, Par 70, SSS 71, Course record 65.
Club membership 1200.
Visitors are welcome, although play is limited on Tue &
difficult on Sat & Sun. Must contact in advance. **Societies**
must book in advance. **Green Fees** terms on application.
Cards ▩ ▩ **Prof** Andrew Gilbert **Course Designer**
Cecil Barcroft **Facilities** ⊗ ⅶ ▮ ▬ ♀ ⚘ 🏠 ⚒ ✐
Location 2m N of Carlow on N9

Hotel ★★★ 68% Dolmen Hotel, Kilkenny Rd, CARLOW
☎ 059 914 2002 40 en suite 12 annexe en suite

TULLOW
Map 01 C3

**Mount Wolseley Hotel, Golf & Country
Club** ☎ 059 9151674 ▤ 059 9152123
e-mail: bmurray@mountwolseley.ie
**A magnificent setting, a few hundred yards from the
banks of the River Slaney with its mature trees and
lakes set against the backdrop of the East Carlow and
Wicklow mountains. With wide landing areas the only
concession for demanding approach shots to almost
every green. There is water in play on eleven holes, with**
Continued

the 11th an all-water carry off the tee of 207 yards.
18 holes, 6786yds, Par 72, SSS 70, Course record 68.
Club membership 350.
Visitors must contact in advance. **Societies** must contact in
advance. **Green Fees** €55 (weekends €75). **Cards** ▩
▩ ▩ ▩ ▩ ▩ **Course Designer** Christy O'Connor
Facilities ⊗ ⅶ ▮ ▬ ♀ ⚘ 🏠 ⚒ 🏡 ⚒ ✐ **Leisure**
hard tennis courts, heated indoor swimming pool, sauna,
solarium, gymnasium, treatment rooms. **Conf** fac available
Corporate Hospitality Days available **Location** 1 mile from
centre of Tullow

Hotel ★★★ 68% Dolmen Hotel, Kilkenny Rd, CARLOW
☎ 059 914 2002 40 en suite 12 annexe en suite

CO CAVAN

BALLYCONNELL
Map 01 C4

Slieve Russell Hotel Golf & Country Club
☎ 049 9526444 & 9526458 ▤ 049 9526640
e-mail: slieve-russell@quinn-hotels.com
**An 18-hole course opened in 1992 and rapidly
establishing itself as one of the finest parkland courses
in the country. The complex incorporates a 9-hole par 3
course and driving range. On the main course, the 2nd
plays across water while the 16th has water
surrounding the green. The course finishes with a 519
yard, par 5 18th.**
18 holes, 6650yds, Par 72, SSS 72, Course record 65.
Club membership 900.
Visitors must book in advance for Saturdays. **Societies**
write or telephone in advance, not allowed Sat. **Green Fees**
not confirmed. **Cards** ▩ ▩ ▩ ▩ ▩ ▩ **Prof** Liam
McCool **Course Designer** Paddy Merrigan **Facilities** ⊗ ⅶ
▮ ▬ ♀ ⚘ 🏠 ⚒ 🏡 ✐ **Leisure** hard tennis courts,
heated indoor swimming pool, sauna, solarium,
gymnasium. **Conf** fac available Corporate Hospitality
Days available **Location** 1.5m E of Ballyconnell

Hotel ★★★★ 70% Slieve Russell Hotel Golf and
Country Club, BALLYCONNELL ☎ 049 9526444
157 en suite

BELTURBET
Map 01 C4

Belturbet Erne Hill ☎ 049 9522287 & 9524044
**Beautifully maintained parkland course with
predominantly family membership and popular with
summer visitors.**
9 holes, 5480yds, Par 68, SSS 65, Course record 64.
Club membership 200.
Visitors must contact in advance. **Societies** must contact
secretary in advance. **Green Fees** not confirmed. **Course
Designer** Eddie Hackett **Facilities** ▮ ▬ ♀ ⚘ 🏠 ⚒ ✐

Hotel ★★★★ 70% Slieve Russell Hotel Golf and
Country Club, BALLYCONNELL ☎ 049 9526444
157 en suite

BLACKLION
Map 01 C5

Blacklion Toam ☎ 072 53024 & 53418 ▤ 072 53418
9 holes, 5614mtrs, Par 72, SSS 69.
Course Designer Eddie Hackett
Telephone for further details

Hotel ★★★ 71% Sligo Park Hotel, Pearse Rd, SLIGO
☎ 071 916 0291 110 en suite

CAVAN   Map 01 C4

County Cavan Drumelis
☎ 049 4331541 & 049 4371313 📄 049 31541
e-mail: info@cavangolf.ie
18 holes, 5634mtrs, Par 70, SSS 69, Course record 64.
Course Designer Eddie Hackett **Location** On Killeshandra
rd,out of Cavan town
Telephone for further details
....

Hotel ★★★ 67% Kilmore Hotel, Dublin Rd, CAVAN
☎ 049 4332288 39 en suite

VIRGINIA   Map 01 C4

Virginia ☎ 049 47235 & 48066
9 holes, 4139mtrs, Par 64, SSS 62, Course record 57.
Club membership 500.
Visitors may not play Thu & Sun. **Societies** must apply in
writing to secretary. **Facilities** 👤 ⛳ 🏨 **Leisure** fishing.
Location By Lough Ramor
....

Hotel ★★★ 61% Conyngham Arms Hotel, SLANE
☎ 041 9884444 16 en suite

CO CLARE

BODYKE   Map 01 B3

East Clare ☎ 061 921322 📄 061 921717
e-mail: eastclaregolfclub@eircom.net
**An 18-hole championship course designed by Arthur
Spring beside Lough Derg, with natural trees and water
on well-drained land. Set on 150 acres of rolling quiet
countryside with superb views of East Clare.**
18 holes, 5922yds, Par 71, SSS 71.
Club membership 652.
Visitors no restrictions unless there is a club competition
or a society playing. **Societies** apply in writing, deposit
required. **Green Fees** not confirmed. **Cards** 🟦 🟥 🟨
🖼 **Course Designer** Dr Arthur Spring **Facilities** ⊗ 〗 🍺
🍷 ♀ 👤 🏠 ⛳ 🛜 🏌 ∅
....

Hotel ★★★ 65% Temple Gate Hotel, The Square, ENNIS
☎ 065 682 3300 70 en suite

CLONLARA   Map 01 B3

Clonlara Golf & Leisure
☎ 061 354141 📄 061 354143
12 holes, 5187mtrs, Par 71, SSS 69.
Course Designer Noel Cassidy **Location** 7m NE of
Limerick
Telephone for further details
....

Hotel ★★★★ 70% Castletroy Park Hotel, Dublin Rd,
LIMERICK ☎ 061 335566 107 en suite

ENNIS   Map 01 B3

Ennis Drumbiggle
☎ 065 6824074 & 6865415 📄 065 6841848
e-mail: egc@eircom.net
**On rolling hills, this immaculately manicured course
presents an excellent challenge to both casual visitors
and aspiring scratch golfers, with tree-lined fairways
and well protected greens.**
18 holes, 5612mtrs, Par 70, SSS 69, Course record 65.
Club membership 1000.

Visitors advisable to contact in advance, course available
Mon-Sat at most times. **Societies** apply in
writing/telephone **Green Fees** €30 (weekends & bank
holidays €35). **Cards** 🟦 🟥 🟨 🖼 **Facilities** ⊗ 〗 🍺
🍷 ♀ 👤 🏠 ⛳ 🏌 ∅ **Conf** Corporate Hospitality Days
available **Location** Close to town, well signposted
....

Hotel ★★★ 65% Temple Gate Hotel, The Square, ENNIS
☎ 065 682 3300 70 en suite

Woodstock Golf and Country Club
Shanaway Rd
☎ 065 6829463 & 6842406 📄 065 6820304
e-mail: woodstock.ennis@eircon.net
**This parkland course stands on 155 acres of land and
includes 4 holes where water is a major hazard. The
course is playable all year and the sand-based greens
offer a consistent surface for putting.**
*Woodstock Golf & Country Club: 18 holes, 5864mtrs, Par
71, SSS 71.*
Club membership 350.
Visitors booking advisable at weekends. **Societies**
advisable to telephone in advance. **Green Fees** 18 holes
€40; 9 holes €20 (weekends €42/€20). **Cards** 🟦 🟥
Course Designer Arthur Spring **Facilities** ⊗ 〗 🍺 🍷 ♀
👤 🏠 ⛳ 🛜 🏌 ∅ **Leisure** heated indoor swimming pool,
sauna, gymnasium. **Location** Off N85
....

Hotel ★★★ 65% Temple Gate Hotel, The Square, ENNIS
☎ 065 682 3300 70 en suite

KILKEE   Map 01 B3

Kilkee East End
☎ 065 9056048 & 9056977 📄 065 9656977
e-mail: kilkeegolfclub@eircom.net
**Well established course on the cliffs of Kilkee Bay.
Mature championship course with a great variety of
challenges - seaside holes, cliff-top holes and holes that
feature well-positioned water hazards.**
18 holes, 6075yds, Par 70, SSS 69, Course record 68.
Club membership 710.
Visitors advance booking advisable. **Societies** apply in
writing/telephone/fax/e-mail **Green Fees** Sept-June €25
(weekends €30); July-Aug €30/€35. **Cards** 🟦 🟥 🟨
🖼 **Course Designer** Eddie Hackett **Facilities** ⊗ 〗 🍺 🍷
♀ 👤 🏠 ⛳ 🏌 ∅ **Leisure** squash, sauna. **Location** On
Cilff-Edge,East End,Kilkee
....

Hotel ★★ 64% Halpin's Townhouse Hotel, Erin St,
KILKEE ☎ 065 9056032 12 en suite

Ocean Cove Golf & Leisure Hotel Kilkee Bay
☎ 065 9083111 📄 065 9083123
e-mail: oceancove1@eircom.net
18 holes, 5265metres, Par 69, SSS 69.
Telephone for further details
....

Hotel ★★ 64% Halpin's Townhouse Hotel, Erin St,
KILKEE ☎ 065 9056032 12 en suite

KILRUSH   Map 01 B3

Kilrush Parknamoney ☎ 065 9051138 📄 065 9052633
e-mail: info@kilrushgolfclub.com
**Parkland course that was extended to 18 holes in the
summer of 1994.**
18 holes, 5986yds, Par 70, SSS 70, Course record 68.
Club membership 500.

Continued   *Continued*

Visitors welcome, contact in advance. **Societies** by prior arrangement. **Green Fees** not confirmed. **Cards** ⊞ ▦ **Course Designer** Arthur Spring **Facilities** ⊗ ⑪ ⓛ ⚑ ♉ ♈ ⚘ ⌂ ⑂ ⚑ ⚐ *ℓ* **Conf** fac available Corporate Hospitality Days available **Location** on main Lahinch/Ballybunion road, 4m from Killimer car ferry. 0.5m from Kilrush on Ennis road.

....

Hotel ★★ 64% Halpin's Townhouse Hotel, Erin St, KILKEE ☎ 065 9056032 12 en suite

LAHINCH   Map 01 B3

Lahinch ☎ 065 7081592 ▤ 065 81592
e-mail: info@lahinchgolf.com
Old Course: 18 holes, 6696yds, Par 72, SSS 73.
Castle Course: 18 holes, 5594yds, Par 70, SSS 70.
Course Designer Alister MacKenzie **Location** 2m W of Ennisstymon on N67
Telephone for further details
....
Hotel ⑪ Kincora Country House & Gallery Restaurant, LISDOONVARNA ☎ 065 7074300
14 en suite

MILLTOWN MALBAY   Map 01 B3

Spanish Point
☎ 065 7084198 ▤ 065 7084263
e-mail: dkfitzgerald@tinet.ie
A 9-hole links course with 3 elevated greens and 4 elevated tees. Overlooking Spanish Point beach. Improvements to the course are planned, the existing course being redesigned and lengthened.
9 holes, 4600mtrs, Par 64, SSS 63, Course record 59.
Club membership 600.
Visitors contact in advance. Not before 1pm Sun. **Societies** apply in writing to the secretary. **Green Fees** terms on application. **Cards** ⊞ ▦ ▦ **Facilities** ⓛ ♉ ♈ ⌂ ⚑ ⑂ ⚘ **Location** 2m SW of Miltown Malbay, on N67
....
Hotel ★★ 64% Halpin's Townhouse Hotel, Erin St, KILKEE ☎ 065 9056032 12 en suite

NEWMARKET-ON-FERGUS   Map 01 B3

Dromoland Castle Golf & Country Club
☎ 061 368444 & 368144 ▤ 061 363355/368498
e-mail: golf@dromoland.ie
Set in 200 acres of parkland, the course is enhanced by numerous trees and a lake. Three holes are played around the lake which is in front of the castle.
18 holes, 6850yds, Par 72, SSS 72, Course record 65.
Club membership 500.
Visitors must contact in advance. **Societies** contact in writing. **Green Fees** €100 per day per 18 holes. **Cards** ⊞ ▦ ▦ ▣ **Course Designer** Ron Kirby & J. B. Carr **Facilities** ⊗ ⑪ ⓛ ♉ ⌂ ⚑ ⑂ ⚑ ⚘ ⚔ *ℓ* **Leisure** hard tennis courts, heated indoor swimming pool, fishing, sauna, solarium, gymnasium. **Conf** fac available Corporate Hospitality Days available **Location** 2m N, on main Limerick/Galway rd
....
Hotel ★★★★★ Dromoland Castle Hotel, NEWMARKET-ON-FERGUS ☎ 061 368144 100 en suite

> **Prices may change during the currency of the Guide, please check when booking.**

SHANNON AIRPORT   Map 01 B3

Shannon ☎ 061 471849 ▤ 061 471507
e-mail: shannongolfclub@eircom.net
18 holes, 6874yds, Par 72, SSS 74, Course record 65.
Course Designer John Harris **Location** 2m from Shannon Airport
Telephone for further details
....
Hotel ★★★ 69% Fitzpatrick Bunratty Hotel, BUNRATTY ☎ 061 361177 115 en suite
4 annexe en suite

CO CORK

BANDON   Map 01 B2

Bandon Castlebernard ☎ 023 41111 ▤ 023 44690
e-mail: bandongolfclub@eircom.net
18 holes, 5663mtrs, Par 70, SSS 69, Course record 66.
Location 2.5km W
Telephone for further details
....
Hotel ★★★ 66% Innishannon House Hotel, INNISHANNON ☎ 021 4775121 12 en suite

BANTRY   Map 01 B2

Bantry Bay Donemark ☎ 027 50579 ▤ 027 53790
e-mail: info@bantrygolf.com
Designed by Christy O'Connor Jnr and extended in 1997 to 18 holes, this challenging and rewarding course is idyllically set at the head of Bantry Bay. Testing holes include the par 5 of 487mtrs and the little par 3 of 127mtrs where accuracy is all-important.
18 holes, 5910mtrs, Par 71, SSS 72, Course record 71.
Club membership 600.
Visitors advance booking recommended. At weekends and bank holidays visitors between 11.30-1.30pm and 3-4.30pm. **Societies** must apply in writing. **Green Fees** not confirmed. **Cards** ⊞ ▦ **Course Designer** Christy O'Connor Jnr/Eddie Hackett **Facilities** ⊗ ⑪ ⓛ ♉ ♈ ⌂ ⚑ ⚑ ⚘ *ℓ* **Location** 3km N of Bantry town on the N71 Glengarrif road
....
Hotel ★★★ 64% Westlodge Hotel, BANTRY ☎ 027 50360 90 en suite

BLACKROCK   Map 01 B2

Mahon Clover Hill ☎ 021 4294280
18 holes, 4862metres, Par 70, SSS 67, Course record 64.
Course Designer Eddie Hackett
Telephone for further details
....
Hotel ★★★★ 72% Rochestown Park Hotel, Rochestown Rd, Douglas, CORK ☎ 021 4890800 160 en suite

BLARNEY   Map 01 B2

Muskerry Carrigrohane
☎ 021 4385297 ▤ 021 4516860
An adventurous game is guaranteed at this course, with its wooded hillsides and the meandering Shournagh River coming into play at a number of holes. The 15th is a notable hole - not long, but very deep - and after that all you need to do to get back to the clubhouse is stay out of the water.
18 holes, 5520mtrs, Par 71, SSS 70.
Club membership 801.   *Continued*

413

Visitors may not play Wed afternoon & Thu morning. Some limited play at weekends after 3.30pm & members hour 12.30-1.30pm daily. Must contact in advance. **Societies** must telephone in advance and then confirm in writing. **Cards** ⊞ ▆▆▆ ▆▆▆ **Prof** W M Lehane **Course Designer** Dr A McKenzie **Facilities** ⊗)Ⅲ ⊾ ▦ ♀ ⚘ 🏠 ⚐ ⚗ **Location** 2.5m W of Blarney

Hotel ★★★★ Hayfield Manor, Perrott Av, College Rd, CORK ☎ 021 4845900 88 en suite

CARRIGALINE   Map 01 B2

Fernhill Hotel & Golf Club
☎ 021 4372226 📄 021 4371011
e-mail: fernhill@iol.ie
18 holes, 5000mtrs, Par 69, SSS 68.
Course Designer M L Bowes **Location** 2m from Ringaskiddy
Telephone for further details

Hotel ★★★★ 72% Rochestown Park Hotel, Rochestown Rd, Douglas, CORK ☎ 021 4890800 160 en suite

CASTLETOWNBERE   Map 01 A2

Berehaven Millcove ☎ 027 70700 📄 027 71957
Scenic seaside links founded in 1902. Moderately difficult with four holes over water. Testing 9 hole course with different tee positions for the back nine. Water is a dominant feature and comes into play at every hole.
9 holes, 2624mtrs, Par 68, SSS 67, Course record 63.
Club membership 150.
Visitors welcome. Please check for major events. **Societies** telephone or write in advance. **Green Fees** €20 per round/day (weekends & bank holidays €25). **Cards** ⊞ ▆▆▆ **Course Designer** Royal Navy **Facilities** ⊗)Ⅲ ⊾ ▦ ♀ ⚘ ⚐ ⚗ **Leisure** hard tennis courts, sauna. **Conf** fac available Corporate Hospitality Days available **Location** 2m from Castletownbere on Glen Garriff Rd

Hotel ★★★ 🍴 Sea View House Hotel, BALLYLICKEY ☎ 027 50073 & 50462 📄 027 51555 25 en suite

CHARLEVILLE   Map 01 B2

Charleville ☎ 063 81257 & 81515 📄 063 81274
e-mail: charlevillegolf@eircom.net

West Course: 18 holes, 6212yds, Par 71, SSS 69, Course record 65.
East Course: 9 holes, 6702yds, Par 72, SSS 72.
Course Designer Eddie Connaughton **Location** 2m W from town centre
Telephone for further details

Hotel ★★★ 🍴 Longueville House Hotel, MALLOW ☎ 022 47156 & 47306 📄 022 47459 20 en suite

CLONAKILTY   Map 01 B2

Dunmore Dunmore, Muckross ☎ 023 33352
9 holes, 4464yds, Par 64, SSS 61, Course record 57.
Course Designer E Hackett **Location** 3.5m S of Clonakilty
Telephone for further details

Hotel ★★★★ 74% The Lodge & Spa at Inchydoney Island, CLONAKILTY ☎ 023 33143 67 en suite

CORK   Map 01 B2

Cork Little Island ☎ 021 4353451 📄 021 4353410
e-mail: corkgolfclub@eircom.net
This championship-standard course is kept in superb condition and is playable all year round. Memorable and distinctive features include holes at the water's edge and in a disused quarry. The 4th hole is considered to be among the most attractive and testing holes in Irish golf.
18 holes, 5910mtrs, Par 72, SSS 72, Course record 67.
Club membership 750.
Visitors may not play 12.30-2pm or on Thu (Ladies Day), and only after 2pm Sat & Sun. **Societies** must contact in advance. **Green Fees** €80 (€90 weekends and bank holidays). **Cards** ⊞ ▆▆▆ ▆▆▆ ▩ **Prof** Peter Hickey **Course Designer** Alister Mackenzie **Facilities** ⊗)Ⅲ ⊾ ▦ ♀ ⚘ 🏠 ⚐ ⚗ ⚑ **Conf** Corporate Hospitality Days available **Location** 5m E, on N25 of Cork City

Hotel ★★★★ 69% Jurys Cork Hotel, Western Rd, CORK ☎ 021 4276622 & 4252700 📄 021 4274477 185 en suite

Fota Island Carrigtwohill
☎ 021 4883700 📄 021 4883713
e-mail: reservations@fotaisland.ie
Set in the heart of a 780-acre island in Cork Harbour. The course is routed among mature woodlands with occasional views of the harbour. The traditional design features pot bunkers and undulating putting surfaces. Fota hosted the Murphys Irish Open in 2001 and 2002.
18 holes, 6500yds, Par 71, SSS 71, Course record 63.
Club membership 400.
Visitors advisable to contact in advance. Metal spikes and blue jeans not permitted. **Societies** contact in advance. **Green Fees** €62-€98. **Cards** ⊞ ▆▆▆ ▆▆▆ **Prof** Kevin Morris **Course Designer** Jeff Howes **Facilities** ⊗)Ⅲ ⊾ ▦ ♀ ⚘ 🏠 ⚐ ▨ ⚗ ⚑ **Conf** fac available Corporate Hospitality Days available **Location** Off N25 E of Cork City. Take exit for Cobh, course 500m on right

Hotel ★★★ 70% Midleton Park Hotel & Spa, MIDLETON ☎ 021 4631767 40 en suite

The Ted McCarthy Municipal Golf Course
Blackrock ☎ 021 294280
18 holes, 4862mtrs, Par 70, SSS 66, Course record 63.
Course Designer E Hackett **Location** 2m from city centre
Telephone for further details

Continued *Continued*

The Ted McCarthy Municipal Golf Course

Hotel ★★★★ 65% Silver Springs Moran Hotel, Tivoli, CORK ☎ 021 4507533 109 en suite

DONERAILE
Map 01 B2

Doneraile ☎ 022 24137 & 24379
9 holes, 5528yds, Par 68, SSS 67, Course record 61.
Location Off T11
Telephone for further details

Hotel ★★★ 65% Springfort Hall Hotel, MALLOW
☎ 022 21278 50 en suite

DOUGLAS
Map 01 B2

Douglas ☎ 021 4895297 📄 021 4895297
e-mail: admin@douglasgolfclub.ie
Well maintained very flat parkland course which has been recently redesigned with panoramic views from the clubhouse.
18 holes, 5607mtrs, Par 72, SSS 69.
Club membership 900.
Visitors Contact in advance. May not play Sat or Sun am or Tues (ladies day). Reserved for members 12.30-2 pm. **Societies** must contact in writing, by end of Jan. **Green Fees** €50 per round (€60 weekends and bank holidays). **Cards** ▩ ▦ **Prof** Gary Nicholson **Course Designer** Peter McEvoy **Facilities** ⊗ ⅲ ⅃ ⅃ 🗗 ♀ ⚲ 🏠 ⚑ ⚐ ⚲ ⚑
Location 6km east of Cork City.

Hotel ★★★★ 69% Jurys Cork Hotel, Western Rd, CORK
☎ 021 4276622 & 4252700 📄 021 4274477 185 en suite

FERMOY
Map 01 B2

Fermoy Corrin Cross
☎ 025 32694 (office) & 31472 (shop) 📄 025 33072
e-mail: fermoygolfclub@eircom.net
A mature 18 hole heathland course facing the slopes of Corrin Hill and set in a profusion of natural heather and gorse and bisected by a road. The course commands panoramic views.
18 holes, 5596mtrs, Par 70, SSS 69.
Club membership 820.
Visitors contact in advance, must telephone in advance for weekends bookings **Societies** advisable to write or telephone in advance. **Green Fees** not confirmed. **Cards** ▩ ▦ **Prof** Brian Moriarty **Course Designer** John Harris **Facilities** ⊗ ⅲ ⅃ 🗗 ♀ ⚲ 🏠 ⚑ 🔧 ⚲ **Location** located off N8 to S of town Route to clubhouse is signposted on N8 on Cork side of town.

Hotel ★★★ 🛏 Longueville House Hotel, MALLOW
☎ 022 47156 & 47306 📄 022 47459 20 en suite

CORK CITY COUNCIL

The Ted McCarthy Municipal Golf Course

Located 5km from Cork City.
This course offers undulating fairways, numerous water hazards and extremely demanding greens.
Green Fees and Societies Welcome.
Restaurant/Bar Service – The Blackrock Inn.

Mahon Golf Course (021) 429 2543

GLENGARRIFF
Map 01 B2

Glengarriff ☎ 027 63150 📄 027 63575
Founded 1935.
9 holes, 2042mtrs, Par 66, SSS 62.
Club membership 300.
Visitors no restrictions **Societies** apply to club. **Green Fees** not confirmed. **Facilities** ⅃ 🗗 ♀ ⚲ ⚑ ⚲ **Location** On N71

Hotel ★★★ 64% Westlodge Hotel, BANTRY
☎ 027 50360 90 en suite

KANTURK
Map 01 B2

Kanturk Fairyhill ☎ 029 50534 📄 029 20951
Scenic parkland course set in the heart of the Duhallow region with superb mountain views. It provides a good test of skill for golfers of all standards, with tight fairways requiring accurate driving and precise approach shots to small and tricky greens.
18 holes, 5721mtrs, Par 71, SSS 69, Course record 68.
Club membership 600.
Visitors Please ring in advance. **Societies** apply in writing or telephone the Secretary at 087 2217510 **Green Fees** not confirmed. **Course Designer** Richard Barry **Facilities** ⊗ by prior arrangement ⅲ by prior arrangement ⅃ 🗗 ♀ ⚲ ⚲ **Conf** Corporate Hospitality Days available **Location** 1m from Kanturk on Fairyhill road, 2m off main Mallow/Killarney road from Ballymacquirke Cross

Guesthouse ♦♦♦♦ Assolas Country House, KANTURK ☎ 029 50015 6 en suite 3 annexe en suite

KINSALE — Map 01 B2

Kinsale Farrangalway ☎ 021 4774722 📠 021 4773114
e-mail: office@kinsalegolf.com
In addition to the existing 9-hole (Ringenane) course, an 18-hole (Farrangalway) course was opened in 1994. Set in unspoilt farmland and surrounded by peaceful rolling countryside, it offers a stiff yet fair challenge to be enjoyed by all standards of golfers. New putting green.
Farrangalway: 18 holes, 6609yds, Par 71, SSS 71, Course record 70.
Ringenane: 9 holes, 5332yds, Par 70, SSS 68.
Club membership 800.
Visitors welcome but may not be able to play at weekends. Contact in advance. **Societies** by reservation **Green Fees** terms on application. **Cards** 💳 💳 **Prof** Ger Broderick **Course Designer** Jack Kenneally **Facilities** ⊗ ⊪ ⅃ 🍴 🏌 ♨ 🛎 🍴 🐎 🛒 ⟟ **Location** On main Cork/Kinsale rd

Hotel ★★★ 69% Trident Hotel, Worlds End, KINSALE ☎ 021 4772301 58 en suite

Old Head ☎ 021 4778444 📠 021 4778022
e-mail: info@oldheadgolf.ie
Opened for play in 1997 and designed by Paddy Merrigan, Ron Kirby and Joe Carr, the Old Head course is spectacularly situated on a promontory jutting out into the Atlantic. As well as bringing the sea and cliffs into play, you have to contend with strong prevailing winds - a fine test for all serious golfers.

18 holes, 6451yds, Par 72, SSS 73.
Club membership 300.
Visitors tee time must be booked in advance. **Societies** pre booking necessary, rates for groups over 24. **Green Fees** 18 holes €250; 36 holes €420. **Cards** 💳 💳 💳 **Prof** Danny Brassil **Course Designer** R Kirby/J Carr/P Merrigan/E Hackett **Facilities** ⊗ ⊪ ⅃ 🍴 🏌 ♨ 🛎 🐎 🛒 ⟟ **Conf** Corporate Hospitality Days available **Location** From Cork city/airport, follow R600 to Kinsale, then signed to golf course

Hotel ★★★ 73% Actons Hotel, Pier Rd, KINSALE ☎ 021 4772135 76 en suite

LITTLE ISLAND — Map 01 B2

Harbour Point Clash Rd
☎ 021 4353094 📠 021 4354408
e-mail: hpoint@iol.ie
A championship-standard course in rolling countryside on the banks of the River Lee at Cork's scenic harbour. A distinctive and testing course for every standard of golfer, providing for a full range of shots in its design. The large undulating greens and difficult par 3s are a feature of this course.
Continued

18 holes, 5883metres, Par 72, SSS 71, Course record 71.
Visitors must contact in advance. **Societies** telephone for bookings. **Green Fees** terms on application. **Cards** 💳 💳 **Prof** Morgan O'Donovan **Course Designer** Patrick Merrigan **Facilities** ⊗ ⊪ ⅃ 🍴 🏌 ♨ 🛎 🍴 🐎 🛒 ⟟ **Conf** fac available **Location** 5m E of Cork, take Rosslare road E from Cork city & exit at Little Island

Hotel ★★★★ 65% Silver Springs Moran Hotel, Tivoli, CORK ☎ 021 4507533 109 en suite

MACROOM — Map 01 B2

Macroom Lackaduve
☎ 026 41072 & 42615 📠 026 41391
e-mail: mcroomgc@iol.ie
A particularly scenic parkland course located on undulating ground along the banks of the River Sullane. Bunkers and mature trees make a variable and testing course and the 12th has an 80-yard carry over the river to the green.
18 holes, 5574mtrs, Par 72, SSS 70, Course record 68.
Club membership 650.
Visitors Booking essential for at all times **Societies** Telephone in advance. **Green Fees** €35 (Mon-Thu early bird until 10.30 €20) (€40 weekends and bank holidays). **Cards** 💳 💳 **Course Designer** Jack Kenneally/Eddie Hackett **Facilities** ⊗ ⊪ ⅃ 🍴 🏌 ♨ 🛎 🐎 🛒 ⟟ **Location** Through castle entrance in town square

Hotel ★★★ 70% Castle Hotel, Main St, MACROOM ☎ 026 41074 60 en suite

MALLOW — Map 01 B2

Mallow Ballyellis
☎ 022 21145 📠 022 42501
e-mail: golfmall@gofree.indigo.ie
Mallow Golf Club was first established in the late 1800s. A well wooded parkland course overlooking the Blackwater Valley, Mallow is straightforward, but no less of a challenge for it. The front nine is by far the longer, but the back nine is demanding in its call for accuracy and the par 3 18th provides a tough finish.

18 holes, 5769metres, Par 72, SSS 71, Course record 67.
Club membership 1250.
Visitors must contact in advance. **Societies** apply in advance. **Green Fees** €35 per round (€40 weekends & public holidays). **Cards** 💳 💳 💳 **Prof** Sean Conway **Course Designer** D W Wishart **Facilities** ⊗ ⊪ ⅃ 🍴 🏌 ♨ 🛎 🐎 🛒 ⟟ **Leisure** hard tennis courts, squash. **Location** 1m E of Mallow town

Hotel ★★★ ♨ Longueville House Hotel, MALLOW ☎ 022 47156 & 47306 📠 022 47459 20 en suite

MIDLETON   Map 01 C2

East Cork Gortacrue
☎ 021 4631687 & 4631273 🖫 021 4613695
e-mail: eastcorkgolfclub@eircom.net
A well wooded course calling for accuracy of shots.
18 holes, 5634yds, Par 69, SSS 66, Course record 64.
Club membership 820.
Visitors may not play Sun mornings. **Societies** must
telephone. **Green Fees** €25 (weekend €30). **Cards** 💳
🔳 **Prof** Don MacFarlane **Course Designer** E Hackett
Facilities ⊗ ⍨ ⅃ ⌁ 🍺 ♀ ⅄ 🏠 ⛳ ⏀ ℂ **Location** on the
A626, 2m north of Midleton on Fermoy Rd.

Hotel ★★★ 70% Midleton Park Hotel & Spa,
MIDLETON ☎ 021 4631767 40 en suite

MITCHELSTOWN   Map 01 B2

Mitchelstown Limerick Rd
☎ 025 24072 & 087 2650110
e-mail: info@mitchelstown-golf.com
**Attractive, gently undulating parkland course set in the
Golden Vale, noted for the quality of the greens, the
magnificent views of the Galtee Mountains and its
friendly atmosphere. Ideal for golfers seeking
tranquility and a golfing challenge.**
18 holes, 5493mtrs, Par 71, SSS 70.
Club membership 600.
Visitors advisable to check in advance (information line
025 24231) **Societies** apply in writing or telephone. **Green
Fees** €25 per round (weekends €30). **Course Designer**
David Jones **Facilities** ⊗ ⅃ 🍺 ♀ ⅄ ⛳ **Location** 0.75m
on Limerick rd from Mitchelstown

Hotel ★★★ ⚶ Longueville House Hotel, MALLOW
☎ 022 47156 & 47306 🖫 022 47459 20 en suite

MONKSTOWN   Map 01 B2

Monkstown Parkgariffe, Monkstown
☎ 021 4841376 🖫 021 4841722
e-mail: office@monkstowngolfclub.com
**Undulating parkland course with five tough finishing
holes.**
18 holes, 5441mtrs, Par 70, SSS 68, Course record 66.
Club membership 960.
Visitors must contact in advance. Not Tue or before 2pm
weekends. **Societies** apply in writing or telephone. Large
groups (24+) should book before Xmas. **Green Fees** €37
per day (weekend €44). **Cards** 💳 🔳 **Prof** Batt Murphy
Facilities ⊗ ⍨ ⅃ 🍺 ♀ ⅄ 🏠 ⛳ ⏀ ℂ **Conf** Corporate
Hospitality Days available **Location** 0.5m SE of
Monkstown village

Hotel ★★★★ 69% Jurys Cork Hotel, Western Rd, CORK
☎ 021 4276622 & 4252700 🖫 021 4274477 185 en suite

OVENS   Map 01 B2

Lee Valley Golf & Country Club Clashanure
☎ 021 7331721 🖫 021 7331695
e-mail: leevalleygolfclub@eircom.net
18 holes, 6434yds, Par 72, SSS 70, Course record 62.
Course Designer Christy O'Connor **Location** 8m from
Cork on Cork/Killarney road N22
Telephone for further details

Lee Valley Golf & Country Club

Hotel ★★★ 70% Castle Hotel, Main St, MACROOM
☎ 026 41074 60 en suite

SKIBBEREEN   Map 01 B2

Skibbereen & West Carbery Licknavar
☎ 028 21227 🖫 028 22994
e-mail: bookings@skibbgolf.com
Slightly hilly course in scenic location.
18 holes, 6004yds, Par 71, SSS 69, Course record 66.
Club membership 700.
Visitors advisable to contact club secretary for dates in
writing. **Societies** apply in writing or telephone. **Green
Fees** not confirmed. **Cards** 💳 🔳 **Course Designer** Jack
Kenneally **Facilities** ⊗ ⍨ ⅃ 🍺 ♀ ⅄ 🏠 ⛳ ⏀ 🛺 ⏀
Conf Corporate Hospitality Days available **Location** 1m
W on Baltimore road

Hotel ★★★ 67% Baltimore Harbour Hotel & Leisure
Cntr, BALTIMORE ☎ 028 20361 64 en suite

YOUGHAL   Map 01 C2

Youghal Knockaverry
☎ 024 92787 & 92861 🖫 024 92641
e-mail: youghalgolfclub@eircom.ie
**For many years the host of various Golfing Union
championships, Youghal offers a good test of golf and is
well maintained for year-round play. There are
panoramic views of Youghal Bay.**
18 holes, 5646mtrs, Par 70, SSS 69, Course record 61.
Club membership 994.
Visitors may not play Wed (Ladies Day) and should
contact in advance for weekends. **Societies** must apply in
writing a few months in advance. **Green Fees** not
confirmed. **Cards** 💳 🔳 **Prof** Liam Burns **Course
Designer** Cd. Harris **Facilities** ⊗ ⍨ ⅃ 🍺 ♀ ⅄ 🏠 ⛳ ⏀ 🛺
⏀ **Location** On N25 between Waterford and Cork

Hotel ★★ 60% Devonshire Arms Hotel and Restaurant,
Pearse Square, YOUGHAL ☎ 024 92827 10 en suite

CO DONEGAL

BALLINTRA   Map 01 B5

Donegal Murvagh, Laghy
☎ 074 9734054 🖫 074 9734377
e-mail: info@donegalgolfclub.ie
**This massive links course was opened in 1973 and
provides a world-class facility in peaceful surroundings.**

Continued

Continued

It is a very long course with some memorable holes, including five par 5s, calling for some big hitting.
18 holes, 6243mtrs, Par 73, SSS 73, Course record 68.
Club membership 750.
Visitors must contact in advance, limited availability at weekends & Mondays **Societies** must contact in advance. **Green Fees** €50 Mon-Thu; €65 Fri-Sun. **Cards** 💳 📧 **Prof** Leslie Robinson **Course Designer** Eddie Hackett **Facilities** ⊗ ⑭ ఏ ⚑ ♀ ⚑ 🏌 ⚑ ∅ **Conf** Corporate Hospitality Days available **Location** 6m S of Donegal on Ballyshannon road

Hotel ★★★ 78% Sand House Hotel, ROSSNOWLAGH
☎ 071 985 1777 55 en suite

BALLYBOFEY   Map 01 C5

Ballybofey & Stranorlar Stranorlar
☎ 074 9131093 📠 074 9130158
A most scenic course incorporating pleasant valleys backed by mountains with three of its holes bordered by a lake. There are three par 3s on the first nine and two on the second. The most difficult hole is the long uphill par 4 16th. The only par 5 is the 7th.
18 holes, 5366mtrs, Par 68, SSS 68, Course record 64.
Club membership 620.
Visitors may play on weekdays. Advisable to book in advance **Societies** contact golf shop **Green Fees** not confirmed. **Facilities** ⊗ ⑭ ఏ ⚑ ♀ ⚑ 🏌 ∅ **Location** 0.25m from Stranorlar

Hotel ★★★ 70% Kee's Hotel, Stranorlar, BALLYBOFEY ☎ 074 913 1018 53 en suite

BALLYLIFFIN   Map 01 C6

Ballyliffin Clonmany ☎ 074 9376119 📠 074 9376672
e-mail: info@ballyliffingolfclub.com
The Old course is a links course with rolling fairways, surrounded by rolling hills and bounded on one side by the ocean. Nick Faldo said 'This is the most natural golf links I have ever played'. It has an old-fashioned charm with its uniquely contoured fairways. The 18-hole Glashedy course (opened summer 1995) offers a modern (and arguably 'fairer') championship test.
Old Links: 18 holes, 6604yds, Par 71, SSS 72, Course record 65.
Glashedy Links: 18 holes, 7135yds, Par 72, SSS 74, Course record 68.
Club membership 1200.
Visitors advisable to telephone in advance. **Societies** telephone in advance. **Green Fees** not confirmed. **Cards** 💳 📧 **Prof** Francis Howley **Course Designer** Tom Craddock/Pat Ruddy **Facilities** ⊗ ⑭ ఏ ⚑ ♀ ⚑ 🏌 ⚑ ∅ ⚐ **Location** from Foyle Bridge, take road to Muff village and on to Quigley's point. Turn left to Carndonagh, 5m to club. Alternatively travel through Buncrana and Clonmany village, 2m to club.

Guesthouse ♦♦♦♦ Mount Royd Country Home, CARRIGANS ☎ 074 914 0163 4 en suite

BUNCRANA   Map 01 C6

Buncrana Municipal Railway Rd, Ballymacarry
☎ 07493 62279 0749320749
e-mail: buncranagc@eircom.net
A 9-hole course with a very challenging par 3 3rd with all carry out of bounds on either side. Situated beside the shores of Lough Swilly.

9 holes, 2125yds, Par 62, SSS 60, Course record 59.
Club membership 200.
Visitors during open competitions only visitors with club handicaps.Telephone in advance to make arrangements for weekends. **Societies** write in advance/telephone. **Green Fees** €13 per round (€8 ladies). **Facilities** ఏ ⚑ ♀ ⚑ 🏌 ∅ **Conf** fac available

Guesthouse ♦♦♦♦ Mount Royd Country Home, CARRIGANS ☎ 074 914 0163 4 en suite

North West Lisfannon, Fahan, buncrana
☎ 074 9361715 📠 074 9363284
e-mail: nwgc@tinet.ie
A traditional-style links course on gently rolling sandy terrain with some long par 4s. Good judgement is required on the approaches and the course offers a satisfying test coupled with undemanding walking.
18 holes, 5968yds, Par 70, SSS 70, Course record 64.
Club membership 580.
Visitors contact in advance for weekends. Wed - Ladies Day **Societies** telephone in advance. **Green Fees** €25 (€30 weekends). **Prof** Seamus McBriarty **Course Designer** Thompson Davy **Facilities** ⊗ ⑭ ఏ ⚑ ♀ ⚑ 🏌 ⚑ ∅ **Location** 1m S of Buncanna

Guesthouse ♦♦♦♦ Mount Royd Country Home, CARRIGANS ☎ 074 914 0163 4 en suite

BUNDORAN   Map 01 B5

Bundoran ☎ 071 9841302 📠 071 9842014
e-mail: bundorangolfclub@eircom.net
This popular course, acknowledged as one of the best in the country, runs along the high cliffs above Bundoran beach and has a difficult par of 70. Designed by Harry Vardon, it offers a challenging game of golf in beautiful surroundings and has been the venue for a number of Irish golf championships.
18 holes, 5688mtrs, Par 70, SSS 70, Course record 67.
Club membership 770.
Visitors must contact in advance for prior booking. **Societies** must contact in advance. **Green Fees** €40 per round (weekend €50). **Prof** David T Robinson **Course Designer** Harry Vardon **Facilities** ఏ ⚑ ♀ ⚑ 🏌 ⚑ ∅ **Location** Just off Main St, Bundoran on the Sligo/Derry road, 22m N of Sligo

Hotel ★★★ 78% Sand House Hotel, ROSSNOWLAGH
☎ 071 985 1777 55 en suite

CRUIT ISLAND   Map 01 B5

Cruit Island Kincasslagh
☎ 074 9543296 📠 074 9548028
A links course on a small island. It is perched along the cliffs overlooking the Atlantic. The course is short but always challenging as the wind blows 90% of the time. It is crowned by a magnificent 6th hole which is played across a cove to an island green. With the prevailing wind in your face and the Atlantic waves crashing in front, it is not for the fainthearted.
9 holes, 4833mtrs, Par 68, SSS 66, Course record 62.
Club membership 350.
Visitors restricted Sun & Thu mornings for Club competitions. **Societies** apply in writing to secretary. **Green Fees** €22 per day (with member €11). **Cards** 💳

Continued   Continued

Course Designer Michael Doherty **Facilities** 🔛 ♨ ♀ ⛱ 𝒞 **Conf** Corporate Hospitality Days available **Location** 8km N of Dungloe

Hotel ★★★ 67% Arnold's Hotel, DUNFANAGHY ☎ 074 913 6208 30 en suite

DUNFANAGHY   Map 01 C6

Dunfanaghy Kill ☎ 074 9136335 📄 074 9136684
e-mail: dunfanaghygolf@eircom.net
Overlooking Sheephaven Bay, the course has a flat central area with three difficult streams to negotiate. At the Port-na-Blagh end there are five marvellous holes, including one across the beach, while at the Horn Head end, the last five holes are a test for any golfer.
18 holes, 5247mtrs, Par 68, SSS 66, Course record 63.
Club membership 335.
Visitors must book in advance, time sheet in operation all year. Societies must telephone in advance. Green Fees terms on application. **Course Designer** Harry Vardon **Facilities** 🔛 ♨ ♀ ⛱ 🏠 🏌 ➤ 🏌 𝒞 **Conf** fac available **Location** On N56

Hotel ★★★ 67% Arnold's Hotel, DUNFANAGHY ☎ 074 913 6208 30 en suite

GREENCASTLE   Map 01 C6

Greencastle Geencastle
☎ 074 9381013 📄 074 9381015
e-mail: info@greencastlegolfclub.net
A typical links course along the shores of Lough Foyle, surrounded by rocky headlands and sandy beaches. In 1992 to celebrate its centenary, the club increased its size from 9 to 18 holes.
18 holes, 5118mtrs, Par 69, SSS 67, Course record 65.
Club membership 750.
Visitors no restrictions. Societies telephone in advance. May not play Sun. **Green Fees** €25/€20 (€35/€25 weekends and bank holidays). **Course Designer** E Hackett **Facilities** ⊗ 🔛 ♨ ♀ ⛱ 𝒞

Hotel ★★★ 70% Quality Hotel Davincis, 15 Culmore Rd, LONDONDERRY ☎ 028 7127 9111 67 en suite

GWEEDORE   Map 01 B6

Gweedore Derrybeg ☎ 075 31140
9 holes, 6201yds, Par 71, SSS 69.
Telephone for further details

LETTERKENNY   Map 01 C5

Letterkenny Barnhill
☎ 074 9121150 📄 074 9121175
The fairways are wide and generous, but the rough, when you find it, is short, tough and mean. The flat and untiring terrain on the shores of Lough Swilly provides good holiday golf. Many interesting holes include the intimidating 1st with its high tee through trees, and the tricky dog-leg of the 2nd hole. The last seven holes are on undulating ground; steep climb from 11th green to 12th tee.
18 holes, 6239yds, Par 70, SSS 71, Course record 65.
Club membership 700.
Visitors preferred Mon-Fri, except Wed evenings after 5pm. Advisable to contact in advance for weekends and bank holidays. Societies apply by writing or telephone. Green Fees terms on application. **Course Designer** Eddie

Hacket **Facilities** ⊗ 🎽 🔛 ♨ ♀ ⛱ 🏠 🏌 ➤ 𝒞 **Conf** fac available **Location** 2m from town on Rathmelton road

Hotel ★★★ 70% Kee's Hotel, Stranorlar, BALLYBOFEY ☎ 074 913 1018 53 en suite

MOVILLE   Map 01 C6

Redcastle Redcastle ☎ 074 9382073 📄 074 9382214
e-mail: redcastle.hotel@oceanfree.net
A testing course enjoying a picturesque setting on the shores of Loch Foyle. The two challenging par 3 holes should be approached with the necessary respect.
9 holes, 3076yds, Par 36.
Club membership 200.
Visitors welcome except club times, advisable to telephone. Societies enquiries welcome by telephone or in writing. **Green Fees** €19 (€25 weekend). **Cards** 💳 💳 💳 **Facilities** ⊗ 🎽 🔛 ♨ ♀ 🏠 🏌 🏌 𝒞 **Leisure** hard tennis courts, heated indoor swimming pool, fishing, sauna, gymnasium. **Conf** fac available **Location** Main Londonderry/Moville road

NARIN   Map 01 B5

Narin & Portnoo ☎ 074 9545107 📄 074 9545107
e-mail: narinportnoo@eircom.net
Seaside links with every hole presenting its own special feature. One of the few natural links layouts remaining, with undulating fairways and greens. Fine views of Gweebarra Bay are visible from the course with an adjacent award winning beach. The links will test a player's iron play, with raised greens a common feature.
18 holes, 5322mtrs, Par 69, SSS 68, Course record 63.
Club membership 700.
Visitors contact in advance for weekend tee times. Societies telephone or email in advance. **Green Fees** €30 per day (€35 weekends & bank holidays). **Course Designer** Harry Vardon **Facilities** 🔛 ♨ ♀ ⛱ 🏠 ➤ 𝒞 **Leisure** blue flag standard beach 200m away. **Location** 6m from Ardara

PORTSALON   Map 01 C6

Portsalon ☎ 074 9159459 📄 074 9159919
e-mail: portsalongolfclub@eircom.net
Another course blessed by nature. The golden beaches of Ballymastocker Bay lie at one end, while the beauty of Lough Swilly and the Inishowen Peninsula beyond is a distracting but pleasant view to the west. Situated on the Fanad Peninsula, this lovely links course provides untiring holiday golf at its best. A redevelopment and extension of the course is currently in progress.
18 holes, 6185mtrs, Par 72, SSS 72, Course record 71.
Club membership 500.
Visitors telephone in advance. Societies telephone in advance. **Green Fees** €35 (€40 weekends & bank holidays). **Cards** 💳 💳 💳 **Course Designer** Pat Ruddy **Facilities** ⊗ by prior arrangement 🎽 by prior arrangement 🔛 by prior arrangement ♨ by prior arrangement ♀ ⛱ 🏌 𝒞 **Conf** Corporate Hospitality Days available **Location** 20m N of Letterkenny

Hotel ★★★ 🏌 75% Fort Royal Hotel, Fort Royal, RATHMULLAN ☎ 074 915 8100 11 en suite 4 annexe en suite

Continued

RATHMULLAN
Map 01 C6

Otway Saltpans ☎ 074 58319
One of the oldest golf courses in Ireland, created in
1861 by British military personnel as a recreational
facility to ease the tedium during the Napoleonic war.
9 holes, 4234yds, Par 64, SSS 60, Course record 60.
Club membership 92.
Visitors welcome. **Societies** contact for details. **Green
Fees** not confirmed. **Facilities** ♀ ⚐ **Conf** Corporate
Hospitality Days available **Location** W shore of Loch
Swilly

Hotel ★★★ 75% Fort Royal Hotel, Fort Royal,
RATHMULLAN ☎ 074 915 8100 11 en suite
4 annexe en suite

ROSAPENNA
Map 01 C6

Rosapenna Downings
☎ 074 9155301 🖹 074 9155128
e-mail: rosapenna@tinet.ie
Dramatic links course offering a challenging round.
Originally designed by Tom Morris and later modified
by James Braid and Harry Vardon, it includes features
such as bunkers in mid-fairway. The best part of the
links runs in the low valley along the ocean. New 18-
hole Sandy Hills Links course opened in June 2003.
Old Tom Morris: 18 holes, 6271yds, Par 70, SSS 71.
Sandy Hills Links: 18 holes, 6356yds, Par 71.
Club membership 200.
Visitors no restrictions. **Societies** must contact in advance.
Green Fees Old Tom Morris: €45 per round (€50
weekend & bank holiday); Sandy Hills Links €60 per
round. **Cards** 🎟 🎟 🎟 🎟 **Course Designer** Old Tom
Morris **Facilities** ⊗ 〗 🕭 🖤 ♀ ⚐ 🎋 🕿 ☕ **ˀ**
Leisure hard tennis courts, heated indoor swimming pool.
Conf fac available **Location** 25m N of Letterkenny

Hotel ★★★ 67% Arnold's Hotel, DUNFANAGHY
☎ 074 913 6208 30 en suite

CO DUBLIN

BALBRIGGAN
Map 01 D4

Balbriggan Blackhall ☎ 01 8412229 🖹 01 8413927
e-mail: balbriggangolfclub@eircom.net
A parkland course with great variations and good views
of the Mourne and Cooley mountains.
18 holes, 5922mtrs, Par 71, SSS 71.
Club membership 650.
Visitors must contact in advance. With member only at
weekends. Tuesdays ladies day. **Societies** must apply in
writing. **Green Fees** terms on application. **Course
Designer** Paramoir **Facilities** ⊗ 〗 🕭 🖤 ♀ ⚐ 🎋 ☕
Location 1km S off Balbriggan on N1

Hotel ★★★ 65% Boyne Valley Hotel & Country Club,
Stameen, Dublin Rd, DROGHEDA ☎ 041 9837737
73 en suite

BALLYBOUGHAL
Map 01 D4

Hollywood Lakes ☎ 01 8433406 🖹 01 8433002
e-mail: austinbrogan@hotmail.com
A parkland course opened in 1992 with large USGA-
type, sand-based greens and tees. There are water
features on seven holes. The front nine requires
Continued

accuracy while the second nine includes a 636yd par 5.
18 holes, 6246mtrs, Par 72, SSS 72, Course record 67.
Club membership 690.
Visitors welcome Mon-Fri but may only play weekends
from 2pm. **Societies** telephone then write in advance.
Green Fees not confirmed. **Cards** 🎟 🎟 **Prof** Sid
Baldwin **Course Designer** Mel Flanagan **Facilities** ⊗ 〗
🕭 🖤 ♀ ⚐ 🎋 🕿 ☕ **ˀ** **Location** 3m off main
Dublin/Belfast road

Hotel ★★★ 70% Marine Hotel, Sutton Cross, DUBLIN
13 ☎ 01 8390000 48 en suite

BRITTAS
Map 01 D4

Slade Valley Lynch Park
☎ 01 4582183 & 4582739 🖹 01 4582784
18 holes, 5388mtrs, Par 69, SSS 68, Course record 65.
Course Designer W Sullivan & D O Brien **Location** 9m
SW of Dublin on N81
Telephone for further details

Hotel ★★★ 66% Downshire House Hotel,
BLESSINGTON ☎ 045 865199 14 en suite
11 annexe en suite

CASTLEKNOCK
Map 01 D4

Elm Green ☎ 01 8200797 🖹 01 8226662
e-mail: elmgreen@golfdublin.com
Located a short distance from Dublin, beside Phoenix
Park, with a fine layout, tricky greens and year round
playability.
18 holes, 5796yds, Par 71, SSS 66, Course record 65.
Club membership 650.
Visitors must book in advance. **Societies** telephone in
advance. **Green Fees** not confirmed. **Cards** 🎟 🎟 🎟
Prof Arnold O'Connor/Paul McGavan **Course Designer**
Eddie Hackett **Facilities** ⊗ 🕭 🖤 ⚐ 🎋 🕿 ☕ **ˀ**
Leisure pitch and putt course. **Conf** fac available
Corporate Hospitality Days available **Location** Off Navan
Rd, 15 mins from city centre

Hotel ★★★ 70% Finnstown Country House Hotel,
Newcastle Rd, Lucan, DUBLIN ☎ 01 6010700 25 en suite
28 annexe en suite

Luttrellstown Castle Dublin15
☎ 01 8089988 🖹 01 8089989
e-mail: golf@luttrellstown.ie
Set in the grounds of the magnificent 560-acre
Luttrellstown Castle estate, this championship course
has retained the integrity of a mature and ancient
parkland. It is renowned for the quality of its greens
and the log-built clubhouse which provides excellent
facilities.
18 holes, 6032mtrs, Par 72, SSS 73, Course record 66.
Club membership 400.
Visitors bookings made in advance only, no denims, soft
spikes only, no trainers. **Societies** must phone in advance.
Green Fees not confirmed. **Cards** 🎟 🎟 🎟 🎟 🎟 **Prof**
Edward Doyle **Course Designer** N Bielenberg **Facilities**
⊗ 〗 🕭 🖤 ♀ ⚐ 🎋 🕿 ☕ **ˀ** **Leisure** hard tennis
courts, heated outdoor swimming pool, fishing, clay
shooting. **Conf** fac available Corporate Hospitality Days
available **Location** Porterstown rd

Hotel ★★★ 70% Finnstown Country House Hotel,
Newcastle Rd, Lucan, DUBLIN ☎ 01 6010700 25 en suite
28 annexe en suite

CLOGHRAN

Map 01 D4

Forrest Little

☎ 01 8401183 & 8401763 ▤ 01 8401000
e-mail: office@forrestlittle.com
Mature parkland course in a scenic setting. A true test of golf for all abilities.
18 holes, 5902mtrs, Par 71, SSS 72, Course record 68.
Club membership 1000.
Visitors preferred weekday mornings. **Societies** welcome Mon & Thu. Apply in advance by writing or telephone.
Green Fees not confirmed. **Prof** Tony Judd **Course Designer** Mr Hawtree snr **Facilities** ⊗ ⅷ ⅼ ▼ ♀ ☎ ⚐ ♂
Location 6m N of Dublin on N1, adjacent to Dublin airport

Hotel ★★★ 70% Marine Hotel, Sutton Cross, DUBLIN 13 ☎ 01 8390000 48 en suite

DONABATE

Map 01 D4

Balcarrick Corballis

☎ 01 8436228 & 8436957 ▤ 01 8436957
e-mail: balcarr@iol.ie
Splendid 18-hole parkland course located close to the sea. A strong prevailing wind often plays a big part on every hole. Many challenging holes, notably the 5th - nicknamed 'Amen Corner'.
18 holes, 6273mtrs, Par 73, SSS 71.
Club membership 750.
Visitors must contact in advance. **Societies** telephone in advance. **Green Fees** terms on application. **Prof** Stephen Rayfus **Course Designer** Barry Langan **Facilities** ⊗ ⅷ ⅼ ▼ ♀ ♨ ☎
★★★ 67% Deer Park Hotel & Golf Courses, HOWTH ☎ 01 8322624 80 en suite

Corballis Public Corballis ☎ 01 8436583

18 holes, 4971yds, Par 65, SSS 64.
Telephone for further details

Hotel ★★★ 67% Deer Park Hotel & Golf Courses, HOWTH ☎ 01 8322624 80 en suite

Donabate Balcarrick ☎ 01 8436346 ▤ 01 8434488

e-mail: info@donabategolfclub.com
Tree lined course extended to 27 holes in 1996. Water comes into play on 8 holes. All greens now USGA standard. Sand based course playable all year.
27 holes, 6068mtrs, Par 72, SSS 73, Course record 66.
Club membership 1200.
Visitors must telephone in advance, restricted Tue/Wed & weekends. **Societies** telephone in advance **Green Fees** €45 (€60 weekends and bank holidays). **Cards** ▦ ▥ ▨ ▨ **Prof** Hugh Jackson **Course Designer** Pat Suttle **Facilities** ⊗ ⅷ ⅼ ▼ ♀ ♨ ☎ ⚐ ♪ ♨ ♂ **Conf**
Corporate Hospitality Days available **Location** 5m N of Dublin Airport on Belfast road. Turn right 1m past Swords and follow signs

Hotel ★★★ 67% Deer Park Hotel & Golf Courses, HOWTH ☎ 01 8322624 80 en suite

Island Corballis ☎ 01 8436205 ▤ 01 8436860

e-mail: islandgc@iol.ie
A genuine old links course surrounded by the Irish Sea, Donabate beach and the Broadmeadow estuary, nestling between the highest sand dunes of any links course in Ireland. The rugged beauty cannot

Continued

fail to impress. An Irish qualifying course for the Open Championship from 2005.

The Island Golf Club
18 holes, 6206mtrs, Par 71, SSS 73.
Club membership 1000.
Visitors must contact in advance. **Societies** telephone in advance **Green Fees** not confirmed. **Cards** ▦ ▩ ▨
Prof Kevin Kelliher **Course Designer** Hackett/Hawtree **Facilities** ⊗ ⅷ ⅼ ▼ ♀ ♨ ☎ ⚐ ♨ ♂ **Conf** fac available
Corporate Hospitality Days available **Location** Take main Dublin/Belfast road N1, pass airport, take turn for Donabate/Portrane, follow signs

Hotel ★★★ 67% Deer Park Hotel & Golf Courses, HOWTH ☎ 01 8322624 80 en suite

DUBLIN

Map 01 D4

Carrickmines Carrickmines ☎ 01 2955972

Meadowland and partly hilly gorseland course.
9 holes, 6063yds, Par 71, SSS 69.
Club membership 600.
Visitors may not play Wed,Sat or bank holidays. **Societies** contact for details. **Green Fees** terms on application.
Facilities ⅼ ▼ ♀ ♨ ♂ **Location** 7m S of Dublin

Hotel ★★★ 68% The Gresham Royal Marine Hotel, Marine Rd, DUN LAOGHAIRE ☎ 01 2801911 103 en suite

Castle Woodside Dr, Rathfarnham

☎ 01 4904207 ▤ 01 4920264
e-mail: office@castlegc.ie
A tight, tree-lined parkland course which is very highly regarded by all who play there.
18 holes, 5732mtrs, Par 70, SSS 70, Course record 63.
Club membership 1350.
Visitors welcome but may not play at weekends & bank holidays. **Societies** must apply in writing 6 months in advance. **Green Fees** €60 per 18 holes. **Cards** ▦ ▥ ▨
Prof David Kinsella **Course Designer** Barcroft-Pickman & Hood **Facilities** ⊗ ⅷ ⅼ ▼ ♀ ♨ ☎ ♂ **Location** Off Dodder Park Road

Hotel ★★★★ 72% Jurys Ballsbridge Hotel, Pembroke Rd, Ballsbridge, DUBLIN 4 ☎ 01 660 5000 303 en suite

Clontarf Donnycarney House, Malahide Rd

☎ 01 8331892 & 8331520 ▤ 01 8331933
e-mail: info.cgc@indigo.ie
The nearest golf course to Dublin city, with a historic building as a clubhouse, Clontarf is a parkland type course bordered on one side by a railway line. Although a relatively short course, its narrow fairways and

Continued

punitive rough call for accuracy off the tee and will test players' golfing skill. There are several challenging holes including the 12th, which involves playing over a pond and a quarry.

18 holes, 5317mtrs, Par 69, SSS 68, Course record 64.
Club membership 1150.
Visitors welcome daily but must contact in advance. **Societies** Tue & Fri. Must contact in advance. **Green Fees** not confirmed. **Prof** Mark Callan **Course Designer** Harry Colt **Facilities** ⊗ ⅜ ⅃ ⅄ ⅄ ⅃ ⅃ ⅃ **Leisure** bowling green, snooker room, golf teaching by pro. **Conf** fac available Corporate Hospitality Days available **Location** 2.5m N via Fairview

....
Hotel ★★★ 63% McEniff Skylon Hotel, Drumcondra Rd, DUBLIN 9 ☎ 01 8379121 88 en suite

Corrstown Corrstown, Kilsallaghan
☎ 01 8640533 & 8640534 ▤ 01 8640537
e-mail: info@corrstown.com
The 18 hole course has a small river meandering through, coming into play at several holes culminating in a challenging island green finish. Orchard course has mature trees and rolling pastureland offering golfers a relaxing enjoyable game.

River Course: 18 holes, 6077mtrs, Par 72, SSS 71, Course record 69.
Orchard Course: 9 holes, 2792mtre, Par 35, SSS 69.
Club membership 1050.
Visitors advisable to contact in advance. May play weekends after 3pm on River Course. Visitors welcome anytime on Orchard Course. **Societies** telephone or write in advance. **Green Fees** €40 per 18 holes (€50 weekends). Orchard course €20 (€30 weekends). **Cards** ▦ ▦ ▬ **Prof** Pat Gittens **Course Designer** Eddie Connaughton **Facilities** ⊗ ⅜ ⅃ ⅄ ⅄ ⅃ ⅃ **Location** 10 minutes W of Dublin Airport via St Margarets

....
Hotel ★★★ 63% McEniff Skylon Hotel, Drumcondra Rd, DUBLIN 9 ☎ 01 8379121 88 en suite

Deer Park Hotel & Golf Course Howth D13
☎ 01 8322624 ▤ 01 8392405
e-mail: sales@deerpark.iol.ie
Claiming to be Ireland's largest golf/hotel complex, be warned that its popularity makes it quite busy at times and only hotel residents and societies can book tee-off times.
St Fintans: 9 holes, 3373yds, Par 37.
Deer Park: 18 holes, 6830yds, Par 72.
Grace O'Malley: 9 holes, 3130yds, Par 35.
Short Course: 12 holes, 1810yds, Par 36.
Club membership 350.

Deer Park Hotel & Golf Course
Visitors no restrictions. There may be delays especially Sun mornings. **Societies** must contact by telephone. **Green Fees** 18 hole €25 (weekend); 9 hole €17. **Cards** ▦ ▦ ▬ ▦ **Course Designer** Fred Hawtree **Facilities** ⊗ ⅜ ⅃ ⅄ ⅄ ⅃ ⅃ ⅃ **Leisure** hard tennis courts, heated indoor swimming pool, sauna. **Conf** fac available Corporate Hospitality Days available **Location** 9m from Dublin, follow coast road via Fairview, Clontarf and Sutton. On right 0.5m before Howth Harbour

....
Hotel ★★★ 70% Marine Hotel, Sutton Cross, DUBLIN 13 ☎ 01 8390000 48 en suite

Edmondstown Edmondstown Rd, Edmondstown
☎ 01 4931082 & 4932461 ▤ 01 4933152
e-mail: info@edmondstowngolfclub.ie
A popular and testing parkland course situated at the foot of the Dublin Mountains in the suburbs of the city. Recently completely renovated and redesigned. All greens are now sand based to the highest standard. An attractive stream flows in front of the 4th and 6th greens calling for an accurate approach shot. The new par 3 17th will test the best golfers and the 5th and 12th require thoughtful club selection to the green.

18 holes, 6111mtrs, Par 71, SSS 73.
Club membership 750.
Visitors must contact in advance as there are daily times reserved for members. Limited times after 3.30pm weekends. **Societies** must contact Angela Sterling (marketing manager) in advance. **Green Fees** €55 per round (€65 weekends).. **Cards** ▦ ▦ ▬ ▣ **Prof** Andrew Crofton **Course Designer** McEvoy/Cooke **Facilities** ⊗ ⅜ ⅃ ⅄ ⅄ ⅃ ⅃ ⅃ **Conf** fac available Corporate Hospitality Days available

....
Hotel ★★★ 67% Jurys Montrose Hotel, Stillorgan Rd, DUBLIN ☎ 01 2693311 178 en suite

Continued

Booking a tee time is always advisable.

Elm Park Golf & Sports Club Nutley House,
Nutley Ln, Donnybrook ☎ 01 2693438 🖹 01 2694505
e-mail: office@elmparkgolfclub.ie

Interesting parkland course requiring a degree of accuracy, particularly as half of the holes involve crossing the stream.

18 holes, 5380mtrs, Par 69, SSS 69, Course record 64. Club membership 1850.

Visitors must contact in advance. **Societies** apply in advance. **Green Fees** terms on application. **Cards** 💳 💳 🖻 **Prof** Seamus Green **Course Designer** Paytrick Merrigan **Facilities** ⊗ 🏊 🖳 🍴 ♀ ⚘ 🛒 ᴪ 🚜 ♂ ⚑ **Leisure** hard and grass tennis courts. **Location** 3m from city centre

....

Hotel ★★★★ 72% Jurys Ballsbridge Hotel, Pembroke Rd, Ballsbridge, DUBLIN 4 ☎ 01 660 5000 303 en suite

Foxrock Torquay Rd, Foxrock
☎ 01 2895668 & 2893992

9 holes, 5667mtrs, Par 70, SSS 69.

Telephone for further details

....

Hotel ★★★ 68% The Gresham Royal Marine Hotel, Marine Rd, DUN LAOGHAIRE ☎ 01 2801911 103 en suite

Grange Rathfarnham ☎ 01 4932889
18 holes, 5517mtrs, Par 68, SSS 69.

Location 6m from city centre
Telephone for further details

....

Hotel ★★★ 67% Jurys Montrose Hotel, Stillorgan Rd, DUBLIN ☎ 01 2693311 178 en suite

Howth St Fintan's, Carrickbrack Rd, Sutton
☎ 01 8323055 🖹 01 8321793
e-mail: secretary@howthgolfclub.ie

A heathland course with scenic views of Dublin Bay. It is hilly and presents a good challenge to the novice or expert golfer.

18 holes, 5618mtrs, Par 72, SSS 69. Club membership 1200.

Visitors contact in advance. May not play Wed and weekends. **Societies** must contact in advance. **Green Fees** €50 per day. **Cards** 💳 💳 💳 🖻 **Prof** John McGuirk **Course Designer** James Braid **Facilities** ⊗ by prior arrangement 🏊 by prior arrangement 🖳 🍴 ♀ ⚘ 🛒 🚜 ♂ **Conf** fac available Corporate Hospitality Days available **Location** 9m NE of City Centre, 2m from Sutton Cross, on Sutton side of Hill of Howth

....

Hotel ★★★ 70% Marine Hotel, Sutton Cross, DUBLIN 13 ☎ 01 8390000 48 en suite

Milltown Lower Churchtown Rd
☎ 01 4976090 🖹 01 4976008
e-mail: info@milltowngolfclub.ie

Level parkland course on the outskirts of the city.

18 holes, 5638mtrs, Par 71, SSS 69. Club membership 1400.

Visitors must contact in advance but may not play weekends. **Societies** apply in writing. **Green Fees** €80 per 18 holes. **Cards** 💳 💳 **Prof** John Harnett **Course Designer** Freddie Davis **Facilities** ⊗ 🏊 🖳 🍴 ♀ ⚘ 🛒 ᴪ ♂ **Location** Lower Churchtown Road, Dublin 14

....

Hotel ★★★★ 72% Jurys Ballsbridge Hotel, Pembroke Rd, Ballsbridge, DUBLIN 4 ☎ 01 660 5000 303 en suite

Newlands Clondalkin
☎ 01 4593157 & 4593498 🖹 01 4593498

18 holes, 5714mtrs, Par 71, SSS 70.

Course Designer James Braid
Telephone for further details

....

Hotel ★★★ 68% Jurys Green Isle Hotel, Naas Rd, DUBLIN 22 ☎ 01 4593406 90 en suite

Rathfarnham Newtown
☎ 01 4931201 & 4931561 🖹 01 4931561
e-mail: rgc@oceanfree.net

Parkland course designed by John Jacobs in 1962.

14 holes, 5815mtrs, Par 71, SSS 70, Course record 69. Club membership 685.

Visitors must contact in advance, by arrangement only. **Societies** restricted to Mon, Thu & Fri. **Green Fees** terms on application. **Prof** Brian O'Hara **Course Designer** John Jacobs **Facilities** 🖳 🍴 ♀ ⚘ 🛒 ♂ **Location** M50 Firhouse/Knocklyon exit

....

Hotel ★★★★ 72% Jurys Ballsbridge Hotel, Pembroke Rd, Ballsbridge, DUBLIN 4 ☎ 01 660 5000 303 en suite

Royal Dublin North Bull Island, Dollymount
☎ 01 8336346 🖹 01 8336504
e-mail: jlambe@theroyaldublingolfclub.com

A popular course with visitors, for its design subtleties, the condition of the links and the friendly atmosphere. Founded in 1885, the club moved to its present site in 1889 and received its Royal designation in 1891. A notable former club professional was Christy O'Connor, who was appointed in 1959 and immediately made his name. Along with its many notable holes, Royal Dublin has a fine and testing finish. The 18th is a sharply dog-legged par 4, with out of bounds along the right-hand side. The decision to try the long carry over the 'garden' is one many visitors have regretted.

18 holes, 6002mtrs, Par 72, SSS 71, Course record 63. Club membership 1000.

Visitors must contact in advance & have handicap certificate. May not play Wed, Sat until 4pm. Restricted Sun. **Societies** must book one year in advance. **Green Fees** €130 per round. **Cards** 💳 💳 💳 **Prof** Leonard Owens **Course Designer** H S Colt **Facilities** ⊗ 🏊 🖳 🍴 ♀ ⚘ 🛒 ᴪ 🚜 ♂ **Location** 3.5m NE of city centre.
See advert on page 424.

....

Hotel ★★★ 67% Longfield's Hotel, Fitzwilliam St Lower, DUBLIN 2 ☎ 01 6761367 26 en suite

St Anne's North Bull Island, Dollymount
☎ 01 8336471
18 holes, 5652mtrs, Par 70, SSS 69.
Telephone for further details

Hotel ★★★ 67% Longfield's Hotel, Fitzwilliam St
Lower, DUBLIN 2 ☎ 01 6761367 26 en suite

St Margaret's Golf & Country Club
St Margaret's ☎ 01 8640400 ▤ 01 8640289
e-mail: sales@stmargaretsgolf.com
**A championship standard course which measures
nearly 7,000 yards off the back tees, but flexible teeing
offers a fairer challenge to the middle and high
handicap golfer. The modern design makes wide use of
water hazards and mounding. The par 5 8th hole is set
to become notorious - featuring lakes to the left and
right of the tee and a third lake in front of the green.
Ryder Cup player, Sam Torrance, has described the
18th as 'possibly the strongest and most exciting in the
world'.**
18 holes, 6917yds, Par 73, SSS 73, Course record 69.
Club membership 260.
Visitors may play any day but must reserve tee time in
advance **Societies** apply in writing or telephone or e-mail.
Green Fees not confirmed. **Cards** ▦ ▬ ▬ ▣ **Prof**
Dacvid O'Sullivan **Course Designer** Craddock/Ruddy
Facilities ⊗ ⅢⅬ ♨ ♀ ⚎ ☎ ⚐ ⚑ ⚒ ⚓ ⚔ { **Location** 9m
NW of city centre. From main airport roundabout take exit
for Belfast, after 500ydss take 1st exit from roundabout to
St Margarets just passed 'Coachman's Innbo

Hotel ★★★ 70% Marine Hotel, Sutton Cross, DUBLIN
13 ☎ 01 8390000 48 en suite

The Royal Dublin Golf Club

**North Bull Island, Dollymount
Tel: 01 8336346   Fax: 01 8336504**

email: jlambe@theroyaldublingolfclub.com
www.theroyaldublingolfclub.com

Visitors from home and abroad are always most welcome here at The Royal Dublin Golf Club. The Club is located on the North East Coast of Dublin approximately 5 km from the city centre and just 15 minutes drive from Dublin Airport.

Enjoy the excellent condition of our Championship Links and particularly the fine and testing closing holes. In particular the decision to try the long carry over the 'garden' is one many golfers have regretted.

There is an excellent Dining Room and a feature of the clubhouse, which is one of the finest in Ireland, is the Grill Room off the locker area – ideally suited for a Golfer in a hurry or after your game of golf, with a wide menu selection (Grill Room – dress informal or Dining Room – jacket and tie). Enjoy the 19th (bar facilities) in the Christy O'Connor Room located on the first floor in the Clubhouse (dress informal) or the Members' Bar (jacket and tie) situated overlooking the 18th green with a panoramic view of the course, sea and surrounding landscape.

Stackstown Kellystown Rd, Rathfarnham
☎ 01 4942338 & 4941993 ▤ 01 4933934
e-mail: stackstowngc@eircom.net
**Pleasant course in the foothills of the Dublin mountains,
affording breathtaking views of Dublin City and Bay.
Mature woodland borders every hole and premium is
placed on accuracy off the tee. In 1999 the course was
remodelled and the mountain streams which run
through the course were harnessed to bring them into
play and provide attractive on-course water features.**
18 holes, 6152yds, Par 72, SSS 72, Course record 68.
Club membership 1092.
Visitors preferred Mon, Thu-Fri & Sun pm. **Societies**
telephone in advance and confirm in writing. **Green Fees**
€35 (€45 Sun). **Prof** Michael Kavanagh **Course Designer**
Shaftrey **Facilities** ⊗ Ⅲ Ⅼ ♨ ♀ ♨ ☎ ⚑ ⚒ ⚓ ⚔ ⚐ **Conf**
fac available Corporate Hospitality Days available
Location South on M50 junct 13, follow signs for
Rathfarnham. At 3rd lights left for Leopardstown and
Ticknock. At next lights, follow road under M50,club 300
metres

Hotel ★★★ 67% Jurys Montrose Hotel, Stillorgan Rd,
DUBLIN ☎ 01 2693311 178 en suite

DUN LAOGHAIRE   Map 01 D4

Dun Laoghaire Eglinton Park, Tivoli Rd
☎ 01 2803916 ▤ 01 2804868
e-mail: dlgc@iol.ie
**This is a well wooded parkland course, not long, but
requiring accurate club selection and placing of shots.
The course was designed by Harry Colt in 1918.**

18 holes, 5313mtrs, Par 69, SSS 68, Course record 63.
Club membership 1118.
Visitors restricted Thu, Sat & Sun. Telephone pro on:
2801694 in advance **Societies** must apply in writing.
Green Fees €55 per 18 holes. **Cards** ▦ ▬ **Prof** Vincent
Carey **Course Designer** Harry Colt **Facilities** ⊗ Ⅲ Ⅼ ♨
♀ ♨ ☎ ⚑ ⚐ **Conf** fac available **Location** 0.75m from
town centre and ferry port

Hotel ★★★ 68% The Gresham Royal Marine Hotel,
Marine Rd, DUN LAOGHAIRE ☎ 01 2801911
103 en suite

KILLINEY   Map 01 D4

Killiney Ballinclea Rd ☎ 01 2852823 ▤ 01 2852823
9 holes, 5655mtrs, Par 70, SSS 70.
Telephone for further details

Hotel ★★★★ 68% Fitzpatrick Castle Hotel, KILLINEY
☎ 01 2305400 113 en suite

Portmarnock

Map 01 D4 | Portmarnock

☎ 01 8462968 📄 01 8462601

U niversally acknowledged as one of the truly great links courses, Portmarnock has hosted many great events from the British Amateur Championship of 1949 and the Canada Cup in 1960, to 12 stagings of the revived Irish Open. Founded in 1894, the championship course offers a classic challenge. Surrounded by water on three sides and laid out in a serpentine fashion, no two successive holes play in the same direction. Unlike many courses which play nine out and nine home, Portmarnock demands a continual discernment of wind direction. The course has some extraordinary holes including the 14th, which Henry Cotton regarded as the best hole in golf; the 15th which Arnold Palmer regards as the best par 3 in the world, and the 5th regarded as the best on the course by the late Harry Bradshaw, 40 years Portmarnock's golf professional and runner-up to AD Locke in the 1949 British Open after playing his ball from an empty bottle of stout.

e-mail: liz@portmarnockgolfclub.ie

Visitors Must contact in advance and confirm in writing. Restricted Sat, Sun and public holidays. Handicap certificate required

Societies Must contact in advance in writing

Green Fees Telephone for details

Facilities

Professional Joey Purcell

Location 12m from Dublin, 1m from village down Golf Rd.

Holes/Par/Course record 27 holes
Old Course: 18 holes, 7182yds, Par 72, SSS73
New Course: 9 holes , 3370yds, Par 37

WHERE TO STAY NEARBY

Hotel
PORTMARNOCK
★ ★ ★ ★ ⓐ ⓐ ⓐ Portmarnock Hotel & Golf Links.
☎ 01 8460611. 99 en suite

Championship Course

KILTERNAN
Map 01 D4

Kilternan Golf & Country Club Hotel
☎ 01 2955559 🖷 01 2955670
e-mail: kgc@kilternan-hotel.ie
Interesting and testing course overlooking Dublin Bay.
18 holes, 5491yds, Par 68, SSS 66, Course record 66.
Club membership 720.
Visitors may not play before 1.30pm at weekends. Contact in advance. **Societies** apply in writing/telephone in advance. **Green Fees** not confirmed. **Cards** 🖿 🖿 🖿 🖿 **Course Designer** Eddie Hackett **Facilities** ⊗ ⫫ 🏌 🍺 ♀ 🔺 🖾 🏌 🦽 ⚌ **Leisure** hard tennis courts, heated indoor swimming pool, sauna, gymnasium.

Hotel ★★★★ 68% Fitzpatrick Castle Hotel, KILLINEY ☎ 01 2305400 113 en suite

LUCAN
Map 01 D4

Hermitage Ballydowd ☎ 01 6265049 & 6268491
e-mail: hermitagegolf@eircom.net
Part level, part undulating course bordered by the River Liffey and offering some surprises.
18 holes, 6034mtrs, Par 71, SSS 71.
Club membership 1100.
Visitors Must contact in advance. **Societies** must telephone well in advance. **Green Fees** €75 per 18 holes. **Cards** 🖿 **Prof** Simon Byrne **Course Designer** J McKenna **Facilities** ⊗ ⫫ 🏌 🍺 ♀ 🔺 🖾 🏌 🦽 ⚌ **Location** On N4

Hotel ★★★ 70% Finnstown Country House Hotel, Newcastle Rd, Lucan, DUBLIN ☎ 01 6010700 25 en suite 28 annexe en suite

Lucan Celbridge Rd ☎ 01 6282106 🖷 01 6282929
e-mail: lucangolf@eircom.net
Founded in 1897 as a 9-hole course and extended to 18 holes in 1988, Lucan involves playing over a lane which bisects the 1st and 7th holes. The first nine is undulating while the back nine is flatter and features water hazards and a 538 metre par 5 18th hole.
18 holes, 5958mtrs, Par 71, SSS 71, Course record 67.
Club membership 780.
Visitors may play Mon, Tue & Fri. **Societies** must apply in writing. **Green Fees** €45. **Course Designer** Eddie Hackett **Facilities** ⊗ ⫫ 🏌 🍺 ♀ 🔺 🐾 🦽 ⚌ **Location** N4 W to Celbridge at rear of Spa Hotel

Hotel ★★★ 64% Lucan Spa Hotel, LUCAN ☎ 01 6280494 71 rms (61 en suite)

MALAHIDE
Map 01 D4

Malahide Beechwood, The Grange
☎ 01 8461611 🖷 01 8461270
e-mail: malgc@clubi.ie

Continued

Main Course: 18 holes, 6066mtrs, Par 71.
Course Designer E Hackett **Location** 1m from coast road at Portmarnock
Telephone for further details

Hotel ★★★★ Portmarnock Hotel & Golf Links, Strand Rd, PORTMARNOCK ☎ 01 8460611 99 en suite

PORTMARNOCK See page 425

RATHCOOLE
Map 01 D4

Beech Park Johnstown ☎ 01 4580522 🖷 01 4588365
e-mail: info@beechpark.ie
Relatively flat parkland with heavily wooded fairways. Famous for its 'Amen Corner' (holes 10 to 13).
Beech Park: 18 holes, 5753mtrs, Par 72, SSS 70, Course record 67.
Club membership 1038.
Visitors may not play weekends, telephone in advance. **Societies** apply in writing. **Green Fees** €40 per 18 holes. **Cards** 🖿 🖿 🖿 **Course Designer** Eddie Hackett **Facilities** ⊗ ⫫ 🏌 🍺 ♀ 🔺 🦽 ⚌ **Conf** Corporate Hospitality Days available

Hotel ★★★ 70% Finnstown Country House Hotel, Newcastle Rd, Lucan, DUBLIN ☎ 01 6010700 25 en suite 28 annexe en suite

RUSH
Map 01 D4

Rush ☎ 01 8438177 (Office) 8437548 (Clubhouse)
🖷 01 8438177
e-mail: info@rushgolfclub.com
Seaside borders three fairways on this links course. There are 28 bunkers and undulating fairways to add to the challenge of the variable and strong winds that blow at all times and change with the tides. There are no easy holes!
Rush Golf Course: 9 holes, 5598mtrs, Par 70, SSS 69.
Club membership 500.
Visitors restricted Wed, Thu, weekends & bank holidays. **Societies** telephone or apply in writing. **Green Fees** €32 per round. **Facilities** ⊗ ⫫ 🏌 🍺 ♀ 🔺 ⚌ **Location** Take exit for Rush on M1 going N.

Hotel 🆄 Holiday Inn Dublin Airport, Dublin Airport, DUBLIN ☎ 01 8080500 249 en suite

SAGGART
Map 01 D4

City West Hotel & Golf Resort
☎ 01 4010500 & 4010878 (shop) 🖷 01 4588565
e-mail: info@citywest-hotel.iol.ie
Course west of Dublin comprising 142 acres at the foothills of the Dublin mountains and built on fine parkland. Well wooded and enjoys natural drainage.
Championship: 18 holes, 6314yds, Par 70, SSS 70, Course record 65.
Executive: 18 holes, 5154yds, Par 65, SSS 69.
Visitors time sheet in operation, telephone in advance. **Societies** apply in writing/telephone in advance. **Green Fees** Championship: €40 per round (weekends €50); Executive €35 (weekend €40). **Cards** 🖿 🖿 🖿 🖿 **Course Designer** Christy O'Connor Jnr **Facilities** ⊗ ⫫ 🏌 🍺 ♀ 🔺 🖾 🏌 🦽 🍴 **Leisure** heated indoor swimming pool, fishing, sauna, solarium, gymnasium. **Conf** fac available Corporate Hospitality Days available **Location** Naas road, southbound N7

Continued

....
Hotel ★★★ 65% Bewley's Hotel Newlands Cross, Newlands Cross, Naas Rd, DUBLIN 22 ☎ 01 4640140 260 en suite

SKERRIES
Map 01 D4

Skerries Hacketstown ☎ 01 8491567 📄 01 8491591
e-mail: skerriesgolfclub@eircom.net
18 holes, 6081mtrs, Par 73, SSS 72.
Location E of Dublin-Belfast road
Telephone for further details

....
Hotel ★★★ 65% Boyne Valley Hotel & Country Club, Stameen, Dublin Rd, DROGHEDA ☎ 041 9837737 73 en suite

SWORDS
Map 01 D4

Swords Open Golf Course Balheary Av, Swords
☎ 01 8409819 & 8901030 📄 01 8409819
e-mail: swordsgc@indigo.ie
Parkland course situated beside the River Broadmeadow in unspoilt countryside, 10 miles from Dublin.

18 holes, 5612mtrs, Par 70, SSS 70, Course record 73.
Club membership 475.
Visitors timesheet bookings available all year, telephone to book, may play at any time **Societies** telephone well in advance. **Green Fees** not confirmed. **Course Designer** T Halpin **Facilities** 🏋 🍺 🛆 ⛳ 🏌 **Location** 5 mins from Swords

....
Hotel ★★★ 63% McEniff Skylon Hotel, Drumcondra Rd, DUBLIN 9 ☎ 01 8379121 88 en suite

TALLAGHT
Map 01 D4

Dublin City Ballinascorney
☎ 01 4516430 📄 01 4598445
e-mail: info@dublincitygolf.com
Set in the valley of Glenasmole, this very scenic course offers a variety of terrain, where every hole is different, many would be considered feature holes.
18 holes, 5535yds, Par 69, SSS 67, Course record 63.
Club membership 350.
Visitors please contact in advance, welcome weekdays and weekends at any time. **Societies** contact for details. **Green Fees** terms on application. **Cards** 💳 🖥 **Course Designer** Eddie Hackett **Facilities** 🏋 🍺 🍴 🛆 ⛳ 🏌 🛆 **Conf** fac available **Location** 8m SW of Dublin city centre, M50 junct 11(Firhouse) club 5 mins on R114

....
Hotel ★★★ 68% Jurys Green Isle Hotel, Naas Rd, DUBLIN 22 ☎ 01 4593406 90 en suite

> **Booking a tee time is always advisable.**

BALLINASLOE
Map 01 B4

Ballinasloe Rosglos ☎ 090 9642126 📄 090 9642538
e-mail: ballinasloegolfclub@eircom.net
Well maintained parkland course, extended from a par 68 to a par 72. With a number of feature holes and two water hazards.
18 holes, 5865mtrs, Par 72, SSS 70, Course record 69.
Club membership 884.
Visitors preferably Mon-Sat, contact in advance. **Societies** contact in advance. **Green Fees** €25 per round;€30 weekends. **Cards** 💳 🖥 **Prof** n **Course Designer** E Hackett/E Connaughton **Facilities** ⊗ by prior arrangement 🍺 by prior arrangement 🏋 by prior arrangement 🍺 by prior arrangement 🍴 🛆 ⛳ 🏌 🛆 ⛳ ℓ **Conf** Corporate Hospitality Days available **Location** 2 miles from Ballinasloe Town, on the Portumna road

....
Hotel ★★ 68% Royal Hoey Hotel, Mardyke St, ATHLONE ☎ 090 647 2924 & 647 5395 📄 090 647 5194 38 en suite

BALLYCONNEELY
Map 01 A4

Connemara ☎ 095 23502 & 23602 📄 095 23662
e-mail: links@iol.ie
This championship links course is situated on the verge of the Atlantic Ocean in a most spectacular setting, with the Twelve Bens Mountains in the background. Established as recently as 1973, it is a tough challenge, due in no small part to its exposed location, with the back 9 the equal of any in the world. The last six holes are exceptionally long and offer a great challenge to golfers of all abilities. When the wind blows, club selection is crucial. Notable holes are the 13th (200 yd par 3), the long par 5 14th, the 15th with a green nestling in the hills, the 16th guarded by water and the 17th and 18th, both par 5s over 500 yds long.

Championship: 18 holes, 6666yds, Par 72, SSS 73, Course record 64.
New: 9 holes, 3012yds, Par 35.
Club membership 970.
Visitors advisable to book in advance. Sun am members only **Societies** telephone or email in advance. **Green Fees** Mon-Thu €50 per round; Fri-Sun €55. **Cards** 💳 🖥 **Prof** Hugh O'Neill **Course Designer** Eddie Hackett **Facilities** ⊗ 🏋 🍺 🍴 🍺 🍴 🛆 🏌 🍴 🛆 ⛳ ℓ **Conf** Corporate Hospitality Days available **Location** 9m SW of Clifden

....
Hotel ★★★ 76% Abbeyglen Castle Hotel, Sky Rd, CLIFDEN ☎ 095 21201 38 en suite

BEARNA
Map 01 B3

Bearna Golf and Country Club Corboley
☎ 091 592677 🖷 091 592674
e-mail: info@bearnagolfclub.com
Set amid the beautiful landscape of the west of Ireland and enjoying commanding views of Galway Bay, the golf course covers more than 100 hectares of unique countryside. This has resulted in generously proportioned fairways, many elevated tees and some splendid carries. Water comes into play at thirteen holes and the final four holes provide a memorable finish. New lakes developed on holes 6, 7 and 10 in 2003 with many other improvements.
18 holes, 5746mtrs, Par 72, SSS 72. Course record 68.
Club membership 600.
Visitors must telephone in advance. Can play at any time **Societies** contact in advance. **Green Fees** €35 Mon-Thu (€45 Fri-Sun and bank holidays). **Cards** 🖃 🖃 🖃 **Prof** Declan Cunningham **Course Designer** Robert J Brown **Facilities** ⊗ ⊞ 🖳 ♥ ♀ ♨ 🖻 ↑ ❀ ♨ ∅ **Location** 5miles W Galway City on Spiddal Rd.

Hotel ★★★ 66% Galway Ryan Hotel, Dublin Rd, GALWAY ☎ 091 753181 96 en suite

GALWAY
Map 01 B4

Galway Blackrock, Salthill
☎ 091 522033 🖷 091 529783
e-mail: galwaygolf@eircom.net
Designed by Dr Alister McKenzie, this course is inland by nature, although some of the fairways run close to the ocean. The terrain is of gently sloping hillocks with plenty of trees and furze bushes to catch out the unwary. Although not a long course, it provided a worthy challenge as the venue of the Celtic International Tournament in 1984 and continues to delight the visiting golfer.
18 holes, 6376yds, Par 70, SSS 71, Course record 67.
Club membership 1050.
Visitors preferred on weekdays, except Tue. **Societies** must apply in writing. **Green Fees** terms on application. **Cards** 🖃 🖃 **Prof** Don Wallace **Course Designer** McKenzie **Facilities** ⊗ ⊞ 🖳 ♥ ♀ ♨ 🖻 ↑ ❀ ∅ **Conf** Corporate Hospitality Days available **Location** 2m W in Salthill

Hotel ★★★ 60% Lochlurgain Hotel, 22 Monksfield, Upper Salthill, GALWAY ☎ 091 529595 13 en suite

Glenlo Abbey Bushypark
☎ 091 526666 🖷 091 527800
e-mail: glenlo@iol.ie
9 holes, 6009mtrs, Par 71, SSS 71.
Course Designer Jeff Howes **Location** On N59 Galway/Clifden road 4km from Galway City Centre **Telephone for further details**

Hotel ★★★★ ⚬⚬ 77% Glenlo Abbey Hotel, Bushypark, GALWAY ☎ 091 526666 46 en suite

GORT
Map 01 B3

Gort Castlequarter ☎ 091 632244 🖷 091 632387
e-mail: info@gortgolf.com
Replacing the original 9-hole course, this new 18-hole course, opened in June 1996, offers golfers a

real challenge. The 564yd 9th and the 516yd 17th are played into a prevailing wind and the par 4 dog-leg 7th will test the best.
18 holes, 5705mtrs, Par 71, SSS 69.
Club membership 1060.
Visitors advisable to contact in advance. Sun am reserved for members. **Societies** apply in writing, telephone, fax or e-mail. **Green Fees** €25 per day (€30 weekends). **Cards** 🖃 🖃 **Course Designer** Christy O'Connor Jnr **Facilities** ⊗ by prior arrangement ⊞ by prior arrangement 🖳 ♥ ♀ ♨ 🖻 ↑ ❀ ♨ ∅

Hotel ★★★ 66% Galway Ryan Hotel, Dublin Rd, GALWAY ☎ 091 753181 96 en suite

LOUGHREA
Map 01 B3

Loughrea Bullaun Rd, Graigue
☎ 091 841049 🖷 091 847472
18 holes, 5261metres, Par 69, SSS 67, Course record 68.
Course Designer Eddie Hackett
Telephone for further details

MOUNTBELLEW
Map 01 B4

Mountbellew Ballinasloe
☎ 0905 79259 🖷 0905 79274
A 9-hole wooded parkland course with two quarries and penalty drains to provide hazards.
9 holes, 5143mtrs, Par 69, SSS 66, Course record 63.
Club membership 400.
Visitors welcome. Contact club if you wish to play at weekends. **Societies** by prior arrangement. **Green Fees** not confirmed. **Facilities** 🖳 ♥ ♀ ♨ ∅ ₹ **Location** Of N63 midway between Roscommon/Galway

Hotel ★★ 68% Royal Hoey Hotel, Mardyke St, ATHLONE ☎ 090 647 2924 & 647 5395 🖷 090 647 5194 38 en suite

ORANMORE
Map 01 B3

Athenry Palmerstown ☎ 091 794466 🖷 091 794971
e-mail: athenrygc@eircom.net
A mixture of parkland and heathland built on a limestone base against the backdrop of a large pine forest. The par 3 holes are notable with a feature hole at the 12th - from an elevated tee played between beech and pine trees.
18 holes, 5687metres, Par 70, SSS 70, Course record 67.
Club membership 1000.
Visitors advisable to telephone in advance, may not play Sun or Sat am. **Societies** must apply in writing, telephone, e-mail. **Green Fees** Apr-Sep: €30 per day Mon-Thu (€35 Fri-Sun). Oct-Mar €25 (weekends €28). **Cards** 🖃 🖃 🖃 **Prof** Raymond Ryan **Course Designer** Eddie Hackett **Facilities** ⊗ ⊞ 🖳 ♥ ♀ ♨ 🖻 ↑ ❀ ♨ ∅ ₹ **Conf** Corporate Hospitality Days available **Location** On R348 to Athenry 10km E of Galway City

Hotel ★★★ 66% Galway Ryan Hotel, Dublin Rd, GALWAY ☎ 091 753181 96 en suite

Galway Bay Golf & Country Club Renville
☎ 091 790503 🖷 091 792510
e-mail: gbaygolf@iol.ie
A championship golf course surrounded on three sides by the Atlantic Ocean and featuring water hazards on a number of holes. Each hole has its own characteristics

Continued

Continued

428

made more obvious by the everchanging seaside winds. The design of the course highlights and preserves the ancient historic features of the Renville Peninsula. The spectacular setting and distractingly beautiful and cleverly designed mix of holes presents a real golfing challenge, demanding total concentration.
18 holes, 6533mtrs, Par 72, SSS 73, Course record 68.
Club membership 280.
Visitors Contact in advance, official handicaps required. **Societies** Telephone in advance. **Green Fees** not confirmed. **Cards** ⊞ ▦ ▭ 🌅 ▦ 🏧 🖳 **Prof** Eugene O'Connor **Course Designer** Christy O'Connor Jnr **Facilities** ⊗ ⅷ ⅏ 🏌 ♀ 🛵 🖆 ⛵ ✍ **Leisure** sauna.
Location N18 S towards Limerick/Shannon, turn right for Oranmore at rdbt, through village, follow signs

Hotel ★★★ 59% Victoria Hotel, Victoria Place, Eyre Square, GALWAY ☎ 091 567433 57 en suite

OUGHTERARD
Map 01 B4

Oughterard ☎ 091 552131 📄 091 552377
e-mail: golfough@iol.ie
18 holes, 6660yds, Par 70, SSS 69, Course record 67.
Course Designer P Merrigan **Location** 1m from Oughterard on N59 from Galway
Telephone for further details

Hotel ★★★ ♨♨ 77% Lough Inagh Lodge Hotel, Inagh Valley, RECESS ☎ 095 34706 & 34694 📄 095 34708 12 en suite

PORTUMNA
Map 01 B3

Portumna ☎ 090 9741059 📄 090 9741798
e-mail: portumnagc@eircom.net
Parkland course with mature trees.
18 holes, 6225mtrs, Par 72, SSS 72.
Club membership 900.
Visitors restricted Sat, no green fees Sunday . **Societies** must contact in writing. **Green Fees** terms on application.
Cards ⊞ ▭ **Prof** Richard Clarke **Course Designer** E Connaughton **Facilities** ⊗ ⅷ ⅏ 🏌 ♀ 🛵 🖆 🏌 🐾 🛒 ✍
Location 2.5m from town on Woodford/Ennis road

Hotel ★★★ 63% County Arms Hotel, BIRR ☎ 0509 20791 24 en suite

RENVYLE
Map 01 A4

Renvyle House Hotel ☎ 095 43511 📄 43515
e-mail: renvyle@iol.ie
Pebble Beach course at Renvyle House is an exceptionally demanding 9-hole course. Exposed to Atlantic winds, crosswinds are a regular feature. A lake comes into play on three holes, one of which drives over the water. On four holes the pebble beach and sea demand precision.
Pebble Beach: 9 holes, 3500yds, Par 36, Course record 34.
Club membership 250.
Visitors Must contact in advance. **Societies** Telephone in advance. **Green Fees** not confirmed. **Cards** ⊞ ▦ 🌅 **Facilities** ⊗ ⅷ ⅏ 🏌 ♀ 🛵 🖆 🐾 ✍ **Leisure** hard tennis courts, heated outdoor swimming pool, fishing.
Location From N59 West, right into Recess, left at . Kylemore, right at Letterfrack, proceed for 5m

Hotel ★★★ 70% Renvyle House Hotel, RENVYLE ☎ 095 43511 68 en suite

TUAM
Map 01 B4

Tuam Barnacurragh ☎ 093 28993 📄 093 26003
18 holes, 5513mtrs, Par 72, SSS 69.
Course Designer Eddie Hackett **Location** 0.5m from town on Athenry road
Telephone for further details

Hotel ★★★ 66% Galway Ryan Hotel, Dublin Rd, GALWAY ☎ 091 753181 96 en suite

CO KERRY

BALLYBUNION
See page 431

BALLYFERRITER
Map 01 A2

Dingle Links ☎ 066 9156255 📄 066 9156409
e-mail: dinglegc@iol.ie
This most westerly golf course in Europe has a magnificent scenic location. It is a traditional links course with beautiful turf, many bunkers, a stream that comes into play on 14 holes and, usually, a prevailing wind.
Dingle Links/Ceann Sibeal Golf Club: 18 holes, 6700yds, Par 72, SSS 71, Course record 72.
Club membership 432.
Visitors telephone in advance. **Societies** must contact in advance. **Green Fees** Nov-Feb €35 per 18 holes (weekends €45); Mar,Apr,Oct €45 (€55); May-Sep €60 (€70). **Cards** ⊞ ▦ ▭ **Prof** Dermot O'Connor **Course Designer** Hackett/O'Connor Jnr **Facilities** ⊗ ⅷ ⅏ 🏌 ♀ 🛵 🖆 ✍ **Leisure** buggies for hire May-Oct. **Location** 1.5m from Ballyferriter

Guesthouse ◆◆◆◆ Gormans Clifftop House & Restaurant, Glaise Bheag, Ballydavid, DINGLE ☎ 066 9155162 9 en suite

CASTLEGREGORY
Map 01 A2

Castlegregory Stradbally
☎ 066 7139444 📄 066 7139958
A links course sandwiched between the sea and a freshwater lake and mountains on two sides. The 3rd hole is visually superb with a 365 yard drive into the wind.
9 holes, 2569mtrs, Par 68, SSS 68, Course record 67.
Club membership 378.
Visitors advisable to contact in advance. **Societies** apply in advance. **Green Fees** €27 per 18 holes, €17 per 9 holes.
Course Designer Dr Arthur Spring **Facilities** ⅏ 🏌 ♀ 🛵 🖆 ✍ **Leisure** fishing. **Location** On Main Tralee/Castlegregory/Conor-pass road, 1km from Stradbally village

Hotel ★★★ 67% Abbey Gate Hotel, Maine St, TRALEE ☎ 066 7129888 100 en suite

GLENBEIGH
Map 01 A2

Dooks ☎ 066 9768205 📄 066 9768476
e-mail: office@dooks.com
Old-established course on the sea shore between the Kerry mountains and Dingle Bay. Sand dunes are a feature (the name Dooks is a derivation of the Gaelic word for sand bank) and the course offers a fine challenge in a superb Ring of Kerry location. Recently redesigned by Martin Hantree. *Continued*

18 holes, 6071yds, Par 70, SSS 68.
Club membership 800.
Visitors must contact in advance. Members time reserved.
Societies contact in advance. **Green Fees** €48 per 18
holes. **Cards** 🌐 💳 💳 **Course Designer** Martin Hantree
Facilities ⊗ ⊬ ᕧ 🏌 ♀ ⚘ 🏠 ℉ ❦ ♂ **Conf** Corporate
Hospitality Days available **Location** On N70, between
Killorglin and Glenbeigh

Hotel ★★★ 70% Gleneagle Hotel, KILLARNEY
☎ 064 36000 250 en suite

KENMARE   Map 01 B2

Kenmare Kilgarvan Rd ☎ 064 41291 📄 064 42061
18 holes, 5615yds, Par 71.
Course Designer Eddie Hackett
Telephone for further details

Hotel ★★★★ ⚲ Park Hotel Kenmare, KENMARE
☎ 064 41200 49 en suite

Ring of Kerry Golf & Country Club

Templenoe ☎ 064 42000 📄 064 42533
e-mail: reservations@ringofkerrygolf.com
**A world class golf facility with spectacular views across
Kenmare Bay. Opened in 1998, the club has gone from
strength to strength and is fast becoming a 'must play'
course for golfers visiting the area. Every hole is
memorable.**

18 holes, 6416yds, Par 72, SSS 71.
Club membership 250.
Visitors advisable to pre-book at weekends. **Societies** book
beforehand by telephone, in writing or by e-mail. **Green
Fees** 18 holes €80; 36 holes €120. **Cards** 🌐 💳 💳
Prof Adrian Whitehead **Course Designer** Eddie Hackett
Facilities ⊗ ⊬ by prior arrangement 🏌 🏌 ♀ ⚘ 🏠 ℉
♂ ❰ **Conf** fac available Corporate Hospitality Days
available **Location** 4m W of Kenmare

Hotel ★★★★ ⚲ Sheen Falls Lodge, KENMARE
☎ 064 41600 66 en suite

KILLARNEY   Map 01 B2

Beaufort Churchtown, Beaufort
☎ 064 44440 📄 064 44752
e-mail: beaufortgc@eircom.net
**A championship standard par 71 parkland course
designed by Dr Arthur Spring. This course is in the
centre of south-west Ireland's golfing mecca. Old ruins
of an 11th century castle dominate the back nine and
the whole course is overlooked by the MacGillycuddy**

Reeks. **The par 3 8th and par 4 11th are two of the most
memorable holes.**

Beaufort

18 holes, 6600yds, Par 71, SSS 72, Course record 68.
Club membership 350.
Visitors booking advisable for weekends. **Societies**
advance booking essential. **Green Fees** €45 (€55
weekends). **Cards** 🌐 💳 💳 💳 💳 💳 **Prof** Hugh
Duggan **Course Designer** Arthur Spring **Facilities** ⊗ ⊬ 🏌
🏌 ♀ ⚘ 🏠 ℉ ♂ **Conf** Corporate Hospitality Days
available **Location** 7m W of Killarney, off N72 w

Hotel ★★★ 68% Castlerosse Hotel, KILLARNEY
☎ 064 31144 121 en suite

Killarney Golf & Fishing Club Mahony's Point
☎ 064 31034 📄 064 33065
e-mail: reservations@killarney-golf.com
**The three courses are parkland with tree-lined
fairways; many bunkers and small lakes provide no
mean challenge. Mahoney's Point Course has a
particularly testing par 5, 4, 3 finish and the courses
call for great skill from the tee. Killarney has been the
venue for many important events, including the 1996
Curtis Cup, and is a favourite of many famous golfers.**
*Mahony's Point: 18 holes, 5826mtrs, Par 72, SSS 72,
Course record 64.*
*Killeen: 18 holes, 6001mtrs, Par 72, SSS 72, Course
record 68.*
Lackabane: 18 holes, 6011mtrs, Par 72, SSS 72.
Club membership 1300.
Visitors advisable to contact in advance. Neat casual dress
required in the clubhouse and on the course. **Societies** must
telephone in advance/apply in writing. **Green Fees** per 18
holes: Mahony's Point €80, Killeen €85, Lackabane €50.
Cards 🌐 💳 💳 💳 💳 **Prof** Tony Coveney **Course
Designer** H Longhurst/Sir Guy Campbell **Facilities** ⊗ ⊬
🏌 🏌 ♀ ⚘ 🏠 ℉ ❦ ♂ ❰ **Leisure** sauna, gymnasium.
Conf Corporate Hospitality Days available **Location** On N
72, Ring of Kerry road

Hotel ★★★★ Aghadoe Heights Hotel, KILLARNEY
☎ 064 31766 56 en suite

KILLORGLIN   Map 01 A2

Killorglin Stealroe ☎ 066 9761979 📄 066 9761437
e-mail: kilgolf@iol.ie
**A parkland course designed by Eddie Hackett as a
challenging but fair test of golf, surrounded by
magnificent views.**
18 holes, 6497yds, Par 72, SSS 71, Course record 68.
Club membership 510.
Visitors pre booking of tee time advisable. Deposit

Continued

Continued

Ballybunion

| Map 01 A3 | Ballybunion |

☎ 068 27146   🖹 068 27387

Hailed for its excellent links courses, Ballybunion is recognised for its fine development of the natural terrain. Mr Murphy built the Old Course in 1906. With large sand dunes and an Atlantic backdrop, Ballybunion offers the golfer an exciting round of golf in a scenic location; but be warned, the Old Course is difficult to play in the wind. President Clinton played Ballybunion on his historic visit to Ireland in 1998. Although overshadowed by the Old Course, the Cashen Course designed by Robert Trent Jones is also world class. Narrow fairways, small greens and large dunes characterise the course.

e-mail: bbgolfgc@ioe.ie

Visitors Must contact in advance. May not play at weekends.

Societies Apply in advance

Green Fees Old Course €125 per round, Cashen Course €85 per round, €160 for both

Facilities ⊗ ⟩〛 🖾 🖥 ♀ 🗴 🖾 🖤 ⚷ ↾

Professional Brian O'Callaghan

Location Sandhill Rd, Ballybunion
(20 miles N of Tralee).

Holes/Par/Course record 36 holes.
Old Course: 18 holes, 6603 yds, Par 71, SSS 72, Course record 67
Cashen Course: 18 holes, 6216 yds, Par 72, SSS 71

WHERE TO STAY NEARBY

Hotels
BALLYBUNION

◆◆◆◆ Cashen Course House
☎ 068 27351. 9 en suite

◆◆◆◆ Tides
☎ 068 27980. 5 en suite

BALLYHEIGE

★★★ ⊚ 66% The White Sands
☎ 066 7133102. 81 en suite

TRALEE

★★★ 69% Meadowlands Hotel
☎ 066 7180444. 56 en suite

★★★ 64% Abbey Gate.
☎ 066 7129888. 100 en suite

Championship Course

required for groups. **Societies** book by telephone, confirm in writing. **Green Fees** €25 (weekends & bank holidays €30). **Cards** ⬜⬜⬜⬜ **Course Designer** Eddie Hackett **Facilities** ⊗ 🏌 🛒 💷 ♀ 👥 🏠 🍴 🐾 🚗 ⚙ **Leisure** fishing. **Location** 3km from Killorglin, on N70 to Tralee

Guesthouse ♦♦♦♦ The Grove Lodge, Killarney Rd, KILLORGLIN ☎ 066 9761157 10 en suite

PARKNASILLA

Map 01 A2

Parknasilla ☎ 064 45122 📠 064 45323

9 holes, 5400mtrs, Par 70, SSS 69.
Course Designer Arthur Spring **Location** 2m E of Sneem village on Ring of Kerry road
Telephone for further details

Hotel ★★★★ 75% Great Southern Hotel, PARKNASILLA ☎ 064 45122 24 en suite 59 annexe en suite

TRALEE

Map 01 A2

Tralee West Barrow ☎ 066 7136379 📠 066 7136008 e-mail: info@traleegolfclub.com
The first Arnold Palmer designed course in Europe, this magnificent 18-hole links is set in spectacular scenery on the Barrow peninsula, surrounded on three sides by the sea. Perhaps the most memorable hole is the par four 17th which plays from a high tee, across a deep gorge to a green perched high against a backdrop of mountains. The back 9 are very difficult and challenging. Not suitable for beginners.
18 holes, 5939mtrs, Par 71, SSS 71, Course record 66.
Club membership 1190.
Visitors may play before 4.20pm on weekdays but only between 7.30-10.30am on Wed & 11am-1.30pm on Sat & 11.30-1pm bank holidays. Must have a handicap certificate and contact in advance. May not play Sun. **Societies** weekdays only; must contact in writing. **Green Fees** €150 per round. **Cards** ⬜⬜⬜ **Prof** David Power **Course Designer** Arnold Palmer **Facilities** ⊗ 🏌 🛒 💷 ♀ 👥 🏠 🍴 ⚙ 🍴 **Location** 8m NW of Tralee off Spa-Fenit Road

Hotel ★★★ 69% Meadowlands Hotel, Oakpark, TRALEE ☎ 066 7180444 58 en suite

WATERVILLE

Map 01 A2

Waterville House & Golf Links
☎ 066 9474102 📠 066 9474482
e-mail: wvgolf@iol.ie
On the western tip of the Ring of Kerry, this course is highly regarded by many top golfers. The feature holes are the par 5 11th, which runs along a rugged

Continued

valley between towering dunes, and the par 3 17th, which features an exceptionally elevated tee. Needless to say, the surroundings are beautiful.
18 holes, 6640yds, Par 72, SSS 72, Course record 65.
Visitors please contact in advance. **Societies** must contact secretary/manager in advance. **Green Fees** €150 per round (€105 before 8am & after 4pm Mon-Thu). **Cards** ⬜⬜ ⬜⬜ **Prof** Liam Higgins **Course Designer** Eddie Hackett/Tom Fazio **Facilities** ⊗ 🏌 🛒 💷 ♀ 👥 🏠 🍴 🐾 🚗 ⚙ ⚙ **Leisure** heated outdoor swimming pool, fishing, sauna. **Location** on the ring of Kerry route (N70) a quarter-mile from Waterville Village.

Hotel ★★★ 76% Butler Arms Hotel, WATERVILLE ☎ 066 9474144 40 en suite

CO KILDARE

ATHY

Map 01 C3

Athy Geraldine ☎ 059 8631729 📠 059 8634710 e-mail: info@athygolfclub.com
The course was upgraded in 2003 to include new tees, new bunkers, a new par 5 with a lake feature and trees have been planted to create a more exacting course.
18 holes, 6159yds, Par 72, SSS 70, Course record 68.
Club membership 800.
Visitors advisable to call in advance, no green fees on Sun **Societies** apply in writing or e-mail to the Hon Secretary **Green Fees** €25 per 18 holes (€35 Sat and bank holidays). **Cards** ⬜⬜ ⬜⬜ **Course Designer** Jeff Howes **Facilities** ⊗ 🏌 by prior arrangement 🛒 💷 ♀ 👥 🚗 ⚙ **Conf** fac available Corporate Hospitality Days available **Location** 1m N of Athy on Kildare road

Guesthouse ♦♦♦♦♦ Coursetown Country House, Stradbally Rd, ATHY ☎ 059 8631101 5 en suite

CARBURY

Map 01 C4

Highfield Highfield House
☎ 046 9731021 📠 046 9731021
e-mail: hgc@indigo.ie
A relatively flat parkland course but with interesting undulations, especially by the fast flowing stream which runs through many holes. The 7th dog-legs over the lake, the 10th is a great par 5 with a challenging green, the 14th par 3 is over rushes onto a plateau green (out of bounds on left) and the 18th par 3 green is tucked between bunkers and a huge chestnut tree.
18 holes, 5707mtrs, Par 72, SSS 69.
Club membership 500.
Visitors welcome, must contact in advance for weekend play. **Societies** telephone or apply in writing. **Green Fees** not confirmed. **Cards** ⬜⬜ **Prof** Peter O'Hagan **Course Designer** Alan Duggan **Facilities** 🛒 💷 ♀ 👥 🍴 🐾 🚗 ⚙ 🍴 **Location** take M4 from Dublin, situated 9m S of Enfield

Hotel ★★★★ 72% Keadeen Hotel, NEWBRIDGE ☎ 045 431666 75 en suite

CASTLEDERMOT

Map 01 C3

Kilkea Castle ☎ 0503 45555 📠 0503 45505
e-mail: kilkeagolfclub@eircom.net
18 holes, 6200mtrs, Par 71, SSS 71.
Telephone for further details

Continued

Kilkea Castle

Hotel ★★★ 70% Seven Oaks Hotel, Athy Rd, CARLOW
☎ 059 913 1308 59 en suite

DONADEA Map 01 C4

Knockanally Golf & Country Club
☎ 045 869322 📠 045 869322
e-mail: golf@knockanally.com
Home of the Irish International Professional Matchplay championship, this parkland course is set in a former estate, with a Palladian-style clubhouse.
18 holes, 6485yds, Par 72, SSS 72, Course record 66. Club membership 500.
Visitors may not play on Sun 8.30am-noon. **Societies** must contact in writing or telephone. **Green Fees** not confirmed. **Prof** Martin Darcy **Course Designer** Noel Lyons **Facilities** **Leisure** fishing. **Location** 3m off main Dublin-Galway road between Kilcock & Enfield

Hotel ★★★ 64% Lucan Spa Hotel, LUCAN
☎ 01 6280494 71 rms (61 en suite)

KILDARE Map 01 C3

Cill Dara Cill Dara, Little Curragh
☎ 045 521295 & 521433
e-mail: cilldaragolfclub@ireland.com
9 holes, 5852mtrs, Par 71, SSS 70, Course record 64.
Location 1m E of Kildare
Telephone for further details

Hotel ★★★★ 72% Keadeen Hotel, NEWBRIDGE
☎ 045 431666 75 en suite

The Curragh Curragh
☎ 045 441238 & 441714 📠 045 441714
A particularly challenging course, well wooded and with lovely scenery all around.
18 holes, 6035mtrs, Par 72, SSS 71, Course record 63. Club membership 1040.
Visitors must contact in advance, preferred on Mon, Wed, Thu & Fri. **Societies** apply in writing. **Green Fees** 18 holes €32 (weekends €40). **Prof** Gerry Burke **Facilities** **Location** Off N7 between Newbridge & Kildare

Hotel ★★★★ 72% Keadeen Hotel, NEWBRIDGE
☎ 045 431666 75 en suite

KILL Map 01 D4

Killeen ☎ 045 866003 📠 045 875881
e-mail: admin@killeengc.ie
Set in pleasant countryside, the attractive course is characterised by its many lakes. It provides a challenge to test the skills of the moderate enthusiast and the more experienced golfer.
18 holes, 5561mtrs, Par 71, SSS 71, Course record 70. Club membership 170.
Visitors please ring for tee-times **Societies** must contact in advance. **Green Fees** not confirmed. **Cards** **Course Designer** Pat Ruddy/M Kelly **Facilities** **Location** Off N7 at Kill signposted

Hotel ★★★ 76% Barberstown Castle, STRAFFAN
☎ 01 6288157 22 en suite

NAAS Map 01 D4

Bodenstown Sallins ☎ 045 897096
Bodenstown: 18 holes, 6132mtrs, Par 71, SSS 71.
Ladyhill: 18 holes, 5428mtrs, Par 71, SSS 68.
Course Designer Richard Mather **Location** 4m from town near Bodenstown graveyard
Telephone for further details

Hotel ★★★ 66% Downshire House Hotel, BLESSINGTON ☎ 045 865199 14 en suite 11 annexe en suite

Craddockstown Blessington Rd
☎ 045 897610 📠 045 896968
e-mail: gaynolan@craddockstown.com
A parkland course with easy walking. A major redevelopment has recently been conmpleted with new tee boxes, 2 new greens, many water features, fairway improvements and the redevelopment of all greenside bunkers.
18 holes, 5726mtrs, Par 71, SSS 69, Course record 66. Club membership 800.
Visitors should ring in advance to verify tee times available, limited at weekends. **Societies** apply in writing. **Green Fees** 18 holes €40. **Cards** **Course Designer** A Spring **Facilities** **Conf** fac available Corporate Hospitality Days available **Location** Off the main dual carriageway (N7/N97), head towards Naas, turn left on to Blessington Road

Hotel ★★★ 59% Ambassador Hotel, KILL
☎ 045 877064 36 en suite

Naas Kerdiffstown
☎ 045 897509 & 874644 📠 045 896109
e-mail: naasgolfclubisdn@eircom.net
Scenic parkland course, well bunkered, with a substantial number of trees; greens are both sand-based and natural. Additional water hazards provide a challenge to golfers of all levels.
18 holes, 5663mtrs, Par 71, SSS 69, Course record 65. Club membership 1200.
Visitors may not play on Sun, Tue or Thu. **Societies** must contact in advance by telephone. **Green Fees** €32 per round (€42 weekends & bank holiday). **Cards** **Course Designer** E Hackett/A Spring/J Howes **Facilities** **Location** 1m from town on Sallins-Johnstown road N7

Hotel ★★★ 66% Downshire House Hotel, BLESSINGTON ☎ 045 865199 14 en suite 11 annexe en suite

Prices may change during the currency of the Guide, please check when booking.

Continued

Woodlands Cooleragh, Coill Dubh
☎ 045 860777 📄 045 860988
9 holes, 6408yds, Par 72, SSS 71.
Course Designer Tommy Halpin **Location** Off the
Clane/Edenderry road
Telephone for further details

Hotel ★★★★ 72% Keadeen Hotel, NEWBRIDGE
☎ 045 431666 75 en suite

STRAFFAN
Map 01 D4

Castlewarden ☎ 01 4589254 & 4589838
📄 01 4588972
e-mail: info@castlewardengolfclub.com
**Founded in 1990, Castlewarden is maturing into a
delightful parkland course with excellent greens.**
18 holes, 6496yds, Par 72, SSS 70.
Club membership 765.
Visitors welcome contact for details. Tues Ladies Day.
Societies by prior application. **Green Fees** not confirmed.
Prof Gerry Egan **Course Designer** Tommy Halpin
Facilities ⊗ ♨ ♂ ♥ ♀ ♨ 🏠 ⛳ 🏌 ♿ ⚙ **Location**
Between Naas/Rathcoole

Hotel ★★★★★ 🏌 The Kildare Hotel & Golf Club,
STRAFFAN ☎ 01 6017200 69 en suite
10 annexe en suite

The K Club ☎ 01 6017300 📄 01 6017399
e-mail: golf@kclub.ie
**New South Course opened in July 2003 alongside North
Course both designed by Arnold Palmer. Both are a
challenge to even the best golfers. Covering 220 acres of
prime Kildare woodland with 14 man-made lakes as
well as the River Liffey to create water hazards.**

*The K Club - North Course: 18 holes, 6526mtrs, Par 74,
SSS 72. Course record 65.*
*The K Club - South Course: 18 holes, 6636mtrs, Par 72,
SSS 72.*
Club membership 540.
Visitors contact in advance to book preferred tee times,
restricted at members times. **Societies** telephone & write in
advance, societies not allowed on Sats & Wed afternoon.
Green Fees terms on application. **Cards** 🌐 💳 💳 💳
Prof John McHenry/Peter O'Hagan **Course Designer**
Arnold Palmer **Facilities** ⊗ ♨ ♂ ♥ ♀ ♨ 🏠 ⛳ 🏌 🏇 ♿
⚙ ⚑ **Leisure** heated indoor swimming pool, fishing, sauna,
solarium, gymnasium. **Conf** Facilities Available Corporate
Hospitality Days Available **Location** From Dublin take N4
and exit R406, entrance to hotel on right in Straffan

Hotel ★★★★★ 🏌 The Kildare Hotel & Golf Club,
STRAFFAN ☎ 01 6017200 69 en suite
10 annexe en suite

CALLAN
Map 01 C3

Callan Geraldine ☎ 056 25136 & 25949 📄 056 55155
e-mail: info@callangolfclub.com
**Meadowland course with well positioned spinneys and
water hazards. Not difficult walking and a good test for
golfers of all standards.**
18 holes, 6422yds, Par 72, SSS 70, Course record 66.
Club membership 800.
Visitors contact in advance. **Societies** must apply in
writing. **Green Fees** not confirmed. **Cards** 🌐 💳 💳
Prof John O'Dwyer **Course Designer** B Moore/J Power
Facilities ⊗ ♨ ♂ ♥ ♀ ♨ 🏠 ⛳ 🏌 ⚙ **Leisure** fishing.
Location 1m from Callan on the Knocktopher Road

Hotel ★★★ 73% Newpark Hotel, KILKENNY
☎ 056 776 0500 111 en suite

KILKENNY
Map 01 C3

Kilkenny Glendine ☎ 056 7765400 📄 056 7723593
e-mail: enquiries@kilkennygolfclub.com
**One of Ireland's most pleasant inland courses, noted
for its tricky finishing holes and its par threes. Features
of the course are its long 11th and 13th holes and the
challenge increases year by year as thousands of trees
planted over the last 30 years or so are maturing. As
host of the Kilkenny Scratch Cup, the course is
permanently maintained in championship condition.
The Irish Dunlop Tournament and Irish Professional
Matchplay Championship have also been held here.**
18 holes, 5925mtrs, Par 71, SSS 70, Course record 68.
Club membership 1368.
Visitors must contact in advance. **Societies** must contact in
advance. **Green Fees** €35 per 18 holes (€40 weekends &
bank holidays). **Cards** 🌐 💳 **Prof** Jimmy Bolger
Facilities ⊗ ♨ ♂ ♥ ♀ ♨ 🏠 ⛳ 🏌 🏇 ♿ ⚙ ⚑ **Location** 1m
from centre on Castlecomer road

Hotel ★★★ 64% Langtons Hotel, 69 John St, KILKENNY
☎ 056 776 5133 14 en suite 16 annexe en suite

THOMASTOWN
See page 435

ABBEYLEIX
Map 01 C3

Abbeyleix Rathmoyle ☎ 0502 31450 📄 0502 30108
A pleasant, parkland 18 hole course.
18 holes, 5557mtrs, Par 72, SSS 70.
Club membership 470.
Visitors welcome weekdays. **Societies** apply in writing.
Green Fees not confirmed. **Course Designer** Mel
Flanagan **Facilities** ⊗ ♂ ♥ ♀ ♨ ⚙ **Location** 0.4m
outside town of Abbeyleix on Ballyroaw road

Hotel ★★★ 73% Newpark Hotel, KILKENNY
☎ 056 776 0500 111 en suite

MOUNTRATH
Map 01 C3

Mountrath Knockanina
☎ 0502 32558 & 32643 (office) 📄 0502 32643
**A picturesque course at the foot of the Slieve Bloom
Mountains. The 18 hole course has fine fairways,**
Continued

Mount Juliet

Map 01 C3

Thomastown

☎ 056 7773064 📄 056 7773078

Venue for the American Express World Golf Championships in 2002 and again in 2004, Mount Juliet's superb 18-hole golf course was designed by Jack Nicklaus. It has also hosted many prestigious events including the Irish Open on three occasions. The course boasts a cleverly concealed drainage and irrigation system, perfect even when inclement weather would otherwise preclude play. It takes advantage of the estate's mature landscape to provide a world-class 72-par challenge for professionals and high-handicap golfers alike. A unique three-hole golfing academy has been added to offer both novice and experienced players ample opportunity to improve their game, while a new 18-hole putting course provides an extra dimension of golfing pleasure and is the venue for the National Putting Championship.

e-mail: golfinfo@mountjuliet.ie

Visitors Welcome, contact in advance

Societies Book in advance by telephone or in writing

Green Fees 18 holes €140–€155 depending on season. Discounts for groups and hotel residents

Facilities ⊗ ⅀ ⅃ ⯑ ⯑ ⯑ ⯑ ⯑ ⯑
⯑ ⯑ ⯑

Conf facilities available; corporate hospitality days available

Professional Sean Cotter

Leisure Tennis, indoor swimming pool, private fishing, sauna, solarium, gym, horse riding, clay target shooting, archery

Location Thomastown (4km south of Thomastown on N9 Dublin / Waterford Rd.)

Holes/Par/Course record 18 holes, 6926 yds, Par 72, SSS 73, Course record 62

Championship Course

WHERE TO STAY NEARBY

Hotels
THOMASTOWN

★★★★ ◉ ◉ ⚓
Mount Juliet Conrad Hotel
☎ 056 7773000. 32 en suite 27 annexe en suite

KILKENNY

★★★★ ◉ 70% Kilkenny River Court
☎ 056 7723388. 90 en suite

★★★ 73% Newpark Hotel
☎ 056 7760500. 111 en suite

★★★ 64% Langton House
☎ 056 7765133. 14 en suite 16 annexe en suite

the **River Nore** flows through the course.
18 holes, 5493mtrs, Par 71, SSS 69, Course record 68.
Club membership 800.
Visitors check for availability at weekends, other days no
problem but safer to check. **Societies** must contact in
advance. **Green Fees** 18 holes €20 (weekends €25); (Dec-
Feb €15). **Facilities** ⊗ by prior arrangement ᴸ ⬛ ♥ ♨ ⚑
⛳ 𝒞 **Location** 1.5m from town on Dublin-Limerick road

Hotel ★★★★ 72% Keadeen Hotel, NEWBRIDGE
☎ 045 431666 75 en suite

PORTARLINGTON   Map 01 C3

Portarlington Garryhinch
☎ 0502 23115 📄 0502 23044
e-mail: portalingtongc@eircom.net
Lovely parkland course designed around a pine forest.
It is bounded on the 16th and 17th by the River Barrow
which makes the back 9 very challenging.
18 holes, 5723mtrs, Par 71, SSS 70, Course record 66.
Club membership 700.
Visitors welcome but restricted Tue-Ladies Day, Sat &
Sun societies and club competitions. Must contact in
advance **Societies** must apply in writing. **Green Fees** not
confirmed. **Cards** 🎫 💳 **Course Designer** Eddie Hackett
Facilities ⊗ ⅲ ᴸ ⬛ ♥ ♨ 🏠 ♥ ♨ 𝒞 **Conf** Corporate
Hospitality Days available **Location** 4m from town on
Mountmellick road

Hotel ★★★★ 72% Keadeen Hotel, NEWBRIDGE
☎ 045 431666 75 en suite

PORTLAOISE   Map 01 C3

The Heath
☎ 0502 46533 & 46045 (office) 📄 0502 46866
e-mail: info@theheathgc.ie
Course noted for its rough heather and gorze furze and
scenic views of the rolling hills of Co Laois.
18 holes, 5857mtrs, Par 71, SSS 70, Course record 67.
Club membership 950.
Visitors contact in advance, preferred on weekdays.
Societies apply in writing to the Administrator **Green Fees**
€18 per 18 holes (€34 weekends and bank holidays).
Cards 🎫 💳 **Prof** Mark O'Boyle **Facilities** ⊗ ⅲ
ᴸ ⬛ ♥ ♨ 🏠 ♨ 𝒞 ⚑ **Location** 4m N on N7

Hotel ★★★★ 72% Keadeen Hotel, NEWBRIDGE
☎ 045 431666 75 en suite

RATHDOWNEY   Map 01 C3

Rathdowney ☎ 0505 46170 📄 0505 46065
e-mail: rathdowneygolf@eircom.net
An 18 hole parkland course, with undulating terrain.
The 17th hole is a tricky par 3, 12th and 15th are
particularly tough par 4s and the 6th is a challenging
par 5 (550yds) into the prevailing wind.
18 holes, 5894mtrs, Par 71, SSS 70, Course record 67.
Club membership 500.
Visitors welcome. Ladies have priority on Wed, Sat & Sun
mornings are reserved for member & societies. **Societies**
must apply in writing and pay deposit to confirm booking.
Green Fees €20 (€25 weekends). **Course Designer**
Eddie Hackett **Facilities** ⊗ by prior arrangement ᴸ ⬛ ♥
♨ ♨ 𝒞 **Location** 0.5m SE. Follow Johnstown signs
from town square

Hotel ★★★ 73% Newpark Hotel, KILKENNY
☎ 056 776 0500 111 en suite

CO LEITRIM

BALLINAMORE   Map 01 C4

Ballinamore ☎ 071 9644346
A very dry and very testing 9-hole parkland course
along the Ballinamore/Ballyconnell Canal. Not busy on
weekdays which makes it ideal for high handicap
golfers.
9 holes, 5680yds, Par 70, SSS 68, Course record 66.
Club membership 300.
Visitors welcome 6 days per week,competition on most
Sundays. Visitors welcome to play in open competitions.
Societies must contact in writing or telephone secretary.
Green Fees terms on application. **Course Designer** A
Spring **Facilities** ⬛ ♨ ♨ **Leisure** fishing. **Location** 2m
from Ballinamore, along Shannon-Erne water-way canal

Hotel ★★★★ 70% Slieve Russell Hotel Golf and
Country Club, BALLYCONNELL ☎ 049 9526444
157 en suite

CARRICK-ON-SHANNON   Map 01 C4

Carrick-on-Shannon Woodbrook
☎ 071 9667015 📄 071 9667015
e-mail: ckgc@eircom.net
A pleasant 9-hole course overlooking the River Shannon.
A fine test of golf for both those with low and high
handicaps. A further 9 holes have recently been added.
9 holes, 5545mtrs, Par 70, SSS 68.
Club membership 400.
Visitors welcome, contact in advance to avoid
competitions. **Societies** must contact in advance. **Green
Fees** not confirmed. **Course Designer** Eddie Hackett
Facilities ⊗ ⅲ ᴸ ⬛ ♥ ♨ ⚑ 𝒞 **Location** 4m W beside N4

Hotel ★★★★ 70% Slieve Russell Hotel Golf and
Country Club, BALLYCONNELL ☎ 049 9526444
157 en suite

CO LIMERICK

ADARE   Map 01 B3

Adare Manor ☎ 061 396204 📄 061 396800
e-mail: info@adaremanorgolfclub.com
An 18-hole parkland course, par 69, in an unusual
setting. The course surrounds the ruins of a 13th-
century castle and a 15th-century abbey.
18 holes, 5800yds, Par 69, SSS 69, Course record 63.
Club membership 750.
Visitors welcome weekdays, weekends only by
arrangement and subject to availability. Advisable to
contact in advance. **Societies** apply in writing or e-mail
Green Fees €35 per round. **Cards** 🎫 💳 **Course
Designer** Ben Sayers/Eddie Hacket **Facilities** ⊗ ⅲ ᴸ ⬛
♥ ♨ 🏠 ⚑ 𝒞 **Location** 10m from Limerick City, on
Killarney road

Hotel ★★★★ 70% Dunraven Arms Hotel, ADARE
☎ 061 396633 75 en suite

LIMERICK   Map 01 B3

Castletroy Castletroy
☎ 061 335753 & 335261 📄 061 335373
e-mail: cgc@iol.ie
Parkland course with out of bounds on the left of the

Continued

first two holes. The par three 13th has a panoramic view of the course and surrounding countryside from the tee and the 18th is a daunting finish, with the drive played towards a valley with the ground rising towards the green. In recent years the club has hosted the finals of the Irish Mixed Foursomes and the Senior Championships.

18 holes, 5854mtrs, Par 71, SSS 70, Course record 65. Club membership 1062.

Visitors must contact in advance & have handicap certificate but may not play Sun or 1-2.30pm weekdays. **Societies** apply in writing. **Green Fees** €40 per 18 holes (€50 Fri-Sun and bank holidays). **Cards** 🔲 🔲 🔲 **Facilities** ⊗ ⅲ ⅇ ♨ ♀ ⚲ ⌂ ⛳ ⚑ ⚒ ✂ **Conf** Corporate Hospitality Days available **Location** 3m from city on Dublin road

....

Hotel ★★★★ 70% Castletroy Park Hotel, Dublin Rd, LIMERICK ☎ 061 335566 107 en suite

Limerick
Ballyclough ☎ 061 415146 📠 061 319219 e-mail: pat.murray@limerickgc.com

Tree-lined parkland course which hosted the 1991 Ladies Senior Interprovincial matches. The club are the only Irish winners of the European Cup Winners Team Championship.

18 holes, 5938mtrs, Par 72, SSS 71, Course record 63. Club membership 1300.

Visitors may not play after 4pm or on Tue & weekends. **Societies** must contact in writing. **Green Fees** terms on application. **Cards** 🔲 🔲 **Prof** Lee Harrington **Course Designer** A McKenzie **Facilities** ⊗ ⅲ ⅇ ♨ ♀ ⚲ ⌂ ⛳ ✂ **Conf** Corporate Hospitality Days available **Location** 3m S on Fedamore Road

....

Hotel ★★★ 73% Jurys Hotel, Ennis Rd, LIMERICK ☎ 061 327777 95 en suite

Limerick County Golf & Country Club
Ballyneety ☎ 61 351881 📠 61 351384 e-mail: lcgolf@ioi.ie

Limerick County was designed by Des Smyth and presents beautifully because of the strategic location of the main features. It has over 70 bunkers with six lakes and several unique design features.

18 holes, 6712yds, Par 72, SSS 74, Course record 70. Club membership 800.

Visitors welcome but prebooking essential. **Societies** book by telephone or in writing. **Green Fees** Mon-Thu €40 per round; Fri-Sun €60. **Cards** 🔲 🔲 🔲 🔲 **Prof** Donal McSweeney **Course Designer** Des Smyth **Facilities** ⊗ ⅲ ⅇ ♨ ♀ ⚲ ⌂ ⛳ ⚑ ⚒ ✂ **Conf** fac available Corporate Hospitality Days available **Location** 5m SE of Limerick on R512

....

Hotel ★★★ 65% Hotel Greenhills, Caherdavin, LIMERICK ☎ 061 453033 18 rms (13 en suite)

NEWCASTLE WEST   Map 01 B3

Killeline
Cork Rd ☎ 069 61600 📠 069 77428 e-mail: killeline@eircom.net

18 holes, 6671yds, Par 72, SSS 68.

Location 0.25m off main Limerick/Killarney route **Telephone for further details**

....

Hotel ★★★★ 70% Dunraven Arms Hotel, ADARE ☎ 061 396633 75 en suite

Newcastle West
Ardagh ☎ 069 76500 📠 069 76511 e-mail: ncwgolf@eircom.net

Course set in 150 acres of unspoilt countryside, built to the highest standards on sandy free draining soil. A practice ground and driving range are included. A signature hole is the par 3 6th playing 185 yards over a lake.

18 holes, 6141yds, Par 71, SSS 72, Course record 67. Club membership 1019.

Visitors advisable to contact in advance, but available most days. **Societies** contact in advance. **Green Fees** terms on application. **Cards** 🔲 🔲 **Prof** Tom Murphy **Course Designer** Dr Arthur Spring **Facilities** ⊗ ⅲ ⅇ ♨ ♀ ⚲ ⌂ ⛳ ✂ ⚑ **Conf** fac available Corporate Hospitality Days available **Location** 2m off N21 between Limerick & Killarney

....

Hotel ★★★★ 70% Dunraven Arms Hotel, ADARE ☎ 061 396633 75 en suite

CO LONGFORD

LONGFORD   Map 01 C4

County Longford
Glack, Dublin Rd ☎ 043 46310 📠 043 47082 e-mail: colonggolf@eircom.net

18 holes, 6044yds, Par 70, SSS 69, Course record 69.

Location E of town **Telephone for further details**

....

Hotel ★★★ 69% Abbey Hotel Conference & Leisure, Galway Rd, ROSCOMMON ☎ 090 662 6240 50 en suite

CO LOUTH

ARDEE   Map 01 D4

Ardee
Townparks ☎ 041 6853227 📠 041 6856137 e-mail: ardeegolfclub@eircom.net

Pleasant parkland course with mature trees and a stream. Five new holes laid out in 1996. The 13th hole is a par 3 over water and is the main feature of the course.

18 holes, 6464yds, Par 71, SSS 72, Course record 64. Club membership 680.

Visitors Must contact Pro on 041 6853227. **Societies** apply by writing/email/phone to Secretary/Manager **Green Fees** €35 per 18 holes (€50 Sat). **Cards** 🔲 🔲 **Prof** Scott Kirkpatrick **Course Designer** Eddie Hackett & Declan Branigan **Facilities** ⊗ ⅇ ♨ ♀ ⚲ ⌂ ⛳ ⚑ ⚒ ✂ **Conf** Corporate Hospitality Days available **Location** exit M1 at

Continued

437

N33 (Ardee/Derry Road) 7km to Ardee town; 400 yrds from Fair Green

Hotel ★★★ 73% Ballymascanlon House Hotel, DUNDALK ☎ 042 9358200 90 en suite

BALTRAY
Map 01 D4

County Louth ☎ 041 9881530 🖹 041 9881531
e-mail: reservations@countylouthgolfclub.com
Generally held to have the best greens in Ireland, this links course was designed by Tom Simpson to have well guarded and attractive greens without being overly dependant on bunkers. It provides a good test for the modern champion, notably as the annual venue for the East of Ireland Amateur Open.
18 holes, 6673yds, Par 72, SSS 72.
Club membership 1342.
Visitors must contact in advance. Societies by prior arrangement. Green Fees €100 per round (€120 weekends). Cards 🔲 🔲 🔲 Prof Paddy McGuirk Course Designer Tom Simpson Facilities ⊗ ⅲ ⅃ ♥ ♀ ⚄ 🛇 ☂ ⚒ ➤ ⚙ ⚡ Leisure hard tennis courts.
Location 5m NE of Drogheda

Hotel ★★★ 61% Conyngham Arms Hotel, SLANE ☎ 041 9884444 16 en suite

DUNDALK
Map 01 D4

Ballymascanlon House Hotel
☎ 042 9358200 🖹 042 9371598
e-mail: info@ballymascanlon.com
A testing 18-hole parkland course with numerous water hazards and two difficult holes through woodland, this very scenic course is set at the edge of the Cooley Mountains.

18 holes, 5548yds, Par 68, SSS 66.
Visitors must telephone in advance to check availability. Societies booking by telephone or letter. Green Fees terms on application. Cards 🔲 🔲 🔲 🔲 🔲 Course Designer Craddock/Ruddy Facilities ⊗ ⅲ ⅃ ♥ ♀ ⚄ 🛇 ☂ ⚒ ➤ ⚙ ⚡ ⚡ Leisure hard tennis courts, heated indoor swimming pool, sauna, gymnasium. Conf fac available Corporate Hospitality Days available Location 3m N of Dundalk on the Carlingford road

Hotel ★★★ 73% Ballymascanlon House Hotel, DUNDALK ☎ 042 9358200 90 en suite

Dundalk Blackrock ☎ 042 9321731 🖹 042 22022
e-mail: dwgc@iol.ie
Championship course with fine views of mountain and sea.
18 holes, 6028mtrs, Par 72, SSS 71.

Club membership 1500.
Visitors must contact in advance and may not play Tue or Sun. Societies must apply in writing in advance. Green Fees not confirmed. Cards 🔲 🔲 Prof Leslie Walker Facilities ⊗ ⅲ ⅃ ♥ ♀ ⚄ 🛇 ☂ ⚒ ⚡ Leisure sauna. Location 2.5m S on coast road from Dundalk

Hotel ★★★ 73% Ballymascanlon House Hotel, DUNDALK ☎ 042 9358200 90 en suite

Killin Park Killin Park
☎ 042 9339303 🖹 042 9331412
Opened in 1991 and designed by Eddie Hackett, this undulating 18-hole parkland course has mature woodland and river features. It provides challenging golf and breathtaking scenery. Bordered on the north side by Killin Wood and on the south by the Castletown River.
Killinbeg Park Golf Course: 18 holes, 5293yds, Par 69, SSS 65, Course record 65.
Club membership 300.
Visitors no restrictions. Societies apply by telephone or in writing in advance. Green Fees €20 per 18 holes (€25 weekends and bank holidays). Course Designer Eddie Hackett Facilities ⊗ by prior arrangement ⅲ by prior arrangement ⅃ ♥ ♀ ⚄ 🛇 ☂ ➤ ⚙ ⚡ Location take Castle Blaney road from Dundalk, turn right at 'Fagans Lounge' and keep to main road until river bridge, Course on left

Hotel ★★★ 73% Ballymascanlon House Hotel, DUNDALK ☎ 042 9358200 90 en suite

GREENORE
Map 01 D4

Greenore ☎ 042 9373212 & 9373678 🖹 042 9383898
e-mail: greenoregolfclub@eircom.net
Situated amidst beautiful scenery on the shores of Carlingford Lough, with views of the Mourne Mountains. The pine trees here are an unusual feature on a semi-links course. There are quite a number of water facilities, tight fairways and very good greens.
18 holes, 6647yds, Par 71, SSS 73, Course record 69.
Club membership 1035.
Visitors must contact in advance at weekends. Societies must contact in advance especially for weekend play. Green Fees €35 per round (€50 weekends & bank holidays). Cards 🔲 🔲 🔲 Prof Mr Robert Giles Course Designer Eddie Hackett Facilities ⊗ ⅲ ⅃ ♥ ♀ ⚄ 🛇 ➤ ⚙ ⚡ ⚡ Leisure Golf lessons available on request but must be pre booked. Conf Corporate Hospitality Days available Location halfway between Dublin and Belfast on M1. Exit at Dundalk, Co Louth. 10m on East Coast road to Earlingford/Greenmore

Hotel ★★★ 73% Ballymascanlon House Hotel, DUNDALK ☎ 042 9358200 90 en suite

TERMONFECKIN
Map 01 D4

Seapoint ☎ 041 9822333 🖹 041 9822331
e-mail: golflinks@seepoint.ie
A premier championship links course of 7,100 yards with a particularly interesting 17th hole.
18 holes, 6420mtrs, Par 72, SSS 74.
Club membership 580.
Visitors phone in advance for restrictions. Societies telephone in advance. Green Fees €40 Mon-Thur; €50 Fri; €60 weekends (half price for 9 holes). Cards 🔲 🔲

Continued   *Continued*

Prof David Carroll **Course Designer** Des Smyth
Facilities ⊗ 〉Ⅲ ⓛ ⓛ ♈ ♀ △ 🛆 ⌇Γ ➘ 🛆 ♂ ໐ **Location** 4m
NE of Drogheda

....

Hotel ★★★ 61% Conyngham Arms Hotel, SLANE
☎ 041 9884444 16 en suite

CO MAYO

BALLINA   Map 01 B4

Ballina Mossgrove, Shanaghy
☎ 096 21050 📄 096 21718
e-mail: ballinagc@eircom.net
Undulating but mostly flat inland course.
18 holes, 6103yds, Par 71, SSS 69, Course record 69.
Club membership 520.
Visitors welcome but may not play Sun before 11.30am.
Societies apply in writing or telephone in advance. **Green
Fees** not confirmed. **Cards** 🖃 🖃 ▦ **Course Designer**
E Hackett **Facilities** ⓛ ♈ ♀ △ ⌇Γ ♂ **Location** 1m
outside town on Bonnocolon Rd

BALLINROBE   Map 01 B4

Ballinrobe Cloonacastle
☎ 094 9541118 📄 094 9541889
e-mail: bgcgolf@iol.ie
**A championship parkland 18 hole course, set in the
mature woodlands of a historic estate at Cloonacastle.
The layout of the course incorporates seven man made
lakes with the river Robe flowing at the back of the 3rd
and 5th greens. Ballinrobe is full of charm and
character typified by the 19th century period residence
now used as the clubhouse.**
18 holes, 6043mtrs, Par 73, SSS 72, Course record 67.
Club membership 650.
Visitors welcome daily, telephone to reserve Tee-time.
Societies must telephone or write to Secretary in advance.
Green Fees terms on application. **Cards** 🖃 ▦ **Prof**
Courtney Cougar **Course Designer** Eddie Hackett
Facilities ⊗ 〉Ⅲ ⓛ ♈ ♀ △ 🛆 ⌇Γ ➘ 🛆 ♂ ໐ **Conf**
Corporate Hospitality Days available **Location** Off N84
onto R331 to Claremorris

BALLYHAUNIS   Map 01 B4

Ballyhaunis Coolnaha ☎ 0907 30014 📄 094 81829
e-mail: tmack@tinet.ie
9 holes, 5413mtrs, Par 70, SSS 68, Course record 68.
Location 3m N on N83
Telephone for further details

BELMULLET   Map 01 A5

Carne Carne ☎ 097 82292 📄 097 81477
e-mail: carngolf@iol.ie
**A wild tumultuous roller-coaster landscape, which has
been shaped into an inspirational links course by Eddie
Hackett.**
18 holes, 6119mtrs, Par 72, SSS 72, Course record 66.
Club membership 460.
Visitors welcome, booking essential to guarantee tee-time.
Societies booking advisable. **Green Fees** €50 per day
(weekends & bank holidays €50 per round). **Cards** 🖃
▦ **Course Designer** Eddie Hackett **Facilities** ⊗ 〉Ⅲ ⓛ ♈
♀ △ 🛆 ⌇Γ 🛆 ♂ **Location** 2m from Belmullet

Carne Golf Course

CASTLEBAR   Map 01 B4

Castlebar Hawthorn Av, Rocklands
☎ 094 21649 📄 094 26088
e-mail: castlebargolf@eircom.ie
18 holes, 5698mtrs, Par 71, SSS 70.
Course Designer Peter McEvoy **Location** 1m from town
on Belcarra road
Telephone for further details

....

Hotel ★★ 64% Welcome Inn Hotel, CASTLEBAR
☎ 094 902 2288 & 902 2054 📄 094 902 1766
40 en suite

CLAREMORRIS   Map 01 B4

Claremorris Castlemacgarrett
☎ 094 93 71527 📄 094 93 72919
e-mail: claremorrisgc@ebookireland.com
**A 18 hole parkland course designed by Tom Craddock,
designer of Druids Glen. It consists of many eye-
catching water features, bunkers, trees and wooded
backgrounds. Noted by golfers for its layout, variation
on each hole and the quality of the sand based greens.**
*Claremorris Golf Course: 18 holes, 6600mtrs, Par 73, SSS
70, Course record 68.*
Club membership 550.
Visitors contact club for availability. **Societies** contact 094
9371527 for details. **Green Fees** Oct-Mar €23/€28 per
round; Apr-Sep €30/€33. **Cards** 🖃 ▦ **Course
Designer** Tom Craddock **Facilities** ⊗ by prior
arrangement 〉Ⅲ by prior arrangement ⓛ ♈ ♀ △ ⌇Γ 🛆 ♂
Location 1.5m from town, on N17 S of Claremorris

....

Hotel ★★★ 63% Belmont Hotel, KNOCK ☎ 094 938
8122 63 en suite

KEEL   Map 01 A4

Achill Achill Island, Westport ☎ 098 43456
e-mail: achillgolfclub@eircom.net
**Seaside links in a scenic location on the edge of the
Atlantic Ocean.**
9 holes, 2723mtrs, Par 70, SSS 66, Course record 69.
Club membership 240.
Visitors welcome but cannot play on some Sundays
Societies must write or telephone in advance. **Green Fees**
terms on application. **Facilities** ♈ △ **Location** 15 Km
towards Keel Village

....

Hotel ★★★ 73% Hotel Westport Conference & Leisure
Centre, Newport Rd, WESTPORT ☎ 098 25122
129 en suite

Continued

439

SWINFORD
Map 01 B4

Swinford Brabazon Park
☎ 094 9251378 📄 094 9251378
e-mail: regantommy@eircom.net
A pleasant parkland course with good views of the beautiful surrounding countryside.
9 holes, 5542mtrs, Par 70, SSS 68.
Club membership 420.
Visitors must contact in advance in peak season. **Societies** must apply in writing or telephone in advance. **Green Fees** terms on application. **Facilities** 🔟 💷 ♀ 🛎 ⚐ **Location** On old Kiltimagh raod, .5 miles from town

Hotel ★★ 64% Welcome Inn Hotel, CASTLEBAR
☎ 094 902 2288 & 902 2054 📄 094 902 1766 40 en suite

WESTPORT
Map 01 B4

Westport Carrowholly
☎ 098 28262 & 27070 📄 098 27217
e-mail: wpgolf@eircom.net
This is a beautiful course with wonderful views of Clew Bay, with its 365 islands, and the holy mountain called Croagh Patrick, famous for the annual pilgrimage to its summit. Golfers indulge in a different kind of penance on this challenging course with many memorable holes. Perhaps the most exciting is the par five 15th, 580 yards long and featuring a long carry from the tee over an inlet of Clew Bay.
18 holes, 6667yds, Par 73, SSS 71, Course record 65.
Club membership 600.
Visitors must contact in advance. No visitors during members times. **Societies** apply in writing or telephone/email well in advance. **Green Fees** €36/€40 per round (weekends €43/€50). **Cards** 💳 💳 💳 **Prof** Alex Mealia **Course Designer** Fred Hawtree **Facilities** ⊗)Ⅲ 🔟 💷 ♀ 🛎 🛎 ⚐ 🐾 🛎 ⚐ 🍷 **Conf** Corporate Hospitality Days available **Location** 2.5m from town on Newport road

Hotel ★★★ 73% Hotel Westport Conference & Leisure Centre, Newport Rd, WESTPORT ☎ 098 25122 129 en suite

CO MEATH

BETTYSTOWN
Map 01 D4

Laytown & Bettystown
☎ 041 9827170 📄 041 28506
e-mail: bettystowngolfclub@utvinternet.com
A very competitive and trying links course, home of famous golfer, Des Smyth.

18 holes, 5652mtrs, Par 71, SSS 70, Course record 65.
Club membership 950.
Visitors may not play 1-2pm. Advisable to contact in advance. **Societies** must contact in writing. **Green Fees** €45 per 18 holes (€55 weekends and bank holidays). **Cards** 💳 💳 **Prof** Robert J Browne **Facilities** ⊗)Ⅲ 🔟 💷 ♀ 🛎 🛎 🐾 ⚐ **Leisure** hard tennis courts. **Location** off N1(M1), turn off at signs for Julianstown/Laytown/Bettystown

Hotel ★★★ 61% Conyngham Arms Hotel, SLANE
☎ 041 9884444 16 en suite

DUNSHAUGHLIN
Map 01 D4

Black Bush Thomastown
☎ 01 8250021 📄 01 8250400
e-mail: golf@blackbush.iol.ie

Black Bush: 18 holes, 6930yds, Par 73, SSS 72.
Agore: 18 holes, 6598yds, Par 71, SSS 69.
Thomastown: 18 holes, 6433yds, Par 70, SSS 68.
Course Designer Bobby Browne **Location** 1.5m from village on Dunshaughlin-Ratoath road
Telephone for further details

Hotel ★★★ 70% Finnstown Country House Hotel, Newcastle Rd, Lucan, DUBLIN ☎ 01 6010700 25 en suite 28 annexe en suite

KELLS
Map 01 C4

Headfort ☎ 046 9240146 📄 046 9249282
e-mail: hgcadmin@eircom.net
The Old Course is a delightful parkland course which is regarded as one of the best of its kind in Ireland. There are ample opportunities for birdies, but even if these are not achieved, provides for a most pleasant game. The New Course is a challenging course with water featuring on 13 of its 18 holes. Not a course for the faint hearted, this is a course for the thinking golfer.
Headfort Golf Club-Old Course: 18 holes, 5973mtrs, Par 72, SSS 71.
Headfort Golf Club-New Course: 18 holes, 6164, Par 72, SSS 74.
Club membership 1608.
Visitors Must contact in advance, timesheets in operation **Societies** must apply in writing. **Green Fees** Old Course: €40 per round (€45 Fri-Sun). New Course; €55per round (€60 Fri-Sun). **Cards** 💳 💳 💳 **Prof** Brendan McGovern **Course Designer** Christy O'Connor jnr **Facilities** ⊗)Ⅲ 🔟 💷 ♀ 🛎 🛎 🐾 🛎 ⚐ **Location** 0.5m 0n N3, E of Kells

Hotel ★★★ 64% Ardboyne Hotel, Dublin Rd, NAVAN
☎ 046 902 3119 29 en suite

Continued

KILCOCK   Map 01 C4

Kilcock Gallow ☎ 01 6287592 🗎 01 6287283
e-mail: kilcockgolfclub@eircom.net
A parkland course with generous fairways, manicured greens and light rough only.
18 holes, 5775mtrs, Par 72, SSS 70, Course record 69.
Club membership 700.
Visitors must contact in advance for weekends, no problem weekdays. **Societies** telephone for dates available. **Green Fees** €25 per 18 holes(€30 Fri-Sun & bank holidays). **Cards** 🏧 **Course Designer** Eddie Hackett **Facilities** ⊗ ⅏ ⅃ ■ ♀ ⚲ ⚒ ✆ **Location** 2m from end of M4

Hotel ★★★ 64% Lucan Spa Hotel, LUCAN ☎ 01 6280494 71 rms (61 en suite)

NAVAN   Map 01 C4

Royal Tara Bellinter
☎ 046 25508 & 25244 🗎 046 25508
e-mail: info@royaltaragolfclub.com
Pleasant parkland course offering plenty of variety. Situated close to the Hill of Tara, the ancient seat of the Kings of Ireland:
New Course: 18 holes, 5757mtrs, Par 71, SSS 70.
Bellinter Nine: 9 holes, 3184yds, Par 35, SSS 35.
Club membership 1000.
Visitors prior arrangement is advisable. Tue is ladies day. **Societies** apply in writing or telephone. **Green Fees** not confirmed. **Cards** 🌐 📠 **Prof** Adam Whiston **Course Designer** Des Smyth **Facilities** ⊗ ⅏ ⅃ ■ ♀ ⚲ 🏠 ✆ ➤ ⚒ ✆ **Conf** fac available Corporate Hospitality Days available **Location** 6m from town on N3

Hotel ★★★ 64% Ardboyne Hotel, Dublin Rd, NAVAN ☎ 046 902 3119 29 en suite

TRIM   Map 01 C4

County Meath Newtownmoynagh
☎ 046 31463 🗎 046 37554
Originally a 9-hole course opened in 1971, it was extended to 18-holes in 1990. It is maturing into a very challenging and formidable parkland course with four testing par 5s. Luxurious clubhouse with panoramic views across the course.
18 holes, 6720mtrs, Par 73, SSS 72, Course record 68.
Club membership 900.
Visitors welcome; some restrictions telephone for details. **Societies** not Sun, enquiries welcome. **Green Fees** not confirmed. **Cards** 🌐 📠 📠 📶 **Prof** Robin Machin **Course Designer** Eddie Hackett/Tom Craddock **Facilities** ⊗ ⅏ ⅃ ■ ♀ ⚲ 🏠 ✆ **Leisure** snooker. **Location** 3m outside Trim on Trim/Longwood rd

Hotel ★★★ 61% Conyngham Arms Hotel, SLANE ☎ 041 9884444 16 en suite

CO MONAGHAN

CARRICKMACROSS   Map 01 C4

Mannan Castle Donaghmoyne
☎ 042 9663308 🗎 042 9663195
Parkland and picturesque, the course features the par 3 2nd to an island green. The short par 4 12th through the woods and the 14th to 18th, all crossing water at

least once. **A test of golf for both amateur and professional.**
18 holes, 6500yds, Par 70, SSS 69.
Club membership 700.
Visitors may play anytime except competition times Sat, Sun & Wed from 2-2.30pm. **Societies** apply in writing to the secretary. **Green Fees** not confirmed. **Course Designer** F Ainsworth **Facilities** ⊗ ⅏ ⅃ ■ ♀ ⚲ ✆ **Location** 4m N

Hotel ★★★ 73% Ballymascanlon House Hotel, DUNDALK ☎ 042 9358200 90 en suite

Nuremore ☎ 042 9671368 🗎 042 9661853
e-mail: nuremore@eircom.net
Picturesque parkland course of championship length incorporating the drumlins and lakes which are a natural feature of the Monaghan countryside. Precision is required on the 10th to drive over a large lake and between a narrow avenue of trees. Signature hole 18th.
18 holes, 6400yds, Par 71, SSS 69, Course record 64.
Club membership 250.
Visitors welcome all times but must contact Maurice Cassidy in advance. **Societies** must contact in advance. **Green Fees** €35 (€42 weeekends and bank holidays). **Cards** 🌐 📠 📠 📶 **Prof** Maurice Cassidy **Course Designer** Eddie Hackett **Facilities** ⊗ ⅏ ⅃ ■ ♀ ⚲ 🏠 ✆ ➤ ⚲ ⚒ ✆ **Leisure** hard tennis courts, heated indoor swimming pool, squash, fishing, sauna, gymnasium. **Conf** fac available Corporate Hospitality Days available **Location** 1m S of Carrickmacross, on main N2

Hotel ★★★★ 75% Nuremore Hotel, CARRICKMACROSS ☎ 042 9661438 72 en suite

CASTLEBLAYNEY   Map 01 C4

Castleblayney Onomy
☎ 042 9740451 🗎 042 9740451
e-mail: rayker@eircom.net
Scenic course on Muckno Park estate, adjacent to Muckno Lake and Hope Castle.
9 holes, 5378yds, Par 68, SSS 66, Course record 65.
Club membership 280.
Visitors no visitors allowed during major weekend competitions. **Societies** must contact in advance. **Green Fees** not confirmed. **Course Designer** Bobby Browne **Facilities** ⅃ ■ ✆ **Leisure** fishing. **Location** Situated on the Hope Castle Estate, in the town of Castleblayney

Hotel ★★★ 73% Ballymascanlon House Hotel, DUNDALK ☎ 042 9358200 90 en suite

CLONES   Map 01 C5

Clones Hilton Park
☎ 047 56017 & 56913 🗎 047 56913
e-mail: clonesgolfclub@eircom.net
Parkland course set in Drumlin country and renowned for the quality of the greens and the wildlife. Due to limestone belt, the course is very dry and playable all year round. There is a timesheet in operation on Saturday and Sunday.
18 holes, 5549mtrs, Par 69, SSS 69, Course record 62.
Club membership 330.
Visitors must contact in advance.Timesheets in operation at weekends. **Societies** telephone in advance. **Green Fees** €25 per round. **Cards** 📠 📠 **Course Designer** Dr Arthur Spring **Facilities** ⊗ ⅏ ⅃ ■ ♀ ⚲ ⚒ ✆ ✆ **Conf** Corporate Hospitality Days available **Location** 3m from Clones on Scotshouse rd

Continued

Continued

Hotel ★★★★ 61% Hillgrove Hotel, Old Armagh Rd, MONAGHAN ☎ 047 81288 44 en suite

MONAGHAN Map 01 C5

Rossmore Rossmore Park, Cootehill Rd
☎ 047 71222
An undulating 18-hole parkland course amidst beautiful countryside.
18 holes, 5590mtrs, Par 70, SSS 69, Course record 68.
Club membership 800.
Visitors must contact in advance, telephone Pro Shop on 047 71222. **Societies** must apply in writing or telephone in advance **Green Fees** not confirmed. **Cards** 🔳 🔳 **Prof** Gareth McShea **Course Designer** Des Smyth **Facilities** ⓑ ♟♀♨🏌🔒🏌 **Leisure** snooker & pool. **Location** 2m S on Cootehill Road

Hotel ★★★★ 61% Hillgrove Hotel, Old Armagh Rd, MONAGHAN ☎ 047 81288 44 en suite

CO OFFALY

BIRR Map 01 C3

Birr The Glenns ☎ 0509 20082 🖺 0509 22155
e-mail: birrgolfclub@eircom.net
The course has been laid out over undulating parkland utilising the natural contours of the land, which were created during the ice age. The sandy subsoil means that the course is playable all year round.
18 holes, 5700mtrs, Par 70, SSS 70, Course record 62.
Club membership 750.
Visitors contact in advance. **Societies** advance contact to secretary. **Green Fees** not confirmed. **Course Designer** Eddie Connaughton **Facilities** ⊗ ⚆ ⓑ ♨♀♨🏌🔒🏌 🏌 ♂ ⚆ **Location** 2 miles W of Birr town en route to Banagher)

Hotel ★★★ 63% County Arms Hotel, BIRR ☎ 0509 20791 24 en suite

DAINGEAN Map 01 C4

Castle Barna ☎ 0506 53384 🖺 0506 53077
e-mail: info@castlebarna.ie
Parkland course on the bank of the Grand Canal. Many mature trees, natural streams and the naturally undulating landscape provide a great challenge for golfers of all abilities.
Castle Barna Golf Course: 18 holes, 5798mtrs, Par 72, SSS 69, Course record 66.
Club membership 600.
Visitors may not play Sun am from 8-12 noon. **Societies** telephone to check availability. **Green Fees** €20 per round (€27 weekends and bank holidays). **Cards** 🔳 🔳 **Course Designer** Alan Duggan/Kieran Monahan **Facilities** ⊗ by prior arrangement ⚆ by prior arrangement ⓑ ♟♀♨🏌 🏌 🏌 ♂ **Conf** Corporate Hospitality Days available **Location** 7m off main Dublin to Galway road (N6) at Tyrellspass.

EDENDERRY Map 01 C4

Edenderry ☎ 046 9731072 🖺 046 9733911
e-mail: enquiries@edenderrygolfclub.com
A most friendly club which offers a relaxing game in pleasant surroundings. In 1992 the course was extended to 18 holes.

18 holes, 6029mtrs, Par 72, SSS 72, Course record 66.
Club membership 700.
Visitors restricted Thu & weekends, ring for times. **Societies** may not play on Thu & Sun; must contact the secretary in writing. **Green Fees** not confirmed. **Course Designer** Havers/Hackett **Facilities** ⊗ ⚆ ⓑ ♟♀♨ ♂ **Conf** fac available Corporate Hospitality Days available **Location** off main Dublin to Edenderry road, 0.75m outside Edenderry on Dublin side

Hotel 🏠 Crookedwood House, Crookedwood, MULLINGAR ☎ 044 72165 8 en suite

TULLAMORE Map 01 C4

Tullamore Brookfield
☎ 0506 21439 🖺 0506 41806
e-mail: tullamoregolfclub@eircom.net
Parkland course set amongst mature hardwood trees on the edge of the town. The visitor is guaranteed delightful scenery, splendid fairways, well manicured rough and superb greens. The course is level and suitable for all ages and abilities.
18 holes, 6196yds, Par 70, SSS 71, Course record 68.
Club membership 1000.
Visitors must contact in advance, restricted on Tue & at weekends. **Societies** must contact in advance. **Green Fees** Mon-Fri €37 per 18 holes (€48 Sat). **Cards** 🔳 🔳 **Prof** Donagh McArdle **Course Designer** James Braid/Paddy Merrigam **Facilities** ⊗ ⚆ ⓑ ♟♀♨🏌🔒🏌 ♂ **Location** 2.5m SW on Kinnity road

Hotel ★★★ 70% Hodson Bay Hotel, Hodson Bay, ATHLONE ☎ 090 6442000 133 en suite

CO ROSCOMMON

ATHLONE Map 01 C4

Athlone Hodson Bay ☎ 0902 92073 🖺 0902 94080
18 holes, 5854mtrs, Par 71, SSS 71, Course record 66.
Course Designer J McAllister **Location** 4m from town beside Lough Ree
Telephone for further details

Hotel ★★★ 70% Hodson Bay Hotel, Hodson Bay, ATHLONE ☎ 090 6442000 133 en suite

BALLAGHADERREEN Map 01 B4

Ballaghaderreen ☎ 094 9860295
Mature 9-hole course with an abundance of trees. Accuracy off the tee is vital for a good score. Small protected greens require a good short-iron plan. The par 3, 5th hole at 178 yards has ruined many a good score.

Continued

Continued

9 holes, 5727yds, Par 70, SSS 67, Course record 68.
Club membership 250.
Visitors no restrictions. **Societies** apply in writing or telephone during office hours. **Green Fees** €15 per day. **Course Designer** Paddy Skerritt **Facilities** ⓑ ♥ ♀ ♧ ♂
Location 2m S of town

BOYLE   Map 01 B4

Boyle Roscommon Rd ☎ 0719 9662594
Situated on a low hill and surrounded by beautiful scenery, this is an undemanding course where, due to the generous fairways and semi-rough, the leisure golfer is likely to finish the round with the same golf ball.
9 holes, 5324mtrs, Par 67, SSS 66, Course record 65.
Club membership 621.
Visitors no restrictions. **Societies** must contact in writing.
Green Fees €15 per day. **Course Designer** E Hackett
Facilities ⊗ by prior arrangement ⅷ by prior arrangement ⓑ ♥ ♀ ♧ ♂ **Location** 2m from Boyle on the Roscommon road

CASTLEREA   Map 01 B4

Castlerea Clonalis ☎ 0907 20068 & 20705
9 holes, 4974mtrs, Par 68, SSS 66, Course record 62.
Location On Dublin/Castlebar road
Telephone for further details
....
Hotel ★★★ 69% Abbey Hotel Conference & Leisure, Galway Rd, ROSCOMMON ☎ 090 662 6240 50 en suite

ROSCOMMON   Map 01 B4

Roscommon Mote Park
☎ 090 6626382 & 26931 🖹 090 6626043
e-mail: rosegolfclub@eircom.net
Located on the rolling pastures of the old Mote Park estate, this recently extended 18-hole course successfully blends the old established nine holes with an exciting and equally demanding new 9-hole lay-out. Numerous water hazards, notably on the tricky 13th, multi-tiered greens and an excellent irrigation to give an all-weather surface.
18 holes, 6290mtrs, Par 72, SSS 70.
Club membership 700.
Visitors contact in advance,especially Sundays. **Societies** apply in writing or telephone. **Green Fees** €30 (€35 weekends). **Course Designer** E Connaughton **Facilities** ⊗ ⅷ ⓑ ♥ ♀ ♧ ♂ ♂ **Location** 0.5m S of Roscommon town
....
Hotel ★★★ 69% Abbey Hotel Conference & Leisure, Galway Rd, ROSCOMMON ☎ 090 662 6240 50 en suite

STROKESTOWN   Map 01 C4

Strokestown Bumlin ☎ 078 33528
Picturesque 9-hole course set in parkland with fine views. A new 9 hole course completed in summer 2001.
9 holes, 2615mtrs, Par 68.
Club membership 250.
Visitors may play any times except during competitions.
Societies apply in writing or telephone at least 2 weeks in advance. **Green Fees** terms on application. **Course Designer** Mel Flanagan **Facilities** ♧ **Location** 1.5m from Strokestown
....
Hotel ★★★ 69% Abbey Hotel Conference & Leisure, Galway Rd, ROSCOMMON ☎ 090 662 6240 50 en suite

CO SLIGO

BALLYMOTE   Map 01 B4

Ballymote Ballinascarrow
☎ 071 9183089 🖹 071 9189210
e-mail: jocon@iol.ie
Although Ballymote was founded in 1940, the course dates from 1993 and has matured well into a parkland course with ample fairways and large greens. It has recently been improved with new tees, 20 bunkers and 2 new greens. The feature par 4 7th hole has been redesigned with the green surrounded by water and Ballinascarrow Lake in the background. A challenging course set in breathtaking scenery.
9 holes, 5302mtrs, Par 70, SSS 68.
Club membership 250.
Visitors no restrictions **Societies** telephone in advance.
Green Fees €20 per day. **Course Designer** Eddie Hacket/Mel Flanagan **Facilities** ♥ ♧ ♂ ♂ Leisure fishing. **Location** 1m N
....
Hotel ★★★ 71% Sligo Park Hotel, Pearse Rd, SLIGO
☎ 071 916 0291 110 en suite

ENNISCRONE   Map 01 B5

Enniscrone ☎ 096 36297 🖹 096 36657
e-mail: enniscronegolf@eircom.net
In a magnificent situation with breathtaking views of mountain, sea and rolling countryside, this course offers some unforgettable golf. The addition of 6 new holes threading a path through the mountainous dunes add an exciting dimension to the 27 hole layout.
27 holes, 6698yds, Par 73, SSS 72, Course record 70.
Club membership 800.
Visitors must book tee times in advance. **Societies** must book in advance. **Green Fees** not confirmed. **Cards** 🌑
🌑 🌑 **Prof** Charlie McGoldrick **Course Designer** E Hackett/Donald Steel **Facilities** ⊗ ⅷ ⓑ ♥ ♀ ♧ ♂ ♂ ♂ ♂ ♂ **Location** 0.5m S on Ballina road

SLIGO   Map 01 B5

County Sligo Rosses Point
☎ 071 9177134 or 9177186 🖹 071 9177460
e-mail: cosligo@iol.ie
Now considered to be one of the top links courses in Ireland, County Sligo is host to a number of competitions, including the West of Ireland Championships and Internationals. Set in an elevated position on cliffs above three large beaches, the prevailing winds provide an additional challenge. Tom Watson described it as 'a magnificent links, particularly the stretch of holes from the 14th to the 17th.' All Ireland Golf Club of the Year 2002.
18 holes, 6043mtrs, Par 71, SSS 72, Course record 67.
Bomore: 9 holes, 2785mtrs, Par 35, SSS 69.
Club membership 1175.
Visitors must contact in advance, available most days except Captains or Presidents days.Deposit required to secure. **Societies** must contact in writing & pay a deposit.
Green Fees Championship Course:€65 per 18 holes Mon-Thur (€80 Fri-Sun and bank holidays). **Cards** 🌑 🌑 🌑
Prof Jim Robinson **Course Designer** Harry Colt **Facilities** ⊗ ⅷ ⓑ ♥ ♀ ♧ ♂ ♂ ♂ ♂ ♂ ♂ **Conf** fac available
Corporate Hospitality Days available **Location** Off N15 to Donegal
Continued

443

Hotel ★★★ 63% Tower Hotel, Quay St, SLIGO
☎ 071 914 4000 58 en suite

Strandhill Strandhill
☎ 071 9168188 ▤ 071 9168811
e-mail: strandhillgc.eircom.net
This scenic course is situated between Knocknarea Mountain and the Atlantic, offering golf in its most natural form amid the sand dunes of the West of Ireland. The 1st, 16th and 18th are par 4 holes over 364 metres in length; the 2nd and 17th are testing par 3s which vary according to the prevailing wind; the par 4 13th is a testing dogleg right. This is a course where accuracy will be rewarded.
18 holes, 5516mtrs, Par 69, SSS 68.
Club membership 450.
Visitors must contact in advance. **Societies** apply in advance. **Green Fees** terms on application. **Cards** 🎫 🎫 **Facilities** ⊗ ⅸ 🖺 ♨ ♀ ♨ 🖻 ⚐ ⚘ ♣ ⚘ *Ø* **Location** 5m from town

Hotel ★★★ 71% Sligo Park Hotel, Pearse Rd, SLIGO
☎ 071 916 0291 110 en suite

TOBERCURRY   Map 01 B4

Tobercurry ☎ 071 85849
e-mail: contacttubbercurry@eircom.net
A 9-hole parkland course designed by Edward Hackett. The 8th hole, a par 3, is regarded as being one of the most testing in the west of Ireland. An exceptionally dry course, playable all year round.
9 holes, 5490mtrs, Par 70, SSS 69, Course record 65.
Club membership 300.
Visitors Advisable to contact in advance of wishing to play at weekends **Societies** telephone in advance **Green Fees** €15 (€20 weekends). **Course Designer** Eddie Hackett **Facilities** ⊗ ⅸ 🖺 ♨ ♀ ♨ *Ø* **Conf** Corporate Hospitality Days available **Location** 0.25m from Tobercurry

CO TIPPERARY

CAHIR   Map 01 C3

Cahir Park Kilcommon ☎ 052 41474 ▤ 052 42717
18 holes, 6350yds, Par 71, SSS 71, Course record 67.
Course Designer Eddie Hackett **Location** 1m from Cahir on the Clogheen road
Telephone for further details

Hotel ★★★ 64% Cahir House Hotel, The Square, CAHIR
☎ 052 42727 41 en suite

CARRICK-ON-SUIR   Map 01 C2

Carrick-on-Suir Garvonne
☎ 051 640047 ▤ 051 640558
e-mail: cosgc@eircom.net
18 holes, 6061mtrs, Par 72, SSS 71, Course record 69.
Course Designer Eddie Hackett **Location** 2m SW
Telephone for further details

Hotel ★★★ 73% Minella Hotel, CLONMEL
☎ 052 22388 70 en suite

> **Looking to try a new course? Always telephone ahead to confirm visitor arrangements.**

CLONMEL   Map 01 C2

Clonmel Lyreanearla, Mountain Rd
☎ 052 24050 & 21138 ▤ 052 83349
e-mail: cgc@indigo.ie
Set in the scenic, wooded slopes of the Comeragh Mountains, this is a testing course with lots of open space and plenty of interesting features. It provides an enjoyable round in exceptionally tranquil surroundings.
18 holes, 6347yards, Par 72, SSS 71.
Club membership 950.
Visitors must contact in advance. **Societies** apply in advance by writing or phone. **Green Fees** terms on application. **Cards** 🎫 **Prof** Robert Hayes **Course Designer** Eddie Hackett **Facilities** ⊗ ⅸ by prior arrangement 🖺 ♨ ♀ ♨ 🖻 ⚐ ⚘ *Ø* **Location** 3m from Clonmel off N24

Hotel ★★★ 73% Minella Hotel, CLONMEL
☎ 052 22388 70 en suite

MONARD   Map 01 B3

Ballykisteen Ballykisteen, Limerick Junction
☎ 062 33333 ▤ 062 52457
18 holes, 6765yds, Par 72, SSS 72.
Course Designer Des Smith **Location** On N24 2m from Tipperary towards Limerick
Telephone for further details

Guesthouse ♦♦♦ Ach-na-Sheen Guesthouse, Clonmel Rd, TIPPERARY ☎ 062 51298 9 rms (7 en suite)

NENAGH   Map 01 B3

Nenagh Beechwood ☎ 067 31476 ▤ 067 34808
e-mail: nenaghgolfclub@eircom.net
A major re-development including 13 new holes completed in 2001, giving a fair test of golf for every golfer irrespective of ability and experience. New sand-based greens guarded by intimidating bunkers are a challenge for even the most fastidious of putters. Excellent drainage and firm surfaces allow play all year round.
18 holes, 6009mtrs, Par 72, SSS 72, Course record 71.
Club membership 1100.
Visitors Mon-Fri only, must contact in advance. **Societies** must apply in writing. **Green Fees** not confirmed. **Cards** 🎫 **Prof** Robert Kelly **Course Designer** Patrick Merrigan **Facilities** ⊗ ⅸ 🖺 ♨ ♀ ♨ 🖻 ⚐ ⚘ ♣ ⚘ *Ø* **Location** 3m from town on old Birr rd

Guesthouse ♦♦♦ Ashley Park House, Ashley Park, NENAGH ☎ 067 38223 & 06738013 ▤ 067 38013 6 rms (5 en suite)

ROSCREA   Map 01 C3

Roscrea Golf Club Derryvale
☎ 0505 21130 ▤ 0505 23410
Course situated on the eastern side of Roscrea in the shadows of the Slieve Bloom mountains. A special feature of the course is the variety of the par 3 holes, most noteworthy of which is the 180 yards 4th, which is played almost entirely over a lake. It is widely recognised that the finishing 6 holes will prove a worthy challenge to even the best players. The most famous hole on the course in the 7th. referred to locally as 'The Burma Road', a par 5 of over 500 yards with the

Continued

fairway lined with trees and 'out of bounds' on the left side.
18 holes, 5750mtrs, Par 71, SSS 70, Course record 66. Club membership 600.
Visitors telephone in advance, on Sun by arrangement. **Societies** apply in writing to Hon Secretary. **Green Fees** €20 (€25 weekends). **Course Designer** A Spring **Facilities** ⊗)Ⅲ ⅃ ♨ ♀ ⌂ ♂ **Conf** Corporate Hospitality Days available **Location** N7, Dublin side of Roscrea

Hotel ★★★ 63% County Arms Hotel, BIRR
☎ 0509 20791 24 en suite

TEMPLEMORE   Map 01 C3

Templemore Manna South
☎ 0504 31400 & 32923 📄 0504 35450
e-mail: johnkm@tinet.ie
Parkland course with many mature and some newly planted trees which offers a pleasant test to visitors without being too difficult. Ideal for holiday makers.
9 holes, 5443mtrs, Par 70, SSS 69, Course record 68. Club membership 330.
Visitors may not play during Special Events. **Societies** must contact in advance. **Green Fees** not confirmed. **Cards** 💳 **Facilities** ⊗)Ⅲ ⅃ ♨ ♀ ♂ **Leisure** hard tennis courts. **Location** 0.5m S of town, beside N62

Hotel ★★★ 63% County Arms Hotel, BIRR
☎ 0509 20791 24 en suite

THURLES   Map 01 C3

Thurles Turtulla
☎ 0504 21983 & 24599 📄 0504 24647
Superb parkland course with a difficult finish at the 18th.
18 holes, 5904mtrs, Par 72, SSS 71, Course record 67. Club membership 1200.
Visitors welcome, limited availability at weekends, Tuesday is Ladies day. **Societies** apply in writing to Hon Secretary. **Green Fees** not confirmed. **Prof** Sean Hunt **Course Designer** Mr J McMlister **Facilities** ⊗)Ⅲ ⅃ ♨ ♀ ♨ 🏠 ⌂ 🏌 ♂ ♆ ⌖ **Leisure** squash, sauna, gymnasium. **Conf** fac available Corporate Hospitality Days available **Location** 1m from town on N62, Cork road

Guesthouse ♦♦♦ Ach-na-Sheen Guesthouse, Clonmel Rd, TIPPERARY ☎ 062 51298 9 rms (7 en suite)

TIPPERARY   Map 01 C3

County Tipperary Golf & Country Club
Dundrum House Hotel, Dundrum
☎ 062 71717 📄 062 71718
e-mail: dundrumh@id.ie
The course had been built into a mature Georgian estate using the features of woodland and parkland adorned by the Multeen River. Designed by Philip Walton. The 13th hole is one of the most testing par 5s in Ireland.
18 holes, 7050yds, Par 72, SSS 72, Course record 70. Club membership 460.
Visitors booking is advisable especially at weekends. **Societies** apply in writing or telephone in advance **Green Fees** not confirmed. **Cards** 💳 💳 💳 **Course Designer** Philip Walton **Facilities** ⊗)Ⅲ ⅃ ♨ ♀ ♨ 🏠 ⌂ 🏌 🏠 ♆ 🏌 ♂ **Leisure** tennis courts, heated indoor swimming pool, fishing, solarium, gymnasium. **Conf** Corporate Hospitality Days available **Location** 7m W of Cashel off N8

Continued

Guesthouse ♦♦♦ Ach-na-Sheen Guesthouse, Clonmel Rd, TIPPERARY ☎ 062 51298 9 rms (7 en suite)

Tipperary Rathanny ☎ 062 51119 📄 062 51119
e-mail: tipperarygolfclub@eircom.net
Recently extended to 18-holes, this parkland course has plenty of trees and bunkers and water at three holes to provide additional hazards.
18 holes, 5761mtrs, Par 71, SSS 71, Course record 66. Club membership 700.
Visitors advisable to contact by phone, weekend play available but limited on Sun. **Societies** apply in writing. **Green Fees** not confirmed. **Prof** Ger Jones **Facilities** ⊗)Ⅲ by prior arrangement ⅃ ♨ ♀ ♨ 🏠 🏌 ♂ ⌖ **Location** 1m S

Guesthouse ♦♦♦ Ach-na-Sheen Guesthouse, Clonmel Rd, TIPPERARY ☎ 062 51298 9 rms (7 en suite)

CO WATERFORD

DUNGARVAN   Map 01 C2

Dungarvan Knocknagranagh
☎ 058 41605 & 43310 📄 058 44113
e-mail: dungarvangc@eircom.net
A championship-standard course beside Dungarvan Bay, with seven lakes and hazards placed to challenge all levels of golfer. The greens are considered to be among the best in Ireland.
18 holes, 6560yds, Par 72, SSS 71, Course record 66. Club membership 900.
Visitors welcome weekdays, booking advisable weekends. **Societies** telephone then write to confim booking. **Green Fees** €31 (weekends & bank holidays €42). **Cards** 💳 💳 **Prof** David Hayes **Course Designer** Moss Fives **Facilities** ⊗)Ⅲ ⅃ ♨ ♀ ♨ 🏠 ♆ 🏌 ♂ **Leisure** snooker. **Location** Off N25 between Waterford & Youghal

Hotel ★★★ 61% Lawlors Hotel, DUNGARVAN
☎ 058 41122 & 41056 📄 058 41000 89 en suite

Gold Coast Golf & Leisure Ballinacourty
☎ 058 44055 📄 058 44055
e-mail: info@goldcoastgolfclub.com
A parkland course bordered by the Atlantic Ocean with unrivalled panoramic views of Dungarvan Bay. The mature tree-lined fairways of the old course are tastefully integrated with the long and challenging newer holes to create a superb course.
18 holes, 6171mtrs, Par 72, SSS 72, Course record 70. Club membership 600.
Visitors book in advance, times available throughout the week. **Societies** apply by telephone in advance. **Green Fees** €35 per 18 holes (€45 weekends). **Cards** 💳 💳 💳 💳 💳 **Course Designer** Maurice Fives **Facilities** ⊗)Ⅲ ⅃ ♨ ♀ ♨ 🏠 ⌂ 🏌 🏠 ♆ 🏌 ♂ ⌖ **Leisure** hard tennis courts, heated indoor swimming pool, sauna, gymnasium. **Conf** fac available **Location** Left of N25, 2m before Dungarvan

Hotel ★★★ 61% Lawlors Hotel, DUNGARVAN
☎ 058 41122 & 41056 📄 058 41000 89 en suite

Use the maps at the back of the guide to help locate a golf course.

West Waterford
☎ 058 43216 & 41475 📠 058 44343
e-mail: info@westwaterfordgolf.com
Designed by Eddie Hackett, the course is on 150 acres of rolling parkland by the Brickey River with a backdrop of the Comeragh Mountains, Knockmealdowns and Drum Hills. The first nine holes are laid out on a large plateau featuring a stream which comes into play at the 3rd and 4th holes. The river at the southern boundary affects several later holes.
18 holes, 6712yds, Par 72, SSS 72, Course record 70. Club membership 400.
Visitors pre book for tee times. **Societies** telephone or write in advance. **Green Fees** €30 per 18 holes (€40 weekends and bank holidays). **Cards** 🌐 💳 **Course Designer** Eddie Hackett **Facilities** ⊗ ⅋ 🏌 🍺 ♀ ⚑ ⛳ ⛱ 🏌 **Leisure** hard tennis courts. **Location** Approx 3m W of Dungarvan, off N25

Hotel ★★★ 61% Lawlors Hotel, DUNGARVAN
☎ 058 41122 & 41056 📠 058 41000 89 en suite

DUNMORE EAST   Map 01 C2

Dunmore East ☎ 051 383151 📠 051 383151
e-mail: dunmoregolf@eircom.net
Overlooking the village of Dunmore East, with panoramic views of the village, bay and Hook peninsula. This course promises to offer idyllic surroundings and challenging golf for the high or low handicap golfer.
18 holes, 5400mtrs, Par 72, SSS 69, Course record 65. Club membership 500.
Visitors welcome, no restrictions. **Societies** telephone in advance. **Green Fees** Apr-Sep €25 per 18 holes (weekends €30); Oct-Mar €20 per 18 holes (weekends €25). **Cards** 🌐 💳 **Prof** James Kane-Nash **Course Designer** W H Jones **Facilities** ⊗ ⅋ 🏌 🍺 ♀ ⚑ ⛳ 🏌 **Location** Follow signs to Dunmore East. After Petrol Stn take left fork. Left at The Strand Inn & 1st right

Hotel ★★★ 65% Majestic Hotel, TRAMORE
☎ 051 381761 60 en suite

LISMORE   Map 01 C2

Lismore Ballyin ☎ 058 54026 📠 058 53338
e-mail: moynihan@eircom.net
Picturesque, tree-dotted, sloping, 9 hole parkland course on the banks of the Blackwater River.
9 holes, 2748mtrs, Par 69, SSS 68. Club membership 350.
Visitors telephone in advance, especially weekends. **Societies** must apply in writing or phone. **Green Fees** €20 per 18 holes. **Course Designer** Eddie Hackett **Facilities** 🏌 🍺 ♀ ⚑ **Location** 1 m from Lismore on Ballyduff Road

Hotel ★★★ 61% Lawlors Hotel, DUNGARVAN
☎ 058 41122 & 41056 📠 058 41000 89 en suite

TRAMORE   Map 01 C2

Tramore Newtown Hill ☎ 051 386170 📠 051 390961
e-mail: tragolf@iol.ie
18 holes, 5918mtrs, Par 72, SSS 72, Course record 65.
Course Designer Capt H C Tippet **Location** 0.5m from Tramore on Dungaruan coast road
Telephone for further details

Hotel ★★★ 65% Majestic Hotel, TRAMORE
☎ 051 381761 60 en suite

WATERFORD   Map 01 C2

Faithlegg Faithlegg
☎ 051 382241 & 086 3840215 📠 051 382664
e-mail: golf@faithlegg.com
Some wicked slopes and borrows on the immaculate greens, a huge 432yd 17th that has a host of problems and a dog-leg approach to the two-tier 18th green are just some of the novel features on this course. Set on the banks of the River Suir, the course has been integrated into a landscape textured with mature trees, flowing parkland and five lakes. Ongoing improvement and development of the course following major work on irrigation and drainage.
18 holes, 6629yds, Par 72, SSS 72, Course record 69. Club membership 440.
Visitors subject to availability, booking advised **Societies** apply in writing or telephone at least a month in advance. **Green Fees** Mon-Thu €45; Fri-Sun €59 (early bird Mon-Fri up to 9am €28). **Cards** 🌐 💳 **Prof** Darragh Tighe **Course Designer** Patrick Merrigan **Facilities** ⊗ ⅋ by prior arrangement 🏌 🍺 ♀ ⚑ ⛳ ⛱ 🏌 **Leisure** hard tennis courts, heated indoor swimming pool, sauna, solarium, gymnasium, full P.G.A. club repair & custom fitting service available. **Conf** fac available **Location** take Dunmore East road from Waterford, passing Waterford Regional Hospital, at fork of road proceed left for Cheekpoint. After 300mtrs turn right under bridge. Club after 3kms

Hotel ★★★ 61% McEniff Ard Ri Hotel, Ferrybank, WATERFORD ☎ 051 832111 98 en suite

Waterford Newrath ☎ 051 876748 📠 051 853405
18 holes, 5722mtrs, Par 71, SSS 70, Course record 64.
Course Designer W Park/J Braid **Location** 1m N
Telephone for further details

Hotel ★★★ 61% McEniff Ard Ri Hotel, Ferrybank, WATERFORD ☎ 051 832111 98 en suite

Waterford Castle The Island, Ballinakill
☎ 051 871633 📠 051 871634
e-mail: golf@waterfordcastle.com
A unique 320 acre island golf course surrounded by the River Suir and accessed by private ferry. The course has four water features on the 2nd, 3rd, 4th and 16th holes with a Swilken Bridge on the 3rd hole. Two of the more challenging holes are the par 4s at the 9th and 12th, the 9th being a 414 yard uphill, dog-leg right. The 456 yard 12th is a fine test of accuracy and distance. The views from the course are superb.
18 holes, 5827mtrs, Par 72, SSS 71, Course record 70. Club membership 770.
Visitors must contact in advance, pre booking required. **Societies** apply in advance. **Green Fees** Winter €41-€49; Summer €49-€59. **Cards** 🌐 💳 **Course Designer** Des Smyth **Facilities** ⊗ ⅋ 🏌 🍺 ♀ ⚑ ⛳ ⛱ 🏌 **Leisure** hard tennis courts. **Conf** fac available Corporate Hospitality Days available **Location** 2m E of Waterford City, on Island approached by private ferry

Hotel ★★★★ Waterford Castle Hotel, The Island, WATERFORD ☎ 051 878203 19 en suite

Booking a tee time is always advisable.

CO WESTMEATH

ATHLONE   Map 01 C4

Glasson Golf & Country Club Glasson
☎ 090 6485120 📄 090 6485444
e-mail: info@glassongolf.ie
Opened for play in 1993 the course has earned a reputation for being one of the most challenging and scenic courses in Ireland. Designed by Christy O'Connor Jnr it is reputedly his best yet! Surrounded on three sides by Lough Ree the views from everywhere on the course are breathtaking. The introduction of a new 29 bedroom luxury hotel has added another dimension to the course.
21 holes, 6664yds, Par 72, SSS 72, Course record 65.
Club membership 220.
Visitors must book in advance. **Societies** book in advance.
Green Fees €55 (Mon-Thur); €60 (Fri & Sun); €70 (Sat) per round. **Cards** 🖃 🎟 🖅 💳 🔜 **Course Designer** Christy O'Connor Jnr **Facilities** ⊗ ⅶ ⅙ ♥ ⅄ ⌂ ⋔ 🛵 🛆 ⚲ **Leisure** chipping green. **Conf** fac available Corporate Hospitality Days available **Location** 6m N of Athlone on N55

Hotel ★★★ 70% Hodson Bay Hotel, Hodson Bay, ATHLONE ☎ 090 6442000 133 en suite

DELVIN   Map 01 C4

Delvin Castle Clonyn
☎ 044 64315 & 64671 📄 044 64315
Situated in the mature parkland of Clonyn Castle, the course is well known for its unique historic setting with a 16th century ruin in the back nine holes and an imposing Victorian castle in the front nine.
18 holes, 5800mtrs, Par 70, SSS 68.
Club membership 400.
Visitors no restrictions. Advance booking recommemded. **Societies** apply in writing in advance. **Green Fees** not confirmed. **Prof** David Keenaghan **Course Designer** John Day **Facilities** ⊗ ⅶ ⅙ ♥ ⅄ ⌂ ⋔ ⚲ **Location** On N52, Dundalk to Mullingar road

Hotel ★★★ 64% Ardboyne Hotel, Dublin Rd, NAVAN ☎ 046 902 3119 29 en suite

MOATE   Map 01 C4

Moate ☎ 0902 81271 📄 0902 81267
18 holes, 5742mtrs, Par 72, SSS 70, Course record 67.
Course Designer B Browne **Location** 1m N
Telephone for further details

Hotel ★★ 68% Royal Hoey Hotel, Mardyke St, ATHLONE ☎ 090 647 2924 & 647 5395 📄 090 647 5194 38 en suite

Mount Temple Mount Temple Village
☎ 0902 81841 & 81545 📄 0902 81957
e-mail: mttemple@iol.ie
A traditionally built, championship course with unique links-type greens and natural undulating fairways. A challenge for all levels of golfers and all year golfing available.
18 holes, 6020mtrs, Par 72, SSS 72, Course record 71.
Club membership 250.
Visitors welcome but must book for weekends. **Societies** telephone in advance. **Green Fees** not confirmed. **Cards**

🖃 🖅 **Prof** David Keenan **Course Designer** Michael Dolan **Facilities** ⊗ ⅶ ⅙ ♥ Wine licence ⅄ ⌂ ⋔ 🛵 ⚲ **Conf** Corporate Hospitality Days available **Location** 5km off N6 to Mount Temple village, 8km from Athlone

Hotel ★★ 68% Royal Hoey Hotel, Mardyke St, ATHLONE ☎ 090 647 2924 & 647 5395 📄 090 647 5194 38 en suite

MULLINGAR   Map 01 C4

Mullingar ☎ 044 48366 📄 044 41499
18 holes, 6406yds, Par 72, SSS 71, Course record 63.
Course Designer James Braid **Location** 3m S
Telephone for further details

Hotel ★★ 68% Royal Hoey Hotel, Mardyke St, ATHLONE ☎ 090 647 2924 & 647 5395 📄 090 647 5194 38 en suite

CO WEXFORD

ENNISCORTHY   Map 01 D3

Enniscorthy Knockmarshall
☎ 054 33191 📄 054 37367
18 holes, 6115mtrs, Par 72, SSS 72.
Course Designer Eddie Hackett **Location** 1m from town on New Ross road
Telephone for further details

Hotel ★★★ 69% Riverside Park Hotel, The Promenade, ENNISCORTHY ☎ 054 37800 60 en suite

GOREY   Map 01 D3

Courtown Kiltennel ☎ 055 25166 📄 055 25553
e-mail: courtown@iol.ie
A pleasant parkland course which is well wooded and enjoys views across the Irish Sea near Courtown Harbour.
18 holes, 5898mtrs, Par 71, SSS 71, Course record 65.
Club membership 1637.
Visitors must contact in advance. **Societies** advisable to contact in advance. **Green Fees** not confirmed. **Cards** 🖃 🖅 **Prof** John Coone **Course Designer** Harris & Associates **Facilities** ⊗ ⅶ ⅙ ♥ ⅄ ⌂ ⋔ 🛵 🛆 ⚲ **Location** 3m from town, off Courtown Road

Hotel ★★★ ♨ Marlfield House Hotel, GOREY ☎ 055 21124 20 en suite

NEW ROSS   Map 01 C3

New Ross Tinneranny ☎ 051 421433 📄 051 420098
Recently extended to 18-holes, this well kept parkland course has an attractive backdrop of hills and mountains. Straight hitting and careful placing of shots is very important, especially on the 2nd, 6th, 10th and 15th, all of which are challenging holes.
18 holes, 5751yds, Par 70, SSS 70.
Club membership 700.
Visitors welcome, booking required for weekend play. **Societies** apply to secretary/manager. **Green Fees** €25 per round(€35 weekends & bank holidays). **Cards** 🖃 🖅 **Course Designer** Des Smith **Facilities** ⊗ ⅙ ♥ ⅄ ⌂ ⚲ **Location** 3m from town centre

Continued   *Continued*

Hotel ★★★ 67% The Cedar Lodge Hotel & Restaurant, Carrigbyrne, Newbawn, NEW ROSS ☎ 051 428386 28 en suite

ROSSLARE
Map 01 D2

Rosslare Rosslare Strand ☎ 053 32203 ▤ 053 32263 e-mail: office@rosslaregolf.com
This traditional links course is within minutes of the ferry terminal at Rosslare, but its popularity is not confined to visitors from Fishguard or Le Havre. It is a great favourite with the Irish too. Many of the greens are sunken and are always in beautiful condition, but the semi-blind approaches are among features of this course which provide a healthy challenge.
Old Course: 18 holes, 6608yds, Par 72, SSS 72, Course record 66.
New Course: 12 holes, 3956yds, Par 46.
Club membership 1000.
Visitors telephone 053 32203 ext3 in advance. **Societies** apply in writing/telephone. **Green Fees** terms on application. **Cards** 🖃 🖳 **Prof** Johnny Young **Course Designer** Hawtree/Taylor **Facilities** ⊗ ⫟ ⤋ ♣ ♟ ♨ 🎋 🏌 🐾 ♨ ♂ **Leisure** sauna. **Location** 6m N of Rosslare Ferry Terminal

Hotel ★★★★ Kelly's Resort Hotel, ROSSLARE ☎ 053 32114 99 annexe en suite

St Helen's Bay Golf & Country Club
St Helens, Kilrane ☎ 053 33234 ▤ 053 33803 e-mail: sthelens@iol.ie
Eighteen hole championship course with an additional 9 holes opened in 2003. Overlooking beach with accommodation on site.
27 holes, 5813mtrs, Par 72, SSS 72, Course record 69.
Club membership 500.
Visitors contact in advance. **Societies** telephone in advance. **Green Fees** not confirmed. **Cards** 🖃 🖳 **Course Designer** Philip Walton **Facilities** ⊗ ⫟ ⤋ ♣ ♟ ♨ 🎋 🏌 🐾 ♂ 🏇 **Leisure** hard tennis courts, golf academy and tuition area. **Location** 5 minutes from the ferryport of Rosslare

Hotel ★★★★ 70% Ferrycarrig Hotel, Ferrycarrig Bridge, WEXFORD ☎ 053 20999 102 en suite

WEXFORD
Map 01 D3

Wexford Mulgannon ☎ 053 42238 ▤ 053 42243
18 holes, 6100yds, Par 72, SSS 70.
Telephone for further details

Hotel ★★★ 73% Talbot Hotel Conference & Leisure Centre, Trinity St, WEXFORD ☎ 053 22566 98 en suite

CO WICKLOW

ARKLOW
Map 01 D3

Arklow Abbeylands ☎ 0402 32492 ▤ 0402 91604 e-mail: arklowgolflinks@eircom.net
18 holes, 5802mtrs, Par 69, SSS 68, Course record 64.
Course Designer Hawtree & Taylor **Location** 0.5m from town centre
Telephone for further details

Hotel ★★★ ♨ Marlfield House Hotel, GOREY ☎ 055 21124 20 en suite

BALTINGLASS
Map 01 D3

Baltinglass Dublin Rd
☎ 059 6481350 ▤ 059 6481842 e-mail: baltinglassgc@eircom.net
18 hole course overlooking Baltinglass town with breathtaking views of the Wicklow Mountains. Abundant mature trees make this course a good test of golf for all levels of handicap.
18 holes, 5912mtrs, Par 71, SSS 71, Course record 68.
Club membership 600.
Visitors advisable to check availability for weekends. **Societies** apply in writing or by telephone. **Green Fees** terms on application. **Course Designer** Lionel Hewston **Facilities** ⊗ ⤋ ♣ ♟ ♨ 🎋 🏌 ♂ **Location** 500 metres N of Baltinglass

Hotel ★★★ 70% Seven Oaks Hotel, Athy Rd, CARLOW ☎ 059 913 1308 59 en suite

BLAINROE
Map 01 D3

Blainroe ☎ 0404 68168 ▤ 0404 69369 e-mail: blainroegolfclub@eircom.net
Parkland course overlooking the sea on the east coast, offering a challenging round to golfers of all abilities. Some holes are situated right on the coast and two holes worth noting are the 14th and the par 3 15th over the lake.
18 holes, 6070mtrs, Par 72, SSS 72, Course record 71.
Club membership 1060.
Visitors must contact in advance. **Societies** must telephone in advance. **Green Fees** not confirmed. **Cards** 🖃 🖳 **Prof** John McDonald **Course Designer** Fred Hawtree **Facilities** ⊗ ⫟ ⤋ ♣ ♟ ♨ 🎋 🏌 ♂ **Conf** Corporate Hospitality Days available **Location** 3 miles S of Wicklow, on coast road

Hotel ★★★★ 69% Tinakilly Country House & Restaurant, RATHNEW ☎ 0404 69274 51 en suite

BLESSINGTON
Map 01 D3

Clarian Tulfarris House Hotel & Country Club ☎ 045 867644 & 867600 ▤ 045 867000
e-mail: info@tulfarris.com
Designed by Paddy Merrigan, this course is on the Blessington lakeshore with the Wicklow Mountains as a backdrop. The use of the natural landscape is evident throughout the whole course, the variety of trees guarding fairways and green approaches.
Tulfarris House Hotel & Golf Resort: 18 holes, 7116yds, Par 72, SSS 74, Course record 68.
Club membership 150.
Visitors tee booking advisable; may not play Sun 8-11.30pm. **Societies** must contact in writing or telephone in advance. **Green Fees** not confirmed. **Cards** 🖃 🖳 🖳 🖾 **Prof** A Williams **Course Designer** Patrick Merrigan **Facilities** ⊗ ⫟ ⤋ ♣ ♟ ♨ 🎋 🐾 🏌 ♂ 🏇 **Leisure** hard tennis courts, heated indoor swimming pool, fishing, sauna, solarium, gymnasium. **Conf** fac available Corporate Hospitality Days available **Location** Via N81, 2m from Blessington village

Hotel ★★★ 66% Downshire House Hotel, BLESSINGTON ☎ 045 865199 14 en suite 11 annexe en suite

> **Use the maps at the back of the guide to help locate a golf course.**

BRAY
Map 01 D4

Old Conna Ferndale Rd
☎ 01 2826055 & 2826766 📠 01 2825611
e-mail: info@oldconna.com
Parkland course set in wooded terrain with panoramic views of Irish Sea and Wicklow mountains.
18 holes, 6550yds, Par 72, SSS 72, Course record 68.
Club membership 1000.
Visitors advisable to contact in advance but may not play weekends. Smart dress essential on course & in clubhouse. **Societies** must telephone well in advance. **Green Fees** €50 per round (weekends €65). **Cards** 💳 💳 **Prof** Michael Langford **Course Designer** Eddie Hackett **Facilities** ⊗ ⅏ ⅃ 🖳 💶 ♀ ⚐ 🕐 ⑂ **Conf** fac available Corporate Hospitality Days available **Location** 2m from Bray

Hotel ★★★ 62% Royal Hotel & Leisure Centre, Main St, BRAY ☎ 01 2862935 91 en suite

Woodbrook Dublin Rd ☎ 01 2824799 📠 01 2821950
e-mail: golf@woodbrook.ie
Pleasant parkland with magnificent views and bracing sea breezes which has hosted a number of events, including the Irish Close and the Irish Open Championships. A testing finish is provided by an 18th hole with out of bounds on both sides.
18 holes, 6017mtrs, Par 72, SSS 71, Course record 65.
Club membership 1200.
Visitors must contact in advance and have a handicap certificate. **Societies** must contact in advance. **Green Fees** €85 per 18 holes (€95 weekends & bank holidays). **Cards** 💳 💳 **Prof** Billy Kinsella **Course Designer** Peter McEvoy **Facilities** ⊗ ⅏ ⅃ 🖳 💶 ♀ ⚐ 🕐 ⑂ **Location** 11m S of Dublin on N11

Hotel ★★★ 62% Royal Hotel & Leisure Centre, Main St, BRAY ☎ 01 2862935 91 en suite

BRITTAS BAY
Map 01 D3

The European Club ☎ 0404 47415 📠 0404 47449
e-mail: info@europeanclub.com
A links course that runs through a large dunes system. Since it was opened in 1992 it is rapidly gaining recognition as one of Irelands Best Courses. Notable holes include the 7th, 13th and 14th.
20 holes, 7210yds, Par 71, SSS 73, Course record 67.
Club membership 100.
Visitors pre-booking advised especially for weekends, no denim. **Societies** must book in advance. **Green Fees** €75 per round Nov-Mar; €125 Apr-Oct. **Cards** 💳 💳 **Course Designer** Pat Ruddy **Facilities** ⊗ ⅏ ⅃ 🖳 ♀ ⚐ 🕐 ⑂ **Conf** Corporate Hospitality Days available **Location** 1m from Brittas Bay Beach

Hotel ★★★★ 69% Tinakilly Country House & Restaurant, RATHNEW ☎ 0404 69274 51 en suite

DELGANY
Map 01 D3

Delgany ☎ 01 2874536 📠 01 2873977
e-mail: delganygolf@eircom.net
An undulating parkland course amidst beautiful scenery.
18 holes, 5480mtrs, Par 69, SSS 68, Course record 61.
Club membership 1070.
Visitors may play Mon, Wed (until 9am), Thu & Fri.

Contact in advance. **Societies** contact in advance. **Green Fees** not confirmed. **Cards** 💳 💳 **Prof** Gavin Kavanagh **Course Designer** H Vardon **Facilities** ⊗ ⅏ ⅃ 🖳 💶 ♀ ⚐ 🕐 ⑂ **Location** 0.75m from village

Hotel ★★★ 62% Royal Hotel & Leisure Centre, Main St, BRAY ☎ 01 2862935 91 en suite

DUNLAVIN
Map 01 D3

Rathsallagh ☎ 045 403316 📠 045 403295
e-mail: info@rathsallagh.com
Designed by Peter McEvoy and Christy O'Connor Jnr, this is a spectacular course which will test the pro's without intimidating the club golfer. Set in 252 acres of lush parkland with thousands of mature trees, natural water hazards and gently rolling landscape. The greens are of high quality, in design, construction and condition.
18 holes, 6916yds, Par 72, SSS 74, Course record 68.
Club membership 280.
Visitors prior booking and neat dress is essential. Metal spikes are prohibited. **Societies** apply in writing or by telephone or e-mail. **Green Fees** €60 per round (€75 Fri-Sat & bank holidays); (reduced rates for hotel residents). **Cards** 💳 💳 **Prof** Brendan McDaid **Course Designer** McEvoy/O'Connor **Facilities** ⊗ ⅏ ⅃ 🖳 💶 ♀ ⚐ 🕐 ⑂ **Leisure** hard tennis courts, sauna, private jacuzzi/steam room. **Conf** fac available Corporate Hospitality Days available **Location** 15m SE of Naas off main Dublin/Carlow road

Hotel ★★★ 66% Downshire House Hotel, BLESSINGTON ☎ 045 865199 14 en suite
11 annexe en suite

ENNISKERRY
Map 01 D4

Powerscourt Powerscourt Estate
☎ 01 2046033 📠 01 2761303
e-mail: golfclub@powerscourt.ie
A free draining course with links characteristics. This championship course with top quality tees and exceptional tiered greens, is set in some of Ireland's most beautiful parkland. The course has an abundance of mature trees and natural features, with stunning views of the sea and the Sugarloaf mountain.
East Course: 18 holes, 5930mtrs, Par 72, SSS 72.
West Course: 18 holes, 5906mtrs, Par 72, SSS 72.
Club membership 920.
Visitors necessary to book in advance. **Societies** necessary to book in advance. **Green Fees** terms on application. **Cards** 💳 💳 **Prof** Paul Thompson **Course Designer** Peter McEvoy **Facilities** ⊗ ⅏ ⅃ 🖳 💶 ♀ ⚐ 🕐 ⑂ **Conf** fac available Corporate Hospitality Days available **Location** Just off N11 to Enniskerry, follow signs for Powerscourt Estate. See advert on page 450.

Hotel ★★★ 62% Royal Hotel & Leisure Centre, Main St, BRAY ☎ 01 2862935 91 en suite

GREYSTONES
Map 01 D3

Charlesland Golf & Country Club Hotel
☎ 01 2874350 & 2878200 📠 01 2874360
e-mail: teetimes@charlesland.com
18 holes, 5963mtrs, Par 72, SSS 72.
Course Designer Eddie Hackett **Location** 1m S of Greystones on the road to Delgany village

Continued

Continued

At Powerscourt you get
a choice of courses.

With two of Ireland's finest golf courses and a new clubhouse located just 12 miles south of Dublin, isn't it time you paid a visit to Powerscourt. Both our courses are open to visitors every day of the week, so why not find out for yourself what makes us one of the country's leading golf locations. Come and shoot a round here, it's always open season.

West Course

POWERSCOURT
GOLF CLUB

East Course

Powerscourt Estate, Enniskerry, Co. Wicklow Tel: +353 1 204 6033 Fax: +353 1 276 1303
email: golfclub@powerscourt.ie www.powerscourt.ie

Druid's Glen

Map 01 D3   Kilcoole

☎ 01 2873600   📄 01 2873699

Druid's Glen from the first tee to the 18th green creates an exceptional golfing experience, with its distinguished surroundings and spectacular views. A masterpiece of inspired planning and golfing architecture, designed by Tom Craddock and Pat Ruddy, it is the culmination of years of preparation, creating a unique inland golf course that challenges and satisfies in equal parts. Special features include an island green on the 17th hole and a Celtic Cross on the 12th. Druids Glen hosted the Murphy's Irish Open in 1996, 1997, 1998 and an unprecedented fourth time in 1999. In 2000 Druids Glen won the title of European Golf Course of the Year and in 2002 it hosted the Seve Trophy. The world's top professionals and club golfers alike continue to enjoy the challenge offered here. A variety of teeing positions are available and there is a practice area, including three full-length 'academy holes'. Individual and corporate members enjoy generous reserved tee times; visitors are very welcome but it is recommended that you book well in advance.

e-mail: info@druidsglen.ie

Visitors Advance booking essential

Societies Advance booking essential

Green Fees Telephone for details

Facilities ⊗ ⫲ 🛒 ☕ ♀ ⛱ 🏠 ⛳ 🐦 🏌 🏍 🎿

Conf Facilities available; corporate hospitality days available.

Professional Eamonn Darcy

Leisure Swimming, sauna, gym

Location 20m S of Dublin, 3m off N11 motorway, immediately S of Glen of the Downs

Holes/Par/Course record 18 holes, 6547 yds, Par 71, SSS 73, Course record 62

WHERE TO STAY NEARBY

Hotels
NEWTOWN MOUNT KENNEDY

🅄 Druids Glen Marriott
☎ 01 2870800. 148 en suite

RATHNEW

★★★★ 🌐 69% Tinakilly Country House & Restaurant.
☎ 0404 69274. 51 en suite

★★★ 🌐 67% Hunters Hotel.
☎ 0404 40106. 16 en suite

Championship Course

Telephone for further details

Hotel ★★★★ 69% Tinakilly Country House &
Restaurant, RATHNEW ☎ 0404 69274 51 en suite

Greystones ☎ 01 2874136 📠 01 2873749
e-mail: secretary@greystonesgc.com
18 holes, 5322mtrs, Par 69, SSS 68.
Course Designer P Merrigan
Telephone for further details

Hotel ★★★★ 69% Tinakilly Country House &
Restaurant, RATHNEW ☎ 0404 69274 51 en suite

KILCOOLE See page 451

KILCOOLE   Map 01 D3

Kilcoole ☎ 01 2872066 2872070 📠 01 2010497
e-mail: admin.kg@eircom.net
**Beautifully manicured nine holes with water features
on five holes. The course is dry and flat with sand based
greens and the Sugarloaf Mountain in the background
provides a pleasing view. Near the sea but well
protected by tree lined fairways.**
9 holes, 5506mtrs, Par 70, SSS 69, Course record 70.
Club membership 400.
Visitors restricted Sat & Sun 8-10am. **Societies** telephone
in advance **Green Fees** not confirmed. **Cards** 🖭 🖭
Facilities ⊗ ⅏ ㄴ ♥ ♀ ♧ 🖂 ✔ **Conf** fac available
Corporate Hospitality Days available **Location** N11
Kilcoole/Newcastle, opposite Druids Glen golf club

Hotel ★★★★ 69% Tinakilly Country House &
Restaurant, RATHNEW ☎ 0404 69274 51 en suite

RATHDRUM   Map 01 D3

Glenmalure Greenane ☎ 0404 46679 📠 0404 46783
e-mail: golf@glenmalure-golf.ie
18 holes, 5300yds, Par 71, SSS 67, Course record 71.
Course Designer P Suttle **Location** 2m W
Telephone for further details

Hotel ★★★ 64% Woodenbridge Hotel, WOODEN
BRIDGE ☎ 0402 35146 23 en suite

ROUNDWOOD   Map 01 D3

Roundwood Newtown, Mountkennedy
☎ 01 2818488 & 2802555 📠 01 2843642
e-mail: rwood@indigo.ie
**Heathland and parkland course with forest and lakes
set in beautiful countryside with views of the coast and
the Wicklow Mountains.**

Continued

---

18 holes, 6685yds, Par 72, SSS 72.
Club membership 160.
Visitors no restrictions **Societies** pre booking necessary.
Green Fees not confirmed. **Cards** 🖭 🖭 🖭 **Facilities** ⊗
⅏ ㄴ ♥ ♀ ♧ ⚐ ✻ 🛒 ✔ **Conf** Corporate Hospitality
Days available **Location** 2.5m off N11 at Newtown
Mountkennedy on N765

Hotel ★★★ 63% The Glendalough Hotel,
GLENDALOUGH ☎ 0404 45135 44 en suite

SHILLELAGH   Map 01 D3

Coollattin Coollattin ☎ 055 29125 📠 055 29125
18 holes, 6148yds, Par 70, SSS 68, Course record 70.
Course Designer Peter McEvoy
Telephone for further details

Hotel ★★★ ♨ Marlfield House Hotel, GOREY
☎ 055 21124 20 en suite

WICKLOW   Map 01 D3

Wicklow Dunbur Rd ☎ 0404 67379
**Situated on the cliffs overlooking Wicklow Bay this
parkland course does not have many trees. It was
extended to 18 holes in 1994, it provides a challenging
test of golf with each hole having its own individual
features.**
18 holes, 5126mtrs, Par 71, SSS 70.
Club membership 500.
Visitors welcome, restrictions on Wed/Thu evening and
Sun. Recommended to call in advance for times **Societies**
contact for details. **Green Fees** not confirmed. **Cards** 🖭
🖭 **Prof** Darren McLoughlin **Course Designer** Craddock
& Ruddy **Facilities** ⊗ ⅏ ㄴ ♥ ♀ ♧ 🖂 ✔

Hotel ★★★★ 69% Tinakilly Country House &
Restaurant, RATHNEW ☎ 0404 69274 51 en suite

WOODENBRIDGE   Map 01 D3

Woodenbridge Woodenbridge, Arklow
☎ 0402 35202 📠 0402 35754
e-mail: wgc@eircom.net
18 holes, 6400yds, Par 71, SSS 70, Course record 71.
Course Designer Patrick Merrigan **Location** 4m NW of
Arklow
Telephone for further details

Hotel ★★★ 64% Woodenbridge Hotel, WOODEN
BRIDGE ☎ 0402 35146 23 en suite

> **Prices may change during the currency of
> the Guide, please check when booking.**

Golf
driving ranges

DRIVING RANGES

DRIVING RANGES

DRIVING RANGES

DRIVING RANGES

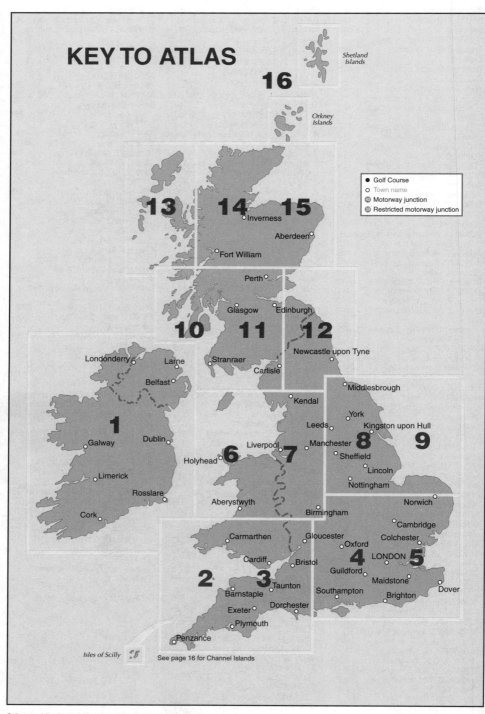

KEY TO ATLAS

16

Shetland Islands

Orkney Islands

Golf Course
Town name
Motorway junction
Restricted motorway junction

13   **14**   **15**

Inverness

Aberdeen

Fort William

Perth

Glasgow   Edinburgh

10   **11**   **12**

Londonderry   Larne   Stranraer   Newcastle upon Tyne

Belfast   Carlisle

Middlesbrough

Kendal

York

Leeds   Kingston upon Hull

1   Liverpool   Manchester   **8**   **9**

Galway   Dublin   Holyhead   **6**   **7**   Sheffield

Limerick   Lincoln

Rosslare   Nottingham

Cork   Aberystwyth   Norwich

Birmingham   Cambridge

Carmarthen   Gloucester   Colchester

Cardiff   Oxford   **4**   LONDON   **5**

2   **3**   Bristol   Guildford   Maidstone

Barnstaple   Taunton   Southampton   Brighton   Dover

Exeter   Dorchester

Plymouth

Penzance

Isles of Scilly   See page 16 for Channel Islands

© Automobile Association Developments Limited 2004

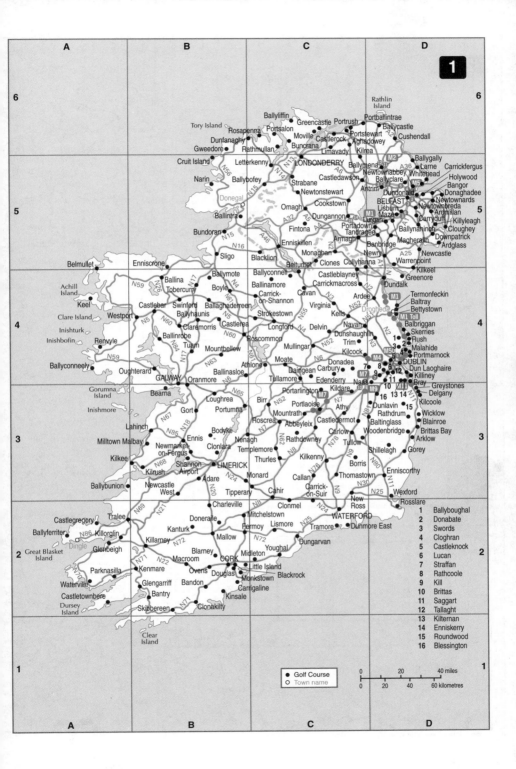

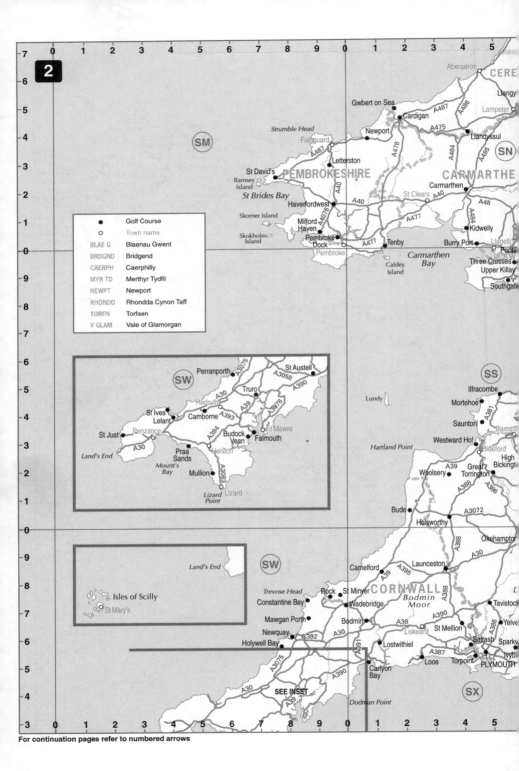

2

●	Golf Course
○	Town name
BLAE G	Blaenau Gwent
BRDGND	Bridgend
CAERPH	Caerphilly
MYR TD	Merthyr Tydfil
NEWPT	Newport
RHONDD	Rhondda Cynon Taff
TORFN	Torfaen
V GLAM	Vale of Glamorgan

SM

SN

SS

SW

SX

CEREDIGION

Aberaeron
Llangy
Lampeter

Gwbert on Sea
Cardigan
Newport
A487
A486
A475
Llandyssul
A484
A485

Strumble Head
Fishguard
Letterston
A481
A478
A40
A476
CARMARTHE
Carmarthen
St Clears
A40

PEMBROKESHIRE

St David's
Ramsey
Island
St Brides Bay
Haverfordwest
A40
A477
A48
A484
Kidwelly

Skomer Island

Milford
Haven
Skokholm
Island
Pembroke
Dock
Pembroke
A477
Tenby
Burry Port
Llanelli
Ponti
Three Crosses
Upper Killay
Southgate

Caldey
Island
Carmarthen
Bay

Perranporth
A3075
St Austell
A3058
A390
Truro
Redruth
A30
A39
A3078
St Ives
Lelant
Camborne
A393
A394
St Just
Penzance
A30
Budock
Vean
St Mawes
Falmouth
Land's End
Praa
Sands
Helston
Mount's
Bay
Mullion
A3083
Lizard
Point
Lizard

Lundy

Ilfracombe
Mortehoe
Saunton
A361
Barnsta
Westward Ho!
Bideford
High
Bickingt
Hartland Point
Woolsery
A39
Great
Torrington
A388
A386
Bude
A3072
Holsworthy

Okehampto
A388
A30

Land's End

Isles of Scilly
St Mary's

Camelford
A39
A395
Launceston
CORNWALL
Tavistoc
Rock
St Minver
Bodmin
Moor
A388
Trevose Head
Constantine Bay
Wadebridge
A390
Mawgan Porth
Bodmin
A38
St Mellion
A386
Yelve
Newquay
A392
A30
Liskeard
Saltash
Sparky
Holywell Bay
A3075
A391
Lostwithiel
A387
Torpoint
Ivyb
Looe
PLYMOUTH
Carlyon
Bay
A30
A39
SEE INSET
Dodman Point

For continuation pages refer to numbered arrows

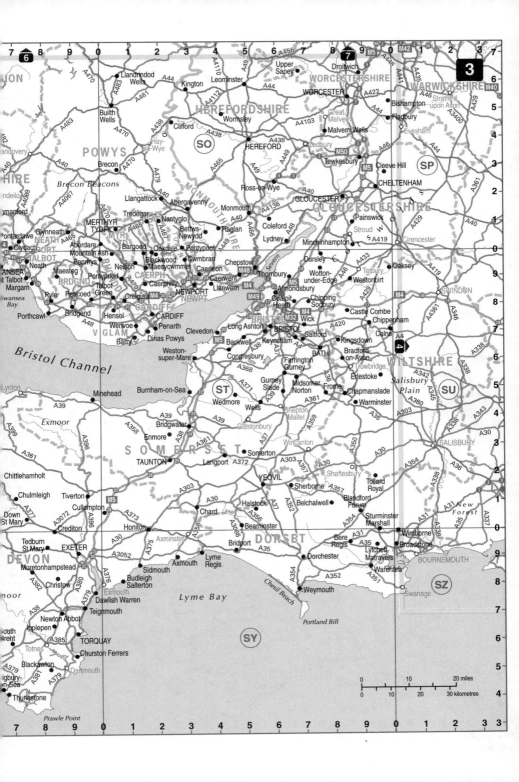

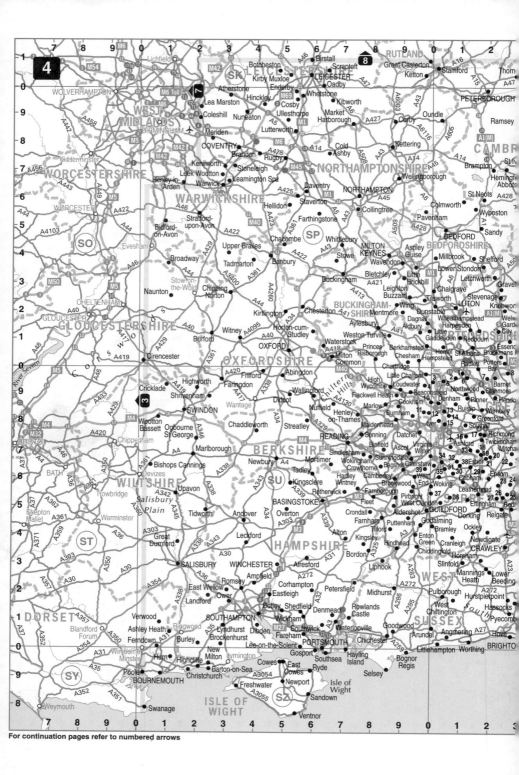

For continuation pages refer to numbered arrows

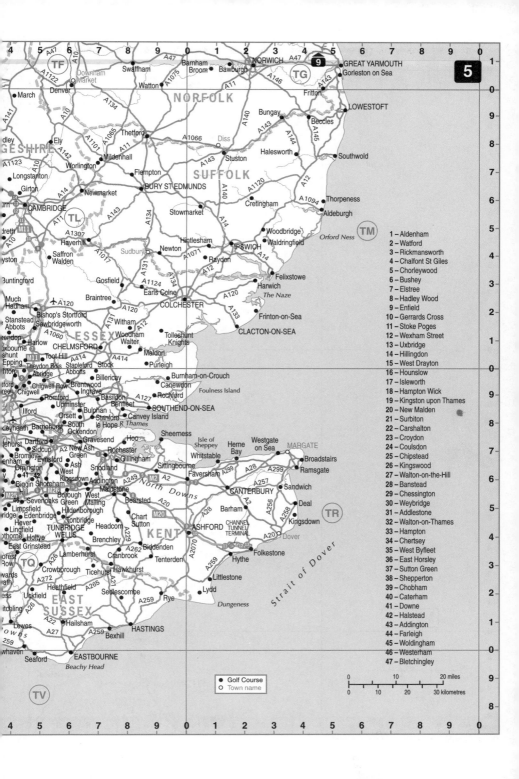

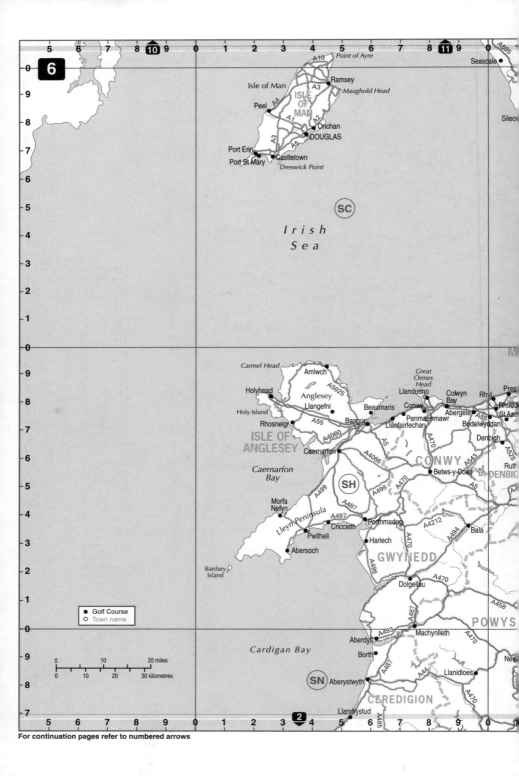

Point of Ayre

Isle of Man

ISLE OF MAN

Maughold Head

Ramsey

A3

A10

A3

Peel

A4

A7

Onchan

DOUGLAS

A2

A1

Port Erin

A3

A5

Castletown

Port St Mary

Dreswick Point

Irish Sea

(SC)

Seascale

A595

Silecı

Golf Course
○ **Town name**

0	10		20 miles
0	10	20	30 kilometres

Carmel Head

Amlwch

A5025

Great Ormes Head

Holyhead

Anglesey

Llandudno

Colwyn Bay

Rhyl

Pres

Llangefni

Holy Island

A55

Beaumaris

Conwy

Abergele

A55

Rhudd

St Asa

Rhosneigr

A4080

Bangor

Penmaenmawr

Bodelwyddan

ISLE OF ANGLESEY

Caernarfon

Llanfairfechan

A5

Denbigh

A470

Caernarfon Bay

A4086

CONWY

A543

A525

A499

(SH)

Betws-y-Coed

A5

Ruth

DENBIG

A498

A470

Morfa Nefyn

A487

A4

Criccieth

A497

Porthmadog

A4212

A494

Bala

Lleyn Peninsula

Pwllheli

Harlech

A470

Abersoch

GWYNEDD

Bardsey Island

A496

Dolgellau

A470

A458

A487

A470

POWYS

Cardigan Bay

Aberdyfi

A493

Machynlleth

A470

Borth

A487

New

(SN)

Aberystwyth

A44

Llanidloes

A470

CEREDIGION

Llanrhystud

A485

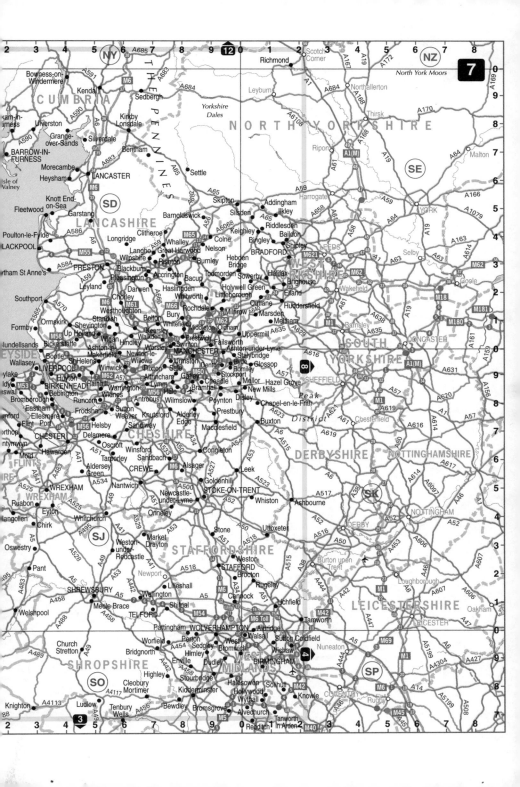

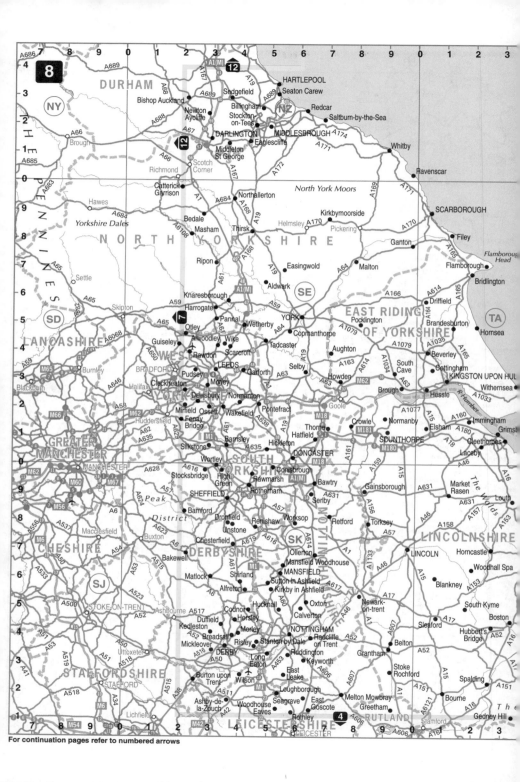

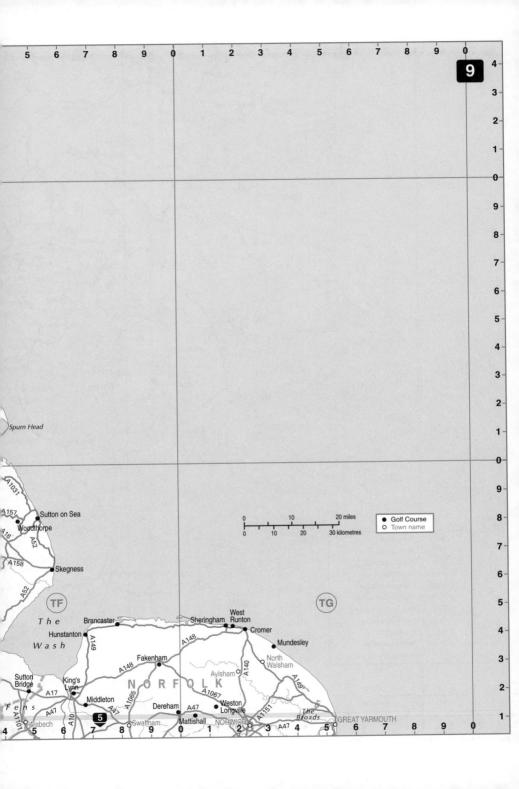

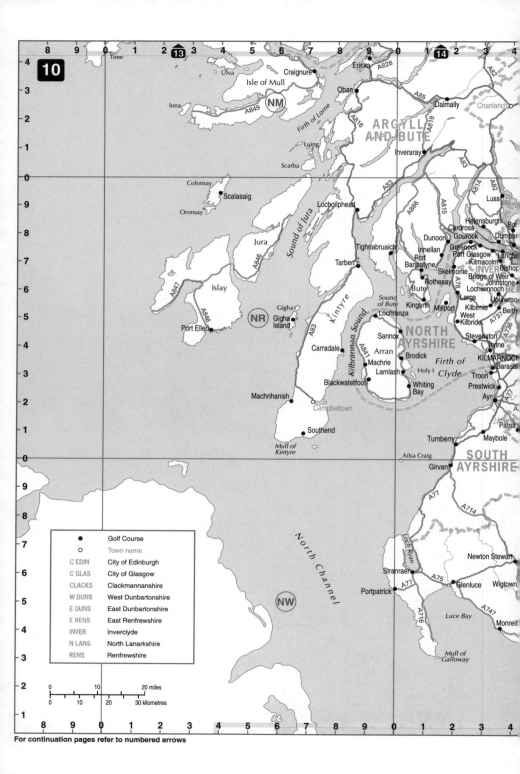

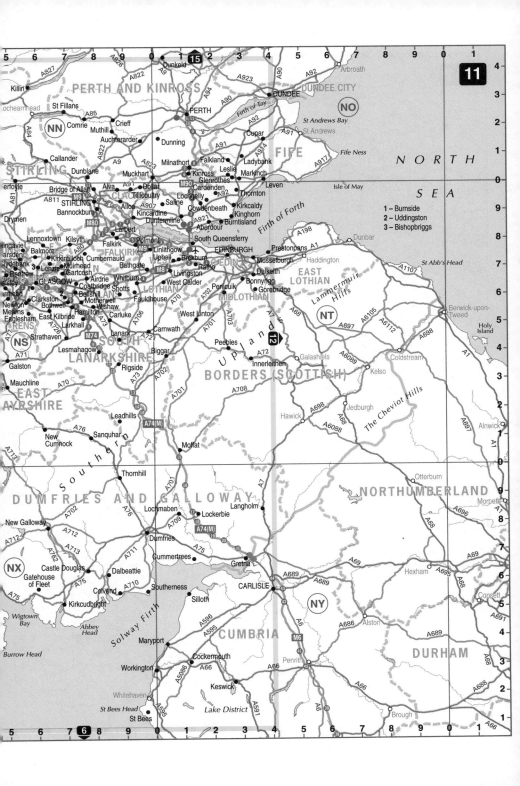

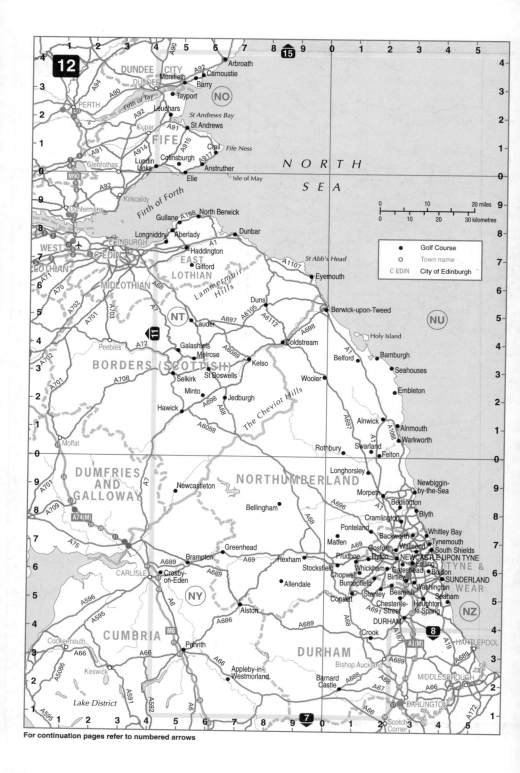

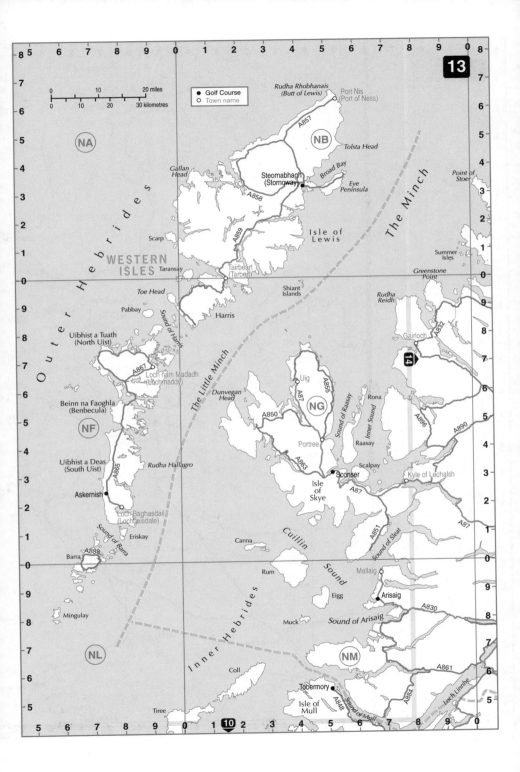

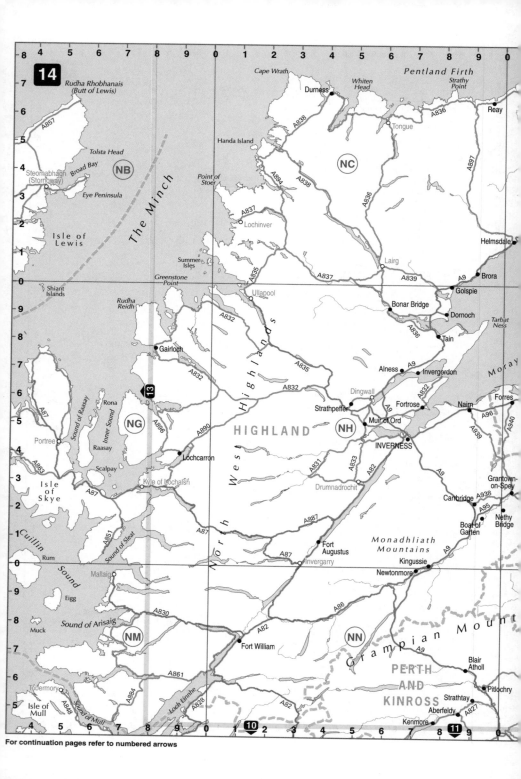

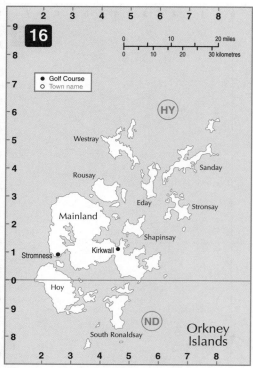

16

Golf Course
○ Town name

HY

Westray

Rousay

Sanday

Eday

Stronsay

Mainland

Shapinsay

Stromness • Kirkwall •

Hoy

ND

South Ronaldsay

Orkney
Islands

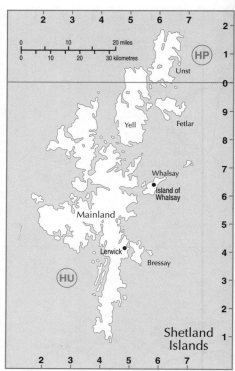

HP

Unst

Yell

Fetlar

Whalsay
Island of
Whalsay

Mainland

Lerwick ○

Bressay

HU

Shetland
Islands

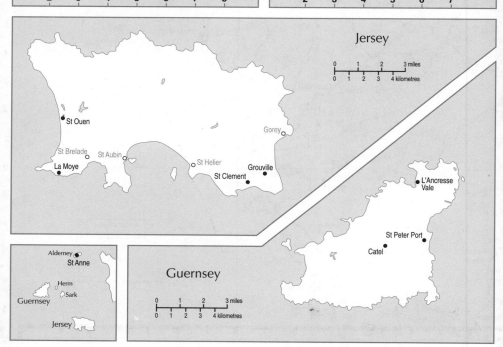

Jersey

St Ouen •

Gorey ○

St Brelade ○   St Aubin ○

St Helier ○   Grouville •

La Moye •

St Clement •

L'Ancresse
Vale •

St Peter Port •

Catel •

Alderney •
St Anne

Herm

Guernsey   ○ Sark

Jersey

Guernsey

Index of Golf Courses

Index *of Golf Courses*

Index *of Golf Courses*

Index *of Golf Courses*

Index *of Golf Courses*

Index of Golf Courses

Index *of Golf Courses*

Index *of Golf Courses*

Index *of Golf Courses*

Index *of Golf Courses*

Index *of Golf Courses*

Index *of Golf Courses*

Lifestyle Collection

SHIRE HOTELS

AA Lifestyle Guides has five golf breaks to give away. We invite you to enter one of five free prize draws. The winner of each free prize draw will enjoy a free golf break consisting of a two night Refresher Break including breakfast and dinner at Cottons Hotel and Spa in Cheshire for two people, plus a free round of golf each at High Legh Park (see entry on page 41)

To enter simply visit **www.pspcomp.com**, click on the picture of the 2005 AA Golf Course Guide enter the competition code GG05 and complete your details on the form.

Terms and conditions apply.

Alternatively you can complete (in capitals please) and return this page to:

AA Golf Guide Prize Draw
AA Publishing
Fanum House (14)
Basing View
Basingstoke RG21 4EA

Title Mr/Mrs/Miss/Ms/other, please state
Initial
Surname
House Name or Number
Street
Town
County
Postcode
Telephone Number
Email

1. Gender male/female
2. Age 18-24 25-44   45-65   65+
3. Age of children in the household <10yrs ___ 10 – 17 years ___
4. Do you have any pets in your household? yes/no
5. AA membership number (if applicable)
6. Have you bought any other travel guides in the last 12 months   yes/no

P.T.O.

7. Please select any of the following leisure activities that are of interest to you :-
Camping and caravanning [ ]
Eating out [ ]
Walking [ ]
Short breaks in the UK [ ]
Short breaks overseas [ ]
Longer break in the UK [ ]
Longer breaks overseas [ ]

The information we hold about you will be used to provide the product(s) and ser-vice(s) requested and for identification, account administration, analysis, and fraud/loss prevention purposes. More details about how that information is used is in our privacy statement, which you'll find under the heading "Personal Information" in our terms and conditions and on our website. Copies are also available from us by post, by contacting our Data Protection Compliance Officer, The AA, Southwood East, Apollo Rise, Farnborough, Hampshire, GU14 0JW
In addition, we may want to contact you about the other products and services from us or our partners. Please tick here if you do NOT want to hear about such prod-ucts. [ ]

Finally, we may want to contact you about other products and services from us or our partners by email, text or multi-media message. Please tick here if you DO want to hear about such products and services. [ ]

*Terms and Conditions

1. A winner will be drawn from each of the five prize draws to take place on the first Monday in each of the following months January, March, May, July and September 2005.
2. Closing date for receipt is midday on the relevant draw date. Final closing date for receipt of entries for the final draw is 1st September 2005
3. Entries received after any draw date, other that the final one, will go forward into the next available draw. Each entry will only be entered in one draw. Only one entry per household [per draw] will be accepted [in relation to all of the draws.]
4. Winner will be notified by post with 14 days of the relevant draw date.
5. Prizes must be booked within date specified on the letter detailing how to redeem the prize. Prizes are bit transferable and there is no case alternative.
6. This prize cannot be use in conjunction with any other discount, promotions or special offer.
7. Each prize consists of 2 nights accommodation for two people in twin or double room, including English breakfast and dinner plus a round of golf for 2 people which needs to be pre-booked via the hotel and will be subject to availability and tee times at the club.
8. Shire Hotels provide all hotel accommodation, services and facilities and AA Publishing is not party to your agreement with Shire Hotels in this regard.
9. No purchase of any AA products is necessary to enter the draws.
10. The prize draw is open to UK residents over the age of 18, other than employ-ees and agents of the Automobile Association or Shire Hotels, members of their households or anyone else connected with the promotion.
11. For a list of winners, please send a stamped, self addressed envelope to AA Lifestyle Guide Winners 2004, AA Publishing, Fanum House 14, Basing View, Basingstoke, Hampshire RG21 4EA.
12. This card must have an appropriate stamp13. Winners may be asked to partici-pate in draw-related publicity.
14. AA does not accept any liability for other parties failure to provide any of the prizes which are the subject of this free prize draw.